The Oxford Handbook of
Social Work in Health and Aging

The Oxford Handbook of
Social Work in
Health and Aging

SECOND EDITION

Daniel B. Kaplan & Barbara Berkman

EDITORS

Oxford University Press is a department of the University of
Oxford. It furthers the University's objective of excellence in research,
scholarship, and education by publishing worldwide.

Oxford   New York
Auckland   Cape Town   Dar es Salaam   Hong Kong   Karachi
Kuala Lumpur   Madrid   Melbourne   Mexico City   Nairobi
New Delhi   Shanghai   Taipei   Toronto

With offices in
Argentina   Austria   Brazil   Chile   Czech Republic   France   Greece
Guatemala   Hungary   Italy   Japan   Poland   Portugal   Singapore
South Korea   Switzerland   Thailand   Turkey   Ukraine   Vietnam

Oxford is a registered trademark of Oxford University Press
in the UK and certain other countries.

Published in the United States of America by
Oxford University Press
198 Madison Avenue, New York, NY 10016

Library of Congress Cataloging-in-Publication Data
   Oxford handbook of social work in health and aging / Daniel B. Kaplan &
Barbara Berkman, editors.—Second Edition.
      pages cm
   Revised edition of Handbook of social work in health and aging, 2006.
   Includes bibliographical references and index.
   ISBN 978-0-19-933695-1 (alk. paper)
   1. Social work with older people—Handbooks, manuals, etc.   2. Medical social work—Handbooks,
manuals, etc.   I. Kaplan, Daniel B., editor.   II. Berkman, Barbara, editor.   III. Title: Handbook of
social work in health and aging.   IV. Title: Social work in health and aging.
   [DNLM: 1. Health Services for the Aged.   2. Aged.   3. Community Health Services.
   4. Social Work—methods.]
   HV1451.O94 2016
   362.1'0425—dc23
   2015009383

We dedicate this book to older adults and their families worldwide, who deserve only the best of social and healthcare services, and to those social workers who strive every day to help them manage their health while maintaining quality of life.

Preface

There is increasing awareness that people are living longer and healthier lives and are redefining the aging experience in terms of family roles, work and volunteerism, and physical, social, and intellectual pursuits. While these trends are welcome, at the same time we must address the multitude of challenges that may impact the physical, social, economic, and emotional well-being of older adults and their families. Professional providers in health, mental health, and aging services have opportunities and responsibilities for assisting the older adult population in confronting these challenges.

The leading causes of morbidity and mortality are almost all related to chronic diseases, resulting in both ongoing limitations in daily functioning and acute episodes of illness over many years. The growing number of elderly with chronic disabling illnesses and the increasing need for rehabilitative services to support independent functioning means that patients and families will require more psychological and social assistance in order to address their problems effectively. Therefore, the goal of healthcare for the older adult is not only to provide state-of-the-art medicine and nursing but also to focus on how the older person can manage his or her health while maintaining quality of life. Thus, we require state-of-the-art social work. Social workers and other health professionals with knowledge in aging will become even more essential to address the complex needs of older people and their families. Elderly people with chronic diseases and activity limitation will represent an increasing percentage of all persons helped by social workers. A growing body of research has shown that social work practice with older adults and their families, once virtually the exclusive concern of social workers in geriatric settings, is increasingly becoming a major focus of care in a range of health and community-based services. We can expect all social workers will deal with combined issues of health and aging regardless of practice specialization.

The 2006 edition of the *Handbook of Social Work in Health and Aging* was the first reference to compile the most up-to-date knowledge, at the time, in a single volume. With the population of older adults increasing, and as new possibilities for their care advanced rapidly, professionals needed an accessible source of specialized information about how best to serve the elderly and their families, and this authoritative handbook was indispensable. While the format and content of the book remain relevant for today's students and practitioners, we recognized that the context of social work in health and aging has shifted. The book's content needed to be updated in order to reflect advances in the knowledge base that guides social work service delivery in health and aging, including enhancements in the theories of gerontology, innovations in clinical interventions, and major recent developments in the social policies that structure and finance healthcare and senior services. In addition, the policy reforms of the 2010 Patient Protection and Affordable Care Act, designed to improve access to and quality of care while reducing costs, set in motion a host of resultant changes in the United States healthcare system. These changes have potentially profound implications for the programs and services that provide care to older adults and their families.

The *Handbook* needed to address these evolving interdisciplinary healthcare programs and services and the broader social work practice environment. Therefore, in 62 chapters and nine section overviews, we bring you the 2nd edition of the *Handbook*. The most experienced and prominent gerontological healthcare scholars in the United States and across the world provide up-to-date knowledge of evidence-based practice guidelines for effectively assessing and treating older adults and supporting their families. The contributing authors paint rich portraits of a variety of populations that social workers serve and the arenas in which they practice, followed by detailed recommendations of best practices for an array of physical and mental health conditions. The volume's unprecedented attention to diversity,

healthcare trends, and implications for research, policy, and education make the publication of such a compendium a major event in the field of gerontological social work.

ORGANIZATION OF THE *HANDBOOK*

The 2nd edition of the *Handbook of Social Work in Health and Aging* is organized around three unifying themes: Part A, Social Work Practice in Health and Aging, including assessments and interventions, settings, and specific services; Part B, Populations Social Workers Serve in Health and Aging, including older adults with chronic physical and mental health conditions, special populations, older adults from diverse cultures, and those in palliative and end-of-life care; and Part C, Policies and Regulations in Health and Aging. Parts A, B, and C are subdivided into sections, each of which contains chapters that focus on similar domains, and each section has a section editor who has written an overview of the chapters in the section.

This *Handbook* is planned as a comprehensive reference text that covers the major areas of social work in health and aging in one volume. The chapters in the *Handbook* present a balanced mix of current evidence-based knowledge and key policy decisions, issues, and trends, as well as research needs. Each chapter has been concisely written, synthesized, and integrated in order to create an overview of the topic. In addition, heuristics are used throughout the *Handbook* to engage the reader and generate quickly and easily consumed knowledge. The authors have given complete references to online resources and contemporary reports. Case studies and vignettes are provided to illustrate concepts, especially in chapters on practice, assessment, special populations, and theory. The ideal way to begin reading this text is to peruse the table of contents, which, we believe, will give the reader a clear, comprehensive view of the field of health and aging. We hope you will be impressed and gratified as you review the depth and wealth of knowledge presented.

Daniel B. Kaplan & Barbara Berkman
Editors

Acknowledgments

We thank our Section Editors, David Biegel, Letha Chadiha, Namkee Choi, Louisa Daratsos, Ruth Dunkle, Nancy Hooyman, Amy Horowitz, Judith Howe, Rosalie Kane, James Lubben, Philip McCallion, Kathleen McInnis-Dittrich, and Philip Rozario. These dedicated, brilliant scholars provided the guidance and skills for what, at times, seemed like a monumental endeavor. Without their support, we doubt this revision would ever have been undertaken. They worked beyond our expectations (and sometimes their own) to update and revise this single volume covering much of the knowledge base on social work in health and aging. We also appreciate and thank our contributors, who wrote exceptional chapters that met our stringent guidelines for conciseness while thoroughly covering their subjects. And finally, we thank the John A. Hartford Foundation of New York City and the Gerontological Society of America for their support of the Hartford Geriatric Social Work Initiative, which has created a rebirth of interest in social work in health and aging and generated a growing network of social work specialists in aging who, with other health professionals, are available to meet the needs of our aging population.

Contents

**Part B
Populations Social
Workers Serve in Health
and Aging**

Part C
**Policies and Regulations
in Health and Aging**

About the Editors

Daniel Kaplan, PhD, LICSW, CSW-G

Dr. Kaplan is a clinical social worker with expertise in mental and neurological disorders. He is an Assistant Professor at Adelphi University School of Social Work. He earned his doctorate at Columbia University School of Social Work and then held an NIMH-funded postdoctoral research fellowship at the Institute for Geriatric Psychiatry at Weill Cornell Medical College. His research includes both intervention and implementation studies that aim to optimize care services, clinical interventions and supportive environments for older adults with mental and neurological disorders living in the community. He also conducts program evaluation research and services for several gerontology leadership and workforce development programs. Dr. Kaplan is a Co-Investigator and the Co-Director of the National Coordinating Center for the Hartford/NASW Gerontological Social Work Supervisors Program. He is the former National Director of Social Services for the Alzheimer's

Foundation of America. He has also worked in an Elder Protective Services and Elder at Risk program. He has developed a number of courses and training programs on advanced clinical practice with individuals with dementia and their families. He holds clinical social work licensure in New York and Massachusetts, as well as an NASW certification in advanced gerontological clinical social work.

Barbara J. Berkman, DSW/PhD

Dr. Barbara Berkman is the Helen Rehr / Ruth Fizdale Professor Emerita of Health and Mental Health at Columbia University School of Social Work, and Research Professor at Boston College Graduate School of Social Work. She has directed 23 federally and foundation supported research projects focusing on issues in gerontology and oncology, and was the Principal Investigator of the Hartford Foundation's Geriatric Social Work Faculty Scholars Program. She is a former President of the Institute for the Advancement of Social Work Research. Dr. Berkman has received many awards and honors for her research and policy efforts in health and aging. In recent years, she received the "2002 Career Achievement Award" from the Association for Geriatric Education in Social Work, and in 2004 was given NASW Foundation's Social Work Pioneer Award. In 2009 she received the Donald P. Kent award from The Gerontological Society of America. Most recently, in 2012, she received the Distinguished Achievement in Cancer Award from the American Cancer Society. In recognition of her major contributions to research and practice, she has been elected a Fellow of The Gerontological Society of America, the New York Academy of Medicine, and The American Academy of Social Work and Social Welfare.

Contributors

Ronald H. Aday, PhD
Professor
Department of Sociology
Middle Tennessee State University

Geri Adler, PhD, LISW-CP
Research Health Scientist
South Central Mental Illness Research, Education
and Clinical Center
Michael E. DeBakey VA Medical Center

Suran Ahn, MSW
Doctoral Student
School of Social Welfare
University at Albany, SUNY

Amy L. Ai, PhD, MS, MA, MSW
Professor
Florida State University College of Social Work, and
Colleges of Medicine, Nursing, and Art and Science
(Psychology)

Gretchen E. Alkema, PhD, LCSW
Vice President, Policy and Communications
The SCAN Foundation

María P. Aranda, PhD, MSW, MPA, LCSW
Associate Professor
School of Social Work
University of Southern California

Sandra K. Atkins, MPA
Vice President, Strategic Initiatives
Partners in Care Foundation

Catherine Ayers, PhD, ABPP
Assistant Professor
Department of Psychiatry
University of California

A.E. Benjamin, PhD, MSW
Professor Emeritus
Department of Social Welfare
UCLA Luskin School of Public Affairs

Barbara J. Berkman, PhD/DSW
Research Professor
School of Social Work
Boston College

Mercedes Bern-Klug, PhD, MSW
Associate Professor
School of Social Work
University of Iowa

Julie Berrett-Abebe, MSW, MA
Doctoral Student
Simmons College School of Social Work

David E. Biegel, PhD, MSW
Henry L. Zucker Professor of Social Work Practice
and Professor of Psychiatry and Sociology
Jack, Joseph and Morton Mandel
School of Applied Social Sciences
Case Western Reserve University

James Boehnlein, MD, MSc
Professor of Psychiatry
Oregon Health and Science University
Associate Director for Education
VA Northwest Network Mental Illness Research,
Education, and Clinical Center (MIRECC)

Robin P Bonifas, PhD, MSW
Associate Professor
School of Social Work
Arizona State University

Christiana Bratiotis, PhD, MSW
Assistant Professor
School of Social Work
Portland State University

Colette V. Browne, Dr.PH, MSW
Professor
Myron B. Thompson School of Social Work
University of Hawaii

Denise Burnette, PhD, MSSW
Professor
School of Social Work
Columbia University

Sandra S. Butler, PhD, MSW
Professor and MSW Coordinator
School of Social Work
University of Maine

Tamara J. Cadet, PhD, MSW, MPH
Assistant Professor
Simmons College School of Social Work

Karen Campbell, LCSW-R
Director, Client Services & The Dr. Lorraine Marchi
Client Assistance Program
Lighthouse Guild International

Edward R. Canda, PhD, MSW, MA
Professor
School of Social Welfare
The University of Kansas

Kim Cassie, PhD, MSSW, MA
Assistant Professor
College of Social Work
University of Tennessee

Letha A. Chadiha, PhD, MSW
Rose C. Gibson Collegiate Professor of Social Work
School of Social Work
University of Michigan

Rosemary Chapin, PhD, MSW
Professor, Director of the Office of Aging and Long
Term Care
School of Social Welfare
University of Kansas

Namkee G. Choi, PhD
Professor and Louis and Ann Wolens Centennial
Chair in Gerontology
School of Social Work
University of Texas

Sherry M. Cummings, PhD
Associate Dean and Professor
College of Social Work
University of Tennessee

Lori R. Daniels, PhD, MSW
Counselor
Portland Vet Center—Readjustment Counseling
Service
Department of Veterans Affairs

Louisa Daratsos, PhD, LCSW
Psychosocial Coordinator for Oncology/Palliative
Care
VA New York Harbor Healthcare System, Brooklyn
Campus

Julie S. Darnell, PhD, MHSA
Associate Professor
School of Public Health
University of Illinois at Chicago

Joan K. Davitt, PhD, MSS, MLSP
Associate Professor
School of Social Work
University of Maryland

Diana M. DiNitto, PhD, ACSW, LCSW, AAC
Cullen Trust Centennial Professor in Alcohol
Studies and Education
School of Social Work
University of Texas

Patricia H. Ducayet, LMSW
Texas State Long-Term Care Ombudsman

Ruth E. Dunkle, PhD, MSW
Professor
School of Social Work
University of Michigan

Charles A. Emlet, PhD, MSW
Professor
Social Work Program
University of Washington

Joy Swanson Ernst, PhD, MSW
Professor of Social Work
Department of Sociology and Social Work
Hood College

Andrea S. Fielding, MSW
School of Social Work
Adelphi University

Richard B. Francoeur, PhD, MSW
Associate Professor of Social Work
School of Social Work
Adelphi University

Colleen Galambos, PhD, MSW
Professor
School of Social Work
University of Missouri

Daniel S. Gardner, PhD, MSW
Associate Professor
Silberman School of Social Work
Hunter College, City University of New York

Zvi D. Gellis, PhD
Professor
School of Social Policy & Practice
University of Pennsylvania

Nancy Giunta, PhD, MSW
Associate Professor
Silberman School of Social Work
Hunter College, City University of New York

Robyn L. Golden, LCSW
Director of Health and Aging
Rush University Medical Center

Judith G. Gonyea, PhD, MSW
Professor
School of Social Work
Boston University

Jan S. Greenberg, PhD, MSW
Professor
School of Social Work
University of Wisconsin

Roberta R. Greene PhD MSW
Professor and Louis and Ann Wolens Centennial
Chair
Gerontology and Social Welfare Emerita
University of Texas

Emily A. Greenfield, PhD
Associate Professor
School of Social Work
Rutgers, the State University of New Jersey

Irene A. Gutheil, DSW
Professor Emeritus
Former Henry C. Ravazzin Professor of Gerontology
Graduate School of Social Service
Fordham University

Trang Hoang, LCSW, PhD
Division Director
Asian and Pacific Islander Mental Health Alliance
Special Service for Groups

Nancy Hooyman, MSW, PhD
Hooyman Professor of Gerontology and Dean
Emeritus
School of Social Work
University of Washington

Amy Horowitz, PhD
Professor and Nicholas J. Lagenfeld Chair in Social
Research
Graduate School of Social Service
Fordham University

Judith L. Howe, PhD
Professor
Brookdale Department of Geriatrics and Palliative
Medicine
Icahn School of Medicine at Mount Sinai

Robert B. Hudson, PhD
Professor
School of Social Work
Boston University

Anne K. Hughes, PhD, MSW
Associate Professor
School of Social Work
Michigan State University

Hae-Sook Jeon, PhD, MSW
Associate Professor
Department of Social Welfare
Kyungpook National University

Rebecca G. Judd, PhD, LMSW-IPR
Assistant Professor
Texas A&M University-Commerce

Jung Sim Jun, MSW
Edward G. & Elizabeth Bower Family Scholar
School of Social Work
University of Missouri

Rosalie A. Kane, PhD, MSW
Professor
Division of Health Policy and Management, School
of Public Health
University of Minnesota

Daniel B. Kaplan, PhD, MSW
Assistant Professor
School of Social Work
Adelphi University

Lenard W. Kaye, DSW, PhD
Director and Professor
Center on Aging and School of Social Work
University of Maine

Bonnie Kenaley, PhD, MSW, RN
Associate Professor
School of Social Work
Boise State University

Kathryn G. Kietzman, PhD, MSW
Research Scientist
UCLA Center for Health Policy Research
UCLA Fielding School of Public Health

Terry L. Koenig, PhD, LSCSW
Associate Professor
School of Social Welfare
University of Kansas

Beverley L. Laubert, MA
Ohio State Long-Term Care Ombudsman

Ji Seon Lee, PhD, MSSW, MPA
Associate Professor and Assoicate Dean
Graduate School of Social Service
Fordham University

Jordan Lewis, PhD, MSW, CPG
Assistant Professor
Indigenous Wellness Research Institute
University of Washington School of Social Work

Lydia W. Li, PhD, MSW
Associate Professor
School of Social Work
University of Michigan

Elizabeth Lightfoot, PhD, MSW
Professor and Doctoral Program Director
School of Social Work
University of Minnesota

James Lubben, PhD
Louise McMahon Ahearn Professor
School of Social Work
Boston College

Wendy Lustbader, MSW
Affiliate Associate Professor
School of Social Work
University of Washington

Kelley R. Macmillan, PhD, MSW
Clinical Associate Professor
School of Social Work
University of Maryland

Ellen K. Mahoney, RN, PhD
Associate Professor
William F. Connell School of Nursing
Boston College

Kevin J. Mahoney, PhD
Professor
School of Social Work
Boston College

Marsha R. Mailick, PhD
Vice Chancellor for Research and Graduate
Education
Vaughan Bascom and Elizabeth M. Boggs Professor
University of Wisconsin

Peter Maramaldi, PhD, MPH, MSW
Professor
Hartford Faculty Scholar & National Mentor
Simmons School of Social Work

Tina Maschi, PhD, LCSW, ACSW
Associate Professor
Graduate School of Social Service
Fordham University

Leah A. Maxwell, MSW
Part-Time Faculty
School of Social Work
University of Maine

Philip McCallion, PhD, ACSW
Professor & Co-Director
Center for Excellence in Aging & Community Wellness
School of Social Welfare
University at Albany

Erin E. McGaffigan, PhD, MSW, MS
Principal
Collective Insight, LLC

Kathleen McInnis-Dittrich, ACSW, PhD
Chair, Older Adults and Families Concentration
Graduate School of Social Work
Boston College

Helen B. Miltiades, PhD
Associate Professor
Department of Social Work Education
California State University

Jong Won Min, PhD, MSW
Associate Professor
School of Social Work
San Diego State University

Phyllis B. Mitzen, AM
Co-Program Director
Center for Long Term Care Reform
Health & Medicine Policy Research Group

Ailee Moon, PhD, MSW
Associate Professor
Department of Social Welfare
Luskin School of Public Affairs
University of California

Carmen Morano, PhD, MSW
Associate Professor
Silberman School of Social Work
Hunter College
City University of New York

Nancy Morrow-Howell, MSW, PhD
Betty Bofinger Brown Distinguished Professor of
Social Policy
Director, Friedman Center for Aging
Washington University

Jean Correll Munn, PhD, MSW
Associate Professor
College of Social Work
Florida State University

Edna Naito-Chan, PhD, MSW
Program Director
Transitional Residence Program
VA Greater Los Angeles Healthcare System

Mitsuko Nakashima, PhD, MSWMatthias
J. Naleppa, MSW, PhD
Professor
School of Economy, Health and Social Work
University of Applied Sciences Bern

Eun Ha Namkung, MSW
Research Assistant
School of Social Work
University of Wisconsin

Adria E. Navarro, PhD, LCSW
Assistant Professor
Department of Social Work
Azusa Pacific University

Holly Nelson-Becker, PhD, MSW
Professor
School of Social Work
Loyola University Chicago

Cara Pappas, ND, ARNP, RN
Assistant Professor
Florida State University College of Nursing, and
College of Social Work

Manoj P. Pardasani, PhD, MSW
Associate Professor and Research Scholar
Graduate School of Social Service
Fordham University

Michael W. Parker, PhD/DSW
Professor
School of Social Work & Executive Board, Center
for Mental Health & Aging
University of Alabama

David A. Patterson Silver Wolf (Adelv unegv Waya),
PhD, MSSW
Assistant Professor
School of Social Work
Washington University

Marcie Pitt-Catsouphes, PhD, MSW
Associate Professor, Director Sloan Center
on Aging & Work
Graduate School of Social Work
Boston College

Lonique R. Pritchett, PhD, LCSW
Clinical Care Coordinator
Michael E. DeBakey VA Medical Center

Michelle Putnam, PhD, MGS
Professor
School of Social Work
Simmons College

Kerry A. Rastigue, JD, MSW
Coordinator of Service Learning
Saginaw Valley State University

Victoria H. Raveis, PhD
Research Professor and Director
Psychosocial Research Unit on Health, Aging and
the Community
College of Dentistry
New York University

Amy Restorick Roberts, PhD, MSSA, LSW
Assistant Professor
Department of Family Studies and Social Work
Miami University

Virginia E. Richardson, PhD, MSW
Professor Emeritus
College of Social Work
The Ohio State University

Joyce Riley, BS, MA
Associate Director (Retired)
Health Administration and Policy Program
University of Maryland

Philip A. Rozario, PhD, MSW
Professor and Director of Doctoral Program
School of Social Work
Adelphi University

Stephanie Elias Sarabia, PhD, LCSW, LCADC
Assistant Professor
Social Work
Ramapo College of New Jersey

Janice Lynch Schuster, MFA
Lead Writer, federal
Magellan Health

Mark Sciegaj, PhD, MPH
Associate Professor
Department of Health Policy and Administration
Pennsylvania State University

Alicia Sellon, MSW
Graduate Research Assistant
School of Social Welfare
University of Kansas

Sherry Sheffield PhD, LCSW-S
Program Director—Behavioral Health Services
Hunt Regional Medical Center

Tazuko Shibusawa, PhD, LCSW
Associate Dean & Director, MSW Program
Silver School of Social Work
New York University

Gayle E. Shier Kricke, MSW
Program Coordinator
Health and Aging
Rush University Medical Center

W. June Simmons, BA, MSW
President and CEO
Partners in Care Foundation

Kelsey Simons, PhD, MSW
Assistant Professor (status only)
Factor-Inwentash Faculty of Social Work
University of Toronto

Gaynell M. Simpson, PhD, MSW
Assistant Professor
School of Social Work
University of Alabama

Charles A. Smith, PhD, LCSW
Assistant Professor
School of Social Work
University of Southern Maine

Margaret M. Souza, PhD, MSW
Associate Professor
Social Sciences
SUNY/Empire State College

Gail Steketee, PhD
Dean and Professor
School of Social Work
Boston University

Cynthia Stuen, PhD, AM
UN Representative
International Federation on Ageing

Fei Sun, PhD, MSW
Assistant Professor
School of Social Work
Arizona State University

Stephanie Swerdlow, MSW
President
Elder Options Inc.

M. Lori Thomas, PhD, MSW, MDiv
Associate Professor
School of Social Work
University of North Carolina

Ronald W. Toseland, PhD, MSW
Distinguished Professor
School of Social Welfare
University at Albany, State University of
New York

Molly J. Tovar, EdD, MAT
Director, Kathryn M. Buder Center for American
Indian Studies & Professor of Practice
School of Social Work
Washington University

Shannon Trecartin, MSW
Doctoral Candidate
College of Social Work
University of Tennessee

Deborah P. Waldrop, PhD, MSW
Professor & Associate Dean for Faculty
Development
School of Social Work
University at Buffalo

Kathleen H. Wilber, PhD, LCSW
Mary Pickford Professor of Gerontology
Davis School of Gerontology
University of Southern California

Alicia M. Wilson, MSW
Adjunct Faculty
School of Social Work
Adelphi University

Stephanie P. Wladkowski, PhD, LICSW
Assistant Professor
School of Social Work
Eastern Michigan University

Jeanine Yonashiro-Cho, MSG
Doctoral Student
Davis School of Gerontology
University of Southern California

Karen Zgoda, MSW, LCSW
Instructor
Bridgewater State University

Sheryl Zimmerman, PhD
Kenan Distinguished Professor
Associate Dean for Doctoral Education
School of Social Work
University of North Carolina

Bradley D. Zodikoff, PhD, LCSW
Associate Dean for Academic Affairs
School of Social Work
Adelphi University

The Oxford Handbook of
Social Work in
Health and Aging

Social Work Practice in Health and Aging

KATHLEEN MCINNIS-DITTRICH
JAMES LUBBEN

SECTION I

Assessments and Interventions

OVERVIEW

This section of the *Handbook* is divided into two sections. The first section examines various facets of assessment; the second provides an overview of practice theories and models most relevant to work with individuals and families.

ASSESSMENTS

In this section, Kathleen McInnis-Dittrich proposes that biopsychosocial assessments are the foundation of social work practice with older adults. Dr. McInnis-Dittrich advises that assessment is both a process and a product. During the process phase, social workers build relationships with the older adult client. The product of assessment becomes the basis of care planning and monitoring change. Rosalie A. Kane provides an overview of standardized measures used in geriatric assessment. Dr. Kane provides a critique of a select group of traditional assessment measures as well as an introduction to some newer measures that should be considered along with the more traditional ones.

THEORIES AND MODELS OF INTERVENTION

Kathleen McInnis-Dittrich describes cognitive-behavioral approaches used most often to treat mild to moderate forms of depression and anxiety in older adults. The basic principles of these approaches have also been adapted to treat more serious conditions such as bipolar disorder, post-traumatic stress disorder, and affective disorders in individuals with mild to moderate dementia. This chapter specifically examines the therapeutic process and application of cognitive-behavioral therapy (CBT) and problem-solving therapy (PST), two evidence-based therapeutic approaches, to treating older adults. The validation approach, while not considered an evidence-based practice in social work intervention, offers a common-sense intervention technique based on cognitive-behavioral principles to manage difficult behaviors in older adults with mild to moderate dementia.

Therapeutic approaches to working with extended family and the power of the group process are the foci of Roberta R. Greene and Joyce Riley's chapter. The authors acknowledge the importance of supporting the well-being of caregivers as part of an ecological and systemic approach to providing services to older adults. Family-centered case management methods for recognizing and alleviating the stressors involved in caring for an aging family member are described in this chapter. The authors include an in-depth discussion of the use of group treatment models for both older adults and caregivers.

Based on the combined perspectives of Erik Erikson's psychosocial theory of human and development and Robert Butler's phenomena of life review, therapeutic reminiscence and facilitated life review offer other choices in clinical interventions as presented in the next chapter by Lori R. Daniels and James Boehnlein. Reminiscence targets the retrieval of specific emotional content, most often positive affect that can moderate negative emotional states. Life review requires a more structured approach and accesses both positive and troublesome emotional memories with the intent of addressing the resolution of negative emotions. The authors compare these interventions, describing the application of each approach to specific clinical case examples.

Rosemary Chapin, Holly Nelson-Becker, Kelley MacMillan, and Alicia Sellon examine new applications to the strengths-based and solution-focused practice model with older adults. The authors note that the strength model offers a unique philosophical view about how social workers can interact with clients to elicit positive outcomes. More specifically, the authors note how the strengths-based approach elicits an activist role for clients in contrast with a more passive role induced by traditional medical models of care.

One of the fastest growing, innovative approaches to working with older adults is that of recognizing and mobilizing an older adult's spirituality, described in the chapter by Holly Nelson-Becker, Edward R. Canda, and Mitsuko Nakashima. The authors propose that development of a spiritually sensitive practice requires a strengths-based approach that includes listening to the profound and diverse questions clients express and demonstrating openness to hear all expressions of grief, longing, confusion, and joy that emanate from the human experience. According to the authors, such practice requires "a hearing of the heart: an ability to hear the pain and the hope in the stories clients tell and an ability to highlight for clients important themes or subtexts of which they may not be fully aware." The authors offer a thoughtful discussion of what clinician and client characteristics are most appropriate for spiritually based interventions.

Kevin J. Mahoney, Erin McGaffigan, Mark Sciegaj, Karen Zgoda, Ellen Mahoney recall the work of Jane Addams to anchor an overview chapter on approaches that empower individuals and communities. The authors review empowerment theory and suggest adaptations for social work practice with older adults. Examples of empowerment interventions were drawn from the nationwide Cash and Counseling research programs carried out by the authors.

SECTION

Assessments

A thorough biopsychosocial assessment is a prerequisite to all social work interventions regardless of a client's age. However, assessing older adults has its unique challenges. This chapter discusses the purpose and function of an assessment emphasizing an older adult's strengths. What an older adult continues to do well serves as the foundation for meeting the challenges facing him or her (Chapin, Nelson-Becker, & MacMillan, 2006). The origin of the request for an assessment and how that origin contributes to an older adult's vulnerability depending on the findings of the assessment process are explored in depth as potential ethical dilemmas for the social worker. The major domains of assessment (physical health, competence in activities of daily living [ADLs], psycho-emotional well-being, social functioning, spirituality, sexuality, and environmental safety) are presented.

THE ROLE OF ASSESSMENT IN SOCIAL WORK PRACTICE

Assessment can be described as sophisticated problem solving. The worker gathers as much information as possible from the individual, and in some cases collaterals, to form preliminary hypotheses about the cause of and possible solutions to challenges facing a client. The use of "challenge" as opposed to "problem" in this definition is intentional. Aging is not a social problem; it is a developmental life stage. In traditional clinical work, the assessment may be presented through a specific theoretical lens, such as psychodynamic, cognitive-behavioral, or the solution-focused perspective. With older adults, assessment is focused more often on his or her specific service and material needs.

Assessment as Both Process and Product

Assessment is both a process and a product. Observing and accurately evaluating an older adult's abilities and needs is a dynamic, ongoing process. For example, early in the course of dementia, limitations in cognitive functioning may be apparent but may not actually impair an older adult's ability to live independently. However, dementia can progress rapidly or be exacerbated by physical illness, quickly becoming incapacitating for that older adult. The evaluative part of the assessment process

KATHLEEN MCINNIS-DITTRICH

Comprehensive Biopsychosocial Assessments: The Foundation of Social Work Practice with Older Adults

1

is continuous and strongly dependent on contextual factors.

Assessment is a product as well. The findings of an assessment serve as the basis for making initial decisions about services or supports that an older adult needs to maintain independence and preserve dignity. It is a constant evolution between what is observed at the "moment in time" of an assessment and the reality that the situation facing the older adult may change quickly.

The social work profession's concern about using evidence-based practice, the use of intervention methods found to be effective as supported by empirical research, suggests a rigorous assessment process is crucial to the selection of an appropriate intervention (Grady & Drisko, 2014). Applying evidence-based practice assumes the clinician has made an accurate identification of the challenges facing the client.

Challenges in Assessing Older Adults

In assessments of children and adolescents, it is common practice to assess individual functioning in comparison with what is considered normal developmental milestones. For example if a child shows no attempt to crawl or walk by 2 years of age or is not able to do so, it suggests the child may have a developmental lag, or at least the possibility should be explored. However, there are no common developmental milestones that cover the broad range of abilities and challenges within the heterogeneous population of older adults. Many older adults show no biopsychosocial limitations until well into their 80s, while others may be showing signs of severe cognitive and physical limitations as early as their 60s. There are 80-year-olds who still run marathons and 70-year-olds who are wheelchair bound. Assessment of the "functional capacity," regardless of the age of the older adult, is the most useful tool in identifying what supports and services may be indicated (Ferri, James, & Pruchno, 2009; Moore, Palmer, Patterson, & Jeste, 2007).

Assessments can be used for very specific purposes in work with older adults. It is tempting to assume that assessments are used primarily to evaluate what older adults cannot do, known as the *deficit* approach to assessment. Instead, contemporary practice with older adults suggests a *strengths* perspective,

in which every effort is made by the social worker to help older adults discover and employ their own strengths; mobilize their capabilities, not deficits; and problem-solve to achieve their own service goals (Chapin, Nelson-Becker, & MacMillan, 2006: Faul et al., 2009). In the absence of significant cognitive impairment, older adults are the experts in what strengths they possess and what challenges they face. Assessments can also be used with older adults to identify, support, and enhance existing functioning. Determining those areas in which older adults are functioning adequately but may benefit from additional support to maintain self-sufficiency supports the goals of maximizing independence and maintaining dignity. Another purpose of assessments is to identify interventions and supports that restore lost functioning.

ETHICAL ISSUES IN ASSESSMENT OF OLDER ADULTS

Two very significant ethical issues may emerge in the process of conducting assessments of older adults: the origin of the request for an assessment and an older adult's vulnerability pending the outcome of the assessment (McInnis-Dittrich, 2014).

The Origin of the Request for Assistance

When an older adult voluntarily requests assistance from a social service agency, the social worker can assume the older adult is self-motivated to obtain supportive services to improve the quality of his or her life. They alone stand to benefit (or not benefit) from their active participation in the change effort. The older adult retains his or her self-determination to select how many or how few services are received. To have one's privacy and right to confidentiality respected by the social worker are reasonable expectations. However, in many cases with older adults, the request for assessment and intervention is not initiated by the older adult but rather by family members, caregivers, neighbors, or even a public servant such as a police officer. The older adult may not be voluntarily participating in the assessment. It is important that the social worker approach the process with a clear understanding of whose goals are being addressed in the assessment and intervention process. Is the older adult a willing participant in the assessment evaluation process? Is the older adult competent to refuse interventions if such are deemed necessary by the assessment? What does the party requesting the assessment expect as the final outcome of the assessment process? Who is the client here? Whose goals are being met? Are these expectations consistent with the social work profession's protection of self-determination even if the older adult has limited capacity? The rights and interests of well-meaning family members or other interested parties do not supersede the rights of the older adult regardless of who originates the request for assistance.

The Vulnerability of the Older Adult: What Does the Older Adult Have to Lose?

If an older adult does not voluntarily request an assessment and the request comes from a family member, it is imperative to ask "What are the stakes for the older adult?" If an older adult wants services, it is in his or her best interest to be honest in identifying challenges and consider services. However, if the assessment is initiated by a family member or other concerned party and the findings may result in a move to a nursing home, what is the incentive for the older adult to be perfectly honest about his or her limitations? The deep-seated fear of losing one's independence and being forced to leave one's home often keeps older adults from either recognizing or admitting functional limitations (Fastame & Penna, 2013). The older adult may go to great lengths to deny, hide, or underestimate the challenges he or she faces. The social worker conducting the assessment needs to be cognizant of the presence and power of this fear. Even a simple assessment may present a threat (real or perceived) to the basic dignity and independence of the older adult. Who is the client?

Clinical Judgment or Standardized Assessment Measures?

Before the domains of a biopsychosocial assessment are presented, it is important to address the issue of how much (or how little) standardized measures should be used in assessments with older adults. An in-depth discussion of the use of standardized measures and the ways such measures can be applied

to each of the components of an assessment are the subjects of the next chapter of this handbook, "Standardized Measures and Geriatric Social Work." There are benefits and limitations to using these tools.

One benefit of using standardized measures is that the instruments have been tested for reliability and validity so the clinician can assume such measures, if applied appropriately, will accurately identify both the strengths and challenges facing any client (Grady & Drisko, 2014). Scores on standardized measures can be interpreted similarly by social workers, psychologists, nurses, and physicians as a form of common language about the older adult's functioning (Moore et al., 2007). Standardized measures such as the Geriatric Depression Scale (Sheikh & Yesavage, 1986), the Mini-Mental Status Exam (Folstein, Folstein, & McHugh, 1975) and measures of ADLs (Katz, Down, Cash, & Grotz, 1970) and instrumental activities of daily living (IADLs; Lawton, 1969), among others that assess physical and mental health, have become standard practices and should be used to complement clinical judgments. However, the increase of home- and community-based care demands equally rigorous measures of social health. The Medical Outcome Study Social Support Scale (Sherbourne & Stewart, 1991), the Lubben Social Network Scale (Lubben, 1988; Lubben et al., 2006), and the UCLA Loneliness Scale (Russell, 1996) are examples of such measures.

The limitations of using such measures include the person conducting the assessment's lack of skill in administering the measure, the over- or underestimation of abilities by older adult or family members in answering questions or completing checklists (Fastame & Penna, 2013), and dishonest answers by either party reflecting their own goals (McInnis-Dittrich, 2014). The social worker needs to be aware of the limitations of each of the standardized measures and take professional responsibility to be trained in their use.

In reality, standardized measures are meant to serve as ways to complement clinical judgment. Social workers are trained to use every clue in the biopsychosocial context to help inform clinical judgments and observations about the older adult. What are you hearing or seeing that helps you understand the older adult? Are the findings of the standard measures consistent with what you observe about the older adult's level of functioning? Are there issues not covered in either a formal assessment protocol or domains of functioning that are reason for concern? What do you need or want to know that you have not been able to find out? Clinical judgment is trained professional intuition and implies that the social worker will follow up with open-ended questions when the answers to questions given by either the older adult or collaterals seem inconsistent or indicative of issues that need further exploration. The combination of clinical judgment and standardized measures offers the best opportunity for an accurate evaluation of an older adult's abilities.

THE PROCESS OF A BIOPSYCHOSOCIAL ASSESSMENT

Conditions for Conducting an Assessment

The ideal place for an assessment to be done is in the older adult's home or primary residence, although this is not always possible. This places the older adults on his or her own turf, which transfers some of the power from the social worker to the older adult. The home setting also provides the social workers with invaluable information to corroborate or challenge information that is obtained either from the older adults directly or through the use of standardized measures.

An older adult should be given every opportunity to optimize his or her functioning during the assessment. Make sure the older adult has access to any assistive devices including glasses, hearing aids, dentures, or mobility devices such as a cane or walker. Minimize any visual or audio distractions. Select a time, if possible, when the older adult is not fatigued or feeling poorly. Older adults need every chance to fare as well as possible in the assessment considering what the consequences might be. It may be necessary to schedule the assessment in a number of shorter time slots if an older adult's health or mental health is compromised (Faul et al., 2009).

Be sensitive to cultural and gender issues that influence the quality of the interaction between the older adult and the social worker (Rose & Chueng, 2012). If English is not the older adult's first language, arrange for a skilled interpreter trained to translate in these kinds of assessments rather than a just someone who speaks the language. Subtle but significant information can be lost in translation if only the language but not the nuance is translated. Some Latina

and Asian women may be extremely uncomfortable sharing deeply personal information with male social workers (Rose & Chueng, 2012). Use family members to gauge what special arrangements may need to be made.

Establishing Rapport with an Older Adult

Establishing good rapport with an older adult is the most critical component of the assessment process. For many older adults, the initial encounter with a social worker will be the first time he or she has come in contact with the social services delivery system. The process of sharing very personal and often times embarrassing information with a total stranger can be intimidating and extremely uncomfortable (Pinsker, Pachana, Wilson, Tilse, & Byrne, 2010; Rose & Chueng, 2012). It is important to slow down the pace of the assessment, giving the older adult a chance to be heard and ask questions. In many respects, the older adult is evaluating the person conducting the assessment as much as vice versa to determine whether he or she will actively engage in the assessment process. Is this person really interested in me? Is he or she willing to listen to me talk about what is important to me? Can I trust him or her to respect me and who I *was* as well as who I *am* now? What happens if I don't do well on this "test?" These types of questions are common in the mind of an older adult. The person conducting the assessment should also expect to be asked a number of personal questions as the older adult gets to know him or her and should be prepared to respond personally and professionally to these questions. The initial conversation with the older adult is an appropriate time to explain the purpose of the assessment and how the information will be used and to reassure the older adult that an assessment looks at both strengths and challenges. If the results of the assessment will be shared with healthcare providers or family members, the person conducting the assessment should be honest about that reality. The older adult should be given every opportunity to show what he or she can do well in addition to identifying those issues that present challenges.

This first phase of the assessment usually involves getting the necessary demographic information for the assessment. This can be integrated into a conversation rather than a strict question and answer format. One approach to starting off the assessment is to ask an older adult what a typical day in his or her life is like. When does he or she get up? How does the older adult take care of the essentials such as bathing and dressing? Is preparing breakfast part of the routine? What does the older adult do all day in terms of activities and interests? What are the highlights of the day as well as those times that are challenging? An older adult's description of the activities of the day can give the social worker wonderful insights as to how an older adult views his or her strengths and challenges as well as providing a general overview of the quality of his or her life. The information shared during this part of the assessment also serves as a valuable segue to questions that come later in the assessment.

COMPONENTS OF A COMPREHENSIVE ASSESSMENT

Most social service agencies have a standard protocol for conducting assessments including the format that the written evaluation should take. A specific format for the assessment is not provided in this chapter but all of the topic areas usually included in an assessment protocol are presented. The discussion of these domains focuses on general questions the social worker might ask that can be used in conjunction with the standardized assessment measures presented in Chapter 2 of this handbook.

Physical Health

In the very beginning of the assessment, the social worker should be acutely aware of any sensory limitations of the older adult. Difficulty in hearing or seeing can compromise the integrity of the entire assessment. Older adults who have a hearing loss may nod and appear to hear you but fail to answer questions appropriately, give inaccurate answers, or ignore questions completely. If an older adult is self-conscious about a hearing loss he or she may deny it exists, making communication very frustrating. Accurately assessing the presence of vision impairment is equally important. A person with sight loss may squint or tilt his or her head or reach out for items in plain sight quite tentatively. He or she may bump into chairs and tables. Hearing and vision impairments often put older adults at high risk for social isolation, one of the most critical challenges

facing older adults (Lubben & Gironda, 2003; Nicholson, 2012).

Although only a physician or nurse can professionally evaluate an older adult's health, it is important to obtain basic medical information about the older adult early in the assessment process. The social worker should match his or her observations about the older adult's physical health against what are considered expected changes associated with the physical aging process. The social worker's first impression of the older adult's health, the observation of any mobility limitations, the presence of instability while walking, and any obvious damage from a stroke or accident are most often a significant part of the first assessment of physical health (Tabloski, 2010). Asking whether the older adult sees a healthcare provider on a regular basis (and for what) as well as getting a list of medications (prescription and over the counter) he or she is taking is critical to understanding physical well-being. Are there any injuries that seem suspicious, as might be the case if the older adult is being physically abused?

It is important to ask an older adult how he or she rates his or her own health. Does he consider himself healthy? What would she identify as major health concerns? What health conditions prevent him or her from doing things he or she would like to do? Self-assessment gives the social worker very powerful insights as to what health limitations the older adult defines as problems and which are simply inconveniences. In other words, what do the physical health problems mean to the older adult, if anything? Clearly some older adults are immobilized both physically and psychologically by what one might consider relatively minor health problems. Others can have very serious health challenges that they hardly seem to notice. Ferri et al. (2009) suggest that an older adult's *perception* of their health status is more important than his or her actual health status.

Competence in Activities of Daily Living

Activities of daily living include the basic tasks of self-care such as eating, toileting, ambulating and transferring, bathing, dressing, and grooming. These functional abilities are influenced by the physical and psychological status of the older adult as he or she interfaces with the demands of everyday living. The inability to perform any of these basic tasks suggests the need for support services and in some cases a more structured living situation. It is critical to ask about each of these activities. Is he or she able to complete the activity with some assistance?

Instrumental activities of daily living are more complicated tasks than ADLs, yet remain basic skills necessary to managing an independent household. These activities include using the telephone, shopping, food preparation, housekeeping skills, independent transportation, administration of medication, and money management. The ability to complete each IADL is assessed on the basis of how much assistance the individual needs ranging from "needs no assistance" to "is not able to complete." Competence in the ADLs and IADLs is among the most important determinant of an older adult's functionality, the key to interpreting an assessment.

In assessing any level of activity, the social worker needs to balance the older adult's response to the question of his or her ability to complete the tasks with a direct observation of whether the older adult's self-assessment is accurate. However, a word of caution is indicated. While self-assessment of one's abilities may be an accurate predictor of mortality and functional ability (Idler & Benyamini, 1997), more frequently self-rating is inaccurate (Fastame & Penna, 2013; Faul et al., 2009; Ferri et al., 2009; Lichtenberg, 2012). As discussed earlier, accurately admitting one's limitations may have very serious consequences, thus there may be a disincentive to being totally honest in identifying limitations.

Psycho-Emotional Functioning

Compiling an accurate picture of an older adult's psycho-emotional well-being starts at the moment the social worker begins interacting with him or her. While talking to the older adult about physical health and functional abilities, the social worker should begin to get a preliminary idea of how he or she is able to process and answer questions, recall factual information, and carry on a logical and coherent conversation.

Even brief conversations can provide insights into an older adult's emotional health as indicated by affect and emotional stability. Ask how the older adult has handled stress in his or her life. What have been the greatest joys or disappointments in life? Does the older adult feel he or she has changed much

since earlier years? The answers will give the social worker insight as to how the older adult is able to mobilize problem-solving skills and maintain mastery in life, indicators of one's personality. How does he or she stay mentally active? How well does the individual feel he or she handles problem solving? Considered basic functional intelligence, problem solving is a trait independent of both education and crystallized intelligence.

An older adult's personal assessment of his or her memory is important to understanding any deterioration in memory function. Does the older adult feel memory loss is more of a problem recently than it was in the past? Does the older adult repeat stories or facts without an awareness of having said something before? An older adult may simply take more time to process a question requiring memory retrieval so the question is more one of speed than ability to remember. Try to determine whether the older adult is concerned about the memory loss, unaware of it, or just accepts it as part of the aging process. Assessing for the presence of dementia may be part of this process if indicated.

Does the older adult appear to be sad or have a flat affect? Does his or her language reflect self-deprecating remarks or a negative self-image? Does the older adult appear openly anxious or depressed? Has the older adult ever considered suicide in a difficult emotional time? What kind of emotional "energy" does the older adult emit (or not)? Observations about these emotional states offer the social worker important insights into the emotional well-being of the older adult.

Social Functioning

The purpose of assessing social functioning is to determine what, if any, social activities the older adult does participate in or would like to and to determine whether there are social supports that can be mobilized to meet social needs. Does the older adult feel lonely or feel alone? Would he or she like more (or less) social interaction? Fewer social supports correlate with higher levels of depression (Vanderhorst & McLaren, 2005). Social functioning may also be deeply affected by losses in the older adult's support system, so it is important to ask about recent (or remote) losses. Who helps the older adult with shopping or running errands (instrumental social support)? Whom does the older adult rely on if he or she needs someone to talk to or is upset (emotional social support)? The presence of even one close emotional friend can help an older adult ease the pain of loneliness and continue to feel connected to others. The ultimate assessment of social functioning is determined by comparing how much social interaction an older adult has with how much he or she wants (Lubben & Gironda, 2003).

Religion and Spirituality

An older adult's spirituality can be an important source of support and has been associated with better mental health, an enhanced ability to cope with life events and improved self-esteem (Nelson-Becker, Nakashima, & Canda, 2006). The social worker should ask specific questions about the older adult's religion, such as What level of involvement does the older adult have with a faith tradition? Does he or she want a stronger connection to a faith community? Spirituality is a broader concept than religion and includes what gives the older adult meaning in his or her life or what gives them hope. It also includes how an older adult might find comfort and connection in thinking about a "greater power," regardless of how that is defined. How does the older adult express that spirituality? How does the older adult's sense of spirituality act as a support in difficult times? Applying spirituality to practice with older adults is explored in depth in Chapter 7 in this handbook: "Spirituality in Professional Practice with Older Adults."

Sexuality

Sexual activity, per se, may or may not be of interest to an older adult. In cases where an older adult is experiencing chronic health challenges or physical limitations, sexual activity may not be possible or may be well beyond the immediate interests of the older adult. The social worker might state "Despite health problems, many older adults continue to be sexually active. Is that important to you?" The older adult's answer will suggest whether the social worker should follow up with other questions about sexual activity, including a question about safe sex. Regardless of sexual activity, sexuality, defined as sexuality, understood to include both gender identity and sexual orientation, remains important regardless of health status. It is important not to assume an older adult is straight, gay, lesbian,

bisexual, or transgendered and to ask directly whether his or her sexual orientation is important to understanding who he or she is. Sexual orientation is particularly important when actual service delivery decisions are made, as some older adults may not be comfortable with service providers who are not comfortable with gay, lesbian, bisexual, or transgendered clients.

Environmental Safety

Falls can be a life-changing event for an older adult, and many falls occur in an older adult's home because of hazards in his or her living space (Pynoos, Steinman, Nguyen, & Bressett, 2012). Assessing the safety of the environment includes observing the general repair of the home or apartment and identifying conditions that need attention to prevent injury from falls or other household mishaps.

Check the living space for furniture, rugs, or clutter in walkways that could cause an older adult to trip and fall. Look for drapery and electrical cords that are difficult to see and easy to stumble over. Do stairs have handrails? Is the home equipped with smoke and carbon monoxide detectors? Does the older adult have an emergency alert device that connects with the local police or fire departments or a hospital if assistance is needed? Does the older adult appear to "hoard" items such as trash, food, or pets? Does the older adult feel safe in the neighborhood? Are there adequate locks on the doors and windows? Too few? Too many?

Using Collaterals to Gather Information

A comprehensive biopsychosocial assessment should include some information gathering from collaterals including family members, friends, and neighbors in some cases. It is important that the older adult both gives you permission to speak with others and knows that you will be asking others about him or her. Family members who have ongoing contact with the older adult can be helpful in identifying those areas in which an older adult is maintaining a high level of functioning and those areas that present a challenge to him or her. How has the older adult changed in the past 6 months or year? Was there a precipitating event such as an illness or a loss that contributed to a loss in functioning? Have there been specific changes in mood, cognitive abilities, or social involvement? Be aware that families have lifelong, unresolved familial issues, and be sensitive to personal agendas that may skew the accuracy of responses. Other collaterals such as lifelong friends, physicians, clergy, or even the postal carrier may have insights that help the social worker clarify strengths and challenges and older adult may face in his or her daily life.

A Final Word on Assessments

By its nature, an assessment requires social workers to ask very personal questions that may be uncomfortable for both client and worker. Personal questions must be asked with exceptional sensitivity and patience on the part of the social worker. Resistance and even hostility can be expected when an older adult has to admit to difficulties and limitations. Any sensitive area should be explored only when it has a direct bearing on the request for services or eligibility for those services. If an older adult asks why certain information is needed, be prepared to tell him or her.

The comprehensive assessment process offers the social worker a valuable opportunity to gather as much information as possible about the older adult in preparation for identifying services and supports that can help the older adult maintain his or her independence. The process and the product of a biopsychosocial assessment should always reflect the importance of self-determination and preserving individual dignity as critical values of the social work profession.

REFERENCES

Chapin, R., Nelson-Becker, H., & Macmillan, K. (2006). Strengths-based and solution-focused approaches to practice. In B. Berkman (Ed.), *Handbook of social work in health and aging* (pp. 789–796). New York: Oxford University Press.

Fastame, M. C., & Penna, M. P. (2013). Does social desirability confound the assessment of self-reported measures of well-being and metacognitive efficiency in young and older adults? *Clinical Gerontologist, 36,* 995–112. doi:10.1080/07317115.2012.749319.

Faul, A. C., Yankeelov, P A, Rowan, N. L., Gillette, P., Nicholas, L. D., Borders, K. W., ... Wiegand, M. (2009). Impact of geriatric assessment and self-management support on community dwelling older adults with chronic illnesses. *Journal of Gerontological Social Work, 52,* 230–249. doi:10.1080/01634370802609288

Ferri, C., James, I., & Pruchno, R. (2009). Successful aging: Definitions and subjective assessment according to older adults. *Clinical Gerontologist, 32,* 379–388. doi:10.1080/07317110802677302

Folstein, M. F., Folstein, S. E., & McHugh, P. R. (1975). Mini-Mental State: A practical method for grading the cognitive state of patients for the clinician. *Journal of Psychiatric Research, 12,* 189–198.

Grady, M. D., & Drisko, J. W. (2014). Thorough clinical assessment: The hidden foundation of evidence-based practice. *Families in Society, 95*(1), 5–14. doi:10.1606/1044-3894.2014.95.2.

Idler, E., & Benyamini, Y. (1997). Self-rated health and morality: A review of twenty-seven community studies. *Journal of Health and Social Health and Social Behavior, 38,* 21–37.

Katz, S., Down, T., Cash, H., & Grotz, R. (1970). Progressive development of the Index of ADL. *The Gerontologist, 10,* 20–30.

Lawton, M. P., & Brody, E. M. (1969). Assessment of older people: Self-maintaining and instrumental activities of daily living. *The Gerontologist, 9*(3), 179–186.

Lichtenberg, P. A. (2012). Misdiagnosis of Alzheimer's disease: Case studies in capacity assessment. *Clinical Gerontologist, 35,* 42–56. doi:10.1080/07317115.2011.626516

Lubben, J. E. (1988). Assessing social networks among elderly populations. *Journal of Family and Community Health, 11*(3), 42–52. doi:10.1097/00003727-198811000-00008

Lubben, J. E., Blozik, E., Gillmann, G., Iliffe, S., Kruse, W. R., Beck, J. C., & Stuck, A. E. (2006). Performance of an abbreviated version of the Lubben social network scale among three European community-dwelling older adult populations. *The Gerontologist, 46,* 503–513. doi:10.1093/geront/46.4.503

Lubben, J. E., & Gironda, M. W. (2003). Centrality of social ties to the health and well being of older adults. In B. Berkman & L. Harootyan (Eds.), *Social work and health care in an aging works: Education, policy, practice, and research* (pp. 319–350). New York, NY: Springer.

McInnis-Dittrich, K. (2014). *Social work with older adults: A biopsychosocial approach to assessment and intervention.* Boston, MA: Pearson.

Moore, D. J., Palmer, B. W., Patterson, & Jeste, D. V. (2007). A review of performance-based measures of functional living skills. *Journal of Psychiatric Research, 41,* 97–118. doi:10.1016/j.jpsychires.2005.10.008

Nelson-Becker, H., Nakashima, M., & Canda, E. (2006). Spirituality in professional helping interventions. In B. Berkman (Ed.), *Handbook of social work in health and aging* (pp. 797–807). New York: Oxford University Press.

Nicholson, N. R. (2012). A review of social isolation: An important but underassessed condition in older adults. *Journal of Primary Prevention 33*, 137–152. doi:10.1007/s10935-012-0271-2.

Pinsker, D. M., Pachana, N. A., Wilson, J., Tilse, C., & Byrne, G. (2010). Financial capacity in older adults: A review of clinical assessment approaches and considerations. *Clinical Gerontologist, 33*, 332–346. doi: 10.1080/07317115.2010.502107

Pynoos, J., Steinman, B. A., Nguyen, A., & Bressett, M., (2012). Assessing and adapting the home environment to reduce falls and meet the changing capacity of older adult. *Journal of Housing for the Elderly, 26*, 137–155. doi:10.1080/02763893.2012.673382

Rose, A. L., & Cheung, M. (2012). DSM-5 Research: Assessing the mental health needs of older adults from diverse ethnic backgrounds. *Journal of Ethnic and Cultural Diversity in Social Work, 21*, 144–167. doi:10.1080/15313204.2012.6743437

Russell, D.W. (1996). UCLA Loneliness Scale (Version 3): Reliability, validity, and factor structure. *Journal of Personality Assessment, 66*, 20–40.

Sheikh, J. I., & Yesavage, J. A. (1986). Geriatric Depression Scale: Recent evidence and development of a shorter version. *Clinical Gerontologist, 5*, 165–173.

Sherbourne, C. D. & Steweart, A. I. (1991). The MOS Social Support Survey. *Social Science and Medicine, 32*, 705–714. doi:10.1016/0277-9536(91)90150-B

Tabloski, P. A. (2010). *Gerontological Nursing* (3rd Ed.). Upper Saddle River, NJ: Prentice-Hall.

Vanderhorst, R. K. M., & McLaren, S. (2005). Social relationships as predictors of depression and suicidal ideation. *Aging and Mental Health, 9*, 517–525.

Standardized assessments are systematic protocols used to gather information using well-defined standard elements and procedures, often yielding information about multiple domains of functioning and well-being. *Standardized measures* go a step beyond assessment to yield scores to describe various attributes of older people and their worlds.

Acronyms for types of measures and specific widely used tools have become a common language for communication within and across professional groups in aging services, though it must seem mysterious jargon to clients. For example, ADL (i.e., the ability to perform activities of daily living; Katz et al., 1963), IADL (instrumental activities of daily living; Lawton & Brody, 1969), and MSQs (mental status questionnaires, a class of measures used to screen for cognitive ability) are well-understood terms in geriatric care teams, as are abbreviations for common measures.

In the early 1980s, this author critiqued assessment tools in aging and coauthored a volume with many measures included (R. A. Kane & Kane, 1981). Preparing an update 20 years later, R. L. Kane and Kane found an exponential increase in measures and in constructs or domains being measured and generated a much longer edited reference book (R. L. Kane & Kane, 2000). By the mid 2010s, creating print compendia of frequently used measures seemed futile—there were too many with too many versions, and they were updated too often. Thus, this chapter contains no copies of measures, and references are offered illustratively rather than for endorsement as "best measures."

ROSALIE A. KANE

Standardized Assessments and Measures in Geriatric Practice

SOCIAL WORK AND STANDARDIZED ASSESSMENT

Social workers often belong to multidisciplinary teams that use standardized tools to assess all clientele. They may be responsible for completing psychological and social portions of the standardized protocol; they may be responsible for completing the whole tool for use of the entire team; or they may use data from an assessment tool completed by a non-social worker, perhaps a nurse. Because of the profession's expertise in establishing rapport and conducting interviews and their frequent responsibility for intake, social workers frequently conduct the entire protocol even in areas outside their scope of practice. Whatever portions social workers complete,

2

they must take the task seriously, scrupulously avoiding introducing bias into collection of data on which they and all team members should be able to rely.

In clinical research, measures are used to establish baseline states, to measure outcomes of interventions, and to adjust results by differences at baseline (known as case-mix differences). In more basic research, measures are used to study inter-relationships among various phenomena. Versions of commonly used assessments are embedded in standardized publicly funded population surveys, occasioning issues when descriptive and epidemiological surveys are updated. If measures are changed, comparisons from earlier dates are compromised, yet failure to change measures to reflect new approaches may limit future information.

Sometimes social workers develop tools to measure outcomes of interest to them. If so, they must adhere to conventional approaches in identifying items, field-testing instruments, establishing their psychometric properties (such as reliability and scalability), testing validity, and establishing norms. Generally, social workers should avoid developing measures unless a thorough search reveals no appropriate extant instruments. But if the scales used by a practice team do a poor or incomplete job of describing phenomena or outcomes of interest to social work practice, then new measures may be needed.

Formal Measurement Properties

Reliability

Reliability means that measures yield consistent information over time and across multiple assessors. *Intra-assessor* reliability means the same rater gets the same results in successive measurement efforts, if the older persons are unchanged in the interim. *Inter-assessor* reliability means that several assessors get the same results when assessing the same individual or phenomenon. When measures entail observations of physical settings or client interactions, raters can simultaneously complete protocols and reliability of results can be tested. With interviews, the interviewer's manner and approach and their interaction with the older person may affect responses. Training and periodic reliability checks can reduce variability and increase reliability. Using a standardized assessment protocol with rigor (e.g., asking questions as written, in the order written, and without skipping items) while maintaining the warmth, rapport, and empathy takes training, experience, and discipline (King, 1997).

Internal scale reliability or *scale consistency* means that the items consistently are associated with each other in a coherent scale. This property is usually measured by item-scale correlation of items, often expressed by a Cronbach's alpha statistic. Factor analysis may be used to eliminate items and improve scale reliability. The goal is high internal reliability (close to .8) but not total convergence.

Validity

Validity refers to the capacity of a measure to accurately reflect the attribute intended to be measured. A measure may be reliable but not valid; an inaccurate bathroom scale may be reliably wrong, and so, too, can the professional judgments or scale results be consistent but inaccurate. Reliability is necessary but not sufficient for validity.

Face validity is a commonsense consideration of whether the scale's items measure what it purports to measure and fully cover the construct measured. *Concurrent validity* means the measure is highly correlated with another previous measure of the same construct. *Discriminant validity* is achieved if the measure correctly identifies those with the trait from those without; for example, a measure of depression applied to a mental health clinic population discriminates if it correctly identifies those with a diagnosis of depression but not those without depression. *Predictive validity* refers to the measure's ability to predict the older person's future status. For example, the single item asking persons to rate their health on a 5-point scale has high predictive ability if those who rate their health as fair or poor have higher mortality 6 months later than those who rate their health using more positive choices.

OTHER DISTINCTIONS AMONG MEASURES

Sources of Information

Information for assessment may come directly from the older person, or from various proxies including family members and paid caregivers. Assessments from proxy respondents are more reliable if the matters assessed are objective and the person responding is in a position to know.

Certainly people with dementia should not be automatically eliminated because they have measurable cognitive impairment. Many seniors with substantial cognitive impairment can reliably and meaningfully provide the information for assessment of their own status, particularly when the domains concern attitudes, opinions, and feelings rather than actual facts about recent activity (Brod, Stewart, Sands, & Walton, 1999; Logsdon, Gibbons, McCurry, & Terri, 1999).

Some well-established tools can approximate mood among those who cannot report it. For example, the MOSES (Multidimensional Observation Scale for Elderly Subjects) yields measures of depression and anxiety and social dimensions like engagement and relationships, based on ratings of a staff member who observes the person for a week. Items are detailed and specific (e.g., how often did X talk about being depressed, look depressed, sound depressed; or how often did X respond to social contacts, how often did he/she initiate social contacts?), and the response categories are based on the number of days the observation was made and the frequency of the behavior on those days (Helmes, Csapo, & Short, 1987). Although rapidly completed, this tool engenders more confidence than simple ratings of whether people are anxious, depressed, or socially engaged. In another example, the Apparent Affect Rating Scale (AARS) is completed by making multiple 5-minute observations of the older person's facial expression to gauge happiness, sadness, anger, anxiety, and engagement (Lawton, Van Haitsma, & Klapper, 1996). Apparent Affect Rating Scale assessors can be trained using videos to achieve high inter-rater reliability. Similarly, numerous measures, sometimes based on detailed observation, are used to identify and classify aggression and agitation among older people with dementia. The Cohen-Mansfield Agitation Inventory (CMAI) (Cohen-Mansfield, Marx, & Rosenthal, 1989) and the Agitation Behavior Mapping Instrument (ABMI) (Cohen-Mansfield, Werner, & Marx, 1989) are well tested, available in many languages, and used worldwide in efforts to establish nonpharmacological treatments for dementia.

Time Reference Point

Assessments must have a time reference; for example, "right now," in the past week, in the past month, in the past 6 months, or "ever in your life." The choice of time frame is important and should be based on the frequency of the measured phenomenon and its nature. If we used "past week" for visits of family, we might misstate family involvement in visiting a nursing home, and if we used "past year" to get information on the ability to dress oneself, we would lose focus on, say, the immediate post-stroke period.

Recording Formats Versus Measures

Some systematic assessments widely used in gerontology are not measures but systematic formats for recording data. The Minimum Data Set (MDS), now federally mandated for assessments at intervals for all nursing home residents, began as such a systematic recording tool (Morris et al., 1990), but gradually came to include post hoc measures and then direct measures. Table 2.1 describes how measures evolved from this standardized assessment and describes its evolving uses and significance). Other examples of a standardized approach to assessment developed to provide systematic information rather than scores include various assessments of values and preferences, such as the Preferences for Everyday Life Inventory (PELI) (Van Haitsma et al., 2013), and tools to assess work with client strengths, such as the Strengths Inventory (Kivnick & Murray, 2001) and the Occupational Profile (Kivnick & Stoffel, 2005).

Scoring

Scores provide a convenient way of summarizing assessment measures. Once scores come into common usage, however, they tend to be treated as though they have objective meaning. Thus, scales should not be chosen by their name alone; the items, response sets, and instructions used to achieve that score should be scrutinized. Two competing impulses are present in scoring assessment batteries: the urge to consolidate and the urge to differentiate, sometimes referred to as *lumping* versus *splitting*. The lumpers may seek a single score to measure a complex, multidimensional construct such as quality of life or psychological well-being, whereas the splitters may prefer to consider a host of subscores. For overall or subscale scores, it may be necessary to weight (or assign more points to) some items as more important than others to the concept measured.

TABLE 2.1 Case Study: Evolution of the Nursing Home MDS and the Social Work Connection

Purpose	• Originally intended to ensure accurate resident assessment as required in federal regulation.
	• MDS now used to select residents for state & federal inspections, to develop case-mix-adjusted payment systems that consider the time involved in a resident's care; and to generate national quality measures that are available electronically to consumers and advocates.
History	• The mandate for the MDS was part of nursing home regulatory reform in 1987.
	• Two iterations of an assessment protocol were developed, MDS 1.0 and MDS 2.0, and by 1999 all nursing homes were required to submit their MDS assessments electronically on a quarterly basis (for some items), annually, and on major change of condition. A "who's who" of measurement experts were part of the initial development under contract with RTI International and many subcontractors.
	• Gradually items were added to the MDS to incorporate the work with posthospital patients receiving rehabilitation, and assessment intervals were added.
	• The current iteration, MDS 3.0, was developed under contract with RAND Corporation and became effective in the fall of 2010.
Standardization	• The Centers for Medicare & Medicaid Services (CMS) provide detailed User Manuals with instructions for all items.
	• A registered nurse is responsible for signing off on all MDS assessments, and typically nursing homes employ an MDS coordinator who directs the process of completing the required items in a timely fashion.
	• Various staff members may be designated to complete MDS sections, but when rating ADL, IADL, behavioral problems, and other such items they are expected to draw their information from consultation with staff on all shifts.
	• MDS 3.0 varied from earlier iterations by containing sections assessing resident preferences, cognitive functioning, depression and mood, pain, and expectation of return to the community by direct interview with residents—the manual specifies when direct interviews may be deemed impossible.
Scores	• MDS began as a standardized way to gather information without scoring.
	• Scales were retroactively developed from the rating data to measure cognitive performance (Morris et al., 1994), social engagement (Mor et al., 1995), and ADL functioning.
	• MDS 3.0 not only includes scales derived from professional raters but also incorporates established measures, including the Brief Interview for Mental Status (BIMS) (Saliba et al., 2012) and a self-reported resident mood measure, the Patient Health Questionnaire (PHQ9) (Kroenke, Spitzer, & Williams, 2002).
Social work roles	• Nursing home social workers often complete MDS sections—typically, they complete sections on social functioning, mood, problem behaviors, resident preferences, and return to the community items. They sometimes do other sections such as ADL functioning.
Issues	• MDS reflects substantial public investment.
	• MDS is now used for multiple purposes, some of which create perverse incentives that may affect the assessment.
	• Although difficult to change, MDS has gradually changed over its 25 years of use.
	• MDS illustrates a publicly funded group of measures that are found in many sectors and are likely to increase over the next decades as care settings become more computerized.
	• Social work practitioners in multiple settings—hospitals from which most nursing home residents are admitted, nursing homes, and HCBS settings to which many resident are discharged—have a stake in the accuracy and adequacy of the MDS tool. These measures influence large components of social work practice with seniors.

ASSESSMENT DOMAINS

Assessment domains refers to the topics or areas to be assessed. In the late 1970s, R. A. Kane and Kane (1981) reviewed standardized assessments in just five domains: physical functioning (referring to abilities to conduct basic and more complex ADLs); physical health; psychological well-being; cognitive functioning; and social functioning. In a sequel about two decades later (R. L. Kane & Kane, 2000), the caveats on the use of assessments were unchanged, but the number of assessment tools available in gerontology and geriatrics had increased dramatically and the number of domains for which serious measurement was available had also multiplied. Domains reviewed by the various contributors included function, health and physiological well-being, cognition, emotions, social functioning, quality of life, values and preferences, satisfaction, religiosity and spirituality, family caregivers, and physical environments. Measurement issues in selected domains are briefly discussed in what follows.

Physiological and Health Domain

This general domain historically comprised lists of symptoms and active and past diagnoses, measures of healthcare use (e.g., hospital days, doctor visits), measures of time unable to perform usual activities because of health, use of common prosthetic and mobility devices, and self-rated health (this single item being an excellent predictor of mortality). Tools are available to screen for and objectively classify common clinical problems or risk factors, such as, among other examples, fall risk (Tinetti, 1986), nutritional status (Pendergast et al., 1989), pressure sores (Goldstone, 1982), delirium (Inouye et al., 2003), and quality of sleep (Hays & Stewart, 1992).

Many tools are now available to measure pain and discomfort. Some type of adjectival rating or visual analog for the subject to rate intensity of pain is typically used along with frequency ratings. Because people with dementia who exhibit aggressive or disturbing behavior are often thought to be suffering from pain of various kinds that they cannot express, the work on an observational pain measure for dementia, PAINAD, is particularly promising (Warden, Hurley, & Volicer, 2003).

Functional Measures

Measures of functional status include measures of basic self-care ADLs, and measures of more complex IADLs. The ADLs usually include bathing, dressing, using the toilet, getting in and out of a chair or bed (called transferring), and eating. Sometimes ADL tools include other items (e.g., grooming, continence), and sometimes they further differentiate among items (dressing can be subdivided into upper and lower body dressing, and eating can be divided into drinking from a cup and eating with a fork and spoon). Some ADL tools tap a lower level

of functioning and examine differential functioning among those confined to their bed. The most common ADL tool was developed by Katz as a 6-item dichotomous rating and later refined in various ways—for example, dropping continence and expanding response options (Katz et al., 1963). More elaborate ADL assessments are used to guide rehabilitation programs, such as the Barthel Index (Mahoney & Barthel, 1965) and the Functional Independence Measure (FIM) (Kidd et al., 1995).

The IADLs typically include functioning at tasks such as cooking, cleaning, laundry, using the telephone, taking medications, driving a car, and using a bus or other transportation. A large number of tasks could be used in an IADL measure. As a measure of outcomes, functional status assumes paramount importance because maintaining, improving, or slowing decline in functioning is a major goal of many services for older people. As an independent variable—that is, something that might influence the outcomes being measured—functional status is almost as ubiquitous as the inevitable age, gender, marital status, and ethnicity as a case-mix adjustor—that is, a way of controlling for variation among the clientele.

With so many tools to measure ADLs, the selection of a specific tool is less important than determining the definitions one is using, the time frame, and the decision rules. Functional measures can be directed at performance (what people actually do) or at capability (what they say that are capable of doing). The ADLs can be based on best performance or average performance in a time period. They can take into account pain, speed, or reported difficulty as criteria for judging that the person can perform the function. Some functional assessors may require that cleaning or dressing be performed to a certain standard of competence. Some tests of functioning involve actual demonstrated performance. Given all these nuances, assessors must choose their strategy carefully based on the purpose of the measure and describe in detail the procedures used and the wording of the stem questions.

Cognitive Functioning

The challenge of measuring cognitive abilities of seniors has resulted in a plethora of instruments, some brief screening tools and others more elaborate. Subdomains of cognition include recent memory, remote memory, attention, judgment, calculation, and problem solving. Tools to measure cognitive functioning have often been developed by and for the use of clinical psychologists. As such, they often entail demonstration of abilities, and their norms and psychometric properties are usually known. Instruments are less well developed to tap upper-level functioning, such as logic, creativity, and wisdom, but even here, some tools are available.

As with ADL measures, within limits, it may not matter which cognitive screening test is used; many are interchangeable, though some seem less likely to alienate the people being tested. Commonly used tools are the Mini-Mental State Exam (MMSE) (Folstein et al., 1975) and versions of the Blessed Test (Blessed, Tomlinson, & Roth, 1968). The MMSE was used extensively in geriatric assessment programs until copyright fees were enforced; then MMSE use dropped off as substitutes were found in the public domain. The Cognitive Performance Test based on the theory of disability of occupational therapist Claudia Allen is a particularly practical staging effort because of its ability to suggest the need for care and support based on the demonstrated performance of common household tasks (Burns & Mortimer, 1994). For example, at early stages, a person can make buttered toast (one of the tasks), including assembling the items needed in the kitchen; at another stage, the person can perform the task if the toaster, bread, and butter are laid out in plain sight; and at a still later stage, the person may be able to make toast if asked to do each subtask separately, and eventually cannot do it at all.

Emotions and Mental Well-Being

Over the past 20 years, question-and-answer tests to gauge emotional well-being have gained acceptance whereas, previously, exclusive reliance was placed on a clinical interview by a qualified mental health professional even for screening. Many domains can be specified for assessment of emotional functioning, including depression, anxiety, hopelessness, and anger, and positive domains such as hope, future orientation, and general psychological well-being. Among the many measures of depressive affect, the best ones overcome the challenge of relying on somatic manifestations of depression that may be associated with illness in old people. Older instruments have largely been supplanted by the Geriatric Depression Scale (Yesavage & Brink, 1983), the CES-D tool used in multisite population studies

(Radloff, 1977), and other recently developed tools. The Affect Balance Scale (Bradburn, 1969) counts both negative and positive emotions and generates two subscales. Another self-report tool that includes positive and negative emotions has been well tested with people with poor cognitive functioning (Brod et al., 1999). For morale and life satisfaction, the two most commonly used tools are variants of the Life Satisfaction Index (Neugarten, Havighurst, & Tobin, 1961) and the Philadelphia Geriatric Center Morale Scale (Lawton, 1972). To tap the positive end of psychological well-being, Ryff and Keyes (1995), developed short scales to tap dimensions such as mastery, sense of purpose, and self-esteem.

Social Functioning

Social functioning includes a wide range of phenomena. The available tools include measures of *social network* (i.e., the structure of a person's relationships and associations—see Lubben, 1988, and Lubben & Girondam, 2003, for examples developed by social workers), *social support* (the extent to which an individual is supported by that network (which is sometimes further divided into physical, emotional, financial, and social support), and *social activity. Social well-being*, which implies a value judgment, is much more difficult to measure as there is no unified body of theory that suggests the right blend of activity, stimulation, and relationships that constitutes social well-being. Moreover, this area is particularly sensitive to cultural and individual variation. The perception of meaningful relationships, of being loved by and loving others, of being trusted by and trusting others, seems pivotal to social well-being, and thus questions about the reciprocal presence of a confidante (someone you trust and turn to, someone who trusts and turns to you) are widely used.

Social functioning as a construct remains highly susceptible to societal values. Being busy and enjoying interaction with others is generally viewed as better than being alone, but many people enjoy solo tasks like reading and doing puzzles. Whereas there is growing evidence to suggest that having someone with whom to relate (even a pet) has some protective effect, it is unreasonable to argue that the level of protection increases with the number of friends. There has been little convergence on satisfactory measures to tap domains of great interest to social work, such as productive aging (sometimes conceptualized as a blend of activities in the labor force, volunteer activities, activities within family, and activities that involve creative expression). Also needed are measures of social integration—that is, participation of older people in the larger community. Other important domains of social functioning amenable to measurement include sexual well-being, occupational well-being, financial well-being, elder abuse, and the list goes on.

Religiousness and Spirituality

Although spiritual well-being has come to be considered a fourth dimension of well-being (along with the physical, psychological, and social spheres identified by the World Health Organization), we have made only small steps toward determining how to measure it. As independent variables, religion, religious practices, and religiosity have been measured. In contrast, spiritual well-being is typically a dependent variable that may or may not be related to religious observances.

Quality of Life

Quality of life (QOL) is a multidimensional construct that has been measured in a variety of ways. Most authorities agree that QOL is a summary of physical, psychological, social, and even spiritual well-being. Health-related quality of life (HRQOL) is contrasted to more general QOL. Further, QOL tools can be identified for specific diagnoses such as stroke, arthritis, and diabetes. Those exploring this topic are referred to three edited books on QOL for older people, which show the progression of thinking about this topic over time and offer a many examples (Abeles, Gift, & Ory, 1994; Birren, Lubben, Rowe, & Deutchman, 1991; Noelker & Harel, 2001).

Values and Preferences

Measures of values and preferences relevant to older people are underdeveloped, though it is encouraging that development of some of these tools is underway. The current practice climate that promotes consumer control and autonomy has enhanced the felt need for measures in this domain. Most of the instruments available, perhaps appropriately, are tools to systematically record information rather than to yield scores.

Satisfaction

Satisfaction is sometimes defined as experience compared with expectations. As such, it is hard to measure because human beings lower their expectations in response to bad experiences. Satisfaction measures often are biased toward the positive, though measurement experts have suggested ways to word items to achieve a greater distribution of responses. Specific tools have been developed to assess satisfaction with healthcare, living conditions, nursing homes, assisted living, and home care—for example, see Geron et al. (2000), who carefully constructed scales to measure four domains of home care satisfaction.

Personality

Personality traits are often difficult to distinguish from mood states and attitudes; the former are relatively fixed, whereas the latter are more likely to change with circumstances and interventions. Personality batteries, the province of psychologists, have been well developed for self-completed tests in younger people but many of the items pertain poorly to older people. Costa and McCrae (1988) have been associated with most work on personality measurement in elderly people—their tool, called the NEO because it originally measured Neuroticism, Extroversion, and Openness—has gone through many revisions and is somewhat of a gold standard but can be used only with permission of its developers. The Big Five personality measure assesses neuroticism, conscientiousness, extroversion/introversion, openness, and agreeableness (John, 1999). This writer and colleagues developed and tested a shortened version of the Big Five, capable of being administered in an interview to frail nursing home residents who could not use self-completed versions. We simplified and reduced items, removed workplace references, and used the anchoring phrase "thinking about the kind of person you have been in your whole life" to avoid getting responses based on current energy levels and capabilities (see Chapter 5 of the final project report, Kane, Pratt, & Schoeneman, 2004, at http://www.hpm.umn.edu/ltcResourceCenter/research/QOL/Final_Report_to_CMS_Volume_1.pdf).

Family Caregiving

Family caregiver measures are abundant. Initially, the main constructs measured were the burden of caregiving, itself a multidimensional construct including various types of burden. Examples include the Montgomery Burden Scales (Montgomery, Ganyea, & Hooyman, 1985); the Zarit Burden Scale (Zarit, Reever, & Back-Peterson, 1980), which is specific to the burden associated with care of a person with Alzheimer's disease; and the multiple short tools developed by Pearlin and colleagues (Pearlin, Mullan, Semple, & Skaff, 1990) to make operational the stress process related to family caregiver outcomes. The Hassles Scale captures the small inconveniences and negative effects of caregiving on a daily basis (Kinney & Stephens, 1989a), and the Uplifts Scale measures more positive effects of family caregiving (Kinney & Stephens, 1989b). Despite the many caregiving measures, some dimensions require development. First, little attention has been given to measuring the actual activities of family care and their intensity and duration. Second, insufficient measures have been developed to assess the care recipient's perspective on the caregiving experience.

Physical Environments

Systematic assessment of physical environments for older people should be an important area for social work, given the profession's focus on the person and the environment. Elaborate approaches are available, the best known being Moos's Multiphasic Environmental Assessment Protocol (Moos & Lemke, 1996), which in its entirety is often too difficult to apply even in research contexts. Some environmental tools have been developed specifically for the assessment of care units in nursing homes, especially special dementia care units; see the Therapeutic Environment Screening Scale (TESS) (Sloane & Mathew, 1990) and the Professional Environmental Assessment Procedure (PEAP) (Lawton et al., 2000). Cutler and colleagues (2006) developed less subjective ways of assessing environments in assisted living and in nursing homes, ways to measure the specific environment of each resident rather than average unit characteristics, and measures of conceptual environmental domains such as function-enhancing features, life-enriching features, controllability of environment, and privacy-enhancing attributes.

MOVING AHEAD—TRENDS AND RESOURCES

Predictably, ever more standardized measures will be used in geriatrics and gerontology, affecting the multidisciplinary and unidisciplinary practice of social workers. Likely, we will see more electronic formats for entering assessment data, calculating scores, and communicating results. As generations of seniors become more computer literate, we may see self-administration of electronic protocols. Governmentally mandated standardized assessments, such as the nursing home MDS described in Table 2.1; the home health tool, called the Outcome and Assessment Information Set (OASIS); and the many state measures used in home and community based services (HCBS) assessment, nursing home preadmission screening, and adult protective services. We can expect more precision in describing behavior and moods of people with dementia who cannot themselves communicate. Social workers will increasingly use the language of the measures and their classifications. This trend can be positive, though social workers should be mindful that concepts important to us may need to be measured more carefully to get the attention they deserve, and that the individual person must never get lost in the standardized measures.

Many measures developed by individual researchers are not copyrighted or are given out without restriction other than the author's request to be kept informed about work with the measure. Measures developed with public money almost always are in the public domain. Many measures are similar to each other and highly correlated—there should be no need to use copyrighted tools with fees for each time the measure is used.

If social workers are looking for measures, or are seeking to understand more about measures they are already using or considering using, what should they do? Books are likely to be out of date on the specifics of measures by the time they are printed, and journal articles are difficult for practitioners to access and typically tell a small part of the story of a particular tool. Fortunately, the Internet provides a great deal of information. Consider the following:

• Googling the name of the tool will likely result in a lot of material about its development and subsequent use. If you don't find the latter, probably it is not extensively used.

- The developers of particular tools such as the NEO personality measures, the Cohen-Mansfield Agitation Inventory, and the Ryff Scales of Psychological Well-being maintain a full record of the development and use of the tools on their own websites with actual tools in various iterations and instruction manuals often available.
- Many websites dedicated to types of tools are worth visiting. The Hartford Institute for Geriatric Nursing at New York University's School of Nursing sponsors a program to consult a geriatric nurse at http://consultgerirn.org/resources. This website is organized by specific geriatric conditions, and contains a great deal of information on tools, their properties, their scoring, and their use history. Since 2000, Brown University has sponsored a website with a toolkit of instruments to measure end-of life care at http://www.chcr.brown.edu/pcoc/toolkit.htm. The Family Caregiver Alliance publishes the Selected Assessment Measures: A Resource Inventory for Practitioners. The latest 2012 version is available online at https://caregiver.org/selected-caregiver-assessment-measures-resource-inventory-practitioners-2012. Of course, websites are uneven in their value, and subject to change, so the Web needs to be approached with some skepticism, but it is still the best resource.
- If you are interested in a particular tool, do not hesitate to contact its developer.

REFERENCES

Abeles, R. P., Gift, H. C., & Ory, M. G. (Eds.). (1994). *Aging and quality of life.* New York, NY: Springer.

Birren, J. E., Lubben, J. E., Rowe, J. C., & Deutchman, D. E. (Eds.). (1991). *The concept and measurement of quality of life in the frail elderly.* San Diego, CA: Academic Press.

Blessed, G., Tomlinson, B. E., & Roth, M. (1968). The association between quantitative measures of dementia and senile change in cerebral gray matter of elderly subjects. *British Journal of Psychiatry, 114,* 797–811.

Bradburn, N. M. (1969). *The structure of psychological well-being.* Chicago, IL: Aldine.

Brod, M., Stewart, A. L., Sands, L., & Walton, P. (1999). Conceptualization and measurement of quality of life in dementia: The Dementia Quality of Life Instrument (DQoL). *The Gerontologist, 39,* 25–35.

Burns, T., & Mortimer, J. A. (1994). The Cognitive Performance Test: A new approach to functional assessment in Alzheimer's disease. *Journal of Geriatric Psychiatry and Neurology, 7,* 46–54.

Cohen-Mansfield, J., Marx, M. S., & Rosenthal, A. S. (1989). A description of agitation in a nursing home. *Journal of Gerontology: Medical Sciences, 44,* M77–M84.

Cohen-Mansfield, J., Werner, P., & Marx, M. S. (1989). An observational study of agitation in agitated nursing home residents. *International Psychogeriatrics, 1,* 153–165.

Costa, J. P. T., & McCrae, R. (1988). Personality in adulthood: A six-year longitudinal study of self-reports and spouse ratings on the NEO PTY Inventory. *Journal of Personality and Social Psychology, 54,* 853–863.

Cutler, L. J., Kane, R. A., Degenholtz, H. B. Miller, M. J., & Grant L. (2006). Assessing and comparing physical environments for nursing home residents: Using new tools for greater specificity. *The Gerontologist, 45*(1), 42–51.

Folstein, M. F., Folstein, S., & McHugh, P. R. (1975). Mini-mental state: A practical method for grading the cognitive state of patients for the clinician. *Journal of Psychiatric Research, 12,* 189–198.

Geron, S. M., Smith, K., Tennstedt, S., Jette, A., Chassler, D., & Kasten, L. (2000). The Home Care Satisfaction Measure: A client-centered approach to assessing the satisfaction of frail older adults with home care services. *Journal of Gerontology: Social Sciences, 55,* S259–S270.

Goldstone, L. A. (1982). The Norton score: An early warning of pressure sores? *Journal of Advanced Nursing, 7,* 419–426.

Hays, R. D., & Stewart, A. L. (1992). Sleep measures. In A. L. Stewart & J. E. Ware (Eds.), *Measuring functioning and well-being: The medical outcomes study approach* (pp. 235–400). Durham, NC: Duke University Press.

Helmes, E., Csapo, K. G., & Short, J. A. (1987). Standardization and validation of the Multidimensional Observational Scale for Elderly Subjects (MOSES). *Journal of Gerontology, 42,* 395–405.

Inouye, S. K., Bogardus, S.T., Vitagliano, G., Desai, M. M., Williams, C. S., Grady, J. N., & Scinto, J. D. (2003). The burden of illness score for elderly persons (BISEP): Cumulative impact of diseases, physiologic abnormalities and functional impairments. *Medical Care, 41,* 70–83.

John, O. P. (1999). The "big five" factor taxonomy: History measurement and theoretical perspectives. In L. A. Pervin (Ed.), *Handbook of personality: Theory and research* (2nd ed., pp. 102–138). New York, NY: Guilford Press.

Kane, R. A., & Kane, R. L. (1981). *Assessing the elderly: A practical guide to measurement*. Lexington, MA: Heath.

Kane, R. A., Kling, K. C., Bershadsky, B., Kane, R. L., Giles, K., Degenholtz, H. B., . . . Cutler L. J. (2003). Quality of life measures for nursing home residents. *Journal of Gerontology: Medical Sciences, 58A,* 240–248.

Kane, R. A., Pratt, M., & Schoeneman, K. (2004). Measures, Indicators, and Improvement of Quality of Life in Nursing Homes: Final Report. White paper submitted to Centers for Medicare & Medicaid Services. Retrieved from: http://www.hpm.umn.edu/ltcResourceCenter/research/QOL/Final_Report_to_CMS_Volume_1.pdf.

Kane, R. L., & Kane, R. A. (Eds.). (2000). *Assessing older persons: Measures, meaning, and practical applications*. New York, NY: Oxford University Press.

Katz, S., Ford, A. B., Moskowitz, R. W., Jackson, B. A., & Jaffee, M. W. (1963). Studies of illness in the aged. The Index of ADL: A standardized measure of biological and psychosocial function. *Journal of the American Medical Association, 185,* 914–919.

Kidd, D., Stewart, G., Baldry, J., Johnson, J., Rossiter, D., Petruckevitch, A., & Thompson, A. J. (1995). The Functional Independence Measure: A comparative validity and reliability study. *Disability and Rehabilitation, 17,* 10–14.

King, C. (1997). Guidelines for improving assessment skills. *Generations, 21,* 73–75.

Kinney, J., & Stephens, M. A. P. (1989a). Caregiver Hassles Scale: Assessing the daily hassles of caring for a family member with dementia. *The Gerontologist, 28,* 328–332.

Kinney, J. M., & Stephens, M. A. P. (1989b). Hassles and uplifts of giving care to a family member with dementia. *Psychology and Aging, 4,* 402–408.

Kivnick, H. Q., & Murray, S. V. (2001). Life Strengths Interview Guide: Assessing elder clients' strengths. *Journal of Gerontological Social Work, 34,* 7–32.

Kivnick, H. Q., & Stoffel, S. A. (2005). Vital involvement practice: Strengths as more than tools for solving problems. *Journal of Gerontological Social Work, 46,* 85–116.

Kroenke K., Spitzer, R. L., & Williams J. B. (2002). The PHQ-9: Validity of a brief depression severity measure. *Journal of General Internal Medicine, 16,* 606–613.

Lawton, M. P. (1972). The dimensions of morale. In Kent, D.P., Kastenbaum, R., & Sherwood, S. (Eds.), *Research, planning and action for the elderly* (pp. 144–165). New York, NY: Behavioral Publications, Inc.

Lawton, M. P., & Brody, E. (1969). Assessment of older people: Self-maintaining and instrumental activities of daily living. *The Gerontologist, 9,* 179–186.

Lawton, M. P., Van Haitsma, K., & Klapper, J. (1996). Observed affect in nursing home residents with Alzheimer's disease. *Journal of Gerontology, 51B,* 3–14.

Lawton, M. P., Weisman, G. D., Sloane, P. D., Norris-Baker, C., Caulkins, M., & Zimmerman, S. I. (2000). Professional environment assessment procedure for special care units for elders with dementing illness and its relationship to the therapeutic environment schedule. *Alzheimer's Disease and Associated Disorders, 14,* 23–38.

Logsdon, R., Gibbons, L. E., McCurry, S. M., & Terri, L. (1999). Quality of life in Alzheimer's disease: Patient and caregiver reports. *Journal of Mental Health and Aging, 5,* 21–32.

Lubben, J. E. (1988). Assessing social networks among elderly populations. *Family Community Health, 11,* 45–52.

Lubben, J. E., & Gironda, M. W. (2003). Centrality of social ties to the health and well being of older adults. In B. Berkman, & L. K. Harootyan (Eds.), *Social work and health care in an aging world* (pp. 319–345). New York, NY: Springer.

Mahoney, F. I., & Barthel, D. W. (1965). Functional evaluation: The Barthel Index. *Maryland State Medical Journal, 14,* 61–65.

Montgomery, R. J. V., Gonyea, J. G., & Hooyman, N. R. (1985). Caregiving and the experience of subjective and objective burden. *Family Relations, 34,* 19–26.

Moos, R. H., & Lemke, S. (1996). *Evaluating residential facilities*. Thousand Oaks, CA: Sage.

Mor, V., Branco, K., Fleishman, J., Hawes, C., Phillips, C., Morris, J., & Fries, B. (1995). The structure of social engagement among nursing home residents. *Journal of Gerontology: Psychological Sciences, 50B,* P1–P8.

Morris, J. N., Fries, B. E., Mehr, D. R., Hawes, C., Phillips, C., Mor, V., & Lipsitz, L. A. (1994). MDS cognitive performance scale. *Journal of Gerontology: Medical Sciences, 49,* M174–M182.

Morris, J. N., Hawes, C., Fries, B. E., Phillips, C. D., Mor, V., Katz, S., . . . Friedlob, A. S. (1990). Designing the National Resident Assessment Instrument for nursing homes. *The Gerontologist, 3,* 293–307.

Neugarten, B. L., Havighurst, R. J., & Tobin, S. S. (1961). The measurement of life satisfaction. *Journal of Gerontology, 16,* 134–143.

Noelker, L. S., & Harel, Z. (Eds.). (2001). *Linking quality of long-term care and quality of life*. New York, NY: Springer.

Pearlin, L. I., Mullan, J. T., Semple, S. J., & Skaff, M. M. (1990). Caregiving and the stress process: An overview of concepts and their measures. *The Gerontologist, 30,* 583–594.

Pendergast, J. M., Coe, R. M., Chavez, M. N., Romeis, J. C., Miller, D. K., & Wolinsky, F. D. (1989). Clinical validation of a nutritional risk index. *Journal of Community Health, 14*, 125–135.

Radloff, L. L. (1977). The CES-D scale: A self-report depression scale for research in the general population. *Applied Psychological Measurement, 1*, 385–401.

Ryff, C. D., & Keyes, C. L. M. (1995). The structure of psychological well-being revisited. *Journal of Personality and Social Psychology, 69*, 719–727.

Saliba, D., Buchanan, J., Edlen, M. O, Streim, J., Ouslander, J., Berlowitz, D., & Chodosh, J. (2012), *Journal of the American Medical Directors Association, 13*, 611–617.

Sloane, P. D., & Mathew, L. J. (1990). Therapeutic environment screen scale. *American Journal of Alzheimer's Disease and Associated Disorders, 5*, 22–26.

Tinetti, M. E. (1986). Performance-oriented assessment of mobility problems in elderly patients. *Journal of the American Geriatrics Society, 34*, 119–126.

Van Haitsma K., Curyto, K., Spector A., Towsley G., Kleban M., Carpenter B., . . . Koren, M. J. (2013). The preferences for everyday living inventory: Scale development and description of psychosocial preferences responses in community-dwelling elders. *The Gerontologist, 53*, 582–595.

Warden, V., Hurley, A. C., & Volicer, L. (2003). Development and psychometric evaluation of the Pain Assessment in Advanced Dementia (PAINAD) scale. *Journal of the American Medical Directors Association, 4*, 9–15.

Yesavage, J. A., & Brink, T. L. (1983). Development and validation of a geriatric depression screening scale: A preliminary report. *Journal of Psychiatric Research, 17*, 37–49.

Zarit, S. H., Reever, K. E., & Back-Peterson, J. (1980). Relatives of the impaired elderly: correlates of feelings of burden. *The Gerontologist, 20*, 649–655.

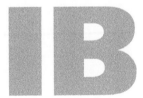

SECTION IB

Interventions

The phrase "cognitive-behavioral" embraces a broad range of therapeutic interventions, ranging from the complicated process of cognitive restructuring to relatively simple behavior management techniques employed in the validation approach. The common denominator of cognitive-behavioral interventions is the focus on the "meaning" of events and words in an older adult's mind and how that meaning influences subsequent emotional and behavioral responses. How events or words are perceived by the older adult determines how he or she feels and consequently behaves. Cognitive-behavioral approaches are used most often to treat mild to moderate forms of depression and anxiety in older adults, although the basic principles of these approaches have been adapted to treat more serious conditions such as bipolar disorder, post-traumatic stress disorder, and affective disorders in individuals with mild to moderate dementia (Sorocco & Lauderdale, 2011). This chapter specifically examines the therapeutic process and application of cognitive-behavioral therapy (CBT) and problem-solving therapy (PST), two evidence-based therapeutic approaches, to treating older adults. The validation approach, while not considered an evidence-based practice in social work intervention, offers a common-sense intervention technique based on cognitive-behavioral principles to manage difficult behaviors in older adults with mild to moderate dementia.

COGNITIVE-BEHAVIORAL THERAPY

Cognitive-behavioral therapy is based on the assumption that cognitive and behavioral responses to events are learned and can be unlearned or replaced by other learned responses (Adler, 1963; J. S. Beck, 1995; Ellis, 1962; James, 2010). This approach involves the process of identifying the relationship between events that occur in an individual's life that generate negative automatic thoughts. These automatic thoughts are the result of a negative view (or cognitive distortion) of one's self, the future, or the environment. Troublesome and self-defeating emotional responses follow such as depression, anxiety, or anger. These emotions may also initiate physiological or behavioral responses that are uncomfortable or destructive to the individual, the behavioral component of the CBT approach. Once an older adult recognizes the triggers for negative automatic responses

KATHLEEN MCINNIS-DITTRICH

Cognitive-Behavioral Interventions

3

that cause emotional and sometimes physical distress, new and more functional patterns of behavior can also be learned.

Cognitive-behavioral therapy is not used with older adults in treating mild to moderate depression or anxiety as frequently as it is used with other age groups. Unfortunately, the therapeutic community (and older adults themselves) may operate on the premise that depression is a normal consequence of the aging process rather than a treatable psychological condition (McInnis-Dittrich, 2014; O'Hara, 2000). There are also lingering Freudian perspectives suggesting that older adults' personality traits and behaviors are too rigid to respond to any kind of psychotherapy (James, 2010; Gallagher-Thompson & Thompson, 2010). In addition to these ageist attitudes, older adults' hesitancy to pursue mental health treatment when depressed or anxious, an overreliance on antidepressants by primary care physicians, and lack of training about its specific application to older adults may also contribute to the underutilization of this therapeutic approach (Berman & Furst, 2011; James, 2010).

An accurate diagnosis of depression or anxiety in an older adult is often challenging. Dementia, delirium, anxiety, and depression often mimic each other, and it may be difficult to clearly determine which of these conditions is present in an older adult (Anderson, 2001; Gallagher-Thompson & Thompson, 2010; McInnis-Dittrich, 2014). Assessment tools shown to be both reliable and valid in assessing older adults include the Beck Depression Inventory (BDI-II; A. T. Beck, Brown, & Steer, 1996), the Center for Epidemiological Studies Depression Scale (CES-D; Radloff, 1977), the Geriatric Depression Scale (GDS; Yesavage et al., 1983), and the Patient Health Questionnaire (PHQ-9; Kroenke & Spitzer, 2002). These tools have both strengths and limitations but are those traditionally used to identify depression and anxiety in older clients (Gallagher-Thompson & Thompson, 2010).

Identifying Older Adults Appropriate for Cognitive-Behavioral Therapy

Even with an accurate diagnosis, the use of CBT is not appropriate for use with all older adults. Late-onset (after age 60) maladaptive thinking and behavior appear to respond better to CBT than those thought

and behavior patterns reinforced from childhood or adolescence (O'Hara, 2000). It is most effective with older adults who are verbal, insightful, and have few, if any, cognitive impairments, even when such impairments are not due to dementia (McInnis-Dittrich, 2014). The ability to engage in abstract thinking and behavior analysis combined with a willingness to complete "homework" assignments are cornerstones of the CBT process. No matter how easily the clinician can see how cognitive distortions are causing the older adult to become depressed or anxious, it is the older adult's insight, not the therapist's that is necessary for an older adult to change emotional and behavioral responses to trigger events.

Cognitive-behavioral therapy has shown limited efficacy in work with older adults who are highly autonomous or have extreme difficulty asking for or receiving help (Mosher-Ashley & Barrett, 1997). Significant cognitive limitations, active abuse of drugs or alcohol, or an extensive history of suicidal behavior also contraindicate the use of CBT (Dautovich & Gum, 2011; Karlin, 2011). An older adult's poor physical health may or may not present an obstacle depending on whether the individual can tolerate the length of therapy sessions or the necessity of keeping behavior records between sessions (James, 2010).

The Cognitive-Behavioral Process

This chapter is not intended to be a detailed presentation of the protocol used in CBT but rather an overview of the therapeutic approach and how it can be adapted to use with older adults. Several excellent in-depth descriptions of CBT have been developed for the clinician who is interested in the specific use of this technique (Gallagher-Thompson & Thompson, 2010; James, 2010; Sorocco & Lauderdale, 2011).

A number of clinicians and researchers have adapted the CBT protocol for specific use with older adults, although the basic structure of this therapeutic technique is preserved in these adaptations (James, 2010; Gallagher-Thompson & Thompson, 2010; Mosher-Ashley & Barrett, 1997). The first stage in the process is the *preparation phase*, in which considerable time is devoted to developing the professional relationship between the older adult and the therapist. Developing a trusting professional relationship between an older adult and a therapist may take longer than with other age groups. This phenomenon is due, in part, to the older adult cohort's sociocultural beliefs about mental health counseling, the compounding influence of multiple losses in an older adult's life, and the past experience of having assumed more passive roles in health and mental health treatment (Reiser et al., 2007). In addition, the age difference between the older adult and the therapist may be significant, leading to the need to be especially sensitive to issues in transference and countertransference as the relationship develops (Gallagher-Thompson & Thompson, 2010). Older adults need to develop a clear understanding of the cognitive-behavioral process along with realis tic expectations of how CBT can help them change the emotional and behavioral responses to negative thought patterns during this phase.

In the *collaboration-identification phase*, the older adult is introduced to the process of identifying the relationships between events, thoughts, and feelings. The therapist explores those situations in which the older adult is aware of being depressed or anxious, helping him or her see how certain situations elicit such feelings based on what the older adult was thinking. For example, in the case of an older widow with mild depression, it is important for her to identify those times when she is acutely aware of her depressed feelings. She may identify Sundays as a particularly difficult time because she is alone on a day associated with family activities. While her son usually calls her on Sunday afternoons, if he does not, she spirals into painful feelings of sadness and of being unloved. She may be thinking "I am not important enough for my son to remember to call. He must not care about me. No one cares about me. Why am I alive if no one cares, not even my children?" In this case, the therapist explores the woman's negative automatic thoughts (I am worthless, ignored, or forgotten) to the event (lack of a phone call) and how those negative thoughts are creating an emotional response (sadness, depression, anger). With the guidance of the therapist, the woman can develop some level of insight into this chain of events. "Homework" that tracks the emotional journey of the older adult throughout the week is often helpful in sensitizing the client to these connections. Elaborate worksheets and suggested homework activities are available from other sources (Gallagher-Thompson & Thompson, 2010; Sorocco & Lauderdale, 2011).

Once events, feelings, and thoughts are identified by the older adult, the therapist can explore the behavioral reaction to this chain of events. For example, even though she welcomes the attention

from her son when he does call later in the week, she is hypercritical and argumentative with him (another behavioral response). When she is able to see that she may be trying to punish her son for his neglect but this unpleasant interaction may be exacerbating the problem of his not calling, she can begin to change the way she responds both emotionally and behaviorally. During this phase, depending on the client's goals, client and therapist may explore negative messages the older adult has received throughout his or her life stages, helping both to understand why reactions to relatively simple events can be so intensely negative. Many of the techniques and skills inherent to a purely psychodynamic approach can supplement the CBT approach in this phase of therapeutic work. Some older adults are interested in considering the origins of negative thinking and are willing to revisit past life experiences that have contributed to the development of that thought process. Others are decidedly not interested in revisiting and gaining insight about past relationships, events, and behaviors. They just don't want to be anxious or depressed at this point in their lives.

An important part of this phase of the CBT process involves helping the older adult examine cognitive distortions (James, 2010). One common form of cognitive distortion is extreme thinking. Examples applicable to the example above would include such statements as "He didn't call me, he doesn't love me, he wouldn't care if I died!" suggesting the woman can only see the extremes in what the lack of a phone call means. Another example of extreme thinking is a tendency for a client to set unrealistically high standards of behavior for others such as "I am his mother! He would call me every day if he really loved me!" Catastrophizing, predicting the absolute worst in every situation whether warranted or not, is considered extreme thinking as well ("He hasn't called today. He must have gotten in a car accident! I told him not to drive so fast!").

Other cognitive distortions include generalizing, in which the person sees a single negative event as evidence that everything is bad, or magnifying negative events at the expense of positive ones. Older adults can get fixated on jumping to conclusions ("He didn't call today. I bet my daughter-in-law won't let him talk to his own mother. I never did like her!") or interpreting another's behavior through the lens of self-reproach ("This is all my fault! I have been a terrible mother. And now as an adult, he is finally seeing that. There are so many things I should have done better with him."). Clearly, these are very simple illustrations of what cognitive distortions look like in client statements but they do demonstrate the range and intensity of distorted thinking as applied to the case under discussion. Left unchallenged, it is easy to see how an older adult can "think" themselves into chronic depression or anxiety. A depressed state can lead an older adult to withdraw and disengage from pleasurable events and interactions. Withdrawal from sources of pleasure and satisfaction reinforce the depressed state in a dangerous downward spiral, threatening both the emotional and physical health of an older adult.

At this point in CBT, the therapist explores how the client can begin the actual *behavioral change phase* of this work by exploring how she can employ corrective behavioral actions to prevent the development of depression as a response to these events. Instead of brooding all day because her son has not called, she can decide to become proactive, empowering herself to do something positive to make herself feel better. Rather than fixating on the thought "He doesn't love me." She can replace the negative automatic thought with "He must be very busy. I should call him and find out how he is doing." Taking such positive steps empowers her to regain mastery over her environment and stop the development of a depressed thought. This corrective action has the added advantage of making the interaction between mother and son more positive for both parties. If she is less difficult when he calls, perhaps he will call more.

In this phase of treatment, therapists often help older adults identify and increase (and in some cases restore) the presence of pleasurable activities in their lives. Part of the cognitive restructuring process involves intentionally substituting negative thoughts with an increase in pleasant experiences (Gallagher-Thompson & Thompson, 2010). That process may begin with simply identifying the kinds of activities an older adult finds pleasurable and increasing intentional use of those activities. As straightforward as that may sound, it is often hard for a depressed or anxious older adults to even recognize that some activities actually do give them pleasurable feelings. These activities may include the simple acts of reading a magazine, visiting with friends, or attending social events, and older adults can be guided to consider a wide range of sensorial and cognitively stimulating activities. The California Older Person's Pleasant Event Schedule (COPPES) has been developed to assist the older adult and the clinician in this identification process (Gallagher-Thompson & Thompson, 2010, p. 213).

The final phase of CBT is the *consolidation and termination phase*. The therapist's task is to consolidate the changes observed during the treatment process. Reviewing how far the older adult has come, discussing what strengths have developed in identifying emotions and thoughts, and reinforcing the belief that he or she can handle future challenges are all part of this process. An older adult needs to leave the therapeutic process confident that he or she has learned the skills to continue to fight depression or anxiety in the future. Termination may present a challenge to the therapist and an older adult client. This time in an older adult's life is fraught with multiple and compounded losses, making older adults particularly sensitive to the difficulty of ending a healthy therapeutic relationship (Karlin, 2011). It may take significantly longer to end the intervention, and therapists should be aware of the possibility of painful reactions on the part of the client.

Adjustments for Using Cognitive-Behavioral Therapy with Older Adults

Therapists experienced in using CBT with older adults recommend several adjustments to the therapeutic protocol (Gallagher-Thompson & Thompson, 2010; James, 2010; Karlin, 2011).

1. Slow down the pace of the therapeutic process both in one's speech and in discussing complex and abstract concepts to compensate for slower cognitive processing speeds present in many older adults. Obviously, do not insult the older adult with simplistic speech patterns. The point here is to give older adults time to process the abstract connections among thoughts, emotions, and behavior inherent to the process of CBT.
2. Use multiple modalities to reinforce concepts and ideas in CBT including whiteboards, written agendas for the therapy session, note cards, diagrams, and so forth. Multimodal presentations help reinforce learning and can be used by older adults in completing homework assignments.
3. Encourage note taking and keeping portfolios of homework and worksheets to serve as written reminders to older adults of work done in

the therapy sessions. Demonstrate the principles of the thought–behavior connection through role-plays or examples.

4. Provide a verbal bridge between therapy sessions to remind the older adult what was covered in the previous session and what will be covered in this session as a memory cue. This may be in the form of therapist and client summaries of what happened in previous sessions or what the therapeutic goals are for the intervention.

5. Redirect the older adult as necessary away from distracted storytelling that is not germane to the therapy issues at hand. Whether the older adult is distracted as a way to avoid confronting difficult material or just likes to tell stories, excessive amounts of this activity are not productive to the therapeutic effort.

6. Begin homework activities in the sessions with the older adult to clarify what you are expecting him or her to do between therapy sessions. If you are asking an older adult to keep an emotional "log" during the coming week, give numerous examples of what you mean and how such a log might look.

The Effectiveness of Cognitive-Behavioral Therapy with Older Adults

The effectiveness of CBT in reducing both anxiety and depression in older adults is widely supported in the mental health research (Arean, 1993; J. G. Beck & Stanley, 1997; Berman & Furst, 2011; Laidlaw et al., 2008; Scogin et al., 2007). O'Hara (2000) found CBT to be especially effective in reducing anxiety when it was combined with relaxation techniques. While working on correcting distortions in thinking, older adults benefited from the immediate anxiety-reducing influence of a variety of relaxation techniques.

Pinquart and Sorenson (2001) found that CBT was more effective in resolving issues in depression and anxiety among older adults than psychoeducational, activity promotion, and cognitive training approaches. Both CBT and psychodynamic approaches significantly improved an older adult's sense of well-being and the clinician's perception of the level of depression in the older adult. Pinquart and Sorenson (2001) suggest CBT is more effective

in the context of individual therapy as opposed to use in a group setting.

These researchers and others (Laidlaw et al., 2008; Zarit & Zarit, 1998) attribute CBT's success to the concrete problem-solving nature of the approach. Although problem-solving therapy (PST) may be incorporated into CBT, it also stands as its own unique therapeutic approach.

PROBLEM-SOLVING THERAPY

As simple as it may sound, the straightforward act of solving a situational or emotional problem using a rational, systematic, and sequential problem-solving model has shown to be an effective therapeutic approach to decreasing emotional stress and improving the quality of life in depressed older adults (Gellis & Bruce, 2009; Gellis & Kenaley, 2008). Problem-solving therapy is considered an evidence-based approach to addressing anxiety and depression in older adults, especially those patients who refuse antidepressants or have complicated medical problems that may contraindicate medication (Bell & D'Zurilla, 2009; Cuijpers, Van Straten, & Warmerdam, 2007; Gellis & Nezu, 2011). In view of the significant number of medications older adults already take, PST is a welcome nonpharmaceutical addition to cognitive-behaviorally based mental health interventions.

The simple goal of PST is to foster adaptive problem-solving *attitudes and behaviors* in older adults. Based on the theory of social problem solving, the "agency" derived from the personal confidence that one can solve problems effectively and having the skills to engage in rational problem solving is known to have a mediating and moderating role in the relationship between stressful life events and the development of depressive or anxious symptoms (Gellis & Nezu, 2011). All challenges facing an individual are viewed within a *problem orientation*, the psychological appraisal of, and emotional reaction to, the possible threat to one's well-being and the likelihood that one can find a solution to the problem. One's problem orientation can be negative or positive. Viewed in a negative orientation, problems such as changes in health, loss of friends to death, or loss of traditional work roles, pose major threats to one's well-being. The problems created by such life events not only can be overwhelming but also can be interpreted as beyond the individual's ability to solve. This frustration and lack of agency contributes to tendency for the older adult to become depressed or anxious.

However, if an older adult can learn to reframe these challenges as opportunities, not problems, and can employ a rational, constructive approach to identifying resources to meet those challenges, perhaps he or she can change the course of stressful events and his or her emotional reactions to the events. The agency created by the confidence in one's ability to meet life's challenges reduces the likelihood that an older adult will have a depressed or anxious response to life events. Gellis and Nezu (2011) see the therapeutic application of basic problem solving techniques as minimizing impulsivity and carelessness, increasing self-confidence in managing life events, and increasing rational goal setting in older adults. The development of these skills in older adults is believed to be a buffer against anxious or depressed feelings.

The Therapeutic Application of the Problem-Solving Model

Problem-solving therapy can be applied in individual clinical work with older adults as a collaborative, nonjudgmental approach to solving problems identified by the older adults, not the therapist. This approach is based on the assumption that the "consumer" of mental health treatment is in the best position to identify what issues he or she wants to address rather than responding to problem areas identified by a therapist. The PST approach serves as the basis for the evidence-based Program to Encourage Active, Rewarding Lives for Seniors (PEARLS), a short-term community intervention aimed at reaching community-dwelling older adults who are or are at high risk for depression (Berman & Furst, 2011). The PST protocol used by PEARLS consists of seven steps applied during each of eight sessions with an older adult (Ciechanowski et al., 2004):

1. *Clarify and identify the problem* including when and where a problem occurs.
2. *Set a realistic goal* that is achievable and has a clear outcome.
3. *Generate multiple solutions*, exploring through brainstorming many different possibilities for achieving the goal.
4. *Evaluate* or compare solutions, considering the pros and cons of each.
5. *Select a feasible solution* that has the best chance of achieving the goal identified by the older adults.
6. *Implement the solution* by identifying the specific steps necessary to put the solution into action.
7. *Evaluate the outcome* as in what worked well and what did not.

The problem-solving model is widely accepted as a way to approach challenges presented in many areas of social work practice and has been used throughout the profession's history as a rational approach to working with individuals, groups, and communities. What is unique about PST's application to older adults is teaching older adults a model for solving their own problems now and in the future. Rationally approaching a challenge and breaking down the solution into manageable steps is a continually applicable skill.

THE VALIDATION APPROACH

Although a cognitive-behavioral or problem-solving approach works well with older adults who still have moderate to high cognitive functioning, it is not recommended for addressing troublesome affect or behavior in older adults presenting with Alzheimer's disease or other dementias. One alternative therapeutic approach for this population is known as the validation approach. Unlike cognitive-behavioral approaches, the validation approach does not try to change the way an older adult interprets stimuli, thus changing his or her affective and physical responses to automatic negative thoughts. Rather, the validation approach tries to understand how the distorted thinking often associated with dementia is actually an older adult's attempt to communicate a need to those around him or her (Feil, 1996). Rather than attempt to reorient older adults with dementia to the correct time and space in their environment (the main focus of reality orientation) the validation approach communicates with the older adult by validating their feelings in whatever time or place is real to them (Day, 1997).

For example, if a widow with dementia keeps asking, "Where is my husband?" even though her husband has been dead for many years, the validation approach would suggest that this statement reflects the woman's need for something such as attention or affection. Rather than correct the woman by reorienting her that she is widowed and her husband gone, the validation response might be, "You must miss your husband very much" or "I know it must be frightening to be alone right now." Rather than interpret the person's statement as a reflection of her confusion, a validation approach interprets the statement as her expression of loneliness or grief that her husband is not with her. The therapeutic benefits of such a statement come from the empathetic, reassuring tone of the respondent and the lack of attempt to argue with or contradict the older adult. It can serve both as a distraction to the older adult to move him or her away from the troubling thought and as a way to minimize agitation. Not only does such an approach appear to de-escalate agitation in confused older adults but also it defuses the anger, resentment, and frustration of caregivers and family members constantly trying to reorient a confused older adult (Day, 1997). Often by the time a family member has "validated" an older adult's question or comment, the older adult has moved on to another topic, avoiding the agitated emotional state often associated with trying to communicate with others.

Is the Validation Approach Effective?

In her clinical social work practice, Feil (1993) did observe improved speech, less regression, less crying, less wandering behavior, and improvements in gait, interactions, and eye contact among older adults with dementia who were treated using the validation techniques. She also found less need for physical or chemical restraints due to the reduction in aggressive and violent behavior. Other observers found that older adults and their families were able to communicate more successfully during visits, resulting in less frustration on the part of both the older adult and the caregivers (Babins, Dillion, & Merovitz, 1988; Fine & Rouse-Bane, 1995). Anecdotal evidence supports the contention that the approach can be effective in defusing potentially catastrophic behaviors by older adults who are agitated, confused, and potentially violent to self and others (Fine & Rouse-Bane, 1995). The primary advantage of the validation approach is that is it relatively safe; no medication or restraints are needed.

However, controlled studies have no statistically significant connection between the use of a validation approach and improvements in behavior among older adults with dementia (Babins, Dillion, & Merovitz, 1988; Morton & Bleathman, 1991; Robb, Stegman, & Wolanin, 1986; Scanland & Emershaw, 1993). In the studies that both supported and refuted the effectiveness of validation as a therapeutic approach, very small, nonrandomized samples were used without matched control groups or the establishment of credible preintervention behavior baselines. Other critics feel that validation techniques contribute to deterioration in the remaining ability of older adults to reorient themselves when confused. The validation approach may have its greatest usefulness in responding to acute behavior problems, as long-term insight into the meaning of a behavior is not a goal (Mcinnis-Dittrich, 2014; Pietro, 2002).

SUMMARY

Therapeutic approaches directed toward correcting patterns of distorted thinking in older adults or empowering them with problem-solving skills offer reasonable alternatives to antidepressants in some older adults experiencing mild to moderate depression or anxiety. While not effective with all older adults, especially those with cognitive limitations imposed by dementias, CBT and PST are evidence-based interventions that can help develop long-term skills that older adults can take beyond the therapeutic setting. The validation approach, while not considered an evidence-based intervention, may offer a common-sense behavioral intervention that can be used by family members and professional helpers in managing responses to older adults with cognitive limitations. All three approaches are powerful illustrations of the connections between an older adult's thought patterns and subsequent behavior.

REFERENCES

Adler, A. (1963). *The practice and theory of individual psychology.* New York, NY: Premier Books.

Anderson, D. N. (2001). Treating depression in old age: The reasons to be positive. *Age and Ageing, 30,* 13–17.

Arean, P. A. (1993). Cognitive behavioral therapy with older adults. *Behavior Therapist, 16,* 236–239.

Babins, L., Dillion, J., & Merovitz, S. (1988). The effects of validation therapy on disoriented elderly. *Activities, Adaptation, and Aging, 12,* 73–86.

Beck, A. T., Brown, G., & Steer, R. A. (1996). *Manual for Beck Depression Inventory-II*. San Antonio, TX: Psychological Corporation.

Beck, J. G., & Stanley, M A. (1997). Anxiety disorders in the elderly: The emerging role of behavior therapy. *Behavior Therapy, 28*, 83–100.

Beck, J. S. (1995). *Cognitive therapy: Basics and beyond.* New York, NY: Guilford Press.

Bell, A. C., & D'Zurilla, T. J. (2009). Problem-solving therapy for depression: A meta-analysis. *Clinical Psychology Review, 29*, 348–353.

Berman, J., & Furst, L. M. (2011). *Depressed older adults: Education and screening.* New York, NY: Springer.

Ciechanowski, P., Wagner, E., Schmaling, K., Schwartz, S., Williams, B., Diehr, P., . . . LoGerfo, J. (2004). Community-integrated home-based depression treatment in older adults: A randomized controlled trail. *Journal of the American Medical Association, 291,* 1569–1577.

Cuijpers, P., van Straten, A., & Warmerdam, L. (2007). Problem solving therapies for depression: A meta-analysis. *European Psychiatry, 22*, 9–15.

Dautovich, N. D., & Gum, A. M. (2011). Cognitive behavioral therapy for late-life depression and comorbid psychiatric conditions. In K. H. Sorocco & S. Lauderdale (Eds.), *Cognitive behavior therapy with older adults: Innovations across care settings.* (pp. 125–156). New York, NY: Springer.

Day, C. R., (1997). Validation therapy: A review of the literature. *Journal of Gerontological Nursing, 23*, 29–34.

Ellis, A. (1962). *Reason and emotion in psychotherapy.* New York, NY: Stuart.

Feil, N. (1993). *The validation breakthrough.* Baltimore, MD: Health Professions Press.

Feil, N. (1996). Validation: Techniques for communicating with confused old-old persons and improving their quality of life. *Topics in Geriatric Rehabilitation, 11*, 34–42.

Fine, J. I., & Rouse-Bane, S. (1995). Using validation techniques to improve communication with cognitively impaired older adults. *Journal of Gerontological Nursing, 21*, 39–45.

Gallagher-Thompson, D., & Thompson, L. W. (2010). *Treating late-life depression: A cognitive-behavioral therapy approach.* New York, NY: Oxford University Press.

Gellis, Z. D., & Bruce, M. L. (2009). Problem solving therapy for subthreshold depression among home health care patients with cardiovascular disease. *American Journal of Geriatric Psychiatry, 18*, 464–474. doi:10.1097/JGP.ob013e3181b21442.

Gellis, Z. D., & Kenaley, B. (2008). Problem solving therapy for depression in adults: A systematic review. *Research on Social Work Practice, 18*, 117–131.

Gellis, Z. D., & Nezu, A. M. (2011). Integrated depression care for homebound medically ill older adults: Using evidence based problem solving therapy. In K. H. Sorocco & S. Lauderdale (Eds.) *Cognitive behavior therapy with older adults: Innovations across care settings* (pp. 391–420). New York, NY: Springer.

James, I. A. (2010). *Cognitive behavioural therapy with older people: Interventions for those with and without dementia.* London, England: Kingsley.

Karlin, B. E. (2011). Cognitive behavioral therapy with older adults. In K. H Sorocco & S. Lauderdale (Eds.) *Cognitive behavior therapy with older adults: Innovations across care settings* (pp. 1–30). New York, NY: Springer.

Kroenke, K., & Spitzer, R. L. (2002). The PHQ-9: A new depression diagnostic and severity measure. *Psychiatric Annals, 32*, 1–7.

Laidlaw, K., Davidson, K., Toner, H., Jackson, G., Clark, S., Law, J., . . . Cross, S. (2008). A randomized controlled trial of cognitive behavior therapy vs. treatment as usual in the treatment of mild to moderate late-life depression. *International Journal of Geriatric Psychiatry, 23*, 843–850.

McInnis-Dittrich, K. (2014). *Social work with older adults: A biopsychosocial approach to assessment and intervention* (4th ed.). Boston, MA: Pearson.

Morton, I., & Bleathman, C. (1991). The effectiveness of validation therapy in dementia: A pilot study. *International Journal of Geriatric Psychiatry, 6*, 327–330.

Mosher-Ashley, M., & Barrett, P. W. (1997). *A life worth living: Practical strategies for reducing depression in older adults.* Baltimore, MD: Health Professions Press.

O'Hara, B. (2000). Cognitive-behavioral treatment of anxiety in late life from a schema-focused approach. *Clinical Gerontologist, 22*, 23–36.

Pietro, M. J. S. (2002). Training nursing assistants to communicate effectively with persons with Alzheimer's disease: A call to action. *Alzheimer's Care Quarterly, 3*, 157–164.

Pinquart, M., & Sorenson, S. (2001). How effective are psychotherapeutic and other psychosocial interventions with older adults? A meta-analysis. *Journal of Mental Health and Aging, 7*, 207–243.

Radloff, L. S. (1977). The CES-D Scale: A self-report depression scale for research in general population. *Applied Psychological Measurement, 1*, 385–401.

Reiser, R., Truong, D., Nguyen, T., Wachsmuth, E., Marquett, R., Feit, A., & Thompson, L. W. (2007). Cognitive behavioral therapy for older adults with bipolar disorder. In D. Gallagher-Thompson, A. Steffen, S. Eperstein, & W. Thompson (Eds.), *Handbook of cognitive behavioral therapies with older adults* (pp. 249–263). New York, NY: Springer.

Robb, S. S., Stegman, C. E., & Wolanin, M. O. (1996). No research versus research with compromised results: A study of validation therapy. *Nursing Research, 35,* 113–118.

Scanland, S. G, & Emershaw, L. E. (1993). Reality orientation and validation therapy: Dementia, depression, and functional status. *Journal of Gerontological Nursing, 19,* 7–11.

Scogin, F., Morthland, M., Kaufman, A., Burgio, Chaplin, W., & Kong, G. (2007). Improving quality of life in diverse rural older adults: A randomized trial of a psychological treatment. *Psychology and Aging, 22,* 657–665.

Sorocco, K. H., & Lauderdale, S. (2011). *Cognitive behavior therapy with older adults: Innovations across care settings.* New York, NY: Springer.

Yesavage, J. A., Brink, T. L., Rose, T. L., Lum, O., Huang, V., Adey, M., & Leirer, V. O. (1983). Development and validation of a geriatric depression screening scale: A preliminary report. *Journal of Psychiatric Research, 17,* 37–49.

Zarit, S. H., & Zarit, J. M. (1998). *Mental disorders in older adults: Fundamentals of assessment and treatment.* New York, NY: Guilford Press.

ROBERTA R. GREENE
JOYCE RILEY

Family and Group Interventions

Despite the dramatic demographic changes known as the longevity revolution and the demonstrated need, older adults continue to receive inadequate mental health care. Mental health professions, including social workers, far too frequently ignore the grand-parental generation, viewing aging as a time of decline. Practitioners also have tended to discount the utility of therapy with older adults, arguing that treatment is not efficacious (Newton, Brauer, Gutmann, & Grunes, 1986; Schneider & Kropf, 1992). Furthermore, professionals continue to debate how to overcome the lag existing in practice, research, education, policy, and planning (Council on Social Work Education [CSWE]/SAGE/SW, 2001; Gatz, 1995). Moreover, research about what therapies work with older adults and their families is just emerging, including information on health, mental health, and social role (Cummings & Kropf, 2009; Table 4.1). At the same time, the allocation of resources to support caregiving families has always been routine among social work practitioners.

Ironically, research about the caregiving process has "flourished, [leading to] an intense concern about its economic, social, and psychological impact" (Pearlin, Mullen, Semple, & Skaff, 1990, p. 583). The information garnered has countered practice trends. The burgeoning of information about the impact of caregiving, and the increased recognition that informal caregiving is a typical family experience, has propelled practitioners and theorists alike to seek interventions that might alleviate caregiver stress (Toseland & Rossiter, 1989). Consequently, family therapy and group treatments have become more commonplace. That is, practitioners have gradually adopted or modified traditional family and group clinical social work approaches thought to be effective with the general population for use with frail older adults and their caregivers. By the mid-1980s, a growing interest in caregiver support began to close the gap between what is known about family functioning and clinical practice (Greene, 2008b). This chapter discusses the development and nature of those social work family and group interventions.

CAREGIVING

Caregiving involves attending to the health, social, and personal care needs of people who are lacking some capacity for self-care. It encompasses the functional capacities of older adults, the caregiving

TABLE 4.1. Effective Interventions With Late Life Social Roles

Chapter	Social Support/ Psycho-Educational Groups	Psychotherapy or Wellness Groups	Individual/Family Psychotherapy	Case Management/ Interdisciplinary Team
End of Life	Enhanced social adjustment of bereaved spouses by reducing depression, and helping to cope	Increased engagement of bereaved spouses by improving role function and mental health		Improved satisfaction and symptom management,
Family Caregivers	Decreased depression and anxiety for caregivers, decreased behavior problems for care recipients, improved caregiver affect, increased caregiver knowledge of resources	Increased general well-being	Decreased/delayed institutionalization of care recipient	
Grandparent Caregivers	Reduced loneliness and isolation by increasing access to services, increasing grandparent skills, and enhancing technology proficiency			Improved grandparent functioning, mental health, access to resources, satisfaction with services
People with DD and Caregivers	Increased future planning, improved caregiver skills, better knowledge for people with DD, and enhanced leisure choices and life satisfaction		Increased family ability to plan for future care issues	Increased future planning efforts and access to services

Adapted from: Cummings, S., & Kropf, N. (2009). Handbook of psychosocial interventions with older adults: Evidence-Based approaches. MA: Routledge. P. 340.

patterns of families, and the use of community-based services (Greene, Dalin, & Lebow, 1991). Daatland (1983) has proposed that family caregiving be seen as a form of social organization that includes the interpersonal relationships and the division of practical tasks: "a truly collective action, depending upon direct and indirect contributions from a number of actors, including the cared for himself" (p. 1).

It is a well-known fact that the majority of older adults who need assistance are cared for by a family member (AARP, 2011). The family transition to providing care for an older adult has become so widespread that Brody (1985) called this phase of the life course "normative family stress" (p. 25). At the same time, as family size among baby boomers shrinks, the availability of family caregivers may be of concern (AARP, 2011).

Caregiving tasks may include direct personal care, such as bathing and grooming, and indirect care, such as cooking, cleaning, and running errands. When an older adult has an acute or chronic illness, caregiving tasks may encompass simple forms of medical treatment such as injections. Usually, a primary caregiver—often a wife,

daughter, or daughter-in-law—assumes major responsibility. The generation of mostly women with direct caregiving responsibilities for two generations is called the sandwich generation; they juggle the responsibilities of mother-caregiver, daughter-caregiver, and worker (Marks, 1998; Stephens, Franks, & Townsend, 1994). In addition, other family and friends, especially male relatives, may assume instrumental caregiving responsibilities, including bill paying (Hash, 2003).

Providing care for an older frail relative is complex and often involves rewards and risks. Rewards include feelings of being useful, appreciated, and satisfied with one's caregiving. Caregivers may also develop a sense of altruism and competence and have the opportunity to share feelings of love and empathy with the care recipient (Toseland & Smith, 2001). In addition, caregivers not only derive benefits, but can maintain resilience (Greene, 2008b). Risks thought to stem from the stress experienced in caregiving may include restrictions on the caregiver's activities, social isolation, reduced paid employment, and emotional difficulties such as depression and anxiety (Toseland & Smith, 2001).

Uncertainty about the older adult's illness or disability as well as the costs associated with such needs as special diets may also increase risks. Still another source of stress for caregivers is having to make end-of-life decisions for the care recipient (Smerglia & Deimling, 1997).

INTERGENERATIONAL FAMILY INTERVENTIONS

Social work practice with older adults and their caregivers is based on knowledge that came to the fore in the 1970s and 1980s about intergenerational family functioning, filial relationships, and the biopsychosocial processes of aging. Theorists who defined inter-generational family dynamics contest the idea that there is a totally isolated nuclear family. Rather, they suggest that family dynamics involve the connecting link between generations based on loyalty, reciprocity, and indebtedness (Boszormenyi-Nagy & Spark, 1973). Research studies on the topic consistently reveal the financial, physical, and emotional reciprocity across generations, taking the form of telephoning, visiting, writing, and showing respect and concern. Care was also found to vary due to cultural factors associated with race/ethnicity, including differences in parent–child relationships and family hierarchy (Lee & Sung, 1998). Diversity dimensions may also include size of household, intergenerational contacts and family support exchanges, gender, cohort group, and socioeconomic status (Tennstedt & Chang, 1998).

Following suit, family therapists suggested that therapy is indicated when a family experiences disagreements about autonomy issues or when the family experiences hidden and unresolved conflicts between generations (Greene, 1989). Autonomy issues encompass the balance between independence and dependence within the family; unresolved conflicts include unsettled scores or arguments. Moreover, it was noted that multigenerational conflicts often arise because of challenges to the family's long-standing interaction patterns, involving a shift in role transitions and family structure (Davey, Murphy, & Price, 2000; Newton & Lazarus, 1992).

Systems theory is frequently used to explore how people interact as a unit, particularly their structure and organization as a group. Systems theory assumes that a family is a functioning whole, with each person in constant interplay with another. Family dynamics is composed of these mutual influences and refocuses

a practitioner's concerns on the here-and-now interactions that provoke difficulties. A family systems approach to family interventions offers the social worker a number of other useful guidelines:

- Assumes the family is a system with unique and discernible structure and communication patterns.
- Defines the boundaries of the family membership and cultural forms.
- Develops a picture of family structure, power relationships, and how roles are differentiated.
- Examines communication patterns to learn about the rules and cultural patterns.
- Determines how responsive the family is to stress as well as its ability to restructure to meet caregiving demands. (Based on Greene, 2008b, p. 224)

The ecological perspective is also used to better understand how a family relates with other social systems. The perspective is based on Bronfenbrenner's (1979) conceptualization of person–environment fit. The ecological perspective lends itself to multisystemic analysis of how client families function and the consideration of what resources may support their endeavors. For example, practitioners work with small-scale microsystems (such as families and peer groups), the connection between systems known as mesosystems (such as the family and healthcare systems), exosystems (the connections between systems that do not directly involve the person, such as Social Security and Medicare), and macrosystems, or overarching large-scale systems, such as legal, political, and value systems.

Social work practice from an ecological perspective focuses on what Gitterman and Germain (1976) termed problems of daily living. It also underscores the need for social workers to promote everyday competence among older adults (Willis, 1991). Research on environmental press suggests that caregiving responsibilities have the potential to negatively affect the mental and physical well-being of the caregiver, be disruptive to marital and family relationships, and cause problems in meeting work and other social responsibilities (Pearlin, Aneshensel, & Leblanc, 1997). These research models make the distinction between primary and secondary stressors. Primary stressors are those associated with the necessities of the caregiving role, such as coping with the behaviors associated with dementia. Secondary stressors are more peripheral to or outside the caregiving role and may involve social or workplace issues of the sandwich generation. Such stressors in caregiving often precipitate families contacting social services agencies. From the ecological perspective, the social worker would determine how well the family fits with the environment, with a view toward ascertaining resource needs; choose intervention strategies congruent with a client's environmental and cultural context; direct interventions at any aspect of the ecosystem; and base interventions on client strengths and expertise (Greene & Barnes, 1998).

INTERVENTION MODELS

Models of geriatric healthcare are based on designs that promote optimal functioning among elders. At the core of this care process are comprehensive assessments used to gather a wide array of information about the quality of an older adult's biopsychosocial functioning (McInnis-Dittrich, 2002). The social worker evaluates the client's capacity to function effectively in his or her environment and to ascertain what resources are needed to improve interpersonal functioning (Greene & Sullivan, 2001). The purpose of the biopsychosocial assessment is to assess functional capacity or everyday competence: the ability of older people to care for themselves, manage their affairs, and live independent, quality lives in their communities (Willis, 1991). The assessment may also include a diagnostic workup, which is an in-depth medical and physical evaluation (McInnis-Dittrich, 2002).

Models of Family Intervention

During the 1980s and 1990s, social workers developed models for working with older adults and their family caregivers. These included the family case management approach for Level I needs (Greene & Kropf, 2009), the auxiliary function model (Silverstone & Burack-Weiss, 1983), and the functional age model of intergenerational family treatment (Greene, 1986, 2001, 2008b).

The family case management approach is a process of assisting families with multiple needs, helping them cope with stress and issues related to the use of multiple service providers (Table 4.2). "The goals of family case management are to mobilize a family's strengths, to marshal resources, and to maximize family functional capacity" (Greene & Kropf, 2009, p. 85). The social worker first engages the family in a

helping relationship and then works with the family to develop and carry out a mutual care plan.

The auxiliary function model (Silverstone & Burack-Weiss, 1983) proposes that the major problems facing frail, impaired older adults are not disease or old age, but the effects these conditions may have on mental and physical functioning. The proponents of this model contended that therapy should be based on a supportive relationship and designed to counter the factors associated with depletion or loss. The major goal of the social worker in this model of intervention is to combat a family's feelings of helplessness in the face of its multiple losses, that is, to convey a sense of hope.

Another example of family-focused intervention is the functional age model of intergenerational family treatment (Greene, 1986, 2001, 2008b). This model can be used to examine caregiving risk and well-being from a systems perspective; it is an approach used to promote a family's caregiving capacity. The model suggests that the social worker understand the "family as a mutually dependent unit with interdependent pasts and futures" (Greene, 2008a, p. 20). As such, it employs a systems approach to intervene with families whose older relative is experiencing interference in performing activities of daily living—those skills that are called on to meet environmental demands. The model comprises assessment and intervention strategies in two domains: the functional age or biopsychosocial functioning of the older adult (Birren, 1969) and the role allocation and life course development of the family.

Functional Age

The central part of the functional age model is the social worker's assessment of the functional age or capacity of the older adult. Functional age is composed of three spheres related to adaptational capacity:

1. Biological age, referring to a client's health-related issues, such as chronic disease, medication effects, and physical concerns, such as energy levels. Decrements in memory, cognition, and judgment also are included in biological age.
2. Psychological age, encompassing affective and rational processes, such as mood, and thought processes, encompassing introspection and the meaning of events.
3. Social age, referring to the role one plays in the social structure, including norms, values, culture, and ethnicity.

TABLE 4.2. Key Features of Family-Focused Social Work Case Management

Family-focused social work requires that the case manager

- Identify the family as the unit of attention
- Assess the frail or impaired person's biopsychosocial functioning and needs within a culturally sound family context.
- Write a mutually agreed on family care plan.
- Refer client systems to services and entitlements not available in the natural support system.
- Implement and coordinate the work that is done with the family.
- Determine what services need to be coordinated on behalf of the family.
- Intervene clinically to ameliorate family emotional problems and stress accompanying illness or loss of functioning.
- Determine how the impaired person and family will interact with formal care providers.
- Integrate formal and informal services provided by the family and other primary groups.
- Offer or advocate for particular services that the informal support network is not able to offer.
- Contact client networks and service providers to determine the quality of service provision.
- Mediate conflicts between family and service providers to empower the family when it is not successful.
- Collect information and data to augment the advocacy and evaluation efforts to ensure quality of care.

Source: Vourlekis and Greene (1992, p. 12).

Family

Along with the assessment of functional age, the social worker also develops an understanding of the family's adapting and coping capacity. The family is viewed as a social system with a high degree of interdependence and interrelatedness (however obscure) that is challenged when an older member has a crisis in functional capacity. The family is assessed from two perspectives:

1. The family as a set of reciprocal roles, including the expectations members share concerning behaviors in a certain situation, such as what a "good" older child does for his or her parent.
2. The family as a developmental unit, referring to the tasks expected of the family as a mutual aid system.

Family development emphasizes that family relationships are more than a combination of individual life cycles. Rather, family members' life stages are intertwined, with the effects of membership, including births, marriages, and deaths, introducing family change over time (McGoldrick, Carter, & Garcia-Preto, 2010).

Group Interventions

Because many older adults are more socially isolated than they were in their younger years, a group approach provides the therapeutic effect of group dynamics (McInnis-Dittrich, 2002). This reaffirmation of the human connection is based on the long-standing tradition of social group work with vulnerable older persons (Saul, 1983) and continues today in efforts of narrative gerontologists and others (Crimmens, 1998; Webster, 2001).

There are a variety of groups appropriate to work with older adults, using an array of theoretical frameworks, such as Yalom and Leszcz's (2005) existential perspective. According to McInnis-Dittrich (2002), group methods may have to be adjusted to account for elders' physical and sensory limitations. The group leader may have to take a more active role, and the pace may be slower. Group interventions may take several forms: group psychotherapy (Zarit & Knight, 1996), based on psychodynamic theory and intended to help clients gain insight; reality orientation groups (Greene, 2008b), based on cognitive frameworks and designed to combat confusion and disorientation among elderly persons; support groups, based on the strengths perspective and intended to share solutions for common problems (Cox & Parsons, 1994); and reminiscing groups, based on Eriksonian life stages and aimed at recalling the past to settle past concerns.

Support Groups

Support groups are based on mutual aid and often provide information about a specific illness (Table 4.3). Support groups for caregivers take many forms and

TABLE 4.3. Forums for Educating and Training Caregivers

Community Workshops and Forums

Provide information about community services, usually single sessions lasting an hour to a day; often sponsored by health and human services organizations.

Lecture Series and Discussion

Lectures given by clinical experts on topics of interest to specific groups of caregivers.

Support Groups

Allows for mutual sharing of information, usually unstructured, and encourages reciprocal and self-help among group members.

Psychoeducational and Skills-Building Groups

Educates members usually in short-term, structured groups by teaching specific problem-solving and coping skills and sharing information about caregiving resources.

Individual Counseling and Training

Focuses on the individual caregivers' needs, helping them deal with the emotional and coping skills needed to be effective in the role and to handle the stresses of caregiving.

Family Counseling

Helps the family system deal with issues related to caregiving that will allow them to sustain the care recipient and maintain family balance and cohesiveness; often connects the family with other resources in the community.

Care Coordination and Management

Educates caregivers on how to perform caregiving roles more effectively and on how to connect with formal caregivers.

Technology-Based Interventions

Uses telephone-mediated groups, computer-mediated groups, and video conferencing to educate and train caregivers.

Source: Toseland and Smith (2001, pp. 10–12).

can reduce caregiver stress by providing a caregiver with respite; reducing loneliness; promoting ventilation of emotions; sharing feelings in a supportive environment; validating, universalizing, and normalizing thoughts, feelings, and experiences; instilling hope; affirming the significance of the caregiver role; educating caregivers about the aging process, resources, or health and disability topics; teaching problem-solving and coping strategies; and fostering the caregiver's capacity for problem solving (Hash, 2003, p. 223).

Reminiscing Groups

One of the most common theoretical frameworks used in group work with older adults and their caregivers is the reminiscing group format. Life review is based on Erikson's (1950) approach to the eighth stage of development, in which the developmental tasks involve resolving the crisis of integrity versus despair. Robert Butler (1963), one of the founding group of geriatric psychiatrists, believed that Erikson's approach provided the insight necessary to frame a life cycle psychiatry to guide psychotherapy

with older adults. He contended that life review is "a progressive return to consciousness of past experiences in an attempt to resolve and integrate them" as well as a means of coming to terms with past conflicts and relationships (p. 65).

Based on his research at the National Institute of Mental Health and his private practice, Butler (1963, p. 237) came to believe that the "possibilities for intrapsychic change may be greater in old age than at any other period in life." He also thought that through therapies that define and seek opportunities, older adults come to terms with life, bear witness, find reconciliation, and achieve integration and transcendence.

Since the inception of Butler's life review therapy, the intervention has been applied with individuals, families, and groups. Its use with families can create a therapeutic milieu in which members can resolve conflict that may accompany various role changes in adulthood, such as shifts in responsibility involved in caregiving (Greene, 1983). There is some evidence that the use of reminiscence therapy can enhance family coping strategies (Comana & Brown, 1998).

Reminiscing groups with older adults can produce or enhance a cohort effect. That is, older adults
find their historical connection and share accomplishments, tribulations, and viewpoints. The purpose may be to support social functioning, uncover
and resolve unconscious conflicts, or ascribe new
meaning to old events (Greene, 2008b). Groups usually consist of no more than 10 people and may be
run for a short period (10 weeks or less) or for as
much as a year. Review content may be prompted by
using visual or artistic devices such as videos, plays,
or drama (Hargrave, 1994).

CONCLUSIONS

Although a number of group and family interventions are now seen as effective, the longevity revolution presses the profession to think about the
aging process and caregiving in a broader context
(Corman & Kingson, 1996; Kiyak & Hooyman, 1999;
Silverstone, 2000). That expanded context embraces
alterations in attitudes toward aging, an increasing
empirically based gerontological knowledge base,
and changing family forms (Bengtson, Giarrusso,
Silverstein, & Wang, 2000; Greene, 2005).

From a research perspective, numerous studies
have emphasized the role of caregiving in reducing
institutional placements. Few studies have examined the effects of programmatic interventions such
as support groups. The strongest research efforts to
date have focused on caregiver burden, stress, and
strain. According to Cairl and Kosberg (1993, p. 86),
this research has provided information on the (1) the
nature and scope of burden or stress experienced by
the caregiver; (2) the variance in the experience of
burden relative to the type of relationship of the caregiver to the frail elderly or the involvement in external
supports; and (3) the potential consequences of the
experience of burden with regard to caregiver tolerance and, more specifically, the propensity to institu-
tionalize. Cairl and Kosberg argue that although this
tradition of research offers a clear picture of caregiver
stress, it does not offer an understanding of whether
burden results in decreased capacity. The baby
boomer generation and information about successful aging compel practitioners to consider caregiving
issues differently (Noonan & Tennstedt, 1997; Rowe
& Kahn, 1998; Stull, Kosloski, & Kercher, 1994). The
negative emphasis on caregiver burden has led some
researchers to call for "a wholesale rethinking about

caregiving experiences and outcomes to include positive aspects of caregiving and positive indicators of
well-being" (Kramer, 1997, p. 218).

REFERENCES

AARP. (2011). *Valuing the invaluable: 2011 Update. The eco-
nomic value of family caregiving in 2009.* Washington,
DC: AARP Public Policy Institute.
Bengtson, V. L., Giarrusso, R., Silverstein, M., & Wang,
H. (2000). Families and intergenerational relation-
ships in aging societies. *Hallyn International Journal
of Aging, 2,* 3–10.
Birren, J. E. (1969). Principles of research on aging.
In J. E. Birren (Ed.), *The handbook of aging and the
individual* (pp. 3–42). Chicago, IL: University of
Chicago Press.
Boszormenyi-Nagy, I., & Spark, G. (1973). *Invisible loyal-
ties.* New York, NY: Harper & Row.
Brody, E. (1985). Parent care as normative family stress.
Gerontologist, 25, 19–29. doi:10.1093/geront/25.1.19
Bronfenbrenner, U. (1979). *The ecology of human devel-
opment.* Cambridge, MA: Harvard University Press.
Butler, R. N. (1963). The life review: An interpretation of
reminiscence in the aged. *Psychiatry, 26,* 65–76.
Cairl, R. E., & Kosberg, J. I. (1993). The interface of bur-
den and level of task performance of caregivers of
Alzheimer's disease patients: Clinical profiles. *Journal
of Gerontological Social Work, 19,* 133–151. doi:10.1300/
J083v19n03_10
Comana, M. T., & Brown, V. M. (1998). The effect of reminiscence therapy on family coping. *Journal of Family
Nursing, 4,* 182–198. doi:10.1177/107484079800400205
Corman, J. M., & Kingson, E. R. (1996). Trends, issues,
perspectives, and values for the aging of the baby
boom cohort. *The Gerontologist, 36,* 15–26. doi:10.1093/
geront/36.1.15
Council on Social Work Education/SAGE-SW. (2001).
*Strengthening the impact of social work to improve the
quality of life for older adults and their families: A blue-
print for the new millennium.* Alexandria, VA: Author.
Cox, E., & Parsons, R. (1994). *Empowerment-oriented
social work practice with elderly.* Pacific Grove,
CA: Brooks/Cole.
Crimmens, E. (1998, fall). Is disability declining among
the elderly? Defining disability and defining trends.
Critical Issues in Aging, (2), 10–11.
Cummings, S., & Kropf, N. (2009). *Handbook of psy-
chosocial interventions with older adults.* New York,
NY: Francis & Taylor.
Daatland, S. O. (1983). Care systems. *Aging and Society,
3*(Pt. 1), 21–33. doi:10.1017/S0144686X00009818

Davey, A., Murphy, M., & Price, S. (2000). Aging and the family: Dynamics and therapeutic interventions. In W. C. Nichols (Ed.), *Handbook of family development and intervention* (pp. 235–252). New York, NY: Wiley.

Erikson, E. (1950). *Child and society.* New York, NY: Norton.

Gatz, M. (Ed.). (1995). *Emerging issues in mental health and aging.* Washington, DC: National Academy Press.

Gitterman, A., & Germain, C. B. (1976). Social work practice: A life model. *Social Service Review, 50,* 3–13. doi:10.1086/643430

Greene, R. R. (1983). Life review: A technique for clarifying family roles in adulthood. *Clinical Gerontologist, 1,* 59–67. doi:10.1300/J018v01n02_07

Greene, R. R. (1986). The functional-age model of inter-generational therapy: A social casework model. In T. L. Brink (Ed.), *Clinical gerontology: A guide to assessment and intervention* (pp. 335–346). New York, NY: Haworth Press.

Greene, R. R. (1989). A life systems approach to understanding parent-child relationships in aging families. *Journal of Family Psychotherapy, 5,* 57–69. doi:10.1300/J287v05n01_05

Greene, R. R. (2001). *Social work with the aged and their families* (2nd ed.). New York, NY: Aldine de Gruyter.

Greene, R. R. (2008a). *Human behavior theory and social work practice* (3rd ed.). New Brunswick, NJ: Aldine Transaction Press.

Greene, R.R. (2008b). *Social work with the aged and their families* (3rd ed.). New Brunswick, NJ: Aldine Transaction Press.

Greene, R. R. (2005). The changing family of later years and social work practice. In L. Kaye (Ed.). *Productive aging* (pp. 107–122). Washington, DC: NASW Press.

Greene, R. R., & Barnes, G. (1998). The ecological perspective, diversity, and culturally competent social work practice. In R. R. Greene & M. Watkins (Eds.), *Serving diverse constituencies: Applying the ecological perspective* (pp. 63–96). Hawthorne, NY: Aldine de Gruyter.

Greene, R. R., Dalin, H., & Lebow, G. (1991). A study of caregiving systems in one community: When and why elders enter a nursing home. *Journal of Jewish Communal Service, 67,* 244–250.

Greene, R. R., & Kropf, N. P. (2009). A family case management approach for level I functioning. In A. Kilpatrick & T. P. Holland (Eds.), *Working with families: An integrative model by level of functioning* (pp. 85–123). Needham Heights, MA: Allyn & Bacon.

Greene, R. R., & Sullivan, W. P. (2001). Putting social work values into action: Use of the ecological perspective with older adults in the managed care arena. *Journal of Gerontological Social Work, 43,* 131–149. doi:10.1300/J083v42n03_08

Hargrave, T. (1994). Using video life reviews with older adults. *Journal of Family Therapy, 16,* 259–268. doi:10.1111/J.1467-6427.1994.00794.x

Hash, K. (2003). Practice with caregivers: Individuals and groups. In M. J. Naleppa & W. H. Reid (Eds.), *Gerontological social work: A task-centered approach* (pp. 203–234). New York, NY: Columbia University Press.

Kiyak, N., & Hooyman, N. (1999). Aging in the twenty-first century. *Hallyn International Journal of Aging, 1,* 56–66. doi:10.2190/HA1.1.e

Kramer, B. (1997). Gain in the caregiving experience: Where are we? What next? *The Gerontologist, 17,* 218–232. doi:10.1093/geront/37.2.218

Lee, Y., & Sung, K. (1998). Cultural influences on caregiver burden: Cases of Koreans and Americans. *International Journal of Aging and Human Development, 46,* 125–141. doi:10.2190/PM2C-V93R-NE8H-JWGV

Marks, N. (1998). Does it hurt to care? Caregiving, work-family conflict, and midlife well-being. *Journal of Marriage and the Family, 60,* 951–966. doi:10.2307/3536337

McGoldrick, M., Carter, B., & Garcia-Preto, N. (2011). *The expanded family life cycle Individual, family, and social perspectives* (4th ed.). Boston, MA: Pearson, Allyn & Bacon.

McInnis-Dittrich, K. (2002). *Social work with elders: A biopsychosocial approach to assessment and intervention.* Boston, MA: Allyn & Bacon.

Newton, N., Brauer, D., Gutmann, D. L., & Grunes, J. (1986). Psychodynamic therapy with the aged: A review. In T. L. Brink (Ed.), *Clinical gerontology: A guide to assessment and intervention* (pp. 205–243). New York, NY: Haworth Press.

Newton, N., & Lazarus, L. W. (1992). Behavioral and psychotherapeutic interventions. In J. E. Birren, R. B. Sloane, & G. D. Cohen (Eds.), *Handbook of mental health and aging* (2nd ed., pp. 699–719). San Diego, CA: Academic Press.

Noonan, A. E., & Tennstedt, S. L. (1997). Meaning in caregiving and its contribution to caregiver wellbeing. *The Gerontologist, 37,* 785–794. doi:10.1093/geront/37.6.785

Pearlin, L. I., Aneshensel, C. S., & Leblanc, A. J. (1997). The forms and mechanisms of stress proliferation: The case of AIDS caregivers. *Journal of Health and Social Behavior, 38,* 223–236. doi:10.1093/geront/10.2307/2955368

Pearlin, L. I., Mullan, J. T., Semple, S. J., & Skaff, M. M. (1990). Caregiving and the stress process: An overview of concepts and their measures. *The Gerontologist, 30,* 583–594. doi:10.1093/geront/30.5.583

Rowe, J. W., & Kahn, R. L. (1998). *Successful aging.* New York, NY: Pantheon.

Saul, S. (1983). *Groupwork with the frail elderly*. New York, NY: Haworth Press.

Schneider, R. L., & Kropf, N. P. (1992). *Gerontological social work*. Chicago, IL: Nelson-Hall.

Silverstone, B. (2000). The old and the new in aging: Implications for social work practice. *Journal of Gerontological Social Work, 33*, 35–50. doi:10.1300/J083v33n04_04

Silverstone, B., & Burack-Weiss, A. (1983). *Social work practice with the frail elderly and their families*. Springfield, IL: Thomas.

Smerglia, V. L., & Deimling, G. T. (1997). Care-related decision-making satisfaction and caregiver well-being in families caring for older members. *The Gerontologist, 29*, 658–665. doi:10.1093/geront/37.5.658

Stephens, M., Franks, M., & Townsend, A. (1994). Stress and rewards in women's multiple roles: The case of women in the middle. *Psychology and Aging, 9*, 45–52. doi:10.1037/0882-7974.9.145

Stull, D. E., Kosloski, K., & Kercher, K. (1994). Caregiver burden and generic well-being: Opposite sides of the same coin? *The Gerontologist, 34*, 88–94. doi:10.1093/geront/34.1.88

Tennstedt, S., & Chang, B. H. (1998). The relative contribution of ethnicity vs. socioeconomic status in explaining differences in disability and receipt of national care. *Journal of Gerontology: Social Sciences, 53B*, 861–870. doi:10.1093/geronb/538.2,S61

Toseland, R., & Rossiter, C. (1989). Group interventions to support family caregivers: A review and analysis. *The Gerontologist, 29*, 438–48. doi:10.1093/geront/29.4.438

Toseland, R., & Smith, T. (2001). *Supporting caregivers through education and training*. Prepared for U.S. Administration on Aging, National Family Caregiver Support Program (NFCSP): Selected Issue Briefs. Washington, DC: US Department of Health and Human Services.

Vourlekis, B. S., & Greene, R. R. (1992). *Social work case management*. Hawthorne, NY: Aldine de Gruyter.

Webster, J. (2001). The future of the past: Continuing challenges for reminiscence research. In G. Kenyon, P. Clark, & B. de Vries (Eds.), *Narrative gerontology* (pp. 159–214). New York, NY: Springer.

Willis, S. L. (1991). Cognition and everyday competence. In K. W. Schaie (Ed.), *Annual review of gerontology and geriatrics* (Vol. 11, pp. 80–109). New York, NY: Springer.

Yalom, I., & Leszcz, M. (2005. *The theory and practice of group psychotherapy*. New York, NY: Basic Books.

Zarit, S., & Knight, B. G. (1996). *A guide to psychotherapy and aging*. Washington, DC: American Psychological Association.

Now as the years roll on
Each time we hear our favorite song
The memories come along
Older times we're missing
Spending the hours reminiscing
Hurry, don't be late, I can hardly wait
I said to myself when we're old
We'll go dancing in the dark
Walking through the park and reminiscing

—Excerpt from "Reminiscing" (1978)
by Graham Goble, The Little River Band[1]

LORI R. DANIELS
JAMES BOEHNLEIN

The Role of Reminiscence
and Life Review
in Healthy Aging

The lyrics from the 1970s hit "Reminiscing" adhere to a commonly held belief that reflecting about one's past experiences occurs only in later adulthood—when older adults share stories of their personal histories, times of yore, and recollections. Gerontology specialists recognize that integrating one's memories in narrative form has benefits toward the improved self-identity, increased life satisfaction, higher emotional well-being, and reduced depression of an aging adult (Bohlmeijer, Roemer, Cuijpers, & Smit, 2007; Cappeliez, O'Rourke, & Chaudhury, 2005; Coleman, 2005; Watt & Cappeliez, 1995; Webster, 1998). There can be significant value, at any age or stage of human development, in sharing stories about one's past experiences and, as we discuss in this chapter, reminiscing and the process of life-review can also serve a valuable function in productive aging.

OPTIMAL AGING AND
THE THEORETICAL BACKGROUND
OF REMINISCENCE

The course of normal aging is often progressively more challenging as one's body, mind, and emotional well-being encounter numerous losses. Characteristics of "optimal aging" include the ability to make choices among alternative strategies while simultaneously compensating for losses throughout the aging processes (Baltes & Baltes, 1990). Successful aging is also bolstered by a positive self-concept when one is able to evaluate one's performance in proper relation to one's physical and mental capacity (Schaie & Willis, 1996).

In the gerontology literature, the term "successful (or optimal) aging" is used frequently but is not consistently defined, and the construct lacks concise and detailed clinical descriptions (Sinnott, 1977). However, a more general description recognizes "optimal aging" as an older adult's ability to function with behavioral flexibility and supportive components of their environment, including maintaining social supports, developing new relationships, using techniques for stress reduction, coping with change, and exercising self-compassion during stressful situations (Phillips & Ferguson, 2013).

There can be an increase in psychological distress because of age-related physical and cognitive changes in later adulthood. Age-related changes and how one interprets these changes can contribute to heightened anxiety over various systemic losses. However, negative interpretations of normal changes can be counteracted by compensatory measures, which can improve an individual's emotional well-being (Whitbourne, 1996). Social workers and other mental health practitioners can facilitate coping methods and/or various different healing interventions to combat emotional or experiential barriers to successful aging.

Reminiscence and Life Review: Concepts and Distinctions

Reminiscence and life review as clinical interventions emerged from Erik Erikson's (1964) psychosocial theory of human development (specifically later-life) combined with Robert Butler's (1963, 1974) explanation of successful aging. The last crisis of Erikson's stages of psychosocial development involves one's *ego integrity* versus *despair*. Ego integrity includes having a sense of dignity, fulfillment, wisdom, and "emotional integration" of one's life (Erikson, 1964, p. 269). Failure to emotionally integrate memories at this stage of older adulthood and accept oneself as one who's made positive contributions in life may result in emotional bitterness, despondence, and poorly developed death-preparation ("despair"). Erikson states that the adult "expresses the feeling that time is now short, too short for the attempt to start another life and to try out alternate roads to integrity" (1964, p. 269). Erikson's theory suggests the key to successful older adulthood—and to feeling satisfied and complete as a human being—is the effective integration of all elements of one's life, both positive and negative (Ingersoll-Dayton & Bommarito, 2006).

It was a common belief for many years that reminiscing about the past was an indication of underlying emotional problems until Butler's (1963) conceptualization of life review (in conjunction with Erikson's [1964] theoretical framework) normalized reminiscence during later life. Butler suggested that reminiscing was a universal, natural occurrence in older adults who are reviewing their life experiences. Thus, facilitating and encouraging one's life review could enhance an older adult's adaptation to changes, consolidate challenges across the life span, and help create meaning from those experiences. For older adults, Butler (1963) also emphasized the utility of reminiscing during more stressful periods of loss.

What is the difference between life-review and reminiscence? Interchangeable use of the terms "life review," "narrative," and "reminiscence" by researchers often has made it difficult to understand what each of these terms means and which parts of these constructs contribute toward improved aging (Watt & Wong, 1991). Without consistent conceptual definitions, it is more challenging to operationally define these constructs in terms of measuring any therapeutic components through research study or assessment.

Both constructs (life review and reminiscence) have therapeutically valuable characteristics. The process of sharing memories is different between the two types of interventions: Reminiscence process is encouraged in a group venue, whereas the life-review process is suggested for one-to-one interactions. According to Haight and Burnside (1993), as summarized in what follows, the most relevant differences between reminiscence and life review are the process, client's role, the practitioner's role, and the outcomes. These authors describe reminiscing as a *process* of clients recalling their memories spontaneously. Reminiscence sharing can be free-flowing, more relaxed, and focused on positive recall. In contrast, life review is a process of clients being directed/guided toward memories, is more structured, uses a life-span approach, discusses issues, is open to unpleasant emotions, has evaluative and integrative emphasis, and allows the individual to reframe the events. Expectations of the *client's role* during reminiscence focus less on the experience of emotional pain, as contrasted with life review, which anticipates emotional pain during the process, including possible disclosure being triggered by a need or crisis. Regarding the *practitioner's role*, the reminiscence intervention focuses more on obtaining data and gathering information, whereas a life-review intervention focuses on the practitioner as a therapeutic listener and emphasizes a client-centered counseling approach, unconditional positive regard, acceptance and caring, and permission for feelings and meanings. Life review focuses on the provider being involved with reframing events, accepting, valuing, and being empathetic about the client's disclosure. The *outcomes* of reminiscence intervention are less directed, focusing more on connecting, socializing, and increasing self-esteem. In contrast, life-review intervention outcomes are more focused on decreasing depression, increasing life satisfaction, allowing for integration of memories, increasing well-being, and increasing self-esteem. With these distinctions being made, life review appears to be more appropriate for addressing memories that are problematic, allowing the therapist's involvement in assisting with these memories, as the *main emphasis* of life review intervention is to facilitate integrity and bypass despair (Haight & Burnside, 1993).

The Taxonomy of Reminiscence

Addressing some of the confusion regarding the construct of reminiscence, Watt and Wong (1991) created a working taxonomy of reminiscence. They described two major types of reminiscence: adaptive and problematic. The adaptive type associated with successful aging is called *integrative reminiscence*, which contrasts with the problematic type called *obsessive reminiscence*. Watt and Wong (1991) proposed for future study a possible change of one's problematic obsessive reminiscence into more integrative reminiscence, thereby potentially shifting one's psychosocial developmental crisis outcome from ego despair toward more ego integrity (Erikson, 1964, 1982). Watt and Wong's taxonomy launched opportunities for researchers to investigate reminiscing and life review using terms that could be measured and investigated toward the development of appropriate clinical interventions (Wong & Watt, 1991).

Coleman (2005) encourages researchers to illuminate the origins of obsessive reminiscence (i.e., uncontrolled recall, sensory immediacy, and failure to rework memories), identifies integrative reminiscence as having clearly beneficial associations, and discusses operationalizing measures within the different types of reminiscence in order to provide

potential for measurement. It is with reminiscence measurement tools, such as the Reminiscence Function Scale (RFS; Webster, 1993) discussed in what follows, that future studies can evolve, including integration with other fields of study (Coleman, 2005).

A meta-analysis of both reminiscence and life-review interventions was conducted, assessing the effectiveness of these methods on psychological well-being across different target groups and treatment settings (Bohlmeijer et al., 2007). Using 15 controlled outcome studies, Bohlmeijer and colleagues found moderate effects on life satisfaction and emotional well-being for simple reminiscence groups (mean effect size = 0.54) and a higher effect-size ($D = 1.04$) for studies focused on life-review interventions. They concluded that older adults reported higher psychological well-being after participating in reminiscence interventions, especially when life review was incorporated. In addition, the meta-analysis found that individual and group formats seem to be equally effective; reminiscence was significantly more effective for community-dwelling participants than those living in nursing homes; and life review had greater effect on psychological well-being than simple reminiscence (Bohlmeijer et al., 2007).

Assessing Reminiscence

Gradually, gerontology experts have been working toward developing a vernacular that best describes reminiscence and can be used across disciplines. These efforts have produced two reminiscence assessment instruments: the Reminiscence Function Scale (Webster, 1993) and the Late Onset Stress Symptomology assessment (LOSS; King, King, Vickers, & Davison, 2007).

Reminiscence Function Scale

The Reminiscence Function Scale (RFS) is a 43-item questionnaire used to assess different types of reminiscence over the course of one's lifetime. Webster (1993) originally created this scale to expand on Wong and Watt's (1991) taxonomy originating from their study of older adults. Webster performed a factor analysis, and factor loadings from the 43 items suggested that reminiscence serves multiple purposes and can be organized into seven discrete functions: (1) boredom reduction, (2) death preparation,

(3) identity/problem solving, (4) conversation, (5) intimacy maintenance, (6) bitterness revival, and (7) teach/inform. Internal consistency of each factor suggests that the RFS is a reliable measure of these functions, with alpha levels ranging from .79 to .89. Webster (1993) also validated this instrument by looking at predictive validity and developmental applications of the RFS in subsequent studies. For predictive validity, he examined the relationship between reminiscence functions (measured with the RFS) and personality traits, with evidence of the RFS correlating at a statistically significant level, especially for function 6 (bitterness revival) with neuroticism personality; function 4 (conversation) correlating with extroversion personality; and function 3 (identity/problem solving) correlating with openness personality traits. In terms of developmental applicability, Webster (1998) looked at age differences of respondents in terms of function 2 (death preparation) and noted an increase of reminiscence with older adults, significantly different than younger adults. Webster later identified through subsequent study an eighth function: identity function (i.e., reminiscing to better define oneself, to understand oneself better), which was split from the problem-solving function (i.e., the use of reminiscence to resolve current problems). He concluded that parallels exist between the RFS and Watt and Wong's (1991) classifications of reminiscence, but the RFS can be used as a tool providing clearer differentiation between each of the above listed functions (Webster, 1993, 1998).

Late Onset Stress Symptomology Scale

King and colleagues (2007) identified a phenomenon called late onset stress symptomatology (LOSS) specifically related to older veterans of military service. Late onset stress symptomatology occurs when older war veterans, who have previously functioned well since military service, begin to exhibit increased military-related reminiscences and emotions later in life. These changes are consistent with age-related stressors such as bereavement, physical decline, and retirement. King et al. developed the LOSS Scale, a 44-item measure that asks true/false questions regarding reminiscence of war experiences and possible delayed onset of memories related to war-time exposure. Thirty-three of the items assess late onset stress symptoms; 11 are "positive" items about war zone experiences. The measure was psychometrically supported for use among older war veterans

who were exposed to stressful war zone events during their early adult years and have functioned successfully with no long-term history of stress-related disorders, but have more recently begun to register combat-related mental health complaints accompanying the aging process. As of this writing, there does not exist a nonveteran ("civilian") version of the LOSS.

REMINISCENCE INTERVENTIONS

In spite of the challenges that exist in defining and measuring reminiscence, it appears that providing opportunities for reminiscing is helpful for older adults (Blankenship, Molinari, & Kunik, 1996; Bohlmeijer et al., 2007; Pasupathi, 2001). Reminiscence groups can be used in both community and institutional settings in order to assist clients—it can increase morale, self-esteem, and life satisfaction as well as allow for an increased sense of control over the environment (Rice, 2005). Reminiscing can be facilitated successfully with older adults through group therapeutic approaches and through "facilitated reminiscence." Group therapy can maximize socialization and social reintegration for older people who are living in either isolated individual housing or in group housing in which residents initiate little social contact on their own (Shulman, 1981). Social interactions can be enhanced with an age-matched cohort that has had similar life experiences. Group members can help each other deal with frequently encountered challenges such as retirement, physical illness, and death of family and friends. Particularly with grief and mourning engendered by death and loss, group members can be supportive models for each other in processing the intense feelings that accompany the loss of close and intimate relationships. Although professional group leaders certainly can facilitate this modeling, the powerful transference among group members that grows out of group collaboration, cohesiveness, compassion, and mutual identification may be the most important factor in the healing process (Boehnlein & Sparr, 1993; Shulman, 1981). Reminiscing older adult group members can feel an increased sense of understanding and support for, other group members as they share their common experiences (Rice, 2005; Shulman, 1981).

Along with the communal support that reminiscence groups can offer, the act of reminiscing has therapeutic value through functions that affect one's memories and their meaning. Hunt and McHale (2008) note that individual narratives developed through interactions between personal memories and sharing these memories in a social venue can be beneficial. In some situations, older adults would otherwise focus heavily on the worst memories (i.e., traumatic events and crises) and the impact of these situations in their lives. Hunt and McHale (2008) advocate that practitioners go beyond the traditional use of reminiscence to use reminiscence in mental health practice. Social workers and mental health professionals can use individual narratives to focus on comparative concepts of time, which recognizes the importance of continuous identity when dealing with an older adult's life stories (Hunt & McHale, 2008).

Structured Reminiscence

This intervention is designed for depressed older people and consists of five weekly 90-minute individual sessions (Fry, 1983). During each session, the clinician helps the client to reminisce about one past upsetting event using a structured format that focuses on eight topical areas, each discussed for 10 minutes. Fry lists these topical areas and provides illustrative questions, some of which include:

- Strong negative and positive feelings associated with the events.
- People, objects, or other experiences related to the event.
- Images or ruminations about the event (e.g., "Were there thoughts you couldn't get rid of although you tried very hard?").
- Fears, anxieties, or hopes related to the event (e.g., "Do you wish certain things would happen that would make you feel better?").
- Unresolved feelings (e.g., "Were there people or situations that you tried very hard to avoid?").
- How time was spent during the event.

As participants reminisce about the event in each of these topical areas, the clinician listens empathically but avoids giving advice or providing evaluative comments, instead allowing for the act of disclosing and sharing to be unencumbered and supported.

Yet another element of reminiscence that can be structured toward specific aspects of one's life could

occur through the construct of self-forgiveness when clients are asked a simple question: "Do you forgive yourself?" When reminiscence is directed in this way, and shared with others, it may play a role in diminishing guilt and enhancing self-acceptance (Ingersoll-Dayton & Krause, 2005).

Positive Core Memories

Designed for nursing home residents, this 12-week group approach is focused on those who are experiencing depression or anxiety (Hyer, Sohnle, Mehan, & Ragan, 2002). During the initial sessions, the clinician works with the group members to identify two or three positive core memories (i.e., challenges and obstacles that were overcome). The clinician encourages group interaction and appreciation for each group member's core memories. Later sessions are devoted to applying the lessons learned from these memories to present-day experiences. Most importantly, the clinician helps clients to identify coping methods they previously have used successfully in order to apply these coping methods to current problems.

Unstructured Reminiscence Group for Trauma Survivors

The following brief clinical case best illustrates how one support group (for former prisoners of war from the European theater during World War II) can facilitate identification of personal mastery through unstructured reminiscing and enhance a sense of trust, purpose, and meaning, helping to make possible altruistic activities and enriched social networks (Boehnlein & Sparr, 1993):

A 66-year-old, married, retired Veteran was referred to the group after developing a mild depression following a relatively mild cerebrovascular accident the previous year. He quickly became a popular member of the group because of his irreverent humor. He was a former infantryman who had been captured during an intense battle in Belgium about 4 months before the end of the war. He was never in the same POW camp for more than a few weeks because he and fellow prisoners were often moved from one makeshift camp to another—the camps were placed adjacent to key installations to discourage allied bombing raids. He developed an apathetic attitude toward survival and lost 80 pounds, which represented 45% of his original body weight. He never regained his original weight and since the war had been plagued with chronic gastrointestinal and neurological problems. During his first year in the group he often discussed his futile search for survivors of his unit. He determined that only 16 of the original 220 unit members had survived the war, but he never was able to locate anyone. Two years after he joined the group he found one member who lived in a retirement community on the East Coast. They began to correspond, leading to an invitation for his wife and him to visit. The two Veterans immediately made a strong connection, and afterward he decided to move across the country, citing the importance of reestablishing a valued friendship and the strong, supportive Veterans' community in that area. After his move, he continued to correspond with the treatment group, and 2 years later he wrote that after a full-time effort he and his friend had located 8 of the 16 survivors. Two of those veterans later moved to the same community. He described the process as emotionally rewarding, similar to being reunited with lost family members. ▨

LIFE REVIEW INTERVENTIONS AND METHODS

Reflecting and assessing one's life is a normative process that all older people undergo as they face their life coming to an end, and can be an adaptive response to aging when used as an opportunity to gain insight and introspection (Coleman, 2005). Therefore, the life-review process can be used to assist those who have numerous difficulties in life and when there are possibilities for change and development. Life review can be used to facilitate normal life transitions and to facilitate treatment for depression, post-traumatic stress disorder, and mild cognitive impairment. Because life review is an intervention, there are no assessment instruments to measure one's level of life reviewing; instead, guidelines are created or used to facilitate the process of life review. There are no reminiscence or life-review interventions that fit all groups, because disparate client needs and variety of treatment settings entail different approaches.

Several life-review interventions were described in the previous edition of this book by Ingersoll-Dayton and Bommarito (2006), and these are again summarized in this section. Based on the expertise of the current authors of this chapter, two additional interventions are also discussed.

Life Review and Experiencing

This 8-week intervention is used to help older people cope with relocation to a nursing home (Haight, Michel, & Hendrix, 1998). Clinicians meet with clients individually using a Life Review and Experiencing Form (LREF; Haight, 1992) to guide the intervention. The LREF is a guide sheet that lists pointed and open-ended questions about a client's life focusing on several life phases: childhood, adolescence, family and home, and adulthood. The questions target important life issues such as relationships, family, and fears and progress chronologically through the life span. The final portion of the form focuses on summary questions (e.g., "What was the hardest thing you had to face in your life?", "What was the proudest moment in your life?") that are intended to help clients assess their lives by acknowledging and integrating their mistakes as well as their contributions. Haight and colleagues (1998) used the LREF with two groups of newly relocated older adults in nursing homes and found that compared with two control groups who had friendly visits, the life-review groups reported significantly less depression, less hopelessness, and higher levels of life satisfaction both immediately after their transition to nursing homes and 1 year afterward. These findings provide evidence that life review has value for those transitioning to nursing home environments.

Life Challenges Interview

This intervention is a 1-hour individual interview designed to help older clients cope with anxiety prior to surgery or other invasive medical procedures (Rybarczyk & Bellg, 1997). The intervention begins by asking clients to recount early memories, and follows themes that emerge in a chronological framework. A unique focus of this interview is identifying specific challenges that the client successfully met in the past. Clinicians ask questions in order to help clients reflect on how life challenges were met and emphasize client strengths and resourcefulness. "Defining moments" are highlighted as reminders of competence in the face of adversity. The session concludes with the development of a collaborative summary of the two or three client strengths and resources that emerge most consistently throughout these stressful situations, which can then be identified as pre-established successes toward facing future challenges, such as impending medical surgeries.

The Life Story Book

This intervention is designed to facilitate life review with older clients with dementia and their caregivers (Haight et al., 2003). Two practitioners meet simultaneously, but separately, with the client and caregiver to develop a book that portrays the life of the client. The caregiver contributes to this effort by locating pictures and mementos. The client selects items from the memorabilia, and the clinician asks the client to describe them. With the client's permission, these sessions are tape-recorded and transcribed. Portions of the transcriptions are then used as captions for the life story book. The clinician encourages the client and caregiver to reminisce about the pictures between sessions as a way of increasing communication and enhancing pleasurable interactions between client and their caregiver. When the book is completed, the client decides whether and how to share it with others outside the caregiving relationship.

Group Life Review for Older Adults

More recently, life review interventions have expanded beyond individual meetings to group venues, overlapping with reminiscence groups. Korte, Drossaert, Westerhof, and Bohlmeijer (2013) studied whether a group structure can be effective with life review. Their study investigated the social aspects of a life-review group intervention in an exploratory, randomized, controlled, qualitative study that assessed outcomes based on the perspective of the client about the benefits and barriers of receiving a life-review intervention in a group setting. Their results suggest that the social processes of life review in a group has numerous benefits, including experiencing a sense of belonging, feeling accepted, learning to express oneself, realizing that others also have problems, being recognized for unique

life experiences, learning from others, and being able to help others. Some negative processes were mentioned, including having difficulties with sharing in a group and experiencing anxiety caused by the prospect of finding no recognition. The researchers categorized three categories of social processes in their life review group: having a good atmosphere, disclosing to peers, and relating to others. Their results identified various social processes facilitating the effects of life-review therapy using a group format (Korte et al., 2013).

Groups, as described earlier, can be structured to facilitate a client's reflections of life experiences. But what if an older adult has troubling memories that are too difficult to think about? A possible dilemma emerges with intrusive traumatic memories accompanying post-traumatic stress disorder (PTSD; American Psychiatric Association [APA], 2013), within the developmental stage of integration versus despair (Erikson, 1964). Case studies have suggested that war veterans diagnosed with PTSD and depression as a client group could benefit from life review (individually or using a group format) given poor mental health outcomes reported from studies on older war veterans (Brooks & Fulton, 2010; Cook & Niederehe, 2007; Daniels, Boehnlein, & McCallion, 2015; Hyer, Summers, Braswell, & Boyd, 1995; Markowitz, 2007).

CONCLUSION

This chapter briefly summarized clinical aspects of reminiscence and methods of both reminiscing groups and life-review interventions that can be applied to enhance the mental health of older adults. Social workers and mental health providers can use the natural inclination to reminisce as a tool to support healthy aging. By modifying the methods presented in order to fit with the needs of specific clients, many options are available to clinical social workers, from individually guided life review to less-structured group reminiscing. The life review can be helpful with the later psychosocial stages of human development that arise within clinical settings with a wide variety of people, including those dealing with dementia, traumatic stress, living transitions, or depression. Readers are encouraged to review the expanding literature about reminiscence and life review, taking into consideration with whom, when, and in what settings these various methods can be useful for older adults (or those of any age) who may benefit emotionally from reflecting on their past life experiences. . . . *"Spending the hours reminiscing."*

NOTE

1. REMINISCING. Words and Music by GRAHAM GOBLE. Copyright © 1978 WHEATLEY MUSIC PTY. LTD. All Rights Administered by WB MUSIC CORP. All Rights Reserved. Used By Permission of ALFRED MUSIC.

REFERENCES

American Psychiatric Association. (2013). Post traumatic stress disorder. In *Diagnostic and statistical manual of mental disorders* (5th ed.). Arlington, VA: Author. doi:10.1176/appi.books.9780890425596.744053

Baltes, P. B., & Baltes, M. M. (1990). Selective optimization with compensation. In P. B. Baltes & M. M. Baltes (Eds.), *Successful aging: Perspectives from the behavioral sciences* (pp 1–34). New York, NY: Cambridge University Press.

Blankenship, L. M., Molinari, V., & Kunik, M. (1996). The effect of a life-review group on the reminiscence functions of geropsychiatric inpatients. *Clinical Gerontologist, 16,* 3–17.

Boehnlein, J. K., & Sparr, L. F. (1993). Group therapy with WWII ex-POWs: Long-term posttraumatic adjustment in a geriatric population. *American Journal of Psychotherapy, 47,* 273–282.

Bohlmeijer, E., Roemer, M., Cuijpers, P., & Smit, F. (2007). The effects of reminiscence on psychological well-being in older adults: A meta-analysis. *Aging and Mental Health, 11,* 291–300. doi:10.1080/13607860600963547

Brooks, M. S., & Fulton, L. (2010). Evidence of poorer life-course mental health outcomes among veterans of Korean War cohort. *Aging and Mental Health, 14,* 177–183. doi:10.1080/13607860903046560

Butler, R. (1963). The life review: An interpretation of reminiscence in the aged. *Psychiatry, 26,* 65–76.

Butler, R. N. (1974). Successful aging and the role of the life review. *Journal of the American Geriatrics Society, 22,* 529–535.

Cappeliez, P., O'Rourke, N., & Chaudhury, H. (2005). Functions of reminiscence and mental health in later life. *Aging and Mental Health, 9,* 295–301. doi:10.1080/13607860500131427

Coleman, P. (2005). Uses of reminiscence: Functions and benefits. *Aging and Mental Health, 9,* 291–294. doi:10.1080/13607860500169641

Cook, J. M., & Niederehe, G. (2007). Trauma in older adults. In M. K. Friedman (Ed.), *Handbook of PTSD: Science and practice* (pp. 252–276). New York, NY: Guilford Press.

Daniels, L. R., Boehnlein, J., & McCallion, P. (2015). Aging, depression, and wisdom: A pilot study of life-review intervention and PTSD treatment with two groups of Vietnam veterans, *Journal of Gerontological Social Work, 58*(4), 420–436.

Erikson, E. (1964). *Childhood and society* (2nd ed.). New York, NY: Norton.

Erikson, E. (1982). *The life cycle completed: A review.* New York, NY: Norton.

Fry, P. S. (1983). Structured and unstructured reminiscence training and depression among the elderly. *Clinical Gerontologist, 1,* 15–37.

Haight, B. K. (1992). Long-term effects of a structured life review process. *Journal of Gerontology, 47,* 312–315. doi:10.1093/geronj/47.5.P312

Haight, B. K., Bachman, D. L., Hendrix, S., Wagner, M. T., Meeks, A., & Johnson, J. (2003). Life review: Treating the dyadic family unit with dementia. *Clinical Psychology and Psychotherapy, 10,* 165–174. doi:10.1002/cpp.367

Haight, B. K., & Burnside, I. (1993). Reminiscence and life review: Explaining the differences. *Archives of Psychiatric Nursing, 7,* 91–98. doi:S0883941709900073

Haight, B. K., Michel, Y., & Hendrix, S. (1998). Life review: Preventing despair in newly relocated nursing home residents short- and long-term effects. *International Journal of Aging and Human Development, 47,* 119–142. doi:10.2190/A011-BRXD-HAFV-5NJ6

Hunt, N., & McHale, S. (2008). Memory and meaning: Individual and social aspects of memory narratives. *Journal of Loss and Trauma, 13,* 42–58.

Hyer, L., Sohnle, S., Mehan, D., & Ragan, A. (2002). Use of positive core memories in LTC: A review. In M. P. Norris, V. Molinari, & S. Ogland-Hand (Eds.), *Emerging trends in psychological practice in long-term care* (pp. 51–90). Binghamton, NY: Haworth Press.

Hyer, L., Summers, M. N., Braswell, L., & Boyd, S. (1995). Posttraumatic stress disorder: Silent problem among older combat veterans. *Psychotherapy, 32,* 348–364. doi:10.1037/0033-3204.32.2.348

Ingersoll-Dayton, B., & Bommarito, A. (2006). Reminiscence and life review. In B. Berkman & D'Ambruoso (Eds.), *Handbook of social work in health and aging,* (pp. 781–788). New York, NY: Oxford University Press.

Ingersoll-Dayton, B., & Krause, N. (2005). Self-forgiveness: A component of mental health in later life. *Research on Aging, 27,* 267–289. doi:10.1177/0164027504274122

King, L. A., King, D. W., Vickers, K. S., & Davison, E. H. (2007). Assessing late-onset stress symptomatology among aging male combat veterans. *Aging and Mental Health*, 11, 175–191. doi:10.1080/13607860600844424

Korte, J., Drossaert, C. H. C., Westerhof, G. J., & Bohlmeijer, E. T. (2013). Life review in groups? An explorative analysis of social processes that facilitate or hinder the effectiveness of life review. *Aging and Mental Health*, 15, 638–646. doi:10.1080/13607863.2013.837140

Markowitz, J. (2007). Post-traumatic stress disorder in an elderly combat veteran: A case report. *Military Medicine*, 172, 659–662.

Pasupathi, M. (2001). The social construction of the personal past and its implication for adult development. *Psychological Bulletin*, 127, 651–672. doi:10.1037/0033-2909.127.5.651

Phillips, W. J., & Ferguson, S. J. (2013). Self-compassion: A resource for aging. *Journals of Gerontology*, 68B, 529–539. doi:10.1093/geronb/gbs091

Rybarczyk, B. D., & Bellg, A. (1997). *Listening to life stories: A new approach to stress intervention in health care*. New York, NY: Springer.

Rice, S. (2005). Group work with elderly persons. In G. A. Greif, *Group work with populations at risk* (2nd ed., pp. 146–158). New York, NY: Oxford University Press.

Schaie, K. W., & Willis, S. L. (1996). *Adult development and aging*. New York, NY: Harper Collins.

Shulman, E. (1981). Integrative counseling with a group. In E. Shulman, *Counseling the aging: An integrative approach* (pp. 144–189). New York, NY: Free Press.

Sinnott, J. (1977). Sex-role inconstancy, biology, and successful aging. *The Gerontologist*, 17, 459–463.

Watt, L. M., & Cappeliez, P. (1995). Reminiscence interventions for the treatment of depression in older adults. In B. K. Haight & J. D. Webster (Eds.), *The art and science of reminiscing: Theory, research, methods, and applications* (pp. 221–232). Washington, DC: Taylor & Francis.

Watt, L. M., & Wong, P. T. P. (1991). A taxonomy of reminiscence and therapeutic implications. *Journal of Gerontological Social Work*, 16, 37–57. doi:10.1300/J083v16n01_04

Webster, J. (1993). Construction and validation of the Reminiscence Function Scale. *Journal of Gerontology*, 48, 256–262. doi:10.1093/geronj/48.5.P256

Webster, J. (1998). Attachment styles, reminiscence functions and happiness in young and elderly adults. *Journal of Aging Studies*, 12, 315–331. doi:10.1016/S0890-4065(98)90006-8

Whitbourne, S. (1996). Psychological perspectives on the normal aging process. In L. E. Carstensen, B. A. Edelstein, & L. Dornbrand (Eds.), *The practical handbook of clinical gerontology* (pp. 3–35). Thousand Oaks, CA: Sage.

Wong, P. T. P., & Watt, L. M. (1991). What types of reminiscence are associated with successful aging? *Psychology and Aging*, 6, 272–279. doi:10.1037/0882-7974.6.2.272

Practitioners searching for more effective methods in working with older adults are combining strengths-based and solution-focused approaches in new ways to improve outcomes. The strengths perspective is a philosophical standpoint that focuses on the inherent resilience in human nature that undergirds much of social work practice. This perspective is especially applicable to work with older adults, who have a lifetime of rich experience that can be used to address current difficulties. Strengths-based and solution-focused approaches are both rooted in the belief that capacity rather than pathology should be the primary focal point of the helping process. Similar to strengths-based focus on the positive, solution-focused approaches identify when the "trouble" did not exist so that the client and the client-situation are not viewed as a problem. Challenges experienced by older adults often require identification of possible solutions, which may include reactivation of social networks and/or modification of the physical environment. Both the strengths perspective and the solution-focused approaches are discussed in this chapter. The vignette that follows provides an example of an older client with whom the approaches were initiated.

ROSEMARY CHAPIN
HOLLY NELSON-BECKER
KELLEY MACMILLAN
ALICIA SELLON

Strengths-Based and Solution-Focused Practice with Older Adults: New Applications

6

Viola Wilson was referred to the Peer Support and Wellness for Older Adults (PSWOA) program by her local hospital's social worker. Mrs. Wilson is a 75-year-old African American woman. She is divorced and living alone. She developed arthritis about 6 years ago and was a participant in an arthritis self-management program at the local community center until she was diagnosed with chronic obstructive pulmonary disease (COPD) and placed on oxygen. She has had trouble managing her COPD and has been readmitted to the hospital several times. In addition, she has been diagnosed with moderate levels of depression and has not gone back to the local community center to participate in the arthritis program or resumed volunteering with her church group. After Mrs. Wilson was readmitted for the third time in 4 months, the hospital's social worker spoke with her about the new PSWOA program in the community, run by Heather Smith, a home- and community-based services social worker at the local Aging and Disability Resource Center (ADRC).Heather had worked at the ADRC for about 2 years when she was asked to begin the new PSWOA program that could benefit some of the older adults in the community who have had difficulty managing their chronic disease and are socially isolated. The PSWOA is a program for older adults at high risk of rehospitalization, and is based on both a peer model and the strengths perspective. Heather had learned about the strengths perspective, which focuses on the individual's strengths and abilities instead of illnesses or problems, and thought it would provide a useful framework for working with the older adults in her community. She also believed the idea of matching older adult participants with volunteers of a similar age would make the program more engaging for both participants and volunteers. Heather's work with Mrs. Wilson is detailed further in the "Applications" section of the chapter. ▓

We first present frameworks of strengths-based principles and solution-focused principles commonly used with older adult populations within a larger strengths perspective. Strengths-based and solution-focused approaches to intervention draw on similar assumptions about practice with older adults. These two approaches work well together and may serve to reinforce each other because they each contain complementary principles that provide client-centered and holistic perspectives for social work practice. Second, we discuss applications of these approaches in various settings to broaden comprehension of the uses of each approach. We also examine how these perspectives contrast with a traditional problem focus in social work generalist practice, and benefits and cautionary notes about use of these perspectives are addressed. We include discussion of recent research implications, focusing on the potential of the strengths-based and solution-focused approaches for improving social work practice for older adults.

STRENGTHS OVERVIEW

The strengths perspective, also referred to as the strengths-based perspective, is a philosophical view about how social workers can interact with clients to elicit positive outcomes (Cowger, 1994; Saleebey, 1997, 2013). When practiced fully, the strengths perspective is an operational stance that puts social work values

into action; it is not just about providing support and motivation. For instance, a social worker utilizing the strengths perspective (1) recognizes the inherent power that individuals can bring to bear on their own lives to achieve their potential; (2) acknowledges the life lessons that will facilitate the journey toward aging well; and (3) engages individuals in a way that promotes the ongoing task of building a mindful and meaningful life.

The strengths model is best understood in comparison with the traditional medical model that socializes the client to be a passive recipient of services largely determined through professional expertise. The strengths perspective serves as an antidote to victim blaming through its focus on dialogue, collaboration, resilience, empowerment, and, ultimately, wholeness as defined by the client (Nelson-Becker, 2013; Saleebey, 2013). Instead of holding a problem or deficit viewpoint, the professional assumes a potentials and possibilities focus that affirms individual hopes and aspirations within the constraints of the current situation.

The strengths perspective seeks to empower people and communities when incorporated into practice, policy, and research settings. For example, as applied to direct practice in a healthcare environment, the strengths perspective leads social workers to consider the multiple influences that shape health status. Social workers are urged to go beyond linear explanations for health and disease and to focus on the capacity of individuals and communities to take an active role in achieving and maintaining health (Weick, 1986). Emphasis is on removing barriers to improving health status and on more effective use of community resources. The strengths perspective also fosters a sense of belonging by recognizing the reciprocity between the client and the social environment even in the most extreme stages of coping with dementia or receiving full personal care. Although these relationships may appear one-sided, there are usually benefits for clients and caregivers as well as helping professionals. The communication between the client, family and friends, and professional helpers and advocates provides insights that improve direct care, empirical research, and policy. For example, in regard to policy development, the strengths perspective leads social workers to work collaboratively with individuals and communities at all stages of policy formulation. Focusing on the individuals' and community's strengths and goals, rather than their deficits, changes not only the policy process but also the final product (Chapin, 2014). Removing barriers to healthcare access and community resources can begin with work to implement policies that would support programs such as the PSWOA and also include empowering consumers to effectively lobby for policies to create the formal services lacking in their community.

The conceptual underpinnings of the strengths perspective reflect a social constructionist approach to reality, which posits that our explanations of all human interactions, including social problems, are based on views of reality that are socially and personally constructed (Berger & Luckmann, 1967; Geertz, 1973; Gergen, 1999). Strengths are as people see them, but seeing them, especially within oneself, can be a difficult task. The phrase "socially and personally constructed" suggests that personal beliefs and group consensus shape what a group of people consider to be real at a given time. Hence, in the strengths perspective, understanding the beliefs and values of the older adult is the beginning point for all further work.

General principles of the strengths perspective (Nelson-Becker, Chapin, & Fast, 2013; Saleebey, 2013) that pertain to older adults include the following:

- All individuals have strengths.
- All experiences, even negative ones, may present opportunities for growth.
- Practitioner diagnosis and the assessment process in direct practice often make assumptions that limit rather than expand capacity.
- Collaboration rather than coercion leads to highly motivated and engaged clients.
- All environments have resources.
- A civil society engages in care for all of its members.

Practice based on these principles always involves a delicate dance of interpretation as one applies them to the web of work with clients and sometimes the people in their environments. However, incorporation of a focus that builds on individual and community strengths and resources, and on forming a collaborative relationship to help them achieve their goals, opens new possibilities for effective practice. A parallel perspective has emerged with the development of the positive psychology movement. Positive psychology, similar to the strengths perspective in social work, emphasizes the value of savoring, or giving weight to positive experience (Bryant, 2003).

The social worker's role is to skillfully create a helping relationship that empowers the client to resolve life struggles, and this suggests an upward and broadening effect that may spill over into other areas.

THE STRENGTHS-BASED APPROACH WITH OLDER ADULTS

The strengths-based approach was initially developed for use with adults served in mental health centers/agencies (Kisthardt, 1993; Rapp, 1998; Saleebey, 2002). A strengths-based perspective has also been successfully extended to social policy and direct practice with older adult populations (Chapin, 1995, 2014; Chapin et al., 2013; Fast & Chapin, 2000, 2002; Nelson-Becker et al., 2013; Tice & Perkins, 1996). These strengths-based approaches reflect the concepts developed by Saleebey and others. Elements presented below have been tailored for work with older adults.

- Discovering and building on strengths of older adults rather than problems will facilitate hope, self-reliance, and personal satisfaction.
- Acknowledging that older adults have the power to learn, grow, and change is fundamental.
- Developing the older adult–social worker relationship is essential to effectively assist the older adult.
- Participating in decisions, making choices, and determining the direction of the helping process is a primary role for the older adult.
- Acquiring resources based on active outreach to the community is a key role for the social worker.

As use of the strengths perspective has increased in practice and research settings, evidence suggests that the strengths perspective can be used in multiple settings with a diverse group of older adults (Chapin et al., 2013; Judge, Yarry, & Orsulic-Jeras, 2010). For example, the strengths-based approach has been used to help educate and provide individuals with dementia and their family caregivers with new skills (Judge, Yarry, & Orsulic-Jeras, 2010). In addition, the strengths approach has been used with older adults living in the community to reduce symptoms of depression and increase quality of life (Chapin et al., 2013). While research into the use of the strengths perspective with older adults is increasing, future studies should use an experimental design where strengths-based case management approaches are treated as independent variables and control for differences in case manager training and case management style (Staudt, Howard, & Drake, 2001).

PHILOSOPHICAL TENETS OF THE SOLUTION-FOCUSED APPROACH

Solution-focused therapy shares common roots with the strengths perspective. Solution-focused therapy traces its origins to work by de Shazer and colleagues (1986; de Shazer, 1988, 1991; Lipchik, 1993, 2002). Central to the solution-focused approach and many therapy models are certain assumptions, discussed below, about the nature of the person, how problems are formed and maintained, how change occurs, and the role of the individual and the social worker in the therapeutic/helping process (Bonjean, 2003; de Shazer et al., 1986).

When using a solution-focused approach, determining cause and effect is not a central goal. Looking for a cause and effect maintains the focus of intervention on the problem or complaint. Just as the name implies, the solution-focused intervention revolves around constructing or identifying solutions. The approach suggests that the solution to the complaint is found in exceptions to the complaint, or those times when the complaint is absent (Bonjean, 2003; de Shazer et al., 1986). The social worker's role is to help the individual identify those exceptions. Hence, assessments focus on those times when life is going well and attempt to find out what was happening that made life satisfactory. In this manner, the solution is separated from the problem and can build on the strengths and positive experiences of the individual.

The solution-focused approach affirms the idiosyncratic nature of the person through the appreciation of his/her subjective experience and worldview (Bonjean, 2003). The social worker's role is to assist individuals in creating their own solutions. In addition, the solution-focused approach makes clear how problems are formed and maintained. All individuals experience difficulties in life; however, the difficulty becomes a complaint when multiple attempts to resolve the problem are ineffective (de Shazer et al., 1986; Nelson-Becker, 2004). A solution-focused approach also has a unique perspective on how change occurs. Constructing or identifying solutions

creates an expectation of change. The expectation of change, or actual change itself, does not have to be great; in fact, any expectation of change is valuable as slight changes influence the interactional pattern between the client and other individuals (Bonjean, 2003; de Shazer et al., 1986).

Finally, the solution-focused approach defines the role of the individual and social worker as a collaboration to establish aims that are based on client values, preferences, and life goals. Solution-focused interventions are client centered: The individual decides what his/her goals are and when enough change has occurred to end the intervention. This client-centered approach to goal setting also de-emphasizes the social worker as the expert and develops a collaborative relationship that is respectful of the individual's life experience, worldview, and capacities (Bonjean, 2003; de Shazer et al., 1986).

Solution-focused approaches have been used in clinical work with older adults and their families, and in case management settings and other direct service interventions (Bonjean, 1997, 2003; Dahl, Bathel, & Carreon, 2000). A solution-focused approach includes principles that guide the social worker's action and are comparable to the strengths perspective principles (Bonjean, 2003). The focus is on the positive elements in one's life, on the solution, and on the future in order to facilitate change toward the older adult's goals:

- Goal attainment is accomplished in the older adult's own unique way, and he or she is able to resourcefully and creatively change.
- The older adult and the social worker are both experts and collaborators.
- Identifying exceptions to the problem enables the older adult and social worker to build or create solutions. An exception is any instance when the older adult does not experience the challenge.

The solution-focused approach emphasizes these principles as fundamental to intervention. Both solution-focused and strengths-based approaches have broad application to work with older adults. They may be easily used in many types of settings, and the fundamental principles, consistent with social work values, are quickly assimilated by social workers at any level of practice.

APPLICATIONS

In this section, we illustrate the application of strengths-based and solution-focused approaches. A challenge for social workers is that many settings use a traditional problem-solving model or a diagnosis is made as a basis for the intervention.

Regardless of the agency auspices or services, the strengths-based/solution-focused assessment lays the foundation for the older adult to develop goals that are personally important and meaningful, and identifies intrapersonal, interpersonal, and social-environmental resources to achieve these goals. The social worker can play multiple roles in helping the older adult define and articulate goals and the changes that will illustrate measurable achievement of the goals. For example, the social worker may work directly with the older adult—helping him/her to identify goals and resources, or the social worker may educate and train older adults to act as peer volunteers and assist other older adults in developing goals and identifying resources. This work emphasizes and supports the self-efficacy, autonomy, and self-determination that are essential to client empowerment and a sense of hope. Since health is often a major area of focus in later years, strengths associated with identifying and managing health goals should especially be highlighted (McMahon & Fleury, 2012).

A number of applications of the strengths approach have been suggested (Schueller, 2010; Shearer, Fleury, Ward, & O'Brien, 2012). These include an active-constructive response that enhances the event or situation by encouraging, retelling, and re-experiencing. This activity is linked to well-being and relationship satisfaction (Gable, Reis, Impett, & Asher, 2004). Another exercise consistent with building strengths includes enhancement of gratitude. This is accomplished by asking older adults to reflect each day on what went well and to write down three gratitude elements or journal entries (Emmons, 2008). This enhances an older adult's ability to balance their feelings about daily occurrences in life. A specific strengths-related exercise invited older adults to identify their signature strengths (Seligman, Steen, Park, & Peterson, 2005). They were then asked to find a new way to engage a key strength each day. Decrease in depressed mood was an outcome of the study.

In the case of Viola Wilson described earlier, the social worker has knowledge of human development

and models of change, a wealth of information about community resources, and the professional skills to train both the peer volunteer and to assist Mrs. Wilson. The expertise the older adult brings to the relationship is from her own life experience, personal strengths, and viewpoints regarding her personal circumstances.

The social worker's use of the strengths perspective can be more fully explicated by examining work with Viola Wilson in more depth. The social worker matched Mrs. Wilson with Evelyn Sanchez, a 70-year-old PSWOA community connector volunteer. Prior to hearing about the PSWOA program, Mrs. Sanchez had been looking for a high-impact volunteer experience that would provide training and an opportunity to learn new skills and be emotionally rewarding and intellectually stimulating.

The social worker accompanied Mrs. Sanchez to the first meeting with Mrs. Wilson. Although she was at first reticent about discussing her medical condition and quality of life, when the social worker explained that the goal of the program was to help Mrs. Wilson identify and achieve some of her own personal goals, Mrs. Wilson began to open up. After the strengths assessment form was explained, Mrs. Sanchez and Mrs. Wilson discussed how they would work together to fill out the form and identify Mrs. Wilson's goals. Mrs. Wilson decided that she wanted to focus on several goals including attending her granddaughter's wedding in 6 months, returning to the arthritis group at the community center, and doing volunteer work with her church again. Together they identified steps necessary to achieve her goals. Because the focus was on goals and solutions that Mrs. Wilson had chosen, she was motivated to take action. Mrs. Wilson's strength assessment is provided in Table 6.1.

As the assessment illustrates, the social worker and peer volunteer learned that Mrs. Wilson had a strong support network. The social worker recognized the importance of using assessment and active listening skills as a means to elicit discussion with the older adult about how she conducted her life prior to the current circumstances and events as well as to review earlier life challenges and responses. The older adult identifies goals, provides her preferred resolution to the challenges she faces, potential solutions to these challenges, and shares her ideas about how she would like to overcome them (Bonjean, 2003). After goals are identified, the older adult is assisted in finding and acquiring necessary formal and informal

TABLE 6.1.   Strengths Assessment

Participant's Name __*Viola Wilson* ____ Date _1_/_10_/_2014_ Volunteer's Name ___*Evelyn Sanchez*_____

	Current Status What do I have going for me?	Individual's Desires/Aspirations What do I want?	Personal/Social Resources What have I used in the past?
Daily Living Situation	*Live alone in my own house. I am able to take care of most of the chores around my house.*	*I would like to stay in my house. I would like to cook more, but sometimes my arthritis makes it hard.*	*I sometimes asked my friends' sons to help me change the light bulbs, and such.*
Physical Activity	*I vacuum and clean once or twice a week.*	*I would like to be more active. My arthritis makes it hard.*	*I used to go to the arthritis self-management program at the community center.*
Social Supports	*I have family and lots of friends at the community center, but I haven't kept in touch. I used to go to church and I volunteered with the women's church group.*	*I would like to attend my granddaughter's wedding and be with my friends at the community center, and at church*	*I have friends at the community center, church, and in my church's women's group.*
Spirituality & Religion	*My religion is a source of hope for me. I belong to the AME Methodist church but haven't been attending*	*I would like to see my friends from church and attend a service every now and then.*	*I was an active church member*
Leisure & Recreational Interests	*I used to spend a lot of time with the women from my church.*	*I would really like to volunteer again with my church's women's group.*	*Received emotional support from my women's church group.*

Modified Strengths Assessment, Copyright © 2003 Chapin and Fast

resources. Focusing on strengths and informal community resources identified in the strengths assessment above, the next step is to assist Mrs. Wilson to reengage with her support systems and to develop new support systems.

Community resources, such as community centers that provide senior services, often provide programs and services that support the health and well-being of older adults. If such programs do not yet exist in the community, or older adults have trouble accessing these services, it is incumbent on the social worker practicing from a strengths perspective to work with community and state agencies to develop policies to see that such services are developed and easily accessible.

Another resource available that could address the depression experienced by Mrs. Wilson is the community integrated behavioral health center, where she would receive both medical and behavioral healthcare services. A behavioral health social worker could use a solution-focused approach to identify the exceptions to the problem (e.g., the depression) by concentrating on prior times when she felt life was going well. S/he could assist Mrs. Wilson to identify possible change opportunities to separate the problem from the solution (Bonjean, 1997). Social workers using the solution-focused approach can

apply their assessment skills to find instances when the problem was not present or when feelings were less intense. For instance, the social worker assessing Mrs. Wilson would learn about the small things that had helped her feel better each day: participating in her arthritis class and working with the other women in her church group. These exceptions could be used to help Mrs. Wilson recognize that there are brief lapses in her feelings of depression and loneliness when she reflects on the enjoyable times and rewarding experiences she has had with friends. The social worker could encourage Mrs. Wilson to think about these exceptions to her emotional pain and use this process to take steps to re-engage with her support network.

Long-term care institutions, such as assisted living and nursing care facilities, also offer many opportunities to apply the strengths and solution-focused perspectives. A social worker working in these locations may help to focus older adults' energy on those activities they found personally meaningful throughout their life and facilitate engagement in those same or similar activities in the new location. Further, as people begin to prepare for end-of-life issues, they can be encouraged to assess their contributions to their families and others and discuss the strengths they discovered that meant the most to them. Courageously discussing their end-of-life preferences is another type of strength that can relieve families of burden and provide clarity (Ko & Nelson-Becker, 2013).

CAUTIONS AND BENEFITS

We believe the strengths-based and solution-focused approaches have great value, particularly for older adults who encounter life challenges with diminished friendship networks, emerging health concerns, and other losses. However, consider these cautions in using these approaches. First, although there is increasing evidence that these approaches offer benefits to older adults, the need exists for more formal research to provide empirical evidence of the specific mechanisms by which these approaches assist older adults in leading more fulfilling lives. There is some evidence for the value of strengths emerging out of positive psychology, as well as in the social work literature, and more is now available specifically related to older adults. However, there has been little discrimination of what type of older adult may benefit and who may not. Future research could include better delineation of how these approaches operate in comparison with other approaches and better evaluation of specific outcomes.

Second, when needs are minimized, a novice worker may lose the sense of urgency to address these needs. There are times when needs are critical and must be immediately addressed. A social worker does well to learn to discriminate when it is appropriate to engage a strengths-based or solution-focused approach and when emergent issues, such as domestic violence or other abuse must be addressed first.

Third, although we believe the approaches discussed here have lasting value and can be used to some extent in nearly every context, it is important to understand that in specific situations other approaches might better meet certain needs. As with any social work approach, no one size fits all. It is important for social workers who work with older adults to become adept at incorporating many models of practice.

We believe there are many merits to integrating strengths and solution-focused perspectives into work with older adult clients. Foremost is that they sharpen the focus on the capacity of older individuals rather than on pathology and disability. The strengths-based and solution-focused approaches do not ignore biological components; the social worker conducts a biopsychosocial assessment and considers biological influences in the larger context of the older adult's social environment. Thus, these perspectives work to counter dominant paradigms in many disciplines that discount the truth that healing generally resides within the individual. The strengths and solution-focused perspectives require workers to assertively look for strengths, resilience, and resourcefulness in their clients as well as the clients' families and environments. Such reframing can initially be a challenge, but social workers can train themselves to see in new ways, and this becomes a skill that develops over time.

The strengths perspective particularly gives voice to populations whose views previously were ignored. Listening to older adults, particularly older adults of oppressed groups, such as people of color, women, gays, lesbians, bisexual and transgender individuals, and people with disabilities, helps social workers understand more clearly how they managed to survive and even thrive in challenging environments. The emphasis on exploring strengths in the context of unique life experiences is beneficial across ethnic, cultural, and economic groups (Chapin, 2001).

Finally, using these perspectives can be energizing for the social worker who practices with older adults. Sometimes, when facing a long litany of challenges rehearsed by older adult clients who often find no redress in formal societal institutions, social workers can become overwhelmed, discouraged, and experience compassion fatigue. The perspectives detailed in this chapter can keep social workers fully engaged as they encourage older individuals to explore their hopes, dreams, and goals and, in the process, replenish their own energy reserves.

CONCLUSION

The strengths perspective and the strengths-based and solution-focused approaches focus on client and community capacity, resilience, and goals. These distinct strategies offer social workers a practice framework that helps them put into action values such as self-determination and social justice. The strengths perspective draws on a long but sometimes neglected tradition in social work of starting where the client is and of honoring the insights into the capacity to identify their own solutions that clients possess. Because older adults bring a lifetime of experience in working out solutions, these approaches can be especially helpful for the gerontological social worker. The next step is for gerontological researchers and practitioners to further elucidate these approaches to determine how the strengths-based and solution-focused approaches can be most effectively implemented in specific settings and conditions.

REFERENCES

Berger, P., & Luckmann, T. (1967). *The social construction of reality*. Garden City, NY: Anchor/Doubleday.

Bonjean, M. J. (1997). Solution-focused brief therapy with aging families. In T. D. Hargrave & S. M. Hanna (Eds.), *The aging family: New visions in theory, practice and reality* (pp. 81–100). New York, NY: Brunner/Mazel.

Bonjean, M. J. (2003). Solution-focused therapy: Elders enhancing exceptions. In J. L. Ronch & J. A. Goldfield (Eds.), *Mental wellness in aging: Strengths-based approaches* (pp. 201–236). Baltimore, MD: Health Professions Press.

Bryant, F. (2003). Savoring beliefs inventory (SBI): A scale for measuring beliefs about savoring. *Journal of Mental Health*, 12, 175–192. doi:10.1080/0963823031000103489

Chapin, R. (1995). Social policy development: The strengths perspective. *Social Work*, 40, 506–514.

Chapin, R. (2001). Building on the strengths of older women. In K. J. Peterson & A. Lieberman (Eds.), *Building on women's strengths: An agenda for the 21st century* (Rev. ed., pp. 169–195). Binghamton, NY: Haworth Press.

Chapin, R. (2014). *Social policy for effective practice: A strengths approach*. London, England: Routledge.

Chapin, R., Sergeant, J. F., Landry, S. T., Leedahl, S. N., Rachlin, R., Koenig, T. L., & Graham, A. (2013). Reclaiming joy: Pilot evaluation of a mental health peer support program for Medicaid Waiver recipients. *The Gerontologist*, 53, 345–352. doi:10.1093/geront/gns120

Cowger, C. D. (1994). Assessing client strengths: Clinical assessment for client empowerment. *Social Work*, 39, 262–268.

Dahl, R., Bathel, D., & Carreon, C. (2000). The use of solution-focused therapy with an elderly population. *Journal of Systemic Therapies*, 19, 45–55. doi:10.1111/j.1545-5300.2000.39408.x

de Shazer, S. (1988). *Clues: Investigating solutions in brief therapy*. New York, NY: Norton.

de Shazer, S. (1991). *Putting difference to work*. New York, NY: Norton.

de Shazer, S., Berg, I. K., Lipchik, E., Nunnally, E., Molnar, A., Gingerich, W., et al. (1986, June). Brief therapy: Focused solution development. *Family Process*, 25, 207–221. doi:10.1111/j.1545-5300.1986.00207.x

Emmons, R. A. (2008). Gratitude, subjective well-being, and the brain. In M. Eid & R. J. Larsen (Eds.), *The science of subjective well-being* (pp. 469–489). New York, NY: Guilford Press.

Fast, B., & Chapin, R. (2000). *Strengths-based care management for older adults*. Baltimore, MD: Health Professions Press.

Fast, B., & Chapin, R. (2002). The strengths model with older adults. In D. Saleebey (Ed.), *The strengths perspective in social work practice* (3rd ed., pp. 143–162). Boston, MA: Allyn & Bacon.

Gable, S. L., Reis, H. T., Impett, E., & Asher, E. R. (2004). What do you do when things go right? The intrapersonal and interpersonal benefits of sharing positive events. *Journal of Personality and Social Psychology*, 87, 228–245.

Geertz, C. (1973). *The interpretation of cultures*. New York, NY: Basic Books.

Gergen, K. (1999). *An invitation to social construction*. Thousand Oaks, CA: Sage.

Judge, K. S., Yarry, S. J., & Orsulic-Jeras, S. (2010). Acceptability and feasibility results of a strength-based skills training program for dementia caregiving dyads. *The Gerontologist*, 50, 408–417. doi:10.1093/geront/gnp138

Kisthardt, W. E. (1993). An empowerment agenda for case management research: Evaluating the strengths model from the consumer's perspective. In M. Harris & H. Bergman (Eds.), *Case management for mentally ill patients: Theory and practice* (pp. 165–182). Langhorn, PA: Harwood.

Ko, E. J., & Nelson-Becker, H. (2013). Does end-of-life decision making matter? Perspectives of the older homeless adults. *American Journal of Hospice and Palliative Medicine*, 31(2), 183–188. doi:10.1177/1049909113482176

Lipchik, E. (1993). "Both/and" solutions. In S. Friedman (Ed.), *The new language of change: Constructive collaboration in psychotherapy* (pp. 25–49). New York, NY: Guilford Press.

Lipchik, E. (2002). *Beyond technique in solution-focused therapy: Working with emotions and the therapeutic relationship*. New York, NY: Guilford Press.

McMahon, S., & Fleury, J. (2012). Wellness in older adults: A concept analysis. *Nursing Forum*, 47, 39–51. doi:10.1111/j.1744-6198.2011.00254.x

Nelson-Becker, H. (2004). Meeting life challenges: A hierarchy of coping styles in African-American and Jewish-American older adults. *Journal of Human*

Behavior in the Social Environment, 10, 155–174. doi:10.1300/J137v10n01_03

Nelson-Becker, H. (2013). Resilience in aging: Moving through challenge to wisdom. In D. S. Becvar (Ed.), *Handbook of family resilience* (pp. 339–357). New York, NY: Springer. doi:10.1007/978-1-4614-3917-2_20

Nelson-Becker, H., Chapin, R., & Fast, B. (2013). The strengths model with older adults: Critical practice components. In D. Saleebey (Ed.), *The strengths perspective in social work practice.* White Plains, NY: Longman.

Rapp, C. A. (1998). *The strengths model: Case management with people suffering from severe and persistent mental illness.* New York, NY: Oxford University Press.

Saleebey, D. (2002). Introduction: Power in the people. In D. Saleebey (Ed.), *The strengths perspective in social work practice* (3rd ed., pp. 1–20). Boston, MA: Allyn & Bacon.

Saleebey, D. (2013). The strengths approach to practice. In D. Saleebey (Ed.), *The strengths perspective in social work practice* (pp. 49–58). New York, NY: Longman.

Schueller, S. M. (2010). Preferences for positive psychology exercises. *Journal of Positive Psychology, 5,* 192–203. doi:10.1080/17439761003790948

Seligman, M. E. P., Steen, T. A., Park, N., & Peterson, C. (2005). Positive psychology progress: Empirical validation of interventions. *American Psychologist, 60,* 410–421. doi:10.1037/0003-066X.60.5.410

Shearer, N. C., Fleury, J., Ward, K. A., & O'Brien, A. M. (2012). Empowerment interventions for older adults. *Western Journal of Nursing Research, 34,* 24–51. doi:10.1177/0193945910377887

Staudt, M., Howard, M. O., & Drake, B. (2001). The operationalization, implementation, and effectiveness of the strengths perspective: A review of empirical studies. *Journal of Social Service Research, 27,* 1–21. doi:10.1300/J079v27n03_01

Tice, C., & Perkins, K. (1996). *Mental health issues and aging: Building on the strengths of older persons.* Pacific Grove, CA: Brooks/Cole.

Weick, A. (1986). The philosophical contest of a health model of social work. *Social Casework, 76,* 551–559.

HOLLY NELSON-BECKER
EDWARD R. CANDA
MITSUKO NAKASHIMA

Spirituality in Professional Practice with Older Adults

7

Older adults typically value the importance of religion and spirituality in their lives. In the United States, adults over age 65 rate the importance of religion higher than any other age group: Between 80% and 90% across surveys consider religion to be very important (Association for Religious Data Archives [ARDA], 2008). Approximately 84% of adults ages 60–69 and 88% over age 70 express a Christian religious affiliation (Pew Forum, 2007), although with immigration other world religious affiliations are increasing though still statistically small. As health and mobility decline in older ages, formal religious participation tends to decrease, but private spiritual expressions (use of prayer; the Bible, other scriptures, and devotional reading; and religious radio/TV) tend to increase (Fitchett, Benjamins, Skarupski, & Mendes, 2013). Because religion and spirituality are often important aspects of their lives, older adults may welcome integration of a spiritual perspective when they interact with formal helpers.

Spirituality has become a focal point for investigation in many gerontological disciplines (Nelson-Becker & Canda, 2008). For example, recent studies about older adults have explored connections between cultural diversity and religiousness (Krause & Bastida, 2009), spirituality as an important resource for well-being (Piderman et al., 2011), collaboration between social work and churches (Pickard & Tang, 2009), and issues related to dying and hospice programs (Cobb, Puchalski, & Rumbold, 2012; Wortman & Park, 2008). Numerous empirical studies have examined the relationship between religion or spirituality and well-being, with about 80% reporting positive correlations between religiousness and greater happiness, life satisfaction, or other measures (Koenig, King, & Carson, 2012; Paloutzian & Park, 2005). In particular, empirical studies of the effects of religion on the health and mental health of older adults, though having mixed outcomes, generally suggest that religious and spiritual practices have salubrious effects on social support, coping, and quality of life at the end of life (Ardelt & Koenig, 2006; Lee, Besthorn, Bolin, & Jun, 2012; Nelson-Becker et al., 2013). These findings imply that religious and spiritual interventions may be valuable resources for social workers in helping to maintain life satisfaction for some older adults.

Development of a spiritually sensitive practice requires a strengths-based approach that includes listening to the profound and diverse questions clients express and demonstrating openness to hear all expressions of grief, longing, confusion, and joy that emanate from the human experience. Spiritually sensitive practice involves the ability to recognize and respond to these expressions with clients, but it does not impose a viewpoint that is contrary to the perspective of the client. It is a hearing of the heart: an ability to hear the pain and the hope in the stories clients tell and an ability to highlight for clients important themes or subtexts of which they may not be fully aware.

SPIRITUALITY: WHAT IS IT?

Spirituality is the search for meaning, purpose, and morality. It develops through relationships with self, others, the universe, and ultimate reality or the ground of being, however a person or group understands this (Canda & Furman, 2010; James, 1902/1961; Tillich, 1963). Transpersonal experience includes the journey within to the deepest nature of oneself as well as the process of fulfilling and transcending the individual self in the context of our connections with others and the universe (Puchalski et al., 2009; Robbins, Chatterjee, & Canda, 2012). It may also include direct mystical experiences with the divine (James, 1902/1961). Individuals and groups may express their spirituality with or without involvement in religious organizations.

Spirituality is expressed through religious involvement somewhat more commonly among older adults compared with younger cohorts (Marler & Hadaway, 2002). Religion refers to organized beliefs, values, rituals, and institutions that are concerned with spirituality, shared by a community, and transmitted through traditions. Older adults, however, in contrast to their often younger social workers, are more likely to be able to define and discuss religion or their practical philosophy of living more easily than they define spirituality, a term they may find unfamiliar or confusing (Nelson-Becker, 2003).

Existentialism refers to a philosophical approach where one's primary task is to find what determines level of meaning in life. This is related to spirituality in terms of the search for meaning and purpose, though is distinct from it in that one often feels a disconnection from any type of transcendent power. Often this may involve an anguished process where prior beliefs no longer seem valid and one begins a search for one's own meaning. Meaning is often conceived in a way that is entirely personal. At the end of life, terminally ill individuals may expand their curiosity in the hope

that this will lead to new self-discovery. This often takes an individual through a process of uncertainty and ambiguity that includes the re-examination of prior understandings to determine what one holds to be true (Nelson-Becker, 2006).

Spiritual care in client care recognizes and supports the holistic need for healing. Spiritual care involves attention to the needs of the soul for compassion (both giving and receiving love), meaning/purpose, hope, faith, and reconciliation. It involves initiating an assessment to determine whether spirituality and/or religion are important to a patient and if so, including these aspects in whatever manner is both important to the client and ethical. In social work, the term "spiritually sensitive practice" includes a reminder for practitioners to listen to spiritual cues. Many times, the spiritual discourse has been a hidden discourse (Nelson-Becker, 2003; Puchalski et al., 2009).

AGING AND THE SPIRITUAL JOURNEY

A natural concomitant of the aging process seems to be a turn toward exploration of the meaning of existence in relation to the universe (Nelson-Becker, 2013). This inner spiritual exploration that coincides with aging is an expected cultural norm across cultures and spiritual traditions. Tornstam (2005) found that older adults often exhibit an increase in transcendent attitudes, including delight in the inner world, less death anxiety, and greater sense of connection to the universe. Older adults approaching the end of life may take this challenge as an opportunity to reflect on the significance of their life, to consider possibilities for what occurs at death or after death, and to grow in wisdom even in the process of dying (Nakashima & Canda, 2005; Nelson-Becker, 2013). Yet others find no appeal in religiosity or spiritual growth that are expressions of explicit spirituality, and maintain secular patterns that they established years earlier.

It is important to note that spiritual struggle and suffering are also expected conditions in the life course (Ai, Pargament, Appel, & Kronfol, 2010; Fitchett & Risk, 2009). Suffering is an intensely personal experience that may be linked to spiritual distress. Although unresolved physical pain, especially when it persists, can and does lead to suffering, spiritual suffering involves hopelessness and profound anguish. Older adults who face serious illness or death may search for answers to their illness that cannot be found and may despair over choices made or future plans that must remain unfinished. Suffering surrounding spiritual questions is particularly difficult for social work and other health professionals, who seldom have training to address this kind of need. In fact, at times the only clear solution, aside from calling pastoral care associates, is to bear witness to this journey that lies apart from all attempts to ignore, manipulate, or control it, and to understand that healing spaces can be created even when the potential for cure is absent.

The remainder of this chapter identifies spiritual needs expressed by older adults and the clinical contexts where they appear. Eleven domains of spirituality useful for assessment are identified and sample questions are provided. The need for self-reflection by social workers and types of spiritually attuned activities useful under different circumstances are discussed. Finally, ethical considerations are presented.

SPIRITUAL NEEDS AND CLINICAL CONTEXTS OF OLDER ADULTS

Spiritual Needs

Spiritual needs pertain to the universal desire to locate meaning and purpose in life. Among many types of spiritual needs, there are three commonly expressed by older adults: the need to create meaning and purpose, the need to become empowered through connection to a higher power/transcendent force or nature, and the need to give and receive support through affiliation.

Continuing old affiliations or making new ones is a way to remain connected to community and continue to make contributions. In older ages, adults typically receive many services; they need to know that they can still make significant contributions to others, whether through sharing wisdom-based stories or imparting knowledge gained as a by-product of lifelong vocational pursuits. They value the support they both receive and provide to others.

Clinical Contexts

There are numerous life challenges across settings where spirituality may be a resource. Older adults particularly value attention to religion and/or spirituality, and this may become more salient during times of health or social crisis. Common contexts for spiritually focused helping activities include coping with chronic or terminal illnesses, bereavement, relocation, and caregiving.

When chronic illness leads to pain or life limitation, older adults often feel discouraged. One active response is to use emotion-focused coping (Lazarus & Folkman, 1984). "Religion helps me in a lot of ways. When I feel that I'm depressed about things, it just seems that I think about how the Lord is able and He rules the world. When I get that feeling, it helps," commented one older African American female study participant (Nelson-Becker, 2005a, p. 58). Social workers may support clients by engaging with their spiritual language and symbolism.

Bereavement is difficult at any age, but losses are magnified in later life when one's life companion dies and friendship networks begin to thin. Spiritual beliefs and practices may bring comfort for those who suffer from the loss of important companions and grapple with the meaning of life and the deaths of their significant others. Spiritual mentors, such as clergy or wise friends and relatives, as well as religious or nonreligious spiritual support groups can provide guidance and social healing.

Older adults who transition to greater levels of care, often in new locations, find it hard to maintain contact with their faith communities. In such cases, religious television and radio programs may take on new significance. Engagement with familiar religious activities, such as prayer, meditation, scripture reading, reciting a mantra or rosary, and attending available religious ceremonies, can be facilitated for interested clients. Spirituality can be a resource that aids in the transition.

Caregiver burden is becoming an increasing concern as older adults live longer with chronic conditions (Centers for Disease Control, 2013). Spirituality has been viewed as a resource for both the caregiver and older person in dealing with multiple physical, emotional, and social demands that contribute to this burden (Craigie, 2007; Kim, Reed, Hayward, Kang, & Koenig, 2011). For example, among many East Asian and East Asian–American communities, older adults are influenced by the Confucian virtue of filial piety to expect family-based care from their adult children (Canda, 2013; Chan et al., 2012). Concurrently, their adult children often feel a sense of obligation and/or genuine loving concern to care for their parents at home. However, contemporary social conditions, such as disruption of extended family households, migration of adult children for work, extended life spans, complicated medical conditions of older family members, and lack of adequate governmental policies and funding for elder care infrastructures, make it difficult for many adult children to fulfill these expectations. This sometimes leads to resentment by parents and exacerbated caregiver burden for children. However, some families are able to create flexible adaptations of filial piety expression. This exemplifies the importance of professional helpers taking into account the specific spiritual and cultural backgrounds of older adults and caregivers and helping them to maximize the potential for mutual benefit through creative approaches to the challenges of aging. Indeed, many people strive to meet the expectations of their own cultural or religious versions of moral expectations for elder care.

SPIRITUAL ASSESSMENT

Many social work agencies now incorporate some questions on religion and spirituality as part of their formal intake process. Usually this takes the form of one or two brief questions surrounding religious affiliation and church/synagogue/spiritual group attendance. In social work and aging, Ortiz and Langer (2002) developed a short protocol for conducting spiritual assessments with older adults. In addition, social work has developed spiritual assessment tools to assist practitioners (Canda & Furman, 2010; Hodge, 2001; Nelson-Becker, 2005b), as have medicine and nursing (Anandarajah & Hight, 2001; Fitchett, 1993; Koenig, 2002; Puchalski & Romer, 2000; Sulmasy, 2002) and psychology (Pargament, 2007). The Fetzer Institute (1999) also has an excellent resource.

Spiritual assessment with older adults should form part of a comprehensive assessment that is ongoing. Some older adults consider religion and spirituality to be private matters, so they may not be forthcoming about these dimensions in the beginning. An essential starting point in spiritually sensitive practice is to create a supportive and collaborative space for older adults to freely reflect on their religious and spiritual views and experiences according to their own interests. For example, a social worker might initiate a conversation in a casual manner by mentioning the presence of a religious painting in the client's room. Such an invitation creates an opportunity to make a smooth transition to a spiritual assessment.

Spiritual assessment can help the social worker to determine whether the client would like to explore spirituality further in counseling with the social worker or referrals to other resources. It is important to adapt these or other suggestions about spiritual assessment to the specific circumstances of the particular older adult's culture, spiritual perspective, interest, comfort level, and readiness. It is best to engage this topic after establishing sufficient rapport with the client to know whether this is relevant. Before embarking on a detailed spiritual assessment, the social worker should ask preliminary questions that open up exploration of the topic. The words "spirituality," "religion," "faith," or other explicit terms are not always necessary. The important point is to indicate openness to this topic and to invite conversation, always being willing to abandon it if the client wishes.

1. What helps you to experience a sense of meaning, purpose, and moral perspective in your life? (Note: If the client mentions spirituality, religion, or faith in any way, this can lead smoothly into the next questions. These questions should be tailored to the style and beliefs of the client. If she/he answers in a way that shows discomfort with terms like "spirituality," "religion," or "faith," assessment can be pursued by using terms and beliefs suggested by the client.)
2. Is spirituality, religion, or faith important in your life? If so, please give examples. If not, please explain why they are not important, or, if you prefer, we do not need to discuss this further. (You can skip to Option 2 in question 4 below).
3. If important to you, what terms for referring to spirituality, religion, or faith do you prefer?
4. Would you like to incorporate spirituality, religion, or faith in our work together? Please explain.

OR Option 2:

Would you like to incorporate the ways of experiencing meaning, purpose, or life satisfaction that you mentioned earlier? Please explain.

Posing these questions is crucial in setting an appropriate framework to customize the questions that are consistent with the client's orientation and needs. In Table 7.1, we present 11 domains of spirituality developed from previously cited sources (see Nelson-Becker, Nakashima, & Canda, 2007) along with examples of questions for use as an assessment

TABLE 7.1. Eleven Domains to Explore During Spiritual Assessment

Domains	Definitions	Relevant Questions
1. Spiritual Affiliation	The formal religious or nonreligious spiritual groups with which the client closely identifies his or her orientation.	• Do you belong to any spiritual/religious group? • What does membership in this group signify to you? • Do you express your spirituality outside of participation in a religious or spiritual support group?
2. Spiritual Beliefs	Perspectives and ideas related to existential issues, the divine, nature, meaning, or purpose in life.	• What religious or spiritual beliefs give you comfort or hope? Describe. • What religious or spiritual beliefs upset you? Describe. • Do you believe in God, a Transcendent Power, or Sacred Source of meaning? • Describe your vision of who God or this Sacred or Higher Power is. • How would your beliefs influence your medical decisions if you became very ill? Would your beliefs interfere with or enhance your medical care in any way? • Do you believe in an afterlife? What does this mean for you now?
3. Spiritual Behavior	The spiritual practices or actions engaged in daily or special occasions such as prayer, meditation, or worship (including both private and public, organizational and nonorganizational).	• What religious or spiritual behaviors do you engage in? • How often do you engage in these religious or spiritual behaviors? • Do you engage in these privately, with family, or in spiritual groups? • What about these behaviors do you find nourishing or undermining?
4. Emotional Qualities of Spirituality	Feelings associated with spiritual beliefs and/or experiences/activities (both positive and negative).	• Have you recently experienced an emotion such as anger, sadness, guilt, joy, love, or relief in the context of religious or spiritual experiences? • What significance, if any, did this have for you? • What feelings did you have in response (to a specific experience)?
5. Values	Moral principles and ethical guidelines derived from spiritual beliefs.	• What are the guiding moral principles and values in your life? • How do these principles guide the way you live?
6. Spiritual Experiences	Private or shared profound transcendent experiences shaping sacred meanings, including both ordinary and altered states of consciousness.	• Have you had any spiritual experiences that communicate special meaning to you? If so, please describe. • Do you experience a connection with spiritual forces such as God, angels, spirits, or deceased loved ones?
7. Spiritual History	Developmental trajectory of spiritual beliefs, values, practices, and experiences. Includes both gradual change and pivotal points involving crisis or life enhancement.	• Were you raised in a spiritual or religious tradition? Do you now practice in the tradition in which you were raised? Describe early experiences and parental involvement. • In what decades of your life were you involved in spiritual practices? Would you rate your involvement as low, medium, or high for each? Were there any change points? • What events in your life were especially significant in shaping your spirituality? • Who encouraged your spiritual or religious practices? • Describe any spiritual breakthroughs that are relevant to you now.

(continued)

TABLE 7.1 Continued

Domains	Definitions	Relevant Questions
8. Therapeutic Change Factors	Unique spiritually focused individual strengths and environmental resources available for healing, growth, and improvement of well-being.	• What might be an object or image that symbolizes/represents your spiritual strengths? • Could you tell me a story of how it helped you to cope with difficulties in the recent past? • How do you see that this particular spiritual strength may help your current problems? • What spiritually based strategies, rituals, or actions have helped you to cope with times of difficulty or to experience healing or growth?
9. Social Support	Assistance and support offered by other individuals and groups that promote client coping and spiritual well-being.	• When you have religious/spiritual concerns and problems, whom do you talk to? • In the past, what types of supports have you received from these people?
10. Spiritual Well-Being	Client's subjective sense of happiness and satisfaction related to his or her spirituality.	• How worthwhile do you find living your current life? Can you tell me more about it? How does this relate to your spirituality? • How does your spirituality help you to find meaning in your life? • How strongly do you feel connected to God/Higher Power/Spiritual/Universe?
11. Extrinsic/ Intrinsic Spiritual Focus	Extrinsic focus: client's spiritual identity and orientation tied to a certain group membership and conformity. Intrinsic focus: client's spiritual identity and orientation that may or may not be tied to a group membership, but is more flexible and relatively self-determined.	• Do you find the teachings and values of your spiritual group similar to or different from your own? Please explain. • How integrated are your spiritual practices with your daily life, apart from spiritual group participation?

Source: Developed from Nelson-Becker, Nakashima, and Canda (2007).

tool or guide. The goal of this guide is to obtain a comprehensive understanding of an older adult's relationship to spirituality.

In conducting an assessment, a worker needs to be ready to frame questions in a manner that the client can easily understand. Conducting a thorough spiritual assessment based on Table 7.1 is quite a formidable task. We recommend that the extent of assessment and selection of questions should be determined by the issues at hand, the setting and nature of the client–worker relationship, and the social worker's clinical expertise. Spiritual assessment may be incorporated into ongoing work with the client if time allows. The simple act of asking these questions to explore the client's spiritual life itself may generate a therapeutic effect, bringing some insights and clarification to issues that are important to the client. Sometimes, simply asking the previous four preliminary questions will be sufficient.

SPIRITUALLY FOCUSED HELPING ACTIVITIES

All social work activities with older adults may be framed within a spiritually sensitive practice approach if the social worker is intentional about his or her own spiritual development and spiritual path. Thus, although the social worker may not use explicit spiritual activities with a client because they are outside the area of focus or the older adult has no interest, the social worker may use implicit spiritual sensitivity in preparing for his or her own interactions. Explicit spiritually focused helping activities help older adults by promoting profound healing or spiritual development. These activities may be associated with a religious organization or a nonreligious support group, or they may be private. A social worker may foster this type of helping indirectly through networking and/or collaboration with religious/spiritual organizations desired by the older adult or directly through exercise of spiritual activities under specific conditions discussed below.

For example, research and clinical experience suggest that mindfulness-based practices can be appropriate for work with elders who are interested and able to engage relaxation, reflection, and focused mental awareness (McBee, 2008). Mindfulness-based practices involve helping people learn how to be aware of themselves in the present moment, with gentleness, clarity, and acceptance, through meditation-related activities (Canda & Furman, 2010; Canda & Warren, 2013; Hick, 2009). This helps people to free themselves from attachment to unhelpful thinking and feelings and to accept and let go of whatever is happening (including physical or emotional discomfort) with minimal distress. These practices are sometimes used by social workers privately to help them manage work-related stress and to enhance clarity in working with clients. They are also frequently used without explicit mention of their Buddhist origin or spiritual ideas. This is often considered desirable in order to keep the benefits of the practices without raising possible discomfort with explicit Buddhist or other spiritual language and beliefs. Sometimes mindfulness practices are used with explicit spiritual intentions (such as encouraging preparation for an optimal dying process) or even linkage with Buddhist meditation, Christian prayer, or other religious practices familiar to the client. The main principle is matching the older client's purposes and sense of comfort and interest.

Table 7.2 designates types of spiritually focused practices and the conditions under which they may be considered for use.

Implicit Spiritual Activities

Spiritually sensitive practice with older adults develops when the social worker relates with the client through genuine respect, unconditional positive regard, empathy, and openness to the client's distinctive spiritual perspective. These relational qualities should be the foundation of both implicit and explicit spiritually focused activities. Spiritual sensitivity requires explicit discussion of spirituality or use of overt spiritually focused activities only when appropriate for the client's goals, interests, and readiness. Section 1 of Table 7.2 indicates some spiritually

focused activities that may be appropriate when the client has not expressed interest in spirituality.

Establishing a personal intention to be fully and spiritually present helps center the social worker for whatever events or situations enter his or her physical, psychological, or emotional space. This type of preparation also is effective in countering compassion fatigue: it provides the ability to be fully connected to the present moment and manage the energy dissipation that often results from empathic engagement with older adults who may experience many forms of pain. Building a work and/or home environment with inviting spaces, artwork, and beauty provides a place where one can release the accumulation of energy that may be absorbed in all facets of direct social work practice. Listening to calming sounds or relaxing music helps build a holding or safety zone. Creating supportive networks with other professionals, friends, and family and engaging in personal renewal strategies such as taking walks in a natural setting also provide a type of inoculation against burnout when work with older adults becomes very complex or sad.

An important task of the social worker is to re-envision the current situation and to assist older clients in reengaging their passions in innovative ways or to develop new ones. There may be a clear moment of enlightenment, when the client reveals the truth he/she most needs to acknowledge. When the mechanism of careful attention is skillfully practiced, the social worker can also attune to other ways of knowing: the intuition, spirit, and artfulness that may help a client shift to a new perspective. This is accomplished well where multichannel listening is engaged. Multichannel listening is listening to the content of what is said, the emotion and manner in which it is said, the spiritual over- or undertones, awareness of the intended audience, and the context of the situation. Stories are shaped in a hermeneutic fashion where the storyteller and the audience form the landscape of memory and meaning (Gadamer, 1971). For older adults, memory has the power to extend the story back in time and reshape it repeatedly as the story moves forward with the aging of the storyteller.

Explicit Spiritual Activities

Spirituality can be engaged explicitly when the older adult has expressed interest in doing so. Sections 2, 3, and 4 of Table 7.2 indicate some explicitly spiritual

TABLE 7.2. Using Spiritually Focused Activities with Older Adults in Social Work

1. Client has not expressed interest in spirituality. (*Implicit Spiritual Sensitivity*)	A. Social worker uses other types of helping activities with client, for example:
	  1. Life review
	  2. Strengths-based interventions
	  3. Cognitive-behavioral techniques
	  4. Other therapeutic styles
	B. Social worker prepares self for therapeutic encounter through private spiritually based activities outside of session, for example:
	  1. Meditation
	  2. Relaxation
	  3. Visualization/imagery (e.g., seeing client surrounded by protective light)
	  4. Spiritual journaling
	  5. Engagement with a spiritual support group for grounding
	  6. Prayer for self-guidance
	C. Social worker engages with client in spiritually sensitive relationship, for example:
	  1. Relates with unconditional positive regard
	  2. Extends sense of hope to client until client can begin to build own
	  3. Listens with ears, mind, and heart to catch the meaning behind client verbalizations and nonverbalizations

2. Client has expressed interest, but social worker does not have relevant expertise or permission for direct use of spiritually focused activities; or social worker–older adult relationship has not yet been deeply established. (*Explicit Spirituality Focused Helping*)	D. Above activities plus (with caution): Social worker refers client to outside spiritual support systems, for example:
	  1. Ministers, rabbis, spiritual mentors with whom client already has relationship
	  2. Church/synagogue/mosque/temple leaders and spiritual teachers/healers congruent with client's expressed religious or spiritual affiliation
	  3. Other systems of potential spiritual support that are consistent with client interests

3. Client has expressed interest, *plus* a spiritually sensitive relationship and practice have been established. (*Explicit Spirituality Focused Helping*)	E. Social worker collaborates with outside spiritual support systems, for example:
	  1. Social worker works directly with outside supports chosen by client (e.g., chaplain or traditional healer) unless there is a concern
	  2. With client approval, social worker works with outside system members generally to build greater support for client or to assist in clarifying and mediating problems
	F. Above activities plus (with caution) direct use of spiritual helping activities by client request, for example:
	  1. Use of insights from spiritual/sacred writing
	  2. Exploration of personal sacred objects/symbols/stories
	  3. Use of art, music, poetry as therapy
	  4. Creation of spiritual map/time line including identification of significant mentors
	  5. Focused relaxation and breathing techniques
	  6. Exploration of forgiveness issues
	  7. Discussion of significant dreams
	  8. Development of rituals/ceremonies
	  9. Reading inspirational texts
	  10. Discussion of attitudes toward death/dying/afterlife
	  11. Reflection on harmful/helpful aspects of spiritual group participation

4. Client has expressed interest, *plus* a spiritually sensitive practice has been established, *plus* social worker has credentials or qualifications for particular activities (*Explicit Spiritually Focused Helping*)	G. Above activities plus (with caution) direct use of technique/therapy/ritual for which social worker is formally sanctioned and client requests, for example:
	  1. Use of prayer/religious ceremony with client when social worker is also a clergy person or recognized leader in the same religious group
	  2. Biofeedback
	  3. Jungian dreamwork
	  4. Body-centered therapy
	  5. Guided visualization
	  6. Meditation with a spiritual focus (such as Zen mindfulness meditation or Christian centering prayer)
	  7. Disciplines for healing and spiritual cultivation such as Reiki, tai chi, or hatha yoga
	  8. Herbalism
	  9. Acupuncture

Source: Adapted from Canda and Furman (1999, p. 254).

activities that may be appropriate depending on the client's goals, the practice situation, and the qualifications of the social worker. Sections 2 to 4 represent increasingly direct levels of engaging spirituality. Greater caution to avoid inappropriate impositions of the social worker's own values and assumptions should be used.

Basic explicit spiritually focused helping activities (section 2) are activities that do not necessarily require special training or supervision. Simply, they may involve referral to outside spiritual support systems. At times, explicit helping may involve advocating for the older adult when the spiritual or religious system itself has been a source of misunderstanding, betrayal, or pain. It may involve collaboration when the older adult asks the social worker to share information or to remain in contact with the spiritual mentor or leader.

If the older adult has expressed interest and a spiritually sensitive relationship is in place (Canda & Furman, 2010), the social worker may include activities such as exploring personal sacred objects/stories or a spiritual time line (section 3). Activities listed as possible choices should be used only if the social worker has competence or expertise with them. Activities in section 4 require that the older adult expresses interest, a spiritually sensitive relationship has been established, and the social worker has credentials or qualifications to conduct the activity (e.g., assisting an older adult to interpret the contents of a dream through Jungian analysis).

Further Ethical Considerations

An important consideration in choosing to be engaged in any type of spiritually focused practice, whether implicit or explicit, involves thinking through ethical issues. Work with older adults involves a self-assessment process. In the context of practice, social workers often encounter situations that help them understand their own values better. They grow as they engage in self-reflection that assists in identifying limitations, biases, and negative attitudes. Achieving value clarity calls one to be open to explore personal understandings and to refine these understandings based on further evidence (Canda & Furman, 2010; Nelson-Becker, 2008). Questions to ask oneself include: What types of experiences have I had that shaped my current reaction? What does this response suggest about my strengths and limits

in regard to this helping situation and generally? Is there something here that I want to work on? If so, what is my plan?

Other principles that are important to consider from an ethical standpoint include respect, client-centeredness, and inclusivity (Canda & Furman, 2010; Canda, Nakashima, & Furman, 2004). Respect in work with older adults includes demonstrating respect for all secondary clients as well as the primary client. Client-centeredness involves honoring the older adult's aspirations, values, and dreams even when they are very different from our own. It means helping clients to achieve their goals, even when we might disagree that a goal is in their best interest. Inclusivity concerns include honoring diverse spiritual expressions even when they are quite different from our own.

Before social workers engage in any type of spiritual helping activity with an older adult, they need to be clear that there is no motive aside from the welfare of the client. For example, if the social worker privately prays for a client with a petition for something that is contrary to the older adult's self-determined goal, this raises concerns about client self-determination and informed consent. Activities need to be performed in a way that honors the older adult and the traditions of the association or organization connected to the activity. Some activities are not permitted to be conducted outside of formal affiliation and authorization with the religious tradition, such as Christian sacraments and indigenous healing ceremonies. For example, unless a social worker is also an ordained or lay minister in a faith tradition that practices administration to the sick, also known as laying on of hands, and the older adult is a member of the same faith tradition or seeks out this ritual, it should not be practiced out of context. The social worker should have competency and skill in the activity, and also permission from the client and the culture or group that is associated with the activity to conduct it.

CONCLUSION

Spiritually focused assessment and helping activities should be included among the strategies social workers use with older adults, especially because spirituality tends to be important to older cohorts. The resources contained in this chapter, a spiritual assessment tool and a guide for when and how to include spiritual helping activities, are intended to be practical applications for social workers interested either in developing a spiritual component in their work with older adults or deepening and extending the spiritual foundation they already employ. Though there has been a surge of research in the areas of religion and spirituality, more specific research should be conducted related to aging (George, Kinghorn, Koenig, Gammon, & Blazer, 2013). Gerontological social workers would benefit from exploring spirituality through dialogue with other practitioners, researchers, educators, and older adults.

REFERENCES

Ai, A. L., Pargament, K. I., Appel, H. B., & Kronfol, Z. (2010). Depression following open-heart surgery: A path model involving interleukin-6, spiritual struggle, and hope under preoperative distress. *Journal of Clinical Psychology, 66*, 1057–1075. doi:10.1002/jclp.20716

Anandarajah, G., & Hight, E. (2001). Spirituality and medical practice: Using HOPE questions as a practical tool for spiritual assessment. *American Family Physician, 63*, 81–88. http://www.aafp.org/journals/afp.html?cmpid=_van_188

Ardelt, M., & Koenig, C. (2006). The role of religion for hospice patients and relatively healthy older adults. *Research on Aging, 28*, 184–215. doi:10.1177/0164027505284165

Association for Religion Data Archives (ARDA). (2008). *Quick stats: US religious surveys*. Retrieved April 14, 2009, from http://www.thearda.com/quickstats/index.asp

Canda, E. R. (2013). Filial piety and care for elders: A contested Confucian virtue re-examined. *Journal of Ethnic and Cultural Diversity in Social Work, 22*(3–4), 213–234. doi:10.1080/15313204.2013.843134

Canda, E. R., & Furman, L. D. (1999). *Spiritual diversity in social work practice: The heart of helping*. New York, NY: Free Press.

Canda, E. R., & Furman, L. D. (2010). *Spiritual diversity in social work practice: The heart of helping* (2nd ed.). New York, NY: Oxford University Press.

Canda, E. R., Nakashima, M., & Furman, L. D. (2004). Ethical considerations about spirituality in social work: Insights from a national qualitative survey. *Families in Society, 85*, 27–35. doi:10.1606/1044-3894.256

Canda, E., & Warren, S. (2013-11-04). Mindfulness-Based Therapy. Encyclopedia of Social Work. Retrieved 13 May. 2015, from http://socialwork.oxfordre.com/

view/10.1093/acrefore/9780199975839.001.0001/acrefore-9780199975839-e-988.

Centers for Disease Control (CDC). (2013). *Assuring healthy caregivers: A public health approach to translating research into practice*. Retrieved August 26, 2013, from http://www.cdc.gov/aging/caregiving/assuring.htm

Chan, C. L. W., Ho, A. H. Y., Leung, P. P. Y., Chochinov, H. M., Neimeyer, R. A., Pang, S. M. C., & Tse, D. M. W. (2012). The blessings and curses of filial piety on dignity at the end-of-life: Lived experience of Hong Kong Chinese adult children caregivers. *Journal of Ethnic and Cultural Diversity in Social Work, 21*, 217–296. doi:10.1080/15313204.2012.729177

Cobb, M., Puchalski, C. M., & Rumbold, B. D. (2012). *Oxford textbook of spirituality in healthcare*. Oxford, England: Oxford University Press. doi:10.1093/med/9780199571390.001.0001

Craigie, F. C. J. (2007). Spiritual caregiving by health care professionals: Physicians, nurses, and other also have important contributions to make. *Health Progress (Saint Louis, Mo.), 88*, 2.

Fetzer Institute. (1999). *Multidimensional measurement of religiousness/spirituality for use in health research*. Kalamazoo, MI: Author.

Fitchett, G. (1993). *Assessing spiritual needs: A guide for caregivers*. Minneapolis, MN: Augsburg Press. doi:10.1002/(SICI)1099-1611(199909/10)8:5<461::AID-PON417>3.0.CO;2-P

Fitchett, G., Benjamins, M. R., Skarupski, K. A., & Mendes, L. C. F. (2013). Worship attendance and the disability process in community-dwelling older adults. *Journals of Gerontology. Series B, Psychological Sciences and Social Sciences, 68*, 235–245. doi:10.1093/geronb/gbs165

Fitchett, G., & Risk, J. L. (2009). Screening for spiritual struggle. *Journal of Pastoral Care and Counseling: JPCC, 66*, 1–12. http://www.jpcp.org/jpcc.htm

Gadamer, H. G. (1971). *Truth and method*. New York, NY: Crossroad.

George, L., Kinghorn, W., Koenig, H., Gammon, P., & Blazer, D. (2013). Why gerontologists should care about empirical research on religion and health: Transdisciplinary perspectives. *The Gerontologist 53*(6), 898–906. doi:10.1093/geront/gnt002.

Hick, S. F. (Ed.). (2009). *Mindfulness and social work*. Chicago, IL: Lyceum Books.

Hodge, D. R. (2001). Spiritual assessment: A review of major qualitative methods and a new framework for assessing spirituality. *Social Work, 46*, 203–214. doi:10.1093/sw/46.3.203

James, W. (1961). *The varieties of religious experience*. New York, NY: Collier Books. (Original work published 1902).

Kim, S. S., Reed, P. G., Hayward, R. D., Kang, Y., & Koenig, H. G. (2011). Spirituality and psychological well-being: Testing a theory of family interdependence among family caregivers and their elders. *Research in Nursing and Health, 34,* 103–115. doi:10.1002/nur.20425

Koenig, H. G. (2002). *Spirituality in patient care: Why, how, when, and what.* Philadelphia, PA: Templeton Foundation Press.

Koenig, H. G., King, D. E., & Carson, V. B. (2012). *Handbook of religion and health.* New York, NY: Oxford University Press.

Krause, N., & Bastida, E. (2009). Religion, suffering, and health among older Mexican Americans. *Journal of Aging Studies, 23,* 114–123. doi:10.1016/j.jaging.2008.11.002

Lazarus, R. S., & Folkman, S. (1984). *Stress, appraisal, and coping.* New York, NY: Springer.

Lee, K. H., Besthorn, F. H., Bolin, B. L., & Jun, J. S. (2012). Stress, spiritual, and support coping, and psychological well-being among older adults in assisted living. *Journal of Religion and Spirituality in Social Work, 31,* 328–347. doi:10.1080/15426432.2012.716287

Marler, P. L., & Hadaway, C. K. (2002). Being religious or being spiritual in America: A zero-sum proposition? *Journal for the Scientific Study of Religion, 41,* 289–300. doi:10.1111/1468-5906.00117

McBee, L. (2008). *Mindfulness-based elder care.* New York, NY: Springer.

Nakashima, M., & Canda, E.R. (2005). Positive dying and resiliency in later life: A qualitative study. *Journal of Aging Studies, 19,* 109–125. doi:10.1016/j.jaging.2004.02.002

Nelson-Becker, H. B. (2003). Practical philosophies: Interpretations of religion and spirituality by African-American and Jewish elders. *Journal of Religious Gerontology, 14,* 85–99. doi:10.1300/J078v14n02_01

Nelson-Becker, H. (2005a). Religion and coping in older adults. *Journal of Gerontological Social Work, 45,* 51–68. doi:10.1300/J083v45n01_04

Nelson-Becker, H. B. (2005b). Development of a spiritual support scale for use with older adults. *Journal of Human Behavior in the Social Environment, 11,* 195–212. doi:10.1300/J137v11n03_10

Nelson-Becker, H. (2006). Voices of resilience: Older adults in hospice care. *Journal of Social Work in End-of-Life and Palliative Care, 2,* 87–106. doi:10.1300/J457v02n03_07

Nelson-Becker, H. (2008). Integrating spirituality in practice: From inner journey to outer engagement. *Journal of Geriatric Care Management, 18,* 10–15. http://www.caremanager.org/members-only/member-resources/gcm-journal/

Nelson-Becker, H. (2013). Resilience in aging: Moving through challenge to wisdom. In Dorothy C. Becvar (Ed.), *Handbook of family resilience* (pp. 339–357). New York, NY: Springer. doi:10.1007/978-1-4614-3917-2_20

Nelson-Becker, H., Ai, L. A., Hopp, F., McCormick, T. R., Schlueter, J. O., & Camp, J. K. (2013). Spirituality and religion in end-of-life care: The challenge of interfaith and cross-generational matters in changing environments. *British Journal of Social Work,* 1–16. doi:10.1093/bjsw/bct110

Nelson-Becker, H., & Canda, E. R. (2008). Spirituality, religion, and aging research in social work: State of the art and future possibilities. *Journal of Religion, Spirituality, and Aging, 20,* 177–193. doi:10.1080/15528030801988849

Nelson-Becker, H. B, Nakashima, M., & Canda, E. R. (2007). Spiritual assessment in aging: A framework for clinicians. *Journal of Gerontological Social Work, 48,* 331–347. doi:10.1300/J083v48n03_04

Ortiz, L. P., & Langer, N. (2002). Assessment of spirituality and religion in later life: Acknowledging clients' needs and personal resources. *Journal of Gerontological Social Work, 37,* 5–21. doi:10.1300/J083v37n02_02

Paloutzian, R. F., & Park, C. L. (2005). *Handbook of the psychology of religion and spirituality.* New York, NY: Guilford Press.

Pargament, K. I. (2007). *Spiritually integrated psychotherapy: Understanding and addressing the sacred.* New York, NY: Guilford Press.

Pew Forum on Religion in the Public Life. (2007). *US religious landscape survey: Chapter 3. Religious affiliation and demographic groups.* Retrieved on April 14, 2009, from http://religions.pewforum.org/reports#

Pickard, J., & Tang, F. (2009). Older adults seeking mental health counseling in a NORC. *Research on Aging, 31,* 638–660. doi:10.1177/0164027509343539

Piderman, K. M., Lapid, M. I., Stevens, S. R., Ryan, S. M., Somers, K. J., Kronberg, M. T., . . . Rummans, T. A. (2011). Spiritual well-being and spiritual practices in elderly depressed psychiatric inpatients. *Journal of Pastoral Care and Counseling: JPCC, 65,* 1–11. http://www.jpcp.org/jpcc.htm

Puchalski, C., Ferrel, B., Virani, R., Otis-Green, S., Baird, P., Bull, J., . . . Sulmasy, D. (2009). Improving the quality of spiritual care as a dimension of palliative care: The report of the consensus conference. *Journal of Palliative Medicine, 12,* 885–904. doi:10.1089/jpm.2009.0142

Puchalski, C. M., & Romer, A. L. (2000). Taking a spiritual history allows clinicians to understand patients more fully. *Journal of Palliative Medicine, 3,* 129–137. doi:10.1089/jpm.2000.3.129

Robbins, S. P., Chatterjee, P., & Canda, E. R. (2012). *Contemporary human behavior theory: A critical perspective for social work* (3rd ed.). Boston, MA: Pearson Allyn & Bacon.

Sulmasy, D. P. (2002). A biopsychosocial-spiritual model of the care of patients at the end of life. *The Gerontologist, 42,* 24–33. doi:10.1093/geront/42.suppl_3.24

Tillich, P. (1963). *The eternal now.* New York, NY: Scribner.

Tornstam, L. (2005). *Gerotranscendence: A developmental theory of positive aging.* New York, NY: Springer.

Wortman J., & Park, C. (2008). Religion and spirituality in adjustment following bereavement: An integrative review. *Death Studies, 32,* 703–736. doi:10.1080/07481180802289507

KEVIN J. MAHONEY
ERIN MCGAFFIGAN
MARK SCIEGAJ
KAREN ZGODA
ELLEN MAHONEY

Approaches to Empowering Individuals and Communities

Jane Addams, once described by FBI director J. Edgar Hoover as the most dangerous woman in America, was born to an upper-class family in 1860 (Specht & Courtney, 1994). Abandoning her social class and the privilege it afforded, Addams dedicated her life to serving the poor. She worked hard to promote international peace and to improve the social conditions that caused poverty. Addams became internationally known for creating Hull House, a settlement house located in a poor, working-class neighborhood in Chicago. She strongly believed the poor were victims of social and economic conditions, so she lived and worked with these neighbors, in their cultural and community contexts, to help them help themselves (Addams, 1910).

Addams is credited with laying the groundwork for what is now called empowerment-based practice in social work. Building on the work of Addams, contemporary empowerment theory grew out of the progressive social movements of the 1960s and 1970s. These social movements, including the women's movement, the Black Power movement, and the welfare rights movement, were founded to change oppressive social conditions in the United States. Acting in accordance with the principle of self-determination, empowered communities and individuals fought for the right to determine their own fates. Micro and macro level interventions of empowerment were designed to better the lives and communities of oppressed peoples and thus ultimately effect a progressive transformation in society (Gutiérrez, Parsons, & Cox, 1998).

Although specific definitions of empowerment abound, it is clear that many social workers are currently examining the significance of power for their clients (Gutiérrez, DeLois, & GlenMaye, 1995). Relying on a definition supplied by Solomon (1976), the National Association of Social Workers (NASM, 2001), as part of their National Committee on Racial and Ethnic Diversity, defines empowerment as essentially an individual's ability to do for himself or herself. This involves fostering a connection between an individual and his or her own power and reaching across cultural barriers to become further empowered. Lee (1994) adds to this definition by stating that the focus of empowerment should be on members of stigmatized groups. Askheim (2003), Boehm and Staples (2002), and Adams (2003) assert that empowerment deals with the transmission of power such that the disempowered take or receive power. In this case, individuals are the experts at using their skills, competencies, and self-determination to act in their best interest. The social worker facilitates this process. The World Bank (2002) defines empowerment in terms of poor people and their expansion of assets and capabilities such that they can assert power over the institutions that affect them.

Empowerment theory today is essentially a broad, yet fairly consistent, collection of concepts, methods, and models designed to develop power in individuals, families, groups, and communities (Gutiérrez et al., 1998). Empowerment theory asserts that there are numerous, perpetuating problems associated with an absence of power. Unequal access to resources, caused by an unequal distribution of power, prevents individuals and groups in oppressed communities from gaining the social goods they need. As a result, vulnerable persons are unable to shield themselves from the negative effects of oppression, including poor functioning in family and community systems.

The absence of power may produce intense feelings and behaviors. Pinderhughes (1994) asserts that individuals who are less powerful may feel less gratified, experience less pleasure and more pain, feel alone, fear their own anger and/or anger at the more powerful, fear abandonment, feel inferior, deprived, or incompetent, and have a strong tendency toward depression. Common behaviors among the less powerful include an inability to impact an external system of the self, projection of acceptable attributes (i.e., smart, attractive, competent) onto the power group, distrust, sensitivity to discrimination, paranoia, isolation, use of passive-aggressive behavior as a defense mechanism, rigidity in behavior to control feelings of powerlessness, striking out or becoming aggressive to avoid feeling powerless, and use of deception.

Major empowerment theorists recommend similar intervention strategies to achieve empowerment, most commonly beginning with an individual and expanding to include sociopolitical systems (Askheim, 2003; Cox & Parsons, 1993; Gutiérrez et al., 1998). At an individual level, a relationship between the social worker and the client is established, linking families to needed services, raising consciousness, and empowering goals and outcomes. Individual goals may include increasing control over one's life, increasing self-confidence, and, as a result of increased knowledge and skills, better self-perception. If these elements are adequately addressed, individuals should be able to take more control over their lives. At a structural level, the focus shifts to community and societal change. Social

workers work with clients to gain knowledge about sociopolitical issues and power structures, develop advocacy skills, learn methods of sociopolitical change, and engage in social action. Fundamentally, work at this level deals with the social structures and power relations that construct barriers to individual and community empowerment. As a result of these interventions, people and communities resolve disempowering situations and thus rebuild and reclaim an empowered status in society. Outcomes of empowerment-based interventions may include changes in self-efficacy, self-awareness, feeling that one has rights, self-acceptance, critical thinking, knowledge, skills, assertiveness, asking for help, problem solving, accessing resources, practicing new skills, lobbying, community organization, collaboration, and political action.

It should be noted that, under the empowerment model, the relationship between social worker and client is based on collaboration and mutual responsibility, not the traditional professional–client relationship (Johnson, 2011; Laverack, 2006). Indeed, the success of the empowerment intervention depends heavily on the success of this relationship, also referred to as a balanced partnership of an egalitarian relationship. As problems of disempowerment are rooted in sociopolitical systems, social workers and clients should act as partners with a common interest in addressing the problem. Using dialogue and critical analysis, the social worker should both work with the client and facilitate the empowerment process of the client. Clients bring just as much valuable expertise to the problem situation as the social worker does.

EMPOWERING THE ELDERLY

The elderly face a unique set of factors that contribute to a loss of power (Cox & Parsons, 1993; Heumann, Winter-Nelson, & Anderson, 2001; Shearer, Fleury, Ward, & O'Brien, 2012; Thompson & Thompson, 2001). At an individual level, the elderly cope with a decline in physical health, increase in mental stress (frequently as a result of depression, loss, and grief), and loss of social support systems, including peers and spouse. Elderly clients may view their problems as unique, personal, and theirs alone to solve. At a social level, many elderly individuals cope with economic loss from retirement, rising healthcare costs, poor housing, discrimination resulting from ageism, loss of status and contributors' roles (i.e., from work and civic activities), political marginalization, continuing sociopolitical disadvantages for members of minority populations, and a disempowering social service model. These factors can interact to produce increased dependency, oppression, learned helplessness, internalization, and powerlessness and ultimately limit elders' independence and ability to actively participate in society. Indeed, due to ageism, an assumption may exist that the elderly need to be cared for and looked after, reducing unique needs to a focus on provision of care.

Elderly people in the United States value independence and privacy as the core of empowerment (Heumann et al., 2001). Many seniors want to age in the home they have known their entire lives; to own that home and manage that household is empowerment. Many prefer not to depend on visiting service providers who gradually usurp more and more decisions for their own convenience.

Accordingly, when the elderly need care, they want efficient outcomes and concrete results (Boehm & Staples, 2002). In terms of empowerment, the elderly tend to focus on their financial situation and ability to maintain it. They also focus on improvements in healthcare, social networks, living conditions, and relations with family and friends. In contrast, social workers often focus on the process of empowerment, rather than the results of the process, thus reinforcing a professional–client relationship. To be considered worthwhile and effective by consumers, the empowerment process should be cost-effective in terms of time and effort and show tangible results.

EMPOWERING INDIVIDUALS: A MICRO LEVEL EXAMPLE

One approach for capturing and describing some of the ways social workers can work to empower individuals and families is through case example. The Cash and Counseling Demonstration and Evaluation (CCDE) shows how older adults and persons with disabilities who needed Medicaid-funded home- and community-based services were given the opportunity to direct and manage those services and the positive results that ensued. The CCDE, funded by the Robert Wood Johnson Foundation and the Office of the Assistant Secretary for Planning and Evaluation in the US Department of Health and Human Services was a test of one of the most unfettered forms of

consumer-directed care: offering elders and younger person with disabilities a cash allowance in place of agency-delivered services. Operating under a research and demonstration waiver granted by the Centers for Medicare and Medicaid Services, 6,700 volunteers from across Arkansas, Florida, and New Jersey participated in this large-scale test; half of them were randomly assigned to manage individualized budgets while the other half remained with traditional agency providers.

Consumers who met project eligibility criteria and expressed interest in participating in CCDE were randomly assigned to participate in the program, managing a cash allowance to purchase services through the state's existing system. The evaluation compared outcomes for consumers receiving traditional service packages with those receiving cash allowances with respect to cost, quality, and satisfaction. The evaluation also examined impacts on informal caregivers and analyzed the experiences of paid workers.

The resulting analysis showed that when Medicaid beneficiaries had the opportunity to direct their personal care services themselves, it significantly increased the proportion of consumers and (paid) caregivers who were very satisfied with their care. The program also reduced some unmet needs for personal assistance services and substantially enhanced consumers' quality of life. Moreover, it produced these improvements without compromising consumer health or functioning (Foster, Brown, Phillips, Schore, & Carlson, 2003). There were no major incidents of fraud or abuse.

The results of the controlled experiment were so positive that the Robert Wood Johnson Foundation, the DHHS Office of the Assistant Secretary for Planning and Evaluation, and the Administration on Aging authorized funding to replicate this approach in 12 additional Medicaid programs between 2004 and 2008. During this same time period two pieces of national legislation were passed to encourage the development of this option in all states, and the Veterans Health Administration began using this model to serve veterans returning from current conflicts as well as aging Veterans. Recent data show that as of 2010 every state had at least one program where people with disabilities could hire their own worker, while 44 states had a program where people could manage a budget for their long-term supports and services. Over 800,000 Americans are participating in such programs.

EMPOWERING INDIVIDUALS: A MEZZO LEVEL EXAMPLE

Peer support, which is the sharing of knowledge and the promotion of skills among individuals with similar life experiences, is a well-established empowerment strategy. Peer support can be informal (e.g., members of a Cash and Counseling focus group staying late to trade phone numbers and lessons learned on managing personal assistance needs) or a publicly funded service (e.g., skills training and advocacy services provided by local independent living centers run by people with disabilities for people with disabilities). Peer support, both informal and paid, has played an important role in the Cash and Counseling model. For instance, peers have assumed informal mentor roles and paid consultant roles for Cash and Counseling participants; trained program participants on how to recruit and train workers; and provided self-determination training for social workers.

Since 2007, the creation of the Cash and Counseling National Participant Network (or the NPN), has expanded the opportunity for Cash and Counseling participants to support one another, inform the design and improvement of programs, and advocate for program sustainability. As of 2013, the NPN had 950 members in 40 states and held teleconferences on a quarterly basis to allow for peer information sharing and support. These teleconferences, as well as routine requests from multiple sources for NPN members to provide a participant perspective at national conferences, has allowed the NPN to influence consumer-directed services at the micro and macro level as a result of empowerment-based practices.

EMPOWERING INDIVIDUALS: A MACRO LEVEL EXAMPLE

Macro level empowerment-based practices should complement social workers' individual or micro level empowerment strategies to ultimately support systems wide transformation. Empowerment is demonstrated at the macro level in a number of ways, one of which is meaningful engagement of program participants, family members, and advocates in the design and improvement of programs (often referred to as stakeholder engagement). Pioneer Cash and Counseling programs deployed a wide range of engagement strategies to design politically palatable programs that were driven by the needs of participants. The success of these programs and their engagement practices pointed to stakeholder engagement as a critical component of the Cash and Counseling model.

As Cash and Counseling programs developed across the country, many administrators struggled to meaningfully engage and empower Medicaid recipients and other stakeholders at the macro level. It is clear that engagement challenges are not limited to Cash and Counseling programs, but the existence of such challenges within an empowerment-based program like Cash and Counseling sheds light on just how difficult empowerment at the macro level can be. While minimal research literature existed on effective stakeholder engagement strategies (McGaffigan, 2011), timely solutions to engagement were needed given this innovative model faced continued objections from traditional-minded decision-makers during tight fiscal climates. Engagement solutions also had broader significance resulting from the 2010 Affordable Care Act mandate to engage stakeholders in a wide variety of healthcare and long-term care innovations.

McGaffigan's (2011) research on stakeholder engagement in Cash and Counseling programs identified three groups of factors that influence empowerment success at the macro (programmatic) level. These factors, which are grouped into people, approach, and environmental categories, influence engagement success on their own and interdependently.

People

Program participants, family members, advocates, and program administrators come with personal values, beliefs, and experiences that influence their perceptions of the importance of engagement and how they approach the engagement process. Participants who are well informed of program and engagement goals, confident in what they have to offer, and communicate effectively their areas of knowledge, confusion, and/or points of frustration will be most effective in an engagement process. Program administrators who are strong communicators, acknowledge participants as experts, constructively address conflict, and emphasize teamwork have been found to be most successful in empowering participants at the macro level.

Process

While program administrators may use various engagement methods (e.g., advisory groups, focus groups, public forums) to engage constituents, there are process factors to consider regardless of approach chosen. For instance, for program participants to be truly empowered, they must be informed. Information must be shared in an accessible format (e.g., large print and simple wording), and in many cases, ahead of meetings to allow for meaningful digestion. Other process considerations include clear and consistent decision-making protocols and communication practices (including follow-up on next steps) to allow trust to develop.

Environment

Open environments are the most conducive to empowerment at the macro level. For instance, research indicates that executive leaders who want to change the status quo, whether it be due to a severe budget deficit, a change in political appointment, or an aggressive push from external advocates, were far more invested in engaging stakeholders through an open and transparent process given their high stakes, and as a result, invested the resources (in both people and process) to make it work.

EMPOWERMENT IN A CHANGING PRACTICE ENVIRONMENT

Empowering individuals via participant-directed approaches is becoming more common at the micro, mezzo, and macro levels. Person-centered planning and participant direction are central elements in the health reform strategies embodied in the Affordable Care Act, and they are spreading in areas as diverse as managed care, behavioral health, and most forms of care integration. Consumers are experts when it comes to their own lives and lifestyles. Our overarching goal as social workers is to help them maintain and improve their independence and dignity. In doing so, we revisit the very roots of social work. We work with the community, in their community, to help them help themselves, and in doing so continue the tradition of Jane Addams.

REFERENCES

Adams, R. (2003). *Social work and empowerment* (3rd ed.). Basingstoke, England: Palgrave Macmillan.

Addams, J. (1910). Twenty Years at Hull-House with Autobiographical Notes. New York: The MacMillan Company.

Askheim, O. P. (2003). Empowerment as guidance for professional social work: An act of balancing on a slack rope. *European Journal of Social Work, 6,* 229–240. doi:10.1080/1369145032000164546

Boehm, A., & Staples, L. H. (2002). The functions of the social workers in empowering: The voices of consumers and professionals. *Social Work, 47,* 449–460. doi:10.1093/sw/47.4.449

Cox, E. O., & Parsons, R. J. (1993). *Empowerment-oriented social work practice with elderly.* Pacific Grove, CA: Brooks/Cole.

Foster, L., Brown, R., Phillips, B., Schore, J., & Carlson, B. L. (2003). Improving quality of Medicaid personal assistance through consumer direction. *Health Affairs, W3,* 162–175. doi:10.1377/hlthaff.w3.162

Gutiérrez, L., DeLois, K., & GlenMaye, L. (1995). Understanding empowerment practice: Building on practitioner-based knowledge. *Families in Society: The Journal of Contemporary Human Services, 76,* 534–542. http://alliance1.org/fis

Gutiérrez, L., Parsons, R., & Cox, E. (1998). *Empowerment in social work practice: A sourcebook.* Pacific Grove, CA: Brooks/Cole.

Heumann, L. F., Winter-Nelson, K., & Anderson, J. R. (2001). The 1999 National Survey of Section 202 Elderly Housing. Washington, DC: AARP. <http://assets.aarp.org/rgcenter/il/2001_02_housing.pdf>

Johnson, M. O. (2011). The shifting landscape of health care: Toward a model of health care empowerment. *American Journal of Public Health, 101,* 265–270. doi:10.2105/AJPH.2009.189829

Laverack, G. (2006). Improving health outcome through community empowerment: A review of the literature. *Journal of Health, Population and Nutrition, 24,* 113–120. http://www.jhpn.net/index.php/jhpn

Lee, J. A. B. (1994). *The empowerment approach to social work practice.* New York, NY: Columbia University Press.

McGaffigan, E. E. (2011). It's not so simple: Understanding participant involvement in the design, implementation, and improvement of Cash & Counseling programs. *Graduate Doctoral Dissertations.* Paper 55.

National Association of Social Workers, NASW National Committee on Racial and Ethnic Diversity. (2001). *NASW standards for cultural competence.* http://www.

socialworkers.org/sections/credentials/cultural_comp.asp

Pinderhughes, E. (1994). Empowerment as an intervention goal: Early ideas. In L. Gutierrez & P. Nurius (Eds.), *Education and research for empowerment practice* (pp. 17–30). Seattle, WA: Center for Policy and Practice Research.

Shearer, N. B. C., Fleury, J., Ward, K. A., & O'Brien, A. (2012). Empowerment interventions for older adults. *Western Journal of Nursing Research, 34,* 24–51. doi:10.1177/0193945910377887

Solomon, B. (1976). *Black empowerment.* New York, NY: Columbia University Press.

Specht, H., & Courtney, M. E. (1994). *Unfaithful angels: How social work has abandoned its mission.* New York, NY: Free Press.

Thompson, N., & Thompson, S. (2001). Empowering older people: Beyond the care model. *Journal of Social Work, 1,* 61–76. doi:10.1177/146801730100100105

World Bank. (2002). *Empowerment and poverty reduction* (D. Narayan, Ed.). Washington, DC: Author.

PHIL McCALLION
NANCY HOOYMAN

SECTION II

Social Work Practice in the Community

OVERVIEW

The time period since the first edition of this handbook has been marked by a number of societal changes, policy developments, and practice innovations that have both changed traditional functions for social workers in aging and heralded the possibility, if not always the reality, of new and higher impact roles. Some of the key contributors are listed here:

1. Increasing recognition that the growing aging population in general and increases in dementia and other chronic conditions in particular are challenging existing care options and presenting increasingly unmanageable financial and care challenges.

2. Implications of the extended resource constraints and loss of employer-provided pensions and retiree health insurance resulting from the Great Recession.

3. The passage of the Affordable Care Act (ACA) with its emphasis on extended coverage, prevention, improved care management, integrated care, cost savings, use of electronic tools, and advancement of evidence-based practices.

4. Merging of the Administration on Aging and the Administration on Community Living (ACL), which is encouraging a single entry point to services, shared delivery models, and planning for the aging and disability constituencies.

5. Recognition of the need for greater collaboration between Medicaid, Medicare, and the ACL in pursuit of the ACA's triple aims of better health, better care, and lower cost.

6. Medicaid reform in an ACA era, when the numbers of people covered is increasing in many states but there is growing emphasis on community-based care and developing new and often privately managed delivery models to support both cost containment and quality maintenance.

7. Reform of long-term services and supports to emphasize maintenance in the community rather than out-of-home placement, planning rather than crisis management, and improved collaboration and communication as exemplified in the ACL's No Wrong Door philosophy.

8. Growing emphasis on self-directed (e.g., consumer- or participant-directed), informed, and integrated approaches to support, which draw from research-based evidence but may also require the redesign of infrastructure, strategies for fidelity and quality assurance, and retraining of both the health and long-term services and supports workforce and the organizations they work for.

9. Greater acknowledgment by healthcare professionals of the social determinants of health and of social work's competence to address issues raised by those determinants.

Looking specifically at healthcare for older adults, there is a distinct shift toward a realignment of healthcare services away from management of acute health episodes toward management and support of chronic conditions. There is a concomitant realization that chronic care management requires better integration between hospital-/clinic-/physician-/health-professional-based services, community supports, and activated participants and family caregivers, thus necessitating a reorientation of both organizations and their workforce (Barr et al., 2003; Coleman et al., 2009).

With this rapidly changing environment in mind, it is appropriate to reconsider the functions of different organizational units in the health and aging network and the types of services social workers are being called on to provide. This section is therefore divided into two subsections: "Settings for Community-Based Practice" and "Social Services Available Through Community Settings."

SETTINGS FOR COMMUNITY-BASED PRACTICE

In the first of the eight chapters in this subsection, Darnell, Golden, Mitzen, and Shier consider how services are being reshaped by the ACA. They review ACA-driven changes of greater emphases on home- and community-based services, long-term-care reform, prevention, care coordination, physical and mental health parity, and Medicaid and Medicare redesign. Their analysis includes consideration of the emerging opportunities for social workers to be more involved in long-term services and supports, patient navigation, and behavioral healthcare coordination. However, they also caution that greater advocacy is needed from social workers to ensure that they are included in such innovations and for the profession to see themselves as bridging between and acting as "interpreters" for the health and community services sectors. Their advice is for greater awareness by social workers of the need to demonstrate social work's value.

In their chapter on hospitals, Judd and Sheffield re-examine the roles of generalized and specialized hospitals particularly in light of dramatic changes associated with ACA, Medicare cost containment, and increasingly complex patient populations. They too argue for helping other stakeholders, including other professional groups, to understand the distinctive contribution of social workers. And they call for social work to position itself to take the lead on new efforts to manage care transitions and complicated discharge planning; to continue advocacy, education, and informational roles; and to build needed evidence on the efficacy of social workers in discharge planning.

Kietzman, Naito-Chan, and Benjamin posit in their chapter on home care that this long-standing community-based aging and health service continues to accrue value, given the growing emphasis on maintaining people with chronic conditions in the community. Yet the role of social work in home care remains underdeveloped, stymied both by a lack of evidence on the effectiveness of social work interventions and the related perception that social work is not a primary or particularly valued home care function. This barrier to greater use of social work is institutionalized in Medicare, where reimbursement for social work services requires an enabling physician order, and in Medicaid, where social work services may only be provided when an individual is receiving other services designed to avoid nursing home placement. The authors do see new social work opportunities with the growing emphasis on person-centered care and improved care coordination and integration, but they too call for the building of an evidence base to support expansion of social work roles.

Another traditional delivery site has been Departments of Public Welfare or Social Services. In their chapter, Ernst and Smith emphasize that social workers most directly reach low-income and vulnerable populations through these agencies. They then argue that social work case management, brokering, and advocacy skills are required to navigate what are likely to be complex bureaucratic structures and increasingly restrictive budgets. They highlight critical skill areas of sensitivity to ageism, the dynamics of adult abuse and neglect, and collaboration within interdisciplinary environments as well as knowledge areas such as the Older Americans Act, income

supports, nursing home placement requirements, and community-based care, including respite. They also include new innovations such as evidence-based health promotion, self-management and falls programs, and greater support of environmental modifications in the home. Finally, they assert that social work in these agencies must offer leadership in addressing guardianship versus self-determination issues and power imbalances with the persons served. In agencies with limited and declining resources, they argue, social workers must advocate to maximize the benefits and services available.

As they look at the changing role of community mental health centers, particularly given the ACA's greater emphasis on integrating behavioral and physical health services, Cummings, Cassie, and Trecartin are concerned that there continues to be lower access by older adults than warranted by reported levels of mental health issues such as depression. They nevertheless are encouraged that greater integration will improve both quality of life and longevity. They argue that more work is needed in identifying mental health concerns among older adults and in helping them and their families to access community mental health center services. Social workers, they posit, are both the most prevalent available staff and the best prepared to address such needs. However, they argue for (1) changes in service delivery to include in-home services at these centers, (2) greater linkages with community medical providers, (3) social work services to become embedded in health homes, and (4) greater staff training on geriatric mental health issues and interventions.

Undoubtedly, the most well established intervention sites for older adults are the approximately 12,000 community senior centers, which as Rosario and Pardasani note, play vital roles in supporting community living and preventing institutionalization. However, that effect is not well documented, which contributes to centers being underfunded. Understanding senior centers also requires consideration of the extent to which they emphasize volunteer activities, social services, and provision of nutrition and how well they are adapting to changing demographics, including the greater diversity among older adults. As demographics and services systems change, the authors posit that a continuing lack of evidence for the value of their role at least fails to make the case for additional funding and potentially places centers in jeopardy.

In a rapidly changing healthcare environment, particularly with the ACA, Simmons, Schuster, and

Atkins argue there must be greater understanding and embeddedness of social work in health maintenance organizations and managed care. In particular, they highlight the opportunity for social work to assume the lead on targeting high-risk, high-cost populations through offering full care coordination as members of interdisciplinary teams and advancing evidence-based and preventive interventions. Additionally, social work must carve out central roles in patient-centered medical homes, preferred provider organizations, and accountable care organizations, thereby contributing to healthcare innovation and improvement of patient outcomes and supporting safe and stable community living. Above all, they maintain that social work must better understand its function in managed, capitated service delivery systems.

Finally, Hudson provides a historical overview of aging network programs, highlighting challenges created by the increased focus on Medicaid-funded home- and community-based services (planning for what) and the increased diversity of the older population (planning for whom, including targeting age-based services to those with greatest need). He then addresses the current challenges created by emerging confluence of aging and disability service delivery by discussing the development of both the aging and the independent living service networks, including their funding and underlying paradigms and how these ideas, resources, and priorities have been combined in Aging and Disability Resource Centers (ADRCs) and the Administration for Community Living. He also considers how self-directed care, the Money Follow the Person program, and other long-term services and supports innovations are driving this contemporary change process.

SOCIAL SERVICES AVAILABLE THROUGH COMMUNITY SETTINGS

In these five chapters, the prevalent social work paradigms and roles in the range of aging, health, and social service setting are described. Naleppa updates his chapter from the previous edition, reviewing the core roles of case managers to include management and support of personal care services, chore and homemaker services, transportation and escort, personal emergency response systems, information and referral, financial management and legal assistance, and nutrition—all services that are largely supported by the Older Americans Act. He differentiates between care and case management and sees the value of case management as well established and ready to respond to the new opportunities offered by ACA.

Morano, Gardner, and Swerdlow agree with the separation of case and care management and address specifically the role of geriatric care managers, typically a privately funded, entrepreneurial approach offering 24-7 availability. Geriatric care managers combine traditional case management activities with individual and family therapy, conflict resolution, and family mediation in what they argue is an approach that is more consumer driven and focused on the extended client system. Nevertheless, they see considerable overlap with traditional case management and a paucity of research on the distinctive contributions of geriatric care managers. They believe that geriatric care management will be a growing role for social workers but that many of its core activities will be absorbed within traditional case management. However, they argue that the 24-7 model of availability will be difficult to replicate in public agencies, suggesting there will continue to be a need for a private enterprise geriatric care manager role.

Maxwell and Kaye report a growing availability of counseling services not only in traditional social work and social service agencies but also in area agencies on aging (AAAs), federally qualified health clinics (FQHCs), community action programs (CAPs), and senior centers. Newly emerging locations include the ADRCs highlighted by Hudson, accountable care organizations and patient-centered medical homes described by Darnell and colleagues and Simmons and colleagues, and traditional and newly emerging behavioral healthcare providers. This growth in options reflects the emphasis on integration of physical and mental health delivery and the desire to maintain people in their own homes and to offer improved case management and wrap-around services. They also highlight new opportunities offered through telehealth initiatives. Arguing that support groups have traditionally been an important intervention mechanism, Maxwell and Kaye underscore social work roles in treatment and behavior change modalities, socialization and educational learning groups, and supportive self-help groups. They anticipate that the wellness visits required under ACA will lead to new demand particularly for disease-specific interventions, health promotion, and trauma and substance abuse-focused services and perhaps new funding for both counseling and support groups.

In a new chapter in this edition, Greenfield and Giunta argue for social work roles in supporting age-friendly community initiatives and recognize that the success of such initiatives relies on community development, community-based agency delivery of services, supportive housing, environmental gerontology and an underlying empowerment perspective. Above all, such initiatives find and build on value in place, locating in specific areas, seeing aging in place as an end goal, deliberately enhancing social and physical environments, and collaborating with multiple stakeholders. They describe naturally occurring retirement communities, villages, community partnerships for older adults, and the WHO Aging Friendly Initiatives. They also point to the challenges for social workers and other stakeholders in promoting and sustaining such initiatives, arguing for measures of effectiveness, a greater emphasis on inclusion, more attention to sustainability, and the identification of best practices. Finally they highlight the micro, mezzo, and macro level issues in these initiatives and the related skills social workers bring to their management.

Gonyea also addresses the aging in place concept and the dilemmas faced by communities and owner and rental housing stock, which was not necessarily designed for an aging population that wishes to remain in homes and communities. She highlights that those living in public housing and those with chronic conditions face greater challenges to aging in place; that is, those with high needs and low levels of resources are more likely to remain in housing that is least prepared to support their aging in place. Such dilemmas are examined in this chapter through an environmental press paradigm; additionally, lack of integration between housing and health agencies is noted as well as their contribution to overcare (often through forced nursing home placement) and undercare for older adults. However, the Olmstead Decision and a growing focus by HUD on understanding how best to house older adults are cited as expanding housing options and identifying best practices in integrating housing and healthcare.

Given the dramatic changes in social services and healthcare delivery, social work leadership is and will be critical to developing the evidence base for new and emerging roles and outcomes. These chapters capture the array of roles from direct care to policy and program development to advocacy that will support older adults and their choices in the years ahead.

REFERENCES

Barr, V. J., Robinson, S., Marin-Link, B., Underhill, L., Dotts, A., Ravensdale, D., & Salivaras, S. (2003). The expanded chronic care model. *Health Care Quarterly, 7,* 73–82.

Coleman, K., Austin, B. T., Brach, C., & Wagner, E. H. (2009). Evidence on the chronic care model in the new millennium. *Health Affairs, 28,* 75–85.

SECTION **IIA**

Settings for Community-Based Practice

INTRODUCTION

The expected growth in the 65 and older population in the coming decades will carry with it a sharp increase in the number of people with functional or cognitive disabilities. Among individuals turning 65, two-thirds are estimated to need either formal or informal care at home, and more than 1 in every 10 will need long-term services and supports (LTSS) for 5 or more years (Kemper, Komisar, & Alecxih, 2005). Thus, as our population ages, especially as baby boomers reach older adulthood, the demand for LTSS is predicted to rise dramatically.

As demand for a range of health and long-term care services among older adults and people with disabilities increases, the policies undergirding these services are changing in response. This chapter reviews recent and unfolding policy activity, considers the impact of these changes on their recipients, and sets forth ways for social workers to adapt to the new healthcare landscape.

HOME- AND COMMUNITY-BASED SERVICES AND LONG-TERM SERVICES AND SUPPORTS

The concept of long-term care emerged in response to the needs of people with limitations in their cognitive capacity or abilities to perform activities of daily living (ADLs), including bathing, dressing, and eating. Historically, people received these services in nursing homes, despite their preference to stay at home and despite the potential savings of public funds that could be achieved by providing these services in the community. Aging policy has been advanced through legislative actions while disability policy has developed in response to lawsuits and their corresponding judicial decisions. These historical differences are summarized in Table 9.1 and provide a context for the changes in LTSS introduced by the Affordable Care Act (ACA).

Medicaid, in effect since 1965, provides an entitlement to health insurance coverage for low-income people. It is the primary payer for LTSS, which includes home health and personal care, as well as services in institutional settings. State Medicaid programs must provide nursing home services for all individuals age 21 or older who need them, and may not limit access to the service or make it subject to waiting lists (US Department of Health and Human

JULIE S. DARNELL
ROBYN L. GOLDEN
PHYLLIS MITZEN
GAYLE E. SHIER

Services and Settings Inspired by the Affordable Care Act

TABLE 9.1. Legislative and Judicial Milestones in Aging and Disability Policy

Year	Milestone	Description
1954	Office on Aging	Arthur Flemming, Director of Health Education and Welfare during the Eisenhower Administration, created the federal Office on Aging. Flemming believed that "older persons need a dream, not just a memory" (Mackelprang & Salsgiver, 1996).
1956	Council on Aging	President Dwight D. Eisenhower created the federal Council on Aging "to coordinate interdepartmental policies and programs in . . . aging and to review existing activities and to make recommendation to meet the pressing needs of older citizens" (McCamman, 1956).
1965	Medicare	Congress created Medicare as a federal health insurance program for persons age 65 and older and persons with disabilities, regardless of income or medical history.
1965	Medicaid	Congress created Medicaid as a joint federal-state health insurance program for certain categories of low-income people.
1965	Older Americans Act (OAA)	The OAA established the Administration on Aging within the Department of Health, Education and Welfare and state Units of Aging to provide LTSS, enabling older people to remain in their communities.
1970	Independent Living	As a student at the University of California, Berkeley, "Father of Independent Living" Ed Roberts founded a disabled students' program with his group, The Rolling Quads. Later he and other advocates started the first Center for Independent Living in Berkeley.
1970	Urban Mass Transit Act	Urban Mass Transit Act required all new mass transit vehicles to be equipped with wheelchair lifts. The organization Americans Disabled for Accessible Public Transit (ADAPT), founded by Wade Blank in 1978, played a key role in establishing 1990 regulations mandating lifts on buses.
1990	Americans with Disabilities Act (ADA)	President George H. W. Bush signed the ADA, the most comprehensive civil rights legislation adopted to prohibit discrimination against and provide comprehensive protection for Americans with disabilities (Mayerson, 1992).
1990	Olmstead Decision	The Supreme Court ruled on Olmstead v. L.C. based on the "integration mandate" in the ADA. Key rulings included: Mental illness is a form of disability; institutional placement perpetuates unwarranted assumptions that people so isolated are unworthy of participating in community life; confinement in an institution severely diminishes everyday life activities.
2007	Money Follows the Person (MFP)	The Centers for Medicare and Medicaid Services (CMS) initiated the MFP Rebalancing Demonstration Grant program and awarded almost $1.5 billion to states proposing to transition more than 34,000 people from institutions into the community over a 5-year period.
2009	Community Living Initiative (CLI)	The US Department of Health and Human Services created the Community Living Initiative to promote federal partnerships in pursuit of furthering the directive of the Olmstead decision. A Coordinating Council guides partnerships.
2009	Aging and Disability Resource Center Program (ADRC)	AOA and CMS collaborated to create ADRCs, single points of entry into the LTSS system for older adults and disabled persons. ADRCs help consumers and families nationwide find information, services, and supports.
2010	Patient Protection and Affordable Care Act (ACA)	President Barack Obama signed the ACA law and the Health Care and Education Reconciliation Act, which together represent a major overhaul of the US health system. Key provisions include individual mandate to purchase insurance with subsidies to make it more affordable; employer mandate to offer coverage; expansion of Medicaid to all persons below 138% of the federal poverty level; minimum benefit standards; elimination of preexisting condition exclusions; reforms to improve quality of care and lower the cost of care.
2012	Administration for Community Living (ACL)	The ACL brings the AOA, the Office on Disability, and the Administration on Developmental Disabilities into a single agency to increase access to community supports and full participation, with focused attention and resources on the unique needs of older Americans and people with disabilities.

Services, Centers for Medicare and Medicaid, n.d.). Early on, advocates became concerned that many people living in nursing homes could live in the community if basic home care supports were available. States worked with the federal government to obtain waivers, or vehicles designed by Medicaid to test new and existing ways to deliver and pay for services, in order to create alternatives to institutionalization for targeted populations, including older adults and persons with disabilities. The concept of "long-term care" then evolved into "LTSS" to encompass services both in institutions and the community.

Home- and community-based services (HCBS) are Medicaid-supported waivers that allow eligible beneficiaries to receive services in their home rather than in more expensive and often less desired institutional settings (US Department of Health and Human Services, Centers for Medicare and Medicaid, 2013a). Such services include transportation, homemaker services, friendly visiting, respite, and home modification. Concerned about the demand for home care services, federal and state legislators limited access to the waiver programs, which resulted in waiting lists.

For older adults and for persons with disabilities LTSS has evolved along different paths. Aging has followed a "top-down" model guided by the Older Americans Act's (OAA) aging network of service delivery systems in each state. The OAA's underlying purpose was to enhance the ability of older individuals to maintain as much independence as possible and to remain in their homes and communities by focusing on income, health, housing, employment, long-term care, retirement, and community service. The disabilities movement, by contrast, has followed a "bottom-up" model emerging from the civil rights turbulence of the 1960s, when significant numbers of people with disabilities demanded access to the mainstream of society. During the early 1970s, Independent Living emerged as a program, a civil rights movement, and a culture, in which people with disabilities designed, operated, and governed their living arrangement with a strict philosophy of consumer control in response to societal discrimination (National Council on Independent Living, n.d.). Advocacy and lawsuits followed hand-in-hand: In 1990, the Americans with Disabilities Act was signed into law, followed by the 1999 landmark Supreme Court decision *Olmstead v. LC* (Mackelprang & Salsgiver, 1996). In the disabilities movement, people needing services are known as "consumers," not clients. Consumers rely on peer counseling to learn how to obtain and use services, and they recruit, hire, manage, and fire their personal care attendants. The primary goals of both aging and disabilities advocates, whether approached top-down or bottom-up, are to reverse the unintended consequences of the Medicaid entitlement to nursing home care, which led to premature or unnecessary institutionalization, and to assure that people have access to the supports they need to remain in their communities.

AFFORDABLE CARE ACT

The 2010 Affordable Care Act (ACA) sets forth comprehensive reforms to the US health system to provide "affordable, quality health care for all Americans and reduce the growth in health care spending" (Patient Protection and Affordable Care Act, 2010). The ACA's organizing principle consists of three pillars—improved access to care, enhanced quality of care, and reduced cost of care. These pillars deliberately parallel the so-called Triple Aim originating from the Institute for Healthcare Improvement, a nonprofit organization focused on promoting healthcare improvement: improve population health, enhance the patient experience, and lower the cost of care (Berwick, Nolan, & Whittington 2008).

Changes to Services Under the Affordable Care Act

The ACA makes several important changes to existing HCBS and LTSS programs serving older adults and persons with disabilities. It strengthens the Money Follows the Person (MFP) program and provides opportunities for more states to participate through September 30, 2016. The purpose of MFP is to:

- Increase the use of HCBS and reduce the use of institutional services;
- Eliminate barriers that restrict Medicaid expenditures to let people get long-term care in their preferred setting;
- Strengthen Medicaid's ability to provide HCBS to people who choose to transition out of institutions; and
- Implement procedures to provide quality assurance and improvement of HCBS (US Department of Health and Human Services Centers for Medicare and Medicaid Services, 2013b).

The ACA also expands the scope of the Community Living Initiative (CLI) and the opportunities available to states to promote and support community living for people with disabilities. This expanded role deepens the focus on the relationship between HCBS and accessible, affordable medical services (US Department of Health and Human Services, 2009). Many of the services needed by older persons to preserve dignity and their ability to live in the community, and those services needed by persons with disabilities to enable them to fully participate in society, are, in fact, identical or similar.

The ACA also creates new initiatives and incentives for states to improve care to older adults and persons with disabilities. For instance, the Balancing Incentives Program (BIP) was created in response to the integration mandate of the Americans with Disabilities Act, as required by the *Olmstead* decision. The program uses a Medicaid enhanced match (i.e., federal matching funds for expenditures, or FMAP, federal medical assistance percentage) to incentivize states that historically spent less than 50% of their Medicaid expenditures on noninstitutional LTSS to provide more noninstitutional LTSS. States must achieve stated goals by September 30, 2015, or be liable for the funds. The goals are to help states transform their long-term care systems by:

- Lowering costs through improved systems performance and efficiency;
- Creating tools to help consumers with care planning and assessment; and
- Improving quality measurement and oversight.

Another ACA initiative is the Community First Choice (CFC) state plan option. The CFC specifies required services and supports to enable people to live in the most integrated setting appropriate to the individual's needs, without regard to the individual's age, nature of disability, or the form of home- and community-based attendant services that the individual requires to have an independent life. Through CFC, states are required to offer hands-on assistance, supervision, or cueing for ADLs, instrumental activities of daily living (IADLs), and health-related tasks. They must also provide services that promote skills necessary for the individual to accomplish these tasks on his or her own, as well as voluntary training on how to select, manage, and dismiss attendants. States implementing the CFC option will receive a 6% increase in their federal match (O'Shaughnessy, 2013).

The ACA's health home state plan option focuses on providing comprehensive care management, care coordination and health promotion, transitional care from inpatient to other settings, individual and family support, and referral to community and social support services for beneficiaries with chronic conditions. Eligible beneficiaries have two or more chronic conditions, or are at risk for a second, or have one serious and persistent mental health condition. A Medicaid match of 90% is available for a 2-year period (O'Shaughnessy, 2013).

Other Key Changes to Medicaid

The ACA expanded Medicaid eligibility to all persons with incomes below 138% of the federal poverty level, but a subsequent Supreme Court ruling on the constitutionality on the ACA found the Medicaid expansion clause to be coercive, thereby giving the states the option to implement it (*National Federation of Independent Business (NFIB) v. Sebelius,* 2012). Following the decision, 23 states have elected (as of December 2013) not to expand Medicaid (Kaiser Family Foundation, 2013).

States have traditionally provided Medicaid benefits to people under a fee for service system. However, the aging population and increased longevity, coupled with chronic health problems, have put new demands on medical and social services. As the number of beneficiaries and covered services have grown, it has become increasingly difficult for states to integrate care across settings. Keeping pace with the latest health information system trends and client-management systems is a challenge for any governmental agency. Given these factors, along with the anticipated growth in Medicaid recipients under the ACA expansion, many states have turned to contracting out to managed care organizations (MCOs) to better coordinate care and control costs.

Under managed care, Medicaid reimbursement or financing systems are changed to a prepaid capitated payment system: The state Medicaid Agency contracts with MCOs, which in turn contract with and reimburse providers. State Medicaid payments to the MCOs are based on a reimbursement rate per individual enrolled in an MCO on a monthly basis, that is, a "per-member per-month" capitated rate. However, in Medicaid Managed Care (MMC), the contracts between the state and MCOs transcend simple reimbursement rates; MCOs are challenged with the important task of integrating primary, acute, and postacute care or bringing together components that were once separate. A successful MCO will integrate the following five healthcare domains:

1. Funding (source and structure of financing healthcare; e.g., Medicaid and Medicare);
2. Administration (regulatory, administrative functions, including eligibility and management of systems resources);
3. Organization (partnerships and relationships within an MCO and with outside community and health entities);
4. Service Delivery (management and systems of delivery, including care coordination);
5. Clinical (consumer health needs, standards of care for certain conditions/diseases, provider-consumer communication) (Kodner & Spreeuwenberg, 2002).

To add to the complexity, states must comply with the federal regulations that govern managed care delivery systems. These regulations include requirements for a managed care plan to have a quality program and provide appeal and grievance rights, reasonable access to providers, and the right to change managed care plans, among others.

As MCOs take over the responsibility to coordinate and manage LTSS services, the networks that have developed and functioned for the past 40 years are changing dramatically. MCOs are required to coordinate a person's care across systems of health care, mental health, social services, aging services, and services for persons with disability. At the same time, these systems and services will no longer contract with the state, but with the MCOs.

The MCOs rely on care management and coordination to maintain control over care and costs. Social workers are employed within MCOs as care managers, and MCOs also contract with private providers of mental health services and care coordination. Understanding how MCOs work and contract is critical for social workers.

Key Changes to Medicare

Medicare has never been a major payer for LTSS, and the ACA does not change Medicare's role in the LTSS arena. Medicare is, however, undergoing an overhaul that will impact beneficiaries. For instance, Medicare Part D's prescription drug coverage gap between the initial coverage limit and the catastrophic-coverage limit—more commonly known as the "Donut Hole"—will be phased out by 2020 through a combination of discounts and subsidies that close the gap. New Medicare provisions remove costs for the majority of preventive health services. In addition, an annual wellness visit to obtain a health risk assessment, medical history, and review of functional level/safety will be fully covered. The ACA also makes changes to improve Medicare quality and cost. For example, it seeks to improve care coordination for "dual eligibles" (i.e., persons eligible for both Medicare and Medicaid) by establishing the Federal Coordinated Health Care Office. It creates the Center for Medicare and Medicaid Innovation (CMMI) to test new payment methods and delivery system models that simultaneously reduce costs and improve quality. And it makes changes to how providers and hospitals are paid to encourage better quality and lower costs through a combination of incentives (e.g., accountable care organizations, or ACOs) and penalties (e.g., hospital readmissions). All together these changes will allow Medicare consumers to have improved access, reduced costs, and enhanced quality of care.

Increased Focus on Prevention

In addition to the improved preventive benefits to Medicare, the ACA contains other provisions to increase the availability of preventive services. It mandates coverage for certain preventive services, offers financial incentives to cover recommended services, and removes patient cost-sharing (copayments, coinsurance, or deductibles) for the majority of preventive health services. Private insurance plans must cover evidence-based screenings and counseling, routine immunizations, childhood preventive services, and preventive services for women. As a joint federal-state program, Medicaid's scope of services, including preventive care, is determined by states within broad federal guidelines. Certain benefits, such as physician services, are mandatory, while others, such as dental care, are optional. The ACA offers financial incentives to states vis-à-vis an enhanced Medicaid match to cover preventive services recommended by the US Preventive Services Task Force and immunizations recommended by the Advisory Committee on Immunization Practices without imposing cost-sharing requirements.

New Emphasis on Care Coordination

The ACA emphasizes care coordination through initiatives such as Patient-Centered Medical Homes and ACOs, and, importantly, includes financial incentives—a significant departure from past efforts—to encourage its widespread implementation. The National Coalition of Care Coordination defines care coordination as "a person- and family-centered, assessment-based, interdisciplinary, multicultural approach to integrating health care and social support services in a cost-effective manner in which an individual's needs and preferences are assessed, a comprehensive care plan is developed, and services are managed and monitored by an evidence-based process which typically involves a designated lead care coordinator" (SCAN Foundation, 2013). Care coordination begins with the patient and their family and is developed based on their needs, values, and goals rather than those of providers. Care coordination comes in many forms with application in numerous healthcare settings, but the majority of effective models include an assessment of patients' needs and resources, enhanced communication across an interprofessional team, and active involvement of patients and caregivers. This process is most often led by a designated care coordinator trained in any number of educational backgrounds, including nurses, social workers, pharmacists, or other disciplines.

The ACA does not explicitly lay out specifications of care coordination, but meeting the ACA's expectations will require effective coordination that includes the services described herein, particularly across transitions of care. New ACA programs incentivize better care as people move from one care setting to another. The Community Based Care Transitions Program (CCTP) provides support for improved care coordination that includes many care coordination activities. The goal of care transitions is to reduce hospital readmissions within 30 days of discharge, which ties CCTP to the Readmissions Reduction Program, a penalty for hospitals with excess hospital readmissions.

Integration of Physical/Mental Health and Mental Health Parity

Mental health needs are often complicated by age-associated changes in physiology, cognition, and social functioning, but mental health and well-being are critical to optimal functioning, physical health, and satisfying social relationships among older adults. Most older adults seek treatment first from their primary care physician, and 50% to 75% of all primary care visits focus on a mental health concern (Eden, Maslow, Le, & Blazer, 2012). Therefore, access to primary care and the identification of mental health issues in that setting are vitally important, as is access to mental health services when a need is identified.

Historically, insurance has been a barrier for both health and mental health services access. Most medical insurance carriers considered mental health to be a preexisting condition, hindering access to affordable healthcare. Under the ACA, people cannot be denied insurance based on a preexisting condition, including a mental health diagnosis. Additionally, the Medicaid expansion will improve access to health and mental health services. Lastly, the ACA requires insurance plans to cover mental health and substance services at an equal rate as that extended to medical care (National Alliance on Mental Illness, 2013).

OPPORTUNITIES AND NEW ROLES FOR SOCIAL WORK

As the ACA moves us from an episodic, disease focus to a chronic care focus, with some attention to social determinants of health, now is an ideal time for social workers to influence the health and well-being of older adults and persons with disabilities.

Home- and Community-Based Services and Long-Term Services and Supports

Primarily organized around the provision of HCBS, consumer-directed services are aimed at empowering older adults and family caregivers, giving them major control over the what, who, and when of needed care. Consumers of HCBS and LTSS recruit, hire, manage, and fire their own employees, as was seen in the disability movement described previously.

Social work can benefit greatly from a shift in focus from case management in which clients are labeled "cases" to a consumer-driven model of practice that acknowledges self-developed empowerment rather than empowerment bestowed by others. Social work and the disability movement have much to offer each other. Social work can contribute decades of experience with the ecology of society and multiple systems. The disability movement can help social work enhance approaches to consumers (clients), better empower oppressed and devalued groups, and understand the needs of people with disabilities (Mackelprang & Salsgiver, 1996).

Patient Navigation

Patient navigation, an approach centered on identifying and removing barriers to the timely diagnosis and treatment of medical conditions, is especially relevant during the post-ACA era, which is characterized by a strong emphasis on patient-centeredness and care coordination.

It is used in diverse healthcare delivery settings across a range of health conditions, most often targeting individuals who are vulnerable due to their membership in a racial/ethnic minority group or low socioeconomic profile. While still evolving, the concept of "patient navigator" dates back nearly 25 years to Dr. Harold Freeman at Harlem Hospital Center in New York City. He used nonprofessional lay "patient navigators" from the community to remove barriers to breast cancer screening, diagnosis, and treatment, including financial, system, and communication-related barriers and personal beliefs (Freeman, 2006).

The need for patient navigation is particularly great among older adults and persons with disabilities who use multiple providers to address complex conditions. These factors put them at risk for suboptimal care resulting from fragmentation, poor communication, or under- or overutilization that could be alleviated or prevented by effective patient navigation.

Social workers have been slow to move into navigator roles, despite considerable overlap in tasks and common ideology (Darnell, 2007). Navigators can help older adult clients gain entry into the health system; become aware of and understand the new coverage options and benefits available to them under the ACA; find a location where needed services are provided; locate a trusted provider; obtain the needed medical, behavioral, rehabilitative, and social services in a timely fashion; become skilled in how to effectively manage their health conditions; learn how to communicate with their providers; and improve their quality of life. This kind of assistance is needed to fully realize ACA's promise. Consider that fewer than half of older adults are up to date with preventive services (Shenson, Bolen, Seeff, Blackman, & Adams, 2005; US Department of Health and Human Services, n.d.) or that only 6% of older adults take advantage of the no-cost Welcome to Medicare benefit (Sloan, Acquah, Lee, & Sangvai, 2012). Likewise, studies suggest that 20% of noninstitutionalized adults with disabilities (and 58% of dual eligibles) have an unmet need for LTSS (Feder, Komisar, & Friedland, 2007; Komisar, Feder, & Kasper, 2005). These low utilization rates and high levels of unmet need illustrate areas where navigators can play a role.

The literature establishing the effectiveness of navigators in serving older adults is limited and reveals mixed results (Manderson, Mcmurray, Piraino, & Stolee, 2012). The varied results are likely influenced by the lack of uniform qualifications among those who carry out patient navigation (e.g., nurses, social workers, lay people, etc.) and the absence of task standardization. Social work's potential contribution to the field of navigation on behalf of older adults and persons with disabilities has yet to be assessed, suggesting an area where future research is sorely needed.

Care Coordination and Mental Health

Many ACA provisions are relevant to care coordination and represent new opportunities for social work involvement, including those in Table 9.2.

The ACA provides support for testing and implementing models that take a person-driven, interprofessional, and coordinated approach. Providers' commitment to access the range of health and social support services that consumers need (and want) will dictate whether or not these new approaches improve care. In addition, providers will need to cooperate and be creative in integrating services to meet the standards of new incentives, acknowledging that older adults and people with disabilities must be engaged in the process and that care coordination is not transactional but, instead, a long-term relationship.

TABLE 9.2. Opportunities for Care Coordination Under the Affordable Care Act

Reform Component	What It Means	What Social Workers Need to Work On
Transitional care and hospital readmission reduction	Funds available for providing transitional care through a cooperative agreement Financial penalties for excess readmissions	Quality and patient safety Care coordination Evidence-based care maps Clinical documentation
Value Based Purchasing	Payment based on performance on core measures	
Hospital Acquired Conditions	1% reduction in payment in top quartile	
Coverage expansion	More patients with insurance	Manage access
Bundled payments	Lump sum payments to providers for 10 conditions	Alignment and partnerships Manage quality *and* cost
Accountable Care Organizations	Manage care of specified beneficiaries; quality/cost; share of cost savings	Manage populations Care coordination Informatics
Patient-centered medical home	Services, structures, and access for continuous and comprehensive care	

Source: Golden (2012). Used with permission.

Social workers could play a role in augmenting the patient's medical encounter, addressing gaps that result from insufficient time, staff, and resources. In this role, social workers could assess patients' psychosocial considerations and their impact on medical status. They could also educate providers on how to best support patient self-management, providing linkage to community-based service providers that can address issues or barriers faced by patients and their caregivers. In addition, social workers could ensure all care team members—both those within the medical setting and those in the community—are sharing information and working together toward achieving patients' goals.

The social work perspective and training makes them ideally suited for new roles as lead care coordinators, particularly with the profession's "person-in-environment" framework and approaches for navigating complex systems. However, the ACA's care coordination provisions neither recognize a role for social workers nor concretely identify social workers in new financial incentives, which mean that the social work profession is at risk of being left out. A clear business case backed by credible evidence is needed to ensure that social workers perform such functions. To date, few evidence-based team models for care coordination incorporate social work participation (Allen, 2012) and those that do (Boult et al., 2011) fail to clearly define a role for social workers.

Increased mental health insurance coverage to millions of individuals under ACA is predicted to result in a greater demand for mental health services,

and for mental health professionals including social workers. Studies show that mental health conditions, such as depression, are more likely to be unnoticed in older adults than younger adults by primary care physicians (Mitchell, Rao, & Vaze, 2010). Social workers can play an important role in filling this gap. This is another opportunity to expand social work's presence in interdisciplinary teams of physicians, nurses, and social workers in medical settings and in the community.

KEY CHALLENGE OF THE AFFORDABLE CARE ACT: FINDING A PLACE FOR SOCIAL WORK

The ACA brings a host of new opportunities within healthcare in in-patient, ambulatory, and administrative settings. However, the social work profession needs to carve out its own role to be included in many of these changes. Social workers must be prepared to advocate on many different levels: for older adults as they attempt to navigate healthcare system changes, for system changes that address the gaps that emerge as the ACA is implemented, and for themselves as professionals to support their valuable contribution to patient outcomes. Social workers will be in a unique position to identify and speak up for vulnerable and marginalized populations. Additionally, social work will need to articulate a clear voice for the profession, securing resources to support its role in care coordination, navigation, mental health, and other areas of practice.

Using their position as a bridge between the medical and community-based social service worlds, social workers are positioned to mobilize resources across multiple settings. Social workers, using their skills in communication, coordination, and motivation, can facilitate cross-institutional collaboration by bringing these two communities together around patient care and systems improvement. This may require social workers to serve as "interpreter" between the medical and the social service world, helping to convey the value each contributes in a way that is understood by these fragmented groups.

Getting to the Table

Getting to the table is the important first step the social worker profession must take in order to carve out and to play a leadership role within the ACA. It is important that social workers be as willing to advocate for themselves in this process as they are for older adults. To get to the table, social workers must effectively communicate and market social work by framing the field in terms understood by other members on the team (physicians, nurses, administrators, financial officers). The message needs to be varied to fit the team's mission and the needs. Partnering with other disciplines is crucial in this process.

Demonstrating social work's value will require both motivational case examples and measurable health outcomes, such as impact on readmissions, emergency department usage, utilization costs, patient compliance, and individual metrics like weight and hemoglobin A1c (blood sugar) levels. While this charge is daunting, real progress in carving out social work roles in healthcare will not be made until these concepts are no longer foreign to community-based service providers. Social workers will be challenged to integrate these medical concepts into how they measure and communicate value while maintaining their integrity and focus on patients as individuals who have a history and identity outside the healthcare system.

Lastly, the profession can only progress if its contribution is seen not as a guild issue but in the social determinants of health and the vital skills social work brings to the team. This is not an argument that "social workers can do it better," but rather an affirmation that "social workers can do it too." Proving this point requires demonstrating the return on investment of social work involvement compared

with not having a social worker. Moreover, the business case should be anchored by identifying how social work helps meet the Triple Aim of better care and better health at a lower cost.

REFERENCES

Allen, H. (2012). Is there a social worker in the house? Health care reform and the future of medical social work. *Health and Social Work, 37,* 183–186.

Berwick, D. M., Nolan, T. W., & Whittington, J. (2008). The triple aim: Care, health, and cost. *Health Affairs, 27*(3), 759–769.

Boult, C., Reider, L., Leff, B., Frick, K. D., Boyd, C. M., Wolff, J. L., . . . Mroz, T. (2011). The effect of guided care teams on the use of health services: Results from a cluster-randomized controlled trial. *Archives of Internal Medicine, 171,* 460.

Darnell, J. S. (2007). Patient navigation: A call to action. *Social Work, 52,* 81–84.

Eden, J., Maslow, K., Le, M., & Blazer, D. (2012). *The mental health and substance use workforce for older adults: In whose hands?* Washington, DC: National Academies Press.

Feder, J. M., Komisar, H. L., & Friedland, R. B. (2007). *Long-term care financing: Policy options for the future.* Washington, DC: Georgetown University Long-Term Care Financing Project.

Freeman, H. P. (2006). Patient navigation: A community based strategy to reduce cancer disparities. *Journal of Urban Health, 83,* 139–141.

Golden, R. L. (2012, October 19). *Breaking down silos of care: Integration of social support services with health care delivery.* Oral Presentation. National Health Policy Forum. Washington, DC.

Kaiser Family Foundation. (2013). *Status of state action on the Medicaid expansion decision.* Retrieved 2014, from http://kff.org/health-reform/state-indicator/state-activity-around-expanding-medicaid-under-the-affordable-care-act/

Kemper, P., Komisar, H. L., & Alecxih, L. (2005). Long-term care over an uncertain future: What can current retirees expect? *Inquiry, 42*(4), 335–350.

Kodner, D. L., & Spreeuwenberg, C. (2002). Integrated care: Meaning, logic, applications, and implications—a discussion paper. *International Journal of Integrated Care, 2.* http://www.ncbi.nlm.nih.gov/pmc/articles/PMC1480401/

Komisar, H. L., Feder, J., & Kasper, J. D. (2005). Unmet long-term care needs: An analysis of Medicare-Medicaid dual eligibles. *Inquiry, 42,* 171–182.

Mackelprang, R. W., & Salsgiver, R. O. (1996). People with disabilities and social work: Historical and contemporary issues. *Social Work, 41*, 7–14.

Manderson, B., Mcmurray, J., Piraino, E., & Stolee, P. (2012). Navigation roles support chronically ill older adults through healthcare transitions: A systematic review of the literature. *Health and Social Care in the Community, 20*, 113–127.

Mayerson, A. (1992). *The history of the ADA: A movement perspective*. Disability Rights Education & Defense Fund. Berkeley, CA. Retrieved from http://dredf.org/news/publications/the-history-of-the-ada/.

McCamman, D. (1956). The Federal-State Conference on Aging. *Social Security Bulletin, 19*, 3.

Mitchell, A. J., Rao, S., & Vaze, A. (2010). Do primary care physicians have particular difficulty identifying late-life depression? A meta-analysis stratified by age. *Psychotherapy and Psychosomatics, 79*, 285–294.

National Alliance on Mental Illness. (2013). *Health reform and mental health*. Arlington, VA. National Alliance on Mental Illness. Retrieved from http://www2.nami.org/Content/NavigationMenu/Inform_Yourself/About_Public_Policy/Issue_Spotlights/NAMI-FactSheet1_HealthReformMH.pdf.

National Council on Independent Living. (n.d.). *About independent living*. Retrieved 2014, from http://www.ncil.org/about/aboutil/

National Federation of Independent Business (NFIB) v. Sebelius (2012). https://www.law.cornell.edu/supremecourt/text/11-393

O'Shaughnessy, C. V. (2013). *Medicaid home- and community-based services programs enacted by the ACA: Expanding opportunities one step at a time*. National Health Policy Forum. Washington, DC: National Health Policy Forum. Retrieved from http://www.nhpf.org/library/background-papers/BP86_ACAMedicaidHCBS_11-19-13.pdf.

Olmstead vs. L.C., 527 U.S. 581 (1999).

Patient Protection and Affordable Care Act, Pub. L. No. 111–148 (2010).

SCAN Foundation. (2013). *Achieving person-centered care through care coordination* (Vol. 8). Long Beach, CA: Author.

Shenson, D., Bolen, J., Seeff, L., Blackman, D., & Adams, M. (2005). Are older adults up-to-date with cancer screening and vaccinations? *Preventing Chronic Disease (serial online), 2*. Retrieved from http://www.cdc.gov/pcd/issues/2005/jul/05_0021.htm.

Sloan, F. A., Acquah, K. F., Lee, P. P., & Sangvai, D. G. (2012). Despite "Welcome To Medicare" benefit, one in eight enrollees delay first use of part B services for at least two years. *Health Affairs, 31*, 1260–1268.

US Department of Health and Human Services. (n.d.). *Older adults*. Retrieved 2014, from http://www.healthypeople.gov/2020/topicsobjectives2020/objectiveslist.aspx?topicId=31

US Department of Health and Human Services. (2009). *Community living initiative*. Retrieved 2013, from http://www.hhs.gov/od/community/index.html

US Department of Health and Human Services Centers for Medicare and Medicaid. (n.d.). *Nursing facilities*. Retrieved 2013, from http://www.medicaid.gov/Medicaid-CHIP-Program-Information/By-Topics/Delivery-Systems/Institutional-Care/Nursing-Facilities-NF.html

US Department of Health and Human Services Centers for Medicare and Medicaid. (2013a). *Home and community-based services*. Retrieved 2013, from http://www.medicaid.gov/Medicaid-CHIP-Program-Information/By-Topics/Long-Term-Services-and-Support/Home-and-Community-Based-Services/Home-and-Community-Based-Services.html

US Department of Health and Human Services Centers for Medicare and Medicaid Services. (2013b). *Money Follows the Person (MFP)*. Retrieved 2013, from http://www.medicaid.gov/Medicaid-CHIP-Program-Information/By-Topics/Long-Term-Services-and-Support/Balancing/Money-Follows-the-Person.html

The purpose of this chapter is to provide readers with an overview of the healthcare delivery landscape in the United States, with a specific focus on hospital settings and older adults. Types of inpatient hospitals and services; older adult's use of acute care settings, payment mechanisms used by older adults for this care, and distinctive concerns older adults and their families have about acute hospital care are briefly described. This chapter concludes with an overview of typical roles and responsibilities of hospital social workers and changes in hospital care as a result of the Patient Protection and Affordable Care Act (ACA).

HEALTHCARE DELIVERY IN THE UNITED STATES

The healthcare system in the United States is multifaceted, complex, and built on a constantly changing landscape consisting of inpatient, outpatient, institutional, and at-home health services that fall along a continuum of care. Older adults (aged 65 and over) are the largest consumer group of healthcare in the United States, and projected population growth suggests a continuation of this trend.

Number and Types of Hospitals

According to an annual survey conducted by the American Hospital Association (2011), there are 5,724 registered hospitals in the United States. These hospitals include any institution accredited as a hospital by The Joint Commission (TJC) or certified as a provider of acute services under Title 18 of the Social Security Act. An institution with a primary function of providing patient services, both diagnostic and therapeutic, for particular or general medical conditions is also included, even if they do not have TJC accreditation or Title 18 certification. Of the registered hospitals, the AHA defines almost 87% (4,973) as community hospitals. These include all nonfederal, short-term general and other special hospitals (obstetrics and gynecology, rehabilitation, orthopedic, and other individually described specialty services), and academic medical centers or other teaching hospitals if they are nonfederal short-term hospitals. The remainder of registered hospitals includes 208 federal government hospitals, 112 nonfederal long-term care hospitals, 421 psychiatric hospitals, and 10 hospital units in institutions

REBECCA G. JUDD
SHERRY SHEFFIELD

Generalized and Specialized Hospitals

such as prison hospitals. Registered acute care hospitals include the following:

- **General:** The primary function is to provide patient services, diagnostic and therapeutic, for a variety of medical conditions.
- **Special**: The primary function is to provide diagnostic and treatment services for patients who have specified medical conditions, both surgical and nonsurgical.
- **Rehabilitation and Chronic Disease**: The primary function is to provide diagnostic and treatment services to physically challenged or disabled individuals requiring restorative and adjustive services.
- **Psychiatric**: the primary function is to provide diagnostic and treatment services for patients who have psychiatric-related illnesses.

The majority of federal government hospitals (151) are Veteran's hospitals, which are part of the large integrated healthcare system that serves over 8.76 million Veterans each year (US Department of Veterans Affairs [VA], n.d.). Social work services are prominent in the VA system, which employs over 9,000 social workers in 26 inpatient and outpatient treatment facilities within six regions across the United States (Beder, Postiglione, & Strolin-Goltzman, 2012).

Hospital Services

Services provided within acute care hospitals consist of diagnosis and treatment of the acute illness that led to hospitalization. Every hospitalized patient receives care from a physician and nursing services. In addition to medical services, auxiliary services encompass physical and occupational therapy, nutritional consultation, social work, and chaplain services. Rehabilitation and psychiatric hospitals provide assessment and longer-term therapy services for patients recovering from disabling medical and psychiatric conditions. Some hospitals have specialized units for geriatric patients that include geropsychiatric evaluation, treatment from staff specialized in working with patients who have dementias, particularly Alzheimer's disease, and other mental disorders that may be associated with advanced aging.

OLDER ADULTS AND ACUTE HOSPITAL CARE

Patients 65 years of age and older make up 13% of the American population, but they account for 38% of all discharges from nonfederal acute hospitals and 48% of the inpatient hospital days of care (Buie, Owings, DeFrances, & Golosinskiy, 2010). According to the US Census Bureau (as cited in Spector, Mutter, Owens, & Limcango, 2012), persons age 65 and older represented 12.5% of the population but accounted for 34.3% of admissions to community hospitals and 89.7% of the nursing home admissions in the United States. In 2012, persons age 65 and older were more likely to have stayed in the hospital overnight in the past 12 months, and rates of hospitalization were more than twice as great for the 85 years and older age group when compared with those 65 to 74 years (US Department Health and Human Services, Centers for Disease Control, [USDHHS CDC], 2012). There is a positive association between multiple chronic conditions and emergency department admissions; additionally, unplanned hospital readmissions are eight times more likely to occur for elder adults with chronic illness (Lehnert et al., 2011). The five primary reasons for adults age 65 and over being admitted to the hospital are heart disease, infections, injuries, digestive disorders, and respiratory disorders, accounting for 59.8% of hospitalizations (Spector et al., 2012). In 2012, persons hospitalized for an unintentional injury were most likely (78%) to have fallen (USDHHS CDC, 2012).

PAYMENT FOR INPATIENT HOSPITAL SERVICES

The healthcare financing system in the United States is a "crazy quilt of programs that, when pieced together, cover to some degree, the majority of the American people" (US National Library of Medicine, 2013, "Module 2," para 6). Medicare and Medicaid usually provide payment for the hospitalization of older adults, at least in part. In 2012, health insurance coverage was nearly universal among persons age 65 and over. Among the 42 million adults over the age 65 in 2012, 20.9 million (50%) had private health insurance and 14.6 million (35%) had Medicare alone, with approximately 1% (371,000 persons) uninsured (USDHHS CDC, 2012).

Medicare

Medicare is the federal health insurance program for over 50 million older and disabled Americans, established by the US Congress in 1965 as Title 18 of the Social Security Act. Eligibility for Medicare depends on individual work history (Social Security eligibility) and reaching age of retirement as defined by the federal government—that is, age 65. In 2012, adults age 65 and older made up 83% of the Medicare population, with 13% age 85 and older (Kaiser Family Foundation, 2012). Coverage options for individuals include Medicare Parts A, B, C, and D (Table 10.1).

The A, B, C, and Ds of Medicare

In most inpatient hospitals, Medicare Part A pays for room and board and services on a prospectively determined rate known as a prospective payment system (PPS). For inpatient general hospitals, reimbursement is based primarily on the patient's diagnosis using a system of diagnostic related groups (DRGs). For inpatient acute rehabilitation settings a formula associated with information obtained on the patient assessment instrument (PAI) and a case mix group (CMG) is used. Amount of payment for the DRG is an estimate of intensity of the patient's care needs, combined with factors that vary by geographic region (e.g., wages, and the cost of goods and services) and some degree of risk adjustment (e.g., for age). Amount of payment for the CMG also include levels of functioning as assessed by licensed physical and occupational therapy. Services are bundled and the hospital receives a global rate that includes all the service an average patient needs. Thus, variations in the types of services that individual patients receive usually make no difference in payment in either a general acute hospital or a rehabilitation hospital (as illustrated by the example below).

> Flora is an 83-year-old woman who spends 4 days in the hospital with a diagnosis of pneumonia. She receives intravenous antibiotics, routine nursing care, and an evaluation by a physical therapist when she complains of stiffness in her left leg, but discharges soon thereafter. Sylvia, Flora's best friend and next-door neighbor, also 83 years old, admits to the hospital the following week with a similar diagnosis. She received similar treatment, but responds more slowly, has difficulty walking without assistance and appears more frail and weaker. Sylvia's son lives in a distant state; is concerned about her living alone and has asked that she move in with him. However, Sylvia refuses. The social worker assesses Sylvia's needs; arranges an evaluation of her home and postdischarge services. Together, Sylvia and her son, and the social worker, in conversation with the physician, agree that Sylvia will return home with follow-up home nursing care and therapy services and that her ability to remain at home will be assessed periodically.

TABLE 10.1. Medicare Categories

Type of Medicare	Eligibility	Coverage
Medicare Part A	Traditional Fee for Service Medicare (FFS), a person becomes eligible if they have earned 41 credits in their work history and reached age of retirement	Hospital Care; Skilled Nursing Facility Care, Hospice, Home Health Services
Medicare Part B	Supplementary medical insurance program. Enrollment in Part B is voluntary, but the majority of people who are entitled to Part A also enroll in Part B.	Medically necessary services or supplies; preventive services (ambulance services, durable medical equipment, inpatient/outpatient mental health, getting a second opinion before surgery)
Medicare Part D	Voluntary benefit where eligible individual chooses to join a Medicare prescription drug plan and pay a monthly premium	Prescription drug plans.
Medicare Part C	Offers an alternative to traditional Medicare where beneficiaries enroll in a private plan	Medicare Advantage Plans (like an HMO or PPO) that include both Part A (hospital insurance) and Part B (medical insurance) provided by private companies approved by Medicare.

Flora and Sylvia received different services, but the hospital receives essentially the same amount of reimbursement for the care provided to each of them. That payment will not specifically reflect Flora's physical therapy services and Sylvia's social work services as these services along with most physicians' services (billed separately) are not reflected in the Medicare payment to the hospital. However, because reimbursement is essentially the same regardless of the patient's length of stay, services that can facilitate earlier discharge can represent a cost savings. While there is little research on the impact of social work services, recent studies have shown social work services to be correlated with reducing a patient's length of stay (Galati, Wong, Morra & Wu, 2011) and with better posthospital outcomes for the patient (Fabbre, Buffington, & Altfeld, 2011).

Patients with multiple, complex medical problems requiring an extended length of stay may need to be a transferred to a specialty hospital known as long-term acute care (LTAC). Medicare reimburses these hospitals using a fixed per diem rate. There are specific criteria for admission to an LTAC, and they generally serve patients on ventilators and/or with chronic open wounds that require on-site wound care specialty services.

Medicaid

The Medicaid program is funded jointly by the federal government and the state. In 2012, it provided healthcare coverage to 65 million low-income people who met specific income, asset, and other eligibility requirements (Congressional Budget Office, 2013). As a condition of receiving federal Medicaid funding, states must provide basic services of inpatient and outpatient hospital care, physician services, skilled nursing care for persons ages 21 and over, and in-home services for persons eligible for skilled care (Kaiser Family Foundation, 2013). States can offer additional programs under Medicaid at their discretion, and some cover services of clinical social workers and case management services provided by social workers. State Medicaid reimbursement for hospitals and individual practitioners can vary widely, with some having PPSs, whereas reimbursement in others reflects costs and/or negotiated rates (Kaiser Family Foundation, 2013).

Medicare beneficiaries who have limited income and resources may get help from Medicaid to pay their Medicare premiums and out-of-pocket medical expenses. Individuals entitled to Medicare Part A and/or Part B and eligible for some form of Medicaid benefit are "dual eligibles." In 2009, 7 million people were "full duals," meaning they qualified for full benefits from both programs, and 2 million were "partial duals" who do not qualify for full Medicaid but qualify to have Medicaid pay some of the costs they incur under Medicare (Congressional Budget Office, 2013). In 2010, 59% of dual eligible enrollees were 65 and older and accounted for 60% of Medicaid spending. As the sickest and poorest covered under Medicare and Medicaid, dual eligible individuals have significantly more serious health conditions such as cognitive or mental impairments, depression, and diabetes than non-dual-eligible Medicare beneficiaries (Young, Garfield, Musumeci, Clemans-Cope, & Lawton, 2013) Although dual eligible beneficiaries accounted for only 14% of Medicaid enrollment in 2010, 36% of all Medicaid expenditures for medical services were made on their behalf, and 33% of Medicare spending in 2009 was for dual-eligible beneficiaries (Young et al., 2013).

Patient Protection Affordable Care Act

In 2011 the Affordable Care Act (ACA) was signed into law and impacts Medicare in several ways. First, it expands on existing coverage including preventive care, cancer screenings, wellness visits, personalized prevention plans, vaccines, and flu shots. In addition, it includes a series of Medicare reforms to improve the quality of care, reform the healthcare delivery system, appropriately price services and modernize financing systems as well as fight waste, fraud, and abuse. Hospital readmissions of the elderly are a prominent target area of the Affordable Care Act through provisions such as The Medicare Hospital Readmissions Reduction Program (HRRP), which provides financial incentives for hospitals to reduce preventable readmissions (Health Policy Briefs, 2013). The HRRP targeted reducing readmissions for patients ages 65 and older with diagnoses of acute myocardial infarction, heart failure, or pneumonia in fiscal years 2013 and 2014. The program was scheduled to expand in 2014 to include elective hip or knee replacement and chronic obstructive pulmonary disease.

Another target area is care delivery for those with chronic illnesses. It is estimated that about 80% of older adults have one chronic condition and 50% have at least two (National Center for Chronic Disease and Prevention and Health Promotion, 2011). In addition, to focus on improvements in how care is delivered, payment reimbursement, and public health expansion, care coordination is also addressed (Volland, Schraeder, Shelton, & Hess, 2013). Care coordination models include *transitional care* and *comprehensive care management*. Transitional care models are time-limited activities designed to coordinate healthcare as patients move between services, typically from hospital to home. In contrast, comprehensive care management models assign a care coordinator to work with a patient who has chronic illnesses in order to reduce risk of hospitalization (Volland et al., 2013). It is suggested that for care coordination to be effectively implemented, interdisciplinary training for health and homecare providers will be key to improving patient outcomes (Volland et al., 2013).

SPECIAL CONCERNS OF OLDER ADULTS WHO ARE HOSPITALIZED

The older adult presents challenges that differ from those of younger patients, as described in what follows. Demonstrated risks to older people during hospitalization include complications such as deconditioning, which is a complex process that results in functional losses following a period of inactivity, delirium, medication interactions, falls and other injuries. Legal and ethical issues are paramount for the older individual who is hospitalized. These include autonomy in decision-making, advanced care directives, confidentiality and end of life care. Financial issues also create special concerns for older hospitalized adults. In addition family caregivers for older individuals have distinctive worries when a loved one enters the hospital.

Risk Associated with Hospitalization

Older adults typically have longer and more frequent hospitalizations with greater severity of illness (Palmer, 2005), increased number of chronic diseases and greater risk to have an injury from a fall. Associated with hospital stays, older adults are at risk

of experiencing a loss of functional independence, falls, delirium, nosocomial infections, adverse drug reactions and pressure ulcer development (National Patient Safety Foundation, 2006; Rudolph & Marcantonio, 2005). Because an elder family member may be physically frail and have dementia, family members and caregivers may feel responsible for staying with the patient at all times to advocate for good care, and experience stress when they are unable to provide 24-hour oversight and assistance.

Family and Caregiver Worries

Hospitalization of an elderly loved one has been shown to create a typology of worry for family members. A study by Li (2005) revealed family members' worries related to the patient's condition, the care received from the health care team; the need for future care the patient provided by the family caregiver and finances. While family caregivers may worry about losing their loved one to death during hospitalization, they may also have unrealistic expectations about the chances for recovery of their loved one or about available services post discharge. In addition, the hospitalization of an elderly individual might signal a physical or cognitive change that will now require the initiation of care or increased care by a family member. Healthcare decisions related to treatment options, end-of-life care, and discharge destinations for those with multiple chronic conditions and physical frailty can create stress for older adults and their family members (Popejoy, 2011).

Legal and Ethical Issues

Individuals in a hospital have federal protections to privacy, confidentiality, and active autonomy in decision-making.

Rosairo is a 75-year-old female immigrant from Ecuador who is admitted to an inpatient rehabilitation facility following surgery for her broken hip. Rosairo does not speak English, but her daughter Yvonne accompanies her and is bilingual. The staff needs to get admission and financial information, the healthcare team needs to complete evaluations and set goals, and the social worker needs to complete an assessment and begin discharge planning. It is suggested to have her daughter interpret for Rosairo or to use a certified nurse's aide (CNA) who is bilingual but works on another hall and does not provide care for Rosairo. ▦

In this case, if Rosairo has not agreed to allow her daughter or a healthcare provider not directly involved in her care to hear her health information, this would be a violation of HIPPA. Most hospitals will use the Language Bank, which is a translation service that will not violate the patient's right to confidentiality, dignity, and autonomy. The social worker can advocate and arrange for the use of a translation service and protect the patient's rights.

Issues of culture and ageism may circumvent an individual's right to privacy and autonomy. In addition, ethical and legal challenges for lesbian, gay, bisexual, and transgender older adults (LBGT) have been brought to the forefront (The White House, 2010).

▦ Ellen, a 65-year-old female, was brought into the emergency department unresponsive after falling and hitting her head. The physician needs an accurate medical history to provide the best of care, however Ellen's family is not present. Ellen's long-time partner, Jane, is in the waiting room, but was informed by the nurse that Ellen's situation cannot be discussed with her until her family is contacted. The social worker is consulted to try to contact family so information can be obtained. The social worker takes a proactive approach and respects the family structure. Therefore, she informs Jane the hospital policy allows her to see Ellen once she stabilizes, and confirms Ellen has made Jane her healthcare agent through an advanced directive. The social worker then provides this information to the physician, who is able to obtain an accurate medical history for Ellen. ▦

As with other marginalized groups, the LGBT population has experienced discrimination and at times abusive care by individuals in the healthcare environment (Conron, Mimiaga, & Landers, 2010; Frost, Lehavot & Meyer, 2011; Lambda Legal, 2010). The Health Insurance Portability and Accountability Act (HIPPA) of 1996 sets rules for healthcare providers about who can look at and receive health information, including friends and relatives. While seemingly straightforward, issues arise when an older individual from a different culture and who speaks a language other than English enters a healthcare setting. Protecting a patient's right to privacy and confidentiality also protects their right of active participation in all decisions about treatment and level of independence.

Financial Concerns

Medicare beneficiaries face considerable out-of-pocket expenses for uncovered services, copayments, deductibles, and part B premiums. Some of these expenses are associated with outpatient rather than inpatient services, but there are significant out-of-pocket costs associated with hospitalization. For instance, beneficiaries are responsible for a deductible for the first day of their hospital stay and for copayments for hospital stays beyond 60 days. Planning for discharge often requires obtaining durable medical equipment, which may require out-of-pocket expenses. The need for continued care either in the home or nursing home often has costs associated as Medicare only reimburses temporarily for skilled nursing care and does not cover costs associated with convalescent care. Often patients and their families are unaware of what Medicare does and does not cover until faced with a healthcare crisis.

HOSPITAL SOCIAL WORK

Formal hospital social work services were first implemented in Massachusetts General Hospital in 1905 and included provision of concrete resources, counseling services, and patient advocacy. Not too different from current roles carried out by social workers, early medical social workers assisted patients with chronic disease management needs, mental health issues, drug and alcohol abuse, physical disabilities, terminal conditions, and accessing extended care services (Cannon, 1913). Because of a growing aging population, availability of healthcare social workers jobs is projected to grow by 34% from 2012 to 2022, much faster than the average for all occupations (Bureau of Labor Statistics, 2012).

The social work role in the hospital is of vital importance in addressing the complex needs of older people and their families. Through the provision of education and information, counseling, advocacy, participation in complex discharge planning, and arranging support services, hospital social workers can positively influence outcomes for the patient, family, and healthcare organizations.

Education and Information

In 2009, the majority of elderly admitted to the hospital from a nursing home returned to a nursing home (76.8%), but 7.0% were discharged to the community; however, 27.2% of hospital admissions from the community were discharged to a skilled nursing facility (Spector et al., 2012). Because the hospitalization of an elderly loved one will most likely result in changes for the patient and the family caregiver(s), the social worker involved in discharge planning must help the caregiver anticipate and plan for posthospital needs and provide support during the transitions from one setting to another.

Counseling and Advocacy

Frequently, end-of-life care decisions are necessary; older adults and their families seek guidance, compassion, and understanding to make the best decisions. Social workers provide support for elders and their family in response to psychological and emotional stresses, and often become involved in grief and bereavement, spiritual issues, and funeral planning (Kramer, 2013). Hospital social workers also intervene for mental health issues such as depression, substance abuse, chronic mental illness, cognitive deficits, and suicide prevention and to address the changes that these conditions will require of the older patient (Clark, 2003).

Complex Discharge Planning: Preventing Hospital Readmissions

Discharge planning is a primary task for most hospital social workers (Judd & Sheffield, 2010) and includes the roles of providing education and information, counseling, and advocacy as well as obtaining tangible resources for the patient after discharge (Levine & Kuerbis, 2002). In a comparison study of predictors for length of stay (LOS) in older patients, the evidence shows that the severity of patients' psychosocial problems was

a significant predictor for longer lengths of stay (LOSs) (Lechman & Duder, 2009).

The older hospitalized patient historically is at high risk for poor postdischarge outcomes including rehospitalization, frequent emergency department visits, and institutionalization (Royer & Mion, 2005). Therefore, care coordination and discharge planning for older patients is a top priority in efforts to reduce readmission rates and is now a quality of care and financial target for Medicare (Silow-Carroll, Edwards, & Lashbrook, 2011), with the reduction of hospital readmissions estimated to save $8.2 billion in 10 years (CMS Office of the Actuary, 2010). Social workers are poised to become a resource for specialized knowledge and serving in transitions of care between the hospital setting and community-based partnerships (Golden, 2011; Lechman & Duder, 2009).

A 2009 meta-analysis (Preyde, Macaulay, & Dingwall) revealed a paucity of social work research evidence regarding the effectiveness of discharge planning; given this, the development and testing of a transitional model is a step toward evidence-based practice. Recognized as an evidence-based model of transitional care by the Administration on Community Living (ACL), the Bridge Model at Rush University is a person-centered, social work–led, interdisciplinary model that emphasizes collaboration among hospitals, community-based providers, and the Aging Network to ensure seamless continuum of health and community care across settings (Fabbre et al., 2011).

SUMMARY

Social work in hospital settings is linked to social work with older adults (Berkman, Rehr, & Volland, 2005; Duffy & Healy, 2011). Those ages 65 and older are the primary consumers of inpatient hospital care in the United States (Buie et al., 2010). The ACA introduces legislation to reform the healthcare delivery system for improving quality of care and reducing costs. Transition care and comprehensive case management models are designed to reduce hospitalizations and readmissions among vulnerable, at-risk adults with chronic illnesses. Social workers are vital members of the healthcare team in the implementation and provision of care between the hospital setting and community for the older adult.

WEB-BASED RESOURCES

- Department of Health and Human Services: Administration for Community Living (formerly Administration on Aging) is an organization for maximizing the independence, well-being, and health of older adults, people with disabilities across the life span, and their families and caregivers.
  http://acl.gov/About_ACL/Index.aspx
- Eldercare Locator is a public service of the US Administration on Aging connecting individuals to services for older adults and their families.
  http://www.eldercare.gov/Eldercare.NET/Public/Index.aspx
- National Senior Citizens Law Center has information about its services, manuals, publications, and information about Social Security and Supplemental Security Income, Medicare, Medicaid, nursing home resident's rights, home care, pension rights, age discrimination and mandatory retirement, and OAA services.
  https://www.nsclc.org/
- National Resource Center on LGBT Aging is the country's first and only technical assistance resource center aimed at improving the quality of services and supports offered to LGBT older adults.
  http://www.lgbtagingcenter.org/
- Society for Social Work Leadership in Health Care is an association dedicated to promoting the universal availability, accessibility, coordination, and effectiveness of healthcare that addresses the psychosocial components of health and illness.
  http://www.sswlhc.org/
- The Bridge Model is a person-centered, social work–led, interdisciplinary model of transitional care.
  http://www.transitionalcare.org/the-bridge-model/

REFERENCES

American Hospital Association. (2011). *Fast facts on US hospitals.* Retrieved from http://www.aha.org/research/rc/stat-studies/fast-facts.shtml

Beder, J., Postiglione, P., & Strolin-Goltzman, J. (2012). Social work in the Veteran's Administration Hospital System: Impact of the work. *Social Work in Health Care, 51,* 661–679. doi:10.1080/00981389.2012.699023

Berkman, B., Rehr, H., & Volland, P. J. (2005). Social work practice with hospitalized elders: Counselors, case managers, and discharge planners. In *Caring for the hospitalized elderly: Current best practice and new horizons: A special supplement to* The Hospitalist, *the official publication of the Society of Hospital Medicine* (pp. 21–24). Retrieved from http://www.hospital-medicine.org/AM/Template.cfm?Section=The_Hospitalist&Template=/CM/ContentDisplay.cfm&ContentFileID=1447

Buie, V. C., Owings, M. F., DeFrances, C. J., & Golosinskiy, A. (2010). National hospital discharge survey: 2006 summary. *Vital Health Statistics, 13,* 1–70. Retrieved from: http://www.cdc.gov/nchs/nhds/nhds_questionnaires.htm

Bureau of Labor Statistics. (2012). *Occupational outlook handbook: Social workers.* Retrieved from http://www.bls.gov/ooh/Community-and-Social-Service/Social-workers.htm#tab-6

Cannon, I. M. (1913). *Social work in hospitals: A contribution to progressive medicine.* New York: NY: Survey Associates.

Centers for Disease Control and Prevention. (2001–2012). *Leading causes of nonfatal injury reports.* Retrieved from http://webappa.cdc.gov/sasweb/ncipc/nfilead2001.html

Clark, E. J. (2003). The Future of Social Work. In R. A. English (Ed.), *Encyclopedia of Social Work* (19th ed., 2003 supplement) (pp. 61–70). Washington, DC: NASW Press.

CMS Office of the Actuary. (2010). *The Affordable Care Act update: Implementing Medicare cost savings, 2–11.* Retrieved from http://www.cms.gov/apps/docs/aca-update-implementing-medicare-costs-savings.pdf

Congressional Budget Office (CBO). (2013). *Dual-eligible beneficiaries of Medicare and Medicaid: Characteristics, health care spending and evolving policies* (Pub No 4374 1-42). Retrieved from http://www.cbo.gov/sites/default/files/cbofiles/attachments/44308_DualEligibles.pdf

Conron, K. J., Mimiaga, M. J., & Landers, S. J. (2010). A population-based study of sexual orientation identity and gender differences in adult health. *American Journal of Public Health, 100,* 1953–1960.

Duffy, F., & Healy, P. (2011). Social work with older people in a hospital setting. *Social Work in Health Care, 50,* 109–123. doi:10.1080/00981389.2010.527786

Fabbre, V. D., Buffington, A. S., Altfeld, S. J., Shier, G. E., & Golden, R. L. (2011). Social work and transitions of care: Observations from an intervention for older adults. *Journal of Gerontological Social Work, 54,* 615–626. doi:10.1080/01634372.2011.589100

Frost, D. M., Lehavot, K., & Meyer, I. H. (2011). *Minority stress and physical health among sexual minorities.* Paper presented at the 119th Annual Convention of the American Psychologist Association.

Galati, M., Wong, H. J., Morra, D., & Wu, R. C. (2011). An evidence-based case for the value of social workers in efficient hospital discharge. *The Health Care Manager*, 30, 242–246. doi:10.1097/HCM.0b013e31822571dd

Golden, R. L. (2011). Coordination, integration, and collaboration: A clear path for social work in health care reform. *Health and Social Work*, 36, 227–228.

Health Policy Briefs. (2013). *Medicare hospital readmissions reduction program*. Retrieved from http://www.healthaffairs.org/healthpolicybriefs/brief.php?brief_id=102

Judd, R. G., & Sheffield, S. (2010). Hospital social work: Contemporary roles and professional activities. *Social Work in Health Care*, 49, 856–871. doi:10.1080/00981389.2010.499825

Kaiser Family Foundation. (2012). *Medicare at a glance: Overview of Medicare*. Retrieved from http://kff.org/medicare/fact-sheet/medicare-at-a-glance-fact-sheet/

Kaiser Family Foundation. (2013). *Medicaid: A primer*. Retrieved from http://kaiserfamilyfoundation.files.wordpress.com/2010/06/7334-05.pdf

Kramer, B. J. (2013). Social workers' roles addressing the complex end-of-life care needs of elders with advanced chronic disease. *Journal of Social Work in End-of-Life and Palliative Care*, 9, 308–330. doi:10.1080/15524256.2013.846887

Lambda Legal. (2010). *When healthcare isn't caring: Lambda Legal's survey on discrimination against LGBT people and people living with HIV*. New York, NY: Author.

Lechman, C., & Duder, S. (2009). Hospital length of stay: Social work services an important factor. *Social Work in Health Care*, 48, 495–504. doi:10.1080/00981380802619360

Lehnert, T., Leicht, H., Heinrich, S., Corrieri, S., Luppa, M., Riedel-Heller, S., & Konig, H.-H. (2011). Review: Health care utilization and costs of elderly persons with multiple chronic conditions. *Medical Care Research and Review*, 68, 387–420.

Levine, C., & Kuerbis, A. (2002). Building alliances between social workers and family caregivers. *Journal of Social Work in Long-Term Care*, 1, 3–17.

Li, H. (2005). Hospitalized elders and family caregivers: A typology of family worry. *Journal of Clinical Nursing*, 14, 308.

National Center for Chronic Disease Prevention and Health Promotion. (2011). *Healthy aging: Helping people to live long and productive lives and enjoy a good quality of life*. Retrieved from http://www.cdc.gov/chronicdisease/resources/publications/aag/pdf/2011/healthy_aging_aag_508.pdf

National Patient Safety Foundation. (2006). *Agenda for research and development in patient safety*. Retrieved from: http://www.npsf.org/download/researchagenda,pdf

Palmer, R. M. (2005) Acute hospital care of the elderly: Making a difference. In *Caring for the hospitalized elderly: Current best practice and new horizons: a special supplement to* The Hospitalist, *the official publication of the society of hospital medicine* (pp. 4–7). Retrieved from: http://www.hospitalmedicine.org/AM/Template.cfm?Section=The_Hospitalist&Template=/CM/ContentDisplay.cfm&ContentFileID=1447

Popejoy, L. (2011). Participation of elder persons, families, and health care teams in hospital discharge destination decisions. *Applied Nursing Research*, 24, 256–262. doi:10.1016/j.apnr.2009.11.001

Preyde, M., Macaulay, C., & Dingwall, T. (2009). Discharge planning from hospital to home for elderly patients: A meta-analysis. *Journal of Evidence-Based Social Work*, 6, 198–216. doi:10.1080/15433710802686898

Royer, M. C., & Mion, L. C. (2005). Involving the older adult and/or family member in discharge planning. In *Caring for the hospitalized elderly: Current best practice and new horizons: A special supplement to* The Hospitalist, *the official publication of the society of hospital medicine* (p. 42). Retrieved from http://www.hospitalmedicine.org/AM/Template.cfm?Section=The_Hospitalist&Template=/CM/ContentDisplay.cfm&ContentFileID=1447

Rudolph, J. L., & Marcantonio, E.R. (2005). Caring for the postoperative patient with delirium. In Caring for the hospitalized elderly: Current best practice and new horizons: a special supplement to The Hospitalist, the official publication of the society of hospital medicine (pp. 8–13). Retrieved from: http://www.hospitalmedicine.org/AM/Template.cfm?Section=The_Hospitalist&Template=/CM/ContentDisplay.cfm&ContentFileID=1447

Silow-Carroll, S., Edwards, J. N., & Lashbrook, A. (2011). *Reducing hospital readmissions: Lessons learned from top-performing hospitals*. Synthesis Report. *The Common Wealth Fund* (Publication 1473 (5), 2–18. Retrieved from: www.commonwealthfund.org

Spector, W., Mutter, R., Owens, P., & Limcangco, P. (2012). *Transitions between nursing home and hospitals in the elderly population*. (Brief # 141) Healthcare Cost and Utilization Project. Retrieved from http://www.hcup-us.ahrq.gov/reports/statbriefs/sb141.pdf

The White House. (2010). *Presidential memorandum—Hospital visitation*. Retrieved from http://www.

whitehouse.gov/the-press-office/presidential-memorandum-hospital-visitation

US Department of Health and Human Services, Center for Disease Control and Prevention (USDHHS CDC). (2012). *Summary health statistics for the U.S. population: National health interview Survey, 2012* (Series 10, number 259). Retrieved from http://www.cdc.gov/nchs/data/series/sr_10/sr10_259.pdf

US Department of Veterans Affairs (n.d.). *Veterans health administration.* Retrieved from http://www.va.gov/health/

US National Library of Medicine. (2013). *Health economics information resources: A self-study course.* Retrieved from http://www.nlm.nih.gov/nichsr/edu/healthecon/02_he_01.html

Volland, P. J., Schraeder, C., Shelton, P., & Hess, I. (2012). The transitional care and comprehensive care coordination debate. *Generations, 36*(4), 13–19.

Young, K., Garfield, R., Musumeci, M., Clemons-Cope, L., & Lawton, E. (2013). Medicaid's role for dual eligible beneficiaries: Issue brief. The Kaiser Commission on Medicaid and the Uninsured. Retrieved from http://kaiserfamilyfoundation.files.wordpress.com/2013/08/7846-04-medicaids-role-for-dual-eligible-beneficiaries.pdf

The practice of social work in home care settings is both important and marginalized, even as home care has become the preferred care option for growing numbers of chronically ill older adults and for reformers seeking to shorten institutional stays and contain the costs of medical care. While professional social work knowledge, skills, and values are well suited to address the needs of home care clients and their caregivers, social work is often viewed as secondary to physician and nursing care, which are typically considered the primary home care services (Berger, 1988; Kane, 1987). The lack of outcome studies on the effectiveness of social work services has contributed to this perception of social work as an ancillary service, and thus to the low use of social workers in home care (Lee & Gutheil, 2003). Nonetheless, the growing field of home care, and healthcare reform provisions passed as part of the Patient Protection and Affordable Care Act of 2010 (P.L. 111-148), provide opportunities for social work to significantly expand its role and contribute to the health and well-being of older adults. This chapter provides an overview of social work practice in home care, including a historical perspective and an analysis of social work's current role and functions and those government policies that have shaped and constrained social work practice. We conclude with a brief discussion of the challenges involved in enhancing the role of social work in home care and some possible solutions.

KATHRYN G. KIETZMAN
EDNA NAITO-CHAN
A. E. BENJAMIN

Home Care Settings

DEFINITIONS

"Home care" refers to services provided by home care organizations, including home health agencies, hospices, homemaker and home care aide agencies, staffing and private-duty agencies, and companies specializing in medical equipment and supplies, pharmaceuticals, and drug infusion therapy. This chapter focuses on home healthcare and homemaker service agencies, which are the most frequent providers of social work services among home care organizations.

Home health care (HHC) is often associated with the type of services provided under the Medicare home health benefit. Medicare may reimburse a range of health and social services delivered at home for eligible older persons who are recovering from illness or injury or are terminally ill and needing medical, nursing, social, or therapeutic treatment and/or assistance with activities of daily living (ADLs).

Activities of daily living are self-care activities that include bathing, dressing, feeding, toileting, and transferring. Assistance with ADLs is known as personal assistance or care. Despite this broad characterization of HHC, older persons actually qualify for Medicare home health because of medical conditions and related assistance needs, while supportive care needs are considered secondary. *Homemaker service agencies*, on the other hand, employ workers who provide personal assistance, that is, help with ADLs, as well as homemaker and chore services, which include assistance with meal preparation, housekeeping, laundry, shopping, and transportation, termed instrumental activities of daily living (IADLs). Older adults requiring these services have ongoing needs related more to functional impairment than medical need; hence, these are supportive rather than medically oriented services. Among public payers, the Medicaid program is the largest funder of supportive services, although this varies widely across states. Importantly, Medicaid covers both home healthcare (a mandatory service) and supportive care (a state-optional service and typical waiver service).

HOME CARE FOR AN AGING SOCIETY

The growth of the home care industry in the United States has been both dramatic and dynamic. In 2010, more than 33,000 providers delivered home care services to about 12 million persons with acute or chronic health conditions, permanent disability, or terminal illness (NAHC, 2010). The 1965 enactment of Medicare and Medicaid legislation has accelerated the growth of the home care industry, as has the steady rise in the numbers of those with disability and chronic illness for whom home care is an increasingly attractive option.

As the risk for chronic illness and disability increases with age, so does the need for assistance with ADLs. Federal data indicate that adults aged 85 years and over were more than seven times as likely as adults aged 65–74 years old to need help with personal care from other people (NHIS; National Center for Health Statistics [NCHS], 2004). Moreover, the NHIS data also show that the proportions of older women and minorities who needed

personal care assistance were higher than for older white men. For those 85 years old and over, 25% of women versus 17% of men reported needing ADL assistance; and the proportion of those needing assistance aged 65 and over was higher for Hispanic (10%) and non-Hispanic black (10%) elders than for non-Hispanic white elders (6%).

HISTORICAL PERSPECTIVE

A century ago virtually all medical care was provided in the home, first by family members, and later by physicians and nurses making house calls (Benjamin, 1993; Cowles, 2003). The provision of services at home is also not new to social work practice. Social work in home care has emerged from two traditions—community-based "friendly visitor" services and hospital social work. Contemporary social work practice has its roots in the 19th century with "friendly visitor" services provided by charitable organizations to the ill and indigent (Brieland, 1995; Romaine-Davis, Boondas, & Lenihan, 1995). Friendly visitations were part of "outdoor relief"—assistance to people who resided in their homes and outside of an almshouse, orphanage, or other residential facility (Barker, 2003). Friendly visitors began as volunteers, then became paid employees of charity organization societies (COSs), and eventually became known as social workers. Their main duties were not very different from social workers in home care today: to investigate homes of indigent families; determine the causes of problems; provide guidance for solving problems; and, in some cases, provide material aid. Eventually, friendly visiting was replaced by the practice of professional social casework, currently referred to as "clinical social work," as the friendly visitors developed greater professionalism, received better training, and improved understanding of the causes of health and social ills (Barker, 2003).

The other progenitor of social work in home care is hospital or medical social work. The role of the hospital social worker was initially modeled after that of the "friendly visitor" in its sympathetic and paternalistic attempt to alleviate social problems (Nacman, 1977). Richard Cabot, a Boston physician, is credited with introducing social work practice in medical settings. Cabot added social workers to his hospital staff in 1905 for the purpose of "augment(ing) the physician's treatment of patients by studying, reporting, and alleviating, to the extent possible, the patients' social problems that interfered with the plan for medical care" (Cabot, 1915, as cited in Caputi, 1978). Cabot's delineation of social work as an ancillary function to medical care continues to resonate to this day in most entitlement programs and healthcare settings. As a result of these efforts by Cabot and others, the nation's first medical social work department was established at Massachusetts General Hospital in 1906, and the American Hospital Association developed the first formal description of medical social work in the mid-1920s (Caputi, 1978; Nacman, 1977; Ross, 1995). It includes the augmentation role suggested by Cabot along with other practice roles: liaison between the physician and patient; liaison between the physician and community resources necessary for continuing patient care; and educator serving as an agent of the physician to promote patient compliance in the medical treatment plan (Caputi, 1978).

By the mid-1950s, a commission of the US Public Health Services called for organized home care programs to provide medical and social services to patients in their homes following hospitalization. Care was to be provided by a team of healthcare professionals through a range of services under a physician's plan of care, including medical, nursing, social work, housekeeping, transportation, medication, and other benefits. Some private health insurance companies became convinced that home care following hospitalization for certain patients could, under institutional and physician oversight, deliver high-quality and cost-effective care. As a result, the introduction of home care coverage by Blue Cross and other private insurers significantly enhanced the visibility and respectability of organized home care programs. Passage of Medicare (Title 18 of the Social Security Act) and Medicaid (Title 19) in 1965, which authorized health insurance for older adults and the medically needy, formally established the role of home care in mainstream healthcare. Moreover, social work was designated as one element of the range of professional services offered in organized home care programs.

HOME CARE POLICY AND FUNDING

In developing home care policy, federal planners embraced the range of services offered through early hospital home care programs, but limited them to the kind of coverage provided by Blue Cross plans. Current home care policy and funding can be conceptualized in terms of two models: the predominant medical or postacute model, represented by HHC and largely financed by Medicare; and the social-supportive model, including personal assistance and homemaker services typically covered by Medicaid and private (out-of-pocket) payment (Benjamin, 1993; Dhooper, 1997).

Medicare and the Medical Model

Established to provide medical care for those 65 years and over, Medicare has played a significant role in the rapid growth of the home care industry. Medicare beneficiaries are the largest consumers of short-term, postacute home healthcare. In 2007, about 70% of the 1.46 million persons receiving home healthcare were Medicare beneficiaries (NCHS, 2010). Medicare's home health benefit is not designed to address long-term care needs or environmental factors influencing illness and recovery. Home care services are initiated by a physician's order and are usually reserved for those who have been recently hospitalized and whose care needs are short-term and intermittent. A Medicare beneficiary can qualify for HHC if he/she meets all of the following conditions.

- Physician decides that beneficiary needs medical care at home, and makes a plan for care at home.
- Beneficiary must need at least one of the following: intermittent (fewer than 7 days each week or less than 8 hours each day over a period of 21 days or less) skilled nursing care, or physical therapy, or speech-language therapy, or continue to need occupational therapy.
- Beneficiary must be homebound (unable to leave home unassisted).
- Home health agency providing care is Medicare-certified (Centers for Medicare and Medicaid Services [CMS], 2011).

Medicare is the only major public program that covers social work services under its home health benefit. But Medicare home health coverage allows beneficiaries to receive medical social work services, home health aide services, and occupational therapy *only* when they are also receiving skilled nursing, physical therapy or speech therapy. Therefore, contingent services such as social work are not provided to all HHC patients, but only when ordered by the physician (Dhooper, 1997). Moreover, Medicare coverage of HHC does *not* include 24-hour-a-day care at home, home-delivered meals, and homemaker services such as cooking, cleaning, and shopping.

Despite its status as an optional home health service, medical social work is characterized by Medicare as a service that is "necessary to resolve social or emotional problems that are or are expected to be an impediment to the effective treatment of the patient's medical condition or his or her rate of recovery" (CMS, 2011). Services provided by HHC social workers can include assessment, community resource planning, counseling services (including discharge planning), short-term therapy (i.e., two to three visits) for family members or caregivers to address problems that "clearly and directly" hinder effective patient treatment, and "other" services approved by physician's orders, such as interventions related to suspected abuse/neglect and suicide risk (CMS, 2011).

Medicaid and Social-Supportive Care

Medicaid—the jointly financed federal and state healthcare program for low-income people—finances a variety of home-based services and accounts for well over half of total public payments for care services delivered in the home (CMS, 2000; Ng, Harrington, & Kitchener, 2010). There are three categories of Medicaid home care: The traditional home health benefit, required in all state plans, reimburses basic home health care and medical equipment; personal care services, an optional benefit provided in about 30 states; and home- and community-based waivers, a flexible package of services offered in all states to a limited number of high-need recipients (National Association of Home Care and Hospice [NAHC], 2010). Personal care involves "semiprofessional" services that assist clients with ADLs, IADLs, or homemaker tasks, and these services may be agency directed or consumer directed. In the latter case, the recipient may hire and supervise their own worker, with payment by a public agency or from a cash account in the consumer's name (Benjamin, 2001; Simon-Rusinowitz, Loughlin, Ruben, Martinez-Garcia, & Mahoney, 2010). Eligibility for personal care services is determined by limitations in functioning due to chronic conditions rather than an acute medical episode.

Under Medicaid waiver programs, clients deemed at high risk for nursing home placement may be provided personal assistance, homemaker services, meals-on-wheels, respite care, transportation, adult daycare, and numerous other services (Goode, 2000). Clients in waiver programs can also receive case management by social workers. However, Medicaid does not pay for social work services provided by home healthcare and homemaker service agencies unless the client is receiving waiver services aimed at reducing nursing home stays.

Funding Sources

Medicare is the largest single payer for home health services, and together Medicare and Medicaid account for as much as 80% of all home health expenditures. Other public funding sources—the Older Americans Act, Title 20 Social Services Block Grants, the Veterans Administration, and the Civilian Health and Medical Program of the Uniformed Services (CHAMPUS)—provide an important but very modest share of home care dollars (National Association for Home Care and Hospice, 2010). Private insurance companies account for less than 10% of overall home care support, while out-of-pocket spending is significant and growing, especially for personal care services.

The Shifting Policy Environment

Significant changes in home care financing were introduced under the Balanced Budget Act (BBA) of 1997, which represents one element of a shifting policy environment in which the place of home care and the role of social work are being shaped. To curb a steady expansion of Medicare home health utilization and the resulting rising costs, the BBA, implemented in 2000, introduced a prospective payment system (PPS) for home health agencies that changed reimbursement from fee-for-service to a flat (capitation) rate based on classification of patient medical condition and associated needs (Cowles, 2003). Psychological and social factors are not included in the case-mix formula that sets capitation payments (Egan & Kadushin, 2005). This payment shift has created incentives for agencies to be more efficient, manage (ration) resources more carefully, and to restore their focus on short-term, postacute medical care (Egan & Kadushin, 2005; McCall, Korb,

Petersons, & Moore, 2003). This has led first to a dramatic decline by 2001 in average visits per Medicare user (i.e., from 73 visits per patient in 1997 to 33 visits per patient in 2001), then a very slow increase over the last decade (i.e., to an average of 36 visits per patient in 2010) (Medicare Payment Advisory Commission [MedPAC], 2013). The mix of services has shifted away from home health aide services (which accounted for 48% of all services in 1997 and only 16% of services in 2010) and toward nursing and the therapies, while leaving social work comparatively unaffected at about one percent of all visits over time (Egan & Kadushin, 2005; MedPAC, 2013).

The shift to capitated payment and embrace of managed care systems has been accelerated by even more dramatic reform within the healthcare system, namely the passage in 2010 of P.L. 111-148, also known as the Affordable Care Act (ACA). The ACA is designed to make health insurance coverage available to an estimated 28 million Americans who were previously uninsured through health insurance exchanges, premium subsidies, and Medicaid expansion (Buettgens, Garrett, & Holahan, 2010). This historic legislation not only targets many Americans currently uninsured but also addresses issues of rising healthcare costs and uncertain quality. Along with the mechanisms for enrollment, the Act authorizes various models for managing costs and enhancing quality, perhaps most notably "patient-centered medical homes" (PCMH) and "accountable care organizations" (ACO). What these approaches share is an emphasis on integrated and coordinated care and the role of interdisciplinary teams. While these are hardly new concepts, they command our attention because models like PCMHs and ACOs have been propelled into the policy and practice spotlight by healthcare reform and because they hold significant promise and challenges for social work practice.

EMERGING MODELS OF CARE

The ACA contains numerous provisions that expand the parameters of healthcare delivery, including where healthcare happens, how it is delivered, who delivers it, and how it will be paid for. These provisions offer many areas of opportunity for social workers to expand their roles in the delivery of health and social care to older adults, especially in home- and community-based settings.

Many of the new models of care that are being proposed, implemented, and tested in healthcare reform include language that emphasizes a "patient- or person-centered" approach to healthcare delivery. The goal of this approach is to place the consumer at the center of the organization and provision of healthcare, which is to be delivered by an interdisciplinary team of healthcare professionals. These care models often expand beyond the delivery of acute and physical health services to integrate the delivery of behavioral health and long-term services, and extend the delivery of care into the home and community. A number of ACA provisions explicitly support person-centered care while also incentivizing states to shift health and social care from institutions to home and community-based care settings (see Table 11.1 for a selected list of Medicaid provisions that encourage person-centered care).

Social Workers and the Delivery of Person-Centered Care

Social workers seem well suited to respond to this call to provide person-centered care in the home and community. A person-in-environment approach that holistically assesses consumer needs and preferences is foundational to social work training. Geriatric social workers have extensive experience working as part of interdisciplinary teams charged with geriatric evaluation and management. A growing body of evidence demonstrates the effectiveness of interdisciplinary teams in improving or maintaining functional status, enhancing quality of life, and improving mental health outcomes for older adults (Boult et al., 2001; Burns et al., 2000, both as cited in Simons, Shepherd, & Munn, 2008).

Social Workers and Care Coordination

The ACA is also concerned with advancing healthcare delivery models that improve care coordination, through provisions that reward positive health outcomes while reducing costs to Medicare and Medicaid (see Table 11.2 for a selected list of ACA provisions that encourage the advancement of care coordination). Social workers are trained to identify and access the broad range of nonmedical and psychosocial resources essential to effective care

TABLE 11.1. Provisions in the Affordable Care Act That Advance Person-Centered Care*

ACA Provision	Description
Health Homes (Section 2703) http://www.medicaid.gov/Medicaid-CHIP-Program-Information/By-Topics/Long-Term-Services-and-Support/Integrating-Care/Health-Homes/Health-Homes.html	A State option in Medicaid for beneficiaries at risk or with multiple chronic conditions that designates a qualified provider or team as their health home, and provides comprehensive, coordinated, *person-centered* healthcare.
Money Follows the Person (Section 2403) http://downloads.cms.gov/cmsgov/archived-downloads/SMDL/downloads/SMD10012.pdf	Extension of demonstration project (until 2019) that helps Medicaid eligible individual's transition from institutions to community-based care.
Community First Choice Option (Section 2401) http://www.gpo.gov/fdsys/pkg/FR-2012-05-07/pdf/2012-10294.pdf	A new State plan option in Medicaid to provide *person-centered* community-based attendant supports and services to individuals with disabilities.
State Balancing Incentives Payment Program (Section 10202) http://www.medicaid.gov/Medicaid-CHIP-Program-Information/By-Topics/Long-Term-Services-and-Support/Balancing/Balancing-Incentive-Program.html	A temporary program provides qualifying states with an increase in their federal match for state expenditures on Medicaid 1915 (c) home- and community-based services (HCBS) waivers, PACE programs, and home health and personal assistance under the Medicaid state plan HCBS costs.

*Selected provisions, adapted from Kietzman (2012).

TABLE 11.2. Provisions in the Affordable Care Act that Advance Care Coordination*

ACA Provision	Description
Accountable Care Organizations (Section 3022) http://www.cms.gov/Medicare/Medicare-Fee-for-Service-Payment/sharedsavingsprogram/Downloads/ACO_Summary_Factsheet_ICN907404.pdf	Organizations of healthcare providers that are charged with improving quality of care while reducing costs; Must demonstrate quality improvements in patient and caregiver experience, care coordination, safety, preventive health, and health of at-risk populations and frail older adults (Andrews et al., 2013)
Community-Based Care Transitions Program (Section 3026) http://innovation.cms.gov/initiatives/CCTP/?itemID=CMS1239313	Partnerships between hospitals and community-based organizations to test models for improving care transitions from the hospital to other settings and reducing readmissions for high-risk Medicare beneficiaries.
State Demonstrations to Integrate Care for Dual Eligible Individuals (Section 3021) http://kff.org/medicaid/fact-sheet/state-demonstration-proposals-to-integrate-care-and-align-financing-for-dual-eligible-beneficiaries/	Demonstration to develop and test approaches to achieve better coordination of care and better health outcomes for Medicaid/Medicare dual eligible individuals.
Independence at Home (Section 3024) http://www.cms.gov/Medicare/Demonstration-Projects/DemoProjectsEvalRpts/Medicare-Demonstrations-Items/CMS1240082.html	A service delivery model for home-bound chronically ill Medicare beneficiaries. Home-based primary care teams are led by a physician or nurse practitioner and may include social work services.

*Selected provisions, adapted from Kietzman (2012).

coordination including food, housing, transportation, assistive equipment, social support, individual and family counseling, and rehabilitation services.

In view of the predominance of the medical model, funding constraints, and a shifting policy environment, some suggest that social workers may be "losing ground" in healthcare (Dhooper, 1997). However, there are models of home care either in place or being proposed that may expand the role of social workers. For example, telehealth programs and psychiatric home care have been discussed as areas where social workers can establish an important clinical role (P. Berkman, Heinik, Rosenthal, & Burke, 1999; Black & Mindell, 1996; Byrne, 1999). The Veterans Health Administration (VHA), the nation's single largest employer of social workers (US Department of Veterans Affairs, 2013), has traditionally defined home care as an interdisciplinary program in which social work plays an integral role. Unlike Medicare-certified HHC, the provision of social work services at the VHA does not require a physician's order and the social worker is considered a core member of the home-based primary care (HBPC) program. The responsibilities of the HBPC social worker include performing initial and ongoing assessment of the interpersonal resources and psychosocial functions of the Veteran and caregiver; identifying psychosocial problems; providing psychosocial treatment; coordinating discharge planning; collaborating with other health professionals; maximizing VA and community resources available to Veterans and caregivers, and educating the HBPC about available resources (Veterans Health Administration [VHA], 2007).

SOCIAL WORK ROLE AND FUNCTIONS

Constraints

The roles of social work in home care have been limited in two important ways by the design of health insurance, both public and private. First, predominance of the medical model limits the range of tasks that insurers will cover to those associated directly with acute episodes. Second, funding constraints perennially confronting the Medicare and Medicaid programs have pressured provider agencies to control costs, often by minimizing or eliminating services (like social work) not considered "core" in home care. It is estimated that by 2019, Medicare payments for home healthcare will be reduced by more than $39.5 billion (Eck, 2010). As noted, Medicare does not require social workers to see all home health patients or to participate in the planning of their care; it only requires that social work services be made available to patients (Dhooper, 1997). Within Medicare-certified home health agencies, social workers make up only 2% of personnel, compared with 43% for nurses (see Table 11.3). Similarly, in 2010, social workers accounted for 1% of Medicare home health visits, compared with 52% for nurses and 33% for therapists (MedPAC, 2013).

Another barrier to the wider use of social work services in home care is the lack of evidence-based research on the effectiveness of social work services. One review of social work practice in long-term care identified 14 articles that included social workers employed in home healthcare, but only two reported efficacy specifically linked to the role of the social worker (Simons et al., 2008). Other studies of social work efficacy in home care are inconclusive (Lee & Gutheil, 2003). However, a growing literature offers evidence of the effectiveness of discharge planning and needs assessment (including psychosocial needs), and this may bode well for social workers, given the increased attention to transitional care and the use of interdisciplinary teams in the delivery of health care (DePalma, 2008).

TABLE 11.3. Home Healthcare Personnel Mix, 2009

Service	Percent
Home Health Aides	20
Professional Nurses	29
Vocational Nurses	14
Physical Therapists	8
Occupational Therapists	3
Social Workers	2
Other	24

Source: Unpublished data on FTEs in Medicare-certified home healthcare agencies for calendar year (CY) 2009 from the Centers for Medicare and Medicaid Services HCFA Center for Information Systems, Health Standards and Quality Bureau (February 2010), as cited in the National Association for Home Care and Hospice report: *Basic Statistics About Home Care, Updated 2010.*

Social Work Functions and Case Management

Social work's emphasis on addressing biopsychosocial needs provides a more expansive and multidimensional perspective than the medical model, which is frequently used by both medically based and psychodynamically based practitioners (B. Berkman & Volland, 1997). Moreover, in home care settings the biopsychosocial perspective is particularly useful to social workers in screening and assessing the needs of home care clients and their families and in identifying effective interventions and needed resources.

The problems commonly faced by home care clients and their families (detailed in Figure 11.1) are diverse and fall into several categories, such as adjustment to illness or disability, behavioral health issues such as depression, caregiver burden and stress, financial problems, and suspected abuse or neglect (Cowles, 2003; Goode, 2000). Using a person-centered approach in addressing these problems, social workers in home care may assume case management roles and design interventions that are appropriate for clients in either HHC or homemaker service agencies.

The National Association for Social Workers (NASW) has long recognized the importance of social work case management through its establishment of social work case management practice standards and specialty practice credentials (NASW, 2013; Yagoda, 2004). Although the role of case manager in HHC is not reimbursable and engenders conflicts with nursing regarding care coordination responsibilities, some case management activities (such as counseling and resource brokering) are reimbursable services under Medicare.

Although not well documented, Medicaid waiver programs may offer more opportunities than HHC programs for social workers to function as case managers. One such opportunity is provided by PACE (Program of All-Inclusive Care for the Elderly), featuring a capitated, comprehensive medical and social service delivery system and integrated Medicare and Medicaid funding to help older adults at risk for institutionalization to continue living at home. In principle, capitated payment allows providers to deliver all services participants need, including social services, rather than limiting them to those reimbursable under Medicare and Medicaid. As of 2012, there were 88 PACE programs operating in 29 states (National PACE Association, n.d.).

In reviewing various models of case management, we have identified several core functions for social workers doing case management in home care settings using a person-centered approach (see Figure 11.1): engagement, biopsychosocial assessment/reassessment, service planning, implementation of service plan, coordination and monitoring of service delivery, advocacy, and termination (Cowles, 2003; NASW, 2013; Raiff & Shore, 1993; Yagoda, 2004).

CHALLENGES AND OPPORTUNITIES FOR SOCIAL WORK PRACTICE

The future of social work practice in home care remains fluid and uncertain. It is constrained by increasingly restrictive reimbursement policies and by a growing interest in adopting a consumer-directed approach to home care services for older people, which may limit the need for case managers (Benjamin, 2001; Simon-Rusinowitz & Hofland, 1993). Use of case management services is further hindered by the lack of screening instruments to identify those who need social work case management (Diwan, Ivy, Merino, & Brower, 2001).

Possible Solutions

Geriatric social work leaders in the areas of health-care policy, practice, research, and education have begun to address some of the challenges confronting social work in home care. For example, two studies have been funded by the John A. Hartford Foundation—one on the relationship between social work education and practice in healthcare (Volland, Berkman, Stein, & Vaghy, 2000) and the other on the impact of the prospective payment system on social work in home healthcare (Lee & Gutheil, 2003; Lee & Rock, 2005). These studies have produced several recommendations, including (1) enhancing social work curriculum content through a greater focus on healthcare practice (including case management), outcomes research, and data management; (2) establishing independent case finding for social work services to replace the current system of dependence on physicians and nurses; (3) developing a clearer definition of social work roles in HHC that is understood by other healthcare professionals; (4) fostering evidence-based research on the effectiveness of social

Home Care Problems Addressed by Social Work Case Management[1]

Access to needed services
(e.g., transportation)
Adjustment to illness/disability
Behavior management of neurocognitive
disorders (e.g., dementia)
Behavioral health issues (e.g., depression)
Caregiver burden/stress
Discharge planning (transition from home
care to other settings/services)
End of life issues (grief, death & dying)

Family conflict
Financial problems
Housing assistance (e.g.,
assisted living)
Legal issues (e.g., advance directives)
Nonadherence to treatment
Safety and level of care issues (e.g., unsafe
environment, need for more supervision)
Social isolation/inadequate social support
Suspected abuse/neglect

Social Work Case Management Functions in Home Care[2]

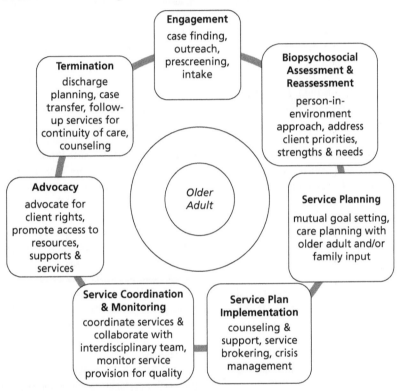

FIGURE 11.1. Person-centered approach to social work case management in home care.

[1]Adapted from Goode (2000).

[2]*Sources:* Cowles (2003), NASW (2013), Raiff and Shore (1993), Yagoda (2004).

work services; and (5) developing screening instruments for social work services for use in HHC.

In light of current constraints, there is enormous potential for expanding the role of social work in home care and for demonstrating the impact of social interventions on health. Without the evidence on impact, however, it has been difficult to make the case for expanded resources to support social work services. To address this, advocates need to identify demonstration programs to test the impact of selected social work interventions with home care clients and to build support for funding both the demonstrations and their evaluation. While a solid evidence base will probably not be sufficient to develop the political support required to enlarge the role of social work in home care, it is certainly necessary if the profession is to expand the service options available to vulnerable populations at home.

REFERENCES

Andrews, C. M., Darnell, J. S., McBride, T. D., & Gehlert, S. (2013). Social work and implementation of the Affordable Care Act. *Health and Social Work*, *38*(2), 67–71. doi:10.1093/hsw/hlt002

Barker, R. L. (2003). *The social work dictionary* (5th ed.). Washington, DC: NASW Press.

Benjamin, A. E. (1993). An historical perspective on home care policy. *Home Health Care Services Quarterly*, *71*, 129–166. http://www.jstor.org/stable/3350277

Benjamin, A. E. (2001). Consumer-direction services at home: A new model for persons with disabilities. *Health Affairs*, *20*, 80–95. doi:10.1377/hlthaff.20.6.80

Berger, R. M. (1988). Making home health social work more effective. *Home Health Care Services Quarterly*, *9*, 63–75. doi:10.1300/J027v09n01_05

Berkman, B., & Volland, P. (1997). Health care practice overview. In R. L. Edwards (Ed.), *Encyclopedia of social work: 1997 Supplement* (pp. 143–149). Washington, DC: NASW Press.

Berkman, P., Heinik, J., Rosenthal, M., & Burke, M. (1999). Supportive telephone outreach as an interventional strategy for elderly patients in a period of crisis. *Social Work in Health Care*, *28*, 63–76. doi:10.1300/J010v28n04_05

Black, J., & Mindell, M. (1996). A model for community-based mental health services for older adults: Innovative social work practice. *Journal of Gerontological Social Work*, *26*, 113–127. doi:10.1300/J083V26N03_09

Brieland, D. (1995). Social work practice: History and evolution. In R. L. Edwards & J. G. Hopps (Eds.), *Encyclopedia of social work* (19th ed., Vol. 3, pp. 2247–2257). Washington, DC: NASW Press.

Buettgens, M., Garrett, B., & Holahan, J. (2010). *America under the Affordable Care Act*. Urban Institute and Robert Woods Johnson Foundation.

Byrne, J. (1999). Social work in psychiatric home care: Regulations, roles, and realities. *Health and Social Work*, *24*, 65–71. http://www.oxfordjournals.org/

Caputi, M. A. (1978). Social work in health care: Past and future. *Health and Social Work*, *3*, 9–29. http://www.oxfordjournals.org/

Centers for Medicare and Medicaid Services (CMS). (2000). *A profile of Medicaid: Chart book 2000*. Retrieved August 19, 2004, from www.cms.hhs.gov/charts/medicaid/2Tchartbk.pdf

Centers for Medicare and Medicaid Services (CMS). (2011). *Medicare benefit policy manual. Ch.7- Home health services* (Rev. 144, May 6, 2011). Retrieved September 27, 2013, at http://www.cms.gov/Regulations-and-Guidance/Guidance/Manuals/downloads/bp102c07.pdf

Cowles, L. A. F. (2003). *Social work in the health field: A care perspective* (2nd ed.). New York, NY: Haworth Social Work Practice Press.

DePalma, J. A. (2008). Evidence to support social work in home care for the elderly. *Home Health Care Management Practice*, *20*, 276–277. doi:10.1177/1084822307310000

Dhooper, S. S. (1997). *Social work in health care in the 21st century*. Thousand Oaks, CA: Sage.

Diwan, S., Ivy, C., Merino, D. A., & Brower, T. (2001). Assessing need for intensive case management in long-term care. *The Gerontologist*, *41*, 680–686. doi:10.1093/geront/41.5.680

Eck, W. (2010). Home care, hospice care, and the Affordable Care Act. *AHLA Connections*, 16–21.

Egan, M., & Kadushin, G. (2005). Managed care in home health: Social work practice and unmet client needs. *Social Work in Health Care*, *41*, 1–18. doi:10.1300/J010v41n02_01

Goode, R. A. (2000). *Social work practice in home health care*. New York, NY: Haworth Press.

Kane, R. A. (1987). Long-term care. In A. Minahan (Ed.), *Encyclopedia of social work* (18th ed., Vol. 2, pp. 59–72). Silver Spring, MD: National Association of Social Workers.

Kietzman, K. G. (2012). Using a "person-centered" approach to improve care coordination: Opportunities emerging from the Affordable Care Act. *Journal of Geriatric Care Management*, *22*, 13–19.

Lee, J. S., & Gutheil, I. A. (2003). The older patient at home: Social work services and home health care. In B. Berkman & L. Harootyan (Eds.), *Social work and health care in an aging society* (pp. 73–95). New York, NY: Springer.

Lee, J. S., & Rock, B. D. (2005). Challenges in the new prospective payment system: action steps for social work in home health care. *Health and Social Work*, *30*, 48–55. PMID: 15847237. http://ucelinks.cdlib.org:8888/sfx_local?sid=Entrez:PubMed&id=pmid:15847237

McCall, N., Korb, J., Petersons, A., & Moore, S. (2003). Reforming Medicare payment: Early effects of the 1997 Balanced Budget Act on postacute care. *Milbank Quarterly*, *81*, 277–303. doi:10.1111/1468-0009.t01-1-00054

Medicare Payment Advisory Commission (MedPAC). (2013). *A data book: Health care spending and the Medicare program, 2012*. Washington, DC: Author.

Nacman, M. (1977). Social work in health settings: A historical review. *Social Work in Health Care*, *2*, 407–418.

National Association for Home Care and Hospice. (2010). *Basic statistics about home care.* Retrieved August 16, 2013, from http://www.nahc.org/Consumer/hcstats.htm

National Association of Social Workers. (2013). *NASW standards for social work case management.* Retrieved September 17, 2013, from www.social-workers.org/practice/standards/sw_case_mgmt.asp

National Center for Health Statistics. (2004). *Early release of selected estimates based on data from the 2003 National Health Interview Survey.* Retrieved June 30, 2004, from www.cdc.gov/nchs/data/nhis/earlyrelease/200406_12.pdf

National Center for Health Statistics. (2010). *Home health patients and hospice care discharges, 2007. National home and hospice care survey.* Retrieved August 15, 2013, from www.cdc.gov/nchs/data/nhhcsd/curhomecare.pdf

National PACE Association. (n.d.). What is PACE? Alexandria, VA: National PACE Association. Retrieved September 18, 2013, from http://www.npaonline.org/website/article.asp?id=12&title=Who,_What_and_Where_is_PACE?

Ng, T., Harrington, C., & Kitchener, M. (2010). Medicare and Medicaid in long-term care. *Health Affairs, 29,* 22–28. doi:10.1377/hlthaff.2009.0494

Raiff, N. R., & Shore, B. (1993). *Advanced case management.* Newbury Park, CA: Sage.

Romaine-Davis, A., Boondas, J., & Lenihan, A. (Eds.). (1995). *Encyclopedia of home care for the elderly.* Westport, CT: Greenwood Press.

Ross, J. W. (1995). Hospital social work. In R. L. Edwards & J. G. Hopps (Eds.), *Encyclopedia of social work* (19th ed., Vol. 2, pp. 1365–1377). Washington, DC: NASW Press.

Simon-Rusinowitz, L., & Hofland, B. F. (1993). Adopting a disability approach to home care services for older adults. *The Gerontologist, 33,* 159–167. doi:10.1093/geront/33.2.159

Simon-Rusinowitz, L., Loughlin, D. M., Ruben, K., Martinez-Garcia, G., & Mahoney, K. J. (2010). The benefits of consumer-directed services for elders and their caregivers in the Cash and Counseling demonstration and evaluation. *Public Policy and Aging Report, 20,* 27–31.

Simons, K., Shepherd, N., & Munn, J. (2008). Advancing the evidence base for social work in long-term care: The disconnect between practice and research. *Social Work in Health Care, 47,* 392–415. doi:10.1080/00981380802258458

US Department of Veterans Affairs. (2013, March). *Do I need a social worker?* Retrieved September 5, 2013, from http://www.va.gov/health/NewsFeatures/2013/March/Do-I-Need-a-Social-Worker.asp

Veterans Health Administration (VHA). (2007, January 31). HBPC (home based primary care) program. In *VHA handbook* (1141.01). Washington, DC: Department of Veterans Affairs.

Volland, P. J., Berkman, B., Stein, G., & Vaghy, A. (2000). *Social work education for practice in health care: Final report.* New York: New York Academy of Medicine.

Yagoda, L. (2004, May). Case management with older adults: A social work perspective. *NASW Aging Practice Update,* 1–3.

Departments of public welfare primarily serve low income and vulnerable adults through programs funded via a combination of federal, state, and local funds. Gerontological social workers need to be aware of challenges facing these programs with respect to providing services to older adults affected by poverty, oppression, and a history of social exclusion. They must be sensitive to issues regarding public support for programs in an era of constricted public resources and increased need for services.

ROLE OF GOVERNMENT IN DELIVERY OF SERVICES TO OLDER ADULTS

The Social Security Act of 1935 was the landmark act that expanded the movement toward many of the social welfare programs in place today. One concept encapsulated in it was the distinction between the universal programs such as Old Age, Survivors and Disability Insurance (OASDI—Title II), which were administered by the federal government, and means-tested programs such as Old Age Assistance (Title I), which were funded by grants to the states and administered by state governments to meet needs as specified by those states, within the broad constraints of the legislation. Title I and later Title XVI (Grants to States for the Aged, Blind, or Disabled) mandated that the cash grant programs include services to help applicants "attain self care" (US Social Security Administration, 2012). Each state set up its own system for delivery of these services, usually through county-level departments of public welfare or social services.

Title XX of the Social Security Act, passed in 1974, allocated sums on the basis of each state's population to use for social services, including protective services to adults and home- and community-based care for the elderly and disabled (US Social Security Administration, 2012). The Omnibus Reconciliation Act of 1981 established the Social Services Block Grant (SSBG) to states and did away with certain mandates regarding priority and low-income recipients, further reducing the availability of funds available for protective services and other services for low-income populations. In 2010, the Elder Justice Act was signed into law as part of the Patient Protection and Affordable Care Act. Provisions related to elder justice, which include specific authorizations for Adult Protective Services

JOY SWANSON ERNST
CHARLES A. SMITH

Departments of Public Welfare or Social Services

(APS), were established as amendments to Title XX of the Social Security Act. Congress has threatened to eliminate the SSBG altogether (Lynch, 2012), and has yet to appropriate funds for implementation of the act despite the inclusion of money for an Elder Justice Initiative in the President's Fiscal Year 2015 budget and Appropriations bill. Other publicly funded programs that assist older adults, including the Supplemental Nutritional Assistance Program, have also been targeted for elimination as a result of efforts to rein in federal spending.

ROLE OF SOCIAL WORKERS IN DEPARTMENTS OF PUBLIC WELFARE/SOCIAL SERVICES

Because of variations in job titles, it is not always possible to identify the social workers in public agencies, and the qualifications necessary to provide and/or oversee social services vary by state and program (Brownell, 2006). Depending on their specific role (e.g., case manager, clinician, program administrator), social workers carry out a variety of functions in departments of public welfare (NASW Center for Workforce Studies, 2011). These services range from direct service to clients (e.g., assessment and determination of eligibility, analysis of social service and support needs, service coordination) to administrative and planning roles within the program management structure. To provide these services, knowledge and expertise in working with older adults is essential.

CHARACTERISTICS OF OLDER ADULTS RELEVANT TO SERVICE PROVISION

Social workers in departments of public welfare need to be aware of current and changing characteristics of the elderly population. Relevant factors that are important to understand include growth in total and relative senior population; disparity as it relates to sex, race/ethnicity, and poverty; functional disability; and availability of caregivers.

Population Growth

In 2010 there were 40.3 million individuals age 65 years and older in the United States, which constituted 13% of the entire US population. Projections

indicate that by 2030 the number of seniors (age 65+) will increase to 72 million, and make up 19.3% of the US population. The oldest-old (i.e., those age 85+) are projected to increase from 5.5 million in 2010 to 19 million in 2050 (328% growth) (US Census Bureau, 2012). This population growth will occur differentially by state and region, with the largest future concentrations of older adults projected to be in rural regions and in the south.

Diversity and Disparities

The older adult population is highly diverse and experiences great disparities. While 57% of seniors age 65 years and older are female, by age 85, 67.4% of the elderly population are women. Additionally, elderly men are more likely to be married or living with domestic partners. This disparity grows with increasing age, and by age 75 and older 47.4% of women report living alone compared with 22.6% of men (US Census Bureau, 2012). Living alone, and the social isolation that often results, has been identified as a major risk factor (after controlling for other factors) for a variety of other problems including depression, somatic health, dementia, and mortality (Greenfield & Russell, 2011; Tilvis, Venla Laitala, Routasalo, & Pitkälä, 2011).

The older adult population is becoming increasingly diverse in terms of race and ethnicity. White non-Hispanics are forecast to decrease from 80% of the senior population (age 65+) down to 64.6% by the year 2040. In that same time period, Black non-Hispanics seniors will increase from 8.5% to 10.5%, Asian non-Hispanics will increase from 3.4% to 6.9%, and Hispanics will increase from 6.9% to 16.2%. Level of poverty is also correlated with race and ethnicity among older adults age 65 and over. While the overall senior poverty rate is 9%, this breaks down to 8.3% among White non-Hispanics, 15.1% among Asian non-Hispanics, 20.5% among Black non-Hispanics, and 20.9% among Hispanics (US Census Bureau, 2012).

Disability

Although a number of studies (e.g., Manton, Gu, & Lamb, 2006) have indicated a long-term significant decline in relative disability rates, disability in the older population has an impact on need and demand for services. National survey data indicate that overall self-reported disability rates for those aged 65 and over dropped from 49% in 1992 to 41% in 2009 (Federal Interagency Forum on Aging-Related Statistics, 2012). Included in that decline is a drop in the percentage of older adults in institutional nursing home placements from 6% in 1992 to 4% in 2009. A caveat to the good news on decline in nursing home rates is an increase in seniors residing in assisted living facilities, which were rare in the early 1990s. When one combines nursing home and assistive living rates, the proportion of older adults in supportive residential housing has remained largely unchanged (Spillman & Black, 2006). In terms of trends in functional disability status, the observed declines in self-reported disability from 1992 to the early 2000s may be a product of increased use of assistive devices, rather than an actual improvement in health (Schoeni, Freedman, & Martin, 2008). Additionally, studies that have looked at waves of cohorts suggest that future waves of seniors may be less healthy than prior cohorts due to the impact of the obesity epidemic (Lakdawalla, Bhattacharya, & Goldman, 2004).

Due to the growth in the oldest-old population, one aspect of disability that has increased dramatically is the number of individuals with dementia. Relative rates of dementia change with advancing age. Among those ages 71–79, only 2.3% of people have dementia. Among those ages 80–89, this figure increases to 18.1%, and among those ages 90 and over it rises again to 29.7% (Plassman et al., 2007). However, relative rates, though not total numbers, of seniors with dementia may be declining as a product of enhanced protective factors, such as greater education attainment (Matthews et al., 2013).

Availability of Caregivers

Family and friends provide the majority of care for older adults who develop functional disabilities. Social workers in departments of public welfare often turn to these informal support networks for assistance when dealing with vulnerable seniors. However, a number of factors are likely to reduce their availability. Due to decline in average family size, fewer adult child caregivers will be available to assist with their "boomer" parents, and greater geographic mobility means that many adult children live far from their aged parents. Women, the traditional providers of informal care, are increasingly active in the workforce and have fewer hours available to

provide assistance. Additionally, increased divorce rates among seniors have eliminated many potential spousal caregivers. Forecasts indicate that by the year 2030 the dependency ratio, which is the proportion of older adults (age 65+) relative to younger adults (ages 20–64), will drop from 4.5 to 2.8 younger adults per senior. This not only indicates a significant reduction in available adult child caregivers but also raises questions about the funding mechanisms to support programs for older adults and suggests that more government-financed long-term care will be needed (Redfoot, Feinberg, & Houser, 2013). Another issue that is germane to public support for programs provided through departments of public welfare is that the legally mandated responsibilities of adult children toward their aging and infirm parents is much less clear than the mandate for parents who are legally obligated to support their minor children (Stiegel, Klem, & Turner, 2007).

Political Influence of Older Population

Support for services provided through departments of public welfare depends in part on the political influence of the constituencies that benefit from those services. The degree and intensity of interest in old-age benefits varies among the older population (Binstock, 2012). As the percentage of the population increases, if older adults continue to vote in numbers that are disproportionate to their numbers in the population, they will retain if not grow in political influence (Brandon, 2012; Pew Research Center for People and the Press, 2006). Polls conducted during the 2012 election revealed that older Americans were strongly opposed to cuts in Medicare, for example, and likely to vote for a candidate for national office based on his or her support for Medicare (Pew Research Center for People and the Press, 2012). However, the extent of political support for the state-funded programs that assist low-income older adults such as energy assistance, in-home aide services, and respite care, is difficult for state lawmakers to predict (Smith, 2011).

PUBLIC PROGRAMS AND SERVICES FOR OLDER ADULTS

Funding determines both the capacity to deliver services and dictates what issues or concerns get preferential treatment over others. The federal government is the largest single source of revenues for programs serving older adults, primarily funneled through Social Security, Medicare, Medicaid, and the Older Americans Act (OAA).

On the state and local levels, governments are faced with mandatory balanced budgets, which coupled with the tax reduction fervor nationally has resulted in static or reduced funding for senior programs. In light of the rapid and continued growth of the senior population, previously inadequate state and local resources are becoming increasingly insufficient to meet needs. The gap between funding and need not only manifests itself in competition among senior programs for scarce resources but also pits different sectors of human services (e.g., child welfare vs. elderly) against each other for funding (Ozawa, 1999). For example, at the federal level APS has had to compete with other programs funded by Title XX funds, including child daycare and vital programs for children (US Government Accountability Office [US GAO], 2011).

Older Americans Act (OAA)

Public agency social workers often use OAA-funded programs as resources for older adult clients in the community. These OAA funds are distributed by the Administration for Community Living (ACL, formerly the Administration on Aging) and are used at the local level to fund a variety of free supportive services for individuals ages 60 and over. The largest block of OAA funds (40.4% in FY2012) went toward nutrition support programs, comprising congregate meals (i.e., meals offered at senior centers that are intended to enhance social connectivity as well as nutrition status) and home-delivered meals (HDMs). The next largest share of OAA funds (22.2%) went to support senior employment programs to assist older individuals in entering or reentering the workforce. Next, at 18.2% were home- and community-based services, including senior centers and home-based services (e.g., personal care). Next in order were 8.2% that went to support services for caregivers; 3.7% that served to enhance information, access, and outreach; and 2.6% that went toward protecting vulnerable older adults (e.g., ombudsman, fraud prevention, and APS). Notably, OAA funds are not prioritized to address disease prevention (1% of funding), chronic disease self-management (0.5% of funding), and Alzheimer and dementia supports (0.2% of OAA funding) (Administration for Community Living, 2013).

Adult Protective Services

The program most associated with aging and departments of public welfare is APS, though these services are sometimes housed within state departments of aging (Brownell, 2006; US GAO, 2011). Adult Protective Services programs respond to and investigate allegations of physical and sexual abuse of elderly and dependent adults, neglect by caregivers, financial exploitation and self-neglect. Adult Protective Services responds to elder abuse that takes place in community settings in all states and responds to institution-based elder mistreatment in some (US GAO, 2011). The majority of cases reported to APS are for self-neglect (Teaster et al., 2006). Adult Protective Services workers also arrange for services, such as guardianship, in-home aide services, and nursing home placement and may provide continuing case management services.

Because of the growth and devastating impact of cases of financial exploitation of elderly and disabled adults, many state departments of social services through their adult services programs have joined forces with other organizations, including financial institutions and law enforcement, to address financial exploitation. One example is Financial Abuse Specialist Teams, which are multidisciplinary teams that address financial abuse of elderly and vulnerable adults (Malks, Schmidt, & Austin, 2002).

States differ on whether APS services are centralized, decentralized, a hybrid, or contracted out to private agencies (Mukherjee, 2011); staffing and training vary by state as well. No federal laws or policies direct how protective services should be delivered, and state statutes differ in terms of the definitions of abuse and what types of abuse are covered, and whether reporting of elder abuse is mandated (Brandl et al., 2006). New York State is the only state without mandated reporting. Within-state differences in service delivery makes the accessibility to and use of the services available through departments of public welfare highly variable and dependent on conditions in local offices (National Adult Protective Services Association and National Committee for the Prevention of Elder Abuse, 2013).

While localized control means that states and counties can determine the response that best fits the needs and resources of their communities, one result is that the United States does not collect uniform data that would help determine trends in reporting. Additionally, there is insufficient evidence-based research and dissemination of best practices to APS agencies, which have limited information on evidence-based practices that would help them address complex cases (US GAO, 2011).

Community-Based Care

Departments of public welfare also provide home- and community-based services aimed at keeping low-income seniors in their homes. While social workers in departments of public welfare are not directly responsible for determining eligibility for Medicare and Medicaid they often play a supportive role in assisting clients to apply for such benefits, such as accessing supplemental funding sources. Increasingly, social workers encounter Medicaid via Medicaid Waivers, which are intended to reallocate (or "rebalance") resources from institutional settings (i.e., nursing homes) and direct them toward community-based services. The structure of Medicaid Waivers is that if an individual is deemed as needing a nursing home level of care (as determined by a nursing assessment), and meeting income and asset thresholds (often through spend-down provisions), that community-based services can be provided up to the cost of the mean Medicaid reimbursement level for that state. Proponents of this approach applaud it as not only enhancing individual's quality of life (QOL) but also leading to reductions in government expenditures (e.g., Kaye, LaPlante, & Harrington, 2009). Other researchers, while not questioning the enhancement of QOL, have cautioned that the "woodwork effect," the inability to accurately predict in advance who will enter a nursing home, and the already present self-selection among older adults against nursing homes makes waiver cost savings unlikely (Van Houtven, Jeffreys, & Coffman, 2008; Weissert, Chernew, & Hirth, 2001; Zarit, Gaugler, & Jarrott, 1999).

Respite care, which entails providing caregivers of disabled older adults a temporary break from their caregiving duties, is supported by a variety of funding sources (e.g., federal, state, local) in part due to the politically favorable nature of its intent (i.e., giving a break to those that "deserve" relief). However, despite its intuitive appeal methodologically rigorous studies have suggested that respite care as implemented in many jurisdictions is not actually effective at reducing caregiver stress and burden because the duration and frequency of the break from caregiving

is of insufficient dosage to make a real difference. Additionally, some studies have suggested that limited subtherapeutic breaks from caregiving may actually lead to increased risk of institutionalization by giving caregivers a taste of what life might be like without the burden of caregiving (Mason et al., 2007).

Nursing Home Placement

While most interventions are intended to reduce or delay institutional placement, in some situations the optimum course of action is nursing home placement. Nursing homes can provide intensive medical supervision that is not possible in home settings in a cost-effective manner. While studies show that older adults have a great fear of institutionalization (e.g., Mattimore et al., 1997), such fears may to some extent be unjustified. Researchers have documented that while depression in nursing homes is higher than in the community, this may be a product of the disabling conditions that led to institutionalization and not the actual nursing home environment itself (Smalbrugge et al., 2006). In addition, institutionalization often does reduce caregiver burden and stress, particularly for dementia caregivers (Gaugler, Hepburn, Mittelman, & Newcomer, 2009).

Income Supports

Departments of public welfare administer federally funded programs that provide assistance to eligible low-income citizens, including many seniors. One program is the Supplemental Nutritional Assistance Program (SNAP). The Low Income Home Energy Assistance Program (LIHEAP) helps households that pay a high proportion of their income for heating or electric bills to meet their needs for home energy. Departments of public welfare also serve grandparent caregivers through provision of Temporary Assistance to Needy Families (TANF) and other benefits for which the children in their care may be eligible (Brownell, 2006).

SPECIAL SKILLS AND CONSIDERATIONS FOR SOCIAL WORKERS IN DEPARTMENTS OF PUBLIC WELFARE

Social workers in departments of public welfare work with older adults who are vulnerable due to physical frailty, acute and chronic health conditions, and cognitive impairment. While certain physical changes are age-related, ageism can create assumptions that impairments are an inevitable part of the aging process. Social workers in departments of public welfare must take responsibility to respect client self-determination and see that older clients receive services and supports that they need and that their conditions are assessed and treated appropriately (Brownell, 2006).

Dynamics of Adult Abuse and Neglect

The situations that APS workers encounter have become increasingly complicated and harder to resolve because they involve multiple types of abuse and addiction and physical and cognitive impairment on the part of the older adults and their caregivers (US GAO, 2011). Lack of detailed knowledge on these issues and ageism can mean that workers in public agencies may not recognize signs and symptoms of abuse. In some states APS workers need more training in recognizing and responding to abuse, and states need to do a better job of defining minimum training standards and preparing their workers, for example, in the areas of collecting evidence and distinguishing signs of physical abuse from normal aging (Strasser et al., 2011). Workers must help victims of abuse and neglect access services as well; one study revealed that victims of neglect and their families had difficulty in accessing support services such as in-home aid services and financial assistance (Choi, Kim, & Asseff, 2009).

Collaboration and Interdisciplinary Environment

The ability to collaborate with other professionals and to work in an interdisciplinary environment or as part of a multidisciplinary team is essential for work in departments of public welfare. Social workers need to be able to communicate clearly their role on a team and to understand the role and functions of other team members, such as medical and law enforcement personnel. Social workers must also use their communication skills to help team members recognize commonalities and differences and to deal with conflict among team members (National

Association of Social Workers, 2013). In particular, there is an increased emphasis on the use of teams in dealing with complex cases of elder abuse and neglect (Twomey et al., 2010). Nine states now have language supporting the use of teams in their APS statutes (Daly & Jogerst, 2013). Elder abuse forensic centers are one example of the use of specialized teams that include representatives from APS (Schneider, Mosqueda, Falk, & Huba, 2010).

INNOVATIVE PRACTICES

In response to changing population needs and research on interventions for older adults, departments of public welfare are often involved in developing, pilot testing, and implementing innovative programs and approaches to serve vulnerable older adults. Examples of programs are listed here:

Chronic Disease Self-Management Program (CDSMP): The Stanford CDSMP is an evidence-based program that has been implemented in a variety of communities by public agency social workers. As with fall prevention programs, CDSMP has demonstrated strong efficacy in trials, and where supervision exists; however, adherence is problematic over time when individuals do not receive support (Jerant, Moore-Hill, & Franks, 2009).

Fall prevention: Approximately 35%–40% of all seniors (age 65+) experience a fall every year, with 2% of all seniors requiring hospitalization due to an injurious fall. A number of evidence-based fall-prevention programs have been developed and demonstrate strong efficacy as long as individuals adhere to the intervention. However, the demonstration projects reveal that a large majority of people stop the intervention after the structured program ends. Periodic follow-ups to provide monitoring and encouragement may be a necessary adjunct (Sherrington et al., 2008).

Environmental modifications: A promising new approach to dealing with functional limitations of older adults in the community is to directly address poor person–environment fit by either modifying the home environment or providing individuals and families with devices and/or training to help them better manage their own needs. A number of interventions using teams of occupational therapists and social workers have demonstrated that such interventions can produce better client outcomes (e.g., increase functional status, decreased fear of falling) while being cost-effective (Sheffield, Smith, & Becker, 2012; Szanton et al., 2011).

ETHICS

In light of the vulnerability of older adults, whose desires for self-determination may be in conflict with family members, agency policies, and even social pressures, social workers in departments of public welfare must be aware of some of the ethical dilemmas that they may confront.

Self-Determination Versus Guardianship

Legally and ethically there is a priority given to individuals' rights to make their own decisions (i.e., self-determination). However, situations arise where the individual, due to illness or incapacity, is unable to make informed decisions on his or her own behalf. In those situations a public agency social worker may be called on to seek legal guardianship of the individual, typically by a family member or friend or through the public guardianship program. The dilemma here is between the autonomy and self-determination of the individual versus protecting safety and well-being.

Power Imbalances

There needs to be a recognition that older adults that come to the attention of public programs/services are almost invariably in a position of diminished power, whereby they are seeking assistance for problems outside their control. Vulnerable seniors may not feel able to advocate for themselves (for fear that they will be denied services) and/or may not be willing to protest about neglect or maltreatment (again out of fear). This dynamic can also be present in the relationship between vulnerable elders and caregivers.

Self-Determination Versus Social Justice

In the broadest sense there are potential (and real) conflicts between the desires of older adults

(self-determination) and the needs of society as a whole (social justice). For example, the overriding desire of older adults, and the political mantra given the electoral influence of older adults, is for "aging in place" (AIP). A dilemma can arise when the desire to age in place (i.e., self-determination) runs into conflict with the interests of the larger society. There are costs associated with assisting people to age in place, including: depreciation of housing stock (property values), exclusion of younger families from housing in urban areas (where elderly are often concentrated), global warming associated with heating/cooling houses that are much larger than a person needs, and allocation of limited public dollars to assist people to remain in settings that may not be a good match to their needs as well as their QOL (Golant, 2008).

CONCLUSION

Public departments of public welfare tend to serve those who are most vulnerable and in greatest need. Projections indicate that not only is the older adult population growing dramatically but also the recent trend of decreasing prevalence of disability may end due to the obesity epidemic, and the availability of informal caregivers is likely to become more limited. All of these factors point to the increasing role of gerontological social workers with public welfare agencies. As such, professionals need to be aware of the statutes, programs, funding streams, and best practices that exist.

REFERENCES

Administration for Community Living. (2013). *Final FY 2013 ACL funding budget information.* Retrieved from http://www.acl.gov/about_acl/budget/ACLFunding Budget2013.aspx

Binstock, R. H. (2012). Older voters and the 2010 U.S. Election: Implications for 2012 and beyond? *Gerontologist, 52,* 408–417. doi:10.1093/geront/gnr118

Brandl, B., Dyer, C. B., Heisler, C. J., Otto, J. M., Stiegel, L. A., & Thomas, R. W. (2006). *Elder abuse detection and intervention: A collaborative approach.* New York, NY: Springer.

Brandon, E. (2012). Why older citizens are more likely to vote. *U.S. News & World Report.* Retrieved from http://money.usnews.com/money/retirement/articles/2012/03/19/why-older-citizens-are-more-likely-to-vote.

Brownell, P. (2006). Departments of public welfare and social services. In B. Berkman (Ed.), *Handbook of social work in health and aging* (pp. 435–443). New York, NY: Oxford University Press.

Choi, N. G., Kim, J., & Asseff, J. (2009). Self-neglect and neglect of vulnerable older adults: Reexamination of etiology. *Journal of Gerontological Social Work, 52,* 171–187. doi:10.1080/01634370802609239

Daly, J. M., & Jogerst, G. J. (2013). Multidisciplinary team legislative language associated with elder abuse investigations. *Journal of Elder Abuse and Neglect, 26*(1), 44–59. doi:10.1080/08946566.2013.782783

Federal Interagency Forum on Aging-Related Statistics. (2012). *Older Americans 2012: Key indicators of well-being.* Washington, DC: Author.

Gaugler, J. E., Hepburn, K., Mittelman, M. S., & Newcomer, R. (2009). Predictors of change in caregiver burden and depressive symptoms following nursing home admission. *Psychology and Aging, 24,* 385–396. doi:10.1037/a0006052

Golant, S. M. (2008). Low-income elderly homeowners in very old dwellings: The need for public policy debate. *Journal of Aging and Social Policy, 20,* 1–28. doi:10.1300/J031v20n01_01

Greenfield, E. A., & Russell, D. (2011). Identifying living arrangements that heighten risk for loneliness in later life: Evidence from the U.S. National Social Life, Health, and Aging Project. *Journal of Applied Gerontology, 30,* 524–534. doi:10.1177/0733464810364985

Jerant, A., Moore-Hill, M., & Franks, P. (2009). Home-based, peer-led chronic illness self-management training: Findings from a 1-year randomized controlled trial. *Annals of Family Medicine, 7,* 319–327. http://www.annfammed.org/

Kaye, S., LaPlante, M. P., & Harrington, C. (2009). Do noninstitutional long-term care services reduce Medicaid spending? *Health Affairs, 28,* 262–272. doi:10.1377/hlthaff.28.1.262

Lakdawalla, D. N., Bhattacharya, J., & Goldman, D. R. (2004). Trends: Are the young becoming more disabled? *Health Affairs, 23,* 168–176. doi:10.1377/hlthaff.23.1.168

Lynch, K. E. (2012). *Social services block grant: Background and funding* (94–953). Washington, DC: Congressional Research Service.

Malks, B., Schmidt, C. M., & Austin, M. J. (2002). Elder abuse prevention: A case study of the Santa Clara County Financial Abuse Specialist Team (FAST) program. *Journal of Gerontological Social Work, 39,* 23–40. http://www.tandfonline.com/toc/wger20/current#.UkpWLmTXhqs

Manton, K. G., Gu, X., & Lamb, V. L. (2006). Long-term trends in life expectancy and active life expectancy in the United States. *Population and Development Review, 32,* 81–106. doi:10.1111/j.1728-4457.2006.00106.x

Mason, A., Weatherly, H., Spilsbury, K., Arksey, H., Golder, S., Adamson, J., . . . Glendinning, C. (2007). A systematic review of the effectiveness and cost-effectiveness of different models of community-based respite care for frail older people and their carers. *Health Technology Assessment, 11*(15), 1–157, iii. http://www.journalslibrary.nihr.ac.uk/hta/volume-11

Matthews, F. E., Arthur, A., Barnes, L. E., Bond, J., Jagger, C., Robinson, L., & Brayne, C. (2013). A two-decade comparison of prevalence of dementia in individuals aged 65 years and older from three geographical areas of England: Results of the Cognitive Function and Ageing Study I and II. *Lancet, 382*(9902), 1405–1412. doi:10.1016/S0140-6736(13)61570-6

Mattimore, T. J., Wenger, N. S., Desbiens, N. A., Teno, J. M., Hamel, M. B., Liu, H., . . . Oye, R. K. (1997). Surrogate and physician understanding of patients' preferences for living permanently in a nursing home. *Journal of the American Geriatrics Society, 45,* 818–824.

Mukherjee, D. (2011). Organizational structure of elder abuse reporting systems. *Administration in Social Work, 35,* 517–531. doi:10.1080/03643107.2011.614532

NASW Center for Workforce Studies. (2011). *Social workers in social services agencies: Occupational profile.* Retrieved from http://workforce.socialworkers.org/studies/profiles/Social Services.pdf

National Adult Protective Services Association and National Committee for the Prevention of Elder Abuse (Producers). (2013). *Elder abuse risk factors podcast, part II.* Retrieved from http://www.youtube.com/watch?v=vjFmViZKfZQ

National Association of Social Workers. (2013). *Quick guide: Making interdisciplinary collaboration work.* NASW Tools and Techniques. Retrieved from http://www.socialworkers.org/assets/secured/documents/practice/interdisciplinarycollaboration.pdf.

Ozawa, M. N. (1999). The economic well-being of elderly people and children in a changing society. *Social Work, 44,* 9–20. http://www.naswpress.org/publications/journals/sw.html

Pew Research Center for People and the Press. (2006). *Who votes, who doesn't, and why.* Retrieved from http://www.people-press.org/2006/10/18/who-votes-who-doesnt-and-why/

Pew Research Center for People and the Press. (2012). *For voters it's still the economy.* Retrieved from http://www.people-press.org/2012/09/24/for-voters-its-still-the-economy/

Plassman, B. L., Langa, K. M., Fisher, G. G., Heeringa, S. G., Weir, D. R., Ofstedal, M. B., . . . Wallace, R. B. (2007). Prevalence of dementia in the United States: The Aging, Demographics, and Memory study. *Neuroepidemiology, 29*, 125–132. doi:10.1159/000109998

Redfoot, D., Feinberg, L., & Houser, A. (2013). *The aging of the baby boom and the growing care gap: A look at future declines in the availability of family caregivers.* Retrieved from http://www.aarp.org

Schneider, D. C., Mosqueda, L., Falk, E., & Huba, G. J. (2010). Elder abuse forensic centers. *Journal of Elder Abuse and Neglect, 22*, 255–274. doi:925746408 [pii] 10.1080/08946566.2010.490137

Schoeni, R. F., Freedman, V. A., & Martin, L. G. (2008). Why is late-life disability declining? *Milbank Quarterly, 86*, 47–89. doi:10.1111/j.1468-0009.2007.00513.x

Sheffield, C., Smith, C., & Becker, M. (2012). Evaluation of an agency-based occupational therapy intervention to facilitate aging in place. *The Gerontologist, 52*, 907–918. doi:10.1093/geronto/gns145

Sherrington, C., Whitney, J. C., Lord, S. R., Herbert, R. D., Cumming, R. G., & Close, J. C. T. (2008). Effective exercise for the prevention of falls: A systematic review and meta-analysis. *Journal of the American Geriatrics Society, 56*, 2234–2243. doi:10.1111/j.1532-5415.2008.02014.x

Smalbrugge, M., Jongenelis, L., Pot, A. M., Eefsting, J. A., Ribbe, M. W., & Beekman, A. T. F. (2006). Incidence and outcome of depressive symptoms in nursing home patients in the Netherlands. *American Journal of Geriatric Psychiatry, 14*, 1069–1076. doi:10.1097/01.jgp.0000224605.37317.88

Smith, E. P. (2011). Policy, politics and population. *State Legislatures, 37*, 17–18.

Spillman, B. C., & Black, K. J. (2006). *The size and characteristics of the residential care population: Evidence from three national surveys.* Retrieved from http://aspe.hhs.gov/daltcp/reports/2006/3natlsur.htm

Stiegel, L., Klem, E., & Turner, J. (2007). *Neglect of older persons: An introduction to legal issues related to caregiver duty and liability.* Washington, DC: American Bar Association Commission on Law and Aging.

Strasser, S. M., Kerr, J., King, P. S., Payne, B. K., Beddington, S., Pendrick, D., . . . McCarty, F. (2011). A survey of Georgia adult protective services staff: Implications for older adult injury prevention

and policy. *Western Journal of Emergency Medicine, 12*, 357–364. http://westjem.com/

Szanton, S. L., Thorpe, R. J., Boyd, C., Tanner, E. K., Leff, B., Agree, E., . . . Gitlin, L. N. (2011). Community aging in place, advancing better living for elders: A bio-behavioral-environmental intervention to improve function and health-related quality of life in disabled older adults. *Journal of the American Geriatrics Society, 59*, 2314–2320. doi:10.1111/j.1532-5415.2011.03698.x

Teaster, P. B., Dugar, T. A., Mendiondo, M. S., Abner, E. L., Cecil, K. A., & Otto, J. M. (2006). *The 2004 survey of state adult protective services: Abuse of adults 60 years of age and older.* Retrieved from http://www.elderabusecenter.org/pdf/2-14-06   FINAL 60+REPORT.pdf

Tilvis, R. S., Venla Laitala, V., Routasalo, P. E., & Pitkälä, K. H. (2011). Suffering from loneliness indicates significant mortality risk of older people. *Journal of Aging Research, 2011*, 1–5. doi:10.4061/2011/534781

Twomey, M. S., Jackson, G., Li, H., Marino, T., Melchior, L. A., Randolph, J. F., . . . Wysong, J. (2010). The successes and challenges of seven multidisciplinary teams. *Journal of Elder Abuse and Neglect, 22*, 291–305. doi:10.1080/0896566.2010.490144

US Census Bureau. (2012). *Statistical abstract of the United States.* Washington, DC: Author.

US Government Accountability Office (US GAO). (2011). *Elder justice: Stronger federal leadership could enhance national response to elder abuse* (GAO-11-208). Washington, DC: Government Printing Office.

US Social Security Administration. (2012). *Compilation of the social security laws.* Retrieved from http://www.socialsecurity.gov/OP_Home/ssact/comp-ssa.htm

Van Houtven, C. H., Jeffreys, A. S., & Coffman, C. J. (2008). Home health care and patterns of subsequent VA and medicare health care utilization for veterans. *The Gerontologist, 48*, 668–678. doi:10.1093/geront/48.5.668

Weissert, W., Chernew, M., & Hirth, R. (2001). Beyond managed long-term care: Paying for home care based on risk of adverse outcomes. *Health Affairs, 20*, 172. doi:10.1377/hltaff.20.3.172

Zarit, S. H., Gaugler, J. E., & Jarrott, S. E. (1999). Useful services for families: Research findings and directions. *International Journal of Geriatric Psychiatry, 14*, 165–177.

Although the majority of the older population has sound mental health, studies indicate that almost 20% experience mental health disorders (Houser, Fox-Grage, & Gibson, 2006). The association between older adult mental disorders and physical illness, poor social support, and disability presents unique challenges for the mental healthcare system. The vast majority of older persons suffering from mental health disorders reside in the community (National Association of Mental Health Planning and Advisory Councils, 2007). Therefore, it is imperative that effective community-based options for mental health treatment be available for older adults. Over the past several decades one community-based option has been community mental health centers (CMHCs), which now serve more than 3.5 million clients per year (Druss et al., 2010). These centers, which gained prominence in the 1960s and 1970s through the support of direct federal funding, received federal funds to provide comprehensive, community-based mental health services to all citizens residing within established catchment areas. Federal mandates directed CMHCs to provide culturally sensitive mental health and substance abuse services and to address the needs of high-priority clients, including the severely mentally ill, older adults, and children. Over time however, CMHCs have been barraged by changing political, social, and economic realities. These realities have brought about significant changes in the CMHCs system. Today, community-based mental healthcare agencies are sustained by a variety of funding mechanisms, provide a diversified array of services, and target various client populations, including older adults. Community mental health centers now typically serve low-income individuals, the majority of whom experience severe mental illness such as schizophrenia, bipolar disorder, and major depressive disorder (Koizumi, Rothbard, Smith, & Mayer, 2011).

EARLY HISTORY: 1963–1980

After World War II, a growing consensus among psychiatrists and others in the mental health community held that psychosocial and psychoanalytic therapy within community settings offered greater treatment efficacy than did mental health treatment within institutionalized settings (Geller, 2000). The discovery of psychotropic medications to treat schizophrenia and other mental health disorders decreased the

SHERRY M. CUMMINGS
KIMBERLY M. CASSIE
SHANNON M. TRECARTIN

Community Mental Health Centers

13

need to house the severely mentally ill in state institutions and heightened professionals' and mental health advocates' interest in community-based treatment. *Action for Mental Health*, a summary report of the Joint Commission on Mental Illness and Health (Appel & Bartemeier, 1961), reflected this sentiment and highlighted the need for community-based mental health services. The newly elected president, John F. Kennedy, read this report and came to believe in the need for a federal mental health policy that would foster the movement from institution-based to community-based mental health services. In 1963, President Kennedy called for a "bold new approach" in the treatment of the mentally ill and recommended that Congress authorize grants to the states for the development of comprehensive CMHCs (Cutler, 2003). His address marked the beginning of the CMHC movement in the United States (Geller, 2000).

Later in 1963, the Mental Retardation Facilities and Community Mental Health Centers Construction Act was signed into law. Because of lobbying from the American Medical Association and congressional opposition, staffing for these centers was omitted from the Act, and only funding for building construction was allocated. However in 1965, under President Johnson, funding amendments for staff were passed. From 1965 through 1970, designated mental health catchment areas across the country began to apply for federal funding to build and develop CMHCs. The original centers were mandated to provide five services: education and consultation, crisis services, and education and consultation. In addition, each center was to serve 75,000 to 200,000 persons in a defined catchment area and continuity of care was to be provided to all clients served (Cutler, 2003). The CMHCs Construction Act stipulated that local communities appoint boards that were composed of mental health professionals, consumers, and family members and were reflective of the community racial, ethnic, and demographic profile to help guide the development of needed services.

In 1975, Congress passed a series of amendments to the CMHCs Construction Act. A new CMHC definition mandated the comprehensiveness and accessibility of mental health service for all clients regardless of ability to pay. The amendments also served to further increase the spectrum of services offered by federally funded CMHCs. Services to older adults and children were required, as were drug abuse services and follow-up services such as

halfway houses. As a result of the original Act and the subsequent amendments, 445 CMHCs were funded between 1968 and 1975 (Smith, 1984). By 1981, when direct federal funding was eliminated, 754 catchment areas nationwide had applied for and received funds for the development of CMHCs (Cutler, 2003).

As the result of the new federal mental health policy and the passage of Medicaid and Medicare, the population of state mental hospitals began to decline rapidly. "Deinstitutionalization," the movement of persons with severe mental health disorders from state hospitals to the community, occurred rapidly throughout the 1960s and 1970s. The intent behind the deinstitutionalization movement was for persons with mental health disorders to receive needed treatment and services in community-based settings. The CMHCs were designed to play a vital role in meeting the needs of and maintaining the severally mentally ill in the community.

However in 1981 President Reagan signed the Omnibus Budget Reconciliation Act (OBRA) (1981), which cut 25% of all CMHC funding and eliminated direct federal funding to CMHCs. The additional monies authorized through the National Mental Health Systems Act (1980) were terminated. Federal funds were converted into block grants to be distributed by the states according to the states' estimates of their citizen' mental health needs. The CMHCs were stripped of their federally qualified status and the previous mental health service requirements established by the CMHCs Construction Act and its subsequent amendments were eliminated. Thus, the new legislative acts dramatically reduced the federal government's involvement in shaping mental health programs and services and shifted this responsibility to states and local communities (Geller, 2000). Following OBRA 1981, the financial status of CMHCs became precarious. In an effort to cope with this reality, CMHCs changed their staffing patterns to include less highly paid personnel, focused their services more on the severely mental ill, and began to experiment with alternate sources of funding (Cutler et al., 2003).

CURRENT SITUATION: SINCE 1981

Currently, the structure of the mental healthcare system is intergovernmental, involving federal, state, and local entities (Coddington, 2001). The federal government, through the Community Mental Health

Services Block Program, awards grants to states to provide community-based mental health service to their citizens in order to enhance functioning and reduce psychiatric hospitalizations. This program works closely with each state to develop a state mental health plan, and states may use block grant monies to fund CMHCs. The assumption underlying the block grant program is that mental health needs vary from state to state as do effective mental health treatment approaches. The block grant supports the grassroots involvement of key stakeholders in mental health services at the local, state, and federal levels. For this reason, each state is required to have a mental health planning council to review and provide input for the state's mental health plan (Substance Abuse Mental Health Services Administration [SAMHSA], 2007). Each state, therefore, establishes its own approach to the structure and funding of community-based mental health treatment. Because of diversity within states' geographic regions, some states have given those at the local level the ability to customize mental health service offerings and organizational structures. Thus, although at one point in time federally funded CMHCs shared a common mandate and offered a required set of services, CMHC programs have increasingly diversified. Decreased federal and state funding over the past several decades coupled with soaring healthcare costs have challenged the stability of centers offering mental health services to the public. In order to respond to changing governmental priorities and evolving market forces, mental health centers have had to put together an increasingly complex array of funding streams including Medicare, Medicaid, fee-for-service, employee assistance contracts, local funding, managed care contracts, and block grant money (Broskowski & Eaddy, 1994). Because each of these funding mechanisms may cover varying services and offer differential reimbursement levels, the type and amount of mental health services offered may vary greatly from center to center.

Beginning in 2014 under the Affordable Care Act (ACA), coverage of mental health and substance use disorder benefits are required at parity with medical benefits for individual and small group plans. Parity requirements are also extended to those plans that previously did not include equivalent health and mental health coverage. The expanded Medicaid option, in which states may choose not to participate, also contains mental health and substance use disorder parity requirements (Beronio, Po, Skopec, &

Gilied, 2013). Due to expanded mental health and substance abuse coverage required by the ACA, CMHCs may experience increased demand for their services, especially among low-income individuals. This growth is expected to be greater in those states opting for the ACA-expanded Medicaid option. The extent and nature of this demand in states developing their own Medicaid plans will vary depending on the mental health coverage included.

Move Toward Integration of Behavioral and Medical Health Care

Despite the availability of treatment at CMHCs, those with severe mental illness (SMI) have life expectancies that that are, on average, 25 years shorter than persons in the general population (Colton & Manderscheid, 2006). The primary contributing factor for increased illness and early death of those with SMI is the lack of access to adequate healthcare. The CMHCs and federal community health centers (CHCs), administered by Health Resources and Services Administration (HRSA), have long realized that the integration of health and mental healthcare services is critical for the effective treatment of underinsured and uninsured (Wells, Morrissey, Lee, & Radford, 2010). Many CMHCs screen for medical illness; but their ability to effectively link clients with affordable medical care or to provide medical services on site has been very limited. Likewise, although depression represents the third most common reason that patients present at CHCs, these centers have been unable to provide effective mental health services to their patients (National Association of Community Health Centers, 2013). Integrated behavioral and medical health services are now recognized as necessary to effectively treat patients and control healthcare costs (Cox, 2007).

In 2003 the importance of close coordination between mental and primary healthcare services was highlighted as a goal in a report by New Freedom Commission on Mental Health, established by President George W. Bush. In 2006, both the National Council on Community Behavioral Health and the National Association of State Mental Health Program Directors called for the development of strategies to improve the medical health of their clients. Some states, such as Missouri, began to develop pilot programs integrating the services of publically funded CMHCs and federally qualified health centers. In 2009 SAMHSA created a program to award grants for the establishment of colocated primary medical services in community-based mental healthcare settings (SAMHSA, 2012). As a result of this funding, a growing number of CMHCs now provide primary and specialty medical health services on-site. In 2011, as a result of ACA, the Public Health Services Act was amended to include grants and cooperative agreements for the development of demonstration projects to establish primary and specialty medical care in community mental health settings (HHS, 2011).

Staffing

In addition to mental healthcare, CMHCs increasingly provide primary healthcare services through onsite screenings or collaborative efforts with community health providers (Druss et al., 2008). These centers are staffed by a variety of health and mental healthcare professionals including social workers, psychologists, psychiatrists, medical care managers, nurses, and physicians (Druss et al., 2011; Schuffman, Druss, & Parks, 2009).

Social workers are the largest providers of mental health services in the United States. There are 52% more clinically trained social workers than counselors, the next largest group of providers (SAMSHA, 2010). Social workers offer a variety of services in CMHCs including psychotherapy, case management, and referrals for needed services (Nguyen, Shibusawa, & Chen, 2012), act as representative payees for clients who cannot manage their own finances (Rosen, Desai, Bailey, Davidson, & Rosenheck, 2001), and collaborate with agencies such as Adult Protective Services and with hospitals to ensure continuation of care (Chang & Greene, 2001). In addition to the provision of mental healthcare, social workers are uniquely positioned in CMHCs to act as advocates for clients in need of health and social services (Faust, 2008).

Community Mental Health Centers and Older Adults

Growing use of CMHCs can be attributed in part to the fact that increasing numbers of older adults are turning to CMHCs for mental healthcare (Druss et al., 2006). For example, between 1999 and 2002,

there was an almost 4% growth in the number of older adults served by CMHCs in California each year (Kaskie, Van Gilder, & Gregory, 2008). Older CMHC clients encompass individuals of all races/ethnicities and living environments, including independent living, board and care homes, and other supportive living situations (Mackin & Arean, 2009; Mackin, Ayalon, Feliciano, & Arean, 2010). A wide age range of older adults use CMHCs. In a study of older California CMHC clients, the average age was almost 74 (Kaskie et al., 2008), but in Texas, over 80% of older adults turning to CMHCs for care were between the ages of 60 and 75 (Karlin & Norris, 2006). In Texas, the average older CMHC client was female, married, a person of color, and living independently in a rural part of the state (Karlin & Norris, 2006). The most common presenting problem for older adults was mood disorders (Kaskie et al., 2008; Kaskie & Szecsei, 2011; Karlin & Norris, 2006). Other common diagnoses include dementia, schizophrenia, alcohol and substance abuse, anxiety, and personality disorders (Kaskie et al., 2008; Kaskie & Szecsei, 2011; Karlin & Norris, 2006).

Despite the growth in older adults turning to CMHCs for care, emerging research suggests that many more could benefit from specialized services available through local CMHCs. In a survey of Medicare beneficiaries aged 65 and over in Iowa, 10% of beneficiaries were diagnosed with one or more psychiatric conditions, but less than half presented for specialty mental health services.

Mental health disorders among older adults are often unrecognized and undertreated. Although the number of older adults using CMHCs is growing, they tend to be underrepresented among CMHC clientele. There are several reasons for the undertreatment of older adults in community-based mental healthcare settings. Many mental health professionals have limited training and experience in differentiating normal age-associated changes from those requiring clinical or medical attention. The lack of adequate geriatric training has created a workforce of practitioners who are not prepared to work with this special population (Alexopoulos et al., 2002; Karlin & Norris, 2006; Qualls, Segal, Norman, Niederehe, & Gallagher-Thompson, 2002). In addition, practitioners may be unable to assess mental health problems and effectively intervene. For example, cognitive impairments are present in many older adults at CMHCs, but are largely unrecognized. Mackin and Arean (2009) found that 60% of older adults at one CMHC suffered from some level of cognitive impairments as measured by the Mattis Dementia Rating Scale-2 administered by neuropsychologists, yet cognitive impairments were recognized and documented in only 17% of the cases.

Second, many older adults, their families, and other potential referral sources for mental health services do not recognize the signs and symptoms of mental health problems (Alexopoulos et al., 2002). Community mental health centers often lack an aggressive outreach program to raise awareness of mental health issues among older adults within the community and generate increased referrals. Third, ageism among staff of CMHCs and other referring professionals can lead to the mistaken belief that mental health problems among older adults are neither preventable nor treatable. Therefore, minimal action is taken to assist older adults exhibiting mental health changes. In addition, many older adults and their families have ageist beliefs that negatively influence their perceptions of the usefulness of mental healthcare for older adults and their decisions to access community mental health services (Graham et al., 2003). Fourth, the social stigma of mental health services and resulting embarrassment or fear inhibits older adult's use of mental health services (Alexopoulos et al., 2002; Graham et al., 2003). Finally, CMHCs are not required to provide home-based services (Chang & Greene, 2001). While some CMHCs provide services in the home, the availability of such services is unpredictable. Home-based evaluations in rural areas tend to be especially difficult for older adults to find. Given that many older individuals suffer declines in mobility and cognition, the failure to provide home-based services or significant transportation for services can be major obstacles to mental healthcare. These issues pose barriers that mental health centers must address in order to increase the accessibility of their services to older persons within their communities.

Referrals

Older adults make the decision to use CMHCs or are referred for mental health services for a variety of reasons. Unfortunately, many wait until their mental condition is exacerbated before seeking services. As stated above, stigma continues to be a major barrier that inhibits self-referral. Older adults with depression report both public and internalized stigma

about help-seeking, with internalized stigma being significantly related to treatment-seeking (Conner et al., 2010). In addition, research indicates that older adults who meet criteria for depressive and anxiety-related disorders are less likely to perceive the need to use mental health services than are younger and middle-aged adults (Klap, Unroe, & Unützer, 2003).

In addition to self-referral, older adults are referred to CMHCs by social workers, hospitals, information and assistance centers, physicians, court systems, faith-based institutions, long-term care facilities, Adult Protective Services, and other agencies (Chang & Greene, 2001; Kent, 1990; Mosher-Ashley, 1994). With the emerging push for collaboration between CHCs and CMHCs, CMHCs are receiving increasing referrals from their CHC partners (Cox, 2007; Druss et al., 2010). Community mental health centers located in resource-rich communities that contain multiple health, mental health and social service facilities also receive increased referrals from sources such as in-patient psychiatric units and senior services agencies (Kaskie et al., 2009). Greater service access may occur as a result of the formal and informal referral system that exists among such agencies.

Since older adults may be reluctant to initiate a mental health referral on their own, it is important that agencies that provide services to the aging population be educated on the warning signs of unmet mental health needs. Just as CMHCs are increasingly training their staff to recognize the signs and symptoms of their clients' physical health needs (Druss et al., 2008; Druss et al., 2010), it is critical that community health center personnel be trained to screen and refer their patients to CMHCs for needed mental health services.

Services Provided

According to the Centers for Medicare and Medicaid (CMM), CMHCs are required to provide a number of services including outpatient services, emergency care services, day treatment or partial hospitalization services, and screening for individuals prior to admission at state mental health facilities (CMM, 2013). In addition, regulations specify that outpatient services must include specialized services for those age 62 and over. Beyond these basic instructions, no further guidelines are provided to explain what kind of specialized services CMHCs should provide to meet the needs of older adults in their communities.

Mental healthcare services typically provided by CMHCs include assessments, case management, support groups, information on community resources, referral to other agencies, medication monitoring, and a variety of therapeutic interventions (Semansky, Hodgkin, & Willging, 2012; Shin, Sharac, & Mauery, 2013). The delivery of telephone-based services is increasingly being used with older adults. Preliminary research on telepsychiatry or telepsychogeriatrics has yielded positive results, but more research among a broader range of clients is needed before definitive conclusions about the effectiveness of such interventions can be made (Ramos-Rios, Mateos, Lojo, Conn, & Patterson, 2012; Ulzen, Williamson, Foster, & Parris-Barnes, 2013).

As noted earlier, there is a growing movement to provide integrated mental health and health services in the community. The type of medical services provided at CMHCs, however, can vary. For example, Washington State has a mental health integration program that includes a disease registry, integrated care management, psychiatric consultations for case managers and primary care physicians, brief psychotherapeutic interventions, medication management, and referrals (Bauer, Chan, Huang, Vannoy, & Unutzer, 2012). Perhaps one of the most innovative examples of integrated care is the Asian American Primary Health Care and Mental Health Bridge Program (BRIDGE) at the Charles B. Wang Community Health Center in New York City's Chinatown. BRIDGE provides culturally appropriate integrated health and mental healthcare to Asian Americans. Services include internal medicine, dental care, mental health, social work, care management, and health education (Nguyen, Shibusawa, & Chen, 2012). While these programs do not target older adults, older adults could readily benefit from such integration of care. Although seeking care from one's primary care physician tends to be free of stigma, seeking mental health services can be viewed negatively. Until research emerges shedding light on the outcomes associated with participation in integrated health and mental health programs, we can only speculate on the possible advantages of these treatment modalities.

FUTURE DIRECTIONS

As the aging population continues to grow, CMHCs will be faced with the challenge of providing mental health services to an increasing number of older clients. In order to meet their needs more effectively, knowledgeable and skilled CMHC staff are essential. Comprehensive training initiatives that included expanded geriatric training are necessary to prepare existing staff to meet older adults' needs. At minimum, all CMHC staff must be trained to recognize symptoms of mental health disorders in older adults. Increased personnel with specialized geriatric training are also needed to provide effective treatment for older adults and their families. Last, in order to maintain their relevance, it will be essential for CMHCs to reach out and develop partnerships with community medical providers. In the future, CMHCs that are able to evolve into health homes that integrate both mental and medical health service provision for their clients will have the greatest opportunity to thrive in the new healthcare environment and to provide continued essential services for low-income clients, those with SMI, and older community-dwelling adults.

REFERENCES

Alexopoulos, G. S., Buckwalter, K., Olin, J., Martinez, R., Wainscott, C., & Krishnan, K. R. R. (2002). Comorbidity of late life depression: An opportunity for research on mechanisms and treatment. *Biological Psychiatry, 52*, 543–558. doi:http://dx.doi.org/10.1016/S0006-3223(02)01468-3

Appel, K. E., & Bartemeier, L. H. (1961). *Action for mental health: Final report of the Joint Commission on Mental Illness and Health.* New York, NY: Basic Books.

Bauer, A. M., Chan, Y. F., Huang, H., Vannoy, S., & Unutzer, J. (2012). Characteristics, management and depression outcomes for primary care patients who endorse thoughts of death or suicide on the PHQ-9. *Journal of General Internal Medicine, 28*, 363–369. doi:http://dx.doi.org/10.1007%2Fs11606-012-2194-2

Beronio, K., Po, R., Skopec, L., & Gilied, S. (2013). *Affordable Care Act expands mental health and substance use disorders benefits and federal parity protections for 62 million Americans.* ASPE Issue Brief, U.S. Department of Health & Human Service. Retrieved from http://aspe.hhs.gov/health/reports/2013/mental/rb_mental.cfm

Broskowski, A., & Eaddy, M. (1994). Community mental health centers in a managed care environment. *Administration and Policy in Mental Health, 21,* 335–352. doi:http://dx.doi.org/10.1007/BF00709481

Centers for Medicare and Medicaid (CMM). (2013). *Community mental health centers.* Retrieved from http://www.cms.gov/Medicare/Provider-Enrollment-and-Certification/CertificationandCompliance/CommunityHealthCenters.html

Chang, V. N., & Greene, R. (2001). Study of service delivery by community mental health centers as perceived by adult protective services investigators. *Journal of Elder Abuse and Neglect, 13,* 25–42. doi:http://dx.doi.org/10.1300/J084v13n03_02

Coddington, D. G. (2001). Impact of political, societal, and local influences on mental health. *Administration and Policy in Mental Health, 29,* 81–87. doi:10.1023/A:1013173016549

Colton, C. W., & Manderscheid, R. W. (2006). Congruencies in increased mortality rates, years of potential life lost, and causes of death among public mental health clients in eight states. *Preventing Chronic Disease, 3,* 1–14. Retrieved from http://s395229360.onlinehome.us/Research/Digest/NLPs/CDConMortality.pdf

Conner, K. O., Copeland, V. C., Grote, N. K., Koeske, G., Rosen, D., Reynolds, C. F., III, & Brown, C. (2010). Mental health treatment seeking among older adults with depression: The impact of stigma and race. *American Journal of Geriatric Psychiatry: Official Journal of the American Association for Geriatric Psychiatry, 18,* 531–543. doi:http://dx.doi.org/10.1097/JGP.0b013e3181cc0366

Cox, L. (2007). The community health center perspective (Cover Story). *Behavioral Healthcare, 27,* 20–23.

Cutler, D. L., Bevilacqua, J., & McFarland, B. H. (2003). Four decades of community mental health: A symphony in four movements. *Community Mental Health Journal, 39,* 381–398. doi:10.1023/A:1025856718368

Druss, B. G., Bornemann, T., Fry-Johnson, Y. W., McCombs, H. G., Politzer, R. M., & Rust, G. (2006). Trends in mental health and substance abuse services at the nation's community health centers: 1998–2003. *American Journal of Public Health, 96,* 1779–1784. doi:http://dx.doi.org/10.2105/AJPH.2005.076943

Druss, B. G., Marcus, S., Campbell, J., Cuffel, B., Harnett, J., Ingoglia, C., & Mauer, B. (2008). Medical services for clients in community mental health centers: Results from a national survey. *Psychiatric Services, 59,* 917–920. doi:http://dx.doi.org/10.1176/appi.ps.59.8.917

Druss, B. G., Silke, A., Compton, M. T., Rask, K. J., Zhao, L., & Parker, R. M. (2010). A randomized trial of medical care management for community mental health settings: The Primary Care Access, Referral, and Evaluation (PCARE) study. *American Journal of Psychiatry, 167,* 151–159. doi:http://dx.doi.org/10.1176/appi.ajp.2009.09050691

Druss, B. G., Silke, A., Compton, M. T., Zhao, L., & Leslie, D. L. (2011). Budget impact and sustainability of medical care management for persons with serious mental illnesses. *American Journal of Psychiatry, 168,* 1171–1178. doi:http://dx.doi.org/10.1176/appi.ajp.2011.11010071

Faust, J. R. (2008). Clinical social worker as patient advocate in a community mental health center. *Clinical Social Work Journal, 36,* 293–300. doi:http://dx.doi.org/10.1007/s10615-007-0118-0

Geller, J. L. (2000). 1950–2000: Fifty years in review. The last half-century of psychiatric services as reflected in psychiatric services. *Psychiatric Services, 51,* 41–67.

Graham, N., Lindesay, J., Katona, C., Bertolote, J. M., Camus, V., Copeland, J. R. M., ... World Health Organization. (2003). Reducing stigma and discrimination against older people with mental disorders: A technical consensus statement. *International Journal of Geriatric Psychiatry, 18,* 670–678. doi:10.1002/gps.876

Houser, A., Fox-Grage, W., & Gibson, M. J. (2006). *Across the states: Profiles of long-term care and independent living.* Washington, DC: AARP Public Policy Institute.

Karlin, B. E., & Norris, M. P. (2006). Public mental health care utilization by older adults. *Administration and Policy in Mental Health and Mental Health Services Research, 33,* 730–736. doi:http://dx.doi.org/10.1007/s10488-005-0003-5

Health and Human Services (HHS). (2011). *Affordable Care Act to support quality improvement and access to primary care for more Americans.* Retrieved from http://www.hhs.gov/news/press/2011pres/09/20110929b.html

Karlin, B. E., & Norris, M. P. (2006). Public mental health care utilization by older adults. *Administration and Policy in Mental Health & Mental Health Services Research, 33,* 730–736. doi:10.1007/s10488-005-0003-5

Kaskie, B., Gregory, D., & Van Gilder, R. (2009). Community mental health service use by older adults with dementia. *Psychological Services, 6,* 56–67. doi:http://dx.doi.org/10.1037/a0014438

Kaskie B., & Szecsei, D. (2011). Translating collaborative models of mental health care for older adults: Using Iowa's experience to inform national efforts. *Journal of Aging and Social Policy, 23,* 258–273. http://dx.doi. org/10.1080/08959420.2011.579501

Kaskie, B., Van Gilder, R., & Gregory, D. (2008). Community mental health service use by older adults in California. *Aging and Mental Health, 12,* 134–143. doi:http://dx.doi.org/10.1080/13607860801942761

Kent, K. L. (1990). Elders and community mental health centers. *Generations, 14,* 19–21.

Klap, R., Unroe, K. T., & Unützer, J. (2003). Caring for mental illness in the United States: A focus on older adults. *American Journal of Geriatric Psychiatry, 11,* 517–524. http://dx.doi.org/10.1097/00019442-200309000-00006

Koizumi, N., Rothbard, A. B., Smith, T. E., & Mayer, J. D. (2011). Communities of color? Client-to-client racial concordance in the selection of mental health programs for Caucasians and African Americans. *Health Care Management Science, 14,* 314–323. http://dx.doi.org/10.1007/s10729-011-9164-9

Mackin, R. S., & Arean, P. A. (2009). Incidence and documentation of cognitive impairment among older adults with severe mental illness in a community mental health setting. *American Journal of Geriatric Psychiatry, 17,* 75–82. http://dx.doi.org/10.1097/JGP.0b013e31818cd3e5

Mackin, R. S., Ayalon, L., Feliciano, L., & Arean, P. A. (2010). Sensitivity and specificity of cognitive screening instruments to detect cognitive impairment in older adults with severe psychiatric illness. *Journal of Geriatric Psychiatry and Neurology, 23,* 94–99. http://dx.doi.org/10.1177/0891988709358589

Mosher-Ashley, P. M. (1994). Referral patterns of elderly clients to a community mental health center. *Journal of Gerontological Social Work, 20,* 5–23. doi:10.1300/J083v20n03_02

National Association of Community Health Centers. (2013). *Clinical issues: Behavioral health.* Retrieved October 4, 2013, from http://www.nachc.com/BehavioralHealth.cfm

National Association of Mental Health Planning and Advisory Councils. (2007). *Older adults and mental health: A time for reform.* DHHS Pub. No. SMAXXXXX. Rockville, MD: Center for Mental Health Services, Substance Abuse and Mental Health.

Nguyen, D., Shibusawa, T., & Chen, M. T. (2012). The evolution of community mental health services in Asian American communities. *Clinical Social Work Journal, 40,* 132–143. http://dx.doi.org/10.1007/s10615-011-0356-z

Qualls, S. H., Segal, D. L., Norman, S., Niederehe, G., & Gallagher-Thompson, D. (2002). Psychologists in practice with older adults: Current patterns, sources of training and need for continuing education. *Professional Psychology: Research and Practice, 33,* 435–442. http://dx.doi.org/10.1037//0735-7028.33.5.435

Ramos-Rios, R., Mateos, R., Lojo, D., Conn, D., & Patterson, T. (2012). Telepsychogeriatrics: A new horizon of mental health problems in the elderly. *International Psychogeriatrics, 24,* 1708–1724. doi:http://dx.doi.org/10.1017/S1041610212000981

Rosen, M. I., Desai, R., Bailey, M., Davidson, L., & Rosenheck, R. (2001). Consumer experience with payeeship provided by a community mental health center. *Psychiatric Rehabilitation Journal, 25,* 190–195. http://dx.doi.org/10.1037/h0095025

Substance Abuse and Mental Health Services Administration (SAMHSA). (2007). *Justification of estimates for appropriations committees.* Retrieved from http://www.samhsa.gov/Budget/FY2008/SAMHSA08CongrJust.pdf

Substance Abuse and Mental Health Services Administration (SAMHSA). (2010). *Mental health, United States, 2008.* HHS Publication No. (SMA) 10-4590, Rockville, MD: Center for Mental Health Services, Substance Abuse and Mental Health Services Administration. Retrieved from http://store.samhsa.gov/shin/content//SMA10-4590/SMA10-4590.pdf

Substance Abuse and Mental Health Services Administration (SAMHSA). (2012). *PPFF-2012-Primary and behavioral health care integration.* Retrieved from http://www.samhsa.gov/grants/2012/sm_12_008.aspx

Schuffman, D., Druss, B., & Parks, J. (2009). State mental health policy: Mending Missouri's safety net: Transforming systems of care by integrating primary and behavioral health care. *Psychiatric Services, 60,* 585–588. doi:http://dx.doi.org/10.1176/appi.ps.60.5.585

Semansky, R. M., Hodgkin, D., & Willging, C. E. (2012). Preparing for a public sector mental health reform in New Mexico: The experience of agencies serving older adults with serious mental illness. *Community Mental Health Journal, 48,* 264–269. doi:http://dx.doi.org/10.1007/s10597-011-9418-5

Shin, P. Sharac, J., & Mauery, D. R. (2013). The role of community mental health centers in providing behavioral health care. *Journal of Behavioral Health*

Services and Research, 40, 488–496. doi:10.1007/
s11414-013-9353-z

Smith, C. J. (1984). Geographic patterns of funding for
community mental health centers. *Hospital and
Community Psychiatry, 35*, 1133–1141.

Ulzen, T., Williamson, L., Foster, P. P., & Parris-Barnes, K.
(2013). The evolution of a community-based telepsychiatry program in rural Alabama: Lessons
learned—A brief report. *Community Mental
Health Journal, 49*, 101–105. doi:10.1007/s10597-012-
9493-2 10

Wells, R., Morrissey, J. P., Lee, I. H., & Radford, A.
(2010). Trends in behavioral health care service
provision by community health centers, 1998–2007.
Psychiatric services (Washington, DC), 61, 759–764.
doi:http://dx.doi.org/10.1176/appi.ps.61.8.759

Since their humble beginnings in 1943 in the Bronx, New York, senior centers in the United States have evolved in their purpose, expanded their services and programs, and diversified their clientele (Jellinek, Pardasani, & Sackman, 2010). Over the years, senior centers have come to occupy a pivotal position within the continuum of care system for older adults, and arguably may have contributed to the postponement of costly institutionalization and maintenance of physical health and well-being among its participants (Department of Health and Human Services [DHSS], 2013). There are an estimated 12,000 senior centers across the United States that offer a variety of programs, which are publicly and/or privately funded, with different staffing levels serving a multitude of older adults (Gelfand, 2006). Senior centers may be popular because they are the embodiment of the belief in the potential for continued human growth in later life and the recognition of the older adult's ambitions, capabilities, and creative capacities (National Council on Aging [NCOA], in Lowy, 1985). Another reason for their popularity is that senior centers have long worked hard to be responsive to the needs of the older adults and community they serve, often meeting this challenge on a shoestring budget, while delivering services and programs in a cost-effective manner (Jellinek et al., 2010).

DEFINITION

Despite the growth in its reach and importance, the definition of what constitutes a *senior center* or *multipurpose senior center* remains a challenge, mainly because of its broad manifest legislative mission to provide programs that will enhance the dignity, maintain the autonomy, and support community participation of seniors (Gelfand, 2006). For example, the reauthorized Older Americans Act defines "multipurpose senior center" as "a community facility for the organization and provisions of a broad spectrum of services" (cited in NCOA, 2011, p. 1) to meet the multiple needs of the older person within his or her community. However, Krout (1998) previously argued that the term "multipurpose senior center" is vague because it could simultaneously refer to the goals and content of programming. Indeed, Pardasani (2004a) found that of the 219 senior centers surveyed in New York State, 57% identified themselves as multipurpose centers, 13.7% as senior clubs, 12.8% as senior centers, and 7.3% as nutrition sites

PHILIP A. ROZARIO
MANOJ P. PARDASANI

Senior Centers

with no standardization on the types of programs offered or the model of service delivery. To this end, Pardasani and Thomson (2012) found that not all senior centers identified themselves as such. Indeed, those centers that adopted service delivery models of community center, life-long learning, continuing care, or café almost never identified themselves as senior centers. Still, most researchers, practitioners, and policymakers agree that a senior center typically serves as a "community focal point . . . where older adults come together for services and activities that reflect their experience and skills, respond to their diverse needs and interests, enhance their dignity, support their independence, and encourage their involvement in and with the center and the community" (Wagner, 1995, p. 4).

LEGAL AUTHORITY AND FUNDING

Although senior centers preexisted the legislation that authorized them, they grew exponentially in the 1970s after the enactment of the groundbreaking Older Americans Act [OAA] of 1965 and its subsequent reauthorizations (Gelfand & Bechil, 1991; Krout, 1998; Lowy, 1985), which signified the federal government's commitment to financing and delivering community-based services to older adults. These centers "grew primarily through locally supported and directed institutions" (Gelfand, 2006, p. 146). Much of the federal funding for multipurpose senior centers and other community-based programs and services is derived from Title III of the OAA, which aims for the development of services and programs at the local level that are "comprehensive and coordinated" and targeted at maintaining the "maximum independence" of older adults (Sec. 301 of the OAA, cited in Gelfand, 2006, p.13). As a result of the OAA, a network of federal and state agencies along with Area Agencies on Aging were charged with the planning, coordinating, and delivery of elder-related services at the local level (DHSS, 2013; Gelfand, 2006; O'Shaughnessy, 2008). Table 14.1 illustrates the publicly funded aging service network.

Despite the impetus of the OAA in creating a network of public and private eldercare services with much potential for impact, observers believe that the law has not been fully realized because of the low funding levels allocated to its implementation (Gelfand & Bechil, 1991; Torres-Gil, Spencer-Suarez, & Rudinica, 2014). Indeed, Torres-Gil et al. (2014) asserted that the OAA's annual budget pales in comparison with that of Social Security or Medicare. For example, the budget for OAA for the fiscal year 2011 was a mere $2 billion, while Social Security was allotted $89.7 billion and Medicare had $295 billion for its expenditure. The budget allocation for 2012 toward the OAA was $2.25 billion, a net decrease of nearly $150,000,000 from 2010. Of this total allocation, $416,476,000 was budgeted for home and community-based supportive services (a very small portion of which is allocated toward the operational expenses of senior centers) and an additional $440,783,000 toward nutritional programs (includes congregate meals served at senior centers and home-delivered meals) (Administration on Aging, 2012). It is also noteworthy that approximately half of all senior

TABLE 14.1. The Aging Services Network

Administration on Aging [A division of the Administration on Community Living]			
State Agencies on Aging (57 agencies)		American Indians, Native Alaskans, and Native Hawaiian Programs	
Area Agencies on Aging (670 agencies)		American Indians, Native Alaskans, and Native Hawaiian Programs	
Programs under Title III that may be offered by Local Service Providers			
Supportive and Caregiver Services	Health and Independent Programs	Elder Rights	Protection of Vulnerable Adults
Local Service Providers: Multipurpose Senior Center*			

*Depending on the funding type and amount, centers may provide the all or any of the above programs in conjunction with their sponsoring agencies or in collaboration with other agencies.
Source: Adapted from information obtained from Gelfand (2006); DHHS (2013); and O'Shaughnessy (2008).

TABLE 14.2. Federal Funding Levels Authorized Under the Older Americans Act Since 2010 Under Title III[a]

Fiscal Year	Home- and Community-Based Supportive Services	Nutrition Service [b]	Preventive Health Service	Chronic Disease Self-Management Education	Family Caregiver Support Services
2010	368,290,000	819,353,000	21,026,000	—[c]	154,197,000
2011	367,611,000	817,835,000	20,984,000	—	153,912,000
2012	366,916,000	816,289,000	20,944,000	10,000,000	153,621,000
2013	369,162,000	821,285,000	21,073,000	—	154,561,000
2014 [Proposed budget]	366,916,000	816,289,000	20,944,000	—	153,621,000

Notes:
[a] These amounts exclude funding allocated/authorized for Native American programs.
[b] Each entry in this column includes congregate meals, home-delivered meals, and nutrition services incentive programs.
[c] No funds were allocated/authorized for these years.
Source: Data for this table were obtained from the Department of Health and Human Services (2013).

centers received some funding for nutritional and preventive health service programs between 2003 and 2008 under title III of the OAA (Wacker & Roberto, 2008). Table 14.2 presents funding levels under Title III, which clearly have not kept up with inflation. The absence of separate funding authorization for senior centers means that they are forced to compete with other community-based eldercare agencies for the same pool of limited funds to run programs under Title III (Krout, 1998; Lowy, 1985). In addition to OAA funding, multipurpose senior centers that are publicly funded may receive governmental funding from other sources including block grants from the Department of Housing and Urban Development and Title XX of Social Security Act. Its original universalistic approach (service to all consumers regardless of financial status) was finally changed in 2000 when the reauthorization of the OAA specified measures for cost-sharing by consumers of these services (Gelfand, 2006).

MODEL OF SENIOR CENTERS

In a survey of senior centers developed after the passage of OAA, Taietz (1976) identified two basic types of senior center models: the social agency model and the voluntary organization model (p. 219). Taietz (1976) believed that each model served a unique but different purpose: the voluntary participation model (such as senior clubs) provided older persons access to social and recreational opportunities, while the social service agency model focused on providing

much needed services to the poor and frail elderly (cited in Wagner, 1995, p. 5). Krout (1998) posited that senior centers adopting the social service agency model primarily served at-risk, low-income, immigrant, and disengaged populations that are in need of services to meet their basic survival needs. On the other hand, he added that the voluntary organization model tended to attract relatively affluent, better educated, and socially active elderly populations. This model focused on recreational and educational programs that allowed for greater self-expression and social action (p. 98). In practice, senior centers may follow a social agency model, a voluntary organization model, or a combination of these models. Pardasani (2004a) found that 37.4% of senior centers in New York State focused mostly on social services, 36% focused mostly on volunteer programs, and the remaining centers had a mixed focus. Hostetler (2011) cautioned that the different models of senior centers, especially those that emphasize consumer choice or customer service, could potentially alienate and exclude the very users who may need and benefit from these programs the most. Still, senior centers may need to rely on an increasing number of older adults in the middle- and upper-income brackets for additional revenue to augment their limited budgets.

One meal per day, funded by the OAA allocations and private contributions from older adults, usually forms the core of a senior center's daily function. Additionally, the five most common categories of senior center programs are nutrition, health and fitness, recreation, volunteer opportunities for older adults, and social services (Aday, 2003; Krout, 1985; Leanse & Wagener, 1975; Pardasani, 2004a). However, the range and types of programs offered by a particular senior center depend largely on the amount and source of funding and staffing levels (Krout, 1998). In some centers, certain programs especially those educational in focus, are peer led, which has the added benefit of tapping into the expertise of older members and reducing expenditures for the center.

In 2009–2010, the National Institute of Senior Centers (NISC) conducted a nationwide survey of senior centers to understand their programmatic and organizational models. This study yielded six emerging models of senior centers: community center, wellness center, lifelong learning/arts, continuum of care/transitions, entrepreneurial model, and the café model (Pardasani & Thompson, 2012). This study provides us many reasons for hope. For one, the uncovering of these diverse models points to the adaptability of the respective senior center to its environmental context. The diverse models underscored the ability of senior centers to evolve and adapt to the changing needs of the older adult population in their environments. A second reason for hope is that these models not only reflect but also may contribute to the changing image of an older adult from a recreation-obsessed retiree to a civically engaged, entrepreneurial, and health-focused individual. Detailed descriptions of these models are provided in Table 14.3.

SENIOR CENTER PARTICIPANTS

Regular attendees of senior centers tend to be Caucasian, single or widowed, older women with low incomes and minimal physical disabilities (Caslyn & Winter, 1999; Krout, 1998; Pardasani, 2004b; Turner, 2004). A study conducted by the New York City Department for the Aging (DFTA) revealed that the average senior center participant is 77 years old, and more likely to be female, born in the United States, English speaking, and to have completed high school (2002). A study of seven senior centers in Arizona found that the majority of participants were White women who lived alone and within 5 miles from these centers (Fitzpatrick, McCabe, Gitelson, & Andereck, 2008). The average mean age of those in the Arizona study was 74 years and the age range was 50–85 years. Similarly, another recent study of New York City senior centers also showed that the average age of

senior center participants was 76, a majority of the participants were relatively healthy, widowed, and lived alone (Giunta, Morano, Parikh, et al., 2012). This has given rise to the belief that senior centers may be the sole source of support and service for the vulnerable or isolated older adults in a community. However, Pardasani and Thompson (2012) found that the participants in the wellness center, café, and entrepreneurial models of senior centers tended to be younger (65–70 years), possessed some college experience, and were actively engaged in their communities.

Reasons generally offered for participation include the need for greater social interaction and companionship (Eaton & Salari, 2005; Krout, 1985, 1988; Pardasani, 2004a; Walker, Bisbee, Porter, & Flanders, 2004). Decreased involvement was found to be linked to chronic health problems, decreased mobility, and lack of transportation to sites (Aday, 2003; DFTA, 2002; Pardasani, 2004a). Jellinek et al. (2010) argued that the needs and interests of those who are unable to participate in senior center programming do not dissipate with age.

BENEFITS OF PARTICIPATION

Health and wellness programs are fast becoming a core interest of many large, multipurpose senior centers, with an increase in health-related interventions (Beisgen & Kraitchman, 2003; Ryzin, 2005). Recent integration of evidence-based interventions in senior centers has focused on prevention of falls and minimization of injury risks (Baker, Gottschalk, & Bianco, 2007; Reinsch, MacRae, Lachenbruch, & Tobis, 1992; Li et al., 2008), walking (Sarkisian, Prohaska, Davis, & Weiner, 2007), resistance training (Manini et al., 2007), line dancing (Hayes, 2006), increasing healthy eating habits (Hendrix et al., 2008a), diabetes self-management (Hendrix et al., 2008b), tai chi (Li et al., 2008), and physical activity and exercise (Fitzpatrick et al., 2008). Most of these interventions were reportedly successful in increasing their targeted participants' awareness of health management and in promoting their healthy behaviors.

There is some evidence that participation in activities typically offered by senior centers (e.g., bingo, trips, arts and crafts, meal, etc.) may be related to the well-being of older adults. Researchers have found that senior center participants have better psychological well-being across several measures

TABLE 14.3. Defining Characteristics of Emerging Senior Center Models

	Community Center	Wellness Center	Lifelong Learning/Arts	Continuum of Care/Transitions	Entrepreneurial Center	Café Program
# of agencies/ model	8	9	5	5	6	2
Consumer Profile	Children, Youth, Adults and Active Older Adults.	Active Older Adults 50+.	Active Older Adults 50+. Working seniors	Older Adults 50+. Specific programs and services for frail and homebound older adults	Active Older Adults 50+.	Active Older Adults 50+.
Organizational Mission and Philosophical Focus	Center for all ages under one roof.	Health & Wellness is a major concern for all seniors.	Seniors want to continue to learn and grow post retirement.	Providing services on a gradual continuum as older adults age.	Seniors want to utilize their skills and expertise post retirement. Utilize senior productivity as sources of income	Provide a noninstitutional, non-age-segregating community gathering space.
Program Design and Offerings	Recreation, Arts & Cultural, Fitness, Meals, Education, After-School, Summer Day Camps, Inter-generation Programs, Grandparent Caregiver Support	Health and Wellness, Meals, Arts & Cultural, Recreation	Education, Travel, Cultural Events, Performing Arts	Recreation, Arts & Cultural, Fitness, Meals, Adult Day Health Centers, Caregiver Respite, Home-bound Support Services, Medical Transportation	Employment Placement, Vocational Training, Hand-crafted goods for sale, Recreation, Arts & Cultural, Fitness, Meals, Education	Café-style meals, Recreational and Health Information programs, Entertainment, Information & Referral
Hours of Operation	Early morning to late evenings- daily. Open on weekends.	Early morning to late evenings- daily. Open on weekends.	Daytime, evening hours, and weekends.	Daytime only.	Early morning to late afternoons.	Breakfast and lunch only. Limited programs in the day-time and early evenings.
Service Sites	One main site	One main site	Multiple	Multiple (including senior centers, home-based and assisted living)	One main site	One main site (café)
Location	Suburban or new developments. Could be in a rural region with a growing population.	Urban or Suburban	Urban or Suburban	Urban or Suburban	Urban, Suburban or Rural	Urban or Suburban
Main Sources of Funding	Public mainly. Partly funded by membership dues.	Mainly funded by membership dues and service fees.	Service Fees	Service fees, private insurance and limited public funding.	Income generated through various services/projects, fundraising and limited public funding.	Service and meal fees, and private fundraising.
Identification as "Senior Center"	No	Sometimes	No	No	Sometimes	No

Source: This table originally appeared in Pardasani and Thompson (2012) and it has been reproduced in its entirety with permission from the authors, who retain its copyright.

than nonparticipants, including depressive symptoms (Choi & McDougall, 2007), friendship formations and associated well-being (Aday, Kehoe, & Farney, 2006), and stress levels (Farone, Fitzpatrick, & Tran, 2005; Maton, 2002). Some studies have shown that participation in senior center programs is related to greater self-esteem, life satisfaction and perceived social support, expanded social networks and reduced isolation, and improved perception of general well-being (Aday et al., 2006; Carey, 2004; Fitzpatrick et al., 2008; Maton, 2002; Meis, 2005; Seong, 2003).

CHALLENGES

The population explosion of older adults is a double-edged sword for the future of senior centers in the United States in that these centers are required to balance the demands of serving an increasingly diverse clientele. In terms of age, this means that senior centers are challenged to maintain their existing clientele while attracting new, younger older adults, as many senior centers have experienced the phenomenon of "aging in place," in that their clientele are likely to be older and long-standing participants (Pardasani & Thompson, 2012). Hostetler (2011) conceptualizes this challenge as "adequately serv[ing] the needs of at-risk seniors while maintaining a broader appeal as a "community focal point" (p. 167). Indeed, in their examination of six innovative and emerging models of senior centers, Pardasani and Thompson (2012) found that many emerging models shied away from using the "senior center" label so as to broaden their appeal to those who may perceive the label as stigmatizing. While this concerted move might be expedient, the more crucial task for senior center directors is to not only combat these ageist tendencies (Hostetler, 2011) but also create an inclusive community for their current and future clientele (Stephens & Kwah, 2009).

In addition to age diversity, senior centers are faced with the challenge of providing services and programs that cater to cultural and linguistic diversity especially in cosmopolitan urban centers with ever growing ethnic minority and migrant populations. Further, in order to meet the challenge of being a focal point for everyone in a community, senior centers have to cater to lesbian, gay, bisexual, and transgender (LGBT) elders and those with different levels of abilities, who may not always be or

feel welcomed in mainstream settings. In New York City, the DFTA has helped establish the first publicly funded senior center (SAGE) that caters to LGBT older adults and another senior center primarily serving visually impaired seniors (VISIONS). These developments highlight the fluid and changing definition of community with respect to older adults that is no longer geographically bound. As the older adult population grows more diverse, senior centers need to adapt to serve various cohorts who may not all live within a specific geographic-service area. While these centers are important in meeting the needs of specific groups, their reach might be limited by the extensiveness of available transportation for their users. Further, these specialized centers might not be viable options in locations around the country with a lower density of targeted subgroups of older adults.

The political and economic developments of the late 20th and early 21st centuries and the increased diversification of the aging population will inevitably challenge the notion of retirement as a time for leisure activities. In a follow-up survey of baby boomers aged 50 and over who were employed in 2010, the AARP Policy Institute (2012) found that about 50% of them were jobless and had difficulties in making ends meet. Such economic hardships will undoubtedly delay their retirement plans as they attempt to recover from the recession, which in turn, may inadvertently impact their ability to enjoy the leisure activities offered at senior centers. It is likely that to meet the ever increasing needs of older adults in the near future, senior centers have to move beyond their current image of serving the leisure needs of older adults and expand their programming to promote job training and employment, volunteering, and caregiving (Rozario, 2006). Indeed, Pardasani and Thomson (2012) observe that the emerging models of innovative senior centers are reflecting this change.

Senior centers, like many publicly funded programs and services, have limited financial resources at their disposal especially in the face of cost-containment and cutting initiatives undertaken by federal and state governments in the face of economic uncertainty. As such, pivotal eldercare services, including senior centers, will have the challenge of meeting greater demands from burgeoning older service users with ever diminishing public funding resources (Fitzpatrick et al., 2008). In the past, senior centers have managed to be responsive to the demands of their users while providing quality services and programs despite limited funds

(Jellinek et al., 2010). However, this lack of funding has affected their ability to renovate and refurbish their aging facilities, which in turn may affect their ability to attract new participants. To circumvent the reduced funding levels, Congress approved a cost-sharing arrangement by users of OAA-funded services in 2000, which may have the unintended effect of stigmatizing these programs (Gelfand, 2006). In turn, Gelfand (2006) argues that the move away from a universal service delivery approach to a means-testing one may potentially impact the acceptability of senior centers to their current and potential participants. A greater challenge for senior centers with limited funds is to recruit and hire capable leadership. Indeed, Stephens and Kwah (2009) underscore the importance of the role of the senior center leadership and the sponsoring agency in creating a welcoming atmosphere for participants and thus, increasing the use of programs offered by the center. For example, they found that good center leadership that focused on the needs of participants by offering food choices can indeed turn the slowest day of the month into its busiest at congregate meal sites.

Although these centers "have long been recognized as conduits for senior programming across the country" (Fitzpatrick et al., 2008), research on their positive impact on center participants' health and well-being remain relatively sparse. Perhaps this is in part due to the difficulty in defining the form and functions of senior centers, which might also contribute to the lack of clear understanding among stakeholders of their role, relevance, and impact (Jellinek et al., 2010). As such, the challenge for researchers and evaluators is to determine the influence of site on the content and impact of programming, specifically whether or not these health and social programs would obtain similar benefits or outcomes if they were offered in a different setting. Researchers and evaluators have to question the comparability of multipurpose senior centers, senior clubs, senior centers, and nutrition sites as well as identify the level of involvement that is necessary for participants to secure the positive benefits of participation. Additionally, we have to ensure comparability at the individual level, because service users might differ from nonservice users in terms of their interests, ability, and access. For example, Mui (1998) found that one-third of Chinese participants of senior centers and congregate meal programs reported that they did not have contact with their friends in the past week. Without evidence of their effectiveness and impact, senior centers may face even more funding cuts as policymakers find ways to reduce the deficit spending and national debt in lean economic times.

In this chapter, we highlighted the background and development of senior centers and their importance in ensuring that older adults not only remain socially connected within their own communities but also receive community-based services that will allow them to delay institutionalization. Notwithstanding their importance, senior centers face many challenges especially in securing adequate funding to expand and upgrade their programs and facilities in order to sustain existing and attract future clientele and to remain inclusive of an increasingly diverse older adult population. Indeed, despite the claims of their usefulness, there is relatively little research that documents the impact of senior centers on their participants, families, and communities they serve. Perhaps like Jellinek et al. (2010), who attempted to delineate the importance of senior centers, we need to ask ourselves to imagine a world without senior centers and the impact of that absence on older adults so that we can begin to document its usefulness in the long-term care system for older adults.

REFERENCES

AARP Public Policy Institute. (2012). *Boomers and the great recession: Struggling to recover.* Washington DC: Author. Retrieved July 31, 2013, from http://www.aarp.org/content/dam/aarp/research/public_policy_institute/econ_sec/2012/boomers-and-the-great-recession-struggling-to-recover-v2-AARP-ppi-econ-sec.pdf

Aday, R. H. (2003). *Identifying important linkages between successful aging and senior center participation.* Joint Conferences of the National Council on Aging/American Society on Aging. March 16, 2003, Chicago, IL.

Aday, R., Kehoe, G., & Farney, L. (2006). Impact of senior center friendships on aging women who live alone. *Journal of Women Aging, 18,* 57–73.

Administration on Aging. (2012). *Justification of estimates for appropriations committee.* Washington, DC: Department of Health and Human Services.

Baker, D., Gottschalk, M., & Bianco, L. (2007). Step by step: Integrating evidence-based fall-risk management into senior centers. *The Gerontologist, 47,* 548–554.

Beisgen, B., & Kraitchman M. (2003). *Senior centers: Opportunities for successful aging.* New York, NY: Springer.

Carey, K. (2004). The lived experiences of the independent oldest-old in community-based programs: A Heideggerian hermeneutical analysis. *Dissertation Abstracts International, A: The Humanities and Social Sciences, 65,* 2366-A (University of Chicago).

Caslyn, R., & Winter, J. (1999). Who attends senior centers? *Journal of Social Service Research, 26,* 53–69.

Choi, N., & McDougall, G. (2007). Comparison of depressive symptoms between homebound older adults and ambulatory older adults. *Aging Mental Health, 11,* 310–322.

Department of Health and Human Services (DHHS). (2013). *Administration on Community Living: Justification of estimates for appropriation committees fiscal year 2014.* Washington DC: Author. Retrieved July 29, 2013, from http://acl.gov/About_ACL/Budget/docs/FY2014_ACL_CJ.pdf

Eaton, J., & Salari, S. (2005). Environments for lifelong learning in senior centers. *Educational Gerontology, 31,* 461–480.

Farone, D., Fitzpatrick, T. R., & Tran, T. (2005). Use of senior centers as a moderator of stress-related distress among Latino elders. *Journal of Gerontological Social Work, 46,* 65–83.

Fitzpatrick, T. R., McCabe, J., Gitelson, R., & Andereck, K. (2008). Factors that influence perceived social and health benefits of attendance at senior centers. *Activities, Adaptation, and Aging, 30,* 23–45.

Gelfand, D. E. (2006). *The aging network: Programs and services* (6th ed.). New York, NY: Springer.

Gelfand, D. E., & Bechil, W. (1991). The evolution of the older Americans Act: A 25-year review of the legislative changes. *Generations, 15,* 19–22.

Giunta, N., Morano, C., Parikh, N. S., Friedman, D., Fahs, M. C., & Gallo, W. T. (2012). Racial and ethnic diversity in senior centers: Comparing participant characteristics in more and less multicultural settings. *Journal of Gerontological Social Work, 55,* 1–17.

Hayes, K. (2006, summer). Line dancing with dementia. *Directors' Quarterly for Alzheimer's and Other Dementia, 7*(3),31–34.

Hendrix, S., Fischer, J., Reddy, S., Lommel, T., Speer, E., Stephens, H., . . . Johnson, M. (2008a). Fruit and vegetable intake and knowledge increased following a community-based intervention in older adults in Georgia senior centers. *Journal of Nutrition for the Elderly, 27,* 27–43.

Hendrix, S., Fischer, J., Reddy, S., Lommel, T., Speer, E., Stephens, H., . . . Johnson, M. (2008b). Diabetes self-management behaviors improved following a community-based intervention in older adults in Georgia senior centers. *Journal of Nutrition for the Elderly, 27,* 44–60.

Hostetler, A. J. (2011). Senior centers in the era of the "third age": Country clubs, community centers, or something else? *Journal of Aging Studies, 25,* 166–176.

Jellinek, I., Pardasani, M., & Sackman, B. (2010). *Twenty-first century senior centers: Changing the conversations* [A study of New York City's senior centers]. New York, NY: Council of Senior Center and Services of New York City, Inc. Retrieved July 29, 2013, from http://cscs-ny.org/files/FINAL-WHOLE-REPORT.pdf

Krout, J. (1985). Senior center activities and services: Findings from a national survey. *Research on Aging, 7,* 455–471.

Krout, J. A. (1998). *Senior centers in America* (5th ed.). New York, NY: Greenwood Press.

Leanse, J., & Wagener, L. (1975). *Senior centers: A report of senior group programs in America.* Washington, DC: National Council on the Aging.

Li, F., Harmer, P., Glasgow, R., Mack, K., Sleet, D., Fisher, J., . . . Tompkins, Y. (2008). Translation of an effective tai chi intervention into a community-based falls-prevention program. *American Journal of Public Health, 98,* 1195–1198.

Lowy, L. (1985). Multipurpose senior centers. In A. Monk (Ed.), *Handbook of gerontological services* (pp. 274–301). New York, NY: Van Nostrand Reinhold.

Manini, T., Marko, M., VanAmam, T., Cook, S., Fernhall, B., Burke, J., & Ploutz-Snyder, L. (2007). Efficacy of resistance and task-specific exercise in older adults who modify tasks of everyday life. *Journals of Gerontology. Series A, Biological Sciences and Medical Sciences, 62,* 616.

Maton, K. (2002). Community settings as buffers of life stress? Highly supportive churches, mutual help groups and senior centers. In T. Revenson, A. D'Augelli, S. French, D. Hughes, & D. Livert (Eds.), *A quarter century of community psychology: Readings from the American Journal of Community Psychology,* (pp. 205–235). New York, NY: Kluwer Academic/Plenum.

Meis, M. S. (2005). Geriatric orphans: A study of severe isolation in an elderly population. *Dissertation Abstracts International, A: The Humanities and Social Sciences, 67,* 2766-A (Fielding Graduate Institute).

Mui, A. C. (1998). Living alone and depression among older Chinese immigrants. *Journal of Gerontological Social Work, 30,* 147–166.

National Council on Aging (NCOA). (2011). *Older Americans Act reauthorization: Multipurpose senior centers for positive aging* [Issue Brief]. Washington, DC: Author. Retrieved July 29, 2013, from http://www.ncoa.org/assets/files/pdf/ OAA-Reauthorization-Senior-Center-Issue-Brief-Sept-2011.pdf

New York City Department for the Aging (DFTA). (2002). *Senior center utilization study.* New York, NY: Author.

O' Shaughnessy, C. V. (2008, April 11). *The aging services network: Accomplishments and challenges in serving a growing elderly population* [Brief Paper]. Washington, DC: National Health Policy Forum. Retrieved on August 2, 2013, from http://www.nhpf.org/library/details.cfm/2625

Pardasani, M. P. (2004a). Senior centers: Focal points of community-based services for the elderly. *Activities, Adaptation, and Aging, 28,* 27–44.

Pardasani, M. (2004b). Senior centers: Increasing minority participation through diversification. *Journal of Gerontological Social Work, 43,* 41–56.

Pardasani, M. P., & Thompson, P. (2012). Senior centers: Innovative and emerging models. *Journal of Applied Gerontology, 31,* 52–77.

Reinsch, S., MacRae, P., Lachenbruch, P., & Tobis, J. (1992). Attempts to prevent falls and injury: A prospective community study. *The Gerontologist, 32,* 450–456.

Rozario, P. A. (2006). Senior centers. In B. Berkman (Ed.), *Handbook of social work in health and aging* (pp. 477–482). New York, NY: Oxford University Press.

Ryzin, J. (2005). Senior centers on the cutting edge. *Innovations in Aging, 34,* 15–20.

Sarkisian, C., Prohaska, T., Davis, C., & Weiner, B. (2007). Pilot test of an attribution retraining intervention to raise walking levels in sedentary older adults. *Journal of the American Geriatrics Society, 55,* 1842–1846.

Seong, N. (2003). The relationship of participation in leisure activity to social support, self-esteem, and stress among elderly senior center members in Seoul, South Korea. *Dissertation Abstracts International, A: The Humanities and Social Sciences, 63,* 2090.

Stephens, R., & Kwah, H. (2009). Critical factors in the successful utilization of senior center meals. *Care Management Journal, 10,* 163–175.

Taietz, P. (1976). Two conceptual models of the senior center. *Journal of Gerontology, 31,* 219–222.

Torres-Gil, F., Spencer-Suarez, K., & Rudinica, (2014). The Older Americans Act and the nexus of aging and diversity. In K. Whitfield & T. Baker (Eds.), *Handbook on minority aging* (pp. 367–377). New York, NY: Springer.

Turner, K. (2004). Senior citizens centers: What they offer, who participates, and what they gain. *Journal of Gerontological Social Work, 43,* 37–47.

Wacker, R. R., & Roberto, K. A. (2008). *Community resources for older adults: Programs and services in a era of change* (3rd ed.). Thousand Oaks, CA: Sage.

Wagner, D. L. (1995). Senior center research in America: An overview of what we know. In National Eldercare Institute on Multipurpose Senior Centers and Community Focal Points, *Senior centers in America: A blueprint for the future* (pp. 3–10). Washington DC: National Council on Aging.

Walker, J., Bisbee, C., Porter, R., & Flanders, J. (2004). Increasing practitioners' knowledge of participation among elderly adults in senior center activities. *Educational Gerontology, 30,* 353–366.

W. JUNE SIMMONS
JANICE LYNCH SCHUSTER
SANDY ATKINS

Health Maintenance Organizations, Managed Care, and the Affordable Care Act

15

THE DRAMATICALLY CHANGING HEALTHCARE ENVIRONMENT

Healthcare costs are an ever increasing portion of the American economy, expanding from 5% in 1960 to 18% in 2013, with projections that it will reach 21% by 2023 (Schoen, Guterman, Zezza, & Abrams, 2013). Despite both Republican and Democratic efforts to curb the spending explosion, costs remain high. And yet for all that America invests in health, compared with other industrialized countries, we continue to experience poor outcomes, including shorter life expectancies, higher infant mortality, and failures in quality of care. More and more, policymakers and healthcare leaders point to wasteful, unnecessary, duplicative, and uncoordinated care as a key driver behind the cost explosion. Many of them now seek to achieve the much-vaunted triple aim of the Affordable Care Act (ACA): better care, better health, and lower costs.

Demographic factors driven by the aging of the baby boomers (those born from 1946 through 1964, or some 80 million Americans), as well as the steady increase in the prevalence of multiple chronic conditions (Anderson & Horvath, 2004) and their associated costs (an estimated 85% of all healthcare costs stem from treating chronic conditions (Robert Wood Johnson Foundation, 2010), threaten to bankrupt and overwhelm the fabric of the healthcare system. Although the slight 2012 slowdown in healthcare spending indicates that innovations of the ACA have perhaps had an effect (Blumenthal & Stremikis, 2013), healthcare spending remains an economic challenge to be solved.

NEW UNDERTANDING OF SOCIAL DRIVERS OF HEALTH

American social policy dramatically lacks balance between what we spend for medical interventions and social services; although both are essential for the care and management of chronic disease, we continue to overinvest in one, and ignore the other. This imbalance is illustrated in Figure 15.1, which shows the total investment (as a percentage of gross domestic product, or GDP) in healthcare and social services among countries of the Organisation for Economic Co-operation and Development (OECD). The blue line, representing healthcare investment, is largest for the United States; only Turkey, Korea, and Mexico spend less on social services than does the

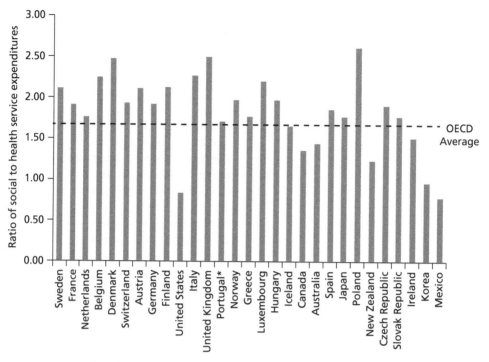

FIGURE 15.1. Ration of Social to Health Service Expenditures among Countries of the Organisation for Economic Co-operation and Development.

Source: Bradley, Elkins, Herrin, and Elbel (2011).

United States. Many assert this is part of the cause for our relatively poor outcomes, despite our high cost and payments per person for healthcare.

To appreciate the significance of this imbalance in investment, one must recognize that chief among the drivers of health outcomes are social and economic factors (i.e., education, employment, income, family and social support, and community safety), followed by health behaviors; access to healthcare and the quality of that care; and the physical environment. Clearly, not all of these factors will be changed or improved by increased investments in medical treatment. In fact, in a survey of 1,000 primary care physicians 85% reported their belief that social needs contribute directly to poor health and that, if it were possible, nearly one out of every seven prescriptions would be to address social needs (Robert Wood Johnson Foundation, 2011). In short, despite long-standing efforts to take a more holistic approach to patient care, as a society we continue to invest in a medical model that fixes parts of care at the expense of caring for the whole person. And this ongoing imbalance, left unchecked, will continue to drive tremendous healthcare costs, particularly as boomers

age, experience illness, and increasingly represent a high-risk, high-cost healthcare population.

TARGETING HIGH-RISK, HIGH-COST POPULATIONS

The ACA includes funding for innovations that encourage healthcare providers and organizations to target and coordinate care in ways that address the multifaceted needs of high-risk, high-cost populations, such as the 5% of the population who use 50% of the healthcare resources (see Figure 15.2). These innovations to ensure effective and efficient care and better outcomes use (1) strategies that offer full care coordination managed by interdisciplinary care teams; (2) mechanisms such as bundled payments and accountable care organizations (ACOs), which aim to move from an episodic model of care to a more planned and structured approach that keeps people well and restores health or slows decline wherever possible; and (3) new models of healthcare, which seek to understand who actually needs care and how to ensure that they receive the right care, in the right place, at the right time.

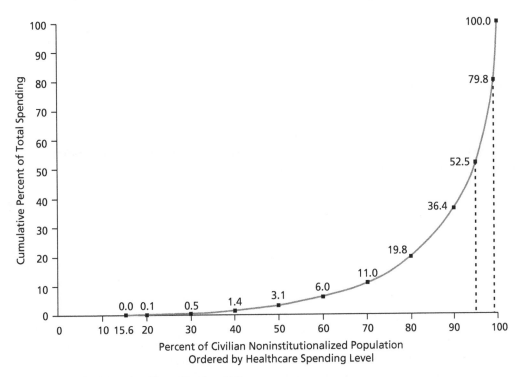

FIGURE 15.2. Distribution of Healthcare Spending, 2008

DRIVERS OF HIGH MEDICAL COST ARGUE FOR BOTH MANAGED APPROACHES AND GREATER USE OF SOCIAL SERVICES

The ACA relies on managing care more effectively and encourages expanding roles for social services with the potential to address so many of the social determinants of health. In this environment, social work has the capacity to augment medical treatment, offering much-needed expertise in comprehensive biopsychosocial and environmental assessment; in working with people to select and implement new, healthier behaviors; and in helping people access needed resources to support better health outcomes. Social workers are skilled in many of the areas in which multiple chronic conditions so often occur, including the special health challenges faced by people with disabilities, or those who live in poverty or who have mental health or substance use disorders. Social workers are also skilled in working with aging people, and those who require long-term services and supports. Social workers have distinctive expertise in working with people in their homes and in their natural environments, and in doing so, can avoid or reduce the costs of intensive, inpatient settings. In

short, as public funds are increasingly reallocated to pay for new approaches to healthcare, social work must be included as a nexus for a partnership with medicine in integrated care and financing systems. Social workers must also become familiar with these new mechanisms and their underlying values, including managed approaches to care.

AFFORDABLE CARE ACT: PAYMENT CHANGE, NEW INCENTIVES, AND EXPANDED ACCESS

The 2010 implementation of the ACA brought crucial provisions aimed at transforming the healthcare system from paying for *volume* to paying for *value*. It also focused on expanding access to care, particularly among the nation's uninsured or underinsured, primarily assuring access through major expansions in insurance coverage options, widening Medicaid eligibility with major federal support, and eliminating exclusion from coverage due to preexisting conditions.

Many provisions of the ACA are changing traditional methods for financing healthcare. All move to strategies that reflect key elements of health maintenance organizations (HMOs) and other managed care models, but coupled now with a new emphasis on measuring outcomes and publicly posting comparative results.

One very powerful and disruptive change has been to adjust payment rates based on quality measures and patient experience. Organizations will be rewarded or penalized for their performance. In addition, various payment redesigns will incentivize new models of care delivery that are more patient-centric and -driven and that will reduce duplication and waste. These new models end long-standing unreasonable incentives to build volume inappropriately. These are transformative dynamics, are emerging rapidly in the current environment, and are also creating a new environment for social work service delivery.

Hospitals will be affected by these payment transformations, too, and will receive penalties and incentives based on their performance on various quality measures; in the future, these financial changes are likely to be applied to physicians and nursing homes as well. Many of these changes have only been made possible by the algorithms and data analytics underlying surging use of big data.

One new example of changes in financial incentives can be seen in the work to reduce avoidable hospital readmissions, an effort that also includes a half-billion-dollar effort funded by the Centers for Medicare and Medicaid (CMS) to identify and correct root causes for readmissions. This work was begun in response to data that found that 20% of Medicare patients were readmitted within 30 days of hospital discharge (Jencks, Williams, & Coleman, 2009), a situation that not only drives increased costs but also heightens patient risk. The CMS will now penalize hospitals that do not reduce avoidable readmissions of Medicare patients, with a 1% reduction in their Medicare payments in 2013, rising to 3% in 2015 (Centers for Medicare and Medicaid Services [CMS], 2014d). In 2012, the penalties targeted three conditions (myocardial infarction, pneumonia, and congestive heart failure), but will expand to seven in 2015, with indications that this will expand to "all cause/all payer" readmissions penalties. These incentives are combined with additional value-based purchasing measurement, and penalties based on hospital measures of quality care. In addition, the public can now readily see these performance measures for itself, by checking the Hospital Compare website. Funding for the related initiatives to support

this shift is coordinated not by hospitals but by community-based organizations, reflecting the social determinants focus previously discussed and the value placed on community-based responses.

Implementation Science, Patient-Centers Outcomes Research, and Innovation Studies

In addition to its effect on healthcare financing, the ACA has stimulated rapid changes in US healthcare policy, practice, and research. Among these changes is increased interest in dissemination, implementation, and improvement science (DII Science), which seeks to understand challenges in implementing change in healthcare practices and how the roles and behaviors of clinicians and stakeholders can advance or prevent the uptake of new models and practice. Growth in DII Science is driven in part by increased health system and policymaker interest in limiting cost while improving quality.

Toward this end, Congress authorized creation of the Patient-Centered Outcomes Research Institute (PCORI) (U.S.H.R. 3590, 2009), which is investing billions in research aimed at providing the best evidence to guide patients and their caregivers in making informed decisions. The ACA also established the CMS Innovation Center (CMMI) (U.S.H.R. 3590, 2009), which is budgeted to receive $1 billion annually for 10 years to identify and support meaningful innovations that improve care and reduce costs. Taken together, these initiatives are additional powerful messages furthering healthcare redesign of care and reimbursement.

Building on Prior Managed Care Approaches

In looking to achieve the triple aim, the ACA has built on lessons learned from decades-old health maintenance organization (HMO) approaches. First created in 1929, HMOs became more prevalent after 1973, when the Nixon administration required businesses with 25 or more employees to offer HMOs as an alternative to traditional insurance (Mueller, 1974). The HMO's successor, the managed care organization (MCO), a more generic term for the model, later emerged as a major factor in healthcare cost containment and quality control.

Since its inception in 1929, managed care has continued to grow across the United States. It is defined as a system that integrates financing and delivery of medical care through contracts with physicians and hospitals to provide comprehensive health services to enrolled members in exchange for a monthly premium. The primary aim of MCOs is to control costs, deliver quality care, and ensure access to healthcare services for enrolled members. Managed care organizations serve as a third party that bridges payers, providers, and patients to provide cost-effective coordinated medical care.

Funding Mechanisms

The term "managed care" emcompasses several financing and organizing models, such as HMOs, preferred provider organizations (PPOs), and point-of-service (POS) financing and delivery of services.

Health maintenance organizations offer prepaid, comprehensive health coverage for hospital and physician services. The HMO is paid monthly premiums or capitated rates by the payers, which include employers, insurance companies, government agencies, and other groups representing covered individuals.

Preferred provider organizations (PPOs) are a partnership of providers, such as a hospital and physician group, that agrees to render particular services to a group of people for discounted rates under contract with a private insurer. A PPO can also be a legal entity, or it may be a function of an already formed health plan, HMO, or PPO. The entity may have a health benefit plan that is also referred to as a PPO. Preferred provider organizations are a common method for managing care while still paying for services through an indemnity plan. Most PPO plans are POS plans, in that they will pay a higher percentage for care provided by providers in the network. However, the insured population may incur out-of-pocket expenses for covered services received outside the PPO if the charge exceeds the PPO payment rate.

Managed care organizations operate under a capitated fiscal structure. This means that providers, whomever or whatever they are, accept a preset payment in exchange for providing healthcare to a group of people. The medical care provider receives a payment for each member in exchange for a comprehensive set of medical services. The rate of service

use by the member does not affect the payment given to the provider—the payment is set, no matter what services are required (or not). This structure is the opposite of the fee-for-service structure, in which each payment is made for specific services.

Managed care arrangements may include a monthly premium per enrolled member (a "per member per month" rate, PMPM). In other scenarios, it includes a case rate, with a maximum payment amount for an episode of care. In all cases, the reimbursement has a cap and is designed to reward providers for being prudent about the care or services provided.

Since its inception, the rate of enrollment of managed care members has continued to rise, with the largest enrollment following the initiation of the Medicaid and Medicare managed care plans. A rapidly expanding variety of managed care arrangements continues to evolve. These include Medicare Hospice, Programs of All-inclusive Care for the Elderly (PACE) and, more recently, shifting Medicaid-eligible persons in a number of states into mandatory managed care.

New Managed Care Reimbursement Approaches

For decades, the healthcare system has operated under these understandings and definitions of managed care. However, with the passage of the ACA, new reimbursement arrangements and trends are rapidly emerging. In the past, except for pioneering managed care organizations (such as Kaiser Permanente and Group Health of Puget Sound, which assumed the dual roles of care and payment), most health organizations/hospitals and physicians were paid separately and health insurers were not involved in managing care.

Blurring Silos and Emerging Integrated Systems

With the ACA, these traditional boundaries have blurred, and this blurring has intensified with the major consolidation of healthcare delivery systems. Many who once operated within the silos of fee-for-service are now joining to take shared risk under capitation arrangements. Sharing risk means that a physician group, hospital, and health plan accept full responsibility for the cost of all care and for meeting quality measures; if they fail to do this successfully, and if the results are too expensive, they bear the financial losses. They are not, as they were in the fee-for-service model, paid ever more to do ever more, with no real improvement in outcomes or care. Major integrated systems are rapidly emerging. Individual freestanding hospitals are diminishing in number, being purchased by larger systems, and physicians, who typically practiced solo or in small groups, are now more often employed by much larger network care systems. Large hospital groups are acquiring physician groups, insurance companies are buying medical practices, and other major healthcare companies are also acquiring physicians and hospitals.

This is a truly transformational change, and one that has led to the relatively new concepts of accountable care organizations (ACOs) and the patient-centered medical home (PCMH).

Accountable Care Organizations/Medicare Shared Savings Programs

Under the provisions of the ACA, the CMS has approved many ACOs. The CMS describes ACOs as "groups of doctors, hospitals, and other health care providers, who come together voluntarily to give coordinated high quality care to their Medicare patients" (CMS, 2014a). The ACOs bring together payment across populations for insurers, physicians, and hospitals as an integrated business operation. These groups share the "risk" of paying for care. A set of measures of success and quality are established and then the organizations are responsible for all costs. If they are successful, they share in the overall savings, but if they overrun on costs, they bear the total losses incurred. This approach is important because it enables hospitals, the highest-cost healthcare sector, to share in the savings from decreased hospitalization, which otherwise would have a negative effect on hospital income.

In some arrangements, such as in an HMO, providers can have greater control over where patients receive their care. In others, the patient population is assigned to but not under full management of the shared savings program. This approach is known as the Medicare Shared Savings Program. To date, approximately 340 of these new organizations have been approved by CMS (CMS, 2014c); most are physician led and serve fewer than 10,000 members. Funding is blended in partnerships that include

physicians, hospitals, and, at times, health insurance companies.

Unlike a traditional fee-for-service model, the program shares savings that accrue from better coordinated and integrated care. But shared savings are hard to achieve, and occur only if the providers deliver care at a lower cost *and* meet targets for 33 quality measures. These measures include patient and caregiver experience, care coordination, patient safety, preventive health services, and improved care for at-risk populations.

Patient-Centered Medical Homes

Patient-centered medical homes offer another model that works to create outpatient care systems that are coordinated and address needs of patients with chronic conditions. They must include care coordination, case management, health promotion, transitional care, patient and family support, and referral to community services and require interdisciplinary teams. According to the National Committee for Quality Assurance (NCQA), which offers certification to PCMHs that meet its standards, they are "a way of organizing primary care that emphasizes care coordination and communication to transform primary care into "what patients want it to be." Medical homes can lead to higher quality and lower costs and can improve patients' and providers' experience of care" (NCQA, 2014). Recently some of these groups are employing social workers or engaging community-based organizations to test expanded care resources to achieve better overall health results at equal or lower costs.

National standards and certification through NCQA enable primary care practices, including community health centers, to target improvement efforts in dimensions as diverse as electronic health records and timeliness standards. The advent of electronic health records (EHRs) or electronic medical records (EMRs) offers the potential not only to track and monitor individual patients in the health system but also to aggregate and assess data about them. While organizations are working to implement such systems, the federal Office of the National Coordinator (ONC) is charged with coordinating efforts, including development of meaningful use standards that will drive interoperable and efficient systems.

Balancing Payment and Outcomes

As noted throughout this chapter, the ACA's primary focus is to expand access to healthcare for millions of previously uninsured or underinsured people. But doing so requires simultaneously reigning in expenses. Toward this end, the ACA includes provisions that change payment structures, with a clear move away from traditional fee-for-service, to a more closely managed and coordinated system with financial checks and balances designed to reward good care and penalize bad. Building on historic models of managed care, the ACA is reimagining the healthcare system to make it more streamlined—and more effective.

Managing Risk—Paying for Outcomes Rather than Procedures—Population Health Management

A key element in all of these efforts is managing risk and consolidating payments to incentivize positive health outcomes, rather than paying for procedures that might or might not be medically necessary. Increased pressure on systems to pay for better results encourages a focus on *population health management*, working to bring best health results across a large population. This approach emphasizes prevention and proactive coordinated care that helps to limit worsening symptoms, engages people in managing their own care, and leads to improved health for all. Managed care organizations, which focus on coordinated, cost-effective care, are designed to complement such an approach.

Bundled Payments

Bundled payments also bring together multiple providers who had previously billed separately for fee-for-service payments. In the bundled payment system, these providers must collaborate and cooperate to provide integrated and complete services for an episode of care under a single capped rate and must also determine how to share savings. Bundled payments broaden the range of interventions covered and give providers greater flexibility in using health dollars to address a broader range of patient needs, including social services and supports.

Managed Care for Dual Eligibles

To date, 15 states have received CMS approval to conduct demonstrations to improve care for dual-eligibles, that is, people who are eligible for both Medicare and Medicaid (California Department of Health Care Services, 2012). These bring into an integrated system people who are at highest risk for health problems and who typically represent a disproportionate amount of healthcare use and costs. The program moves the risk for nursing home care under Medicaid to health plans, and so further transforms incentives, with the aim of keeping people out of nursing homes and in their own communities.

In such programs, the focus is less about treating or curing people, and more on helping stabilize complex medical situations, prevent worsening symptoms that might lead to hospitalization or institutionalization, reduce suffering, and maintain function. Doing so both improves quality of life and directly helps to delay and minimize the length of time these individuals live in healthcare settings. These demonstrations include social work coordination of community resources and services with medical care and treatment.

Building Social Work Roles and Services in Emerging Systems of Care

Better care coordination with more effective links to social services would appear to be a cornerstone of any efforts to rebalance the healthcare spending equation and address the effects of social determinants of health, especially when those drivers continue to lead people to poor health, worsening situations, and ever greater costs. For the millions of boomers aging with multiple chronic conditions, efforts to manage those conditions will, of necessity, include addressing these drivers, as well as focusing on the kinds of prevention and care that can enable older adults to remain at home and out of the hospital. Chief among the groups to be reached by better coordinated care and social services will be those who are dual eligible.

Creating the better system that is required by ACA means that medicine and health systems must engage with social work to build more regional systems of care based on public-private partnerships. These aim to meet patients and families' specific needs and complement investments in best health outcomes for those who can most benefit from social work skills and services.

In a managed care/ACA environment, the ability to assure continued safe and stable community living, to reduce inappropriate use of 911 and hospitals, and to help people and their families avoid long-term placement in nursing homes are both increasingly valued and a challenge for the redesign of social work and other community-based services.

An example of a services redefinition for this population has been developed at Partners in Care Foundation (*Partners*) in Los Angeles (Figure 15.3). It is designed to advance the discussions with healthcare providers and payers in the changing environment on issues that are increasingly critical for social work and uses a business model outlined in the chart below.

Partners is structured around assessments and care coordination, evidence-based self-management, and building efficient provider networks support programs, which target individuals with immediate needs and risks for whom a rapid response and brief intervention can have lasting and valuable economic and clinical outcomes.

The Community-Based Care Transitions Project funded by CMS is one model for similar partnerships. Funding is now being provided to over 100 community-based organizations nationwide to test ways to reduce and prevent hospital readmissions among Medicare beneficiaries (CMS, 2014b). In these models, community partners who had previously seldom communicated about patients and clients have now joined forces to identify those at risk of readmission and are using evidence-based interventions. In these interventions, staff see individuals in the hospital to connect and engage for a follow-up home visit, and then monitor and coach those individuals at home to better self-manage and navigate their healthcare system.

Review of medications is a key element to keeping people at home, and HomeMeds (www.HomeMeds.org) is an example of a social work medication review completed in partnership with pharmacists. It deploys specially trained social workers to the home, where they use their skills in comprehensive assessment and patient engagement, along with software support and pharmacist backup, to help patients manage complex medications. HomeMeds uses social work outreach and involvement as an "eyes and ears" for medical care, to see whether patients are able to take medications as prescribed, safely, and effectively. Social workers can then also bring an environmental and self-management assessment to alert clinicians, patients, and families to typically "invisible" risks and challenges in self-care and help to develop solutions.

Social care coordination/case management is a social work strategy that has been used for years, and that now enjoys an opportunity for more widespread use and impact. Social work strategies

Evaluation, Risk Screening, Care Coordination, and Coaching	Evidence-Based Self-Management	Provider Networks for Efficient Delivery System
Short- and Long-Term Service Coordination and SNF Diversion	Chronic Disease Self-Management Program	Evidence-Based Leadership Council
Adult Day Health Authorization	Chronic Pain Self-Management Program	Regional Evidence-Based Program Delivery Network
HomeMeds	Diabetes Self-Management Program	Long-Term Services & Supports Network
Care Transitions Interventions	A Matter of Balance	Care Transitions Provider Network
Home Safety Evaluation	Savvy Caregiver	
Home Palliative Care Coordination	Powerful Tools for Caregivers	
	Arthritis Foundation Walk with Ease	
	UCLA Memory classes	

FIGURE 15.3 Partners in Care Foundation Service Offerings and Initiatives for Healthcare Partnerships.

will be especially important in helping the roll-out of Dual Eligible Demonstrations, where skills at gaining access in order to visit people at home and assess their challenges will facilitate finding opportunities and services that enable individuals to remain independent at home. Under the dramatic shift to managed care and ACA-driven health system mobilization of community care resources to reduce suffering and decline, the role of social work will be even more essential to managing costs in the new integrated environment. Additionally, social work will be an essential component of a cutting-edge managed care system of the populations with multiple chronic conditions and functional impairments.

Evidence-Based Self-Management Programs

The middle column in Figure 15.3 addresses the broad arena of evidence-based self-management for better health outcomes. People who live with multiple chronic conditions can greatly benefit from learning strategies of self-management for their illness. Toward this end, individuals must address not only the specific medical regime required to manage their illnesses but also the lifestyle and behavior issues that exacerbate it. Learning to manage these conditions often requires insight and awareness as well as the use of skills that social workers can teach. This kind of whole-life approach to care is essential to the workings of managed care programs and their use of interdisciplinary teams. Indeed, the US Administration for Community Living (ACL) has made extensive investments in spreading evidence-based self-management programs, and has laid the groundwork on which to build and expand such programs.

SOCIAL WORK: EMERGING PARTNER IN COST-EFFECTIVE HEALTHCARE

Rapidly evolving new medical structure managed care approaches and financing arrangements require that social work quickly understand where and how it can be applied and integrated. This will be challenging. There is a continuing risk for the medicalization of aging, and social work may not yet understand the complex administrative structures now in play,

including its role in the managed approaches to care underpinning the ACA.

Competition for the redeployment of medical funds among healthcare professional groups and other stakeholders in these structures is fierce, with many players vying for increasingly limited resources. Social work will not be successful in this environment unless its leaders articulate, define, and communicate to stakeholders in medicine and healthcare payment its roles and value proposition. Critical selling points are its competence in engaging community resources, ability to work within interdisciplinary structures, attention to social determinants of health issues, and willingness to reorganize its own approach to services with a stronger emphasis on population health, prevention, and use of evidence-based interventions.

In closing, America faces an urgent question: How can we better care for the most vulnerable among us in ways that do not bankrupt our society or ignore their plight? Social work may not offer all of the answers to this complex issue, but it certainly offers a foundation for so much of what needs to be done.

REFERENCES

Anderson, G., & Horvath, J. (2004). The growing burden of chronic disease in America. *Public Health Reports*, 119, 263–270. doi:10.1016/j.phr.2004.04.005.

Blumenthal, D., & Stremikis, K. (2013, September 17). Getting real about health care value [Web log post]. *Harvard Business Review*. Retrieved from http://blogs.hbr.org/2013/09/getting-real-about-health-care-value/

Bradley, E. H., Elkins, B. R., Herrin, J., & Elbel, B. (2011). Health and social services expenditures: Associations with health outcomes. *BMJ Quality and Safety*, 20, 826–831. doi:10.1136/bmjqs.2010.048363

California Department of Health Care Services. (2012). *State demonstrations to integrate care for dual eligibles: Demonstration proposal.* Retrieved from https://www.cms.gov/Medicare-Medicaid-Coordination/Medicare-and-Medicaid-Coordination/Medicare-Medicaid-Coordination-Office/Downloads/CAProposal.pdf

Centers for Medicare and Medicaid Services (CMS). (2014a). *Accountable care organizations.* Retrieved from http://www.cms.gov/Medicare/Medicare-Fee-for-Service-Payment/ACO/

Centers for Medicare and Medicaid Services (CMS). (2014b). *Community-based care transitions program.* Retrieved from http://innovation.cms.gov/initiatives/CCTP/

Centers for Medicare and Medicaid Services (CMS). (2014c). *Program news and announcements.* Retrieved from http://www.cms.gov/Medicare/Medicare-Fee-for-Service-Payment/sharedsavingsprogram/News.html

Centers for Medicare and Medicaid Services (CMS). (2014d). *Readmissions reduction program.* Retrieved from http://www.cms.gov/Medicare/Medicare-Fee-for-Service-Payment/AcuteInpatientPPS/Readmissions-Reduction-Program.html

Jencks, S. F., Williams, M. V., & Coleman, E. A. (2009). Rehospitalizations among patients in the Medicare fee-for-service program. *New England Journal of Medicine, 360,* 1418–1428. doi:10.1056/NEJMsa0803563

Mueller, M. S. (1974). *Notes and brief reports: Health Maintenance Organization Act of 1973.* Division of Economic and Long-Range Studies, 35–39. Retrieved from http://www.ssa.gov/policy/docs/ssb/v37n3/v37n3p35.pdf

National Committee for Quality Assurance. (2014). *Patient-centered medical home recognition.* Retrieved from http://www.ncqa.org/Programs/Recognition/PatientCenteredMedicalHomePCMH.aspx

Robert Wood Johnson Foundation. (2011). *Health care's blind side, the overlooked connection between social needs and good health: Summary of findings from a survey of America's physicians.* Retrieved from http://www.rwjf.org/content/dam/farm/reports/surveys_and_polls/2011/rwjf71795

Robert Wood Johnson Foundation. (2010). *Chronic care: Making the case for ongoing care.* Retrieved from http://www.rwjf.org/content/dam/farm/reports/reports/2010/rwjf54583

Schoen, C., Guterman, S., Zezza, M. A., & Abrams, M. K. (2013). *Confronting costs: Stabilizing U.S. health spending while moving toward a high performance health care system.* The Commonwealth Fund Commission on a High Performance Health System. Retrieved from http://www.commonwealthfund.org/~/media/Files/Publications/Fund%20Report/2013/Jan/1653_Commission_confronting_costs_web_FINAL.pdf

US House of Representatives 3590. 111th Congress: Patient Protection and Affordable Care Act. (2009). Retrieved from http://www.govtrack.us/congress/bills/111/hr3590

More than many other social policy constituencies, older Americans have long benefited from the presence of planning agencies at both the state and substate levels. Passage of the Older Americans Act (OAA) in 1965 not only created the Administration on Aging (AOA) in the federal government, but also authorized creation of State Units on Aging (SUAs). Amendments to the OAA in 1972 mandated creation throughout the country of substate regional planning bodies, Area Agencies on Aging (AAA). Initially using OAA funds (and, later, Medicaid and state-level appropriations), these agencies contracted with local service providers to fund social, nutritional, transportation, legal, and other direct services to residents of their planning and service areas. Since the late 1970s, this array of agencies has constituted what has since become known as "the aging network." Over the years, this network has grown in scope and responsibilities, but its resource base has remained relatively stagnant even as the older population has grown and younger adults with disabilities have become clients of many network agencies around the country.

DEVELOPMENT OF AREA AGENCIES AND THE AGING NETWORK

In its nearly half-century existence, this network has evolved in important ways. In its nascent stage, the aging network engaged in basic start-up and capacity-building activities. By the 1980s, the network was well established, widely recognized, and had come to represent a substate and local political presence unique among population-based human services constituencies. Beginning in the late 1980s and continuing to this day, the network has been increasingly drawn into the large and challenging world of community-based long-term care.

EARLY DEVELOPMENTS

Both rational and political elements lie behind creation of area agencies (Hudson, 1974). Passed with considerable fanfare in 1965, the OAA was better understood as symbolic rather than substantive legislation. The initial appropriation for FY 1966 was $7.5 million, and the fledgling SUAs could use no more than $15,000 each for state-level

ROBERT B. HUDSON

Social Service and Health Planning Agencies

16

administration. By 1969, total funding had risen to $23 million, with the amount available for their own operations having risen to $25,000 (Hudson, 1973). States were encouraged to appropriate additional funds, but as Congressman John Brademas noted in hearings in 1969, Nebraska was typical in contributing no more than 16 cents per older resident to augment the federal funds. By the early 1970s, criticism of the OAA, AOA, and the SUAs was widespread; one report spoke of "rampant tokenism" (Greenblatt & Ernst, 1972), and another was titled "The Administration on Aging—Or a Successor?" (Sheppard, 1971).

Against this backdrop, a White House Conference on Aging was convened in 1971, bringing some 4,500 older Americans to Washington to press for additional federal programming across a range of aging-related arenas, including social services. In a moment of high political theater, President Nixon—as a means of deflecting attention from his opposition to a proposed 20% increase in Social Security benefits—seized on the OAA as a vehicle for showing his commitment to the well-being of senior citizens. To the surprise of nearly everyone in the auditorium, Nixon announced:

> We want to begin by increasing the present budget of the Administration on Aging nearly five-fold—to 100 million dollars. Now, you may wonder where I got that number because . . . it was 80 million dollars last night, and I decided why not 100 million dollars! (White House Conference on Aging [WHCoA], 1971)

In light of this surprise announcement, there immediately arose a need to address planning and administrative problems seen as endemic among both the AOA and the SUAs. The answer lay in drawing on a "substate planning strategy" then in vogue within the Department of Health, Education, and Welfare. This led to creation of the AAAs through the 1972 amendments to the Act. Being "closer to the people," these agencies were seen as better positioned to set priorities and engage in a meaningful planning process. Beyond creation of the AAAs, amendments in 1972 and 1973 also created a new elderly nutrition program (centrally involving the AAAs) and a new Older Americans Community Service Employment program (involving a delicate distribution of contracts between the SUAs and "federal contractors," including such aging-based interest groups as the American Association of Retired Persons, Green Thumb, the National Council of Senior Citizens, and the National Council on Aging). While many SUA directors and Democrats had objected to creation of AAAs—fearing they would further weaken the SUAs—enactment of the employment program and dramatic appropriations increases swept away the opposition. Ultimately, overall appropriations for the OAA rose to $227 million in 1974, $324 million in 1976, $749 million in 1978, and $919 million by 1980.

LATER DEVELOPMENTS

By the late 1970s, the aging network was firmly in place. In addition to the 57 SUAs (including territories, and the District of Columbia), 655 AAAs had come into being, funding thousands of direct service providers. The 1980s represented a period of consolidation for the network. Funding under the OAA essentially leveled off at roughly $1 billion ($993 million in 1980) and has grown only modestly in the years since. Thus, while the OAA appropriation for 2007 was $1.8 billion, that is actually less than the 1980 amount of $2.5 billion, which is what the 1980 amount would be today in inflation-adjusted dollars (Burgess & Applebaum, 2009).

Additional legislative changes over this time period included new authorizations for in-home services for frail elders, the Long-Term Care Ombudsman Program, health education and illness prevention programs, programs for preventing elder abuse and neglect, and a heightened emphasis on the needs of older people with the greatest economic and social needs. New attention was also brought to bear on intergenerational concerns and the needs of those providing care to the frail elderly. This latter effort was institutionalized in 2000 with passage of the Family Caregivers Support Act, the most significant legislative addition to the OAA in 30 years. These developments (and their relative priorities) are reflected in the title and functional expenditure totals under the Act, which totaled $1.9 billion in 2012 (US Congressional Research Services, 2013):

Title II—Administration on Aging	$43.2 million
Title III B—Supportive Services	366.9 million
Title III C—Nutrition Services	816.3 million
Title III D—Health Promotion	20.9 million
Title III E—Family Caregiver Services	153.6 million
Title IV—Health, Independence, Longevity	7.7 million
*Title V—Community Service Employment	448.3 million
Title VI—Grants to Native Americans	34.0 million
Title VII—Elder Rights Protection	21.8 million

*Administered by the US Department of Labor.

Organizationally, two major—and somewhat contradictory—changes have taken place in recent years. Under President Clinton, the Commissioner on Aging's position—charged with administering the OAA—was elevated to the rank of Assistant Secretary for Aging within the Department of Health and Human Services. However, in 2012 under President Obama, the AOA was folded into a new Administration for Community Living housing a number of constituent populations. This administrative consolidation was controversial among some aging advocates, who worried that it might represent a lessening of AOA's access and influence. A similar concern was expressed nearly 30 years ago when the AOA was removed from the secretary's office and placed in a new Office of Human Development Services with several other service populations. That the current Assistant Secretary for Aging will also head the new ACS has allayed some of the advocates' concerns.

The most recent programmatic developments find the aging network increasingly enmeshed in the world of long-term healthcare and social services. Moreover, the responsibilities (and titles) of many State and Area Agencies on Aging have expanded to include younger adults requiring long-term services and supports (LTSS). While there are wide variations in aging responsibilities and capacities across the nation, these new responsibilities and clients have taken the network well beyond the modest confines of OAA funding to involve them with the much larger Medicaid and Medicare programs (Kunkel & Lackmeyer, 2008).

PLANNING CHALLENGES

Social and health planning for the nation's aging population has long been a complicated endeavor. Questions about the planning function tap into different dimensions. The first centers on comprehensiveness, the most basic question being whether the public sector should take on the task of "planning" for the well-being of millions of older people. Or, if not all older people, whom among them should it plan for? And, if such planning is to be undertaken, at what level(s) of government should it take place? Second, should planning in aging be organized by population or by function, that is, should it be conducted centrally by an "aging planning agency" or should planning be organized along functional lines such as health, transportation, income, or housing, with the needs of older persons being addressed in conjunction with those of the larger population?

Most recently, the traditional concept of planning—organizing and coordinating various entities and directing their combined activities in a centralized manner—has encountered the participant- or consumer-directed services alternative. In this new paradigm, individual-level decision-making reverses the "direction" of planning, substituting a "bottom-up" model for the earlier "top-down" one. In the words of Doty et al. (2012, p. 33), "with our increasingly diverse older population, flexible long-term care delivery is all the more necessary."

As the network has become increasingly involved with the long-term care world, planning activities have become increasingly complicated. As network agencies grapple with a range of programs, facilities, and initiatives scattered throughout the nation's long-term care "system," they find themselves somewhat like the tail trying to lead the dog. Network budgets are extremely modest, and planning functions are only a small part of network activities (Burgess & Applebaum, 2009). Heavy investments by network agencies in long-term care activities also leave fewer resources to direct toward more able seniors residing in the community, even though attention to their concerns has long been a mandate under the OAA Title I. Addressing the needs of younger adults with disabilities presents an additional strain, both in terms of services volume and in the "services paradigm," wherein the two populations have very different ideas about the overall purposes of LTSS and the manner in which they should be administered.

Finally, the locus of service delivery remains a significant challenge to planning efforts. These new initiatives have generated a shift in the balance of care from skilled nursing facilities to home- and community-based services (HCBS) (Kane et al., 1998), a move that has propelled network agencies into the LTSS arena. As noted in what follows, however, the number of programs and the variety of players in the community care world and the emergent consumer-driven model have made any kind of centralized planning difficult to achieve if not, in many circles, an unwarranted undertaking.

Planning for Whom: Eligibility

Because the very notion of "planning" is marginally suspect in the American political culture, no one has called for policy-relevant blueprint planning for the future of the older population. Symbolically, Title I of the OAA resolves to improve most aspects of older people's lives, but it is little more than a wish-statement. Medicare and Medicaid are larger and more concrete programs, directing over $500 billion annually in federal funding to older adults, but they have no formal planning component to them.

Formal planning for the aged has been left largely to the network of aging agencies operating under the OAA. Although these programs are neither purely symbolic nor especially large, thorny questions around planning have long arisen here as well (Justice, 1997). Because there is no formal means testing under the OAA, a nominal case can be made that all older people are eligible for planning services. Resource constraints preclude such broad-based efforts, but in selected areas, such as nursing home ombudsman programs and elder abuse and neglect services, SUAs and AAAs have assumed population-wide intervention roles.

For roughly the Act's first 20 years, what transpired for the most part, however, was that administrators of OAA programs at all levels of government struggled with how to best target their limited resources. During bouts of OAA reauthorization, debate centered on this question. Early guidelines that centered on "those with greatest economic and social need" later evolved into an enumeration centered on older populations of color, those living in rural areas, and those who were frail or disabled (Hasler, 1990). Apart from these often being

overlapping categories, important selection questions remained: Is being over age 70 or 75 "to be disadvantaged"?, What proportion of services should be directed to older populations of color?, What is an adequate measure of "social need?", and so forth.

Beyond these relatively nuanced distinctions, the energies and resources of the aging services network beginning in the 1980s have clearly gravitated toward those elders who could be deemed especially vulnerable by one measure or another. And this is a far different emphasis from that found in the planning and services network's early years. In global terms, this transition was largely about moving away from early efforts under the OAA directed at providing socialization and educational opportunities for older people living in the community (including, for example, funds for senior center construction and operation) toward concerted efforts centered on allowing frail older people to remain at home or in other community settings rather than being relegated to skilled nursing facilities or other institutional placements.

The most recent and equally important chapter in eligibility standards for these agencies began largely during the late 1980s. First, network agencies lessened emphasis on service provision from relatively well elders in the community toward those in danger of institutional placement, and, second, many states extended coverage of the vulnerable and frail old to also include younger adults with disabilities. In this way, the "eligibility axis" began to swing from elders in various circumstances to adults of all ages with disabilities. Thus, in 30 states today, the SUA is charged with serving both elderly and adult disabled clients (Kunkel, Lackmeyer, Straker, & McGrew, 2008). Indeed, the long-standing moniker State Units on Aging has been modified in those states to reflect the added focus on persons with disabilities, and the national trade association has changed its name from National Association of State Units on Aging (NASUA) to National Association of State Units on Aging and Disability (NASUAD).

This partial shift under the OAA from (nominally, at least) serving all elders to largely serving (1) elders with functional impairments and presumably low income and (2) younger adults with disabilities is of both philosophical and programmatic importance. For half a century, old age was essentially understood as a proxy for need, and eligibility for a host of programs was age based (at 60, 62, or 65). Recent developments affecting the aging network in the

HCBS world represents a curtailing of chronological age as a sole or even primary basis for eligibility and moves decidedly in the direction of providing benefits to adults of all ages who are disabled or functionally impaired. As seen below, this evolution has also created planning conundrums in prioritizing and organizing the benefits that recipients should receive (Kane, 2012).

Planning for What: Program Benefits

The substance as well as the targets of planning efforts has been subject to controversy and evolution in the three decades of the aging planning and services network. One subject of debate has long been the degree to which the network should concentrate its efforts on services delivery and coordination on broader advocacy efforts directed at the so-called functional arenas not under its purview. Major efforts were made in the late 1960s and 1970s to undertake advocacy or "leadership planning" wherein SUAs and AAAs would press health, transportation, and other agencies to direct more of their efforts (and comparatively larger budgets) to better serving older people (Binstock, Cherington, & Woll, 1974). Activities of this kind were undertaken with limited success, but the odds were long that new, small, and constituency-based agencies could meaningfully move the agendas of these larger bureaucratic entities (Hudson & Veley, 1974).

In the years before the advent of the AAAs, services planning was rudimentary at best, with the nascent SUAs seeking to distribute small community grants across their states in ways that were both programmatically and politically defensible. With the coming of the AAAs and the very significant increase in OAA funding, new efforts were made to coordinate as well as fund service provision. Toward this end, the AAAs themselves were forbidden to engage in direct service delivery. As with the question of client eligibility, efforts were made to prioritize services, moving from an original list of 18 discrete services found in the 1973 amendments later to a three-part listing of access, in-home, and legal services and the requirement that at least 50% of their Title III funds be used for these purposes. Pressures from the network later led to this provision being softened so that an "adequate proportion" of their funds were used for these purposes (Hudson, 1994).

During the 1970s and early 1980s, these debates had centered almost exclusively on social services alone. By the mid-1980s, however, pressures increased to add more health-related services to the mix. In this way, the larger reality of the aging of the population and, in particular, the aging of the older population began to impact directly the aging planning and services network. The programmatic mandate of the aging network agencies began shifting toward developing HCBS to maximize the possibilities for older residents' "independent living." The political mandate came from officials who wanted to please constituents, save money, or, if possible, both.

The principal impetus to network involvement in HCBS was implementation of a Medicaid waiver program, beginning in 1981. These state-based waivers typically allow states to by-pass statewide income eligibility requirements in order to develop regionally or site-specific community service alternatives. Services such as home health, case management, personal care, and adult day healthcare, which traditional Medicaid cannot offer in noninstitutional settings, and which OAA funds alone are not sufficient to support, are now offered nationwide. By the turn of the century, such programs for older adults and persons with disabilities are administered under the auspices of the SUA in 21 states, and in an additional 12 states these programs served elderly persons alone (NASUA, 2004).

While the benefits for older people and people with disabilities may be, or at least appear to be, the same—for example, information, transportation, assistive devices—differing philosophies of purpose continue to differentiate a given benefit. A long-standing presumption that frail elders need "to be taken care of" and services should be designed to do so contrasts with the more mainstream purpose put forth in the disability community, namely, that resources should be self-directed by the individual often working with peers rather than professionals and that the consumer (not understood as a client) should have power and be in control around services decision-making. As Kane (2012, p. 9) puts it, "The dominant paradigm in services to elders has been to meet unmet needs. The dominant paradigm in disability services is to compensate for disability so people may live as fully as possible." Kane goes on to say that the "normalization" effort by the disability community may be having an effect on elder services as consumer choice initiatives are implemented and evaluated. But the separate philosophical bases have organizational consequences that in many settings have not yet been overcome (Kane, 2012; Kunkel, Lackmeyer, Straker, & McGrew, 2008).

Planning by Whom: Organization of the Delivery System

From both a planning and a political perspective, what has made the aging services delivery system nearly unique in the social services arena is the vertically integrated network represented by AOA, the SUAs, the AAAs, and the host of direct service agencies with whom the state and area agencies contract. The creation of this network is the lasting legacy of Arthur S. Fleming, who served as AOA commissioner under Richard Nixon and who saw in the newly formed AAAs a political as well as a services infrastructure for the old. Political and programmatic advantage was seen in the "vertical" protection afforded regional and local agencies by federal and state-level legislative, regulatory, and accountability language requiring that monies be spent for the old (and later persons with disabilities) in specified ways. Planners and providers in other service domains are in many respects envious of this aging-based services system and have sought at times to emulate it (Grason & Guyer, 1995).

Even in this earlier period, however, there were drawbacks to this organization of aging services. As noted, the larger functionally oriented systems, such as health, mental health, and transportation, operated outside of this network. Two particular problems arose. Much as the aging network might lobby these agencies to do more for its older client base, the network has little leverage to move them in that direction. Moreover, these larger agencies, having seen that there was aging services network in place, were induced to do less rather than more for older consumers. Transportation provides one example, where a regional bus service may not have felt it necessary to tailor its routes and schedules to older riders because the aging network might have been providing specialized bus or van services to older people (e.g., the "OATS" program [Older Americans Transportation Service] program in rural Missouri).

Public health provides a second example. A turn-of-the-century study, *The Aging States Project: Promoting Opportunities for Collaboration Between the Public Health and Aging Networks* (Chronic Disease Directors and National Association

of State Units on Aging [CDD and NASUA], 2003), found coordination between the two networks quite limited. The SUA respondents identified several issues that are critical to health promotion among older adults that they felt not to be sufficiently recognized by state health departments (SHDs). Even more to the point, the report finds that "there appears to be widespread confusion about which agency in a state has lead responsibility for health promotion and disease prevention for older adults" (CDD and NASUA, p. 24). As the authors note, there is some irony in health departments' limited role in aging-related activities in that decades of public health successes may have more to do with the numerical rise of the old than any other single factor.

State and local officials have long struggled with how to integrate these "vertical functional autocracies" (Wright, 1972) into broader service agendas such as those in transportation or health. Because more particularistic agencies, such as those in aging, may be constrained (or protected, depending on one's vantage point) by federal law and regulation, it has often been difficult for general purpose government officials (mayors, county commissioners, governors) to coordinate otherwise interrelated services agendas. Thus in the case of health, federal funding, usually from the Centers for Disease Control, is often disease-specific rather than population specific.

In its first phase, the network was largely successful in creating its own planning and services domain, albeit unevenly and with very modest resources. A second phase of inducing other agencies to pay more attention met with more limited success, the network actors largely lacking the requisite resources and unable to provide incentives needed to prod other major agencies in a new or expanded direction. However, a third phase has now emerged, that of playing a key role in the planning and administering community-based LTSS for vulnerable elders and persons with disabilities.

State-level activities of this sort had begun as early as the late 1970s, and were then greatly expanded through the Medicaid Long-Term Care waiver of 1982, which made Medicaid funds available for community-based as well as institutionally based services. Major impetus then came through passage of the Americans with Disabilities Act in 1990 and the *Olmstead* Supreme Court decision, ruling that people should not be required to live in institutions to have medical needs met unless community alternatives were not available. Such alternatives were increasingly available, brought on by governors hoping they could save Medicaid dollars by transitioning people out of nursing homes, by self-advocates and/or family members determined to get least restrictive care for themselves or their loved ones, and by policy reformers in Washington and in the states, determined to devise and promote organizational arrangements that would address both the volume of community-based alternatives and their quality (O'Shaughnessy, 2011).

There may still be a lack of adequate funding for HCBS, but there has been no lack of attention in policy circles to try to rationalize the financing and delivery system. In 1980, there was a 10-state Channeling Demonstration project designed to see whether community care could be cost-effective; the results were not conclusive, but the demonstration itself gave impetus to nascent state-level efforts around HCBS. Cash and Counseling programs developed in the 1990s allowed beneficiaries to employ, pay, and fire care providers, including paid family members (Mahoney, 2004). Planning and coordination lay at the heart of a series of initiatives beginning early in the last decade under President Bush's larger New Freedom Initiative, which led to federal grants to the states for Real Choice Systems Change. A few years later, the Center for Medicare and Medicaid Services (CMS) and the AOA launched Aging and Disability Resource Centers (ADRCs), and OAA amendments in 2006 required their establishment in all states. Two models of ADRCs were developed, technical assistance centers were established, and the CMS and AOA have imposed quite stringent guidelines to the AAAs and the Independent Living Centers that administer the program at the substate level. There are now more than 340 ADRC sites, about one-third of which are statewide (O'Shaughnessy, 2011). Yet, as with the AAA planning experience dating back to the mid-1970s, there remains great variation across the country in agency design and capacity, and as with OAA programs generally, they are subject to the vagaries of local politics, preferences, and capacity, to say nothing of the new assertiveness of most people with disabilities and many elders themselves.

Further complicating planning—though doubtlessly providing important options—is the Money Follows the Person (MFP) initiative. Launched at the state level and later given federal support through the Deficit Reduction Act of 2005 and the Affordable Care Act (ACA) in 2010, MFP aims to remove patients from skilled nursing facilities and facilitate their return to a "qualified residence" in the community (Reinhart, 2012). By 2011, over 50,000 persons had been resettled in community settings, though only one-third of them were elders. Community placement of many elders, such as those with Alzheimer's disease, has been relatively slow due to a mixture of level of frailty, lack of available workforce, and suitable residences (assisted living residency is prohibited).

Lastly, the major paradigm shift in the organization and direction of health and social services over the past 15 years has undergirded much of these developments. The earlier era of professionally based top-down case management has been increasingly supplanted by consumer-driven initiatives, borrowed largely from the disability community. In lieu of an agency-based social worker or care manager designing, arranging, financing, and assessing a service package—following what DeJong (1979) calls the medical model and rehabilitation paradigm, the new model places the consumer (nee client) in charge of service and provider choice (see Table 16.1). In short, the direction of services for these populations has gone from top-down to bottom-up. While many cautionary comments have been sounded by this "ultimate devolution" (often by agency-based professionals), at least one rigorous three-state evaluation has found high levels of consumer satisfaction and positive health and social outcomes (Doty et al., 2012).

PRESSING ISSUES IN SOCIAL AND HEALTH SERVICES PLANNING

The aging planning and services network has gone through growth, consolidation, and, most recently, redefinition phases. For many network agencies, it is hard to exaggerate the two shifts in their organizational environments, first, during the period c. 1970–1985, when they tried to take the lead in system changes, and second, since the late 1980s, when they have been directly involved in the dense and tangled arena of HCBS. The first of these periods was marked by a role of symbolic affirmation, a limited programmatic mandate, and resources adequate to the relatively modest tasks at hand; the second by attempting with very modest resources to play a lead role in issues associated with the recently discovered "aging of America"; and the last

TABLE 16.1. The Independent Living and Traditional Paradigms

	Medical Model and Rehabilitation Paradigm	Independent Living and Disability Paradigm
Definition of Problem	physical or mental impairment; lack of vocational skill (in the VR system); lack of abilities	dependence on professionals, family members & others; it is the attitudes & environments that are hostile & need fixing
Locus of Problem	in the individual (individuals are sick and need to be "fixed")	in the environment; in the medical and/or rehabilitation process itself; disability is a common part of the human condition
Solution to the Problem	professional intervention; treatment	1. civil rights & advocacy 2. barrier removal 3. self-help 4. peer role models & peer support 5. consumer control over options & services
Social Role	individual with a disability is a "patient" or "client"	individual with a disability is a "consumer," "customer" or "user" of services and products
Who Controls	Professionals	"consumer" or "individual"
Desired Outcomes	maximum self-care (or "ADLs"—activities of daily living); gainful employment (in the vocational rehabilitation system)	independence through control over ACCEPTABLE options for everyday living in an integrated community

Source: DeJong (1979).

with trying to simultaneously maximize consumer choice, save states money, and centrally involve the informal care world (families and friends) at the partial expense of the formal (agency-based) system.

These developments bring into question the role of planning, at least in the centralized vein in which it is often addressed. In the emerging model, responsiveness to client preferences trumps accountability as determined through the formal agency-based procedures. Planning and accountability measures remain very much in place further up the healthcare continuum involving interactions between acute and chronic care systems (furthered by stringent procedures being gradually put in place through provisions under the ACA). But further down the chain where management of long-term frailty and disability are in question, formal planning mechanisms have been substantially supplanted by consumer preference and control. As they continue to expand, it will be critical to determine how well ADRCs accommodate themselves to this new environment. As has long been the case with AAAs, some ADRCs may be little more than information and referral agencies while others may choose to actively coordinate provider activities. Thus, planning may continue, but "the rubber will be closer to the road" than was true a generation ago.

REFERENCES

Binstock, R. H., Cherington, C. M., & Woll, P. (1974). Federalism and leadership-planning: Predictions of variance in state behavior. Gerontologist, 14, 114–121. doi:10.1093/geront/14.2.114

Burgess, M., & Applebaum, R. (2009). The aging network in today's economy. Generations, 33, 40–46.

Chronic Disease Directors and the National Association of State Units on Aging. (2003). The aging states project: Promoting opportunities for collaboration between the public health and aging networks. Atlanta, GA: Centers for Disease Control and Prevention.

DeJong, G. (1979) Independent living: From social movement to analytic paradigm. Archives of Physical and Medical Rehabilitation, 1, 435–446.

Doty, P., Mahoney, K. J., Simon-Rusinowitz, L., Sciegaj, M., Selkow, I., & Loughlin D. M. (2012). How does Cash and Counseling affect the growth of participant-directed services? Generations, 36, 28–36.

Grason, H., & Gruyer, B. (1995). Rethinking the organization of children's programs: Lessons from the elderly. Milbank Quarterly, 73, 565–598. http://dx.doi.org/10.2307/3350286

Greenblatt, E., & Ernst, T. (1972). The Title III Program: Field impressions and policy options. Gerontologist, 12, 189–194. http://dx.doi.org/10.1093/geront/12.2_Part_1.191

Hasler, B. S. (1990). *Reporting of minority participation under Title III of the Older Americans Act.* Washington, DC: American Association of Retired Persons.

Hudson, R. B. (1973). *Client politics and federalism: The case of the Older Americans Act.* Paper presented to the Annual Meeting of the American Political Science Association, New Orleans.

Hudson, R. B. (1974). Rational planning and organizational imperatives: Prospects for area planning in aging. *Annals of the American Academy of Social and Political Science, 413,* 41–54. http://dx.doi.org/10.1177/000271627441500104

Hudson, R. B. (1994). The Older Americans Act and the defederalization of community-based care. In P. Kim (Ed.), *Services to the aging and aged.* New York, NY: Garland.

Hudson, R. B., & Veley, M. (1974). Federal funding and state planning: The case of the state units on aging. *Gerontologist, 14,* 122–128. http://dx.doi.org/10.1093/geront/14.2.122

Justice, D. (1997). The aging network: A balancing act between universal coverage and defined eligibility. In R. B. Hudson (Ed.), *The future of age-based public policy.* Baltimore, MD: Johns Hopkins University Press.

Kane, R. A. (2012). Thirty years of home and community-based services: Getting closer and closer to home. *Generations, 36,* 6–13.

Kane, R. A., Kane, R. A., Ladd, R. C., & Nielsen Veazie, W. (1998). Variation in state spending for long-term care: Factors associated with more balanced systems. *Journal of Health Politics, Policy, and Law, 23,* 363–390.

Kunkel, S. R., & Lackmeyer, A. (2008). Evolution of the Aging Network: Modernization and long-term care initiatives. *Public Policy and Aging Report, 18,* 19–25.

Kunkel, S. R., Lackmeyer, A., Straker, J. K., & McGrew, K. B. (2008). *N4a 2007 Aging Network Survey Reports.* Scripps Gerontology Center, Miami University.

Mahoney, K. (2004). Determining personal care consumers' preferences for a consumer-directed Cash and Counseling option: Survey results. *Health Services Research, 39,* 643–644. http://dx.doi.org/10.1111/j.1475-6773.2004.00249.x

National Association of State Units on Aging. (2004). *Forty years of leadership: The dynamic role of State Units on Aging.* Washington, DC: NASUA.

O'Shaughnessy, C. (2011). Aging and Disability Resource Centers can help consumers navigate the maze of long-term care services and supports. *Generations, 35,* 64–68.

Reinhart, S. (2012). Money Follows the Person: Un-burning bridges and facilitating a return to the community. *Generations, 369,* 52–58.

Sheppard, H. (1971). *The Administration on Aging—Or a successor?* Report to the Special Committee on Aging, United States Senate.

US Congressional Research Services. (2013). *Funding for the Older Americans Act and other aging services programs.* Washington, DC: Author.

White House Conference on Aging (WHCoA). (1972). *Toward a national policy on aging.* Washington, DC: Author.

Wright, D. (1972). The states and intergovernmental relations. *Publius, 1,* 19–28. http://dx.doi.org/10.2307/3329469

Social Services Available Through Community Settings

Case management is a process commonly characterized by a series of activities undertaken to address a client's lack of resources and required services. This chapter provides basic information on case management, primarily focusing on services frequently accessed and coordinated by geriatric case managers working in community settings.

MODELS OF CASE MANAGEMENT

Case management is defined by the Commission for Case Manager Certification (CCMC) as a "collaborative process that assesses, plans, implements, coordinates, monitors and evaluates the options and services required to meet the clients health and human service needs. It is characterized by advocacy, communication, and resource management and promotes quality and cost-effective interventions and outcomes" (CCMC, 2013b). Using a more basic and consumer-driven definition, the Case Management Society of America (CMSA) describes it as follows: "Case managers work with people to get the health care and other community services they need, when they need them, and for the best value" (CMSA, 2005, p. 1).

Case management consists of a series of activities that a case manager undertakes together with clients and, in many cases, their caregivers. Core functions of geriatric case management typically include access to the case management program, screening, a thorough multidimensional needs assessment, the development and coordination of a care plan, access and linkage to the required resources, monitoring of the services coordinated, and a regular reassessment (Austin, 2013; CMSA, 2010). Additional case management tasks often include resource indexing, interagency coordination, advocacy, and collection of data on practice outcomes (Naleppa & Reid, 2003; Rothman, 1994). Clinical case management should be considered a key intervention approach in gerontological social work (Morrow-Howell, 1992).

An extensive range of geriatric case management models exists and has been tested and evaluated during the past three decades. In her comparative analysis of community-based case management models, Hyduk (2002) classifies programs into service provider–initiated models and demonstration models. Examples of service provider–initiated models include health maintenance organization (HMO) case management, community-based long-term care

MATTHIAS J. NALEPPA

Case Management Services

(CBLTC), outpatient geriatric evaluation and management (GEM), postacute case management, and physician practice case management (Hyduk, 2002).

Demonstration projects were created as a response to problems in the service delivery system that included structural fragmentation, duplication and discontinuity of services, and lack of integrating mechanisms. Single-service responses (e.g., acute medical care, skilled nursing facilities, or home health services) alone could not solve the growing problem, which led to the development of several system alternatives of structural integration (merging funding and services into a single system) and service integration (referral systems, care coordination, and case management). A waiver program established through the Omnibus Budget Reconciliation Act of 1981 made it possible to combine healthcare, personal care, and case management costs (Quinn, 1993). Examples of waiver demonstration projects include the On Lok project in San Francisco and its successor projects (i.e., the Program of All-Inclusive Care for the Elderly [PACE]), the Multi-Purpose Senior Services Project (MSSP) in California, and the Nursing Home Without Walls project in New York state. Another set of demonstration projects, the National Long-Term Care "Channeling" Demonstrations, were started in 1980 by the federal government in an effort to direct services to elderly persons who were considered at high risk for entering a nursing home. Two types of channeling projects were implemented. In the basic channeling model, case managers were considered brokers of services, that is, their primary responsibility was to assist elderly clients to access and coordinate services. The financial channeling model, on the other hand, applied pooled funding and financial caps (Applebaum & Austin, 1990).

Another demonstration project, the social health maintenance organization (S/HMO), began in the mid-1980s. These organizations were created through the Deficit Reduction Act of 1984 (Applebaum & Austin, 1990; Quinn, 1993). Differing from many other demonstration projects, the S/HMOs incorporated acute and long-term care and covered elderly clients with all levels of functioning (Abrahams, Capitman, Leutz, & Macko, 1989). All of the demonstration projects incorporated some form of case management (Applebaum & Austin, 1990; Zawadski, 1984).

In a more recent model, an accountable care organization (ACO) is in charge of the quality and cost of care in a certain geographic locale. As professionals in these organizations, case managers can "potentiate" the success for clients of the program (Mullahy, 2014). In patient-centered medical homes (PCMH), another medical-based approach that integrates case and care management, a team of specialists, usually led by a physician, focuses on coordinating care in a patient-focused way (Mullahy, 2014)

PROFESSIONAL ORIENTATION AND ROLES OF CASE MANAGERS

While there has been some debate between the social work and nursing professions in the past over the "ownership" of case management, social work, nursing, and other healthcare workers are the primary professional reference groups of case managers. Licenses are not mandatory in all states, a growing number of employers require licenses or certification for their case managers (CCMC, 2013a).

A survey of the members of the National Association of Professional Geriatric Care Managers (NAPGCM) indicates that approximately two-thirds of geriatric case managers hold a master's degree (American Association of Retired Persons [AARP], 2005). The two largest professional groups providing geriatric case management were licensed social workers (37%) and licensed nurses (30%). Several credentials and certifications are available for geriatric case managers (AARP, 2005). The National Academy of Certified Case Managers (NACCM) confers the care manager certified (CMC) credential, and the Commission of Case Management Certification (CCMC) offers the certified case manager (CCM) credential. Both require a postsecondary degree in a field related to the practice requirements, as well as certain additional prerequisites. The National Association of Social Workers (NASW) offers two case management credentials, the certified social work case manager (C-SWCM) for applicants with a BSW degree and the certified advanced social work case manager (C-ASWCM) those with an MSW degree (NASW, 2013).

The roles of case managers and the models of staffing can vary considerably. The most basic case management staffing option is the individual generalist case manager, that is, the same professional carrying out the complete set of functions from intake through service coordination and monitoring, with a high degree of authority. The benefit is that the client has one practitioner to relate to. A second common approach is the multidisciplinary case management team approach, which combines professional expertise from various disciplines. Frequently the multidisciplinary team takes over some case management functions, such as assessment, while linkage and coordination is carried out by one team member. Comprehensive service centers that provide and coordinate a range of services under one roof could be considered a third approach. Examples of this approach can be found in pioneering case management programs such as On Lok and PACE (Kane, Illston, & Miller, 1992).

The survey by the AARP assessed the services that geriatric care managers directly provide to their clients. The most common services include finding services for clients (95%), arranging services (94%), family and social support assessment (94%), functional assessment (90%), health status assessment (73%), development of care plans (93%), and management of care plan (90%). Family counseling services were included in the service mix of 70% of the respondents (AARP, 2005).

FINDING A CASE MANAGER

Case managers typically work for nonprofit service providers, private case management agencies, or as self-employed private geriatric case managers. Common nonprofit agencies providing case management include local Area Agencies on Aging (AAAs), home health care providers, hospitals, senior or family service agencies, and other human services providers such as the Veterans Administration. Private case management agencies and private geriatric case managers provide their services for a fee, while fees for nonprofit providers range from free to integrated with other service delivery costs and fee-for-service.

Professional case managers as well as referrals for case management or care coordination programs can be found through local AAAs, hospitals and healthcare providers, senior centers, HMOs, and Medicaid offices. Several online services are available to assist in locating case managers and case management resources, for example, the websites of the eldercare locator (www.eldercare.gov), Family Care America (www.familycareamerica), the AAAs (www.n4a.org), and the National Association of Professional Geriatric Care Managers (NAPGCM; www.caremanager.org). The

NAPGCM website includes a guide for clients and caregivers on how to select and interview geriatric case managers.

COMMON SERVICES IN CASE MANAGEMENT

Many services available to elderly clients residing in the community are created, authorized, and funded through the Older Americans Act (OAA). First enacted in 1965 and signed into law by President Lyndon B. Johnson, the OAA has been amended several times since, most recently in 2006. Some, but not all, of the services coordinated by case managers and presented in this chapter are funded directly or indirectly through the mandates of the OAA. The remainder of this chapter focuses on such services, addressing the areas of personal care, homemaker and chore services, transportation, personal emergency response systems, information and referral programs, financial assistance, and nutrition programs.

PERSONAL CARE SERVICES

According to the Administration on Aging (AOA), approximately 27% of the elderly population living in the community have problems with performing at least one activity of daily living (ADL). Moreover, approximately every third elderly person experiences one or more disability (AOA, 2011). Consequently, a great need exists for services that assist elderly individuals who are residing in the community with home and personal care tasks.

An older adult's need for assistance with personal care can range from light household chores to specialized personal care. Professional and trained nonprofessional workers are involved in the delivery of personal care. *Homemakers* assist with household chores, cleaning, laundry, errands, and shopping (see also the following section). They do not provide any healthcare–related services. A *personal care aide* will assist with household chores, personal care, and ambulating. The *home health aide* may assist with household chores but can also provide personal care, medication management, and monitoring of medical status. *Licensed practitioner nurses* (LPNs) and *registered nurses* (RNs) monitor vital signs, dispense medication, and provide other skilled nursing services.

CHORE SERVICES AND HOMEMAKER SERVICES

It is common for elderly clients to need support with home maintenance and housecleaning. Problems with heavy housecleaning are frequently encountered with clients who are otherwise independent enough to continue living on their own. Several approaches can be taken to address this need. Informal support systems, such as family members or local community groups, are often relied on for help with both light and heavy housecleaning. Professional cleaning services, some specializing in housecleaning for elderly persons, may also be available. Case manager tasks include reviewing informal support systems for possible help with housecleaning, trying to enlist help from the informal support network, and educating clients about formal service options for housecleaning.

Chore and *homemaker services* are generally offered by religious groups, nonprofit agencies, and private agencies and usually require a fee for service. Chore services typically provide assistance with heavy housework, such as snow shoveling, mowing, and small home repairs, while homemaker services help with light housework, such as laundry, cleaning, and sometimes cooking.

Elderly clients are often unable to carry out parts of regular maintenance or required repairs, which can lead to safety problems and deteriorating conditions that may lead to the condemnation of the house. Common reasons for not undertaking needed maintenance include high costs, inability to repair due to poor health, and not knowing how to undertake repairs. Not only low-income but also middle-income elderly often require assistance. Types of formal assistance with repairs include neighborhood conservation programs, emergency repair programs, repair and maintenance programs, and weatherization. However, many smaller repair and maintenance jobs may be undertaken by local private businesses.

TRANSPORTATION AND ESCORT SERVICES

Transportation and *escort services* encompass a wide variety of service options that aim at increasing the mobility of older adults living in the community. Transit services range from the regular bus or train system to specialized senior transportation. The most common transportation service options include regular bus service (fixed-route system), deviated route systems, paratransit or demand-responsive systems, incidental transit, and escort services (Naleppa & George, 2013).

Funding and legal authority for transportation services are provided through the mechanisms of a wide variety of laws and regulations. The Social Security Act, Title 19 (Medicaid) regulates the transportation of low-income elderly persons to and from medical appointments. The OAA, Title 3, provides funding for transportation to senior centers, congregate meals sites, and medical appointments. Title 3 of the Intermodal Surface Transportation Efficiency Act of 1991, also called the Federal Transit Act, mandates reduced off-peak fares for elderly riders and provides capital purchase assistance for operators transporting elderly and disabled riders. The most important legislation impacting the transportation of older adults, however, is probably the Americans with Disability Act of 1990 (ADA), providing protection from discrimination against persons with disabilities, including elderly persons with a disability. The ADA mandates, for example, that all new buses must be wheelchair accessible. Fixed-route systems must be offered to persons with disabilities who are unable to use the regular bus system by providing a comparable paratransit system.

In a *fixed-route system*, public transportation or traditional transit services follow a predetermined route and schedule. The *deviated-route system* describes a transit system that generally follows a fixed route but will deviate from this route if a qualified rider requests it.

Paratransit describes transportation services that use smaller buses and vans and provide transportation to older adults and persons with disabilities. Usually they follow a *demand-responsive* approach, that is, a rider makes a request for transportation by phone and is either picked up in front of the home (curbside or at the door) or, in some cases, inside the home. Some demand-responsive systems require an advance request up to a day ahead of time, while others respond in an immediate time frame.

Incidental transit describes the transportation services provided by social service agencies to their clients, such as an adult daycare center that operates a van to transport its clients to and from the program site.

Escort and errand services are usually offered through private and nonprofit providers. In addition to personal transportation, they often provide other services as well, such as accompanied walks, companionship, and light housekeeping.

A wide range of transportation services have been described in this section. At the same time, the National Cooperative Highway Research Program (NCHRP) estimates that close to 90% of older adults rely on automobiles, as driver or passenger, for transportation. In rural and suburban areas, about two-thirds of older adults depend on driving themselves (NCHRP, 2006).

PERSONAL EMERGENCY RESPONSE SYSTEMS

Personal emergency response systems (PERS) are devices that can be activated to send a signal to an emergency contact if a person is in distress. A trained professional answers the distress call immediately, usually over a speaker system integrated into the transponder unit in the home. The responder assesses the situation and activates the appropriate emergency response. If there is no response by the elderly person, an emergency response team is dispatched to the person's home. Two types of PERS are common, a push button worn around the neck or wrist or a push-button or pull-cord device placed on the wall, usually in the bedroom or bathroom.

Two additional procedures can provide added security to older adults living at home. Telephone reassurance is a procedure in which a volunteer makes a daily phone call at a predetermined time to ensure that the elderly person is well. In case the person does not respond, a call is made to an emergency contact. A so-called vial-of-life can provide vital information about the person to the emergency responders. A sticker is positioned at a place that will be seen by an emergency response professional when entering the home, alerting him or her to the fact that a small vial with vital information such as blood type, chronic health problems, and medications used can be found inside the refrigerator.

INFORMATION AND REFERRAL

In 1965, in an effort to improve the knowledge of resources available to older adults living in the community, a mandate by the OAA, funded through OAA, Title 3-B, created information and referral (I & R) services. The goals of these services can be summarized as follows: offering up-to-date information on local services for older adults; providing information on assistive technology; assessment and linkage to appropriate services; monitoring service delivery; and a focus on all older persons living in the community (Wacker & Roberto, 2014).

Local AAAs implement and coordinate I & R services in different ways, with some offering the services themselves and others contracting with outside providers. Some communities house their I & R efforts in public libraries or government institutions. In other communities, I & R services are provided through private or nonprofit organizations.

Examples of I & R efforts on the national level are the 2-1-1 Initiative, the Eldercare Locator, and the National Center for Benefits Outreach and Enrollment (NCBOE). The 2-1-1 initiative, modeled after the 9-1-1 emergency phone number, is a program with the goal of making information and referral data on health and human services available to callers on an around-the-clock basis (Wacker & Roberto, 2014). Using the Eldercare Locator, a consumer can easily obtain information about services in his or her community by providing the ZIP code and type of need for which services are requested. The NCBOE aims at helping low-income seniors and persons with disabilities to locate and access benefits and services (Wacker & Roberto, 2014).

FINANCIAL MANAGEMENT AND LEGAL ASSISTANCE

Daily money management is a service that assists older persons in managing their finances and coordinating other paperwork. Daily money managers (DMMs) help with balancing checkbooks, paying bills, reconciling medical statements, and organizing personal records. They ensure that bills are paid in a timely fashion and intervene on their client's behalf in Medicare and health insurance matters. Some DMMs also provide accounting and income tax preparation, as well as relocation management.

Eldercare attorneys are licensed attorneys who specialize in legal services for older adults. On a fee-for-service basis, they assist elderly clients and their families with estate planning, preparing wills and trusts, establishing a durable power of attorney and advance healthcare directives, long-term care planning, guardianship, and Medicare and Medicaid issues. The American Bar Association provides lawyer referral and information services and volunteer lawyer panels.

NUTRITION PROGRAMS

Nutrition programs for older adults include nutritional screening, home-delivered meals and meals-on-wheels, food stamps, congregate meals, emergency food services, and food banks, as well as shopping assistance programs and grocery delivery. The goal of these nutrition programs is to provide older adults with a healthy diet and to prevent malnutrition and inadequate food intake. Several of the nutrition programs are administered through the OAA (originally OAA, Title 4, and now OAA, Title 3).

Wacker and Roberto (2014) summarize factors that affect the nutritional status in elderly persons as physical (e.g., cognitive status, chronic and acute illness, oral and dental health problems, medication usage, digestive system) and psychosocial (economic status, ethnicity, social supports, access to nutrition programs, advanced age). Moreover, age-related changes to taste and smell may impact food intake.

The National Nutrition Screening Initiative is a program offered by organizations such as the American Academy of Family Physicians, the American Dietetic Association, and the National Council on the Aging to improve the nutritional status of older adults (Wacker & Roberto, 2014). A widely used and well-established screening instrument for nutritional assessment among older adults is the Mini Nutritional Assessment (MNA), which comes in a 6-item and an 18-item questionnaire format (Bauer, Kaiser, Anthony, Guigoz, & Sieber 2008). Nutrition programs that receive funding through the OAA require a nutritional screening, and certain nutritional standards apply. For example, hot meals offered at congregate meals sites and through home-delivered meals programs should provide at least one-third of the recommended daily nutritional allowance for adults.

The OAA, Title III, established the Elderly Nutrition Program, and it provides funding for congregate nutrition services and home-delivered meals. Congregate meals programs funded through the OAA provide one hot meal per day for at least 5 days a week. Only a few congregate meals sites offer breakfast or dinner. Congregate meals programs can be found in a range of community settings such as senior centers and churches. Many congregate meals sites provide nutritional screening, information, and education, and other community-based long-term care services. They also serve an important social function for their visitors.

Meals-on-wheels and home-delivered meals programs are offered by community, county, and nonprofit providers. They are targeted at older adults who cannot prepare meals themselves and are not able to visit a congregate meals site. Home-delivered meals programs receiving funding through the OAA must provide delivery of at least one meal per day to the person's home for at least 5 days a week. According to Wacker and Roberto (2014), the costs of these meals is covered by a little over one-third through OAA funding and about two-thirds through other funding such as local, state, and federal sources and private donations. Volunteers deliver meals to the elderly person's home. Home-delivered meals programs usually ask for a donation and have a sliding fee scale.

Food stamps are an income-based nutrition program available to low-income older adults. The aim of food stamps is to reduce malnutrition among all low-income populations. Any person receiving Supplemental Security Income benefits also qualifies for food stamps. Food stamps can be used in regular grocery stores, and, with the exception of some items, the person can decide what to purchase with them.

Emergency food services and food banks are also targeted toward low-income populations. Food banks receive food donations from a variety of sources and distribute them to those in need, including older adults. The Emergency Food Assistance Program (TEFAP) and the Commodity Supplemental Food Program (CSFP) are administered by the Department of Agriculture's Food and Nutrition Service. Both programs provide low-income persons with basic food items such as butter, flour, cereal, rice, and vegetables at no cost.

Shopping assistance programs and grocery delivery aim to help older adults who are living independently but lack transportation or have mobility problems. A variety of shopping assistance programs have been established by communities, volunteer organizations, and similar groups. In most programs, a volunteer escorts the older adult to the store, assists with shopping, and then accompanies the older adult to his or her home. A growing number of grocery stores also provide grocery delivery. Usually the elderly person calls in his or her order or orders online, and the groceries are delivered the same day by a volunteer. Some grocery stores offer grocery delivery to all customers for a fee.

This chapter focused on an overview of some of the primary services coordinated through geriatric case management. Additional information on some of these programs can be found in other chapters in this section.

REFERENCES

Abrahams, R., Capitman, J., Leutz, W., & Macko, P. (1989). Variations in care planning practice in the Social/HMO: An exploratory study. *Gerontologist, 29,* 725–736.

Administration on Aging (AOA). (2011). *A profile of older Americans: 2011.* Washington DC: Author.

American Association of Retired Persons (AARP). (2005). *Geriatric care managers: A profile of an emerging profession.* Washington, DC: Author. http://re-search.aarp.org/il/dd82_care.html

Americans with Disability Act of 1990, 42 U.S.C. §12101 et seq.

Applebaum, R. A., & Austin, C. D. (1990). *Long-term care case management: Design and evaluation.* New York, NY: Springer.

Austin, C. D. (2013). Case management. In E. Capezuti, E. L. Siegler, & M. Mezey (Eds). *The encyclopedia of elder care: The comprehensive resource on geriatric and social care* (3rd ed.). New York, NY: Springer.

Bauer, J. M., Kaiser, M. J., Anthony, P., Guigoz, Y., & Sieber, C. C. (2008). The Mini Nutritional Assessment: Its history, todays practice, and future perspectives. *Nutrition in Clinical Practice, 23,* 388–396. doi:10.1177/0884533608321132

Case Management Society of America (CMSA). (2005). *Case management leadership coalition adopts consumer definition of case management.* Little Rock. AR: Author. Retrieved May 12, 2013, from http%3A%2F%2Fwww.cmsa.org%2FIndividual%2FNewsEvents%2FPressReleases%2Ftabid%2F267%2Fctl%2FViewPressRelease%2Fmid%2F1004%2FPressReleaseID%2F19%2FDefault.aspx&anno=2

Case Management Society of America (CMSA). (2010). *Standards of practice for case managers.* Little Rock, AR: Author.

Commission for Case Manager Certification (CCMC). (2013a). *Growing trend: Case management licensed required and paid for by more employers.* Issue Brief 1, 1–6. Retrieved May 12, 2013, from http://ccmcertification.org/sites/default/files/downloads/2011/3.%20Growing%20trend%2C%20case%20managers%20desired%2C%20volume%201%2C%20issue%201.pdf

Commission for Case Manager Certification (CCMC). (2013b). Philosophy and definition of case management. Retrieved May 12, 2013, from http://ccmcertification.org/about-us/about-case-management/definition-and-philosophy-case-management

Deficit Reduction Act of 1984, P.L. 98-369 (98 Stat. 494).

Hyduk, C. A. (2002). Community-based long-term care case management models for older adults. *Journal of Gerontological Social Work, 37,* 19–47.

Intermodal Surface Transportation Efficiency Act of 1991, Pub. L. No. 102-240, 105 Stat. 1914.

Kane, R., Illston, L., & Miller, N. (1992). Qualitative analysis of the Program of All-Inclusive Care for the Elderly (PACE). *Gerontologist, 32,* 771–780.

Morrow-Howell, N. (1992). Clinical case management: The hallmark of gerontological social work. *Journal of Gerontological Social Work, 18,* 119–131.

Mullahy, C. M. (2014). *The case manager's handbook, 5th edition.* Burlington, MA: Jones & Bartlett Learning.

Naleppa, M. J., & George, M. (2013). Transportation. In E. Capezuti, E. L. Siegler, & M. Mezey (Eds). *The encyclopedia of elder care: The comprehensive resource on geriatric and social care* (3rd ed.). New York, NY: Springer.

Naleppa, M. J., & Reid, W. J. (2003). *Gerontological social work: A task-centered approach.* New York, NY: Columbia University Press.

National Association of Social Workers. (2013). *NASW professional social work credentials and advanced practice specialty certifications.* Washington, DC: Author. Retrieved May 12, 2013, from https://www.socialworkers.org/credentials/

National Cooperative Highway Research Program (NCHRP). (2006). *Estimating the impacts of aging population on transit ridership.* Fairfax, VA: ICF.

Older Americans Act of 1965, Pub. L. No. 89-73, 42 U.S.C. §3001 et seq., as amended or reauthorized.

Omnibus Budget Reconciliation Act of 1981, Pub. L. No. 97-35, 95 Stat. 357, 5 U.S.C. §8340 et seq., as amended.

Quinn, J. (1993). *Successful case management in long-term care.* New York, NY: Springer.

Rothman, J. (1994). *Practice with highly vulnerable clients: Case management and community-based service.* Englewood Cliffs, NJ: Prentice Hall.

Wacker, R. R., & Roberto, K. A. (2014). *Community resources for older adults: Programs and services in an era of change* (4th ed.). Thousand Oaks, CA: Sage.

Zawadski, R. T. (1984). Research in the demonstrations: Findings and issues. *Home Health Care Services Quarterly, 4,* 209–228.

CARMEN MORANO
DANIEL S. GARDNER
STEPHANIE SWERDLOW

Geriatric Care Management

There is no universally accepted definition of geriatric care management. This is, in part, because the specific roles and functions of care management vary widely, based on the population served, care setting, consumer needs and preferences, model of care (e.g., private, public, independent, or agency-based), agency mandates, and the care manager's professional discipline (e.g., social work, nursing, or rehabilitative medicine). Despite these differences, geriatric care managers share a goal of helping older adults and families who face complex medical, psychological, and social challenges to access and use vital community resources and optimize individual and family functioning (Morano & Morano, 2006). Geriatric care management (GCM) is a client-centered partnership that supports comprehensive individual and family assessment, care planning, advocacy, crisis intervention, family mediation, resource and service linkage, and active care coordination (Knutson & Langer, 1998; Robinson, 2000). The model is grounded in a commitment to strengths-based, consumer-directed care that engages all members of the client system in care planning and service delivery (Doty, Mahoney, & Sciegaj, 2010).

As recently as 2008 there was little, if any mention of GCM in social work practice texts (McInnis-Dittrich, 2013). The National Association of Social Workers (NASW) has not yet specifically defined geriatric care management, but defines case management as "a mechanism for ensuring a comprehensive program that will meet an individual's need for care by coordinating and linking components of a service delivery system" (NASW, 2013). The NASW developed standards for case management practice and offers two levels of case manager certification that are accepted by NAPGCM toward care management certification (NASW, 2013).

While the terms "case management" and "care management" are often used interchangeably (cf., Bodie-Gross & Holt, 1998), some distinctions between the two modalities are noteworthy. Unlike case management, GCM often follows a private, entrepreneurial service model. Although this approach may appear to contravene traditional social work ethics that discourage making a profit from the provision of services, the model affords GCMs a high degree of autonomy from agency policies and constraints, and emphasizes the provision of high quality, cost-effective services that best meet the unique needs and preferences of clients and families. Contrasting case management programs that, for example, provide services during office hours on weekdays, client-centered care management services are usually provided 24 hours a day, 7 days a week. And while public case managers often carry caseloads as large as 100 clients, private geriatric care managers seldom carry more than 25 families (Morano & Morano, 2006).

Care management also includes expanded roles and services that are not typically covered by traditional case managers, such as individual and family therapy, family mediation, and conflict resolution (Cress, 2011). Case management and geriatric care management both begin with biopsychosocial assessment of the older adult, but the latter emphasizes a more comprehensive assessment of the consumer's familial, social, and community strengths and resources, exploring systemic dynamics and connections between family functioning and the consumer's presenting problems. Comprehensive geriatric assessment (CGA) is critical to the development of a care plan that meets the distinctive biopsychosocial needs of the consumer and family, ensures coordination of care across multiple systems, and maximizes the older adult's independent functioning and ability to age in place (Aronson & Kennedy, 1998; Hurria & Balducci, 2009).

Perhaps the principal difference between geriatric care management and case management is in their fundamental philosophies, which for the former is an explicitly consumer-directed, person-centered approach that is, at times, resisted by traditional case managers (Doty, Mahoney, & Sciegaj, 2010). The consumer-driven philosophy requires greater focus on the care preferences of the individual client and their family support system than in case management, increased access to the care manager, and a broader set of knowledge and skills to perform a more comprehensive set of tasks and activities for the extended client system (McInnis-Dittrich, 2004; Parker, 1998).

DEVELOPMENT OF GERIATRIC CARE MANAGEMENT

Geriatric care management traces its roots back to the emergence of the social work profession in the late 19th century. Closely related to case management,

a core method in clinical social work, care management draws on the legacies of Mary Richmond, the Settlement House movement, and the state Boards of Charity that coordinated programs and services for the poor and infirm (Frankel & Gelman, 2011). Geriatric care management was pioneered in the early 1980s by private social workers who sought to fill a gap in services to assist and advocate for a growing population of vulnerable older adults and their families. Although consistent with the traditional values of case management, GCM has expanded the role of case manager and geriatric social worker, and played a pivotal role in advancing contemporary trends toward person-centered, consumer-directed care throughout the life span (Doty, Mahoney, & Sciegaj, 2010).

Geriatric care management developed as a setting of practice in response to significant trends during the past half century: an expanding population of older adults living with complex physical and psychosocial needs, changing family structures and increased geographic mobility, and intensifying specialization and fragmentation in healthcare and community-based services (Coleman et al., 2004; Wagner et al., 2001). Early geriatric care managers recognized there was a growing cohort of older adults who—while ineligible for public assistance and supports—lacked access to resources that would help them function optimally and live independently. Despite having financial means, these elders were increasingly falling through the cracks, experiencing unnecessary declines in physical and mental health, exhausting their savings, and overusing costly health and supportive services (e.g., emergency room visits, hospitalizations, and nursing home admissions). In response to these concerns, social workers and nurses formed the organization currently known as the National Association of Private Geriatric Care Managers (NAPGCM) in 1985 (Cress, 2011).

From its inception, NAPGCM distinguished GCM from traditional case management and worked to establish and support the emerging field. Over the past 20 years, NAPGCM, now known as the National Association of Professional Geriatric Care Managers, evolved from a trade association into a professional organization of over 2,000 members with the primary purpose of advancing and ensuring quality in the provision of GCM (Aging Life Care Association, 2015). Toward this end, they partnered with several aging and disability organizations in 1996 to create the National Academy of Certified Care Managers (NACCM), an independent authority that developed and administered the first GCM credential based on a standardized and validated exam, the care manager certified (CMC; Parker & McNattin, 2002). Currently, care managers must possess a masters degree and hold at least one of four approved certifications in order to qualify as a certified geriatric care manager (see Appendix I).

GERIATRIC CARE MANAGEMENT SETTINGS

There is a dearth of documentation about the number of practicing geriatric care managers and the settings in which they practice (Morano & Morano, 2006). The lack of data about the extent of GCM is complicated by the overlap between case management and care management (and care coordination, care transitions, and other closely related functions) and by the wide range of settings in which GCM is provided. Geriatric care managers include self-employed solo practitioners who work out of home offices, employees of private or public, for-profit or nonprofit, institutional and community-based organizations such as hospitals, home health agencies, or governmental health and social service agencies (e.g., Area Agencies on Aging or municipal and state health and human services divisions). While there has been significant growth in all settings, the majority of geriatric care managers remain private practitioners in small, entrepreneurial organizations (Morano & Morano, 2006).

Data from NAPGCM suggest that approximately 62% of their members are full-time care managers working as either a solo practitioner or with one other care manager, and approximately 27% are affiliated with agencies employing three to five full-time care managers (Knutson & Langer, 1998). Approximately 83% of geriatric care managers work in private, for-profit settings. In addition to these solo or boutique practice settings, there has been a recent growth in the number of larger, for-profit models, and in the public and private not-for-profit organizations. As the population continues to age and the scope of practice for GCM expands to include older adults who have intellectual and physical disabilities, severe and chronic mental illness, and substance use disorders, the number of care managers and types of settings will undoubtedly continue to grow.

REGULATION AND OVERSIGHT

Geriatric care management is not a regulated field of practice; anyone who can qualify for and afford a local business license can develop a GCM practice. The NAPGCM sets standards for the credentials an individual must have to become a member of the association (see Appendix II). In the 1990s, the National Academy of Certified Case Managers (NACCM) developed four levels of certification: care manager certified (CMC), certified case manager (CCM), certified advanced social work case manager (C-ASWCM), and certified social work case manager (C-SWCM). Just as there are operational differences in the definitions of care and case management, there is also a significant difference between their credentials (Parker & McNattin, 2002). While individuals with a high school diploma and 12 years of supervised work in the field of care management were eligible to be certified as care managers, CCM credentialing required all applicants to hold a master's degree in their profession (i.e., social work, nursing, etc.).

There are currently no public entities or policies providing oversight or regulation for the practice of GCM. The only oversight is provided by state licensing and title regulations of the practice of social work, nursing, and psychology. These provisions sanction oversight of the professions but not the practice of GCM. Additional professional oversight is provided by professional standards and codes of ethics of various professional associations (Parker & McNattin, 2002). Unfortunately, this arrangement leaves geriatric care managers who do not identify with their professional associations unregulated and unaccountable.

The NAPGCM also established standards of practice and policies for addressing client or collegial grievances for its members. These standards were developed based on standards of practice and ethics from professional associations (i.e., social work, nursing, medicine, psychology). Areas of oversight addressed by NAPGCM include confidentiality, defining the care manager's primary "client" (e.g., family caregiver or older adult), and potential conflicts of interest. Consumers and colleagues can refer a care manager to the association's peer review committee to review formal complaints about violations to the NAPGCM Code of Ethics or standards (NAPGCM, 2013). This grievance process is not, however a dispute-resolution mechanism or a means to pursue legal or financial remedies, as contract disputes involving consumers are generally outside the organization's purview. As GCM continues to grow, there will be an increasing need for formal oversight, regulation, and licensing to ensure professional quality and to protect consumers and providers.

CORE FUNCTIONS AND PROCESSES

There is a great deal of diversity in the services geriatric care managers offer and the ways in which they operationalize these services (see Appendix II). A survey of the membership of NAPGCM members identified 10 core functions provided by care managers: assessment, care management, information and referral, advocacy, placement, caregiver support, education, crisis intervention, counseling, and entitlements (Knutson & Langer, 1998). Regardless of setting, most care managers perform the following distinct GCM functions:

Inquiry/Case Finding

In private fee-for-service settings, geriatric care managers often spend a great deal of time exploring the referrer's concerns, explaining GCM, and assessing the appropriateness of the service. During the inquiry phase, the care manager provides information about services and associated fees. In the not-for-profit model, the care manager might spend less time explaining why care management is the appropriate service and more time explaining the menu of services available.

Assessment. Conducting a comprehensive geriatric assessment is a hallmark of GCM (Hurria & Balducci, 2009). Beginning with a visit to the consumer's home or a consult with the family member or other referrer, the care manager conducts a thorough, multidimensional assessment of the entire client system, exploring family dynamics, constructing a family genogram, and learning about the strengths and challenges of the family/caregiver system. A strengths-based assessment of the consumer includes a functional assessment and the impact of illness and treatment on the consumer and family caregivers (Gallo et al., 2000; Green, 2002). The elder's ability to perform activities of

daily living (i.e., bathing, grooming, dressing, and walking) and instrumental activities of daily living (shopping, driving, money management) can be assessed by the use of standard measures and scales. Comprehensive assessment includes a mental status assessment of cognitive and psychiatric functioning, signs of depression and anxiety, and caregiver stress and burden. In addition, care managers assess environmental (home or current residence), financial, legal, and social needs on an ongoing basis.

Care Planning

Although there has been some effort to develop GCM protocols for specific types of presenting situations (e.g., the consumer's health/functional status or chronic conditions), the development of the care plan varies a great deal. The challenge is often balancing the consumer's wishes with issues of safety, affordability, practicality, and feasibility (Jackson, 2000). As in other forms of case management, the care manager must be knowledgeable about current community resources and entitlements, including eligibility and application procedures, and be clinically astute, creative, persistent, and flexible when developing a plan of care. Smaller case loads and more frequent contact with the consumer afford GCM greater opportunities to develop creative and flexible care plans.

Given its consumer-driven approach, identifying mutually agreed-on needs and proposing appropriate interventions is of central importance in GCM. The use of a written care plan with clearly articulated concerns, goals, care preferences, and interventions is essential to successful outcomes. Care plans that are not clarified in writing can lead to confusion and misunderstanding that eventually undermine the care management process. Creative and often nontraditional interventions can be helpful in addressing complex psychosocial needs. For example, an intervention to decrease the consumer's level of depression and increase his or her socialization may require a more social atmosphere, such as going to lunch, hitting golf balls, or shopping. Beginning with a nonthreatening, more social venue can overcome resistance and build a productive relationship with the consumer that helps to facilitate some of the more difficult tasks that may arise.

Brokering Versus Providing Services

While some GCM agencies provide their consumers with a comprehensive list of potential referrals, others make the contact and arrange for the services. Some care managers, especially in larger corporate settings, directly provide all of these services (Parker & McNattin, 2002). Each model has advantages and disadvantages. Care managers who act as brokers can shop and select from multiple service providers, while care managers at in-house, "one-stop shopping" agencies can provide a seamless and integrated network of services.

Care Management

The care management process refers to the ongoing engagement of the client in building a therapeutic relationship around identified areas of need. Private, fee-for-service models often have the advantage of fewer restrictions on time needed to develop effective working relationships, and care managers use a variety of techniques to engage with clients and families. Throughout the process, the geriatric care manager continuously evaluates progress, makes appropriate adjustments to the care plan, anticipates future needs, and provides the client and family with support and guidance to maintain the consumer's well-being and quality of life.

Culturally Relevant Services

Cultural sensitivity and culturally competent practice are central to the client-centered, consumer-directed approach of GCM. Beginning with cultural assessment, care managers explore and respect the unique values, beliefs, strengths, and needs of the consumer and family that are essential for inclusive, culturally relevant care planning and care coordination for vulnerable elders and their caregivers. A sizable literature suggests differences in access to and utilization of health and social services among the growing population of elders from diverse ethnic and racial backgrounds and older adults from different age cohorts (Dunlop, Manheim, Song, & Chang, 2002; Gardner & Gelman, 2013). In addition, GCM attends to social and cultural differences in practice with men (Kosberg & Morano, 2000), and with lesbian, gay, bisexual, and transgender (LGBT) elders (Cahill, 2002; Healy, 2002; Sullivan, 2002).

POPULATIONS SERVED

Although the majority of their consumers are older adults, care managers also help people living with physical and developmental disabilities, traumatic brain injury, severe mental illness, and a broad range of complex chronic or serious illnesses. Care managers are often skilled in working with people of all ages, and can assist parents who are caring for young or middle-aged adult children with disabilities to plan for the current and future needs of their adult child.

Geriatric care management agencies, especially the private fee-for-service agencies, serve a relatively small niche segment of the population. Given that the fee structure of the private agency can range from $75 to $300 per hour, the client population is primarily those with higher income families and it is often the adult children who are seeking services on behalf of parent(s) who have some degree of physical and/or cognitive impairment. Although there has been some growth in long-term care insurance providers offering a care management benefit, the majority of GCM services remain private pay. The lack of Medicare and third-party reimbursement limits the older adults who can afford GCM services. In addition, the need to rely on financial assistance from family members may limit the autonomy of older consumers and compromise the ability to provide participant-centered consumer-directed care. This ethical dilemma is one that was identified early on and is specifically addressed in the NAPGCM Standards of Practice (see www.caremanager.org).

SOCIAL WORK ROLES

Historically, many of the social work roles in the GCM setting are similar to those in traditional case management settings. The roles for geriatric care managers vary by setting, agency context, level of education, and worker experience.

Care Manager Assistant

Care manager assistants and care coordinators are responsible for working with the care manager to implement the care plan. Depending on the size and scope of the agency, this can involve accompanying clients to medical appointments, negotiating with service providers, coordinating care, and reconciling insurance-related issues. Care manager assistants and care coordinators generally work under the supervision of the lead geriatric care manager.

Clinical Supervisor

Clinical supervision of the geriatric care manager varies from setting to setting. The authors strongly support the idea that every care manager should be engaged in individual or group supervision, and if practicing in larger agencies, participate in weekly care planning team conferences. Care managers who are sole proprietors are strongly encouraged to contract for clinical supervision or meet regularly with colleagues to discuss cases and clinical, ethical, and business concerns.

Interdisciplinary Team Member

For geriatric care managers, interdisciplinary practice is an essential method and setting of practice (Netting, 1998). Given the fragmentation of healthcare services (Coleman et al., 2004; Wagner et al., 1999) and complex needs of older adults, the roles of navigator/guide across systems and translator across different disciplines in the healthcare team are often the most important and demanding roles of the social work care manager.

Advocate

Effective care management requires advocating for consumers with multiple healthcare systems (e.g., hospitals, insurance companies, and public agencies) and providers. Social work geriatric care managers can draw on an ecological systems perspective that facilitates active brokering and intervention on behalf of the entire client system across health and social service systems and communities.

Family Mediator

Family history, preexisting family conflicts, and the complex demands of caring for a seriously ill parent or older relative can cause difficulties that complicate family communication and decision-making. While some GCM agencies refer the client and family to an outside family therapist or psychologist, many GCM agencies employ clinical social workers as family mediators. Social workers possess the education and training in systems, group work, and family therapy needed to open communication and facilitate healthier family dynamics that disrupt client well-being.

Administrator/Entrepreneur

Geriatric care managers who are solo practitioners often perform all clinical, administrative, and marketing functions, and bear the sole responsibility for maintaining the well-being of consumers and the business (Modigliani, 2004). The administrative role includes everything that needs to be done to remain in operation. Developing budgets, business and marketing plans, hiring and supervision of staff, developing the care management protocol (clinical forms, fee structures, etc.), handling all inquiries, and developing relationships with other providers and referral sources are just some of the administrative roles that must be handled. When asked about the biggest challenge in starting a GCM business, a former president of NAPGCM stated: "Marketing, marketing, marketing." This is particularly important in a setting of practice that is still new and relatively misunderstood by many consumers and healthcare providers (White, 2004).

CONCLUSION

Geriatric care management continues to grow as a setting of practice, and social workers will likely continue to play an important role in the development of the field. Given trends toward greater development of community-based long-term care services, care coordination and person-centered, consumer-directed care mandated by the Affordable Care Act and public policies on health and human services (Darnell, 2013), GCM roles and functions will grow and become more professionally regulated.

As consumer-driven GCM models proliferate, it is likely that the public sector will incorporate aspects of care management into traditional case management settings, and roles for social workers in these settings will greatly expand. One challenge in providing GCM in the public sector will be ensuring the provision of the intensive, individualized, 24/7 model of care that currently exists in the private, fee-for-service models. But as an increasing population of older adults lives longer with complex chronic conditions and needs, the need for highly skilled geriatric care managers will expand well into the 21st century.

SUGGESTED WEBSITES

http://caremanagement.dce.ufl.edu

The University of Florida Division of Continuing Education and Center for Gerontological Studies offer a certificate in GCM, designed to enhance the ability of health and social service professionals to manage the care of the elderly in a variety of settings. The program is currently offered to geriatric care professionals, care and case managers, registered nurses, social workers, and members of other health-related professions who are involved in care of the elderly.

www.acmaweb.org

The American Case Management Association (ACMA) is a nonprofit organization that supports the practice of hospital/health system case management. The ACMA provides resources for interdisciplinary collaboration for case managers and students training to be case managers.

www.cmsa.org

The Case Management Society of America is an international, nonprofit organization dedicated to the support and development of case management through educational forums, networking opportunities, and legislative involvement. The CMSA's mission is to promote the growth and value of case management and support the evolving needs of the case managers.

www.caremanager.org

The National Association of Professional Geriatric Care Managers (NAPGCM) is a nonprofit, professional organization of practitioners whose goal is the advancement of dignified care for older adults and their families. The NAPGCM is committed to maximizing the independence and autonomy of elders while striving to ensure the provision of the highest quality and most cost-effective health and human services.

www.naccm.net

The National Academy of Certified Care Managers (NACCM) works to ensure the provision of "quality and competent care management practice," through a validated, standardized examination process that tests the skills, knowledge, and practice ethics of professional care managers.

www.ctcommunitycare.org

Connecticut Community Care, Inc. (CCCI), is a nonprofit agency that provides care management and long-term care services to chronically ill people and their caregivers, and assists them in remaining as independent as possible in the most cost-effective manner. In addition to direct services, the CCCI is a leader in the field of GCM education.

APPENDIX I

National Association of Geriatric Care Management Membership Criteria

Category	Number of Members	Rights and Criteria
Affiliate	117	A non-voting industry supporter of NAPGCM who is not primarily in the direct practice of care management as defined by NAPGCM, but has an interest in the field, medical equipment supplier, physician, etc.
Associate	592	A non-voting member who meets the criteria for membership in the Certified Geriatric Care Manager category, but does NOT currently hold one of the NAPGCM-Approved Certifications.
Certified	1011	Holds one of 4 recognized certificates* 1) a Baccalaureate, Master's or Ph.D. degree with at least one degree held in a field related to care management, i.e. social work, counseling, nursing, mental health, psychology or gerontology; 2) primarily engaged in the direct practice, administration or supervision of client-centered services to the elderly and their families; 3) two years post degree supervised experience in the field of care management OR 1) Non-degreed RNs and other individuals with a Baccalaureate, Masters or Ph.D. degree who are primarily engaged in the direct practice, administration or supervision of client-centered services to the elderly and their families; 2) Three years supervised experience in the field of care management.
Emeritus	32	A non-voting member who is retired from the active practice of Care Management and has been an NAPGCM member in good standing at the Certified Geriatric Care Manager (or its equivalent) level for a minimum of five (5) years
Fellows	37	Includes voting members currently practicing in care management. Members of with 8- years of NAPGCM membership at the Associate Geriatric Care Manager Level or higher. Holds one of the four-NAPGCM recognized certifications for five (5) years while maintaining membership at the Certified Geriatric Care Manager level, Prior to 2010 criteria: Master's or Ph.D. in any field with at least one degree held in a field related to care management, such as counseling, nursing, mental health, social work; eligible for inclusion in the NAPGCM Leadership Academy Annual Renewal is contingent on commitment to making significant contributions to NAPGCM in accordance with criteria set forth by NAPGCM
Provisional	101	A non-voting member who meets the educational criteria for membership in the Certified Geriatric Care Manager category, but does NOT have the required 2- or 3-years of experience and does NOT hold one of the NAPGCM-Approved Certifications; 2) Primarily engaged in the direct practice, administration or supervision of client-centered services to the elderly and their families; 3) Currently working on obtaining two years of supervised experience OR a Non-degreed RNs and other individuals with a Baccalaureate, Masters or Ph.D. degree; are primarily engaged in the direct practice, administration or supervision of client-centered services to the elderly and their families; and working on obtaining three years supervised experience in care management
Student	37	A non-voting member who is presently enrolled in an undergraduate, graduate or a certificate program from an accredited University or College with an interest in geriatric care management.

* Approved Certificates
Care Manager Certified (CMC)—from the National Academy of Certified Care Managers (NACCM)
Certified Case Manager (CCM)—from the Commission for Case Manager Certification (CCMC)
Certified Advanced Social Work Case Manager (C-ASWCM)—from the National Association of Social Workers (NASW)
Certified Social Work Case Manager (C-SWCM)—from the National Association of Social Workers (NASW)

Appendix II
Case and Care Management

Definitions and Core Functions

DEFINITIONS OF CASE MANAGEMENT AND CARE MANAGEMENT

CASE MANAGEMENT			CARE MANAGEMENT (NAPGCM, 2013)
Rose & Moore (1995)	*Rothman* (2002)	*Naleppa and Reid* (2003)	
Outreach; assessment of needs; services or treatment planning; linking and referring; monitoring	Access and Intake assessment; goal setting; intervention planning; resource identification; indexing; formal linkage; informal linkage; monitoring; reassessment; outcome evaluation; interagency coordination; counseling; therapy; advocacy	Identify target problems; set goals; develop task alternatives; evaluate potential obstacles select and contract tasks; implement tasks; evaluate tasks	Case Finding Assessment Care Planning and problem-solving Care Monitoring Education and advocacy Family caregiver coaching Consultation Housing (home safety and housing options) Home care services Entitlements
			Medical management Advocacy (i.e. medical appointments) Legal (expert opinion in court hearings and referral to elder law attorneys) Financial (i.e., LTC financing) Facilitator (i.e., communication between doctor, client, and family) Socialization, providing opportunity for client to engage in social, recreational, or cultural activities that enrich the quality of life.

Source: Adapted from Knutson and Langer (1998).
*Identified by more than 70% of respondents to NAPGCM membership survey as the top 10 services.

CASE VS GERIATRIC CARE MANAGEMENT

Function	CASE MANAGEMENT	CARE MANAGEMENT
Case Finding	Participants referred or self-referred	Referral sources (physicians, lawyers, trust officers, social service agencies) are actively marketed
Assessment	**Comprehensive geriatric assessment** Focused primarily/exclusively on participant	Includes participant and all members of the caring support system
Care Planning	**Person-centered and** focused on participant goals, preferences Range of support services is limited by resources, agency policy and to public sector aging services	Includes all members participating in the assessment process Participants determine range and use of services Private and public sectors of aging services network
Case Monitoring	**Ongoing assessment and monitoring of service plan** Case loads limit frequency of visits Duration and frequency of monitoring determined by agency based specified criteria	Monitoring is determined in collaboration with participant and care manager Duration and frequency determined by consumer and support system preference
Education and Advocacy	**Education and Advocacy** Access to programs provided by lead agency Advocacy is limited by agency auspices	**Education and Advocacy** Access to programs and services is expanded to broader range of customized services
Family engagement	Case managers have traditionally had a limited role in working with family members. Participant directed programs are now adapting to include coaching	Care managers advocate on behalf of participant and their social support system *Family caregiver coaching* Has always been an important activity role for the care manager
Consultation	Guided by auspices of agency Case manager limits consultation to presenting problem Limited resources at their disposal	Consultation can include the following areas Housing Safety and housing options; Home care services; Entitlements Medical management; Advocacy; Legal; Financial (i.e., LTC financing); With physician, participant, and family; Socialization; social, recreational, and cultural activities to improve quality of life.

REFERENCES

Aging Life Care Association. (2015). Aging Life Care Association History. Retrieved from http://www.aginglifecare.org/ALCA/About_ALCA/History/ALCA/About_Us/History.aspx?hkey=f87eb2d0-ab2f-4b68-9c12-b2c3eaa2fd4d

Aronson, M., & Kennedy, J. (1998) Assessment: The linchpin of geriatric care management. *Geriatric Care Management Journal, 8*, 11–14.

Bodie-Gross, E., & Holt, E. (1998). Care and case management summit: The white paper. *Geriatric Care Management Journal, 8*, 22–24.

Cahill, S. (2002). Long-term care issues affecting gay, lesbian, bisexual and transgender elders. *Geriatric Care Management Journal, 12*, 4–6.

Coleman, E., Smith, J., Frank, J. C., Sung-Joon Min, S.-J., Parry, C., & Kramer, A. M., (2004). Preparing patients and caregivers to participate in care delivered across settings: The care transitions intervention. *Journal of American Geriatrics Society, 52*, 1817–1825. doi:http://dx.doi.org/10.1111/j.1532-5415.2004.52504.x

Cress, C. J. (2011). *Handbook of geriatric care management* (3rd ed.). Gaithersburgh, MD: Jones & Bartlett Learning.

Darnell, J. S. (2013). Navigators and assisters: Two case management roles for social workers in the Affordable Care Act. *Health and Social Work, 38*, 123–126. doi: http://dx.doi.org/10.1093/hsw/hlt003

Doty, P., Mahoney, K. J., & Sciegaj, M. (2010). New state strategies to meet long-term care needs. *Health Affairs, 29*, 49–56. http://dx.doi.org/10.1377/hlthaff.2009.0521

Dunlop, D. D., Manheim, L. M., Song, J., & Chang, R. W. (2002). Gender and ethnic/racial disparities in health care utilization among older adults. *Journals* of *Gerontology Series B: Psychological Sciences and Social Sciences, 57,* S221–S233. http://dx.doi.org/10.1093/geronb/57.4.S221

Frankel, A., & Gelman, S. (2011). *Case management: An introduction to concepts and skills, 3rd edition.* Chicago, IL: Lyceum Books, Inc.

Gallo, J. J., Fulmer, T., Paveza, G. J., & Reichel, W. (2000). *Handbook of geriatric assessment* (3rd ed.). Gaithersburg, MD: Aspen.

Gardner, D., & Rosenthal Gelman, C. (2013). Aging: Racial and ethnic groups. In T. Mizrahi & L. Davis (Eds.), *Encyclopedia of Social Work, Online Edition.* New York: Oxford University Press.

Green, R. (2002). *Social work with the aged and their families.* New York, NY: de Gruyter. http://dx.doi.org/10.2307/584330

Healy, T. (2002). Culturally competent practice with lesbian elders. *Geriatric Care Management Journal, 12,* 9–13.

Hurria, A., & Balducci, L. (Eds.). (2009). *Geriatric oncology: Treatment, assessment and management.* New York, NY: Springer.

Jackson, J. (2000). *Health care without Medicare.* Lenox, MA: Solarian Press.

Knutson, K., & Langer, S. (1998). Geriatric care managers: A survey on long-term chronic care. *Geriatric Care Management Journal, 8,* 9–13.

Kosberg, J. I., & Morano, C. (2000). Cultural considerations in care management with older adults. *Geriatric Care Management Journal, 10,* 24–30.

McInnis-Dittrich, K. (2004). Social work with elders: A biopsychosocial approach to assessment and intervention, 2nd edition. Boston, MA: Pearson Allyn & Bacon.

McInnis-Dittrich, K. (2013). *Social work with older adults: Advancing core competencies* (4th ed.). Boston, MA: Pearson.

Modigliani, S. (2004). Starting and maintaining a solo practice. *Geriatric Care Management Journal, 14,* 11–13.

Morano, C., & Morano, B. (2006). Geriatric care management settings. In B. Berkman (Ed.), *Handbook of social work in health and aging* (pp. 445–455). New York, NY: Oxford University Press.

National Association of Social Workers (NASW). (2013). *NASW standards for social work case management.* Retrieved from http://www.socialworkers.org/practice/naswstandards/CaseManagementStandards2013.pdf

Netting, F. E. (1998). Interdisciplinary practice and the geriatric care manager. *Geriatric Care Management Journal, 8,* 20–24.

Parker, M. (1998). Positioning care management for future health care trends. *Geriatric Care Management Journal, 8,* 4–8.

Parker, M., & McNattin, S. (2002). *Past, present and future trends in care management.* NAPGCM.

Robinson, M. M. (2000). Case management for social workers: A gerontological approach. In N. Kropf, R. Schneider, & A. Kisor (Eds.), *Gerontological social work.* Belmont, CA: Brooks/Cole.

Sullivan, J. (2002). Notes from the field: Care management with GLBT elderly. *Geriatric Care Management Journal, 12,* 14–15.

Wagner, E., Austin, B., Davis, C., Hindmarsh, M., Schaefer, J., & Bonomi, A. (2001). Improving chronic illness care: Translating evidence into action. *Health Affairs, 20,* 64–78. doi:http://dx.doi.org/10.1377/hlthaff.20.6.64

Wagner, E. H., Davis, C., Schaefer, J., Von Korff, M., & Austin, B. (1999). A survey of leading chronic disease management programs: Are they consistent with the literature? *Managed Care Quarterly, 7*(3), 56–66.

White, M. (2004). The business of care management: Reflections from experts. *Geriatric Care Management Journal, 14,* 3–6.

LEAH MAXWELL
LENARD W. KAYE

Counseling, Treatment, and Support Services

HISTORICAL AND PHILOSOPHICAL CONTEXT

Counseling and support services for older adults have reflected changing philosophies over time. For much of the 1900s, especially prior to 1945, the prominent interventive philosophy emphasized decline, incapacity, and impairment in the older adult. The 1960s saw the passage of the Older Americans Act of 1965 (OAA, 1965), which, for the first time, legislated an extensive range of social services as rights for older adults. Since then, albeit gradually, an increasingly optimistic or positive orientation to service intervention with older adults has been evidenced.

In 2011, the baby boom generation (those born between 1946 and 1964) began turning 65 years old. These individuals, nearly 78 million strong, are reaching their 65th birthdays at the rate of approximately 10,000 a day across the United States. In general, the baby boom generation has more education, is more active, and is staying in the work force longer than previous generations (Federal Interagency Forum on Aging Related Statistics [FORUM], 2012).

Baby boomers also reflect greater diversity than any prior generation of older Americans. In 2010, one-fifth of older adults were members of racial or ethnic minority groups. However, by the year 2050, 42% of the older adult population will be members of a racial or ethnic minority group (SAMSHA, 2013c). Historically, Latino and black older adults have received less mental healthcare and accessed fewer outpatient and specialist services, despite equivalent or higher rates of depressive symptomology (Jimenez, Cook, Bartels, & Alegría, 2013). Aging American Indians are also a rapidly growing population, with an estimated 1.3 million age 55 years or older projected by 2020 (Goins & Pilkerton, 2010).

It is in the context of these shifting profiles of the aging population that we consider the range of clinical counseling, treatment, and support services available to older adults.

COUNSELING SERVICES

Because social work skill levels and practice abilities vary from practitioner to practitioner, depending on training, education, and experience, for the purposes of this chapter, "counseling services" is used as an encompassing term to describe a variety of direct services ranging from traditional psychotherapy to consumer and financial counseling services.

Classic techniques of counseling intervention include supportive counseling, where the worker uses supportive listening techniques to help the client feel understood; financial counseling, in which the worker helps the client set a budget or plan for future expenses; and eligibility or entitlements counseling, where the worker helps the client understand which social service programs, benefits, and services he or she may be eligible for. Typically, a person with an undergraduate degree in social work provides these services (Kirst-Ashman & Hull, 2012). Options counseling, a principal goal of the nation's Aging and Disability Resource Centers (ARDCs), is a process in which older adults and their families are supported while making decisions about long-term services and supports with particular importance placed on individual need, preference, value, and circumstance (Alecxih & Blakeway, 2012). Evidence-based behavioral health counseling is another form of treatment services often accessed by older adults. This type of counseling service is typically provided by a person with a master's degree and specialized training in mental health treatment.

The counseling programs outlined above are often paired with other services, including assessment, case management, referral, and care coordination (National Council on the Aging [NCOA], 2001). Sometimes peers or volunteers may provide these services, through the network of Retired and Senior Volunteer Programs (RSVP), Senior Companion Programs, or local community telephone reassurance and friendly visitor programs. Many agencies provide counseling and support services via telephone hotlines. The Alzheimer's Association, with local offices situated throughout the United States, staffs a 24-hour support and referral service for persons with Alzheimer's disease and their caregivers. The Alzheimer's Association also employs clinical professionals to provide more in-depth counseling support. The Alzheimer Disease Education and Referral Center (ADEAR) of the National Institutes on Aging (NIA) also provides telephone support and referral services for caregivers of persons with Alzheimer's disease. Both provide online support options, including current information about the disease, caregiver support, and discussion forums.

Geriatric care managers may also provide counseling services. These are commonly master's level professionals in helping professions who have demonstrated competencies in geriatric case management and who are affiliated with a professional care management association. Geriatric care managers are often self-employed or employed by a private fee-for-service organization. Many are members of the National Association of Professional Geriatric Care Managers (Parker & McNattin, 2002).

Faith-based counseling programs are also an option for many elders. Faith communities, with long histories of social and spiritual support, are beginning to consider their formal role in the health and well-being of their members. Buijs and Olson (2001) describe faith communities as ideal settings for a focus on health and health promotion, citing traditional values of support, personal skills, and social justice. Pastoral counselors and ministers provide counseling services, often on a sliding fee scale, or make such service available at no cost to members of their faith communities.

Counseling Service Locations

Older adults access counseling and support services through a combination of public and private, community-based, and institutional organizations. The counseling services system consists of private providers funded by third-party insurers and private-pay consumers, and publicly mandated, not-for-profit, and privately owned providers funded by the federal government, as well as states, counties, and municipalities. Institutional or facility-based counseling services include those provided by acute and long-term providers such as Veteran's hospitals, centers, and homes; residential treatment centers; and adult foster or family care, boarding, and group homes.

Community-based counseling services are offered in a variety of settings including social service agencies, care management agencies, senior centers, Area Agencies on Aging (AAAs), community action programs (CAPs), Aging and Disability Resource Centers (ARDCs), federally qualified health centers (FQHCs), accountable care organizations (ACOs), primary care homes, and behavioral healthcare providers (Substance Abuse and Mental Health Services Administration [SAMSHA], 2012).

Many older adults wish to stay in their home and community as long as possible as they age. In April of 2012, the US Department of Health and Human Services created the Administration for

Community Living (ACL), which now oversees the Administration on Aging (AOA), the Office of Disability Services, and the Administration on Intellectual and Developmental Disabilities within a single agency. The ACL embraces the belief that "All Americans—including people with disabilities and seniors—should be able to live at home with the supports they need, participating in communities that value their contributions—rather than in nursing homes or other institutions" (USDHHS, 2012).

In accordance with this charge, community-based counseling services are offering integrated physical healthcare, wellness and prevention activities, and behavioral healthcare programs at greater rates than ever before (SAMSHA, 2013b). Behavioral healthcare programs may include suicide prevention; evidenced-based treatment for depression; prevention and early intervention for substance use disorders, including alcohol and prescription medication abuse; psychotherapy; treatment for PTSD; crisis services; case management; and home-based "wraparound" services. Services may be offered at a central location, or may be delivered in the elder's home.

At the same time, increasing use of video, telehealth, and Internet technology has figured in making such services more available remotely. The Health Resources and Services Administration (HRSA) defines telehealth as "the use of electronic information and telecommunications technologies to support long-distance clinical health care, patient and professional health-related education, public health and health administration." While further research is ongoing in the field of telehealth to determine efficacy compared to traditional "face to face" services, the literature highlights cost benefits and increased access to services for older adults, particularly in rural, underserved areas with shortages of providers and fewer transportation resources (Alkema, Wilber, Shannon, & Allen, 2007; Backhaus et al., 2012).

SUPPORT GROUPS

Support groups are another type of counseling and treatment service available in the aging services system. The beginning of social work group practice was evidenced in the late 19th and early 20th centuries, where the focus was on mutual aid and democratic processes to change the social environment and address the needs of tenement dwellers (Garvin, 1997). During those early days of social work

practice, social groups for older adults flourished in the settlement houses, community centers, homes for the aged, and state mental institutions. Crowded conditions and limited staffing made groups an effective and efficient vehicle to meet the needs of older residents (Toseland, 1995). Today, group work with older adults is informed by a well-established theory base, range of services provided, and roles that social workers can assume.

There are many different types of groups used in social work practice. Most groups fall into one of two categories in terms of purpose: groups that provide direct treatment or service to their members and those that do not. Groups that meet for purposes other than direct service, sometimes called task-centered or work groups, are created to do just what their name implies—complete a specific task or set of objectives, not to focus on the individual needs of their members (Kirst-Ashman, 2000).

In contrast, social work treatment-centered groups meet to focus on the individual needs of the members. Examples of treatment-centered groups include therapy groups, education groups, socialization groups, and self-help and support groups. Treatment-centered groups may have an open or closed membership, depending on the needs and intent of the group. Referral to the group may or may not be required, depending on program philosophy, participant eligibility, and funding source requirements.

Some treatment groups tend to be time limited, such as therapy or education groups, while others are more likely to be ongoing, as long as members express interest in continuing the program. Often socialization groups have open admission policies, as do some support groups. Social work roles in these groups will vary depending on the needs and structure of each group. Possible social work roles include facilitator, leader, or consultant (Kirst-Ashman & Hull, 2012).

Types of Social Work Treatment Groups

Therapy groups focus on changing participant behaviors. Membership may be determined based on a particular treatment issue, age group, or location, or the profile of a given agency's client base. Membership may be open or closed. Treatment theory rationale will also vary based on group need, outcome-based indicators, social worker training, and agency orientation. Typically, the social worker may assume more of a leadership role in treatment groups, particularly in the early stages of group formation. Therapy groups with elders may focus on such topics as reminiscence, coping with loss, depression, anxiety, PTSD, or other mental health diagnosis and/or brief treatment for substance use disorders (McInnis-Dittrich, 2002).

Rather than focusing on changing behavior, education groups are formed to provide education to the membership concerning a particular issue or topic. In education groups, the social worker commonly assumes the role of teacher or trainer, often using a formal curriculum or plan of presentation (Kirst-Ashman & Hull, 2012). Examples of education groups for older adults include those teaching new computer skills at the library media lab, healthy cooking for one at the local community meal site, managing diabetes skills at the health clinic, and parenting skills for older relatives providing care to younger relatives, at the university daycare.

Sometimes groups exist to serve the social and recreational needs of their members. These socialization groups usually draw together members who have similar interests in companionship, sharing interests, or learning something new. In these groups, the social worker's role is that of facilitator, encouraging participation and active communication between members, assisting in planning activities, and gathering needed information and resources. Many older adults join travel or interest-based groups held at senior centers and nursing facilities sponsored by social work agencies, or hosted by informal older adult networks (Toseland, 1995).

Life Long Learning Institutes (LLIs) or senior colleges are another type of supportive educational group increasingly available to older adults. Either institutionally driven by a college or university, with curriculum planned and delivered by higher education staff, or member driven, with curriculum planned and delivered by older adult peers, LLI's provide a wide range of liberal arts and cultural programs for older adults, typically for modest membership fees and tuition (Brady, Holt, & Welt, 2003). Older adults reported benefits of participating in an LLI include intellectual challenge, increased nurture and support in a community, increased self-esteem, and opportunities for spiritual renewal (Lamb & Brady, 2005) while peer teachers reported the

benefits of teaching to include an increased opportunity to volunteer and facilitate exploratory learning (Choi, 2009).

Support groups meet to provide encouragement and a safe environment for members to share their experiences. Support groups for older adults may address a particular type of loss, difficult life experience, or health issue, such as widowhood, employment transition, or chronic illness. They may also provide opportunities for particular subgroups of older adults, such as older women, to strengthen their informal networks and experience a sense of personal empowerment (Kaye, 1997b). In support group facilitation, elements of therapeutic growth, socialization, and educational learning may be used separately or combined at different points in time (McInnis-Dittrich, 2002). The term "support group" is also used to describe self-help groups, which differ in their formal structure, likely having member facilitators, and may or may not follow a social work theoretical orientation. Twelve-step groups like Alcoholics Anonymous (AA) or Gamblers Anonymous (GA) are examples of self-help groups that older adults may use. In any case, the term "support group" usually indicates a group that is attentive to the emotional needs of the membership as they pertain to a particular life event or challenge.

FUNDING FOR COUNSELING SERVICES AND SUPPORT GROUPS

Counseling services and group work with older adults receive funding in a variety of ways. Private agencies provide services through private insurance and participant copayments. Many community social service agencies provide counseling treatment as part of billable social work practice, depending on state and federal regulations, through private insurance, Medicaid, and Medicare programs. Agencies may also incorporate funds for treatment groups in their special federal and state grant requests, or charge clients fees to participate.

Public Sources of Support

The OAA, most recently amended in 2006, also provides a source of funding for certain counseling and support services (USDHHS, 2011). Under Title III (Grants for State and Community Programs About Aging), part B (Supportive Services and

Senior Centers), the OAA authorizes funding for the screening and provision of health services (including mental health) and information and assistance services, case management services, and adult day-care/day health, as well as other services (Langer & Tirrito, 2004).

Title III, Part D (Disease Prevention and Health Promotion Services), provides for health risk assessments, routine health screening, nutritional counseling, depression care management, exercise and fitness programs, chronic disease self-management programs, home injury control services, educational programs on prevention and treatment of age- related disease and conditions, and counseling regarding social services (Langer & Tirrito, 2004; National Health Policy Forum, 2012).

Medicare, the federal health insurance program for people 65 and over and people with certain disabilities or end-stage renal disease, underwent many changes with the passage of the Medicare Prescription Drug, Improvement and Modernization Act (MMA) of 2003. The Medicare Improvements for Patients and Providers Act of 2008 provided increased outreach to Medicare beneficiaries, especially those classified as low-income, and mandated greater coordination of Medicare benefits information provided to older Americans. It also reduced the coinsurance payments required of Medicare beneficiaries for outpatient mental health services so that they would be more in line with the required coinsurance payments for other outpatient medical services. The Affordable Care Act of 2010 (ACA) increased access by Medicare beneficiaries to preventive health services at low or no cost and will eliminate the Medicare Part D "doughnut hole" by 2020.

Similarly, Medicaid is another federal health insurance program that covers people with low incomes, pregnant women, children, teenagers, and people who are aging, blind, or disabled. Funds are distributed to states, which then set eligibility and service provision levels. In order for states to receive federal funds, Title 19 of the Social Security Act (Grants to States for Medical Assistance Programs, 1965) requires that certain basic services be offered to eligible recipients, including hospitalization, physician services, and nursing services. States may also provide home- and community-based care waiver services to eligible individuals through the Medicaid program, including case management, treatment of mental health and substance use disorders, personal care services, respite care services, adult day health services, homemaker/home health aide services, rehabilitation, and so on.

The ACA is making several important changes to Medicare and Medicaid during the next several years that will affect the range of covered services available to older adults. One of the most important new services of particular significance to older adults is the availability of annual wellness visits. It is anticipated that social workers and allied health professionals will have an important role to play in helping the influx of new patients and continuing patients, in particular, navigate their way within an enhanced healthcare system by performing case management, health coaching, and counseling functions focused on assisting older clients plan for long-range preventive care.

Local Sources of Support

Often self-help groups or support groups will find an organizational sponsor that is willing to make an in-kind donation of space, while members take turns bringing snacks and sharing material costs (if any). Faith communities may regularly hold groups as part of their community outreach, relying on laity donation for support. While some self-help groups are affiliated with national parent organizations, for many member-driven groups, fundraising is the sole responsibility of the group.

Community centers and YM/YWCAs may charge a fee to join the organization; afterward, participants pay minimal amounts per event or may only need to cover the cost of supplies for particular groups. Typically, senior discounts or scholarships are available. These types of community organizations may also hold fundraising events and capital campaigns in the local business community, as well as receiving support from charitable organizations such as the United Way.

COUNSELING SERVICES AND SUPPORT GROUPS FOR OLDER ADULTS TYPICAL OF MANY COMMUNITIES

In many communities in the United States, a diversity of counseling services and supports are available for older adults, including disease-specific supports, health education programs, and mental health and substance use treatment services.

Disease-Specific Supports

For many communities, support groups and self-help groups are commonly available for people seeking disease-specific supports. Such groups are sometimes offered in affiliation with a local hospital or rehabilitation center as well as through community faith-based organizations and consumer-driven advocacy groups; support group locations and schedules are often published in the local newspaper. The regional Area Agency on Aging should also have a good listing of local resources.

Evidenced-based practices (EBP) are becoming more and more prevalent in aging services. The ACL/AOA began its evidenced-based prevention program in 2003 and the Evidenced-Based Disease and Disability Prevention Program (EBDDP) in 2007 to improve older adult's access to programs that are proven effective in reducing risk of disability, injury, and disease (USDHHS, 2013). Nationally recognized, disease-specific models that exist in many communities may include, but are not limited to: A Matter of Balance, a program developed at Boston University, to reduce fear of falling and increase activity; Healthy IDEAS (Identifying Depression Empowering Activities for Seniors), developed by Baylor College of Medicine's Huffington Center on Aging; and Stanford University's Chronic Disease Self-Management Program, a group-based intervention designed to increase self-confidence in ability to manage how health problems affect lives (NCOA, 2013). New York University's Alzheimer's Disease Center found group therapy intervention for couples, one of whom was diagnosed with Alzheimer's, was beneficial to both members of the relationship (Auclair, Epstein, & Mittelman, 2009).

Health Education

In the past, older adults were often not seen as appropriate candidates for health promotion and education programs because goals invariably included long-term change. As the focus of health education for older adults has shifted to prevention of illness and injury, the maintenance of present functioning, and enhancement of health, this treatment bias has lessened (See, for example, Phelan, Williams, Snyder, Sizer Fitts, & LoGerfo, 2006).

Health education programs promote healthy choices. Education may be provided through organized groups and health fairs or incorporated into existing programming. Groups may be disease specific, such as those targeting a reduction in high blood pressure or building bone density, or encompass a whole-body perspective. A general health promotion group may include sessions on healthy lifestyles and health promotion, chronic disease prevention, nutrition, exercise, and medication education (Huang, Chen, Yu, Chen, & Lin, 2002). Health education groups are found at hospitals, health centers, skilled nursing facilities, senior centers, and elsewhere in the community. Participants should always consult with their physician before beginning any diet and exercise change.

Treatment of Mental Health Disorders

For many older adults, particularly in rural areas, mental health treatment is both inconsistently available and underutilized (Bane & Bull, 2001). Although stigma and embarrassment may prevent elders from seeking treatment, many elders simply do not have access to specialized mental health services, the resources available to pay for such services, or the appropriate types of services available in the community. Service providers themselves face deficits in needed funding, lack of interagency collaboration, and chronic worker shortages. The field of social work needs to continue to attract students and professionals to the field of aging generally, and geriatric mental health services, in particular. In 2005, only 9% of a sample of licensed NASW members identified aging as their field of practice (Wang & Chonody, 2013).

Recognizing this need, services like the University of Washington Health Promotion Research Center's Program to Encourage Active, Rewarding Lives (PEARLS) are designed to identify depressed elders in the community and provide home-based services to alleviate symptoms. It is delivered in the home through nontraditional mental health settings such as senior centers and Area Agencies on Aging (Steinman, Hammerback, & Snowden, 2012).

Outreach on the part of the social worker in the form of mental health education groups or informational sessions can be helpful (Bane & Bull, 2001) when seeking to inform the community of treatment availability. The use of "gatekeepers," that is, nontraditional supports like local businesses, hairdressers, and utility service persons, can provide useful referral information to older adults they come in contact with (Bartsch & Rodgers, 2009).

Counseling and support services to lesbian, gay, bisexual, and transgender (LGBT) older adults are areas of importance in the aging field. Like other older adults, LGBT adults face changes related to their physical, emotional, and social needs. However, as Hughes, Harlod, and Boyer report (2011), LGBT adults may face not only increased health risks (for example, the long-term health effects of hormones used by a transgendered person) but also disparities in accessing elder care services, due to homophobia and heterosexism, and higher rates of mental health and substance use disorders (Kertzner, Barber, & Schwartz, 2011). Partnered LGBT older adults may face problems accessing healthcare and other financial benefits afforded to heterosexual married couples (Muzacz & Akinsulure-Smith, 2013).

Aging Veterans also have counseling and support service needs. In 2010, almost 9 million veterans were age 65 or older (Seligowski et al., 2012). While a rich database confirms the effects of wartime trauma on Veterans, the field is now starting to explore Late-Onset Stress Symptomology (LOSS). The concept of LOSS reflects the phenomenon of Veterans exposed to highly stressful combat situations, subsequently functioning well over their lifetime without history of chronic stress-related disorders, and years later beginning to exhibit symptomology when faced with special challenges associated with the aging process (King, King, Vickers, Davison, & Spiro, 2007).

Evidence-based behavioral health counseling techniques are often used with older adults to treat mental health needs. These include the PEARLS program, cognitive-behavioral therapy (CBT), behavioral therapy, problem-solving therapy (PST), Depression Identification and Empowerment Activities (IDEAS), interpersonal therapy, screening and brief intervention for substance use disorders, and screening for and treatment of post-traumatic stress disorder (PTSD) (Krishna et al., 2011; Samad, Brealey, & Gilbody, 2011, SAMSHA, 2013a).

Reminiscence, also known as life review, may also be a helpful tool in the social work counselors' practice with older adults. Life review group work with older adults reinforces a sense of life meaning and improves social relationships (Adamek, 2003).

Reminiscence can be used to help group members share experiences and weave a sense of mutual understanding among members.

Treatment for Substance Use Disorders

Older adults with substance use disorders, including problem drinking and prescription drug abuse, are now recognized as a growing population of concern. As the nation's population ages, the number and proportion of older adults with alcohol and substance use disorder problems are expected to rise.

For many adults, continuing moderate alcohol use may cause significant health-related problems as they age. Health risks linked to alcohol abuse include hypertension, congestive heart failure, liver disease, stroke, and alcohol-induced dementia (SAMSHA, 2011a). Stowell, Chang, Bilt, Stoehr, and Ganguli (2008) found older adults are also among largest users of benzodiazepines, medications typically prescribed for anxiety and sleep problems. With misuse, cognitive decline, risk of falls, and development of dependence may occur (SAMSHA, 2011b).

Ruffin and Kaye (2004) note that many older adults with substance use issues may respond particularly well to treatment practices that are nonconfrontational, focus on coping and skill building, and offer links to health resources. In this respect, group therapies or self-help groups may be particularly helpful for many older adult drinkers.

CONCLUSION

Counseling and support services will likely be used by increasing proportions and numbers of older adults in the years ahead. Leading-edge baby boomers will represent a generation increasingly familiar and comfortable with using counseling and support group services. There will be less stigma attached to their usage.

Even so, certain subgroups of older adults including older men, those residing in rural and frontier communities, the LGBT community, and certain ethnic and racial minority groups are expected to continue to exhibit lower levels of participation in counseling and support services programming. Barriers that will likely continue to influence help-seeking behaviors by these and other segments of the older adult population are the varying degrees of ageism and discrimination exhibited by service providers as well as an older individuals' need for control and self-reliance, the desire for privacy, stoicism and pride, and the tendency to minimize their problems. Still other older adults' use of counseling services will be impeded by economic hardship and geographic isolation (Kaye, 1997a; Thompson & Kaye, 2013). As the older adult population becomes increasingly diverse, such services will need to reflect high levels of sensitivity to the myriad of needs expressed and issues faced by a heterogeneous community of elders.

A positive, strengths-based, productive aging philosophy needs to be reflected in the interventions made available to future cohorts of older adults. A productive aging philosophy is one that emphasizes older adults remaining connected to their communities and the world around them. It will emphasize participatory, person-centered care in which older patients and clients have an active voice in developing their personalized plan of care. It recognizes the importance of including strategies that promote disease prevention and health and wellness promotion. Such a philosophy also reflects appreciation for an older adult's capacity for continued learning and personal growth and development as well as their need for social interaction, continued civic engagement, and autonomy.

REFERENCES

Adamek, M. E. (2003). Late-life depression in nursing home residents: Social work opportunities to prevent, educate, and alleviate. In B. Berkman & L. Harootyan (Eds.), *Social work and health care in an aging society: Education, policy, practice and research* (pp. 15–47). New York, NY: Springer.

Alecxih, L., & Blakeway, C. (2012). Deciding on care options in the digital age. *Generations, 36,* 77–82.

Alkema, G. E., Wilber, K. H., Shannon, G. R., & Allen, D. (2007). Reduced mortality: The unexpected impact of a telephone-based care management intervention for older adults in managed care. *Health Services* Research, *42,* 1632–1650. doi:10.1111/j.1475-6773.2006.00668.x

Auclair, U., Epstein, C., & Mittelman, M. (2009). Couples counseling in Alzheimer's disease: Additional clinical findings from a novel intervention study. *Clinical Gerontologist, 32,* 130–146. doi:10.1080/07317110802676809

Backhaus, A., Agha, Z., Maglione, M. L., Repp, A., Ross, B., Zuest, D., ... Thorp, S. R. (2012). Videoconferencing psychotherapy: A systematic review. *Psychological Services, 9,* 111–131. doi:10.1037/a0027924

Bane, S., & Bull, C. (2001). Innovative rural mental health service delivery for rural elders. *Journal of Applied Gerontology, 20,* 230–240. doi:10.1177/073346480102000207

Bartsch, D. A., & Rodgers, V. K. (2009). Senior Reach outcomes in comparison with the Spokane Gatekeeper Program. *Case Management Journals, 10,* 82–88. doi: 10.1891/1521-0987.10.3.82

Brady, E., Holt, S. R., & Welt, B. (2003). Peer teaching in lifelong learning institutes. *Educational Gerontology, 29,* 851–868. doi:10.1080/716100364

Buijs, R., & Olson, J. (2001). Parish nurses influencing determinants of health. *Journal of Community Health Nursing, 18,* 13–23. doi:10.1207/S15327655JCHN1801_02

Choi, I. (2009). The meaning of older adults' peer teaching: A phenomenological study. *Educational Gerontology, 35,* 831–852. doi:10.1080/03601270902973573

Federal Interagency Forum on Aging Related Statistics. (2012). Older Americans 2012, Key indicators of well-being. Federal Interagency Forum on Aging-Related Statistics. Washington, DC: U.S. Government Printing Office.

Garvin, C. D. (1997). Group treatment with adults. In J. R. Brandell (Ed.), *Theory and practice in clinical social work* (pp. 315–342). New York, NY: Simon and Schuster.

Goins, R., & Pilkerton, C. S. (2010). Comorbidity among older American Indians: The native elder care study. *Journal of Cross-Cultural Gerontology, 25,* 343–354. doi:10.1007/s10823-010-9119-5

Huang, L., Chen, S., Yu, Y., Chen, P., & Lin, Y. (2002). The effectiveness of health promotion education programs for community elderly. *Journal of Nursing Research: JNR, 10,* 261–270. doi: 10.1097/01.JNR.0000347607.68424.f9

Hughes, A. K., Harold, R. D., & Boyer, J. M. (2011) Awareness of LGBT aging issues among aging services network providers. *Journal of Gerontological Social Work, 54,* 659–677. doi: 10.1080/01634372.2011.585392

Jimenez, D. E., Cook, B., Bartels, S. J., & Alegría, M. (2013). Disparities in mental health service use of racial and ethnic minority elderly adults. *Journal of the American Geriatrics Society, 61,* 18–25. doi:10.1111/jgs.12063

Kaye, L. W. (1997a). Informal caregiving by older men. In J. I. Kosberg & L. W. Kaye (Eds.), *Elderly men: Special problems and professional challenges* (pp. 231–249). New York, NY: Springer.

Kaye, L. W. (1997b). *Self-help support groups for older women.* Washington, DC: Taylor and Francis.

Kertzner, R. M., Barber, M. E., & Schwartz, A. (2011). Mental health issues in LGBT seniors. *Journal of Gay and Lesbian Mental Health, 15,* 335–338. doi:10.1080/1 9359705.2011.606680

King, L. A., King, D. W., Vickers, K., Davison, E. H., & Spiro, A. (2007). Assessing late-onset stress symptomatology among aging male combat veterans. *Aging and Mental Health, 11,* 175–191. doi:10.1080/13607860600844424

Kirst-Ashman, K. K. (2000). *Human behavior, communities, organizations, and groups in the macro social environment: An empowerment approach.* Belmont, CA: Brooks/Cole.

Kirst-Ashman, K. K., & Hull, G. H., Jr. (2012). *Understanding generalist practice* (6th ed.) [Kindle Version]. Retrieved from http://www.amazon.com/ gp/product/B00B7L9M0A/ref=kinw_myk_ro_title

Krishna, M., Jauhari, A., Lepping, P., Turner, J., Crossley, D., & Krishnamoorthy, A. (2011). Is group psychotherapy effective in older adults with depression? A systematic review. *International Journal of Geriatric Psychiatry, 26,* 331–340. doi:10.1002/gps.2546

Lamb, R., & Brady, E. (2005). Participation in lifelong learning institutes: What turns members on? *Educational Gerontology, 31,* 207–224. doi:10.1080/03601270590900936

Langer, N., & Tirrito, T. (Eds.). (2004). *Aging education: Teaching and practice strategies.* Lanham, MD: University Press of America.

McInnis-Dittrich, K. (2002). *Social work with elders: A biopsychosocial approach to assessment and intervention.* Boston, MA: Allyn and Bacon.

Muzacz, A. K., & Akinsulure-Smith, A. M. (2013). Older adults and sexuality: Implications for counseling ethnic and sexual minority clients. *Journal of Mental Health Counseling, 35,* 1–14.

National Council on Aging (NCOA). (2001, summer). *A national survey of health and supportive services in the aging network.* Washington, DC: Author.

National Council on Aging (NCOA). (2013). *Empowering older people to take more control of their health through evidence-based prevention programs: A capping report.* Washington, DC: National Council on Aging.

National Health Policy Forum. (2012). *The basics. Older Americans Act of 1965: Programs and Funding.* National Health Policy Forum. Washington, DC: U.S. Government Printing Office.

Older Americans Act of 1965 (OAA). (1965, July 14). Public Law 89-73. 89th Congress, H.R. 3708.

Parker, M., & McNattin, S. P. (2002, August 6). *Past, present and future trends in care management.* Tucson, AZ: Author.

Phelan, E. A., Williams, B., Snyder, S. J., Sizer Fitts, S., & LoGerfo, J. P. (2006). A five state dissemination of a community-based disability prevention program for older adults. *Clinical Interventions in Aging, 1,* 267–274.

Ruffin, L., & Kaye, L. W. (2004, May/June). Alcohol and aging: Do ask, do tell. *Social Work Today, 4,* 24–27.

Samad, Z., Brealey, S., & Gilbody, S. (2011). The effectiveness of behavioural therapy for the treatment of depression in older adults: A meta-analysis. *International Journal of Geriatric Psychiatry, 26,* 1211–1220. doi:10.1002/gps.2680

Seligowski, A. V., Pless Kaiser, A., King, L. A., King, D. W., Potter, C., & Spiro, A. (2012). Correlates of life satisfaction among aging veterans. *Applied Psychology: Health and Well-Being, 4,* 261–275. doi:10.1111/j.1758-0854.2012.01073.x

Steinman, L., Cristofalo, M., & Snowden, M. (2012). Implementation of an evidence-based depression care management program (PEARLS): Perspectives from staff and former clients. *Preventing Chronic Disease, 9,* 110250. doi: http://dx.doi.org/10.5888/ pcd9.110250.

Stowell, K. R., Chang, C. H., Bilt, J., Stoehr, G. P., & Ganguli, M. (2008). Sustained benzodiazepine use in a community sample of older adults. *Journal of the American Geriatrics Society, 56,* 2285–2291. doi:10.1111/j.1532-5415.2008.02011.x

Substance Abuse and Mental Health Services Administration, Center for Behavioral Health Statistics and Quality (SAMHSA). (2011a). *The TEDS report: Older adult admissions reporting alcohol as a substance of abuse: 1992 and 2009.* (SAMSHA Publication No: TEDS11-1115). Retrieved from http://store.samhsa.gov/product/Older-Adult-Admissions-Reportin g-Alcohol-as-a-Substance-of-Abuse-1992-and-2009/ TEDS11-1115

Substance Abuse and Mental Health Services Administration, Center for Behavioral Health Statistics and Quality (SAMHSA). (2011b). *The NSDUH report: Illicit drug use among older adults.* Retrieved from http://www.samhsa.gov/data/2k11/ WEB_SR_013/WEB_SR_013.htm

Substance Abuse and Mental Health Services Administration (SAMHSA). (2012). *Older Americans behavioral health issue brief 1: Aging and behavioral health partnerships in the changing health care environment.* Retrieved from National Council on Aging website: http://www.ncoa.org/improve-health/center-for-healthy-aging/ content-library/ Older-Americans- IssueBrief1_ServicesNetwork_508_ 12JUN07_dr.pdf

Substance Abuse and Mental Health Services Administration (SAMHSA). (2013a) *Older Americans behavioral health issue brief 6: Depression and anxiety: Screening and intervention.* Retrieved from National Council on Aging website: http://www.ncoa.org/improve-health/ center-for-healthy-aging/ content-library/IssueBrief_6_ DepressionAnxiety_Color.pdf

Substance Abuse and Mental Health Services Administration (SAMHSA). (2013b). *Older Americans behavioral health issue brief 10: Expanding home- and community-based behavioral health services for older adults.* Retrieved from National Council on Aging website: http://www.ncoa.org/improve-health/center-for-healthy-aging/content-library/Issue-Brief-10-Expanding-Grantee.pdf

Substance Abuse and Mental Health Services Administration (SAMHSA). (2013c). *Older Americans behavioral health issue brief 11: Reaching diverse older adult populations and engaging them in prevention services and early interventions.* Retrieved from National Council on Aging website: http://www.ncoa.org/improve-health/ center-for-healthy-aging/ content-library/Issue-Brief-11-Reaching-and-Engaging.pdf

Thompson, E. H., Jr., & Kaye, L. W. (2013). *A man's guide to healthy aging: Stay smart, strong, and active.* Baltimore, MD: Johns Hopkins University Press.

Tirrito, T. (2004). Program and services for older adults: A national and international focus. In N. Langer & T. Tirrito (Eds.), *Aging education: Teaching and practice strategies* (pp. 1–36). Lanham, MD: University Press of America.

Title XIX of the Social Security Act. (1965). United States Code as §1396–1396v, subchapter xix, chapter 7, Title 42.

Toseland, R. W. (1995). *Group work with the elderly and family caregivers.* New York, NY: Springer.

US Department of Health and Human Services, Administration on Aging (USDHHS). (2011). *Historical evolution of programs for older Americans.* Retrieved from http://www.aoa.gov/AOA_programs/OAA/resources/History.aspx

US Department of Health and Human Services (USDHHS). (2012). *A statement from Secretary Sebelius on the Administration for Community Living* [Press Release]. Retrieved from http://www.hhs.gov/news/press/2012pres/04/20120416a.html

US Department of Health and Human Services, Administration on Aging (USDHHS). (2013). *Evidence-based prevention program fact sheet.* Retrieved from http://www.aoa.gov/AoARoot/Press_Room/Products_Materials/pdf/fs_EvidenceBased.pdf

Wang, D., & Chonody, J. (2013). Social workers' attitudes toward older adults: A review of the literature. *Journal of Social Work Education, 49,* 150–172.

A social worker partners with a librarian to add a chronic disease self-management series to the library's programming. Older neighbors engage the mayor to walk through Main Street together to identify ways to make the city easier to navigate on foot. Community leaders meet monthly to strategize on ways to facilitate collaboration among local providers of health and social services.

Despite their variety, these scenarios exemplify what can happen when a group works together to undertake a community aging initiative. Age-friendly community initiatives, also known as age-friendly initiatives, are explicit efforts among diverse stakeholders to make local social and physical environments more conducive for people to remain in their own homes and communities safely and comfortably and with a high quality of life in their later years. This chapter describes age-friendly community initiatives as a relatively new and growing area within community services for older adults and identifies key challenges and opportunities that make research, policy, and practice concerning these initiatives especially relevant for social work.

BACKGROUND

Despite prevailing cultural myths that Americans aspire to relocate to a vacation destination in later life (Freedman, 1999), research consistently finds that most adults in the United States have a strong preference to remain living in their own homes and communities (Keenan, 2010). This phenomenon of "staying put" in later life is referred to as aging in place. Aging in place has been defined more formally as older adults being able to remain in their own homes and communities for as long as they so desire, even when faced with significant life challenges, such as declining health, widowhood, or limited income.

Communities and broader service delivery systems across the United States are poorly designed to support individuals' desire to age in place. Barriers include social factors—such as economic insecurity and lack of access to valued roles for older adults—as well as physical factors—such as poor transit in communities that have limited walkability (Scharlach & Lehning, 2013). Moreover, many older adults do not use existing community-based services for reasons such as not knowing that services exist, perceived stigma around their use, and lack of transportation to get to services (Schoenberg,

EMILY A. GREENFIELD
NANCY GIUNTA

Age-Friendly Community Initiatives

20

Coward, & Albrech, 2001). More generally, there is growing recognition that the United States lacks a comprehensive system of long-term services and support, given a primary reliance on family caregivers to support older adults in their own homes, as well as limited provisions through Medicaid for the most vulnerable (Commission on Long-Term Care, 2013).

Historically, the Older Americans Act (OAA) has served as the focal piece of national legislation underlying services for aging in place. The law was initially passed in 1965 alongside Medicare and Medicaid as part of the "Great Society" legislation. While the purpose of Medicare and Medicaid was to ensure affordable medical care for older adults, the OAA was introduced to address the lack of local community services by establishing grants for states to identify, plan, and implement social services in local communities. Since its initial passage, the OAA has been amended several times to strengthen a network of community-based services for older adults, including senior centers, legal services, case management, caregiver support, and home-delivered and congregate meals (Gelfand, 2006). Today, the national aging network infrastructure includes over 600 Area Agencies on Aging, nearly 250 Tribal organizations, and several Native Hawaiian organizations (Administration on Aging, n.d.a).

Relative to this longer-standing aging network, age-friendly community initiatives have emerged more recently. Naturally Occurring Retirement Community Supportive Service Programs (NORC Programs)—which began in the mid-1980s—have been credited as the first of its kind (Grantmakers in Aging [GIA], 2013). More than 20 years later, in 2009, researchers collected information from 124 age-friendly community initiatives throughout the United States (Lehning, Scharlach, & Price Wolf, 2012). Additionally at the time of publishing this chapter, Grantmakers in Aging (GIA)—a nonprofit organization for groups making charitable grants in aging—maintains a database of over 200 initiatives (http://www.giaging.org/programs-events/community-agenda/community-agenda-database).

CORE FEATURES OF AGE-FRIENDLY COMMUNITY INITIATIVES

Age-friendly community initiatives share elements that are rooted within paradigms from diverse disciplines. These perspectives include community development (Butterfield & Chisanga, 2008), service delivery by community-based nonprofits (Bailey & Koney, 1996), empowerment (Gutierrez, Parsons, & Cox, 1998), supportive housing (Golant, 2006), and environmental gerontology (Wahl, Iwarsson, & Oswald,

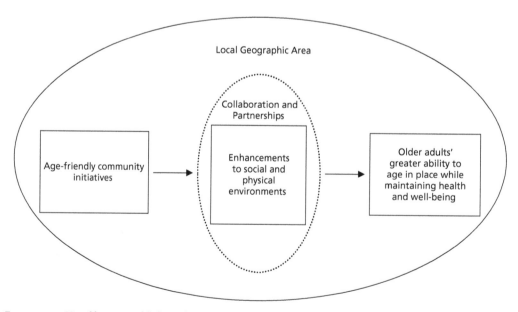

FIGURE 20.1 Visual heuristic of defining features shared across age-friendly community initiatives.

2012). Given these diverse perspectives—in addition to the relative newness of age-friendly community initiatives, the decentralized manner in which they have developed, as well as their deliberate design to be responsive to the localities in which they are implemented—age-friendly community initiatives vary greatly from each other. At the same time, core similarities unify this area. Figure 20.1 provides a visual heuristic of these similarities in terms of an overarching program model.

1. *Targeting a defined and local geographic area*: Whereas many traditional aging services are organized and delivered across expansive geographic areas—such as counties or regions—age-friendly community initiatives are typically developed within a specific locality, such as a town, neighborhood, or cluster of apartment buildings. Most typically, age-friendly community initiatives emerge within a local community—a place where residents share not only a geographic connection to each other but also a sense of identity and belonging (Chaskin, 1997). By rooting themselves within such communities, the initiatives are better positioned to engage people in actions to benefit the community as a whole.

2. *Specifying aging in place and promoting health and well-being as an end goal*: Age-friendly community initiatives share a focus on aging in place as at least one of their primary goals. Other common goals of age-friendly community initiatives include enhancing older adults' social integration, contribution, and feelings of connection to their communities (Alley, Liebig, Pynoos, Banerjee, & Choi, 2007), as well as potentially improving communities for people of all ages (World Health Organization [WHO], 2007).

3. *Engaging in deliberate activities to enhance social and/or physical environments*: Most initiatives include strategic activities that are intended to make social and physical environments more amenable to aging in place (Fitzgerald & Caro, 2013). Social environments include relationships, social networks, and formal organizations within the locality that affect aging in place, such as information-sharing channels among neighbors, the extent to which service providers are aware of each others' activities, and how organizations engage older adults with their activities. Physical environments targeted by age-friendly community initiatives include both the natural and built environment, such as prompt snow removal from curbside bus stops or changing the timing of stoplights to make main street areas more walkable.

4. *Collaborating with multiple stakeholders*: By their very nature, community initiatives require inclusion of a cross-section of community stakeholders for sufficient engagement to occur. Diverse stakeholders offer a range of perspectives on identifying issues critical to community members, as well as designing and implementing solutions to facilitate aging in place. Though community stakeholders might vary in their degree of participation, they are included in the collective ownership of a community initiative (Bolda, Saucier, Maddox, Wetle, & Lowe, 2006). Stakeholders might be private citizens, social service or healthcare providers, government officials or other public sector representatives, business owners, representatives from builders' associations or utility companies, local public school districts, and arts organizations. Engaging older adults as leading stakeholders in age-friendly community initiatives ensures that they are not viewed simply as service recipients or by their deficits, but as a resource in the community that can contribute knowledge, history, and social capital (McDonough & Davitt, 2011).

Over the past decade, scholars have developed several frameworks to characterize ways in which age-friendly community initiatives differ from each other. Bookman (2008) proposed five dimensions along which to compare age-friendly community initiatives, including (1) the type of locale in which they are implemented (e.g., urban or suburban), (2) the income level of residents, (3) the degree of cultural and linguistic diversity of the communities, (4) who initiates them (e.g., organizations, older adults), and (5) how they are funded (e.g., by public funds, private foundations, membership fees). Guided by ecological systems theory, Greenfield (2012) developed a framework for characterizing aging-in-place initiatives more broadly in terms of features through which they intend to promote aging in place; these include (1) whether the initiatives prioritize social versus physical environments, (2) whether they occur more proximally (e.g., within a neighborhood) or distally (e.g., within a larger municipality), (3) in which social institutions they originate (e.g., social services versus healthcare), (4) the extent to which older adults are involved as leaders, (5) the degree to which subgroups of older adults are targeted, and (6) whether they aim to engage older adults at specific times of life changes. Furthermore, Lehning, Scharlach, and Price Wolf (2012) used descriptions from more than 100 age-friendly community initiatives and categorized them according to five types: communitywide planning models, consumer-driven support networks, cross-sector systems change, residence-based support services, and single-sector services. Most recently, GIA summarized 11 networks that support the development of age-friendly community initiatives, noting where they have been implemented, their sponsor and funders, and when they started (GIA, 2013).

EXAMPLES OF AGE-FRIENDLY COMMUNITY INITIATIVES

To further illustrate similarities and differences across age-friendly community initiatives, four of these models are briefly summarized here: NORC programs, Villages, Community Partnerships for Older Adults, and the World Health Organization's Age-Friendly Initiative. These models are selected because they have been implemented most widely across the United States, are the focus of systematic research, and differ from each other in substantively important ways.

NATURALLY OCCURRING RETIREMENT COMMUNITY SUPPORTIVE SERVICES PROGRAMS

"NORC programs" is shorthand for a model more formally known as Naturally Occurring Retirement Community Supportive Services Programs, which is also sometimes referred to as "NORC-SSPs." Since the founding of the first NORC program in New York City in 1986 (Altman, 2006), advocates have secured local, federal, and private philanthropic support to implement the model throughout New York City and State as well as nationally. To date, approximately 100 NORC programs have been implemented, with about half located in New York. The NORC program model developed from the idea that many older adults reside in communities not planned as senior housing, yet over time a significant proportion of the residents aged in place. The model involves identifying such communities and

developing partnerships among stakeholders within the area—including older adults, service providers, building owners and managers, and local government officials—to meet local needs to support aging in place and enhance older adults' quality of life (Bedney, Schimmel, Goldberg, Kotler-Berkowitz, & Bursztyn, 2010; Vladeck, 2004).

Findings from a 2012 national survey of NORC programs provide an overview of their characteristics (Greenfield, Scharlach, Lehning, Davitt, & Graham, 2013). Most NORC programs are part of a lead organization, typically a nonprofit organization, which develops the NORC program as part of their portfolio of aging services. The programs facilitate a variety of services through a combination of professional staff, volunteers, and community referrals, such as a central telephone number to request services, health education and promotion, preventive health services, professional coordination of services, and recreational activities.

Rigorous study of NORC programs' impact on older adults is limited. A study based on a convenience sample of older adults involved with NORC programs across 24 different sites in the United States found that the vast majority of respondents agreed that NORC programs led them to socialize more, enhanced their knowledge of community services, and increased their ability to age in place (Bedney et al., 2007).

VILLAGES

Villages share important similarities with NORC programs, including efforts to coordinate voluntary and formal support systems, to enhance older adults' social capital and civic engagement, and to enhance the availability, accessibility, and affordability of existing services (Greenfield, Scharlach, Lehning, & Davitt, 2012). Nevertheless, Villages are distinct from other age-friendly community initiatives in that they are typically founded and led by older adults themselves rather than by service providers. They also are intended to be funded through membership dues more so than government funds, grants, or fees for individual services (Scharlach, Graham, & Lehning, 2012). Beacon Hill Village is credited as the first Village, which was founded in 2001 within a neighborhood of Boston, Massachusetts. At that time, a group of long-time residents convened to discuss systematic ways that they could support each other's desire to age in place (McWhinney-Morse, 2009). The Village model is currently considered the fastest-growing community aging initiative (GIA, 2013). Since the model's initial development, at least 100 Villages have opened across the United States and globally, with more than 120 in development (Village to Village Network, 2014).

The 2012 national survey referenced above also provides an overview of how Villages have been implemented nationally (Greenfield et al., 2013). Most Villages are stand-alone organizations and nearly always provide a central telephone number to access services; assistance with activities, such as transportation and home repair; and recreational activities. In contrast to related models, such as NORC programs, Village services are often provided by community volunteers of all ages.

Although there are very few studies that use data from Village members, a study in California involving 418 older adults across multiple sites provides preliminary data on self-reported impact. Results indicated that approximately 84% of the members surveyed felt that they know more people than they used to, 46% reported it easier to take care of themselves, and approximately 28% reported feeling that they are more likely to be able to stay in their own homes as they get older because of the Village. Overall, findings indicated that greater engagement with Village activities and services—such as more frequent participation in social activities—was associated with greater self-reported impact (Graham & Scharlach, 2013).

COMMUNITY PARTNERSHIPS FOR OLDER ADULTS

Community Partnerships for Older Adults (CPFOA), a national program of The Robert Wood Johnson Foundation, awarded 15 Community Partnerships (CPs) of $900,000 each between 2002 and 2010 to develop and implement a local strategic plan to improve older adults' lives (Robert Wood Johnson Foundation, 2011). Incorporating the principle that there is no one-size-fits-all model to meet the complex needs of older adults in a diverse society, each CP was encouraged to develop a locally tailored approach to plan, implement, and evaluate efforts to improve local systems to better meet the needs of elders (Giunta & Thomas, 2013). Each community created an individualized strategic plan with substantial input from a broad range of stakeholders, including older adults, social and medical service providers, public offices such as planning and zoning, and local businesses. This led to a variety of approaches to address the long-term support needs within each community (Bolda, Saucier, Maddox, Wetle, & Lowe, 2006).

Several CPs promoted broadly defined "age friendly" initiatives, while others focused on specific issues such as care transitions, workforce development, transportation, or neighborhood safety. Some partnerships planned to create stand-alone initiatives that would become sustainable on their own after support from the CPFOA national program was completed. Others planned to sustain their partnerships as ongoing initiatives under various auspices such as independent nonprofit organizations or as a program within a local nonprofit or public agency (usually the Area Agency on Aging). Aging Together, a regional community partnership consisting of five counties in rural Virginia, is an example of a partnership that has sustained a leading role in facilitating collaboration across organizational auspices to promote information and resource sharing, caregiver support, civic engagement through volunteerism and social interaction, and access to an array of health and wellness services. Aging Together operates with substantial volunteer resources and minimal paid staff (Aging Together, n.d.). In Atlanta, however, the CPFOA initiative incubated programs that would become independently sustainable without facilitation by the CP.

It is difficult to estimate the number of people who have been served by the CPFOA program. The national initiative, implemented over a 9-year timeline, allowed for each CP to hold a variety of roles in its community, including catalyst and facilitator. The national program office was flexible in its reporting requirements, which recognized each community's need to focus on assessing its process as well as outcomes. After the national CPFOA initiative came to a close, the communities continued their efforts to teach and learn from one another through the creation of a "staying connected" network, with conference calls, webinars, and a website (cpfoastayingconnected.typepad.com/). Thirteen communities of the original 15 communities have participated in this network (Robert Wood Johnson Foundation, 2011).

World Health Organization's Age-Friendly Initiative

In response to the aging and urbanization of the global population, the WHO introduced the Age-Friendly City initiative. The initial stage of the WHO initiative used a participatory research approach to develop indicators of an age-friendly city. Using the results of focus groups with older adults, caregivers, and service providers in 33 cities worldwide, WHO (2007) created *Global Age-Friendly Cities: A Guide* as a tool for cities to assess their level of age-friendliness. The guide describes the characteristics of age-friendliness within eight key areas: outdoor spaces and buildings; transportation; housing; social participation; respect and social inclusion; civic participation and employment; communication and information; and community support and health services. Using this framework, the purpose of the Age-Friendly Cities initiative is to address locally both social and environmental factors that contribute to healthy and active aging.

Following the publication of the guide in 2007, the WHO established the Global Age-Friendly Cities Network so that cities could share best practices and information with each other (WHO, 2012). Cities that participate in this global network agree to assess their level of age-friendliness, design a plan to improve social and environmental factors related to age-friendliness, and commit to implement the plan and reassess over time. In 2012, the AARP partnered with the WHO to facilitate the network of Age-Friendly Cities across the United States The state offices of AARP work to identify communities that might be eligible to join the global network. As of the end of 2013, the initiative was underway in 21 local communities across 13 states, with Portland, Oregon, and New York City having the longest history in the program (AARP, 2012). While resources for enrollment, implementation, and evaluation of initiatives are included on the AARP Livable Communities website (e.g., Kihl, Brennan, Gabhawala, List, & Mittal, 2005), aggregate data on program outcomes are not yet available.

CHALLENGES FOR THE FIELD

Despite the growing prominence of these models, age-friendly community initiatives face similar challenges that require leadership in policy, practice, and research. These challenges include concerns in the following areas:

1. *Effectiveness.* Although a multitude of innovative initiatives have been introduced in local communities for decades, little scholarship has focused on examining the outcomes of such initiatives. To examine their effectiveness, it is necessary to clearly determine for whom a particular initiative is developed, what potential outcomes are anticipated, and what processes of change are intended (Giunta & Thomas, 2013). Another challenge in determining the effectiveness of age-friendly community initiatives is that these collaborative initiatives typically take a substantial amount of time to achieve outcomes, particularly at a population level. Although there are exceptions, funders traditionally have not supported initiatives for the length of time necessary to evaluate long-term impact on communities (El Ansari & Weiss, 2006). The WHO initiative described above is one of the exceptions (see WHO, 2007).

2. *Inclusivity.* Related to the challenge of understanding the effectiveness of community initiatives is the challenge to include diverse and sometimes underrepresented community membership in the design and implementation of initiatives. Of particular importance are elders of color; those who have immigrated; lesbian, gay, bisexual, and transgender (LGBT) elders; and rural elders. All of these groups face risks of economic insecurity and social isolation (e.g., Fredriksen-Goldsen et al., 2013). Therefore, inclusion of these historically marginalized groups is necessary to promote healthy aging for all elders.

3. *Sustainability.* For the most part, the development of age-friendly community initiatives has been spurred by funding from organizations outside of the US federal government, including private foundations, think tanks, local governments, and individual citizens (Scharlach, 2012). The only explicit federal funding for age-friendly community initiatives as a whole in the United States was through the Community Innovations for Aging in Place Program (CIAIP), which was part of the 2006 Reauthorization of the Older Americans Act (OAA). After receiving over 200 applications, the US Administration on Aging (AOA) made grants ranging from $265,000 to $500,000 to 14 communities throughout the United States to

engage in collaborative efforts to support aging in place (AOA, n.d.b). Appropriations for the program ended after Fiscal Year 2011 (R. Goldberg, personal communication, 1/2/14), and at the time of writing this chapter, it is unclear whether the CIAIP will be included as part of future OAA reauthorization. Limited public support for age-friendly community initiatives—particularly at the federal and state levels—suggest challenges around developing stable funds (Scharlach & Lehning, 2013). This need is likely especially acute for initiatives that seek to (1) serve communities with fewer resources, (2) address issues for older adults with more complex and intensive care needs, and (3) remain a stand-alone initiative and not be folded into a larger organization or network of providers.

4. *Identifying and disseminating best practices.* There is still much to learn about how best practices can be developed and replicated both within and across communities, or how existing practices may be identified and examined as models for potential replication. This is a ripe area for applied cross-disciplinary gerontological research. Some questions for practitioners, policymakers, and researchers that have yet to be fully explored include What community characteristics are necessary for effective implementation of age-friendly community initiatives? Is it possible to identify and match specific models with particular communities? How can diverse stakeholders within communities develop successful collaborations and partnerships? How are communities teaching and learning from each other about their successes and challenges? What models and frameworks used in sectors or disciplines less traditionally aligned with aging could help inform the design and implementation of age-friendly community initiatives?

OPPORTUNITIES FOR SOCIAL WORK

The role of social workers in age-friendly community initiatives has not been systematically examined. Nevertheless, because age-friendly community initiatives are typically led by public and nonprofit organizations, where social workers often work, the initiatives are likely to become an increasingly salient employment setting for social workers with expertise in health and aging. Moreover, many of the principles of age-friendly community initiatives fit ideally with core social work values and orientations. These principles include:

1. *A strengths-based perspective.* Social work's strengths perspective encourages placing individuals' and groups' talents, aspirations, and potential at the forefront of practice and, in the process, addressing problems (Weick & Chamberlain, 1997). Age-friendly community initiatives draw on this insight in practice by offering an alternative to longer-standing formal systems of care for older adults, which have been designed in large part to respond to crises and address individuals' unmet needs (Vladeck, 2004). Implicit in age-friendly community initiatives is the idea that communities—both in terms of their physical design and the social relationships embedded within them—have the potential to become even better places for aging in place. Moreover, many of the initiatives' inclusion of older adults as partners and leaders of community change exemplifies not only a strengths perspective but also processes of empowerment(McDonough & Davitt, 2011). At the community level, the impact of age-friendly community initiatives on enhancing community strengths can be long-lasting, even after start-up funding subsides. For example, the Age-Friendly New York City initiative (one of the WHO/AARP Age-Friendly Communities) introduced "senior hours" at a local public swimming pool in East Harlem by partnering with the New York City Department of Parks and Recreation. Given the popularity of the program, senior hours were added to 14 other pools citywide. This change demonstrates how age-friendly community initiatives can build strengths beyond the projected scope or timeline of an initial project when they can be incorporated into the existing infrastructure of communities.

2. *Focus on social relationships.* One of social work's core values, as articulated by the National Association of Social Work's Code of Ethics (2008), is the centrality of human relationships within processes of change. Age-friendly community initiatives rely on strengthening relationships among various people—including older adults, service providers, government officials, and

other community volunteers—to enhance the well-being of individuals, organizations, and communities alike (Giunta & Thomas, 2013; Greenfield, 2013). Social workers' expertise in bridging people and organizations from different backgrounds is especially apropos for the diverse range of collaborations that age-friendly community initiatives typically involve.

3. *Diverse levels of practice.* Social work is known for its diverse range of activities across all levels of person–environment systems. Using Zastrow's (2010) framework on three types of social work practice, age-friendly community initiatives demand professionals who are skilled across these domains:

- Micro-level practice involves working one-on-one with an individual, such as through counseling or casework. Social workers in age-friendly community initiatives that have a direct service component—such as NORC programs and Villages—are especially likely to utilize direct practice skills.

- Mezzo-level practice involves working with families and other small groups. Age-friendly community initiatives typically include a variety of groups, such as social activities for older adults, partners' groups, coalitions, and advisory committees. Social workers can use group work skills to facilitate and lead these diverse groups.

- Macro-level practice involves work with larger groups, such as organizations and communities as a whole, as well as pursuing changes in social policies. Social workers' expertise at community organizing and nonprofit management is essential for planning, implementing, and sustaining age-friendly community initiatives. Social workers are well poised to become involved with age-friendly community initiatives not only one community at a time, but also to advance this field more broadly, such as by contributing to research on the field as a whole and by engaging in local and national policy advocacy to support the expansion and maintenance of the models.

4. *Serving as a vehicle for innovation in service delivery.* Social workers are responsible for responding to contexts—such as changing demographics within communities as well as scientific and technological developments—that influence practice and the effectiveness of service delivery systems (Council on Social Work Education, 2008). Age-friendly community initiatives are purposefully designed to be responsive to changing circumstances within a local community. Social workers' sensitivity to both local and broader trends within aging services—such as the nationwide development of evidence-based programs to promote older adults' health and well-being—and within the older population—such as its growing racial/ethnic diversity—is well suited for age-friendly community initiatives that must respond to these shifting circumstances.

In summary, it is both the challenges and opportunities surrounding age-friendly community initiatives that make this area of research, policy, and practice a relevant and critical area for social work leadership. Social work's unique attention to individual well-being within a social context makes it essential that the profession work collaboratively with other disciplines to optimize the potential of these models on behalf of aging individuals, families, and communities locally and beyond.

REFERENCES

AARP (2012). *AARP's network of age-friendly communities: An institutional affiliate of the WHO global network of age-friendly cities and communities.* http://www.aarpinternational.org/events/agefriendly2012

Administration on Aging (AOA). (n.d.a). *Older Americans Act.* Retrieved January 24, 2014, from http://www.aoa.gov/AOA_programs/OAA/

Administration on Aging (AOA). (n.d.b). *Community innovations for aging in place.* Retrieved January 24, 2014, from http://www.aoa.gov/AoA_programs/HCLTC/CIAIP/index.aspx

Aging Together. (n.d.). *Aging together: Five communities creating choices.* Retrieved January 24, 2014, from http://www.agingtogether.org/

Alley, D., Liebig, P., Pynoos, J., Banerjee, T., & Choi, I. H. (2007). Creating elder-friendly communities: Preparations for an aging society. *Journal of Gerontological Social Work, 49,* 1–18. doi:10.1300/J083v49n01_01

Altman, A. (2006). The New York NORC-Supportive Service Program. *Journal of Jewish Communal Services, 81,* 195–200.

Bailey, D., & Koney, K. M. (1996). Interorganizational community-based collaboratives: A strategic response to shape the social work agenda. *Social Work, 41*, 602–611. doi:10.1093/sw/41.6.602

Bedney, B. J., Goldberg, R. B., & Josephson, K. (2010). Aging in place in naturally occurring retirement communities: Transforming aging through supportive service programs. *Journal of Housing for the Elderly, 24*, 304–321. doi:10.1080/02763893.2010.522455

Bedney, B. J., Schimmel, D., Goldberg, R., Kotler-Berkowitz, L., & Bursztyn, D. (2007). *Rethinking aging in place: Exploring the impact of NORC Supportive Service Programs on older adult participants*. http://www.norcs.org/local_includes/downloads/19711.pdf

Bolda, E. J., Saucier, P., Maddox, G. L., Wetle, T., & Lowe, J. I. (2006). Governance and management structures for community partnerships: Experiences from the Robert Wood Johnson Foundation's community partnerships for older adults program. *The Gerontologist, 46*, 391–397. doi:10.1093/geront/46.3.391

Bookman, A. (2008). Innovative models of aging in place: Transforming our communities for an aging population. *Community, Work and Family, 11*, 419–438. doi:10.1080/13668800802362334

Butterfield, A. K., & Chisanga, B. (2008). Community development. In T. Mizrahi & L. E. Davis (Eds.), *Encyclopedia of social work* (20th ed., Vol. 1, pp. 375–381). Washington, DC, and New York: NASW Press and Oxford University Press.

Chaskin, R. J. (1997). Perspectives on neighborhood and community: A review of the literature. *Social Services Review, 71*, 521–547. doi:10.1086/604277

Commission on Long-Term Care. (2013). *Report to the Congress*. http://ltccommission.lmp01.lucidus.net/wp-content/uploads/2013/12/Commission-on-Long-Term-Care-Final-Report-9-26-13.pdf

Council on Social Work Education. (2008). *Educational policy and accreditation standards*. Retrieved from http://www.cswe.org/File.aspx?id=13780

El Ansari, W., & Weiss, E. S. (2006). Quality of research on community partnerships: Developing the evidence base. *Health Education Research Theory and Practice, 21*, 175–180. doi:10.1093/her/cyh051

Fitzgerald, K. G., & Caro, F. G. (2013). An overview of age-friendly cities and communities around the world. *Journal of Aging and Social Policy*. Online advance access. doi:10.1080/08959420.2014.860786

Fredriksen-Goldsen, K. I., Emlet, C. A., Kim, H.-J., Muraco, A., Erosheva, E. A., Goldsen, J., & Hoy-Ellis, C. P. (2013). The physical and mental health of lesbian, gay male and bisexual (LGB) older adults: The role of key health indicators and risk and protective factors. *The Gerontologist, 53*, 664–675. Advance online publication. doi:10.1093/geront/gns123

Freedman, M. (1999). *Prime time: How baby boomers will revolutionize retirement and transform America*. Cambridge, MA: Perseus Books Group.

Gelfand, D. E. (2006). *The aging network: Programs and services* (6th ed.). New York, NY: Springer.

Giunta, N., & Thomas, M. L. (2013). Integrating assessment and evaluation into partnership initiatives: Lessons from the Community Partnerships for Older Adults. *Journal of Applied Gerontology*. Online advance access. doi:10.1177/0733464813487587

Golant, S. M. (2006). Supportive housing for frail, low-income older adults: Identifying needs and allocating resources. *Generations, 29*, 37–43.

Graham, C. L., & Scharlach, A. E. (2013, November). *Village research: Previous findings, current projects, and future directions*. Paper presented at a pre-conference workshop for the annual meeting of the Gerontological Society of America.

Grantmakers in Aging (GIA). (2013). *Age-friendly communities: The movement to create great places to grow up and grow old in America*. http://www.giaging.org/programs-events/community-agenda/community-agenda-resources

Greenfield, E. A. (2012). Using ecological frameworks to advance a field of research, practice and policy on aging-in-place initiatives. *The Gerontologist, 52*, 1–12. doi:10.1093/geront/gnr108

Greenfield, E. A. (2013). Community aging initiatives and social capital: Developing theories of change in the context of NORC Supportive Service Programs. *Journal of Applied Gerontology*. Online advance access. doi:10.1177/0733464813497994

Greenfield, E. A., Scharlach, A., Lehning, A. J., & Davitt, J. K. (2012). A conceptual framework for examining the promise of the NORC program and Village models to promote aging in place. *Journal of Aging Studies, 26*, 273–284. doi:10.1016/j.jaging.2012.01.003

Greenfield, E. A., Scharlach, A. E., Lehning, A. J., Davitt, J. K., & Graham, C. L. (2013). A tale of two community initiatives for promoting aging in place: Similarities and differences in the national implementation of NORC programs and Villages. *The Gerontologist, 53*, 928–938. doi:10.1093/geront/gnt035

Gutierrez, L. M., Parsons, R., & Cox, E. O. (1998). *Empowerment in social work practice: A sourcebook*. Pacific Grove, CA: Brooks/Cole.

Keenan, T. A. (2010). *Home and community preferences of the 45+ population*. Washington, DC: AARP.

Kihl, M., Brennan, D., Gabhawala, N., List, J., & Mittal, P. (2005). *Livable communities: An evaluation guide.* http://assets.aarp.org/rgcenter/il/d18311_communities.pdf

Lehning, A. J., Scharlach, A. E., & Price Wolf, J. (2012). An emerging typology of community aging initiatives. *Journal of Community Practice, 20,* 293–316. doi:10.1080/10705422.2012.700175

McDonough, K., & Davitt, J. (2011). It takes a village: Community practice, social work and aging-in-place. *Journal of Gerontological Social Work, 54,* 528–541. doi:10.1080/01634372.2011.581744

McWhinney-Morse, S. (2009). Beacon Hill Village. *Generations, 33,* 85–86.

National Association of Social Workers. (2008). *Code of ethics of the National Association of Social Workers.* Washington, DC: NASW Press.

Robert Wood Johnson Foundation. (2011). *Community partnerships for older adults: An RWJF national program, program results report.* Retrieved from http://www.rwjf.org/content/dam/farm/reports/program_results_reports/2011/rwjf71882

Scharlach, A. E. (2012). Creating aging-friendly communities in the United States. *Ageing International, 37,* 25–38. doi:10.1007/s12126-011-9140-1

Scharlach, A. E., Graham, C. L., & Lehning, A. J. (2012). The "Village" model: A consumer-driven approach for aging-in-place. *The Gerontologist, 52,* 418–427. doi:10.1093/geront/gnr083

Scharlach, A. E., & Lehning, A. J. (2013). Ageing-friendly communities and social inclusion in the United States of America. *Ageing and Society, 33,* 110–136. doi:10.1017/S0144686X12000578

Schoenberg, N. E., Coward, R. T., & Albrech, S. L. (2001). Attitudes of older adults about community-based services: Emergent themes from in-depth interviews. *Journal of Gerontological Social Work, 35,* 3–19. doi:10.1300/J083v35n04_02

Village to Village Network. (2014). *About VtV Network.* Retrieved from http://www.vtvnetwork.org/content.aspx?page_id=22&club_id=691012&module_id=65139

Vladeck, F. (2004). *A good place to grow old: New York's model for NORC supportive service programs.* New York, NY: United Hospital Fund.

Wahl, H.-W., Iwarson, S., & Oswald, F. (2012). Aging well and the environment: Toward an integrative model and a research agenda for the future. *The Gerontologist, 1,* 306–313. doi:10.1093/geront/gnr154.

Weick, A., & Chamberlain, R. (1997). Putting problems in their place: Further exploration in the strengths perspective. In D. Saleebey (Ed.), *The strengths perspective in social work practice* (2nd ed., pp. 39–48). New York: Longman.

World Health Organization (WHO). (2007). *Global age-friendly cities: A guide.* Geneva, Switzerland: Author.

World Health Organization (WHO). (2012). *Good health adds life to years: Global brief for World Health Day 2012.* Geneva, Switzerland: Author.

Zastrow, C. (2010). *The practice of social work: A comprehensive worktext* (9th ed.). Belmont, CA: Brooks/Cole, Cenage Learning.

JUDITH G. GONYEA

Housing, Health, and Quality of Life

21

Housing, or the need for shelter, is one of our most basic human needs. For most people, however, housing is about much more than a physical space or structure. Rather, a home serves multiple functions and has a deeper meaning. A home offers individuals a safe haven and protection from the intrusion of the outside world. One's home and neighborhood are a crucial piece of one's self-identity and evoke a sense of belonging. For many older adults, a home is a highly cherished symbol of their independence and dignity (Rowles & Chaudhury, 2005).

Achieving a "secure old age" for most Americans depends on three pillars: an adequate retirement income, quality healthcare, and appropriate and affordable housing. However, many of the nation's housing policies and programs for older Americans have been developed and implemented with little reference to this population's healthcare or supportive service needs. This disconnect between the two fields of healthcare and housing, particularly the failure of our nation to develop an affordable and effective community-based, long-term care system, has placed some older citizens at risk of losing their homes and, for others, led to their being inappropriately housed and/or facing premature institutionalization.

This chapter focuses primarily on older adults living in the community in conventional housing—either as homeowners or renters—which is where the vast majority of America's seniors reside. A key theme emphasized throughout this chapter is that the diversity of America's senior population requires a wide range of dwelling types and assistive supports that meet or match their household sizes, budgets, and physical, cognitive, and/or mobility limitations. Despite the historical disconnect between the two fields—healthcare and housing—several recent trends suggest grounds for optimism. There does appear to be growing recognition that our nation must pursue a more comprehensive or holistic approach to protecting older citizens' health and housing security if we are to ensure America's seniors a safe, secure, and dignified old age. Social workers can play a pivotal role through advocacy on both the clinical and macro levels in promoting affordable and appropriate housing options that maximize all older Americans' ability to "age successfully" and achieve their full potential.

DEMOGRAPHIC TRENDS, HOUSING, AND "AGING IN PLACE"

Central to "successful aging" is having appropriate and affordable housing. The dramatic growth in America's older population has drawn attention to the challenges our nation will confront in meeting seniors' housing needs both now and in the near-term future. One in every eight Americans is currently age 65 or older; however by 2030 demographers estimate that 72 million individuals, or almost one if every five Americans, will be among the ranks of the elderly. Further, it is the oldest-old whose numbers are growing the fastest. By 2050, the oldest-old will make up 24 percent of older Americans and 5% of all Americans (Federal Interagency Forum on Aging-Related Statistics [FIRARS], 2012).

These longevity gains will profoundly affect America's housing market, as chronic health conditions, which lead to a loss of function and mobility, increase with age. Although only about 18% of persons ages 65 to 74 living in the community report difficulty with functional limitations such as the ability to walk or climb stairs, 31% of persons 75 to 84 and 54% of persons age 85 and older residing in the community report having at least one functional limitation (Congressional Budget Office, 2013). Thus, for many older Americans, particularly the oldest-old, the aging process will bring changing realities in personal health, functional abilities, and necessary living accommodations. This will have important implications for the housing industry and housing policy and will undoubtedly require the attention of federal, state, and local planners.

Income disparities present among today's older population will unfortunately continue to exist as the baby boom generation ages. Currently 9% of older Americans are living in poverty, although women and persons of color face a much greater risk of poverty in old age than do White men. For both genders and across all racial/ethnic groups, the risk of poverty increases with advanced age (i.e., 75 and older) and living alone (FIFARS, 2012). The interactive effects of gender, race, and living arrangement on poverty risk are underscored by the fact older Asian, Black, and Hispanic women living alone are the most economically vulnerable (Gonyea, 2005). About 3 out of every 10 older Asian and Black women and 4 out of every 10 older Hispanic women living alone fell below the official federal poverty line in 2010 (FIFARS, 2012).

Recognizing the diversity of America's graying population is important, as seniors' housing choices vary by characteristics such as age, income, race/ethnicity, marital status, availability of children, and need for assistance. Yet, despite the heterogeneity of America's older population, research has consistently shown that our nation's seniors overwhelmingly prefer to remain in their longtime homes. The AARP has consistently found that about 85% want to *age in place*—that is, they wish to stay in their own homes and, if that is not possible, at least remain within their communities as they grow older (AARP, 2010). Collectively, these surveys suggest that we must work to transform our local communities to become more aging-friendly or livable communities that meet the needs of residents of all ages—from the very young to the very old.

The concept of aging in place was adopted originally as a strategy to prevent the premature or inappropriate institutionalization of older adults; thus, the focus was primarily on the reconfiguration of seniors' physical space or services so that they could live safely and comfortably within their own homes. In recent years, however, the aging-in-place lens has been broadened to include the development of community-wide responses, which create a comprehensive array of programs and services offering seniors the opportunity to maximize their social engagement. In essence, the aging-in-place perspective now recognizes that while a home is one's anchor, we must look beyond it to how the senior in that home is able to connect to his or her neighborhood and community (Gonyea & Burnes, 2013).

The majority of American cities and towns, however, have not engaged in strategic plans to address the implications of this aging demographic shift. This lack of preparedness was documented in the 2005 national survey, *The Maturing of America: Getting Communities on Track for an Aging Population.* Less than half (46%) of the responding local communities indicated that they had started planning to address the needs of their future aging populations, including their housing needs (National Association of Area Agencies on Aging, 2007). Replicated in 2010, *The Maturing of America II* survey revealed that, as a result of the nation's weak economy, the majority of localities identified "only limited progress" in advancing the goal of creating more aging-friendly communities. Many cited only being able to "hold the line" in maintaining existing programs and services (National Association of Area Agencies in Aging,

2011). Yet, despite current fiscal challenges, there is a growing movement toward the adoption of a broader aging-in-the-community or an aging-friendly community orientation.

HOW AMERICAN SENIORS ARE HOUSED

As previously noted, national data underscore that the vast majority of older Americans reside in conventional housing—that is, in their own homes or apartments within their community versus in age-restricted senior communities or assisted living residences. Similarly, only a very small percentage of the nation's seniors currently live in skilled nursing facilities, although this figure does rise dramatically with advanced old age. Only 1.1% of persons ages 65 to 74 and 3.5% of persons ages 75 to 84 reside in nursing homes; however, 13.2% of persons age 85 and older are nursing home residents (Administration on Aging, 2012). Burr and Mutcher (2007) explored the influence of individual and community factors on residential independence among older adults using two waves of the National Survey of Families and Households. Their results revealed that, in terms of individual-level variables, older adults with better functional status, greater economic resources, and more children were better able to maintain their independence and less likely to live or die in a nursing home. Yet, they also found that residing in areas that had higher levels of geriatric health services, net other contextual or individual characteristics, also increased the likelihood of an elder's independence. Thus, their study suggests the importance of expanding micro-level approaches to understanding seniors' community living arrangements to include an assessment of macro- or community-level factors.

Of the 25.1 million US households headed by older adults (defined as age 65 or older) in 2011, slightly more than one-quarter were found in central cities, approximately half were in the suburbs, and slightly less than one-quarter were in rural areas. Nationally, about three out of four older households resided in single-family homes, about one in five lived in multiunit structures, and approximately one in 20 lived in mobile or manufactured homes (US Census Bureau, 2013a). A sizable proportion, 28% of community-based older adults, lived alone or in one-person households in 2011; however, there was a significant gender difference, and chance of living alone rose dramatically with age. Among individuals age 75 and older, approximately 23% of men and 47% of women lived alone.

The nation's older population has a very high rate of homeownership; of US households headed by seniors (age 65-plus) in 2011, 81% were homeowners and 19% were renters (Administration on Aging, 2012). Housing, therefore, represents a central component of the financial portfolios of many older Americans; the median housing equity for older homeowners in 2011 was $125,000 (Engelhardt, Ericksen, & Greenhalgh-Stanley, 2013). Significant racial disparities exist in home ownership rates across the life course, with Whites having a higher rate of homeownership compared with African Americans in all age groups. The impacts of cumulative or lifelong disadvantage on homeownership become evident in a comparison of the background characteristics of these two groups of older Americans: owners and renters. Older owners are more often White and married, possess more years of formal education, and have greater annual household incomes than older renters (Engelhardt et al., 2013). Although African Americans currently represent only 8.5% of the US total older population, they disproportionately make up 20% of older US renters. In stark contrast to older homeowners, 68% of older renters were not married, 27% were high school dropouts, and their median annual household income was $16,582 in 2011 (Engelhardt et al., 2013).

Older renters are viewed as primarily consisting of two groups: individuals with a lifetime of low income and often never having owned a home; and, wealthier individuals with prior home ownership who now are renting. Some of the nation's most vulnerable seniors live in public or subsidized rental housing. Slightly more than 6% of older renters currently live in these subsidized units; in fact, more than one-third of the households receiving Housing and Urban Development (HUD) assistance are headed by an older person (defined by HUD as age 62 or older). Elders in subsidized housing are disproportionately African American (38%) and Hispanic (16%), relative to their representation in the US older population. Most public housing tenants live alone and have very limited economic resources; the average reported income of older applicants for subsidized rental units is only about $10,000 (Parsons, Mezuk, Ratliff, & Lapane, 2011).

Chronic health problems are also more prevalent among elders in public housing. Their rate of disability is twice that of other community-dwelling seniors, with more than half of elders in subsidized housing reporting difficulty with daily activities compared with about one-quarter of older adults in other independent community settings (Redfoot & Kochera, 2004). Faced with few housing options, most older public housing residents age in place. Fifteen percent of senior public housing households are headed by someone age 85 or older compared with 9% of households nationwide. Research suggests, however, that a significant proportion of elders in federally subsidized housing may be exiting prematurely into nursing homes primarily due to minimal economic resources, particularly those in the Housing Choice Voucher Program (Parsons et al., 2011).

Residential mobility declines throughout our lives; only about 3% of seniors change residences in any given year (US Census Bureau, 2013b). In 2011, the median length of time older homeowners had lived in their current home was 24 years, almost a quarter of a century. Aging in place means that the housing stock in which seniors live is also aging; yet, the majority of seniors live in dwellings that are in good condition. The American Housing Survey (AHS) does, however, identify a segment of the 65-and-older households that are "at risk" in terms of their housing costs and quality. Approximately 11% of older owners and 22% of older renters were defined by HUD as having "priority problems," as determined by paying more than 50% of their monthly income on their housing costs or occupying dwellings with "severe physical problems" in 2011. Another 19% of older owners and 32% of older renters were labeled by HUD as having "moderate problems," defined as a housing cost burden of 30% to 49% of their monthly income or occupying dwellings with "moderate physical problems" in 2011 (US Census Bureau, 2013a).

The interrelationship between the aging individual and his or her aging dwelling can create or exacerbate health problems. As Lawler (2001) notes, a circular relationship exists between health and housing:

When a living environment is affordable and appropriate, an aging individual is more likely to remain healthy and independent. When an individual maintains good health, he or she is more able to keep up with the maintenance of his or her living environment. As the

population ages in an aging housing stock, it becomes difficult to distinguish a health concern from a housing concern. (p. 1)

Poor health and a fixed income may result in an older homeowner or renter being unable to perform and/or purchase home repairs, while substandard housing conditions may further compromise an individual's health. For example, confronted with diminished strength and/or energy and escalating prescription drug expenses, a senior may neglect replacing a broken or malfunctioning stove or refrigerator. However, having a broken stove or refrigerator may result in a poor diet and exacerbate existing health problems, such as diabetes or hypertension.

ENVIRONMENTAL CHALLENGES AND HOUSING DECISIONS

Individuals choose living arrangements to meet their physical and social needs based on the resources available to them. Relocation or migration *triggers* are often characterized in terms of *push factors* and *pull factors*. Push factors are life events or circumstances that loosen individuals' attachment to their current residences and lead them to consider relocation. Pull factors are life events or circumstances that occur at another location and draw an individual toward a new residence (Wiseman, 1980). The specific push and pull factors that influence housing decisions vary across the life course. Although the primary push or reason older adults seek alternative housing arrangements is escalating health problems and the need for assistance with the activities of daily living, these difficulties may be further compounded by declining economic and/or social resources. The death of a spouse is often a push factor, particularly if the frail elder lives alone and does not have caring family members nearby. Loss of a spouse may also reduce or end some sources of income, thus creating greater financial burden for the widow(er) in meeting household expenses (e.g., utility bills, property taxes) and forcing a relocation or move. It is important to remember, however, that there is a great deal of diversity in the disablement process or the pathway to disability. Pull factors might be the opportunity to relocate closer to one's adult children, the availability of a lower-rent apartment in a safer neighborhood, or the chance to move into a single-story dwelling closer to public transportation.

Individuals' environments include not only their homes but also their neighborhoods. Neighborhoods, as well as local policies and programs, present both opportunities and constraints to older residents as they age, including access to resources such as public transportation, parks, senior centers, doctors, groceries, and pharmacies. Using the 1972–1992 Panel Study of Income Dynamics, Sabia (2008) found that not only were diminished physical well-being and changes in family composition negatively associated with aging in place but also increases in property taxes and utility costs contributed to elders' relocation decisions. Yet, as previously noted, most seniors age in place, and, if they do relocate the vast majority—approximately 80%—are local moves; only about 1% of seniors move across state lines (Schafer, 2000). Those seniors who do migrate longer distances (e.g., Florida, Arizona) are typically younger, healthier, and wealthier. While there is a slight rise in relocation after the age of 85, this typically reflects the growing mismatch between an individual's assistance needs and his or her physical space.

The environmental press paradigm articulated by Lawton and Nahemow (1973) focuses on the "fit" of older persons with their home environments and stresses that an individual's ability to function may be either enhanced or impeded by one's immediate environment. Verbrugge and Jette (1994) noted that disability has two aspects: *intrinsic ability* and *actual ability*. Intrinsic ability refers to an individual's abilities regardless of the environment, whereas actual ability focuses on how a person's intrinsic abilities interact with one's social and physical environment. In fact, a growing body of literature suggests that environmental interventions or physical manipulations of the home environment (e.g., home modifications, home repairs, assistive technologies) can improve seniors' quality of life and/or postpone or prevent functional decline in older adults (Hudson & Cohen; 2010; Seplaki et al., 2013).

Despite evidence of such benefits, over 1 million senior households, particularly the households headed by the very old, report needing home modifications (Pynoos, Caraviello, & Cicero, 2009). The 2011 AHS revealed that 23% of older households reported difficulties using their kitchen either in terms of reaching and/or opening cabinets, using the countertop and/or operating the stove The AHS survey also found that 25% of older householders faced challenges in either getting to their bathroom, using the sink or turning on/off faucets, and/or getting into

or out of a bathtub or shower (US Census Bureau, 2013a). However, as dwellings age and incomes dwindle, seniors' out-of-pocket home modification expenses are more typically for replacing worn-out systems and critical repairs rather than for modifications. In fact, the top three identified barriers to home modification are: inability to do it oneself, prohibitive costs, and lack of skilled and trustworthy providers (Bayer & Harper, 2000). Yet, given the existing level of unmet home modification need, coupled with the reality that the United States adds less than 2% yearly to the new housing stock, it is critical that we develop strategies to make home modifications more available and work to retrofit existing housing to meet seniors' needs (Pynoos et al., 2009).

LINKING HEALTHCARE AND HOUSING

Addressing the *suitability of fit* between seniors' assistance needs and their environments to maximize their competence also requires that the older adults be able to access the informal and formal services they require. Despite the fact that the health and housing concerns of seniors are highly interrelated, our current systems of health and housing delivery are typically independent and separate services. This lack of integration or coordination between these two systems—that is, the failure of the United States to develop an integrated approach to community-based long-term care—creates challenges for frail seniors who are seeking to remain in the community. Lawler (2001) notes that because of this disconnect between healthcare and housing, seniors are often faced with two equally undesirable choices as they become frailer—*overcare* or *undercare*:

> They are often forced to choose between entering an expensive, restrictive elderly institution before the need arises, or remaining in their homes alone, to face the pressures of rising medical expenses and a deteriorating shelter while on a fixed income. (p. 5)

Some policy trends suggest, however, some grounds for optimism. First, the US Supreme Court decision in *Olmstead v. L.C.* (1999), affirming the right of persons of all ages with disabilities to live and receive services in the least restrictive setting they desire if at all possible, gave further impetus to government coordination in the creation of a more holistic system of care. Second, there has been a growing convergence between the government's focus on cost containment and its encouragement of self- and community-based care and seniors' desire to age in place within their own homes. Indeed, it has increasingly been recognized that for most older Americans, the home is the primary setting in which long-term care occurs. In 1999, Congress, under the mandates of Public Law 106-7-4, established the Commission on Affordable Housing and Health Facilities Needs for Seniors in the 21st Century. In June 2002, the Commission issued the report *A Quiet Crisis in America*, in which it stated a vision for America:

> The Seniors Commission believes that all older Americans should have an opportunity to live as independently as possible in safe and affordable housing and in their communities of choice. No older person should have to sacrifice his or her home or an opportunity for independence to secure necessary health care and supportive services. (p. 6)

The report's extensive testimony and research, however, underscored that achieving this vision would not be easy. Identified barriers include a long history of policy disconnects between the health and housing fields, poor communication, differing vocabulary, limited opportunities to interact between healthcare and housing professionals, and different financing and regulatory structures for the two domains. Ultimately, the commission developed five principles to guide its policy recommendations:

Preserve the existing housing stock.

Expand successful housing projection, rental assistance programs, home- and community-based services, and supportive housing models.

Link shelter and services to promote and encourage aging in place.

Reform existing federal financial programs to maximize flexibility and increase housing production and health and service coverage.

Create and explore new housing and service programs, models, and demonstrations. (p. 62)

After its release of its 1999 groundbreaking report *Housing Our Elders* (US Department of Housing and Urban Development [HUD], 1999), HUD initiated several more comprehensive programs focused on integrating health and housing services. For example, the HUD Service Coordinator Program, in which the coordinator acts as a broker of community services for seniors, was expanded in 2001 to allow these professionals to work with seniors in the surrounding communities as well as residents of the HUD multifamily developments. Recognizing that low-income seniors might also benefit from assisted living environments, in 2001 HUD made available funds for the conversion of some of its multifamily developments to assisted living facilities (ALFs) to promote vulnerable elders' ability to age in place. More recently, the Section 202 Supportive Housing for the Elder Act of 2010 (Public Law No: 11-372), which was signed into law on January 4, 2011, modernized HUD's Section 202 Support Housing for the Elderly Program through encouraging maintenance and rehabilitation of existing senior housing, streaming the construction process for new units, and expanding service coordination and assisted living options. Importantly, it creates a new category of housing (service enriched housing) under the Assisted Living Conversion Plan (ALCP), which permits nonlicensed facilities that provide supportive services, either directly or through a recognized and experienced third party, to be eligible grantees. Further, under this legislation, owners are now permitted to establish a preference for homeless elders in tenant selection.

Yet, despite these advances, overcoming the existing regulatory, structural, financing, and implementation barriers to develop a comprehensive approach to the health and housing needs of lower-income older Americans continues to be a challenge. Further, there is a very high level of unmet need for publicly subsidized housing. One estimate suggests that there are at least nine older adults waiting for each occupied unit of affordable senior housing (National Coalition for the Homeless, 2007). HUD's Section 8 Rental Assistance Programs, which allows individuals to rent in the private market and apply for a subsidy to their rent, either have long waiting lists or are closed to new applicants (Burt, Pearson, & Montgomery, 2006). Finally, Engelhardt and his colleagues' (2013) comparative analysis of the 2000 and 2010 Health and Retirement Study (HRS) data underscores the declining availability of affordable rental housing for older American households during the past decade. In 2000, about 30% of older renters spent more than 30% of their annual gross income on rent; however, by

2010, this figure grew to 44% of older renters having such a high rent-to-income ratio. To solve this problem through income programs, Engelhardt and his colleagues calculate that "the approximately 2.8 million renter households [spending more than 30% of the annual gross income on rent] would need a $25.2b increase in aggregate income (i.e., an average income increase of $8,997, median of $8,000) to bring their rent-to-income ratios down to the 30-percent standard." Alternatively, they report that if a voucher program was targeted toward these 2.8 million households to address the gap between 30% of their current income and their rents, it would cost "approximately $7.5 billion per year or an average annual household subsidy of $2,699" (Engelhardt et al., 2013, p. 41).

IMPLICATIONS FOR SOCIAL WORK PRACTICE

In addition to their aspiration to age in place, the importance of home to seniors is evident by the fact that, particularly for the very old, it is the physical space in which they spend the vast majority of their time and most of their daily activities occur (Horgas, Wilms, & Baltes, 1998; Moss & Lawton, 1982). For older people who may be coping with multiple personal losses (e.g., death of a spouse, declines in physical health), one's home can offer a sense of normalcy and coherence about one's personhood (Rubenstein, 1989). The social work profession's emphasis on strengths-based and empowerment-oriented paradigms suggests a commitment to honor seniors' desires to age in place.

Currently, older adults experience a number of difficulties as they attempt to negotiate the separate systems of health and housing services to maintain quality of care as they age. As noted in the Seniors Commission (2002) report,

> The ultimate consumer—the senior citizen— faces the daunting task of obtaining care from these two disconnected sources. Confronted with complex entry requirements, insurance coverage limitations, and high costs, many seniors become overwhelmed just when they need help the most. (p. 19)

Social workers, positioned in community agencies, can play a critical role in accessing and coordinating services that allow older persons to live in their own residences and communities as long as possible, despite frailty and/or debilitating health conditions. Moreover, social workers can identify those older individuals who are at risk for housing instability. Within public housing, social workers often play a sensitive but critical role in facilitating the needs of the older residents and the housing management. One of the primary reasons for older adults' eviction from public housing is behavioral problems. Eviction is often a tragic outcome for these vulnerable older adults who have few alternative housing options.

The social work profession's person-in-the environment perspective fits well with understanding the importance of place in older persons' lives. Through their professional orientation and clinical training, social workers are both attuned to and skilled in assessing the environment-behavior interaction—that is, the interaction between the senior's home environment and his or her well-being and daily life functioning. Social workers' clinical assessments of the suitability of fit, however, must extend beyond a focus strictly on how the home and neighborhood environments enhance or impede the senior's *functionality* and *security* to examine their impact on the older adult's level of *comfort* and *social connection*, as well as *personhood*.

It is evident that clinical assessments must incorporate both objective and subjective aspects of the environment to understand seniors' perceived quality of life. It is critical to gain an understanding of how the older adults themselves assess the suitability of fit between their homes and neighborhood environments and needs and their preferences and expectations for future living arrangements. Moreover, social workers must strive to understand how older persons' assessments of their current environment, as well as future housing choices, are influenced by the context and meaning of their past environments, life-course changes, and the disablement process (Golant, 2003; Robison & Moen, 2000). Also key is sensitivity to how an individual's assessment of suitability of fit and housing expectations may be shaped by one's cultural values and norms. Although these distal experiences are not typically included in clinical assessments, failure to frame seniors' housing choices as a process may seriously jeopardize treatment plans.

Attention has generally been focused on how environment supports or impinges on seniors' physical or cognitive health. It is also important to understand the impact of the home environment on mental health. The degree to which an older adult with a disabling condition is able to use the home environment to assert some control over the circumstances of daily life may affect his or her sense of self-efficacy and lead to higher morale (Gitlin, 2003; Schulz, Heckhausen, & O'Brien, 1994). In addition, the extent to which the home environment supports opportunities for social interaction or engagement may positively impact the older person's quality of life.

Older adults express confusion about the meaning of many of the types of housing options such as assisted living, supportive housing, adult care facilities, life care communities, continuing care facilities, and reverse mortgages. Social workers can play a valuable role in educating seniors about housing options so that they are able to exercise informed choices.

As a profession that has historically engaged in interdisciplinary practice, social workers can also contribute to community-based efforts to forge stronger linkages between healthcare and housing programs. For example, as highlighted in the Seniors Commission Report, the two worlds of healthcare and housing are even separated by language and vocabulary. Aging in place and community living for healthcare professionals is about beds, lengths of stay, and insurance, as well as the seniors' activities of daily living skills and ability to access and pay for community services. In contrast, housing professionals typically speak about these issues in terms of dwelling units, turnovers, and subsidies, as well as the seniors' income as a percentage of area median income (AMI) (Seniors Commission, 2002).

Finally, on the local, state, and federal levels, social workers can actively advocate for policies that promote a more comprehensive and holistic approach to community-based long-term care, which is a critical component of creating more aging-friendly communities. Central to this advocacy are the issues of affordability and accessibility, if we as a nation are to create a system of care that works effectively for *all* older citizens. A secure retirement for both current and future generations of older Americans requires all three pillars to be in place—appropriate and affordable housing, adequate income, and quality healthcare. It is vital to recognize that throughout the life course a home is one's anchor to one's community.

REFERENCES

AARP. (2010). *Home and community preferences of the 45+ population.* Retrieved from http://assets.aarp.org/rgcenter/general/home-community-services-10.pdf

Administration on Aging. (2012). *Profile of older Americans: 2012.* Retrieved from http://www.aoa.gov/Aging_Statistics/Profile/2012/docs/2012profile.pdf

Bayer, A., & Harper, L. (2000). *Fixing to stay: A national survey of housing and home modification issues.* Retrieved from http://assets.aarp.org/rgcenter/il/home_mod.pdf.

Burr, J. A., & Mutcher, J. E. (2007). Residential independence among older persons: Community and individual factors, *Population Research Policy Review, 26,* 85–101. doi:10.1007/s1113-007-9022-0.

Burt, M. R., Pearson, C. L., & Montgomery, A. E. (2006). *Homelessness: Prevention strategies and effectiveness.* Hauppauge, NY: Nova Science Publishers, Inc.

Congressional Budget Office. (2013, June). *Rising demand for long-term services and supports for elderly people.* Retrieved from http://www.cbo.gov/sites/default/files/cbofiles/attachments/44363-LTC.pdf

Engelhardt, G. V., Eriksen, M. D., & Greenhalgh-Stanley, N. (2013). *A profile of housing and health among older Americans.* Retrieved from http://housingamerica.org/RIHA/RIHA/Publications/86310_13205_RIHA_Senior_Housing_Paper.pdf

Federal Interagency Forum on Aging-Related Statistics (FIFARS). (2012). *Older Americans 2012: Key indicators of well-being.* Retrieved from http://www.aging-stats.gov/main_site/default.aspx

Gitlin, L. N. (2003). Conducting research on home environments: Lessons learned and new directions. *The Gerontologist, 43,* 628–637. doi:10.1093/geront/43.5.628

Golant, S. M. (2003). Conceptualizing time and behavior in environmental gerontology: A pair of old issues deserving new thought. *The Gerontologist, 43,* 638–638. doi:10.1093/geront/43.5.638

Gonyea, J. G. (2005). The economic well-being of older Americans and the persistent divide. *Public Policy and Aging Report, 15,* 1–11. doi:

Gonyea, J. G., & Burnes, K. (2013). Aging well at home: Evaluation of a neighborhood-based pilot project to "Put connection back in community." *Journal of Housing for the Elderly, 27,* 333–347. doi:10.1080/02763893.2013.813425

Horgas, M. A., Wilms, H.-U., & Baltes, M. M. (1998). Daily life in very old age: Everyday activities as expression of successful living. *Gerontologist, 43,* 556–568. doi:10.1093/geront/38.5.556

Hudson, D. L., & Cohen, M. E. (2010). Intelligent agents in home health care. *Annals of Telecommunication*, *65*, 593–600. doi:10.1007/s12243-010-0170-6.

Lawler, K. (2001). *Aging in place: Coordinating housing and health care provision for America's growing elderly population* (Working Paper W01-03). Cambridge, MA: Joint Center for Housing Studies of Harvard University.

Lawton, M. P., & Nahemow, L. (1973). Ecology and the aging process. In C. Eisdorfer & M. P. Lawton (Eds.), *The psychology of adult development and aging* (pp. 619–674). Washington, DC: American Psychological Association. doi:10.1037/10044-020

Moss, M., & Lawton, M. P. (1982). Time budgets of older people: A window on four life styles. *Journal of Gerontology*, *37*, 115–123. doi:10.1093/geronj/37.1.115

National Association of Area Agencies on Aging. (2011). *The maturing of America: II. Communities moving forward for an aging population*. Retrieved from http://www.n4a.org/files/MOA_FINAL_Rpt.pdf

National Association of Area Agencies on Aging. (2007). *The maturing of America—Getting communities on track for an aging population*. Retrieved from http://www.n4a.org/pdf/MOAFinalReport.pdf

National Coalition for the Homeless. (2007, August). *Homelessness among elderly persons, NCH Fact Sheet #15*. Retrieved from http://www.nationalhomeless.org

Parsons, P. L., Mezuk, B., Ratliff, S., & Lapane, K. L. (2011). Subsidized housing not subsidized health: Health status and fatigue among elders in public housing and other community settings. *Ethnicity and Disease*, *21*, 85–90.

Pynoos, J., Caraviello, R., & Cicero, C. (2009). Lifelong housing: The anchor in aging-friendly communities. *Generations*, *33*, 26–31.

Redfoot, D., & Kochera, A. (2004). Targeting services to those most at risk: Characteristics of residents in federally subsidized housing. *Journal of Housing for the Elderly*, *18*, 141. doi:10.1300/J081v18n03_06

Rowles, G. D., & Chaudhury, H. (2005.) *Home and identity in late life: International perspectives*. New York, NY: Springer.

Robison, J. T., & Moen, P. (2000). A life-course perspective on housing expectations and fits in late midlife. *Research on Aging*, *22*, 499–532.

Rubenstein, R. L. (1989). The home environments of older people: A description of the psychosocial processes linking person to place. *Journal of Gerontology: Social Sciences*, *44*, S45–S53. doi:10.1093/geronj/44.2.S45

Sabia, J. J. (2008). There's no place like home: A hazard model analysis of aging in place among older homeowners in the PSID. *Research on Aging*, *30*, 3–35. doi:10.1177/0164027507307919.

Schafer, R. (2000). *Housing America's seniors* (Report 00-01). Cambridge, MA: Joint Center for Housing Studies at Harvard University.

Schulz, R., Heckhausen, J., & O'Brien, T. (1994). Control and the disablement process in the elderly. *Journal of Social Behavior and Personality*, *9*, 130–152.

Seniors Commission. (2002, June). *A quiet crisis in America: A report to Congress by the Commission on Affordable Housing and Health Facility Needs for Seniors in the 21st Century*. Washington, DC: Government Printing Office. portal.hud.gov/hudportal/documents/huddoc?id=DOC_13078.pdf

Seplaki, C. L., Agree, E. M., Weiss, C. O., Szanton, S. L., Bandeen-Roche, K., & Fried, L. P. (2013). Assistive devices in context: Cross-sectional association between challenges in the home environment and use of assistive devices for mobility. *The Gerontologist*, *54*, 651–660. doi:10.1093/geront/gnt030

US Census Bureau. (2013a). *2011 American housing survey for the United States—Complete set of tables*. Retrieved from http://www.huduser.org/portal/datasets/ahs.html

US Census Bureau. (2013b). *Geographic mobility*. Retrieved from http://www.census.gov/hhes/migration/data/cps/cps2013.html

US Department of Housing and Urban Development (HUD). (1999, November). *Housing our elders*. Washington, DC: Author. Retrieved from http://archives.hud.gov/news/1999/elderlyfull.pdf

Verbrugge, L., & Jette, A. (1994). The disablement process. *Social Science and Medicine*, *38*, 11–24. doi:10.1016/0277-9536(94)90294-1

Wiseman, R. F. (1980). Why older people move: Theoretical issues. *Research on Aging*, *2*, 141–154. doi:10.1177/016402758022003

ROSALIE A. KANE

SECTION III

Social Work Practice in Long-Term Residential Care

OVERVIEW

Social workers have a long history of working in residential settings for older people, and a record of advocacy for the well-being of their residents. As a practice field for social work, residential care is dominated by nursing homes because a half-century of federal rules require social services in nursing homes. But wherever social workers practice with older people and their families, they must be keenly aware of the residential options available to older people who need care and the typical stresses involved with deciding to relocate to a residential care setting and living in one. Such settings are part of the backdrop of family life of older people with whom social workers might work as clinicians in many health, mental health, and social service settings, or as case managers. This section deals with social work practice and advocacy for clients in group residential care settings.

The choices people make about where to live in their later years may affect the amount, type, and costs of support needed and available to them at a crucial period of need. An older person's home should surely be a place of comfort and an expression of personal identity, and the environs of that home should help define that older person's community. In this spirit, social workers and others tend to share the goal that the wide range of group living settings where older people receive care, including nursing homes, be not only "homelike" but also actually home. The chapters in this section illustrate many different ways that social workers might try to realize that aspiration, while also working toward high quality for the healthcare in the settings.

In the section's first chapter, I ruminate on a century or so of developments relevant to older people receiving care in settings other than their own home, present a selected history of social work leadership in this sector, and offer a somewhat idiosyncratic view of current challenges and opportunities. For the chapter, I drew liberally on my own research from 1978 to 2014, which examined the emerging adult foster home and assisted living industries in Oregon and nationally, developed and tested resident-reported quality of life in nursing homes, studied the effectiveness of emerging Green House and small-house nursing homes, and compared and critiqued nursing home regulations and their relationships—positive and negative—to resident autonomy. (PDFs for much of this research are found at http://www.hpm.umn.edu/ltcresourcecenter/, and

the comparative website on regulations is at http://www.hpm.umn.edu/ltcresourcecenter/.)

The next chapter, by Sheryl Zimmerman, Jean Munn, and Terry Koenig, provides an overview of assisted living, broadly defined as all group residential settings not licensed as nursing homes where care is provided. This chapter suggests the difficulty in making sharp distinctions between nursing homes and assisted living, or between assisted living and home care, and discusses recent federal efforts to determine what should be considered an institution and thus be ineligible for reimbursement under Medicaid waiver programs, which fund alternatives to institutions. As of July 2014, assisted living for seniors still "counted" as community care, but the issue is unsettled. Zimmerman and colleagues point out social workers are more likely to provide services to assisted living residents than to practice as employees of these settings, but the chapter itemizes the many ways social workers can make a positive difference for assisted living residents.

The next chapter by Robin Bonifas, Mercedes Bern Klug, and Kelsey Simons updates the corresponding chapter in the first edition with an incisive discussion of the role and context of social work in nursing homes. It is informed by national-level and state-level research describing patterns of social work practice in nursing homes. The nursing home is a large and growing employment site for social workers prepared at the bachelor's or master's level, though the authors point out that some homes—more in some states than in others—still do not employ qualified or full-time social workers in homes with fewer than 120 beds. The chapter is punctuated by brief case examples showing that practice in nursing homes demands depth and a wide range of skills to meet needs in a complex setting with a diverse clientele.

The six authors of the two chapters on nursing homes and assisted living—Bonifas and colleagues and Zimmerman and colleagues, respectively—are all social workers engaged in research within nursing homes and assisted living and disseminating practice ideas and protocols based on evidence. Bonifas, Bern Klug, and Simons have each conducted research to map the terrain of psychosocial care in nursing homes, and all three are leaders in a creating a network of social work educators, policymakers, and practitioners in nursing homes and a national webinar series, hosted by Bern Klug at Iowa, to disseminate excellence in nursing home social work (see National Nursing Home Social Work

Network, http://clas.uiowa.edu/socialwork/nursing-home-social-work-network). Sheryl Zimmerman has for decades led multidisciplinary research efforts to classify the range of assisted living settings and to improve quality in both assisted living and nursing homes, and she established a collaborative of residential providers of all types and licensure as a locus for practice-based research; she also founded the Assisted Living Interest Group at the Gerontological Society of America, which has provided a multidisciplinary forum for research planning and dissemination.

The following chapter, on the Long-Term Care Ombudsman Program, is coauthored by Patricia Ducayet, State Ombudsman of Texas and in 2014 president of the National Association of State Ombudsman, and Beverly Laubert, State Ombudsman of Ohio and in 2014 national chair of Advancing Excellence in America's Nursing Homes (see Advancing Excellence in America's Nursing Homes (http://www.nhquality-campaign.org/). Ombudsmen do not work *for* nursing homes or assisted living settings but rather work *in* them on behalf of residents. The chapter explains how the statutorily mandated mission to resolve complaints in nursing homes and residential care settings has evolved. It adroitly describes the many ways social work skills can be and are used within the ombudsman program, and the process of moving between individual and systems advocacy and using cases to identify causes and drive issues home to the public.

Wendy Lustbader and Carter Catlett Williams update their chapter on the culture change movement in nursing homes and the work of the Pioneer Network (formerly the Nursing Home Pioneers). Williams, widely credited as the visionary who began the culture change movement, is the lifetime convener of the Pioneer Network and a magnificent example of a social worker as change agent. Lustbader, a prolific author, is an articulate voice for humanizing nursing homes as places to live and work, and respecting seniors wherever they live (for videos and resource materials from the Pioneer Network, see https://www.pioneernetwork.net/).

To conclude the section, Geri Adler and Lonique Pritchett describe the residential care programs within or funded by the Veterans Administration (VA). The VA services have evolved considerably since the last edition of the *Handbook*. Adler and Pritchett admirably clarify this complex landscape of programs and eligibilities. Their chapter discusses VA-owned nursing homes, now called Community Living Centers (CLCs) because of their focus on quality of life; State Veterans Homes; the contract nursing home program whereby veterans are supported in community non-VA nursing homes; and medical foster homes, a newer residential option. The VA continues to be a major employer of social workers and an important laboratory for the development of care models for seniors.

Taken together, all chapters in this section illustrate the fluidity in residential care and the continued blurring of lines between in-home services and services in group residential settings and between nursing home and hospital. Nursing homes are doing two distinct kinds of business—short-term posthospital care and long-stay care—and are challenged to meet separate demands. Assisted living is in an unsettled territory between nursing homes and home care, and it is meant to give the intensive level of care of nursing homes while offering resident control and amenities associated with home care. However, critics suggest some assisted living is as institutional as nursing homes but with less expert or intensive care available. Some assisted living facilities resemble nursing homes, whereas others are hard to distinguish from senior independent housing with home care providers frequently on the scene. The ombudsman program by statute works on behalf of nursing home and assisted living residents, but is finding new arrangements involving managed care and hospitals on the one hand, and assisted living and home care on the other, thus requiring new advocacy approaches and partners. Social workers—as practitioners, administrators, policymakers, advocates, regulators, and researchers—will need to carefully monitor changing residential care settings and try to shape and respond to changes in ways that best support the health and well-being of older people and their families.

The most basic human needs include a dwelling-place for shelter and food and drink to sustain life. When older people's care needs become too difficult or expensive to arrange and coordinate in their private homes, a move to a group residential setting where the care is provided may seem sensible or inevitable. In the United States, residential care falls in two general categories: nursing facilities (NFs) and assisted living (AL). In this chapter, "AL" is used for any non-NF care setting; names and definitions vary by state and within a state, including AL facility, AL residence, residential care facility, family care home, adult foster home, domiciliary care home, and others. Nursing facilities provide residentially based services for seniors with substantial care needs. They are licensed by states and certified federally to receive Medicare and Medicaid payments, and about 50% of their funding comes from government subsidy, mostly through Medicaid programs. Nursing facilities are subject to detailed federal quality standards, and often additional or more stringent state standards; federal inspections are largely delegated to state inspectors (known as "the surveyors"). In contrast, AL is largely funded through private payments, and licensing and quality monitoring requirements vary widely. This chapter discusses the evolution of both NFs and ALs, with attention to contributions of social workers historically and currently. The history illuminates opportunities and challenges for social workers in the future as they work toward better outcomes for residents.

ROSALIE A. KANE

A Social Work Perspective on the History and Future of Residential Care

HISTORICAL EVOLUTION OF NURSING FACILITIES

Before the industrial revolution and until the late 19th and early 20th century, older people made few residential choices. If they needed constant or frequent nursing care and help to manage their households and activities, they largely relied on family or hired help. Society was more agrarian, life expectancy was shorter, and family members who provided care often lived in the older person's home. With the growth of cities and factories, the waves of foreign immigration in the 19th century, and internal migration to the cities from other parts of the United States, life became more complex and more people with needs began to fall outside the protection of families and local communities. The first organized social services appeared at the end of the 19th century in the form of charity organization societies and settlement houses.

Like orphanages and mental hospitals, NFs had a common ancestor in the poorhouse—a stigma-ridden, last refuge for "indoor relief" for bereft people of all ages whose support fell to the parish or the county. Professional social work also is rooted in poor laws, poorhouses, and parish relief. Historically speaking, a pleasant "homelike" atmosphere was *not* a goal for indoor relief, and "outdoor relief" (i.e., cash, in-kind goods, or services to people living independently) was a less-favored form of charity.

With the gradual differentiation of social welfare programs and facilities by the early 20th century, frail elderly people were perceived as comparatively deserving of respect and care. Charitable (usually sectarian) organizations established the first homes for the aged at the turn of the 20th century. Also, in many states, local governments maintained a system of county homes, which largely became old age homes as other populations (e.g., children, mentally ill, blind or deaf people) were served by more specialized state programs. In the 1930s, older people with care needs increasingly lived in private boarding homes, partly because residents of various public institutions were ineligible for income payments from the new Social Security program. With more effective healthcare technology and the rising age and health needs of seniors, some boarding homes eventually became more medically oriented and converted to health-related facilities. The post–World War II period saw a boom in for-profit NFs, stimulated by construction payments for NFs and medical assistance payments in the 1950s to support poor people in NFs. Unfortunately, these new settings, though meant to be lifelong homes, were modeled on hospitals of the time with bedrooms on both sides of long corridors, shared rooms, and few amenities or hallmarks of home.

Elias Cohen (1974), an attorney and social worker, identified six periods in the development of NFs through colonial times and up to post-1965. From today's historical vantage point, the 6th phase reaches to 1987. From 1965 to 1987, NFs expanded rapidly, punctuated by frequent quality and business scandals and subsequent regulatory reactions. Some smaller, more homelike NFs, colloquially called "mom-and-pops," were forced out of business during the 1960s and 1970s because of increasing NF standards. In some states, local citizen advocacy

groups arose to plead for NF reform, and in 1975 the National Citizens' Coalition for Nursing Home Reform was founded for advocacy at the national level. In the early 1980s, the Reagan administration proposed deregulation of nursing homes, and advocates responded with outrage. An Institute of Medicine (IOM) committee was tasked with examining the relationship between regulation and quality in NFs. This process resulted in comprehensive recommendations to strengthen the regulatory system (Institute of Medicine [IOM], 1986), most of which were embedded in the Nursing Home Reform Act of 1987.

NURSING HOME REFORM ACT OF 1987

Under the Nursing Home Reform Act of 1987, also known as OBRA 1987, quality standards were strengthened overall and new separate standards were created for quality of life, residents' rights, and resident assessment. Quality assessment for compliance with standards was overhauled: Surveyors were required to interview or observe residents directly rather than rely solely on NF records, inspection intervals were modified to introduce a modicum of surprise, and a two-phase inspection process was developed with an extended survey for facilities showing problems at initial screening. Enforcement of standards was strengthened to encourage intermediate sanctions short of license removal (ranging from fines to admission holds) and to classify facility problems (called "deficiencies") by scope and severity. Use of physical restraints in NFs had already been challenged, partly because of the leadership of social worker Carter Catlett Williams, but OBRA 87 codified new limitations on their use and prohibited using medications to control resident behavior (so-called chemical restraints).

Initial implementation of OBRA 87 took more than a decade. The tumultuous period from 1987 to 2014 is characterized by several thrusts, at times contradictory. Efforts to strengthen regulations and regulatory compliance, which were part of OBRA implementation, coexisted with encouragement of increasing capacity for internal leadership in NFs and with promoting consumer direction in NFs and ALs. Efforts to reduce the use of NFs coexisted with efforts to create competitive marketplaces for informed consumers. Milestones included:

- A resident assessment instrument (RAI) and Minimum Data Set (MDS) were developed and tested, and by 1999 all NFs needed to electronically submit MDS data. The third iteration, MDS 3.0, became effective in October 2013. This MDS was eventually used to derive quality indicators (later called quality measures), to create payment systems based on resident needs, and to guide NF inspections.
- In the late 1990s, the Centers for Medicare and Medicaid Services (CMS) developed a national website to permit consumers and their advisers to compare NFs, using findings from the state regulatory surveys, nurse staffing data collected in tandem with the surveys, and national MDS-derived quality indicators (see website http://www.medicare.gov/nursinghomecompare/search.html). Some state regulatory agencies developed their own additional Web-based quality report cards.
- By 2000, the CMS had in place a system to classify NF problems by scope and severity; "immediate jeopardy" is the highest severity category, and scope refers to whether the problem, however severe, affects many residents, and whether it is recurrent. By 2007, the CMS created a "special focus facility initiative," publishing the names of the worst facilities at the lowest end of the distribution in each state; these facilities were closely monitored and subject to at least twice as many inspections until the status was lifted or (if they failed to improve) the facility was dropped from federal reimbursement.

CULTURE CHANGE

On the culture change front, the Pioneer Network, founded in 1995, ushered in a movement toward transformed nursing homes. Innovations piloted under the culture change banner fell into three categories: (1) Changing physical environments, typically to make them smaller and more normalized (e.g., creating neighborhoods in NFs and increasing private rooms); (2) Empowering decision-making among frontline staff members such as nurse's aides; and (3) Instituting a person-centered care philosophy. In almost two decades, the culture change movement reframed the public conversation about nursing homes, although the actual transformation of facilities is a slow process thus far affecting only a small minority of homes and sometimes in small ways. Milestones include:

- The Eden Alternative was developed (Thomas, 1999) to combat resident boredom, loneliness, and lack of meaning. Its environmental hallmarks include the inclusion of plants and animals. More fundamentally, the Eden Alternative also calls for individualized care, permanent assignment of staff to residents, and flattened hierarchies with more authority afforded to unlicensed staff.
- Thomas also conceptualized the trademarked Green House model of NFs, first implemented in Tupelo, Missouri, in 2003 (Rabig, Thomas, Kane, Cutler, & McAlilly, 2006). Green Houses are small self-contained houses for 7–12 residents; each is licensed as part of an NF, where certified nurse's aides (CNAs) work within a broadened job description beyond their regular personal care duties, including cooking and serving meals, light housekeeping, household laundry, and activity assistance. All professionals required in NFs, including social workers, form a clinical support team to assist the elders and the CNAs. A quasi-experimental evaluation of the first Green House NF in Tupelo showed benefits in residents' psychological and social well-being, family satisfaction, and staff well-being, with no concomitant drop in quality of care (Cutler & Kane, 2009; Kane, Lum, Cutler, Degenholtz, & Yu, 2007; Lum, Kane, Cutler, & Yu, 2008).
- By 2014, more than 25 Green House NF projects were operating, ranging from 1 to 22 houses, and a larger number of similar small-house NFs were operating without the trademark. Some of these programs were within the Veterans Administration (VA), which embraced the culture change movement, renaming their NFs as Community Living Centers (CLCs) and encouraging small-house and neighborhood construction models in all new CLCs and State Veterans Homes.
- In 1998, CMS funded a study to develop and test measures of quality of life (QOL) for NF residents, resulting in self-reported outcome measures on 11 domains of QOL (comfort, security, relationships, meaningful activity, enjoyment, functional competence, dignity, privacy,

individuality, autonomy, and spiritual well-being (Kane et al., 2003). People with dementia were often able to reliably report on their QOL.

- By the end of the 20th century, although not relinquishing its quality of care mission, the CMS became supportive of culture change and mandated that their Quality Improvement Organizations advance culture change. CMS and some state regulators also used civil monetary penalty funds to encourage culture change.

SPECIALIZATION AND MARKET FORCES

Other trends characterize the period, some a response to efforts to hold down government costs of NFs, and some resulting from efforts to make hospital stays for older people more efficient or effective. One result was more specialization within NFs.

- Dementia special care units (SCUs) sprang up to offer (and market) more appropriate care to people with dementia, but also to contain persons with disturbing behavior in locked areas. The Alzheimer's Association pushed for the care in SCUs to live up to its "special" name and added price, and to lobby for dementia-friendly facilities. In the mid-1980s, the National Institute of Aging funded a series of cooperative studies to explore the true benefits and costs of dementia SCUs.
- Post–acute care units, sometimes called transitional care units (TCUs), evolved to serve Medicare-funded residents for rehabilitation and recuperation after hospital discharge. These TCUs were encouraged by hospital incentives to shorten hospitalizations and maximize their revenue under Medicare prospective payment systems.
- Many states established moratoria on new NF development and stringent "certificate of need" standards for adding beds so they could limit the effect of residents spending down their private money and ending on public support. States were also working to change the balance between their long-term care expenditures on NFs compared with long-term care expenditure in the community, and limiting the NF supply promoted that goal.

HISTORICAL EVOLUTION OF ASSISTED LIVING

Starting in about 1985, the AL sector began to evolve from simple residential care settings offering "three hots and a cot" and little care to a differentiated industry with many ALs developing a capacity for care at the NF level. After 1982, states could apply for waivers of Medicaid rules to cover a variety of home- and community-based services (HCBS) as alternatives to NFs for consumers who qualified financially for Medicaid and functionally for an NF-level of disability. During the 1980s, many states covered care in AL under HCBS waivers; housing and board costs were billed to residents, who paid out of SSI payments and other income (only hospitals and NFs can include room and board in a daily rate). Uncoupling room and board from care could be seen as a positive development, making AL care more like home care, and permitting more price transparency for consumers.

Emergence of alternative residential care settings was sometimes encouraged by state policy. During the recession of the 1980s, for example, Oregon offered incentives for its overhoused, underemployed citizens to open adult-foster care (ADC) homes, defined as private homes in residentially zoned areas approved for up to five residents. The care portion was covered under HCBS waivers for those who qualified, and case managers working for local government, often social workers, managed the package. With minimum regulation, these homes grew rapidly, serving both private-pay residents (two-thirds of the customers in the first decade) and Medicaid-waiver clientele (Kane, Kane, Illston, Nyman, & Finch, 1991).

With ready availability of construction loans, purpose-built ALs, including apartment-type ALs, expanded rapidly in the 1990s, and publicly traded AL companies emerged (Kane & Wilson, 1993). Idealists who first planned modern ALs aimed for settings offering consumers autonomy, privacy, and dignity in single-occupied apartments while also making a high level of care and service available. Oregon's model, for example, required a minimum of studio apartments with kitchenettes, full bathrooms, and locking doors, and provision of three daily meals and ongoing assistance with personal care and routine nursing. Oregon-style AL was expected to be a genuine alternative to NFs, rather than a lower level of care for people with lesser needs. Therefore, AL personnel, in this model of care, provided two-person transfers, helped with toileting, and served residents with dementia. However, other states envisaged a continuum, and developed admission and retention rules for AL that forced discharge to higher settings for those residents whose needs for care reached a specified threshold (Wilson, 2007).

Assisted living occupies an unsettled and controversial place in public policy. As neither institutions nor private homes, ALs caused some confusion in the marketplace, raising issues about who should be admitted to ALs, what kinds of care they should receive, how medical practitioners should serve in these settings, and what responsibility governments should have for both payment and quality oversight. If the housing component of the AL model is truly seen as separate from the services component, then the Fair Housing Act should apply and residents should not be evicted because of disability. If AL is a *health facility*, then discharge cannot be forced when resident disability exceeds the perceived capability of the program. Depending on the AL program and the state where it is licensed, residents may be able to receive services from any combination of facility staff, outside home care providers, private duty personnel hired by the consumers, and volunteering family members, which complicates advocacy efforts focused on staff-to-resident ratios.

Despite periodic, highly publicized exposés on the quality of care, the AL sector seems to be the preferred choice of private-pay customers. This has led some critics to deplore a growing two-class system, where low-income individuals are in NFs and persons of means either avoid NFs entirely or have very short stays before their deaths (Hernandez & Newcomer, 2007).

CRITIQUES OF RESIDENTIAL CARE SETTINGS

Soon after Medicare was enacted, NFs were likened to *total institutions*, where inmates are processed in batches and subject to rules designed for the benefit of the organization, not the clientele (Goffman, 1961). Nursing facilities are criticized for lack of privacy and amenities, and for rigid routines and rules that remove control from residents and even threaten their sense of identity (Tobin, 1999). In the post-OBRA period, anthropologists, ethicists, and ethnographic researchers highlighted these problems, and the difficulties faced by NF staff who wished

to develop primary relationships with residents, exercise judgment, and nurture residents' quality of life. The phrase *bed-and-body work*, first articulated by Gubrium (1975), perfectly captures how nurses' aides seemed to be rewarded only for completion of concrete tasks, and were not expected to spend, or rewarded for, time conversing with residents.

But AL has also been critiqued. Some consumer advocates claim that ALs overcharge and underserve residents and consign them to NFs once their needs exceed the service the AL wants to provide or that the older person can afford. Also, though HCBS waivers are for care outside institutions, some ALs may seem institutional in nature. Kane and Cutler (2009) identified five factors that make a group residential setting more institutional and less community-like: institutional scale and design features; lack of private space or a convention of privacy; inability of residents to control their schedules, activities, and associations with others inside the settings; inability of residents to experience integration with the wider community in which the settings are located; and lack of resident control over whether they remain in the setting. Advocates for younger people with disabilities argue that any setting housing more than four residents is, by definition, an institution. Some advocates for seniors counter that an AL complex composed of private apartments dramatically differs from a group home and belongs in the HCBS category regardless of the number of apartments in the complex. Assisted living residents, however, are rarely offered a rental agreement that protects them against eviction (or *discharge*, in medical terms) even if their condition worsens. Advocates sometimes insist that residents with NF-level needs should have OBRA protections even in AL. However, if AL settings adopt the rules, routines, and conventions of NFs, other commentators fear that they will lose the very characteristics that made them popular to seniors.

Residential care services for seniors can be envisaged as a three-legged stool (see Figure 22.1), where each leg is made up of two prongs. Leg 1 is the residential environment, where the two prongs are private space and public space. Leg 2 is service capacity, where one prong is specialized services and the other prong is the capacity for routine services such as bathing assistance, toileting assistance, and routine nursing care like medication management. The routine services must be managed in-house, and some are not amenable to scheduling but depend on the on-call availability of help. Specialty services such as

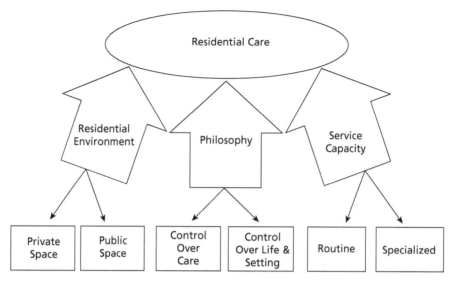

FIGURE 22.1 Three-legged stool model for evaluating attributes of any residential care setting.

Source: This model was developed by Keren Brown Wilson, Portland, Oregon, and is described in Kane, Kane, and Ladd (1998).

psychiatric care, speech therapy, pharmacy services, and the like may be brought in "as needed." Leg 3 is a philosophy that emphasizes consumer control, where one prong is resident control over the amount, type, and timing of care, and the other prong is resident control over what happens in their private space—who enters, how furnishings are arranged, what is done there, and when. Though this model was first developed for AL, it is a heuristic device that can be used to set aspirations and compare successes of both ALs and NFs.

SOCIAL WORK AND RESIDENTIAL CARE

Historically, towering figures in social work have addressed the urgency of psychosocial care in NFs, such as Carter Catlett Williams, already mentioned. A few other examples illustrate the point.

Elaine Brody was early to recognize the trauma of moving to an institution. She called for an emphasis on strengths, not deficits (Brody & Contributors, 1974). During her career at the Philadelphia Geriatric Center, Brody illuminated important concepts such as the need to avoid excess disability and the likelihood that some aggressiveness and grumpiness among NF residents, including those with dementia, could represent life-prolonging strengths rather than behavior problems requiring intervention or medication. This thinking counters the idea that helping

residents "adjust" to the nursing home as they find it is the goal of social work intervention.

Herbert Shore, a NF administrator and social worker from Dallas, Texas, called for individualizing and humanizing the NF environment. In an edited book in which he wrote many chapters (Leeds & Shore, 1964), he suggested approaches for transforming dining routines, developing more intellectual and learning-oriented activities, and eliciting resident feedback and opinions about the programs. Reporting to his board of directors in 1970 (Shore 1970, quoted by Kane, 2001), his language anticipated the culture change movement by two decades:

Older people *need* security—economically (in terms of shelter, housing, and spending money), physically (in terms of medical care and adequate diet), and socially (in terms of status, friendship, and belonging). Older people *want* recognition—for what they can do mentally and manually, for their capacity to make a contribution to their community, country, and world, for social and political consciousness, and their ability to plan for themselves. Older people want response: to be liked for what they are, to hold friends and make new acquaintances; and older people want new experiences and adventures: to continue to learn and grow and develop, to enjoy the new and different, to extend interests, expand horizons, satisfy curiosity, to create for expression in artistic and aesthetic areas. . . . Like every other human being, they need social contact. (p. 301)

Shore also suggested that staff members "need to be secure in self, gain satisfaction in giving, and must receive recognition, love, and compensation" (Kane, 2001, p. 301) as a condition for meeting consumer needs. Shore deplored cultural hang-ups on who does what (Kane, 2001, p. 301), foreshadowing the universal worker ideas of today. Shore's teachings mirror the principles enunciated by the Pioneer Network, largely founded by Carter Catlett Williams, another visionary social worker whose antirestraint crusade was mentioned earlier.

In yet another example, Charles C. Fahey developed practical tools to help NFs develop ethical decision-making. Fahey, a priest, social worker, and NF administrator, is the past president of the American Association of Homes and Services for the Aged (now Leading Age) and the founder of the Third Age Center at Fordham University. In the current decade, Monsignor Fahey (2003) introduced the concept of *intermittent, progressive frailty* as the challenge that residential facilities contend with as they provide support to older residents. As an ethicist, Fahey deplored narrow legalistic formulations about advanced directives and argued about the importance of each older person having someone to stand by them and help them negotiate and live with the effects of intermittent progressive frailty.

TRENDS AND CHALLENGES

The Quality Conundrum

What of quality? At the turn of the century, a 2001 IOM report (Wunderlich & Kohler) found that although NF quality of care had markedly improved since OBRA 1987, care problems remained and little progress had been made in improving resident QOL. A recent federal report describes high prevalence of adverse events such as falls, dehydration, and bedsores (Office of the Inspector General [OIG], 2014). Care problems seem intractable despite the energy directed at monitoring quality in the post-OBRA era.

The Affordable Care Act of 2010 included numerous provisions related to NFs, including a mandate for NFs to implement quality assurance and performance improvement (QAPI), already in place for other types of healthcare providers. Under QAPI, each NF must develop a system for quality management that involves all shifts, departments, and programs, and incorporates all front-line staff including nurses' aides and other unlicensed personnel, to improve quality of care, QOL, and resident choice. Nursing facilities are expected to monitor their own quality over time on multiple parameters and to include meaningful resident and family involvement in that process. They are to set data-driven priorities for performance improvement projects tailored to their own problems. The projects themselves are expected to follow the Plan-Do-Study-Act cycle for testing innovations and adopting change when needed. The NF staff is expected to develop a capacity for conducting root cause analysis to identify potential systemic problems that underlie quality shortfalls.

Quality assurance and performance improvement sets high expectations for a sector that is often underfunded and stressed with immediate care demands. Meanwhile, the labor-intensive inspections for minimum quality continue, and, paradoxically, the CMS is charged to develop a rule for facility-driven QAPI. Providers are concerned that the current survey system will penalize rather than reward them for identifying their problems. For more on the CMS's QAPI resources, see http://www.cms.gov/Medicare/Provider-Enrollment-and-Certification/QAPI/NHQAPI.html. Advancing Excellence in America's Nursing Homes, a voluntary initiative originally launched by the Commonwealth Fund and now encouraged by the CMS, also offers tools to improve services on specific illustrative parameters—see https://www.nhqualitycampaign.org/.

There is no escaping the reality that quality is a concept with many dimensions, some of which are in conflict with others. For example, the Pioneer Network asserts, as a principle, that "risk-taking is a normal part of adult life" (https://www.pioneernetwork.net/AboutUs/Values/, last visited September 21, 2014). The corollary is that these values should be accepted by professionals, but putting this tolerance of risk into operation is difficult when safety is also a predominant goal, especially in highly regulated settings. The challenge is to support quality of care without unduly restricting the movements and lives of residents, and to give adequate legitimacy and attention to QOL domains as critical outcomes.

Transition Programs

The CMS funded Nursing Facility Transition projects starting in 2001, and these were meant to help states promote discharges from NFs to the community. Federal and state policy makers continue to develop initiatives to reduce the use of NFs, including diversion programs to prevent NF admissions in the first place, and transition programs to encourage longer-stay residents to return to the community. The federal Money Follows the Person (MFP) program is in place in almost all states and provides monetary incentives in the form of Medicaid matched funding for states that achieve discharges of long-stay NF residents. States have also begun their own transition initiatives to help discharge privately paying residents who may get "stuck" in an NF after being admitted for rehabilitation. Such programs are motivated by the twin goals of helping more residents live where they wish and decreasing the number of persons who "spend down" to Medicaid eligibility while in NFs.

Social workers are involved in all sides of NF transition programs. Nursing facility social workers have responsibility for arranging discharges. Community social workers, who are sometimes associated with the Area Agencies on Aging, also work directly with residents and families to achieve the discharge and sometimes to assist in the immediate weeks or months after discharge. County social workers often serve as case managers to assist low-income residents in transitions. New forms of team-based work are emerging between NF social workers and community social workers. Nursing facility social workers who are deeply committed to the culture change movement and turning NFs into true homes may experience cognitive dissonance in simultaneously helping long-stay residents leave the facility.

Uncertain Future of Residential Services

The NFs of 2014 are products of the various funding streams for payment and the policies that create pressures on hospitals. They also are products of policies to reduce institutional care, which link NFs (the institution) with ALs (the alternative). The NF now has two major lines of service: intensive posthospital rehabilitation and care, and long-term living services. The two coexist uneasily. It is possible that the continuing care of persons with intermittent progressive frailty, in Fahey's terms, will be increasingly managed at home or in alternative home-like residential sectors. But as disability levels rise for HCBS clients, these sectors will inevitably change and perhaps be more highly regulated. As policy analysts and advocates, social workers can help create this new future. As practitioners, they are challenged to serve their clients while standing on ground that seems to be constantly shifting. In the 1970s and 1980s, social work practice in hospitals was flourishing; today many social work departments have downsized or disappeared. In 2014, social work practice in NFs is becoming more nuanced and effective, whereas social workers are more likely to interact with ALs as case managers or community practitioners rather than as AL staff. It is predictable that the ground will continue to shift, and social workers will need to remain nimble in order to serve consumers of residential care settings.

CONCLUDING NOTE: FUTURE OF SOCIAL WORK IN RESIDENTIAL CARE

In the last few decades social workers have been visible as leaders in residential care, whether as consumer advocates (Freeman, 2000), developers of better models of dementia care (Gwyther, 2001), performance improvement experts, or practice-oriented researchers on specific topics such as minimizing the harm in resident-to-resident aggression (Bonifas, 2015) and improving palliative and end-of-life care in NFs (Bern-Klug, 2010).

Social workers will continue to reinvent themselves in their care for older people in residential settings. In direct practice, they may use a fuller array of individual, family, and group interventions. More social workers will occupy roles beyond the job title "social worker." In NFs, they may be administrators, program developers, or unit coordinators, and may be responsible for staff training, spiritual programming, activities, and volunteer coordination. In ALs, they may be administrators, community liaisons, or marketers. They are likely to be at the forefront of the struggles for innovation and reform. Because of their wide variety of job titles and roles, social workers may need to be proactive to find reference groups from their own profession to help sharpen their skills and guide their work. The social work profession's long-standing mission—assisting the individual in the environment—is crucial in group residential settings where the adjustment of the environment (including rules and policies) may be as critical as the adjustment of individuals. Social workers can be a resource for helping individuals to make connections inside and outside the residential setting, which will foster feelings of continuity and meaningfulness in their lives. In that pursuit, no policy or practice that might affect the ways older adults perceive the world of residential settings should be considered too undignified to justify the social worker's attention—lost and stolen articles, clothing mangled in the laundry, residents who are not using dentures or hearing aids and the like—may seem simple concrete issues but all need skilled attention and system-building to prevent their occurrence and remediate the problems when they do occur.

In keeping with the pioneering work of Herbert Shore, Elaine Brody, Carter Williams, Charles Fahey, and many others, today's social workers must remember that older people in group residential settings wish for and deserve to experience lives that are as normal and as enriched as possible. Like those earlier leaders, social workers cannot gloss over the shock and losses felt when moving into a group residential setting, a move that is rarely made without ambivalence. Moreover, even while facilitating varied therapies, social workers need to understand that adherence to a therapeutic regimen will not fully determine the meaningfulness of life for residents. An overarching goal for social workers practicing in these settings should be to help residents feel that the place where they live and receive care is truly their home.

REFERENCES

Bern-Klug, M. (Ed.). (2010). *Transforming palliative care in nursing homes: The social work role.* New York, NY: Columbia University Press.

Bonifas, R. P. (2015). Resident-to-resident aggression in nursing homes: Social work involvement and collaboration with nursing colleagues. *Health and Social Work.* doi: 10.1093/hsw/hlv040.

Brody, E. M., & Contributors. (1974). *A social work guide for long-term care facilities.* Washington, DC: Government Printing Office.

Cohen, E. (1974). An overview of long-term care facilities. In E. M. Brody & Contributors (Eds.), *Social work guide for long-term care facilities.* Washington, DC: Government Printing Office.

Cutler, L. J., & Kane, R. A. (2009). Post-occupancy evaluation of a transformed nursing home: The first four Green House® nursing homes. *Journal of Housing for the Elderly, 23,* 304–334.

Fahey, C. J. (2003). Culture change in long-term care facilities: Changing the facility or changing the system? *Journal of Social Work and Long-Term Care, 2,* 35–51.

Freeman, I. C. (2000). Uneasy allies: Nursing home regulators and consumer advocates. *Journal of Aging Policy, 11,* 127–135.

Goffman, E. (1961). *Asylums: Essays on the social situation of mental patients and other inmates.* Garden City, NY: Anchor Books.

Gubrium, J. F. (1975). *Living and dying at Murray Manor.* New York, NY: St. Martin's.

Gwyther, L. (2001). *Caring for people with Alzheimer's disease: A manual for facility staff.* Washington, DC: American Health Care Association and Alzheimer's Association.

Hernandez, M., & Newcomer, R. (2007). AL and special populations: What do we know about differences in use and potential access barriers? *The Gerontologist, 47*(Suppl 1), 110–117.

Institute of Medicine (IOM). (1986). *Improving the quality of care in nursing homes.* Washington, DC: National Academy Press.

Kane, R. A. (2001). Long-term care and a good quality of life: Bring them closer together. *The Gerontologist, 41,* 293–304.

Kane, R. A., & Cutler, L. J. (2009). Promoting home-like characteristics and eliminating institutional characteristics in community-based residential care settings. *Senior Housing and Care Journal, 17,* 15–37.

Kane, R. A., Kane, R. L., Illston, L. H., Nyman, J., & Finch, M. D. (1991) Adult foster care for the elderly in Oregon: A mainstream alternative to nursing homes? *American Journal of Public Health, 81,* 1113–1120.

Kane, R. A., Kane, R. L., & Ladd, R. C. (1998). *The heart of long-term care.* New York, NY: Oxford University Press.

Kane, R. A., Kling, K. C., Bershadsky, B., Kane, R. L., Giles, K., Degenholtz, H. B., . . . Cutler, L. J. (2003). Quality of life measures for nursing home residents. *Journal of Gerontology: Medical Sciences, 58A,* 240–248.

Kane, R. A., Lum, T., Cutler, L. J., Degenholtz, H. B., & Yu, A.-C. (2007). Resident outcomes in small-group-home nursing homes: A longitudinal evaluation of the initial Green House program. *Journal of the American Geriatrics Society, 55,* 832–839.

Kane, R. A., & Wilson K. B. (1993). *Assisted living in the United States: A new paradigm for residential care for frail older persons.* Washington, DC: AARP.

Leeds, N., & Shore, H. (Eds.). (1964). *Geriatric institutional management.* New York, NY: Putnam.

Lum, T. Y., Kane, R. A., Cutler, L. J., & Yu, T.-C. (2008). Effects of Green House® nursing homes on resident families. *Health Care Financing Review, 30,* 37–51.

Office of the Inspector General (OIG). (2014). *Adverse events in skilled nursing homes: National incidence among Medicare beneficiaries.* DHS, Office of the Inspector General, February 2014, OEI-06-11-00370.

Rabig, J., Thomas, W., Kane, R. A., Cutler, L. J., & McAlilly, S. (2006). Radical redesign of nursing homes: Applying the Green House concept in Tupelo, MS. *The Gerontologist, 46,* 533–539.

Thomas, W. H. (1999). *The Eden alternative handbook: The art of building human habitats.* Sherburne, NY: Summer Hill.

Tobin, S. S. (1999). *Preservation of self in the oldest years.* New York, NY: Springer.

Wilson, K. B. (2007). Historical evolution of AL in the United States, 1979 to the present. *The Gerontologist, 47*(Suppl 1), 8–22.

Wunderlich, G. S., & Kohler, P. O. (2001). *Improving the quality of long-term care.* Washington, DC: National Academy Press.

SHERYL ZIMMERMAN
JEAN MUNN
TERRY KOENIG

Assisted Living Settings

23

Assisted living (AL) is a term applied to a wide array of residential care settings for older adults. In the broadest sense, these long-term services and supports (LTSS) include all group residential programs not licensed as nursing homes that provide personal care in activities of daily living (ADLs) and can respond to unscheduled needs for assistance (Kane & Wilson, 1993). In theory, the term AL also conveys values that underlie the manner in which care is provided. Thus, AL has come to refer to a *setting* of long-term care that combines housing and supportive services in a homelike environment and that promotes a distinct *philosophy* of care. The field of AL is a complex one, because as a setting of care AL embodies a diversity of residential types and as a philosophy of care it espouses principles that are inconsistently in practice (Zimmerman, Sloane, & Eckert, 2001). To understand the distinction between setting and philosophy, as well as the current state of AL and the needs of its residents, it is helpful to consider the evolution of AL within the field of LTSS.

ASSISTED LIVING AS A SETTING AND A PHILOSOPHY OF CARE

Non-nursing-home residential care for older adults was first recognized in the United States in the 1940s, as small "mom-and-pop" homes and later as senior housing (Morgan, Eckert, & Lyon, 1995). Over time, there was a growing awareness of a gap in the "continuum" of long-term care between residential settings that catered to older adults who had functional impairments and nursing facilities that catered to the chronically ill. This awareness reflected the combined impact of growing numbers of older adults, a shortage of nursing home beds, increasing costs of nursing home care, the better health of new generations of older adults, and dissatisfaction with nursing home care (Bishop, 1999; Borra, 1986; Korcok, 1987). Thus, the need was recognized for a new model of care that would provide an "invisible support system" in a residential setting (Sullivan, 1998). The utility of this concept drew investment from nursing home chains that saw the opportunity to use AL as a feeder for their nursing level of care, into which residents could be transferred as impairment increased. At the same time, market pressure created a stand-alone AL industry, intended to provide increasingly higher levels of care to enable aging in place and avoid nursing home transfer if possible (Mollica, 2001a; Thompson &

Marinaccio, 1997). Over time, a diversity of residential settings that provide or bring in supportive services, including settings otherwise named adult foster care, personal care homes, sheltered housing, homes for adults, board and care, residential care facilities, and domiciliary care (among others), have come to be known as AL.

On a purist level, AL was intended to refer to those settings that embrace the philosophy of care explicated by the Assisted Living Quality Coalition (1998). The coalition set forth 17 philosophies related to care and quality of life that they recommended be reflected in an AL community's mission, policies, and procedures, including offering personalized, quality supportive services; maximizing independence and individuality; assuring dignity, respect, privacy, and choice; involving residents in policy decisions; providing full consumer disclosure before move in; and ensuring that the residential emphasis avoids characteristics of an "institutional" setting (Assisted Living Quality Coalition, 1998). The challenge in conceptualizing AL, however, is that while the industry promotes certain goals, the term is used by communities (whether licensed or unlicensed) that do not subscribe to this philosophy, and it is not always used by those that do. The result is that there is no single accepted definition of AL or guidelines for how to operationally distinguish it from other forms of care.

This controversy notwithstanding, as of 2010 there were an estimated 31,100 licensed, registered, or certified AL residences in the United States, housing almost 750,000 older adults (Park-Lee et al., 2011). It should not be assumed that availability is similar across the country, however, as there is an almost sixfold difference in capacity between the highest and lowest states; specifically, the average capacity in Michigan, Oregon, Idaho, Wisconsin, and Washington is 62 units per 1,000 people age 65 or older, compared with just 11 units per 1,000 people age 65 or older in Nevada, Michigan, West Virginia, Louisiana, and the District of Columbia (Mollica, Houser, & Ujvari, 2012). The charge for AL also varies; the average monthly rate in 2012 was $3,550, but it was as high as $5,933 in the District of Columbia and as low as $2,344 in Arkansas (MetLife Mature Market Institute, 2012).

Diversity also is evident in resident need. One-quarter of residents do not need support with ADLs, but almost 36% require assistance with one or two ADLs, and 38% require assistance with three to five ADLs—the most common being support with bathing and dressing, which describes more than one-half of AL residents (Caffrey et al., 2012). As many as 90% of residents have cognitive impairment, up to two-thirds or more of whom have dementia depending on the exact setting and the manner of dementia ascertainment (Zimmerman et al., 2007). This diversity in care and increasing levels of resident need have raised concerns related to the quality of care and spurred activity to regulate AL (Kane & Wilson, 2001). It is to these regulatory activities that we now turn.

ASSISTED LIVING REGULATION

Unlike nursing homes, there is no overarching federal regulatory body for AL; instead, individual states define, license, regulate, fund, and oversee AL. In consequence, the regulatory environment is variable and not always transparent to consumers. Further complicating the matter is that regulatory terminology varies across states; that is, while the majority of states refer to these residences as AL, others use terms such as "residential care," "boarding homes," "enriched housing programs," "homes for the aged," "personal care homes," and others (Polzer, 2011).

Between 2000 and 2012, virtually every state addressed issues of AL regulation, doing so with regulatory models ranging from those that are highly defined and prescriptive with detailed criteria to those that are broad and general, using criteria as nonspecific as "meeting resident needs." The dynamic nature of the field is evident in that in 2012 alone, 18 states made changes in their regulations, half of which were considered major; for example, more than one state changed reporting requirements, survey procedures, thresholds for resident admission and retention, medication management, staffing, and assessment (Polzer, 2013).

Simply stated, there are four models of state AL licensure (Mollica, Wilson, Ryther, & Lamarche, 1995). The *institutional models* reflect a more traditional board-and-care philosophy of AL, with minimum building and unit requirements (e.g., bedrooms and bathrooms may be shared). The *housing and services model* allows for a wide range of services in apartment-type settings, thereby differentiating AL from traditional board-and-care homes. The *service model* focuses on the services provided by licensed personnel rather than on the structure of the residences themselves. Finally, an *umbrella model* covers a variety of housing and services with names such as residential care, congregate care, and adult care homes, as well as AL.

Four areas that have received notable attention within the regulatory models are the living unit, the residents (including admission and retention criteria), staffing requirements, and services. The existence of state-based regulation should not be taken to assume homogeneity within states with reference to these areas, however, or any other component of AL care. Instead, the criteria set parameters for care, and providers have the latitude to structure and provide care as they see fit within those guidelines.

The Living Unit

The living unit is one of the most controversial areas included in regulations, in large part because many consider private rooms to be definitional of AL (Assisted Living Workgroup, 2003). Board-and-care homes meet minimal requirements, allowing for shared bedrooms and bathrooms. Regulations more focused on the AL philosophy, however, emphasize privacy and a homelike atmosphere and specify single-occupancy and apartment-style living. As of 2010, 23 states required the provision of apartment-style units, and 40 allow units to be shared (Mollica, 2009). The most recent information (2010) indicates that unrelated individuals share only 3% of all AL units (Mollica, Houser, & Ujvari, 2012).

The Residents

Admission and retention criteria set parameters on the extent to which AL residents are allowed to reside and age in place, and so in large part describe the resident population. Typically, these criteria refer to the extent of support and care required for healthcare, function, cognition, and behavior (e.g., posing a danger to self or others). Across the states, criteria range from little specification to very specific exclusionary criteria related to needs for assistance, although in some states acceptable levels of need may be as high as those necessitating 24-hour nursing care as long as supportive services, including from third-party providers, are available (Polzer, 2013).

Given the evolution of AL as an alternative to nursing homes for individuals who need supportive, but not nursing, care, AL is serving an increasingly vulnerable population. Their residents present an increasing number and breadth of chronic medical problems such as high blood pressure (57%), heart disease (34%), and arthritis (27%). Furthermore, and of special relevance to social work, 28% of AL residents have depression and 42% have dementia (Caffrey et al., 2012). Regulations are not silent regarding care for these individuals, as approximately three-quarters of states specify requirements related to serving residents with dementia, including staff training, enclosed areas to accommodate wandering, and special safety provisions; many also address dementia special care units (Polzer, 2011).

The Staff

Resident care needs are met by the staff who work in these residences, but staffing requirements vary across states. For example, minimum staffing levels range from one staff person per 40 residents (Missouri) to one staff person per 6 residents (Alabama). The majority of states require that staffing be "sufficient to meet the needs of residents in the facility," allowing managers to decide the exact level, and the complaint and survey process to assure that it is adequate (Hodlewsky, 2001).

To serve as an administrator in an AL residence, an individual must be at least 18 to 21 years of age, and some states require a high school diploma or its equivalent. Stricter requirements are found in Connecticut, which requires that administrators be a registered nurse (RN) and New York, which requires administrators to have a master's degree in social work (MSW). Requirements for direct care staff are variable, in that some states simply specify that staff must have experience, or a specific number of hours of training (e.g., Alabama) while others are more explicit in terms of the focus of that training (e.g., Arkansas, South Carolina; Bentley, Sabo, & Waye, 2003).

The Services

Services required or allowed under regulation include medical services (e.g., general physician, podiatry, dentistry, nursing), social services, and support services, such as barber or beauty services (Zimmerman, Eckert, & Wildfire, 2001). In 2010, 39% of AL residences provided skilled care by licensed nurses (Park-Lee et al., 2011), reflecting the increasing acuity of the residents who live in AL.

While nearly all AL residences provide basic services (e.g., health monitoring, incontinence care, social activities), other services available are related, at least in part, to residence size, with larger residences more likely to provide occupational and physical therapy, counseling services, and case management (Park-Lee et al., 2011).

In addition to services provided in the residence, third-party services are common. They may be contracted by the resident or the residence itself. The two most common third-party services are home health-care (e.g., skilled nursing, occupational and physical therapy) and hospice. Both treat the AL residence as the resident's primary home and provide the same services they do to community-dwelling individuals. Regulations in 35 states specify that home health services be allowable, although there again is variability, such as whether services need to be of a time-limited nature or expressly not interfere with services provided to other residents (Bentley et al., 2003).

ASSISTED LIVING FUNDING

With the growth of AL and its provision of services to impaired older adults, there has been an increasing trend toward the public subsidy of AL. In 1998, 32 states provided funding for AL services, a number that increased to 41 by 2003 (Bentley et al., 2003). By 2009, 19% of AL residents received Medicaid funding, reflecting an increase of 9% between 2007 and 2009, and of almost 44% between 2002 and 2009 (Mollica, 2009). By 2010, 43% of residences had at least one resident who had some or all of his or her services paid by Medicaid (Park-Lee et al., 2011).

Methods of actual payment are diverse, with states providing payment as a flat rate or tiered rate or in accordance with care plans or resident case mix. The most common source of Medicaid funding is the Medicaid 2176 Home- and Community-Based Care Waiver (Department of Health and Human Services, Centers for Medicare and Medicaid Services, 2014), which is available to beneficiaries who qualify for skilled nursing home care and meet income eligibility criteria (Bentley, Sabo, & Waye, 2003; Mollica, 2001b), although other sources of state funding also exist (Mollica, 2009). A few states allow room and board to be covered, but most do not. Paying for room and board constitutes an ongoing controversy because AL is a residential setting based on a social model rather than a medical model of care and room

and board traditionally have been excluded from Medicaid coverage. Specific reimbursement strategies for AL have evolved as the industry has developed, but not without controversy. Most recently, the Centers for Medicare and Medicaid Services (CMS) specified that Medicaid funding would be available only in instances when person-centered care is provided in a setting that is integrated into the community (Department of Health and Human Services, 2014).

ISSUES IN ASSISTED LIVING

In a field as evolving and variable as AL, a multitude of issues are of interest to the social work community. The eight addressed here relate to the quality of care: small AL and disparities in access and quality; consumer education; dementia care; family involvement; autonomy, negotiated risk, and aging in place; recognizing and treating psychosocial needs; continuing care retirement communities (CCRCs) and transition, and end-of-life care.

Small Assisted Living and Disparity in Access and Quality

While 90% of AL residents live in communities that have at least 11 beds, 50% of all AL communities have 10 or fewer beds (Park-Lee et al., 2011). Smaller AL settings serve an important role as they tend to provide care for more functionally and cognitively impaired residents than do other AL settings; furthermore, while African Americans are rarely resident in AL, smaller settings house proportionately more African Americans (17%) than other settings (6%–8%; Zimmerman, Gruber-Baldini, Sloane, et al., 2003), but they tend to score less well on some ratings of environmental quality (Howard et al., 2002). Indeed, early board-and-care type AL primarily served low-income older adults who could not live independently and relied on Medicaid, SSI, or other state and federal government funds. As AL grew and the business community recognized it as a profit-making opportunity, a schism developed between modest residences catering to those of lesser means and more upscale AL serving residents able to afford substantial private-pay rates (Kane & Wilson, 2001). As a consequence, the AL industry has been largely private pay and unaffordable for low- or moderate-income persons, and due to these economic and other social factors, the proportion of AL residents who are minorities is minimal (i.e., 46%–71% of facilities have no African American residents; Howard et al., 2002). Fortunately, new efforts have promoted affordable AL, including use of Medicaid Home and Community-Based Services (HCBS) waiver monies, which may better balance availability and quality.

Consumer Education

As AL has evolved, the fact that consumers are unaware of the diversity of available options has become a matter of concern. In consequence, recommendations have been issued to promote widespread publicly available information about AL that would include information about specific services and supports, survey results, verified complaints, rating scales, and consumer outcomes such as satisfaction; the need for state mandates to promote such reporting, and the utility to have independent, reputable, unbiased organizations disseminate this information, are important considerations (Zimmerman, Cohen, & Horsford, 2013).

Dementia Care

Some AL communities offer a dementia special care unit, but a minority (14%) of all residents reside there (Zimmerman, Sloane, & Reed, 2015). However, the evidence is not persuasive that special care promotes better outcomes for residents with dementia (Zimmerman, Anderson, et al., 2013) and so, instead, best practices are advised.

Family Involvement

The majority of AL residents have family members who remain involved in their lives and oversee their welfare. However, this oversight comes at a cost, as compared with families of individuals who reside in nursing homes, AL families feel more burdened in their caregiving responsibilities, even though they visit less often (Port et al., 2005; Zimmerman, Cohen, et al., 2013). Therefore, prospective AL residents and families might be encouraged to consider the family's ability to visit and monitor care, and their ability to tolerate burden.

Autonomy, Negotiated Risk, and Aging in Place

The philosophy of AL is to promote control and choice, yet doing so can be a liability to providers if control and choice impede resident safety. Negotiated risk agreements are signed agreements between residents and providers which expressly state that the resident chooses to accept certain risks associated with care in order to maximize preferences (e.g., the choice to not adhere to dietary restrictions or medication schedules). Although many states have incorporated negotiated risk as part of their regulation, they are met by objections from the nursing home industry because they reduce nursing home admissions (Mollica, 2001b). Balancing autonomy, safety, and quality of life in AL is an ongoing challenge, and one of definite interest to the social worker (Kissam, Gifford, More, & Patry, 2003).

Recognizing and Treating Psychosocial Needs, Including Dementia

Based on national data, almost one-quarter (23%) of AL residents have moderate cognitive impairment, and one-fifth (19%) have severe impairment (Zimmerman, Sloane, & Reed, 2015); in addition, 28% have symptoms of depression (Caffrey et al., 2012). In consideration of the limited staff training requirements noted earlier, there is cause to believe that AL providers are not expert in the care of these conditions and that there is room for social work services in AL.

Continuing Care Retirement Communities and Transitions in Care

Continuing care retirement communities (CCRCs) offer a range of housing and supportive services on one campus, typically including independent living, AL, and nursing home care. In most cases, individuals cannot move directly into the AL wing; instead, they first reside in an independent living unit and transition to AL when they require supportive care. Today, there are approximately 1,900 CCRCs (Zarem, 2010). The issue related to AL in CCRCs is that while the range of services purportedly conveys the sense of "aging in place" as individuals transition across levels of care, evidence suggests that the move from independent living to AL in CCRCs is perceived as disempowering, disruptive, and fraught with tension (Shippee, 2009; Zimmerman Dobbs, Roth, Goldman, Peeples, et al., 2014), similar to other transitions in care.

End-of-Life Care

A less-appreciated component of AL care is that as the number of residents living there has increased, so too has the number of residents dying there: approximately 14% of AL residents die annually (Zimmerman et al., 2005). Issues relevant to end-of-life care in AL include pain and symptom management (Caprio et al., 2008), spiritual care (Daaleman, Williams, Hamilton, & Zimmerman, 2008), advance care planning (Daaleman et al., 2009), and communicating with healthcare providers (Biola et al., 2007), among others.

SOCIAL SERVICES IN ASSISTED LIVING

While staff in some AL communities counsel residents on matters related to Supplemental Security Income, Social Security, and Medicaid (a service referred to as "social services counseling" in the National Survey of Residential Care Facilities), and more than one-half report providing case management (although the specific nature of these services is not addressed; Park-Lee et al., 2011), social work's presence in AL has been and remains uneven and infrequent. Instead, when social services are provided for AL residents, they tend to be provided by geriatric care managers or mental health consultants not directly employed by the AL residence, and by ombudsmen. Ombudsman programs provide oversight to AL residences, address complaints made by or on behalf of residents, and support resident rights such as related to freedom and privacy. Some of the recognized parallels between ombudsman programs and social work include an emphasis on serving vulnerable or marginalized populations, meeting residents where they are and proceeding at a pace appropriate for them, providing mediation and conflict resolution, and maximizing residents' quality of life (Dakin, Quijano, & McAlister, 2010).

The lack of sufficient psychosocial services in AL is evident based on findings from one study that

25% of residents with dementia were not recognized as such (Samus et al., 2013); and from another study of more than 2,000 residents from 193 AL residences that over one-third of residents displayed symptoms of depression, which was a risk factor for both discharge to a nursing home and mortality (Watson, Garrett, Sloane, Gruber-Baldini, & Zimmerman, 2003); and because there is concern that rates of severe and persistent mental illness among AL residents will be a growing challenge (Dakin, Quijano, & McAlister, 2010). Clinical social workers and other mental health professionals who work in or consult to AL residences are equipped to assess and treat mental health challenges as well as matters related to end-of-life care planning and engaging the family system (Spitzer, Neuman, & Holden, 2004).

Another area in which social workers could be especially influential relates to helping older adults and their families at the time they are making the decision to move into AL (Ball, Perkins, Hollingsworth, Whittington, & King, 2009; Koenig, Lee, Macmillan, Fields, & Spano, 2013). The decision to move is not always easy, and often raises competing values such as reduced autonomy and increased safety; at this transition, social workers can help prospective residents and families address these concerns (Spano & Koenig, 2003). At this same time, the social worker's ability to assess mental health needs and foster communication among the resident, family members, and staff in the development and implementation of resident care plans could be especially helpful (Ingersoll-Dayton, Schroepfer, Pryce, & Waarala, 2003; Kruzich & Powell, 1995). Another important social work role is to help families anticipate the caregiving task they will continue to do after move-in (e.g., monitoring care and handling finances), and establish supports if necessary; after move-in, social workers might ease the tensions that sometimes exist between families and AL staff (Zimmerman, Cohen, et al., 2013). Indeed, AL administrators who employed social workers in their residences recognized the importance of role of social workers serving as a resident advocate and mental health assessor/counselor, as well as providing important services related to decision-making, transition, family social work, and care planning (Fields, Koenig, & Schoeny-Dabelko, 2012; Koenig, Lee, Fields, & Macmillan, 2011). In many ways, the philosophical principles of the AL model of care support the current and future role of social workers in these settings.

In addition to recognizing this viable social work role within AL, it is important to note that some social workers who are not directly employed by AL settings already provide services to their residents and families, such as case managers for Medicaid waiver programs and hospital discharge planners who facilitate AL placement. However, these workers may not understand the variability of AL services and the overlap of these residents with those of nursing homes; as a result, they may not be as expert as necessary to provide optimal social work services. Consequently, there remains a need to consider the development of a true AL social worker. Unfortunately, the inherent challenge in this quest is to secure the financial buy-in of public entities and profit-making companies to support the work. Thus, a goal of AL research should be to determine the true utility of—and therefore have an impact on the future existence of—the currently largely fictional AL social worker.

REFERENCES

Assisted Living Quality Coalition. (1998). *Assisted living quality initiative: Building a structure that promotes quality*. Washington, DC: Public Policy Institute, American Association of Retired Persons.

Assisted Living Workgroup. (2003). *Assuring quality in assisted living: Guidelines for federal and state policy, state regulation, and operations*. A report to the US Senate Special Committee on Aging. Washington, DC: Author.

Ball, M. M., Perkins, M. M., Hollingsworth, C., Whittington, F. J., & King, S. V. (2009). Pathways to assisted living: The influence of race and class. *Journal of Applied Gerontology, 28*, 81–108.

Bentley, L., Sabo, S., & Waye, A. (2003). *Assisted living state regulatory review*. Retrieved November 2, 2013, from http://www.ahcancal.org/ncal/resources/Documents/2003_reg_review.pdf

Biola, H., Sloane, P. D., Williams, C. S., Daaleman, T. P., Williams, S. W., & Zimmerman, S. (2007). Physician communication with family caregivers of long-term care residents at the end of life. *Journal of the American Geriatrics Society, 55*, 846–856. http://dx.doi.org/10.1111/j.1532-5415.2007.01179.x

Bishop, C. E. (1999). Where are the missing elders? The decline in nursing home use, 1985 and 1995. *Health Affairs, 18*, 146–155. http://dx.doi.org/10.1377/hlthaff.18.4.146

Borra, P. C. (1986). Assisted living a timely alternative. *Provider, 12*, 14, 16–17.

Caffrey, C., Sengupta, M., Park-Lee, E., Moss, A., Rosenoff, E., & Harris-Kojetin, L. (2012). *Residents living in residential care facilities: United States, 2010*. NCHS data brief, no 91. Hyattsville, MD: National Center for Health Statistics. Retrieved November 2, 2013, from http://www.cdc.gov/nchs/data/databriefs/db91.pdf

Caprio, A. J., Hanson, L. C., Munn, J. C., Williams, C. S., Dobbs, D., Sloane, P. D., & Zimmerman, S. (2008). Pain, dyspnea, and the quality of dying in long-term care. *Journal of the American Geriatrics Society, 56*, 683–688. http://dx.doi.org/10.1111/j.1532-5415.2007.01613.x

Daaleman, T. P., Williams, C. S., Hamilton, V. L, & Zimmerman, S. (2008). Spiritual care at the end of life in long-term care. *Medical Care, 46*, 85–91.

Daaleman, T. P., Williams, C. S., Preisser, J. S., Sloane, P. D., Biola, H., & Zimmerman, S. (2009). Advance care planning in nursing homes and assisted living communities. *Journal of the American Medical Directors Association, 10*, 243–251. http://dx.doi.org/10.1016/j.jamda.2008.10.015

Dakin, E., Quijano, L. M., & McAlister, C. (2010). Assisted living facility administrator and direct care staff views of resident mental health concerns and staff training needs. *Journal of Gerontological Social Work, 54*, 53–72.

Department of Health and Human Services, Centers for Medicare and Medicaid Services. (2014). Medicaid program; state plan home and community-based services, 5-year period for waivers, provider payment reassignment, and home and community-based setting requirements for community first choice and home and community-based services (HCBS) waivers, final rule. *Federal Register, 79*, 2947–3039. Retrieved June 5, 2014, from http://www.gpo.gov/fdsys/pkg/FR-2014-01-16/pdf/2014-00487.pdf

Fields, N. L., Koenig, T. L., & Schoeny-Dabelko, H. I. (2012). Resident transitions to assisted living: A role for social workers. *Health and Social Work, 37*, 147–154.

Hodlewsky, R. T. (2001). Staffing problems and strategies in assisted living. In S. Zimmerman, P. D. Sloane, & J. K. Eckert (Eds.), *Assisted living: Needs, policies and practices in residential care for the elderly*. Baltimore, MD: Johns Hopkins University Press.

Howard, D. L., Sloane, P. D., Zimmerman, S., Eckert, J. K., Walsh, J., Buie, V. C., ... Koch, G. G. (2002). Distribution of African Americans in residential care/assisted living: More evidence of racial disparity? *American Journal of Public Health, 92*, 1272–1277.

Ingersoll-Dayton, B., Schroepfer, T., Pryce, J., & Waarala, C. (2003). Enhancing relationships in nursing homes through empowerment. *Social Work, 48*, 420–424. http://dx.doi.org/10.1093/sw/48.3.420

Kane, R., & Wilson, K. B. (Eds.). (1993). *Assisted living in the United States: A new paradigm for residential care for frail older persons?* Washington, DC: Public Policy Institute, American Association of Retired Persons.

Kane, R., & Wilson, K. B. (2001). *Assisted living at the crossroads: Principles for its future.* Portland, OR: Jessie F. Richardson Foundation.

Kissam, S., Gifford, D. R., More, V., & Patry, G. (2003). Admission and continued-stay criteria for assisted living facilities. *Journal of the American Geriatrics Society, 51*, 1651–1654. http://dx.doi.org/10.1046/j.1532-5415.2003.51519.x

Koenig, T. L., Lee, J. H., Fields, N. L., & Macmillan, K. R. (2011). The role of the gerontological social worker in assisted living. *Journal of Gerontological Social Work, 54*, 494–510.

Koenig, T. L., Lee, J. H., Macmillan, K. R., Fields, N., & Spano, R. (2013). Older adult and family member perspectives of the decision-making process involved in moving to assisted living. *Qualitative Social Work, 0*(00), 1–16. Retrieved from http://qsw.sagepub.com/content/early/2013/02/22/147332501347 5468.full.pdf+html

Korcok, M. (1987). "Assisted living": Developing an alternative to nursing homes. *Canadian Medical Association Journal, 137*, 843–845.

Kruzich, J. M., & Powell, W. E. (1995). Decision-making influence: An empirical study of social workers in nursing homes. *Health and Social Work, 20*, 215–222.

Met-Life Mature Market Institute. (2012). *Market survey of long-term care costs: The 2012 Metlife market survey of nursing home, assisted living, adult day services, and home care costs.* Retrieved December 1, 2013, from https://www.metlife.com/assets/cao/mmi/publications/studies/2012/studies/mmi-2 012-market-survey-long-term-care-costs.pdf

Mollica, R. (2001a). The evolution of assisted living: A view from the states. *Caring, 20*, 24–26.

Mollica, R. (2001b). State policy and regulations. In S. Zimmerman, P. D. Sloane, & J. K. Eckert (Eds.), *Assisted living: Needs, policies and practices in residential care for the elderly* (pp. 9–33). Baltimore, MD: Johns Hopkins University Press.

Mollica, R. (2009). *State Medicaid reimbursement policies and practices in assisted living.* Retrieved November 2, 2013, from http://www.ahcancal.org/ncal/resources/documents/medicaidassistedlivingreport.pdf

Mollica, R., Houser, A., & Ujvari, K. (2012). *Assisted living and residential care in the United States.* Insight on the Issues, 58. Retrieved November 2, 2013, from http://www.aarp.org/content/dam/aarp/research/public_policy_institute/ltc/2012/residential-care-insight-on-the-issues-july-2012-AARP-ppi-ltc.pdf

Mollica, R., Wilson, K. B., Ryther, B. S., & Lamarche, H. J. (1995). *Guide to assisted living and state policy.* Retrieved November 2, 2013, from http://aspe.hhs.gov/daltcp/reports/1995/alspguide.pdf

Morgan, L. A., Eckert, J. K., & Lyon, S. M. (Eds.). (1995). *Small board-and-care homes: Residential care in transition.* Baltimore, MD: Johns Hopkins University Press.

Park-Lee, E., Caffrey, C., Sengupta, M., Moss, A. J., Rosenhoff, E., & Harris-Kojetin, L. G. (2011). *Residential care facilities: A key sector in the spectrum of long-term care providers in the United States.* NCHS data brief No. 78. Hyattville, MD: National Center for Health Statistics.

Polzer, K. (2011). *Assisted living state regulatory review, 2011.* Washington, DC: National Center for Assisted Living. Retrieved November 2, 2013, from http://www.ahcancal.org/ncal/resources/documents/2011a ssistedlivingregulatoryreview.pdf

Polzer, K. (2013). *Assisted living state regulatory review, 2013.* Washington, DC: National Center for Assisted Living. Retrieved November 2, 2013, from http://www.ahcancal.org/ncal/resources/Documents/2013_reg_review.pdf

Port, C. L., Zimmerman, S., Williams, C. S., Dobbs, D., Preisser, J. S., & Williams, S. (2005). Families filling the gap: Comparing family involvement for assisted living and nursing home residents with dementia. *The Gerontologist, 45*(Spec 1), 87–95. http://dx.doi.org/10.1093/geront/45.suppl_1.87

Samus, Q. M., Onyike, C. U., Johnston, D., Mayer, L., McNabney, M., Baker, A. S., . . . Rosenblatt, A. (2013). 12-month incidence, prevalence, persistence, and treatment of mental disorders among individuals recently admitted to assisted living facilities in Maryland. *International Psychogeriatrics, 25*, 721–731. http://dx.doi.org/10.1017/S1041610212002244

Shippee, T. P. (2009). "But I am not moving": Residents' perspectives on transitions within a continuing care retirement community. *The Gerontologist, 49*, 418–427. http://dx.doi.org/10.1093/geront/gnp030

Spano, R., & Koenig, T. (2003). Moral dialogue: A worker-client interactional model. *Social Thought, 22*, 91–104. http://dx.doi.org/10.1300/J131v22n01_07

Spitzer, W. J., Neuman, K., & Holden, G. (2004). The coming of age for assisted living care: New options for senior housing and social work practice. *Social Work in Health Care, 383*, 21–45.

Sullivan, J. G. (1998). Redefining long term care. *Contemporary Long Term Care, 21,* 60–64.

Thompson, J. M., & Marinaccio, L. (1997). Improve continuity of care through collaboration: The growth of assisted living provides opportunities for nursing homes. *Balance, 1,* 14–15.

Watson, L., Garrett, J. M., Sloane, P. D., Gruber-Baldini, A. L., & Zimmerman, S. (2003). Depression in assisted living: Results from a four-state study. *American Journal of Geriatric Psychiatry, 11,* 534–542.

Zarem, J. E. (2010). *Today's continuing care retirement community.* Retrieved December 1, 2013, from http://www.leadingage.org/uploadedFiles/Content/Consumers/Paying_for_Aging_Services/CCR Ccharacteristics_7_2011.pdf

Zimmerman, S., Anderson, W., Brode, S., Jonas, D., Lux, L., Beeber, A., . . . Sloane, P. (2013). Systematic review: Effective characteristics of characteristics of nursing homes and other residential long-term care settings for people with dementia. *Journal of the American Geriatrics Society, 61,* 1399–1409. http://dx.doi.org/10.1111/jgs.12372

Zimmerman, S., Cohen, L. W., & Horsford, C. (2013). Group proposes public reporting for assisted living. *Provider,* December. Retrieved from http://www.providermagazine.com/ archives/2013_Archives/Pages/1213/Group-Proposes- Public-Reporting-For-Assisted-Living.aspx

Zimmerman, S., Cohen, L. W., Reed, D., Gwyther, L. P., Washington, T., Cagle, J. C., . . . Sloane, P. D. (2013). Comparing families and staff in nursing homes and assisted living: Implications for social work practice. *Journal of Gerontological Social Work, 56,* 535–553. http://dx.doi.org/10.1080/01634372.2013.811145

Zimmerman, S., Dobbs, D., Roth, E., Goldman, S., Peeples, A., & Wallace, B. (2014). Promoting and protecting against stigma in residential settings. *The Gerontologist, 00*(00-Advanced Access), 1–13. doi:10.1093/geront/gnu058

Zimmerman, S., Eckert, J. K., & Wildfire, J. B. (2001). The process of care. In S. Zimmerman, P. D. Sloane, & J. K. Eckert (Eds.), *Assisted living: Needs, policies and practices in residential care for the elderly* (pp. 198–223). Baltimore, MD: Johns Hopkins University Press.

Zimmerman, S., Gruber-Baldini, A. L., Sloane, P. D., Eckert, J. K., Hebel, J. R., Morgan, L. A., Stearns, S. C., Wildfire, J., Magaziner, J., Chen, C., & Konrad, T. R. (2003). Assisted living and nursing homes: Apples and oranges? *Gerontologist, 43*(Spec. 2), 107–117.

Zimmerman, S., Sloane, P. D., & Eckert, J. K. (2001). The state and quality of assisted living. In L. S. Noelker & Z. Harel (Eds.), *Linking quality of longterm care and quality of life.* New York, NY: Springer.

Zimmerman, S., Sloane, P. D., Eckert, J. K., Gruber-Baldini, A. L., Morgan, L. A., Hebel, R., . . . Chen, C. K. (2005). How good is assisted living? Findings and implications from an outcomes study. *Journal of Gerontology Social Sciences, 60B,* 195–204. http://dx.doi.org/10.1093/geronb/60.4.S195

Zimmerman, S., Sloane, P. D., & Reed, D. (2014). Dementia prevalence and care in assisted living. *Health Affairs, 33,* 658–666. doi:10.1377/hlthaff.2013.1255.

Zimmerman, S., Sloane, P. D., Williams, C. S., Dobbs, D., Ellajosyula, R., Braaten, A., . . . Kaufer, D. I. (2007). Residential care/assisted living staff may detect undiagnosed dementia using the Minimum Data Set Cognition Scale (MDS-COGS). *Journal of the American Geriatrics Society, 55,* 1349–1355.

ROBIN BONIFAS

MERCEDES BERN-KLUG

KELSEY SIMONS

Nursing Homes

Case Example 1

Mr. Johnson has terminal lung cancer and is expected to live for only a few months. He retains capacity for most decisions and wants the freedom to eat foods for pleasure, despite the fact that he is at risk for aspiration from food entering his lungs. The nursing home social worker must navigate Mr. Johnson's right to self-determination, even if his choice increases the risk of choking or aspiration pneumonia, and the facility administrator's concerns regarding legal liability.

Case Example 2

Mrs. Albright fell at home and broke her hip. After a spending a week in the hospital, she was transferred to a nursing home for a short rehabilitative stay. She is adamant about returning to her apartment and complains that she could recuperate better in bed rather than doing physical therapy "exercises." Tensions are high among her family members, with conflict regarding her continued safety at home and how she can afford necessary services; everyone is anxious about what the future holds. The nursing home social worker must help Mrs. Albright and her family to understand the rehabilitative process, sort out available options, and develop realistic plans for the future.

Case Example 3

Ms. Terrez has a developmental disability and has resided in institutional settings since she was 25 years old. Now at age 70, she has announced that she has a boyfriend, a male resident at the same facility, and they want to engage in sexual intimacy. Her legal guardian is adamantly against this relationship. The nursing home social worker must help mediate the positions of all parties as well as uphold facility policies and meet federal regulations regarding resident safety.

Social workers seeking a practice setting serving functionally and socially vulnerable older adults with complex needs in an ever-changing interdisciplinary context need look no further than America's nursing homes (NHs). Despite the rise in availability of assisted living facilities and home care options, NHs remain an essential component of the healthcare continuum, and a common setting for gerontological social work practice (Whitaker, Weismiller, & Clark, 2005). As illustrated above, individuals served by NHs and their situations are tremendously diverse.

Nursing homes are residential healthcare settings providing two distinct types of services: (1) long-term supportive care such as nursing, pharmacy, nutrition, housekeeping, recreational activities, and social services to address residents' basic biopsychosocial functional needs (Jones, Dwyer, Bercovitz, & Strahan, 2009), and (2) short-term rehabilitative care to persons who are recovering from acute conditions following hospitalization with associated medical complexity and multiple comorbidities. Facilities are licensed at the state level and most are also certified to receive federal Medicare payments for short-term skilled care and/or Medicaid payments for long-term care of persons who qualify because of financial and care needs. Of the 15,671 certified NHs in 2013, 92% were both Medicare *and* Medicaid certified (American Health Care Association [AHCA], 2013). In exchange for licensure and certification status, NHs must comply with state and federal regulations that stipulate standards for quality of care, residents' rights, quality of life, and many other categories (see Department of Health and Human Services, Office of Inspector General, 2003). Indeed, NHs are among the most heavily regulated industries in the country; importantly, many standards to which they are accountable are strongly connected to social work values. For example, requirements include promoting care that maintains or enhances residents' dignity, assuring that residents who display mental or psychosocial adjustment difficulties receive appropriate treatment and services, and providing residents with services that reasonably accommodate their individual needs and preferences (Centers for Medicare and Medicaid Services [CMS], 2013).

Nursing homes are complex systems with multiple levels including individual, family, organizational, and community; familiarity with each level increases the likelihood that the social worker can function smoothly and be a strong asset to both the setting and its residents. Effective NH social workers understand the needs and strengths of residents, families, and staff and possess the skills to assess residents' psychosocial needs and develop plans of care to effectively meet identified needs. They understand the roles of other staff members, can participate effectively as part of an interdisciplinary team, and are able and willing to advocate for residents' quality of care and quality of life. Furthermore, effective social workers understand the NH as an organization operating within the larger community and within the context of state and federal policies. Any of these system levels can be a target for social work intervention. Social workers have much to offer older adults and families given the profession's focus on overall quality of life, person-in-environment perspective, competencies in counseling and care coordination, and commitment to advocacy on behalf of individuals and families. This chapter describes (1) the characteristics of NH residents and their psychosocial needs, (2) the social work role and function in NHs, and (3) the characteristics of NHs and industry trends.

TABLE 24.1 Age Distribution of US Nursing Home Residents, 2013

(Total Number of Residents = 1,414,959)

Age	Percent	
< 30	0.6	
31–64	15.4	
65–74	16.1	
75–84	27.5	
85–95	35.5	68%
95+	5.1	

Source: CMS (2013a).

NURSING HOME RESIDENTS AND PSYCHOSOCIAL NEEDS

Although less than .5% of the US population lives in a NH (US Census Bureau, 2011), and NH occupancy rates and the number of certified NHs have declined slightly over recent years (Harrington, Olney, Carrillo, & Kang, 2012; CMS, 2012), more than 1.3 million people receive care in a NH on any given day (AHCA, 2013). Moreover, the number of persons who receive NH services at some time during the year is twice as high, amounting to approximately 3 million persons. Because the likelihood of living in an NH increases with age, and the older adult segment of the population is increasing, the demand for NH care is expected to expand in coming decades. While adults of all ages may receive NH care, over two-thirds are age 75 and over, as reported in Table 24.1.

Two-thirds (66%) of NH residents are women, about half (46%) are widowed, and three-fourths (77%) are white (CMS, 2013a). The number of racially diverse residents is likely to increase in tandem with the changing racial profile of the US population, including growing numbers of Asian and Hispanic Americans (US Census Bureau, 2004). Efforts to improve care for marginalized groups have been called for in light of disparities in the quality of NH care by residents' race and socioeconomic status (Mor, Zinn, Angelelli, Teno, & Miller, 2004).

Due to the availability of more community long-term care options tailored to the fewest needs among those in NHs, individuals with a high level of need are concentrated in NHs. As such, over the past decade the amount of care needed by NH residents has increased. Over 90% receive help with getting dressed, 56% with eating, 87% with using the toilet, and 84% with transferring (CMS, 2013). In addition, the majority of residents (87%) have moderately or severely impaired cognitive skills that impact their daily decision-making, 50% have a diagnosis of depression, 27% anxiety disorder, and 11% a diagnosis of psychotic disorder (CMS, 2013). Cognitive impairment and physical frailty are particularly common among the long-stay population; in contrast, but also challenging, short-term rehabilitative residents tend to have complex health needs and unstable chronic conditions. Compromised physical and mental functioning contributes to increased needs.

Psychosocial Needs

The psychosocial issues that residents bring with them to the NH setting and those that arise within the context of the NH stay can result from losses, an increase in dependency, and changes in support systems. A limited number of psychosocial needs are assessed as part of the Minimum Data Set (MDS), a federally mandated part of resident assessment in NHs since 1990 that is currently in its third version. Psychosocial issues captured by MDS 3.0 include mood, with particular attention to depressive symptoms including suicidal ideation, behavior, preferences in daily routine, and discharge planning. A more comprehensive list of psychosocial needs has been published by Vourlekis, Gelfand, and Greene (1992) and further defined in order of importance by Bonifas (2007); this list is presented in Table 24.2.

SOCIAL WORK ROLE AND FUNCTIONS

Regulatory Context

Current federal regulations implemented in 1990 include the requirement that NHs identify the medically related social and emotional/psychosocial needs of each resident and develop a plan to help each resident adjust to the social and emotional aspects of illness, treatment, and the NH stay. Social work services are covered as part of the overall facility operating costs, and NHs with more than 120 beds must employ at least one full-time qualified social worker. Nursing homes with less than 120 beds are not required to employ a full-time social worker but must still meet residents' psychosocial needs. In the NH context, a qualified social worker is someone with a social work degree or an "educational equivalent" such as a degree in psychology or counseling. Federal regulations require states to observe their own rules pertaining to licensure of healthcare professionals, including social workers in nursing facilities; however, some states exempt nursing homes from meeting such social work licensure requirements. Considerable research indicates that one-half to two-thirds of social service staff have degrees in social work (Bern-Klug et al., 2009; Kruzich & Powell, 1995; Quam & Whitford, 1992; Simons, 2006; Vinton, Mazza, & Kim, 1998; Vourlekis, Bakke-Friedland, & Zlotnik, 1995), and most are not licensed (Bern-Klug et al., 2009; Simons, 2006). Simons, Connolly and colleagues (2012) call for a differentiation of professional social work services from paraprofessional social services. In this chapter, we use the term "social services department" to include both professional or degreed social work staff members and paraprofessional social service staff members.

TABLE 24.2 Nursing Home Residents' Psychosocial Needs: Social Work Perspective

1. Opportunity for structured dialogue between families/residents and home personnel concerning care management.

2. Maintaining contact with friends, associates, and community ties outside the home.

3. Recognition by staff that "difficult behavior," including aggressiveness and withdrawal/apathy, may signify emotional distress; interventions based on a specific understanding of that distress.

4. Security that appropriate care will be in place at points of transition whether into, within, or out of the home.

5. Family collaboration in care planning and decision-making.

6. Help with fears and anxieties that may occur throughout the stay in the home.

7. Emotional support for family members.

8. Assurance that care and resources that are supposed to be provided/available, in fact, are.

9. Independence in functioning and the opportunity to do for oneself whenever possible, whatever the level of functioning.

10. Emotional support and assistance in coping with transition of move to the nursing home.

11. Ongoing relatedness and intimacy with family and loved ones.

12. Orientation to the home, its staff, policies, and procedures, including rights, responsibilities, and grievances.

13. Help with feelings of loss that occur throughout the stay in the home.

14. Choice concerning important daily routines.

15. Help with financial planning and decision-making prior to coming to the home and assistance in locating and accessing financial resources at any point during the stay in the home.

16. Opportunity for formal feedback to home personnel on level of satisfaction with aspects of home care.

17. Specific help in preparing for and coping with death.

18. Recognition of status and wholeness of one's life history.

19. Recognition and opportunity for expression of religious/ethnic/cultural identity.

20. Structured social and group interaction opportunities inside and outside the home.

21. Informal social opportunities with other residents.

22. Opportunity and assistance as needed with access to activities and events within the home that are diverse enough to match each resident's capabilities and interests.

23. Help with acquiring or replacing needed personal belongings or other practical transactions.

24. Contributing to the life and functioning of the nursing home community.

25. Family/resident input into survey/certification and accreditation processes.

Sources: Bonifas (2007); Vourlekis, Gelfand, and Greene (1992).

Social Service Staffing and Caseloads

Nursing home social services departments are predominantly small, with 43% to 58% employing only one staff member (Bern-Klug et al., 2009; Simons, 2006). As a result, an NH social worker's typical caseload ranges in size from 90 to 120 residents (Bern-Klug, Kramer, Sharr, & Cruz, 2010; Simons, 2006). The caseload size is cause for concern, because in a national survey of NH social services directors, the majority indicated one full-time staff member could meet the psychosocial needs of no more than 60 long-term care residents or 20 short-term residents requiring rehabilitation services (Bern-Klug et al., 2010). Likewise, analysis of national NH quality data has identified that lower levels of qualified social service staff is associated with poorer quality psychosocial services (Zhang, Gammonley, Paek, & Frahm, 2008). Similarly, a Washington State study documented negative psychosocial outcomes when NH social work caseloads were higher than 70 residents (Bonifas, 2008).

Nursing Home Social Work Practice

The National Association of Social Workers' (NASW, 2003) standards for practice in long-term care settings provide guidelines for NH social worker qualifications that exceed federal regulations. The NASW standards place greater emphasis on professionalization by recommending that all social work staff have either a BSW or an MSW degree.

National Association of Social Workers Guidelines

Years of professional, conceptual and empirical effort have led to a well-articulated model of NH social workers' roles and functions. In 1993, the NASW developed an important consensus statement on the mission and roles of the NH social work practitioner. These practice guidelines embrace a comprehensive intervention domain that includes the resident, the resident's family, facility staff, and the organizational environment. Emphasis is placed on direct services that promote psychosocial well-being and interdisciplinary collaborative efforts to "foster climate, policy, and routines" that respect residents' cultural diversity, individual uniqueness, dignity, independence, and choice (NASW, 1993).

In addition, the NASW's *Standards for Social Work Services in Long-Term Care Facilities* (2003), although not exclusive to NH practice, provides guidance regarding the necessary and appropriate functions for social workers including "advocacy, care planning, discharge planning and documentation; participation in policy and program planning; quality improvement; staff education pertaining to social services; liaison to the community; and consultation to other staff members" (p. 13). Such responsibilities challenge the professional social worker to use a range of clinical, organizational, and research skills in working directly with residents and their families, and indirectly with facility staff, as well as to develop organizational policies to improve psychosocial outcomes and quality of life for residents. More recently, recommendations from the NASW and the US Department of Veterans' Affairs have been merged by experts in the field to inform the 15 best practice social work functions in long-term care facilities (Simons et al., 2012), listed in Table 24.3.

In conjunction with practices described, NH social workers address specialized areas of resident

TABLE 24.3 Best Practice Social Work Role Functions in Long-Term Care Facilities

1. Psychosocial assessment of residents and family members as a basis for interdisciplinary care planning and intervention.

2. Resident and family education related to illness, including teaching coping and problem-solving skills to maintain or enhance psychosocial functioning.

3. Provision of, or referral for, mental health services.

4. Coordination of discharge planning and follow-up with the resident, family, interdisciplinary team, and community service providers.

5. Documentation of resident's psychosocial status, initial and ongoing, progress notes, review of treatment goals, and so forth.

6. Case management services to facilitate coordination and continuity of care and to assist residents and families with obtaining necessary services in the home or in the community.

7. Psychosocial interventions with individuals, families, and groups related to a range of health, social, and emotional needs.

8. Crisis intervention.

9. Liaison to family members, including coordination-of-care planning meetings.

10. Advocating with and for residents within the long-term care facility and system to ensure greater choice, quality of life, and quality of care. This may include consultation with the facility ombudsman.

11. Assisting with end-of-life planning, including legal and health-related matters.

12. Serving as a staff resource for training staff in nonpharmacological approaches to managing problem behaviors.

13. Participation in resident and family council as requested.

14. Supervision of fieldwork students.

15. Participation in independent or collaborative research projects.

Source: Simons, Connolly et al. (2012).

need. Thus, they can effectively contribute to staff training in areas such as residents' rights, cultural competency, and mental health services.

Resident Rights

Nursing home social workers often provide training to residents, families, and staff about federally established resident rights, which include (1) non-discrimination in admission and care regardless of source of payment; (2) freedom from unnecessary physical and chemical restraints; (3) the right to be informed about all care and to participate in care planning; (4) freedom from verbal, sexual, physical, and mental abuse, corporal punishment, and involuntary seclusion; (5) the right to personal property, access to the telephone, and privacy of mail; and (6) the right to share a room with a spouse who is also a resident of the facility (Knee & Vourlekis, 1995).

Cultural Competence

Social workers can also play an important role in supporting residents, family, and staff in developing cultural competence. Culturally sensitive and competent practice requires awareness and understanding of the culturally distinctive aspects of residents' attitudes, preferences, and behaviors. For example, family members' feelings about the placement decision may vary culturally (Fitzgerald, Mullavey-O'Byrne, & Clemson, 2001; Kolb, 2003), and resident preferences regarding the end of life can be influenced by culture (Ejaz, 2002; Field, Maher, & Webb, 2002; Ingersoll-Dayton, Saengtienchai, Kespichayawattana, & Aungsuroch, 2004). Cultural competence skills are also called for when working with members of other underrepresented groups in the NH setting including younger adults, men, and individuals who are gay, lesbian, bisexual, or transgender.

In many regions of the country, significant numbers of direct care staff are members of recent immigrant groups, who are therefore serving elderly individuals from cultures different from their own. Social workers can be helpful in recognizing and mediating cultural differences between staff members and residents or between family and staff members in an effort to prevent misunderstandings and conflicts. Case examples 4 and 5 illustrate the complex cultural issues social workers negotiate in NH settings.

Case Example 4

Mr. Perez is an American Indian, and in his culture it is considered taboo to discuss death and preferences for life-sustaining efforts should his heart stop beating; however, his condition has declined rapidly and the physician is concerned that attempts at resuscitation would be harmful and result in ventilator dependency. The family is weary of hospitals and technology in general. The nursing home social worker must help staff understand Mr. Perez's cultural perspective and also help explain the implication of resuscitation efforts to the family.

Case Example 5

Mrs. Basha, an Islamic woman, passed away this morning and the family wishes to engage in the bathing and enshrouding rituals of their faith before she is transported to the funeral home. The process may take hours, the resident's roommate is uncomfortable with the situation, and there are two patients at the hospital waiting to be transferred to the facility's one available room. There is no Muslim staff in the facility, and no one is familiar with the necessity of these rituals. The social worker must provide timely education while also exploring options to address the concerns of the roommate as well as the pending admissions from the hospital.

Mental Health Services

Social workers will be best prepared for the provision of psychosocial care if they are skilled in identifying and addressing residents' mental health conditions. The Department of Veterans Affairs (2001) recommends that its NH social workers screen for mental disorders and provide, if appropriately credentialed, individual, group, and family counseling. However, given the great need for mental health services in NHs and the typically high caseloads, it is more likely that residents with intensive needs will be referred to external providers for mental health services. Therefore, the social worker may more often be viewed as part of a team of mental health providers, serving as a first point-of-contact for the resident and his or her family and tasked with recognition of need and appropriate referral, rather than as the sole provider of mental health treatment (Beaulieu, 2002). Indeed, a recent survey of NH social services directors indicates 90% frequently plan interventions for individuals who are depressed, but only 52% regularly provide counseling or psychotherapy to residents with depression or other mood disorders; 25% do not provide such interventions at all (Bern-Klug & Kramer, 2013).

Practice Realities and Issues

The NH social work research and practice literature has been valuable in explaining and reinforcing the highly skilled nature of social work functions for administrators, policy makers, and consumers. Even so, NH social workers confronting the realities of practice are likely to encounter problems of role overload and role expectations (Greene, Vourlekis, Gelfand, & Lewis, 1992). Significant barriers to direct service exist, such as extensive paperwork and being assigned responsibilities in addition to provision of psychosocial care (Department of Health and Human Services, 2003). A total focus on individual residents' needs may inhibit practitioners from advocating for changes at the NH level in order to bring about greater quality of life for all residents.

Despite these limitations, there is evidence of consistency in implementation of the central elements of the social work role. Practitioners in Washington State report their highest frequency functions were (1) psychosocial assessment; (2) collaboration with multidisciplinary staff; (3) assessing factors related to mood and behavioral symptoms; (4) intervening to reduce emotional distress; (5) assisting residents to adjust to the facility; and (6) mediating issues among residents, families, and staff (Bonifas, 2007). National research corroborates these findings, as well as highlighting discharge planning and end-of-life planning as being among social workers' most frequent core functions (Bern-Klug & Kramer, 2013).

Emphasizing Social Work's Role in Quality Improvement

Social work processes and interventions, while conceptually sound, lack empirically demonstrated links to clinical outcomes. To date, only a few studies connect NH social workers' efforts to resident-centered outcomes. For example, Morrison, Chichin, Carter, Burack, and Meier (2005) demonstrated that NH social workers could improve the documentation of resident advance care plans and identify their treatment preferences. Bonifas (2011) found that balanced attention to both psychosocial assessment duties and psychosocial intervention duties is associated with positive resident outcomes. More research is needed to document the effectiveness of social work services. This evidence is crucial for visibility, accountability, and credibility in this setting, where the professionalization of social services remains uneven and incomplete, and budget-constrained administrators need compelling reasons to hire more (or higher-cost) social service providers. In addition, social work's role in quality improvement must extend to evaluating interventions designed to bolster residents' quality of life. For example, social workers have much to contribute in terms of assessing the impact of interventions such as training front-line staff in psychosocial care; instituting procedural changes that promote greater choice, dignity, and individuality; and implementing protocol-driven quality improvement approaches, like person-centered dementia care.

CHARACTERISTICS OF NURSING HOMES AND INDUSTRY TRENDS

The number of beds in an NH can range from less than 10 to more than 200; between the years 2006 and 2010 US NHs averaged 108.5 beds (Harrington, Carrillo, Dowdell, Tang, & Blank, 2011). This average is important given federal requirements for a full-time social worker in facilities with more than 120 beds: The average NH is smaller than this and may not be held to this standard depending on whether state regulations meet or exceed these federal rules. Two-thirds of NHs are located in urban areas (Bowblis, Meng, & Hyer, 2013), and an increasing majority are for-profit (CMS, 2012). Many for-profit NHs are also owned by chain organizations where the same company owns two or more facilities. For-profit chain ownership has been associated with increased concerns about poor quality (Harrington, Olney, Carrillo, & Kang, 2012). Encouragingly, more facilities are embracing the cultural change movement, which emphasizes more individualized care, humanizing neighborhood settings rather than medically centered units or wards, and empowering direct care workers to make independent decisions that promote quality of care as well as job satisfaction (see Chapter 26 by Lustbader and Williams in this section).

Nursing homes continue to be affected by overall healthcare financing and policy trends, examples of which are discussed in what follows (see Chapter 25, "The Long-Term Care Ombudsman Program"; Chapter 26, "Culture-Change in Long-Term Care"; and Section V, "Older Adults in Palliative and End-of-Life Care").

Hospital Diagnosis-Related Groups and Managed Care

A major change, the introduction of diagnosis-related groups (DRGs) occurred in the 1980s. This change dramatically altered how Medicare pays hospitals for patient care. With the introduction of DRGs, hospitals are paid a set amount per diagnosis group, regardless of how long the patient is in the hospital. Another major change has been the growth of managed Medicare in subsequent years. Both of these funding reorganizations have contributed to a decrease in the number of days patients spend in the hospital, a subsequent growing emphasis on NHs for the provision of rehabilitative services, and increases in medical acuity and care needs among NH residents (Zinn, Mor, Feng, & Intrator, 2007). Case example 6 illustrates challenges that may arise for NH social workers in providing services to rehabilitative clients. Beginning in the late 1990s, conversion from a Medicare fee-for-service payment system to a fixed per diem rate, also know as a prospective payment system, or PPS, resulted in the closure of many NHs that could not withstand the loss of revenue associated with the changing payment structure (Bowblis, 2011; Rahman, Zinn, & Mor, 2013).

Case Example 6

Mrs. Collins was admitted to the nursing facility for rehabilitation following hip surgery. She has made excellent progress, but is not yet ready for discharge. She wants to go home, despite the fact that her insurance will still cover her stay. Her husband is her caregiver and expresses concern that she is not strong enough to return home yet. She is becoming irritable with staff and has started declining physical and occupational therapy. The social worker must help identify Mrs. Collins's wishes and values while also considering the need for a safe discharge.

Money Follows the Person (MFP)

More recently, MFP Medicaid demonstrations have been implemented across all but five states. The goal of the MFP demonstrations is to help rebalance the services and supports (LTSS) system away from institutionalized care, where a majority of Medicaid LTSS funding has been allocated in the past, toward home- and community-based services (HCBS). Originally authorized as part of the Deficit Reduction Act of 2005, passage of the Patient Protection and Affordable Care Act (Affordable Care Act, or ACA, 2010) has extended MFP demonstrations through 2016. As of August 2012, these demonstrations have been able to relocate over 25,000 people from institutions to community settings. However, challenges have been reported in identifying affordable housing and arranging HCBS for people with complex needs (O'Shaughnessy, 2013; Williams et al., 2013). Facility social workers often need to collaborate on discharge plans with MFP providers.

The Affordable Care Act

Provisions within the ACA have introduced additional expectations for NHs, including greater transparency and accountability regarding operational factors that impact quality and also requirements for reporting such information to the public. Among the most significant changes are: (1) improvements to the *Nursing Home Compare* website, which contains NH-level information about care provided and resident status; (2) requirements for NHs to disclose how revenues are applied (i.e., toward direct care or elsewhere); (3) more accurate reporting regarding nurse staffing; and (4) enhanced quality assurance processes including the introduction of quality assurance performance improvement (QAPI) strategies. There are also provisions for increasing dementia and abuse prevention training and to expand the system of background checks to prevent theft, abuse, and other forms of crimes committed against residents (Wells & Harrington, 2013). To keep apprised of the ACA developments in NHs, readers are encouraged to refer to the National Consumer Voice for Quality Long-Term Care website.

CONCLUSION

Nursing home social work practice presents worthy challenges to the practitioner and to the profession. For the practitioner, managing the demands and expectations of a large caseload and an extensive practice mission and role requires an ability to initiate, prioritize, and teach others how to make the best use of social work skills and time. Social work interventions that can have an impact on the organization appear to be underutilized, or at least not well documented in the professional literature. Obtaining a better "working picture" of macro social work practice that targets organizational and environmental change would be beneficial for practitioners, educators, and policy makers and ultimately to residents.

The nursing home is both an institution and a potential community. The difference lies in the meaning given and uses made of the structures, rules, roles, and routines that constitute the home's functioning. Social work has much to contribute toward the quality of life of individual residents and their family members as well as to the organizational community.

ADDITIONAL NURSING HOME SOCIAL WORK RESOURCES

- National Consumer Voice for Quality Long-Term Care http://www.theconsumervoice.org
- Advancing Excellence in America's Nursing Homes http://www.nhqualitycampaign.org/
- Center for Aging & Disability Education and Research (CADER) http://www.bu.edu/cader/who-we-are/
- The National Association of Social Workers (NASW) http://www.naswdc.org/
- National Center for Gerontological Social Work Education http://www.cswe.org/CentersInitiatives/GeroEdCenter.aspx
- National Nursing Home Social Work Network http://clas.uiowa.edu/socialwork/nursing-home-social-work-network

ACKNOWLEDGMENTS

Dr. Betsy Vourlekis (Professor Emeritus, University of Maryland, Baltimore County, School of Social Work) is acknowledged for her work on the first edition of this chapter (2006) and Paige Hector, LMSW (Paige Ahead Healthcare Education & Consulting), for her thoughtful comments on and additions to this edition.

REFERENCES

American Health Care Association (AHCA). (2013, September). *Trends in nursing facility characteristics.* Accessed November 22, 2013, from http://www.ahcancal.org/research_data/trends_statistics/Pages/default.aspx

Beaulieu, E. M. (2002). *A guide for nursing home social workers.* New York, NY: Springer.

Bern-Klug, M., & Kramer, K. W. O. (2013). Core functions of nursing home social services departments in the United States. *Journal of the American Medical Directors Association, 14,* e1–7. doi: 10.1016/j.jamda.2012.09.004.

Bern-Klug, M., Kramer, K. W. O., Chan, G., Kane, R., Dorfman, L. T., & Sanders, J. B. (2009). Characteristics of nursing home social services directors: How common is a degree in social work? *Journal of the American Medical Directors Association, 10,* 36–44.

Bonifas, R. P. (2007). Multilevel factors related to survey deficiencies in psychosocial care in Washington state skilled nursing facilities. *Dissertation Abstracts International Section A: Humanities and Social Sciences, 68,* 3588–3734.

Bonifas, R. P. (2008). Nursing home work environment characteristics: Associated outcomes in psychosocial care. *Health Care Financing Review, 30,* 19–33.

Bonifas, R. P. (2011). Multi-level factors related to deficiencies in psychosocial care in skilled nursing facilities. *Journal of Gerontological Social Work, 54,* 203–223. doi: 10.1080/01634372.2010.538817

Bowblis, J. R. (2011). Ownership conversion and closure in the nursing home industry. *Health Economics, 20,* 631–644. doi: 10.1002/hec.1618

Bowblis, J. R., Meng, H., & Hyer, K. (2013). The urban-rural disparity in nursing home quality indicators: The case of facility-acquired contractures. *Health Services Research, 48,* 47–69. doi: 10.1111/j.1475-6773.2012.01431.x

Centers for Medicare and Medicaid Services (CMS). (2012). *Nursing home data compendium, 2012 edition.* Retrieved from http://www.cms.gov/

Medicare/Provider-Enrollment-and-Certification/
CertificationandComplianc/downloads/nursing-
homedatacompendium_508.pdf

Centers for Medicare and Medicaid Services (CMS).
(2013a). *MDS-frequency report for third quarter 2013*.
Retrieved November 24, 2013, from http://www.
cms.gov/Research-Statistics-Data-and-Systems/
Computer-Data-and-Systems/Minimum-Data-Set-
3-0-Public-Reports/Minimum-Data-Set-3-0-
Frequency-Report.html

Centers for Medicare and Medicaid Services (CMS).
(2013b). *Minimum Data Set 3.0 frequency report
(second quarter 2013)*. Retrieved from http://www.
cms.gov/Research-Statistics-Data-and-Systems/
Computer-Data-and-Systems/Minimum-Data-Set-
3-0-Public-Reports/Minimum-Data-Set-3-0-
Frequency-Report.html

Department of Health and Human Services, Office
of Inspector General. (2003). Conditions of
Participation for Long Term Care Facilities (42 CFR
Part 483, Subpart B). *Psychosocial services in skilled
nursing facilities*. Retrieved from http://oig.hhs.gov/
oei/reports/oei-02-01-00610.pdf

Department of Veterans Affairs, Office of Social Work
Service. (2001). *Social worker functions in long-term
care settings*. Available from the Department of
Veterans Affairs, Office of Social Work Service,
Washington, DC, 20011.

Ejaz, F. K. (2002). The influence of religious and personal values on nursing home residents' attitudes
toward life-sustaining treatments. *Social Work in
Health Care, 32*, 23–39.

Field, A., Maher, P., & Webb, D. (2002). Cross-cultural
research in palliative care. *Social Work and Health
Care, 35*, 523–543.

Fitzgerald, M. H., Mullavey-O'Byrne, C., & Clemson, L.
(2001). Families and nursing home placements:
A cross-cultural study. *Journal of Cross-Cultural
Gerontology, 16*, 333–351.

Greene, R. R., Vourlekis, B. S., Gelfand, D. E., & Lewis,
J. S. (1992). Current realities: Practice and education
needs of social workers in nursing homes. *Geriatric
Social Work Education, 18*, 39–54.

Harrington, C., Carrillo, H., Dowdell, M., Tang, P. P., &
Blank, B. W. (2011, October). *Nursing facilities, staffing, residents and facility deficiencies, 2005 through
2010*. Retrieved from www.theconsumervoice.org/
sites/default/files/OSCAR-2011-final.pdf

Harrington, C., Olney, B., Carrillo, H., & Kang, T.
(2012). Nurse staffing and deficiencies in the largest
for-profit nursing home chains and chains owned by
private equity companies. *Health Services Research,
47*, 106–128. doi: 10.1111/j.1475-6773.2011.01311.x

Ingersoll-Dayton, B., Saengtienchai, C.,
Kespichayawattana, J., & Aungsuroch, Y. (2004).
Measuring psychological well-being: Insights from
Thai elders. *The Gerontologist, 44*(5), 596–605.

Jones, A. L., Dwyer, L. L., Bercovitz, A. R., & Strahan,
G. W. (2009). *The National Nursing Home
Survey: 2004 overview*. Retrieved from www.cdc.
gov/nchs/data/series/sr_13/sr13_167.pdf

Knee, R. I., & Vourlekis, B. S. (1995). Patient rights. In
Encyclopedia of social work (19th ed., pp. 1802–1810).
Washington, DC: NASW Press.

Kolb, P. (2003). *Caring for our elders: Multicultural experiences with nursing home placement*. New York,
NY: Columbia University Press.

Kruzich, J. M., & Powell, W. E. (1995). Decision-making
influence: An empirical study of social workers
in nursing homes. *Health and Social Work, 20*,
215–222.

Mor, V., Zinn, J., Angelelli, J., Teno, J. M., & Miller, S. C.
(2004). Driven to tiers: Socioeconomic and racial
disparities in the quality of nursing home care.
Milbank Quarterly, 82, 227–256.

Morrison, R. S., Chichin, E., Carter, J., Burack, M. L., &
Meier, D. E. (2005). The effect of a social work intervention to enhance advance care planning documentation in the nursing home. *Journal of the American
Geriatrics Society, 53*, 290–294.

National Association of Social Workers (NASW).
(1993). *NASW clinical indicators for social work and
psychosocial services in nursing homes*. Washington,
DC: Author.

National Association of Social Workers (NASW). (2003).
*Standards for social work services in long-term care
facilities*. Washington, DC: Author.

O'Shaughnessy, C. V. (2013, May 10). *Money Follows
the Person (MFP) rebalancing demonstration: A work in progress*. National Health Policy
Forum background paper No. 85. Retrieved from
http://www.nhpf.org/uploads/announcements/
BP85_MFP_05-10-13.pdf

Patient Protection and Affordable Care Act, 42 U.S.C. §
18001 (2010).

Quam, J. K., & Whitford, G. S. (1992). Educational needs
of nursing home social workers at the baccalaureate
level. *Geriatric Social Work Education, 18*, 143–156.

Rahman, M, Zinn, J. S., & Mor, V. (2013). The impact
of hospital-based skilled nursing facility closures
on rehospitalizations. *Health Services Research, 48*,
499–518. doi: 10.1111/1475-6773.12001.

Simons, K. (2006). Organizational characteristics influencing nursing home social service directors' qualifications: A national study. *Health and Social Work,
31*, 266–274. doi: 10.1093/hsw/31.4.266

Simons, K., Bern-Klug, M., & An, S. (2012). Envisioning quality psychosocial care in nursing homes: The role of social work. *Journal of the American Medical Directors Association, 13*, http;//dx.doi.org/10.1016/j.jamda.2012.07.016

Simons, K., Connolly, B., Bonifas, R., Allen, L., Bailey, K., Downes, D., & Galambos, C. (2012). Psychosocial assessment of nursing home residents via MDS 3.0: Recommendations for social service training, staffing, and roles in interdisciplinary care. *Journal of the American Medical Directors Association, 13*, 190.e9–190.e15. doi: 10.1016/j.jamda.2011.07.005

U. S. Census Bureau. (2004). Hispanic and Asian Americans increasing faster than overall population. Retrieved June 25, 2004, from http://www.census.gov/ Press-Release/www/releases/archives/race/001839.html.

U. S. Census Bureau. (2011). 2010 Census briefs. The older population: 2010. Retrieved from http://www.census.gov/prod/cen2010/briefs/c2010br-09.pdf.

Vinton, L., Mazza, N., & Kim, Y. (1998). Intervening in family-staff conflicts in nursing homes. *Clinical Gerontologist, 19*, 45–67.

Vourlekis, B. S., Bakke-Friedland, K., & Zlotnik, J. L. (1995). Clinical indicators to assess the quality of social work services in nursing homes. *Social Work in Health Care, 22*, 81–93.

Vourlekis, B. S., Gelfand, D. E., & Greene, R. R. (1992). Psychosocial needs and care in nursing homes: Comparison of views of social workers and home administrators. *The Gerontologist, 32*, 113–119.

Wells, J., & Harrington, C. (2013, January). *Implementation of Affordable Care Act provisions to improve nursing home transparency, care quality, and abuse prevention.* Kaiser Family Foundation publication #8406. Retrieved from http://kaiserfamilyfoundation. files.wordpress.com/2013/02/8406.pdf

Whitaker, T., Weismiller, T., & Clark, E. (2005, March). *Assuring the sufficiency of the front-line workforce: A national study of licensed social workers.* Retrieved from http://www.naswdc.org/resources/workforce/files/NASW_SWCassuring_3.pdf

Williams, S. R., Morris, E., Orshan, B., Denny-Brown, N., Kehn, M., & Ross, J. (2013, July 30). *Money Follows the Person demonstration: Overview of state grantee progress, July to December 2012.* Retrieved from http://www.mathematica-mpr.com/publications/PDFs/health/mfp_july-dec2012_progress.pdf

Zhang, N., Gammonley, D., Paek, S., & Frahm, K. (2008). Facility service environments, staffing, and psychosocial care in nursing homes. *Health Care Financing Review, 30*, 5–17.

Zinn, J., Mor, V., Feng, Z., & Intrator, O. (2007). Doing better to do good: The impact of strategic adaptation on nursing home performance. *Health Services Research, 42*, 1200–1218.

PATRICIA H. DUCAYET
BEVERLEY L. LAUBERT

Long-Term Care Ombudsman Program

Residents in long-term care (LTC) facilities have every right to expect excellence and make their voices heard. As mandated by the Older Americans Act (OAA), the mission of the Long-Term Care Ombudsman Program (LTCOP) is to resolve problems and advocate for the rights of these residents. Thus LTC ombudsmen confidentially investigate and work to resolve complaints on behalf of residents in LTC facilities, and serve as a public advocate for them. In 2013, there were 16,513 nursing homes and 53,376 assisted living or similar board-and-care facilities (Administration on Aging AOA], 2013), the major constituency for whom the ombudsman advocates at both the individual and system levels.

EARLY HISTORY

The LTCOP's roots are in the 17th century Swedish model of hearing and responding to citizen complaints about government (Harris-Wehling, Feasley, & Estes, 1995). Nursing homes expanded rapidly after 1965, when they were provided with a predictable source of revenue through Medicare and Medicaid. Standards for the quality of nursing homes were adopted in the 1970s in response to identification of severe problems. In 1971, President Nixon established eight initiatives to improve nursing home care, one of which called for "state investigative ombudsman units." Thus, the LTCOP began as a pilot in 1972 when five states (ID, MI, PA, SC, and WI) were awarded demonstration grants. In 1975, Commissioner on Aging Arthur Flemming invited proposals from all states to develop community LTCOP programs, and in 1978, the LTCOP was established as part of the OAA. Commissioner Flemming envisaged the LTCOP as different from the classic model of ombudsmen as only neutral mediators; from the outset they were cast as both individual problem-solvers and public advocates.

The National Citizens Coalition for Nursing Home Reform (NCCHNR), in 2010 renamed the Consumer Voice for Quality Long-Term Care, emerged simultaneously with LTCOP. The NCCNHR was formed because of public concern about substandard care in nursing homes. In 1975, Elma Holder, its founder, organized representatives of 12 state citizen advocacy groups to attend a national nursing home industry conference to deliver a message to the industry about the need for serious reform in nursing home conditions. These advocacy organizations then developed a platform of common concerns and founded NCCNHR to represent a consumer voice at the national level.

LEGISLATIVE AUTHORITY

The LTCOP was mandated by the Older Americans Act in 1978, and three major reauthorizations in 1987, 1992, and 2000 strengthened the program (see summary in Table 25.1). Over the years these changes expanded the program scope, provided ombudsmen with legal access to residents, and positioned the program within a group of elder justice initiatives. Significant changes in 2000 included guidelines for conflicts of interest, emphasis on coordination with local law enforcement officers, clarifying funding allocation and levels, continuation of the National Ombudsman Resource Center (discussed later); enabling acceptance of voluntary contributions, and a new focus on family caregivers (Turnham, 2000). Today LTCOP programs operate in all 50 states, the District of Columbia, Guam, and Puerto Rico. Thus, the legal foundation for LTCOP has been periodically strengthened and the program has achieved greater recognition as a critical component of advancing the quality of elder care in the United States.

Ombudsman and NCCNHR advocacy helped shape the 1987 Nursing Home Reform Act, commonly referred to as OBRA 87, which in turn strengthened the role of LTCOP. After the Reagan administration moved to reduce regulations in nursing homes and weaken their enforcement, advocates pushed for an Institute of Medicine (IOM) review before implementation of pending changes, urged that an advocate be appointed to the IOM committee (namely, Iris Freeman, an ombudsman and social worker); conducted and publicized an influential study of consumer views on quality (Spalding 1985), and convened a national NCCNHR working conference where one-third of the invited delegates were nursing home residents whose participation was facilitated by ombudsmen. Among its other reforms, OBRA 87 required that state licensing agencies' contact the ombudsman as part of routine information gathering about a facility, and invite the ombudsman to contribute information in the annual inspection process, for example, during resident meetings with inspectors, and inspectors' exit interviews with the facility staff. These provisions created a structured role for the LTC ombudsman in the inspection process, while raising ombudsman awareness about regulatory processes and facility problems.

In 1993, the NCCNHR received a grant from the AOA to operate a National Long-Term Care Ombudsman Resource Center (NORC) to assist in implementation of the LTCOP. (The NORC is defined in and funded under the OAA, and the grant to NCCNHR is extended with AOA grant cycles.) The NORC provides support, technical assistance, and training to state LTC ombudsman programs and their networks to enhance the knowledge, skills, and capacity of ombudsman programs (for more detail see http://www.ltcombudsman.org).

TABLE 25.1 Changes in LTCOP in Major Reauthorizations of the Older Americans Act

1981	Expanded ombudsman coverage to include board and care homes, also known as assisted living. The name was, therefore, changed from Nursing Home Ombudsman to Long-Term Care Ombudsman.
1987	Required states to provide access to residents and residents' records, assure immunity for the good faith performance of their duties, and prohibit willful interference with the official duties of an ombudsman and/or retaliation against an ombudsman, resident, or other individual for assisting LTCOP representatives in the performance of their duties.
1992	Strengthened the program and transferred it to a new title in the act, Title VII, Vulnerable Elder Rights Protection Activities, which also included programs for prevention of elder abuse, neglect, and exploitation; the state elder rights and legal assistance development program; and an outreach, counseling, and assistance program (which was subsequently deleted).
2000	Retained and updated ombudsman provisions in Titles II, III, and VII, including guidelines for conflicts of interest, the importance of coordinating services with local law enforcement officers, funding allocation patterns, current funding levels, the continuation of the National Ombudsman Resource Center, policies on accepting voluntary contributions, and a new focus on family caregivers.
2006	Retained all provisions in Title VII. A change was made to the base year in reference to the ombudsman minimum funding requirement.

In 1982 Medicaid home-and community-based services waivers allowed for coverage of low-income nursing-home eligible persons in alternative community settings, and, thereafter, the number of homes offering heavy care has expanded dramatically. In most states, ombudsman services to nursing home residents are better developed than those to AL residents because nursing homes operate under uniform federal regulations and the LTCOP has federally protected access to facilities, residents, and resident records. In contrast, AL operates in various forms within states and functions under a variety of state regulations. Further, AL settings may not be identifiable or licensed at the state level. As these alternative residential settings grow and serve more people with complex medical needs similar to nursing home residents, the LTCOP has been challenged to better reach and serve AL residents.

MISSION AND STRUCTURE

Ombudsmen implement their mission by investigating and resolving complaints voiced by, or on behalf of, residents of LTC facilities; educating providers and the public about the preferences, needs, and rights of residents; and advocating at individual and systems levels. Numerous studies and reports about the LTCOP identify the importance of its structure, which establishes an Office of the State Long-Term Care Ombudsman in each state, and affirms the intent for an independent, state-led advocacy service.

By Congressional intent, the administration and functions of the State Long-term Care Ombudsman Program are distinct. For instance, unlike most Older Americans Act programs, this is a statewide program and is not designed for area agencies on aging or other locally designated organizations to establish their own unique programs with policies and procedures that differ from the state program. Much of the structure and the operational guidelines of the program are specified in the federal law. (Barker, Hunt, Merrill, & Smetanka, 2011)

Every state must have a full-time state ombudsman who heads the Office of the State Long-Term Care Ombudsman (hereafter the Office). The state ombudsman designates organizations and individuals to carry out the functions of the office. Given

that the OAA created a structure with State Units on Aging (SUAs) in all states, the SUA is the most common location for a state ombudsman to operate, but host agencies for the program and designated entities vary. In 2011, 15 states and Puerto Rico operated ombudsman programs within an independent SUA (e.g., a department of aging), 22 states and Guam operated within an SUA in an umbrella health and human services agency; 3 states operated in a part of the umbrella state agency separate from the SUA; 4 operated in an independent agency of state government, and 6 states and the District of Columbia designated agencies from outside state government to house the state ombudsman (Barker, Hunt, Merrill, & Smetanka, 2011).

Individual ombudsmen may be employed by the state-level organization or by other designated agencies, including Area Agencies on Aging (AAAs). The program framers were keenly interested in involving communities in the LTCOP (Hunt, 2008). Thus, most state structures include local or regional ombudsman programs, and most states augment paid staff with community volunteers who visit facilities as representatives of the office. Research suggests that volunteer ombudsmen fill a service gap between professionals and clients, add to the LTCOPs oversight effect, heighten regulatory activity, improve care, challenge corporate and government policies that are not in residents' best interests, and are appreciated by residents (Harris-Wehling et al., 1995; Nelson, Huber, & Walter, 1995; Nelson, Netting, Huber, & Borders, 2004). Regardless of who directly employs representatives and whether they are paid or volunteer, all representatives are accountable to the state ombudsman, who oversees program operations and leads the systems advocacy of the office. At the national level, a new position of Director of the Office of Long-term Care Ombudsman Programs was filled in 2010. That milestone raised the stature, importance, and visibility of the LTCOP nationwide.

In 1995, the IOM conducted a major review of the LTCOP, pointing out that effectiveness is influenced by organizational structure, including degree of independence, management of conflicts of interest, and funding levels (Harris-Wehling et al., 1995). In 2002, the National Association of State Long-Term Care Ombudsman Programs (NASOP) convened a large group of stakeholders to build on this IOM work and create a blueprint for the future. The blueprint continues to guide NASOP on issues such as effective systems advocacy, data reporting requirements, program effectiveness, standards of practice, and best practices in training and other program operations. Evidence of public policy advocacy and standards of practice are available at NASOP's website at www.nasop.org.

PROGRAM ADVOCACY

The OAA creates a broad range of responsibilities for an ombudsman, all of which relate to the advocacy roles. Required activities include:

- resolving individual complaints on behalf of residents;
- supporting the development of resident and family councils;
- representing the interests of residents before governmental agencies;
- seeking administrative, legal, and other remedies to protect residents; and
- monitoring and commenting on laws, regulations, and policies impacting residents.

These responsibilities naturally intertwine. An ombudsman cannot well represent a resident's interests without understanding the individual complaints that grew out of that interest. An ombudsman cannot effectively comment on a regulation without investigating the existing administrative and legal remedies that currently apply. And an ombudsman cannot support the development of a family council without first understanding the rights a council has to form.

Individual Advocacy

The investigatory, educational, and advocacy work of the LTCOP are vital to address breakdowns in

quality of care or other conditions affecting resident quality of life. Good quality of life depends on high-quality physical, emotional, and social care in a positive culture within the home. To advance resident well-being, ombudsmen monitor facility practices and conditions, speak out for those who cannot speak for themselves, and empower those needing support to express their wishes.

Ombudsmen are best known for investigating and resolving complaints made by or on behalf of individual residents (see Table 25.2). In 2013, 37% of all complaints were reported by residents themselves. Families, legal surrogates, friends, other agencies, and facility staff may also report problems to the LTCOP. Ombudsmen themselves may also initiate complaints, and in 2013, 13% percent of complaints were ombudsman-initiated). Maintaining a regular ombudsman presence in LTC facilities is an essential practice. This permits establishing relationships and rapport with residents and staff, and provides opportunities to identify and resolve problems quickly and informally (see Table 25.2).

Ombudsmen gather information through interviews, observation, and sometimes review of documents to determine whether a complaint can be verified and to gather evidence leading to possible root causes of the problem. Even when the facts differ from the original complaint, ombudsmen work to resolve problems to the satisfaction of the complainant. Staying grounded in the resident's interests, even when a complainant is someone other than a resident, requires the ombudsman to attempt communication with any resident on whose behalf a complaint was filed. Residents will sometimes inform the ombudsman that this complainant's concern is not theirs, and in those cases, the ombudsman places the resident's wishes first.

TABLE 25.2 Number and Type of Complaints by Facility Type for 2013

	Nursing Homes	Assisted Living and Similar Board and Care	Total Complaints
Care, such as response to requests for help	35,139	9,380	44,519
Autonomy, choice, preference, exercise of rights, including privacy	16,616	6,313	22,929
Environment, quality of life	11,701	5,989	17,690
Systems, such as Medicaid, Medicare, and regulatory functions	9,875	4,337	14,212
Admission, transfer, and discharge, eviction	10,609	3,306	13,915

Source: AOA (2013).

Ethical dilemmas are frequently encountered in ombudsman advocacy. Confidentiality is a hard and fast statutory requirement of the LTCOP, and ombudsmen are often challenged to be creative in resolving problems while protecting the identity of the resident. Ombudsmen are taught to meet in a private space and to visit with numerous residents while in the facility to avoid a single person being identified as a complainant. Cameras in public spaces such as hallways and living areas are fairly common, and several states allow residents to install cameras in their bedrooms and apartments, so ombudsmen must vary their visitation strategies when needed to ensure confidentiality in accordance with resident wishes. Maintaining confidentiality in small LTC facilities is a particular challenge. When a home has five private bedrooms, and perhaps only one resident with the ability to communicate complaints, it is impossible to avoid a resident being identified as the ombudsman's source, and an ombudsman may exercise the option of serving as the complainant and providing supporting evidence rather than exposing a resident. Direction from the resident is at the heart of the LTCOP, and advocates can become frustrated when they cannot proceed without consent of their client. However, ombudsmen do not simply ignore problems. Investigation may lead to other residents who have similar complaints and want the help of the ombudsman to resolve them, which can result in the same positive outcome for the resident who did not provide consent to reveal his or her identity.

When ombudsmen hear the same or similar complaints from many residents or repeatedly over time, their approach to investigation and resolution addresses the system within the home that is somehow failing. For example, tracing back to the root cause of complaints about residents falling may lead to solutions such as consistent assignment of staff, a positive workplace practice that emphasizes the importance of individualized understanding of resident needs and patterns based on knowing the resident. If a resident has a pattern of waking at midnight to use the restroom, a consistently assigned nursing assistant can be aware of that pattern and stand by proactively to prevent a fall. The ombudsman may also advocate for dim floor-level lighting that helps the resident see the floor and furniture to avoid a fall. By using a holistic approach to resolving problems, the ombudsman achieves a sustained improvement that can have positive impact on multiple residents.

Ombudsman effectiveness is partly measured by national reporting data on resolution of complaints. Outcomes include fully resolved to the complainant's satisfaction, partly resolved to the complainant's satisfaction, referral of the complaint to another entity, withdrawn complaints, and complaints that could not be resolved. In 2013, 73% of the programs' 190,592 complaints nationwide were either fully or partially resolved to the satisfaction of the resident or complainant.

Systems Advocacy

Individual complaint work drives much of the LTCOP systems work. Ombudsmen are taught to use program data as a driver for educating the public and policy makers on residents' concerns. Data adds context and scope to case-based stories. For example, in 2013, the California state ombudsman successfully increased the amount of fines imposed on facilities that interfere with an ombudsman's performance of official duties, having demonstrated to the state legislature that interference had increased and that the current penalty amounts were an insufficient deterrent. This example also demonstrates the need for local and state ombudsmen to coordinate their work on issues so that the state ombudsman is aware of the challenges faced by ombudsmen with daily resident contact.

Finding partners with a shared interest for consumer protection and rights is often more influential than the LTCOP acting alone on an issue. Effective systems advocacy can be bolstered by a coordinated advocacy effort. For example, the Washington state ombudsman, in partnership with the AARP and the provider association of private residential care homes, used her program's knowledge and legal counsel to find a sponsor for a bill to protect the interests of residents in the state's adult family homes. The legislation included a consumer website with plain language information about facility quality, imposition of logical remedies to regulatory violations, training requirements for special care designations, and a standard disclosure form for potential residents prior to admission. Still, sometimes ombudsmen can be a lone voice in opposition to provider interests, reinforcing the need for good data collection and responsible data use to inform the public. Sometimes, ombudsmen use contacts within the media to raise public awareness of issues and illustrate the needs of residents.

Preventing Abuse and Neglect

In 2013, ombudsmen received 13,690 complaints regarding abuse and neglect, making it the sixth most frequent category of ombudsman complaints. While some states require the ombudsman to investigate abuse and neglect, and a few are also required to be the first responders to such complaints, others refer all abuse and neglect allegations to the state's regulatory agency for investigation. The differences in state implementation strategies lead to significant differences among state LTCOPs, and such differences also skew state complaint numbers.

Investigation of abuse and neglect is resource-intensive. Typically, the state regulatory agency and law enforcement are called in to take action against the provider and the individual perpetrators of abuse. In many states, the Adult Protective Services also has jurisdiction in facilities. The ombudsman role includes assuring that residents are protected from further abuse or neglect, assuring that their individual care plans included any needed psychological support and treatment of injuries, and looking for issues in the home's practice and environment that might prevent such abuse from occurring.

Unannounced ombudsman visits to facilities at varying times help prevent abuse and neglect. During visits, besides already cited advantages, the ombudsman can assist family and resident councils to recognize risk factors such as residents who are isolated or whose ability for self-advocacy is impaired by dementia. Ombudsmen also train facility staff as another deterrent to abuse; using person-centered care strategies, developing empathy for residents,

and learning how to intervene with coworkers under stress can prevent situations from escalating to abuse.

Additional Advocacy Strategies

The LTCOP representatives also meet with resident and family councils as a way to engage and empower residents to make recommendations to the home's administration and use their strength in numbers influence administrators and owners. Ombudsmen also provide over 300,000 consultations to individuals each year, in which they provide information to individuals seeking assistance with public benefits, inquiring about regulatory requirements such as staffing, or inquiring how to evaluate an AL facility for a parent. They also provide consultation to facilities. These and other examples are detailed in Table 25.3.

Regulatory enforcement is not part of the ombudsman role, and with that comes the flexibility to take action with only the constraints of residents' and consumers' interests. Ombudsmen's power lies in their ability to persuade and advocate. All ombudsmen, paid or volunteer, have the authority to enter any LTC facility and access all residents and, with residents' permission, access medical records to investigate a complaint. Although they are not enforcers, ombudsmen invariably use regulations to leverage their requests and arguments.

SOCIAL WORK IN THE OMBUDSMAN PROGRAM

The responsibilities of a representative of the LTCOP ombudsman fit well with the ethical principles of social

TABLE 25.3 Ombudsman Activities in Addition to Complaint Handling for 2013

Activity (number of contacts, sessions, or activities)	Total
Providing information to and participation in resident group and exit interviews of the licensing inspection process of LTC facilities	19,879
Meetings with resident councils	21,812
Meetings with family councils	2,371
Community education	11,506
Training for ombudsman staff and volunteers	11,318
Training for facility staff	5,424
Information and consultation to individuals	332,630
Consultation to facility staff	129,718

Source: AOA (2013).

workers: namely, service, social justice, respect for the dignity and worth of the person, the importance of human relationships, integrity, and competence (National Association of Social Workers [NASW], 2014). They also fit skills that social workers may have in casework, group work (e.g., for resident and family council development), community development, planning, and advocacy. According to an informal survey by the authors, in 2014 over 300 employees within state ombudsman offices, regional and local ombudsman offices, the NORC at Consumer Voice, and the AOA Office of the Ombudsman had social work backgrounds. Other leaders in the ombudsman programs have legal backgrounds, or have been administrators or policy analysts—social work is not the exclusive profession in the LTCOP, but can have a distinctive and important voice both in leadership and direct work in facilities.

All advocates need expertise in conflict resolution, social systems, and systems change. The LTCOP offers an opportunity for social workers interested in planning, shaping social policy, and research. Work with elected officials and the media is also part of the LTC ombudsman role.

Social worker ombudsmen may feel conflicted on issues of confidentiality. In many states, mandated reporting laws require licensed social workers to report any suspicion of abuse, neglect, or exploitation to the proper authorities for investigation. However the OAA requires the ombudsmen to obtain resident or complainant consent before releasing names. The federal law regarding the ombudsman's duty to protect confidentiality is more stringent than state laws, and the ombudsman—regardless of state licensure status as a social worker—must follow LTCOP procedures. Without consent, the ombudsman's options are limited. State policies should provide for procedures when the resident is unable to provide consent and other limited circumstances when, in accordance with procedures, the ombudsman may be able to file a report of abuse, neglect, or exploitation on behalf of the resident without consent. Thorough training on the subject and on state policies and procedures are essential to the federal law being implemented as required.

Ombudsman Work with Facility Social Workers

Social workers within LTC facilities and ombudsmen can have frequent contact. Within a facility, social workers are responsible for each resident's psychological and social assessment when they first move in and on a regular basis. When the assessment is thorough and person-centered, it informs the social worker and facility of the needs and preferences of a resident. Ombudsmen are likely to seek assistance of facility social workers when a resident reports a complaint about their mood, family conflict, opportunities for social engagement, needed medical appointments, and the plan of care.

Both LTC facility social workers and ombudsmen are change agents and advocates who promote residents' dignity, self-determination, and psychological and social well-being. But the LTC facility social worker's role can be complicated by demands of the facility. Many social workers in LTC facilities also act as the admissions coordinator or marketer, which can conflict with responsibilities to advocate for residents. Social workers' abilities to make pro-resident changes are sometimes limited by their ancillary status in medically oriented facility settings. Social workers may find themselves with conflicting interests between residents' wishes and employers' interests, especially when it comes to risk management and efficiency. In situations when a social worker encounters a conflict of professional roles, the ombudsmen may be called on to support the wishes of residents (Nelson, Netting, Huber, & Borders, 2001).

OMBUDSMAN CHALLENGES

Numerous challenges present obstacles to effective ombudsman programs, including systemic problems such as funding shortfalls and conflicts of interest caused by organizational placement, as well as case-by-case considerations for the impact of dimished intellectual capacity for decision making and conflicting priorities among surrogate decision makers. Additionally, the importance of advocacy in this emotional work requires effective coping and stress management techniques and the ability to strike a delicate balance between diplomacy and assertiveness.

Inadequate Funding

Depending on where the ombudsman is housed, there may be limitations on the ombudsman role to pursue funding. Some local and state ombudsman programs do not conduct fundraising activities, or are limited in their ability to influence how funds are allocated within their agency or appropriated by state and federal legislatures. In other cases fundraising supports added programs, for example, to recruit and train volunteers, develop educational programs and materials, and lobby for legislation to benefit residents of LTC facilities. At the state level, state ombudsmen often compete for limited resources. For example, although state LTCOPs have been mandated to serve AL residents since 1981, federal appropriations have never included a separate allocation for this service. This places the responsibility with the state ombudsman to lobby for state revenue, with some states successfully obtaining the funds needed, and others needing to spread their federal funding across nursing homes and AL facilities. Also, though 13 states authorize and 12 require their offices to serve those receiving Medicaid-waiver service in their own home, three states have given the office no additional funds for the mandated expansion.

Conflicts of Interest

Conflicts of interest can be lurking in many cases and at all levels of the system, including the organizational placement of the office. As the LTC system changes, and shrinking OAA funding leads AAAs to seek funds through Medicaid, managed care, and special projects that require collaboration with hospitals and nursing home providers, the placement of the LTCOP is growing ever-more complicated. In the mid-2000s, states began consolidating government agencies into large umbrella organizations, resulting in numerous offices of the state LTC ombudsman being placed in an agency where adult protective services, regulatory services, or both, are performed. This is in direct conflict with conflict of interest provisions of the OAA and poses serious risk to the integrity of ombudsman programs.

Consider the impact of the office located within an organization that also regulates LTC facilities. Ombudsman perspectives often differ from regulatory perspectives, and ombudsmen frequently hear and express criticism about the outcome of a regulatory investigation. The ombudsman is obligated to represent the resident's interests to regulators, including criticizing insufficient investigation of complaints. At the same time, ombudsmen want to maintain a good working relationship with

regulators. This relationship can be difficult regardless of the ombudsman's organizational placement, but if the office is located within the same agency as regulators, representatives may be pressured not to criticize regulatory functions or the agency, and residents could lose their independent public advocate.

Advocacy for Residents Without Decision-Making Capacity

A cornerstone of the ombudsman program is adhering to the preferences of residents. One of the greatest challenges ombudsmen face is assuring that they know what the resident wants, including whether they want the ombudsman to investigate a problem, talk to a provider, or review their record. When diminished capacity from dementia or another condition prevents getting these answers from residents, a surrogate may be involved. Surrogate decision-makers can be helpful to the ombudsman, but another challenge arises in assuring that the surrogate is considering the preferences the person would express if able. Not uncommonly, family members may disagree with each other or with court-appointed guardians, and credentialed guardians may make decisions contrary to the wishes of family members who may know the resident better. This challenge complicates ombudsmen's complaint-handling process and requires educating surrogates about ethical decision-making principles. It also places ombudsmen in the awkward position of thinking about the resident's "best interests," which is incongruous with ombudsmen's training and code of ethics.

Effective Advocacy Under Stress

Ombudsmen tend to be compassionate people who go the extra mile to help residents achieve their desired outcomes. Caring and compassion can take a toll on the advocate. Even the most effective advocate can find that personal feelings impede their advocacy. Responsive, supportive supervision is essential to helping ombudsmen recognize when they are at risk of crossing a boundary and how to set limits. Time can also help the ombudsman and others involved gain helpful perspective on a problem when emotions are running high.

Effective ombudsmen strike a delicate balance of being friendly, yet firm. Ombudsmen need to be comfortable engaging in conflict, yet diplomatic enough to develop and nurture professional relationships with residents, families, other advocates, regulators, facility staff, and provider associations to influence better care. The nature of advocacy work attracts direct, devoted, and assertive individuals. Ineffective ombudsmen are those comfortable with the status quo who may be hesitant to advocate against systemic odds.

FUTURE CONSIDERATIONS

Ombudsman programs can be expected to adapt to a shifting landscape in long-term care as state and federal policies evolve to respond to new health care delivery and reimbursement models.

Home Care Advocacy

Federal and state governments have financial and political incentives to create a system where individuals can receive nursing-facility-level services in their own homes. The Centers for Medicare and Medicaid Services (CMS) issued federal regulation in 2014 that defines community settings and requires states to develop implementation plans that outline the state's transition to compliance with the 2014 regulation. Ombudsman involvement in the development of the state plans will be important to protect the interests of those receiving care in their own homes. As various models are explored to shift services out of institutional settings, more state ombudsman programs are likely to venture into home and community ombudsman work.

Managed Care

Managed care theoretically promises better coordination of benefits and services, enhanced benefits, cost savings, and a connection between payment and quality. Ombudsman programs with early experience with managed care have found that the fulfillment of the promise is often dependent on contracts between public funding systems, managed care plans, and providers. Contracts are complicated and ombudsmen have to understand them in order to apply advocacy strategies to resolve individual problems for residents (and, in some cases, home care consumers).

Another confounding factor is how roles of once-familiar systems will change in a managed care environment. In the traditional fee-for-service model in a nursing home, if a resident has complaints about care, the ombudsman may use a care plan meeting as a resolution strategy. If the problem is not resolved through education or negotiation with the nursing home, an option is to refer the problem to the regulatory agency. In a managed care environment, the care coordinator may want to be included in care plan meetings, which could create scheduling challenges and delays in resolution. If the problem is not resolved, the ombudsman has to determine whether to refer to the state regulatory agency or the managed care plan's quality assurance staff or to assist the resident with a formal grievance or appeal process.

Blurred Lines Between Hospital and Nursing Homes

Many nursing homes emphasize provision of subacute care after hospitalization. Also reimbursement systems impose performance measures that create disincentives for nursing homes to seek hospital care for residents. Hospitals are admitting fewer people, opting to provide care in observation units in order to avoid reimbursement sanctions for frequent rehospitalization. When all these factors come together, the ombudsman will find it more challenging to draw a bright line at the door of the "long-term care" facility. As nursing homes and hospitals become mutually dependent to meet performance measures, solutions to problems in the nursing home may require ombudsmen to step into hospital settings to carry out advocacy on behalf of the resident. Once again, the ombudsman will need to learn a new, complex system and stretch their resources across new settings.

REFERENCES

Administration on Aging (AOA), US Department of Health and Human Services. (2013). *Ombudsman reporting tool two-year comparison report.* National Ombudsman Reporting System (NORS). Obtained from personal communication with Louise Ryan, Ombudsman Program Specialist for the US Administration for Community Living/ Administration on Aging, April 28, 2014.

Barker, J., Hunt, S., Merrill, D., & Smetanka, L. (2011). *The State Long-Term Care Ombudsman Program: Primer for state agency directors and executive staff.* Washington, DC: National Association of

States United for Aging and Disabilities, National Ombudsman Resource Center.

Harris-Wehling, J., Feasley, J. C., & Estes, C. L. (1995). *Real people, real problems: An evaluation of the long-term care ombudsman programs of the Older Americans Act.* Washington, DC: Institute of Medicine, Division of Health Care Services.

Hunt, S. (2008). *Curriculum resource material for local long-term care ombudsmen.* Washington, DC: National Ombudsman Resource Center. Retrieved May 2014 from http://www.theconsumer-voice.org/about

National Association of Social Workers (NASW). (2014). *NASW code of ethics.* Retrieved June 9, 2014, from https://www.socialworkers.org/pubs/code/code.asp

Nelson, H. W., Huber, R., & Walter, K. L. (1995). The relationship between volunteer long-term care ombudsmen and regulatory nursing home actions. *The Gerontologist, 35,* 509–514.

Nelson, H. W., Netting, F. E., Huber, R., & Borders, K. (2001). The social worker-ombudsman partnership: A resident-centered model of situational conflict tactics. *Journal of Gerontological Social Work, 35,* 65–82.

Nelson, H. W., Netting, F. E., Huber, R., & Borders, K. (2004). Factors affecting volunteer ombudsman efforts and service duration: Comparing active and resigned volunteers. *Journal of Applied Gerontology, 23,* 309–323.

Spalding, J. (1985). *A consumer perspective on quality of care: The residents point of view. Analysis of residents' discussions.* Washington, DC: National Citizens Coalition for Nursing Home Reform.

Turnham, H. (2000). Older Americans Act amendments of 2000, H.R. 782 and S. 1536: Reauthorization of the Older Americans Act. Retrieved May 29, 2004, from http://www.ltcombudsman.org//uploads/OAA Summary.htm

In healthcare settings, the social worker's role has always been clear: to oppose the narrow scope of physical care, to reveal the person behind the patient or resident, and to assist that person to achieve the best possible life for him or her. Necessarily, other members of the healthcare team have focused on pathology. When the acute care hospital model was transposed onto nursing homes in the 1960s (Vladeck, 1980), social workers faced a further need to advocate for the nonphysical dimensions of life that impart wholeness, even when the overarching model of care pointed in narrower directions.

The restraint-free movement in nursing homes, which began in the 1980s, exemplified this approach. Research confirmed what many social workers already knew on a clinical basis: that physical restraint was destructive to both body and spirit. A social worker, Carter Catlett Williams, working closely with nurse researchers and others, was a leader in this change movement (Williams, 1989a, 1989b, 1997).

As a direct outgrowth of this work, Williams and nurse Sarah Burger of the National Citizens' Coalition for Nursing Home Reform identified a small group of providers in long-term care who were practicing approaches radically different from those of the traditional nursing home. They were brought together in 1997 through the coordinating work of Rose Marie Fagan, an ombudsman in Rochester, New York (Fagan, Williams, & Burger, 1997). During this gathering, long-existing practices and those that had been newly initiated were probed to define the *culture* of the nursing home as "expressed in its traditions, style of leadership, social networks, patterns of interaction, relations with the outer community, degree of connectedness to the natural world, use of language, and ways in which the community celebrates and mourns" (Lustbader, 2001). These innovators were then challenged to identify a common set of values and principles to guide future change efforts. The values and principles were:

- Know each person
- Each person can and does make a difference
- Relationship is the fundamental building block of a transformed culture
- Respond to spirit, as well as mind and body
- Risk taking is a normal part of life
- Put person before task
- All elders are entitled to self-determination wherever they live

WENDY LUSTBADER
CARTER CATLETT WILLIAMS

Culture Change in Long-Term Care

26

- Community is the antidote to institutionalization
- Do unto others as you would have them do unto you
- Promote the growth and development of all
- Shape and use the potential of the environment in all its aspects: physical, organizational, psychosocial/spiritual
- Practice self-examination, searching for new creativity and opportunities for doing better
- Recognize that culture change and transformation are not destinations but a journey, always a work in progress

Throughout the culture change process, these and other initiatives have been bolstered by the Nursing Home Reform Law of 1987 (often referred to as OBRA), which, in addition to establishing the resident's right to be free of physical restraint, requires nursing homes to "provide services and activities to attain or maintain the highest practicable physical, mental, and psychosocial well-being of each resident in accordance with a written plan of care which . . . is initially prepared, with participation to the extent practicable of the resident or the resident's family" (Nursing Home Reform Amendments of the Omnibus Budget Reconciliation Act of 1987, Public Law 100–203).

This chapter depicts how social workers continue to play a key role in changing the nursing home culture from one in which dignity has been forfeited for the sake of care into one in which dignity is affirmed and meaning can be restored.

THEORETICAL BACKGROUND

To abide being in a hospital, a patient must accept being seen primarily in terms of a problem list. Members of the healthcare team come to the bedside and address the specific problems that stand between the patient and going home. The goal, *going back home*, is shared by all, except—occasionally—visiting family members who may be exhausted from caregiving. The patient surrenders to the will of the body and tries to heed instructions from those who claim to be advocating for the body's best possible recovery from the insult of the illness.

Arthur Frank, a sociologist who has written extensively about illness, insists that to be fully human, "a person must be recognized *as* fully human by someone else" and that "recognition becomes a

thing: something given, or extracted, and then held as one's own." He claims that medical settings that deprive us of such recognition are dangerous places on the level of the soul:

> In a secular society we seek to evade asking what makes life meaningful in conditions of suffering, when intactness is permanently jeopardized and bodily integrity gone. When suffering no longer allows this question to be evaded, but when lack of spiritual resources do not allow it to be answered either, that is the existential crisis of illness. Because so few of us can answer what our lives are for, we fear those who pose this question, whether they pose it explicitly or through the implicit witness of their suffering bodies. This fear then leads to withholding recognition of the existential suffering of the ill. (Frank, 1991)

When someone ends up residing in a traditional nursing home, to be addressed repeatedly in terms of a medical problem list is to cease to exist as a person. There is no homecoming to anticipate that will bring relief from this nothingness. There are few objects in the environment that suggest meaning or affirm personal identity. This *is* home, yet it feels like the opposite. One researcher, striving to define *home*, found through interviews with nursing home residents that it is "a whole that cannot be broken down into parts without losing the sense of meaning of the whole" and that the experience of home "thus acts as a center to the individual's existence: it provides meaning in a chaotic world and lies at the core of human existence" (Carboni, 1990).

Maggie Kuhn, the founder of the Gray Panthers, was interviewed in the mid-1970s about the fragmented care her brother received in the last months of his life. Her observations about his hospital stay contain the elements of how healthcare roles could be made responsive to all dimensions of a person's experience, regardless of the setting.

> My brother died after being hospitalized for three months. . . . There was a succession of six different nurses who saw him. Each spent a few seconds—a couple of minutes at the most—but nobody looked at him as a whole person. . . . There was no primary nursing care, where one nurse looks at the whole case. It was the nurse's aides who had more continuous

contact with him and who saw to it that he was looked after. How accurate can the reports be when each primary nurse is responsible for an incredible number of patients, with very little time to spend with each? The charge nurse who was supervising never came to visit him. The one person who was the kindest and most loving was a priest. He came to visit every day and was a friend to everyone—Catholic and non-Catholic. ... Pastoral skills should be transferable to other fields ... (and) providers ought to be encouraged to function as teams, not pyramids of power topped by physicians. (Hessel, 1977)

Shifting these "pyramids of power" turns out to be the essence of a transformed culture of long-term care. Those who have the most contact with the ill person, the nurse's aides, must be given a primary voice on the healthcare team, and the locus of control must be returned to the individual, rather than retained by the institution and its staff. This shift requires a revision, at a deep systemic level, of organizational structures, professional roles, and practices for hiring, training, and supervising staff. Only then can someone in need of daily assistance receive such help without forfeiting the ordinary freedoms of which dignity is comprised.

FLATTENED HIERARCHIES

In any institutional structure, deep transformation of the status quo is almost always accompanied by heated disagreements and burgeoning resentments, especially at the beginning of the process. Social workers make a primary contribution to the change process at the outset by ensuring that such feelings and perceptions are voiced and resolved openly. Otherwise, negative feelings tend to go underground, where they exert a corrosive effect and bring change to a standstill. For instance, an administrator declaring in a facility-wide memo "all opinions are respected" differs greatly from one instituting management practices that ensure a respectful reception for all points of view, including the negative, and guarantee that divergent opinions are heard from the bottom up.

Warning against a top-down approach, many culture change advocates emphasize that "everyone must be involved in the process" and that this can be achieved "only when management encourages the voices of residents and staff" (Fagan, 2003). Culture change tends to advance fundamentally as soon as certified nursing assistants (CNAs) are given multiple avenues for voicing their points of view and employing their intimate knowledge of the people they assist. To accomplish this, some nursing homes are implementing learning circles, an Eden Alternative concept introduced by William Thomas, one of the original leaders of the culture change movement.

> Learning circles are small groups of people who meet regularly to learn about and discuss areas of concern with the purpose of planning ways to resolve issues. Learning circles can be initiated for neighborhood work teams, residents, residents and work teams, families, leadership/management, or any configuration of people who have a need to communicate regularly.... In a learning circle, participants take turns one-by-one expressing their thoughts, preferences and opinions. After everyone has spoken, the topic is opened for discussion. (Norris-Baker, Doll, Gray, & Kahl, 2003)

The Eden Alternative was one of the first culture change models to insist on placing decision-making as close to residents as possible, ensuring that residents could determine their own daily schedules and make their own choices about eating, bathing, dressing, and mobility. Certified nursing assistants were empowered to respond to spontaneous wishes and to carry residents' unmet desires back to the care team for further consideration, particularly when loneliness, boredom, or emptiness was at stake. Fostering specific changes that proceed from the point of view of residents and those who serve them so closely produces the right conditions for transforming a sterile monoculture into a warm, human habitat (Thomas, 1994). The Eden model further suggests providing anonymous ways for direct care workers to give feedback to management, as a counter to common barriers such as shyness and shame about writing or speaking skills (Thomas, 1999).

Researchers have found that, given an efficacious voice in how their own care teams are managed, CNAs tend to stay longer, display more positive attitudes about their work, and treat residents with more kindness (Eaton, 1998). Brewster Place, a nursing home in Topeka, Kansas, began including a CNA in each of their job interview teams, reasoning that this person would be working directly with the candidate selected for the job. They also established self-directed teams in which CNAs negotiate their own schedules and work out on-the-job conflicts through learning circles. After these changes, Brewster Place's turnover rate went "from over 100% to 56%," and they anticipated the rate would be lower over time as their workforce becomes more and more stable (Norris-Baker et al., 2003).

Staff turnover and the resulting need to fill staff shortages with temporary agency help are some of the costliest burdens that nursing homes with traditional management practices must bear. Conversely, a changed management culture can lead to cost efficiencies because staff who are more satisfied with their work environment stay longer and become more adept at what they do. At the same time, those who receive assistance from these satisfied workers benefit hugely from the opportunity to know and be known by the people they depend on so intimately.

FLUID PROFESSIONAL ROLES

Striving to foster cross-training and a dynamic exchange of skills across disciplines is another major social work contribution to culture change. Kevin Bail, a social worker who contributed to the formative stages of culture change, served as a neighborhood coordinator at Providence Mt. St. Vincent in Seattle, one of the earliest pioneering facilities. Instead of traditional nurse-managed units, this facility established neighborhoods of 12 to 20 residents run by coordinators who did not have to be nurses. The idea was to use nursing expertise where it was essential, such as in wound care management, and to open up the role definition of *coordinator* to include those with special skills in community building among staff and residents (Bail, 1999).

All professions benefit from increased fluidity in role definition and flexible management structures that support the strengths that each discipline contributes to the team. Yeatts and Seward (2000) studied self-managed work teams in a midsize nursing home in Wisconsin. One of the teams in the study consisted of eight central people in the facility's management structure, "the nursing home administrator; the directors of nursing, social work, and mental health; the assistant directors of nursing and social work; and the managers of grounds and dietary." The other two teams in the study were each made up of three

CNAs. Interestingly, the high-performing team was the one in which the CNAs made their own decisions about resident care, often in quick "stand-up" meetings in the hallway. Observers found that these team members "held a high level of respect for one another and one another's viewpoints." In the low-performing team, care decisions were being made by the RN in charge, with "almost no decision-making at the team level." The RN is quoted as saying, "The main difference between before and now is that now I provide explanations of what's happening, why decisions are being made."

The RN's perception of change in this example relates to the provision of explanations for her decisions to her CNA staff. In effect, she admits that previously she would not have taken the time to say why she had chosen one course of action rather than another. The fact that supervisory structures had not been altered and staff still could not make their own decisions based on immediate knowledge of residents' needs demonstrates how a superficial change in practice is often enacted, rather than true culture change for which a change in systems is necessary. A deeper shift would have been to transform her RN role into one of supporting the decisions made by her staff and providing her expert guidance whenever the CNAs were grappling with an arena of care beyond their scope of practice.

A CARING ATMOSPHERE

Social workers often excel at group process, working hard to promote effective teamwork at staff meetings and during casual encounters between nursing home staff. Sandy Meyers, a social worker in an urban nursing home, attends as much to how a team meeting feels as to the content of the discussion. She writes, "The key is for caregivers to be in touch with feelings, vulnerabilities, and anxieties, and to use the resources of a supportive environment to transform these into positive experiences for our work" (Meyers, personal communication, 2002). Similarly, in his pioneering work on dementia care, Tom Kitwood observes:

> Care is much more than a matter of individuals attending to individuals. Ideally, it is the work of a team of people whose values are aligned, and whose talents are liberated in achieving a shared objective. It is unlikely that this will happen just by chance; if teambuilding

is neglected it is probable that staff will form their own small cliques, and begin to collude in avoiding the less obvious parts of care. Some developmental group work may be necessary in order to facilitate self-disclosure and to lower interpersonal barriers. ... A rough boundary should be drawn between issues that are genuinely work-related, and those of a more personal kind (which might need to be dealt with through counselling outside the workplace). However, it is appropriate for supervision to provide some kind of "containment" for painful feelings arising directly from work. (Kitwood, 1997)

Facilitating self-disclosure and lowering interpersonal barriers has long been a strength that social workers bring to the healthcare team. When the preservation of dignity is at stake, these social work skills become vital in prompting staff to identify ways that they may be inadvertently detracting from residents' lives. Just as important, social workers often help staff speak up about their own needs for recognition and affirmation, as well as the hurt that ensues when these needs are not met. Such discussions serve to lessen team sabotage, such as calling in sick unnecessarily, being overly critical of others' mistakes, and backbiting others on the team rather than speaking directly.

Supporting the well-being of nursing assistants becomes critical when they must minister to sorrowful junctures in residents' lives. While giving a bath, for example, a nursing assistant may wash a bereaved person's hair so tenderly that long-pent-up tears emerge and finally receive comfort. Because grief heals when it is received by a caring other, nursing assistants often become central to promoting the mental and emotional health of those they assist. Researchers have found that "proven methods for improving mental health treatment and the quality of life for nursing home residents exist, but they rely on the skill and adequacy of nursing assistants" (Beck, Doan, & Cody, 2002).

Social worker Cathy Unsino was one of the first to affirm and develop this role in the transformed culture, finding that improved communication between shifts helped nursing assistants convey important breakthroughs in residents' emotional lives and to exchange ideas on ways to best individualize the care they were providing (Unsino, 1998). Researchers have confirmed that when social workers and other professionals take the time to teach compassionate

responses to residents and family in distress, they help direct-care workers empathize with those "who may be demanding as they deal with profound loss" and show them how not to "personalize these demands" (Beck et al., 2002).

PUTTING THE PERSON BEFORE THE TASK

Culture change becomes most telling in the personal aspects of residing in a nursing home. Joanne Rader, a nurse who is one of the leaders of the culture change movement, has long asserted that the goals in bathing and dressing "are to keep decision making very close to the resident and to help that person maintain the highest possible level of independence and function." When someone refuses to bathe, the caregiver "needs to determine what must be cleaned for compelling health reasons and have the skills to identify and carry out the most pleasant, least invasive way to do it." In a changed culture of care, the nursing assistant would not simply walk away from someone who said "no" to a standardized bath but would work with other team members to devise an individualized solution in keeping with that person's dignity and lifelong habits. Thus, the experience becomes pleasant for both the giver and receiver.

> If the job is viewed strictly as a number of tasks to be completed on a group of bodies (washing, dressing, feeding, changing) day after day, there is little reward and caregiving will be seen as an unattractive field of work. If instead, the job is viewed and supported as an opportunity to enter into meaningful and caring relationships with people in need of assistance, it provides a way to be of service to others, and can be quite attractive. To recruit and retain good caregivers, the organizational system should be set up to support relationship and caring. (Rader, McKenzie, Hoeffer, & Barrick, 2002)

The transformed culture celebrates the uniqueness of each person as a fundamental principle, particularly the need to individualize care in its most minute details. It takes time to get to know someone's idiosyncratic preferences and habits, rather than imposing standardized practices that seem to make the institution run more efficiently. To respect someone's autonomy, personal knowledge and understanding must take the place of routine practices, or the care can quickly revert to a deprivation of basic human rights under the guise of "doing what's best."

Rosalie Kane, one of the first to study everyday life in nursing homes, cites the case of a woman in her 80s who preferred returning to prison to remaining in a nursing home. She had taken up residence there as a result of a fall while out on probation. Kane observes, "Unable to tolerate the shared room and the confused environment, she committed a technical parole violation and returned to prison where she had a room of her own. . . . [The fact that she] preferred a prison to a nursing home is a severe indictment of our national provisions for the frail elderly." Kane points out that infringements of personal autonomy "are so commonplace and efforts to protect agreed-upon areas of autonomy so unsuccessful that many observers have come to accept rather severe limits in personal autonomy as the *way things are*" (Kane, 1990).

A SENSE OF COMMUNITY

Relationships are at the heart of life and must also be central to a care setting that wishes to promote well-being for those who live and work there (Williams, 1999). This key principle in a transformed culture emphasizes the importance of establishing and maintaining a sense of community. Barry Barkan, one of the pioneers in culture change, insists on "the conscious and consistent cultivation of a community developed with the intention of connecting people to who they are, to one another and to a positive vision of what it means to be an elder in this culture" (Barkan, 2003).

First at Jewish Home for Aging Parents in Oakland, California, and later at his former nursing home, Live Oak Living Center, Barkan applied his model to create community in nursing homes; it included a community organizer position (which could be filled by any staff member with the skills, including a social worker) and a daily meeting of the entire community of as many residents, staff, and visitors as possible. To observe a community meeting at Live Oak Regenerative Community when Barkan was administrator, was to witness staff, residents, and family members respecting and beholding each other's humanity. For instance, residents' spouses who still live at home are encouraged to attend community

meetings at the nursing home, thus becoming active participants in the life lived there. They develop relationships with other residents and staff that expand their feeling of being welcomed and appreciated each time they visit. Staff attending such meetings and joining in the discussions gain knowledge of residents on dimensions of life far beyond the needs of the body, while the residents become acquainted with aspects of staff members' lives beyond the work that they do (Barkan, 1995).

Bringing family members' input into care discussions is another component of transforming a care setting into a community. Advocating for families has been a long-standing social work practice in most care settings, but the transformed culture seeks to integrate the family's knowledge of the person into what happens for their relative on a daily basis. Relatives provide valuable life history information, as well as details about individual preferences, accelerating staff's capacity to know the people they assist. Lisa Gwyther, a social work pioneer in dementia care, points out that "families appreciate the opportunity to get to know the special staff over time, and to share observations and tricks with the hands-on staff." She emphasizes how family members understand the variability and unpredictability of people with dementia, because they tend to be aware from their own caregiving that "what works today may not work tonight or tomorrow" and that "the best teacher is often experience with each patient over time" (Gwyther, 1985).

The need to be embraced by a community is most urgent for people with Alzheimer's disease and the other forms of dementia. They are often unable to convey their habits and preferences, and it is imperative for their caregivers to communicate what is known with one another. How each person with dementia is best calmed, which kinds of touch yield comfort, and particular ways to bring good cheer must be passed among staff and visitors alike. Astrid Norberg, a researcher in Sweden, declares that people with dementia suffer when they come to feel "disconnected, disintegrated, and homeless" and urges researchers and practitioners to consider how dementia is being experienced by each individual and to see each person's behavior as a meaningful expression of this experience. This approach contrasts dramatically with the prevailing tendency to study and manage "behavioral disturbances." Eloquently, Norberg depicts an attitude toward people with dementia that affirms each person's value and uniqueness while interacting on the level of feelings (Norberg, 2001), another principle of culture change.

ETHICAL PROBLEM SOLVING

Social workers in healthcare settings are often called on when ethical dilemmas leave a care team stymied and unable to move forward. For instance, a nursing home may have someone they term a *problem resident* who gets along with no one. Each roommate placed with this person complains to family members, who in turn demand a room change for their relative. Finally, the nursing home social worker may be asked to find someone to put in that room who has no family to provide noisy advocacy and therefore will have no choice but to abide the situation. One researcher portrays a social worker often faced with these predicaments who "does not like to move people around like dominoes" and therefore "tries her best to match people well and to handle problems creatively" (Kane, 1990).

Such situations are rife with tough ethical issues. Should the needs of the institution ever supersede the needs of the individual? What about the rights of a resident who is unable to complain or has no advocates from outside the facility? Should a social worker obey an instruction from a supervisor that is unethical? Social work as a profession possesses an extensive code of ethics, yet to invoke inconvenient ethical issues to an administrator pressured by budgetary considerations can provoke conflict or imperil one's job standing in traditional settings. In a facility striving to transform its culture, however, a social worker would be able to bring the values and principles of culture change to the fore and function as part of a team whose philosophy and ethics accord with social work ethics.

Instead of seeking to impose a solution on the problem resident, a transformed culture calls for including this resident, direct-care staff, and family members in an open discussion of options. It is more respectful to inform someone of the difficulties others are experiencing than to assume that this person is incapable of change. Occasionally, such a person may seize on this opportunity to deal with problems that have beset other relationships, grateful for the chance to learn more compatible behaviors. In other instances, the social worker's creative problem solving may include input from direct care staff on other shifts who can identify concerns not apparent to daytime observers. Addressing these concerns may resuscitate the relationship between a current pair of roommates, making the upheaval of a room change unnecessary. In a transformed culture, solutions are sought under the principles that behavior has meaning and that each person can, and does, make a difference. The fact that it is often time-consuming to arrive at such individualized solutions is recognized and respected by administrators who perceive culture change as an ongoing process, rather than a firm set of protocols.

BARRIERS AND OPPORTUNITIES

In *Aging: The Fulfillment of Life*, Henri Nouwen and Walter Gaffney argue that "care is more than helping people to accept their fate." They claim that all aspects of personhood must be engaged, and that this process requires honest engagement between the generations on issues many prefer to avoid.

> Real care includes confrontation. Care for the aging, after all, means care for all ages, since all human beings—whether they are ten, thirty, fifty, seventy, or eighty years old—are participating in the same process of aging. Therefore, care for the aging means, more often than not, confronting all men and women with their illusion of immortality out of which the rejection of old age comes forth. (Nouwen & Gaffney, 1974)

Acknowledging this reality, leaders in the culture change movement recognize that long-term care evolves in a wider cultural context than that of the facilities where care takes place. Restoring meaning and life satisfaction to the lives of frail elders ultimately must have its basis in the lives elders led prior to the constraints illness imposes. To this end, the Pioneer Network for Culture Change declares in its vision statement: "In-depth change in systems requires change in the individual's and society's attitudes toward aging and elders; change in elders' attitudes toward themselves and their aging; change in the attitudes and behavior of caregivers toward those for whom they care and change in governmental policy and regulation."

The immediate goal is to create warm, home-like environments, where sources of dignity can be renewed and individual identity can be expressed, despite losses mandated by illness or frailty. In American nursing homes, the change process has been steady but slow. Staff still entrenched in the traditional culture of control over those receiving care frequently react as if they have a lot to lose as residents gain autonomy and jurisdiction over their own lives. Simultaneously, the prospect of more satisfying work roles and happier residents motivates many to abide the "subtle and difficult art" of the transformation process, remembering that "warmth demands persistence, patience, forgiveness, tolerance and respect," virtues that "flourish only when cultivated" (Thomas, 2003). Social workers will continue to be the chief cultivators of such warmth, charged as the profession always has been with honoring the individual as the starting place of service to others.

REFERENCES

Bail, K. (1999, March). Views presented at the Pioneer Network Retreat, San Francisco, CA.

Barkan, B (1995). The regenerative community: The Live Oak Living Center and the quest for autonomy, self-esteem, and connection in elder care. In L. M. Gamroth, J. Semradek, & E. M. Tornquist (Eds), *Enhancing autonomy in long-term care: Concepts and strategies* (pp. 169–192). New York, NY: Springer.

Barkan, B. (2003). The Live Oak Regenerative Community: Championing a culture of hope and meaning. In A. Weiner & J. Ronch (Eds.), *Culture change in long term care* (pp. 197–229). Binghamton, NY: Haworth Social Work Practice Press.

Beck, C., Doan, R., & Cody, M. (2002, Spring). Nursing assistants as providers of mental health care in nursing homes. *Generations, 26*, 66–71.

Carboni, J. (1990). Homelessness among the institutionalized elderly. *Journal of Gerontological Nursing, 16*, 32–38.

Eaton, S. (1998). *Beyond unloving care: Linking work organization and patient care quality in nursing homes.* Presented at the Academy of Management Annual Meeting, San Diego, CA.

Fagan, R. (2003). Pioneer Network: Changing the culture of aging in America. In A. Weiner & J. Ronch (Eds.). *Culture change in long term care* (pp. 125–140). Binghamton, NY: Haworth Social Work Practice Press.

Fagan, R., Williams, C., & Burger, S. (1997). *Meeting of pioneers in nursing home culture change: Final report.* Lifespan of Greater Rochester.

Frank, A. (1991, November 14–16). *The quality of recognition: Suffering and illness in the Hegelian aftermath.* Paper presented at the International Consensus Conference on Doctor-Patient Communication, Toronto, Ontario, Canada.

Gwyther, L. (1985). *Care of Alzheimer's patients: A manual for nursing home staff.* Washington, DC: American Health Care Association.

Hessel, D. (Ed.). (1977). *Maggie Kuhn on aging: A dialogue.* Philadelphia, PA: Westminster.

Kane, R. (1990). Everyday life in nursing homes: The way things are. In R. Kane & A. Caplan (Eds.), *Everyday ethics: Resolving dilemmas in nursing home life* (pp. 3–20). New York, NY: Springer.

Kitwood, T. (1997). *Dementia reconsidered: The person comes first.* Buckingham, UK: Open University Press.

Lustbader, W. (2001). The Pioneer challenge: A radical change in the culture of nursing homes. In L. Noelker & Z. Harel (Eds.), *Linking quality of long-term care and quality of life.* New York, NY: Springer.

Norberg, A. (2001). Communication in the care of people with severe dementia. In M. L. Hummert & J. F. Nussbaum (Eds.), *Aging, communication, and health: Linking research and practice for successful aging* (pp. 157–173). Mahwah, NJ: Erlbaum.

Norris-Baker, L., Doll, G., Gray, L., & Kahl, J. (2003). *Pioneering change: An illustrative guide to changing the culture of care in nursing hones with examples from the PEAK initiative.* Manhattan, KS: The Galichia Center on Aging, Kansas State University.

Nouwen, H., & Gaffney, W. (1974). *Aging: The fulfillment of life.* New York, NY: Image.

Rader, J., McKenzie, D., Hoeffer, B., & Barrick, A. (2002). Organizing care within the institution or home. In A. L. Barrick, J. Rader, B. Hoeffer, & P. Sloane, (Eds.), *Bathing without a battle: Personal care of individuals with dementia* (pp. 117–124). New York, NY: Springer.

Richards, M., Hooyman, N., Hansen, M., Brandts, W., Smith-DiJulio, K., & Dahm, L. (1985). *Choosing a nursing home: A guidebook for families.* Seattle: University of Washington Press.

Thomas, W. (1994). *The Eden Alternative: Nature, hope, and nursing homes.* Columbia: University of Missouri.

Thomas, W. (1999). *The Eden Alternative handbook: The art of building human habitats.* Shelburne, NY: Summer Hill.

Thomas, W. (2003). Evolution of Eden. In A. Weiner & J. Ronch (Eds.), *Culture change in long term care.* Binghamton, NY: Haworth Social Work Practice Press.

Unsino, C. (1998). *Staff and organizational development: A process for changing the culture in long term* care. Paper presented at the annual meeting of the National Citizens' Coalition for Nursing Home Reform, Washington, DC.

Vladeck, B. (1980). *Unloving care: The nursing home tragedy*. New York, NY: Basic Books.

Williams, C. (1989a). The experience of long term care in the future. *Journal of Gerontological Social Work, 14*, 3–18. http://dx.doi.org/10.1300%2FJ083 V14N01_02

Williams, C. (1989b). Liberation: Alternative to physical restraint. *The Gerontologist, 29*, 5. http://dx.doi.org/1 0.1093%2Fgeront%2F29.5.585

Williams, C. (with Finch, C.). (1997). Physical restraint: Not fit for woman, man or beast. *Journal of the American Geriatrics Society, 45*, 773–775.

Williams, C. (1999). *Relationships: The heart of life and long term care*. Paper presented at the American Society on Aging conference, Quality of care in nursing homes: The critical role of the nursing assistant, Philadelphia, PA.

Yeatts, D., & Seward, R. (2000) Reducing turnover and improving health care in nursing homes. *The Gerontologist, 40*, 358–363. http://dx.doi.org/10.1093 %2Fgeront%2F40.3.358

GERI ADLER

LONIQUE R. PRITCHETT

Long-Term Care in the Veterans Administration

27

The Veterans Health Administration (VHA) is a major provider of care to older Veterans. Like the US population, the Veteran population is growing older. Korean-War and Vietnam-era Veterans represent a significant percentage of the total Veteran population, increasing the need for geriatric and long-term care (National Center of Veterans Analysis and Statistics, 2013; Department of Veterans Affairs [DVA], 2011). In fiscal year (FY) 2011, Veterans 65 years and older made up over 40% of the Veteran population; estimates put the number of Veterans 85 years and older as increasing 20% between 2010 and 2019 (DVA, 2011). In response to this growing population of older Veterans, the VHA provides a full complement of institutional and non-institutional long-term-care services (Vandenberg, Bergofsky, & Burris, 2010).

Helping to meet the needs of the burgeoning aging Veteran population are VHA social workers. Beginning with 36 social workers in 1926, the VHA now employs over 11,000, most master's prepared, making it the largest employer of social workers in the United States (DVA, 2014; Manske, 2006). Although VHA social workers work with Veterans of all ages, for many the complex needs of older Veterans are a major focus. Whether they work in oncology, mental health, dementia care, or acute medicine, VHA social workers daily encounter older Veterans facing a myriad of biopsychosocial challenges.

This chapter highlights the roles of VHA social workers, especially those involved in residential services for older people, explains eligibility criteria, and discusses long-term care options aimed at older Veterans. Residential and home-based long-term-care alternatives are available, depending on each Veteran's unique situation. Residential long-term care options include:

- Community Living Centers (CLCs), which are VHA-owned and -operated nursing homes. These were formerly known as Nursing Home Care Units. The name change reflects the cultural change toward resident-centered care and emphasis on quality of life that has been transforming VA nursing homes;
- Community nursing homes (CNHs), where qualifying Veterans may receive care under contracts from the VA;
- State Veterans Homes, which are operated by State governments with construction costs,

standard-setting, and health services provided in large part by the VHA; and

- Medical foster homes, VHA-inspected and -approved facilities for veterans who lack a caregiver to meet their needs.

Home-based long-term care services provided by the VHA include adult day healthcare, home-based primary care, home hospice care, and home respite care (Karlin, Zeiss, & Burris, 2010; Vandenberg et al., 2010).

ROLES OF VETERANS HEALTH ADMINISTRATION SOCIAL WORKERS

Veterans Health Administration social workers provide a rich variety of services to older Veterans and their families. They fulfill critical roles and act in many capacities, ranging from clinical to administrative. While their activities vary by program, specialization, setting and position, VHA social workers must possess strong social work skills and knowledge of the complex VHA healthcare system. Their responsibilities include the following:

- Advocacy,
- Assessment,
- Case management,
- Crisis intervention,
- Discharge planning,
- Family and caregiver support,
- Psychotherapy, and
- Training. (National Association of Social Workers [NASW], 2012; DVA, 2014)

Advocacy

Veterans Health Administration social workers are advocates. They work to ensure that all Veterans have equal access to available resources and opportunities needed for optimal mental and healthcare services and they recommend changes to programs and policies that negatively affect their clients. Veterans Health Administration social workers are responsible for advocating on behalf of the needs of all Veterans, particularly those who are disenfranchised or vulnerable, by helping them negotiate the goals of their care and access needed medical resources (NASW, 2012).

Assessment

Veterans Health Administration social workers require strong assessment skills. An assessment is a dynamic, interactive process whereby social workers evaluate strengths, potential resources, and obstacles to identify supports and interventions that maximize the older Veteran's potential (McInnis-Dittrich, 2005). During an interview, social workers ask questions about recent life events, living arrangements, family relationships, coping skills, social-support networks, and use of community resources. Legal issues, including powers-of-attorney, financial planning, and advanced directives, are explored. This information is synthesized and used to develop an acceptable and appropriate plan of care (NASW, 2012). Veterans Health Administration social workers have an important role in advance care planning. They review or create advanced directives that ensure that Veterans' wishes are clear and carried out as desired. They also offer education, guidance, and assistance on completing and filing advanced directives in Veterans' medical records (NASW, 2012).

Case Management

As case managers, VHA social workers coordinate and monitor care and services for Veterans with complicated health situations. Veterans Health Administration case managers provide resource navigation by facilitating access to a range of financial, housing, health, mental health, education, and community resources across the continuum of services within and outside the VHA. Case-management services are available for all Veterans but have a greater impact among those who have complex medical or mental health problems or who are at increased risk for hospitalization.

Crisis Intervention

Veterans Health Administration social workers often find themselves in situations that require urgent attention. Crises, such as the unexpected death of a loved one or diagnosis of a terminal illness, can cause high levels of stress for older Veterans and their families. During these situations, social workers must often work quickly to assist Veterans and their families to acquire much-needed resources and provide short-term counseling.

Discharge Planning

As discharge planners, VHA social workers play a vital role in easing the Veteran's transition back home or to another healthcare facility. While the Veteran is hospitalized, social workers assess his/her support system, available resources, life situation, and equipment needs for discharge while also serving as a liaison to the family, keeping them apprised of the Veteran's progress and postdischarge plans.

An important element of discharge planning is brokering services. Working with the Veteran, family, and medical team, social workers identify resources for follow-up care. Whether a Veteran is going home or transferring to another healthcare facility, social workers help to make the transition as smooth as possible by identifying resources, within the VHA or in the community, that are best suited to that Veteran's situation. When Veterans are unable to return home, VHA social workers can recommend and locate alternative-care options. Veterans Health Administration social workers must be knowledgeable about both VHA and community programs services.

Family and Caregiver Support

Veterans Health Administration social workers often collaborate with families of older Veterans. They provide families and caregivers with guidance and assistance during hospital stays and outpatient visits. Caregivers can be overwhelmed by caring for their aging relative. Social workers can provide emotional, social, and spiritual support to caregivers individually or in groups. Veterans Health Administration social workers can often be seen leading family support groups, such as for caregivers of Veterans with dementia.

Psychotherapy

Clinical social workers provide psychotherapy with individuals, groups, and families. These social workers often are part of outpatient mental health programs. During sessions, the clinicians can address emotional, behavioral, and mental health needs.

Training Social Work Students

The VHA is affiliated with more than 100 graduate schools of social work and trains more than 600 students annually. Interns are assigned to units throughout VHA medical centers, including the community living centers, inpatient acute care, and outpatient mental health. Interns in geriatric placements develop skills in assessment, workload management, and documentation, as well as specialized aging-related knowledge (Adler, 2006).

ELIGIBILITY

Eligibility for VHA healthcare depends on several factors, including the nature of a Veteran's discharge from military service (i.e., honorable, dishonorable), length of service, service-connected disability, income level, and available VHA resources (DVA, 2013c).

Service-Connected Disability

A service-connected disability is a disease or injury sustained or aggravated by a Veteran during active military service. Service-connected disabilities are assigned a rating (0%–100%), based on the impact of the disability on daily functioning. Veterans with greater levels of impairment receive higher disability ratings and, therefore, higher VA disability compensation. This tax-free monthly disability compensation varies greatly, depending on the degree of the disability and the number of eligible dependents. Overall, Veterans with a service-connected disability rating of 30% or higher are eligible for additional compensation for spouses and/or dependents. Veterans with certain severe disabilities, such as spinal cord or traumatic brain injury, may be eligible for additional special monthly compensation. In addition to monthly compensation, service-connected Veterans are entitled to receive additional benefits, such as medical care, vocational rehabilitation, and/or adaptive equipment or homes (DVA, 2013c).

Means Testing

Veterans who do not receive a service-connected disability or pension payment or who have special eligibility (such as a former Prisoner of War) must complete a financial assessment, or Means Test, to determine their enrollment status and copayment responsibilities. Based on the results of their Means Test, and prior income year total gross household income plus net worth, Veterans are assigned a Priority Group. Priority Groups range from 1 to 8, with 1 being the highest priority for enrollment. Veterans who are in lower Priority Groups may be required to pay copayments for care and medications. Given limited federal funds, Priority Groups ensure that certain groups of Veterans are able to be enrolled before others (DVA, 2013c).

RESIDENTIAL LONG-TERM CARE SETTINGS

As summarized above, CLCs, CNHs, and State Veterans Homes are three major residential long-term care options for eligible older Veterans. These programs differ in several ways, including their locations and cost to the VHA and to the Veteran.

Community Living Centers

There are over 130 VHA-operated nursing homes, now called CLCs (Williamson, 2011). They are colocated at VHA medical center campuses and provide care to more than 46,000 elderly and disabled Veterans annually (Williamson, 2011; DVA, 2013a). In FY 2010 the VA spent over $3.3 billion for care at these facilities (Williamson, 2011).

Beginning in 2005, the VHA began a paradigm shift and culture transformation in how it delivered nursing home care to Veterans (Hojlo, 2010). One of the first signs of change was renaming all VHA nursing homes or units as CLCs. A person-centered care approach replaced the medical model of care, whereby the VHA began a process to improve residents' quality of life and quality of care while simultaneously improving staff autonomy and satisfaction (Hojlo, 2010; Sullivan et al., 2013). Key elements of CLCs include the following:

- Resident-centered and individualized care practices,
- A home-like environment, and
- Changes in workplace practices to include consistent staffing and self-scheduling. (Hojlo, 2010)

Veterans can reside at a CLC for short stays of 90 days or less or long stays, greater than 90 days. In FY 2010, over 90% of residents admitted to CLCs were considered short-stay. Often these Veterans were receiving rehabilitative or restorative care or awaiting transfer to another facility (Williamson, 2011). If CLC residents continue to receive rehabilitation, they will typically go to the hospital units for the service, and they may well have received excellent specialized in-patient rehabilitation in a VA hospital unit before entering the CLC. The VA rehabilitation units do not aspire to be residential, avoiding some of the confusion surrounding postacute care in CNHs as described in Chapter 24 by Bonifas, Bern-Klug, and Simons. Longer stays are available to Veterans who meet eligibility criteria, require end-of-life care, need extensive rehabilitation, or are unable to be maintained in or are inappropriate for other residential options (Vandenberg et al., 2010; Williamson, 2011).

Community Nursing Home Program

In 1965 the VHA began to offer nursing-home care under contracts. The goal of the CNH program is to provide Veterans with short- and long-term institutional care at facilities in their communities. In FY 2012 expenditures for the CNH totaled about $614 million (Office of the Inspector General, 2013). The length of a Veteran's contract depends on eligibility and medical need. Some Veterans who require nursing-home care for a service-connected disability may be eligible for coverage for an indefinite period of time. Veterans ineligible for indefinite coverage may extend their stay by privately paying for care or pursuing Medicare or Medicaid.

Veterans Health Administration staff, often social workers, provide oversight to CNHs. They conduct an annual review to ensure a facility meets VHA nursing-home operation and quality-of-care standards (Office of the Inspector General, 2013; Vandenberg et al., 2010). Most Veterans under a contract must be visited monthly by a social worker or nurse (DVA, 2004; Vandenberg et al., 2010).

State Veterans' Homes

State Veterans' Homes augment the VHA's ability to provide a continuous residence for Veterans in need of long-term care. These facilities are owned and operated by a state. The VHA contributes a percentage of the cost of construction or renovation or per diem charges (Vandenberg et al., 2010). Eligibility and admission criteria vary by state. The VHA assures provision of quality care through VHA inspections, audits, and reconciliation of records conducted by the local VHA medical center (Vandenberg et al., 2010).

Medical Foster Home

Medical foster homes are another alternative to institutionalization available to improve quality of life for older Veterans who are unable to live independently and have no caregiver available to meet their needs. The homes are inspected and approved by the VA, although foster home residents can include nonveterans. The target population for medical foster homes is Veterans who meet nursing-home level of care; are unable to live independently because of functional, cognitive, or psychosocial impairment; prefer a non-institutional setting for long-term care; and have the financial resources or eligibility for VHA benefits to pay for care on an ongoing basis. Veterans are cared for in a private or rented home in the community where they receive 24-hour supervision and personal assistance (DVA, 2009b, 2013b). Their medical needs are met by the home-based primary care team (Edes, 2010). The program services are typically coordinated by social workers.

Home-Based Long-Term Care

Eligible Veterans can also receive home-based long-term care, whereby Veterans receive services to help maintain their ability to live in their own home. The following list describes some of the VHA's home-based programs and services:

- **Adult Day Health Care (ADHC) Centers** are a long-term care option for Veterans, usually frail elders and functionally impaired, who are at risk of institutionalization and who have caregivers in need of respite. In congregate settings, ADHCs provide health maintenance, rehabilitative services, socialization, and caregiver support to assist Veterans to remain in their homes. They are staffed by an interdisciplinary team that includes a social worker. Some ADHCs are available on-site at VHA medical centers or at contract facilities (DVA, 2009a).

- **Home-Based Primary Care** offers healthcare services to Veterans who are bedridden or homebound with conditions that make them unsuitable for management in outpatient clinics. Services are delivered by an interdisciplinary team that often includes a social worker (Davidson, 2009).

- **Homemaker/Home Health Aide** provides health-related services for service-connected Veterans needing nursing-home care; provided by public and private agencies under a system of case management, this service is usually coordinated by a social worker (Vandenberg et al., 2010).

- **Respite Care** is designed to give the family of Veterans a break from day-to-day caregiving responsibilities. Respite services can be offered at a Veteran's home or another setting, such as a CNH or an ADHC (DVA, 2008). Social workers' responsibilities regarding respite care vary by their position. For example, an outpatient social worker might arrange for a Veteran to have a short-term stay at a CLC or, conversely, refer to and arrange for participation at a contract ADHC.

- **Hospice and Palliative Care** provides treatment to relieve pain and control symptoms in a respectful, culturally appropriate manner. Both offer comfort care; however, Veterans needing palliative care do not need a diagnosis of a terminal illness (DVA, n.d.). Hospice and palliative care is available to Veterans in outpatient and inpatient settings depending on individual preferences and needs. In hospice and palliative care, social workers play a pivotal role in meeting the complex psychosocial and medical needs of seriously ill Veterans. They are often members of interdisciplinary teams, providing leadership and offering Veterans and their families support and assistance with issues related to late life, grief, and bereavement.

CONCLUSION

The roles of social workers in the VHA today reflect current trends in models of care, with social workers expanding their activities to provide assistance to patients in a broad spectrum of venues and to their families. Because of its size and the number of social workers it employs, the VHA will continue to be in the forefront of developing innovative geriatric-care options. Consequently, it is expected to continue to be an important employment setting for social workers and an important resource.

REFERENCES

Adler, G. (2006). Geriatric field education in social work: A model for practice. *Educational Gerontology*, 32, 707–719. doi: 10.1080036012706006835439

Davidson, L. (2009). Healthcare for U.S. veterans: Is the system sufficient? *Internet Journal of Healthcare Administration*, 7.

Department of Veterans Affairs (DVA). (n.d.). *VHA website*. Retrieved October 18, 2013, from http://www.va.gov/GERIATRICS/Guide/LongTermCare/Hospice_and_Palliative_Care.asp

Department of Veterans Affairs (DVA). (2004). *VHA community nursing home oversight procedures*. VHA handbook 1143.2. Washington, DC: Department of Veterans Affairs.

Department of Veterans Affairs (DVA). (2008). *Respite care*. VHA handbook 1140.02. Retrieved October 25, 2013, from www1.va.gov/vhapublications/ViewPublication.asp?pub_ID=1802

Department of Veterans Affairs (DVA). (2009a). *Adult day health care*. VHA handbook 1141.03. Retrieved October 24, 2013, from www1.va.gov/vhapublications/ViewPublication.asp?pub_ID=2086

Department of Veterans Affairs (DVA). (2009b). *Medical foster home procedures*. VHA handbook 1141.02. Retrieved October 24, 2013, from http://vaww1.va.gov/vhapublications/ViewPublication.asp?pub_ID=2111

Department of Veterans Affairs (DVA). (2011). *Strategic plan refresh 2011–2015*. Office of the Secretary, Washington, DC.

Department of Veterans Affairs (DVA). (2013a). *Guide to long term care (CLC): Community living centers (VA nursing homes)*. Updated October 4, 2013. Retrieved September 1, 2013, from http://www.va.gov/GERIATRICS/Guide/LongTermCare/VA_Community_Living_Centers.asp

Department of Veterans Affairs (DVA). (2013b). *Guide to long term care (Medical foster homes)*. Updated October 4, 2013. Retrieved September 3, 2013, from http://www.va.gov/geriatrics/guide/longtermcare/medical_foster_homes.asp

Department of Veterans Affairs (DVA). (2013c). *Health benefits home*. Updated October 13, 2013. Accessed October 15, 2013. Available at http://www.va.gov/healthbenefits/

Department of Veterans Affairs (DVA). (2014). *VA social work*. Updated April 11, 2014. Retrieved from http://www.socialwork.va.gov/

Edes, T. (2010). The VA's medical foster home program. *Generations, 34*, 99–101.

Hojlo, C. (2010). The VA's transformation of nursing home care: From nursing homes to community living centers. *Generations, 34*, 43–48.

Karlin, B. E., Zeiss, A. M., & Burris, J. F. (2010). Providing care to older Americans in the Department of Veterans Affairs. *Generations, 34*, 6–8.

Manske, J. E. (2006). Social work in the Department of Veterans Affairs: Lessons learned. *Health and Social Work, 31*, 233–238.

McInnis-Dittrich, K. (2005). *Social work with elders: A biopsychosocial approach to assessment and intervention*. Boston, MA: Allyn & Bacon.

National Association of Social Workers (NASW). (2012). *Standards for social work practice with service members, veterans, and their families*. Washington, DC: NASW Press.

National Center of Veterans Analysis and Statistics. (2013). *Veteran population*. Updated June 25, 2013. Retrieved October 11, 2013, from https://www.va.gov/vetdata/Veteran_Population.asp

Office of the Inspector General. (2013, March 29). *Veterans Health Administration: Audit of the community home program*. Report No. 11-00331-160. Washington, DC: Veterans Health Administration.

Sullivan, J. L., Shwartz, M., Burgess, J. F., Jr., Pekoz, E. A., Christiansen, C. L., Gerena-Melia, M., & Berlowitz, D. (2013). Person-centered care practices and quality in Department of Veterans Affairs nursing homes: Is there a relationship? *Medical Care, 51*, 165–171. doi: 10.1097/MLR.06013e3182763230

Vandenberg, P., Bergofsky, L. R., & Burris, J. F. (2010). The VA's systems of care and veterans under care. *Generations, 34*, 13–19.

Williamson, R. B. (2011). *VA community living centers: Actions needed to better manage risks to Veterans' quality of life and care* (GAO-12-11). Washington, DC: Government Accounting Office.

Populations Social Workers Serve in Health and Aging

B

AMY HOROWITZ

SECTION I

Older Adults with Chronic Physical and Health Conditions

OVERVIEW

Social work practice with older adults, whether or not specifically focused on health issues, requires knowledge of the range of age-related health conditions and physical disabilities that older adults may confront, and especially requires an appreciation of the impact of these conditions on the well-being of both the older adult and their family members. This section contains seven chapters that address the major health conditions experienced by significant numbers of older adults. Each chapter addresses the evidence base in terms of prevalence, risk factors, characteristics of the condition, treatment options, psychosocial impact on older adults and their families, and considerations for social work practice.

Cynthia Stuen and Karen Campbell underscore that sensory *impairments* in later life resulting from age-related vision and hearing disorders need to be distinguished from normal age-related sensory *changes*. The former can have profound functional and psychological consequences for older adults, yet are often accepted as a normal part of aging, which acts as a barrier to older adults seeking services. Social workers need to be aware of both the stigma that is often attached to "blindness" and "deafness" and the network of rehabilitation services that provide options for maximizing function through both training and adaptive devices.

Helen Miltiades and Lenard W. Kaye review the major orthopedic diseases and associated conditions, including the predictors and consequences of both falls and fear of falling among older adults. They highlight the important role that social workers can play in encouraging active lifestyles among older adults as both a preventive approach and one that can minimize the disability associated with orthopedic problems.

Michelle Putnam and Stephanie P. Wladkowski look at disability in later life across health conditions. They argue for the social model of disability, defining disability as a function of environmental conditions as much as it is a function of individual characteristics. The authors address issues related to two populations: adults aging *with* a disability and those aging *into* disability. These two populations experience many of the same social and cultural barriers in daily life but, like older adults living with HIV/AIDS, seem to fall into the cracks between competing service systems.

Tamara J. Cadet, Julie Berrett-Abebe, and Peter Maramaldi focus on cancer and aging. They emphasize that trends in prevalence and treatment are changing the perception and experience of cancer from an inevitable terminal condition to a chronic disease that is largely age related. The authors also highlight that while older adults have the highest prevalence of many forms of cancer they also have the lowest rate of screening, a challenge for both social service and healthcare providers to address.

Amy L. Ai and Cara Pappas examine age-related cardiovascular disease, one of the most prevalent conditions and a major cause of mortality in older cohorts. One of the major themes in this chapter is the close relationship between the emotional health of the older individual and the morbidity and mortality associated with cardiovascular conditions.

Diabetes is also an extremely prevalent and potentially life-threatening condition among older adults, and, as the chapter authors Richard B. Francoeur and Alicia M. Wilson stress, can lead to significant systemic complications, including cardiovascular problems, vision disorders, neuropathy, and cognitive impairment. Sensitivity to cultural diversity in terms of food preferences and choices and the meaning attached to diabetes is especially important in assessment and treatment of diabetes among minority elders.

Charles A. Emlet and Anne K. Hughes note that HIV/AIDS, a disease that has not been historically associated with aging, is increasingly relevant to gerontological social work practice as increased life expectancy has resulted in emerging populations of older adults who are aging with this health condition. However, there is a vast disconnect between the healthcare system addressing persons living with HIV/AIDS and the aging service network, leaving older adults with less than optimal care.

There are several themes that emerge from these thoughtful reviews that have implications for social work practice with older adults. First, it is clear that physical and mental health have strong, reciprocal relationships. That is, age-related health conditions and impairments place the older adult at greater risk of mental health problems, especially depression. Depression, in turn, is a major risk factor for increased disability, further morbidity, and increased mortality in life-threatening illnesses. Evidence is mounting that, regardless of the particular condition, attention to the psychological consequences of age-related disease and disability is a critical component of overall care.

Second, health conditions of older adults affect the entire family system. Family members sometimes suddenly find themselves in caregiving relationships with their older relatives and, as other chapters in this volume also underscore, often experience extensive stress as a result of the physical and psychological demands of caregiving. Further, families often need information and education about the nature of the condition affecting their older relative, as well as help negotiating the typically fragmented systems of acute, rehabilitative, and long-term community and/or institutional care. Social work practice with older adults with health problems is clearly a family affair.

Third, it is evident that risk is not evenly distributed and that there are significant health disparities among older adults. Although not universal, African Americans, Latinos, and other ethnic groups often have higher rates of disease and disability when compared with Caucasians. Some differences apparently have a physiological base (e.g., higher rates of glaucoma among African Americans); others are clearly a function of societal inequities in access to care, as well as socioeconomic characteristics associated with less access to health education and healthy food choices and thus poorer health behaviors (e.g., obesity, smoking) that increase risk of conditions such as cardiovascular disease and diabetes. Advocacy on the individual and policy level is a critical component of social work practice with these diverse populations.

Fourth, social work practice with older adults with chronic health conditions increasingly involves working with multidisciplinary health teams and across systems of care and service networks. That is, older adults with health conditions often move in and out of the different sectors of the healthcare system—acute care, rehabilitative care, home care systems, and long-term care facilities—and not necessarily in linear fashion. Furthermore, providing care for particular subgroups often means coordinating aging network services with, for example, services available from mental health, disability and rehabilitation, and specialty health (e.g., HIV/AIDS) service networks. Cross-disciplinary and interdisciplinary skills coupled with a broad base of knowledge of intervention options, are increasingly critical to the social worker's repertoire.

Finally, the authors have identified an increase in evidence-informed practices targeted to older adults with chronic health conditions but, concurrently, highlight the need for well-designed, controlled intervention studies that test service models (e.g., mental health interventions in healthcare settings, models to enhance self-care, family support programs) targeted to improving the care and enhancing the quality of life for older adults with chronic health conditions and impairments.

The emotional effects of macular degeneration often seem more troublesome than the physical ones. Anger? Depression? Yes. Several fellow sufferers told me that they had sought help from therapists but found that few, if any were expert at dealing with our problems.

—Henry Grunwald, former editor of TIME Inc. (2003, p. 103).

Most of us who lose hearing in adulthood, of whom I am one, do experience diminished hearing as impairment, as disability, as lost competence. Few of us have sign language fluency and, even if we do, most of our family and friends are "culturally hearing" and cannot use a manual language for communication. We too were raised "culturally hearing," but now are no longer able to use sound to interact feely and comfortably with others. Relationships that once were effortless are no longer easy.

—The late Laurel Glass, professor emerita (2003, p. 106).

Groups of people—at dinners, meetings, cocktail parties . . . groups turn into faceless blurs. Worse is I can't see who is speaking and my longstanding hearing impairment becomes a greater handicap. Talk about sensory deprivation! I've been dealt a double whammy.

—Helen Handel Hyman, freelance writer (2003, p. 109).

CYNTHIA STUEN
KAREN CAMPBELL

Older Adults with Age-Related Sensory Loss

Sensory impairment has a profound impact on older persons, affecting their health, mental health, and quality of life status. In providing social work services to older adults, recognition and attention to age-related sensory loss, particularly vision and hearing, is important. The difference between the normal changes in sensory systems and those that are caused by age-related disorders should be basic knowledge for gerontological social workers, who must also recognize that, for many older adults, sensory losses occur in the context of other, comorbid health conditions. While sensory loss may not

be life threatening in comparison with cancer or heart disease, it may be the condition that most impacts the older person's quality of life.

This chapter focuses mainly on the continuum of loss of vision and hearing. The emphasis is on older adults who acquire an age-related sensory loss in later life, not on the population of older persons who are aging with an early-onset sensory loss. Large numbers of older persons experience varying degrees of vision loss and/or hearing loss that can have a profound impact on their quality of life as well as ability to access information, health, and human services.

Attention is first given to normal changes and disease-related impairments and their prevalence. An overview of the specialized service systems of vision rehabilitation and aural rehabilitation and the functional and psychosocial consequences of sensory losses is presented, followed by a discussion of the implications for social work practice and policy concerns. Case vignettes highlight the importance of recognizing the impact of sensory loss in clinical practice.

VISION IMPAIRMENT

All people experience normal changes in vision, usually beginning in their 40s. The most common, normal, age-related vision change is presbyopia. The lens of the eye becomes denser, less elastic, and more yellow, and the effect is that it is harder to focus on near-vision tasks such as reading. It is correctable with reading glasses or bifocal, trifocal, or progressive lenses. Another normal age-related change is that one's pupils become smaller; therefore older adults need more light than younger cohorts. There is a slower reaction time in adjusting to changing illumination levels, and generally older adults have diminished contrast sensitivity and colors appear less vivid, more faded. All of these normal changes generally occur gradually and can either be accommodated to or corrected with regular prescription glasses or contacts.

Vision impairments, on the other hand, typically result from eye disease and are not part of normal age-related vision changes. The most common age-related eye disorders are macular degeneration, glaucoma, diabetic retinopathy, and cataract. The functional impact of each of these conditions, which can occur independently or in combination, is of concern for social workers interacting with older adults.

The Lighthouse National Survey on Vision Loss: The Experience, Attitudes and Knowledge of Middle-Aged and Older Americans (The Lighthouse, 1995), a telephone survey conducted by Louis Harris and Associates, documented that 17% of adults aged 65–74 and 26% of adults age 75 years and older self-reported a vision impairment. The Alliance for Eye and Vision Research (2012) reports that nearly one in four people age 80 and older is either blind or visually impaired.

There is evidence of vision health disparities by race, ethnicity, gender, socioeconomics, disability status, rehabilitation, and access to care. For example, age-related vision impairment is higher among women, even when age adjusted, and is higher among African and Hispanic Americans than it is among their White counterparts except for age-related macular degeneration. Glaucoma and diabetic retinopathy are particularly more prevalent for non-White older persons (Zambelli-Weiner, Crews, & Friedman, 2012). Given the dramatic projected growth of the minority elderly population and also persons with diabetes over the next few decades, this needs urgent attention in terms of early identification and treatment. Disparities by race/ethnicity, education, and economic status among the major eye disorders that affect aging adults requires heightened awareness and response from professionals across disciplines (Zhang et al., 2012).

Cataract, which is the most prevalent of age-related eye diseases, affects nearly 20.5 million people in the United States age 40 and over (www.nei.nih.gov/eyedata/cataract.asp#3). A cataract causes a clouding of the normally clear lens of the eye; this clouding reduces the passage of light to the eye. Things look hazy and blurred, and there is increased sensitivity to glare (see Figure 28.1-A, which shows normal vision, and Figure 28.1-B, which simulates overall blur). Removal of the cataract can be a successful surgical procedure. However not every older person is a candidate for surgery. In these cases a person has very reduced visual function.

Diabetic retinopathy affects over 4 million persons aged 40 and over in the United States, according to the National Eye Institute (www.nei.nih.gov/eyedata/diabetic.asp#4). In addition to overall blur, one may have very hazy, distorted, or splotchy vision caused by leaking blood vessels in the eyes resulting from diabetes (see Figure 28.1-C, hazy, spotty vision). Laser treatment to seal the leaking blood vessels in

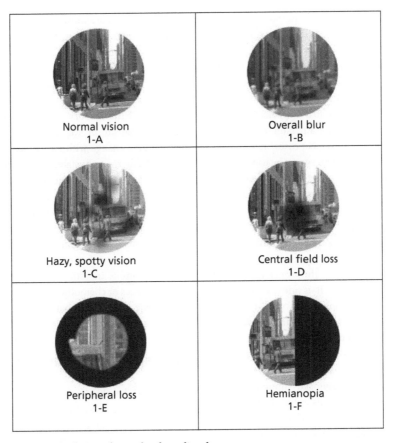

FIGURE 28.1 Composite simulation of age-related eye disorders.

the eye may arrest the leakage, but wherever the laser seals a blood vessel, scar tissue results, and one is unable to see through the scar tissue. Fluctuation in visual ability, sometimes by the hour, is not uncommon, as it is affected by one's blood sugar level. There is no cure for diabetes, and uncontrolled diabetes can lead to total loss of vision; hence, early and prompt intervention is critical.

According to the National Eye Institute, age-related macular degeneration (AMD), another common age-related impairment, affects 2 million adults age 50 and over (www.nei.nih.gov/eyedata/amd.asp). It is far more prevalent among Caucasian than Black or Hispanic persons. In this condition, one's central field of view is obliterated so reading, performing any near-distance task, and recognizing faces are very challenging (see Figure 28.1-D, central field loss). There are two forms of the disorder. Dry AMD is the most common form (estimated to be 85%–90% of cases) and usually progresses slowly. The less common form is Wet AMD; it is more

threatening to vision because at the early stages, tiny new blood vessels grow under the retina and leak fluid, which causes distorted central vision. A press release issued April 30, 2012, by the Director of the National Eye Institute reported that two drugs widely used to treat Wet AMD, Avastin and Lucentis, had been tested with National Eye Institute research funding and were found to improve vision when administered monthly or as needed. There is no cure for macular degeneration at this time; however, these treatments are a major milestone in improving vision lost to patients with Wet AMD (www.nei.nih.gov/news/pressreleases/043012.asp).

Glaucoma affects more the 2.7 million people age 40 and over in the United States. It is strongly related to age and race and is more common in women than in men (www.nei.nih.gov/eyedata/glaucoma.sp#4). It is most prevalent among aging adults and among African Americans. Glaucoma has the opposite functional impact of AMD; it takes away the peripheral or side field of vision, but leaves the central vision intact. The cause is unknown, but glaucoma gradually destroys the cells of the optic nerve that carry information from the eye to the brain. As the nerve cells die, vision is slowly lost at the periphery of the visual field (see Figure 28.1-E, peripheral field loss). Glaucoma is often referred to as the "silent thief of sight" because the loss happens so gradually that it may take years for a person to realize the loss of peripheral vision. In most cases, medications, laser treatments, and/or surgery can be used to slow or arrest the loss of vision, but the disease cannot be prevented. The loss of peripheral vision affects safe mobility in the home and community.

Hemianopia is another type of field loss that gerontological social workers need to understand. Hemianopia is the loss of half of one's visual field in both eyes; it may affect the upper half, lower half, or right or left half. It is most common in persons who have experienced a stroke, tumor, or trauma to the head. The most common defect is right homonymous hemianopia, which occurs in corresponding halves of the right field of vision (see Figure 28.1-F, hemianopia). It can often be overlooked and not diagnosed among persons who have had a stroke. This type of loss affects reading, because the person does not realize there is still a half page or line remaining and wonders why nothing is making sense. Movement and safe mobility are also impacted if half of one's visual field is missing.

HEARING IMPAIRMENT

There is a strong relationship between age and reported hearing loss. According to the National Institute on Deafness and other Communication Disorders (NIDCD), 30% of adults 65–74 years old and 47% of adults 75 years and older have a hearing loss (www.nidcd.nih.gov/health/statistics/pages/quick/aspx). Hearing loss is more prevalent among men than women.

Hearing loss can be classified as a disorder of conducive central auditory processing or of sensorineural processing. A conducive disorder is impairment in the transmission of sound to the inner ear, which can be caused by a build-up of cerumen (wax) or otosclerosis (a growth). Central auditory processing disorders are problems at the level of the brain, and speech discrimination is a problem in these conditions (Strawbridge, Wallhagen, Shema, & Kaplan, 2000).

Older adults are most susceptible to age-related atrophy that diminishes the reception of high-frequency sounds, especially among men, and low-frequency sounds especially among women; both compromise the understanding of speech. This sensorineural loss that accompanies aging is called presbycusis. The sensory structures within the balance mechanism of the inner ear also undergo degenerative change with age, which contributes in part to the dizziness, instability, and falls so common among older adults (Weinstein, 2003).

Hearing loss can also be caused by a number of other factors including exposure over long periods to work or recreational noise, genetic factors, trauma, metabolic disease in organs such as the kidney, vascular disease, or infections. Another high risk for older persons is ingestion of medications such as some diuretics or chemotherapy treatments that have an ototoxic effect—one that is damaging to hearing and balance (Weinstein, 2003).

DUAL SENSORY IMPAIRMENT

Having both hearing impairment and vision impairment, referred to as dual sensory impairment, is quite prevalent and creates a special challenge for social workers, particularly in the area of communication. A study conducted by Lighthouse International based on the secondary analysis of the Longitudinal Study of Aging Version 5 dataset found that 35% of adults age 70 and older reported some degree of vision impairment and 42% reported some hearing impairment, with 21% having both a visual and hearing impairment. African and Hispanic Americans were found to be at greater risk for both single and dual sensory impairments (Brennan, 2003).

Negative outcomes in several domains related to sensory impairment have been documented. Having a vision impairment alone or a dual sensory impairment accounts for greater functional disability, a higher risk for falls, more informal help received in instrumental activities of daily living and personal activities of daily living, dissatisfaction with social interactions, and more healthcare use (Brennan, 2003). As Schneider et al. (2011) document in a literature review of this topic, dual sensory impairment diminishes communication and well-being and can cause depression, reduced independence, social isolation, cognitive impairment, and mortality. These data are significant because the population of older persons is increasing with the baby boom cohorts entering retirement and with increases in longevity.

VISION AND HEARING LOSS IN THE NURSING HOME SETTING

Nursing home populations have a much higher rate of hearing and vision impairments. The rate of moderate or severe vision impairment among nursing home residents was reported at over 50% in a study by Horowitz and Balistreri (1994). Another study by Horowitz (1994) showed that even in the context of multiple chronic impairments, vision impairment significantly contributed to functional disability among older persons living in an institutional healthcare environment. Rein et al. (2006) documented that while only 4.3% of the population age 65 and over lives in nursing homes, that number rises to 16% of those who are visually impaired and 40% of those who are blind. A previous study of nursing home residents found that impaired vision and hearing independently predicted lower levels of social engagement and less time spent in leisure activities (Resnick, Fries, & Verbrugge, 1997).

Recognizing vision and/or hearing impairments in the nursing home setting is important to ensure that older persons maintain their maximum independence. Stuen (1994) documented a successful three-part strategy, including a training video, to introduce nursing home personnel to the field of vision rehabilitation.

VISION REHABILITATION: A TEAM APPROACH

What results most commonly from the age-related eye disorders previously described is partial sight or low vision, although some disorders, if untreated, can lead to total blindness. When there is no treatment, medicine, or surgery to correct vision to the normal range, one is said to have *low vision*. A team approach can be very helpful in treating the patient with low vision. Often, the first step is for the person to be evaluated by a low vision specialist, an ophthalmologist or optometrist with specialized training, who can prescribe appropriate optical and nonoptical aids. The other members of the vision rehabilitation team include the rehabilitation therapist or occupational therapist, who helps an individual learn techniques to remain independent at home, at work, and in the community. An orientation and mobility specialist teaches people with vision loss to move safely indoors and outdoors using any residual vision, auditory cues, or other techniques such as using a white cane or a dog guide. Social workers provide services including individual or group counseling around adjustment to the vision loss, including associated depression and/or anxiety, or concrete services, for example, helping older adults access community resources and government programs such as Social Security Disability.

Once hearing impairment is recognized and the medical factors explored, usually by an otolaryngologist, to make sure there is no treatment or surgery that can restore the hearing to a normal range, an older adult should have an audiological assessment by an audiologist. The goal of the assessment is to identify the areas in which the hearing loss is impacting the older persons and to find appropriate hearing technologies and also referrals for counseling to help the person overcome the hearing handicap.

Hearing aids are not the only resources available to older persons; there are also other hearing assistance technology systems. Some of the reasons cited as to why someone does not acquire aids are cost and cosmetic considerations and older persons not feeling the need even though those around them may disagree (Montano, 2003). One of the simplest, least costly assistive listening devices is a hand-held battery-operated amplification device. There are also infrared and FM systems that use light wave technology to transmit sound directly from the source to the listeners.

Every state has an office or commission that addresses rehabilitation for people who are visually impaired. There are also not-for-profit vision rehabilitation agencies throughout the United States. Senior Site, a website maintained by the American Foundation for the Blind and VisionAware, provides answers to questions about vision problems and also identifies services in local areas—one can input a state or province and find services nearby www.visionaware.org/section.aspx?FolderID=11. The vision rehabilitation field itself, until very recently, has not embraced the growing population of older adults who are in need of their services. Historically, the vision rehabilitation field focused its service delivery on children and vocationally bound adults.

Access to audiologists can be found through the American Speech, Language and Hearing

Association at www.asha.org/proserv. Gerontological social workers should familiarize themselves with the resources in their locale that serve older adults with vision and/or hearing loss.

SOCIAL WORK AND PSYCHOSOCIAL ADJUSTMENT TO SENSORY LOSS

Empowerment of the individual and the right to self-determination are central values of both social work and independent living, however social work approaches it from the professional's involvement in the client or patient's care. Weick, Rapp, Sullivan, and Kisthardt (1989) propose a strengths-based practice approach with older adults who experience sensory loss. This approach gives attention to the strengths and positive capacities people have rather than focusing on their deficits.

Hearing impairment affects one's ability to communicate with others and can have a serious impact on interpersonal relationships. Research has shown that hearing loss is associated with less satisfaction with life, loss of independence, isolation, depression, and anxiety (Mehta, 2003). Weinstein (2003) reports that hearing loss in older adults restricts multiple dimensions of quality of life including functional status and cognitive, emotional, and social functioning.

Similarly, research on the impact of vision impairment on older persons documents that it may significantly disrupt patterns of behavior and social interaction in a broad range of psychological domains such as self-concept, self-awareness, and social domains including communication, mobility, work, and recreation (Brennan & Cardinali, 2002). The loss of vision in later life has a strong relationship with functional disability (Horowitz, 1994).

SOCIAL WORK: CLINICAL IMPLICATIONS

Depression and anxiety can be major problems among older adults and older persons who experience a functional disability are at increased risk of depression (Blazer, 2003):

> "I feel panicky when I have to leave the house . . . sometimes I don't go out for days because I feel so anxious and overwhelmed."

Some people have a preexisting mental health condition, and often the vision or hearing loss can exacerbate these symptoms.

> "My depression was under control and then the doctor told me there is nothing she can do about my vision loss and now I'm depressed again."

Horowitz (2003) draws attention to the unique situation of an older person who has functioned for a lifetime as fully sighted and hearing and then loses vision and hearing later in life, noting the profound impact it can have on the older person's well-being, identity, and core sense of self. Gender roles, ethnicity, and cultural and religious attitudes about disability often play a large part in how people adjust and cope with the vision/hearing loss:

> "My family is over-protective but I'm a grown man . . . I've worked all my life taking care of family . . . now they have to take care of me and I don't feel like a real man anymore."

Disability is a key risk factor for the onset of depressive symptoms, and depression in turn creates a risk for both physical illness and functional disability. There is a strong relationship between age-related vision impairment and, to a somewhat lesser extent, hearing impairment and late-life depression. Among community-dwelling elderly, rates of depression range from 8% to 16% (Blazer, 2003), while between one-fourth and one-third of all visually impaired have been found to report clinically significant depressive symptoms. Horowitz, Reinhardt, and Kennedy (2005) documented that among the older population seeking vision rehabilitation services, 7% had a current major depression, and 26.9% met the criteria for subthreshold depression. Progression of vision loss from normal to blind is associated with more than 1.5-fold increased odds of depression and injury and 2.5- to 3-fold increased odds of use of skilled nursing facilities and long-term care (Javitt, Zhiyuan, & Wilke, 2007) In a recent study, adults with diabetes who have dual sensory impairment and limitations in their physical functioning were more likely to report symptoms of depression (Loprinzi, Smit, & Pariser, 2013).

If a patient is in denial about sensory loss, severely depressed, or anxious, she or he may not be able to move forward with the adjustment and will be much less likely to use vision rehabilitation services. In these cases, counseling is very important to address the loss and grief associated with the vision and/or hearing impairment. At times, a referral to a psychiatrist for medication may be necessary.

Horowitz and Reinhardt (2000) proposed two primary explanations for this particularly strong relationship between sensory impairment and depression. One is that even a moderate vision impairment impacts daily task accomplishment and far too few older persons with vision impairment are aware of or receive vision rehabilitation services to learn new ways of accomplishing daily tasks independently. The second reason is the patient's subjective experience. This relationship to functional disability is supported by some studies for persons with hearing impairment (Strawbridge et al., 2000), but in some studies there is no increase in functional disability related to hearing impairment (Wallhagen, 2001).

A support group member disclosed:

"I'd rather be dead than lose my vision . . . how will I manage . . . I'm all alone since my husband died and I'm terrified to leave my house."

While hearing loss makes communication and social interaction more difficult, the loss of reading and driving may become very traumatic for older persons with vision impairment:

A support group member disclosed to the group that she was still driving her car even though her doctor told her she should stop. She was very distressed because driving represented not only her independence in this case but was the only way she felt she could see friends, socialize, and have any quality of life. Other members of the support group who had already given up driving were able to offer suggestions, support and strongly encourage her to take the steps to keep herself and others safe.

Counseling by social workers in individual, family, and/or group sessions is an important therapeutic intervention for older adults who experience hearing and/or vision loss. Involvement of the family, friends, and formal and informal caregivers can also be useful to provide information on the nature of the sensory loss and its impact on daily functioning.

PRACTICE IMPLICATIONS

Social workers need to educate themselves about the normal age-related vision and hearing changes and must know how to identify/screen older persons for referral for specialized vision and aural assessment/rehabilitation. The Functional Vision Screening Questionnaire is a 15-item (yes/no) questionnaire that may be filled out by the older person or read aloud. It is available for social workers to use in determining whether a client has probable vision impairment and needs referral (Horowitz, Teresi, & Cassels, 1991). The 10-item Hearing Handicap Inventory can be useful to assess whether the older person has a hearing impairment and needs referral (Ventry & Weinstein, 1982). Social workers can also avail themselves of depression and anxiety screening tools that can be helpful in assessment of the older client (see Chapter 36 for more information on interventions for depression and anxiety, "Mental Health Disorders in Later Life," for reference to screening tools for depression and anxiety).

It is also critical to understand that the acceptance of and adjustment to vision loss is a process and this process takes time. Elizabeth Kubler-Ross identifies five stages of grief in her book *On Death and Dying* (1997); these stages can be a conceptual model for assisting clients through this process. It is also important to understand that these stages are not linear and that clients move through them at their own pace. Often, social workers are pressured by agencies to move clients through the process as quickly as possible, but this can be detrimental to the client and may actually produce more resistance and delay the process.

Hearing loss can have a profound impact on quality of life for older adults and on their cognitive, emotional, and social function. Hearing loss interferes with face-to-face and long-distance communication, alters psychosocial behavior, strains family relations, limits the enjoyment of daily activities, jeopardizes physical well-being, and interferes with communication/understanding across the spectrum of health diagnosis, treatment, and management (Weinstein, 2003). Of course aural rehabilitation is essential, but social workers need to address the hearing impairment at the outset of interactions with the client. It is important to ask the individual in any initial assessment about hearing difficulties, what causes problems for the individual, and what one can do to reduce the stress that the hearing loss creates.

The environment where the older person is seen can be critical for the social worker dealing with an older adult with hearing impairment. In the office setting, controlling the ambient noise and/or providing privacy at a front desk is important if the patient cannot hear a person speaking, especially when that person is conveying private information. Asking the hearing impaired person to repeat back information such as time of next appointment is a good strategy.

Family Involvement

Involvement of family in the rehabilitation process has historically been absent, as the traditional model of rehabilitation has focused primarily on the individual. While research has documented the importance of family in providing emotional and instrumental support, their involvement in vision rehabilitation has been limited. However, there is a growing literature to support the importance and involvement of family and friends in the rehabilitation process (Reinhardt, Boerner, & Benn, 2003).

A family-focused model requires a fundamental shift whereby family members participate in the rehabilitation process without diminishing the autonomy of the older person with a sensory impairment. In some cases, helping the older adult deal with his or her relative is the most important intervention (Stuen, 1999). Social workers should assess the family and friend networks of the older person with a sensory impairment to determine whether they will be potential supporters or detractors of the rehabilitation process. The key is to recognize the family dynamics, the cultural differences, and the dynamics of the social network to enable supportive behaviors that will contribute to maximizing the independent functioning of the older adult and promote the general well-being of the entire family system. Support groups for sighted spouses or partners can also be effective to improve their communication with their visually impaired partners and enhance their functioning in everyday life.

CONCLUSION

Vision and/or hearing loss affects a large number of older persons. It is incumbent on social workers to become familiar with the normal and age-related disorders and help older persons access appropriate interventions and remain socially engaged. The goal is to maximize functional independence, prevent excess or unnecessary disability, and enhance quality of life for older persons with sensory loss. The disability arena is a specialized area for social workers to consider working in. There is a tremendous need for social workers to be educated and knowledgeable about sensory loss in order to be competent gerontological practitioners, as vision loss and/or hearing impairments are very prevalent, especially with the aging baby boomer generation, and all areas of practice will be impacted.

REFERENCES

Alliance for Eye and Vision Research. (2012). *The silver book: Vision loss: Vol. II. Chronic disease and medical innovation in an aging nation*. Rockville, MD: Author.

Blazer, D. G. (2003). Depression in late life: Review and commentary. *Journals of Gerontology: Medical Sciences, 58A*, 249–265.

Brennan, M. (2003). Impairment of both vision and hearing among older adults: Prevalence and impact on quality of life. *Generations, 27*, 52–56.

Brennan, M., & Cardinali, G. (2002). The use of pre-existing and novel coping strategies in adapting to age-related vision loss. *The Gerontologist, 40*, 327–334.

Glass, L. (2003). Entendre fr: to hear, to understand. A personal perspective on hearing loss. *Generations, 27*, 105–107.

Grunwald, H. (2003). Twilight: Losing light, gaining insight. *Generations, 27*, 1102–1104.

Horowitz, A. (1994). Vision impairment and functional disability among nursing home residents. *The Gerontologist, 34*, 316–323.

Horowitz, A. (2003). Depression and vision and hearing impairments in later life. *Generations, 27*, 32–38.

Horowitz, A., & Balistreri, E. (1994). *Field initiated research to evaluate methods for the identification and treatment of visually impaired nursing home residents. Final report: Part II. Research methods and results*. New York, NY: The Lighthouse.

Horowitz, A., & Reinhardt, J. P. (2000). Mental health issues in visual impairment: Research in depression, disability and rehabilitation. In B. M. Silverstone, M. Lang, B Rosenthal, and E. E. Faye (Eds.), *The lighthouse handbook on vision impairment and vision rehabilitation* (Vol. 2, pp. 1089–1110). New York, NY: Oxford University Press.

Horowitz, A., Reinhardt, J. P., & Kennedy, J. (2005). Major and subthreshold depression among older adults seeking vision rehabilitation services. *American Journal of Geriatric Psychiatry*, *13*, 180–187. http://dx.doi.org/10.1176/appi.ajgp.13.3.180

Horowitz, A., Teresi, J. E., & Cassels, L. A. (1991). Development of a vision screening questionnaire for older people. *Journal of Gerontological Social Work*, *17*, 37–56.

Hyman, H. K. (2003). Out of sight: A personal journey through ten months of blindness. *Generations*, *27*, 108–110.

Javitt, J. C., Zhiyuan, J., & Wilke, R. J. (2007). Association between vision loss and higher medical care costs in Medicare beneficiaries: Costs are greater for those with progressive vision loss. *Ophthalmology*, *114*, 238–245. http://dx.doi.org/10.1016/j.ophtha.2006.07.054

Kubler-Ross. E. (1997). *On death and dying.* New York, NY: Scribner.

Loprinzi, P. D., Smit, E., & Pariser, G. (2013) Association among depression, physical functioning, and hearing and vision impairment in people with diabetes. *Diabetes Spectrum*, *26*, 6–15. http;//dx.doi.org/10.2337/diaspect.26.1.6

Mehta, K. M. (2003) Prevalence and correlates of anxiety symptoms in well-functioning older adults: Findings from the Healthy Aging and Body Composition Study. *Journal of the American Geriatrics Society*, *51*, 499–504. http://dx.doi.org/10.1046/j.1532-5415.2003.51158.x

Montano, J. J. (2003). Available and emerging technologies on hearing loss: An ecological approach. *Generations*, *27*, 71–77.

Rein, D. B., Zhang, P., Wirth K. E., Lee, P. P., Hoerger, T. J., McCall, N., . . . Saaddine, J. (2006). The economic burden of major adult visual disorders in the United States. *Archives of Ophthalmology*, *124*, 1754–1760.

Reinhardt, J. P., Boerner, K., & Benn, D. (2003). Predicting individual change in support over time among chronically impaired older adults. *Psychology and Aging*, *18*, 770–779. http://dx.doi.org/10.1037/0882-7974.18.4.770

Resnick, H. E., Fries, B. E., & Verbrugge, L. M. (1997). Windows to their world: The effect of sensory impairments on social engagement and activity time in nursing home residents. *Journals of Gerontology: Social Sciences*, *52B*, S135–S144.

Schneider, J. M., Gopinath, B., McMahon, C. M., Leeder, S. R., Mitchell, P., & Wang, J. J. (2011). Dual sensory impairment in older age. *Journal of Aging and Health*, *23*, 1309–1324. http://dx.doi.org/10.1177/0898264311408418

Strawbridge, W. J., Wallhagen, M. I., Shema, S. J., & Kaplan, G. A. (2000). Negative consequences of hearing impairment in old age: A longitudinal analysis. *The Gerontologist*, *40*, 320–326.

Stuen, C. (1994). *Field initiated research to evaluate methods for the identification and treatment of visually impaired nursing home residents. Final report: Part I.* New York, NY: The Lighthouse.

Stuen, C. (1999). *Family involvement: Maximizing rehabilitation outcomes for older adults with a disability.* New York, NY: Lighthouse International.

The Lighthouse. (1995), *The Lighthouse National Survey on vision loss: The experience, attitudes and knowledge of middle-aged and older Americans.* New York, NY: Author.

Ventry, I., & Weinstein, B. (1982). The Hearing Handicap Inventory for the elderly: A new tool. *Ear Hearing*, *3*, 128–134. http://dx.doi.org/10.1097/00003446-198205000-00006

Wallhagen, M. I. (2001). Comparative impact on hearing and vision impairment on subsequent functioning. *Journal of the American Geriatrics Society*, *49*, 1086–1092. http;//dx.doi.org/10.1046/j.1532-5415.2001.49213.x

Weick, A., Rapp, C., Sullivan, W. P., & Kisthardt, W. (1989). A strengths perspective for social work practice. *Social Work*, *34*, 350–354.

Weinstein, B. E. (2003). A primer on hearing loss in the elderly. *Generations*, *27*, 15–19.

Zambelli-Weiner, A., Crews, J. E., & Friedman, D. S. (2012). Disparities in adult vision health in the United States. *American Journal of Ophthalmology*, *154*, S23–S30.

Zhang, X., Cotch, M. F., Ryskulova, A., Primo, S. A., Nair, P., Chou, C.-F., . . . Saaddine, J. B. (2012). Vision health disparities in the United States by race/ethnicity, education, and economic status: Findings from two nationally representative surveys. *American Journal of Ophthalmology*, *154*, S53–S62.

This chapter considers major orthopedic diseases, associated conditions, and challenges they pose for older adults, their families, and the social workers and other healthcare professionals who work with them. Recommendations are offered for social work practitioners who are likely to work with older adults with orthopedic diseases and with those who are at risk for falls, fractures, and joint replacements.

OSTEOPOROSIS

Osteoporosis is a systemic skeletal disease characterized by low bone mass and deterioration of bone tissue, with a consequent increase of bone fragility and susceptibility to fracture. An estimated 10 million people have osteoporosis (National Osteoporosis Foundation, 2007). More than 2 million osteoporotic fractures, totaling 17 million in care occur each year (Burge et al., 2007). Often, individuals suffer additional fractures. Age, low calcium intake, family history, vitamin D deficiency, hypogonadism in men, steroid use for inflammatory conditions, alcoholism, tobacco use, and diabetes all increase the risk of developing osteoporosis (Moyad, 2003).

Although osteoporosis has been historically considered an "older, Caucasian, women's" disease, 1 to 1.5 million African American women have osteoporosis (American Association of Clinical Endocrinologists Osteoporosis Task Force, 2003). African American and Caucasian women share similar risk factors for osteoporosis, however, African American women are less likely to be screened and receive appropriate treatment. Misconceptions concerning the prevalence and risk factors for osteoporosis among the African American community and physicians may contribute to this healthcare disparity (Curtis et al., 2009).

Similarly there is emerging awareness of male osteoporosis; approximately 2 million men aged 50 and older have osteoporosis (Campion & Maricic, 2003). For perspective, a man's lifetime risk of developing prostate cancer is lower than his risk of experiencing an osteoporotic fracture (Seeman, 2004). Although the risk of osteoporotic fractures is lower for men than women, the mortality rate for men is higher (Seeman, 2004). Furthermore, large national studies on treatment modalities for male osteoporosis have not been conducted (Herrera et al., 2012). The American College of Physicians asserts male osteoporosis is substantially underdiagnosed,

HELEN MILTIADES
LENARD W. KAYE

Musculoskeletal Health and Functional Capabilities in Older Adults

undertreated, and inadequately researched (Qaseen et al., 2008). Missed diagnosis and undertreatment may be due to poor physician-to-physician communication, a lack of awareness that osteoporosis is prevalent in older men and premenopausal women, and adverse reactions to prescription osteoporosis medication (Neuner, Zimmer, & Hamel, 2003). Older adults and their caregivers need to be encouraged to advocate for osteoporosis testing. Unfortunately, many elders are unaware of their osteoporosis risk.

Osteoporosis is one of the more preventable diseases. Calcium, vitamin D supplements, and exercise have been shown to be effective in maintaining bone health. Bone Builders is an evidence-based, osteoporosis exercise program that relies on mild weight training to increase muscular strength and bone density (see bonebuilders.org). Balance training is a key class component. Bone Builders is designed to prevent and even reverse osteoporosis, while at the same time improving balance to protect against falls and fractures and increasing energy levels and a sense of well-being. Weekly discussions about osteoporosis-related health topics are an educational component. Classes in many communities are frequently affiliated with a Retired and Senior Volunteer Program, an Area Agency on Aging, or a local healthcare organization (Thompson & Kaye, 2013).

Another evidence-based program is A Matter of Balance. This award-winning program developed by Boston University's Roybal Center for the Enhancement of Late-Life Functioning is designed to help manage falls and increase activity levels. These classes help seniors learn to view falls as controllable, set goals for increasing activity, make changes to reduce fall risks at home, and exercise to increase both strength and balance. A Matter of Balance has received national awards from the American Society on Aging and the National Association of Area Agencies on Aging for innovation and quality (Thompson & Kaye, 2013).

The hallmark of osteoporosis treatment is bisphosphonates; hormone replacement therapy (HRT) is no longer recommended since the Women's Health Initiative reported a link between HRT and various cancers (Zarowitz, 2006). Hormone replacement therapy has been shown to increase bone mineral density and reduce the risk of fractures. Even so, the risks and benefits of HRT should be weighed by patients considering this treatment. See Table 29.1 for more information.

ARTHRITIS

Arthritis refers to 100 different diseases affecting the joints. Arthritis and rheumatoid arthritis are characterized by joint inflammation; the latter is considered an autoimmune disorder. Both are associated with joint stiffness, swelling, and pain. Arthritis is the most common self-reported condition among older persons. An estimated 50 million adults in the United States have arthritis, with projections indicating 67 million adults will have arthritis by 2030 and activity limitations projected to affect 25 million people (Cheng, Hootman, Murphy, Langmaid, & Helmick, 2010; Hootman & Helmick, 2006). Higher prevalence rates for arthritis are associated with age, lower educational attainment, female gender, obesity, and smoking (Cheng et al., 2010).

Arthritis is the leading cause of disability for middle-aged and older persons. People with arthritis have varying degrees of difficulty walking, lifting and carrying items, climbing stairs, and generally maintaining their household. Arthritis is consistently associated with increased risk of functional decline and reduced chance of functional improvement (Porell & Miltiades, 2001). Arthritis-related disability increases with age, obesity, lifestyle choices (e.g., smoking, alcohol use, lack of exercise), and comorbidity and for ethnic/racial minorities and individuals who lack or have inadequate health insurance coverage (Song et al., 2007).

Due to arthritis-related pain, many older adults avoid social and physical activity. Not surprisingly, depression is quite prevalent among persons with arthritis (Sheehy, Murphy, & Barry, 2006). Other health risks include increased dependence, poor health, loss of joint motion, comorbidity, and consequently diminished quality of life (Penninx et al., 2001). Unfortunately, half of arthritis sufferers believe arthritis-related symptoms are a normal part of aging.

Since 2007 there have been attempts to pass the Arthritis Prevention, Control, and Cure Act, which in part supports national arthritis prevention programs. Most older adults with arthritis do not participate in self-management programs despite evidence of their effectiveness. Self-management programs are designed to empower individuals to manage their health conditions through education, self-management principles, exercise, psychological support, behavioral goal setting, and improving communication with health providers. Individuals

TABLE 29.1 Additional Information

The Arthritis Foundation is the largest nonprofit organization dedicated to the prevention, control, and cure of arthritis through advocacy, research, and public health promotion strategies. http://www.arthritis.org/
The Arthritis Society is Canada's only not-for-profit organization devoted solely to funding and promoting arthritis research, programs, and patient care. http://www.arthritis.ca/page.aspx?pid=1055
The National Institute of Arthritis and Musculoskeletal and Skin Diseases supports research into the causes, treatment, and prevention of arthritis and musculoskeletal diseases. http://www.niams.nih.gov
Arthritis Research UK promotes medical research into the causes, treatments, and cures of arthritic conditions. This site provides over 80 downloadable publications. http://www.arthritisresearchuk.org/
The US Administration on Aging provides an English and Spanish version of an arthritis self-management program. http://www.aoa.gov/AoARoot/AoA_Programs/HPW/ARRA/
Medline Plus provides news, research, and consumer information on arthritis. http://www.nlm.nih.gov/medlineplus/arthritis.html
OsteoArthritis Research Society International is a nonprofit, scientific organization promoting and encouraging fundamental and applied research ton osteoarthritis and its treatment. http://oarsi.org
The American College of Rheumatology is the professional organization of rheumatologists and associated health professionals. http://www.rheumatology.org/
The American Geriatrics Society provides tools for healthcare providers who assist older adults who suffer from falls, as well as fall prevention resources for patients and caregivers. http://www.americangeriatrics.org/health_care_professionals/clinical_practice/clinical_guidelines_recommendations/2010/
The National Osteoporosis Foundation is dedicated to osteoporosis and bone health. http://www.nof.org/

who participate in self-management programs experience a reduction in depression, anxiety, pain, and disability (Nuñez, Keller, & Der Ananian, 2009). Self-management support is provided in community settings, and social workers are vital team members who coach, educate, link clients to needed services, and increase clients' self-efficacy for self-management behaviors.

An exercise regimen is an important vehicle for maintaining physical functioning among elders with arthritis. Tai chi (Gallagher, 2003), aerobic and resistance training (Penninx et al., 2001), and fitness walking (Hughes et al., 2004) all show promise in decreasing the pain and stiffness associated with arthritis. In fact, women who believe they can control their exercise behavior do have higher levels of functional performance (Gaines, Talbot, & Metter, 2002). An effective treatment for pain in the later stages of osteoarthritis is joint replacement.

FALLS

Falls are a frequent occurrence among older adults. Rubenstein (2006) estimates 40% of people aged 65 and older experience a fall; 3% are hospitalized, and of those 50% die within a year. A combination of environmental, physical, and psychological factors increase fall risk. Modifiable risk factors include lower body weakness, gait and balance difficulties, poor vision, polypharmacy, and home hazards (Rubenstein & Josephson, 2006). Age, White ethnicity, fall history, incontinence, and living alone also increase fall risk (Ganz, Bao, Shekelle, & Rubenstein, 2007; Yamashita, Jeon, Bailer, Nelson, & Mehdizadeh, 2011). For the oldest-old, being male, in poor health, using assistive devices for ambulation, stroke history, alcohol consumption, and a high body mass index all increase fall risk (Grundstrom, Clare, Guse, & Layde, 2012).

Falls have serious health consequences. In 2006 there were 2.1 million emergency room visits by older adults due to falls; 30% were admitted for further care, with an average hospital stay of 5 days (Owens, Russo, Spector, & Mutter, 2009). Forty-one percent had a fracture; the most common (15%) was an upper extremity fracture (arm), followed by a hip fracture (12%) (Owens et al., 2009). The majority of older adults who experience fall-related fractures and other injuries have yet to recover their prefall functional levels 1 year later (Kempen et al., 2003).

A multifaceted approach to interventions is the most effective method of fall prevention. Multicomponent exercise programs emphasizing balance, strength training, flexibility, and endurance have been shown to decrease the rate of falls (Karlsson, Vonschewelov, Karlsson, Cöster, &

Rosengen, 2013). Tai chi, one of the most effective exercises, increases self-efficacy and reduces the risk and fear of falling (Wolf et al., 2003). Contrary to popular belief, walking programs do not appear to reduce fall risk (Gillespie et al., 2012).

Accidental falls make up 25% to 45% of all falls and occur due to environmental hazards, such as loose floor mats, inadequate lighting, clutter, and absence of handrails/grab bars (Rubenstein & Josephson, 2006). Home hazard modification is effective in reducing falls for the oldest-old who are primarily home bound and may suffer vision loss (Gillespie et al., 2012). Medication review to identify risks associated with polypharmacy, the use of psychotropic medications, and potential side effects such as dizziness also reduces fall rates (Karlsson et al., 2013). Other effective interventions include evaluating footwear and reducing outdoor activities under icy and rainy conditions (Gao & Abeysekera, 2004; McKiernan, 2005). Unmet need for personal assistance services has also been associated with falls (LePlante, Kaye, Kang, & Harrington, 2004). It is important to encourage older adults to see a healthcare provider for disease management, particularly health conditions related to falls. Older adults should also be encouraged to supplement their diet with calcium and Vitamin D to maintain healthy bones.

HIP FRACTURES

In 2007, 531,000 adults aged 65 and older were hospitalized due to fractures; almost 50% were hip fractures (Hall, DeFrances, Williams, Golosinskiy, & Schwartzman, 2010). By 2030, the number of hip fractures is projected to rise to 289,000 (Stevens & Rudd, 2013). A decrease in hip fractures among older women is expected due to greater awareness concerning osteoporosis and advances in medical treatment; however, a 52% increase in hip fractures is expected for men (Stevens & Rudd, 2013). The majority of hip fracture patients do not regain their prefracture levels of mobility (Kempen, Scaf-Klomp, Ranchor, Sanderman, & Ormel, 2001). Mortality rates are also high; older adults with hip fractures are two to three times more likely to die than their same-aged peers (Farahmand, Michaëlsson, Ahlbom, Ljunghall, & Baron, 2005).

Currently, 70% of all hip fractures are sustained by women (Stevens & Rudd, 2013). Men are less likely than women to experience a hip fracture because advancing age and gender (female) are key risk factors (Walter, Lui, Eng, & Covinsky, 2003). Additional risk factors include white ethnicity, cognitive decline, difficulty transferring, limitations on activities of daily living, and lower body limitations (Walter et al., 2003). Nursing home residents who are able to transfer independently or who wander are more likely to experience hip fractures and falls (Cesari et al., 2002; Gregg, Pereira, & Caspersen, 2000). This creates a challenge for caregivers, who must balance an older adult's right to autonomy with the need to create a safe environment.

The average length of hospitalization for a hip fracture is a week; stroke history, renal failure, and delayed surgery all increase length of stay (Brown, Olson, & Zura, 2013). Forty percent of hip fracture patients are discharged to a residential facility; a year later, 25% to 33% remain in long-term care (Magaziner et al., 2000). After an approximately 8-week rehabilitation period, older adults not in residential facilities are discharged home. Postoperative management techniques related to increased recovery and ambulatory ability include medical management by a geriatrician, physical and occupational therapies, and weight/strength training (Chudyk, Jutai, Petrella, & Speechley, 2009). Additionally, higher levels of functional ability prior to fracture influences recovery (Hawkes, Wehren, Orwig, Hebel, & Magaziner, 2006). Depression, anxiety, and pain are barriers to recovery (Oh & Feldt, 2000). Older adults with cognitive impairment or comorbidity experience limited functional recovery (Hawkes et al., 2006; Wang & Emery, 2002).

Multiple interventions exist to prevent hip fractures. Use of hip protectors in nursing homes has been shown to reduce the incidence of hip fractures (Meyer, Warnke, Bender, & Mühlhauser, 2003). Exercise that strengthens muscles and improves balance and gait stability reduces falls and subsequently hip fractures (Wolf et al., 2003). Increasing bone mineral density through calcium supplementation, Vitamin D, and nutrition also reduces hip fractures (Woolf & Akesson, 2003).

HIP AND KNEE REPLACEMENT

Total joint arthroplasty/replacement (TJA) is the treatment choice for end-stage arthritis of the hip or knee once pain and disability can no longer be medically managed (Holtzman, Khal Saleh, & Kane,

2002). Revision arthroplasty is a surgical procedure to replace a failing joint implant, and thus is not elective. A population-based study of Medicare beneficiaries found 61,568 patients had primary hip replacement and 13,483 had revision hip replacement in 1 year (Mahomed et al., 2003). By 2030, projections show an increase of 174% for total hip arthroplasy and up to 673% for total knee arthroplasty (Kurtz, Ong, Lau, Mowat, & Halpern, 2007). Medicare patients most likely to undergo a primary hip replacement are older, female, and Caucasian and have higher incomes (Mahomed et al., 2003). The average length of hospital stay for hip replacement is 4 to 5 days. Almost 50% were discharged to a short-term hospital or other facility, 30% were discharged home, and 20% were discharged home with home healthcare (Hervey et al., 2003). Increasingly younger patients are opting for joint replacement. This trend appears to be in part physician preference for the higher reimbursement rates of private versus Medicare insurance and in part an increasing desire by the baby boom generation to maintain an active lifestyle (Ravi et al., 2012).

Various factors influence recovery. Older adults in poor preoperative health who have functional ability impairments and moderate to severe pain do not reach the same postoperative level of functional ability as less severely impaired older adults (Holtzman et al., 2002). Age, revision hip arthroplasty, male gender, low income, Black ethnicity, comorbidity, and a diagnosis of rheumatoid arthritis are all associated with adverse outcomes and/or mortality (Mahomed et al., 2003). In a comprehensive review, Ethgen, Bruyere, Richy, Dardennes, and Reginster (2004) concluded hip and knee arthroplasty improves health and physical functioning. Older age was not a barrier to functional improvement.

Even after controlling for access to medical care and socioeconomic status, Whites are more likely than ethnic/racial minority elders to have total joint replacements despite greater prevalence and severity of functional impairment (Ang, Monahan, & Cronan, 2008). Upon review, Nwachukwu, Kenny, Losina, Chibnik, and Katz (2010), concluded ethnic/racial minority elders have more postoperative complications than Whites and may need more social support as well as longer stays at acute rehabilitation facilities.

Spousal caregivers require assistance with the changes in social roles and the healthcare complexities of recovery. Increased dependence and assistance with activities of daily living and instrumental activities of daily living are common immediately after

knee or hip replacement but often abate after rehabilitation. Because individual healing trajectories vary, older adults who undergo knee or hip replacement often underestimate the pain and length of recovery time. Older adults express insecurity and impatience with the healing process; their caregivers express difficulty balancing increased household and personal assistance tasks (Showalter, Burger, & Salyer, 2000). The social worker will want to be aware that the dynamics of caregiving under these circumstances may be different from many other situations where the presence of chronic conditions, by definition, precludes full recovery and a return to independent functioning by the older adult.

Education on postoperative functional abilities and explanation of the rehabilitation process reduces length of stay and decreases medication use and anxiety. Assistive devices that allow older adults to manipulate the environment and regain independence ease the recovery transition period (Showalter et al., 2000). Exercise prior to surgery decreases postoperative pain and increases self-reported function only for hip replacement surgery (Gill & McBurney, 2013), whereas participating in rehabilitation programs post surgery hastens functional recovery and decreases stiffness and pain for various joint replacement surgeries (Moffet et al., 2004). Self-efficacy, the belief that one can perform the rehabilitation exercises, increases compliance and speeds rehabilitation (Moon, 2000).

IMPLICATIONS FOR GERONTOLOGICAL SOCIAL WORK PRACTICE

Disease prevention and health promotion represent natural functions of professional social work practice at all levels (Rizzo & Seidman, n.d.). A social worker's attitudinal orientation and skill set is naturally inclined to be sensitive to physical and mental health challenges, including those surrounding musculoskeletal health and functional capacity, that confront diverse populations varying in terms of gender, race, ethnicity, nationality, sexual orientation, and age. The customary focus of direct service (micro-practice) social workers on promoting self-help strategies by discouraging risky and promoting healthy behaviors including proper nutrition and exercise reflects the profession's emphasis on general well-being as compared with restricting itself to narrow medical concerns (Dhooper, 2012). Direct service social workers are also well attuned to promoting awareness of available community resources in the areas of health education and interventions that address health risks. Their skills in information collection and dissemination contribute well to social workers performing these functions effectively and efficiently.

Gerontological social workers are often members of multidisciplinary teams that address medical, psychosocial, and functional limitations of a frail older person in order to develop a coordinated plan of care. When serving older adults with musculoskeletal health issues, social workers will benefit from having a basic understanding of orthopedic diseases, injuries, and procedures, including accompanying symptoms and available treatments, and of their role as a member of the healthcare team. They should maintain, or have direct access to others who have the necessary healthcare and referral resources, in order to organize and facilitate the intricate process of case management and determine long-term care requirements and optimal placement for elders who are suffering from functional impairments. A geriatric case manager often coordinates recommended intervention strategies, assists with the social, financial, environmental, and spiritual components that influence an older adult's health, and follows up with monitoring patient progress. Understanding the multiple issues presented by orthopedic diseases and conditions will allow the social worker to be effective in helping older adults maintain health, independence, and an active lifestyle for as long as possible.

At the mezzo (organizational) practice level, social workers commonly bring their expertise to influence health promotion interventions at various stages in their evolution including planning, design, resource procurement, implementation, administration and management, marketing, and evaluation.

Finally, macro (policy level) practice social workers are natural catalysts who are frequently well positioned to advocate for change in laws and regulations at various levels of government that impact individual and population health. They can also engage in research inquiry that seeks to determine the efficacy of particular forms of health promotion and illness prevention programming. Social work educators and trainers are strategically positioned to share evidence-based practices, translate conceptual principles into promising practices, and help others acquire critical applied skills, knowledge, and

informed behaviors in the areas of health promotion and illness prevention (Dhooper, 2012).

REFERENCES

American Association of Clinical Endocrinologists Osteoporosis Task Force. (2003). American Association of Clinical Endocrinologists medical guidelines for clinical practice for the prevention and treatment of postmenopausal osteoporosis: 2001 edition, with selected updates for 2003. *Endocrine Practice*, 9, 544–564. Retrieved August 10, 2013, from http://www.thecmafoundation.org/projects/pdfs/womenshealth/Osteoporosis%20treatment%20guideline.pdf

Ang, D. C., Monahan, P. O., & Cronan, T. A. (2008). Understanding ethnic disparities in the use of total joint arthroplasty: Application of the health belief model. *Arthritis and Rheumatology*, 59, 102–108. doi.org/10.1002/art.23243

Brown, C. A., Olson, S., & Zura, R. (2013). Predictors of length of hospital stay in elderly hip fracture patients. *Journal of Surgical Orthopaedic Advances*, 22, 160–163. doi:10.3113/JSOA.2013.0160

Burge, R., Dawson-Hughes, B., Solomon, D. H., Wong, J. B., King, A., & Tosteson, A. (2007). Incidence and economic burden of osteoporosis-related fractures in the United States, 2005–2025. *Journal of Bone and Mineral Research*, 22, 465–475. doi:10.1359/jbmr.061113

Campion, J. M., & Maricic, M. J. (2003). Osteoporosis in men. *American Family Physician*, 67, 1521–1526.

Cesari, M., Landi, F., Torre, S., Onder, G., Lattanzio, F., & Bernabei, R. (2002). Prevalence and risk factors for falls in an older community-dwelling population. *Journals of Gerontology: Medical Sciences*, 57A, M722–M726. doi:10.1093/gerona/57.11.M722

Cheng, Y. J., Hootman, J. M., Murphy, L. B., Langmaid, G. A., & Helmick, C. G. (2010). Prevalence of doctor-diagnosed arthritis and arthritis-attributable activity limitation—United States, 2007–2009. *Morbidity and Mortality Weekly Report*, 59, 1261–1265.

Chudyk, A. M., Jutai, J. W., Petrella, R. J., & Speechley, M. (2009). Systematic review of hip fracture rehabilitation practices in the elderly. *Archives of Physical Medicine and Rehabilitation*, 90, 246–262. doi:10.1016/j.apmr.2008.06.036

Curtis, J. R., McClure, L. A., Delzell, E., Howard, V. J., Orwall, E., Saag, K. G., . . . Howard, G. (2009). Population-based fracture risk assessment and osteoporosis treatment disparities by race and gender. *Journal of General Internal Medicine*, 24, 956–962. doi:10.1007/s11606-009-1031-8

Dhooper, S. S. (2012). *Social work in health care: Its past and future* (2nd ed.). Thousand Oaks, CA: Sage.

Ethgen, O., Bruyere, O., Richy, F., Dardennes, C., & Reginster, J. Y. (2004). Health-related quality of life in total hip and total knee arthroplasty: A qualitative and systematic review of the literature. *Journal of Bone and Joint Surgery, 86A*, 963–974. http://jbjs:

Farahmand, B. Y., Michaëlsson, K., Ahlbom, A., Ljunghall, S., & Baron, J. A. (2005). Survival after hip fracture. *Osteoporosis International, 16*, 1583–1590. doi:10.1007/s00198-005-2024-z

Gaines, J. M., Talbot, L. A., & Metter, E. J. (2002). The relationship of arthritis self-efficacy to functional performance in older men and women with osteoarthritis of the knee. *Geriatric Nursing, 23*, 167–170. doi:10.1067/mgn.2002.125420

Gallagher, B. (2003). Tai chi chuan and qigong: Physical and mental practice for functional mobility. *Topics in Geriatric Rehabilitation, 19*, 172–182. doi: 10.1097/TGR.ob013e31828aa443

Ganz, D. A., Bao, Y., Shekelle, P. G., & Rubenstein, L. Z. (2007). Will my patient fall? *Journal of the American Medical Association, 297*, 77–86. doi:10.1001/jama.297.1.77

Gao, C., & Abeysekera, J. A. (2004). A systems perspective of slip and fall accidents on icy and snowy surfaces. *Ergonomics, 47*, 573–598. doi:10.1080/0014013 0410081658718

Gill, S. D., & McBurney, H. (2013). Does exercise reduce pain and improve physical function before hip or knee replacement surgery? A systematic review and meta-analysis of randomized controlled trials. *Archives of Physical Medicine and Rehabilitation, 94*, 164–176. doi:10.1016/j.apmr.2012.08.211

Gillespie, L. D., Robertson, M. C., Gillespie, W. J., Sherrington, C., Gates, S., Clemson, L. M., & Lamb, S. E. (2012). Interventions for preventing falls in older people living in the community. *Cochrane Database of Systematic Reviews, 9*: CD007146. doi:10.1002/14651858.CD007146.pub3

Gregg, E. W., Pereira, M. A., & Caspersen, C. J. (2000). Physical activity, falls and fracture among older adults: A review of the epidemiologic evidence. *Journal of the American Geriatric Society, 48*, 883–893. doi:10.1111/jgs.12438

Grundstrom, A. C., Clare, E., Guse, C. E., & Layde, P. M. (2012). Risk factors for falls and fall-related injuries in adults 85 years of age and older. *Archives of Gerontology and Geriatrics, 54*, 421–428. doi:10.1016/j.archger.2011.06.008

Hall, M. J., DeFrances, C. J., Williams, S. N., Golosinskiy, A., & Schwartzman, A. (2010). *National Hospital Discharge Survey: 2007 summary.* National health statistics reports: no 29. Hyattsville, MD: National Center for Health Statistics.

Hawkes, W. G., Wehren, L., Orwig, D., Hebel, J. R., & Magaziner, J. (2006). Gender differences in functioning after hip fracture. *Journal of Gerontology: Medical Sciences, 61A*, 495–499. doi:10.1093/gerona/61.5.495

Herrera, A., Lobo-Escolar, A., Mateo, J., Gil, J., Ibarz, E., & Gracia, L. (2012). Male osteoporosis: A review. *World Journal of Orthopedics, 18*, 223–234. doi:10.5312/wjo.v3.i12.223

Hervey, S. L., Purves, H. R., Guller, U., Toth, A. P., Vail, T. P., & Pietrobon, R. (2003). Provider volume of total knee arthroplasties and patient outcomes in the HCUP-Nationwide Inpatient Sample. *Journal of Bone and Joint Surgery, 85A*, 1775–1783. http://jbjs:

Holtzman, J., Khal Saleh, M. S., & Kane, R. (2002). Effect of baseline functional status and pain on outcomes of total hip arthroplasty. *Journal of Bone and Joint Surgery, 84*, 1942–1948. http://jbjs:

Hootman, J. M., & Helmick, C. G. (2006). Projections of U.S. prevalence of arthritis and associated activity limitations. *Arthritis and Rheumatism, 54*, 266–229. http://onlinelibrary.wiley.com/journal/10.1002/(ISSN)1529-0131

Hughes, S. L., Seymour, R. B., Campbell, R., Pollak, N., Huber, G., & Sharma, L. (2004). Impact of the fit and strong intervention on older adults with osteoarthritis. *The Gerontologist, 44*, 217–228. doi:10.1093/geront/44.2.217

Karlsson, M. K., Vonschewelov, T., Karlsson, C., Cöster, M., & Rosengen, B. E. (2013). Prevention of falls in the elderly: A review. *Scandinavian Journal of Public Health, 41*, 442–454. doi:10.1177/1403494813483215

Kempen, G., Ormel, J., Scaf-Klomp, W., van Sonderen, E., Ranchor, A., & Sanderman, R. (2003). The role of perceived control in the process of older people's recovery of physical functions after fall-related injuries: A prospective study. *Journal of Gerontology: Psychological Sciences, 58B*, P35–P41. http://psychsocgerontology.oxfordjournals:

Kempen, G., Scaf-Klomp, W., Ranchor, A., Sanderman, R., & Ormel, J. (2001). Social predictors of recovery in late middle-aged and older persons after injury to the extremities: A prospective study. *Journal of Gerontology: Social Sciences, 56B*, S229–S236. doi:10.1093/geronb/56.4.S229

Kurtz, S., Ong, K., Lau, E., Mowat, F., & Halpern, M. (2007). Projections of primary and revision hip and knee arthroplasty in the United States from 2005 to 2030. *Journal of Bone and Joint Surgery, 89*, 780–785. doi:10.2106/JBJS.F.00222

LePlante, M. P., Kaye, H. S., Kang, T., & Harrington, C. (2004). Unmet need for personal assistance services: Estimating the shortfall in hours of help and adverse consequences. *Journal of Gerontology: Social Sciences, 59*, S98–S108. doi:10.1093/geronb/59.2.S98

Magaziner, J., Hawkes, W. J., Hebel, R., Zimmerman, S. I., Fox, K. M., Dolan, M., . . . Kenzora, J. (2000). Recovery from hip fracture in eight areas of function. *Journals of Gerontology, Series A: Biological Sciences and Medical Science, 55*, M498–M507. doi:10.1093/gerona/55.9.M498

Mahomed, N. N., Barrett, J. A., Katz, J. N., Phillips, C. B., Losina, E. L., Robert, A., . . . Baron, J. A. (2003). Rates and outcomes of primary and revision total hip replacement in the United States Medicare population. *Journal of Bone and Joint Surgery, 85*, 27–32. http://jbjs:

McKiernan, F. E. (2005). A simple gait-stabilizing device reduces outdoor falls and nonserious injurious falls in fall-prone older people during winter. *Journal of the American Geriatrics Society, 53*, 943–947. doi:10.1111/j.1532-5415.2005.53302.x

Meyer, G., Warnke, A., Bender, R., & Mühlhauser, I. (2003). Effect on hip fractures of increased use of hip protectors in nursing homes: Cluster randomised controlled trial. *British Medical Journal, 326*, 76. doi:10.1136/bmj.326.7380.76

Moffet, H., Collet, J. P., Shapiro, S. H., Paradis, G., Marquis, F., & Roy, L. (2004). Effectiveness of intensive rehabilitation on functional ability and quality of life after first total knee arthroplasty: A single-blind randomized controlled trial. *Archives of Physical Medicine and Rehabilitation, 85*, 546–556. doi:10.1016/j.apmr.2003.08.080

Moon, J. B. (2000). Relationships among self-efficacy, outcome expectancy, and postoperative behaviors in total joint replacement patients. *Orthopaedic Nursing, 19*, 77–85. doi:10.1097/00006416-200019020-00011

Moyad, M. A. (2003). Osteoporosis: A rapid review of risk factors and screening methods. *Urologic Oncology: Seminars and Original Investigations, 21*, 375–379. doi:10.1016/S1078-1439(03)00140-6

National Osteoporosis Foundation (NOF). (2007). *America's bone health: The state of osteoporosis and low bone mass in our nation.* Washington, DC: Author.

Neuner, J. M., Zimmer, J. K., & Hamel, M. B. (2003). Diagnosis and treatment of osteoporosis in patients with vertebral compression fractures. *Journal of the American Geriatrics Society, 51*, 483–491. doi:10.1046/j.1532-5415.2003.51156.x

Nuñez, D. E., Keller, C., & Der Ananian, C. (2009). A review of the efficacy of the self-management model on health outcomes in community-residing older adults with arthritis.

Worldviews on Evidence-Based Nursing, 6, 130–148. doi:10.1111/j.1741-6787.2009.00157.x

Nwachukwu, B. U., Kenny, A. D., Losina, E., Chibnik, L. B., & Katz, J. N. (2010). Complications for racial and ethnic minority groups after total hip and knee replacement: A review of the literature. *Journal of Bone and Joint Surgery, 92*, 338–345. doi:10.2106/JBJS.I.00510

Oh, H., & Feldt, K. (2000). The prognostic factors for functional recovery in elders with hip fracture. *Nursing and Health Sciences, 2*, 237–242. doi:10.1046/j.1442-2018.2000.00065.x

Owens, P. L., Russo, C. A., Spector, W., & Mutter, R. (2009). Emergency department visits for injurious falls among the elderly, 2006: Statistical Brief #80. In *Healthcare Cost and Utilization Project (HCUP) statistical briefs* [Internet]. Rockville (MD): Agency for Health Care Policy and Research. Retrieved from http://www.ncbi.nlm.nih.gov/books/NBK53603/

Penninx, B. W., Messier, S. P., Rejeski, W. J. K., Williamson, J. D., DiBari, M., Cavazzini, C., . . . Pahor, M. (2001). Physical exercise and the prevention of disability in activities of daily living in older persons with osteoarthritis. *Archives of Internal Medicine, 161*, 2309–2324. doi:10.1001/archinte.161.19.2309

Porell, F. W., & Miltiades, H. B. (2001). Access to care and functional status change among aged Medicare beneficiaries. *Journal of Gerontology: Social Sciences, 56B*, S69–S83. doi:10.1093/geronb/56.2.S69

Qaseen, A., Snow, V., Shekelle, P., Hopkins, R., Jr., Forciea, M. A., & Owens, D. K. (2008). Screen for osteoporosis in men: A clinical practice guideline from the American College of Physicians. *Annals of Internal Medicine, 148*, 680–684. doi:10.7326/0003-4819-148-9-200805060-00008

Ravi, B., Croxford, R., Reichmann, W. M., Losina, E., Katz, J. N., & Hawker, G. A. (2012). The changing demographics of total joint arthroplasty recipients in the United States and Ontario from 2001 to 2007. *Best Practices and Research Clinical Rheumatology, 26*, 637–647. doi:10.1016/j.berh.2012.07.014

Rizzo, V. M., & Seidman, J. (n.d.). *Health promotion and aging: Section 3: The role of social work in promoting health.* Washington, DC: Council on Social Work Education.

Rubenstein, L. Z., & Josephson, K. R. (2006). Falls and their prevention in elderly people: What does the evidence show? *Medical Clinics of North America, 90*, 807–824. doi:10.1016/j.mcna.2006.05.013

Seeman, E. (2004). *Osteoporosis in men: The silent epidemic strikes men too.* International Osteoporosis Foundation. Retrieved July 12, 2013, from http://www.

iofbonehealth:sites/default/files/PDFs/WOD%20 Reports/osteoporosis_in_men_2004_english.pdf

Sheehy, C., Murphy, E., & Barry, M. (2006). Depression in rheumatoid arthritis—Underscoring the problem. *Rheumatology*, *45*, 1325–1327. doi:10.1093/rheumatology/kel231

Showalter, A., Burger, S., & Salyer, J. (2000). Patient's and their spouses' needs after total joint arthroplasty: A pilot study. *Orthopaedic Nursing*, *19*, 49–57. http://journals.lww.com/orthopaedicnursing/pages/default.aspx

Song, J., Chang, H. J., Tirodkar, M., Chang, R. W., Manheim, L. M., & Dunlop, D. D. (2007). Racial/ethnic differences in activities of daily living disability in older adults with arthritis: A longitudinal study. (2007). *Arthritis and Rheumatism*, *57*, 1058–1066. doi:10.1002/art.22906

Stevens, J. A., & Rudd, R. A. (2013). The impact of decreasing U.S. hip fracture rates on future hip fracture estimates. *Osteoporosis International*, *24*, 2725–2728. doi:10.1007/s00198-013-2375-9

Thompson, E. H., Jr., & Kaye, L. W. (2013). *A man's guide to healthy aging: Stay smart, strong, and active*. Baltimore, MD: Johns Hopkins University Press.

Walter, L. C., Lui, L., Eng, C., & Covinsky, K. E. (2003). Risk of hip fracture in disabled community-living older adults. *Journal of the American Geriatrics Society*, *51*, 50–55. doi:10.1034/j.1601-5215.2002.51009.x

Wang, X., & Emery, L. J. (2002). Cognitive status after hip replacement. *Physical and Occupational Therapy in Geriatrics*, *21*, 51–64. doi:10.1300/J148v21n01_04

Wolf, S. L., Barnhart, H. X., Kutner, N. G., McNeely, E., Coogler, C., & Xu, T. (2003). Reducing frailty and falls in older persons: An investigation of tai chi and computerized balance training. *Journal of the American Geriatric Society*, *51*, 1794–1803. doi:10.1046/j.1532-5415.2003.51566.x

Woolf, A., & Akesson, K. (2003). Preventing fractures in elderly people. *British Medical Journal*, *327*, 89–95. doi:10.1136/bmj.327.7406.89

Yamashita, T., Jeon, H., Bailer, A. J., Nelson, I. M., & Mehdizadeh, S. (2011). Fall risk factors in community-dwelling elderly who receive Medicaid-supported home and community-based care services. *Journal of Aging and Health*, *23*, 682–703. doi:10.1177/0898264310390941

Zarowitz, B. J. (2006). Management of osteoporosis in older persons. *Geriatric Nursing*, *27*, 16–18. doi:10.1016/j.gerinurse.2005.12.001

MICHELLE PUTNAM
STEPHANIE P. WLADKOWSKI

Aging and Functional Disability

In the past, aging and functional disability have often been synonymous. Growing older meant physical decline. Now, we no longer make this assumption. While the experience of functional disability still remains common in later life, when and how disability is experienced has changed. This chapter presents an overview of the demographics of functional disability in later life, discusses the ways in which disability is conceptualized, describes factors that influence healthy aging and community participation among older adults with functional disability, presents the current policy context for providing supports and services related to functional disability, and identifies ways that social workers can help facilitate positive health and participation outcomes for older adults with functional disabilities. Our goals are to present a context for understanding the opportunities older adults have to meet their individual healthy aging objectives and to encourage professional social workers to learn more about factors that shape this context.

DEMOGRAPHIC OVERVIEW OF FUNCTIONAL LIMITATION IN LATER LIFE

In 2011, 36.8% of all persons aged 65 and older in the United States—or about 14.7 million, reported having an ambulatory, self-care, and/or independent living disability based on estimates from the Census Bureau's American Community Survey (ACS) (Erickson, Lee, & von Schrader, 2013). Rates of reported disability increase with age. Based on 2006–2008 ACS data, disability prevalence is 69% for those age 85–89, 83% of those age 90–94 years, and 91% of adults age 95 and older (He & Muenchrath, 2011). In recent decades, disability incidence rates have been declining for the overall older adult population (Schoeni, Freedman, & Martin, 2008); however, with the increasing size of the older adult population, the total number of older adults with disabilities is growing. Additionally, the greater prevalence of multiple chronic disease means that older adults are likely to have more than one health condition that effects disability status (Hung, Ross, Boockvar, & Sui, 2012).

Disability rates, both prevalence and incidence, differ between minority and majority population groups. For example, prevalence of disability is 43% for African Americans age 65 and older, 51%

for Native Americans and Alaskan Natives, 32% for Asian Americans, and 42% for persons identifying as Hispanic compared with 36% for Caucasian older adults (Erickson et al., 2013). Disability rates are similar for older men and women. Higher disability rates are also found within the gay, lesbian, bisexual, and transgender older population (Fredriksen-Goldsen et al., 2011) and immigrant populations (Choi, 2011).

Socioeconomic factors (i.e., education and income) have been found to explain much of the racial/ethnic disparities in disability rates of older adults (Fuller-Thomson, Nuru-Jeter, Minkler, & Guralnik, 2010). Childhood socioeconomic status has also been linked to disability in later life (Bowen, 2009). However functional limitation itself can have a significant influence on an individual's financial status; that is, over their lifetimes, persons experiencing disability in early and midlife (ages 18–64) have historically had about a 50% lower rate of employment (US Bureau of Labor Statistics, 2013), a higher likelihood of living in poverty (US Census Bureau, 2012), and higher out-of-pocket healthcare expenditures (Pumkam, Probst, Bennett, Hardin, & Xirasagar, 2013) than their age-based peers who have not experienced disability.

FUNCTIONAL DISABILITY AND HEALTHY AGING

Despite the fact that many reports on aging continue to equate disability with poor health and loss of independence (Centers for Disease Control [CDC], 2013), "healthy aging" is still a relevant concept for older adults with disability. For the majority, withdrawal from prior activities is related more to a lack of appropriate personal and environmental supports than the functional limitation itself.

Viewing Disability as a Contextual Situation, Not a Personal Health Limitation

Definitions and theories of disability and how it occurs differ. The historical medical model of disability focused mainly on the person who is experiencing disability, seeking to identify biological and physiological factors contributing to limitations in physical function (Bickenbach, 1993). This viewpoint of disability is still quite visible today, particularly in clinical social work settings. Social models of

disability move beyond a person-centered view to include social and physical environmental factors in the determination of disability (World Health Organization, 2001). This model underlies several current global aging initiatives including the World Health Organization's Active Ageing framework, which describes personal, social, environmental, and institutional determinants (such as supports and services) that influence opportunities for health, participation, and security in later life (World Health Organization, 2007a). These frameworks influence how persons with disability are categorized and counted as well as what types of programs and services are designed to meet their needs.

Social models of disability have gained wider acceptance over time. The core premise of social models of disability is that disability is a situation, not a characteristic. That is, individuals have a certain set of (in this case) physical capabilities, and their environments have a specific set of "demands" or requirements. If an individual's capabilities and the environment's demands are not in sync, then it is likely that the person will experience some level of disability. A simple example of this is an older man living in a city who is unable to carry his groceries home from a local store who will experience disability related to that task. If the grocery story offers delivery, then the situation is not disabling. In this situation, the man continues to have a physical impairment that limits his carrying ability, but that limitation does not create disability in and of itself.

Using this framework, we begin our discussion of healthy aging by looking at a range of factors that influence the experience of disability among older adults. In this discussion, we recognize two distinct populations of older adults with disabilities. The first comprises persons who "age into" physical disability; that is, individuals who experience substantial functional impairment for the first time in later life. The second population comprises individuals who are "aging with" physical disability; included in this group are people who first experienced disability during childhood, youth, or middle adulthood as a result of conditions such as polio, multiple sclerosis, spinal cord injury, cerebral palsy, rheumatoid arthritis, or spina bifida, to name a few. The difference between these populations occurs mainly with regard to when, how, and for how long they have experienced disability. For many adults aging with disability, the experience of disability has shaped their life course by influencing their ability to work, to engage with others in their communities, and to live independently.

FACTORS INFLUENCING HEALTHY AGING AND COMMUNITY PARTICIPATION

Health and Wellness

Health and wellness is defined by persons with disabilities as including a range of factors such as health behaviors, social contribution, and access to healthcare (Putnam et al., 2003). Assessments of health and wellness include broad outcome measures such as self-rated health, depression, and life satisfaction as well as specific indicators such as level of physical activity (Lowry, Vallejo, & Studenski, 2011) and loneliness (Coyle & Dugan, 2012). Over the past decade a growing body of evidence has demonstrated that management of diet and regular exercise (Sung et al., 2013), reductions in smoking and alcohol consumption (Lui, Woodrow, Louck-Atkinson, Buehler, West, & Wang, 2013), and social engagement (Lee & Kim, 2013), among other factors, support improved health and wellness outcomes for individuals experiencing functional limitations. Thus older adults with disabilities often report feeling healthy and feeling like they can do the activities they would like to do (Thompson, Zack, Krahn, Andresen, & Barile, 2012).

There are many national organizations that coordinate health-promoting programs. Examples include Building Health Communities for Active Aging (US Environmental Protection Agency, 2007), the Administration on Aging (AOA), and the National Council on Aging Center for Health Aging (NCOA). Social workers are positioned to work both on an individual and community level in such organizations to promote healthy aging for older adults. For example, social workers can assess an individual's nutrition or physical activity needs as well identify any barriers to accessing resources. Social workers can advocate for healthy options and build alliances with nutritional programs such as the Supplemental Nutrition Assistance Program (SNAP) and home-delivered nutrition to ensure healthy options are available. It is important for professionals to engage older adults in evaluating their own health and wellness needs and personal goals. Once goals are identified, social workers can help implement a variety of interventions. Examples include using

music or art therapy to alleviate symptoms of depression or anxiety (McInnis-Dittrich, 2009); physical and occupational therapy to maximize abilities, providing information about supportive resources, such as taking public transportation (Rosenbloom, 2009), using adaptive equipment, or connecting to an online community (Rosso, Taylor, Tabb, & Michael, 2013). All these interventions are consumer focused, allowing for individuals' behaviors and preferences to be addressed and appropriate personal or environmental modifications made.

Social Support

The use of social supports, both formal (programs and services) and informal (family and friends), are common strategies to mediate the potential negative consequences of functional impairment and disability. Lack of social support has been linked to significantly worse health and quality of life outcomes among older adults (White, Philogene, Fine, & Sinha, 2009). Social support can include practical support, informational support, and emotional support. Practical support is generally considered tangible, physical support (e.g., assistance with transfers, preparation of meals, etc.). Informational support is generally considered to be advice or guidance. Social workers often serve in this role, offering a range of assistance from providing referrals to services, to counseling individuals in the self-direction of their own services, to taking the lead as case manager of a client's health and care services. Peers (individuals with the same or similar disability) provide this type of informational support as well. Provision of emotional support is generally taken on by family members and peer groups, who help provide everyday opportunities to be a member of a group and moral support during difficult times, although social workers occasionally assist with these activities as well.

Often, social workers help develop and implement social support programs, including peer support and training for families and caregivers. Peer support programs such as those sponsored by nonprofits like the Alzheimer's Association and the National Multiple Sclerosis Society, are frequently cited as important contributors to successful rehabilitation and after-care treatment models for chronic conditions including heart disease (Kang-Yi & Gellis, 2010) and spinal cord injury (Sakakibara, Hitzig, Miller, & Eng, 2012). In addition, such programs have been found to have both short- and long-term positive effects in areas such as coping (Greenglass, Fiksenbaum, & Eaton, 2006) and maintaining functional ability (Orsega-Smith, Payne, Mowen, Ho, & Godbey, 2007). Being providers of social support has also been shown to have positive effects on the well-being of older adults with functional impairments (Ristau, 2011).

Social and Productive Engagement

There is a growing body of evidence indicating that active social engagement provides significant health benefits for older adults with functional limitations. Broadly defined, social engagement may include interacting with friends and family, participation in community organizations and events, and engaging in leisure activities (Berkman, Glass, Brissette, & Seeman, 2000). Productive engagement can be thought of broadly as meaningfully contributing to community life in a socially and/or economically valued way (Hinterlong, 2008). Positive outcomes related to greater social activity engagement include increased quality and length of life for older adults (Levasseur, Desrosiers, & Noreau, 2004). However, older adults with functional impairments may encounter various personal, social, and physical barriers that reduce their levels of participation.

For adults aging with and aging into disability, personal barriers to social engagement and productive contribution may include mental or physical health issues related to living with disability such as chronic depression, pain, fatigue, or ill health (Rosso, Taylor, Tabb, & Michael, 2013). In addition, individuals may lack social support that encourages continuous engagement (Cotter & Sherman, 2008). Common social and physical barriers include lack of accessible environments and accommodations in social settings. Lack of resources such as accessible parking, appropriate walking surfaces, and the provision of seating may influence whether or not a person with functional limitation attempts to participate in an activity. Technology-based supports such as telephone or Internet can enhance a sense of connectedness with friends and family (Rosso et al., 2013) and provide a sense of community (Sum, Matthews, Pourchasem, & Hughes, 2009) for older adults living at home. Regarding productive engagement in employment, flexible work schedules,

ergonomic workspaces, easily accessed buildings, and sensitive colleagues all have the potential to impact engagement.

Age-Friendly Cities is an international movement to support aging with and aging into disability (World Health Organization, 2007c). Making cities age-friendly is a commitment to provide structures and services to support and increase a sense of well-being and contributions for all citizens and to enhance an active aging process. An age-friendly city supports the physical, social, behavioral, economic, physical, and personal determinants of each individual's unique aging process (World Health Organization, 2007b).

Housing and Community Integration

"Aging in place" is the traditional term used to describe aging adults living in familiar home environments. The goal of aging in place at home is often threatened by the high number of environmental barriers present in the homes of individuals who experience functional limitations. Mismatches between the home environment and the physical capacity of older adults tend to be high (Seplaki et al., 2013). Common barriers in the home include items that are located out of reach, stairs, appliance or electrical controls that are difficult to manage, and safety issues such as slippery floors (Stark, Landsbaum, Palmer, Somerville, & Morris, 2009). In addition, the home environment may interfere with the use of some adaptive devices, such as the use of wheelchairs or walkers on uneven surfaces, rugs, or on stairs (Seplaki et al., 2013). In 2011, 2.2 million people in the United States reported using a wheelchair, while 6.4 million people used a cane, walker, or crutches for mobility assistance (US Census Bureau, 2013) With the numbers of persons in need of assistive devices, assessing potential barriers is critical.

Given that most older adults prefer to age in place, many intervention strategies target modifying home environments to make them more accessible or accommodating or introducing assistive technology (AT) such as adaptive equipment that make it possible to accomplish tasks such as dressing or communicating (Center for Technology and Aging, 2010). Occupational therapists and other trained professionals conduct individual assessments and are able to evaluate homes and determine appropriate changes to make. Widening doorways, installing shower grab bars, and changing door handles are frequent suggestions. Environmental modification strategies such as these are important intervention strategies to help manage chronic healthcare conditions, maintain or improve functioning, increase independence, ensure safety (Agree & Freedman, 2011), reduce the need to relocate to institutional facilities (Jutkowitz, Gitlin, Pizzi, Lee, & Dennis, 2012), and even reduce the costs of personal care services (Stark et al., 2009).

While AT is often highly valued by adults for its facilitation of independent living, participation, and well-being, the process of obtaining AT is often frustrating and costly (Lenker, Harris, Taugher, & Smith, 2013). In addition, the possibility of disuse or "abandonment" of AT by individuals due to the complexity of use or embarrassment related to using something different may occur (Scherer, Craddock, & Mackeogh, 2011). Social workers can help assess and address reasons why AT is not used and whether other options for support are available.

Transportation

Older adults who are unable to drive often rely on family members, friends, public transportation, taxis, and paratransit programs to get to community destinations (Lehning, 2011). Specialized transportation services are available for destinations such as medical offices, but the availability for transportation for activities such as shopping, physical activities, or other social engagements are typically nonexistent, further increasing social isolation (Hunter et al., 2013). In addition, many older adults with functional limitations experience difficulty using public bus or metro systems given the duration of wait, limitations in seating, and distance to transportation stops (Marx, Davis, Miftari, Salamone, & Weise, 2010). Overall, low-cost services to transport adults with functional impairments to social engagements, community activities, and during evening hours are extremely limited in most communities. Transportation is often the missing link between participation in community activities and becoming isolated and home bound.

Despite extensive evidence of unmet transportation needs, policy and program advances remain limited. Much available evidence suggests that the majority of older adults prefer driving themselves or using a car to reach their given destination (Marx et al., 2010). Losing one's driver's license is a significant life event and can often dissuade an individual from attempting alternative modes of transportation. Transportation solutions range from public education programs highlighting the use of paratransit to specialized transport programs to serve rural communities (Hunter et al., 2013). Many federal initiatives are aimed at improving the accessibility and quality of transportation services, including United We Ride and the National Consortium on the Coordination of Human Services Transportation. In addition, several states (Colorado, Washington, New York, Oklahoma, Oregon, Kentucky, Pennsylvania, Missouri, and Georgia) have adopted "brokered" or coordinated transportation systems (Burkhardt, 2012) between consumers and providers to fill the gaps between private and public transportation.

Discrimination: Physical, Social, and Cultural Barriers

Adults with disabilities of all ages are subject to prejudice and discrimination. Experiences with prejudice and discrimination among persons aging into disability may be different from experiences among persons aging with a disability. For the latter group, the duration of bias may be longer, and it may affect or have affected aspects of their lives differently (e.g., limiting opportunities in employment, housing, and ability to engage in community activities). In some cases, it may be difficult to distinguish bias against disability from ageism, as ageist beliefs tend to incorporate prejudice against physical and mental impairments commonly found among older adults (Anderson, Richardson, Fields, & Harootyan, 2013).

Despite these differences in experience, adults aging with and aging into disability face many of the same physical, social, and cultural barriers, including inaccessible environments, pervasive stereotypes, discriminatory actions (Meyer, 2010), and general lack of education and respect for physiological difference (Klein & Liu, 2010). Interventions to reduce discrimination include educational training for professionals (Putnam, 2012), age-related diversity awareness trainings for the broader public (NCOA, 2013), and increasing opportunities for community participation and community integration for persons aging with and aging into disability (Ruggiano, 2012).

Broader Program and Policy Issues

There is a web of social welfare policies that broadly support healthy aging and community participation for older adults with functional impairments. Although distinct in their origins and scope, taken together they form a foundation for developing, implementing, and evaluating programs and services for adults aging with and aging into disability. Key policies include the Older American's Act, Medicare, Medicaid, the Rehabilitation Act, and the Americans with Disabilities Act. Services and supports provided under these legislative acts all support community living and attempt to limit unnecessary institutionalization of older adults.

Older adults with physical disability may be eligible for services and supports across the range of programs and service networks. Eligibility requirements are typically related to age, disability status, income level, and type of service or support need. Centers for Independent Living (CILs), established through the Rehabilitation Act of 1978 offer peer-counseling, advocacy, independent living skills training, and information and referral (National Council on Independent Living [NCIL], 2013). Many CILs also offer expertise in home modification and AT. These CIL services are available to all persons with disabilities regardless of age. Adults aged 60 and older are eligible for a wide variety of programs and services provided through the Older American's Act such as transportation assistance, low-cost meals or meal delivery, health and wellness screenings, and assistance with some home healthcare needs and home repairs among others. Medicare and Medicaid are both insurance programs. Medicare is a federally run insurance program with near universal coverage of all older adults (CMS, 2013a). It pays for acute as well as some extended care and medical equipment. The Medicaid insurance program is a federal–state partnership, providing insurance to lower-income individuals including older adults. Medicaid insurance covers a range of long-term services and supports through an array of program options ranging from participant-directed services to managed care (CMS, 2013b).

Since around 2010, there has been a dramatic shift toward community-based provision of long-term services and supports to older adults. This shift was institutionalized in 2013 with the creation of the Administration for Community Living, the umbrella agency for the Administration on Aging, Administration on Intellectual and Developmental Disabilities, and the Center for Disability and Aging Policy (Administration for Community Living [ACL], 2013). This shift is in line with both international and national initiatives to improve the capacity for older adults, including those with functional limitations, to remain active participants in their local communities.

THE ROLE OF THE SOCIAL WORKER

When working with older adults experiencing disability, one of our challenges as professionals is to understand the range of factors that influence healthy aging and determine what types of interventions are needed for persons who are not reaching their own healthy aging goals. Social workers bring much knowledge and skill to this endeavor. However, the wide array of issues that factor into fostering healthy aging and community participation often requires partnering with professionals such as occupational therapists, psychologists, physicians, recreational counselors, public administrators, and policy makers to further interventions at the individual, community, or policy levels. In this area, we have many research and practice gaps. As noted earlier, there are often substantial differences in how disability is viewed and understood based on which field of knowledge scholars and professionals are trained in. Only recently have we begun to view people with disabilities and older adults as having similar interests and needs. Much of the research on interventions and strategies to improve quality of life for older adults with functional limitations has been conducted either for older adults or for younger persons with disabilities—despite their similar outcome interests of good health and wellness and participating in their communities. As policies change and demographics shift, developing partnerships and building bridges across service agencies and organizations will become increasingly important for understanding the needs of older adults aging with and aging into disability and the programs and professionals available to help meet these needs. To do so effectively, scholars and practitioners need to work together to employ successful models of collaboration. There is a substantial role for social workers to play in fostering cross-population and cross-network connections that support effectively working with older adults with functional limitations to meet their own goals for successful aging. We strongly encourage those working with older adults experiencing disability to do so.

REFERENCES

Administration for Community Living (ACL). (2013). *Individuals with disabilities.* Retrieved from http://www.medicaid.gov/Medicaid-CHIP-Program-Information/By-Population/People-with-Disabilities/Individuals-with-Disabilities.html

Agree, E. M., & Freedman, V. A. (2011). A quality-of-life scale for assistive technology: Results of a pilot study of aging and technology. *Physical Therapy, 91,* 1780–1788. doi:10.2522/ptj.20100375

Anderson, K. A., Richardson, V. E., Fields, N. L., & Harootyan, R. A. (2013). Inclusion or exclusion? Exploring barriers to employment for low-income older adults. *Journal of Gerontological Social Work, 56,* 318–334. doi:10.1080/01634372.2013.777006

Berkman, L. F., Glass, T., Brissette, L., & Seeman, T. E. (2000). From social integration to health: Durkheim in the new millennium. *Social Science and Medicine, 51,* 843–857, doi:S0277953600000654

Bickenbach, J. (1993). *Physical disability and social policy.* Toronto, ON: University of Toronto Press.

Bowen, M. E. (2009). Childhood socioeconomic status and racial differences in disability: Evidence from the Health and Retirement Study (1998–2006). *Social Science and Medicine, 69,* 433–441. doi:10.1016/j.socscimed.2009.06.006

Burkhardt, J. E. (2012). Outside the box: New models for transportation partnerships. In J. F. Coughlin & L. A. D'Ambrosio (Eds.), *Aging America and transportation: Personal choices and public policy* (pp. 217–232). New York, NY: Springer.

Center for Technology and Aging. (2010). *Assistive technology for functional improvement.* Retrieved from http://www.techandaging.org/Assistivedraft TechnologyReview.pdf

Centers for Disease Control (CDC). (2013). *The state of aging and health in America 2013.* Retrieved from http://www.cdc.gov/features/agingandhealth/state_of_aging_and_health_in_america_2013.pdf

Centers for Medicare and Medicaid Services (CMS). (2013a). *I have a disability.* Retrieved from http://www.medicare.gov/people-like-me/disability/disability.html

Centers for Medicare and Medicaid Services (CMS). (2013b). *Individuals with disabilities.* Retrieved from http://www.medicaid.gov/Medicaid-CHIP-Program-Information/By-Population/People-with-Disabilities/Individuals-with-Disabilities.html

Choi, S. (2011). Testing healthy immigrant effects among late life immigrants in the United States: Using multiple indicators. *Journal of Aging and Health, 24,* 475–506. doi:10.1177/0898264311425596

Cotter, K. A., & Sherman, A. M. (2008). Love hurts: The influence of social relations on exercise self-efficacy for older adults with osteoarthritis. *Journal of Aging and Physical Activity, 16,* 465–483.

Coyle, C. E., & Dugan, E. (2012). Social isolation, loneliness and health among older adults. *Journal of Aging Health, 24,* 1346–1363. doi:10.1177/0898264312460275

Environmental Protection Agency. (2007). *Building healthy communities for active aging national recognition program.* Retrieved from http://depts.washington.edu/harn/tools/10strategies.pdf

Erickson, W., Lee, C., & von Schrader, S. (2013). *Disability statistics from the 2011 American community survey (ACS).* Ithaca, NY: Cornell University Employment and Disability Institute (EDI). Retrieved from www.disabilitystatistics.org

Fredriksen-Goldsen, K. I., Kim, H. J., Emlet, C. A., Muraco, A., Erosheva, E. A., Hoy-Ellis, C. P., . . . Petry, H. (2011). *The aging and health report: Disparities and resilience among lesbian, gay, bisexual, and transgender older adults.* Seattle, WA: Institute for Multigenerational Health. Retrieved from http://caringandaging.org/wordpress/wp-content/uploads/2011/05/Full-Report-FINAL-11-16-11.pdf

Fuller-Thomson, E., Nuru-Jeter, A., Minkler, M., & Guralnik, J. M. (2010). Black-white disparities in disability among older Americans: Further untangling the role of race and socioeconomic status. *Journal of Aging and Health, 22,* 677–698.

Greenglass, E., Fiskenbaum, L., & Eaton, J. (2006). The relationship between coping, social support, functional disability and depression in the elderly. *Anxiety, Stress, and Coping, 19,* 15–31. doi:10.1080/14659890500436430

He, W., & Muenchrath, M. (2011). *90+ in the United States: 2006–2008 American Community Survey.* Retrieved from http://www.census.gov/prod/2011pubs/acs-17.pdf

Hinterlong, J. E. (2008). Productive engagement among older Americans: Prevalence, patterns, and implications for public policy. *Journal of Aging and Social Policy, 20,* 141–164.

Hung, W. W., Ross, J. S., Boockvar, K. S., & Siu, A. L. (2012). Association of chronic diseases and impairments with disability in older adults: A decade of change? *Medical Care, 50.* doi:10.1097/MLR.0b013e318245a0e0

Hunter, R. H., Sykes, K., Lowman, S. G., Duncan, R., Satariano, W. A., & Belza, B. (2013). Environmental and policy change to support healthy aging. *Journal of Aging and Social Policy, 23,* 354–371, doi:10.1080.0 8959420.2011.605642

Jutkowitz, E., Gitlin, L. N., Pizzi, L. T., Lee, E., & Dennis, M. P. (2012). Cost effectiveness of a home-based intervention that helps functionally vulnerable older adults age in place at home. *Journal of Aging Research, 2012.* http://www.hindawi.com/journals/jar/2012/680265/cta/. doi:10.1155/2012/680265

Kang-Yi, C. D., & Gellis, Z. D. (2010). A systematic review of community-based health interventions on depression for older adults with heart disease. *Aging and Mental Health, 14,* 1–19. doi:10.1080/13607860903421003

Klein, J., & Liu, L. (2010). Ageism in current practice: Experiences of occupational therapists. *Physical and Occupational Therapy in Geriatrics, 28,* 334–349. doi:10.3109/02703181.2010.532904

Lee, E.-K. O., & Kim, J. (2013). Physical and social activities of older adults with functional limitations. *Activities, Adaptation and Aging, 37,* 99–120. doi:10.1 080/01924788.2013.784851

Lehning, A. J. (2011). City governments and aging in place: Community design, transportation and housing innovation adoption. *The Gerontologist, 52,* 345–356. doi:10.1093/geront/gnr089

Lenker, J., Harris, F., Taugher, M., & Smith, R. (2013). Consumer perspectives on assistive technology outcomes. *Disability and Rehabilitation: Assistive Technology, 8,* 373–380. doi:10.3109/17483107.2012.74 9429

Levasseur, M., Desrosiers, J., & Noreau, L. (2004). Is social participation associated with quality of life of older adults with physical disabilities? *Disability and Rehabilitation, 26,* 1206–1213. doi:10.1080/096382804 1233127037AM6MDLFToWAH1RCN

Lowry, K. A., Vallejo, A. N., & Studenski, S. A. (2012). Successful aging as a continuum of functional independence: Lessons from physical disability models of aging. *Aging and Disease, 3,* 5–15.

Lui, F., Woodrow, J., Loucks-Atikinson, A., Buehler, S., West, R., & Whan, P. P. (2013). Smoking and alcohol consumption patterns among elderly Canadians with mobility disabilities. *BMC Research Notes, 6,* 218–227. doi:10.1186/1756-0500-6-218

Marx, J., Davis, C., Miftari, C., Salamone, A., & Weise, W. (2010). Developing brokered transportation for seniors and people with disabilities. *Journal of Gerontological Social Work, 53,* 449–466. doi:10.108 0/01634372.2010.487886

McInnis-Dittrich, K. (2009). *Social work with older adults* (3rd ed., pp. 179–197). Boston, MA: Pearson Education.

Meyer, H.-D. (2010). Culture and disability: Advancing comparative research. *Comparative Sociology, 9,* 157–164. doi:10.1163/156913210X12536181350999

National Council on Aging (NCOA). (2013). *Making a difference for older Americans: 1950–today.* Retrieved from http://www.ncoa.org/about-ncoa/ncoa-history.html

National Council on Independent Living (NCIL). (2013). *Reauthorization of the Rehabilitation Act: Passage of S. 1356.* Retrieved from http://www.ncil.org/rehabact/

Orsega-Smith, E. M., Payne, L. L., Mowen, A. J., Ho, C., & Godbey, G. C. (2007). The role of social support and self-efficacy in shaping the leisure time physical activity in older adults. *Journal of Leisure Research, 39,* 705–727.

Pumkam, C., Probst, J. C., Bennett, K. J., Hardin, J., & Xirasagar, S. (2013). Health care expenditures among working-age adults with physical disabilities: Variation by disability spans. *Disability Health Journal, 6,* 287–297. doi:10.1016/j.dhjo.2013.03.002

Putnam, M. (2012). Can aging with disability find a home in gerontological social work? *Journal of Gerontological Social Work, 55,* 91–94. doi:10.1080/01634372.647581

Putnam, M., Geenen, S., Powers, L., Saxton, M., Finney, S., & Dautel, P. (2003). Health and wellness: People with disabilities discuss barriers and facilitators to well being. *Journal of Rehabilitation, 69,* 37–45.

Ristau, S. (2011). People do need people: Social interaction boosts brain health in older age. *Generations: Journal of the American Society on Aging, 35,* 70–76.

Rosenbloom, S. (2009). Meeting transportation needs in an aging-friendly community. *Generations: Journal of the American Society on Aging, 33,* 33–48.

Rosso, A. L., Taylor, J. A., Tabb, L. P., & Michael, Y. L. (2013). Mobility, disability, and social engagement in older adults. *Journal of Aging and Health, 25,* 617–637. doi:10.1177/0898264313482489

Ruggiano, N. (2012). Consumer direction in long-term care policy: Overcoming barriers to promoting older adults' opportunity for self-direction. *Journal of Gerontological Social Work, 55,* 146–159. doi:10.108 0/01634372.2011.638701

Sakakibara, B. M., Hitzig, S. L., Miller, W. C., & Eng, J. J. (2012). An evidence-based review on the influence of a spinal cord injury on subjective quality of life. *Spinal Cord, 50,* 570–578. doi:10.1038/sc.2012.19

Scherer, M. J., Craddock, G., & Mackeogh, T. (2011). The relationship of personal factors and subjective well-being to the use of assistive technology devices. *Disability and Rehabilitation, 33,* 811–817. doi:10.3109/09638288.2010.511418

Schoeni, R. F., Freedman, V. A., & Martin, L. G. (2008). Why is late-life disability declining? *Milbank Quarterly, 86,* 47–87. doi:10.1111/j.1468-0009.2007.00513.x.

Seplaki, C. L., Agree, E. M., Weiss, C. O., Szanton, S. L., Bandeen-Roche, K., & Fried, L. P. (2013). Assistive devices in context: Cross-sectional associations between challenges in the home environment and use of assistive devices for mobility. *The Gerontologist, 54,* 1–10. doi:10.1093/geront/gnt030

Stark, S., Landsbaum, A., Palmer, J., Somerville, E. K., & Morris, J. C. (2009). Client-centered home modifications improve daily activity performance of older adults. *Canadian Journal of Occupational Therapy, 76,* 235–245.

Sum, S., Matthews, R. M., Pourchasem, M., & Hughes, I. (2009). Internet use as a predictor of sense of community in older people. *CyberPsychology and Behavior, 12,* 235–239. doi:10.1089/cpb.2008.0150

Sung, C., Chiu, C.-Y., Lee, E.-J., Bezyak, J., Chan, F., & Muller, V. (2012). Exercise, diet, and stress management as mediators between functional disability and health-related quality of life in multiple sclerosis. *Rehabilitation Counseling Bulletin, 56,* 85–95.

Thompson, W. W., Zack, M. M., Krahn, G. L., Andresen, E. M., & Barile, J. P. (2012). Health-related quality of life among older adults without functional limitations. *American Journal of Public Health, 102,* 496–504. doi:10.2105/AJPH.2011.300500

US Census Bureau. (2012). *America's with disabilities: 2010. Household economic studies.* Retrieved from http://www.census.gov/prod/2012pubs/p70-131.pdf

US Census Bureau. (2013). *Disability.* Retrieved from http://www.census.gov/people/disability/

US Bureau of Labor Statistics. (2013). *Persons with a disability: Labor force characteristics–2012.* Retrieved from http://www.bls.gov/news.release/pdf/disabl.pdf

White, A. M., Philogene, G. S., Fine, L., & Sinha, S. (2009). Social support and self-reported health status of older adults in the United States. *American Journal of Public Health, 99,* 1872–1878. doi:10.2105/AJPH.2008.146894.

World Health Organization. (2001). *International classification of functioning, disability and health: Final draft, full version.* Retrieved from http://www.sustainable-design.ie/arch/ICIDH-2Final.pdf

World Health Organization. (2007a). *Active ageing: A policy framework.* Retrieved from http://www.who.int/ageing/publications/active_ageing/en/

World Health Organization. (2007b). *Checklist of essential features of age-friendly cities.* Retrieved from http://www.who.int/ageing/publications/Age_friendly_cities_checklist.pdf

World Health Organization. (2007c). *Global age-friendly cities: A guide.* Retrieved from http://www.who.int/ageing/publications/Global_age_friendly_cities_Guide_English.pdf

Following heart disease, cancer is the second leading cause of death in the United States (Siegel, Naishadham, & Jemal, 2013). Annual cancer projections indicate that more than 580,000 people will die of cancer in 2013; that is, approximately 1,600 people are expected to die from some form of cancer every day (American Cancer Society [ACS], 2013). During the same year, more than 1.6 million people are projected to be newly diagnosed with invasive cancer (Siegel et al., 2013). If cancer rates follow current patterns, cancer incidence will double over the next half-century, with almost 3 million newly diagnosed cases in the year 2050 (Hayat, Howlader, Reichman, & Edwards, 2007). Once diagnosed, an individual is considered to be a "survivor" for the remainder of her or his life (National Cancer Institute [NCI], 2013a). In 2012 (the most recent year for which data are available), it was estimated that 13.7 million people, or 4% of the US population, were survivors of cancer. Of the almost 14 million survivors, 15% had survived 20 years or longer (NCI, 2013b). For many people, especially older people, cancer has taken on characteristics of a chronic disease.

Older people bear a disproportionate cancer burden in the United States. As a result, cancer is now classified as a disease of older adults (Institute of Medicine [IOM], 2013). Although older individuals have the highest incidence rates for almost all cancers, they have the lowest rates of screening procedures of proven efficiency. Recent data indicate that between 2006 and 2010, 53% of all newly diagnosed malignant tumors and 69% of cancer deaths occurred in people age 65 and older (NCI, 2013c).

CANCER DEFINED

Cancer is a disease characterized by uncontrolled and abnormal cell growth that often invades nearby tissue. Cancer cells can spread through the lymphatic system and the bloodstream. There are five main types of cancer (NCI, 2013d):

- Carcinoma begins in the skin or tissues that line or cover the internal organs.
- Sarcoma begins in the bone, cartilage, fat, muscle, blood vessels, or other connective tissue.
- Leukemia starts in blood-forming tissue, such as bone marrow, and floods the blood system with abnormal blood cells.

TAMARA J. CADET
JULIE BERRETT-ABEBE
PETER MARAMALDI

Older Adults with Cancer

31

- Lymphoma is a type of cancer that begins in the cells of the immune system.
- Central nervous system cancers start in the tissues of the brain and spinal cord.

Cancer can occur in almost all of the organs and anatomic sites of the human body, and certain types of cancer are more lethal than others (ACS, 2013a).

Common Types of Cancer

The leading causes of cancer deaths in individuals over 65 are lung, colorectal (CRC), prostate, and pancreas for men and lung, breast, colorectal, gynecological, and pancreas for women (Siegel et al., 2013). This section reviews each of these cancers briefly, acknowledging that an entire volume could be dedicated to each.

Lung Cancer

Lung cancer is the leading cause of cancer deaths for both men and women over 60 years old, accounting for approximately 30% of all cancer deaths in this age group (Siegel et al., 2013). The probability of developing lung cancer is 1 in 15 for men and 1 in 20 for women, aged 70 and older (Siegel et al., 2013).

Cigarette smoking is major risk factor:

- Risk is significantly increased based on the duration, quantity, and age at onset and age of cessation.
- Smoking tobacco causes about 9 out of 10 cases of lung cancer in men and about 8 out of 10 cases of lung cancer in women (NCI, 2013e).
- Environmental factors such as asbestos, radon gas, chromate, nickel, polyhydrocarbons, and alkylating compounds are known to increase the risk of lung cancer (NCI, 2013f).

Diagnosing the stage of lung (and other types of cancer) is a highly technical procedure that is often complicated by multiple or overlapping classification systems and conflicting clinical approaches to staging at diagnosis. Advanced stage at diagnosis is directly related to lower survival rates.

Lung cancer is commonly known for its high incidence rate and poor prognosis. The 5-year survival rates for distant metastasis of advanced stage at diagnosis are only 4%, compared with

earlier-stage diagnosis with 53.5% survival rates for those with localized tumors that have not spread (NCI, 2013g).

Lung cancer is generally divided into two groups: small cell and non–small cell:

- Small cell lung cancer:

  - Cells appear small and round when viewed under the microscope
  - Metastasizes slowly and can be treated effectively at early-stage diagnosis

- Non–small cell lung cancer (NSCLC):

  - Includes squamous cell carcinoma, adenocarcinoma, and large cell carcinoma
  - Approximately 75% to 80% of all lung cancers are NSCLC (Jemal et al., 2007)
  - Current treatments do not cure NSCLC. These cancers are often found at an advanced stage due to rapid growth
  - Early detection leads to higher survival rates

Despite the debate about effectiveness, the United States Preventive Services Task Force (USPSTF) recently recommended that individuals at high risk for lung cancer (current or recent smokers aged 55 to 79 years old who have a smoking history of 30 pack-years or greater get a low-dose CT scan every year (see Box 31.1) (USPSTF, 2013). Diagnosis of lung cancer is made through:

- Sputum Cytology
- Bronchoscopy
- Biopsy
- Transthoracic Needle Therapy

Surgical resection offers the greatest chance of cure for many types of lung cancer, provided

---

Text Box 31.1
Screening Tests for Lung Cancer

- Chest radiography
- Sputum
- Low-dose spiral computed tomography (CT) (effectiveness remains controversial)

Text Box 31.2
Common Side Effects of Radiation Therapy

- Fatigue
- Loss of appetite
- Nausea
- Vomiting
- Lowered numbers of blood cells

Text Box 31.3
Risk Factors for Breast Cancer Among Older Women

- Advancing age
- Family history and genetic predisposition
- Higher estrogen levels
- Early age at menarche
- Late menopause
- Benign breast disease
- Dense breasts
- Alcohol use
- Number of or late pregnancies
- Hormone replacement therapy
- Exposure to radiation

the disease has not metastasized to other parts of the body. Adjuvant chemotherapy or radiation therapy is offered to reduce recurrence of the disease. Preoperative chemotherapy is offered for those at more advanced stages before attempting to perform curative resection. At the inoperable stage, radiation therapy has been the most common form of treatment, although it carries certain risks which should be explained to patients (see Box 31.2).

Since the mid-2000s, researchers have learned more about the changes in lung cancer cells that help them grow. As a result, targeted therapies such as Erlotinib have been developed. Erlotinib blocks epidermal growth factor receptor (EGFR) from signaling the cell to grow, and can be effective for individuals whose NSCLC cells have too much EGFR (ACS, 2013b).

Breast Cancer

Breast cancer is the second leading cause of cancer death in women age 65 and older, with approximately 41% of newly diagnosed cases occurring in this age group (NCI, 2013h). The probability of developing breast cancer is 1 in 202 for women before age 40 and 1 in 15 for women at age 70 or older (Siegel et al., 2013). Women over 65 account for as much as 57.6% of breast cancer mortality. The highest incidence rates for breast cancer are seen in women between ages 65 and 74 (20.7%).

A woman's risk of developing breast cancer (see Box 31.3) is greatly increased if she has a mutation in the BRCA1 or BRCA2 gene. These hereditary genes account for 5%–10% of all breast cancers (NCI, 2013i), and may warrant consideration of risk reduction options (see Box 31.4).

For women age 50 and older, the 5-year survival rates from 2003–2009 were:

- 99.3% for localized breast cancer
- 83.7% for regional lymph nodes
- 21.9% for distal metastases

The 5-year overall survival rate for women age 75 and older with early-stage breast cancer is about 47% (Howlader et al., 2013). Despite national conversations on screening recommendations, breast cancer screening remains important for older women. The ACS recommends annual mammograms starting at the age of forty and the 2009 USPTF recommends biannual mammograms for women ages 50–74 (Bellizzi, Breslau, Burness, & Waldron, 2011). Screening strategies for the early detection of breast cancer also include self-examination and clinical breast examination performed by a healthcare

Text Box 31.4
Options to Reduce Risk of Breast Cancer for Women with an Identified Genetic Mutation

- Screening
- Prophylactic surgery
- Chemoprevention

Text Box 31.5
Other Common Breast Cancer Treatment Approaches

- Radiation therapy
- Hormonal therapy
- Chemotherapy

Text Box 31.6
Known Risk Factors for Prostate Cancer

- Advancing age
- African American race/ethnicity
- Family history
- High fat diet (ACS, 2013b)

---

professional. Suspicious screening results are followed up by biopsy to confirm a positive diagnosis.

There are two general types of surgery to treat breast cancer: breast-sparing or breast-conserving surgery and mastectomy. For women diagnosed at an early stage of breast cancer, breast-sparing surgery combined with radiation therapy results in the same survival rates as for those who have mastectomy.

Breast-sparing surgery:

- A procedure intended to remove the breast cancer but not the breast itself
- Types of breast-sparing surgery include:

  - Lumpectomy (removal of the lump)
  - Quadrantectomy (removal of one quarter, or quadrant, of the breast)
  - Segmental Mastectomy (removal of the cancer as well as some of the breast tissue around the tumor and the lining over the chest muscles below the tumor)

Despite risks and more recent controversy associated with its use, hormonal therapy such as tamoxifen or aromatase inhibitors have been known to be effective for older women who cannot tolerate surgery and/or as adjuvant therapy for individuals who have completed surgery, chemotherapy, and/or radiation (see Box 31.5). The American Society of Clinical Oncology (ASCO) currently recommends the use of hormonal therapy for women who have hormone receptor positive breast cancer (ASCO, 2010).

Prostate Cancer

Although the occurrence of prostate cancer is rare in men younger than 40 years, incidence rates double during each subsequent decade of life for all men, and for African American men compared with White men (Howlader et al., 2013). Men 65 and older

account for 57.5% of all prostate cancer and 70% of all prostate cancer mortality (NCI 2013i). The probability of developing prostate cancer is 1 in 7,964 for men under 40 and 1 in 8 for men aged 70 and older (Siegel et al., 2013).

Prostate cancer starts in the prostate gland, which is located at the base of the penis, just below the bladder and in front of the rectum, and which produces seminal fluid. At the beginning stage, it does not endanger life, as the disease remains localized in the gland. The 5-year survival rate of localized prostate cancer is 100%, compared with 28% for distant metastases (NCI, 2013i). Without early detection and appropriate treatment, prostrate cancer can spread to other organs and cause death (Howlader et al., 2013). Routine screening tests such as the serum prostrate specific antigen and the digital rectal examination lead to early detection. However, the USPSTF currently recommends against routine PSA screening, stating that expected harms outweigh potential benefits (USPSTF, 2012). If these tests are completed and are suspicious, follow-up tests include sonogram (also known as ultrasound) and biopsy. Biopsy is the most invasive but most effective means of detecting prostate cancer.

Risk factors for prostate cancer are well understood (see Box 31.6), but the exact etiology of prostate cancer is not known, making preventive behaviors difficult to recommend.

In general, prostate cancer treatment is divided into three categories based on the extent of the cancer (NCI, 2013l).

1. Localized prostate cancer—Potentially curable through prostatectomy and various forms of irradiation therapy. These treatments carry significant risks of side effects, including acute cystitis, urinary retention, impotence, blood loss, and incontinence.
2. An advanced state of the cancer—Although prostate cancer does not spread to other tissues or

organs, local metastasis in the pelvic area makes prostatectomy or irradiation therapy less effective.

3. Metastatic prostate cancer—About 30% of prostate cancers are metastatic at the time of diagnosis. Prognosis is poor, and hormonal therapy is one of the treatment options (NCI, 2013l).

Colon/Rectum Cancer

Although cancer of the colon and rectum are clinically differentiated, they are discussed under the rubric of "colorectal cancer." Colorectal cancer is the second most common cancer for older men and women, and its incidence and mortality rates increase with age. The probability of developing CRC is 1 in 24 for men aged 70 and older and 1 in 26 for women aged 70 and older (Siegel et al., 2013).

Eighty percent of CRC is known to develop from adenomatous polyps that take approximately 5 to 10 years to become malignant. As many as 1 in 3 people have adenomatous polyps by their mid-50s. As of October 2008, the USPSTF recommends routine screening for adults between the ages of 50 and 75 (USPSTF, 2008).

Various detection strategies are available (see Box 31.7), but fecal occult blood testing (FOBT) is the most cost-effective and commonly used screening test for CRC. A positive FOBT should be followed by a colonoscopy. Colonoscopy is the most expensive but the preferred screening procedure because it allows for the clinical examination of the entire colon and immediate biopsy of suspicious tissue.

Approximately 75% of CRC patients had no known risk factors prior to diagnosis (see Box 31.8). The best preventive strategy is to remove premalignant polyps. The 5-year survival rate is 90% for early diagnosis with localized malignancy. Survival drops to 70% for regional metastases and 12.5% for distal metastases (NCI, 2013j).

Text Box 31.7
Current Colorectal Cancer Detection Strategies

- Digital rectal examination
- Fecal occult blood testing (FOBT)
- Sigmoidoscopy
- Colonoscopy

Text Box 31.8
Risk Factors for Colorectal Cancer

- Increased age
- Personal history of CRC or ulcerative colitis (Crohn's disease)
- family history of CRC or familial adenomatous polyposis in a first-degree relative
- history of breast, ovarian, or uterine cancer

Treatment options (see Box 31.9) include the removal of colorectal tumors along with adjacent bowel, blood vessels, and lymphatics through en-bloc surgical resection, as well as adjuvant chemotherapy that may be offered after surgery. Other standard chemotherapies such as capecitabine are given depending on staging and comorbidities. Targeted therapies such as avastin are also more widely being used to treat advanced CRCs (ACS, 2013a). Finally, a complete or partial colectomy is a treatment option for CRC.

Gynecologic Cancers

There are five main types of cancer that develop in women's reproductive organs (see Box 31.10) (Centers for Disease Control and Prevention [CDC], 2013). Of those five, uterine and ovarian cancers are the most common in the United States, with uterine being the fourth most common cancer diagnosis and ovarian the tenth most common cancer diagnosis for women. Ovarian cancer is the fifth leading cause of cancer death for women, while uterine is the eighth (Siegel et al., 2013). As with other cancer diagnoses discussed in this chapter, age is a risk factor for development of gynecologic cancers. For example, the risk of developing uterine cancer is 1 in 1,348 before age 40 and 1 in 80 for those 70 and older (Siegel et al., 2013).

Text Box 31.9
Common Treatment Approaches

- Surgery
- Chemotherapy

Text Box 31.10
Gynecological Cancers

- Cervical
- Ovarian
- Uterine
- Vaginal
- Vulvar

Text Box 31.11
Pancreatic Cancer Risk Factors

- Advanced age
- Smoking
- Diet
- Medical Conditions (chronic pancreatitis, diabetes, cirrhosis)
- Family history
- Environmental agents (ACS, 2013a; NCI, 2010)

Cervical cancer is largely preventable and treatable in developed countries. The main cause of cervical cancer is the human papillomavirus (HPV); there is a vaccine to prevent HPV as well as an effective screening method (PAP test) to detect cancerous/precancerous cells at an early stage and thus improve outcomes and survival (CDC, 2013). *Ovarian and uterine cancers* are traditionally treated with surgery, chemotherapy, radiation, and hormonal therapies. As with other cancers, recent advances have been made in treatment with targeted therapies such as avastin (ACS, 2013c). Physical complications of ovarian cancer and side-effects from treatments can have a significant negative impact on ovarian cancer survivors' quality of life and interpersonal relationships. Common issues include sexual functioning and satisfaction, body-image, relational strain, feelings of isolation, and psychological distress (Roland, Rodriguez, Patterson, & Trivers, 2013).

Pancreatic Cancer

The pancreas is located near the stomach and the small intestine. It produces several hormones used in regular digestion of food (NCI, 2010). In contrast to the downward trend in rates for most other cancer sites over the past decade, pancreatic cancer death rates have slowly been increasing among men and women in the United States. It is the fourth leading type of cancer death for both men and women, accounting for 5%–7% of cancer deaths. Advanced age is a significant risk factor for pancreatic cancer (see Box 31.11), with the likelihood of developing pancreatic cancer in the next 10 years approximately four times higher at age 70 than at age 50 (ACS, 2013a). Because pancreatic cancer tends to be aggressive in nature, most cases (53%) are detected at an advanced stage, and the 5-year survival rate for pancreatic cancer when diagnosed at advanced stage is only 2% (NCI, 2013l).

Just as with other cancer cases, older adults account for a significant portion of pancreatic cancer patients. Most (67%) pancreatic cancer cases are detected in individuals over the age of 65 years, with the median age at diagnosis of 71 years (Howlader et al., 2013). Because the symptoms of pancreatic cancer are not specific, screening and diagnostic tests (see Box 31.12) are often delayed.

Individuals with pancreatic cancer typically seek out medical attention due to:

- Jaundice
- Weight loss
- Epigastric and back pain
- Fatigue
- Loss of appetite
- Glucose intolerance

Patients may also report diarrhea, constipation, bloating, flatulence, chills, dizziness, or muscle pains (ACS, 2013a).

Pancreatic treatment remedies are offered individually or in combination based on the degree of

---

Text Box 31.12
Screening Tests for Pancreatic Cancer

- Computerized axial tomography (CAT scan)
- Endoscopic retrograde cholangiopancreatography (ERCP)
- Magnetic resonance imaging
- Biopsy (ACS, 2013a)

morbidity (ACS, 2013a). Surgery remains the only treatment that offers a chance of cure for pancreatic cancer patients. People with advanced pancreatic cancer usually undergo surgery to remove a small part of the pancreas. This is followed by postoperative adjuvant chemotherapy. Patients with inoperable pancreatic cancer that has not spread to other organs often receive radiation therapy and chemotherapy. Targeted therapies, such as Erlotinib (described earlier), may also be used with gemcitabine among pancreatic cancer patients with metastatic disease. The most severe cases of distal metastatic pancreatic cancer are treated with chemotherapy, targeted therapies, and/or palliative care, which provides symptom management and psychosocial support (ACS, 2013a).

CANCER DISPARITIES

Demographic projections indicate that while the number of non-Hispanic Whites over the age of 65 years will double by the year 2050, the number of Blacks will triple and Hispanics over the age of 65 year will increase 11-fold (Gerst-Emerson & Burr, 2013). In addition, the number of Asians will increase approximately 15% (Federal Interagency Forum on Aging-Related Statistics, 2010). As a result of the increase in the older ethnic minority population, an increase in cancer incidence and mortality is expected for these populations. Thus, the disproportionate cancer burden on these populations is expected to increase as well due to low participation in early detection tests (Jemal, Siegal, Xu, & Ward, 2010). African Americans have the highest death rates from cancer than any other racial or ethnic population. Specifically, the cancer mortality rate is 33% higher than among White males and 16% higher than among White females (ACS, 2013a). Overall, Hispanics have a lower incidence of most commonly diagnosed cancers compared with non-Hispanic Whites. However, they are more likely to be diagnosed with an advanced stage of cancer disease (ACS, 2012). Similar to Hispanics/Latinos, Asian Americans and Pacific Islanders have the lowest overall cancer rates. However, this population has the highest liver cancer incidence and death rates for liver cancer for all racial and ethnic groups for both sexes. Specifically, the incidence and mortality rates for Asian American and Pacific Islanders are approximately twice the rate among non-Hispanic Whites and 20% higher than

Hispanics, who have the second highest rates (ACS, 2013a).

PSYCHOSOCIAL CONSIDERATIONS

Understanding cancer, its treatment, posttreatment recovery, and maintenance are directly associated with an older individual's physical and cognitive ability. Comorbid conditions contribute to the physical and emotional impact of the cancer. If an individual is experiencing a condition with symptoms more severe than those accompanying the cancer, she or he may be less motivated to take treatment action. This is an especially important consideration in early-stage diagnosis, when relatively little or no discomfort may be experienced. Treatment delays and noncompliance with prevention, screening, and treatment regimens introduce the risk of metastases, which may result in less favorable prognosis for cure, survival, and quality of life after treatment. The delay or noncompliance phenomenon may be exacerbated by cognitive impairments.

Clinicians must consider symptom management and possible side effects or complications related to treatments. Pain management, possible physical impairments, effects on social relationships, psychological and emotional distress, nutritional issues, and financial burdens must all be considered in the context of the patient's age and resources. Older cancer patients require considerable support to achieve positive health outcomes from the treatment as well as to achieve an acceptable quality of life.

Physical/Cognitive Functioning

Impaired physical and cognitive capacities may complicate the treatment of older people with cancer. Some older people may experience chemotherapy as intolerable and require special medical attention (Hurria et al., 2011). Cancer treatments must be established through careful individualized assessments that reflect comorbid and other physical conditions (Extermann & Hurria, 2007). Malnutrition, anemia, and neutropenia can result from the negative effects of chemotherapy and require careful attention and monitoring. Older patients' physical impairments, including of hearing, speech, and literacy, may influence their activities of daily living (ADLs), such as cooking, dressing, bathing, shopping, taking medications, and visiting hospitals for treatment, and therefore directly affect prognosis (Extermann & Hurria, 2007).

Older patients with cognitive impairments may be unable to convey their needs and physical condition to healthcare providers. The inability to assess and/or convey one's own physical condition may have a direct outcome on diagnosis, treatment, and maintenance (Hart-Johnson & Green, 2010). Pain assessment and management are critical components of cancer care and quality of life. In addition to behavioral observations, clinicians should use pain assessment tools for people with cognitive impairments (Hart-Johnson & Green, 2010). Pain assessment tools include a numerical rating scale (NRS), in which a respondent is asked to choose a number from 0-10; a verbal descriptor scale (VDS), in which a respondent is asked to choose word that best describes pain, such as "no pain" to "worst pain imaginable"; and the Pain Assessment in Advanced Dementia (PAINAD) Scale, in which clinicians use structured observational data to assess pain (Herr et al., 2006; Warden, Hurley, & Volicer, 2003).

Emotional/Psychological Responses

Cancer produces a range of emotional and psychological distress, often related to specific functional impairments. Fear, anxiety, sleep disturbance, depression, and avoidance often surface due not only to symptoms and side effects of treatment, such as surgery and chemotherapy, but to the looming fear of recurrence or death that is prevalent in older patients (Deimling, Kahana, Bowmon, & Schaefer, 2002). It is common for patients to consider themselves disfigured or maimed by surgery. A colostomy patient may live in horror of leakage, especially during the initial stages of adjustment. Similarly, a woman post mastectomy may experience distress concerns related to body-image and self-esteem, while a man post treatment for prostate cancer may feel embarrassed by issues of incontinence and erectile dysfunction. Attention should also be paid to the psychological adjustment after cancer surgeries, which can be complicated by concerns related to body image, embarrassment, and interpersonal relationships. Cavalier attitudes about appearance or self-consciousness not mattering to an older person should be monitored and addressed by clinicians at every juncture

of service provision in the medical setting and the patient's community.

Older cancer patients may be twice as old as their providers. It is important for providers to be sensitized to the vitality of older people. A younger provider approaching an older cancer patient as someone who has lived out her or his years is behaving inappropriately, unethically, and potentially detrimentally to a patient's prognosis. The despair of older women experiencing surgery for breast cancer should not be minimized because of their age. Neither should providers minimize an older man's concerns about side effects of prostate cancer treatment (Sharp, Blum, & Aviv, 2004). Emotional and psychological assessments and appropriate support must be offered to meet the emotional and psychological needs of older cancer patients.

Social/Financial Resources

Limited financial and social resources may influence treatment decisions and outcomes among older people with cancer (Balducci, 2003). Financial burdens become a critical issue for older adults with cancer, due to their out-of-pocket medical expenses. Visiting the treatment site, securing outpatient medications, receiving home care, and obtaining needed medical supplies are formidable tasks and additional worries for the older patient (Haley, 2003). Treatment planning must include accessible services, including a visiting nurse, community supports, and financial assistance—all critical aspects of treatment for older cancer patients (Cancer Care, 2004). Lack of social support and restrictions on activity have a direct impact on the effectiveness of treatment and can cause emotional and psychological distress among older cancer patients (Koretz & Reuben, 2003). Positive social support including family members, participation in religious communities, and personal spiritual beliefs are associated with resiliency among older adults with cancer (Pentz, 2005) and should be part of the treatment planning.

Social Work

Social workers are uniquely situated to help patients communicate with medical oncologists, to understand the disease and treatment options, and to explore emotional and social issues related to the specific cancer in the patients' psychosocial circumstances. Clinical social workers can provide older cancer survivors and caregivers comprehensive counseling and clinical case management that are responsive to the medical, environmental, and economic conditions during initial diagnosis, treatment, and discharge into the community (Haley, 2003). Conversely, the social worker communicates the patient's situation, understanding of the disease, and treatment options back to the interdisciplinary team. Geriatric considerations, particularly as they relate to quality of life in survivorship, are particularly important. The 2007 IOM report highlights the importance of meeting the psychosocial needs of cancer patients and promotes the importance of the social work role on the multidisciplinary team (IOM, 2007).

Social workers in cancer care settings provide crisis intervention, evidence-based individual and family counseling, support group facilitation, and end of life/bereavement support. Specific evidence-based interventions include cognitive-behavioral therapy, stress-management, and psychoeducation to treat anxiety and depression (Jacobsen & Jim, 2008), group therapy to reduce isolation and address common fears (Herschbach et al., 2010), and mindfulness and problem-solving therapy to improve coping with illness (Ledesma & Kumano, 2009). As members of interdisciplinary teams specializing in specific cancer types, clinical social workers' expertise in all aspects of the disease, including side effects of treatment, pain management, and assessment of self-care needs, helps patients navigate the complex medical terrain and bridge the gap between the biomedical and psychosocial aspects of the disease.

In addition, a comprehensive oncology social work approach will provide older cancer patients, families, and caregivers with an overview of services and resources available that include cultural considerations. Social work approaches must include the patients' and families cultural values and beliefs regarding cancer screening, diagnosis, and treatment. A culturally grounded psychosocial assessment can help both treatment teams and families anticipate and prepare for all aspects of cancer screening, diagnosis, treatment, and, when needed, palliation.

SUMMARY

During their youth, older individuals may have lived through a time in history when a cancer diagnosis was virtually a death sentence. Technological advances in cancer screening, diagnosis, and treatment have resulted in unprecedented cancer survivorship. So great are the numbers of survivors and the duration of survivorship, that cancer—in some cases—can be reframed as a chronic condition. This should not confuse the fact that a cancer diagnosis assaults every aspect of a person's being—especially older people. Unless a patient is significantly debilitated by a comorbid condition, other physical conditions must not interfere with continued cancer screening, treatment, and maintenance. Older cancer patients require special consideration to help them understand the disease and its treatment, to remove barriers to treatment and maintenance, and to monitor not only the disease but also patients' physical and cognitive functioning during survivorship. Social workers are uniquely positioned to provide and promote quality and integrated biopsychosocial care to older adults diagnosed with cancer.

REFERENCES

American Cancer Society (ACS). (2012). *Cancer facts & figures for Hispanics/Latinos—2012–2014.* Retrieved September 15, 2013, from http://www.cancer.org/acs/groups/content/@epidemiologysurveilance/documents/document/acspc-034778.pdf

American Cancer Society (ACS). (2013a). *Cancer facts & figures, 2013.* Retrieved September 21, 2013, from http://www.cancer.org/acs/groups/content/@epidemiology-surveilance/documents/document/acspc-036845.pdf

American Cancer Society (ACS). (2013b). *What are the risk factors for prostate cancer?* Retrieved September 27, 2013, from http://www.cancer.org/cancer/prostatecancer/detailedguide/prostate-cancer-risk-factors

American Cancer Society (ACS). (2013c). *Targeted therapies for ovarian cancer.* Retrieved January 20, 2014, from http://www.cancer.org/cancer/ovariancancer/detailedguide/ovarian-cancer-treating-targeted-therapy

American Society of Clinical Oncology (ASCO). (2010). *ASCO clinical practice guideline: Update on adjuvant endocrine therapy for women with hormone receptor-positive breast cancer.* Retrieved October 1, 2013, from http://www.asco.org/ institute-quality/

asco-clinical-practice- guideline- update-adjuvant-endocrine- therapy-women-hormone

Balducci, L. (2003). New paradigms for treating elderly patients with cancer: The Comprehensive Geriatric Assessment and Guidelines for Supportive Care. *Journal of Supportive Oncology*, 1(Suppl. 2), 30–37.

Bellizzi, K. M., Breslau, E. S., Burness, A., & Waldron, W. (2011). Prevalence of cancer screening in older, racially diverse adults: Still screening after all these years. *Archives of Internal Medicine*, 171, 2031–2037. doi:10.1001/archinternmed.2011.570

Cancer Care. (2004). *Working with an older person who has cancer*. Retrieved December 21, 2004, from http://www.cancercare.org/FPEducationalPrograms/FPEducationalPrograms.cfm?ID=3553&c=394.

Centers for Disease Control and Prevention (CDC). (2013). *Gynecologic cancers*. Retrieved January 20, 2014, from http://www.cdc.gov/cancer/gynecologic/index.htm

Deimling, G. T., Kahana, B., Bowmon, K. F., & Schaefer, M. L. (2002). Cancer survivorship and psychological distress in later life. *Psycho-Oncology*, 11, 479–494. doi:10.1002/pon.614

Extermann, M., & Hurria, A. (2007). Comprehensive geriatric assessment for older patients with cancer. *Journal of Clinical Oncology*, 25, 1824–1831. doi:10.1200/JCO.2007.10.6559

Federal Interagency Forum on Aging-Related Statistics. (2010). *Older Americans 2010: Key indicators of well-being*. Retrieved March 20, 2012, from http://www.agingstats.gov/agingstatsdotnet/Main_Site/Data/2010_Documents/Docs/OA_2010.pdf

Gerst-Emerson, K., & Burr, J. A. (2013). The demography of minority aging. In K. Whitfield & T. Baker (Eds.), *Handbook of minority aging* (pp. 387–404). New York, NY: Springer.

Haley, W. E. (2003). Family caregivers of elderly patients with cancer: Understanding and minimizing the burden of care. *Journal of Supportive Oncology*, 1(Suppl. 2), 25–29.

Hart-Johnson, T. A., & Green, C. R. (2010). Physical and psychosocial health in older women with chronic pain: Comparing clusters of clinical and nonclinical samples. *Pain Medicine*, 11, 564–574. doi:10.1111/j.1526-4637.2010.00803.x

Hayat,M.J.,Howlader,N.,Reichman,M.E.,&Edwards,B.K. (2007). Cancer statistics, trends, and multiple primary cancer analyses from the Surveillance, Epidemiology, and End Results (SEER) Program. *Oncologist*, 12, 20–37. doi:10.1634/theoncologist.12-1-20

Herr, L., Coyne, P. J., Manworren, R., McCaffery, M., Merkel, S., Peolosi-Kelly, J., . . . American Society for Pain Management Nursing. (2006). Pain assessment in the nonverbal patient: Position statement with clinical practice recommendations. *Pain Management Nursing*, 17, 44–52.

Herschbach, P., Book, K., Dinkel, A., Berg, P. Waadt, S., Duran, G., . . . Henrich, G. (2010). Evaluation of two group therapies to reduce fear of progression in cancer patients. *Supportive Care in Cancer*, 18, 471–479. doi:10.1007/s00520.009.0696.1

Howlader, N., Noone, A. M., Krapcho, M., Garshell, J., Neyman, N., Altekruse, S. F., . . . Cronin, K. A. (eds). SEER Cancer Statistics Review, 1975-2012, National Cancer Institute. Bethesda, MD, http://seer.cancer.gov/csr/1975_2012/, based on November 2014 SEER data submission, posted to the SEER web site, April 2015.

Hurria, A., Togawa, K., Mobile, S. G., Owusu, C., Keplin, H. D., Gross, C. P., . . . Tew, W. P. (2011). Predicting chemotherapy toxicity in older adults with cancer: A prospective multicenter study. *Journal of Clinical Oncology*, 29, 3457–3465. doi:10.1200/JCO.2011.34.7625

Institute of Medicine (IOM). (2007). *Cancer care for the whole patient: Meeting psychosocial health needs*. Washington, DC: National Academy of Science.

Institute of Medicine (IOM). (2013). *Delivering high-quality cancer care: Charting a new course for a system in crisis*. Washington, DC: National Academy of Science.

Jacobsen, P. B., & Jim, H. S. (2008). Psychosocial interventions for anxiety and depression in adult cancer patients: Achievements and challenges. *CA: Cancer Journal for Clinicians*, 58, 214–230. doi:10.3322/CA.2008.0003

Jemal, A., Siegel, R., Ward, E., Murray, T., Xu, J., & Thun, M. J. (2007). Cancer statistics, 2007. *CA: A Cancer Journal for Clinicians*, 57, 43–66.

Jemal, A., Siegel, R., Xu, J., & Ward, E. (2010). Cancer statistics, 2010. *CA: A Cancer Journal for Clinicians*, 60, 277–300. doi:10.3322/caac.20073

Koretz, B., & Reuben, D. B. (2003). Instruments to assess functional status, In C. K. Cassel, R. M. Leipzig, H. J. Cohen, E. B. Larson, & D. E. Meier (Eds.), *Geriatric medicine: An evidence based approach* (4th ed., pp. 185–194), New York, NY: Springer.

Ledesma, D., & Kumano, H. (2009). Mindfulness-based stress reduction and cancer: Meta-analysis. *Psycho-Oncology*, 18, 571–579. doi:10.1002/pon.1400

National Cancer Institute (NCI). (2010). *What you need to know about cancer of the pancreas*. Retrieved September 27, 2013, from http://www.cancer.gov/cancertopics/wyntk/pancreas/page1/AllPages

National Cancer Institute (NCI). (2013a). *Estimated US cancer prevalence counts: Definitions*. Retrieved September 21, 2013, from http://cancercontrol.cancer.gov/ocs/prevalence/definitions.html

National Cancer Institute (NCI). (2013b). *Office of cancer survivorship*. Retrieved September 12, 2013, from http://cancercontrol.cancer.gov/ocs/ocs_factsheet.pdf

National Cancer Institute (NCI). (2013c). *SEER stat fact sheets: All sites*. Retrieved September 21, 2013, from http://seer.cancer.gov/statfacts/html/all.html

National Cancer Institute (NCI). (2013d). *Defining cancer*. Retrieved September 21, 2013, from http://www.cancer.gov/cancertopics/cancerlibrary/what-is-cancer

National Cancer Institute (NCI). (2013e). *Lung cancer prevention*. Retrieved September 27, 2013, from http://www.cancer.gov/cancertopics/pdq/prevention/lung/Patient/page3#Keypoint5

National Cancer Institute (NCI). (2013f). *Harms of smoking and health benefits of quitting*. Retrieved September 27, 2013, from http://www.cancer.gov/cancertopics/factsheet/Tobacco/cessation

National Cancer Institute (NCI). (2013g). *SEER fact stat sheet: Lung and bronchus*. Retrieved September 21, 2013, from http://seer.cancer.gov/statfacts/html/lungb.html

National Cancer Institute (NCI). (2013h). *SEER fact stat sheet: Breast*. Retrieved September 21, 2013, from http://seer.cancer.gov/statfacts/html/breast.html

National Cancer Institute (NCI). (2013i). *SEER fact stat sheet: Prostate*. Retrieved September 21, 2013, from http://seer.cancer.gov/statfacts/html/prost.html

National Cancer Institute (NCI). (2013j). *Treatment options by stage*. Retrieved September 27, 2013, from http://www.cancer.gov/cancertopics/pdq/treatment/prostate/Patient/page5#Section_195

National Cancer Institute (NCI). (2013l). *SEER fact stat sheet: Colon and rectum*. Retrieved September 21, 2013, from http://seer.cancer.gov/statfacts/html/colorect.html

Pentz, M. (2005). Resiliency among older adults with cancer and the importance of social support and spirituality-faith. *Journal of Gerontological Social Work, 44*, 3–22. doi:10.1300/J083v44n03_02

Roland, K. C., Rodriguez, J. L., Patterson, J. R., & Trivers, K. F. (2013). A literature review of the social and psychological needs of ovarian cancer survivors. *Psycho-Oncology, 22*, 2408–2418. doi:10.1002/pon.3322

Sharp, J. W., Blum, D., & Aviv, L. (2004). Elderly men with cancer: Social work interventions with prostate cancer. *Cancer Care*. Retrieved December 21, 2004, from http://www.cancercare.org/FPEducationalPrograms/FPEducationalPrograms.cfm?ID=3251&c=395.

Siegel, R., Naishadham, D., & Jemal, A. (2013). Cancer statistics, 2013. *CA: A Cancer Journal for Clinicians, 63*, 11–30. doi:10.3322/caac.21166

US Preventive Services Task Force (USPSTF). (2008). *Screening for colorectal cancer*. Retrieved on September 21, 2013, from http://www.uspreventiveservicestaskforce.org/uspstf08/colocancer/colors.htm

US Preventive Services Task Force (USPSTF). (2012). *Screening for prostate cancer*. Retrieved on September 27, 2013, from http://www.uspreventiveservicestaskforce.org/prostatecancerscreening/prostatecancerfact.pdf

US Preventive Services Task Force (USPSTF). (2013). *Screening for lung cancer: Draft*. Retrieved on September 27, 2013, from http://www.uspreventiveservicestaskforce.org/draftrec.htm

Warden, V., Hurley, H. C., & Volicer, V. (2003). Development and psychometric evaluation of the pain assessment in advanced dementia (PAINAD) scale. *Journal of the American Medical Directors Association, 4*, 9–15.

According to the US Census Bureau (2010), the number of older adults (aged > 65) in the United States (US) has reached 40.3 million, or 13.0% of the total population. In just 5 years, their number will outnumber children up to 5 years of age and, by 2050, the senior population is projected to double (North & Sinclair, 2012; WHO, 2010). The aging population will continue to increase, which is associated with a considerably increased incidence of chronic diseases, especially age-related cardiovascular disease (CVD). Cardiovascular disease includes a number of conditions such as coronary heart disease (CHD), ischemic attack in the brain (stroke), high blood pressure (HBP, or hypertension), irregular heart beat (arrhythmia), and congestive heart failure (CHF). Correspondingly, the nation's healthcare spending is projected to increase by 25% due to shifts in chronic diseases and aging (Centers for Disease Control [CDC] & Merck, 2007). Social workers must enhance their knowledge of CVD to improve their practice with the elderly. This chapter presents the immense impact of age-related CVD on society and disadvantaged populations, its important mental health comorbidity, and recommendations for social work practice.

CARDIOVASCULAR DISEASES IN AN AGING SOCIETY

In the US, CHD, stroke, and HBP are among the top 15 reasons for disability, with an estimated $45 million in costs for Americans (CDC, 2012). Age is a primary risk factor for CVD, as 42.2 million elderly have one or more types of this chronic disease (Schiller, Lucas, & Peregoy, 2011). An estimated 70% of the 60–79 age group has some chronic form of CVD (Kochanek, et al., 2012). The incidence increases with age as 83% of men and 87% of women have CVD in the 80+ age group (American Heart Association [AHA], 2013). The elderly CVD population is more likely to use social services provided by social workers and other providers (e.g., rehabilitation) than their younger counterparts.

Cardiovascular disease is the number one killer of all American subpopulations, irrespective of gender and race/ethnicity (AHA, 2013). Since 1900 (except 1918), CVD accounted for more deaths than any other major cause of death in the United States. In 2009, CVD accounted for 1 of every 3 deaths or 32.3% (787,931) of all 2,437,163 deaths. The most critical age

AMY L. AI

CARA PAPPAS

Older Adults with Cardiovascular Diseases

32

for CVD-related death is 75 and older, during which 66% of all CVD deaths occur. Coronary heart disease is one of the deadliest forms of CVD in that more than half of all cardiac events are the result of CHD in Americans age 75 and older. An estimated 80% of people who die from CHD are older than 65 years old, and over half (55% men, 64% women) have no previous symptoms (AHA, 2013).

Approximately every 44 seconds, an American will have a heart attack or myocardial infarction (MI), a common CHD outcome, and 15% will not survive (AHA, 2013). However, the mortality rate from sudden cardiac death has decreased due to medical and surgical treatment advances. Dracup et al. (2008) showed improved survival rates with a MI, if treatment begins within the first hour. Unfortunately, if one survives a heart attack, there is still a chance of mortality in the first year. People with a history of an MI, are four to six times more at risk of experiencing sudden death, compared with the general population (AHA, 2013).

Congestive heart failure is a common, progressive CVD in the elderly resulting in poor health outcomes and one of the most costly diagnoses (Annema, Luttik, & Jaarsma, 2009). Over 1 million patients are hospitalized with CHF per year, costing Medicare more than $17 billion (Rosamond et al., 2008). At least 50% of those patients will be readmitted to the hospital within 6 months (Chun et al., 2012; Joynt, Orav, & Jha, 2011). Most CHF patients have a history of hypertension, or HBP, as well, and by 2030, the prevalence of progressing to CHF will increase by 25% along with a 120% increase in costs (AHA, 2013).

High blood pressure is the most prevalent form of CVD, affecting both elderly women (57%) and men (54%; Federal Interagency Forum on Aging-Related Statistics, 2010; McDonald, Hertz, Unger, & Lustik, 2009). One of the worst consequences of HBP is stroke, a leading cause of serious long-term disability in the United States (AHA, 2013). Stroke can have a devastating impact on elderly patients and their families, resulting in longer hospital stays, disability requiring assisted living or nursing home placement, and increased risk of mortality (Russo, Felzani, & Marini, 2011; Saposnik & Black, 2009). The estimated stroke prevalence is 6% for Americans aged between 60 and 79 years and increases to approximately 13% after the age of 80 (AHA, 2013). Social workers must be aware that there are considerable CVD disparities in racial/ethnic minority groups in the United States, especially for HBP and the top disabling

condition, stroke (Ai & Pappas, under review). For example, Blacks (4.6 per 1,000 persons) lead in CHF incidence, followed by Hispanics (3.5) (AHA, 2013). Hypertension is the leading health problem disproportionately affecting Blacks (AHA, 2013). In addition, strokes affect minorities at a greater incidence (Blacks at 3.9% and American Indians/Alaska Natives at 5.9%) and are more deadly for these minorities when compared with Whites (AHA, 2013).

THE MENTAL HEALTH COMORBIDITY OF CARDIOVASCULAR DISEASE

Traditional CVD risk factors have included age, gender, family history, lifestyle, and medical comorbidities. A growing body of studies, however, has associated psychological factors with CVD recurrence and mortality (Pan, Sun, Okereke, Rexrode, & Hu, 2011; Rutledge, Reis, Linke, Greenberg, & Mills, 2006; Yusuf et al., 2004). Depression, in particular, has shown to be a reliable predictor of poor short- and long-term health outcomes in CVD patients (Pan et al., 2011; Whooley et al., 2008). Over 100 studies have reported a coexisting prevalence of depression in 20% to 35% of CHD patients (Lichtman et al., 2008). In general, among older adults with CVD, an estimated one out of every five patients has depression (Albus, 2010). Frasure-Smith and Lespérance (2006) found depression occurring three times more often in patients who have had an acute MI than in the general population. A meta-analysis linked depression with CHD-related mortality, especially 3 years after an initial assessment (Barth, Schumacher, & Herrmann-Lingen, 2004), and with post-MI mortality and CV events (van Melle et al., 2004).

Anxiety disorders have shown a positive correlation with risk, progression, or recurrence of CVD (Shibeshi, Young-Xu, & Blatt, 2007; Thurston, Rewak, & Kubzansky, 2013). In a German study, symptoms of anxiety were a strong predictor for subsequent adverse cardiovascular events (Rothenbacher, Hahmann, Wust, Koenig, & Brenner, 2007). In another study, anxiety was identified among one-third of 913 unstable angina (UA) and MI patients and considered persistent in 50% of the identified cases (Grace, Abbey, Irvine, Shnek, & Stewart, 2004). Further, among forms of anxiety disorders (American Psychiatric Association, 2013), clinical studies have related panic, generalized, and phobic disorder with poor prognosis among patients with CHD (Ai, Rollman, & Berger, 2010; Rothenbacher et al., 2007). Of CHF patients, 38%–70% showed some forms of anxiety; however, if CHF symptoms such as shortness of breath or signs of fluid overload were present, the anxiety levels reported were 60% higher than those of asymptomatic patients.

Recent research reported that combined anxiety and depressive symptoms increased the risk of CVD patients experiencing a stroke or cerebrovascular death by 50%–70%, compared with those who had no preexisting history of CVD (Hamer, Kivimaki, Stamatakis, & Batty, 2012). However, others showed no positive correlation between chronic anxiety disorders and risk of stroke incidence (Surtees, Wainwright, Luben, Wareham, & Beingham, 2008). Levels of postoperative depression and anxiety were highly correlated, while both predicted their levels even 2.5 years following open-heart surgery (Ai, Ladd, et al., 2010). Evidence suggests that anxiety has a negative impact on prognosis in CHD patients, independent of depression (Rothenbacher et al., 2007; Shibeshi et al., 2007). Nevertheless, the role of anxiety as a causal risk factor remains inconclusive, and the American Heart Association has thus only recommended routine depression screening for all CHD patients (Lichtman et al., 2008).

Mental health symptoms also manifest in the process of and affect the outcomes of open-heart surgery treatments for advanced heart diseases. Among patients undergoing cardiac surgery, the incidence of depression varies among studies between 7.5% and 47% preoperatively and 19% and 61% postoperatively (Pignay-Demaria, Lesperance, Demaria, Frasure-Smith, & Perrault, 2003). Increased feelings of anxiety continue throughout the inpatient operative course (McKenzie, Simpson, & Stewart, 2010). Reported more often by women than by men (Hunt-Shanks, Blanchard, & Reid, 2009), depression symptom levels remained stable before and after surgery (Pignay-Demaria et al., 2003) and predicted short-term postoperative global functioning and mental fatigue (Ai, Peterson, Bolling, & Rodgers, 2006; Ai, Peterson, et al., 2007). Anxiety has been associated with incidents of postoperative pain (DiMattio & Tulman, 2003; Utriyaprasit & Moore, 2005), less long-term relief of cardiac symptoms, increased risk of hospital readmissions (Oxlad, Stubberfield, Stuklis, Edwards, & Wade, 2006), and poorer quality of life (Pignay-Demaria et al., 2003) in patients undergoing such procedures. Patients

with continued postoperative anxiety have worse long-term psychological outcomes (Boudrez & De Backer, 2001; Gallagher, McKinely, & Dracup, 2003).

For middle-aged and older patients, coronary artery bypass graft (CABG) is the most common (~500,000 per year; AHA, 2013) open-heart surgical procedure, but it is also a stressful event for patients and their families. Although cardiac surgery can save lives and improve cardiac function, all patients must be fully informed before the operation about related side effects and risks (Ai, Hopp, Tice, & Koenig, 2013). An earlier study found an inverse relationship between age and preoperative distress in cardiac surgery patients (Plach, Napholz, & Kelber, 2003). A new finding, however, shows no age influence on either depression or anxiety 2.5 years postoperatively, when race and marital status were controlled for (Ai, Ladd, et al., 2010). Research has also documented that perioperative depressive symptoms occurred in 25% of 963 patients who underwent CABG and contributed to impaired functional status (Mallik et al., 2005).

To date, the link between mental health symptoms and CVDs does not point to a clear direction of causality (Ai, Rollman, et al., 2010; Mosovich et al., 2008). Interdisciplinary research has now focused more on multiple psychophysiological pathways between mental and cardiac health and mechanisms in these associations. These include health-related behaviors, stress, negative emotions (e.g., anger, hostility), autonomic nervous system regulation, platelet activation, hypothalamic-pituitary-adrenal axis activity, and inflammatory processes (Ai, Appel, & Pasic, 2008). Studies have linked hostility and/or anger with increased carotid arterial stiffness in older adults (Anderson, Metter, Hougaku, & Najjar, 2006), ischemia syndrome and increased CHD events in women undergoing angiograph (Krantz, Olson, Francis, & Phankao, 2006; Olson et al., 2005), subclinical atherosclerosis in low-socioeconomic-status individuals (Merjonen et al., 2008), and stroke (Williams, Nieto, Sanford, Couper, & Tyroler, 2002). Behavioral scientists have begun to unfold the interplay among stressors, negative emotions, and biophysiological biomarkers between external challenges and CVDs (Ai et al., 2008). Preoperative stress-sensitive biomarkers predicted negative emotions and hospital stay after surgery (Ai, Hall, et al., 2012; Ai, Lee, & Kabbie, 2014). Contrary to the recent evidence, the influence of psychosocial stressors and mental health on cardiac disease remains underrecognized in healthcare, thereby signifying the importance of interdisciplinary approaches to effectively addressing CVD related mental health issues.

SOCIAL WORK ASSESSMENT AND INTERVENTION WITH CARDIOVASCULAR DISEASE

Without an identified "cure," the key to the prognosis, functioning, and the quality of life in CVD patients with mental health symptoms may lie in the appropriate multidisciplinary assessment and disease management. At the micro level, using standardized measurements for both symptoms and psychosocial well-being can enhance comprehensive evaluation and help gauge patients' perceptions of their health status. Ai, Rollman, et al. (2010) recommended a list of tools for social work assessment of CVDs. These measures include, but are not limited to the following:

- MacNew Heart Disease Health-Related Quality of Life questionnaires (physical limitations, emotional function, and social function, as well as physical signs and symptoms of CVD; Hofer, Lim, Guyatt, & Oldridge, 2004),
- Patient Health Questionnaire (PHQ-9; Kroenke, Spitzer, & Williams, 2001),
- Heart Patients Psychological Questionnaire (subjective well-being, incapacitation, dysphoria, and social inhibition; Erdman, 1982), and
- Minnesota Living with Heart Failure Questionnaire (quality of life; Hunt et al., 2001).

Further, there are other tools to measure stress (Cohen, Kamarck, & Mermelstein, 1983) and negative emotions (Cook & Medley, 1997). These tools enable social workers to capture the comprehensive impacts of CVDs from the patient's perspective as an effective care-team member. The whole-person oriented assessment can position the social worker in readiness for an effective action plan between the patient and the care team to address multilevel needs through a multidisciplinary intervention. Additionally, to improve care outcomes, it is essential for providers to improve management and organizational design of care based on team support (Thombs et al., 2008). The chronic care model (CCM), proposed by Wagner et al. (2001), is an evidence-based guideline for giving high-quality chronic disease care for patients. This is accomplished through the healthcare system including community, self-management support, delivery system design, decision support, and clinical information (also see Ai, Rollman, et al., 2010). A meta-analysis of 37 programs, involving 12,355 primary care patients with an effect size of 0.25 (95% confidence interval: 0.18–0.32), have demonstrated the effectiveness of this model for improving care outcomes of chronic conditions (Gilbody, Bower, Fletcher, Richards, & Sutton, 2006) at a lower total cost of care (Simon et al., 2007). Such effectiveness has been supported by evidence gathered in cardiac patients (Rollman et al., 2009).

Social workers should also understand psychosocial protectors. Social support, adaptive coping, positive faith factors, and life-style modification may improve symptomatology and well-being (Ai, Park, Huang, Rodgers, & Tice, 2007; Hall, 2007; Hartman-Shea, Hahn, Kraus, Cordts, & Sevransky, 2011; McCormick, Engelberg, & Curtis, 2007; Pirraglia, Peterson, Williams-Russo, Gorkin, & Charlson, 1999; Sykes, Hanley, Boyle, & Higginson, 2000). Perceived personal control was related to less risk of a new cardiac event following the first percutaneous transluminal coronary angioplasty (PTCA) (Helgeson & Fritz, 1999) and, more recently, to eudaemonic well-being (e.g., greater spiritual relatedness and vitality) of cardiac surgery patients (Ai, Hopp, et al., 2013; Ai, Wink, & Shearers, 2012). A study has linked hope with the survival advantage of stroke patients (Lewis, Dennis, O'Rourke, & Sharpe, 2001). Preoperative high hope also predicted less anxiety 2.5 years after open-heart surgery (Ai, Ladd, et al., 2010). In open-heart surgery patients, social involvement, social support, and comfort in religion were significant predictors of low mortality (Oxman, Freeman, & Manheimer, 1995) and postoperative mental health symptoms (Ai, Peterson, et al., 2007).

Regarding the motivating function of spirituality among adults with heart conditions, many cultural legacies have related the heart to the mind and spirituality. English physician William Harvey (1578–1657), in 1628 the first in the West to correctly describe the systemic circulation and the physical function of the heart, assumed a connection between the heart and the mind (e.g., a sense of pleasure, hope, or fear). French philosopher Blaise Pascal in his famous *Pensées* stated: "The heart has its reasons which reason does not know" (cited by Ai et al., 2008). An American poet, Henry Wadsworth Longfellow, wrote:

> The heart hath its own memory like the mind,
> And in it are enshrined
> The precious keepsakes, into which is wrought
> The giver's loving thought. (cited by Ai, 1996)

In Asian medicine, the heart is highly sensitive to abrupt emotional stress; it was believed to be "an organ of the mind" (Ai et al., 2008). Follow-up studies showed the contribution of prayer coping to postoperative mental health at 1 year (Ai, Dunkle, Peterson, & Bolling, 1998) and to less depression or to high vitality at 2.5 years after cardiac surgery (Ai, Ladd, et al., 2010; Ai, Wink, et al., 2012).

The benefit is not limited to traditional faiths. Feeling reverence in sacred secular contexts predicted fewer complications and shorter hospitalization following cardiac surgery (Ai, Wink, et al., 2012; Ai et al., 2009). This fact suggests the need to be attentive to spiritual diversity in patients with varied cultural backgrounds and to the underlying mechanisms, such as spirituality-based positive emotions. Given the evident positive effect of spirituality in cardiac care and in minority cultures, social workers could mobilize spiritual resources to better address existential needs of older CVD patients. They should help patients to identify their inner strengths, such as faith, deepest values, willpower, hope, and positive emotions/attitudes in their coping with difficulties in the cardiac disease process (Ai et al., 2008; Anandarajah & Hight, 2001). Tools for measurement of this strength perspective include, but are not limited to the following:

- Hope (Snyder et al., 1991),
- Post-traumatic growth (Tedeschi & Calhoun, 1996),
- Using prayer for coping (Ai, Peterson, Bolling, & Koenig, 2002),
- Perceived spiritual support with diverse faiths under the domain of eudaemonic well-being (Ai, Tice, Peterson, & Huang, 2005; Ai, Hopp, et al., 2013; Ai, Wink, et al., 2009).

Spirituality-relevant intervention is especially important for African Americans as part of their cultural strengths (Ai, Lemieux, et al., 2013; Williamson & Kautz, 2009). Such culturally appropriate approaches (e.g., ceremonies and rituals) can also bring about positive influences for Native American patients with cardiac problems and other related health concerns (Hodge & Limb, 2010; Kalenderian, et al., 2009).

Furthermore, stress management is an important tool for social work intervention. Stress is a known cardiac risk factor and has gained increasing attention in recent years (Mosovich et al., 2008). Stress can be classified as work-related stress, financial stress, subacute life stress, and acute stress. Socioeconomic stressors, commonly faced by underserved minorities, can trigger negative emotions, a predictor for poor cardiac health (Merjonen et al., 2008). Researchers also pointed to the lack of skills for managing social stressors as a risk factor for CVDs (Mosovich et al., 2008). Blacks with low socioeconomic status (financial stress) often use high-effort coping styles to meet stressful demands (also called "John Henryism," see Wikipedia), which in turn predicted CVDs and negative emotional and physiological arousal (Whitfield et al., 2006). Integrative therapies (tai chi, yoga, qigong, and mindfulness types of meditation) from Eastern cultural traditions are now being investigated in CVD patients as effective stress-management tools. These "soft" approaches can be considered as part of social work interventions with CVD patients who are experiencing stress but may not be physically capable of Western-style exercise.

In addition, gerontological social workers should engage in the promotion of health behaviors that can prevent the CVD-related functional declination, disability, and fatality. Adopting healthier behaviors, such as regular physical activity, eating a healthy diet, quitting tobacco, and promoting regular health screenings can dramatically reduce a person's CVD risk (AHA, 2013; CDC & Merck, 2007). Nonadherence in HBP, a negative health behavior, is associated with minority status and related factors (e.g., SES, stress/job strain, low access to care), in addition to lifestyle-diet and BMI (Bosworth et al., 2006; Bosworth et al., 2008; Minor, Wofford, & Wyatt, 2008). This should be an educational component for social work training. For effective psychosocial prevention, risks such as obesity, physical inactivity, smoking, chemical dependency, and abuse or neglect must also be addressed via promotion of healthy lifestyles and exercise.

Finally, as team members, gerontological social workers may need to educate older patients and other healthcare professionals about the importance of a contextual biopsychosocial-spiritual approach to cardiac care. The integration of culturally sensitive clinical models of care, with awareness of structural, political, and economic disparities and advocacy for equal access to care, is a challenge to which we must rise in conventional medical care to promote the quality of life for cardiac patients (American Geriatrics Society, Geriatrics Interdisciplinary Advisory Group, 2006; Simons, Bonifas, & Gammonley, 2011).

ACKNOWLEDGMENT

The cardiac study of Amy L. Ai was supported by National Institute on Aging Grant 1 RO3 AGO 15686-01, National Center for Complementary and Alternative Medicine Grant P50 AT00011, a grant from the John Templeton Foundation, and the Hartford Geriatric Faculty Scholars Program. The opinions expressed in this chapter are those of the authors and do not necessarily reflect the views of these organizations.

REFERENCES

Ai, A. L. (1996). Psychosocial adjustment and health care practices following coronary artery bypass surgery (CABG). *Dissertation Abstracts International: Section B: The Sciences and Engineering, 57*, 4078.

Ai, A. L., Appel, H., & Pasic, J. (2008). Mental health comorbidity in cardiovascular disease: Implications for interdisciplinary intervention. In L. Sher (Ed.), *Psychological factors and cardiovascular disorders: The role of psychiatric pathology and maladaptive personality features* (pp. 311–338). Hauppau, NY: Nova Science.

Ai, A. L., Dunkle, R. E., Peterson, C., & Bolling, S. F. (1998). The role of private prayer in psychosocial recovery among midlife and aged patients following cardiac surgery. *The Gerontologist, 38*, 591–601.

Ai, A. L., Hall, D., & Bolling, S. F. (2012). Interleukin-6 and hospital length of stay after open-heart surgery. *Biological Psychiatry and Psychopharmacology, 14*, 79–82.

Ai, L. A., Hopp, F., Tice, T. N., & Koenig, H. (2013). Enhanced existential relationship in light of eudaemonic tradition and religious coping of middle-aged and older cardiac patients. *Journal of Health Psychology, 18*, 368–382.

Ai, A. L., Ladd, K. L., Peterson, C., Cook, C., Shearer, M., & Koenig, H. G. (2010). Long-term adjustment after surviving open-heart surgery: The effect of using prayer for coping replicated in a prospective design. *The Gerontologists, 50*, 798–809.

Ai, A. L., Lee, K., & Kabbie, M. (2014). Body affects mind? Preoperative biological predictors for postoperative psychiatric symptoms in cardiac patients. *Journal of Behavioral Medicine, 37*, 289–299.

Ai, A. L., Lemieux, C., Richardson, R., Tice, T. N., Plummer, C., Huang, B., & Ellison, C. (2013). Character strengths and deep connections: Spiritual-secular pathways to resilience among black and white H-KR volunteers. *Journal for Scientific Study of Religion, 52*, 537–556.

Ai, L. A., & Pappas, C. (under review). Aging and health disparities in relation to cardiovascular diseases: Endorsing social-behavioral care. Manuscript under review.

Ai, A. L., Park, C., Huang, B., Rodgers, W., & Tice, T. N. (2007). Psychosocial mediation of religious coping: A prospective study of short-term psychological distress after cardiac surgery. *Personality and Social Psychology Bulletin, 33*, 867–882.

Ai, A. L., Peterson, C., Bolling, S. F., & Koenig, H. (2002). Private prayer and optimism in middle-aged and older patients awaiting cardiac surgery. *The Gerontologist, 42*, 70–81.

Ai, A. L., Peterson, C., Bolling, S. F., & Rodgers, W. (2006). Depression, faith-based coping, and short-term postoperative global functioning in adult and older patients undergoing cardiac surgery. *Journal of Psychosomatic Research, 60*, 21–28.

Ai, A. L., Peterson, C., Tice, T. N., Huang, B., Rodgers, W., & Bolling, S. F. (2007). The influence of prayer coping on mental health among cardiac surgery patients: The role of optimism and acute distress. *Journal of Health Psychology, 12*, 580–596.

Ai, A. L., Rollman, B. L., & Berger, C. S. (2010). Co-morbid mental health symptoms and heart diseases: Can health care and mental health care professionals collaboratively improve the assessment and management? *Health and Social Work, 35*, 27–38.

Ai, A. L., Tice, T. N., Peterson, C., & Huang, B. (2005). Prayers, spiritual support, and positive attitudes in coping with the 9-11 national crisis. *Journal of Personality, 73*, 763–792.

Ai, L. A., Wink, P., & Shearers, M. (2012). Fatigue of survivors following cardiac surgery: Positive influences of preoperative prayer coping. *British Journal of Health Psychology, 17*, 724–742.

Ai, A. L., Wink, P., Tice, T. N., Bolling, S. F., Wasin, A., & Shearer, M. (2009). Prayer and reverence in naturalistic, aesthetic, and socio-moral contexts predicted fewer complications following coronary artery bypass. *Journal of Behavioral Medicine, 32*, 570–581.

Albus, C. (2010). Psychological and social factors in coronary heart disease. *Annals in Medicine, 42,* 487–494.

American Geriatrics Society, Geriatrics Interdisciplinary Advisory Group. (2006). Interdisciplinary care for older adults with complex needs: American Geriatrics Society position statement. *Journal of the American Geriatrics Society, 54,* 849–852.

American Heart Association (AHA). (2013). Heart disease and stroke statistics-2013 update: A report from the American heart association. *Circulation, 127,* e6–e245.

American Psychiatric Association. (2013). *Diagnostic and statistical manual of mental disorders* (5th ed.). Washington, DC: Author.

Anandarajah, G., & Hight, E. (2001). Spirituality and medical practice: Using the HOPE questions as a practical tool for spiritual assessment. *American Academy of Family Physicians, 63,* 81–89.

Anderson, D. E., Metter, E. J., Hougaku, H., & Najjar, S. S. (2006). Suppressed anger is associated with increased carotid arterial stiffness in older adults. *American Journal of Hypertension, 19,* 1129–1134.

Annema, C., Luttik, M. L., & Jaarsma, T. (2009). Reasons for readmission in heart failure: Perspectives of patients, caregivers, cardiologists, and heart failure nurses. *Heart and Lung: The Journal of Acute and Critical Care, 38,* 427–434.

Barth, J., Schumacher, M., & Herrmann-Lingen, C. (2004). Depression as a risk factor for mortality in patients with coronary heart disease: A meta-analysis. *Psychosomatic Medicine, 66,* 802–813.

Bosworth, H. B., Dudley, T., Olsen, M. K., Viols, C. I., Powers, B., & Goldstein, M. K. (2006). Racial differences in blood pressure control: Potential explanatory factors. *American Journal of Medicine, 119,* 9–15.

Bosworth, H. B., Olsen, M. K., Neary, A., Orr, M., Grubber, J., & Svetkey, L. (2008). Take Control of Your Blood pressure (TCYB) study: A multifactorial tailored behavioral and educational intervention for achieving blood pressure control. *Patient Education/ Counseling, 70,* 338–347.

Boudrez, H., & De Backer, G. (2001). Psychological status and the role of coping style after coronary artery bypass graft surgery: Results of a prospective study. *Quality of Life Research, 10,* 37–47.

Centers for Disease Control and Prevention (CDC). (2012). Prevalence of stroke: United States, 2006–2010. *Morbidity Mortality Weekly Report, 61,* 379–382.

Centers for Disease Control and Prevention (CDC) and the Merck Company Foundation. (2007). *The state of aging and health in America.* Whitehouse Station, NJ: Merck Company Foundation.

Chun, S., Tu, J. V., Wijeysundera, H. C., Austin, P. C., Wang, X., Levy, D., & Lee, D. S. (2012). Lifetime analysis of hospitalizations and survival of patients newly-admitted with heart failure. *Circulation: Heart Failure, 5,* 414–421.

Cohen, S., Kamarck, T., & Mermelstein, R. A. (1983). Global measure of perceived stress. *Journal of Health and Social Behaviors, 24,* 385–396.

Cook, W. W., & Medley, D. M. (1997). Proposed hostility and pharisaic-virtue scales for the MMPI. *Journal of Applied Psychology, 38,* 414–418.

DiMattio, M. J. K., & Tulman, L. (2003). A longitudinal study of functional status and correlates following coronary artery bypass graft surgery in women. *Nursing Research, 52,* 98–107.

Dracup, K., McKinley, S., Doering, L. V., Riegel, B., Meischke, H., Moser, D. K., . . . Paul, S. M. (2008). Acute coronary syndrome: What do patients know? *Archives in Internal Medicine, 168,* 1049–1054.

Erdman, R. A. M. (1982). Medische Psychologische Vragenlijst voor Hartpatiënten [Medical psychological questionnaire for cardiac patients]. Lisse: Swets en Zeitlinger.

Federal Interagency Forum on Aging-Related Statistics. (2010). *Older Americans 2010: Key Indicators of Well-Being.* Washington, DC: US Government Printing Office.

Frasure-Smith, N., & Lespérance, F. (2006). Depression and anxiety as predictors of 2-year cardiac events in patients with stable coronary artery disease. *Archives of General Psychiatry, 65,* 62e–71.

Gallagher, R., McKinely, S., & Dracup, K. (2003). Effects of a telephone counseling intervention on psychosocial adjustment in women following a cardiac event. *Heart and Lung, 32,* 79–87.

Gilbody, S., Bower, P., Fletcher, J., Richards, D., & Sutton, A. J. (2006). Collaborative care for depression: A cumulative meta-analysis and review of longer-term outcomes. *Archives in Internal Medicine, 166,* 2314–2321.

Grace, S. L., Abbey, S. E., Irvine, J., Shnek, Z. M., & Stewart, D. E. (2004). Prospective examination of anxiety persistence and its relationship to cardiac symptoms and recurrent cardiac events. *Psychotherapy and Psychosomatics, 73,* 344–352.

Hall, N. (2007). We care don't we? *Social Work in Health Care, 44,* 55–72.

Hamer, M., Kivimaki, M., Stamatakis, E., & Batty, G. D. (2012). Psychological distress as a risk factor for death from cerebrovascular disease. *Canadian Medical Association Journal, 184,* 1461–1466.

Hartman-Shea, K., Hahn, A. P., Kraus, J. F., Cordts, G., & Sevransky, J. (2011). The role of the social worker in the adult critical care unit: A systematic review of the literature. *Social Work in Health Care, 50*, 143–157.

Helgeson, V. S., & Fritz, H. L. (1999). Cognitive adaptation as a predictor of new coronary events after percutaneous transluminal coronary angioplasty. *Psychosomatic Medicine, 61*, 488–495.

Hodge, D. R., & Limb, G. E. (2010). A Native American perspective on spiritual assessment: The strengths and limitations of a complementary set of assessment tools. *Health and Social Work, 35*, 121–131.

Hofer, S., Lim, L. Guyatt, G., & Oldridge, N. (2004). The MacNew heart disease health-related quality of life instrument: A summary. *Health and Quality of Life Outcomes, 2*, 1–8.

Hunt, S. A., Baker, D. W., Chin, M. H., Cinquegrani, M. P., Feldman, A. M., Francis, G. S., . . . Smith, S. C. (2001). ACC/AHA guidelines for the evaluation and management of chronic heart failure in the adult: Executive summary. *Circulation, 104*, 2996–3007.

Hunt-Shanks, T., Blanchard, C., & Reid, R. D. (2009). Gender differences in cardiac patients: A longitudinal investigation of exercise, autonomic anxiety, negative affect and depression. *Psychology, Health and Medicine, 14*, 375–385.

Joynt, K. E., Orav, E. J., & Jha, A. K. (2011). Patient race, site of care, and 30-day readmission rates among elderly Americans. *JAMA, 305*, 675–681.

Kalenderian, E., Pegus, C., Francis, C., Goodwin, N., Jacques, H. S., & Lasa, D. (2009). Cardiovascular disease urban intervention: Baseline activities and findings. *Journal of Community Health, 34*, 282–287.

Kochanek, K, Xu, J., Murphy, S., Minino, A., & Kung, H. (2012). *Deaths: Final data for 2009*. National Vital Statistics Reports, 60, 1–117. Hyattsville, MD: National Center for Health Statistics. http://www.cdc.gov/nchs/data/nvsr60/nvsr60_03.pdf

Krantz, D. S., Olson, M. B., Francis, J. L., & Phankao, C. (2006). Anger, hostility, and cardiac symptoms in women with suspected coronary artery disease: The Women's Ischemia Syndrome Evaluation (WISE) study. *Journal of Women's Health, 15*, 1214–1223.

Kroenke, K., Spitzer, R. L., & Williams, J. B. (2001). The PHQ-9: Validity of a brief depression severity measure. *Journal of General Internal Medicine, 16*, 606–613.

Lewis, S. C., Dennis, M. S., O'Rourke, S. J., & Sharpe, M. (2001). Negative attitudes among short-term stroke survivors predict worse long-term survival. *Stroke, 32*, 1640–1645.

Lichtman, J. H., Bigger, J. T., Jr., Blumenthal, J. A., Frasure-Smith, N., Kaufmann, P. G., Lesperance, F., . . . Froelicher, E. S. (2008). Depression and coronary heart disease: Recommendations for screening, referral, and treatment: A science advisory from the American Heart Association Prevention Committee of the Council on Cardiovascular Nursing, Council on Clinical Cardiology, Council on Epidemiology and Prevention, and Interdisciplinary Council on Quality of Care and Outcomes Research: Endorsed by the American Psychiatric Association. *Circulation, 118*, 1768e–1775.

Mallik, S., Krumholz, H. M., Lin, Z. Q., Kasl, S. V., Mattera, J. A., . . . Vaccarino, V. (2005). Patients with depressive symptoms have lower health status benefits after coronary artery bypass surgery. *Circulation, 111*, 271–277.

McCormick, A. J., Engelberg, R., & Curtis, J. R. (2007). Social workers in palliative care: Assessing activities and barriers in the intensive care unit. *Journal of Palliative Medicine, 10*, 929–937.

McDonald, M., Hertz, R. P., Unger, A. N., & Lustik, M. B. (2009). Prevalence, awareness, and management of hypertension, dyslipidemia, and diabetes among United States adults aged 65 and older. *Journal of Gerontology Series A: Biological Sciences and Medical Sciences, 64A*, 256–263.

McKenzie, L. H., Simpson, J., & Stewart, M. (2010). A systematic review of pre-operative predictors of post-operative depression and anxiety in individuals who have undergone coronary artery bypass graft surgery. *Psychology, Health and Medicine, 15*, 74–93.

Merjonen, P., Pulkki-Raback, L., Puttonen, S., Keskivaara, P., Juonala, M., Telama, R., . . . Keltikangas-Jarvinen, L. (2008). Anger is associated with subclinical atherosclerosis in low SES but not in higher SES men and women: The cardiovascular risk in young Finns study. *Journal in Behavioral Medicine, 31*, 35–44.

Minor, D., Wofford, M., & Wyatt, S. B. (2008). Does socioeconomic status affect blood pressure goal achievement? *Hypertension Report, 10*, 390–397.

Mosovich, S. A., Boone, R. T., Reichenberg, A., Bansilal, S., Shaffer, J., Dahlman, K., . . . Farkouh, M. E. (2008). New insights into the link between cardiovascular disease and depression. *International Journal of Clinical Practice, 62*, 423–432.

North, B. J., & Sinclair, D. A. (2012). The intersection between aging and cardiovascular disease. *Circulation Research, 110*, 1097–1108.

Olson, M. B., Krantz, D. S., Kelsey, S. F., Pepine, C. J., Sopko, G., Handberg, E., . . . Merz, C. N. B. (2005). Hostility scores are associated with increased risk of cardiovascular events in women undergoing coronary angiography: A report from the

NHLBI-sponsored WISE study. *Psychosomatic Medicine, 67,* 546–552.

Oxlad, M., Stubberfield, J., Stuklis, R., Edwards, J., & Wade, T. D. (2006). Psychological risk factors for cardiac-related hospital readmission within 6 months of coronary artery bypass graft surgery. *Journal of Psychosomatic Research, 61,* 775–781.

Oxman, T. E., Freeman, D. H., & Manheimer, E. D. (1995). Lack of social participation or religious strength and comfort as risk factors for death after cardiac surgery in the elderly. *Psychosomatic Medicine, 57,* 5–15.

Pan, A., Sun, Q., Okereke, O. I., Rexrode, K. M., & Hu, F. B. (2011). Depression and risk of stroke morbidity and mortality: A meta-analysis and systematic review. *JAMA, 306,* 1241–1249.

Pignay-Demaria, V., Lesperance, F., Demaria, R. G., Frasure-Smith, N., & Perrault, L. P. (2003). Depression and anxiety and outcomes of coronary artery bypass surgery. *Annals of Thoracic Surgery, 75,* 314–321.

Pirraglia, P, A., Peterson, J. C., Williams-Russo, P., Gorkin, L., & Charlson, M. E. (1999). Depressive symptomatology in coronary artery bypass graft surgery patients. *International Journal of Geriatric Psychiatry, 14,* 668–680.

Plach, S. K., Napholz, L., & Kelber, S. T. (2003). Depression during early recovery from heart surgery among early middle-age, midlife, and elderly women. *Health Care for Women International, 24,* 327–339.

Rollman, B. L., Belnap, B. H., LeMenager, M. S., Mazumdar, S., Schulberg, H. C., & Reynolds, C. F. (2009). The bypassing the blues treatment protocol: Stepped collaborative care for treating post-CABG depression. *Psychosomatic Medicine, Journal of Biobehavioral Medicine, 71,* 217–230.

Rosamond, W., Flegal, K., Furie, K., Go, A., Greenlund, K., Haase, N., . . . Hong, Y. (2008). Heart disease and stroke statistics–2008 update: A report from the American Heart Association Statistics Committee and Stroke Statistics Subcommittee. *Circulation, 117,* e25–e146.

Rothenbacher, D., Hahmann, H., Wust, B., Koenig, W., & Brenner, H. (2007). Symptoms of anxiety and depression in patients with stable coronary heart disease: Prognostic value and consideration of pathogenetic links. *European Journal of Cardiovascular Preventive Rehabilitation, 14,* 547–554.

Russo, T., Felzani, G., & Marini, C. (2011). Stroke in the very old: A systematic review of studies on incidence, outcome, and resource use. *Journal of Aging Research, 2011,* 108785.

Rutledge, T., Reis, V. A., Linke, S. E., Greenberg, B. H., & Mills, P. J. (2006). Depression in heart failure: A meta-analytic review of prevalence, intervention effects, and associations with clinical outcomes. *Journal of American College of Cardiology, 48,* 1527–1537.

Saposnik, G., & Black, S. (2009). Stroke Outcome Research Canada (SORCan) Working Group. Stroke in the very elderly: Hospital care, case fatality and disposition. *Cerebrovascular Disease, 27,* 537–543.

Schiller, J., Lucas, J., & Peregoy, J. (2011). Summary health statistics for U.S. adults: National Health Interview Survey. *Vital and Health Statistics, 10,* 1–217.

Shibeshi, W. A., Young-Xu, Y., & Blatt, C. M. (2007). Anxiety worsens prognosis in patients with coronary artery disease. *Journal of American College of Cardiology, 49,* 2021–2027.

Simon, G. E., Katon, W. J., Lin, E. H. B., Rutter, C., Manning, W., Von Korff, M., . . . Young, B. A. (2007). Cost-effectiveness of systematic depression treatment among people with diabetes mellitus. *JAMA Psychiatry, 64,* 65–72.

Simons, K., Bonifas, R., & Gammonley, D. (2011). Commitment of licensed social workers to aging practice. *Health and Social Work, 36,* 183–195.

Snyder, C. R., Harris, C., Anderson, J. R., Holleran, S. A., Irving, L. M., Sigmon, S. T., . . . Harney, P. (1991). The will and the ways: Development and validation of an individual-differences measure of hope. *Journal of Personality and Social Psychology, 60,* 570–585.

Surtees, P. G., Wainwright, N. W. J., Luben, R. N., Wareham, N. J., & Beingham, S. A. (2008). Psychological distress, major depressive disorder, and risk of stroke. *Neurology, 70,* 788–794.

Sykes, D. H., Hanley, M., Boyle, D. M., & Higginson, J. D. (2000). Work strain and the post-discharge adjustment of patients following a heart attack. *Psychology and Health, 15,* 609–623.

Tedeschi, R. G., & Calhoun, L. G. (1996). The Posttraumatic Growth Inventory: Measuring the positive legacy of trauma. *Journal of Trauma Stress, 9,* 455–471.

Thombs, B. D., de Jonge, P., Coyne, J. C., Whooley, M. A., Fasure-Smith, N., Mitchell, A. J., . . . Ziegelstein, R. C. (2008). Depression screening and patient outcomes in cardiovascular care: A systematic review. *JAMA, 300,* 2161–2171.

Thurston, R. C., Rewak, M., & Kubzansky, L. D. (2013). An anxious heart: Anxiety and the onset of cardiovascular diseases. *Progress in Cardiovascular Diseases, 55,* 524–537.

US Census Bureau. (2010). *An older and more diverse nation by midcentury.* Retrieved from http://www.census.gov/newsroom/releases/archives/population/cb08-123.html

Utriyaprasit, K., & Moore, S. M. (2005). Recovery symptoms and mood in Thai CABG patients. *Journal of Transcultural Nursing, 16,* 97–106.

van Melle, J. P., de Jonge, P., Spijkerman, T. A., Tijssen, J. G., Ormel, J., van Veldhuisen, D. J., & van den Berg, M. P. (2004). Prognostic association of depression following myocardial infarction with mortality and cardiovascular events: A meta-analysis. *Psychosomatic Medicine, 66,* 814–822.

Wagner, E. H., Austin, B. T., Davis, C., Hindmarsh, M., Schaefer, J., & Bonomi, A. (2001). Improving chronic illness care: Translating evidence into action. *Health Affairs, 20,* 64–78.

Whitfield, K. E., Brandon, D. T., Robinson, E., Bennett, G., Merritt, M., & Edwards, C. (2006). Sources of variability in John Henryism. *Journal of National Medical Association, 98,* 641–647.

Whooley, M. A., de Jonge, P., Vittinghoff, E., Otte, C., Moos, R., Carney, R. M., . . . Browner, W. S. (2008). Depressive symptoms, health behaviors, and risk of cardiovascular events in patients with coronary heart disease. *JAMA, 300,* 2379e–2388.

Wikipedia. (2014). *John Henryism.* Retrieved from http://en.wikipedia.org/wiki/John_Henryism,02/12/2014

Williams, J. E., Nieto, F. J., Sanford, C. P., Couper, D. J., & Tyroler, H. A. (2002). The association between trait anger and incident stroke risk: The atherosclerosis risk in communities (ARIC) study. *Stroke, 33,* 13–20.

Williamson, W., & Kautz, D. D. (2009). "Let's get moving: Let's get praising": Promoting health and hope in an African American church. *Association of Black Nursing Faculty, 20,* 102–105.

World Health Organization. (2010). *Global status report on noncommunicable diseases, 2010.* Geneva, Switzerland: Author.

Yusuf, S., Hawken, S., Ounpuu, S., Dans, T., Avezum, A., Lanas, F., . . . Lisheng, L. (2004). Effect of potentially modifiable risk factors associated with myocardial infarction in 52 countries (INTERHEART study). *Lancet, 364,* 937–952.

RICHARD B. FRANCOEUR
ALICIA M. WILSON

Social Work Practice with Older Adults to Prevent and Control Diabetes and Complications

33

INTRODUCTION

Diabetes, formally referred to as diabetes mellitus, is an international epidemic that has touched the lives of approximately 366 million people across the world, with 25.8 million living in the United States alone (International Diabetes Federation, 2013a; World Health Organization, 2011). According to the Centers for Disease Control and Prevention, 7 million Americans are currently unaware that they are living with the disease, which has led diabetes to join hypertension as a "silent killer" (Centers for Disease Control and Prevention, 2011). While most individuals are able to live and function for many years with the disease, diabetes can take an enormous toll on a person's health and quality of life. This concern is especially critical for the elderly population, as diabetes mellitus in older adults is commonly associated with an increased risk of developing cognitive impairment, kidney disease, bone frailty, depression, dementia, poor vision, slurred speech, and sleep disorders, among other health conditions. These conditions are major obstacles in the treatment and care of adults with diabetes (Araki & Ito, 2003; Cigolle, Langa, Kabeto, Tian, & Blaum, 2007; Edson, Sierra-Johnson, & Curtis, 2009). Currently, diabetes is one of the most prevalent medical conditions affecting the elderly population, with 10.9 million Americans age 65 and older having the disease (Centers for Disease Control and Prevention, 2011).

Diabetes is becoming one of the leading causes of death and disability in the United States. In 2011, the World Health Organization projected that by 2030 diabetes will be the seventh leading cause of death. Without effective prevention and self-care management programs, the burdens of diabetes will continue to increase globally. Given these statistics, it is in the best interest of social workers to become knowledgeable about the impacts of diabetes and its complications in older populations in order to implement effective services for older adults and for their families, friends, and communities that support them. In addition, through psychoeducation interventions and by modeling effective coping strategies, social workers can assist their clients and caregivers in preventing the onset of this debilitating disease and in gaining control after it is diagnosed (Grey, 2000). This chapter highlights some of the risk factors associated with diabetes and explains how social workers can help older adults cope with the challenges triggered by diabetes through interventions such as psychoeducation and self-management classes.

WHAT IS DIABETES?

The American Diabetes Association (ADA, 2012, p. S64) defines diabetes mellitus as "a group of metabolic diseases characterized by hyperglycemia resulting from defects in insulin secretion, insulin action, or both." Type 1 diabetes mellitus (T1DM) accounts for approximately 5% to 10% of all diagnosed cases of diabetes; it is also referred to as insulin-dependent diabetes or juvenile-onset diabetes. Type 2 diabetes mellitus (T2DM) is the most common form of diabetes, accounting for approximately 90% to 95% of all diagnosed cases, and is frequently referred to as noninsulin-dependent diabetes or adult-onset diabetes. Whereas individuals with T1DM need insulin injections to survive, this is not typically true for individuals with T2DM, who can control hyperglycemia through a careful diet, exercise regimen, and oral medication (ADA, 2012). Diabetes mellitus is a complicated condition, with several risk factors that contribute to the development of the condition, including but not limited to, obesity, age, race, and genetic factors (ADA, 2012).

COMPLICATIONS AND RISK FACTORS ASSOCIATED WITH DIABETES

Diabetes and its complications has become one of the major causes of death around the world. In 2011, approximately 4.6 million people between 20 and 79 years of age died from diabetes (International Diabetes Federation, 2013b). There are several complications associated with diabetes that pose major threats to the health and quality of an individual's life, often leading to increasing disability, higher healthcare costs, and mortality (Debono & Cachia, 2007).

The two major types of diabetes complications are categorized as macrovascular and microvascular. Macrovascular complications include cardiovascular disease such as heart attacks, strokes, and peripheral vascular disease. Peripheral vascular disease can lead to bruises or injuries that do not heal and ultimately lead to amputation (Debono & Cachia, 2007). Currently, cardiovascular disease is the primary cause of death for patients living with diabetes (International Diabetes Federation, 2013b). In a 10-year study, researchers learned that diabetic men and women

were two to four times more likely to experience incidence of heart disease than men and women who were not diabetic (Folsom et al., 2003). Within the last 30 years, the number of diabetic women who died from heart and blood vessel diseases increased 23%, compared with the 27% drop in cardiovascular deaths for women without diabetes (ADA, 2013). The correlation of cardiovascular diseases and diabetes was so high that the study concluded healthcare providers of diabetic individuals should manage their health as if they already had coronary heart disease according to recommendations by the National Cholesterol Education Program (Folsom et al., 2003).

Microvascular complications of the smallest blood vessels constitute the second category of medical complications prevalent in older adults with diabetes. Microvascular complications include nervous system damage resulting in painful nerves in the feet, hands, and legs (neuropathy). Renal system damage prevents waste removal, resulting in excess fluid from the bloodstream along with kidney disease (nephropathy) and eye damage (retinopathy). Most microvascular complications can be prevented or managed if the individual is able to control their glycemic levels (Huang, John, & Munshi, 2009). Currently, diabetic retinopathy is the leading cause of blindness in the United States, with 12,000 to 24,000 new cases developing a year (Fong et al., 2004). The strongest predictor for development and progression of retinopathy is the duration of diabetes. Although as many as 21% of individuals with T2DM have retinopathy on initial diagnosis, preventing diabetic retinopathy is possible in older adults with diabetes. Achieving consistent control over the diabetes is one of the most important factors in preventing progression of retinopathy in older adults (Morisaki et al., 1994). While obesity is not a complication, obesity is one of the most important risk factors leading to individuals being diagnosed with T2DM (Ford, Williamson, & Liu, 1997). It is well documented that both obesity and diabetes can contribute to high blood pressure and high cholesterol levels, which often lead to heart disease. As a result, most studies claim older adults with diabetes and obesity are more likely to suffer an early death, which has caused many clinicians to focus on diabetes in obese clients (Carnethon et al., 2012). A recent study reveals a more nuanced understanding, however. Researchers in this study observed the relationship between weight and fatality in 2,625 adults with T2DM; they discovered that when individuals with diabetes were normal weight, they tended to have a greater proportion of body fat to muscle, and these normal-weight individuals had more difficulty metabolizing their sugar and creating insulin (Carnethon et al., 2012). Thus, being overweight predisposes older adults to develop diabetes, but once diabetes is diagnosed, developing and maintaining a higher proportion of muscle to fat is important, which may result in weight gain. This finding suggests a dual focus for social workers: (1) educating older adults who are overweight to prevent the onset of diabetes; and (2) screening older adults diagnosed with diabetes both when obesity is accompanied by low muscle mass and when weight is normal to below normal, to reduce risk for increasing disability and mortality. Since advanced diabetes complications typically present with low weight, such as insulin resistance, which is the main factor for cardiovascular disease, it is important that individuals be consistently measured for insulin sensitivity and fat mass. Social workers can assist in this area by motivating both groups of clients to engage in exercise and exercise programs and to change their eating habits in order to replace fat with muscle, thus either preventing or slowing the development of T2DM.

PSYCHOLOGICAL FACTORS

Diabetes is a lifelong condition that drastically affects the lives not only of the patient but also the patient's family and friends. Like any chronic illness, individuals upon diagnosis are forced to reevaluate their life. It is common for individuals to wonder whether their life will ever be the same. Can they still work or enjoy life as they previously did? The process of understanding how to care for diabetes can cause individuals to become depressed or feel loss of control over their lives (Patterson, Thorne, Crawford, & Tarko, 1999; Wild, Roglic, Green, Sicree, & King, 2004). People with diabetes are two to three times more likely to suffer from depression (Golden et al., 2008). Psychological disorders such as depression correlate with reduced medication compliance, physical activity participation, and consistency of good eating habits. These behaviors and smoking contribute to poor glycemic control, which puts individuals at greater risk for disease related complications and poor health outcomes (Golden et al., 2008; Naik et al., 2012; Petrak et al., 2005). Through counseling and psychoeducation, social workers can help the client and family to accept the diagnosis and learn different ways to cope by sharing their emotional and physical challenges from diabetes (Naik et al., 2012; Robles-Silva, 2008; Schneider et al., 2011).

The following case study portrays the challenges that many clients with diabetes experience and illustrates how behavioral health coaching can assist clients in managing their physical and emotional health.

Daniel, Age 62

Daniel was a disabled Veteran, divorced, and living alone at the time of treatment initiation. At baseline, he reported feeling stuck in daily routines (e.g., poor diet, lack of exercise) that he considered unhealthy as measured using the Patient Health Questionnaire (PHQ-9) a nine-item Likert scale to measure depressive symptoms. Individuals who score 10 or greater have clinically significant depressive symptoms. Daniel also reported problems falling and staying asleep, which interfered with the daytime activities necessary to effectively manage his diabetes. His moderately high baseline markers for HbA1c (8.8) and PHQ-9 were likely a result of these factors. In order to determine whether Daniel's diabetes was under control based on the American Diabetes Association's recommendation of an HbA1c of 7% or less, researchers used the HbA1c test to evaluate his average blood glucose concentration over a 3-month period. Daniel expressed a great deal of stress and worry over potential complications of his condition, especially because several of his family members had experienced diabetes-related complications. Additionally, he found social situations that involved eating to be difficult, given his dietary restrictions, and admitted to occasional interpersonal difficulties caused by low frustration tolerance and poor stress management.

In *assessing* Daniel, his coach recognized lifestyle problems common to uncontrolled diabetes and *advised* that simple lifestyle modifications would make a big difference in overall well-being. While coaches can vary in different agencies, they are often recruited from the mental health field and trained to develop clinical care goals and action plans that support the treatment plan. The dyad (counselor and client) *agreed* to begin with a fitness goal of walking ¼ mile 5–6 days per week, which Daniel successfully increased to 1 mile as he progressed through the program. In addition to addressing physical goal barriers, such as pain from a leg injury that caused sleep problems, Daniel's coach *assisted* him by helping him identify emotional concerns that could impede goal attainment. Daniel became open to practicing relaxation techniques during coaching sessions and established a goal to incorporate them in his daily life. In *arranging* for prolonged goal maintenance, his coach emphasized the need to identify barriers to his goals and encouraged him to share his diabetes experiences with others to help improve his social connections. At the conclusion of the treatment, Daniel realized notable 6-month changes, including moderate yet clinically significant improvement in HbA1c (drop of 0.9 from baseline) and marked reductions in depression (PHQ-9 score improved 14 points) and diabetes distress (PAID score improved 37.5 points) (Naik et al., 2012, pp. 7–8). ▨

———

This narrative is a good example of the issues that social workers confront in their daily practice. Social workers and other members of the multidisciplinary team work directly with clients like Daniel, and they must determine ways to draw on client strengths and relieve or ameliorate their problems. Supervisors assist social workers and counselors who bring questions and insights about possibilities for helping people in these situations, and administrators, program developers, and social policy planners work indirectly with clients facing difficulties from diabetes. These practitioners should come to appreciate and expect that clients with diabetes typically face a range of issues and challenges, such as the ones Daniel presents, which should motivate them to develop, organize, and finance services accordingly.

THE ROLE OF THE SOCIAL WORKER

How should social workers think about the problems presented in Daniel's case? The primary role of the social worker is to explore with elderly clients their understanding of the disease as well as how to best manage the disease. There are several assessments that social workers can use that identify barriers clients face. The Diabetes-Specific Quality of Life Scale (DSQOLS) is a 64-item questionnaire that focuses on treatments goals and perceived burden of diabetes. The Questionnaire on Stress in Patients with Diabetes and the Type 2 Diabetes Symptom Checklist were designed to evaluate the levels of stress and burden

associated with diabetes. Key interview questions are summarized in Table 33.1. For a list of questionnaires used to assess diabetes quality of life and their effectiveness (Polonsky, 2000), visit http://journal.diabetes.org/diabetesspectrum/00v13n1/pg36.htm.

Prior to choosing a questionnaire or asking certain questions, social workers must have a clear understanding of their clients and the barriers that culture may impose. It is essential to understand the learned values and beliefs that make up cultures, as this will explain why some clients often appear resistant when they are not. For example, the literature informs us that in the Hispanic culture individuals rely heavily on family support. As a result, when elderly members lack family support, such as adult children taking them to medical appointments, they are more likely to lack professional care (Beyene, Becker, & Mayen, 2002). A social worker who is aware of this characteristic of Hispanic culture would ask elderly Hispanic clients how they plan on getting to doctor visits. Another example is the belief by most Native Americans that unless diabetes presents with physical symptoms, there should not be concern about having the actual disease (Cavanaugh, Taylor, Keim, Clutter, &

TABLE 33.1 Selected Open and Semistructured Questions

Questions

1. How would you describe your overall health?
2. Where do you seek help if you have health problems?
3. If you do not have insurance where do you seek help?
4. What are the signs and symptoms of diabetes?
5. What do you think causes diabetes?
6. Can diabetes be prevented?
7. How would you know if you had diabetes?
8. Tell me the story of your diabetes?
9. What role do you think stress plays in developing diabetes?
10. Has your diabetes changed how you are able to take care of yourself? How?
11. Once a person has diabetes, how long does it last?
12. Can a person do anything to manage or control diabetes?
13. Have you heard about any ways of managing or controlling diabetes? What are the approaches you have heard about? Have you tried any of these approaches?
14. Thinking about these different ways of managing diabetes, would you say they worked for you or not? Why do you think they worked/didn't work for you? How did they help? How long did they work?
15. How do you know you are taking good care of yourself?
16. How do you believe you could change your health in the future?

TABLE 33.2 Cultural Perceptions of Health and Diabetes Among Different Populations

Native American Populations

- Some Native American men are not concerned with their diagnosis of diabetes unless there is a physical manifestation of the illness (Cavanaugh et al., 2008).
- Several Native American women considered a person to have poor health only if they are unable to perform their daily tasks. If one is able to get around, they are considered pretty healthy (Keim, Taylor, Sparrer, Van Delinder, & Parker, 2004).
- Ojibway, a tribe located in Canada, believe that diabetes is a "white man's sickness" (McLaughlin, 2010).
- Many American Indian tribes believe that by talking about a deformity or disability they may speak it into existence (Pichette, Garrett, Kosciulek, & Rosenthal, 1999).
- American Indian women are responsible for providing meals that satisfy the entire family. If their health requires dietary changes, they find it unacceptable to put their needs above the wants or needs of the family unit, greatly reducing the likelihood of behavior modification (Keim et al., 2004).

African American Populations

- Most African American adults with T2DM do not believe that diabetes is a permanent condition (Calvin et al., 2011).
- African American women who identify as sole caregivers find it extremely hard to manage their stress level, which has a major effect on their self-care of diabetes (McKenzie & Skelly, 2010).
- African Americans with less education have more difficulty engaging in self-monitoring activities (Karter, Ferrara, Darbinian, Ackerson, & Selvy, 2000).
- African American women reported that spirituality is a source of emotional support and a positive influence on their health that contributes to better life satisfaction when dealing with the challenges associated with diabetes (Chin, Polonsky, Thomas, & Nerney, 2000).
- Several African Caribbean participants diagnosed with T2DM expressed mistrust of medications prescribed to treat diabetes as they believe that the medication will induce more harm than good or even cause complications of diabetes (Brown, Avis, & Hubbard, 2007).

Hispanic/Latino Populations

- Many Hispanic clients diagnosed with diabetes tend to hide their disease due to the social stigma surrounding diabetes (Weiler & Crist, 2009).
- There is a strong correlation between a lack of family support and managing diabetes self-care (Hu, Amirehsani, Wallace, & Letvak, 2013).
- Many Hispanic patients expressed they encountered difficulty in changing their dietary habits due to large family gatherings where it is consider rude to refuse food offered by family and friends (Hu, Amirehsani, Wallace, & Letvak, 2013).
- Older Latina women view decline of health as a natural progression of aging. As a result, it is expected in the Latino culture that the family will care for the elderly. When elderly members lack family support, they are more likely to lack professional care (Beyene, Becker, & Mayen, 2002).

Asian American Populations

- The Chinese often encourage family members with diabetes to increase their consumption of cultural foods to strengthen their constitution although it has been reported that these food items contradict medical diabetes diet restrictions (Ho, Chesla, & Chun, 2011).
- In some cultures (e.g., Asian Indians), modesty is highly valued and as such diabetic patients often will not visit healthcare providers unless they are of the same sex (Ananth, 1984).
- One of the biggest inhibitors when accessing medical care is the ability to communicate with medical providers. According to the President's Advisory Commission on Asian Americans and Pacific Islanders, many Vietnamese, Korean, and Chinese American households are linguistically isolated, a classification referring to households in which none of the members 14 years of age or older speak English very well (Kramer, Kwong, Lee, & Chung, 2002).
- Japanese Americans believe that those who retained a more Oriental diet such as rice, tofu, green tea, and fish are less likely to be diagnosed with diabetes (Araki et al., 2012)
- Chinese Americans are largely influenced by Eastern medicine that promotes that disease can be prevented and controlled by balancing one's yin and yang, emphasizing harmony, and maintaining a level of respect (Hoeman, Ku, & Ohi, 1996).

Geraghty, 2008). These beliefs shape how social workers tailor culturally sensitive psychoeducation to specific cultural communities so that community members come to appreciate the seriousness of diabetes and learn about prevention and diabetes symptoms, the importance of healthy living, and following up with doctor visits. This includes culturally relevant foods, as food plays a crucial role in many social and religious functions. As a result, individuals may not be as willing to eliminate or reduce these foods from their diet. In this case it would be helpful if the social worker works with the client to make wise food choices a majority of the time (Tripp-Reimer, Choi, Skemp Kelley, & Enslein, 2001). A brief literature review of cultural perceptions of health and diabetes among different populations can be found in Table 33.2. Finally, the ADA website (www.diabetes.org) is an excellent resource for culturally specific resources written in different languages.

TREATMENT AND PREVENTION

Treatment and prevention teaches older adults with diabetes and family caregivers how to provide self-care and prevent further complications. The social worker aims to enhance the motivation and capacities of clients and family caregivers to manage the diabetes and any co-occurring conditions and to reduce the chances of complications. Through individual, family, or group counseling involving psychoeducation, and psychotherapeutic modalities such as cognitive-behavioral interventions, social workers can assist clients with diabetes change their lifestyle and reduce environmental barriers that contribute to the disease. In this role, social workers can promote healthy eating choices, smoking cessation, physical activity to lose weight and build muscle, and medication management. At the community level, social workers can advocate for more self-management and training classes in nontraditional settings, work with insurance companies, and encourage the community-at-large to support change in their members (Huang, John, & Munshi, 2009; Norris et al., 2002).

One strategy for social work practice is suggested by a study in which clients with diabetes who had the ability to set goals around nutrition, exercise, and glucose monitoring showed greater improvement in their health and work performance (Schneider et al., 2011). Life coaches trained in diabetes care, motivational interviewing, and stages of change helped clients to create short- and long-term goals that were self-driven to empower clients to change (Naik et al., 2012; Schneider et al., 2011). Using motivational interviewing and stages of change during weekly sessions, life coaches helped clients to create SMART goals (i.e., goals that are Specific, Measurable, Attainable, Realistic, and Timed) such as "I will attend the gym for 1 hour each time, 12 times a month." Goals often focused around checking glucose, monitoring meal portions, scheduling and attending doctor visits, exercise, and managing medication. The study concluded that clients who created their goals were more successful, leading to higher satisfaction (Schneider et al., 2011). Social workers, other counselors, and health providers can mutually refer clients with diabetes (e.g., Naik et al., 2012), and with the post-MSW training and certification, some social workers may also serve as life coaches. Social workers, in consultation with these other professionals, can help clients create SMART goals as a plan to overcome barriers and establish supports for preventing or managing diabetes.

When developing different types of treatments, social service agencies must be creative. For hard-to-reach clients, social workers will have to bring culturally sensitive materials to clients in contrast to the traditional route, where clients seek out the information. For example, if a social service agency wanted to educate Caribbean adults with diabetes on how to prevent further complications or about nutrition counseling, social workers could conduct a psychoeducation class on food preparation and portion requirements at a local community center, faith-based organization, or pharmacy (Lenzi & Lipman, 2013; Norris et al., 2002). In the Naik et al. (2012) study, the researchers conducted ten 30- to 45-minute sessions via telephone for a total of 12 weeks. During those sessions participants discussed any barriers that they faced during the week, their next steps, and how they would manage their self-care for the following week. This intervention helped participants such as elderly adults with multiple complications as well as participants who did not have the means to travel or were unwilling to travel to access care. These participants found the intervention to be extremely helpful, with many planning to continue to set goals after the intervention ended in order to take charge of their own health. In another study, coaches used e-mail to assess how participants were meeting their goals, provide tools for clients to update their progress, and schedule daily reminders for tasks such as foot care, exercising, eating wisely, and taking medication (Schneider et al., 2011).

It is recommended that elderly adults should participate in 30–45 minutes of physical activity at least three times a week. Exercise and nutrition are important to improve muscle strength in elderly adults and in creating new habits of reducing or eliminating foods that could increase their chances of cardiovascular disease or high blood pressure. Social workers in agency settings could create programs that involve physical activities or connect with outside agencies that have programs, as well as integrate periodic in-home visits. Daily in-home glucose monitoring is also necessary to stave off risk of dementia, poor vision, and slurred speech (Edson, Sierra-Johnson, & Curtis, 2009). Social workers can send e-mails or text messages, or make phone calls, to help clients get into the habit of attending to medication management and foot care in order to improve diabetes symptoms and reduce glucose sugar levels. While these more concrete factors are important and must be discussed with clients, social workers cannot forget their interrelationships with the psychological complications associated with diabetes. There is mounting evidence that social and emotional support can have positive effects on diabetes care, prevention of complications, and well-being in older adults (Tripp-Reimer et al., 2001). Periodic home visits may be valuable for assessing these interrelationships for individual clients.

Social workers engaging with older adults and their caregivers need to develop more culturally sensitive written materials that incorporate client values and belief systems. Social workers should also provide education and information sessions in more nontraditional settings, because hard-to-reach clients interested in care may not know how to access it and may lack critical information about handling diabetes complications. Providing psychoeducation to employers would teach organizations how to promote healthy living and to support employees with diabetes or who serve as family caregivers. Using motivational interviewing and SMART goal setting, social workers can increase diabetes awareness and provide older adults with effective information and resources to care for their physical and emotional well-being.

REFERENCES

American Diabetes Association (ADA). (2012). Diagnosis and classification of diabetes mellitus. *Diabetes Care, 35*(Suppl 1), S64–S71. doi:10.2337/dc12-s064

American Diabetes Association (ADA). (2013). *Living with diabetes: Coronary heart disease.* Retrieved September 1, 2013, from http://www.diabetes.org/living-with-diabetes/women/coronary-heart-disease.html

Ananth, J. (1984). Treatment of immigrant Indian patients. *Canadian Journal of Psychiatry, 29,* 490–493.

Araki, A., & Ito, H. (2003). Development of elderly diabetes burden scale for elderly patients with diabetes mellitus. *Geriatrics and Gerontology International, 3,* 212–224. doi:10.1111/j.1444-1586.2003.00084.x

Araki, S., Nishio, Y., Araki, A., Umegaki, H., Sakurai, T., Limuro, S., . . . Japanese Elderly Intervention Trial Research Group. (2012). Factors associated with progression of diabetic nephropathy in Japanese elderly patients with type 2 diabetes: Sub-analysis of the Japanese elderly diabetes intervention trial. *Geriatric and Gerontology International, 12*(Suppl. 1), S127–S133. doi:10.1111/j.1447-0594.2011.00820.x

Beyene Y., Becker, G., & Mayen, N. (2002). Perception of aging and sense of well-being among Latino elderly. *Journal of Cross-Cultural Gerontology, 17,* 155–172. doi:10.1023/A: 1015886816483

Brown, K., Avis, M., & Hubbard, M. (2007). Health beliefs of African-Caribbean people with Type 2 diabetes: A qualitative study. *British Journal of General Practice, 57,* 461–469.

Calvin, D., Quinn, L., Dancy, B., Park, C., Fleming, S. G., Smith, E., & Fogelfeld, L. (2011). African Americans' perception of risk for diabetes complications. *Diabetes Educator, 37,* 689–698. doi:10.1177/0145721711416258

Carnethon, M. R., De Chavez, P. J., Biggs, M. L., Lewis, C. E., Pankow, J. S. Bertoni, A. G., . . . Dyer, A. R. (2012). Association of weight status with mortality in adults with incident diabetes. *Journal of the American Medical Association, 308,* 581–590. doi:10.100/jama.2012.9282

Cavanaugh, C. L., Taylor, C. A., Keim, K. S., Clutter, J. E., & Geraghty, M. E. (2008). Cultural perceptions of health and diabetes among Native American men. *Journal of Health Care for the Poor and Underserved, 19,* 1029–1043. doi:10.1353/hpu.0.0083

Centers for Disease Control and Prevention. (2011). *National diabetes fact sheet: National estimates and general information on diabetes and prediabetes in the United States, 2011*. Retrieved September 1, 2013, from http://www.cdc.gov/diabetes/pubs/pdf/ndfs_2011.pdf

Chin, M. H., Polonsky, T. S., Thomas, V. D., & Nerney, M. P. (2000). Developing a conceptual framework for understanding illness and attitudes in older, urban African-Americans with diabetes. *Diabetes Educator, 26*, 439–449. doi:10.1177/014572170002600311

Cigolle, C. T., Langa, K. M., Kabeto, M. U., Tian, Z., & Blaum, C. S. (2007). Geriatric conditions and disability: The health and retirement study. *Annals of Internal Medicine, 147*, 156–164. doi:10.7326/0003-4819-147-3-200708070-00004

Debono, M., & Cachia, E. (2007). The impact of diabetes on psychological well being and quality of life: The role of patient education. *Psychology, Health and Medicine, 12*, 545–555. doi:10.1080/13548500701235740

Edson, E. J., Sierra-Johnson, J., & Curtis, B. (2009). Diabetes and obesity in older adults: a call to action. *Reviews in Clinical Gerontology, 19*, 135–147. doi:10.1017/S0959259809990128

Folsom, A. R., Chambless, L. E., Duncan, B. B., Gilbert, A. C., Pankow, J. S., & Atherosclerosis Risk in Communities Study Investigators. (2003). Prediction of coronary heart disease in middle-aged adults with diabetes. *Diabetes Care, 26*, 2777–2784. doi:10.2337/diacare.26.10.2777

Fong, D. S., Aiello, L., Gardner, T. W., King, G. L., Blankenship, G., Cavallerano, J. D., . . . Klein, R. (2004). Retinopathy in diabetes. *Diabetes Care, 27*, s84–s87. doi:10.2337/diacare.27.2007.S84

Ford, E. S., Williamson, D. F., & Liu, S. (1997). Weight change and diabetes incidence: Findings from a national cohort of US adults. *American Journal of Epidemiology, 146*, 214–222.

Golden, S. H., Lazo, M., Carnethon, M., Bertoni, A. G., Schreiner, P. J., Diez Roux, A. V., . . . Lyketsos, C. (2008). Examining a bidirectional association between depressive symptoms and diabetes. *Journal of the American Medical Association, 299*, 2751–2759. doi:10.1001/jama.299.23.2751

Grey, M. (2000). Interventions for children with diabetes and their families. *Annual Review of Nursing Research, 18*, 149–170.

Ho, E. Y., Chesla, C. A., & Chun, K. M. (2011). Health communication with Chinese Americans about type 2 diabetes. *Diabetes Educator, 38*, 67–76. doi:10.1177/0145721711428774

Hoeman, S. P., Ku, Y. L., & Ohl, D. R. (1996). Health beliefs and early detection among Chinese women. *Western Journal of Nursing Research, 18*, 518–533.

Hu, J., Amirehsani, K., Wallace, D. C., & Letvak, S. (2013). Perceptions of barriers in managing diabetes: Perspectives of Hispanic immigrant patients and family members. *Diabetes Educator, 39*, 494–503. doi:10.1177/0145721713486200

Huang, E. S., John, P., & Munshi, M. N. (2009). Multidisciplinary approach for the treatment of diabetes in the elderly. *Aging Health, 5*, 207–216. doi:10.2217/ahe.09.3

International Diabetes Federation. (2013a). *Diabetes atlas: Global burden*. Retrieved August 26, 2013, from http://www.idf.org/print/diabetesatlas/5e/the-global-burden

International Diabetes Federation. (2013b). *Diabetes atlas: Mortality*. Retrieved August 26, 2013, from http://www.idf.org/diabetesatlas/5e/mortality

Karter, A. J., Ferrara, A., Darbinian, J. A., Ackerson, L. M., & Selby, J. V. (2000). Self monitoring of blood glucose: Language and financial barriers in a managed care population with diabetes. *Diabetes Care, 23*, 477–483. doi:10.2337/diacare.23.4.477

Kramer, E., Kwong, K., Lee, E., & Chung, H. (2002). Cultural factors influencing the mental health of Asian Americans. *The Western Journal of Medical, 176*, 227–231.

Lenzi Martin, A., & Lipman, R. D. (2013). The future of diabetes education: Expanded opportunities and roles for diabetes educators. *Diabetes Educator, 39*, 436–446. doi:10.1177/0145721713486526

McKenzie, C., & Skelly, A. H. (2010). Perceptions of coronary heart disease risk in African American women with type 2 diabetes: A qualitative study. *Diabetes Educator, 36*, 766–773. doi:10.1177/01457217 10374652

McLaughlin, S. (2010). Traditions and diabetes prevention: A healthy path for Native Americans. *Diabetes Spectrum, 23*, 272–277. doi:10.2337/diaspect.23.4.272.

Morisaki, N., Watanabe, S., & Kobayashi, J. (1994). Diabetic control and progression of retinopathy in elderly patients: Five-year follow up study. *Journal of the American Geriatrics Society, 42*, 142–145.

Naik, A. D., White, C. D., Robertson, S. M., Armento, M. E., Lawrence, B., Stelljes, L. A., & Cully, J. A. (2012). Behavioral health coaching for rural-living older adults with diabetes and depression: An open pilot of the HOPE study. *BMC Geriatrics, 12*, 1–11. doi:10.1186/1471-2318-12-37

Norris, S. L., Nichols, P. J., Caspersen, C. J., Glasgow, R. E., Engelgau, M. M., Jack, L., Jr., . . . Task Force on Community Preventive Services. (2002). Increasing diabetes self-management education in community settings. *American Journal of Preventive Medicine, 22*, 39–66.

Patterson, B., Thorne, S., Crawford, J., & Tarko, M. (1999). Living with diabetes as a transformational experience. *Qualitative Health Research, 9*, 786–802. doi:10.1177/104973299129122289

Petrak, F., Herpertz, S., Albus, C., Hirsch, A., Kulzer, B., & Kruse, J. (2005). Psychosocial factors and diabetes mellitus: Evidence-based treatment guidelines. *Current Diabetes Reviews, 1*, 255–270. doi:10.2174/1573 39905774574329

Pichette, E. F., Garrett, M. T., Kosciulek, J. F., & Rosenthal, D. A. (1999). Cultural identification of American Indians and its impact on rehabilitation services. *Journal of Rehabilitation, 65*, 3–10.

Polonsky, W. H. (2000). Understanding and assessing diabetes-specific quality of life. *Diabetes Spectrum, 13*, 36–41.

Robles-Silva, L. (2008). The caregiving trajectory among poor and chronically ill people. *Qualitative Health Research, 18*, 358–368. doi:10.1177/104973230 7313753

Schneider, J. I., Hashizume, J., Heak, S., Maetani, L., Rude Ozaki, R., & Leong Watanabe, D. (2011). Identifying challenges, goals and strategies for success for people with diabetes through life coaching.

Journal of Vocational Rehabilitation, 34, 129–139. doi:10.3233/JVR-2010-0541

Taylor, C., Keim, K. S., Sparrer, A., Van Delinder, J., & Parker, S. (2004). Social and cultural barriers to diabetes prevention in Oklahoma American Indian women. *Prevention Chronic Disease, 1*, 1–10. Retrieved from http://www.cdc.gov/pcd/issues/2004/apr/03_0017.htm

Tripp-Reimer, T., Choi, E., Skemp Kelley, L. S., & Enslein, J. C. (2001). Cultural barriers to care: Inverting the problem. *Diabetes Spectrum, 14*, 13–22. doi:10.2337/diaspect.14.1.13

Weiler, D. M., & Crist, J. D. (2009). Diabetes self-management in a Latino social environment. *Diabetes Educator, 35*, 285–292. doi:10.1177/0145721708329545

Wild, S., Roglic, G., Green, A., Sicree, R., & King, H. (2004). Global prevalence of diabetes: Estimates for the year 2000 and projections for 2030. *Diabetes Care, 27*, 1047–1053. doi:10.2337/diacare.27.5.1047

World Health Organization. (2011). *Diabetes.* Retrieved August 30, 2013, from http://www.who.int/mediacentre/factsheets/fs312/en/

This chapter presents an overview of social work practice considerations that arise when HIV disease and aging intersect. The intersection of aging and HIV/AIDS creates a complexity for providers that can be challenging. Medical and/or social service practitioners frequently fail to identify and adequately serve HIV-infected older adults; thus, HIV-infected persons over 50[1] often remain hidden and their needs unaddressed. Despite recent advances in understanding this population, stigma (including ageism, homophobia, and HIV stigma) and lack of knowledge remain barriers to appropriate service provision. Throughout this chapter older adults living with HIV disease (including AIDS) are identified using the acronym OALH.

HIV-related advocacy, service provision, and policy analysis are compatible with social work because of our focus on forming productive partnerships with disenfranchised, oppressed, and marginalized populations (Shernoff, 1990). Examining and advocating for older adults impacted by HIV disease falls well within the role of advocacy and the promotion of social justice for oppressed and marginalized populations (Poindexter, 2010). Systems of care for people living with HIV and for older adults continue to be separate and fragmented, resulting in OLAH falling "through the cracks."

OLDER PERSONS WITH HIV

CHARLES A. EMLET
ANNE K. HUGHES

Older Adults with HIV/AIDS

Advances in the clinical management of HIV disease, including the introduction of antiretroviral therapy (ART) in the mid-1990s, have altered HIV from a deadly disease to one that can be managed successfully (Kirk & Goetz, 2009). HIV disease is increasingly recognized as a disease impacting older adults. Data from the Centers for Disease Control and Prevention (CDC) indicate that the number of adults age 50 and over living with HIV continues to grow (CDC, 2013a). By 2015, half of all persons living with HIV in the United States will be age 50 or over (High et al., 2012). This growth is due to the intersection of incidence and prevalence; that is, the continued new diagnoses of HIV among older adults (currently 17% of all new infections) (Administration on Aging, 2012), along with aging of long-term survivors (Kirk & Goetz, 2009). This trend is best exemplified by the CDC's surveillance data, where we see increasing overall numbers of adults aged 50 and older living with HIV. Between 2007 and 2009 the prevalence of HIV among older adults increased from 209,433 to 256,259. This reflects an increase in the rate per 100,000 from 240.9 to 280.6 in only 2 years. Racial and ethnic disparities exist in the aging population, as older African Americans and Hispanic/Latinos have rates of HIV infection 12.6 and 5 times, respectively, the rates of their White peers (CDC, 2013a).

BIOLOGICAL ASPECTS OF AGING WITH HIV/AIDS

Aging with HIV disease has a clear biological/physiological component. While there is not room in this chapter to discuss all these issues in depth, we have chosen to focus on several important physiological elements including disease management, late diagnosis, comorbidities, cognitive decline, and medication adherence.

Disease Management

Research suggests that OALH are more likely to receive a late diagnosis of HIV than their younger counterparts (CDC, 2013a). Late diagnosis is defined as receiving an AIDS diagnosis within 12 months of an HIV diagnosis, indicating long-term and unidentified infection. In 2009, at the time of HIV infection diagnosis, 41.5% of older adults were classified as stage 3 (having AIDS) (CDC, 2013a). Late diagnosis results in untreated HIV infection, acceleration of HIV symptoms, increased morbidity and mortality, and decreased effectiveness of antiretroviral therapy. Lack of clinical suspicion by providers and the parallel lack of identifying at-risk behavior among older adults themselves add unnecessarily to the potential of late diagnosis of HIV among older people.

Comorbidities

For older people, life can require the adjustment to and living with both HIV-related and age-related comorbidities. An increased number of comorbid health conditions among those living with HIV have been associated with increased age (Weiss, Osorio, Ryan, Marcus, & Fishbein, 2010), while age and comorbidity have been associated with decreased physical function (Oursler et al., 2011) and decreased physical health quality of life (Fredriksen-Goldsen, Emlet, et al., 2013). The issues of comorbidity among OALH are extremely complex. Conditions can be

comorbid with HIV (i.e., hepatitis C, renal disease, peripheral neuropathy, and cancer) or associated with antiretroviral therapy (e.g., hyperlipidemia, cardiovascular disease, and diabetes), or can be non-HIV-related conditions associated with aging, such as chronic pulmonary disease, arthritis, and cardiovascular disease (Weiss et al., 2010). Mental health (especially depression) and substance abuse concerns are also common comorbidities.

Cognitive Decline

Cognitive decline can occur among OALH for many reasons: normal aging, direct HIV infection, psychiatric disorders, substance abuse, non-HIV-related neurodegenerative diseases, opportunistic infections, and medication side effects (Skapik & Treisman, 2007). HIV-associated dementia (HAD) is three times more likely to occur in older than in younger adults with HIV (High, Valcour, & Paul, 2006). Changes in memory, attention, verbal skills, and other executive functions are common among OALH, regardless of the cause. Decreased neurocognitive functioning has been implicated in poor medication adherence among OALH (Barclay et al., 2007). Neuropsychological testing should be used to assess cognitive decline in this population; however, use of the Mini Mental State Examination (MMSE) is not recommended as it is not sensitive to HIV-related cognitive problems (Skapik & Treisman, 2007).

Pharmaceutical Treatment

Antiretroviral medications suppress the ability of the HIV virus to replicate, keeping a person's viral load down and protecting immune function. They function most effectively when patients strictly adhere to the prescribed regimen. Most OALH have been found to have better adherence rates than their younger counterparts (Hinkin et al., 2004), however adherence worsens in the presence of cognitive impairment. HIV-positive persons tend to be able to adhere to their medication protocols better when they receive and perceive supportive interest from healthcare providers (Powell-Cope et al., 1998). Comorbidity can mean juggling many complex medication protocols that may result in confusion about which cognitive or physical symptoms are caused by which conditions (Manfredi, 2002). Social workers should be familiar with the importance of medical and pharmaceutical adherence, because viral suppression increases longevity.

Psychosocial Aspects of Aging with HIV/AIDS

Many OALHs face numerous and serious psychosocial challenges that can be exacerbated by the aging process. Social isolation, stigma, and depression are some of the primary psychosocial issues faced by this population. Because OALH have a high likelihood of living alone (Fredriksen-Goldsen, Emlet, et al., 2013; Grov, Golub, Parsons, Brennan, & Karpiak, 2010), they may be more socially isolated than their HIV-negative age counterparts (Cahill & Valadez, 2013). A recent study of social isolation among OALH found increased social isolation to be associated with increased hospitalizations and mortality (Greysen et al., 2013).

Stigma

HIV stigma continues to be a major and well-documented social problem among older populations living with HIV (Emlet, 2006; Foster & Gaskins, 2009; Haile, Padilla, & Parker, 2011). HIV stigma is a complex array of intrapersonal and interpersonal experiences including enacted stigma (prejudice/discrimination), internalized stigma (the internal acceptance of negative attributes and beliefs about people living with HIV), and anticipated stigma (the anticipation of enacted stigma, resulting anxiety and fear) (Earnshaw & Chaudoir, 2009). Stigma is associated with negative outcomes, including depression, poorer quality of life, lack of disclosure, and loneliness (Grov et al., 2010; Haile et al., 2011). Many OALH face the potential of duel stigma based on age and HIV status (Emlet, 2006). This phenomenon has been termed "layering," which occurs when one experiences stigma from HIV and from other personal characteristics, such as sexual orientation, age, race, or ethnicity (Reidpath & Chan, 2005). Social workers who are working with OALH must assess the experiences of stigma among this population and carefully consider the intersection of HIV stigma and other forms of discrimination when considering psychosocial support and advocacy. In a recent study of HIV stigma among older Canadians, Emlet, Brennan, and colleagues

(2013) noted the importance of social support and mastery as means of counteracting the negative impacts of stigma.

Mental Health Needs

Mental health concerns, particularly depression and substance abuse, are common among OALH. While in the general population depression risk decreases with age, the opposite is true for OALH. Rates of depression as high as 50% have been identified in various studies (Brennan, Karpiak, & Cantor, 2009; Frontini et al., 2012; Justice et al., 2004). Rates of substance use and abuse among OALH are higher than those of older HIV-negative individuals (Justice et al., 2004). Use of illicit substances was identified by 20% of one sample of OALH (Frontini et al., 2012), with the majority reporting the use of marijuana or cocaine. Both mental health status and substance use can be risk factors for HIV infection and can also occur as a result of the crisis associated with an HIV diagnosis. Social workers need to monitor both as they offer services to OALH.

Social and Interpersonal Resources

While OALH face numerous challenges in biological and psychological realms, strengths and resilience can aid in adjustment and serve as protective factors against the deleterious impacts of HIV disease. Interpersonal and intrapersonal factors have been associated with decreased psychological distress and improved quality of life in this population. Social support has been repeatedly found to benefit older, HIV-positive adults. Studying 378 older adults living with HIV in Ontario Canada, Emlet, Brennan, and colleagues (2013) found emotional and informational social support to be associated with decreased HIV stigma. These findings parallel Logie and Gadalla (2009), who found a negative relationship between HIV stigma and social support. Recently Fredriksen-Goldsen, Emlet, et al. (2013) found increased social support to be a protective factor associated with improved mental health quality of life among 226 older gay and bisexual men living with HIV disease in the United States.

Research has also noted the importance of intrapersonal characteristics including mastery, optimism and spirituality. Moore and colleagues (2013) found optimism and mastery to be associated with improved self-rated successful aging, as well as physical and psychological functioning in OALH. Mastery has also been associated with reduced stigma in HIV-positive older Canadians (Emlet, Brennan, et al., 2013). Recent inquiry into HIV disease has identified the importance of resilience as a means of coping and managing HIV (De Santis, Florom-Smith, Vermeesch, Barroso, & DeLeon, 2013; Emlet, Tozay, & Raveis, 2011). Social workers need to ensure that their assessment processes identify and capitalize on strengths and resilience in this population, as often the focus has been on the deleterious effects of this disease.

SPECIFIC CONCERNS AND RESPONSES

Older adults living with HIV/AIDS are heterogeneous, and it is important to consider that subgroups within this population may have special concerns and responses that will require an approach to service delivery that honors these experiences. In this section we highlight several of these issues, including the episodic nature of the illness and resultant continued grief and loss, decisions about disclosure, and the need for safe behavior assessment and education. As you consider the information that follows, consider also that the following subgroups within the older HIV-positive population may have differential responses: gay men who have suffered multiple losses; women infected by a (perhaps long-term) partner who she was unaware was HIV-positive; African American older adults affected by ageism, racism, and HIV; people infected at a younger age and aging with HIV; people infected in older age and aging with HIV or AIDS; and serodiscordant couples.

Living with Episodic Disability, Grief, and Adjustment

While the success of HAART has extended longevity for people living and aging with HIV, it has at the same time created uncertainty related to physical, emotional and social determinants of health (O'Brien, Bayoumi, Strike, Young, & Davis, 2008). This uncertainty can create and extend periods of crisis and require new approaches to service provision. Solomon, O'Brien, Wilkins, and Gervais (2014) have concluded that OALH may experience age-related uncertainties including episodic health challenges,

providers who are uninformed about aging and HIV, financial uncertainty (including issues of disability and retirement), and questions about who will care for them. Additionally, OALH who were diagnosed prior to the advent of HAART may continue to have unresolved issues of grief, loss, and survivor's guilt, having lost friends, lovers, or partners, or having been "at death's door" themselves (Emlet, 2013). Social workers should be observant for serial and serious HIV-related crises in the lives of those they serve, and respond with immediacy, sensitivity, and flexibility. Many of the uncertainties discussed here can trigger significant existential crises that will require support and/or referral to mental health treatment.

Need for Safe Behavior Assessment and Education

Because of deeply ingrained ageist attitudes and misinformation, providers are often blind to the possibility that an older person is at risk for or has HIV. Stereotypes that older people are asexual, heterosexual, do not inject drugs, and do not employ sex workers fuel this lack of awareness. Social workers should strive to forge a climate conducive to discussing health concerns, including HIV status and risk. Adults over the age of 65 have the lowest HIV testing rates in the United States (Nguyen & Holodniy, 2008); thus social workers can be a valuable resource in connecting older clients with information about local testing sites. Studies of HIV-positive older adults have found concerning rates of unsafe sexual practices. Of sexually active OALH in one large study, 41% had unprotected sex (Brennan, Karpiak, & Cantor, 2009), while another study found that 33% of their sample did not use condoms when sexually active (Lovejoy et al., 2008). Social workers must be knowledgeable about prevention and risk issues and offer services to reduce secondary infection (an HIV-positive individual infecting another person), also known as prevention for positives (CDC, 2013b).

Concerns About Disclosure

The disclosure of one's HIV status is a significant challenge at any age. Disclosure may open the door to support and care but also to possible stigma and discrimination. A meta-analysis of HIV disclosure found those who disclosed their status received increased social support (Smith, Rossetto, & Peterson, 2008). In a qualitative study of 19 older women, Psaros and colleagues (2012) noted what they called the disclosure dilemma, which was characterized by a strong sense of obligation to disclose HIV status and the inherent fear of reactions to disclosure. Social workers need to engage openly and nonjudgmentally with those who may be experiencing disclosure dilemmas, whether the issue is with family, friends, providers, or current or potential sexual partners. Social workers can help older persons practice approaching others about painful topics or being assertive with physicians and others using various forms of rehearsal or coaching.

GENERAL PRACTICE IMPLICATIONS

When working with OALH, social workers can offer information on HIV transmission, sexual safety, pathogenesis, treatment, and adherence; care management, crisis intervention, and referrals; supportive individual, dyadic, family, or group counseling; legal services; concrete services and logistical help; and benefits advocacy. In addition to the social work responses to the concerns discussed above, the general practice considerations discussed in this section may help in designing services for HIV-infected older persons and HIV-affected caregivers.

Offering Specific Outreach and Services

Practitioners in the Aging Network, hospitals and clinics, and AIDS Service Organizations should strive to identify the concerns of OALH so that they can be steered to the most appropriate services. Older people can feel out of place in AIDS Service Organizations, which they perceive as geared to younger people, and in the Aging Network, which has historically been unwelcoming to persons with HIV. Social workers within AIDS Service Organizations should be proactive in addressing the specific needs of this population. Likewise, gerontological social workers should ask older people, in a way that is nonjudgmental and normalizing, whether they have any HIV-related concerns they wish to discuss, and make sure that staff are adequately trained regarding HIV.

Inviting Individual Participation

Social workers need to gently open the door so that older persons can discuss their sexual and drug histories, HIV status, and caregiving realities. It helps to ask people about their knowledge and experience with HIV as a matter of course, just as you would approach any other health concern. Modeling discussion of difficult subjects, such as sexual health and HIV risk, helps to normalize this practice and may even encourage older adults to proactively address them with their healthcare providers (Hughes, 2013). Gerontological social workers can begin by identifying those service applicants and recipients who have HIV concerns. HIV practitioners can ask HIV-positive persons about their social networks and identify older caregivers who may need information and support.

Older HIV-Affected Caregivers

Although HIV/AIDS is no longer considered a terminal disease, partners and loved ones of OALH may still find themselves in a caregiving relationship. For example, Fredriksen-Goldsen, Kim, and Goldsen (2011) found that more than one-quarter of lesbian, gay, bisexual, and transgender (LGBT) older adults in a national survey were in caregiving roles. Midlife and older caregivers can experience stress as they work to balance multiple needs, and consequently their own emotional, financial, and physical stability can be at risk (Leblanc, London, & Aneshensel, 1997). Social workers need to be sensitive to the needs of caregivers and be aware of the possibility that caregivers have historically experienced or are currently experiencing enacted and/or secondary stigma.

Assessment

A social worker who is working with an HIV-affected or HIV-infected older person should first acknowledge the intense struggle inherent in the situation. It is then necessary to conduct a mutual, comprehensive, culturally competent and HIV-knowledgeable assessment, including both assets and needs. Assessments should include HIV as well as aging concerns. Table 34.1 provides nine domains that should be considered and included in an assessment of older adults impacted by HIV disease.

TABLE 34.1 Assessment Domains

Domain	Older Persons with HIV/AIDS
Physical Functioning	Comorbidity may result in decline in functioning from various sources. Functioning may decline more rapidly and more sporadically with HIV disease than typical chronic diseases associated with aging. Some data suggest that functional dependence is more important than diagnosis in determining reactions to illness and quality of life. Assessments should include a thorough accounting of HIV-related issues as well as comorbidities and their associated functional decline.
Cognitive/Affective	Cognitive decline in older adults may be due to a variety of factors including dementias normally associated with aging in addition to HIV dementia. Consider use of instruments or questions designed to detect HIV-associated cognitive decline. See Valcour, Paul, Chiao, Wendelken, and Miller (2011) for discussion of appropriate instruments.
Strengths and Resilience	Older adults living with HIV disease routinely express feelings of resilience in the midst of a long-term declining illness. Self-mastery, social support, spirituality, and contextualizing HIV are important factors associated with intrapersonal and interpersonal strengths in this population. Strengths and resilience should be an integral part of the assessment process.
Social Support	Older adults with HIV/AIDS, depending on their history, may have limited contact with biological family. Additionally, social supports common to younger persons with HIV, such as parents and even siblings, may be unavailable to older adults due to death or frailty of family members. Both quality as well as quantity of social relationships could be considered as part of the assessment process.
Sexual and Drug Health	Taking sexual and drug histories with older adults requires an understanding of cohort terminology and may require altering language typically used with younger clients. Ageist attitudes among professionals about sexuality and drug use must be recognized. Research indicates that older, HIV-positive adults continue to be sexually active and engage in at-risk sexual and drug use behavior. Nonjudgmental and nonageist approaches are critical.
Spirituality	Older adults may need assistance with disclosing diagnosis to clergy or may need to locate spiritual resources that are HIV sensitive. Individuals may have broken ties with religious organizations from the past who engaged in "blaming" behaviors. Spirituality is an important component to resilience among HIV-positive older adults and should be included in the assessment process.
Immune Function	Senescence of the immune system (aging process) may serve to accelerate the decline of CD4 T-cells that are diminished through HIV. Older adults will need to be educated about the importance of CD4 and viral load and may need to be assisted with regular and ongoing testing.
Disclosure	Determine whom the client has disclosed their HIV status to. This may include various family members, friends, healthcare providers, clergy, and coworkers. The client may need help assessing the pros and cons of disclosure to a variety of individuals and/or groups.
Caregiver well-being	Caregivers (including partners) of individuals with HIV suffer from many of the same physical, emotional, financial, and social burdens of other caregivers. In addition, associative stigma may exist, depending on the disclosure of the care receiver's HIV status.

SERVICE DELIVERY SYSTEMS

People living with HIV/AIDS can access services from a variety of sources including private, community based, and governmental. Service needs can be addressed through numerous systems including health (physical and mental), home care, rehabilitation, and pharmaceutical services. Many OALH may have Medicare coverage due to their age or disability status. Medicare Part D covers prescription medications, including those used to manage HIV disease. Social work responses will depend on the OALH's perceptions of his or her needs, as well as the local availability of services. Professionals working with OALH must be familiar with the range of services from both the Aging Network and the HIV Network.

HIV Network Services

Services for persons of all ages living with HIV may be provided through public health and social services, university medical centers and clinics, and AIDS Service Organizations (ASOs) supported through the Ryan White CARE Act. The Ryan White Comprehensive AIDS Resources Emergency [CARE] Act (PL101-381) of 1990 was the first federal service delivery mechanism to aid persons with HIV. The Act was reauthorized in 2009 as the Ryan White HIV/AIDS Treatment Extension Act of 2009 (PL 111-87), and funds programs that provide services to those with HIV/AIDS who are uninsured or underinsured and who lack financial resources to pay for HIV care. AIDS Service Organizations are community-based agencies developed to ensure the delivery of health-related and social services to HIV-affected individuals and families (Burrage & Porche, 2003). AIDS Service Organizations may not specifically target older adults, and this may serve as a barrier for some older adults. Research suggests that ASOs do not uniformly understand the risks and impact of HIV on older adults (Wood, 2013). The Ryan White HIV/AIDS Treatment Extension Act includes the AIDS Drugs Assistance Programs (ADAPs), which provide HIV-related medications to those who do not have drug coverage and are an essential resource for older adults who do not yet qualify for Medicare.

The Aging Network

The Older Americans Act (OAA) of 1965 created the Administration on Aging (AOA) and authorized grants to States for community planning and services programs. The OAA created the aging network, which includes 57 State Units on Aging and approximately 650 Area Agencies on Aging. Currently, through the newly established Administration for Community Living (ACL), providers in the aging network will be increasingly able to provide services to younger, disabled adults. This integration will expand the availability and access of Aging and Disability Resource Centers, while

continuing to serve older adults through established programs (Hooyman, Mahoney, & Sciegaj, 2013). While gerontological social workers are commonly knowledgeable about services available under the aging network, many area agencies on aging are not familiar with the needs of OALH. Emlet, Gerkin, and Orel (2009) surveyed Area Agencies on Aging in Washington State and found that while the majority agreed that serving older adults impacted by HIV was part of their mission, only 16% offered some type of HIV education to consumers. Continued efforts to improve knowledge and programming from both the HIV and aging service delivery sectors are needed.

SUMMARY

When working with HIV-infected older persons, social workers need to be creative and flexible. HIV-positive persons, as well as older persons, often do not fare well in the complexity of human services and healthcare provision. Social workers must monitor their own attitudes and behaviors related to ageism and HIV stigma, along with other prejudgments, so that the helping relationship does not become another place where people suffer from maltreatment and misunderstanding.

Over the past three-plus decades, we have learned a great deal about the needs of and the differences among older adults living with HIV disease. Social work has contributed substantially to this knowledge base. Research is beginning to examine the "positive" side of aging with HIV through studies on resilience. From there, we can develop intervention strategies that improve care for this vulnerable population, while learning from those who are doing well naturally. The development of evidence-based practice models through intervention studies is a reasonable next step for the profession.

SUGGESTED RESOURCES

Administration on Aging (AOA)

http://www.aoa.gov/AoAroot/AoA_Programs/HPW/
    HIV_AIDS/GrayingHIVAIDS.aspx
- Webinar on services available to the aging services network on positive aging and prevention.

http://www.aoa.gov/AoARoot/AoA_Programs/HPW/HIV_AIDS/index.aspx
- Links to HIV testing sites, health centers, and community aging organizations. Website includes HIV/AIDS and aging resources.

http://www.aoa.gov/AoARoot/AoA_Programs/HPW/HIV_AIDS/toolkit.aspx
- Resources and materials to use in promotion of HIV/AIDS education for older adults.

http://www.aoa.gov/AoARoot/AoA_Programs/OAA/How_To_Find/Agencies/find_agencies.aspx
- Find a local State or Area Agency on Aging. Searchable by state, then county.

ACRIA (AIDS Community Research Initiative of America)

http://www.ageisnotacondom.org/index.html
- Website has facts about HIV/AIDS, aging, and sexuality. Includes resources and links to publications regarding OALH.

Centers for Disease Control and Prevention (CDC)

http://www.cdc.gov/hiv/library/reports/surveillance/2010/surveillance_Report_vol_18_no_3.html
- CDC surveillance report specifically on HIV in adults age 50 and over.

National Institute on Aging

http://www.nia.nih.gov/health/publication/hiv-aids-and-older-people
- Basic information about HIV and aging.

Ryan White HIV/AIDS Program

http://hab.hrsa.gov/abouthab/aboutprogram.html
- Basics about local and state HIV programs, factsheets, a glossary, and details about coverage offered by the Ryan White program.

National Resource Center on LGBT Aging

http://www.lgbtagingcenter.org/resources/index.cfm?a=1
- Information to aging service providers on creating LGBT-affirming organizations and working with older members of the LGBT community. Site has a section on HIV and aging.

Professional Association of Social Workers in HIV and AIDS (PASWHA)

www.paswha.org
- This is a professional membership organization for social workers who provide service at all levels in the field of HIV/AIDS social work. Website access is restricted to members.

NOTE

1. When the CDC began monitoring incidence and prevalence of AIDS in 1982, age was reported by categories with the oldest category being "over 49". Older persons became defined as 50-plus years.

REFERENCES

Administration on Aging (AOA). (2012). *The graying of HIV/AIDS: Community resources for the aging network.* Retrieved from http://www.aoa.gov/AoAroot/AoA_Programs/HPW/HIV_AIDS/GrayingHIVAIDS.aspx

Barclay, T. R., Hinkin, C. H., Castellon, S. A., Mason, K. I., Reinhard, M. J., Marion, S. D., . . . Durvasula, R. S. (2007). Age-associated predictors of medication adherence in HIV-positive adults: Health beliefs, self-efficacy, and neurocognitive status. *Health Psychology, 26*, 40–49. doi:10.1037/0278-6133.26.1.40

Brennan, M., Karpiak, S. E., & Cantor, M. H. (2009). *Older adults with HIV: An in-depth examination of an emerging population.* Hauppauge, NY: Nova Science.

Burrage, J., & Porche, D. (2003). AIDS service organization partnerships: A method to assess outcomes of community service organizations for vulnerable populations. *Journal of Multicultural Nursing and Health, 9*, 7–12.

Cahill, S., & Valadez, R. (2013). Growing older with HIV/AIDS: New public health challenges. *American Journal of Public Health, 103*, e7–e15. doi:10.2105/AJPH.2012.301161

Centers for Disease Control and Prevention (CDC). (2013a, February). *Diagnoses of HIV infection among adults aged 50 years and older in the United States and dependent areas, 2007–2010.* HIV Surveillance Supplemental Report, 18. Retrieved from http://www.cdc.gov/hiv/topics/surveillance/resources/reports/#supplemental

Centers for Disease Control and Prevention (CDC). (2013b). *Prevention with persons with HIV.* Retrieved from http://www.cdc.gov/hiv/prevention/programs/pwp/

De Santis, J. P., Florom-Smith, A., Vermeesch, A., Barroso, S., & DeLeon, D. A. (2013). Motivation, management, and mastery: A theory of resilience in the context of HIV infection. *Journal of the American Psychiatric Nurses Association, 19*, 36–46. doi:10.1177/1078390312474096

Earnshaw, V. A., & Chaudoir, S. R. (2009). From conceptualizing to measuring HIV stigma: A review of HIV stigma mechanism measures. *AIDS and Behavior, 13*, 1160–1177. doi:10.1007/s10461-009-9593-3

Emlet, C. A. (2006). "You're awfully old to have this disease": Experiences of stigma and ageism in adults 50 years and older living with HIV/AIDS. *The Gerontologist, 46*, 781–790. doi:10.1093/geront/46.6.781

Emlet, C. A. (2013, May). *"I'm happy in my life now, I'm a positive person" Discovering resilience among older adults living with HIV.* Fulbright lecture presented at Dalhousie University, Halifax, Nova Scotia, Canada, May 6, 2013.

Emlet, C. A., Brennan, D., J., Brennenstuhl, S., Rueda, S., Hart, T. A., Rourke, S. B. & the OHTN Cohort Study Team. (2013). Protective and risk factors associated with stigma in a population of older adults living with HIV in Ontario, Canada. *AIDS Care, 25*, 1330–1339. doi:10.1080/09540121.2013.774317

Emlet, C. A., Gerkin A., & Orel, N. (2009). The graying of HIV/AIDS: Preparedness and needs of the aging network in a changing epidemic. *Journal of Gerontological Social Work, 52*, 803–814. doi:10.1080/01634370903202900

Emlet, C. A., Tozay, S., & Raveis, V. H. (2011). "I'm not going to die from the AIDS": Resilience in aging with HIV disease. *The Gerontologist, 51*, 101–111. doi:10.1093/geront/gnq060

Foster, P. P., & Gaskins, S. W. (2009). Older African Americans' management of HIV/AIDS stigma. *AIDS Care, 21*, 1306–1312. doi:10.1080/09540120902803141

Fredriksen-Goldsen, K. I., Kim, H.-J., & Goldsen, J. (2011). *The aging and health report: Resilience and disparities among lesbian, gay, bisexual and transgender older adults—Preliminary findings.* Seattle, WA: Institute for Multigenerational Health.

Fredriksen-Goldsen, K. I., Emlet, C. A., Kim, H.-J., Muraco, A., Erosheva, E. A., Goldsen, J., & Hoy-Ellis, C. P. (2013). The physical and mental health of lesbian, gay male and bisexual (LGB) older adults: The role of key health indicators and risk and protective factors. *The Gerontologist, 53*, 664–675. Advance online publication. doi:10.1093/geront/gns123

Frontini, M., Chotalia, J., Spizale, L., Onya, W., Ruiz, M., & Clark, R. A. (2012). Sex and race effects on risk for selected outcomes among elderly HIV-infected patients. *Journal of the Association of Physicians in AIDS Care, 11*, 12–15. doi:10.1177/1545109711404947

Greysen, S. R., Horwitz, L. I., Covinsky, K. E., Gordon, K., Ohl, M. E., & Justice, A. E. (2013). Does social isolation predict hospitalization and mortality among HIV+ and uninfected older veterans? *Journal of the American Geriatric Society, 61*, 1456–1463. doi:10.1111/jgs.12410

Grov, C., Golub, S. A., Parsons, J. T., Brennan, M., & Karpiak, S. E. (2010). Loneliness and HIV-related stigma explain depression among older HIV-positive adults. *AIDS Care, 22*, 630–639. doi:10.1080/09540120903280901

Haile, R., Padilla, M. B., & Parker, E. A. (2011). "Stuck in the quagmire of an HIV ghetto": The meaning of stigma in the lives of older black gay and bisexual men living with HIV in New York City. *Culture, Health and Sexuality, 13*, 429–442. doi:10.1080/1369 1058.2010.537769

High, K. P., Brennan-Ing, M., Clifford, D. B., Cohen, M. H., Currier, J., Deeks, S. G. . . . . Volberding, P. (2012). HIV and aging: State of knowledge and areas of clinical need for research. A report to the NIH Office of AIDS Research by the HIV and Aging Working Group. *Journal of Acquired Immune Deficiency Syndromes, 60*, S1–S18. doi:10.1097/QAI.0b013e31825a3668

High, K. P., Valcour, V., & Paul, R. (2006). HIV infection and dementia in older adults. *Clinical Infectious Diseases, 42*, 1449–1454. doi:10.1086/503565

Hinkin, C. H., Hardy, D. J., Mason, K I., Castellon, S. A., Durvasula, R. S., Lam, M. N., & Stefaniak, M. (2004). Medication adherence in HIV-infected adults: Effect of patient age, cognitive status, and substance abuse. *AIDS, 18*, S19–S25. doi:10.1097/00002030-200401001-00004

Hooyman, N., Mahoney, K., & Sciegal, M. (2013). Preparing social workers with person-centered and participant-directed services for the changing aging and disability network. *Journal of Gerontological Social Work, 56*, 573–579. doi:10.1080/01634372.2013.837296

Hughes, A. K. (2013). Mid-to late-life women and sexual health: Communication with health care providers. *Family Medicine, 45*, 252–256.

Justice, A. C., McGinnis, K. A., Atkinson, J. H., Heaton, R. K., Young, C., Sadek, J . . . VACS 5 Project Team. (2004). Psychiatric and neurocognitive disorders among HIV-positive and negative veterans in care: Veterans aging cohort five site study. *AIDS, 18,* S49–S59. doi:10.1097/00002030-200418001-00008

Kirk, J. B., & Goetz, M. B. (2009). Human immunodeficiency virus in an aging population: A complication of success. *Journal of the American Geriatrics Society, 57,* 2129–2138. doi:10.1111/j.1532-5415.2009.02494.x

LeBlanc, A. J., London, A. S., & Aneshensel, C. S. (1997). The physical costs of AIDS caregiving. *Social Science Medicine, 45,* 915–923. doi:10.1016/S0277-953600002-6

Logie, C., & Gadalla, T. M. (2009). Meta-analysis of health and demographic correlates of stigma towards people living with HIV. *AIDS Care, 21,* 742–753. doi:10.1080/09540120802511877

Lovejoy, T. I., Heckman, T. G., Sikkema, K. J., Hansen, N. B., Kochman, A., Suhr, J. A., . . . Johnson, C. J. (2008). Patterns and correlates of sexual activity and condom use behavior in persons 50-plus years of age living with HIV/AIDs. *AIDS and Behavior, 12,* 943–956. doi:10.1007/s10461-008-9384-2

Manfredi, R. (2002). HIV disease and advanced age: An increasing therapeutic challenge. *Drugs and Aging, 19,* 647–669. doi:10.2165/00002512-200219090-00003

Moore, R. C., Moore, D. J., Thompson, W. K., Vahia, I. V., Grant, I., & Jeste, D. V. (2013). A case-controlled study of successful aging in older HIV-infected adults. *Journal of Clinical Psychiatry, 74,* 417–423. doi:10.4088/JCP.12m08100

Nguyen, N., & Holodniy, M. (2008). HIV infection in the elderly. *Clinical Interventions in Aging, 3,* 453–472. doi:10.2147/CIA.S2086

O'Brien, K. K., Bayoumi, A. M., Strike, C., Young, N. L., & Davis, A. M. (2008). Exploring disability from the perspective of adults living with HIV/AIDS: Development of a conceptual framework. *Health and Quality of Life Outcomes, 6:* 76, 1–10. doi:10.1186/1477-7525-6-76

Oursler, K. K., Goulet, J. L., Crystal, S., Justice, A. C., Crothers, K., Butt, A. A . . . Sorkin, J. D. (2011). Association of age and comorbidity with physical function in HIV infected and uninfected patients: Results of the Veterans Aging Cohort Study. *AIDS Patient Care and STDs, 25,* 13–20. doi:10.1089/apc.2010.0242

Poindexter, C. C. (2010). *Handbook of HIV and social work: Principles, practice and populations.* Hoboken, NJ: Wiley.

Powell-Cope, G. M., Turner, J. G., Brown, M. A., Holzemer, W. L., Corless, I. B., Inouye, J., & Nokes, K.M. (1998). *Perceived health care providers' support and HIV adherence.* International Conference on AIDS, 12:592 (abstract no. 32354).

Psaros, C., Barinas, J., Robbins, G. K., Bedoya, C. A., Safren, S. A., & Park, E. R. (2012). Intimacy and sexual decision making: Exploring the perspective of HIV positive women over 50. *AIDS Patient Care and STDs, 26,* 755–760. doi:10.1089/apc.2012.0256

Reidpath, D. D., & Chan, K. Y. (2005). A method for the quantitative analysis of the layering of HIV-related stigma. *AIDS Care, 17,* 425–432. doi:10.1080/095401 20412331319769

Shernoff, M. J. (1990). Why every social worker should be challenged by AIDS. *Social Work, 35,* 5–8.

Skapik, J. L., & Treisman, G. J. (2007). HIV, psychiatric comorbidity, and aging. *Clinical Geriatrics, 15,* 26–36. http://www.clinicalgeriatrics.com/

Smith, R., Rossetto, K., & Peterson, B. (2008). A meta-analysis of disclosure of one's HIV-positive status, stigma and social support. *AIDS Care, 20,* 1266–1275. doi:10.1080/09540120801926977

Solomon, P., O'Brien, K., Wilkins, S., & Gervais, N. (2014). Aging with HIV and disability: The role of uncertainty. *AIDS Care, 2,* 240–245. doi:10.1080/09 540121.2013.811209

Valcour, V., Paul, R., Chiao, S. Wendelken, L. A., & Miller, B. (2011). Screening for cognitive impairment in human immunodeficiency virus. *Clinical Infectious Diseases, 53,* 836–842. doi:10.1093/cid/cir524

Weiss, J. J., Osorio, G., Ryan, E., Marcus, S. M., & Fishbein, D. A. (2010). Prevalence and patient awareness of medical comorbidities in an urban AIDS clinic. *AIDS Patient Care and STDs, 24,* 39–48. doi:10.1089=apc.2009.0152

Wood, A. M. (2013). A generation skipped: An exploratory study of HIV/AIDS education and prevention services for older adults. *Research in the Sociology of Health Care, 31,* 217–246. doi:10.1108/S0275-4959(2013)0000031012

RUTH E. DUNKLE

SECTION II

Older Adults with Mental Health Conditions

OVERVIEW

The World Health Organization reports that more that 20% of adults over age 60 live with a mental or neurological disorder. With 6.6% of all disabilities attributed to these, it is important to understand the nature of these disorders and the most successful treatment approaches. Unfortunately, mental health problems are often underidentified by professionals and older adults. Even when these problems are identified, they are undertreated by healthcare professionals.

More than half of those over age 65 with a recognized mental health or substance abuse disorder have unmet service needs. They typically seek help from their primary care physician for physical problems. When they do receive help for mental health issues they are either over or undertreated. These unmet needs can result from poor professional training and lack of available services due to inadequate funding for services. Further, lack of care coordination among professionals as well as the stigma older persons face when they seek treatment contributes to the persistence of mental health problems. These problems take on greater significance in the face of the fact that evidence shows that treatment for mental disorders among older adults works when the disorders are accurately diagnosed and treated.

The President's New Freedom Commission on Mental Health, Older Adults Subcommittee, outlined barriers preventing older adults from accessing appropriate mental health care (Bartels, 2003). The committee identified three overarching issue, areas: (1) access and continuity of care, (2) quality of care, and (3) workforce capacity and caregiver supports (Mental Health America, 2011). The chapters in this section examine four prevalent mental health disorders of older adults: dementia, depression and anxiety, substance abuse, and hoarding. Each chapter deals with the etiology of the disorder as well as successful treatment strategies and where possible addresses the treatment barriers identified by the President's committee. The roles of the social worker and other health professionals are identified with practice guidelines described.

Because dementia is a complicated medical problem, many professionals are involved in the care of the patient as well as the family. Toseland, Parker and Ahn, in their chapter, note that while more women are diagnosed with dementia, it is not because of greater susceptibility but rather because there is a larger number of older women. Cognitive as well as physical functioning is affected, and these debilities advance with time. Social workers are involved in all arenas of the disease from assessment to the intervention planning process with the patient and their family members. Intervention strategies focused on prevention, remediation, and support are used by social workers, who play a central role with the person with dementia and their family through the older person's decline and ultimate death. Because of the wide range of different domains of the disease that affect mental, emotional, physical, and social functioning, social workers help the person with dementia and the person's family in the community as well as in institutional settings.

The chapter authored by Gellis and Kenaley deals with the disorders of depression and anxiety, prevalent among older adults and associated with negative outcomes. As common as these disorders are, many barriers to receiving adequate and appropriate care exist. Inadequate recognition and treatment of the problems by practitioners as well as those suffering with these disorders contribute to the service delivery problems. The care system also restricts the time allocated per patient, further barring a person from receiving an appropriate amount of care. With medical illnesses associated with depression and anxiety such as heart disease and dementia, it is important to appropriately diagnoses and treats these disorders. Psychosocial as well as pharmacological interventions are effective in their treatment. The research conducted to better understand the racial and ethnic differences that contribute to the likelihood of elders seeking treatment for depression indicates that Mexican Americans as well as African Americans have lower odds of receiving treatment than do others.

Due to the increasing number of older adults, coupled with a more liberal attitude among older people toward substance use, abuse and misuse are expected to increase as the baby boomer generation ages. The chapter written by Shibusawa and Sarabia focuses on three types of substance abuse issues among older adults: abuse and misuse of prescription drugs, alcohol abuse, and illicit drug use. While significantly more men than women abuse alcohol, little is known about ethnic variation. Drug dependence, on the other hand, is more common among women. Most detection of drug and alcohol abuse is noticed in the workplace, a less common arena for older adults. But with older adults seeing their doctor on a more regular basis, it is recommended that screening for alcohol abuse occur in a medical setting. Important components of the screening process are reviewed. It is recognized, though, that often the abuse is confused with problems of dementia and depression. Treatment success, greater among older than younger adults, is described.

With the increasing recognition of hoarding as a problem, the fifth edition of the *Diagnostic and Statistical Manual of Mental Disorders* created a diagnostic criteria for hoarding disorder, defined as difficulty parting with possessions due to the urge to save them, resultant clutter in living areas, and distress or impairment as a result of the first two symptoms. In their chapter, Bratiotis, Ayers and Steketee describe the features of hoarding behavior and its prevalence, onset, and course among older adults. While onset of this disorder is early in life, typically during childhood and adolescence and rarely in old age, it persists across the lifespan. Impairment in activities of daily living as well as in medical and social arenas persists among persons who hoard, which is exaggerated by limited motivation to seek help and low insight into problems. There are standardized instruments for hoarding behaviors to assess aspects of this disorder as well as health and cognitive status. Clinical trials that examine treatment for hoarding disorder typically focus on middle-aged adult samples. Cognitive-behavioral therapy modules exist for

treatment of the disorder but need to be modified for older adults, who often experience cognitive deficits. To date, there are no randomized clinical trials for the treatment of hoarding disorder among older adults. A combination of intervention strategies is suggested as the most successful approach for treating hoarding disorder in older people.

Taken together, these chapters provide comprehensive coverage of the scope of each of these four common mental health problems faced in older age. Common themes include comorbidity, contrasting older adults to younger people, and comparing gender and racial ethnic variation among people with the disorder. Evidence-based treatment approaches are described where they exist.

REFERENCES

Bartels, S. J. (2003). Improving the system of care for older adults with mental illness in the United States: Findings and recommendations for the President's New Freedom Commission on Mental Health. *American Journal of Geriatric Psychiatry, 11,* 486–497.

Mental Health America. (2011). Position statement 35: Aging well. Alexandria, VA: Mental Health America. Retrieved June 3, 2015 from http://www.mentalhealthamerica.net/positions/aging-well.

RONALD W. TOSELAND
MICHAEL PARKER
SURAN AHN

Older Adults
with Dementia

35

Dementia is very difficult to cope with because it affects both mental and physical functioning progressively, until death. Dementia is the major reason why people are placed in nursing homes. In the middle stage of dementia, those with the disease sometimes lash out at people who are trying to help them. The purpose of this chapter is to provide an overview of the social work (SW) role in the care of persons with dementia (PWD). The SW role includes providing services and support to PWD to help them cope with the disease, to families giving support (FGS), and to others who care for PWD.

BACKGROUND

"Dementia" comes from the Latin term *de mens* or "out of mind." It is used to describe a group of symptoms and syndromes characterized by multiple cognitive deficits of sufficient severity to interfere with daily activities and social relationships (American Psychiatric Association, 2013). Typically, the symptoms gradually progress as an increasing number of brain cells become impaired until death. Although progressive, the course of dementia and the time to death is quite variable. Because dementia affects many areas of functioning, the assessments and interventions of social workers (SWS) should focus on the whole person. They should include emotional, physical, psychological, social, and spiritual functioning of PWD and their caregivers. Because of the progressive nature of the disease, advance planning is essential.

About 50% to 60% of dementia in the elderly is caused by Alzheimer's disease, and about 20% is caused by cardiovascular disease. Other causes include Parkinson's disease, Pick's disease, Huntington's disease, and Creutzfeldt-Jakob's disease, traumatic brain injury, Down syndrome, HIV/AIDS, and alcoholism (American Psychiatric Association, 2013; Kane, Ouslander, & Abrass, 2004; Zarit & Zarit, 2007). Other diseases and delirium may produce symptoms that are similar to those of dementia, so a careful differential diagnosis is essential.

Approximately 5.2 million persons have Alzheimer's disease and other dementias in the United States (Alzheimer's Association, 2013). The prevalence of dementia increases rapidly with advancing age. For example, it has been estimated that one in nine persons have dementia over 65, but almost 1 in 3 have dementia over age 85. The prevalence of dementia varies by gender and racial/ethnic status. Almost two-thirds of people with dementia are women, but this is because women live longer, not because they have a higher incidence of dementia at any given age. African Americans and Hispanics also have a much higher prevalence of dementia, but this is likely due to health conditions such as high blood pressure and diabetes, leading to vascular dementia. Lower education levels, poverty, and poor nutrition may also account for some of the difference. Because of the aging of the population, the prevalence of dementia is expected to increase dramatically in the next several decades (Alzheimer's Association, 2013). Therefore, SWS can expect to encounter an increasing number of PWD and their caregivers in future years.

Dementia causes profound changes in a person's functional abilities. The essential feature of dementia is memory impairment, but at least one of the following cognitive disturbances must also be present: aphasia (vague or empty speech), apraxia (impaired ability to execute motor functioning), agnosia (failure to recognize or identify objects), and disturbance in executive function such as the ability to think abstractly and to plan, initiate, sequence, monitor, and implement complex behavioral sequences (American Psychiatric Association, 2013). As dementia progresses, behavioral disturbances often arise. Psychiatric symptoms may also occur, causing personality changes, depression, anxiety, delusions, or hallucinations.

ASSESSMENT

The first step when working with PWD is to conduct a thorough assessment of the situation (Table 35.1). If a diagnosis of dementia has not already been established, the SWS' role is to help PWD get an accurate diagnosis. Dementia is diagnosed by ruling out other physical illnesses that may be causing the symptoms, by history taking that establishes progressive memory loss, and by advanced brain imaging. Therefore, it is important to have referral sources of physicians who specialize in dementia (Kane et al., 2004; Toseland, Derico, & Owen, 1984). Referrals can also be made to memory clinics and Alzheimer's disease assistance centers.

When making an assessment, SWS should use a reliable and valid measure to assess the level of cognitive impairment such as the Mini Mental Status

TABLE 35.1 A Comprehensive Geriatric Assessment

- Medical History
- Physical Exam:
  - vital signs
  - behavior and appearance
  - sensory (ears/eyes)
  - dental
  - skin
  - chest/cardiovascular
  - abdomen/genitourinary
  - extremities
  - neurological
- Laboratory Assessment
- Mental Status Exam
- Spirituality Assessment
- Environmental Assessment
- Functional Assessment
  - ADLs
    - feeding
    - dressing
    - ambulation
    - toileting
    - bathing
    - continence
    - grooming
    - communication
  - IADLs
    - writing
    - reading
    - cooking, cleaning, shopping, climbing stairs, using telephone, managing medication, managing money
- Social Service Assessment
  - family dynamics
  - service needs
  - resource needs
  - benefits
  - legal issues (e.g., power of attorney, healthcare proxy)
  - advance care planning: functional needs
  - advance care planning: medical and end-of-life preferences

Exam (Folstein, Folstein, & McHugh, 1975). Social workers may also want to use other instruments, such as the Global Deterioration Scale, to determine the stage of disease progression (Reisberg, Ferris, & deLeon, 1982). To help with intervention planning, the assessment should include determining the current stage of the disease.

Part of the role of SWS in the early stage of work with PWD and caregivers is to provide support as they go through the process of accepting the diagnosis and understanding its implications. Social workers provide information to help PWD and their caregivers understand the consequences of the diagnosis for functional abilities. According to Kaplan (1996), caregivers of dementia patients go through the following states of adjustment: denial and making excuses for the person's behavior; overinvolvement and overcompensation for the person's losses; anger over the loss, frustration about the inability to halt the disease progression, and embarrassment caused by the person's behavior; guilt about the inability to accommodate and fully meet the person's behavior and care needs; and grieving and acceptance. At the same time, it is equally important to acknowledge and point out the resiliencies and strengths that caregivers display during each stage of adjustment (Coon, 2012).

During the assessment process it is important to work with the primary caregiver and other family and nonfamily caregivers. Kuhn (2013) suggests that at least one family member of individual PWD should be helped to step into a leadership role. This person takes overall responsibility for ensuring the well-being of the PWD, avoids undermining the remaining abilities of the person, and encourages the active involvement of others interested in the person's well-being. However, because caregiving frequently involves primary and secondary FGS, an important role for SWS is to help these individuals to define their roles, to cooperate in care planning and decision-making, and to negotiate and resolve conflicts as they occur (Toseland, Haigler, & Monahan, 2011).

Once a diagnosis of dementia has been confirmed, SWS can proceed with the assessment and intervention planning process. A comprehensive assessment should consider the medical, physical, social, emotional, psychological, practical, and spiritual aspects of PWD's functioning and that of their caregivers.

Physical Functioning and Dementia

Dementia has a profound impact on functional abilities—language and speech, motor ability, and judgment and reasoning. Measures of functional status can be used to assess basic activities of daily living (ADLs) such as bathing and toileting and also higher-level instrumental activities of daily living (IADL) such as managing money and driving. In early stages of dementia, SWS' roles include helping PWD and their caregivers to make adaptations in their environment that help them compensate for memory loss. In the middle stages of dementia, functional assessments help SWS teach caregivers tailored communication strategies that compensate for the specific impairments in language and speech of individual PWD. In later stages, SWS' roles focus on assessing caregiver's abilities to continue to provide assistance to PWD to provide information about community services such as day care and home care, and supportive housing, continuing care communities, and nursing home placement. This information helps reassure PWD and caregivers that help is available if needed.

Psychological and Emotional Impact of Dementia

Emotional lability and emotional problems are common among PWD and their caregivers. Caregivers often struggle emotionally as they reflect on the continual cognitive decline that inevitably leads to profound changes in PWD. Social workers can help caregivers by providing support and reassurance and developing long-term care plans that address medical, legal, financial, spiritual, and grief and loss issues. They provide emotional support as well as assistance with practical issues such as behavior problems and family work to avoid or reduce conflicts and coordinate family meetings to determine who is responsible for different parts of the care plan and the safety of the PWD. Because people cope in many different ways with emotional challenges, a careful assessment of the emotional concerns of PWD and their caregivers is essential to guide intervention efforts. Some PWD and their caregivers may, for example, benefit from early-stage dementia support groups (Yale, 1995). Others may benefit from individual or family counseling to alleviate emotional problems (Knight, 2004; Qualls & Knight, 2006).

Psychological impairments can occur in all disease stages. In early and middle stages, depression and anxiety are common. There are some good resources for counseling depressed and anxious older adults, who can still benefit from psychotherapeutic intervention in the early and early-middle stage of dementia (Fiske, Wetherell, & Gatz, 2009; Qualls & Knight, 2006). In later stages, psychotic symptoms such as agitation, hallucinations, and delusions may occur. Pharmacologic treatment may help, but the use of psychotropic medications is complicated; some medications, such as the benzodiazepines, make dementia worse. Therefore, it is essential for SWS to work with psychiatrists who are familiar with the treatment of PWD.

Behavioral problems, common in the middle stage, are often the result of inappropriate environmental stimulation or poor pain management. Therefore, it is important for SWS to conduct a careful assessment of the way caregivers interact with the PWD and of the physical comfort of the PWD before assuming that behavioral symptoms are due to psychiatric problems. Because of the adverse effects of some psychotropic medications, it is preferable to use nonpharmacological approaches whenever possible (Callaway, 1998; Zarit & Talley, 2013; Zarit & Zarit, 2007).

The Social Impact of Dementia

Socially, the PWD often becomes isolated. Dementia causes problems in word finding, sentence structure, and executive functioning, resulting in a decreasing ability to communicate. As dementia progresses, it becomes increasingly difficult to understand what the person is trying to communicate. Even close FGS may become frustrated or angry and short-tempered. Caregivers may feel it is too difficult to take the person out in public or have visitors. When visitors do come, they may find it difficult to interact with the PWD. Apathy and lethargy are common problems experienced by PWD in the middle stage of dementia, contributing further to isolation.

Often caregivers become socially isolated as they increasingly have to be available around the clock to make sure the PWD is safe. Therefore, SWS should encourage caregivers to care for themselves. It is also important for caregivers and PWD to make use of informal and formal services as part of the care plan. Social workers can teach caregivers communication skills and activities, described later in this chapter, to continue engagement as PWD skills deteriorate and dementia progresses.

Practical Aspects of Care

Another important SW assessment and intervention role is to help with the practical aspects of care planning and management. Social workers assess the capacity of PWD and their caregivers to get practical needs met. For example, SWS frequently become involved in helping the PWD and FGS understand the role of Medicaid and Medicare and other programs such as food stamps. This assistance may include helping caregivers with questions about eligibility and with required application procedures that might include investigating the availability of well-trained dementia sitters. Social workers also frequently become involved in planning for future needs. They may help those with mild dementia and their caregivers develop healthcare proxies and advance directives regarding medical care wishes if they become incapacitated. They may also encourage caregivers and PWD who still have the capacity to update wills, powers of attorney, and financial arrangements and to plan for the assistance that will be needed during later stages of dementia.

The Role of Religion and Spirituality

Many families confronted with the effects of dementia find strength in their spiritual beliefs and the support they receive from their communities of faith and are often comforted by clergy with a theology that reminds them of God's remembrance and sustenance of them (Houston & Parker, 2011). The early stage of dementia is a good time to help persons express what type of religious or spiritual support, if any, they would like as their symptoms progress. This may include continued or renewed contact with organized religions, or other spiritual practices. Social workers can help PWD to articulate preferences for medical care and funeral arrangements that reflect religious and spiritual values.

Attending to Caregiver Needs

A comprehensive biopsychosocial and environmental assessment should consider the needs of all FGS and other persons involved with the PWD. In some families, for example, a diagnosis of dementia can rekindle or exacerbate long-standing family conflicts. In others, it can bring FGS closer together. One or more family meetings are often helpful to assess the strengths and weaknesses of the family system in planning for the future, in problem solving, and in resolving conflicts and differences of opinion about care options and roles (Toseland et al., 2011). Zarit and Talley (2013) point out that understanding, accepting, and coming to terms with the dementing illness of a family member may be a long, slow process that varies significantly for individual FGS. Families giving support are faced not only with the prospect of providing care over the long-term, but also with the emotional challenge of coming to grips with the gradual loss of their loved one and changing expectations about the relationship they will have with the person as disease processes progress (Cox, 2007; Zarit & Talley, 2013). SWS have an important role to play in helping individual FGS and the entire family system cope with these emotional adjustments.

INTERVENTION ROLES

Social workers can play a variety of roles when working with PWD. These roles can include consultant, coordinator, and care manager. As consultants, SWS utilize the expertise and skills of PWD and their FGS. They rely heavily on the input of PWD and their caregivers during both assessment and care planning. Social workers assume that caregivers and PWD will take primary responsibility for the day-to-day implementation and monitoring of the care plan. After a period of consultation during which the assessment is conducted and a care plan is made, SWS check periodically to ensure that the care plan is being implemented and that problems and issues are addressed as they arise.

As care coordinators, SWS take greater responsibility for implementing the care plan they have developed with FGS and PWD. Social workers help to link PWD and caregivers to needed community resources and services and help to ensure that these services are received in a timely and consistent way. Once services are in place, the care coordinator's role is to ensure that services continue to meet ongoing needs that are responsive to changing circumstances as dementia progresses. The care coordinator role is frequently used by SWS who are called on to work with persons with moderate dementia. Care coordination is also frequently needed in situations where caregivers cannot assume great responsibility because of distance or other issues.

As care managers, SWS often do care planning for isolated PWD without family who are moderately or severely cognitively impaired. In this role, SWS can involve neighbors or other non-kin in the care planning and implementation process. Care managers help distant or less involved caregivers and PWD by putting services in place that remove some or all of the responsibility for day-to-day care. Typically, in the care management role SWS implement care plans by coordinating health and social services from different providers and by providing services themselves. They maintain regular and frequent contact with the PWD and any caregivers to ensure that appropriate care is delivered in a timely fashion. They also advocate for services to fill needs that are not being fully met. Overall, the focus of care management is to keep the person living at home for as long as possible in a safe and comfortable setting. When needs become too great, care managers' roles include helping to place the PWD in more sheltered environments such as assisted living.

INTERVENTION STRATEGIES

There are a wide variety of intervention strategies that can be used to help PWD and their caregivers cope with the disease. These can be classified into strategies focused on prevention, remediation, and support. Although an extensive discussion of these strategies is beyond the scope of this chapter, a brief overview is presented here.

The label "prevention" is not meant to imply that there are intervention strategies that can prevent or reverse the course of dementing illnesses. At this time, there are no such strategies. There are, however, intervention strategies that can slow the course of dementia and mitigate some of its harmful side effects. There are medications that can temporarily slow the course of dementia in some persons, but there are still no medications that have a lasting effect (Schwarz, Froelich, & Burns, 2012). Callaway (1998) provides an overview of pharmacological treatment from a SW perspective, and Schwarz et al. (2012) have completed a review of the results of more recent clinical drug trials. Some reviews are written in language easily understood by practicing SWS and include medications not only to treat cognitive loss but also to treat depression, agitation, delusions, and hallucinations (e.g., Kawas, 2003; Schwarz et al., 2012). The SW role in pharmacology management is to help PWD and their caregivers obtain appointments with geriatricians, neurologists, and psychiatrists familiar with PWD who can help them determine the best course of pharmacological treatment of symptoms of dementia. In general, it is thought that pharmacological agents to treat cognitive loss are most effective if they are administered in early dementia. Therefore, SWS can play an important role in urging PWD and their caregivers to have medication reviews as early as possible and to take medications as prescribed.

Another type of preventive intervention consists of cognitive stimulation programs. Early attempts include reality orientation, reminiscence, and remotivation therapy. The efficacy of these approaches for PWD is limited (Kasl-Godley & Gatz, 2000; Spector, Davies, Woods, & Orrell, 2000; Zarit & Zarit, 2007). Cognitive stimulation and training programs that have focused on cognitive deficits in episodic memory, language, and numerical skills have also been attempted (Hopper et al., 2012). Social workers also implement interventions to structure the environment of PWD by providing external cognitive aides to enhance memory. These interventions include suggesting specific places to store keys and other items used daily, medication organizers, the use of labels and color coding, and similar memory aides.

Apathy and lack of engagement are major problems for PWD, particularly during middle and late stages of the disease, problems that can be vexing to FGS. Programs to maintain communication and to stimulate interaction have been developed (e.g., Eggenberger, Heimerl, & Bennett, 2013; Passalacqua & Harwood, 2012; Toseland & McCallion, 1998). Table 35.2 present some areas of content around which strategies for enhancing and maintaining caregiver communication could be developed. For example, caregivers should expect a PWD to believe and say things that are unreasonable and illogical, so, if possible, they need to find a way to avoid arguing or correcting a PWD unnecessarily. They can learn to ask themselves, "Does it really matter?" Other strategies for maintaining communication with PWD at early, moderate, and severe stages of the disease can be found in Toseland and McCallion (1998).

Memory albums and memory charts can be used to stimulate reminiscence and life review and to engage PWD whose language abilities may be quite limited. Memory albums are small photo albums with pictures of important people, places, and events from the distant past that are particularly meaningful to the PWD. Simple words describing each picture are placed underneath the picture or on the opposite page of the photo album. Memory charts are larger boards that contain photographs and simple words in different panels that can be placed where a PWD spends a considerable amount of time. Memory albums and memory charts are particularly effective for engaging persons with moderate and severe dementia. Remedial intervention strategies include those that are focused on emotional and psychological problems and personality changes that are frequently observed in early- and middle-stage dementia. They can also be focused on agitation and behavior problems that are commonly encountered in moderate to severe stages of dementia.

Most remedial approaches to agitation and behavior problems rely on some form of behavioral analysis, with caregivers becoming behavior detectives identifying when problems occur and the antecedents and consequences of behavior. The idea is to find out precisely when behaviors occur and to try to determine the underlying needs that are not being met. Caregivers can be encouraged to identify antecedents that may stimulate the behavior and consequences that maintain the behavior. Based on these data, the environment can often be modified so that the comfort of the PWD is restored. Simple strategies such as making the room cooler or warmer, engaging the person in an activity, reducing noise or other stimulation, and reassurance and attention to positive behaviors often help reduce behavior problems (Zarit & Talley, 2013).

Another useful framework to reduce emotional and psychological problems is the progressively lowered stress threshold (PLST) model originally developed by Hall and Buckwalter (1987). Adapted from stress adaptation and coping models, the PLST model identifies clinical triggers such as fatigue, change in routine, inappropriate stimulation, and internal and external demands that exceed the capacities of the PWD. According to PLST, these triggers can lead to a sudden decline in functional ability. The PLST model recommends establishing daily routines, making environmental modifications, minimizing fatigue, managing inappropriate stimuli, minimizing affective responses, decreasing excessive demands, limiting physical triggers, and improving communication and behavior management strategies (Buckwalter et al., 1999).

TABLE 35.2 General Communication Guidelines

1. Begin all communications by first ensuring that you are relaxed and are conveying that you are relaxed.

    One technique to get rid of stress has been called deep breathing. This is a method of breathing for relaxation. This technique should not take more than approximately 2 minutes.

    • Concentrate on one spot in your stomach.

    • Concentrate on the flow of your breath as you inhale.

    • Concentrate on the flow of your breath as you exhale.

    • Focus on your breathing as you repeat this procedure several times slowly.

    • Visualize your breath going in through your nose, into the center of your body, and out again.

2. Reduce background noise and other distractions and stimuli.

3. Ensure that there is adequate lighting for the PWD or move to a brighter location.

4. If the PWD usually wears glasses or a hearing aid, try to have the PWD use them. However, do not argue if the PWD does not want to wear them.

5. Speak in a slow, calm, respectful manner and keep the pitch of your voice low.

6. Avoid speaking to the PWD as if he or she were a child.

7. Even when the PWD has severe language problems, never assume that he or she does not understand you. Always assume that he or she will understand at least some of the information you are attempting to convey.

8. Do not talk about the PWD with others as if the PWD is not there.

9. Sit at the same eye level as the PWD to show that your attention is focused on him or her.

Poor pain management that can cause behavior problems and agitation can be addressed with a careful review of physical causes (e.g., arthritis pain), and this should be undertaken before behavioral intervention programs are initiated. A number of helpful books give directions on how to handle a variety of specific behavior problems, including but not limited to apathy, combativeness, food refusal, insomnia, resistance to care, and wandering (e.g., Hoffman & Platt; 1991; Mahoney, Volicer, & Hurley, 2000; Rau, 1993). There are also many resources that address apathy as well as behavioral and sleep problems (Cohen-Mansfield, 2000; Cooper et al., 2012; Gallagher, Odenheimer, & Kunik, 2011; Gallagher-Thompson & Steffen, 2008; Karlin, Visnic, McGee, & Teri, 2013; Kiosses, Teri, Velligan, & Alexopoulos, 2011; Mace & Rabins, 2011; McCurry, LaFazia, Pike, Logsdon, & Teri, 2012; Potts & Potts, 2013; Zarit & Zarit, 2007).

Social workers have a vital role to play in supporting PWD and caregivers through the inevitable decline to death that is the ultimate result of dementia. In the early stages of dementia, support may take the form of affirming the coping abilities of PWD and their caregivers. In later stages, reassurance and gentle touch can be used by caregivers, and strategies to continue verbal and nonverbal engagement can be

implemented by engaging and stimulating whatever aspects of long-term memories and language abilities remain intact. Supportive interventions also include family care planning and problem-solving meetings, supportive counseling and reassurance, and assistance with community and institutional options for care as dementia advances. Support groups for caregivers and persons in early and moderate stages of dementia can be used for in-person meetings as well telephone, video, and Internet groups (Blom, Bosmans, Cuijpers, Zarit, & Pot, 2013; Cooper et al., 2012; Logsdon et al., 2010; Toseland & Larkin, 2011; Toseland, Naccarato, & Wray, 2007; Toseland & Rivas, 2012).

CONCLUSIONS

Because it affects many different aspects of emotional, physical, mental, social, and spiritual functioning, dementia is a very challenging disease to cope with for the person afflicted and for FGS. Social workers are called on to play a vital role in supporting and assisting PWD and their FGS in many different community and institutional settings. During assessment and intervention, it is essential for SWS to take a broad view of the PWD and their family and other caregivers. The SW profession is ideally suited for this role, working alone and in conjunction with other disciplines to help PWD and their FGS cope with the devastating impact of this disease.

REFERENCES

American Psychiatric Association. (2013). *Diagnostic and statistical manual of mental disorders* (5th ed., text rev.). Arlington, VA: American Psychiatric Publishing. doi:10.1176/appi.books.9780890425596

Alzheimer's Association. (2013). *2013 Alzheimer's disease facts and figures*. Chicago, IL: Alzheimer's Association Public Policy Office, 1–69. doi:10.1016/j.jalz.2013.02.003

Blom, M., Bosmans, J. E., Cuijpers, P., Zarit, S. H., & Pot, A. M. (2013). Effectiveness and cost-effectiveness of an Internet intervention for FGS of people with dementia: Design of a randomized controlled trial, *BMC Psychiatry, 13*, 17–24. doi:10.1186/1471-244X-13-17.

Buckwalter, K. C., Gerdner, L., Kohout, F., Hall, G. R., Kelly, A., Richards, B., & Sime, M. (1999). A nursing intervention to decrease depression in FGS of PWD. *Archives of Psychiatric Nursing, 13*, 80–88. doi:10.1016/S0883-941780024-7

Callaway, J. (1998). Psychopharmacological treatment of dementia. *Research on Social Work, 8*, 452–474. doi:10.1177/104973159800800405

Cohen-Mansfield, J. (2000). Nonpharmacological management of behavioral problems in PWD: The TREA model. *Alzheimer's Care Quarterly, 1*, 22–33. http://journals.lww.com/actjournalonline/pages/default.aspx

Coon, D. W. (2012). Resilience and family caregiving. *Annual Review of Gerontology and Geriatrics, 32*, 231–249. doi:10.1891/0198-8794.32.231

Cooper, C., Mukadam, N., Katona, C., Lyketsos, C., Ames, D., Rabins, P., . . . Livingston, G. (2012). Systematic review of the effectiveness of non-pharmacological interventions to improve quality of life of people with dementia, *International Psychogeriatrics, 24*, 856–870. doi:10.1017/S1041610211002614

Cox, C. (2007). *Dementia and social work practice: Research and intervention*. New York, NY: Springer.

Eggenberger, E., Heimerl, K., & Bennett, M. (2013). Communication skills training in dementia care: A systematic review of effectiveness, training content, and didactic methods in different care settings. *International Psychogeriatrics, 25*, 345–358. doi:10.1017/S1041610212001664

Fiske, A., Wetherell, J., & Gatz, M. (2009). Depression in older adults. *Annual Review of Clinical Psychology, 5*, 363–389. doi:10.1146/annurev.clinpsy.032408.153621

Folstein, M., Folstein, S., & McHugh, P. (1975). Mini-Mental State: A practical method for grading the cognitive state of patients for the clinicians. *Journal of Psychiatric Research, 12*, 189. doi:10.1016/0022-395690026-6

Gallagher, K. S., Odenheimer, G., & Kunik, M. E. (2011). Treating sleep problems in dementia caregivers based on parent-child interventions. *American Journal of Alzheimer's Disease and Other Dementias, 26*, 366–372. doi:10.1177/1533317511412048

Gallagher-Thompson, D., & Steffen, A. (2008). *Handbook of behavioral and cognitive therapies with older adults*. New York, NY: Springer.

Hall, G. R., & Buckwalter, K. C. (1987). Progressively lowered stress threshold: A conceptual model for care of adults with Alzheimer's disease. *Archives of Psychiatric Nursing, 1*, 399–406.

Hoffman, S., & Platt, C. (1991). *Comforting the confused: Strategies for managing dementia*. New York, NY: Springer.

Hopper, T., Bourgeois, M., Pimentel, J., Qualls, C., Hickey, E., Frymark, T., & Schooling, T. (2012). An evidence-based systematic review on cognitive interventions for individuals with dementia. *American Journal of Speech-Language Pathology, 22*, 126. doi:10.1044/1058-0360(2012/11-0137

Houston, J. M., & Parker, M. (2011). *A vision for the aging church: Renewed ministry to and from seniors*. Downers Grove, IL: Inter-Varsity Press.

Kane, R., Ouslander, J., & Abrass, I. (2004). *Essentials of clinical geriatrics* (5th ed.). New York, NY: McGraw-Hill.

Kaplan, M. (1996). *Clinical practice with caregivers of dementia patients*. Washington, DC: Taylor & Francis.

Karlin, B., Visnic, S., McGee, J. S., & Teri, L. (2013). Results from the multisite implementation of STAR-VA: A multicomponent psychosocial intervention for managing challenging dementia-related behaviors of veterans. *Psychological Services, 11*, 200–208. doi:10.1037/a0033683

Kasl-Godley, J., & Gatz, M. (2000). Psychosocial interventions for individuals with dementia: An integration of theory, therapy, and a clinical understanding of dementia. *Clinical Psychological Review, 20*, 755–782. doi:10.1016/S0272-735800062-8

Kawas, C. (2003). Early Alzheimer's disease. *New England Journal of Medicine, 349*, 1056–1063. doi:10.1056/NEJMcp022295

Kiosses, D., Teri, L., Velligan, D., & Alexopoulos, G. (2011). A home-delivered intervention for depressed, cognitively-impaired, disabled elders. *Journal of Geriatric Psychiatry, 26*, 256–262. doi:10.1002/gps.2521

Knight, B.G. (2004). *Psychotherapy with older adults* (3rd ed.). Thousand Oaks, CA: Sage.

Kuhn, D. (2013). *Alzheimer's early stages: First steps for families, friends and caregivers* (3rd ed.). Alameda, CA: Hunter House.

Logsdon, R., Pike, K., McCurry, S., Hunter, P., Maher, J., Snyder, L., & Teri, L. (2010). Early-stage memory loss support groups: Outcomes from a randomized controlled clinical trial. *Journal of Gerontology: Series B: Psychological Sciences and Social Sciences, 65B*, 691–697. doi:10.1093/geronb/gbq054

Mace, N., & Rabins, P. (2011). *The 36-hour day: A family guide to caring for people who have Alzheimer disease, related dementias, and memory loss* (5th ed.). Baltimore, MD: Johns Hopkins University Press.

Mahoney, E., Volicer, L., & Hurley, A. (2000). *Management of challenging behaviors in dementia.* Baltimore, MD: Health Professions Press.

McCurry, S., LaFazia, D., Pike, K., Logsdon, R., & Teri, L. (2012). Development and evaluation of a sleep education program for older adults with dementia living in adult homes. *American Journal of Geriatric Psychiatry, 20*, 494–504. doi:10.1097/JGP.0b013e318248ae79

Passalacqua, S., & Harwood, J. (2012). VIPS communication skills training for paraprofessional dementia caregivers: An intervention to increase person-centered dementia care. *Clinical Gerontologist, 35*, 425–445. doi:10.1080/07317115.2012.702655

Potts, D., & Potts, E. (2013). *A pocket guide for the Alzheimer's caregiver.* Tuscaloosa, AL: Dementia Dynamics.

Qualls, S., & Knight, B. (2006). *Psychotherapy for depression in older adults.* Hoboken, NJ: Wiley.

Rau, M. (1993). *Coping with communication challenges in Alzheimer's disease.* San Diego, CA: Singular.

Reisberg, B., Ferris, S., & deLeon, M. (1982). The global deterioration scale for assessment of primary degenerative dementia. *American Journal of Psychiatry,* 139, 1136–1139. http://ajp.psychiatryonline.org/article.aspx?articleid=160021

Spector, A., Davies, S., Woods, B., & Orrell, M. (2000). Reality orientation for dementia: A systematic review of the evidence of effectiveness from randomized controlled trials. *The Gerontologist, 40*, 206–212. doi:10.1093/geront/40.2.206

Schwarz, S., Froelich, L., & Burns, A. (2012). Pharmacological treatment of dementia, *Current Opinion in Psychiatry, 25*, 542–550. doi:10.1097/YCO.0b013e328358e4f2

Toseland, R., Derico, A., & Owen, M. (1984). Alzheimer's disease and related disorders: Assessment and intervention. *Health and Social Work, 9*, 212–228. doi:10.1093/hsw/9.3.212

Toseland, R., Haigler, D., & Monahan, D. (2011). *Education and support programs for caregivers.* New York, NY: Springer.

Toseland, R., & Larkin, H. (2011). Developing and leading telephone groups. *Social Work with Groups, 34*, 21–34. doi:10.1080/01609513.2010.526091

Toseland, R., & McCallion, P. (1998). *Maintaining communication with PWD.* New York, NY: Springer.

Toseland, R., Naccarato, T., & Wray, L. (2007). Telephone groups for older persons and FGS: Key implementation and process issues. *Clinical Gerontologist, 31*, 59–76. doi:10.1300/J018v31n01_05

Toseland, R., & Rivas R. (2012). *An introduction to group work practice* (7th ed.). Needham Heights, MA: Allyn & Bacon.

Yale, R. (1995). *Developing support groups for individuals with early-stage Alzheimer's disease: Planning, implementation, and evaluation.* Baltimore, MD: Health Professions Press.

Zarit, S. H., & Talley, R. C. (Eds.). (2013). *Caregiving for Alzheimer's disease and related disorders: Research, practice, policy.* New York, NY: Springer.

Zarit, S. H., & Zarit, J. M. (2007). *Mental disorders in older adults: Fundamentals of assessment and treatment* (2nd ed.). New York, NY: Guilford Press.

Introduction

Depression and anxiety disorders are common in older adults. These disorders are associated with impaired functioning, disability, and high service use and costs. Co-occurrence of depression and anxiety is common with chronic diseases. Effective psychological and pharmacological treatments are available. However, too often, depression and anxiety disorders are underdiagnosed or are not optimally treated. This chapter presents an update on the state of knowledge on depression and anxiety disorders in later life, focusing on prevalence, comorbidity, and effective evidence-based treatments.

DEPRESSION IN LATER LIFE

Depression is a frequent cause of psychological distress in older adults and significantly decreases quality of life (Gellis, 2009). Inadequate recognition and treatment of these problems at the individual level has important implications for social services, medical and mental health service use, and the allocation of healthcare resources. Less than half of elders with depression seek professional treatment from social workers, psychologists, or primary care physicians, with the majority stating that they would not seek mental health treatment in the future (Conner et al., 2010). Racial and ethnic backgrounds contribute to the likelihood of elders seeking professional treatment. Mexican Americans have lower odds for receiving any type of depression therapy despite reporting high depression severity scores (Gonzalez et al., 2010). However, African Americans are less likely to seek mental health services due to issues of mistrust and a lack of confidence in outcomes of such treatment compared with their White counterparts (Conner et al., 2010).

The provision of mental healthcare to older adults poses a unique set of service barriers. Individual barriers to seeking treatment include stigma, denial of an emotional problem, fear of health insurance loss, financial insecurity, embarrassment, isolation, being declared incompetent, language barriers, and lack of culturally sensitive programs (Center for Mental Health Services, 2004; Conner et al., 2010; Pepin, Segal, & Coolidge, 2009). Managed care is increasingly restricting the time spent by physicians with patients. Primary care physicians often report feeling too pressured for time to investigate mental

ZVI D. GELLIS

BONNIE KENALEY

Mental Health Disorders in Later Life

health problems in older people (Mitchell, Vaze, & Rao, 2009).

Prevalence of Depression Disorders

Depression is a serious medical illness in older adults and can range on a severity continuum from mild to moderate to severe. The presentation of symptoms may be mild in that they do not meet criteria for a depression disorder or manifest as severe with catatonic or psychotic features (American Psychiatric Association, 2013). The prevalence estimates of major depression in large-scale community elderly studies are generally low, ranging from 1% to 4.6% compared with younger cohorts, with higher prevalence among women (Fiske, Wetherell, & Gatz, 2009). In medically ill older adults, estimates for major depression range from 10% to 43%, with an additional 23% experiencing significant depressive symptoms (Fiske et al., 2009). Late-life depression is associated with increased risk of lifetime chronic depression (Murphy & Byrne, 2012). The prevalence rate for dysthymia is about 2% (Lee et al., 2012). Prevalence rates for minor depression range from 10% to 30% in older community-dwelling adults (Hybels & Blazer, 2003; Thota et al., 2012) and approximately 5% to 9% in adults seen by primary care physicians (Meeks, Vahia, Lavretsky, Kulkarni, & Jeste, 2011).

In home healthcare settings, estimates range from 6.4% to 13.5% for major depression and 27.5% for subthreshold depression (Bruce et al., 2002; Gellis, 2010; Shao, Peng, Bruce, & Bao, 2011). Depression is twice as prevalent in home healthcare as in primary care (Brown, Kaiser, & Gellis, 2007). In long-term care settings prevalence rates for major depression can range from 12% to 30%, and clinically significant depressive symptoms range from 12% to 35% (McDougall, Matthews, Kvaal, Dewey, & Brayne, 2007). Prevalence rates for major and minor depression in assisted living facilities are estimated at 14% (Watson, Zimmerman, Cohen, & Dominik, 2009) and 14%–42% in nursing homes (Djernes, 2006).

While prior research (Zalaquett & Stens, 2006) has shown no significant racial or ethnic differences in prevalence rates for depression, a controlled trial (Steffens, Fisher, Langa, Potter, & Plassman, 2009) found clear racial differences in depression scores measured by the Composite International Diagnostic Interview (CIDI; Kessler et al., 1998). White and Hispanic older adults experienced nearly three times the prevalence of depression compared with African Americans (Steffens, Fisher, Langa, Potter, & Plassman, 2009). As many as 15% of older Latinos, 12% of older Asian Americans, and 10% of older African Americans meet criteria for minor depression (Arean & Alvarez, 2001).

Marital status differences have also been reported, with widowed, separated, or divorced older people having higher prevalence rates of major depressive disorders (Chou & Cheung, 2013) than those who were married. Rates for depression appear to be higher in older women than older men (Vink, Aartsen, & Schoevers, 2009).

A significant risk factor of late-life depression is suicide. Older adults account for 20% of all suicides and have a higher completion rate compared with younger cohorts, yet they make up only 13% of the population (Center for Disease Control and Prevention, 2013). The most common demographic correlates of suicide are older age, male gender, white race, and unmarried status (Lapierre et al., 2011). For older females and males aged 65 years and older, suicide rates were elevated with a ratio of 150 suicides per 100,000 (Lapierre et al., 2011). In the United States, White males age 85 and older have the highest suicide completion rates (45 per 100,000; Centers for Disease Control and Prevention, 2013). A systematic review of elderly suicide prevention programs revealed that gender-specific distinctions play a role in the seeking of treatment, with men less inclined to seek medical services (Lapierre et al., 2011).

Comorbidity of Depression in Older Adults

Depression has been found to be associated with the presence of comorbid medical conditions. Approximately one-quarter (24.8%) of individuals with one or two medical conditions experience depression; whereas 27.7% of individuals with three or four medical conditions manifest depressive symptoms (Spangenberg, Forkmann, Brahler, & Glaesmer, 2011). Medical illnesses known to be associated with depression include heart disease, asthma, hypothyroidism, stroke and dementia, hypertension, diabetes, cancer, chronic pain, and osteoarthritis (Chou & Cheung, 2013; Gellis et al., 2012; McCarthy et al., 2009). The most common psychiatric comorbid disorder associated with depression is anxiety, with 47% of all individuals with late-life depression experiencing anxiety (Beekman et al., 2000). Negative outcomes of depression and comorbid conditions include poor health, poor social support, impaired functional status, increased disability, and mortality (Brown, Kaiser, & Gellis, 2007; Lyness et al., 2006; Preyde & Brassard, 2011). Increase healthcare use is a risk for late-life depression and comorbid disorders, including increased and unplanned hospital stays, and increased emergency department visits (Kang-Yi & Gellis, 2010, Preyde & Brassard, 2011). In the presence of other medical problems, older adults with late-life depression also incur slower recovery rates from illnesses and increased mortality (Murphy & Byrne, 2012).

EVIDENCE-BASED INTERVENTIONS

Psychosocial Interventions

A large body of evidence supports the use of various types of psychotherapy in the treatment of depression in older adults (Thorp et al., 2009). Manualized depression interventions that have been modified for older adults include cognitive-behavioral therapy (CBT), problem-solving therapy (PST), behavioral therapy, cognitive bibliotherapy, brief psychodynamic therapy, and life review therapy and have met evidence-based guidelines (Dickens et al., 2013). Several meta-analyses reported that psychotherapeutic interventions such as CBT, PST, and interpersonal and reminiscence therapy were more effective than placebo in improving depressive symptoms among older adults (Peng, Huang, Chen, & Lu, 2009; Wilson, Mottram, & Vassilas, 2008). Collaborative care models in primary care (e.g., IMPACT) have demonstrated greater improvement in depression symptoms and reduced suicidal ideation as compared with Primary Care Physician (PCP) treatment alone (Katon, Unutzer, Wells, & Jones, 2010). Several randomized controlled trials in nonspecialty mental health settings such as home healthcare tested the effectiveness of home-based PST in depressed medically ill older adults (Gellis & Bruce, 2010; Gellis et al., 2007; Gellis & Kenaley, 2008). Overall robust evidence exists for reduction in depressive symptoms over time relative to usual care. Older patients with late-life depression who received PST also reported higher quality of life, life satisfaction,

and problem-solving ability compared with patients who received standard home healthcare (Gellis et al., 2007).

To address individual and geographic barriers and reduce health costs, telehealth applications (defined as remote patient monitoring, Internet, audio, and video technologies to provide medical and mental health services) have been used for the past five decades (van den Berg, Schumann, Kraft, & Hoffmann, 2012). Depression treatment has been shown to be effective when integrated with telehealth technology among depressed older adults with comorbid diseases (Gellis & Kang-Yi, 2012; van den Berg et al., 2012). A recent randomized trial of the Tele-HEART program providing remote patient monitoring of cardiac disease symptoms and integrated depression care found a 50% reduction in depression symptoms over a 3-month period and cost reductions in emergency department use over a 12-month period (Gellis et al., 2012).

Past research examined the use of Internet and telephone therapy to provide depression treatment with positive outcomes (Speck et al., 2008). Since telephone therapy is generally not covered by reimbursement models, cost-benefits must be taken into consideration. Kiosses, Arean, Teri, and Alexopoulos (2010) examined the PATH depression intervention compared with usual care for cognitively impaired depressed elderly and found that depression significantly decreased over 12 weeks compared with usual care. In another randomized control trial with 138 older adults, age 50 years, participants received either PST and behavioral activation (PEARLS) or usual care, with reported improvements in depressive symptomatology for the intervention (Ciechanowski et al., 2004). The Healthy IDEAS study, examining the impact of an intervention for depression delivered by case managers in community-based agencies to 94 high-risk, diverse older adults, found that at 6 months, participants improved their knowledge significantly on how to obtain help for their depression, reported increased activity, and reported reduced pain (Quijano et al., 2007).

There is evidence that psychosocial interventions alone, including CBT and PST, are effective with older populations including minorities (Horell, 2008). Problem-solving therapy has proven efficacy among older adults in reducing depressive symptoms of moderate severity and impairment in executive functioning (Arean et al., 2010; Gellis & Nezu, 2011). Brief depression interventions by nonmedical practitioners have demonstrated effectiveness for homebound, frail, and medically ill populations (Gellis et al., 2007). Adjunct written educational materials for patients and family members have been shown to improve medication adherence and clinical outcomes (Wilson et al., 2008). In a series of randomized controlled trials, Gellis and colleagues (Gellis & Bruce, 2010; Gellis et al., 2012; Gellis et al., 2007; Gellis et al., 2008; Gellis et al, 2014) found robust effects in treating geriatric depression using 6 sessions of PST delivered by social workers and nurses. Other researchers found similar effects using 12 sessions of PST (Arean et al., 1993). Problem-solving therapy can also be used by therapists of different theoretical orientations (Gellis et al., in press).

Pharmacological Interventions

Antidepressants are reported as safe first-line treatment of depression in older adults (Chemali, Chahine, & Fricchione, 2009). Yet, as older adults are prescribed medications for medical diseases, the likelihood of self-medication, multiple drug use, drug–drug interactions, and unpleasant side effects increases. Common side effects of SSRIs include nausea, diarrhea, weight changes, sexual dysfunction, gastrointestinal bleeding, and hyponatremia (Chemali et al., 2009). Nonadherence to medications, especially antidepressants by older adults with major depression, is a major concern in treatment management (Grenard et al., 2011). In fact, between 24% and 28% of older adults are nonadherent (Keaton et al., 2009).

Biological Interventions

Since the mid-2000s, several advances have been made in the use of biological treatment modalities for late-life depression. Recent evidence reports positive outcomes using high-dose right unilateral electrode placement (RUL) brief pulse ECT, resulting in milder cognitive side-effects, yet having equal efficacy compared with bilateral electrode placement (BL) ECT and greater efficacy compared with lower doses of RUL ECT (Alexopoulos & Kelly, 2009).

Vagus nerve stimulation (VNS) plus treatment as usual (TAU) has shown efficacy in treating resistant depression when compared with treatment as usual (Alexopoulos & Kelly, 2009). Another new and efficacious advancement is the use of deep brain stimulation (DBS), which stimulates portions of the basal ganglia, resulting in reduction of symptoms or remission of depression.

ANXIETY DISORDERS IN LATER LIFE

Anxiety disorders are prevalent in older adults with estimated rates as high as 14% and even higher in healthcare settings (Pinquart, Duberstein, & Lyness, 2007). Clinically significant symptom prevalence estimates range from 20% to 24% among older adults (Bryant, Jackson, & Ames, 2008). The prevalence of anxiety disorders among older adults is a serious public health issue, yet, they remain underdiagnosed and undertreated (Simning, Conwell, Fisher, Richardson, & van Wijngaarden, 2012).

Anxiety disorders are often comorbid with common age-related chronic conditions such as cardiac disease, chronic pain, COPD, dementia, and Parkinson's disease (Wolitzky-Taylor, Castriotta, Lenze, Stanley, & Craske, 2010). Research has reported that personality traits such as neuroticism and external locus of control, poor coping strategies, previous mental health problems, and stressful life events are risk factors related to both incidence and prevalence of anxiety in later life (Djernes, 2006).

Recognition of Anxiety in Older Adults

Recognizing an anxiety disorder in an older person poses several challenges. Aging brings with it a higher prevalence of certain medical conditions, realistic concern about physical problems, and a higher use of prescription medications. As a result, separating a medical condition from physical symptoms of an anxiety disorder is more complicated in an older adult. Diagnosing anxiety in individuals with dementia can be difficult, too: agitation typical of dementia may be difficult to separate from anxiety; impaired memory may be interpreted as a sign of anxiety or dementia, and fears may be excessive or realistic depending on the person's situation.

Prevalence of Anxiety Disorders in Later Life

Anxiety disorders appear to be the most common class of psychiatric disorder among older people, more prevalent than depression or severe cognitive impairment (Bryant et al., 2008). A recent review by Wolitzky-Taylor and colleagues (2010) reported prevalence estimates ranging from 3.2% to 14.2% for anxiety disorders in older adults. The National Comorbidity Survey-Replication (NCS-R) reported 7% of older adults (65 and older) met the anxiety disorder criteria within the past year (Kessler et al., 2005). One study involving interviews with nearly 6,000 people nationwide reported a lifetime prevalence rate of 15.3% for DSM-IV-diagnosed anxiety disorders in respondents over age 60 (Kessler et al., 2005). Another study of approximately 500 community-dwelling tri-ethnic elders reported prevalence rates of 11.3% in Blacks, 12.4% in Hispanics, and 21.6% in non-Hispanic Whites age 75 and older (Ostir & Goodwin, 2006).

Generalized anxiety disorders (GAD) and phobias account for most anxiety disorders in later life (Wolitzky-Taylor et al., 2010). Prevalence estimates for GAD among older adults range from 1.2% to 7.3% (Bryant et al., 2008). Estimates of social phobia among older adults are relatively low, ranging from 0.6 to 2.3% (Wolitzky-Taylor et al., 2010). Several reviews summarized the prevalence of specific anxiety disorders in older community-based epidemiological samples as follows: phobias, including agoraphobia and social phobia, 0.7%–12.0%; GAD, 1.2%–7.3%; obsessive-compulsive disorder, 0.1%–1.5%; and panic disorder, 0%–0.3% (Vink et al., 2008; Wolitzky-Taylor et al., 2010).

The prevalence of subthreshold anxiety syndrome, including symptoms that do not meet criteria for a specific disorder, may be as high as 26% among older adults (Grenier et al., 2011). This includes anxiety symptoms associated with common medical conditions such as asthma, thyroid disease, coronary artery disease, and dementia, as well as adjustment disorders following significant late-life stressors such as bereavement or caregiving (Bryant et al., 2008).

Psychosocial Interventions for Anxiety Disorders in Later Life

The efficacy of evidence-based psychosocial interventions has been tested using randomized trials for geriatric anxiety and reviewed with emerging evidence of support for their use. Recent meta-analyses found that behavioral treatments for older persons with anxiety symptoms were on average significantly more effective than active control conditions (Gould, 2012; Thorp et al., 2009). No differences on gender, diagnostic targets, or treatment duration emerged in the analyses, suggesting that both women and men can benefit from behavioral interventions Treatments that are effective for anxiety disorders and symptoms included CBT and relaxation training (Wolitzky-Taylor et al., 2010).

Pharmacological Treatment for Anxiety Disorders

Anxiolytic medications, including benzodiazepines, are the most common treatment for late-life anxiety, likely because older patients present to primary care centers (Ravindran & Stein, 2010). Benzodiazepine users are also more likely than nonusers to experience accidents requiring medical attention due to increased risk of falls, hip fractures, and automobile accidents (Ravindran & Stein, 2010). Older patients taking benzodiazepines are also more likely to develop disabilities in both mobility and activities of daily living (ADLs) (Davidson et al., 2010). Benzodiazepines can impair memory and other cognitive functions and can also cause interactions with other drugs, and toxicity (Davidson et al., 2008). Although SSRIs are often used to treat geriatric anxiety, they can also cause side effects such as frequent falls, hyponatremia, weight loss, sexual dysfunction, and drug interactions (Arfken, Wilson, & Aronson, 2001; Herrmann, 2000; Kirby & Ames, 2001; Mort, 1999).

CONCLUSIONS

Depression and anxiety disorders are prevalent in later life and associated with negative outcomes. Depression disorders can exhibit as a spectrum disorder with subsyndromal symptoms not meeting full criteria for a major depressive disorder; however, the subsyndromal symptoms can be serious and may require further assessment. Effective brief treatments are available. Geriatric anxiety prevalence rates are high and are associated with poor functioning, emotional distress, and sleep problems. Various treatments including CBT and relaxation training are generally more effective than active control conditions.

REFERENCES

Alexopoulos, G., & Kelly, R. E. (2009). Research advances in geriatric depression. *World Psychiatry, 8*, 140–148.

American Psychiatric Association. (2013). *Diagnostic and statistical manual of mental disorders* (5th ed.). Washington, DC: Author.

Arean, A., & Alvarez, J. (2001). Prevalence of mental disorder, subsyndromal disorder and service use in older disadvantaged medical patients. *Interpersonal Journal of Psychiatry in Medicine, 31*, 9–24.

Arean, P. A., Perri, M. G., Nezu, A. M., Schein, R. L., Christopher, F., & Joseph, T. X. (1993). Comparative effectiveness of social problem-solving therapy and reminiscence therapy as treatments for depression in older adults. *Journal of Consulting and Clinical Psychology, 61*, 1003–1010. doi.org/10.1037/0022-0 06X.61.6.1003

Arean, P. A., Raue, P., Mackin, R. S., Kanellopoulos, D., McCulloch, C., & Alexopoulos, G. S. (2010). Problem-solving therapy and supportive therapy in older adults with major depression and executive dysfunction. *American Journal of Psychiatry, 167*, 1391–1398. doi.org/10.1176/appi.ajp.2010.09091327

Arfken, C. L., Wilson, J. G., & Aronson, S. M. (2001). Retrospective review of selective serotonin reuptake inhibitors and falling in older nursing home residents. *International Psychogeriatrics, 13*, 85–91. doi:10.1017/S1041610201007487

Beekman, A. T., deBeurs, E., van Balkom, A. J., Deeg, D. J., van Dyck, R., & van Tilburg, W. (2000). Anxiety and depression in later life: Co-occurrence and communality of risk factors. *American Journal of Psychiatry, 157*, 89–95.

Brown, E. L., Kaiser, R. M., & Gellis, Z. D. (2007). Screening and assessment of late life depression in home healthcare: Issues and challenges. *Annals of Long Term Care, 15*, 27–32.

Bryant, C., Jackson, H., & Ames, D. (2008). The prevalence of anxiety in older adults: Methodological issues and a review of the literature. *Journal of Affective Disorders, 109*, 233–250. doi.org/10.1016/j.jad.2007.11.008

Bruce, M. L., McAvay, G. J., Raue, P. J., Brown, E. L., Meyers, B. S., Keohane, D. J., . . . Weber, C. (2002). Major depression in elderly home health care patients. *American Journal of Psychiatry, 159*, 1367–1374. doi:10.1176/appi.ajp.159.8.1367

Center for Disease Control and Prevention. (2013). *Web-based injury statistics query and reporting system.* Retrieved from http//:www.cdc.gov/ncip/wisqars/default.htm

Center for Mental Health Services, Substance Abuse and Mental Health Services Administration. (2004). *Community integration for older adults with mental illnesses: Overcoming barriers and seizing opportunities.* DHHS Pub. No. (SMA) 05-4018. Retrieved from http://www.taadas.org/publications/prodimages/Community%20Integration%20for%20Older%20Adults%20with%20Mental%20Illnesses%20Overcoming%20Barriers%20and%20Seizing%20Opportunities.pdf

Chemali, Z., Chahine, L., & Fricchione, G. (2009). The use of selective serotonin reuptake inhibitors in elderly patients. *Harvard Review of Psychiatry, 17*, 242–253. doi.org/10.1080/10673220903129798

Chou, K., & Cheung, C. (2013). Major depressive disorder in vulnerable groups of older adults, their course and treatment, and psychiatric comorbidity. *Depression and Anxiety, 30*, 528–537. doi.org/10.1002/da.22073

Ciechanowski, P., Wagner, E., Schmailing, K., Schwartz, S., Williams, G., Diehr, P., . . . LoGerfo, J. (2004). Community-integrated home-based depression treatment in older adults: A randomized controlled trial. *Journal of the American Medical Association, 291*, 1569–1577. doi.org/10.1001/jama.291.13.1569

Conner, K. O., Copeland, V. C, Grote, N., Koeske, G., Rosen, D., Reynolds, C. F., & Brown, C. (2010). Mental health treatment seeking among older adults with depression: The impact of stigma and race. *American Journal of Geriatric Psychiatry, 18*, 531–543. doi.org/10.1097/JGP.0b013e3181cc0366

Davidson, J., Zhang, W., Connor, K., Ji, J., Jobson, K., Lecrubier, Y., . . . Versiani, M. (2010). Review: A psychopharmacological treatment algorithm for generalized anxiety disorder (GAD). *Journal of Psychopharmacology, 24*, 3–26. doi:10.1177/0269881108096505

Dickens, C., Cherrington, A., Adeyemi, I., Roughley, K, Bower, P., Garrett, C., . . . Coventry, P. (2013). Characteristics of psychological interventions that improve depression in people with coronary heart disease: A systematic review and meta-regression.

Psychosomatic Medicine, 75, 211–221. doi.org/10.1097/PSY.0b013e31827ac009

Djernes, J. (2006). Prevalence and predictors of depression in populations of elderly: A review. *Acta Psychiatrica Scandinavica, 113,* 372–387. doi.org/10.1111/j.1600-0447.2006.00770

Fiske, A., Wetherell, J., & Gatz, M. (2009). Depression in older adults. *Annual Review of Clinical Psychology, 5,* 363–389. doi:10.1146/annurev.clinpsy.032408.153621 doi.org/10.1111/j.1532-5415.2010.03220.x

Gellis, Z. D. (2009). Evidence-based practice in older adults with mental health disorders. In A. Roberts (Ed.) *Social work desk reference* (2nd ed., pp. 843–852). New York, NY: Oxford.

Gellis, Z. D. (2010). Depression screening in medically ill homecare elderly. *Best Practices in Mental Health, 6,* 1–16.

Gellis, Z. D., & Bruce, M. L. (2010). Problem solving therapy for subthreshold depression in home health-care patients with cardiovascular disease. *American Journal of Geriatric Psychiatry, 18,* 464–474. doi.org/10.1097/JGP.0b013e3181b21442

Gellis, Z. D., & Kang-Yi, C. (2012). Meta-analysis of cardiac rehabilitation interventions on depression outcomes among older adults. *American Journal of Cardiology, 110,* 1219–1224. doi.org/10.1016/j.amjcard.2012.06.021

Gellis, Z. D., & Kenaley, B. (2008). Problem solving therapy for depression in adults: A systematic review. *Research on Social Work Practice, 18,* 117–131. doi:10.1177/1049731507301277

Gellis, Z. D., Kenaley, B., McGinty, J., Bardelli, E., Davitt, J., & Ten Have, T. (2012) Impact of telehealth intervention on heart and chronic respiratory failure medically ill patients. *The Gerontologist, 52,* 541–552. doi:10.1093/geront/gnr134

Gellis, Z. D., McGinty, J., Horowitz, A., Bruce, M., & Misener, E. (2007). Problem solving therapy for late life depression in home care elderly: A randomized controlled trial. *American Journal of Geriatric Psychiatry, 15,* 968–978. doi.org/10.1097/JGP.0b013e3180cc2bd7

Gellis, Z. D., McGinty, J. Tierney, L., Burton, J., Jordan, C., Misener, E., & Horowitz, A. (2008). Randomized controlled trial of problem-solving therapy for minor depression in home care. *Research on Social Work Practice, 18,* 117–131. doi:10.1177/1049731507301277

Gellis, Z. D., & Nezu, A. T. (2011). Integrating depression treatment for homebound medically ill older adults: Using evidence-based problem-solving therapy. In K. Sorocco & S. Lauderdale (Eds.), *Cognitive behavior therapy with older adults: Innovations across care settings* (pp. 391–420). New York, NY: Springer.

Gellis, Z. D., Solomon, P., Wiesel-Cullen, S., Lukens, J., Gleba, J., Zalucki, D., & Huz, S.(2014). Dissemination of evidence-based depression care for community-dwelling older adults. *Best Practices in Mental Health, 10,* 1–15.

Gonzalez, H., Vega, W., Williams, D., Tarraf, W., West, B., & Neighbors, H. (2010). Depression care in the United States. *Archives of General Psychiatry, 67,* 37–46. doi:10.1001/archgenpsychiatry.2009.168

Gould, R. (2012). Efficacy of cognitive behavioral therapy for anxiety disorders in older people: A meta-analysis and meta-regression of randomized controlled trials. *Journal of the American Geriatrics Society, 60,* 218–229. doi:10.1111/j.1532-5415.2011.03824

Grenard, J., Munjas, B., Adams, J., Suttorp, M., Maglione, M., McGlynn, E., & Gellad, W. (2011). Depression and medication adherence in the treatment of chronic diseases in the United States: A meta-analysis. *Journal of General Internal Medicine, 26,* 1175–1182.

Grenier, S., Preville, M., Boyer, R., O'Connor, K., Beland, S. G., Potvin, O., . . . Scientific Committee of the ESA Study. (2011). The impact of DSM-IV symptom and clinical significance criteria on the prevalence estimates of subthreshold and threshold anxiety in the older population. *American Journal of Geriatric Psychiatry, 19,* 316–326.

Herrmann, N. (2000). Use of SSRIs in the elderly: Obvious benefits but unappreciated risks. *Canadian Journal of Clinical Pharmacology, 7,* 91–95.

Horell, S. (2008). Effectiveness of cognitive behavioral therapy with adult ethnic minority clients: A review. *Professional Psychology Research and Practice, 39,* 160–168.

Hybels, C., & Blazer, D. (2003). Epidemiology of late life mental disorders. *Clinical Geriatric Medicine, 19,* 663–696. doi.org/10.1016/S0749-0690(03)00042-9

Kang-Yi, C. D., & Gellis, Z. D. (2010). Systematic review of community-based health interventions on depression for older adults with heart disease. *Aging and Mental Health, 14,* 1–19. doi.org/10.1080/13607860903421003

Katon, W., Unutzer, J., Wells, K., & Jones, L. (2010). Collaborative depression care: History, evolution and ways to enhance dissemination and sustainability. *General Hospital Psychiatry, 32,* 456–464. doi.org/10.1016/j.genhosppsych.2010.04.001

Keaton, D., Lamkin, N., Cassidy, K., Meyer, W., Ignacio, R., Aulakh, L., . . . Sajatovic, M. (2009). Utilization of herbal and nutritional compounds among older adults with bipolar disorder and with major depression. *International Journal of Geriatric Psychiatry, 24,* 1087–1093. doi.org/10.1002/gps.2227

Kessler, R. C., Berglund, P., Demler, O., Jin, R., Merikangas, K. R., & Walters, E. E. (2005). Lifetime prevalence and age-of-onset distributions of DSM-IV disorders in the national comorbidity survey replication. *Archives of General Psychiatry, 62*, 593–602. doi.org/10.1001/archpsyc.62.6.593

Kessler, R. C., Wittchen, H. C., Abeson, J. M., McGonagle, K., Schwarz, N., Kendler, K. S., ... Zhao, S. (1998). Methodological studies of the Composite International Diagnostic Interview (CIDI) in the US National Comorbidity Survey. *International Journal of Methods in Psychiatric Research, 7*, 33–55.

Kiosses, D., Arean, P., Teri, L., & Alexopoulos, G. (2010). Home-delivered Problem Adaptation Therapy (PATH) for depressed, cognitively impaired, disabled elders: A preliminary study. *American Journal of Geriatric Psychiatry, 18*, 988–989. doi.org/10.1097/JGP.0b013e3181d6947d

Kirby, A. D., & Ames, D. (2001). Hyponatraemia and selective serotonin re-uptake inhibitors in elderly patients. *International Journal of Geriatric Psychiatry, 16*, 484–493. doi:10.1002/gps.367

Lapierre, S., Erlangsen, A., Waern, M., DeLeo, D., Oyama, H., Scocco, P., ... Quinett, P. (2011). A systematic review of elderly suicide prevention programs. *Crisis, 32*, 88–98.

Lee, S. Y., Franchetti, M. K., Imanbayev, A., Gallo, J. J., Spira, A., & Hochang, B. L. (2012). Non-pharmacological prevention of major depression among community-dwelling older adults: A systematic review of the efficacy of psychotherapy interventions. *Archives of Gerontology and Geriatrics, 55*, 522–529. doi.org/10.1016/j.archger.2012.03.003

Lyness, J. M., Moonseong, H., Datto, C. J., Have, R. T., Katz, I. R., Drayer, R., ... Bruce, M. L. (2006). Outcomes of minor and subsyndromal depression among elderly patients in primary care settings. *Annals of Internal Medicine, 144*, 496–506.

McCarthy, L. H., Bigal, Marcelo, E., Katz, M., Derby, C., & Lipton, R. B. (2009). Chronic pain and obesity in elderly people: Results from the Einstein Aging Study. *Journal of the American Geriatrics Society, 57*, 115–119.

McDougall, F., Kvaal, M., Dewey, M., & Brayne, M. (2007). Prevalence and symptomatology of depression in older people living in institutions in England and Wales. *Age and Ageing, 36*, 562–568. doi.org/10.1093/ageing/afm111

Meeks, T. W., Vahia, I. V., Lavretsky, H., Kulkarni, G., & Jeste, D. V. (2011). A tune in "a minor" can "b major": A review of epidemiology, illness course, and public health implications of subthreshold depression in older adults. *Journal of Affective Disorders, 129*, 126–142. doi.org/10.1016/j.jad.2010.09.015

Mitchell, A., Vaze, A., & Rao, S. (2009). Clinical diagnosis of depression in primary care: A meta-analysis. *Lancet, 374*, 609–619. doi.org/10.1016/S0140-6736(09)60879-5

Mort, J. R. (1999). Selective serotonin reuptake inhibitors (SSRIs) and falls in the elderly depressed patient. *South Dakota Journal of Medicine, 52*, 201–202.

Murphy, J., & Byrne, G. (2012). Prevalence and correlates of the proposed DSM-5 diagnosis of chronic depressive disorder. *Journal of Affective Disorders, 139*, 172–180.

Ostir, G. V., & Goodwin, J. S. (2006). Anxiety in persons 75 and older: Findings from a tri-ethnic population. *Ethnicity and Disease, 16*, 22–27.

Peng, X., Huang, C., Chen, L., & Lu, Z. (2009). Cognitive behavioral therapy and reminiscence techniques for the treatment of depression in the elderly: A systematic review. *Journal of International Medical Research, 7*, 975–982. doi.org/10.1177/147323000903700401

Pepin, R., Segal, D. L., & Coolidge, F. L. (2009). Intrinsic and extrinsic barriers to mental health care among community-dwelling younger and older adults. *Aging and Mental Health, 13*, 769–777. doi.org/10.1080/13607860902918231

Pinquart, M., Duberstein, P., & Lyness, J. (2007). Effects of psychotherapy and other behavioral interventions on clinically depressed older adults: A meta-analysis. *Aging and Mental Health, 11*, 645–657. doi.org/10.1080/13607860701529635

Preyde, M., & Brassard, K. (2011). Evidence-based risk factors for adverse health outcomes in older patients after discharge home and assessment tools: A systematic review. *Journal of Evidence-Based Social Work, 8*, 445–468.

Quijano, L., Stanley, M., Petersen, N., Casado, B., Steinberg, E., Cully, J., & Wilson, N. (2007). Healthy IDEAS, A depression intervention delivered by community-based case managers serving older adults. *Journal of Applied Gerontology, 26*, 139–156. doi.org/10.1177/0733464807299354

Ravindran, L., & Stein, M. (2010). The pharmacologic treatment of anxiety disorders: A review of progress. *Journal of Clinical Psychiatry, 71*, 839–848. doi.org/10.4088/JCP.10r06218blu

Shao, H., Peng, T., Bruce, M., & Bao, Y. (2011). Diagnosed depression among Medicare home health patients: National estimates of prevalence and key characteristics. *Psychiatric Services, 62*, 538–540. doi:10.1176/aapi.ps.62.5.538.

Simning, A., Conwell, Y., Fisher, S. G., Richardson, T. M., & van Wijngaarden, E. (2012). The characteristics of anxiety and depression symptom severity in older adults living in public housing. *International Psychogeriatrics, 24*, 614–623.

Spangenberg, L., Forkmann, T., Brahler, E., & Glaesmer, H. (2011). The association of depression and multimorbidity in the elderly: Implications for the assessment of depression. *Psychogeriatrics, 11*, 227–234.

Speck, V., Cuijpers, P., Nyklicek, I., Smits, N., Riper, H., Keyzer, J., & Pop, V. (2008). One year follow-up results of a randomized controlled clinical trial on internet-based cognitive Depressive Disorders in Older Adults behavioural therapy for subthreshold depression in people over 50 years. *Psychological Medicine, 38*, 635–639.

Steffens, D. C., Fisher, G. G., Langa, K. M., Potter, G. G., & Plassman, B. L. (2009). Prevalence of depression among older Americans: The Aging, Demographic and Memory Study. *International Psychogeriatrics, 21*, 879–888.

Thorp, S., Ayers, C., Nuevo, R., Stoddard, J., Sorrell, J., & Wetherell, J. (2009). Meta-analysis comparing different behavioral treatments for late life anxiety. *American Journal of Geriatric Psychiatry, 17*, 105–115. doi:10.1097/JGP.0b013e31818b3f7e

Thota, A., Sipe, T., Byard, G., Zometa, C., Hahn, R., McKnight-Elly, L., ...Williams, S. (2012). Collaborative care to improve the management of depressive disorders: A community guide systematic review and meta-analysis. *American Journal of Preventive Medicine, 42*, 525–538. doi.org/10.1016/j.amepre.2012.01.01

Van den Berg, N., Schumann, M., Kraft, K., & Hoffmann, W. (2012). Telemedicine and telecare for older patients: A systematic review. *Maturitas, 73*, 94–114. doi.org/10.1016/j.maturitas.2012.06.010

Vink, D., Aartsen, M., & Schoevers, R. (2008). Risk factors for anxiety and depression in the elderly: A review. *Journal of Affective Disorders, 106*, 29–44. doi.org/10.1016/j.jad.2007.06.005

Watson, L. C., Zimmerman, S., Cohen, L. W., & Dominik, R. (2009). Practical depression screening in residential care/assisted living: Five methods compared with gold standard diagnoses. *American Journal of Geriatric Psychiatry, 17*, 556–564. doi.org/10.1097/JGP.0b013e31819b891c

Wilson K., Mottram P., & Vassilas, C. (2008) Psychotherapeutic treatments for older depressed people. *Cochrane Database Systematic Reviews, 23*: CD004853.

Wolitzky-Taylor, K., Castriotta, N., Lenze, E., Stanley, M., & Craske, M. (2010). Anxiety disorders in older adults: A comprehensive review. *Depression and Anxiety, 27*, 190–211. doi:10.1002/da.20653

Zalaquett, C., & Stens, A. (2006). Psychosocial treatments for major depression and dysthymia in older adults: A review of the research literature. *Journal of Counseling and Development, 84*, 192–201. doi.org/10.1002/j.1556-6678.2006.tb00395.x

Alcohol and substance abuse and misuse among older adults are expected to increase rapidly with the aging of the baby boomers, a cohort with more liberal attitudes toward substance abuse than previous cohorts (Gfroerer, Penne, Pemberton, & Folsom, 2003). Substance abuse among older adults, however, has remained underdiagnosed and undertreated and has been referred to as an invisible epidemic (US Department of Health and Human Services, 1998). This chapter focuses on three types of substance abuse among older adults: alcohol abuse, abuse and misuse of prescription drugs, and illicit drug use.

ALCOHOL ABUSE

Although alcohol abuse declines with age, it is estimated that up to 15% of community-dwelling older adults abuse alcohol (Bartels, Blow, Brockman, & Van Citters, 2005). According to the 2005 and 2006 National Survey on Drug Use and Health, 13% of men and 8% of women age 65 years and older reported at-risk alcohol use (two or more drinks per day on average within past 30 days), and 14% of men and 3% of women reported binge drinking (five or more drinks on same occasion on at least 1 day within 30 days) (Blazer & Wu, 2009).

Aging can lower physical tolerance for alcohol, and exacerbate problems such as high blood pressure, memory loss, and mood disorders (National Institute of Alcohol Abuse and Alcoholism [NIAAA], 2013). The NIAAA recommends that older adults consume no more than seven drinks in a week because of physical changes associated with aging (NIAAA, 2013).[1] As with younger populations, alcohol abuse and dependence are more common among older men than women. Approximately four times more older men than women abuse alcohol (US Department of Health and Human Services, 1998). There has been a paucity of research on alcohol abuse among ethnic elders, and further studies are needed given the rapid increase in the number of ethnic elders (Andrews, 2008; Cummings, Bride, & Rawlins-Shaw, 2006).

Older adults who abuse alcohol can be categorized into early- and late-onset groups (Benshoff, Harrawood, & Koch, 2003). It is estimated that two-thirds of older adults are early-onset drinkers who developed alcohol problems while young (Rigler, 2000). These adults suffer from various physical and psychological consequences of long-term alcohol abuse such as malnutrition, osteoporosis, decreased

TAZUKO SHIBUSAWA
STEPHANIE SARABIA

Older Adults with Substance/Alcohol Abuse Problems

37

TABLE 37.1 Risk Factors for Alcohol and Substance Abuse Among Older Adults

Depression/Anxiety	Homebound	Retirement
Loss and bereavement	Chronic pain	Loss of employment
Social isolation	Loss of physical mobility	New caregiving role
Living alone	Loss of spouse or partner	

red blood cell production, increased cancer risk, myopathy, hypertension, hepatitis, pancreatitis, stroke, dementia, esophagitis/gastritis, and depression (Centers for Disease Control [CDC] 2012; NIAAA, 2012). As presented in Table 37.1, late-onset drinking is often precipitated by life events such as retirement, death of a spouse or partner, loss of status, and chronic health problems as well as loneliness and depression (Rigler, 2000). Studies also indicate that older women may be at greater risk of developing alcohol use disorders later in life than older men (Blow & Barry, 2002). The prognosis for later-onset drinkers is better than that for early-onset drinkers because the former have not suffered from the physical and psychological consequences of long-term abuse (Benshoff et al., 2003).

MISUSE OF PRESCRIPTION AND OVER-THE-COUNTER MEDICATION

Older adults consume large amounts of prescription drugs and over-the-counter (OTC) medications. They are estimated to spend $15 billion annually on prescription drugs, which is four times the amount of younger populations (US Department of Health and Human Services, 1999). It is important to distinguish between the terms *misuse* and *abuse*. Misuse refers to the inappropriate use of medications and includes underuse, overuse, or erratic use (US Department of Health and Human Services, 1999). Misuse can be caused by difficulties with reading and following prescription labels, keeping track of medications, and taking inappropriate dosages. Vision and hearing loss can increase the misuse of prescription and OTC medication among older adults.

Abuse, on the other hand, refers to nontherapeutic use of medications (National Institute on Drug Abuse [NIDA], 2014). Psychoactive drugs tend to be more misused than other medications (Simoni-Wastila, Zuckerman, Singhal, Briesacher, & Hsu, 2005). Benzodiazepines, which are prescribed

for conditions such as insomnia, anxiety, and chronic pain, are prescribed widely among older adults, can be addictive, and have been associated with confusion, cognitive losses, depression, and increase in falls (Blow & Barry, 2012).

Older women are more likely than men to receive psychoactive drugs, and drug dependence is more common among older women than men (Blow & Barry, 2012). Pharmaceutical companies target aging women with prescription drug advertising, which results in some women pressuring their physician for various medications (Stevens, Andrade & Ruiz, 2009; White & Kilbourne, 2006). Studies have also found that physicians prescribe mood-altering medications more to older women than any other age or gender group (Blow & Barry, 2002; Simoni-Wastila & Yang, 2006), and prescription drug misuse is expected to continue to increase among women (Rider, 2006; Sarabia & Martin, 2013). Although OTC and prescribed medications are considered to be safer than illicit drugs (Manchikanti, 2006), prescription drugs have caused more deaths than heroin and cocaine combined (CDC, 2011).

Vignette #1

Sam is a 68-year-old single gay man who lived alone since the death of his partner almost 10 years ago. Sam scheduled an appointment with a nurse practitioner at his primary care office because he had hurt his hip from a fall. Shortly after his hip injury Sam began having severe headaches, nausea, and vomiting. Sam told the nurse practitioner that he felt exhausted and achy as if he had the flu. He was also having significant trouble sleeping, and his friends at the senior center complained that he was moody, which was out of character for him.

The nurse practitioner found out that Sam had always had difficulty sleeping. When his partner was alive, having a beer at night was enough to help him fall asleep. But since the death of his partner, his sleep troubles worsened, and Sam began taking OTC Benadryl to help him fall asleep. Over the years Sam slowly increased the amount of Benadryl to four or five pills per night as well as taking a swig of Nyquil. When Sam hurt his hip, his physician prescribed muscle relaxers and pain medication. While filling these prescriptions the pharmacist noticed that Sam was also buying Benadryl and told him he should not take the Benadryl while taking the medications his physician prescribed. The nurse practitioner concluded that Sam had become dependent on the Benadryl and Nyquil combination, and his symptoms were a result of withdrawal when he suddenly stopped after seeing the pharmacist. ▪

ILLICIT DRUG ABUSE AND DEPENDENCE

Historically, older adults have used fewer illicit drugs such as marijuana, cocaine, and heroin than have younger populations. Recent studies, however, cast doubt on the "maturing out" theory, which contends that people age out of illicit drug use or die prematurely from abuse (Prins, 2008). According to the National Household Survey on Drug Abuse (NHSDA), adults ages 50–59 have doubled their use of illicit drugs from 2002 (2.7%) to 2010 (5.8%) (Substance Abuse and Mental Health Services Administration [SAMHSA], 2011). Analysis of substance abuse treatment admissions from 1998 through 2006 also suggests that treatment admissions with a primary diagnosis related to alcohol use has remained consistent, whereas treatment admissions for a primary drug use disorder have grown steadily (Duncan, Nicholson, White, Bradley, & Bonaguro, 2010). Researchers have attributed this surge in illicit drug use among aging adults to the aging of the baby boomer birth cohort (Duncan et al., 2010; Gfroerer et al., 2003). Furthermore, methadone treatment and needle exchange have added to the longevity of heroin and/or injection drug users, resulting in an increase in the number of older adults who use illicit drugs. In addition, there are a number of older adults who start to use crack cocaine for the first time after age 50 (Johnson & Sterk, 2003).

EFFECTS OF ALCOHOL AND SUBSTANCE ABUSE ON OLDER ADULTS

Older adults have a decreased tolerance for alcohol and drugs. Their bodies do not absorb food and drugs as well as they did in their younger years. Because of reduced body mass and body water, slowed metabolism, and decreased absorption rate in the gastrointestinal system, alcohol and drugs remain in the body for longer periods of time and at higher rates of concentration (Benshoff et al., 2003). Accordingly, alcohol, prescription drugs, and illicit drugs have stronger effects on older adults than for younger adults, especially when they are used in combination. Depression is often comorbid with alcohol and substance abuse; mood and anxiety disorders can be exacerbated by alcohol or drug use. Prescription or OTC medication misuse or combining drugs with alcohol can lead to decreased functional capacity and cognition, including impairment of memory and attention, excessive sedation, delirium, and greater risk for falling (Benshoff et al., 2003). Psychoactive medication when taken with alcohol can have serious consequences. For example, benzodiazepines when mixed with alcohol can result in decreased alertness, impaired judgment, respiratory failure, and falls and accidents (US Department of Health and Human Services, 1998).

The makeup of the female body makes abusing substances a more dangerous habit for women. Because women have more body fat, less muscle mass, and a slower metabolism than men, not only do their bodies contain less water to dilute alcohol but also alcohol remains in their bodies longer and at higher levels (NIAAA, 2011). Several negative effects, commonly referred to as a *telescoping effect*, stem from this gender disparity. Women advance more quickly into addiction and develop cirrhosis more quickly than men (Hernandez-Avila, Rounsaville, & Kranzler, 2004). As women age their body fat increases, and this disparity also continues to increase over time (Kerr-Correa, Igami, Hiroce, & Tucci, 2007). It is, therefore, recommended that aging women have a maximum of one drink each day if at all, which is half the recommendation for men (US Department of Health and Human Services, 2009).

TABLE 37.2 Signs of Possible Alcohol and Substance Abuse in Older Adults

Dementia	Depression/Anxiety	Mood Swings, Irritability
Dulling of senses	Recent memory loss	Disorientation
Slowed thought process	Swelling	Inflammation of joints
Indigestion	Malnutrition	Heart disease
Changes in sleep patterns	Changes in eating habits	Lack of energy
Loss of short-term memory	General loss of interest	Social isolation
Unexplained accidents/falls	Self-neglect	Tremors

IDENTIFICATION OF ALCOHOL AND SUBSTANCE ABUSE

Although alcohol abuse by older adults is less prevalent than in younger populations, it is more difficult to detect, particularly because the workplace is where alcohol and drug problems are frequently discovered. In particular, older women are more likely to drink alone and at home, which rarely results in driving under the influence (DUI) or other legal charges that can be a catalyst into treatment (Briggs, Magnus, Lassiter, Patterson, & Smith, 2011). Older adults who are White, female, or of upper middle-class backgrounds are less likely to be identified as having a problem because they do not fit the stereotype of someone who has an alcohol or drug problem. The trend toward shorter medical visits and the shortage of providers with training in geriatric medicine also serve as barriers to the detection of alcohol and substance problems (US Department of Health and Human Services, 1998).

Healthcare providers are often ill trained in detecting substance use disorders (NIAAA, 2005b), and questions about alcohol and substance use are rarely included in routine intake sessions in healthcare and social service settings. Symptoms of alcohol and substance abuse often present as age-related conditions (see Table 37.2), including insomnia, gastrointestinal problems, sexual dysfunction, forgetfulness, dementia, and depression, further deterring service providers from exploring the possibilities of alcohol and substance abuse (NIAAA, 2005a). Moreover, studies cite poor health resulting from substance use as the most common catalyst for aging women entering substance abuse treatment (Satre, Gordon, & Weisner, 2007; Schutte, Moos, & Brennan, 2006). The healthcare system must address the increase in older adults with alcohol and drug problems, especially in primary care settings (Corley, Gray, & Yakimo, 2006; Wang & Andrade, 2013).

Patient-related deterrents to identifying alcohol and drug problems in older adults include a lack of awareness or denial. In addition, older adults in general are reluctant to seek nonmedical help such as counseling and mental healthcare because of stigma and shame. This stigma and shame also contribute to elders hiding their use, resulting in family members never realizing that their loved one is abusing substances.

Perhaps not surprisingly, caregivers and healthcare professionals often shy away from confronting the older adult or referring him/her for treatment. Some believe that older adults should not be forced to give up a lifelong habit that is one of the few pleasures left for them to enjoy. Thus, forcing abstinence would be cruel. Another reason for inaction is a mistaken assumption that alcohol and substance abuse treatment is not effective for older adults. Research, however, indicates that older adults have better outcomes for treatment than younger adults (Oslin, Pettinati, & Volpirelli, 2002).

Vignette #2

Mary is a 70-year-old married woman with three adult children. Mary had been an active volunteer in her local hospital's gift shop since her youngest daughter, who is mentally disabled, moved into an independent living arrangement over 10 years ago. Mary is known for her cooking and she prepares meals for neighbors who are ill, her grandchildren's favorite desserts, and homemade sauce for her adult children to keep in their freezers. Almost 5 years ago, Mary's eldest son was diagnosed with terminal esophageal cancer. During his illness, treatment, and eventual death, Mary had trouble accepting the circumstances. She became angry, discontinued her volunteer work, and demanded that her disabled daughter leave her independent living situation and return home. Mary's husband felt powerless and went along with all her requests in an attempt to appease her. Mary's surviving daughters and grandchildren found that Mary had become difficult, demanding, and no longer kept up with the housework. Mary's family also noticed that she wasn't taking care of herself. She no longer made her weekly beauty salon appointments for her hair and nails, and she would often smell badly from not showering regularly or changing her clothes. She was also beginning to have trouble remembering appointments. Mary's family thought she might be depressed or that she was getting too old to keep up with housework, so they hired a housekeeper to come in a few times a week to cook and clean for Mary and her husband. After a few weeks the housekeeper contacted the family. The housekeeper had found several vodka bottles hidden around the house, most of them empty. Mary's family had no idea that Mary had been drinking vodka daily for years.

SCREENING INSTRUMENTS

As Corley and colleagues (2006) note, primary care, where elders most often seek help, is an ideal setting to screen elders for substance abuse. Screening instruments that have been used with older adults include the CAGE, Short Michigan Alcohol Screening Test-Geriatric Version (SMAST-G),[2] and the Alcohol Use Disorders Identification Test (AUDIT) (US Department of Health and Human Services, 1998). The SMAST-G comprises items that address issues related to aging such as increased drinking following death and losses. Screening tests are recommended by SAMHSA as part of the Screening, Brief Intervention, Referral to Treatment (SBIRT) procedure (Naegle, 2012).

The CAGE is used commonly in assessment and evaluations and has been used by physicians examining older patients (Fleming, 2001). The CAGE questions are:

1. Have you ever tried to **C**ut down on your drinking?
2. Do you become **A**nnoyed when others ask you about your drinking?
3. Do you every feel **G**uilty about your drinking?
4. Have you ever used alcohol in the morning, taking an "**E**ye-opener?"

These questions need to be modified when inquiring about prescription of OTC medicine misuse and abuse (US Department of Health and Human Services, 1998), and services providers should conduct follow-up with a more detailed assessment of alcohol abuse if a client answers affirmatively to any of the questions. Screening also needs to be conducted in a nonjudgmental manner and as part of a health assessment to lessen the sense of stigma for older adults.

AGE-SPECIFIC TREATMENT FOR ALCOHOL AND SUBSTANCE ABUSE

Intervention and treatment for alcohol and substance abuse depend on the severity of the problem and include educational sessions, outpatient care, residential care, and psychiatric hospitalization (US Department of Health and Human Services, 1999). It is important that all levels of intervention be tailored to meet the physical, psychological and social needs of older adults (Corley et al., 2006). Programs serving older adults need to:

1. identify and address stressors that are related to the aging process, such as loss and bereavement;
2. assess and understand alcohol and substance abuse problems in the context of the life stage of the older adult;
3. focus on enhancing (or rebuilding) the client's social support network;
4. assist clients in restoring a sense of self-worth by helping them to develop or maintain activities of interest;
5. refer clients to services that are age-sensitive and age-appropriate such as Alcoholics Anonymous for seniors;
6. attend to aspects of the older adult's life such as nutrition, activities of daily living, and physical functioning;
7. link clients with medical and social services such as housing, transportation, and senior programs,

8. maintain a flexible treatment program that meets the changing physical, psychological, and social needs of the clients; and

9. provide treatments that are culturally and linguistically appropriate for ethnic and sexual minority elders.

Because older adults are reluctant to receive help, developing a trusting relationship is especially important, as is a nonjudgmental attitude on the part of the service provider. Alcohol and substance abuse treatment for older adults also need to be less confrontational than interventions for younger populations (Finfgeld-Connett, 2004; Simoni-Wastila & Yang, 2006). Barriers to treatment must also be addressed before referring older adults for services. Facilities must be able to accommodate functional disabilities such as ambulation problems. Transportation to programs must be secured, and special accommodations need to be made for older adults with vision and hearing losses. Service providers must also attend to financial resources so that older adults can pay for treatment.

INTERVENTIONS AND TREATMENT

Single session educational interventions have been effective for older adults who are not aware that they are consuming too much alcohol or misusing medications (US Department of Health and Human Services, 1998). Some practitioners use the CAGE screening questions to educate older adults about alcohol consumption while reviewing the results of the screening. Interventions for older adults who misuse prescription or OTC medications include creating medication checklists and home visits by care providers to remove unwanted pills from the home (US Department of Health and Human Services, 1998).

Treatments that embrace a nonjudgmental and least-restrictive approach include a combination of motivational interviewing (MI), cognitive-behavioral therapy (CBT), brief interventions (BI), and harm reduction (HR) (Briggs et al., 2011). Motivational interviewing attends to where the person is at in their change process with a compassionate and nonconfrontational approach, and is optimal for older adults who may experience considerable shame associated with their use (Simoni-Wastila & Yang, 2006). Interventions from

MI and CBT, such as identifying the pros and cons of use, can give older adults the tools to reduce their use to healthy levels. Furthermore, brief interventions can be delivered by a host of professionals in the medical and social service fields, including social workers, who can implement these treatments where they serve elders. Recent research has found considerable success integrating substance abuse screening, assessment, education, and intervention using brief interventions in a primary care of hospital setting (Briggs et al., 2011). Two evidence-based approaches for older adults are Screening, Brief Intervention, and Referral to Treatment (SBIRT) and the Gerontology Alcohol Project (GAP) (Briggs et al., 2011). The SBIRT approach is conducted in up to five sessions of assessment, advice, education, and referral in settings convenient to an older population including emergency rooms, primary care offices, and in their homes (Schonfeld et al., 2010). Similarly, GAP draws on the techniques of MI and CBT to reduce substance use to healthier levels (Finfgeld-Connett, 2004). These approaches do not require abstinence but rather strive for healthier use of substances, which can be more appealing to older adults (Finfgeld-Connett, 2004).

Withdrawal from alcohol can be a life-threatening medical emergency for older adults with significant physical dependency on alcohol. Hospitalization is recommended for the detoxification of older adults because of potential medical complications (US Department of Health and Human Services, 1998). One medication that has been proven effective in reducing cravings for alcohol when used in conjunction with counseling is naltrexone, which has been reported to be safe for older adults (Barrick & Connors, 2002).

CONCLUSION

Older adults with alcohol and substance abuse problems are less likely to be recognized by healthcare providers than are younger populations because the former's symptoms are often mistaken for problems that are associated with aging, such as dementia and depression. The high prevalence of older adults who receive prescription medication also exacerbates the risk of medication misuse and abuse. Furthermore, family members' lack of awareness of the problem and denial on the part of elders deter them from receiving appropriate treatment.

Research indicates that once elders are in treatment they have better outcomes than younger adults. Evidenced-based treatment such as the SBIRT and GAP, which are tailored to the specific needs of older adults, have been proven to be effective in treating alcohol and drug abuse among this population. With the changing demographics and increase in the number of older adults who are at risk for alcohol and substance abuse, it is important for social workers not only to be able to able to identify the symptoms and signs of problematic substance use but also to be competent in providing age-appropriate treatment interventions.

RESOURCES

Brochure for Consumers

US Department of Health and Human Services. Substance Abuse and Mental Health Services Administration. *As you age . . . A guide to aging, medicines, and alcohol.* http://store.samhsa.gov/product/As-You-Age-A-Guide-to-Aging-Medicines-and-Alcohol/SMA04-3940

Books

Barry, K. L., Oslin, D. W., & Blow, F. C. (2001). *Alcohol problems in older adults: Prevention and management.* New York, NY: Springer. http://www.springerpub.com/product/9780826114037#.UkxKtRbU7lI

Beecham, M. (2002). *Elderly alcoholism: Intervention strategies.* Springfield, IL: Thomas.

Gurnack, A. M., Atkinson, R., & Osgood, N. (Eds.). (2001). *Treating alcohol and drug abuse in the elderly.* New York, NY: Springer. http://dx.doi.org/10.1017/S1041610202258603

Websites

Aging and Addiction. *Helping Older Adults Overcome Alcohol or Medication Dependence.* http://agingandaddiction.net/

International Center for Alcohol Policies. *23. Alcohol and the Elderly.* http://www.icap.org/PolicyTools/ICAPBlueBook/BlueBookModules/23AlcoholandtheElderly/tabid/181/Default.aspx

NIH. *Alcohol Use and Older Adults.* http://nihseniorhealth.gov/alcoholuse/alcoholandaging/01.html

NIAAA. *Older Adults and Alcohol.* http://pubs.niaaa.nih.gov/publications/olderAdults/olderAdults.htm

NIAAA. *Helping People Who Drink Too Much: A Clinician's Guide.* http://pubs.niaaa.nih.gov/publications/Practitioner/CliniciansGuide2005/clinicians_guide.htm

NIH. *Alcohol Use and Older Adults.* http://nihseniorhealth.gov/alcoholuse/alcoholandaging/01.html

Substance Abuse and Mental Health Administration. *At Any Age, It Does Matter: Substance Abuse and Older Adults* (online course). http://captus.samhsa.gov/access-resources/any-age-it-does-matter-substance-abuse-and-older-adults

Substance Abuse and Mental Health Administration. *Get Connected! Linking Older Adults with Medication, Alcohol and Mental Health Resources.* http://www.samhsa.gov/aging/docs/GetConnectedToolkit.pdf

Substance Abuse and Mental Health Administration. *Substance Abuse Relapse Prevention for Older Adults: A Group Treatment.* http://store.samhsa.gov/shin/content//SMA05-4053/SMA05-4053.pdf

Substance Abuse and Mental Health Administration. *Treatment Improvement Protocol* [TIP] Series 26. Center for Substance Abuse Treatment (1998). http://store.samhsa.gov/product/TIP-26-Substance-Abuse-Among-Older-Adults/SMA12-3918

Substance Abuse and Mental Health Administration. *Rethinking the Demographics of Addiction: Helping Older Adults.* http://store.samhsa.gov/product/Rethinking-the-Demographics-of-Addiction-Helping-Older-Adults-Find-Recovery/DVD184

Videos

Council on Social Work Education. *The Greying Elephant in the Room.* http://www.cswe.org/Publications/CSWEPressDVDs/56444.aspx

Multijurisdictional Counter Drug Task Force Training. *Drug Abuse & the Baby Boomer Generation.* https://mctft.icfwebservices.com/webcasts/w.aspx?ID=587

NOTES

1. One drink refers to 12 ounces of beer, 1.5 ounces of distilled spirits, or 5 ounces of wine.

2. The SMAST-G is available at http://www.ssc.wisc.edu/wlsresearch/pilot/P01-R01_info/aging_mind/Aging_AppB5_MAST-G.pdf

REFERENCES

Andrews, C. (2008). An exploratory study of substance abuse among Latino older adults. *Journal of Gerontological Social Work, 51*, 87–108. doi:http://dx.doi.org/10.1080/01634370801967570

Barrick, C., & Connors, G. J. (2002). Relapse prevention and maintaining abstinence in older adults with alcohol-use disorders. *Drugs and Aging, 19,* 583–594. doi:http://dx.doi.org/10.2165/00002512-200219080-00004

Bartels, S., Blow, F., Brockman, L., & Van Citters, A. (2005). *Substance abuse and mental health among older Americans: The state of knowledge and future directions.* Older Americans Substance Abuse and Mental Health Technical Assistance Center: US Department of Health and Human Services, Substance Abuse and Mental Health Services Administration, Center for Substance Abuse and Prevention. Retrieved from http://www.samhsa.gov/aging/SA_MH_%20AmongOlderAdultsfinal102105.pdf

Benshoff, J. J., Harrawood, L. K., & Koch, D. S. (2003). Substance abuse and the elderly: Unique issues and concerns. *Journal of Rehabilitation, 69,* 43–48. http://www.questia.com/library/1G1-102024782/substance-abuse-and-the-elderly-unique-issues-and

Blazer, D. G., & Wu, L.-T. (2009). The epidemiology of at-risk and binge drinking among middle-aged and elder community adults National Survey on Drug Use and Health. *American Journal of Psychiatry, 166,* 1162–1169. doi:http://dx.doi.org/10.1176/appi.ajp.2009.09010016

Blow, F. C., & Barry, K. L. (2002). Use and misuse of alcohol among older women. *Alcohol Research and Health, 26,* 308–315. http://www.niaaa.nih.gov/publications/journals-and-reports/alcohol-research

Blow, F. C., & Barry, K. L. (2012). Alcohol and substance misuse in older adults. *Current Psychiatry Reports, 14,* 310–319. doi:http://dx.doi.org/10.1007/s11920-012-0292-9

Briggs, W. P., Magnus, V. A., Lassiter, P., Patterson, A., & Smith, L. (2011). Substance use, misuse, and abuse among older adults: Implications for clinical mental health counselors. *Journal of Mental Health Counseling, 33,* 112–127. http://www.amhca.org/news/journal.aspx

Centers for Disease Control and Prevention (CDC). (2011). *Policy impact: Prescription painkiller overdoses.* Atlanta, GA: Author. Retrieved from http://www.cdc.gov/homeandrecreationalsafety/rxbrief/

Centers for Disease Control and Prevention (CDC). (2012). *Alcohol and public health.* Retrieved from http://www.cdc.gov/alcohol/fact-sheets/alcohol-use.htm

Corley, C., Gray, M., & Yakimo, R. (2006). Substance abuse networks. In B. Berkman & D'Ambrusio, S. (Eds.), *Handbook of social work in health and aging* (pp. 509–518). New York, NY: Oxford University Press. doi:10.1093/acprof:oso/9780195173727.001.0001

Cummings, S., Bride, B., & Rawlins-Shaw, A. (2006). Alcohol abuse treatment for older adults: A review of recent empirical research. *Journal of Evidence-Based Social Work, 31,* 79–99. doi:http://dx.doi.org/10.1300/J394v03n01_05

Duncan, D. F., Nicholson, T., White, J. B., Bradley, D. B., & Bonaguro, J. (2010). The baby boomer effect: Changing patterns of substance abuse among adults ages 55 and older. *Journal of Aging and Social Policy, 22,* 237–248. doi:http://dx.doi.org/10.1080/08959420.2010.485511

Finfgeld-Connett, D. L. (2004). Treatment of substance misuse in older women using a brief intervention model. *Journal of Gerontological Nursing, 30,* 30–37. http://www.healio.com/journals/jgn

Fleming, M. (2001). Identification and treatment of alcohol use disorders in older adults. In A. M. Gurnack, R. Atkinson, & N. Osgood (Eds.), *Treating alcohol and drug abuse in the elderly* (pp. 85–108). New York, NY: Springer. doi:http://dx.doi.org/10.1017/S1041610202258603

Gfroerer, J., Penne, M., Pemberton, M., & Folsom, R. (2003). Substance abuse treatment need among older adults in 2020: The impact of the aging baby-boomer cohort. *Drug and Alcohol Dependence, 69,* 127–135. doi:http://dx.doi.org/10.1016/S0376-8716(02)00307-1

Hernandez-Avila, C. A., Rounsaville, B. J., & Kranzler, H. R. (2004). Opioid-, cannabis- and alcohol-dependent women show more rapid progression to substance abuse treatment. *Drug and Alcohol Dependence, 74,* 265–272. doi:http://dx.doi.org/10.1016/j.drugalcdep.2004.02.001

Johnson, W. A., & Sterk, C. E. (2003). Late-onset crack users: An emergent HIV risk group. *Journal of Acquired Immune Deficiency Syndromes, 33,* S229–S232. doi:http://dx.doi.org/10.1097/00126334-200306012-00022

Kerr-Correa, F., Igami, T. Z., Hiroce, V., & Tucci, A. M. (2007). Patterns of alcohol use between genders: A cross-cultural evaluation. *Journal of Affective Disorders, 102,* 265–275. doi:http://dx.doi.org/10.1016/j.jad.2006.09.031

Manchikanti, L. (2006). Prescription drug abuse: What is being done to address this new drug epidemic? Testimony before the subcommittee on criminal justice, drug policy and human resources. *Pain Physician, 9,* 287–321. http://www.painphysicianjournal.com

Naegle, M. A. (2012). Alcohol use screening and assessment for older adults. *Try This: Best Practices in Nursing Care to Older Adults.* Retrieved from http://consultgerirn.org/uploads/File/trythis/try_this_17.pdf

National Institute on Alcohol Abuse and Alcoholism (NIAAA). (2005a). *Social work education for the prevention and treatment of alcohol use disorders: Older adults and alcohol problems.* Retrieved from http://pubs.niaaa.nih.gov/publications/Social/Module10COlderAdults/Module10C.html

National Institute on Alcohol Abuse and Alcoholism. (2005b). *Brief interventions.* Retrieved March 7, 2012, from http://pubs.niaaa.nih.gov/publications/AA66/AA66.pdf

National Institute on Alcohol Abuse and Alcoholism (NIAAA). (2011). *Women and alcohol.* Retrieved from http://pubs.niaaa.nih.gov/publications/womensfact/womensFact.pdf

National Institute on Alcohol Abuse and Alcoholism (NIAAA). (2012). *Older adults and alcohol.* Retrieved from http://pubs.niaaa.nih.gov/publications/olderAdults/olderAdults.htm

National Institute on Alcohol Abuse and Alcoholism (NIAAA). (2013). *Older adults.* Retrieved from http://www.niaaa.nih.gov/alcohol-health/special-populations-co-occurring-disorders/older-adults

National Institute on Drug Abuse (NIDA). (2014). *What is prescription drug abuse?* Retrieved from http://www.drugabuse.gov/publications/research-reports/prescription-drugs/what-prescription-drug-abuse

Oslin, D. W., Pettinati, H., & Volpirelli, J. R. (2002). Alcoholism treatment adherence: Older age predicts better adherence and drinking outcomes. *American Journal of Geriatric Psychiatry, 10,* 740–747. doi:http://dx.doi.org/10.1097/00019442-200211000-00013

Prins, E. (2008). "Maturing out" and the dynamics of the biographical trajectories of hard drug addicts. *Forum Qualitative Sozialforschung/Forum: Qualitative Social Research, 9*(1), Article 30, 1–39. Retrieved from http://www.qualitativeresearch.net/index.php/fqs/article/view/322/705

Rider, M. B. (2006). Alcohol and analgesic use in the baby boomer cohort. *Dissertation Abstracts International: Section B: The Sciences and Engineering, 67,* 1–125. http://trace.tennessee.edu/utk_graddiss/1851

Rigler, S. K. (2000). Alcoholism in the elderly. *American Family Physician, 61,* 1710–1716. http://www.aafp.org/journals/afp.html?cmpid=_van_188

Sarabia, S. E., & Martin, J. I. (2013). Aging effects on substance use among midlife women: The moderating influence of race and substance. *Journal of Social Work Practice in the Addictions, 13,* 417–435. doi:10.1080/1533256X.2013.842799.

Satre, D. D., Gordon, N. P., & Weisner, C. (2007). Alcohol consumption, medical conditions, and health behavior in older adults. *American Journal of Health Behavior, 31,* 238–248. doi:http://dx.doi.org/10.5993/AJHB.31.3.2

Schonfeld, L., King-Kallimanis, B. L., Duchene, D. M., Etheridge, R. L., Herrera, J. R., Barry, K. L., & Lynn, N. (2010). Screening and brief intervention for substance misuse among older adults: The Florida BRITE Project. *American Journal of Public Health, 100,* 108–114. doi:http://dx.doi.org/10.2105/AJPH.2008.149534

Schutte, K. K., Moos, R. H., & Brennan, P. L. (2006). Predictors of untreated remission from late-life drinking problems. *Journal of Studies on Alcohol, 67,* 354–363. http://www.jsad.com

Simoni-Wastila, L., Zuckerman, I. H., Singhal, P. K., Briesacher, B., & Hsu, V. P. (2005). National estimates of exposure to prescription drugs with addiction potential in community dwelling elders. *Substance Abuse, 26,* 33–42. http://www.springer.com/psychology/journal/11226

Simoni-Wastila, L., & Yang, H. K. (2006). Psychoactive drug abuse in older adults. *American Journal of Geriatric Pharmacotherapy, 4,* 380–394. http://www.ajgeripharmacother.com

Stevens, S. J., Andrade, R. A., & Ruiz, B. S. (2009). Women and substance abuse: Gender, age, and cultural considerations. *Journal of Ethnicity in Substance Abuse, 8,* 341–358. doi:http://dx.doi.org/10.1080/15332640903110542

Substance Abuse and Mental Health Services Administration. (2011). *Results from the 2010 National Survey on Drug Use and Health: Summary of national findings,* NSDUH Series H-41, HHS Publication No. (SMA) 11-4658. Rockville, MD: Substance Abuse and Mental Health Services

Administration. Retrieved from http://www.samhsa.gov/data/nsduh/2k10nsduh/2k10results.htm

US Department of Health and Human Services. (1998). *Substance abuse among older adults.* Treatment Improvement Protocol (TIP) Series 26. DHHS Publication No. SMA 98-3179. Rockville, MD: Substance Abuse and Mental Health Services Administration. http://www.ncbi.nlm.nih.gov/books/NBK64419/

US Department of Health and Human Services. (1999). *Mental health: A report of the surgeon general.* Retrieved from http://www.surgeongeneral.gov/library/

US Department of Health and Human Services (2009). *Substance abuse treatment: Addressing the specific needs of women.* Treatment Improvement Protocol (TIP) Series 51. DHHS Publication No. SMA 09-4426. Rockville, MD: Substance Abuse and Mental Health Services Administration. http://www.ncbi.nlm.nih.gov/books/NBK83252/

Wang, Y. P., & Andrade, L. H. (2013). Epidemiology of alcohol and drug use in the elderly. *Current Opinion Psychiatry, 26,* 343–348. doi:10.1097/YCO.0b013e328360eafd

White, W. L., & Kilbourne, J. (2006). American women and addiction: A cultural double bind. *Counselor, 7,* 46–50. http://www.counselormagazine.com

INTRODUCTION

Early definitions of hoarding included the acquisition of and failure to discard a large number of possessions of often limited value, excessive clutter precluding the use of household spaces, and significant distress or impairment in functioning caused by the hoarding (Frost & Hartl, 1996). The fifth edition of the *Diagnostic and Statistical Manual of Mental Disorders* (American Psychiatric Association, 2013) created a diagnostic criteria for hoarding disorder (HD), defined as difficulty parting with possessions due to urges to save them, resultant clutter in living areas, and distress or impairment as a result of the first two symptoms. Excessive acquiring is included as a specifier that may or may not be present.

Psychiatric comorbidities are common in older adults with HD (Ayers, Saxena, Golshan & Weatherall, 2010; Diefenbach, DiMauro, Frost, Steketee, & Tolin, 2012). In an older adult community-based sample with a primary diagnosis of HD, Ayers et al. (2010) found that mood disorders were the most frequent comorbid condition (28% major depressive disorder, 22% dysthymia), followed by anxiety disorders (16% obsessive-compulsive disorder, 11% post-traumatic stress disorder, 5% generalized anxiety disorder, 5% social phobia, 5% agoraphobia). Diefenbach et al. (2012) reported similar patterns of comorbidity in a sample aged 60 and older, although the frequency of comorbid disorders was somewhat higher (51% major depressive disorder, 23% generalized anxiety disorder, 23% social phobia, 18% obsessive-compulsive disorder) compared with Ayers and colleagues' findings.

Prevalence of Hoarding Disorder in Older Adults

Epidemiological reports estimate the prevalence of clinically significant hoarding symptoms from 2% (Iervolino et al., 2009) to 5% (Samuels et al., 2008) in adult community samples. In older adults, Samuels et al. (2008) found that hoarding symptoms were three times more prevalent in older versus younger adults, but other studies have no association between hoarding prevalence and age (Fullana et al., 2010; Mueller, Mitchell, Crosby, Glaesmer, & de Zwaan, 2009; Timpano et al., 2011). Nonetheless, a moderately high frequency of hoarding has been reported among older adults living in medically supported settings compared

CHRISTIANA BRATIOTIS
CATHERINE AYERS
GAIL STEKETEE

Older Adults Who Hoard

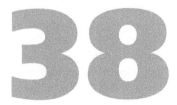

407

with community populations. For example, 25% of senior daycare participants and 15% of nursing home residents exhibited hoarding symptoms (Marx & Cohens-Mansfield, 2003). It is possible that actual rates of clinically significant hoarding do not increase with age, but rather that the manifestations of HD become more challenging to cope with as people age. Indeed, as noted in what follows, hoarding symptom severity seems to increase with age (Ayers et al., 2010).

Onset and Course of Older Adult Hoarding

Hoarding symptoms typically onset during childhood and adolescence, and onset in later life is rare (e.g., Grisham, Frost, Steketee, Kim, & Hood, 2006; Tolin, Meunier, Frost, & Steketee, 2010). Among a small community-based sample of older adults, most reported that hoarding symptoms began early in life (Ayers et al., 2010). Although some older adults in this study reported a midlife onset after a stressful life event, a careful review of their symptoms at each decade of life indicated that all study participants actually experienced hoarding symptoms during childhood or adolescence. Because some older adults may not be accurate in reporting about their hoarding symptoms, clinicians seeking to understand the course of hoarding behavior may need to carefully review their history to tie specific hoarding symptoms (difficulty discarding, acquiring, clutter) to early events in their lives (e.g., educational experiences, family events). Late-life onset of hoarding has been reported in people diagnosed with dementia or schizophrenia (Hwang, Tsai, Yang, Liu, & Liring, 1998; Poyurovsky, Bergman, & Weizman, 2006). However, it is unclear whether participants met criteria for HD as a mental health disorder or whether the symptoms resulted from cognitive or behavioral effects of their primary condition (e.g., dementia).

The retrospective study conducted by Ayers et al. (2010) indicated that older adults with HD reported increased severity of their hoarding behaviors in each decade of life. Mild symptoms were reported in young adulthood and progressed to moderate levels in midlife and to severe symptoms in older adult years. These data mirror

findings for middle-aged adults in two previous studies that also indicated a worsening course after childhood (Grisham et al., 2006; Tolin, Meunier, Frost & Steketee, 2010).

IMPAIRMENT IN FUNCTIONING

Activities of daily living are significantly compromised in older adults with HD (Ayers, Scheisher, Liu, & Wetherell, 2012; Steketee, Schmalisch, Dierberger, DeNobel, & Frost, 2012). Older adults who hoard find it difficult to carry out basic activities such as moving within their home, finding particular objects, preparing meals, and even sleeping in their beds (Ayers, Scheisher, et al., 2012). A study by Kim, Steketee, and Frost (2001) found that the homes of older adults who hoard had nonfunctioning appliances and significant plumbing problems, and the adults experienced difficulty using essential rooms in the house. Phone interviews with geriatric service workers with hoarding people in their caseload and who had visited the homes of these clients indicated that 80% of the clients with hoarding in their caseload experienced substantial impairment in movement through the home; 70% were unable to use their sofa, 45% could not use their refrigerator, and 10% could not use their toilet. Older adults with physical disabilities reported significant challenges navigating through their homes and were at increased risk of falls due to tripping on clutter (Bratiotis, Sorrentino Schmalisch & Steketee, 2011; Diefenbach et al., 2012).

Medical Impairment

Chronic and severe medical conditions are common among adults who hoard, often leading to increased use of healthcare services (Tolin, Frost, Steketee, Gray, & Fitch, 2008). Far less is known about the extent to which older adults with HD have similar health patterns, as many older adults do not receive regular medical care. A community-based study by Ayers et al. (2010) indicated that older adults with HD report frequent chronic and age-related illnesses. Problems from illness are magnified in hoarders by their increased mismanagement of medications and poor dietary habits (Ayers, Schiehser, et al., 2012; Diefenbach, DiMauro, Frost, Steketee, & Tolin, 2012). In addition, dust or insect/rodent infestations commonly found in hoarded homes may exacerbate chronic medical conditions such as emphysema (Turner, Steketee, & Nauth, 2010).

Social Impairment

Because many older adults live alone and are socially isolated, the dangerous living conditions that result from hoarding behavior often remain unseen and unknown (Kim et al., 2001). It is not clear whether social isolation precedes hoarding symptoms or is, at least in part, a consequence of them. Likewise, older adults may resist engagement in intervention services due to shame, guilt, embarrassment, or fear of being reported to authorities, knowing this could lead to the end of their ability to live independently.

Family Burden and Interference

Family members of individuals with HD express feeling burdened by the individual's symptoms (Tolin, Frost, Steketee, & Fitch, 2008) and may view the hoarding behavior as more problematic than does the person who hoards (Tolin, Fitch, Frost & Steketee, 2010). Geriatric service workers reported that approximately 21% of older adult hoarding clients were referred by family and friends for assistance compared with only 3% who were self-referred (Kim et al., 2001). This discrepancy may occur because family members are strongly invested in a particular outcome (e.g., removing clutter, moving the hoarder to assisted living) that is in opposition to the desires of the hoarder. Tompkins and Hartl (2009) suggest that this differing viewpoint about appropriate interventions and outcomes may lead to familial alienation.

Insight

Low insight may also account for the limited motivation of individuals with HD to seek help (see Bratiotis et al., 2011). Studies have demonstrated low awareness in those who hoard, including older adults, that their behaviors are abnormal or are causing problems for themselves or for other people (Kim et al., 2001; Tolin, Frost, Steketee, Gray, & Fitch, 2008).

ASSESSMENT AND DIAGNOSIS

Assessing and diagnosing HD can present some challenges with both middle-aged and older adults. Lack of awareness of hoarding as being problematic and reluctance to divulge embarrassing information, as well as concurrent medical and/or cognitive problems, can lead to inaccurate reporting. A comprehensive diagnostic assessment is recommended, especially as most older adults have comorbid health and mental health problems (e.g., major depression, anxiety disorders) that complicate the picture. Multiple sources of information are most useful, including an individual interview, one or more home visits, family and agency reports to evaluate symptom severity and impairment in functioning, and assessment of cognitive status and areas of functioning. Guidelines for assessment and strategies for overcoming evaluation barriers are given below.

Assessment of Hoarding Symptom Severity

Standardized instruments for hoarding behavior assess the person's acquisition, urges to save, ability to discard, and overall clutter. These tools were developed for adult populations and have been used with older samples but their reliability and validity have not been tested specifically in this population. Older adults have been able to complete the standard measures described below, although accommodations may be necessary for some elders, such as using large print or visual markings on self-report questionnaires and repeating questions on interview measures to ensure accurate understanding.

The Saving Inventory-Revised (SI-R; Frost, Steketee, & Grisham, 2004) is an extensively validated 23-item self-report measure that assesses clutter, acquisition, and difficulty discarding. This questionnaire is widely used and takes most clients approximately 10 minutes to complete. Another standard measure of symptom severity is the Hoarding Rating Scale (HRS; Tolin, Frost, & Steketee, 2010), a brief 5-item questionnaire that assesses the salient HD features of clutter, difficulty discarding, acquisition, distress, and functional impairment. This measure can be completed as a self-report form or in an interview and is helpful as an initial screening tool, especially for patients who cannot tolerate lengthy assessments. Both instruments are commonly used to assess outcomes following treatment for hoarding symptoms.

The Activities of Daily Living for Hoarding scale (ADL-H; Frost, Hristova, Steketee, & Tolin, 2013) determines the extent to which 16 activities of daily living such as dressing, bathing, and preparing meals are affected by the hoarding problem. Finally, the Clutter Image Rating scale (CIR; Frost, Steketee, Tolin, & Renaud, 2008) comprises a series of nine photographs with varying levels of clutter. The client selects the picture that best represents the volume of clutter in the rooms (living room, kitchen, and bedroom) in his/her home. In addition to assessing the volume of clutter, the CIR can help gauge awareness of illness by comparing the client's responses to those of a home visitor.

Diagnostic Assessment of Hoarding and Comorbidity

The Structured Interview for Hoarding Disorder (SIHD; see Mataix-Cols, Billotti, Fernandez de la Cruz, & Nordsletten, 2013) is a semistructured interview that uses DSM-5 criteria to diagnose HD and also helps clinicians make a differential diagnosis with regard to other sources of hoarding symptoms, such as obsessive-compulsive disorder and autism spectrum disorders. This instrument also includes an assessment of risk.

Assessment of co-occurring mental health conditions requires clinicians to administer a comprehensive diagnostic interview. Among several options, the Mini-International Neuropsychiatric Interview (Sheehan et al., 1998), known as the MINI, is among the briefest options with reasonable reliability among trained interviewers. Comorbid conditions can be further characterized through geriatric-specific symptom severity measures, such as the Geriatric Depression Scale (Yesavage et al., 1983). Determining the presence of disorders that can mimic hoarding is particularly important to avoid misdiagnosis and misapplication of therapeutic strategies. For example, in older adults, the presence of clutter may be due not to HD but to another condition, such as depression (client lacks motivation or desire to discard) or dementia (client is unable to organize; repetitive behaviors may mimic saving). A careful assessment is necessary to make a differential diagnosis of HD.

Assessment of Health Status

Physical limitations and medical comorbidities may further complicate health and safety hazards caused by hoarding behaviors. Assessment of environmental risks, functioning, and disability is critical when working with older adults. Environmental assessment may include fire hazards, home infestations and structural problems, and sanitation concerns (Dong, Simon, Mosqueda, & Evans, 2011). The Home Environment Index is a 15-item measure to assess the extent of squalid conditions within the home (HEI; Rasmussen, Steketee, Frost, Tolin, & Brown, 2013). Another useful environmental measure is the HOMES Multidisciplinary Hoarding Risk Assessment, a checklist that can be used to determine the level of risk in five domains: health, obstacles in the home, mental health, endangerment, and structure/safety (Bratiotis et al., 2011). Geriatric-specific assessments such as the Function and Disability Instrument (FDI; Jette et al., 2002) are recommended for patients with physical illnesses (e.g., arthritis); this instrument examines how disability affects the frequency of performing social and personal activities. The FDI also indicates how disability may limit a person's ability to perform activities in the home and community.

Assessment of Cognitive Status

The cognitive capacity of older adults with HD has significant implications for intervention outcomes (Ayers, Bratiotis, Saxena, & Wetherell, 2012). Before beginning treatment, a brief screen of cognitive abilities using an instrument such as the Montreal Cognitive Assessment (MoCA; Nasreddine et al., 2005) may be helpful. The MoCA assesses impairment in attention, concentration, and executive functioning, providing information about functional disability and potential barriers to intervention that may require further investigation using a complete neuropsychological battery. Clinicians should consider dividing a lengthy neurocognitive evaluation into multiple sessions to avoid client fatigue and frustration. A comprehensive assessment including hoarding severity, health and functional status, and cognitive dysfunction helps formulate a comprehensive treatment from which appropriate interventions can follow.

INTERVENTION

Clinical trials examining treatments for HD have focused on middle-aged adult samples (e.g., Tolin, Frost, & Steketee, 2007; Steketee, Frost, Tolin, Rasmussen, & Brown, 2010). The older adult HD treatment intervention literature is divided into community-based/case management interventions and therapeutic treatments (cognitive-behavioral therapy, or CBT). These interventions differ greatly, as community-based/case management approaches aim to mitigate the interfering consequences of hoarding, whereas CBT aims to treat HD symptoms and their presumed causal factors. Much of the literature on CBT for HD in older adults reports case study findings, although some open trials have been published and a controlled trial is ongoing at this time (e.g., Ayers, Bratiotis, et al., 2012).

Community-Based Harm Reduction and Clean-Out Efforts

One commonly used intervention for older adult hoarding is a community-based case management approach that emphasizes harm reduction and clearing the clutter from the home (Tompkins, 2011). Harm reduction strategies seek to mitigate immediate safety concerns resulting from clutter by reducing the volume of possessions accumulated through excessive acquiring and difficulty discarding. A harm reduction plan is coordinated by a case manager, who leads a team of diverse professionals with the goal of helping the older adult remain in his or her home and neighborhood, improving the safety of the home and fostering empowerment in the individual (Tompkins, 2011; Whitfield et al., 2011). Use of a community multidisciplinary task force can be especially helpful in implementing a harm reduction intervention (Bratiotis et al., 2011).

Although commonly used for late-life hoarding, home clean-outs are not a recommended form of intervention. Clean-outs can be initiated by the older adult, family members, or social service agencies in order to reduce or eliminate the clutter. Variations on this strategy include partial clearing of rooms in the home, clearing out the entire home, or providing assistance in clearing to the person who hoards (Kim et al., 2001). Clean-outs focus only on the environment by removing the clutter, but fail to address

the older adult's emotional state, beliefs about possessions, skills and capacity, or their social support system. Social service staff reports of interventions using home clean-outs indicated no change in 55% of the clients with hoarding and a worsening of symptoms in 8% (Kim et al., 2001). These findings suggest that such efforts are ineffective for chronic hoarding problems. Partial clearing efforts showed mixed results, as some patients were able to keep their homes clutter-free, but the majority relapsed, had no change, or worsened. Clearing the entire home most often resulted in complete recluttering (Kim et al., 2001).

Cognitive-Behavioral Therapy

A number of older adult HD case studies in the literature illuminate the complexities of working with older adults who hoard (e.g., Cermele, Melendez-Pallitto, & Pandina, 2001; Franks, Lund, Poulton, & Caserta, 2004). Cermele et al. (2001) described the successful treatment of a 72-year-old women with 6 months of CBT following Frost and Hartl's (1996) model. The goal of treatment was to reduce the patient's emotional attachment to items and strong beliefs about her possessions and improve her decision-making capacity. Their intervention started with a detailed assessment of clutter, followed by intervention planning sessions, and gradually by a decluttering intervention conducted by a team of therapists and a case manager (Cermele et al., 2001).

Recent larger-scale investigations of older adults with HD include a case series analysis (Turner et al., 2010) and an uncontrolled study (Ayers, Wetherell, Golshan, & Saxena, 2011). The case series conducted by Turner et al. (2010) tested an intervention adapted from Steketee and Frost's (2007) specialized CBT for HD. Treatment included motivational enhancement strategies and skills training such as problem solving, decision-making about possessions, practice discarding, and some cognitive restructuring. Of 11 participants, 6 older adults with an average age of 72 completed treatment; they reported statistically significant reductions improvement in clutter according to mean scores on the pictorial CIR. Additionally, significant improvements also occurred in daily functioning and reduction of safety concerns according to the ADL-H scale. Though the results of this study were promising, Turner and colleagues noted that the generalizability of the findings are limited by the small sample size and discrepancies in elders' and clinicians' ratings of insight and hoarding severity.

Ayers and colleagues conducted a larger open trial using Steketee and Frost's (2007) specialized CBT for HD with 12 older adult participants who had an average age of 74 years old (Ayers et al., 2011). They reported mixed results: Average reductions of hoarding symptoms ranged from 14% to 20% on the self-reported SI-R, but only three participants were categorized as treatment responders and two participants showed an increase in hoarding severity. The three participants who demonstrated significant improvement in hoarding severity relapsed by the 6-month follow-up visit (Ayers et al., 2011).

A follow-up study with 12 older adults (mean age = 67) with an age-adapted manualized treatment produced significant improvement (Ayers et al., 2014). The treatment included specific skills in calendar use, task completion, problem solving, flexible thinking, and planning to address problems in executive functioning. The adapted treatment also emphasized exposure over cognitive therapy techniques. Overall hoarding symptoms improved significantly and by an average of 38% on the SI-R. These findings are promising but highlight the need for studies with larger sample sizes, multimethod assessments, and specialized hoarding protocols adapted to older adult populations.

Treatment Modifications

As earlier noted, older adults with HD often experience cognitive deficits that impair their ability to make use of core CBT modules. Accordingly, these older adults may benefit from a specialized CBT that emphasizes cognitive rehabilitation to remediate cognitive deficits and exposure to discarding/acquiring to promote habitation of discomfort while discarding and not acquiring possessions. Beginning with cognitive remediation may enhance the effectiveness of the CBT (Ayers et al., 2011; Mackin, Areán, Delucchi, & Mathews, 2011) and improve treatment engagement and homework compliance (Ayers, Bratiotis, et al., 2012) as older clients learn to work around their cognitive deficits (e.g., excessive use of visual cues) and enhance areas of cognitive weakness (e.g., repeated practice with problem-solving strategies).

One HD protocol for older adults dedicates the first 6 sessions to increasing cognitive flexibility with modules on problem solving, planning, and prospective memory (Ayers, Bratiotis, et al., 2012). The remaining 14 sessions are dedicated to exposure therapy for discarding and not acquiring, adapted for elderly participants by using mainly in vivo (rather than imagined) exposures (Ayers, Bratiotis, et al., 2012). Steketee and Frost's (2007) manual combined cognitive therapy methods with exposure to challenge beliefs, but Ayers and colleagues suggest that this combination may be too challenging for older adults (Ayers, Bratiotis, et al., 2012; Ayers et al., 2010).

Treatment accommodations for health status and energy limitations may be needed for older adult clients (Eckfield, 2011; Eckfield & Wallhagen, 2011). Exposure exercises may require the therapist and others to assist with discarding, sorting, and organizing items and carrying boxes or bags. Research on treatment of older adults with HD suggests that symptoms improve when cognitive impairments are directly addressed, cognitive therapy techniques are simplified, exposures constitute the majority of treatment, and treatment accommodations are provided for clients.

BARRIERS TO TREATMENT IN OLDER ADULTS

Non-compliance with treatment protocols among older adults is associated several factors, including difficulty attending sessions and completing treatment homework assignments, impaired executive functioning, and challenges associated with insufficient income, housing stability and transportation.

Treatment Session and Homework Compliance

Compliance with treatment and homework are predictors of symptom improvement (Tolin et al., 2007). In older adults who hoard, noncompliance may result from homework assignments that are too difficult, ill health or physical limitations that prevent completion of the assignment, or deficits in executive functioning (e.g., difficulty prioritizing, planning, and organizing). Older adults reported feelings of guilt, sadness, and embarrassment when they do not complete homework in their HD treatment (Ayers, Bratiotis, et al., 2012). Clinicians must determine the skill level required for homework assignments and make necessary adjustments to ensure that the older adult can comply.

Another challenge to treatment progress is the patient's unwillingness to adhere to the session agenda. While using a manualized CBT treatment study, clinicians reported that some clients preferred to talk about feelings rather than follow the structured session outline (Ayers, Bratiotis, et al., 2012). Advancing treatment goals requires a fine balance—clinicians need to let clients express their feelings for a limited amount of time and then gently but firmly guide them back to the session agenda. Directly addressing poor compliance with homework assignments and session structure may enhance treatment outcomes for older adults with HD (Gilliam et al., 2011).

Neurocognitive Deficits

Several studies have reported neurocognitive deficits among adults with HD (e.g., Hartl et al., 2004; Grisham, Brown, Savage, Steketee, & Barlow, 2007; Grisham, Norberg, Williams, Certoma, & Kadib, 2010; Wincze, Steketee, & Frost, 2007). Only recently has the cognitive status of older adults with HD been examined (Mackin et al., 2011). Older adults with HD and cormorbid depression showed a variety of deficits in executive functioning—categorizing, maintaining attention, using feedback, abstract thinking, set-shifting, maintaining a cognitive set, generating hypotheses, selecting strategies, inhibiting incorrect responses, monitoring performance, strategic planning, flexible thinking, and organized searching were all impaired. Further, older participants with HD and no comorbid Axis I disorders performed significantly worse than their nonpsychiatric peers in several domains of executive function, including concentration, mental control, working memory, set shifting, inhibition, and cognitive flexibility (Ayers, Wetherell, et al., 2013). Interestingly, executive functioning was strongly correlated with the severity of hoarding symptoms.

These executive functioning impairments are evident throughout treatment for HD in aging clients. Cognitive inflexibility may manifest in repeated use of the same problem-solving strategy despite obvious indications of its ineffectiveness (Ayers, Bratiotis, et al. 2012). Moreover, the older adult client may not have the ability to brainstorm new solutions to their problems. These difficulties are furthered by challenges with organization and categorization (Ayers, Bratiotis, et al., 2012).

Practical Challenges

Low income, housing problems such as relocation to senior housing, and transportation problems may also be barriers to treatment for older adults with HD (Ayers, Bratiotis, et al., 2012; Kim et al., 2001; Steketee et al., 2012). Older adults who no longer drive may have difficulty getting to treatment sessions because they rely on public transportation or on transportation provided by others. This may discourage older adults from pursuing treatment or adversely affect their attendance or timeliness. Clinician assistance in problem solving transportation arrangements with friends and family members may ease these difficulties.

Many older adults are unable to afford treatment. Clinicians with specialized training in HD treatment may not accept Medicare, and paying out of pocket for a specialist may be a hardship for older adult clients. Exploring free or sliding scale treatment options, possibly through research studies, may reveal an older adult's only avenue to receive care.

CONCLUSION AND FUTURE IMPLICATIONS

Older adults with HD may suffer from severe consequences that threaten their health, autonomy, and safety. The consequences of hoarding seem to worsen with age as older adults decline physically and develop comorbid medical conditions that impair their daily functioning. A combination of changing social roles due to aging and strains on social relationships due to hoarding may lead late-life hoarders to become socially isolated. Hoarding disorder is a serious psychiatric condition impacting all areas of life for the older adult. Social support systems, communities, and social service agencies must work collaboratively to help mitigate these outcomes (see Bratiotis et al., 2011).

To date, there are no published randomized controlled trials of treatment for older adults with HD. Additionally, research on the use of psychotropic medications in older adults who hoard may improve our understanding of how best to help people with this complex disorder. A combination of intervention strategies (e.g., pharmacotherapy plus CBT plus case management) may provide the most benefit, but more information on the usefulness of each of these intervention options is needed.

REFERENCES

American Psychiatric Association. (2013). *Diagnostic and statistical manual of mental disorders* (5th ed.). Washington, DC: Author.

Ayers, C. R., Bratiotis, C., Saxena, S., & Wetherell, J. L. (2012). Therapist and patient perspectives on cognitive-behavioral therapy for older adults with hoarding disorder: A collective case study. *Aging and Mental Health, 16,* 915–921.

Ayers, C. R., Saxena, S., Espejo, E., Twamley, E., Granholm, E., & Wetherell, J. L. (2014). Novel treatment for geriatric hoarding disorder: An open trial of cognitive rehabilitation paired with behavior therapy. *American Journal of Geriatric Psychiatry, 22,* 248–252. doi:10.1016/j.jagp.2013.02.010.

Ayers, C. R., Saxena, S., Golshan, S., & Wetherell, J. L. (2010). Age at onset and clinical features of late life compulsive hoarding. *International Journal of Geriatric Psychiatry, 25,* 142–149.

Ayers, C. R., Scheisher, D., Liu, L., & Wetherell, J. L. (2012). Functional impairment in geriatric hoarding participants. *Journal of Obsessive-Compulsive and Related Disorders, 1,* 263–266.

Ayers, C. R., Wetherell, J. W., Schiehser, D. Almklov, E., Golshan, S., & Saxena, S. (2013). Executive functioning in older adults with hoarding disorder. *International Journal of Geriatric Psychiatry, 28,* 1175–1181. doi:10.1002/gps.3940.

Ayers, C. R., Wetherell, J. L., Golshan, S., & Saxena, S. (2011). Cognitive-behavioral therapy for geriatric compulsive hoarding. *Behaviour Research and Therapy, 49* 689–694.

Bratiotis, C., Sorrentino Schmalisch, C., & Steketee, G. (2011). *The hoarding handbook: A guide for human service professionals.* New York, NY: Oxford University Press.

Cermele, J. A., Melendez-Pallitto, L., & Pandina, G. J. (2001). Intervention in compulsive hoarding: A case study. *Behavior Modification, 25,* 214–232.

Diefenbach, G. J., DiMauro, J., Frost, R. O., Steketee, G., & Tolin, D. F. (2013). Characteristics of hoarding in older adults. *American Journal of Geriatric Psychiatry, 21,* 1043–1047. doi:10.1016/j.jagp.2013.01.028

Dong, X., Simon, M. A., Mosqueda, L., & Evans, D. A. (2011). The prevalence of elder self-neglect in a community-dwelling population hoarding, hygiene,

and environmental hazards. *Journal of Aging and Health, 24,* 507–524.

Eckfield, M. (2011, May). *The influence of aging on the process of accumulation: A qualitative study of older adults with hoarding and cluttering behaviors.* PowerPoint presented at Doctoral Dissertation Defense, University of California at San Francisco School of Nursing.

Eckfield, M., & Wallhagen, M. (2011, November). *Influences of aging on hoarding and cluttering behaviors.* Poster session presented at the Gerontological Society of America's Annual Scientific Meeting, Boston, MA.

Franks, M., Lund, D. A., Poulton, D., & Caserta, M. S. (2004). Understanding hoarding behavior among older adults: A case study approach. *Journal of Gerontological Social Work, 42,* 77–107.

Frost, R. O., & Hartl, T. L. (1996). A cognitive-behavioral model of compulsive hoarding. *Behaviour Research and Therapy, 34,* 341–350.

Frost, R. O., Hristova, V., Steketee, G., & Tolin, D. F. (2013). Activities of daily living in hoarding disorder (ADL-H). *Journal of Obsessive Compulsive and Related Disorders, 2,* 85–90.

Frost, R. O., Steketee, G., & Grisham, J. (2004). Measurement of compulsive hoarding: Saving inventory-revised. *Behavior Research and Therapy, 42,* 1163–1182.

Frost, R. O., Steketee, G., Tolin, D. F., & Renaud, S. (2008). Development and validation of the clutter image rating. *Journal of Psychopathology and Behavioral Assessment, 30,* 193–203.

Fullana, M. A., Vilagut, G., Rojas-Farreras, S., Mataix-Cols, D., de Graaf, R., Demyttenaere, K., . . . Alonso, J. (2010). Obsessive–compulsive symptom dimensions in the general population: Results from an epidemiological study in six European countries. *Journal of Affective Disorders, 124,* 291–299.

Gilliam, C. M., Norberg, M. M., Villavicencio, A., Morrison, S., Hannan, S. E., & Tolin, D. F. (2011). Group cognitive-behavioral therapy for hoarding disorder: An open trial. *Behaviour Research and Therapy, 49,* 802–807.

Grisham, J. R., Brown, T. A., Savage, C. R., Steketee, G., & Barlow, D. H. (2007). Neuropsychological impairment associated with compulsive hoarding. *Behaviour Research and Therapy, 45,* 1471–1483.

Grisham, J. R., Frost, R. O., Steketee, G., Kim, H., & Hood, S. (2006). Age of onset of compulsive hoarding. *Journal of Anxiety Disorders, 20,* 675–686.

Grisham, J. R., Norberg, M. M., Williams, A. D., Certoma, S. P., & Kadib, R. (2010). Categorization and cognitive deficits in compulsive hoarding. *Behaviour Research and Therapy, 48,* 866–872.

Hartl, T. L., Frost, R. O., Allen, G. J., Deckersbach, T., Steketee, G., Duffany, S. R., & Savage, C. R. (2004). Actual and perceived memory deficits in individuals with compulsive hoarding. *Depression and Anxiety, 20,* 59–69.

Hwang, J. M. D., Tsai, S., Yang, C., Liu, K., & Liring, J. (1998). Hoarding behavior in dementia: A preliminary report. *American Journal of Geriatric Psychiatry, 6,* 285–289.

Iervolino, A. C., Perroud, N., Fullana, M. A., Guipponi, M., Cherkas, L., Collier, D. A., & Mataix-Cols, D. (2009). Prevalence and heritability of compulsive hoarding: A twin study. *American Journal of Psychiatry, 166,* 1156–1161.

Jette, A. M., Haley, S. M., Coster, W. J., Kooyoomjian, J. T., Levenson, S., Heeren, T., & Ashba, J. (2002). Late life function and disability instrument: I. development and evaluation of the disability component. *Journals of Gerontology Series A Biological Sciences and Medical Sciences, 57,* 209–216.

Kim, H., Steketee, G., & Frost, R. O. (2001). Hoarding by elderly people. *Health Social Work, 26,* 176–184.

Mackin, R. S., Areán, P. A., Delucchi, K. L., & Mathews, C. A. (2011). Cognitive functioning in individuals with severe compulsive hoarding behaviors and late life depression. *International Journal of Geriatric Psychiatry, 26,* 314–321.

Marx, M. S., & Cohen-Mansfield, J. (2003). Hoarding behavior in the elderly: A comparison between community-dwelling persons and nursing home residents. *International Psychogeriatrics, 15,* 289–306.

Mataix-Cols, D., Billotti, D., Fernandez de la Cruz, L., & Nordsletten, A. E. (2013). The London field trial for hoarding disorder. *Psychological Medicine, 43,* 837–847. doi.org/10.1017/S0033291712001560

Mueller, A., Mitchell, J. E., Crosby, R. D., Glaesmer, H., & de Zwaan, M. (2009). The prevalence of compulsive hoarding and its association with compulsive buying in a German population-based sample. *Behaviour Research and Therapy, 47,* 705–709.

Nasreddine, Z. S., Phillips, N. A., Bédirian, V., Charbonneau, S., Whitehead, V., Collin, I., ... Chertkow, H. (2005). The Montreal Cognitive Assessment, MoCA: A brief screening tool for mild cognitive impairment. *Journal of the American Geriatrics Society, 53,* 695–699.

Poyurovsky, M., Bergman, J., & Weizman, R. (2006). Obsessive-compulsive disorder in elderly schizophrenia patients. *Journal of Psychiatric Research, 40,* 189–191.

Rasmussen, J., Steketee, G., Frost, R. O., Tolin, D. F., & Brown, T. A. (2014). Assessing squalor in hoarding: The Home Environment Index. *Community Mental Health Journal, 50,* 591–596. doi:10.1007/s10597-013-9665-8

Samuels, J. F., Bienvenu, O. J., Grados, M. A., Cullen, B., Riddle, M. A., Liang, K., ... Nestadt, G. (2008). Prevalence and correlates of hoarding behavior in a community-based sample. *Behaviour Research and Therapy, 46,* 836–844.

Sheehan, D. V., Lecrubier, Y., Sheehan, K. H., Amorim, P., Janavs, J., Weiller, E., ... Dunbar, G. C. (1998). The Mini-International Neuropsychiatric Interview (MINI): The development and validation of a structured diagnostic psychiatric interview for DSM-IV and ICD-10. *Journal of Clinical Psychiatry, 59*(Suppl 20), 22–33.

Steketee, G., & Frost, R. O. (2007). *Compulsive hoarding and acquiring: Therapist guide.* New York, NY: Oxford University Press.

Steketee, G., Frost, R. O., Tolin, D. F., Rasmussen, J., & Brown, T. A. (2010). Waitlist-controlled trial of cognitive behavior therapy for hoarding disorder. *Depression and Anxiety, 27,* 476–484.

Steketee, G., Schmalisch, C. S., Dierberger, A., DeNobel, D., & Frost, R. O. (2012). Symptoms and history of hoarding in older adults. *Journal of Obsessive-Compulsive and Related Disorders, 1,* 1–7.

Timpano, K. R., Exner, C., Glaesmer, H., Rief, W., Keshaviah, A., Brahler, E., & Wilhelm, S. (2011). The epidemiology of the proposed DSM-5 hoarding disorder: Exploration of the acquisition specifier, associated features, and distress. *Journal of Clinical Psychiatry, 72,* 780–786.

Tolin, D. F., Fitch, K., Frost, R. O., & Steketee, G. (2010). Family Informants' Perceptions of Insight in Compulsive Hoarding. *Cognitive Therapy & Research 34,* 69–81.

Tolin, D. F., Frost, R. O., & Steketee, G. (2007). An open trial of cognitive-behavioral therapy for compulsive hoarding. *Behaviour Research and Therapy, 45,* 1461–1470.

Tolin, D. F., Frost, R. O., & Steketee, G. (2010). A brief interview for assessing compulsive hoarding: The hoarding rating scale-interview. *Psychiatry Research, 178,* 147–152.

Tolin, D. F., Frost, R. O., Steketee, G., & Fitch, K. (2008) Family burden of compulsive hoarding: Results of an Internet survey. *Behaviour Research and Therapy, 46,* 434–443. doi:10.1016/j.brat.2007.12.008

Tolin, D. F., Frost, R. O., Steketee, G., Gray, K. D., & Fitch, K. E. (2008). The economic and social burden of compulsive hoarding. *Psychiatry Research, 160*, 200–211.

Tolin, D. F., Meunier, S. A., Frost, R. O., & Steketee, G. (2010). Course of compulsive hoarding and its relationship to life events. *Depression and Anxiety, 27*, 829–838.

Tompkins, M. A. (2011). Working with families of people who hoard: A harm reduction approach. *Journal of Clinical Psychology, 67*, 497–506.

Tompkins, M. A., & Hartl, T. L. (2009). *Digging out: Helping your loved one manage clutter, hoarding, and compulsive acquiring.* Oakland, CA: New Harbinger.

Turner, K., Steketee, G., & Nauth, L. (2010). Treating elders with compulsive hoarding: A pilot program. *Cognitive and Behavioral Practice, 17*, 449–457.

Whitfield, K. Y., Daniels, J. S., Flesaker, K., & Simmons, D. (2011). Older adults with hoarding behaviour aging in place: Looking to a collaborative community-based planning approach for solutions. *Journal of Aging Research, 2012* (Article ID 205425). http://dx.doi.org/10.1155/2012/205425

Wincze, J. P., Steketee, G., & Frost, R. O. (2007). Categorization in compulsive hoarding. *Behaviour Research and Therapy, 45*, 63–72.

Yesavage, J. A., Brink, T. L., Rose, T. L., Lum, O., Huang, V., Adey, M., & Leirer, V. O. (1983). Development and validation of a geriatric depression screening scale: A preliminary report. *Journal of Psychiatric Research, 17*, 37–49.

DAVID E. BIEGEL

SECTION III

Special Older Adult Populations

OVERVIEW

The heterogeneity of the aging population is well recognized. This section of the handbook is intended to provide an understanding of the characteristics, needs, and practice issues for social work with particular at-risk subpopulations of older persons. Specifically, the section focuses on the following issues: (1) the role of work and voluntarism among older adults; (2) characteristics and service needs of the oldest old; (3) family caregivers to older and disabled adults; (4) issues of older prisoners in state and federal prisons; (5) an overview of the extent of poverty and homelessness among at-risk elderly persons; (6) mistreated and neglected older adults; and (7) older adults with intellectual and developmental disabilities.

The first chapter, by Marcie Pitt-Catsouphes and Nancy Morrow-Howell, discusses the value of productive engagement of older persons in society and the need for social workers and others to address barriers to such engagement in order to maximize the involvement of older adults in productive roles. Today many older adults are working beyond the traditional retirement age with almost one-fifth of persons 65 and older still in the labor force, with the majority of whom are in full-time positions. It is estimated that about one-quarter of older adults volunteer, a rate that is somewhat lower than for younger adults. However, elderly who do volunteer commit more time volunteering than younger adults. The authors present a number of action steps that social workers can take to promote productive aging and thus help to positively shape the health and well-being of older adults.

The second chapter, by Ruth Dunkle and Hae-Sook Jeon, discusses the fastest-growing group of older adults, the oldest old, those elderly individuals who are 85 years and older. This group is projected to constitute one-fifth of the population 65 years and older by 2050. The authors describe the demographic and socioeconomic characteristics of the oldest-old population as well as their mental and physical health needs and need for social support. They note that the oldest old have more combined health and mental health problems with fewer financial and social resources to address these problems than do other older adults. Implications for mental health service delivery and caregiving are presented.

The third chapter, by Michael Parker and colleagues, focuses on family caregiving with older and disabled adults. Over two-thirds of older Americans will need long-term care, and almost 90% of them will receive care from an unpaid family member. Data show that the gaps in our formal care system leave family caregivers who provide care to older and disabled persons more vulnerable. The authors of this chapter discuss the impact of caregiving on the caregiver, with particular attention to caregiving with older adults with developmental disabilities or serious mental illness. Interventions to address caregiver needs are presented together with a list of national and state resources for practitioners and caregivers.

The fourth chapter, by Tina Maschi and Ron Aday, addresses the issue of older adults who are incarcerated. The number of such individuals has been steadily rising during the past two decades. By 2015 there were 200,000 incarcerated individuals aged 50 years and older (16% of all prisoners), the age that correctional officials usually consider to be an older adult. The authors point out the significant need for social and health services for the diverse population of older adults in state and federal prisons, noting that there are higher physical and mental health costs for older as compared with younger prisoners. They present information about a variety of innovative programs in prison and post-prison release that foster the health and well-being of older adults and call for social workers to use research, practice, and advocacy to address the needs of older persons in prison and upon their release.

The fifth chapter, by David E. Biegel and Amy Restorick Roberts, demonstrates that although rates of poverty are lower for elderly than for nonelderly adults, there are large differences in the rates of poverty among subgroups of elderly persons. In particular, older elderly persons, women, elders living alone, racial and ethnic elders, and homeless elderly persons have higher rates of poverty than other elders. The authors present a framework for examining service delivery barriers on system, community, agency staff, and individual and family levels. They also offer recommendations to address identified barriers and to strengthen practice and service delivery among women, racial and ethnic minorities, rural elderly persons, and the homeless elderly.

The sixth chapter, by Joy Swanson Ernst, focuses on social work practice with elders who have been mistreated or neglected, a problem area that has only been recognized within the past several decades. Elder abuse is a significant problem, it is estimated that one in ten elder adults has been mistreated or neglected. Elder abuse encompasses physical abuse, sexual abuse, emotional or psychological abuse, neglect and abandonment, financial or material exploitation, and self-neglect. Whether an act is considered abusive or neglectful is defined based on intentionality, severity, intensity, frequency, and consequences. Ernst reviews theories of causation of elder mistreatment as well as the characteristics of perpetrators and victims. A major emphasis of the chapter is the presentation of specific assessment and intervention strategies for social workers to use in working with elders when maltreatment is suspected.

The seventh chapter, by Elizabeth Lightfoot and Philip McCallion, focuses on older adults with intellectual and developmental disabilities. Given their increasing life expectancy, the current population of over 600,000 adults with intellectual/developmental disabilities is expected to double by the year 2030. This chapter discusses the paradigm shift in service provision for people with intellectual/developmental disabilities that has occurred and health concerns for this population arising from their great longevity. In discussing the role of social workers in serving persons with intellectual/developmental disabilities, the authors discuss the impact of a number of important issues including Alzheimer's disease and other dementias, residential living options, community participation and retirement, family caregiving, end of life and grief, and rights and advocacy.

Overall, the chapters in this section of the *Handbook* elucidate the importance for social workers of understanding the particular circumstances of at-risk populations of elderly persons. Roles for social workers in working with these populations include needs assessment, counseling, developing linkages with informal support systems, and advocacy while recognizing both intragroup and intergroup differences.

MARCIE PITT-CATSOUPHES
NANCY MORROW-HOWELL

New Paradigms of Paid and Unpaid Work: Employment and Voluntarism for Older Adults in the 21st Century

INTRODUCTION

The aging of the population is arguably one of the most significant transformations shaping economic, social, and policy experiences in the 21st century. Consider:

- The numbers of adults 65 and older in the US was 35 million in 2000. This number is expected to reach 83.7 million by 2050 (Werner, 2011; US Census Bureau, 2012). These shifts will translate into not only increased demand for programs and services but also increased pressure for new types of opportunities that engage older adults in a wide range of activities.
- The gift of longevity has been accompanied by extended good health for many. The National Health Interview Survey found that the three-fourths (76%) of those 65 and over assessed their own health as being "good, very good, or excellent" during the period of 2008–2010 (Federal Interagency Forum on Aging-Related Statistics, 2012).
- By definition, increases in longevity means that adults will have more years to live and support themselves in the post-65 years. Survey research indicates that the number of older adults who provide financial assistance to their young adult children is on the rise (Parker & Patten, 2013). Unfortunately, only a minority of older adults have the savings needed to complement public supports (e.g., Social Security) and pensions that they receive (AARP, 2013). It has become an economic imperative for many to work past the traditional retirement age of 65. With a focus on the most vulnerable, social workers will need to continue to advocate for resources that provide economic security needed for well-being.
- Work—both paid and unpaid volunteering—has been woven in the fabric of the everyday lives of Baby Boomers throughout their older adult years. Having found meaning in their work, it should not be surprising that older adults often indicate that they would like to continue to contribute value to the world around them. Following in the tradition of Saleebey (2012), social workers can articulate new visions of older adults as community assets.
- Nonprofit organizations are under pressure to develop new approaches for staffing their projects. Social workers can be at the vanguard of

the development of new models of service delivery, and can tap into the significant numbers of older adults who say that they want to contribute to social change efforts and community-based initiatives but who want to use their skills and expertise if they volunteer.

A number of profound questions emerge from these new trends in aging, including: What do older adults *want* to do with their added years? What do our families and communities *expect* that older adults will do with these additional healthy years? What does an aging society *need* from the older adult population, in terms of fulfilling social and productive roles?

In this chapter, we discuss perspectives about aging that resonate with social work's asset orientation.

We focus particular attention on two important productive roles that increasing numbers of older adults are assuming (or are continuing to assume) in their later adult years: paid work and unpaid work (volunteering and civic engagement). We focus on these roles because there are indications that both paid work and volunteering can have beneficial impacts on the health of those older adults (Heaven et al., 2013; Luoh & Herzog, 2002).

PERSPECTIVES ON AGING

The time has come for thought leaders—including social workers who carry the banner for asset perspectives about vulnerable populations—to embrace new perspectives about aging. These new perspectives cast aside the assumption that older adulthood is only a time of prefrailty, which precedes the frailty of elderhood (Walston et al., 2006). Rather, the new perspectives focus on the addition of relatively healthy years when people have the capacity and desire to make valued contributions to families, friends, and communities. Over the past few decades, there has been growing discussion about a new life phase experienced by "younger" older adults: those who have transitioned from the midlife demands of child rearing and so-called career jobs and who also continue to have good health (see Moen, 2011; James & Wink, 2007; Laslett, 1991; Neugarten, 1974). While some of used the term "The Third Age" to describe this new stage, others have called it "the crown of life" (James & Wink, 2007).

Several new conceptual frameworks have been proposed in an effort to capture the asset perspectives encapsulated in the third age paradigm, such as healthy aging (Butler, 2010; Robinson, Novelli, Pearson, & Norris, 2007), positive aging (Hill, 2005), and successful aging (Rowe & Kahn, 1998; Havighurst, 1961). Butler and Gleason (1985) introduced the concept of productive aging to draw attention to the capacity of the older population to continue to contribute to society. The concept galvanized an advocacy movement as well as a scholarly agenda aimed at documenting the contributions of older adults as workers, volunteers, caregivers, and custodial grandparents as well as determining how engagement could be maximized through program and policy reforms. A compelling aspect of the productive aging perspective is the dual focus on positive outcomes to society as well as the older individual. Further, scholars have argued that we need older adults to stay productively engaged. In certain industries (such as healthcare), there will be labor shortages, demanding the retention of older workers. In the face of reduced public expenditure for social service organizations, we will need more volunteers. And, with the rise of the oldest-old, we will need a larger force of caregivers. Thus, our society most likely will require the productive engagement of older adults, and Robert Butler (1997) argued for the extension of work life and volunteer roles, for the benefit of society as well as the individual.

Scholars speculate that the productive engagement of older adults can lead to many positive societal outcomes, such as leveraging the talents of experienced workers, volunteers, and caregivers; reducing some of the pressure on postretirement income; promoting a stronger civil society; and supporting stronger families. There is a large literature that documents the effects of these activities on the older adults themselves. In general, working and volunteering has been demonstrated to be health promoting for older adults, although circumstances and contexts matter a great deal. For example, the negative health effects of caregiving are widely documented (Talley & Crews, 2007), although positive outcomes have also been described as well (Roth et al., 2013).

Currently, the potential contributions of older adults are limited by ageist attitudes, outdated organizational structures, and ineffective policies. Social workers, as clinicians, program developers, and policy analysts, should take an active part in transforming aging societies to maximize the involvement of older adult in these productive roles.

NEEDS, EXPECTATIONS, AND OPPORTUNITIES: PAID EMPLOYMENT FOR OLDER ADULTS

Changes in the labor force participation rates of older adults in the United States compel our attention. Data from the Current Population Survey suggests that from 1977 to 2007, the employment rate of workers 65 and older increased 101% (compared with a 59% increase in the total employment for those aged 16 and older in the United States). This change was particularly notable for women 65 and older, whose labor force employment rate increased 147% over that time period (US Bureau of Labor Statistics, 2008). In 2012, nearly 1 of every 5 people age 65 and older (18.5% of people in that age bracket) were in the labor force, with a majority of these holding full-time positions (US Bureau of Labor Statistics, 2008, 2012).

Mor Barak (1995) has identified four sets of reasons that older adults remain at the workplace: financial (including both earnings as well as benefits with financial value), personal (for example positive psychological outcomes including an improved sense of self-esteem as well as feelings of satisfaction related to accomplishments), social (including both work-based relationships as well as more broad social status derived from the work role), and generative (including opportunities to pass work-related knowledge and wisdom forward to younger people). It is important to remember that these reasons are not mutually exclusive and that most people indicate that each of these factors (to some extent) contributes to their decisions to remain in the labor force (Smyer, Besen, & Pitt-Catsouphes, 2009).

Brown, Aumann, Pitt-Catsouphes, Galinksy, and Bond (2010) analyzed data collected from people who had previously retired but then reentered the workforce. Health was the reason cited by the higher percentage of people (33%) for having previously retired. The reasons for returning including financial reasons (53% "wanted to retire more comfortably," 18% found that their "income from other sources was insufficient," and 6% "needed health insurance"); personal (31% "would be bored if they were not working," 18% wanted to "feel productive, useful, and helpful,"

15% had jobs that were "fun, enjoyable"); and social (13% "wanted to interact with people"). Importantly, some people reported that their desire to maintain well-being was a motivator to remain in the labor force, with 12% indicating they wanted to stay physically/mentally active. Clearly, as older adults cycle in and out of the labor force, the basic concept of "retirement" has become quite muddled and can now describe a time of life that includes paid work.

There are different ways for older adults to continue to participate in the labor force, such as (1) staying with the same employer in the current job but with changes in some of the assigned work responsibilities so that the job fits better with the preferences of the older worker; (2) staying with the current employer but switching to a different job that is better aligned with the older worker's priorities; (3) staying with the same employer but negotiating a phased retirement agreement with the employer that work hours would be reduced over a specified period of time before the person retires from the organization; (4) finding a new employer who has a job that is a better fit with the older worker's needs (possibly a "bridge job" as discussed by Cahill, Giandrea, and Quinn, in press, 2006); and (5) leaving the current employer to become self-employed (Rogoff, 2007). One challenge facing social work professionals and older adults themselves is that our workplace systems—the practices and cultures of work that affect all aspects of the employment experiences (from hiring to transitions out of a particular work situation)—have not yet caught up with the changes in the patterns of older adults labor force attachment. This is what Riley, Kahn, and Foner (1994) call the structural lag.

Encore.org is an organization that offers a model for engaging the skills and competencies of older adults, and putting those talents to use for purpose work that has an impact on one of today's complex social problems. In her book, *The Encore Career Handbook: How to Make a Difference in the Second Half of Life*, Alboher (2013) observes that it may be normative for adults in midlife/older adults to engage in a "search for purpose, passion, and a paycheck that coalesces into an encore career—continued work that combines personal meaning with social purpose" (p. 3). This new mental image of active older adults stands in sharp contrast to outdated assumptions of older adults who prematurely disengage from meaningful work. Furthermore, the work of organizations such as Encore.org helps leaders in the social service sector to consider how the involvement of older adults can help agencies address expected labor force shortages.

There is a substantial body of literature that examines the complex relationships between work and health (see Lindeboom & Kerkhofs, 2009). It has been difficult for researchers to fully account for cohort effects (factors that might be unique to a specific population group), interpret subjective health status reports, and disentangle the bidirectional effect of health status on decisions about labor force participation (and vice versa). However, there is some evidence that retirement—particularly so-called involuntary retirement—can have a negative impact on physical and mental health (Dhaval, Rashad, & Spasojevic, 2008; James & Spiro, 2007). For many, the impact of work on health may reflect whether the person is extending labor force participation voluntarily ("because they want to") or not ("because they have to").

There are a number of ways that social workers might be able to enhance the well-being of older workers, such as:

- Offering services to unemployed older adults who find it takes them longer to reenter the workforce compared with their younger counterparts
- Engaging older adults in lifelong learning opportunities so that they have marketable skills into their older adult years
- Providing supports through services such as Employee Assistance Programs (EAPs) that help older employees to cope with work-related stress and transitions
- Helping older employees with elder care responsibilities access services through employer-sponsored work-life programs
- Responding to age bias and discrimination through diversity initiatives at the workplace
- Coaching older adults who face employment transitions, whether the transition is to full or partial retirement or to other paid work
- Helping older adults access workplace-based wellness programs to maintain health and stamina, manage chronic disease, and reduce the risk of injuries
- Working with employers to expand older adults' "workability," which is understood as achieving a good fit between the work environment, job demands, workplace supports, and the individual's skills and health status (Gould, Ilmarinen, Järvisalo, & Koskinen, 2008). As noted by

McLoughlin, Taylor, and Bohle (2011), social workers might consider changing job characteristics that can affect workability as one way to improve the well-being of older adults who are in the labor force.

EXPECTATIONS AND OPPORTUNITIES: UNPAID WORK EXPERIENCES

Volunteering is a productive role that has always been available to older adults in their "retirement years." Volunteering is discretionary and can accommodate the schedules of older adults who value more flexibility, fitting into the leisure ethic that has dominated our vision of late life since the 1960s. And volunteering has always been a socially desirable activity, bringing positive recognition and rewards to older adults. Yet this history has limited the potential of older adults in these highly valuable and potentially demanding roles; and as described above in regard to paid work, structural lag has negatively affected the involvement of older adults in unpaid work.

It is estimated that 24.4% of older adults in the United States volunteer; yet, this rate is lower than the rate among younger adults (for 35–44 year olds, the rate is 31.6%) (US Bureau of Labor Statistics, 2013). There are several reasons for this drop in rates of volunteering in later life, despite the gain in discretionary time. First of all, younger adults engage in volunteering related to the work and educational organizations in their lives. For example, parents volunteer at their children's schools and employees sign up for service events offered through the workplace. Older adults are more often separated from these institutions and are less likely to be asked to get involved (Independent Sector, 2000). Older adults are most likely to volunteer for religious organizations, institutions that they remain connected to, despite their age. Health problems are not likely to affect volunteering until later than commonly believed (AARP, 2003).

The promising news is that when an older adult is asked to volunteer, they are more likely to get involved (Independent Sector, 2000). Also, once in volunteer roles, older adults commit more time, reporting a median of 90 hours a year, while the 45–54 age group reports 52 hours a year, and those 55–64 years report 56 hours (US Bureau of Labor Statistics, 2013). It is important to note that these numbers only include formal volunteering with organizations. When informal volunteering, or helping others outside an organization, is counted, these numbers are higher. Zedlewski and Schaner (2006) estimated from the Health and Retirement Survey that 33% of respondents aged 55 years and over engaged in formal volunteering and 52% engaged in informal volunteering.

Older adults with more personal and social resources volunteer—those with more education, income, health, social support, and social connections (Tang, 2006). Lower rates of volunteering among lower socioeconomic and ethnic groups can be attributed to disparities in economic and health resources and competing demands of caregiving and working (McBride, 2007). Motivations to volunteer differ between older and younger adults. Older adults report more of a service orientation and the desire to give back and be generative, while younger adults are more interested in the social and career development aspects of volunteering (Musick & Wilson, 2008). However, in both groups, there is evidence that volunteering increases personal and social resources and can lead to new civic and work engagements (Morrow-Howell, McCrary, Lee, & McBride, 2011).

There is speculation that baby boomers will volunteer at higher rates in later life than previous cohorts because, as a group, they have higher levels of education and they had their children later in life (which keeps them involved in volunteering at educational institutions and child-related activities into later ages). They may stay attached to the employment sector longer, through part-time work, and part-time work is associated with the highest levels of volunteer involvement (Foster-Bey, Grimm, & Dietz, 2007). A poll by the National Governor's Association in 2008 documented that two-thirds of older adults not currently engaged in volunteer service express a desire to become engaged (National Governors Association, 2008). All of these signs point to the potential to grow the volunteer labor force and bring more older adults into service to the public and non-profit sector.

Structural lag between organizational practices and social policies and the abilities and desires of the older population have constrained the participation of older adults in civic service. Over the last two decades, advocates and scholars alike have pointed out that older volunteers are not given the types of challenging work that their experience and dedication enables them to do. And there has not been adequate outreach and institutional support to bring them into and support them in volunteer positions. Emergent practices have the potential to maximize the engagement of older adults in unpaid volunteer work. These include the expansion of online resources for locating volunteer opportunities (see volunteermatch.com and comingofage. org); the diversification of work arrangements to allow for more flexibility and choice; the more serious exploration of volunteer work in retirement transitional planning; and the development of incentives to offset costs and reward service. For example, some municipalities offer a reduction in property taxes for volunteer service in the public schools. The Serve America Act of 2010 (S. 3487) amended AmeriCorps regulations, allowing for the educational stipend associated with volunteer service to be transferred to children, grandchildren, and foster children.

A long list of health and well-being outcomes has been associated with volunteering: decreased mortality (Ayalon, 2008), increased physical function (Hong & Morrow-Howell, 2010; Lum & Lightfoot, 2005), increased self-reported health (Luoh & Herzog, 2002), decreased depressive symptoms (Musick & Wilson, 2003), improved cognitive function (Carlson et al., 2009), and increased life satisfaction (Van Willigen, 2000). Further, there is some evidence that older adults with fewer personal and social resources may experience greater positive effects compared with better-resourced counterparts. There are many explanations for the positive effects of volunteering, including increased physical, social, and cognitive activity (Fried et al., 2004); role enhancement and role accumulation (Greenfield & Marks, 2004; Hao, 2008); and the altruistic nature of the activity (Piliavin & Siegl, 2007).

Given that our society will likely need more volunteers to support the missions of public and nonprofit agencies, social workers in these agencies must be foresighted and creative to promote the engagement of older volunteers. Social workers traditionally have supervised and managed volunteers; and the need for this expertise has never been greater. Additionally, social workers can promote the health and well-being of older adults by encouraging engagement in volunteer roles. Social workers can develop or expand programs and policies aimed at maximizing the engagement of the aging population in volunteer roles.

RECOMMENDATIONS AND CONCLUSIONS

Practitioners and researchers alike have noted that the loss of roles as one ages can pose threats to physical and emotional well-being. Decades ago, Burgess (1960) warned us about the perils when aging becomes a "roleless role."

The challenge and opportunity of aging in the 21st century is to engage older adults as fully as possible in roles and activities that are valued by society and that are meaningful to the older adults themselves. Reflecting some of the precepts of activity theory (Chambre, 1984; Longino & Karet, 1982; Lemon, Bengtson, & Peterson, 1972) and role identity theory (Stryker & Burke, 2000), "engaged aging" recognizes that older adults can derive physical and emotional health benefits from involvement in activities that are valued both by society and by the older adults themselves. The engaged aging framework challenges the assumption that involvement in any activities keeps older adults "busy" and "connected." As discussed by Matz-Costa, Besen, James, and Pitt-Catsouphes (2012), older adults who participate in activities associated with work and volunteer roles *without* this psychological engagement may experience lower well-being than if they had not been involved at all.

Paradigms associated with engaged aging help social work practitioners to remember that the overarching goal is to partner with older adults so that they can focus on roles and activities that are satisfying to them and on roles that (on average) energize them more than drain energy from them. Using this perspective, social workers can work with older adults and organizations that want to access the talents of these older adults. The engaged aging framework also focuses attention on the quality of the role experience; enhancing role quality means that older adults need to have access to supports and the resources necessary for people to respond to and cope with the demands of the roles. Health and well-being can be jeopardized when role demands exceed the resources needed to meet the demands (Karasek & Theorell, 1990).

In conclusion, there are a number of action steps that social workers can take to positively shape the health and well-being of older adults.

- Promote age-friendly organizations that welcome older adults as they pursue paid and unpaid work roles.
- Support age-friendly community initiatives that not only offer supportive services so that older adults can age-in-place but also increase the opportunities for older adults to engage in paid and unpaid work. For example, some community-based age-friendly initiatives include job fairs and career counseling for older adults. In regard to volunteering, Village and naturally occurring retirement community (NORC) models include volunteer programs to engage older residents in providing services to each other. Many advocate that these age-friendly communities be reconceptualized as "communities of all ages," because these transformed communities support both older and younger people.
- Seek out innovations in universal design (for instance in areas such as housing, transportation, and job structures) that benefit people at every stage of the life course.
- Provide leadership for intergenerationalism—efforts that capitalize on the positive outcomes associated with positive interactions among people of different ages. Social workers should be at the vanguard of documenting the health and mental health benefits of age diversity in the workplace, in the volunteer labor force, in educational settings, and in residential arrangements.

These new directions have the potential to augment healthy aging as a result of the productive engagement of older adults.

REFERENCES

AARP. (2003). *Multicultural study 2003: Time and money: An in-depth look at 45+ volunteers and donors.* Washington, DC: Author.

AARP. (2013). *2013 Retirement confidence survey: A secondary analysis of the findings from respondents age 50+.* Washington, DC: AARP. Retrieved from http://www.aarp.org/content/dam/aarp/research/surveys_statistics/general/2013/2013-Retirement-Confidence-Survey-A-Secondary-Analysis-of-the-Findings-from-Respondents-Age-50-Plus-AARP-rsa-gen.pdf

Alboher, M. (2013). *The encore handbook: How to make a living and a difference in the second half of life.* New York, NY: Workman.

Ayalon, L. (2008). Volunteering as a predictor of all-cause mortality: What aspects of volunteering really matter? *International Psychogeriatrics, 20,* 1000–1013. doi:10.1017/S1041610208007096

Brown, M., Aumann, K., Pitt-Catsouphes, M., Galinsky, E., & Bond, J. T. (2010). *Working in retirement: A 21st century phenomenon.* New York, NY: Families and Work Institute. Retrieved from http://familiesandwork.org/site/research/reports/workinginretirement.pdf

Burgess, E. W. (1960). *Aging in western societies.* Chicago, IL: University of Chicago Press.

Butler, R. N. (1997). Living longer, contributing longer. *Journal of the American Medical Association, 278,* 1372–1374.

Butler, R. N. (2010). *The longevity prescription. The 8 proven keys to a long, healthy life.* New York, NY: Avery.

Butler, R. N., & Gleason, H. P. (1985). *Productive aging.* New York, NY: Springer.

Cahill, K. E., Giandrea, M. D., & Quinn, J. F. (2015). Retirement patterns and the macroeconomy, 1992–2010: Prevalence and determinants of bridge jobs, phased retirement, and re-entry among three recent cohorts of older Americans. *The Gerontologist, 55,* 384–403. doi:10.1093/geront/gnt146

Cahill, K. E., Giandrea, M. D., & Quinn, J. F. (2006). Retirement patterns from career employment. *The Gerontologist, 46,* 514–523. doi:10.1093/geront/46.4.514

Carlson, M. C., Erickson, K., Kramer, A., Voss, M., Bolea, N., Mielke, M., . . . Fried, L. (2009). Evidence for neurocognitive plasticity in at-risk older adults: The experience corps program. *Journal of Gerontology: Biological Sciences, 64,* 1275–1282. doi:10.1093/gerona/glp117

Chambre, S. M. (1984). Is volunteering a substitute for role loss in old age? An empirical test of activity theory. *The Gerontologist, 24,* 292–298. doi:10.1093/geront/24.3.292

Dhaval, D., Rashad, I., & Spasojevic, J. (2008). The effects of retirement on physical and mental health outcomes. *Southern Economic Journal, 75,* 497–523.

Federal Interagency Forum on Aging-Related Statistics. (2012). *Older Americans: Key indicators of well-being.* Washington, DC: US Government Printing Office. Retrieved from http://www.agingstats.gov/agingstatsdotnet/Main_Site/Data/2012_Documents/Docs/EntireChartbook.pdf

Foster-Bey, J., Grimm, R., & Dietz, N. (2007). *Keeping baby boomers volunteering: A research brief on volunteer retention and turnover.* Washington, DC: Corporation for National and Community Service.

Fried, L. P., Carlson, M. C., Freedman, M., Frick, K. D., Glass, T. A., Hill, J., . . . Zeger, S. (2004). A social model for health promotion for an aging population: Initial evidence on the Experience Corps model. *Journal of Urban Health: Bulletin of the New York Academy of Medicine, 81,* 64–78. doi:10.1093/jurban/jth094

Gould, R., Ilmarinen, J., Järvisalo, J., & Koskinen, S. (Eds.). (2008). *Dimensions of work ability: Results of the health 2000 survey.* Helsinki, Finland: Finnish Center for Pensions.

Greenfield, E. A., & Marks, N. F. (2004). Formal volunteering as a protective factor for older adults' psychological well-being. *Journal of Gerontology, 59B,* S258–S264. doi: 10.1093/geronb/59.5.S258

Hao, Y. (2008). Productive activities and psychological well-being among older adults. *Journal of Gerontology, 63B,* S64–S72.

Havighurst, R. J. (1961). Successful aging. *The Gerontologist, 1,* 8–13. doi:10.1093/geront/1.1.8

Heaven, B., Brown, J. J. E., White, M., Errington, L., Mathers, J. C., & Moffatt, S. (2013). Supporting well-being in retirement through meaningful social roles: Systematic review of intervention studies. *Millbank Quarterly, 91,* 222–287.

Hill, R. D. (2005). *Positive aging. A guide for mental health professionals and consumers.* New York, NY: Norton.

Hong, S. I., & Morrow-Howell, N. (2010). Health outcomes of Experience Corps: A high-commitment volunteer program. *Social Science and Medicine (1982), 71,* 414–420. doi: 10.1016/j.socscimed.2010.04.009

Independent Sector. (2000). *America's senior volunteers.* Washington, DC: Author.

James, J. B., & Spiro, A., III. (2007). The impact of work on the psychological health and well-being of older Americans. In J. B. James and P. Wink (Eds.), *The crown of life: Dynamics of the early postretirement period* (pp. 153–173). New York, NY: Springer.

James, J. B., & Wink, P. (Eds.). (2007). *The crown of life: Dynamics of the early postretirement period.* New York, NY: Springer.

Karasek, R., & Theorell, T. (1990). *Healthy work. Stress, productivity, and the reconstruction of working life.* New York, NY: Basic Books.

Laslett, P. (1991). *A fresh map of life: The emergence of the third age.* Cambridge, MA: Harvard University Press.

Lemon, B. W., Bengtson, V. L., & Peterson, J. A. (1972). An exploration of the activity theory of aging: Activity types and live satisfaction among in-movers to a retirement community. *Journal of Gerontology, 27,* 511–523. doi:10.1093/geronj/27.4.511

Lindeboom, M., & Kerkhofs, M. (2009). Health and work of the elderly: Subjective health measures, reporting errors and endogeneity in the relationship between health and work. *Journal of Applied Econometrics, 24,* 1024–1046. doi: 10.1002/jae.1077

Longino, C. F., & Kart, C. S. (1982). Explicating activity theory: A formal replication. *Journal of Gerontology, 37*, 713–722. doi:10.1093/geronj/37.6.713

Lum, T. Y., & Lightfoot, E. (2005). The effects of volunteering on the physical and mental health of older people. *Research on Aging, 27*, 31–55. doi:10.1177/0164027504271349

Luoh, M. C., & Herzog, A. R. (2002). Individual consequences of volunteer and paid work in old age: Health and mortality. *Journal of Health and Social Behavior, 43*, 490–509. doi: 10.2307/3090239

Matz-Costa, C., Besen, E., James, J. B., & Pitt-Catsouphes, M. (2014). The differential impact of multiple levels of productive activity engagement on psychological well-being in middle and later life. *The Gerontologist, 54*, 277–289. doi:10.1093/geront/gns148

McBride, A. (2007). Civic engagement, older adults, and inclusion. *Generations, 30*, 66–71.

McLoughlin, C., Taylor, P., & Bohle, P. (2011). Promoting worker resilience over the lifecourse. In B. Resnick, L. P. Gwyther, & K. A. Roberto (Eds.), *Resilience in aging: Concepts, research, and outcomes* (pp. 121–132). New York, NY: Springer. doi:10.1007/978-1-4419-0232-0

Moen, P. (2011). A life course approach to the third age. In D. C. Carr & K. Komp (Eds.), *Gerontology in the era of the third age* (pp. 13–22). New York, NY: Springer.

Mor Barak, M. E. (1995). The meaning of work for older adults seeking employment: The generativity factor. *International Journal of Aging and Human Development, 41*, 325–533. ERIC number: EJ524143

Morrow-Howell, N., McCrary, S., Lee, Y. S., McBride, A. M. (2011). *Experience Corps: Pathway to new engagement.* CSD Research Brief 11-11. St. Louis, MO: Washington University, Center for Social Development.

Musick, M. A., & Wilson, J. (2003). Volunteering and depression: The role of psychological and social resources in different age groups. *Social Science and Medicine, 56*, 259–269.

Musick, M. A., & Wilson, J. (2008). *Volunteering: A social profile.* Bloomington: Indiana University Press.

National Governors Association. (2008). *Increasing volunteerism among older adults: Benefits and strategies for states.* Washington, DC: Author.

Neugarten, B. (1974). Age groups in American society and the rise of the young-old. *Annals of the American Academy of Political and Social Sciences, 415*, 187–198. doi: 10.1177/000271627441500114

Parker, K., & Patten, E. (2013). *The sandwich generation: Rising financial burdens for middle-aged Americans.* Washington, DC: Pew Research Center. Retrieved from http://www.pewsocialtrends.org/files/2013/01/Sandwich_Generation_Report_FINAL_1-29.pdf

Piliavin, J. A., & Siegl, E. (2007). Health benefits of volunteering in the Wisconsin longitudinal study. *Journal of Health and Social Behavior, 48*, 450–464.

Riley, M. W., Kahn, R. L., & Foner, A. (Eds.). (1994). *Age and structural lag: Society's failure to provide opportunities for work, family, and leisure.* New York, NY: Wiley.

Robinson, M., Novelli, W., Pearson, C., & Norris, L. (Eds.). (2007). *Global health and global aging.* San Francisco, CA: Jossey-Bass.

Rogoff, E. (2007). Opportunities for entrepreneurship in later life. *Generations, 31*, 90–95.

Roth, D., Haley, W., Hovater, M. Perkins, M., Wadley, V., & Judd, S. (2013). Family caregiving and all-cause mortality: Findings from a population-based propensity-matched analysis. *American Journal of Epidemiology, 178*, 1571–1578. doi:10.1093/aje/kwt225

Rowe, J. W., & Kahn, R. L. (1997). Successful aging. *The Gerontologist, 37*, 433–440. doi: 10.1093/geront/37.4.433

Saleebey, D. (2012). *The strengths perspective in social work practice* (6th edition). Boston, MA: Pearson.

Smyer, M., Besen, E., & Pitt-Catsouphes, M. (2009). Boomers and the many meanings of work. In Hudson, R. B. (Ed.). *Boomer bust? Economic and political issues of the graying society* (pp. 3–16). Westport, CT: Greenwood.

Stryker, S., & Burke, P. J. (2000). The past, present, and future of an identity theory. *Social Psychology Quarterly, 63*, 284–297. doi: 10.2307/2695840

Tang, F. (2006). What resources are needed for volunteerism? A life course perspective. *Journal of Applied Gerontology, 25*, 375–390. doi:10.1177/0733464806292858

Talley, R., & Crews J. (2007). Framing the public health of caregiving. *American Journal of Public Health. Public Health, 97*, 224–228.

US Bureau of Labor Statistics. (2008). *Older workers: Are there more older people in the workplace?* Retrieved from http://www.bls.gov/spotlight/2008/older_workers/

US Bureau of Labor Statistics. (2012). *Household data annual averages: Employment status of the civilian noninstitutional population by age, sex, and race.* Retrieved from http://www.bls.gov/cps/cpsaat03.pdf

US Bureau of Labor Statistics (2013). *Volunteering in the United States.* Retrieved from www.bls.gov/news.release/pdf/volun.pdf

US Census Bureau (2012). *2012 National Population Projections: Summary Tables.* Retrieved from https://

www.census.gov/population/projections/data/national/2012/summarytables.html

Van Willigen, M. (2000). Differential benefits of volunteering across the life course. *Journal of Gerontology, Social Sciences, 55B,* 308–318. doi:10.1093/geronb/55.5.S308

Walston, J., Hadley, E. C., Ferrucci, L., Guralnik, J. M., Newman, A. B., Studenski, S. A. . . . Fried, L. P. (2006). Research agenda for frailty in older adults: Toward a better understanding of physiology and etiology: Summary from the American Geriatrics Society/National Institute on Aging research conference on frailty in older adults. *Journal of the American Geriatrics Society, 54,* 991–1001. doi:10.1111/j.1532-5415.2006.00745.x

Werner, C. A. (2011). *The older population: 2010.* Washington, DC: United States Census Bureau. Retrieved from http://www.census.gov/prod/cen2010/briefs/c2010br-09.pdf

Zedlewski, S. R., & Schaner, S. G. (2006). *Older adults engaged as volunteers.* The Retirement Project, Perspectives on Productive Aging No. 5. Washington, DC: Urban Institute.

INTRODUCTION

As the demographic landscape of the world changes, researchers and practitioners are curious about those who live well beyond their life expectancy; those we call the oldest old. In this chapter, we report findings in the main areas of sociodemographic factors, function, mental health, health, social support, and caregiving. Where possible, findings regarding the oldest old (85+) are compared with the young-old (65–74) and the old-old (75–84) as well as the subgroups within the "oldest-old" category (85–89, 90–100, and 100+).

SOCIODEMOGRAPHICS

The increase in life expectancy and the decline in fertility have contributed to the aging society in developed countries. With the aging of the baby boomers, American society has grown old rapidly, resulting in a dramatic increase in the demographic projections for the oldest old. The oldest old, the fastest growing age group, will constitute 21.5% of the US population 65 years and over and is projected to be 4.3% of the overall population by 2050 (US Census Bureau, 2012). Figure 40.1 graphically displays the population distribution by age and sex in 1950, 2000, and 2050 (Shrestha & Heisler, 2011). The coming decades bring many more people into the oldest-old age groups that will be the most populous age group in 2050.

Race

By 2020, there will be 6.6 million people aged 85 and over in the United States, representing 1.93% of total population (US Census Bureau, 2012). As shown in Table 40.1, among the oldest old, the majority of people were non-Hispanic Whites, compared with Blacks, Hispanics, and Asians (US Census Bureau, 2012). Even though this racial composition reflects much less diversity than the younger population in 2010, the racial diversity among the oldest old is projected to increase in coming decades (US Census Bureau, 2012). In 2050, 81% of the oldest old are projected to be White, whereas Hispanics will make up 15% of this age group, Blacks 10%, and Asians 6% (US Census Bureau, 2012).

RUTH E. DUNKLE

HAE-SOOK JEON

The Oldest Old

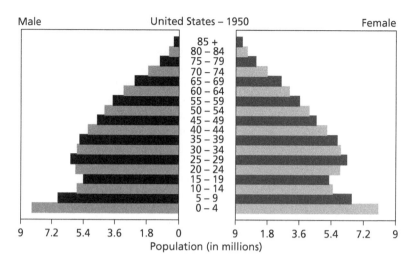

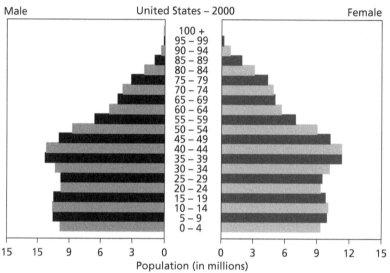

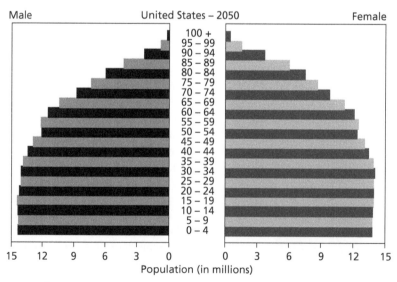

FIGURE 40.1 Continued

Gender

Gender disparity becomes more remarkable with advancing age. As shown in Table 40.2, in 2010, among the population aged 85 and over 67% percent are women and 33% are men, whereas among the young-old 54% are women and 46% are men (US Census Bureau, 2012). The extreme gender gap in advancing age poses more challenges for elderly women than men. For instance, elderly women are more likely to be widowed, economically disadvantaged, physically frail, and institutionalized than their male counterparts (Federal Interagency Forum on Aging-Related Statistics, 2012; He & Muenchrath, 2011). While the gender gap is expected to continue over the next decades, the extreme gender gap among the oldest old is projected to narrow in 2050 (Table 40.2). There are also gender differences by race among the oldest old: Males make up 41% of elders among the Hispanic population, 36.5% among Non-Hispanic Whites, and 33.5% among Blacks in 2011 (US Census Bureau, 2012a). Gender disparity is lower among the Hispanic oldest old than any other racial counterpart.

Marital Status

The pattern of marital status is changing with advancing age as well. As shown in Table 40.3, in 2010, 18% of women and 58% of men among the oldest old are married, 73% and 35% are widowed, respectively. The oldest old men are three times as likely as women to be married (Federal Interagency Forum on Aging-Related Statistics, 2012).

Living Arrangements

Living arrangements vary by gender for the oldest old aged 90 and over. In 2006–2008, 53% of the oldest old men lived in a household with others and 30% lived alone. In contrast, 32% of the oldest old women lived in a household with others and 40% lived alone. The proportion of oldest old living in institutions such as skilled nursing homes is 14.5% for the oldest old men and 25.5% for the oldest old women (He & Muenchrath, 2011). Although most of the oldest old live in the community, people in this age group constitute the largest proportion of skilled nursing facility residents. In 2010, 42% of nursing home residents were over the age of 85, compared with 28% for elders aged 75–84 and 13% for those aged 65–74 (Werner, 2011).

Socioeconomic Status

With advancing age, the poverty rate among older adults is increasing, indicating that the oldest old are more likely to be poor. In 2010, the poverty rate among the oldest old was 12%, while the proportion of those in poverty among the young-old and old-old was 8% and 9%, respectively (Federal Interagency Forum on Aging-Related Statistics, 2012). The poverty rates are related to race and gender among the older population aged 75 and over compared with the young-old. In 2010, non-Hispanic White men aged 75 and over had a poverty rate of 5.4%, compared with 13.3% of Black, 14.5% of Hispanic, and 15.8% of Asian counterparts. Older Black women (24.7%) and Hispanic women (22.4%) aged 75 and over are

Figure 40.1 Age-Sex Structure of the United States in Years 1950, 2000, and 2050.

Source: CRS extractions from US Census Bureau, International Data Base (IDB), http://www.census.gov/ipc/www/idb/country.php. Reprinted from Shrestha and Heisler (2011)Notes: US data are based on official estimates and projections. Population estimates for 1950–1999 are based on the resident population plus the armed forces overseas. Population estimates for 2000–2008 are for the resident population and are based on Census 2000. The estimates are produced using vital statistics through 2007 and survey data on international migration (supplemented with administrative data) through 2007. Population data in the IDB for 2009–2050 are projections of the resident population. The projections originate with a base population from Census 2000 and are produced using a cohort-component method—the most common method used for age structure projections because they take into account potential differences in the rates of mortality, fertility, and migration at different ages. Projections are based on historical trends in vital statistics data through 2003 and administrative data on legal immigration through 2002. Census 2010 has been completed and preliminary data were released in December 2010; however, population projections have not yet been updated with these data. (See http://www.census. gov/ipc/www/idb/country.php.)

TABLE 40.1 Older Population by Race

2010	65 and Over		Young-Old		Old-Old		Oldest Old	
	number*	percent	number*	percent	number*	percent	number*	percent
White	34926	(86.8%)	18312	(85.3%)	11424	(87.8%)	5189	(90.2%)
Non-Hispanic White	32243	(80.2%)	16735	(78.0%)	10607	(81.5%)	4902	(85.2%)
Black	3418	(8.5%)	1975	(9.2%)	1046	(8.0%)	397	(6.9%)
American Indian and Alaska Native	235	(0.6%)	148	(0.7%)	66	(0.5%)	20	(0.4%)
Asian	1333	(3.3%)	833	(3.9%)	387	(3.0%)	113	(2.0%)
Native Hawaiian and Other Pacific Islander	39	(0.1%)	25	(0.1%)	11	(0.1%)	3	(0.1%)
Hispanic	2858	(7.1%)	1685	(7.9%)	868	(6.7%)	305	(5.3%)
Total	40229	(100%)	21463	(100%)	13015	(100%)	5751	(100%)

2050	65 and over		Young-Old		Old-Old		Oldest Old	
White	68055	(76.9%)	29931	(74.6%)	22633	(77.0%)	15491	(81.4%)
Non-Hispanic White	51772	(58.5%)	21854	(54.5%)	17093	(58.2%)	12825	(67.4%)
Black	10553	(11.9%)	5170	(12.9%)	3402	(11.6%)	1982	(10.4%)
American Indian and Alaska Native	918	(1.0%)	446	(1.1%)	293	(1.01%)	180	(0.9%)
Asian	7541	(8.5%)	3778	(9.4%)	2618	(8.9%)	1145	(6.0%)
Native Hawaiian and Other Pacific Islander	219	(0.2%)	111	(0.3%)	72	(0.2%)	35	(0.2%)
Hispanic	17515	(19.8%)	8698	(21.7%)	5945	(20.2%)	2871	(15.1%)
Total	88547	(100%)	40113	(100%)	29393	(100%)	19041	(100%)

*Numbers in Thousands
Source: Vincent and Velkog (2010); US Census Bureau (2008)

TABLE 40.2 Older Population by Gender and Age

2010	65 and Over		Young-Old		Old-Old		Oldest Old	
	number*	percent	number*	percent	number*	percent	number*	percent
Men	17,292	(42.9%)	9,938	(46.3%)	5,461	(42.0%)	1,893	(32.9%)
Women	22,937	(57.1%)	11,525	(53.7%)	7,554	(58.0%)	3,859	(67.1%)
Total	40,229	(100.0%)	21,463	(100.0%)	13,015	(100.0%)	5,752	(100.0%)
2050	65 and Over		Young-Old		Old-Old		Oldest Old	
Men	39,917	(45.1%)	19,162	(47.8%)	13,297	(45.2%)	7,458	(39.1%)
Women	48,630	(54.9%)	20,951	(52.2%)	16,096	(54.8%)	11,583	(60.8%)
Total	88,547	(100.0%)	40,113	(100.0%)	29,393	(100.0%)	19,041	(100.0%)

*Numbers in Thousands
Source: US Census Bureau, Statistical Abstract of the United States (2012)

more likely to live in poverty than non-Hispanic White women (9.7%) (Federal Interagency Forum on Aging-Related Statistics, 2012).

Educational attainment, one of the crucial determinants for socioeconomic status, increases over time among older population. For example, in 2000, 70% of those aged 65 and over had at least a high school education as compared with 80% in 2010 (Federal Interagency Forum on Aging Related Statistics, 2012). Yet, there are age and race differences in educational attainment. The proportion of those with at least a high school education is lower among the oldest-old (73.1%) than young-old (84.5%) and old-old (77.1%) in 2011 (US Census Bureau, 2012a). Even though there were no significant gender differences for high school graduates, men were more likely to have a bachelor's degree among older populations (US Census Bureau, 2012a). Racial differences in educational attainment exist among older adults. Eighty four percent of non-Hispanic Whites and 74% of Asians completed at least a high school education, while 65% of Blacks and 47% of Hispanics received

TABLE 40.3 Marital Status by Age and Gender Among Older Adults (2010)

	Elderly Men		
	Young-Old	Old-Old	Oldest Old
Total	100%	100%	100%
Married	78.0%	73.2%	58.3%
Widowed	6.4%	17.2%	34.6%
Divorced	11.0%	6.1%	3.9%
Never married	4.5%	3.5%	3.2%
	Elderly Women		
	Young-Old	Old-Old	Oldest Old
Total	100%	100%	100%
Married	55.9%	38.1%	18.0%
Widowed	24.0%	50.4%	72.9%
Divorced	15.0%	7.9%	4.7%
Never married	5.1%	3.6%	4.5%

Source: Federal Interagency Forum on Aging-Related Statistics (2012)

a high school education (Federal Interagency Forum on Aging-Related Statistics, 2012).

Life Expectancy

Life expectancy increased significantly during the 20th century from 49 years in 1900 to 78.5 in 2009 at birth. At age 85, the average life expectancy of 4 years in 1900 increased to 6.7 years by 2009 (Federal Interagency Forum on Aging-Related Statistics, 2012). Life expectancy differed by race, but the gap declined with age. In 2009, life expectancy at birth was 78.8 for White Americans and 74.5 for Black Americans. At age 65, the difference between White Americans and Black Americans decreased to 1.3 years. Among those who survive to age 85, however, Black Americans can expect to live an average of 0.2 more years than White Americans (Federal Interagency Forum on Aging-Related Statistics, 2012). In addition, gender differences in life expectancy exist across all age groups. Life expectancy at birth was 76 for men and 80.9 for women in 2009. The life expectancy among women who survive to age 85 was also higher than men (7 for women and 5.9 for men) (Federal Interagency Forum on Aging-Related Statistics, 2012).

Mental Health

The oldest old are at high risk for mental disorders due to multiple functional disabilities, medical illness, and increasing vulnerabilities to various stressors with age resulting from declining health and dwindling social relationships (Borson, Bartels, Colenda, Gottlieb, & Meyers, 2001). Depression, one of the most common mental health problems among older populations, varies by age and gender, but there are no significant racial or ethnic differences in prevalence rates for depression (Zalaquett & Stens, 2006). The oldest old report higher levels of depressive symptoms than the young-old. In 2008, the proportion of the oldest old with clinically relevant depressive symptoms was 18.3%, while the percentage of younger older age groups ranged between 11.9% and 14.6% (Federal Interagency Forum on Aging-Related Statistics, 2012). In a longitudinal study of the American oldest old, the participants reported increasing depressive symptoms with age (Dunkle, Roberts, & Haug, 2001; Jeon & Dunkle, 2009). Although literature supports the notion that

the oldest old in the United States present higher levels of depressive symptoms (Federal Interagency Forum on Aging-Related Statistics, 2012), the prevalence of clinically diagnosable depression among this population is not clear. Even though gender is an important predictor of depressive symptoms among older adults, the difference narrows for the oldest old due to a rapid increase of depressive symptoms among oldest old men. In 2008, 18.9% of the oldest old men and 17.9% of the oldest old women reported depressive symptoms, whereas only 10% of old-old men reported depressive symptoms compared with 17.5% of old-old women (Federal Interagency Forum on Aging-Related Statistics, 2012).

Suicide is strongly associated with depression among older adults (Alexopoulos, 2005) and was the 10th leading cause of death in 2011 (Hoyert & Xu, 2012). Even though the rates of suicide in the United States among the oldest old have declined from 22.2 per 100,000 in 1990 to 17.6 in 2010, suicide rates among the oldest old are higher than for the old-old and young-old (17.6, 15.7, and 13.7 per 100,000, respectively) (National Center for Health Statistics, 2013). Risk factors of suicide in later life are linked to various factors that older adults face as they age, such as cognitive impairment, psychiatric and physical illness, stressful life events, and others (Conwell, Orden, & Caine, 2011). With historically high rates of suicide among the baby boom cohort reaching age 65, it is estimated that the suicide rate in late life will increase (Conwell et al., 2011). White men aged 85 and over in the United States have the highest suicide rates of any other age or ethnic group (National Center for Health Statistics, 2013). Erlangsen, Bille-Brahe, and Jeune (2003) examined suicide trends among young-old aged 65 to 79 and the oldest old in Denmark who committed suicide for the period 1972–1998. They found that the suicide level among the oldest old remained very high, while that of the young-old declined. Their study also showed that the oldest old used determined suicide methods such as hanging or jumping compared with young-old, indicating that suicide intention is stronger with advancing age.

Worry is another significant factor influencing mental health. Examining worry in the sample of the oldest old aged 85 and over living in the community in a 9-year period, Dunkle et al. (2001) found that worry was low at the initial interview but significantly increased over the 9 years of the study. For example, the oldest old in their 80s worried about the health of family members, not having enough personal energy, or about forgetting things. When they reached their 90s, they worried about a wide range of issues including their health and memory problems in addition to health of family members and neighborhood crime (Jeon, Dunkle, & Roberts, 2006).

With advancing age, dementia incidence continues to increase exponentially in both men and women among the oldest old (Corrada, Brookmeyer, Paganini-Hill, Berlau, & Kawas, 2010). Hebert and colleagues estimated that the number of the oldest old aged 85 and over with Alzheimer's disease (AD) was 1.8 million, making up 38.3% of the 4.7 million people aged 65 or older with AD dementia (Hebert, Weuve, Scherr, & Evans, 2013). It is estimated that the number of individuals with AD dementia in 2050 will increase to 13.8 million in 2050, with 7 million over age 85 (Hebert et al., 2013), imposing caregiving burden at the individual level as well as the public health cost at the social level.

HEALTH

The health of the elderly has improved as demonstrated by declining mortality and less prevalent disability in the oldest ages. With the ability to treat disease and chronic conditions, the prevalence of most diseases has decreased and the inventions of more sophisticated assistive devices allow elders to live more independently (Jacobsen, Kent, Lee, & Mather, 2011).

After age 45, issues of disability and declining functional ability become a concern for many. Disability is defined as a substantial limitation in a major life activity, according to the 1990 Americans with Disabilities Act and is the most commonly used indicator of health among older people (He & Muenchrath, 2011). With advancing age, many major health problems such as cancer, osteoporosis, dementia, and limitations on activities of daily living (ADLs) tend to be observed in those over the age of 85 (Administration on Aging, US Department of Health and Human Services, 2010). There are significant differences in disability among subgroups of elders with increasing age; 69.2% of those 85–89 have a disability compared with 82.7% in the 90–94 age group and 91.2% in those over 95 years of age (Freedman, Schoeni, Martin, & Cornman, 2007). More than one-half of all female and almost 40% of male non-institutionalized Medicare enrollees over

age 85 are unable to perform any one of the five physical functions (stoop/kneel, reach over head, write/grasp small objects, walk two to three blocks, or lift 10 lbs.). In 2009, 70% of males and 66% of females of noninstitutionalized Medicare enrollees over age 85 had limitations in instrumental ADLs (IADLs) and received personal assistance (Administration on Aging, 2010). The proportion of the oldest old with respondent-assessed health status varies by racial groups. At age 85 and over, 30.6% of non-Hispanic Whites reported fair or poor health, while 45.8% of Blacks and 48.2% of Hispanics rated their health as fair or poor (Federal Interagency Forum on Aging-Related Statistics, 2012).

Even with the identification of functional problems among the oldest old and their increase with advancing age, disability does not always result. Recent figures from the 2011 Census of the United States indicate that less than two-fifths (36.6%) of those over age 65 are disabled. While ADL and IADL disabilities are more extensive in the oldest-old age group than among those who are younger, there are a number of chronic conditions such as paralysis, numbness, and diabetes that are more common among nonelderly age groups (Takagi, Davey, & Wagner, 2013). The most common chronic condition among the oldest old is dementia, with 40% being afflicted by some form of dementing illness (Yaffe et al., 2011).

With age being positively associated with physical difficulty, it is not surprising that the oldest old have the highest levels of physical and cognitive disability. (Administration on Aging, US Department of Health and Human Services, 2010). It should be noted, though, that old age disability declined in recent decades in the United States (Schoeni, Freedman, & Martin, 2008). Since 1984, the number of years a person may expect to live disability free is on the rise (Crimmins, Hayward, Hagedorn, Saito, & Brouard, 2009), but reduced mortality among the disabled has kept the disability prevalence higher among the elderly than it would have been otherwise (Crimmins & Beltrán-Sánchez, 2011).

SOCIAL SUPPORT

There is a demonstrated positive association between social involvement and health in very late life (Cherry et al., 2013) even in the face of evidence that network size shrinks over time for the oldest old (Dunkle et al., 2001; Litwin, 2011). This may be due to a relationship selection process that seems to occur among the very old as explained by the emotional selectivity theory (Carstensen, Fung, & Charles, 2003).

This shrinking social network is even greater for centenarians than octogenarians because of the age-related decline (Randall, Martin, McDonald, & Poon, 2010). Data from the Georgia Centenarians Study indicate a significant difference between these two groups on receiving instrumental support. Centenarians reported more help with household chores and meal preparation and were less likely to rely on a relative or community agency than octogenarians. One possible explanation is that their relatives are also old and in need of help themselves. The lack of agency use could be due to transportation problems faced by centenarians. They were also more likely to rely on a friend and more likely to receive instrumental support from paid help whether in a nursing home or in the community. It appears that centenarians with higher levels of social resources experience a steeper decline in IADLs. With the possibility that social resources influence health through such processes as sense of control, mastery, or self-efficacy (Antonucci, Birditt, & Akiyama, 2009), it has been suggested that social resources can erode over time (Krause, 2006) as a result of too much support, which reduces self-esteem and perceived control (Newsom & Schulz, 1998).

IMPLICATION FOR SERVICE DELIVERY AND FUTURE RESEARCH

In many ways, those who are very old are not very different in their needs than other older people. What does make them different is their heterogeneity of needs. The oldest old experience more health and certain mental health problems simultaneously and as a group have fewer health, financial, and social resources to deal with the problems they face. Researchers have only begun to examine service needs of the oldest old and the resources that they bring to their health and mental health needs.

Mental Health Service Delivery

With increasing numbers of older adults with mental health problems, demand for mental health services is expected to increase. Interestingly, mental health services are underutilized among older adults compared with general medical services (Quinn, Laidlaw, & Murray, 2009). This may be due to a number of factors such as cohort beliefs, stigmatizing attitudes related to mental illness and aging (Crisp, Gelder, Goddard, & Meltzer, 2005), lack of familiarity with mental health services, and ageism from the individual as well as the culture (Laidlaw, Thompson, Dick-Siskin, & Gallagher-Thompson, 2003). Evidence supports the use of various types of psychotherapy in the treatment of depression in older adults (Dickens et al., 2013; Thorp et al., 2009).

Depression in older people can be difficult to diagnose due to comorbid symptoms and anxiety and substance abuse use disorders (Skoog, 2011). In addition, mood problems are seen as part of the aging process (Wetherell et al., 2004). The result is a decrease in mental healthcare with increasing age because of lower perceived need (Garrido, Kane, Kaas, & Kane, 2009). Primary care is typically the best place for older people to raise mental health issues (Robb, Chen, & Haley, 2002), but they are less likely to be referred to specialized mental healthcare (Verhaak et al., 2009). In fact, older adults accepting treatment for depression prefer counseling and psychotherapy over pharmacotherapy (Hindi, Dew, Albert, Lotrich, & Reynolds, 2011) and prefer receiving this treatment in a primary care versus specialty settings (Arean, Hegel, & Reynolds, 2001).

Caregiving

Significant increase in the prevalence and incidence of dementia among the oldest old has imposed a great burden on informal caregivers as well as the public healthcare system. Dementia caregiving is more complicated and burdensome than nondementia caregiving, as dementia affects cognitive, behavioral, and affective functioning. Dementia caregivers experience caregiver burden because of the higher prevalence of behavioral and psychological symptoms (Rocca et al., 2010). In addition, the behavioral and psychological symptoms of people with dementia add to the greater cost of care (Murman et al., 2002) and a more rapid rate of institutionalization (Phillips & Diwan, 2003). The issue of caregiver burden is associated with caregiver anxiety as well as depression, but this can be mediated by the coping strategies used by the caregiver. Garcia-Alberca et al. (2013) suggest that interventions used by the caregiver to reduce the behavioral and psychological symptoms should emphasize engagement strategies rather than disengagement strategies, as this results in less depression and anxiety among caregivers and fewer neuropsychiatric symptoms among dementia patients.

Related to the issue of need for assistance is a focus on the availability of caregivers, those who can provide support. Changes in family life have made caregiving by family members more difficult. For instance, the divorce rate has increased since the early 1960s with recent estimates indicating that nearly half of female baby boomers will have been divorced by the time they are 65, compared with less than one-fifth of those born before 1925. These high levels also affect men, so that more people will live without a spouse, the person most likely to provide care in a marital relationship (Jacobsen et al., 2011). In large part, caregivers are family members (Miller, Allen, & Mor, 2009), with female family members most likely to be caregivers, as they constitute two-thirds of family caregivers (Wolff & Kasper, 2006).

When the care recipient is the oldest old, the spouse and children are also likely to be old (Takagi et al., 2013). Because of this, the caregivers often face similar problems as the older care recipient. Among these very old people, this may mean that the social support network shrinks due to death and illness of the caregivers themselves. Caregivers for the oldest old are less likely to be sole caregivers, and the oldest old are more likely to use formal care services and formal caregivers (Takagi et al., 2013). The stress of caregiving, though, was higher for adult children who cared for their oldest-old parents than was the stress for the spouse who was providing care.

Social Support

Social support interventions can improve the health of adults (Uchino, 2009). Expanding or creating networks can generate an increase in instrumental, emotional, and informational support resources that can impact the health of the oldest old, who are more likely to experience health-related decline that can result in the need for assistance and/or support (Cherry et al., 2013). All too often, social support is not seen as a primary intervention for healthy individuals but only those experiencing psychological, behavioral or medical problems. Evidence shows that maintaining social support reduces the probability of health problems developing (Kaplan, 2000) and receiving social support is a key link to health (Neely et al., 2006). A comprehensive assessment of the quality and quantity of social support is recommended prior to any intervention in the social support arena.

CONCLUSION

Caregiving networks of the oldest old may significantly differ from those of younger generations (Takagi et al., 2013), but unfortunately only limited information exists on the family life and caregiving issues of the oldest old (Freeman, Kurosawa, Ebihara, & Kohzuki, 2010). In addition, there is a need to include a variety of cultural groups in large longitudinal studies that can track the influence of stress and coping variables over a longer period of time (Knight & Sayegh, 2010). Increasing numbers of the oldest old will pose challenges for healthcare systems (Christensen, Doblhammer, Rau, & Vaupel, 2009). By learning who these very old people are, where they live, whom they care about, and what health issues they face, practitioners can begin to develop more relevant services to meet the health and care needs of the very old.

REFERENCES

Administration on Aging, US Department of Health and Human Services. (2010). *A profile of older Americans: 2010*. Retrieved from http://www.aoa.gov/AoARoot/Aging_Statistics/Profile/2010/index.aspx

Alexopoulos, G. S. (2005). Depression in the elderly. *Lancet, 365*, 1961–1970. doi:10.1016/S0140-673666665-2

Arean, P. A., Hegel, M. T., & Reynolds, C. F. (2001). Treating depression in older medical patients with psychotherapy. *Journal of Clinical Geropsychology, 7*, 93–104. doi:10.1023/A:1009581504993

Antonucci, T. C., Birditt, K. S., & Akiyama, H. (2009). Convoys of social relations: An interdisciplinary approach. In V. L. Bengston, D. Gans, N. M. Putney, & M. Silverstein (Eds.), *Handbook of theories of aging, second edition* (pp. 247–260). New York, NY: Springer.

Borson, S., Bartels, S. J., Colenda, C. C., Gottlieb, G. L., & Meyers, B. (2001). Geriatric mental health services research: Strategic plan for an aging population: Report of the Health Services Work Group of the American Association for Geriatric Psychiatry. *American Journal of Geriatric Psychiatry, 9,* 191–204. doi:10.1097/00019442-200108000-00002

Carstensen, L. L., Fung, H. H., & Charles, S. T. (2003). Socioemotional selectivity theory and the regulation of emotion in the second half of life. *Motivation and Emotion, 27,* 103–123. doi:10.1023/A:1024569803230

Cherry, K. E., Walker, E. J., Brown, J. S., Volaufova, J., LaMotte, L. R., Welsh, D. A., . . . Frisard, M. I. (2013). Social engagement and health in younger, older, and oldest-old adults in the Louisiana Healthy Aging Study. *Journal of Applied Gerontology, 32,* 51–75. doi:10.1177/0733464811409034

Christensen, K., Doblhammer, G., Rau, R., & Vaupel, J. (2009). Ageing populations: The challenges ahead. *Lancet, 374,* 1196–1208. doi:10.1016/S0140-6736(09)61460-4

Conwell, Y., Van Orden, K., & Caine, E. D. (2011). Suicide in older adults. *Psychiatric Clinics of North America, 34,* 451–468. doi:10.1016/j.psc.2011.02.002

Corrada, M. M., Brookmeyer, R., Paganini-Hill, A., Berlau, D., & Kawas, C. H. (2010). Dementia incidence continues to increase with age in the oldest old: The 90+ Study. *Annals of Neurology, 67,* 114–121. doi:10.1002/ana.21915

Crimmins, E. M., & Beltrán-Sánchez, H. (2011). Mortality and morbidity trends: Is there compression of morbidity? *Journals of Gerontology: Psychological Sciences, 66B,* 75–86. doi:10.1093/geronb/gbq088

Crimmins, E. M., Hayward, M. D., Hagedorn, A., Saito, Y., & Brouard, N. (2009). Change in disability-free life expectancy for Americans 70 years old and older. *Demography, 46,* 627–646. doi:10.1353/dem.0.0070

Crisp, A., Gelder, M., Goddard, E., & Meltzer, H. (2005). Stigmatization of people with mental illnesses: A follow-up study within the Changing Minds campaign of the Royal College of Psychiatrists. *World Psychiatry, 4,* 106–113. Retrieved from http://www.ncbi.nlm.nih.gov/pmc/articles/PMC1414750/

Dickens, C., Cherrington, A., Adeyemi, I., Roughley, K., Bower, P., Garrett, C., . . . Coventry, P. (2013). Characteristics of psychological interventions that improve depression in people with coronary heart disease: A systematic review and meta-regression. *Psychosomatic Medicine, 75,* 211–221/ doi. ORG/10.1097/PSY.OBO13E31827AC009

Dunkle, R. E., Roberts, B., & Haug, M. (2001). *The oldest old in everyday life: Self perception, coping with change, and stress.* New York, NY: Springer.

Erlangsen, A., Bille-Brahe, U., & Jeune, B. (2003). Differences in suicide between the old and the oldest old. *Journals of Gerontology, 58B,* S314–S322. doi:10.1093/geronb/58.5.S314

Federal Interagency Forum on Aging-Related Statistics. (2012). *Older Americans 2012: Key indicators of well-being.* Retrieved from http://www.agingstats.gov/Main_Site/Data/2012_Documents/docs/EntireChartbook.pdf

Freedman, V. A., Schoeni, R. F., Martin, L. G., & Cornman, J. C. (2007). Chronic conditions and the decline in late-life disability. *Demography, 44,* 459–477. doi:10.1353/dem.2007.0026

Freeman, S., Kurosawa, H., Ebihara, S., & Kohzuki, M. (2010). Caregiving burden for the oldest old: A population based study of centenarian caregivers in Northern Japan. *Archives of Gerontology and Geriatrics, 50,* 282–291. doi:10.1016/j.archger.2009.04.008

Garcia-Alberca, J. M., Cruz, B., Lara, J. P., Garrido, V., Lara, A., Gris, E., & Gonzalez-Herero, V. (2013). The experience of caregiving: The influence of coping strategies on behavioral and psychological symptoms in patients with Alzheimer's disease. *Aging and Mental Health, 17,* 615–622. doi:10.1080/13607863.2013.765833

Garrido, M. M., Kane, R. L., Kaas, M., & Kane, R. A. (2009). Perceived need for mental health care among community-dwelling older adults. *Journals of Gerontology: Psychological Sciences, 64B,* 704–712. doi:10.1093/geronb/gbp073

He, W., & Muenchrath, M. N. (2011). *90+ in the United States: 2006–2008: American Community Survey reports.* ACS-17. Retrieved from https://www.census.gov.edgekey.net/prod/2011pubs/acs-17.pdf

Hebert, L. E., Weuve, J., Scherr, P. A., & Evans, D. A. (2013). Alzheimer disease in the United States (2010–2050) estimated using the 2010 census. *Neurology, 80,* 1778–1783. doi:10.1212/WNL.0b013e31828726f5

Hindi, F., Dew, M. A., Albert, S. M., Lotrich, F. E., & Reynolds, C. F. (2011). Preventing depression in later life: State of the art and science circa 2011. *Psychiatric Clinics of North America, 34,* 67–78. doi:10.1016/j.psc.2010.11.008

Hoyert, D., & Xu, J. (2012). Deaths: Preliminary data for 2011. *National Vital Statistics Reports, 6,* 1–52. National Center for Health Statistics Retrieved from http://198.246.124.29/nchs/data/nvsr/nvsr61/nvsr61_06.pdf

Jacobsen, L. A., Kent, M., Lee, M., & Mather, M. (2011). America's aging population. *Population Bulletin, 66,* 1–20. Retrieved from http://www.prb.org/pdf11/aging-in-america.pdf

Jeon, H.-S., & Dunkle, R. E. (2009). Stress and depression among the oldest-old: A longitudinal analysis. *Research on Aging, 31,* 661–687. doi:10.1177/0164027509343541

Jeon, H.-S., Dunkle, R. E., & Roberts, B. L. (2006). Worries of the oldest-old. *Health and Social Work, 31*, 256–265. doi:10.1093/hsw/31.4.256

Kaplan, R. M. (2000). Two pathways to prevention. *American Psychologist, 55*, 382–396. doi:10.1037/0003-066X.55.4.382

Knight, B. G., & Sayegh, P. (2010). Cultural values and caregiving: The updated sociocultural stress and coping model. *Journals of Gerontology: Psychological Sciences, 65B*, 5–13. doi:10.1093/geronb/gbp096

Krause, N. (2006). Social relationships in late life. In R. H. Binstock, L. K. George, S. J. Cutler, J. Hendricks, & J. H. Schulz (Eds.), *Handbook of aging and the social sciences* (6th ed., pp. 181–200). Burlington, MA: Academic Press.

Laidlaw, K., Thompson, L. W., Dick-Siskin, L., & Gallagher-Thompson, D. (2003). *Cognitive behaviour therapy with older people*. Hoboken, NJ: Wiley.

Litwin, H. (2011). Social relations and well-being in very late life. In L. Poon & J. Cohen-Mansfield (Eds.), *Understanding well-being in the oldest-old* (pp. 213–226). New York, NY: Cambridge University Press.

Miller, E. A., Allen, S. M., & Mor, V. (2009). Commentary: Navigating the labyrinth of long-term care: Shoring up informal caregiving in a home- and community-based world. *Journal of Aging and Social Policy, 21*, 1–16. doi:10.1080/08959420802473474

Murman, D. L., Chen, Q., Powell, M. C., Kuo, S. B., Bradley, C. J., & Colenda, C. C. (2002). The incremental direct costs associated with behavioral symptoms in AD. *Neurology, 59*, 1721–1729. doi:10.1212/01.WNL.0000036904.73393.E4

National Center for Health Statistics. (2013). *Health, United States 2012: With special feature on emergency care*. Retrieved from http://www.cdc.gov/nchs/data/hus/hus12.pdf

Neely, L. C., Lakey, B., Cohen, J. L. Barry, R., Orehek, E., Abeare, C. A., & Mayer, W. (2006). Trait and social processes in the link between social support and affect: An experimental, laboratory investigation. *Journal of Personality, 74*, 1015–1045. doi:10.1111/j.1467-6494.2006.00401.x

Newsom, J. T., & Schulz, R. (1998). Caregiving from the recipient's perspective: Negative reactions to being helped. *Health Psychology, 17*, 172–181. doi:10.1037/0278-6133.17.2.172

Phillips, V. L., & Diwan, S. (2003). The incremental effect of dementia-related problem behaviors on the time to nursing home placement in poor, frail, demented older people. *Journal of American Geriatrics Society, 51*, 188–193. doi:10.1046/j.1532-5415.2003.51057.x

Quinn, K. M., Laidlaw, K., & Murray, L. K. (2009). Older peoples' attitudes to mental illness. *Clinical Psychology and Psychotherapy, 16*, 33–45. doi:10.1002/cpp.598

Randall, G., Martin, P., McDonald, M., & Poon, L. (2010). Social resources and longevity: Findings from the Georgia Centenarian Study. *Gerontology, 56*, 106–111. doi:10.1159/000272026

Robb, C., Chen, H., & Haley, W. E. (2002). Ageism in mental health and health care: A critical review. *Journal of Clinical Geropsychology, 8*, 1–12. doi:10.1023/A:1013013322947

Rocca, P., Leotta, D., Liffredo, C., Mingrone, C., Sigaudo, M., Capellero, B., . . . Bogetto, F. (2010). Neuropsychiatric symptoms underlying caregiver stress and insight in Alzheimer's disease. *Dementia and Geriatric Cognitive Disorders, 30*, 57–63. doi:10.1159/000315513

Schoeni, R. F., Freedman, V., & Martin, L. (2008). Socioeconomic and demographic disparities in trends in old-age disability. In D. Cutler & D. Wise (Eds.), *Health at older ages: The causes and consequences of declining disability among the elderly*. Chicago, IL: University of Chicago Press.

Shrestha, L., & Heisler, E. (2011). *The changing demographic profile of the United States*. Congressional Research Service. Retrieved from http://www.fas.org/sgp/crs/misc/RL32701.pdf

Skoog, I. (2011). Psychiatric disorders in the elderly. *Canadian Journal of Psychiatry, 56*, 387–397.

Takagi, E., Davey, A., & Wagner, D. (2013). (In)formal Support and unmet needs in the National Long-Term Care Survey. *Journal of Comparative Family Studies, 44*, 437–453. http://urn.kb.se/resolve?urn=urn:nbn:s e:hj:diva-21743

Thorp, S., Ayers, C., Nuevo, R., Stoddard, J., Sorrell, J., & Wetherall, J. (2009) Meta-analysis comparing different behavioral treatments for late life anxiety. *American Journal of Geriatric Psychiatry, 17*, 105–115. doi: 10.1097/JGP.0b013e31818b3f7e

Uchino, B. N., (2009). Understanding the links between social support and physical health: A life-span perspective with emphasis on the separability of perceived and received support. *Perspectives on Psychological Science, 4*, 236–255. doi:10.111/ j.1745-6924.209.01122.x

US Census Bureau. (2012). *Statistical abstract of the United States: 2012*. Retrieved from http://www.census.gov/compendia/statab/overview.html

US Census Bureau. (2012a). *Current population survey: Annual social and economic supplement, 2011*. Internet release date: November 2012. Retrieved from http://www.census.gov/population/age/data/ 2011.html

Verhaak, P. F., Prins, M. A., Spreeuwenberg, P., Draisma, S., van Balkom, T. J., Bensing, J. M., . . . Penninx, B. W. (2009). Receiving treatment for common mental disorders. *General Hospital Psychiatry, 31,* 46–55.

Werner, C. A. (2011). *Census briefs: The older population: 2010.* Retrieved from http://www.census.gov/prod/cen2010/briefs/c2010br-09.pdf

Wetherell, J. L., Kaplan, R. M., Kallenberg, G., Dresselhaus, T. R., Sieber, W. J., & Lang, A. J. (2004). Mental health treatment preferences of older and younger primary care patients. *International Journal of Psychiatry in Medicine, 34,* 219–233. doi:10.2190/QA7Y-TX1Y-WM45-KGV7

Wolff, J. L., & Kasper, J. D. (2006). Caregivers of frail elders: Updating a national profile. *The Gerontologist, 46,* 344–356. doi:10.1093/geront/46.3.344

Yaffe, K., Middleton, L. E., Lui, L.-Y., Spira, A. P., Stone, K., Racine, C., & Kramer, J. H. (2011). Mild cognitive impairment, dementia, and their subtypes in oldest old women. *Archives of Neurology, 68,* 631–636. doi:10.1001/archneurol.2011.82

Zalaquett, C., & Stens, A. (2006). Psychosocial treatments for major depression and dysthymia in older adults: A review of the research literature. *Journal of Counseling and Development, 84,* 192–201. doi.org/10.1002/j.1556-6678.2006.tb00395.x

MICHAEL W. PARKER

JAN S. GREENBERG

MARSHA R. MALICK

GAYNELL M. SIMPSON

EUN HA NAMKUNG

RONALD TOSELAND

Caregivers to Older and Disabled Adults

4 1

Worldwide declining birthrates in many developed and some developing countries, rising life expectancies in most countries, increases in multigenerational households, young adult migration, increased female labor-force participation, and other factors are challenging economic, religious, geopolitical, and *familial* stability (Whittington & Kunkel, 2013). These changes are having a profound impact on the backbone of long-term care in the United States, the American family caregiver (CG). According to the National Alliance for Caregiving (NAC, 2009), over 65 million CGs are providing care to someone who is ill, disabled, or aged. Parker and Patten (2013) indicate that 39% of US adults are providing care, up from 30% in 2010. Approximately 70% of older Americans will need long-term care, and 87% of them will receive it from unpaid family CGs. The number of older Americans needing long-term care will double by 2050 (Rousseau, Firth, & Jankiewicz, 2013). Although leading gerontologists are calling for local, age-friendly initiatives such as proactive disaster planning for vulnerable adults (Beard & Warth, 2013; Parker et al., in press), the MetLife Foundation (2011) reports that most communities in the United States are not making age-friendly progress. Local religious groups have been slow to respond to the needs of CGs in their aging congregations (Parker et al., in press). Gaps in formal care continue to leave family CGs to older and disabled persons more vulnerable (Institute of Medicine, 2008). Clearly, the demographics of aging in the United States and many other countries accentuate the importance of identifying tailored strategies to prepare and support the many different types of family CGs of older and disabled individuals.

The primary purpose of this chapter is to provide information to social workers and others who work with different kinds of family CGs. We describe why some CGs of physically and cognitively impaired, frail older adults respond well to the caregiving experience, while others suffer from physical and mental health difficulties. We review the special issues faced by older adult CGs of people with developmental disabilities or serious mental illnesses. Then, we describe evidence-based CG interventions, including the growing trend of CG programs offered by employers by describing, as an example, a Web-based intervention program offered to the faculty and staff of three universities. In conclusion, we list a sample of state and national resources for practitioners and CGs.

443

VARIABLE CAREGIVER REACTIONS

Although there is evidence that caregiving can be a gratifying experience, there is more data suggesting the adverse effects of family caregiving. Cross-sectional studies comparing CGs with non-CGs reveal many negative reactions (e.g., Adams, 2008). Researchers have established that CGs are more likely than non-CGs to report higher levels of anxiety and stress (Marquez, Bustamante, Kozey-Keadle, Kraemer, & Carrion, 2012), sleep disturbance (Castro et al., 2009), psychological distress (Savla, Almeida, Davey, & Zarit, 2008), and negative appraisals of events (Soskolne, Halevy-Levin, & Ben-Yehuda, 2007). In a meta-analysis, Pinquart and Sorensen (2003) report that CGs have higher levels of stress and depression and lower levels of subjective well-being and self-efficacy than non-CGs.

Yet, according to a review of longitudinal studies on CGs of stroke patients, levels of depression and psychological well-being among CGs stabilize over time (Gaugler, 2010). In fact, Berger et al. (2005) found depression lessened over time among family CGs of dementia patients. Thus, it is well established that while caregiving has short-term, adverse effects on psychological and social well-being, over time there is mounting evidence of considerable heterogeneity with respect to the long-term effects of caregiving on psychological and social well-being. Several studies suggest that religious beliefs and practices may reduce CG stress by helping CGs to reframe the caregiving situation and give greater meaning and purpose to it (e.g., Haley et al., 2004).

Studies on the effect of caregiving on physical health have been less conclusive. Some studies report serious adverse physical effects. For example, female CGs often report significantly poorer self-rated health, greater physical functioning limitations, and more negative physical symptoms, compared with non-CGs (e.g., Marquez et al., 2012). Other research has demonstrated that CGs have lowered immune responses, disturbed metabolic responses, and an increased allostatic load (e.g., Gouin, Glaser, Malarkey, Beversdorf, & Kiecolt-Glaser, 2012). However, other studies have reported that caregiving has little impact on health or may even be associated with better health. Soskolne et al. (2007) did not find differences in the number of diseases and use of prescription medications among CGs and non-CGs, and others report that the physical health of CGs remains relatively stable or improves over time (e.g., Gaugler, 2010).

Overall, caregiving appears to have a smaller effect on physical health than on psychosocial health. Pinquart and Sorensen's (2003) meta-analysis estimated that whereas caregiving status explains about 8% of the variance in depressive symptoms, it explained only about 1% of physical health variance. Thus, the literature indicates that there is considerable heterogeneity in the long-term effects of different aspects of CGs' lives.

In an attempt to explain the heterogeneity in response to caregiving, researchers have investigated a broad range of factors. Some have focused on gender. Despite the evidence of male involvement (Kramer & Thompson, 2005), the NAC (2009) estimates that 66% of CGs are female. While balancing work with multiple caregiving duties, female CGs manage the most difficult caregiving tasks (Reinhard, Levine, & Samis, 2012). For example, 95% of CGs to aging veterans are women, and veterans suffer more often from traumatic brain injury, paralysis, and stress disorders (NAC, 2010). Women provide more hours of care and more hands-on help with caregiving tasks and report more behavioral problems with care recipients than men (Lahaie, Earle, & Heymann, 2013) while experiencing higher burden, depression, poorer physical health, and lower self-efficacy (Pinquart & Sorensen, 2003).

Considering race, Pinquart and Sorensen (2005) concluded that African American (AA) CGs had lower levels of depression and CG burden compared with their White counterparts, but others have found that psychological well-being is dependent of the CG's living situation and their access to supportive resources, implying that socioeconomic status (SES) may be the real determining factor (e.g., Hilgeman et al., 2009). Some studies have found that AA CGs do not differ from Whites with respect to physical health (e.g., Clay et al., 2013). Other factors that likely affect the variability of CG reactions include the type and severity of the illness of the care recipient, long-term familial relationships, personality traits, coping skill, and norms of filial piety (e.g., Parker et al., 2003). Care recipients with stroke, dementia, and other conditions that cause mental as well as physical deterioration are much more burdensome to CGs of those with physical problems (see Chapter 35, "Older Adults with Dementia").

Less is also known about how work roles interact with the role of caregiving to affect the well-being of CGs. Lee, Walker, and Shoup (2001) found that respondents occupying the dual roles of CG and employee reported higher levels of depressive symptoms than those occupying only one of these two roles. Yu-Nu, Yea-Ing Lotus, Min-Chi, and Pei-Shan (2011) found that poorer health and well-being was associated with difficulty reconciling work and caregiving roles. Yet, Cannuscio and colleagues (2004) found no effect of employment on depression for employed female CGs aged 46–71. Thus, much remains to be learned about whether employment and other previously mentioned factors amplify or dampen the effects of caregiving stress on social, mental, and physical health outcomes.

OLDER ADULTS AS CAREGIVERS TO ADULTS WITH DEVELOPMENTAL DISABILITIES OR SERIOUS MENTAL ILLNESS

A less common type of caregiving is provided by aging parents who have an adult child with disabilities (Pruchno & Meeks, 2004). In this section, we focus on older CGs of adults with developmental disabilities or mental illness because these two groups of CGs face overlapping caregiving responsibilities, yet at the same time have distinctly different caregiving experiences because of differences in the age of onset of the disorder, the trajectory of the life course of the illness, and societal stigma associated with nature of the disability (Greenberg, Seltzer, & Greenley, 1993).

Several cross-sectional studies report no differences between CGs of adults with developmental disabilities and non-CGs with respect to physical health (Caldwell, 2008) and mental health (Llewellyn, McConnell, Gething, Cant, & Kendig, 2010) or a process of adaptation to the stresses of caregiving (Heller, Caldwell, & Factor, 2007). However, data from the Wisconsin Longitudinal Survey (WLS), which followed a random sample of high school seniors over a 50-year period, suggest that effects of caregiving may only become apparent as parents move from midlife to old age (e.g., Seltzer et al., 2011). Specifically, there were no differences in the physical health and psychological well-being of WLS parents of adults with developmental disabilities and parents with typically developing adult children when both groups of parents were in their mid-50s. However, by early old age, parental CGs had poorer health and functional abilities than similarly aged parents of adult children without caregiving responsibilities. In analyses of data from the Survey of Mid-Life in the United States, Seltzer and colleagues (2009) found that midlife parents of children with development disabilities who spent more time with their children had lower levels of cortisol than a comparison group of parents who had typically developing children.

Whereas the effects of caregiving on aging parents of adult children with developmental disabilities appears later in the parent's life course, there is a growing body of research on aging parents of adult children with serious mental illness indicating that the toll of caregiving is evident by midlife and continues unabated into early old age. In a study comparing midlife parents caring for a child with developmental disabilities, midlife parents of adults children with a serious mental health problem, and midlife parents whose adult children did not have disabilities, parents of adults with mental health problems had elevated levels of physical health symptoms and depression (Seltzer et al., 2001). Barker, Greenberg, Seltzer, and Almeida (2012) found that on days when midlife and aging parents of adults with mental illness experienced elevated levels of stress, they had increased levels of cortisol upon waking in the morning and their cortisol declined less during the day, evidence of a poorly regulated pattern of cortisol expression, which might lead to compromises in CG health. Studies focusing on lifelong parenting for adult children with bipolar disorder similarly find that both midlife and aging parental CGs report poorer health, higher levels of depressive symptoms, and a greater number of somatic symptoms (Aschbrenner, Greenberg, & Seltzer, 2009).

There is a large and growing literature indicating that formal and informal supports are a significant resource for caregivers of the elderly (e.g., Lai & Thomson, 2011; Roth, Perkins, Wadley, Temple, & Haley, 2009; Sherman, Webster, & Antonucci, 2013), and social support has had a similar positive effect for aging parental CGs. Caldwell (2008) found that unmet service needs contribute to poor health of female family CGs of adults with developmental disabilities. Other studies found that informal social support predicted decreased depression (e.g., Benson & Karlof, 2009) and better health (Llewellyn et al., 2010) and well-being (Smith, Seltzer, & Greenberg, 2012) among CGs of adults with developmental disabilities or mental illness. Less social support also predicted higher levels of burden (Biegel, Ishler, Katz, & Johnson, 2007) and depressive symptomology (Biegel, Katz-Saltzman, Meeks, Brown, & Tracy, 2010) among CGs of women with co-occurring mental and substance use disorders. The strengthening of formal and informal social support for aging parent CGs of adults with disabilities should therefore be an important target of interventions.

CAREGIVER INTERVENTIONS

Originating with the seminal works of Horowitz (1985), Toseland and Rossiter (1989), and Biegel, Sales, and Schulz (1991), family caregiving has been described as an unanticipated, unplanned transition for adult children from the role of adult child or spouse to a new, often unfamiliar relationship with a frail parent or partner. This transition from the familiar to the new is thought to begin the caregiving journey. Some CGs are drawn insidiously into the process because of a parent's progressive disability, while others enter dramatically following a significant health event (fall or stroke) that renders a previously healthy parent dependent.

One of the most difficult challenges the gerontological community faces is how to translate and sustain the best evidence-based CG support programs into community settings. Only recently have there been concerted efforts to translate evidence-based, CG support programs to communities (e.g., Burgio et al., 2009; Parker et al., 2007). Many intervention studies have addressed successfully the multidimensional needs of CGs in order to reduce the negative and enhance the positive outcomes of eldercare giving (e.g., Melis et al., 2008). Reviews of the literature indicate that participation in individual and group intervention programs with CGs and the use of daycare and other community resources for care recipients can be effective in supporting the family CG's efforts to maintain cognitively and physically impaired older persons in community settings (Toseland, Haigler, & Monahan, 2011; Zarit & Talley, 2013). Some studies indicate that CG support programs can delay nursing home placement and reduce healthcare costs for care recipients, but much more work needs to be done on the cost effectiveness of CG support and education programs (Toseland et al., 2011).

Caregiving intervention research has focused largely on psychoeducational, psychosocial, and respite treatments for family CGs (e.g., Burgio, Stevens, Guy, Roth, & Haley, 2003). Guided by theoretical CG models, the majority of these interventions have targeted multiple stressors faced by CGs. Prime targets have included problem behaviors exhibited by the person with functional impairment and lack of social support for the CG (e.g., Sorensen, Pinquart, & Duberstein, 2002). Generally, interventions have produced small to moderate effects on clinical outcomes such as depression and burden (Schulz, Martire, & Klinger, 2005). These findings suggest that interventions are most effective when they target specific

outcome variables (e.g., depression) with a high dose of treatment specifically designed to address the CG's need (Zarit, Kim, Femia, Almeida, & Klein, 2013). However, Schulz et al. (2005) reported that while combined interventions that targeted multiple CG challenges produced significant improvement in CG knowledge, skill, and satisfaction, there was only moderate success in reducing burden and depression. There are also new evidence-based attempts to reach out to caregivers using telephone, video, and Internet programs (e.g., Glueckauf & Noel, 2011; Blom, Bosmans, Cuijpers, Zarit, & Pot, 2013).

EMPLOYER-GENERATED CAREGIVER PROGRAMS

The NAC (2009) reports that that over 70% of family CGs are employed full- or part-time. Working CGs add additional costs for the employer because of their decreased productivity, increased absenteeism, and higher turnover rate (Coughlin, 2010). Albert and Schulz (2010) indicate that when employed CGs provide 20 hours or more care per week, it represents a tipping point that often results in major work adjustments. Further, they report that employed CGs have more stress-related illnesses and use their company's healthcare plans more often, resulting in an 8% differential in increased healthcare costs between caregiving and non-caregiving employees, and potentially costing US employers an additional $13.4 billion per year. Many large employers are concluding that it is in the best interests of their organizations and their employees to develop eldercare benefit programs that also use wellness initiatives.

Now that a number of studies have demonstrated that caregiving is an expensive human resource problem (e.g., NAC, 2009), attention has increasingly focused on developing employer-generated eldercare initiatives that benefit the organization and support employed CGs (Crewe & Chipungu, 2006). Although programs vary, one of the most common approaches offers contracted, call-in services to geriatric care managers, a service typically coordinated through the organization's human resource department. Marketing employer-sponsored programs represents a significant challenge, as preliminary findings suggest that contracts for geriatric call-in services have been underused. Other options include multicomponent programs, seminars, and Internet links to state and national programs and resources. One less expensive approach uses the Internet and related technologies (e.g., Glueckauf & Noel 2011). If properly managed, new technologies (Internet, telephone, and video conferencing) can help overcome some of the limitations associated with the local, long-term care systems (Toseland & Larkin, 2011). For example, the Department of Veteran Affairs is increasingly using telemedicine strategies to reach rural CGs of aging veterans.

A WEB-BASED, EMPLOYER-GENERATED CAREGIVER INTERVENTION PROGRAM

As an example of the use of new technology, we describe a Web-based intervention program, supported by the human resource departments of three major universities (Parker, in press), and initially designed for military families and later for other organizations (Parker, Church, & Toseland, 2006). Parker and an interdisciplinary team of geriatric professionals conducted a series of studies to develop a Web-based assessment, intervention, and education program for elder care and late-life planning (e.g., Myers et al, 2004; Parker, Call, Dunkle, & Vaitkus, 2002). Taken from the military's "family care plan" required prior to deployment (Parker & Martin, 2003), the adapted Internet program (AgeReady) enables employed CGs and older employees to work at their own pace and schedule. Using scoring algorithms based on the trans-theoretical model of change, the program assists older employees and CGs to review a landscape of over 40 possible tasks associated with caregiving and longer life, and to develop a personalized long-term care plan consisting of completed tasks in four areas (legal, medical, familial, and emotional-spiritual) (Parker et al., 2006). Movie clips about specific tasks, interviews with experts, and avatars are used to help motivate people to action—the completion of specific task(s)—and the scoring algorithms help employees prioritize which task(s) to complete first and to control the dosage level of information. This is strategically important because many adult children entering a caregiving trajectory are not motivated to complete necessary tasks because their parents are relatively healthy or because they are disengaged for other reasons. Concise intervention prescriptions and links to vetted state and national websites provide CGs with ongoing, evidenced-based, state of science information about important aspects of caregiving that CGs

might not have considered. The program supports professional consultation and promotes the idea that caregiving is an ongoing process that involves reassessment of completed and uncompleted tasks as the functional and health status of the elder changes. Adjunctive components to the program like call-in, geriatric care management services can be added, along with workshops on specific topics (e.g., successful aging) and teleconferencing with organizations like the Family Caregiver Alliance.

CONCLUSION

The research literature on the effects of caregiving leads to four overall conclusions. First, there is compelling evidence that caregiving has long-term effects on mental and physical health. Research on the biological mechanisms by which caregiving takes its toll is still in its infancy; still, it holds great promise to shed light on the causal mechanisms by which caregiving affects well-being. Second, the experience of caregiving is uniquely shaped by the position of the CG in the larger sociocultural context; by many other variables related to the type and trajectory of care recipient health problem(s), such as gender, race/ethnicity, spirituality and religious support, and socioeconomic and employment status; and by other factors. Therefore, clinicians should treat all CGs as unique individuals with heterogeneous needs and responses to interventions that must be tailored by careful assessment and care planning. Third, the effects of caregiving are not static. They vary over time, resulting in either adaptation and resiliency or the further depletion of CGs' capacity. The collection of genetic samples in many of the newer, large-scale aging studies provides an opportunity to examine the role of genetics as an explanatory mechanism for the heterogeneity in the caregiving outcomes over the life course. Still, biology is not destiny, and timely interventions in cognitive, behavioral, emotional, and environmental realms can make an important difference in the quality of life for CGs. Thus, a broadly focused biopsychosocial and environmental systems perspective is imperative for effective clinical practice with CGs. This includes a pressing need to identify new evidence-based strategies and technologies to support and prepare family CGs because they serve as the backbone of our long-term care system. The employer-generated program described in this chapter is just one very promising, proactive approach to the use of new technologies for meeting this need. This and other innovative telephone, video conferencing, and streaming Web-based telehealth technologies, like those being used by the VA, are now more widely available and provide clinicians with new venues to transcend distance to empower help CGs and care recipients to address the many difficult tasks they face over the life course.

RESOURCES

Description	Web Address
AARP Caregiving	www.aarp.org/home-family/caregiving
Administration on Aging	www.aoa.gov
AgeLab at MIT	agelab.mit.edu
Alliance for Aging Research	www.agingresearch.org
Alzheimer's Association	www.alz.org
American Society on Aging	www.asaging.org
Benefit Checkup	www.benefitscheckup.org
Caregiver Action Network	www.caregiveraction.org
CDC Emergency Preparedness for Older Adults	www.cdc.gov/aging/emergency
Eldercare Locator	www.eldercare.gov
Elderweb	www.edlerweb.com
Fall Prevention Center of Excellence	www.stopfalls.org
Family Caregivers and Professionals Working Together	www.nextstepincare.com
Family Caregiver Alliance+	www.caregiver.org
Fisher Center for Alzheimer's Research Foundation	www.alzinfo.org
Gerontological Society of America	www.geron.org
Hospice Foundation of America	www.hospicefoundation.org
Independent Transportation Network	www.itnamerica.org
Medicare	www.medicare.gov
National Age in Place Council	www.ageinplace.org
National Alliance for Caregiving	www.caregiving.org
National Association for Home Care and Hospice	www.nahc.org
National Association of Area Agencies on Aging *	www.n4a.org
National Association of Professional Geriatric Care Managers	www.caremanager.org
National Association of States United for Aging and Disability**	www.nasuad.org
National Council on Aging	www.ncoa.org
National Institute on Aging	www.nia.nih.gov
National Respite Coalition Task Force	www.archrespite.org
National Resource Center on LGBT Aging	www.lgbtagingcenter.org
A Nation in Motion—Orthopedic Resources	www.anationinmotion.org
Public Health Emergency Preparedness	www.phe.gov
Rosalynn Carter Institute for Caregiving	www.rosalynncarter.org
Social Security Administration	www.seniors.gov
VA Caregiver Support Services^	www.caregiver.va.gov

* Contains contact information for local agencies within each state
** Contains contact information for state agencies on aging
+ Contains numerous fact sheets that provide relevant information on all aspects of caregiving
^ Includes multiple resources to get oriented with caregiving

REFERENCES

Adams, K. B. (2008). Specific effects of caring for a spouse with dementia: Differences in depressive symptoms between caregiver and non-caregiver spouses. *International Psychogeriatrics, 20*, 508–520. doi:http://dx.doi.or/10.1017/s1041610207006278

Albert, S. M., & Schulz, R. (2010, February). *New insights and innovations for reducing health care costs for employers.* Retrieved from http://tinyurl.com/osr3l3q

Aschbrenner, K. A., Greenberg, J. S., & Seltzer, M. M. (2009). Parenting an adult child with bipolar disorder in later life. *Journal of Nervous and Mental Disease, 197*, 298–304. doi:10.1097/NMD.06013e3181a206cc

Barker, E. T., Greenberg, J. S., Seltzer, M. M., & Almeida, D. M. (2012). Daily stress and cortisol patterns in parents of adult children with a serious mental illness. *Health Psychology, 31*, 130–134. doi:10.1037/a0025325

Beard, J. R., & Warth, L. (2013). Building an age-friendly world, one city at a time. *Aging Today, 34*, 7.

Benson, P. R., & Karlof, K. L. (2009). Anger, stress proliferation, and depressed mood among parents of children with ASD: A longitudinal replication. *Journal of Autism and Developmental Disorders, 39*, 350–362. doi:10.1007/s10803-008-0632-0

Berger, G., Bernhardt, T., Weimer, E., Peters, J., Kratzsch, T., & Frölich, L. (2005). Longitudinal study on the relationship between symptomatology of dementia and levels of subjective burden and depression among family caregivers in memory clinic patients. *Journal of Geriatric Psychiatry and Neurology, 18*, 119–128.

Biegel, D. E., Ishler, K. J., Katz, S., & Johnson, P. (2007). Predictors of burden of family caregivers of women with substance use disorders or co-occurring substance and mental disorders. *Journal of Social Work Practice in the Addictions, 7*, 25–49. doi:10.1300/J160v07n01_03

Biegel, D. E., Katz-Saltzman, S., Meeks, D., Brown, S., & Tracy, E. M. (2010). Predictors of depressive symptomatology in family caregivers of women with substance use disorders or co-occurring substance use and mental disorders. *Journal of Family Social Work, 13*, 25–44. doi:10.1080/10522150903437458

Biegel, D. E., Sales, E., & Schulz, R. (1991). *Family caregiving in chronic illness.* Newbury Park, CA: Sage.

Blom, M., Bosmans, J. E., Cuijpers, P., Zarit, S. H., & Pot, A. M. (2013). Effectiveness and cost-effectiveness of an Internet intervention for family caregivers of people with dementia: Design of a randomized controlled trial. *BMC Psychiatry, 13*, 17–24. doi:10.1186/1471-244X-13-17.

Burgio, L., Stevens, A., Guy, D., Roth, D. L., & Haley, W. E. (2003). Impact of two psychosocial interventions on White and African American family caregivers of individuals with dementia. *The Gerontologist, 43*, 568–579. doi:10.1093/geront/43.4.568

Burgio, L., Collins, I., Schmid, B., Wharton, T., McCallum, D., & DeCoster, J. (2009) Translating the REACH caregiver intervention for use by area agency on aging personnel: The REACH OUT program *The Gerontologist, 49*, 103–116. doi:10.1093/geron/gnp012

Caldwell, J. (2008). Health and access to health care of female family caregivers of adults with developmental disabilities. *Journal of Disability Policy Studies, 19*, 68–79. doi:10.1177/1044207308316093

Cannuscio, C. C., Colditz, G. A., Rimm, E. B., Berkman, L. F., Jones, C. P., & Kawachi, I. (2004). Employment status, social ties, and caregivers' mental health. *Social Science and Medicine, 58*, 1247–1256. doi:10.1016/s0277-953600317-4

Castro, C. M., Lee, K. A., Bliwise, D. L., Urizar, G. G., Woodward, S. H., & King A. C. (2009). Sleep patterns and sleep-related factors between caregiving and non-caregiving women. *Behavioral Sleep Medicine, 7*, 164–179. doi:10.1080/15402000902976713

Clay, O. J., Grant, J. S., Wadley, V. G., Perkins, M. M., Haley, W. E., & Roth, D. L. (2013). Correlates of health-related quality of life in African American and Caucasian stroke caregivers. *Rehabilitation Psychology, 58*, 28–35. doi:10.1037/a0031726

Crewe, S., & Chipungu, S. (2006). Services to support caregivers of older adults. In S. Berkman & S. D'Ambruoso (Eds.), *Handbook of social work in health and aging* (pp. 539–550). New York, NY: Oxford University Press.

Coughlin, J. (2010). Estimating the impact of caregiving and employment on well-being. *Outcomes and Insights in Health Management, 2*, 1–7.

Gaugler, J. E. (2010). The longitudinal ramifications of stroke caregiving: A systematic review. *Rehabilitation Psychology, 55*, 108–125. doi:10.1037/a0019023

Glueckauf, R. L., & Noel, L. T. (2011). Telehealth and family caregiving: Developments in research, education, policy and practice. In R. W. Toseland, D. H. Haigler, & D. J. Monahan (Eds.), *Education and support programs for caregivers: Research, practice, policy* (pp. 85–106). New York, NY: Springer. doi:10.1007/978-1-4419-8031-1

Gouin, J.-P., Glaser, R., Malarkey, W. B., Beversdorf, D., & Kiecolt-Glaser, J. (2012). Chronic stress, daily stressors, and circulating inflammatory markers. *Health Psychology, 31*, 264–268. doi:10.1037/a0025536

Greenberg, J. S., Seltzer, M. M., & Greenley, J. R. (1993). Aging parents of adults with disabilities: The gratifications and frustrations of later-life caregiving. *The Gerontologist, 33,* 542–550.

Haley, W. E., Gitlin, L. N., Wisniewski, S. R., Mahoney, D. F., Coon, D. W., Winter, L., . . . Ory, M. (2004). Well-being, appraisal, and coping in African-American and Caucasian dementia caregivers: Findings from the REACH study. *Aging and Mental Health, 8,* 316–329. doi:10.1080/13607860410001728998.

Heller, T., Caldwell, J., & Factor, A. (2007). Aging family caregivers: Policies and practices. *Mental Retardation and Developmental Disabilities Research Reviews, 13,* 136–142. doi:10.1002/mrdd.20138

Hilgeman, M. M., Durkin, D. W., Sun, F., DeCoster, J., Allen, R. S., Gallagher-Thompson, D., & Burgio, L. D. (2009). Testing a theoretical model of the stress process in Alzheimer's caregivers with race as a moderator. *The Gerontologist, 49,* 248–261. doi:10.1093/geron/gnp015

Horowitz, A. (1985) Sons and daughters as caregivers to older parents: Differences in role performance and consequences. *The Gerontologist, 25,* 612–617. doi:10.1093/geront/25.6.612

Institute of Medicine of the National Academics. (2008, April) *Retooling for an aging America: Building the health care workforce.* Retrieved from http://tinyurl.com/7kcjofw

Kramer, B. J., & Thompson, E. H. (2005). *Men as caregivers.* Amherst, NY: Prometheus Books.

Lahaie, C., Earle A., & Heymann J. (2013). An uneven burden: Social disparities in adult caregiving responsibilities, working conditions, and caregiver outcomes. *Research on Aging, 35,* 243–274. doi:10.1177/0164027512446028

Lai, D. L., & Thomson, C. C. (2011). The impact of perceived adequacy of social support on caregiving burden of family caregivers. *Families in Society: The Journal of Contemporary Social Services, 92,* 99–106.

Lee, J. A., Walker, M., & Shoup, R. (2001). Balancing elder care responsibilities and work: The impact on emotional health. *Journal of Business and Psychology, 16,* 277–291.

Llewellyn, G., McConnell, D., Gething, L., Cant, R., & Kendig, H. (2010). Health status and coping strategies among older parent-carers of adults with intellectual disabilities in an Australian sample. *Research in Developmental Disabilities, 31,* 1176–1186. doi:10.1016/j.ridd.2010.08.00

Marquez, D. X., Bustamante, E. E., Kozey-Keadle, S., Kraemer, J., & Carrion, I. (2012). Physical activity and psychosocial and mental health of older caregivers and non-caregivers. *Geriatric Nursing, 33,* 358–365. doi:10.1016/j.gerinurse.2012.03.003

Melis, R. F., Van Eijken, M. J., Teerenstra, S., Van Achterberg, T., Parker, S. G., Borm, G. F., & Olde Rikkert, M. G. M. (2008). A randomized study of a multidisciplinary program to intervene on geriatric syndromes in vulnerable older people who live at home (Dutch EASYcare Study). *Journals of Gerontology, 63A,* 283–290.

MetLife Foundation. (2011, June). *The maturing of America: Communities moving forward for an aging population.* Retrieved from http://www.n4a.org/files/MOA_FINAL_Rpt.pdf

Myers, D. R., Roff, L. L., Harris, H. W., Klemmack, D. L., & Parker, M. W. (2004). A feasibility study of a parent care-planning model with two faith-based communities. *Journal of Religion, Spirituality and Aging, 17,* 39–53. doi:10.1300/J496v17n01_03

National Alliance for Caregiving. (2009, November). *Caregiving in the U.S. 2009.* Retrieved from http://www.caregiving.org/data/Caregiving_in_the_US_2009_full_report.pdf

National Alliance for Caregiving. (2010, November). *Caregivers of veterans—Serving on the homefront.* Retrieved from http://www.caregiving.org/data/2010_Caregivers_of_Veterans_FULLREPORT_WEB_FINAL.pdf

Parker, M., Dunn, L., MacCall, S., Park, N., Martin, S., & Koenig, H. (in press). Helping to unite an aging southern community: A multifaceted Internet directory and survey project involving local congregations, agencies and universities. *Journal of Social Work and Christianity.*

Parker, M. W., Call, V. A., Dunkle, R., & Vaitkus, M. (2002). "Out of sight" but not "out of mind": Parent contact and worry among senior ranking male officers in the military who live long distances from parents. *Military Psychology, 14,* 257–277. doi:10.1207/S15327876MP1404_3

Parker, M. W., Call, V. A., Toseland, R., Vaitkus, M., Roff, L., & Martin, J. A. (2003). Employed women and their aging family convoys: A life course model of parent care assessment and intervention. *Journal of Gerontological Social Work, 40,* 101–121. doi:10.1300/J083v40n01_07

Parker, M., Church, W., & Toseland, R. (2006). Caregiving at a distance. In B. Berkman & S. D'Ambruoso (Eds.), *Handbook of social work in health and aging* (pp. 391–406). New York, NY: Oxford University Press.

Parker, M. W., & Martin, J. A. (2003). Caring for an aging parent is a military family affair. *Geriatric Care Management Journal, 13,* 2. Retrieved from http://www.caremanager.org/education-central/digital-resources/

Parker, K., & Patten, E. (2013, January 30). *The sandwich generation: Rising financial burdens for middle-aged Americans.* Retrieved from http://www.pewsocial-trends.org/2013/01/30/the-sandwich-generation/

Parker, M. W., Powers, R., Roff, L. L., Ford, B., Hollingsworth, M., Winstead, D., & Dyer, C. (2007, April). *Evacuation of the frail elderly during Katrina: Lessons and solutions.* Paper presented at Forensic Psychiatry Post Katrina: Lessons Learned Post Disaster conference. New Orleans, LA.

Pinquart, M., & Sorensen, S. (2003). Differences between caregivers and non-carers in psychological health and physical health: A meta-analysis. *Psychology and Aging, 18,* 250–267. doi:10.1037/0882-7974.18.2.250

Pinquart, M., & Sorensen, S. (2005). Ethnic differences in stressors, resources, and psychological outcomes of family caregiving: A meta-analysis. *Gerontologist, 45,* 90–106. doi:10.1093/geront/45.1.90

Pruchno, R. A., & Meeks, S. (2004). Health-related stress, affect, and depressive symptoms experienced by caregiving mothers of adults with a developmental disability. *Psychology and Aging, 19,* 394–401. doi:10.1037/0882-7974.19.3.394

Reinhard, S. C., Levine, C., & Samis, S. (2012). *Home alone: Family caregivers providing complex chronic care.* Retrieved from http://www.aarp.org/ppi

Roth, D. L., Perkins, M., Wadley, V. G., Temple, E. M., & Haley, W. E. (2009). Family caregiving and emotional strain: Associations with quality of life in a large national sample of middle-aged and older adults. *Quality of Life Research: An International Journal of Quality of Life Aspects of Treatment, Care and Rehabilitation, 18,* 679–688. doi:10.1007/s11136-009-9482-2

Rousseau, D., Firth, J., & Jankiewicz, A. (2013). A short look at long-term care for seniors. *JAMA, 310,* 786–787. doi:10.1001/jama.2013.1676

Savla, J., Almeida, D. M., Davey, A., & Zarit, S. H. (2008). Routine assistance to parents: Effects on daily mood and other stressors. *Journals of Gerontology, 63B,* S154–S161.

Schulz, R., Martire, L. M., & Klinger, J. N. (2005). Evidence-based caregiver interventions in geriatric psychiatry. *Psychiatric Clinics of North America, 28,* 1007–1038. doi:10.1016/j.psc.2005.09.003

Seltzer, M. M., Almeida, D. M., Greenberg, J. S., Savla, J., Stawski, R. S., Hong, J., & Taylor, J. L. (2009). Psychological and biological markers of daily lives of midlife parents of children with disabilities. *Journal of Health and Social Behavior, 50,* 1–15.

Seltzer, M. M., Floyd, F. J., Song, J., Greenberg, J. S., & Hong, J. (2011). Midlife and aging parents of adults with intellectual and developmental disabilities: Impacts of lifelong parenting. *American Journal on Intellectual and Developmental Disabilities, 116,* 479–499. doi:10.1352/1944-7558-116.6.479

Seltzer, M. M., Greenberg, J. S., Floyd, F., Pettee, Y., & Hong, J. (2001). Life course impacts of parenting a child with a disability. *American Journal of Mental Retardation, 106,* 265–286.

Sherman, C., Webster, N. J., & Antonucci, T. C. (2013). Dementia caregiving in the context of late-life remarriage: Support networks, relationship quality, and well-being. *Journal of Marriage And Family, 75,* 1149–1163.

Smith, L., Seltzer, M., & Greenberg, J. (2012). Daily health symptoms of mothers of adolescents and adults with Fragile X Syndrome and mothers of adolescents and adults with autism spectrum disorder. *Journal of Autism and Developmental Disorders, 42,* 1836–1846. doi:10.1007/s1007/s10803-011-1422-7

Sorensen, S., Pinquart, M., & Duberstein, P. (2002). How effective are interventions with caregivers? An updated meta-analysis. *Gerontologist, 42,* 356–372. doi:10.1093/geront/42.3.356

Soskolne, V., Halevy-Levin, S., & Ben-Yehuda, A. (2007). The context of caregiving, kinship tie and health: A comparative study of caregivers and non-caregivers. *Women and Health, 45,* 75–94.

Toseland, R., & Rossiter, C. (1989) Group interventions to support family caregivers: A review and analysis. *The Gerontologist, 29,* 438–448. doi:10.1093/geront/29.4.438

Toseland, R. W., Haigler, D. H., & Monahan, D. J. (2011). *Education and support programs for caregivers: Research, practice, Policy.* New York, NY: Springer. doi:10.1007/978-1-4419-8031-1

Toseland, R. W., & Larkin, H. (2011). Developing and leading telephone groups. *Social Work with Groups, 34,* 21–34. doi:10.1080/01609513.2010.526091

Whittington, F. J., & Kunkel, S. R. (2013). Think globally, act locally: The maturing of a worldwide science and practice of aging. *Generations, 37,* 6–11.

Yu-Nu, W., Yea-Ing Lotus, S., Min-Chi, C., & Pei-Shan, Y. (2011). Reconciling work and family caregiving among adult-child family caregivers of older people with dementia: Effects on role strain and depressive symptoms. *Journal of Advanced Nursing, 67,* 829–840. doi:10.1111/j.1365-2648.2010.05505

Zarit, S. H., & Talley, R. C. (Eds.). (2013). *Caregiving for Alzheimer's disease and related Disorders: Research, practice, policy.* New York, NY: Springer.

Zarit, S. H., Kim, K., Femia, E. E., Almeida, D. M., & Klein, L. C. (2013). The effects of adult day services on family caregivers' daily stress, affect and health: Outcomes from the DaSH study. *The Gerontologist, 47,* 775–788. doi:10.1093/geront/47.6.775

*Prison is a hard place. Pure
Hell! As long as you are in
khaki, you are considered
non-human. The elder suffer
the most because there isn't
much for them, us. I have the
starts of osteoporosis and seeing how some people young
and old are treated makes me
suffer and deal with it. Overall
it's horrible and wouldn't wish
this on my worst enemy.*
—Quote from a 66-year-old woman
in prison

GLOBAL SCOPE OF THE PROBLEM

The steady rise of the mass incarceration of the
elderly is international in scope but is particularly
problematic in the United States, which has the largest incarceration rate per capita (American Civil
Liberties Union [ACLU], 2012). As of 2009, prisoner
population rates per 100,000 were 760 in the United
States, 624 for Russia, 153 in the United Kingdom,
119 in China, and 116 in Canada (Organization for
Economic Co-operation and Development [OECD],
2010). Of the 2.3 million persons in custody in the
United States, 16% (*n* = 200,000) are aged 50 and
older (Guerino, Harrison, & Sabol, 2011). In global
corrections, the number of incarcerated adults aged
50 and older varies and has been steadily increasing
over the past two decades (Aday, 2003; Carstairs &
Keon, 2009). Incarcerated older adults, aged 50 and
older, represent about 20% (2,800) of Canada's total
inmate population of 14,000 (Hale & Swiggum, 2011).
In Australia, of the 19,082 general population of prisoners, 7.4% (1,412) are aged 50 and older (Grant,
1999); in England and Wales, incarcerated adults
aged 50 and older represent almost 11% (6,417) of the
total prison population (Ministry of Justice, 2010).

THE HIGH COST OF PUNISHMENT POLICIES

Two major factors have contributed to the global
rise in aging people in prison: increases in the aging
population coupled with the long-term aftermath
of stricter sentencing and parole policies from the
1980s (Aday, 2003). In the United States, for example,
the number of aging people in prison is expected to
increase to 20% between 2010 and 2030 (US Census

TINA MASCHI
RON ADAY

The Crisis of Aging People in Prison: Forging a Social Work Response to the Social Determinants of Health and Justice

Bureau, 2010). In addition, conservative criminal justice policies implemented in the 1980s resulted from stricter public and legislative policies, such as restrictive drug and habitual offenders laws (Aday & Krabill, 2012). This conservative shift toward extreme punishment resulted in adjudicated offenders receiving longer mandatory minimum prison sentences including an increase in the number of life sentences without parole. Many current advocacy efforts argue that these sentences are unjust and disproportionate to the crimes committed (Human Rights Watch [HRW], 2012). Currently, the global prison system is ill-prepared to address the growing numbers of incarcerated elderly, especially those aged 65 and older, which increases the likelihood that costs for specialized long-term care or palliative and end-of-life care will continue to strain budgets and resources (Maschi, Marmo, & Han, 2014; Maschi, Viola, & Sun, 2013).

Specific to people aging in prison, institutional expenditures for medical care, especially those with serious illness, disabilities, or terminal illnesses, are common (United Nations Office on Drugs and Crime [UNODC], 2009). For example, in the United States, costs such as medical, mental health, and dental care constitute a large percentage of correctional budgets, and a disproportionate numbers of older adults use these services. Human Rights Watch reports that the costs of healthcare increase with age. In the United States, the average annual cost of care for the average prisoner is approximately $5,500, but the cost is twice as much for prisoners aged 55 to 59 ($11,000) and eight times as much for prisoners aged 80 and over ($40,000; HRW, 2012).

VARYING DEFINITIONS OF AGE

According to the United Nations (UN), "older prisoners," including those with mental and physical disabilities and terminal illnesses, constitute a special needs populations and are thus subject to special international health, social, and economic practice and policy considerations (UNODC, 2009). The age at which individuals are defined as "older" or "elderly" differs across countries. Many societies view the age of 65 as older because that is when most individuals are eligible to receive full pension or social security benefits. However, this age designation is not uniform across the world, because age has different meanings in various cultures (UNODC, 2009). Similarly, the age at which a prisoner is defined as "older" or "elderly" varies across different countries. For example, in Australia, the age 50 is designated as older in prison. Although it varies among states, incarcerated persons in the United States may be classified as "older adult" or "elderly" as early as age 50 (HRW, 2012). Other countries, such as the United Kingdom, designate age 60 to 65 as older. Canada has a two-tiered system in which "older" in prison is age 50 to 64 years and "elderly" is age 65 and above (UNODC, 2009).

In general, this lower age classification reflects the fact that the average prisoner may experience accelerated decrements in their health status equivalent to community-dwelling adults who are 15 years older (ACLU, 2012; Loeb, Steffensmeier, & Lawrence, 2008). This process of accelerated aging is corroborated by evidence from international prison studies showing that older adults in prison have significantly higher rates of physical and mental health decline compared with younger prisoners or older adults of a comparative age in the community (Aday, 2003; Maschi, Kalmanofsky, Westcott, & Pappacena, 2015; Maschi, Viola, & Sun, 2013). This rapid decline of incarcerated older adults' health has been attributed largely to their high-risk personal histories; chronic health conditions; and poor health practices such as poor diets and tobacco, alcohol, and substance abuse; as well as the stressful conditions of prison confinement, such as prolonged exposure to overcrowding, social deprivation, and prison violence (Aday & Krabill, 2012). These combined personal and social environmental risk factors significantly increase the likelihood of the early onset of serious physical and mental illnesses, including dementia, among people in prison (Maschi, Kwak, Ko, & Morrissey, 2012).

DIVERSITY AMONG OLDER ADULTS IN PRISON

As illustrated in case vignettes found in Box 42.1, adults aged 50 and older are a diverse population, which has implications for social work and interprofessional prevention, assessment, and intervention with older adults in the criminal justice system. A holistic portrait of older adults in prison reveals a diverse population that

---

Box 42.1
Case Vignettes

Jorge is a 56-year-old male from Puerto Rico and the youngest of nine children. He has a history of trauma and criminal offending that has included the unexpected death of his father at age 5, childhood sexual victimization, poverty, prostitution, drug dealing, substance abuse (heroin addiction), and recidivism (incarcerated two times). At age 17, he reported committing armed robbery to support his heroin addiction and was sentenced to 20 years in prison. During his prison term, he continued to use drugs. He violated parole within 15 months of release after being charged with sexual offense of a minor and possession of controlled dangerous substances and, as a result, is now serving his second and current 45-year sentence. In prison, he has spent 8 of the past 15 years in solitary confinement. He perceives prison as "an overcrowded monster" designed to hold, degrade, and punish people. He views the staff as disinterested and disengaged and is despondent over the limited access to counseling and education rehabilitative services. Jorge was diagnosed with cancer 6 months ago while in prison and is projected to receive parole in 14 years when he is in his late 70s. He has not had any contact with family in over 5 years and reports feeling depressed.

Mary is a 64-year-old, Caucasian, Catholic woman who is incarcerated in a maximum security facility for women. She identifies herself as a lesbian. As a child, she experienced the divorce of her parents, abandonment by her mother, and sexual, physical, and verbal abuse by her father, whom she described as having serious mental health issues. At age 25, Mary married a man 10 years younger, had two children, and divorced. This is her first criminal conviction, and she is serving a 10-year prison sentence (85% minimum) for conspiracy and the attempted murder of her abusive husband, which she describes as in self-defense. She has a medical history of hypertension, vision impairment, and osteoporosis that makes it difficult for her to walk or use a top bunk bed. At age 64, Mary's extensive dental problems have resulted in a premature need for dentures. She describes her current prison experience as "degrading, especially the way correctional officers treat inmates." Although she reports feelings of depression and despair, Mary reports that she copes with her prison experience by "finding meaning" in it through spirituality. Despite her ill health, Mary is resistant to using prison healthcare services. Her projected parole date is in 2 years, when she will be 66 years old. Because of the distance, Mary has not had any in-person visits with her family members since her incarceration but corresponds monthly by mail with her two adult children and four grandchildren every 3 months by phone. She says that she misses her family immensely.

---

disproportionately reflects vulnerable populations based on characteristics such as age, race, sex, disability or veteran status, and gender identity and sexual orientation. For example, in the US prison population aged 50 and older, the vast majority are men (96%) compared with women (4%) and are disproportionately from racial ethnic groups (Black = 45%, Latino = 11%, other = 10%) compared with Whites (43%; Guerino et al., 2011). Health status also varies; some individuals have functional capacity, while others suffer from disabilities or serious, chronic, and terminal illnesses such as HIV/AIDs, cancer, and dementia or mental health (e.g., depression, anxiety, psychosis) and substance use problems (Maschi, Sutfin, & O'Connell, 2012).

The majority report a history of victimization (especially the lesbian, gay, bisexual, and transgender [LGBT] population); grief and loss; chronic stress prior to and during prison, including veterans exposed to combat; and varying levels of coping and social support (Maschi, Viola, Morgen, & Koskinen, 2013; Sampson & Laub, 2003). Family relationships also vary among older people in prison. Many incarcerated elders are married or partnered, divorced/separated, or widowed. Many elders in prison also are parents and grandparents, and separation from their families may be a significant form of distress, especially for older women (Aday & Krabill, 2011, Maschi, Viola, & Morgen, 2013).

Histories of cumulative trauma and stress are an important consideration among older people in prison, especially older women (Aday & Krabill, 2011). Older adult men and women on average reported three adverse life experiences that occurred in the community or in prison. These experiences, including events from childhood, often cause lingering subjective distress that influences their current state of health and well-being. Their life history trajectories also suggest that lack of power, inability to access services and justice often proceed imprisonment, and the trauma of incarceration may only exacerbate mental distress and lead to adverse stress responses (Maschi, Viola, & Koskinen, 2015, 2011; Maschi, Gibson, Zgoba, & Morgen, 2011; Maschi, Morgen, Zgoba, Courtney, & Ristow, 2011). Evidence also suggests that experiences of trauma and stress vary by age. For example, One study examined significant differences in lifetime experiences of trauma and stress between incarcerated young adults aged 18 to 24 ($n = 38$) and adults aged 50 and older ($n = 2$). They found that incarcerated older adults were more likely to report experiencing a natural disaster, life-threatening illness, or the death of a loved one, whereas their younger counterparts were more likely to report histories of witnessing physical assault (Maschi, Gibson, Zgoba, & Morgen, 2011).

Another important issue with implications for social work and health is variation in length of prison term and preparedness for prison placement and community reintegration. The major types of older people in prison include the long termer (a person with 20 or more years served), the lifer (life sentence), older people who recidivated (one or more prior incarcerations), and the older person who committed a crime in later life (first convicted in old age). Regardless of their age at release, formerly incarcerated older adults experience collateral consequences of incarceration and ageism post release that create barriers to accessing health, economic, and social care services, such as healthcare (including nursing home placement), housing, employment, housing, and social welfare benefits (Aday, 2003; Maschi & Koskinen, 2015).

FORGING AN INTEGRATED HEALTH AND JUSTICE RESPONSE

When considering the important transition of bridging older adults in prison to their families and communities, issues of the right to health and elder and intergenerational justice can be raised. The pathways to prison vary for older adults. However, a common thread among this group is that their experiences often include one or more cumulative disadvantages or inequalities such as social disadvantage based on age, race, education, socioeconomic status, gender, disability, or legal or immigration status. These accumulated disadvantages can influence individuals' access to health and social services, economic resources, and justice across the life course. As the grassroots human rights movement is gaining momentum in its advocacy for the rights of rights of older prisoners, including their right to access healthcare and justice, the social work and interprofessional practice community is challenged to think creatively and out of the concrete "prison" box on how to coordinate effective intersectoral collaboration, holistic care, and care transitions for older adults in prison and post release.

We argue that the social determinants of health disparities (e.g., poverty, chronic stress, poor nutrition) and justice involvement coupled with poor social conditions of confinement for older adults are a form of elder abuse and neglect (World Health Organization [WHO], 2012). The WHO (2012) defines elder abuse as a "a single, or repeated act, or lack of appropriate action, occurring within any relationship where there is an expectation of trust which causes harm or distress to an older person" (p. 1). Elder abuse may take many forms, including physical, sexual, psychological, and emotional abuse; financial exploitation; and intentional or unintentional neglect, including medical neglect (United Nations [UN], 2012). Chronic victimization, medical neglect, and lack of rehabilitation services and discharge planning exacerbate physical and mental illnesses and are a violation of human rights, especially the rights to health, well-being, social security, family, culture, and safety, including protection from torture or cruel and unusual punishment or elder abuse (UN, 1948). The existence of abuse and neglect of elders, including in prison, suggests an area where social work could take a leading advocacy role.

UNITED NATIONS GUIDELINES: BLUEPRINTS FOR ACTION

The Report of the United Nations High Commissioner for Human Rights (UN, 2012) asserts special consideration for older adults in prison due to their common experiences of accumulated or aggravated disadvantages before, during, and after prison. Fundamental to human rights values are dignity and respect for all persons and the indivisible and interlocking holistic relationship of all human rights in civil, political, economic, social, and cultural domains (UN, 1948). In the Convention on the Rights of Older Persons, rights are framed in terms of equality, respect, autonomy, and dignity (UN, 2012). Areas of protections of older persons that are underscored for those in prison include age discrimination; legal capacity and equal recognition before the law; conditions of institutional and home-based long-term care; violence and abuse; access to productive resources, work, food, and housing; social protection and the right to social security; the right to health and palliative and end-of-life care; disabilities in old age; and access to justice and legal rights. The UN classifies "older prisoners" as a special needs population along with racial/ethnic minorities, persons with disabilities or terminal illnesses, LGBT individuals, and death row inmates, with specific nonbinding guidelines for their treatment, including care transitions (UNDOC, 2009).

Existing UN documents, such as the Standard Minimum Rules on the Treatment of Prisoners (UN, 1977) and the *Handbook for Prisoners with Special Needs* (UNDOC, 2009), provide nonenforceable guidelines that address the needs of older prisoners. These guidelines include access to prison rehabilitation, physical and mental healthcare, geriatric-specific care, family programming, and community linkages to services. The community reintegration or resettlement of older people with their families is a critical issue. The collateral consequences of incarceration, such as lack of family contact and inability to access housing, healthcare, employment, and social security and benefits, make it challenging for older adults to readjust, especially those with longer or life prison terms (Aday, 2005; Higgins & Severson, 2009). Individual prisons, states, and countries can use these guidelines to determine to what extent their programming addresses quality of life and safety for their aging prison population.

REALIZING RIGHTS: PROMISING COMPASSIONATE POLICIES AND LAWS

Some of these UN guidelines regarding elders in prison may be seen in "compassionate" policies and laws in some countries. For example, in the United States federal and state policies on geriatric release are often referred to as discretionary parole, inmate furloughs,

or medical or compassionate release policies. Since 2009, these geriatric release provisions included one more of the following criteria: minimum age, physical or mental health status, and minimum sentence and low-level criminal risk clauses. However, there are barriers to their effective implementation, even for older, infirm, and seriously ill older adults in prison, which impinges on their right to dignity and respect even when dying. These barriers include the poor design of the laws (e.g., narrow eligibility criteria), implementation procedures (e.g., bureaucratic red tape), and the reluctance of politicians to remedy the situation due to public pressure (Chiu, 2010).

In 1998, the US Supreme Court held in *Pennsylvania Dept. of Corrections v. Yeskey, 524 U.S. 206* (1998) that the Americans with Disabilities Act (ADA) applies to persons in prisons and jails. Prison wardens in the United States stated that compliance with the Americans with Disabilities Act inadvertently improved their services for older prisoners (National Institute of Corrections [NIC], 2010). The ADA-compliant standards in prisons have included environmental modifications such as handrails in inmate cells, showers, hallways, and communal settings. Some prisons have created specialized geriatric services to best ensure comprehensive services for incarcerated older adults (Harrison, 2011).

PROMISING PRACTICE INNOVATIONS

There are no guarantees that well-being of older adults will be protected after they are released from prison. For example, older adults who served long prison sentences may experience institutionalization (e.g., not knowing how to survive outside of prison; Davies, 2011). Community reintegration success for older adults may be complicated by health and/or mental health issues; lack of family and peer support; substance use; lack of available community medical, mental health, and substance abuse services; lack of financial resources; and lack of access to social welfare benefits (including retirement), suitable housing options such as assisted living and nursing homes, and available transportation (Williams, McGuire, Lindsay, Baillargeon, Cenzer, Lee, & Kushel, 2012).

Some older adults who are released from prison may have limited functional capacities and may need assistance with activities of daily living, such as taking care of personal hygiene and clothing. Other seriously or terminally ill older adults may need long-term institutional care, such as placement in a nursing home. Some terminally ill older adults may need hospice placement in the community to address their palliative and end-of-life care needs (Mesurier, 2011). However, barriers to placement in nursing homes and hospices may exist due to the stigma and discrimination against individuals with criminal offense histories, especially for more serious offenses, such as arson and sex crimes (Maschi & Koskinen, 2015). For able-bodied older adults, attainment of employment or job training is another factor that makes successful community reintegration challenging, as a criminal history may create barriers to attaining employment (Maschi, Morgen, Viola, Westcott, & Koskinen, 2014).

Despite these health and social care challenge of justice-involved older adults, promising practices have emerged across the globe that are guided by human rights principles that promote the health and well-being of older adults. There are some global innovative prison and community reintegration for older adults and their families. Promising practices often include comprehensive case management; medical, mental health, substance abuse, family, and social services; housing; education or vocational training; spiritual counseling; exercise and creative arts programs; psychoeducation, and financial, employment and/or retirement counseling. Program-specific aspects include one or more of the following: age- and cognitive-capacity-sensitive environmental modifications (including the use of segregated units), interdisciplinary staff and volunteers trained in geriatric-specific correctional care, complementary medicine, specialized case coordination, the use of family and inmate peer supports and volunteers, mentoring, and self-help peer support or advocacy group efforts. Due to space limitations, only select international programs are highlighted here.

The True Grit Program (United States)

The True Grit Program in Nevada (United States) is a prison-based structured living program that attempts to foster older prisoners' well-being. The program, set in a geriatric sociocultural environment, was designed to enhance physical health (using creative arts, recreational and physical therapy activities); mental and social well-being (using group and individual therapy), human agency and empowerment (using self-help modalities), spiritual well-being (using a prison chaplain and volunteers), and successful community reintegration (using discharge planning).

Research evidence suggests the program is effective in increasing psychological and social well-being while in prison (Harrison, 2011). The program also shows a 0% recidivism rate for program graduates (Maschi, Viola, Harrison, & Harrison, 2014). For a detailed description of the program components and sample intervention plan see Box 42.2 and Table 42.1

Hocking Correctional Facility (United States)

The Hocking Correctional Facility (HCF) in Ohio addresses the prison and community reintegration needs of older prisoners. Offering one-stop wrap-around services, it includes a prerelease program that provides inmates with information on social security or welfare benefits, job-seeking skills, housing placement services, employment training, property maintenance skills, self-care and psychoeducational classes (for topics that address age-related issues, such as the physical, psychological, and social processes of aging), and general education and literature courses. The facility also provides staff training with knowledge and skills to deal effectively with geriatric populations, including those with chronic and terminal illnesses. Community reintegration is an active component of services so that older adults have the necessary resources, including an approved placement in a nursing home if an older adult's declining health status necessitates this placement (Aday & Krabill, 2012).

The California Men's Colony (United States)

California Men's Colony in San Luis Obispo, California (medium secure care facility), has a dementia unit that can be described as a "peer support" program. The program aides consist of six volunteer inmates or "social aides." Their role is to act as "buddies" to fellow prisoners with dementia. Their responsibilities include to ensure they receive medical care, provide social support, and provide protection, because in prison older adults with cognitive disorders are vulnerable to victimization (Ubelacker, 2011).

Recoop (England)

The Resettlement and Care for Older Ex-Offenders (Recoop) is a program that promotes older adults' health and well-being by providing care, resettlement, and rehabilitation services to older offenders and ex-offenders. It does so through the provision of

Box 42.2
Program Components

1. **Diversion activities.** Diversion activities are a major segment of the program. Crocheting, knitting, beading, and latch-hook rug-making provide activity that is not only cognitively stimulating, but affords excellent physical therapy for arthritic hands and fingers

2. **Culturally responsive cognitive interventions.** Cognitive interventions include creative writing, Spanish-language study group, ethnodrama, and a cultural arts group. The groups produce a newsletter and poetry journal, which are edited by the group members.

3. **Substance abuse/addictions groups.** Weekly meetings of 12-step groups including Alcoholics Anonymous, Narcotics Anonymous, and Sexual Compulsives Anonymous, which are facilitated by volunteer sponsors.

4. **Psychoeducation.** Weekly seminars are held that address aging, health and wellness, sexuality, life skills, cooking, menu-planning and healthy life choices, or other relevant activities.

5. **Animal assisted therapy/end-of-life care.** Volunteers provide animal-assisted therapy (individually and in groups). Animal-assisted therapy targets physical, occupational, speech and psychotherapies, special education, pain management issues, and end-of-life support.

6. **Physical exercise.** Program participants are scheduled for daily exercise activities. These activities include wheelchair softball, basketball, or volleyball; aerobics, tennis, measured-distance walking, weight-lifting, stationary bicycle, billiards, ping-pong, horseshoes, or dancing.

7. **Peer support groups/Vet-to-Vet.** Veteran Volunteers assist members with writing and producing artwork about their war experiences.

8. **Spiritual wellness.** Spiritual wellness consists of traditional religious activities by staff or volunteers or peer support members. Bereavement services are provided for when the death of a family member or peer in prison occurs.

9. **Correctional mental health activities.** Formal correctional programs facilitated by both staff and community volunteers are available to program participants. These programs include victim awareness, stress management, anger management, conflict resolution, relationship skills, health-related recovery, commitment to change, trauma and recovery, addictions prevention education, sex offender treatment, parenting and grandparenting classes, and special populations programs.

10. **Prison legal services.** Prison legal services provide program participants access to pro bono lawyers and social workers who are versed in elder and prison rights and law and case management services. Program participants can seek consultation or representation for appeals based on sentencing, parole release, or geriatric, medical, and compassionate release. The prison ombudsman represents cases of interpersonal victimization and institutional abuse. Community advocates who monitor cases based on the Prison Rape Elimination Act also are available to incarcerated persons at the facility, including program participants.

11. **Family visiting programs.** The family visiting program provides extended time with family members, which includes spouses and partners, children, and grandchildren. Families can request transportation services from faith-based volunteers if there is no access to public transportation to get to the facility. An option for televisiting was available for participants, such as Mary, whose family lived at a distance that did not enable them to visit her in person. For participants without family members that can visit, peer visits and volunteer visitors can be arranged based on request.

12. **Restorative justice/reconciliation and forgiveness groups/long termers and lifers group.** The program also offers a session for reconciliation and forgiveness. It uses a narrative style writing and group reflection for individuals to process their crime, especially violent or sexual offenses that resulted in the harm or death to another person or persons. For participants with life sentences, a weekly lifers group is offered.

13. **Education and Vocational Training.** Program participants may choose from a range of vocational services to obtain GED or high school diplomas, college degrees, and vocational training in occupations, such as the culinary arts and select trades.

14. **Discharge planning.** Volunteers provide members with information and referrals concerning their eventual release from prison. This includes collaboration with nonprofit organizations, halfway houses, resources for potential employment, and other assistance, such as veterans or disability benefits.

support services, advocacy, financial advice, mentoring on issues such as employment and training, and advice on housing and health that will enable them to take control of their lives and remain free from reoffending while minimizing social isolation (Cooney & Braggins, 2010).

Reintegration Effort for Long-Term Infirm and Elderly Federal Offenders' (RELIEF) Program (Canada)

The RELIEF Program was established in 1999 to facilitate the transition of elderly and infirm prisoners into the community. The program was designed based on human rights and social justice values of dignity and worth of the person and respect to the dying. The program trains formerly incarcerated people and caregivers to provide compassionate peer support to the formerly incarcerated persons who are dying (Maschi, Viola, & Sun, 2013).

BUILDING BRIDGES

Older adult prisoners and their families and communities have the right to care transitions that foster health and well-being, safety, and family bonds. Yet, a combination of individual, family, and community vulnerabilities often complicates the building of bridges between prison and community for them. The context with which incarcerated people experience their reentry is critical: Income, employment, housing, safety, and access to health and social services influence the likelihood for successful reintegration within communities (La Vigne & Cowan, 2005). During incarceration, the ability to be employed and contribute to partners and children, and to provide for the health and welfare of families, impacts prisoners' anticipatory stress (Maschi & Koskinen, 2013; Maschi, Morrissey, & Leigey, 2013). Released prisoners can expect to earn no more than half of what they made before incarcerated, and the impact on families cannot be overstated; research shows that family income is a major indicator of future success for children, and combined with the associated school problems children with an incarcerated parent experience, the intergenerational costs become incalculable (Pew Charitable Trusts [PCT], 2010).

Thus, for older adults in prison, especially women, who still have responsibility for children younger than 18, moving from prison to work takes on even more import than it might otherwise, whether they reside with the children or not. Over 10% of those returning to prison for violations are sent back because of the inability to pay child support (PCT, 2010). Despite this, even for those persons who would normally be approaching "retirement age," work takes on increased significance because they often have no other income or family support for retirement. Therefore, programs and policies that support work initiatives and training, or provide support from community-based coalitions that bridge the formerly incarcerated and employers, are critical to securing and sustaining employment.

Within the prison population there are those who are at greater risk for recidivism, especially those who were homeless, suffer from physical and/or mental health issues, or present with alcohol or drug use at time of offense. Programs that combine rehabilitation services with employment and housing demonstrate higher levels of reentry success and lower levels of drug relapse (PCT, 2010). Providing disease prevention programs and consistent medical care during incarceration and anticipating transitions to community-based care, including health homes designed for vulnerable Medicaid beneficiaries, or Accountable Care Organizations for elderly who suffer from chronic conditions, is critical for removing health barriers that prevent newly released prisoners from seeking employment, housing, or renewed family and community relationships. Improving care during incarceration is an important step toward reducing overall costs of incarceration and reentry; costs for care during incarceration are two to eight times higher for those between the ages of 55 to 80 (Maschi, Viola, & Sun, 2013). Policy changes are also required at the federal and state level if we are to truly have any success at reintegrating the formerly incarcerated. Currents laws and policies often bar the formerly incarcerated from employment opportunities and receipt of government benefits that provide housing, education, and even food stamps and limit opportunity for removing criminal records and histories (Maschi, Morgen, Viola, Wescott, & Koskinen, 2014; Western, 2008).

RECOMMENDATIONS

The biggest challenge for social work and other interdisciplinary efforts is to be competent at working in

TABLE 42.1 Intervention Plan

Intervention	Jorge	Mary
Treatment Goals	1. Increase holistic well-being. 2. Reduce disciplinary infractions to zero	1. Increase holistic well-being. 2. Increase preparedness for community reintegration
Programming Assigned		
Arts-Based Diversion Activities	X	X
Culturally Responsive Cognitive Interventions	X	X
Substance Abuse/Addictions Groups	X	X
Psychoeducation	X	
Animal Assisted Therapy	X	X
End-of-Life Care/Grief and Bereavement		
Physical Exercise	X	X
Peer Support Groups/Vet to Vet		
Spiritual Wellness	X	X
Mental Health Activities	X	X
Prisoner Legal Services & Victim Rights	X	X
Family/Peer/Volunteer Visiting Program	X	X
Restorative Justice/Reconciliation/ Forgiveness	X	X
Education and Vocational Training	X	X
Discharge Planning		X
Lifers and Long Termers Group	X	

collaboration at the intersection of the aging, social service, public health, and criminal justice sectors of care. Although the extent to which some skills are used depends on where a professional is "positioned" in the system (e.g., clinical social worker in prison, reentry program administrator), it involves having competencies in aging (gerontological practice), physical and mental health assessment and intervention, case management, interdisciplinary collaboration, discharge planning, and legal and policy issues. Due to the complex health, social, legal, moral issues raised by justice involved older adults, an interdisciplinary response that includes doctors, nurses, psychologists, spiritual counselors, social workers, peer companions, family, and communities is critical. The promising programs outlined above

are just some examples as to how service provider can provide access to services to incarcerated and formerly incarcerated elders that fosters their over well-being. Professionals, such as social workers or nurses, who conduct needs assessments or provide transitional services, can identify the potential barriers in their local communities and identify community-based organizations and members who can help address them.

Older people are generally considered at low risk for reoffending. Official statistics suggest that compared with younger inmates, older inmates have the lowest likelihood of recidivating (Langan & Levin, 2002). Given this low risk, the policy and programming initiatives outlined are viable options for communities and service providers to incorporate in

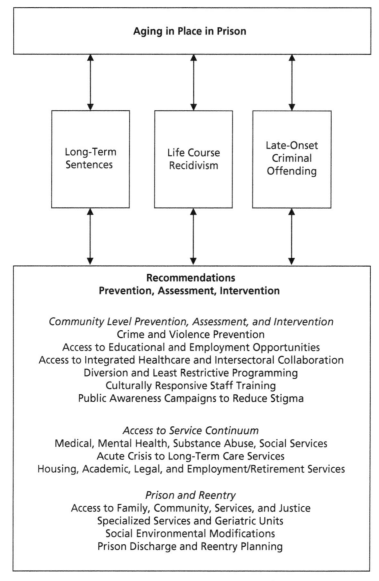

FIGURE 42.1 Prevention, assessment, and intervention planning for older adults at risk of and/or involved in the criminal justice system.

their service provision. However, there are more conservative monitoring approaches, such as the use of ankle bracelets, allow for alternative to incarceration diversion programs or the early release of older prisoners. Alternative to incarceration and diversion strategies are much less expensive than warehousing older in prison. Community-based programs compared to corrections are in a better position with the professional workforce and resources to more readily address trauma, mental health, and health issues commonly found in the older population. It

also would greatly reducing the costs associated with caring for older people in correctional facilities. The establishment of geriatric units for elder in prison provide the option to separate from the younger prison population, better provide for their age specific special needs. However, it is critical for correctional staff members who work to receive specialized training to effectively provide care for the incarcerated aging population (Dawes, 2009).

The best-case scenario for prevention is for social workers to use research, practice, and advocacy to address health and justice disparities experienced by elders. Older adults reentering the community should be provided services that match their complexity of needs (see Figure 42.1). Providing needed resources early enough in the process, such as access to social security benefits or housing, may make a significant difference toward successful reintegration (Higgins & Severson, 2009). Lawyers can provide services for many older adults in prison who need legal representation, such as in the case of disabilities or victimization or medical neglect while in prison. Human rights and legislative advocates can assist with ongoing policy and system reform efforts.

Providing a seamless bridge between prison and community not only is a key component of providing individual, family, and community cohesion; health; and well-being (Snyder, van Wormer, Chada, & Jaggers, 2009) but also may be key to reducing the $60 billion in reentry costs that are positioned to increase as more prisoners age with complex health- and social care needs (Nunez-Neto, 2008). The promising programs highlighted in this chapter suggest that even correctional staff can triumph over attitudinal and systemic barriers to treat incarcerated older adults and their families with dignity and respect and help make communities safer. If we are to follow our mission, social work must take a leading role in developing services and advocating on behalf of and with incarcerated and formerly incarcerated older adults and their families and communities.

ONLINE RESOURCES

ACLU Report: *At America's Expense: The Mass Incarceration of the Elderly.* https://www.aclu.org/criminal-law-reform/americas-expense-mass-incarceration-elderly

Be the Evidence Project White Paper: *Aging Prisoners: A Crisis in Need of Intervention.* https://sites.google.com/site/betheevidenceproject/white-paper-aging-prisoner-forumHuman

Human Rights Watch Report: *Old Behind Bars.* http://www.hrw.org/reports/2012/01/27/old-behind-bars-0

National Institute of Corrections Report: *Effectively Managing Aging and Geriatric Offenders.* http://nicic.gov/Library/024363

United Nations Office on Drugs and Crime: *Handbook for Prisoners with Special Needs.* http://www.unhcr.org/refworld/docid/4a0969d42.html

Vera Institute Report: *Aging Prisoners, Increasing Costs, and Geriatric Release.* http://www.vera.org/sites/default/files/resources/downloads/Its-about-time-aging-prisoners-increasing-costs-and-geriatric-release.pdf

World Health Organization. *Final report: World Conference on the Social Determinants of Health.* http://www.who.int/sdhconference/resources/wcsdh_report/en/index.html

REFERENCES

Aday, R. H. (2003). *Aging prisoners: Crisis in American corrections.* Westport, CT: Praeger.

Aday, R. H. (2005). Aging prisoners' concerns toward dying in prison. *OMEGA-Journal of Death and Dying, 52,* 199–216.

Aday, R. H., & Krabill, J. (2011). *Women aging in prison: A neglected population in the prison system.* Boulder, CO: Rienner.

Aday, R., & Krabill, J. (2012). Older and geriatric offenders: Critical issues for the 21st Century. In L. Gideon (Ed.), *Special needs offenders in correctional institutions* (pp. 203–233). Thousand Oaks, CA: Sage.

American Civil Liberties Union (ACLU). (2012). *At America's expense: The mass incarceration of the elderly.* Washington, DC: Author.

Carstairs, B., & Keon, D. (2009). *Canada's aging population: Seizing the opportunity report.* Ontario: Canada: Special Senate Committee on Aging. Retrieved from http://www.parl.gc.ca/Content/SEN/Committee/402/agei/rep/AgingFinalReport-e.pdf

Chiu, T. (2010). *It's about time: Aging prisoners, increasing costs, and geriatric release.* New York, NY: Vera Institute of Justice.

Cooney, F., & Braggins, J. (2010). *Doing time: Good practice with older people in prison—The views of prison staff.* London, England: Prison Reform Trust.

Davies, M. (2011). The reintegration of elderly prisoners: An exploration of services provided in England and Wale. *InternetJournal of Criminology,* 1–32. Retrieved from http://www.internetjournalofcriminology.com/davies_the_reintegration_of_elderly_prisoners.pdf

Dawes, J. (2009). Ageing prisoners: Issues for social work, *Australian Social Work, 62*(2), 258–271.

Grant, A. (1999). *Elderly inmates: Issues for Australia.* Canberra ACT 2601, Australia. Retrieved from http://www.aic.gov.au/documents/7/0/B/%7B70B4E5D4-3F91-416B-8670-0E3E4A1FF2AC%7Dti115.pdf

Guerino, P., Harrison, P., & Sabol, W. (2011). *Prisoners in 2010*. US Department of Justice, Bureau of Justice Statistics. Retrieved from http://bjs.ojp.usdoj.gov/content/pub/pdf/p10.pdf

Hale, L., & Swiggum, C. (2011, March). Older prisoners pose new challenges for Canada's prisons. *UBC Journalism News Service*. Retrieved from http://thethunderbird.ca/2011/03/31/older-prisoners-pose-new-challenges-for-canadas-correctional-service/

Harrison, M. (2011). *A promising practice—True grit*. Paper presented at the Public Forum Aging Prisoners: A Crisis in Need of Intervention, Fordham University, New York, NY, November 2011.

Higgins, D., & Severson, M. (2009). Community reentry and older adult offenders: Redefining social work roles. *Journal of Gerontological Social Work Roles, 52*, 784–802.

Human Rights Watch (HRW). (2012). *Old behind bars: The aging prison population in the United States*. Retrieved from http://www.Human Rights Watch.org/reports/2012/01/27/old-behind-bars

La Vigne, N. G., & Cowan, J. (2005). *Mapping prisoner reentry: An action research Guidebook*. Washington, DC: Urban Institute, Justice Policy Center.

Langan, P. A., & Levin, D. J. (2002). Recidivism of prisoners released in 1994. Bureau of Justice Statistics Special Report, June 2002, NCJ 193427, 1-16. Washington, DC: US Department of Justice Office of Justice Programs. Retrieved from http://www.bjs.gov/content/pub/pdf/rpr94.pdf

Loeb, S. J., Steffensmeier, D., & Lawrence, F. (2008). Comparing incarcerated and community-dwelling older men's health. *Western Journal of Nursing Research, 30*, 234–249.

Maschi, T., Gibson, S., Zgoba, K., & Morgen, K. (2011). Trauma and life event stressors among young and older adult prisoners. *Journal of Correctional Health Care, 17*, 160–172.

Maschi, T., Kalmanofsky, A., Westcott, K., & Pappacena, L. (2015). *An Analysis of United States Compassionate and Geriatric Release Laws: Towards a Rights-Based Response for Diverse Elders and Their Families and Communities*. New York, NY: Be the Evidence Press, Fordham University. Available at: www.beetheevidence.org

Maschi, T., & Koskinen, L. (2015). Co-constructing community: A conceptual map for reuniting aging people in prison with their families and communities. *Traumatology*, doi:10.1037/trm0000026

Maschi, T., Kwak, J., Ko, E. J., & Morrissey, M. (2012). Forget me not: Dementia in prisons. *The Gerontologist, 52*(2), 441–451. doi:10.1093/geront/gnr131

Maschi, T., & Marmo, C., & Han, J. (2014). Palliative care in prison: A content analysis of the literature. *International Journal of Prisoner Health, 10* (3), 172–197.

Maschi, T., Morgen, K., Westcott, K., Viola, D., & Koskinen, L. (2014). Aging, incarceration, and employment prospects: Recommendations for practice and policy reform. *Journal of Applied Rehabilitation Counseling, 45*(4), 44–55.

Maschi, T., Morgen, K., Zgoba, K., Courtney, D., & Ristow, J. (2011). Trauma, stressful life events, and post traumatic stress symptoms: Do subjective experiences matter? *The Gerontologist, 51*(5), 675–686. doi:10.1093/geront/gnr074

Maschi, T., Morrissey, M., & Leigey, M. (2013). The case for human agency, well-being, and community reintegration for people aging in prison: A statewide case analysis. *Journal of Correctional Healthcare, 19*, 194–210. doi:10.1177/1078345813486445

Maschi, T., Suftin, S., & O'Connell, B. (2012). Aging, mental health, and the criminal justice system: A content analysis of the literature. *Journal of Forensic Social Work, 2*, 162–185.

Maschi, T., & Viola, D., Harrison, M., & Harrison, W. (2014). Bridging community and prison for older adults and their families: Invoking human rights and intergenerational family justice. *International Journal of Prisoner Health, 19*(1), 1–19.

Maschi, T., Viola, D., & Koskinen, L. (2015). Trauma, stress, and coping among older adults in prison: Towards a human rights and intergenerational family justice action agenda. *Traumatology*. Advance online publication. http://dx.doi.org/10.1037/trm0000021

Maschi, T., Viola, D., & Morgen, K. (2013). Trauma and coping among older adults in prison: Linking empirical evidence to practice. *The Gerontologist, 54*(5), 857–867. doi:10.1093/geront/gnt069.

Maschi, T., Viola, D., Morgen, K., & Koskinen, L. (2013). Trauma, stress, grief, loss, and separation among older adults in prison: The protective role of coping resources on physical and mental wellbeing. *Journal of Crime and Justice, 38*(1), 113–136. doi:10.1080/0735648X.2013.808853.

Maschi, T., & Viola, D., Morgen, K., Harrison, M. T., Harrison, W., & Koskinen, L. (2014). Bridging community and prison for older adults and their families: Invoking human rights and intergenerational family justice. *International Journal of Prisoner Health, 19*(1), 1–19.

Maschi, T., Viola, D., & Sun, F. (2013). The high cost of the international aging prisoner crisis: Well-being as the common denominator for action. *The Gerontologist, 53*, 543–554. doi:10.1093/geront/gns125

Mesurier, R. (2011). Supporting older people in prison: Ideas for practice. Retrieved from http://www.ageuk.org.uk/documents/en-gb/for-professionals/government-and-society/older%20prisoners%20guide_pro.pdf?dtrk=true

Ministry of Justice. (2010). *Offender management caseload statistics* 2009. London, England. Retrieved from http://www.justice.gov.uk/publications/statistics-and-data/prisons-and-probation/omcs-annual.htm

National Institute of Corrections (NIC). (2010). *Effectively managing aging and geriatric offenders.* Retrieved April 1, 2011, from http://nicic.gov/Library/024363

Nunez-Neto, B. (2008). *Offender reentry: Correctional statistics, reintegration into the community, and recidivism.* Retrieved from http://lieberman.senate.gov/assets/pdf/crs/offenderreentry.pdf

Organization for Economic Co-operation and Development (OECD). (2010). *Factbook.* Retrieved from http://www.oecdlibrary.org/economics/oecd-factbook-2010_factbook-2010-en

Pennsylvania Department of Corrections v. Yeskey, No. 97-634 (U.S. June 15, 1998).

Pew Charitable Trusts (PCT). (2010). *Collateral costs: Incarceration's effect on economic mobility.* Washington, DC: Author.

Sampson, R., & Laub, J. (2003). Life-course disasters? Trajectories of crime among delinquent boys followed to age 70. *Criminology, 41,* 555–592.

Snyder, C., van Wormer, K., Chada, J., & Jaggers, J. (2009). Older adult inmates: The challenges for social work. *Social Work, 54,* 117–124.

Ubelacker, S. (2011). *Program trains inmate caregivers to watch over aging prisoners with dementia.* Retrieved August 1, 2011, from http://www.breitbart.com/article.php?id=cp_imtmi6k6c1&show_article=1

US Census Bureau. (2010). *U.S. popclock projection.* Retrieved from http://www.census.gov/main/www/popclock.html

United Nations (UN). (1948). *The universal declaration of human rights.* Retrieved from http://www.un.org/en/documents/udhr/

United Nations (UN). (1977). *Standard minimum rules for the treatment of prisoners.* Retrieved from http://www2.ohchr.org/english/law/treatmentprisoners.htm

United Nations (UN). (2012). *Report of the United Nations High Commissioner for Human Rights.* Substantive session, 23–27, July 2012 Geneva.

United Nations Office on Drugs and Crime (UNODC). (2009). *Handbook for prisoners with special needs.* Retrieved from http://www.unhcr.org/refworld/docid/4a0969d42.html.

Western, B. (2008). *From prison to work: A proposal for a national prisoner reentry program.* Washington, DC: The Brookings Institution. Retrieved from http://scholar.harvard.edu/brucewestern/files/12_prison_to_work_western.pdf

Williams B., McGuire J., Lindsay R., Baillargeon J., Cenzer I., Lee, S., & Kushel, M. (2010). Coming home: health status and homelessness risk of older pre-release prisoners. *Journal of Gerontological Internal Medicine, 25,* 1038–1044.

World Health Organization (WHO). (2012). *Ageing and life course.* Retrieved from http://www.who.int/ageing/projects/elder_abuse/en/.

INTRODUCTION

Despite the advent of a variety of federal level income support and social service programs that have had positive effects in reducing the extent of poverty of older adults, poverty and homelessness among the elderly is still a significant problem. Given the heterogeneity of the elderly population, poverty is of particular concern among elderly women, elders who are 75 years and older, elders of color, and elderly persons living in rural communities. This chapter reviews the extent of poverty and homelessness among the elderly and discusses the characteristics and needs of vulnerable older populations. Of significant concern to social workers is the underuse of health, mental health, and social services by older people, especially by those at-risk populations most in need. A framework for conceptualizing service delivery barriers, and practice and service delivery recommendations to address identified barriers are presented.

EXTENT OF POVERTY AMONG THE ELDERLY IN THE UNITED STATES

Poverty rates among adults age 65 years and over have been steadily falling since 1965, from about 30% of the overall elderly population being below the poverty line to 9.1% of elderly persons below the poverty line in 2012 (US Census Bureau, 2013a).[1] This significant drop in poverty rates among the elderly is principally due to the increases in Social Security benefits and the advent of federal Medicare and other safety net programs (Bok, 1996; Hungerford, Rassette, Iams, & Koenig, 2001/2002). The rate of poverty among elderly persons in the United States is now lower than the poverty rates of both children under 18 years of age and nonelderly adults (US Census Bureau, 2013a). It should be noted, however, that poverty rates for the elderly in the United States, especially for elderly women and elderly women who live alone, are considerably higher than for elderly citizens of European industrialized nations (Smeeding & Sandstrom, 2004).

The declining rates of overall elderly poverty in the United States have been interpreted by some to indicate that we no longer have to be concerned with elders in poverty, however, examining a cross-sectional view of overall poverty of elderly persons can be misleading for several reasons. First,

DAVID E. BIEGEL
AMY RESTORICK ROBERTS

Impoverished and Homeless Older Adults

the elderly population is very heterogeneous, with higher poverty rates among vulnerable elderly subpopulations. Second, there is a failure to consider the "near poor," or those individuals whose incomes are below 150% of the poverty line with significant income needs (Bogdon, Katsura, & Mikelsons, 2001). Third, this approach does not provide any information about elders' cumulative chances of being poor during their elder years, the duration of their poverty, or their chances of escaping from poverty and thus does not provide an accurate picture of the degree to which elderly individuals experience poverty during their later years.

HETEROGENEITY OF POVERTY RATES AMONG THE ELDERLY

As can be seen in Table 43.1, which is based on census data from 2012, there are large differences in the rates of poverty among subgroups of elderly persons. Thus, older elderly persons, women, elders living alone, and racial and ethnic minorities have higher rates of poverty than other elders (US Census Bureau, 2013c). For example, the poverty rate for elderly individuals who live alone is almost double the poverty rate for elders overall, while the poverty rate for Black elderly and elders of Hispanic origin is twice as high as the poverty rate for White elders. In addition, the poverty rates for elderly Blacks, Asians, and individuals of Hispanic origin are all higher than nonelderly adults in these racial and ethnic groups (US Census Bureau, 2013c).

As can be seen in Table 43.1, poverty rates for women are higher than those for men (except for Asians), and for older as compared with younger elderly individuals. The rates of poverty for elderly persons living alone are much higher among Blacks, Asians, and elders of Hispanic origin as compared with White elders. The poverty rate for females living alone among Black and Hispanic elderly is higher than that of males for these two racial/ethnic groups.

"Near Poor" Elders

The "near poor," those with incomes less than 150% of the poverty rate, often have incomes too high to qualify for public assistance, yet too low to cover their housing, food, transportation, and healthcare needs. As can be seen in Table 43.1, overall there are twice

as many elders living in "near poverty" than elders who are under the poverty level. Overall, one-fifth of all elders live near the poverty line. Table 43.1 also shows the same patterns for near poverty as for poverty reported above, with higher near-poverty rates among elders who are 75 years and older, female elders, racial and ethnic elders, elders living alone, and combinations of these variables.

Women

The poverty rate data presented earlier have demonstrated the higher poverty rates of elderly women as compared with elderly men, with older women from racial and ethnic minority groups being at greatest risk for poverty and near poverty. A number of variables that impact the risk for women becoming poor have been identified in the literature, including divorce, widowhood, increased longevity, intermittent work histories, greater likelihood of living alone, lower likelihood of receiving pension income, and lower wages (Anzick & Weaver, 2001; Goldberg, 2010; Kingson & Williamson, 2001; Rupp, Strand, & Davies, 2003). Marital status in particular has a significant impact on the income of elderly women (Ozawa, 1997; Sevak, Weir, & Willis, 2004), with widowhood being a significant risk factor for older women's transition into poverty (Sevak et al., 2004).

Racial and Ethnic Minorities

The higher levels of poverty of elders of color is of increasing concern, given the fact that the non-White elderly population is growing at a faster rate than that of the White elderly population. It is projected that one-quarter of the elderly population will be non-White by the year 2025. With significantly higher rates of poverty among adults aged 45 to 54 years, the growing percentage of minority elderly in the future will mean growing numbers of elderly individuals without adequate financial assets (Binstock, 1999). Higher rates of poverty among racial and ethnic elderly individuals are also associated with greater deficits in education, lower self-reported health status, greater physical impairment, less access to healthcare, underuse of healthcare services, and inadequate housing (Binstock, 1999; Reed, Hargreaves, & Cassil, 2003; Whitfield & Baker, 2014).

TABLE 43.1 Poverty Ratio for Persons 65 Years and Older by Race: 2012

Population Group	Percent Below 100% of Poverty	Percent Below 150% of Poverty
65 and Over (All races)	9.1	20.9
65–74	7.9	17.3
75 and over	10.6	25.6
Males	6.6	15.9
65–74	6.6	14.2
75 and over	6.7	18.5
Females	11.0	24.9
65–74	9.1	20.0
75 and over	13.3	30.7
Living Alone (65 and over)	17.3	38.5
Male	13.0	30.2
Female	19.3	42.5
65 and Over (White)	7.8	19.3
65–74	6.7	15.5
75 and over	9.2	24.1
Males	5.6	14.4
65–74	5.5	12.7
75 and over	5.7	16.9
Females	9.6	23.2
65-74	7.8	18.0
75 and over	11.7	29.3
Living Alone (65 and over)	15.2	36.3
Males	10.6	27.5
Females	17.3	40.4
65 and Over (Black)	18.2	33.5
65–74	16.1	29.4
75 and over	21.2	39.7
Males	14.0	26.9
65–74	14.6	25.4
75 and over	12.8	29.6
Females	21.2	38.3
65–74	17.3	32.6
75 and over	26.4	45.8
Living Alone (65 and over)	30.4	52.7
Males	25.5	44.7
Females	33.2	57.1
65 and Over (Hispanic Origin)	20.6	38.9
65–74	20.7	37.7
75 and over	20.6	40.7

(continued)

TABLE 43.1 Continued

Population Group	Percent Below 100% of Poverty	Percent Below 150% of Poverty
Males	19.1	36.3
65–74	20.6	35.0
75 and over	16.7	38.3
Females	21.8	40.9
65–74	20.7	39.8
75 and over	23.4	42.4
Living Alone (65 and over)	40.7	45.8
Males	37.0	44.5
Females	42.7	46.4
65 and Over (Asian)	12.3	22.4
65–74	9.3	19.2
75 and over	16.8	27.3
Males	12.3	22.2
65–74	9.1	17.5
75 and over	18.3	30.6
Females	12.2	22.6
65–74	9.4	20.6
75 and over	15.9	25.2
Living Alone (65 and over)	25.2	45.8
Males	27.5	44.5
Females	24.2	46.4

Rural Elderly

Rates of poverty among elderly persons living in nonmetropolitan areas are consistently higher than those of elderly persons living in metropolitan communities. Using data from Current Population Surveys, 1999–2009, Slack & Rizzuto (2013) report that between 1999 and 2009, poverty among non-metropolitan elderly individuals averaged 14.1% as compared with 10.8% in metropolitan areas. Nonmetropolitan elderly individuals are more likely to become poor than metropolitan elders, even after controlling for other confounding variables such as race, education, marital status, and widowhood (McLaughlin, & Jensen, 1995). Elders in rural communities have lower lifetime earnings, fewer Social Security benefits, less pension coverage, and less likelihood of enrollment in the Supplemental Security Income program (Glasgow & Brown, 1998;

McLaughlin & Jensen, 1993). Despite greater anticipated service needs, fewer services are available and used in rural communities due to lack of governmental resources, lower population densities, shortages of trained professionals, and high levels of individuals' self-reliance (Krout, 1998). In addition, migration of younger populations away from rural communities may weaken the informal social networks of elderly persons remaining in those communities (Glasgow, 1993).

HOMELESS OLDER ADULTS

Homelessness is defined in different ways in the literature, although most commonly it describes an unmet need for stable housing caused by poverty and unaffordable housing. Older adults experiencing homelessness may be sheltered (living in an emergency shelter or transitional housing program), or unsheltered and living in a place unsuitable for human habitation such as the streets, abandoned buildings, or vehicles (US Department of Housing and Urban Development [HUD], 2011a). These older members of the homeless population include both the chronically homeless population that is aging and older adults who experience homelessness for the first time in later life.

Within the homeless population, there are differing characteristics between younger and older groups of older adults. Typically, the younger group of the homeless (age 50 to 64 years) are considered homeless "older adults" (Corporation for Supportive Housing & HEARTH, 2011; National Coalition for the Homeless, 2009), whereas the older group (age 65 and above) are referred to as homeless "elders." Although the "older adult" category is chronologically younger, their healthcare needs and functional status are equivalent to adults who are from 10 to 20 years older in the general population (Gelberg, Linn, & Mayer-Oakes, 1990). Due to unmet physical health, mental health, and substance use treatment needs, homeless adults age 50 years and older have a mortality rate three to four times higher than the general population (O'Connell, 2005). Sadly, the younger group of homeless older adults are denied access to age-qualified government safety net programs for housing, healthcare, and poverty alleviation.

The Sixth Annual Homeless Assessment Report to Congress (HUD, 2011a) described 40,750 sheltered homeless people age 62 and older (4.2% of the overall sheltered population), while 204,191 (14.9%) of the sheltered homeless were age 51 to 61 (HUD, 2011b). Taken together, these figures suggest that approximately 250,000 older adults experience homelessness over the course of a year. The same report described an upward trend in the proportion of sheltered homeless older adults age 51 to 61 (18.9% in 2007 compared with 22.3% in 2010). The relatively low incidence of homelessness among the elderly may be attributable to their lower average life expectancy, as well as the increased availability of subsidized senior housing at age 62, and Medicare and Social Security benefits at age 65 (Corporation for Supportive Housing & HEARTH, 2011).

Projections of future increases in the elderly homeless population are troubling. The National Alliance to End Homelessness estimated that the elderly homeless population will increase by 33% from 44,172 in 2010 to 58,772 in 2020, and it will more than double in size between 2010 and 2050, when over 95,000 elderly

persons are projected to be homeless (Sermons & Henry, 2010, p. 3). Factors contributing to these projections include the aging of the baby boomers, the aging chronically homeless population (about half of the chronically homeless population were born between 1954 and 1964, according to Culhane, Metraux, and Bainbridge [2010]), and the higher risk of homelessness among the poor (as stated earlier, 9.1% of adults 65 and older were living below the official poverty line in 2012) (US Census Bureau, 2013c).

Subpopulations of Elderly Homeless

As defined by the US Department of Housing and Urban Development (HUD, 2011b), a "chronically homeless" person is defined as an individual or family head of household with a disabling condition who "has been homeless and living or residing in a place not meant for human habitation, a safe haven, or in an emergency shelter continuously for at least one year or on at least four separate occasions in the last 3 years, where each homeless occasion was at least 15 days" (p. 75967). Chronically homeless older adults often have multiple complex physical health, mental health, and substance use problems in addition to a need for housing, while seniors living on a fixed income may be pushed into first-time homelessness due to a lack of affordable housing. These homeless elders face a number of challenges in addition to the lack of affordable housing, including increased physical frailty, chronic disease, impaired mental function, loneliness, and isolation (HEARTH, 2009).

Risk Factors and Problems Pertaining to Homelessness

There are many causes for homelessness among the elderly. First, housing instability results from the combination of income and savings relative to the affordability of housing costs. Nearly 50% of older persons in 2011 spent more than one-fourth of their income on housing costs (Administration on Aging, 2012). Seniors are becoming more burdened with the cost of housing, particularly for those who rent or own homes with mortgages (Harrell, 2011). In 2007, 21% of all older adult households experienced a severe housing burden, requiring more than 50% of their income to cover housing expenses, according to the National Alliance to End Homelessness

(Sermons & Henry, 2010). Indicators of the demand for affordable housing include a 3- to 4-year waiting list (National Coalition for the Homeless, 2009) and "a serious shortage" of permanent supportive housing (US Interagency Council on Homelessness, 2010).

A multitude of other factors interact in complex ways and place some older adults at greater risk for homelessness than others. Older adults living alone are not only more likely to be poor but also more likely to become homeless (Crane, et al., 2005). Those who develop functional impairments from physical health issues, cognitive impairment, mental illness, or substance abuse are more likely to become homeless (Garibaldi, Conde-Martel, & O'Toole, 2005). Additional risk factors include job loss and prolonged unemployment, living alone, and going through a life transition, such as widowhood, divorce, or domestic violence (HEARTH, 2009).

SERVICE DELIVERY BARRIERS

A variety of barriers to the use of health, mental health, and social services by at-risk older people and their family caregivers have been identified in the literature (Barrio et al., 2008; Biegel, Farkas, & Song, 1997; Casado, van Vulpen, & Davis, 2011; Yeatts, Crow, & Folts, 1992). These barriers are often the greatest for subgroups of the most vulnerable elders in poverty. Biegel and colleagues (Biegel & Farkas, 1989; Biegel, Johnsen, & Shafran, 1997) have categorized service delivery barriers on four different levels—system, agency staff, community, and individual and family (see Table 43.2). This framework highlights the places where barriers occur, in order to guide the development of interventions at the proper locations to address these barriers and thus improve practice and service delivery to elders in need. In addressing barriers to service delivery to older people, we believe it is important to focus on all four levels.

Though the four levels of barriers are applicable to any type of service, the specific barriers identified in Table 43.2 vary to some degree depending on the type of service as well as the vulnerable elderly subpopulations. For example, a barrier such as lack of services is a greater problem in rural as compared with urban communities, while past experiences with discrimination and lack of culturally competent service providers pertain particularly to minority older populations.

Systems-level barriers refer to deficits at the service agency and at the agency network level that are impacted by political, economic, and social forces that shape the development of agency services and funding for such services. An example of a systems-level barrier is the lack of permanent supportive housing available for homeless older adults. Staff-level barriers are the levels of knowledge, skills, attitudes, and behaviors of agency staff, which could involve a lack of professional commitment and the tendency to treat minority elders without regard to their unique life experiences. Community-level barriers can discourage the use of formal professional services while endorsing only the use of informal helpers and community-based organizations (e.g., neighborhood associations, self-help groups, ethnic and fraternal organizations) (Biegel, Johnsen, & Shafran, 1997). Individual-level barriers refer to personal and family attitudes and behaviors that influence elders' use of community services. Such attitudes and behaviors may stem from negative prior experiences by minority individuals when accessing a variety of service delivery systems. For health-related services, evidence suggests that ethnicity plays an important role in the conceptualization of illness (Hall & Tucker, 1985; Urdaneta, Saldana, & Winkler, 1995), how ethnic elders define illness, and their knowledge of service delivery systems.

PRACTICE AND SERVICE DELIVERY RECOMMENDATIONS

In order to fully address and remedy the widespread health and psychosocial ramifications of economic hardship of at-risk elders in poverty, a multidimensional approach targeting all four barrier levels presented above—system, staff, community, and individual/family—is required. Recommendations are, therefore, directed toward these levels as they pertain to the needs of poor elderly women, racial and ethnic minorities, rural residents, and the homeless elderly.

One of the greatest barriers to service delivery, affecting all at-risk elderly, is the lack of knowledge about the problems and needs of poor elders, at both the system and staff levels. This barrier is significant as it contributes to the development and delivery of services that do not adequately meet the needs of this population. A second barrier, at the staff level, involves the provision of services by professionals who lack the specialized knowledge and skills needed to attend to older adults in poverty, including a specialized

TABLE 43.2 Program and Service Delivery Barriers for Elders in Poverty

System Level (Agency and agency network deficits)

- Lack of linkages with informal networks
- Lack of linkages with other service systems and providers
- Financial (cost of services)
- Lack of permanent supportive housing for homeless older adults
- Lack of respite and transitional housing programs for homeless older adults
- Lack of services/lack of specialized services
- Inappropriately designed services
- Location of services/transportation issues

Staff Level (Knowledge, skills, attitudes, and behaviors of staff)

- Lack of non-English-speaking staff members
- Lack of cultural competency of agency staff members/insensitive service providers
- Lack of knowledge of problems/needs of elders in poverty
- Lack of training to address specific problems of the elderly
- Staff is not reflective of the racial and ethnic diversity of the population to be served
- Ageism

Community Level (Attitudes toward service use by lay helpers and organizations/relationships between lay helpers and professional services)

- Discouragement of formal help-seeking
- Lack of knowledge of agency services
- Lack of relationships with service providers
- Unwillingness to recognize/define "problems" of elders in poverty

Individual/Family Level (Personal and family attitudes and behaviors toward service use)

- Physical, mental, or cognitive limitations of at-risk elderly (e.g., homeless) to access and navigate through the complex social welfare system
- Language barriers/lack of proficiency in English
- Past/present experiences with racism, racial/ethnic or age discrimination
- Past negative experiences with service use/distrust of service providers
- Negative attitudes toward seeking help—stigma, fear, embarrassment, shame, confidentiality concerns
- Discouragement of service use by family members
- Belief that treatment/services will not be effective
- Preference for use of family care and other informal networks
- Lack of knowledge of services
- Accessibility issues—concern about transportation, location of services, cost of services
- Concern about acceptance by agency staff
- Unaware of need for services/Denial of problems

knowledge of gerontological social work and of the resources (both formal and informal) available to support homeless elderly, older women, racial and ethnic minorities, and rural clients. Equally important is a thorough understanding of the experience of being poor in older adulthood, including a familiarity with the risk factors and implications of poverty, an awareness of the barriers these older adults face, and the cumulative effects of lifelong discrimination (e.g., racial, class, gender, and now age discrimination).

Elderly Women

Elderly women are especially vulnerable to the risks of poverty. Those who are particularly vulnerable to these effects are divorced, widowed, or single women over the age of 70 and living alone. Minority and rural women are the most vulnerable. While a large majority of those in poverty rely on Social Security to survive, women and widows generally receive the fewest benefits on account of their low-wage histories and major interruptions in their employment history. At the staff level, social workers should be aware of the unique issues facing older women, including their financial constraints, and understand that while many would prefer to continue working, greater numbers of them are leaving the workforce prematurely because of health problems (Perkins, 1992). In addition to health and financial barriers, elderly women are subject to gender discrimination and social isolation. With this awareness, the social worker's primary role should be to assess the older woman's financial and health status, the social supports she has in place, and her ability to afford healthcare. Social workers should recognize that if discrimination figured prominently in her early life, she may have little faith in "the system" and may be reluctant to accept services.

Recommendations at the individual level might involve resource counseling and provision to support women who are socially isolated (e.g., widows and childless older women) through enrollment at a senior center, a support group for widows, a volunteer home visitor program, or some other social or religious organization that appeals to the client. Social work advocacy may be necessary to ensure the client is not assuming any excess costs for enrollment or transportation. At the community level, social workers can disseminate information at churches, community centers, and social organizations about resources available to support socially isolated older adults, widows, or those who are frail. At the system level, agencies should discuss collaborative efforts to serve at-risk elders.

Racial and Ethnic Minority Elders

When the older person's ethnicity differs from that of the provider, the helping process becomes even more complex. Intervention with ethnic minorities, regardless of their economic status, requires a specific set of skills and competencies in order to respond in a manner that is culturally sensitive, relevant, and empowering. A central feature of culturally sensitive social work is the provider's capacity for self-insight to initially identify any bias that might interfere with client assessment and treatment. Equally important is an acknowledgment of one's own values and the conceptualization of health, illness, help-seeking, treatment, and quality of life through the client's perspective (Sotomayor, 1997). While it is important to acquire knowledge about the ethnic group, it is even more important to recognize and understand within-group diversity. Therefore, a comprehensive evaluation of the older adult's values and attitudes is necessary, including the elder's self-perceptions regarding his/her affiliation to the racial/ethnic group.

Failed attempts at outreach might be the result of two barriers in particular: (1) the provider, whose ethnic identity does not match the client's, and (2) the service offered, which does not cater to members of the client's ethnic group. Recommendations at the staff level involve hiring a diverse group of staff representing a variety of ethnic backgrounds, using multilingual staff as resources to provide translation and interpretation when necessary, providing in-service staff training and education to nonminority staff regarding cultural sensitivity, incorporating activities and meals that appeal to minority consumers, and including minority representatives on the advisory board of the agency (Yeatts et al., 1992). A community-level recommendation would involve the provision of services to ethnic minority elders in a familiar and culturally sensitive location, such as a church or ethnic organization.

Rural Elders

Social work in rural regions also presents a unique set of challenges in delivering services, especially to at-risk groups, including the oldest old, racial and ethnic minority elders, and older women. Older adults living in nonmetropolitan settings have fewer community resources, especially specialized services, therefore, they experience greater deprivation than do urban elderly (Coward, Duncan, & Netzer, 1993; Glasgow & Brown, 2012; Krout, 1994). An awareness of the minimal services for older adults, the inadequate transportation available, and the social isolation of rural elders, lends appreciation for the struggle of seniors and providers and an understanding of the creativity necessary to ameliorate conditions.

Interventions should incorporate the community's preference for services, using flexibility and multimethod approaches, and build on the strengths and resources already present in these rural areas. The goal is to maximize these resources through efficient service coordination and coalition building, using existing relationships with local leaders and the private sector to offer services that promote personal autonomy and dignity (Krout, 1998). Of particular relevance to these points is that a majority of care in rural communities is provided by family members, who also need support (Stoller & Lee, 1994). Given the above considerations, social workers should attempt to address all barrier levels to overcome obstacles to access and use of services, such as the reluctance on the part of the older adult to access community resources, the lack of availability of specialized services and professionals, and the lack of variety in services that are offered. Satellite senior centers can provide outreach to socially isolated older persons, and public health nurses can provide health screening and education to frail seniors through local churches. Area Agencies on Aging can use their relationships with area hospitals and nursing homes to increase the availability and array of home health services that could be offered to at-risk elders and could also link with other Area Agencies on Aging to develop housing coalitions to increase housing resources for older adults (Krout, 1989).

Homeless Elderly

At the system level, there is a great need for more affordable and subsidized housing options for seniors. For older adults who are currently homeless, permanent supportive housing offers a promising approach to end homelessness. This comprehensive model combines affordable housing with supportive services for homeless older adults, providing affordable housing with deep subsidies, tolerant property management, care management, and evidence-based service models (Corporation for Supportive Housing & HEARTH, 2011). Along with stable housing, permanent supportive housing links individuals to holistic and ongoing supportive services.

Outreach services connect older adults at risk of homelessness to available resources within the local community. A better coordinated system of housing, healthcare, and income support plus increased supportive services as people become older and more frail are essential to support independent living for older adults at risk of homelessness (Corporation for Supportive Housing & HEARTH, 2011; National Coalition for the Homeless, 2009; Schill & Daniels, 2003). In terms of the delivery of services, providers who serve homeless older adults recommend having multiple services available in one location with a multidisciplinary approach in the assessment and evaluation of clients to connect clients with transitional housing quickly and provide outreach to older adults living on the streets or at-risk for homelessness (HUD, 2003). Intensive case management services are effective in helping homeless older adults access and benefit from social service, income support, and healthcare programs.

SUMMARY

In summary, despite reductions in overall poverty rates for the past four decades, very old individuals, women, racial and ethnic minorities, and rural elderly residents are at significantly greater risk for poverty, with the population of at-risk poor elderly individuals increasing at a faster rate than that of the elderly population as a whole. In addition, we have noted the significant barriers to the use of health, mental health, and social services by older adults, and have presented strategies for social workers to help address these barriers on system, staff, community, and individual and family levels.

NOTE

1. Only a few changes have been made in the computation of the poverty rate since it was first adopted in 1969. The US Census bureau is researching a new measure that takes into account government assistance programs for low-income individuals and families. Using this calculation, in 2012, the poverty rate for elderly persons 65 years and older would have been 14.8% rather than 9.1% (US Department of Commerce, 2013b).

REFERENCES

Administration on Aging. (2012). *Profile of older Americans*. Retrieved from http://www.aoa.gov/AoARoot/Aging_Statistics/Profile/2012/11.aspx

Anzick, M. A., & Weaver, D. A. (2001). *Reducing poverty among elderly women*. ORES Working Paper Series, No. 87. Washington, DC: Social Security Administration, Office of Policy.

Barrio, C., Palinkas, L. A., Yamada, A., Fuentes, D., Criado, V., Garcia, P., & Jeste, D. V. (2008). Unmet needs for mental health services for Latino older adults: Perspectives from consumers, family members, advocates, and service providers. *Community Mental Health Journal, 44,* 57–74.

Biegel, D. E., & Farkas, K. (1989). *Mental health and the elderly: Service delivery issues.* Cleveland, OH: Monograph Series, Western Reserve Geriatric Education Center, Case Western Reserve University.

Biegel, D. E., Farkas, K., & Song, L. (1997). Barriers to the use of mental health services by African-American and Hispanic elderly persons. *Journal of Gerontological Social Work, 29,* 23–44.

Biegel, D. E., Johnsen, J. A., & Shafran, R. (1997). Overcoming barriers faced by African-American families with a family member with mental illness. *Family Relations, 46,*163–178.

Binstock, R. H. (1999). Public policies and minority elders. In M. L. Wykle & A. B. Ford (Eds.), *Serving minority elders in the 21st century* (pp. 5–24). New York, NY: Springer.

Bogdon, A. S., Katsura, H., & Mikelsons, M. (2001). Exploring the housing assistance needs of elderly renters. *Journal of Housing for the Elderly, 15,* 111–130.

Bok, D. (1996). *The state of the nation: Government and the quest for a better society.* Cambridge, MA: Princeton University Press.

Casado, B. L., van Vulpen, K. S., & Davis, S. L. (2011). Unmet needs and community-based services among frail older Americans and their caregivers. *Journal of Aging and Health, 23,* 529–553.

Corporation for Supportive Housing & HEARTH. (2011). *Ending homelessness among older adults and elders through permanent supportive housing.* Revised Policy Paper Prepared for the National Leadership Initiative to End Elder Homelessness. Retrieved from http://www.csh.org/wp-content/uploads/2012/01/Report_EndingHomelessness AmongOlderAdultsandSeniors ThroughSupportiveHousing_ 112.pdf

Coward, R. T., Duncan, R. P., & Netzer, J. K. (1993). The availability of health care resources for elders living in nonmetropolitan persistent low-income counties in the South. *Journal of Applied Gerontology, 12,* 368–387.

Crane, M., & Byrne, K., Fu, R., Lipmann, B., Mirabelli, F., Rota-Bartelink, A., . . . Warnes, A. M. (2005). The causes of homelessness in later life: Findings from a three-nation study. *Journal of Gerontology: Social Sciences, 60B,* S152–S159.

Culhane, D. P., Metraux, S., & Bainbridge, J. (2010). *The age structure of contemporary homelessness: Risk period or cohort effect?* Penn School of Social Policy and Practice Working Paper, 1–28.

Garibaldi, B., Conde-Martel, A., & O'Toole, T. P. (2005). Self-reported co-morbidities, perceived needs, and sources for usual care for older and younger homeless adults. *Journal of General Internal Medicine, 20,* 726–730.

Gelberg, L., Linn, L. S., & Mayer-Oakes, S. A. (1990). Differences in health status between older and younger homeless adults. *Journal of the American Geriatrics Society, 38,* 1220–1229.

Glasgow, N. (1993). Poverty among rural elders: Trends, context, and directions for policy. *Journal of Applied Gerontology, 12,* 302–319.

Glasgow, N., & Brown, D. L. (1998). Older, rural, and poor. In R. T. Coward, & J. A. Krout (Eds.), *Aging in rural settings: Life circumstances and distinctive features* (pp. 187–207). New York, NY: Springer.

Glasgow, N., & Brown, D. L. (2012). Rural ageing in the United States: Trends and contexts. *Journal of Rural Studies, 28,* 422–431.

Goldberg, G. S. (2010). *Poor women in rich countries.* New York, NY: Oxford University Press.

Hall, L. E., & Tucker, C. M. (1985). Relationships between ethnicity, conceptions of mental illness, and attitudes associated with seeking psychological help. *Psychological Reports, 57,* 907–916.

Harrell, R. (2011). *Housing for older adults: The impacts of the recession.* AARP Public Policy Institute. Retrieved from http://assets.aarp.org/rgcenter/ppi/liv-com/insight53.pdf

HEARTH. (2009). *The importance of service-enriched housing.* Retrieved from http://www.hearth-home.org/media/hearth_research09.pdf

Hungerford, T., Rassette, M., Iams, H., & Koenig, M. (2001/2002). Trends in the economic status of the elderly, 1976–2000. *Social Security Bulletin, 64,* 12–22.

Kingson, E. R., & Williamson, J. B. (2001). Economic security policies. In R. H. Binstock & L. K. George (Eds.), *Handbook of aging and the social sciences.* New York, NY: Academic Press.

Krout, J. A. (1989). *Senior centers in America.* Westport, CT: Greenwood Press.

Krout, J. A. (1994). *Providing community-based services to the rural elderly.* Thousand Oaks, CA: Sage.

Krout, J. A. (1998). Services and service delivery in rural environments. In R. T. Coward & J. A. Krout (Eds.), *Aging in rural settings: Life circumstances and distinctive features* (pp. 247–266). New York, NY: Springer.

McLaughlin, D. K., & Jensen, L. (1993). Poverty among older Americans: The plight of nonmetropolitan elders. *Journals of Gerontology: Social Sciences, 48,* S44–S54.

McLaughlin, D. K., & Jensen, L. (1995). Becoming poor: The experiences of elders. *Rural Sociology, 60,* 202–223.

National Coalition for the Homeless. (2009). *Homelessness among elderly persons*. Retrieved from http://www.nationalhomeless.org/factsheets/Elderly.pdf

O'Connell, J. (2005). *Premature mortality in homeless populations: A review of the literature*. Nashville, TN: National Health Care for the Homeless Council.

Ozawa, M. N. (1997). *Income and net worth of the elderly in the United States*. Report to the International Longevity Center, Japan. St. Louis, MO: Washington University, George Warren Brown School of Social Work.

Perkins, K. (1992). Psychosocial implications of women and retirement. *Social Work*, 37, 526–532.

Reed, M., Hargraves, J. L, & Cassil, A. (2003). *Unequal access: African-American Medicare beneficiaries and the prescription drug gap*. Issue Brief No. 64, Center for Studying System Change.

Rupp, K., Strand, A., & Davies, P. S. (2003). Poverty among elderly women: Assessing SSI options to strengthen social security reform. *Journal of Gerontology, Social Sciences*, 58B, S359–S368.

Schill, M. H., & Daniels, G. (2003). *State of New York City's housing and neighborhoods: An overview of recent trends*. Policies to promote affordable housing: Proceedings of a conference cosponsored by the Federal Reserve Bank of New York and New York University's Furman Center for Real Estate and Urban Policy. *Economic Policy Review*, 9, 5–17. Retrieved from http://www.newyorkfed.org/research/epr/2003n2.html

Sermons, M. W., & Henry, M. (2010). *Demographics of homelessness series: The rising elderly population*. Homeless Research Institute: National Alliance to End Homelessness. Retrieved from http://www.endhomelessness.org/library/entry/demographics-of-homelessness-series-the-rising-elderly-population

Sevak, P., Weir, D. R., & Willis, R. J. (2004). *The economic consequences of a husband's death: Evidence from the HRS and AHEAD*. Ann Arbor: University of Michigan.

Slack, T., & Rizzuto, T. E. (2013). Aging and economic well-being in rural America: Exploring income and employment challenges. In N. Glasgow & E. H. Berry (Eds.), *Rural aging in 21st century America*. Dordrecht, Netherlands: Springer.

Smeeding, T. M., & Sandstrom, S. (2004). *Poverty and income maintenance in old age: A cross-national view of low income older women*. Syracuse, NY: Syracuse University.

Sotomayor, M. (1997). Aging: Racial and ethnic groups. In *Encyclopedia of social work* (Supplement, pp. 26–36). Washington, DC: NASW Press.

Stoller, E. P., & Lee, G. R. (1994). Informal care of rural elders. In R. T. Coward, C. N. Bull, G. Kukulka, & J. M. Galliher (Eds.), *Health services for rural elders* (pp. 33–64). New York, NY: Springer.

Urdaneta, M. L., Saldana, D. H., & Winkler, A. (1995). Mexican-American perceptions of severe mental illness. *Human Organization*, 54, 70–77.

US Census Bureau. (2013a). *Income, poverty and health insurance coverage in the United States: 2012*. P60-245. Washington, DC: US Department of Commerce, Economics and Statistics Administration, US Census Bureau.

US Census Bureau (2013b). *The research supplemental poverty measure: 2012*. P60-247. Washington, DC: US Department of Commerce, Economics and Statistics Administration, US Census Bureau.

US Census Bureau (2013c). *Current population survey, 2013: Annual social and economic supplement*, 1–330. Washington, D.C.: US Census Bureau. Retrieved from https://www.census.gov/prod/techdoc/cps/cpsmar13.pdf

US Department of Health and Human Services, Health Resources and Services Administration. (2003). *Homeless and elderly: Understanding the special health care needs of elderly persons who are homeless*. Retrieved from http://bphc.hrsa.gov/policiesregulations/policies/pdfs/pal200303.pdf

US Department of Housing and Urban Development (HUD). (2011a). *Homeless emergency assistance rapid transition to housing: Emergency solutions grants program interim rule*. Federal Register: Rules and Regulations, Vol. 76, No. 233, December 5, 2011. Retrieved from http://hudhre.info/documents/HEARTH_ESGInterimRule&ConPlanConforming Amendments.pdf

US Department of Housing and Urban Development (HUD). (2011b). *The 2010 annual homeless assessment report to Congress*. Retrieved from https://www.onecpd.info/resources/documents/2010HomelessAssessmentReport.pdf

US Interagency Council on Homelessness. (2010). *Opening doors: Federal strategic plan to prevent and end homelessness*. Retrieved from http://www.usich.gov/resources/uploads/asset_library/Opening%20Doors%202010%20FINAL%20FSP%20Prevent%20End%20Homeless.pdf

Whitfield, K. E., & Baker, T. A. (Eds.). (2014). *Handbook of minority aging*. New York, NY: Springer.

Yeatts, D. E., Crow, T., & Folts, E. (1992). Service use among low-income minority elderly: Strategies for overcoming barriers. *The Gerontologist*, 32, 24–32.

With distressing frequency, the news media carry stories about older adults who have been mistreated, physically abused, neglected, financially exploited, or otherwise victimized. Social workers who work with older adults in hospitals and healthcare settings, home health agencies, mental health and substance abuse agencies, corrections, and multigenerational families in the child welfare system may come across older adults who have been mistreated or neglected by caregivers or other family members. Other older adults, who are able to care for themselves, may live or come into contact with others who mistreat, take advantage of, or exert undue influence over them.

Knowledge of the incidence, prevalence, risk factors for, and evidenced-based interventions to address elder mistreatment lags behind that of other fields. Social workers must develop knowledge to enhance prevention and detection of elder mistreatment and interventions that preserve self-determination and enhance quality of life (US Government Accountability Office [GAO], 2011). This chapter presents definitions, prevalence data, and information on theoretical models and risk factors and outcomes of abuse. Models for assessment and intervention in elder abuse highlight the multi-faceted ways to address the problem. Table 44.1 lists websites that provide reliable information on definitions, research, and intervention strategies.

DEFINITIONS AND INDICATORS OF MISTREATMENT

JOY SWANSON ERNST

Mistreated and Neglected Older Adults

Older adults can be mistreated or neglected at home and in institutions, or they can neglect themselves. Defined broadly, elder abuse is "any form of mistreatment that results in harm or loss to an older person" (National Committee for the Prevention of Elder Abuse, 2008, para 1). It encompasses different subtypes—physical abuse, sexual abuse, emotional or psychological abuse, neglect, abandonment, financial or material exploitation, and self-neglect (see Table 44.2).

Definitions of elder mistreatment must consider issues related to age (there is no universally accepted definition of the point when a person becomes "elder"), health and functional status of victim, gender, whether the abuse occurred in the home or in a facility, and the relationship between the victim and the abuser (Brandl et al., 2006). Some elder abuse is domestic or intimate partner violence (Nerenberg, 2008).

TABLE 44.1 Web Resources

Center of Excellence on Elder Abuse and Neglect	http://www.centeronelderabuse.org/
National Center on Elder Abuse	http://www.ncea.aoa.gov/
Cornell Project on Elder Abuse and Neglect	http://cornellaging.org/elderabuse/
Ageless Alliance	http://www.agelessalliance.org/
National Clearinghouse on Abuse in Later Life	http://www.ncall.us/
National Committee for the Prevention of Elder Abuse	http://www.preventelderabuse.org/
National Adult Protective Services Association	http://www.napsa-now.org/
International Network for the Prevention of Elder Abuse	http://www.inpea.net/

While legal responses to elder mistreatment depend on state laws, the research community has made efforts to develop standardized definitions. The National Research Council defined elder mistreatment as being perpetrated by a person in a "trust relationship" to the older adult, which excludes crimes perpetrated by strangers. The perpetrator is someone with whom the older person has an ongoing, committed partnership, familial, or other type of trust relationship (Bonnie & Wallace, 2003).

This definition excludes self-neglect. However, Adult Protective Services (APS) programs, which respond to reports of the abuse and neglect of vulnerable older adults, deal with more cases of self-neglect than any other type. Self-neglect is generally included when discussing practice with mistreated and neglected older adults. Neglect and self-neglect present unique challenges because they represent the failure to provide care rather than the perpetration of physical and emotional injury (Institute of Medicine [IOM] and National Research Council [NRC], 2013).

Older adults are often mistreated in multiple ways. The term "hybrid financial exploitation" encompasses situations where financial exploitation co-occurs with physical abuse and/or neglect

TABLE 44.2 Types and Definitions of Elder Mistreatment

Type	Definition
Physical abuse	Inflicting, or threatening to inflict, physical pain or injury on a vulnerable elder, or depriving them of a basic need.
Sexual abuse	Nonconsensual sexual contact of any kind, coercing an elder to witness sexual behaviors.
Emotional or psychological abuse	Inflicting mental pain, anguish, or distress on an elder person through verbal or nonverbal acts.
Neglect	Refusal or failure by those responsible to provide food, shelter, healthcare, or protection for a vulnerable elder.
Abandonment	The desertion of an elderly person by an individual who has assumed responsibility for providing care for an elder.
Financial or material exploitation	Illegal taking, misuse, or concealment of funds, property, or assets of a vulnerable elder.
Self-neglect	The behavior of an elderly person that threatens his/her own health or safety. Self-neglect generally manifests itself in an older person as a refusal or failure to provide himself/herself with adequate food, water, clothing, shelter, personal hygiene, medication (when indicated), and safety precautions. Excludes a situation in which a mentally competent older person makes a conscious and voluntary decision to engage in acts that threaten his/her health or safety as a matter of personal choice.

Source: http://www.ncea.aoa.gov/faq/index.aspx

(Jackson & Hafemeister, 2011). The term "polyvictimization" has been introduced as a way to conceptualize and respond to abuse of older adults (Jackson & Mulford, 2013).

EXTENT OF THE PROBLEM

Available data suggests that 1 in 10 older adults in the United States are mistreated or neglected (US Government Accountability Office [US GAO], 2011). A study of community-dwelling older adults found that the past year prevalence of all types of mistreatment studied was 11.4%; the prevalence of potential neglect was 5.1%, financial mistreatment, 5.2%, emotional mistreatment, 4.6%, physical abuse, 1.6%, and sexual abuse, 0.6%. Except for physical abuse, there were no differences in prevalence by race or ethnicity (Acierno et al., 2010).

A study that combined a population-based survey of community-dwelling older adults with a study of elder abuse (excluding self-neglect) reported to community-based agencies in New York State found a wide discrepancy between rates for reported and unreported mistreatment. The total cumulative incidence rate (number of new cases in the past year) of self-reported elder abuse was 76 per 1,000. Major financial exploitation was the most common form of mistreatment (41.1 per 1,000), followed by physical abuse (22.4 per 1,000), neglect (18.2 per 1,000), and psychological/verbal abuse (16.4 per 1,000) (Lifespan of Greater Rochester Inc. et al., 2011). The total cumulative prevalence rate (any elder abuse event at any time since turning age 60) was 141.2 per 1,000. The prevalence rate was nearly 24 times greater than the number of cases referred to social service, law enforcement, or legal authorities that have the responsibility to assist older adult victims. These agencies reported that emotional abuse was the most common form of mistreatment, while financial abuse was most frequently self-reported (Lifespan of Greater Rochester Inc. et al., 2011).

Studies of cases reported to APS or known to service providers for the aging highlight that the service system must also respond to cases of self-neglect. The 2004 survey of state APS, the most recent study available, revealed that in 32 of the 50 states there were 253,426 incidents involving elder abuse (including self-neglect) in 2003. Self-neglect accounted for 26.7% of all reported cases and 37.2% of substantiated cases (Teaster et al., 2006).

Statistics on older adults who are mistreated in long-term care facilities are scarce. Studies that rely on case records, reports of family members, and the observations of nursing assistants show that verbal mistreatment, neglect, and physical abuse by staff towards residents occur at varying rates (Castle, Ferguson-Rome, & Teresi, 2013). In Michigan, 21% of family members of nursing home residents reported at least one incident of neglect during the past 12 months (Zhang et al., 2011). A major concern is resident-to-resident abuse in skilled nursing and assisted living facilities (Castle et al., 2013; Rosen, Pillemer, & Lachs, 2008).

THEORIES OF ELDER MISTREATMENT

A number of theories attempt to explain elder mistreatment (Burnight & Mosqueda, 2011; Castle et al., 2013; Jackson & Hafemeister, 2013). The National Research Council's sociocultural model of mistreatment accounts for victim and perpetrator characteristics, the factors that characterize their interactions including power and control dynamics, and the micro- and macro-level context in which the mistreatment occurs (Bonnie & Wallace, 2003). Burnight and Mosqueda (2011) identified four different theoretical approaches: interpersonal (social exchange, caregiver stress, and dyadic discord theories); intrapersonal (social learning theory); sociocultural (power and control theory); and multisystemic (ecological and sociocultural context theories). The latter category supports the inclusion of victim, perpetrator, dyad, and environmental characteristics. These syntheses draw attention to the difficulty in accounting for different pathways by which elder mistreatment occurs. However, without adequate theory development, knowledge development cannot happen (Jackson & Hafemeister, 2013).

Caregiver stress has been a popular causal explanation for elder abuse, but focus on it has led to intervention strategies that may inadvertently blame the victim or minimize the need for offenders to be accountable (Brandl & Raymond, 2012). However, because research on caregiver characteristics is scarce, further research on the role of caregiver stress in elder abuse is needed (Dong, Chen, Chang, & Simon, 2013). The prospect of older adults aging with disabilities for extended periods, fewer available family members, and the reduction of government support means increased caregiving obligations. For example, older adults and their adult children may have to renegotiate their commitments to each other as circumstances change and competing demands emerge, creating a context where abuse or neglect could occur (Lowenstein, 2010).

Theories that focus on both victims and perpetrators do not account for the occurrence of self-neglect. Self-neglect has been described as a geriatric syndrome because it shares characteristics with common health conditions of older adults such as frailty, pressure ulcers, falls, incontinence, delirium, and declining functional status that have multiple causes and affect quality of life and disability status (Pavlou & Lachs, 2006). One model links self-neglect to executive dysfunction, which results from combinations of the syndromes of aging including cardiovascular disease, dementia, and diabetes (Dyer, Goodwin, Pickens-Pace, Burnett, & Kelly, 2007). Another conceptual model highlights how self-neglect encompasses both physical and psychological aspects of the individual and environmental aspects (Iris, Ridings, & Conrad, 2010).

RISK FACTORS AND OUTCOMES

The older adults at risk for abuse vary depending on the elder's life circumstances, health status, functional abilities, and disability status. However, the characteristics of older adults, considered alone, are insufficient explanations for the occurrence of elder abuse and neglect (Tomita, 2006). Research has identified characteristics of victims, perpetrators, the nature of their relationship, and the immediate social environment as well as the larger social environment that are reliably associated with elder mistreatment and neglect, including self-neglect (Johannesen & LoGiudice, 2013). Taken together, population-based studies, studies conducted with samples from clinics or social service agencies such as APS, and exploratory studies of older adults give social workers information to use when assessing risk for mistreatment.

Characteristics of Mistreated Older Adults

Common victim characteristics include health problems, limitations in functional abilities, cognitive impairment, and depression.

With respect to functional abilities, a study of community-dwelling older adults identified potentially harmful caregiving behavior that mostly consisted of verbal and emotional mistreatment and found that the older adult's higher need for care predicted higher levels of mistreatment by caregivers (Beach et al., 2005). Several studies have found an association between neglect and the older person's ability to perform activities of daily living (ADLs) and instrumental activities of daily living (IADLs) (see, e.g., Fulmer et al., 2005).

Cognitively impaired older adults who verbally abuse or physically assault their caregivers risk being verbally mistreated or physically abused (Paveza et al., 1992; Wiglesworth et al., 2010). Abuse of adults who are not cognitively impaired or care dependent by a spouse or other family member is domestic violence, which requires a different intervention than the mistreatment of adults who are vulnerable due to cognitive impairment (IOM and NRC, 2013).

Mistreated and neglected older adults are often socially isolated, with low social support predictive of every type of mistreatment except financial exploitation in one study (Acierno et al., 2010). Elder mistreatment and self-neglect are risk factors for mortality (Dong et al., 2009), with higher mortality risk associated with those who are more depressed and have lower levels of social engagement and smaller social networks (Dong, Simon, Beck, et al., 2011). The relationship between self-neglect and mortality is stronger for African Americans than for White older adults (Dong, Simon, Fulmer, et al., 2011). Mortality risk is also higher for community-dwelling middle-aged and older women who reported past year physical and verbal abuse than for women who did not reveal abuse (Baker et al., 2009).

Characteristics of Perpetrators

The perpetrator's relationship to the victim, substance abuse, mental health problems, social isolation, and unemployment are associated with elder mistreatment (Bonnie & Wallace, 2003; Nerenberg, 2008). While research has uncovered perpetrator characteristics associated with different types of mistreatment, understanding of the perpetrators' perspective is lacking (Dong et al., 2013).

The majority of perpetrators of elder mistreatment are family members or acquaintances. The percentages of perpetrators who used substances at the time of the most recent incident of mistreatment ranged from 21.4% of the perpetrators of emotional mistreatment to 51.6% of the perpetrators of physical abuse; this incidence of probable substance abuse is higher among perpetrators of mistreatment than substance abuse among the general population (Acierno et al., 2010). Among cases reported to APS in Milwaukee, the perpetrator was most often an adult child, 20.9% had a substance abuse problem, and 14.1% were identified as having a mental illness (Thomson et al., 2011).

A study of family caregivers of older adults with dementia found that neglectful caregivers were more socially isolated and had higher perceived burden then non-neglectful caregivers; those who abused were more likely to report role limitations due to emotional problems (Wiglesworth et al., 2010). Another study of caregiver/care recipient dyads found that the caregiver's impairments in ADLs and physical symptoms were predictive of provision of lower quality care, which could lead to neglect (Beach et al., 2005). In cases reported to APS the perpetrators of physical abuse and "hybrid financial exploitation" were more likely than the perpetrators of caregiver neglect to be "parasitic abusers" who depend on the older adult for financial or other support (Jackson & Hafemeister, 2011).

Perpetrators of abuse in nursing homes are more likely to be other residents than staff members (IOM and NRC, 2013). Teaster, et al. (2004) found that the majority of perpetrators of sexual abuse of 82 adults aged 60 and older were other nursing home residents.

Characteristics of the Social Environment

Societal attitudes that may contribute to mistreatment and neglect of older adults include ageism, sexism, destructive attitudes toward the elderly, and greed (Tomita, 2006). For example, ageism may prevent those in contact with older adults from recognizing sexual abuse (Jones & Powell, 2006).

CULTURAL AND ETHNIC DIFFERENCES

Awareness of factors that influence conceptualizations of elder abuse in different cultural contexts helps the social worker respond more effectively and sensitively (Patterson & Malley-Morrison, 2006).

A study of elderly Korean immigrants used a vignette to determine whether respondents identified financial abuse and whether they would seek help (Lee & Eaton, 2009). While most identified the situation as abusive, American-born Korean Americans were more likely to express willingness to seek help, while Asian-born immigrants were more likely to tolerate or characterize the problem and its resolution as a family matter. In another study, rates of financial and psychological mistreatment were higher for African American than for non–African American older adults (Beach, Schulz, Castle, & Rosen, 2010). These findings are consistent with earlier studies that demonstrate that differences in the definitions of and tolerance for abusive behavior differ among different groups of minority elders in the United States (Tomita, 2006).

The reluctance of older adults who do not want the abuse uncovered for fear of involvement of APS or law enforcement hampers both research and intervention in elder abuse. An example of underreported mistreatment in one ethnic group comes from a study of the prevalence of abuse and neglect among non–cognitively impaired Spanish-speaking Latinos in Los Angeles. The data were collected by *promotores*, or Latino health workers, who are not mandated reporters in California. Findings revealed that 40.4% of the sample of 198 was abused, neglected, or financially exploited, with 22.7% experiencing severe abuse. Two percent reported the abuse to APS (DeLiema, Gassoumis, Homeier, & Wilber, 2012).

STRATEGIES FOR INTERVENTION

Social workers may find that older adults are reluctant to report mistreatment or accept help because they fear losing their independence or the relationship with the abuser. Social workers need the ability to assess risk of abuse in addition to the older person's cognitive ability, decision-making capacity, executive functioning, and ability to carry out ADLs. Strategies for intervention depend on characteristics of the abuse and the older victim.

The response to elder abuse—prevention, identification, and intervention—is constrained by laws, policies, and practices at the federal, state, and local level. The aging, health, and criminal justice systems have established ways to prevent elder abuse and to intervene when it occurs. Since the mid 2010s, efforts to create a wide-ranging response to elder mistreatment that relies on cooperation among different service systems, which have different roles in response, have been initiated (Ernst & Brownell, 2013). A challenge is that interventions to address elder abuse lack solid research that demonstrates their effectiveness (Ploeg, Fear, Hutchison, MacMillan, & Bolan, 2009).

The strategies that have been used to address elder abuse include APS, domestic violence prevention, a public health approach, victim advocacy, and restorative justice (Nerenberg, 2008). The social worker's awareness of these is important, as the philosophy and theoretical orientation behind each strategy differs as well.

The Elder Justice Act (EJA), signed into law in 2010, is the first national law to create mechanisms for federal involvement and funding. The EJA provides support for the Long-Term Care Ombudsman Program, which responds to abuse and neglect in skilled nursing facilities. It authorizes the first federal funding for state and local APS programs and funding for Elder Abuse Forensic Centers. The Act established the Elder Abuse Coordinating Council, representatives from federal agencies who oversee the federal government's response to elder abuse, and an expert Advisory Board on Elder Abuse, Neglect, and Exploitation. To date, no appropriations have been allocated to fund authorized services (National Adult Protective Services Association, 2013).

Prevention and Early Detection Strategies

The programs funded by the Older Americans Act provide primarily preventive services to those age 60 years of age and older through state offices for the aging and county- and regional-based Area Agencies on Aging. These systems address spouse and partner abuse for older adults who are not functionally disabled or cognitively impaired where the abuse has not escalated to the level of a crime through preventive activities such as educational programs, caregiver support groups, and public service announcements to raise community awareness (Ernst & Brownell, 2013).

Programs that train professionals (e.g., doctors, financial institution employees, and the clergy) and community members (e.g., employees of senior centers and doormen) to recognize signs of potential abuse or neglect increase detection and response. The range and type of training available has expanded (Gironda et al., 2010). *The Geriatric Pocket Doc*, designed for social workers, police, and others who have regular contact with older adults, is one example of a tool that includes a guide to common geriatric disorders and medications plus definitions, examples of, and ways to assess for different types of elder abuse (Mosqueda, 2012).

Screening Tools

A number of screening instruments to assess elder mistreatment have been developed to be used in hospitals and other settings and to assess for risk when abuse and neglect are reported to APS (Fulmer, Guadagno, Dyer, & Connolly, 2004). While existing tools have shortcomings, and many require specialized training and time to complete (Anthony, Lehning, Austin, & Peck, 2009), efforts to develop self-report screening tools have shown promise (Conrad, Iris, Ridings, Langley, & Anetzberger, 2010; Conrad, Iris, Ridings, Langley, & Wilber, 2010).

Adult Protective Services

In most states, social workers are legally mandated to report suspected elder mistreatment. Adult Protective Services responds to reports of elder abuse that takes place in community settings in all states and responds to institution-based elder mistreatment in some states (US GAO, 2011). Adult Protective Services uses intervention models such as case management, crisis intervention, and guardianships and other involuntary services including removal to a hospital or skilled nursing facility. Adult Protective Services assumes that victims lack the capacity to care for themselves or protect themselves from harm, whether the harm is coming from their own inability to care for themselves (self-neglect) or from others (abuse or neglect). Most state elder abuse mandatory reporting systems are based on the premise that older adults need protection by the state if they are being harmed by others, are unwilling to accept services, and meet some predetermined criteria for diminished capacity to make informed decisions on their own behalf (Ernst & Brownell, 2013).

Adult Protective Services workers also serve as investigators who are called on to collect evidence that may be used to prosecute perpetrators (Nerenberg, 2008). One barrier in bringing cases to justice is that elderly victims may not want the perpetrator, often an adult child, prosecuted, though they would like the perpetrator to receive help (Jackson & Hafemeister, 2012). Adult Protective Services workers have also expressed concern that in some types of cases, such as neglect, the involvement of law enforcement may do more harm than good.

Criminal Justice and Domestic Violence Service Systems

The interventions provided through the criminal justice system and within the domestic violence service network include law enforcement, prosecution of elder abuse cases, and victims' services programs (Ernst & Brownell, 2013). While relatively rare, there are programs to provide temporary shelter to victims of elder abuse (Reingold, 2006). Older victims of domestic violence face barriers in receiving help from shelters for abused women and other domestic violence services if those agencies do not have the expertise to respond to their age-related needs (Kilbane & Spira, 2010). Nonresidential programs include victim and perpetrator psychoeducational support groups and legal services for the elderly. These service models assume that victims have the capacity to make decisions about the relationship with their abusers.

Collaboration and Multidisciplinary Teams

A variety of team approaches have addressed mistreatment (Twomey et al., 2010), although they have not been systematically evaluated (Dong, Chen, Chang, & Simon, 2013). Elder abuse forensic centers provide multidisciplinary expertise to aid in the resolution of complex cases (Schneider, Mosqueda, Falk, & Huba, 2010). The Family Care Conference model, piloted in several Native American communities, involves a structured family meeting attended by the older person, family members, and involved agencies. The goal of the meeting is to develop a plan that will provide for the protection of the older adult while meeting the needs and desires of the family unit (Holkup, Salois, Tripp-Reimer, & Weinert, 2007).

Legal teams have been established to bring perpetrators to justice. Police officers can work with victim advocates within the domestic violence realm. Fatality review teams can assist in identifying forensic markers for elder mistreatment. Strategies that would promote victim advocacy and supports for local, state, and federal prosecutors in their efforts to detect, investigate, and prosecute elder abuse are also needed (Connolly, 2010).

CONCLUSION

While advocates, practitioners, and researchers have made progress on raising awareness of elder mistreatment, more information about prevalence, risk factors, perpetrator characteristics, and evidenced-based interventions are needed in order to ensure that older adults will be able to live safely and with dignity. With its values of self-determination and social justice, the social work profession is pivotal in responding to the mistreatment and neglect of older adults. Social workers must be open to the possibility of mistreatment, respond sensitively to adults who may have been abused, and advocate for research that will increase knowledge of risk factors and interventions that will address all facets of this problem.

REFERENCES

Acierno, R., Hernandez, M. A., Amstadter, A. B., Resnick, H. S., Steve, K., Muzzy, W., & Kilpatrick, D. G. (2010). Prevalence and correlates of emotional, physical, sexual, and financial abuse and potential neglect in the United States: The National Elder Mistreatment Study. *American Journal of Public Health, 100*, 292–297. doi: 10.2105/AJPH.2009.163089

Anthony, E. K., Lehning, A. J., Austin, M. J., & Peck, M. D. (2009). Assessing elder mistreatment: Instrument development and implications for adult protective services. *Journal of Gerontological Social Work, 52*, 815–836. doi: 915858527 [pii]10.1080/01634370902918597

Baker, M. W., LaCroix, A. Z., Wu, C., Cochrane, B. B., Wallace, R., & Woods, N. F. (2009). Mortality risk associated with physical and verbal abuse in women aged 50 to 79. *Journal of the American Geriatrics Society, 57*, 1799–1809. doi: 10.1111/j.1532-5415/2009.02429.x

Beach, S. R., Schulz, R., Castle, N. G., & Rosen, J. (2010). Financial exploitation and psychological mistreatment among older adults: Differences between African Americans and non-African Americans in a population-based survey. *The Gerontologist, 50,* 744–757. doi: 10.1093/geront/gnq053

Beach, S. R., Schulz, R., Williamson, G. M., Miller, L. S., Weiner, M. F., & Lance, C. E. (2005). Risk factors for potentially harmful informal caregiver behavior. *Journal of the American Geriatrics Society, 53,* 255–261.

Bonnie, R. J., & Wallace, R. B. (Eds.). (2003). *Elder mistreatment: Abuse, neglect, and exploitation in an aging America.* Washington, DC: National Academies Press.

Brandl, B., Dyer, C. B., Heisler, C. J., Otto, J. M., Stiegel, L. A., & Thomas, R. W. (2006). *Elder abuse detection and intervention: A collaborative approach.* New York, NY: Springer.

Brandl, B., & Raymond, J. A. (2012). Policy implications of recognizing that caregiver stress is not the primary cause of elder abuse. *Generations, 36,* 32–39.

Burnight, K., & Mosqueda, L. (2011). *Theoretical model development in elder mistreatment* (2005-IJ-CX-0048). Washington, DC: US Department of Justice.

Castle, N., Ferguson-Rome, J. C., & Teresi, J. A. (2013). Elder abuse in residential long term care: An update to the 2003 National Research Council report. *Journal of Applied Gerontology, 34,* 407–433. doi: 10.1177/0733464813492583

Connolly, M. T. (2010). Where elder abuse and the justice system collide: Police power, *parens patriae*, and 12 recommendations. *Journal of Elder Abuse and Neglect, 22,* 37–93. doi: 10.1080/08946560903436338

Conrad, K. J., Iris, M., Ridings, J. W., Langley, K., & Anetzberger, G. J. (2010). Self-report measure of psychological abuse of older adults. *The Gerontologist, 51,* 354–366. doi: gnq103 [pii] 10.1093/geront/gnq103

Conrad, K. J., Iris, M., Ridings, J. W., Langley, K., & Wilber, K. H. (2010). Self-report measure of financial exploitation of older adults. *The Gerontologist, 50,* 758–773. doi: 10.1093/geront/gnq054

DeLiema, M., Gassoumis, Z. D., Homeier, D. C., & Wilber, K. H. (2012). Determining prevalence and correlates of elder abuse using *promotores*: Low income immigrant Latinos report high rates of abuse and neglect. *Journal of the American Geriatrics Society, 60,* 1333–1339. doi: 1 0.1111/j.1532-5415.2012.04025.x

Dong, X., Chen, R., Chang, E.-S., & Simon, M. (2013). Elder abuse and psychological well-being: A systematic review and implications for research and policy—A mini review. *Gerontology, 59,* 132–142. doi: 10.1159/000341652

Dong, X., Simon, M. A., Beck, T. T., Farran, C., McCann, J. J., Mendes De Leon, C. F., . . . Evans, D. A. (2011).

Elder abuse and mortality: The role of psychological and social well-being. *Gerontology, 57,* 549–558. doi: 10.1159/000321881

Dong, X., Simon, M. A., Fulmer, T., Mendes De Leon, C. F., Hebert, L. E., & Beck, T. (2011). A prospective population-based study of differences in elder self-neglect and mortality between black and white older adults. *Journal of Gerontology: Biological Sciences, 66A,* 695–704.

Dong, X., Simon, M., Mendes De Leon, C., Fulmer, T., Beck, T., Hebert, L., . . . Evans, D. (2009). Elder self-neglect and abuse and mortality risk in a community-dwelling population. *JAMA: Journal of the American Medical Association, 302,* 517–526.

Dyer, C. B., Goodwin, J. S., Pickens-Pace, S., Burnett, J., & Kelly, P. A. (2007). Self-neglect among the elderly: A model based on more than 500 patients seen by a geriatric medical team. *American Journal of Public Health, 97,* 1671–1676.

Ernst, J. S., & Brownell, P. J. (2013). The United States of America. In A. Phelan (Ed.), *International perspectives on elder abuse.* London, UK: Routledge.

Fulmer, T., Guadagno, L., Dyer, C. B., & Connolly, M. T. (2004). Progress in elder abuse screening and assessment instruments. *Journal of the American Geriatrics Society, 52,* 297–304.

Fulmer, T., Paveza, G., VandeWeerd, C., Fairchild, S., Guadagno, L., Bolton-Blatt, M., & Norman, R. (2005). Dyadic vulnerability and risk profiling for elder neglect. *The Gerontologist, 45,* 525–534.

Gironda, M. W., Lefever, K., Delagrammatikas, L., Nerenberg, L., Roth, R., Chen, E. A., & Northington, K. R. (2010). Education and training of mandated reporters: Innovative models, overcoming challenges, and lessons learned. *Journal of Elder Abuse and Neglect, 22,* 340–364. doi: 925751056 [pii] 10.1080/08946566.2010.490188

Holkup, P. A., Salois, E. M., Tripp-Reimer, T., & Weinert, C. (2007). Drawing on wisdom from the past: An elder abuse intervention with tribal communities. *The Gerontologist, 47,* 248–254.

Institute of Medicine (IOM) and National Research Council (NRC). (2013). *Elder abuse and its prevention: Workshop summary.* Washington, DC: National Academies Press.

Iris, M., Ridings, J. W., & Conrad, K. J. (2010). The development of a conceptual model for understanding elder self-neglect. *The Gerontologist, 50,* 303–315. doi: gnp125 [pii] 10.1093/geront/gnp125

Jackson, S. L., & Hafemeister, T. L. (2011). Risk factors associated with elder abuse: The importance of differentiating by type of maltreatment. *Violence and Victims, 26,* 738–757. doi: 10.189/0886-6708.26.6.738

Jackson, S. L., & Hafemeister, T. L. (2012). How do abused elderly persons and their adult protective services caseworkers view law enforcement involvement and criminal prosecution, and what impact do these views have on case processing? *Journal of Elder Abuse and Neglect, 25,* 254–280. doi: 10.1080/08946566.2012 .751843

Jackson, S. L., & Hafemeister, T. L. (2013). *Understanding elder abuse: New directions for developing theories of elder abuse occurring in domestic settings.* Retrieved October 1, 2013, from http://www.ncjrs.gov/pdffiles1/ nij/241731.pdf

Jackson, S. L., & Mulford, C. F. (2013). *The complexity of responding to elder abuse demands the use of multidisciplinary teams.* Retrieved from http:// www.nccdglobal.org/blog/the-complexity-of-responding-to-elder-abuse-demands-the-use-of-multidisciplinary-teams

Johannesen, M., & LoGiudice, D. (2013). Elder abuse: A systematic review of risk factors in community-dwelling elders. *Age and Ageing, 42,* 292–298.

Jones, H., & Powell, J. L. (2006). Old age, vulnerability and sexual violence: Implications for knowledge and practice. *International Nursing Review, 53,* 211–216. doi: 10.1111/j.1466-7657.2006.00457.x

Kilbane, T., & Spira, M. (2010). Domestic violence or elder abuse? Why it matters for older women. *Families in Society, 91,* 165–170. doi: 10.1606/1044-3894.3979

Lee, H. Y., & Eaton, C. K. (2009). Financial abuse in elderly Korean immigrants: Mixed analysis of the role of culture on perception and help-seeking intention. *Journal of Gerontological Social Work, 52,* 463–488. doi: 10.1080/01634370902983138

Lifespan of Greater Rochester, Inc., Weill Cornell Medical College of Cornell University, & New York City Department for the Aging. (2011). Under the radar: New York State elder abuse prevalence study, 1–142. Retrieved from http://www.ocfs.state.ny.us/ main/reports/Under%20the%20Radar%2005%20 12%2011%20final%20report.pdf

Lowenstein, A. (2010). Caregiving and elder abuse and neglect—Developing a new conceptual perspective. *Ageing International, 35,* 215–227. doi: 10.1007/ s12126-010-9068-x

Mosqueda, L. (2012). *Geriatric pocket doc: A resource for non-physicians* (2nd ed.). Irvine, CA: Center of Excellence on Elder Abuse and Neglect, University of California, Irvine.

National Adult Protective Services Association. (2013). *The Elder Justice Act.* Retrieved December 10, 2013, from http://www.napsa-now.org/policy-advocacy/ eja-implementation/

National Committee for the Prevention of Elder Abuse. (2008). *What is elder abuse?* Retrieved October 1, 2013, from http://www.preventelderabuse.org/ elderabuse/

Nerenberg, L. (2008). *Elder abuse prevention: Emerging trends and promising strategies.* New York, NY: Springer.

Patterson, M., & Malley-Morrison, K. (2006). A cognitive-ecological approach to elder abuse in five cultures: Human rights and education. *Educational Gerontology, 32,* 73–82. doi: 10.1080/03601270500338666

Paveza, G. J., Cohen, D., Eisdorfer, C., Freels, S., Semla, T., Ashford, J. W., . . . Levy, P. (1992). Severe family violence and Alzheimer's disease: Prevalence and risk factors. *The Gerontologist, 32,* 493–497.

Pavlou, M. P., & Lachs, M. S. (2006). Could self-neglect in older adults be a geriatric syndrome? *Journal of the American Geriatrics Society, 54,* 831–842. doi: 10.1 111/j.1532-5415.2006.00661.x

Ploeg, J., Fear, J., Hutchison, B., MacMillan, H., & Bolan, G. (2009). A systematic review of interventions for elder abuse. *Journal of Elder Abuse and Neglect, 21,* 187–210. doi: 10.1080/08946560902997181

Reingold, D. A. (2006). An elder abuse shelter program: Build it and they will come, a long term care based program to address elder abuse in the community. *Journal of Gerontological Social Work, 46,* 123–135.

Rosen, T., Pillemer, K., & Lachs, M. (2008). Resident-to-resident aggression in long-term care facilities: An understudied problem. *Aggression and Violent Behavior, 13,* 77–87. doi: 10.1016/j. avb.2007.12.001

Schneider, D. C., Mosqueda, L., Falk, E., & Huba, G. J. (2010). Elder abuse forensic centers. *Journal of Elder Abuse and Neglect, 22,* 255–274. doi: 925746408 [pii] 10.1080/08946566.2010.490137

Teaster, P. B., Dugar, T. A., Mendiondo, M. S., Abner, E. L., Cecil, K. A., & Otto, J. M. (2006). *The 2004 survey of state Adult Protective Services: Abuse of adults 60 years of age and older.* Retrieved August 31, 2007, from http://www.elderabusecenter.org/pdf/2-14-06 FINAL 60+REPORT.pdf

Thomson, M. J., Lietzau, L. K., Doty, M. M., Cieslik, L., Williams, R., & Meurer, L. N. (2011). An analysis of elder abuse rates in Milwaukee County. *Wisconsin Medical Journal, 110,* 271–276.

Tomita, S. (2006). Mistreated and neglected elders. In B. Berkman (Ed.), *Handbook of social work in health and aging* (pp. 219–230). New York, NY: Oxford University Press.

Twomey, M. S., Jackson, G., Li, H., Marino, T., Melchior, L. A., Randolph, J. F., . . . Wysong, J. (2010). The successes and challenges of seven multidisciplinary teams. *Journal of Elder Abuse and Neglect, 22,* 291–305. doi: 10.1080/0896566.2010.490144

US Government Accountability Office (US GAO). (2011). *Elder justice: Stronger federal leadership could enhance national response to elder abuse* (GAO-11-208). Washington, DC: Government Printing Office.

Wiglesworth, A., Mosqueda, L., Mulnard, R., Liao, S., Gibbs, L. M., & Fitzgerald, W. (2010). Screening for abuse and neglect of people with dementia. *Journal of the American Geriatrics Society, 58,* 493–500. doi: 1 0.1111/j.1532-5415.2010.02737.x

Zhang, Z., Schiamberg, L. B., Oehmke, J., Barboza, G. G., Griffore, R. J., Post, L. A., . . . Mastin, T. (2011). Neglect of older adults in Michigan nursing homes. *Journal of Elder Abuse and Neglect, 23,* 58–74. doi: 10.1080/0894 6566.2011.534708

ELIZABETH LIGHTFOOT
PHILIP MCCALLION

Older Adults with Intellectual and Developmental Disabilities

45

BACKGROUND

Developmental disabilities are a diverse group of physical and/or mental impairments that begin anytime up until 22 years of age and are usually lifelong. Developmental disabilities limit a person's capacity to engage in major life activities, such as independent living, mobility, language, learning, working, decision-making, and self-care. In the United States, there is a precise federal definition of a developmental disability (Table 45.1). Common diagnoses that often fall under the definition of developmental disabilities include intellectual disability (Table 45.2), autism, cerebral palsy, hearing impairment, vision impairment, and attention-deficit hyperactivity disorder (ADHD). There are currently about 4 million people in the United States with an intellectual/developmental disability.

The issues surrounding aging with an intellectual/developmental disability have received more attention due to both increased longevity and an increased focus on the rights and quality of life issues of people with disabilities overall. In 1930, the average life span for a person with an intellectual/developmental disability in the United States was only about 20 years (Carter & Jancar, 1983). More recently, people with Down syndrome have an average life expectancy of around 60 years, and for people with other types of intellectual/developmental disabilities it approaches 70 years (Janicki, Dalton, Henderson, & Davidson, 1999). In 2000, there were approximately 641,000 adults with intellectual/developmental disabilities over the age of 60 in the United States (Heller, Janicki, Hammel, & Factor, 2002), and this is expected to double by the year 2030 (Factor, Heller & Janicki, 2012).

In the late 20th century a major paradigm shift commenced in service provisions for people with intellectual/developmental disabilities. Services used to be provided primarily in institutions, with professionals making the primary decisions on where and how a person would live. Now services are more consumer-driven and community-based. Growing numbers of people with intellectual/developmental disabilities are living in the community in their own homes, working in real jobs for real wages, and participating in leisure activities of their choice. *Person-centered planning*, which involves supporting people with intellectual/developmental disabilities to make choices about how they live their lives, has increased self-determination. Although supports for

TABLE 45.1   US Federal Definition of Developmental Disabilities

The Developmental Disabilities Assistance and Bill of Rights Act of 2000 defines a "developmental disability" as a severe, chronic disability of an individual 5 years of age or older that:

1. Is attributable to a mental or physical impairment or combination of mental and physical impairments
2. Is manifested before the individual attains age 22
3. Is likely to continue indefinitely
4. Results in substantial functional limitations in three or more of the following areas of major life activity:
   (i) Self-care
   (ii) Receptive and expressive language
   (iii) Learning
   (iv) Mobility
   (v) Self-direction
   (vi) Capacity for independent living
   (vii) Economic self-sufficiency
5. Reflects the individual's need for a combination and sequence of special, interdisciplinary, or generic services, supports, or other assistance that is of lifelong or extended duration and is individually planned and coordinated.

community living have not developed at the same rate as the desire for community living, they have expanded greatly.

Likewise, roles of social workers and social service organizations have changed dramatically. Social workers previously were primary assessors of needs and decision makers for services and now support individuals with intellectual/developmental disabilities to make their own choices, coordinate or broker services, and assist in advocacy for appropriate services. Disability service providers have moved away from being institution-based service providers and are now more likely to be community support organizations—providing supports to live, work, and interact in the community (Lightfoot, Hewitt, & Sauer, 2004). This trend toward community-based supports and person-centered planning fits with the social work values of self-determination and respect for the dignity of all people (National Association of Social Workers, 2008). Effective social workers need to be knowledgeable about this paradigm shift as well as federal and state laws and policies that protect the rights of people with intellectual/developmental disabilities and fund community-based services (Table 45.3), program options that provide people with intellectual/developmental disabilities with adequate supports, and the organizations that work to enact progressive legislation (Table 45.4).

HEALTH AND HEALTH DISPARITIES

Social workers need to be aware of health concerns associated with aging with intellectual/developmental disabilities. These include not only the normal health trajectory of older people with intellectual/developmental disabilities, but also health disparities they experience accessing healthcare, preventative care, and health promotion. As people with intellectual/developmental disabilities are living much longer, they are now experiencing age-related health conditions similar to other older people. Individuals with intellectual/developmental disabilities also have a greater variety of healthcare needs compared with those of the same age and gender in the general

TABLE 45.2   Language Matters

Intellectual Disability
An intellectual disability is a type of developmental disability that includes limitations in intellectual functioning and adaptive behavior. The terminology in the field of intellectual/developmental disabilities has been continuously changing in an attempt to increase both respect and preciseness. The term "intellectual disability," used internationally, has recently been adopted by many US advocacy, research, and governmental agencies as a more appropriate and respectful synonym for "mental retardation." However, many federal and state programs in the United States are still currently using the older term.
People-First Language
The most important aspect in the use of language is to try to avoid labeling individuals (e.g., "He is blind") or using words with negative connotations (e.g., "stroke victim") or words regarded as slurs (e.g., "handicapped"). In the United States, many people with disabilities advocate using "people-first language." People-first language puts the person before the disability, and it describes what a person *has* or *uses*, not what a person *is* (e.g., "person with an intellectual disability" rather than "mentally retarded person"; "he uses a wheelchair" rather than "he is confined to a wheelchair"; "people with disabilities" rather than "the disabled").

population (US Department of Health and Human Services, 2002):

- Higher rates of chronic conditions such as dementia (vanSchrojenstein, Metsemakers, Haveman, & Crebolder, 2000)
- Different patterns of co-occurring conditions such as mental health concerns as compared with other older adults (McCarron et al., 2013).
- Higher rates of unhealthy lifestyles (McCarron et al., 2013)
- Higher levels of medication use (Haveman et al., 2009).

While there is training for health professionals about working with people with intellectual/developmental disabilities, there is less emphasis on working with older adults with intellectual/developmental disabilities. Thus, many medical professionals are not familiar with their typical health and functioning issues (Haveman et al., 2010; Messinger-Rapport & Rapport, 1997), and these poorly prepared health professionals may miss health problems in persons with intellectual/developmental disabilities (McCarron et al., 2013). In addition, there are often communication barriers to receiving appropriate care (Scheepers et al., 2005). A final barrier is health rationing. Many people with intellectual/developmental disabilities

TABLE 45.3 Major US Federal Disability Laws

Americans with Disabilities Act of 1990 (ADA)
Prohibits discrimination on the basis of disability in employment, state and local government, public accommodations, commercial facilities, transportation, and telecommunications.

Section 504 of the Rehabilitation Act of 1973
Prohibits discrimination on the basis of disability in programs that receive federal funds.

Developmental Disabilities Assistance and Bill of Rights Act
Provides federal funding to developmental disabilities councils, protection and advocacy agencies, and university centers on excellence in developmental disabilities.

The Fair Housing Act Amendments of 1988
Prohibits discrimination in housing on the basis of disability.

The Civil Rights of Institutionalized Persons Act (CRIPA)
Authorizes the US attorney general to investigate conditions of confinement at state and local government institutions, including institutions for people with developmental disabilities.

TABLE 45.4 Organizations Serving Older People with Developmental Disabilities

Administration on Developmental Disabilities
The federal organization responsible for implementation of the Developmental Disabilities Assistance and Bill of Rights Act.
http://www.acf.hhs.gov/programs/add/

American Association on Mental Retardation (AAMR)
Promotes progressive policies, sound research, effective practices, and universal human rights for people with intellectual disabilities.
http://www.aamr.org/

The ARC
A national organization providing information, support, advocacy, and research for people with developmental disabilities and their families, including older people.
www.thearc.org

Canadian Association for Community Living
National Canadian organization for people with intellectual disabilities and their families.
www.cacl.org

Foundation for People with Learning Disabilities (UK)
Provides research, develops projects, and provides information on people with intellectual disabilities (called learning disabilities in the United Kingdom).
http://www.learningdisabilities.org.uk

International Association for the Scientific Study of Intellectual Disabilities
An international scientific organization that promotes worldwide research and exchange of information on intellectual disabilities and has a special interest group on aging.
http://www.iassid.org/

Rehabilitation Research and Training Center on Aging with Developmental Disabilities, University of Illinois at Chicago
Conducts research and provides technical assistance and information on aging with developmental disabilities.
http://www.uic.edu/orgs/rrtcamr/index.html

Self-Advocates Empowering Ourselves
A national organization of self-advocates that provides training, information, and support for individuals and self-advocacy organizations.
http://www.sabeusa.org/

United Cerebral Palsy
A national organization dedicated to improving independence, productivity, and full citizenship of people with cerebral palsy.
http://www.ucp.org/

have been denied access to some forms of medical care, most notably access to organ transplants, because of their disability (National Work Group on Disability and Transplantation, 2004). Social workers need to advocate for access to appropriate healthcare for older people with intellectual/developmental disabilities.

Social workers also have a role advocating for health promotion. People with intellectual/developmental disabilities are still more likely to have sedentary lifestyles and poor nutrition (Braunschweig et al., 2004; Heller et al., 2002), they do not access health promotion to the same extent as peers without disabilities, and health promotion programs seldom target people with intellectual/developmental disabilities (McCarron et al., 2013). Health promotion activities can help avoid Type 2 diabetes, osteoporosis, and coronary heart disease (Perkins & Moran, 2010; Heller, Hsieh, & Rimmer, 2004). In addition, involvement in volunteering can help improve health and mental health outcomes for older people (Lum & Lightfoot, 2005).

THE CHALLENGE OF ALZHEIMER'S DISEASE AND OTHER DEMENTIAS

Older age in people with intellectual/developmental disabilities may also mean exposure to Alzheimer's disease and other dementias. This is particularly true for older people with Down syndrome, who are uniquely at risk of developing Alzheimer's dementia at earlier ages. Current estimates are that 15%–40% of persons with Down syndrome over the age of 35 years present with symptoms of dementia and their related declines are precipitous. Onset is also earlier, with the mean age of dementia in persons with Down syndrome being estimated at 51.3 years (McCarron et al., 2013).

Responses to Alzheimer's disease for people with intellectual/developmental disability have tended to be reactive rather than proactive, with unanswered questions regarding how resources and skills may best be pooled and what service models/developments need to be undertaken and by whom (Bigby, McCallion, & McCarron, in press; McCallion et al., 2012). A question remains as to what care setting is most useful in responding to dementia in terms of both cost-effectiveness and quality of life outcomes. Differences in philosophies, terminologies, fiscal arrangements, and priorities complicate these issues (Bigby et al., in press; McCallion & Kolomer, 2003; Wilkinson, Janicki, & Edinburgh Working Group on Dementia Care Practices (EWGDCP), 2002). Even less is known about the impact and needed

supports for family caregivers (McCallion, Nickle, & McCarron, 2005). There is a need for evidence-based models for care if resolution is to be realized, institutionalization and reinstitutionalization avoided, quality of life maintained, and costs contained (McCallion et al., 2011).

The inevitable decline associated with dementia challenges the intellectual/developmental disabilities programming philosophy largely focused on supporting and promoting the independence of persons who are in jobs and interested and ready for community participation (McCallion et al., 2011). Also, funding assumptions of fixed needs are challenged by new needs, for example, 24-hour staffing where overnight staff were not previously needed, frequent hospitalizations and emergency room use as symptoms of both dementia and comorbidities increase, and environmental management challenges such as falls, wandering, and safety concerns occur (Bigby et al., in press). Responses to these new challenges are too rarely planned and are often unprepared for end-stage disease even when maintaining a person in place is intended (Janicki et al., 2002; McCallion et al., 2005). Service redesign for dementia continues to be needed at individual, staff, residential/programming unit, and organizational levels (McCallion & McCarron, 2004; McCallion et al., 2011).

RESIDENTIAL OPTIONS

Community-based living arrangements have expanded rapidly. The US Supreme Court solidified this trend toward community-based residential options with its *Olmstead* decision, which guaranteed the rights of individuals with disabilities to live in the community or in the most integrated setting feasible (*Olmstead et al. v. L.C. et al.*, 1999). Most community-based living options are in the form of small group homes or shared homes and apartments with staff providing flexible supports. However, the formal system of residential living options for older people with disabilities is currently well beyond capacity (NCD, 2011). The number of older individuals on waiting lists is growing. A greater emphasis on caregiver supports, proactive environmental modifications to support aging in place, embedding knowledge about intellectual/developmental disabilities in general population healthcare and social services systems, and strategies to bridge general population and intellectual/developmental disability service systems may reduce the need for such placements (Bigby et al., in press).

Despite the growth in residential options, the most common living arrangement for adults with intellectual/developmental disabilities is living with family members. It is estimated that in the United States about 72% of adults with intellectual/developmental disabilities live with their families, and about 25% of the family caregivers are over age 60 (Braddock et al., 2013; Fujiura, 2012). For these adults, the types of residential supports available include respite care, personal care assistance, and in-home healthcare. However, the needs for these services are much greater than their availability, and the waiting lists for these community-based supports are long. As states continue to redesign services to be responsive to the *Olmstead* decision and as the Centers for Medicare and Medicaid Services (CMS) Balancing Incentive Payments Program and Medicaid Waivers reshape long-term services and supports away from residential to genuinely community-based options, there are growing opportunities for people to live, spend their days, work, and participate in their community (Bigby et al., in press; Perez, 2012). These legislative and regulatory changes provide significant advocacy opportunities for social workers.

For those older people already in formal care, aging in place requires early detection, clinical supports to help staff provide appropriate care, program adaptations that fit an individual's changing functional level, and environmental adaptations such as ramps or alarm systems (Janicki, McCallion, & Dalton, 2002). Despite many advocates' preference for the aging in place model, many group homes do not have the training, finances, or other resources available to offer this option. It remains to be seen how the public policy forces of *Olmstead* and the CMS advance the reality of aging in place. Again social workers have an opportunity to ensure that they have such an effect.

COMMUNITY PARTICIPATION AND RETIREMENT

Adults with intellectual/developmental disabilities are becoming increasingly involved in their communities, including working and participating in leisure activities. As people age, they vary on how they wish to continue community involvement, whether through continued work, retirement, or volunteer activities. Retirement is still uncommon for older persons with intellectual/developmental disabilities. As many are still not working at jobs with competitive wages, retirement may signify a shift in activities that allows increased leisure time, rather than finishing their careers and receiving retirement benefits (Heller, 1999).

Many older people with intellectual/developmental disabilities simply continue to work past the typical retirement age (Sutton, Sterns, & Schwartz-Park, 1993) or stay in their current day activity programs (McGlinchey, McCallion, Burke, Carrol, & McCarron, 2012). Often, they like the structure of their current programs (Mahon & Mactavish, 2000) and worry that changing to a new activity or program would result in the loss of friends and/or income (Bigby et al., 2011; Judge, Walley, Anderson, & Young, 2010). However, older persons and their families may not be aware that retirement options exist that allow for continued engagement. For example, some of the larger intellectual/developmental disability support providers provide retirement options, such as supported volunteering or recreational opportunities. There are also attempts to encourage existing senior programs, such as senior centers or senior parks and recreation programs, to be more inclusive, such as through mentoring programs (Chng, Stancliffe, Wilson, & Anderson, 2012). However, new retirement options are still limited and altogether unavailable in many areas.

FAMILY CAREGIVING

Family caregiving has always been and continues to be the most prevalent care of adults with intellectual/developmental disabilities, and many of those caregivers are themselves aging (Braddock et al., 2013; Fujiura, 2012). Over 70% of individuals with intellectual and developmental disabilities live with their families (Fujiura, 2012), at least 20% live with siblings (Bigby et al., in press), and many more receive supports from siblings regardless of where they live (Zendell, 2011).

Changing Family Roles

Siblings have always played a role in the care of their family members with intellectual disability (McCallion & Toseland, 1993). Burke et al. (2012) report that female siblings in close relationships with or living close to their brother or sister are more likely to assume higher levels of caregiving when parents are no longer able. However, Zendell (2011) in a national survey sample found a much fuller range of caregiving roles for siblings regardless of gender (Zendell, 2010).

In addition, there are changing gender roles among parents. Traditionally, women were the primary caregivers for persons with intellectual/developmental disabilities— fathers worked to support the family, while mothers stayed at home. In the aging years there were reports that these patterns continued, with fathers unlikely to take on additional responsibilities (Essex, Seltzer, & Krauss, 1999). These gender patterns are now changing. An important concern for social workers, therefore, is not to stereotype families and fathers, as there is evidence that fathers feel isolated and judged by assumptions that caregiving is a mother's role (McCallion & Kolomer, 2003; Fujiura, 2012).

Culturally Competent Caregiver Support

While persons of all cultures have intellectual/developmental disabilities, families of some cultural groups are less likely to receive services from public disabilities agencies (McCallion & Grant-Griffin, 2000). Mainstream disabilities agencies have been found to poorly accommodate the needs of diverse families (McCallion & Grant-Griffin, 2000). Social workers must recognize and harness the strengths offered by locally based multicultural agencies, and be open to family structures and ways of caring that are different from their own and recognize that different values and structures may mean that different services are necessary (McCallion & Grant-Griffin, 2000).

Aging Competent Caregiver Services

To date, care of aging persons with intellectual/developmental disabilities and supports for their caregivers have remained largely within the purview of disabilities service providers. National Family Caregiver programs, funded by the Administration on Aging/Administration on Community Living have included such family caregivers as a targeted population for Area Agencies on Aging. Social workers must continue to play key roles in addressing

identified cross-agency barriers. New solutions and genuine integration will require sustained advocacy by social workers and others.

Transition Challenges

When persons with intellectual/developmental disabilities were not expected to live into old age there was a reasonable expectation that parents would outlive their offspring and offer a lifetime of care. Instead aging parents now increasingly cope with their own health problems and eventual death (Heller & Factor, 2008). Conversely, there has been a long-standing concern that social workers and other professionals do not recognize the caregiving strength of family members even as they cope with their own diminishing health (McCallion & Toseland, 1993). Further, workers may view the mutual emotional and financial support they often encounter as not in the best interest of the individual with intellectual/developmental disabilities (McCallion & Kolomer, 2003). A priority for social workers is to assist families to have formal arrangements in place for the adult when his or her parent becomes incapacitated and/or dies.

Long-Term Planning for Adults with Intellectual/Developmental Disabilities

Parents are often averse to creating detailed future care plans for their adult children with intellectual/developmental disabilities (Bigby et al., in press; Heller & Factor, 1991). Stress, concerns for safety, and anxiety all contribute to reluctance to make concrete plans including speaking of future living arrangements with other family members (McCallion & Kolomer, 2003). There are four types of long-term plans: explicit succession plans transferring the responsibilities of overseeing care of the adult with intellectual/developmental disabilities to an appointed person; implicit succession plans; financial plans; and residential plans.

The issue of planning for guardianship is also important. While family member or state guardianship used to be the norm for people with intellectual/developmental disabilities, it is now used more specifically to protect individual rights. For example, an individual may need either a full, partial, or temporary guardian, such as for help in managing finances or need for medical care. Planning for guardianship is often discussed in the context of future health-care planning. An individual with an intellectual/developmental disability who cannot express an understanding of a complicated medical issue cannot demonstrate consent. This necessitates some arrangement of surrogate medical decision-making, depending on an individual's ability to understand and make complicated medical choices. Although guardianship can help protect individuals with intellectual/developmental disabilities, such as in allowing them to access medical care, it also limits self-determination. Other complicated issues that individuals and parents might want to plan for include advance directives, such as a living will.

A key role for social workers going forward will be in helping families to understand that the future may not be about movement to an out-of-home setting. Instead they will need help to explore maintenance in their existing home; accessing of services for both the individual with a intellectual/developmental disability and themselves; involvement of other family members, neighbors, and friends through "circles of support" (O'Brien & O'Brien, 1998); and the purchasing of services from a range of providers (Bigby et al., in press; Hewitt et al., 2010).

END OF LIFE AND GRIEF

Hospice and palliative care for adults with intellectual/developmental disabilities have come to the fore only in recent years. However, there are concerns regarding the lack of knowledge of how to effectively communicate with a dying person with an intellectual/developmental disability and of appropriate bereavement supports for caregivers (Ng & Li, 2003). The lack of experience of service providers means that aggressive approaches to care may be overly prolonged (McCallion & McCarron, 2004), and the limited experiences of caring for persons with intellectual/developmental disabilities among palliative and hospice staff may equally hamper provision of services (Ryan & McQuillan, 2005).

Social workers may play an important role in bridging the disability and hospice/palliative care service systems and in determining and advocating for choices of the person and in supporting their family, other persons with intellectual/developmental disabilities they live with, and other caregivers before and after the death. There is a need to recognize the unique strengths of disability staff in providing supports to people with intellectual/developmental disabilities, and of the staff in hospice and palliative care for their expertise in symptom management, despite lack of knowledge of the unique communication and other needs of people with disabilities. Social workers can potentially assist in reevaluating the skill mix among staff in disability care settings as more persons present with chronic and terminal illness.

There is long-standing belief both that persons with an intellectual/developmental disability do not experience the range of emotions of others including feelings of grief and, conversely, that they will not be able to "manage" the associated feelings (Yanok & Beifus, 1993). These beliefs are often used by family and staff to justify not informing persons with an intellectual/developmental disability of the death of parents and for not involving them in funerals and other mourning rituals (Todd, 2004). Not having experienced death and mourning means that many persons with intellectual/developmental disabilities might poorly understand death and not be prepared for their own deaths. There is evidence that persons with intellectual/developmental disabilities do indeed understand the finality of death and feel personal loss and grief. However, being shielded from funerals, and even the announcement of death, may mean that people with intellectual/developmental disabilities do not have opportunities to express their grief. While symptoms of normal grief typically occur within 1 month of the bereavement and do not exceed 6 months' duration, for persons with intellectual/developmental disabilities later onset and longer duration of grief symptoms are more likely (McCallion et al., 2012). Social workers may play critical roles both in ensuring involvement of people with intellectual/developmental disabilities in death rituals for persons they feel connected to and consideration in advance of the care the individual would like when they themselves approach death, as well as offering education on the unique presentation of grief among people with intellectual/developmental disabilities and in advocacy for the support of staff, families, and peers when a death occurs.

RIGHTS AND ADVOCACY

The push for rights for people with intellectual/developmental disabilities has come from national advocacy groups, such as the National Association for Retarded Citizens (ARC); self-advocacy groups, such as People First; and many individuals and relatives of people with intellectual/developmental disabilities. While the social work profession was not historically in the forefront of the disability rights movement (Mackelprang & Salsgiver, 1996), many social work professionals are now involved in supporting systems-level changes.

Of particular importance for older people with intellectual/developmental disabilities is the worldwide self-advocacy movement, a movement *of* mostly younger people with intellectual/developmental disabilities. Participation in self-advocacy has generally not been encouraged among older adults in this population, though self-advocacy organizations are beginning to look more closely into issues of aging (Levitz, 1999). As individuals' degree of community inclusion and self-determination is linked with their ability to advocate for what they want and need (Herr & Weber, 1999), social workers should encourage older people with intellectual/developmental disabilities to become or continue to be involved in self-advocacy.

NEW DIRECTIONS FOR SOCIAL WORK PRACTICE

Social workers who embrace the paradigm shift that has occurred in the field of intellectual/developmental disabilities will find themselves well situated to support older persons with intellectual/developmental disabilities to

- Live quality lives,
- Have more control of their lives,
- Participate in the community,
- Receive appropriate healthcare,
- Access appropriate assistive technology, and
- Cope with grief and loss associated with aging.

Social workers also have an important role in assisting older people with intellectual/developmental disabilities and their family members to plan together regarding the future. Finally, social workers can be involved in building coallitions among providers for more effective services and in advocating for civil rights, adequate funding, and a more consumer-directed, community-based service system. Social work researchers can help design and evaluate new models for providing services and

supports to older people with intellectual/developmental disabilities in the 21st century. This will be particularly important, as the next cohort of older people will have grown up with more involvement in the community, and retirement and community residential options will be more in demand. The values and skills of social workers are ideal for supporting the new paradigm of service provision and supports for older people with intellectual/developmental disabilities.

REFERENCES

Bigby, C., McCallion, P., & McCarron, M. (in press). Serving an elderly population. In M. Agran, F. Brown, C. Hughes, C. Quirk, & D. Ryndak (Eds.), *21st century issues for individuals with severe disabilities: Ensuring quality services and supports in challenging times*. Baltimore, MD: Brookes.

Bigby, C., Wilson, N., Balandin, S., & Stancliffe, R. (2011). Disconnected expectations: Staff, family and supported employee perspectives about retirement. *Journal of Intellectual and Developmental Disability, 36*, 167–174. doi:10.3109/13668250.2011.598852.

Braddock, D., Hemp, R., Rizzolo, M. C., Tanis, E. S., Haffer, L., Lulinski, A., & Wu, J. (2013). *State of the states in developmental disabilities, 2013*. Washington, DC: American Association on Intellectual and Developmental Disabilities.

Braunschweig, C., Gomez, S., Sheean, P., Tomey, K., Rimmer, J., & Heller, T. (2004). Nutritional status and risk factors for chronic disease in urban-dwelling adults with Down syndrome. *American Journal on Mental Retardation, 109*, 186–193. doi:10.1352/0895-8 017(2004)109<186:NSARFF>2.0.CO;2.

Burke, M. M., Taylor, J. L., Urbano, R., & Hodapp, R. M. (2012). Predictors of future caregiving by adult siblings of individuals with intellectual and developmental disabilities. *American Journal of Intellectual and Developmental Disabilities, 117*, 33–47. doi:10.1352/1944-7558-117.1.33.

Carter, G., & Jancar, J. (1983). Mortality in the mentally handicapped: A fifty year survey at State Park Group Hospitals (1930–1980). *Journal of Mental Deficiency Research, 27*, 143–156.

Chng, J., Stancliffe, R., Wilson, N., & Anderson, K. (2012). Engagement in retirement: An evaluation of the effect of active mentoring on engagement of older adults with intellectually disability in mainstream community groups. *Journal of Intellectual Disability Research, 57*, 1130–1142, doi:10.1111/j.1365-2788.2012.01625.x

Essex, E. L., Seltzer, M. M., & Krauss, M. W. (1999). Differences in coping effectiveness and well being among aging mothers and fathers of adults with mental retardation. *American Journal on Mental Retardation, 104,* 545–563. doi.org/10.1352/0895-8017 (1999)104≤0545:DICEAW≥2.0.CO;2

Factor, A., Heller, T., & Janicki, M. (2012). *Bridging the aging and developmental disabilities services networks: challenges and best practices* Chicago, IL: Institute on Disability and Human Development, University of Illinois at Chicago.

Fujiura, G. T. (2012). *Structure of intellectual disability and developmental disabilities households in the United States.* Presentation at AAIDD Annual Meeting, Charlotte, NC.

Haveman, M., Heller, T., Lee, L., Maaskant, M., Shooshtari, S., & Strydom, A. (2010). Major health risks in aging persons with intellectual disabilities: An overview of recent studies. *Journal of Policy and Practice in Intellectual Disabilities, 7,* 59–69. doi. org/10.1111/j.1741-1130.2010.00248.x

Heller, T. (1999). Emerging models. In S. S. Herr & G. Weber (Eds.), Aging, rights and quality of life: Prospects for older people with developmental disabilities. Baltimore, MD: Brookes.

Heller, T., & Factor, A. (1991). Permanency planning for adults with mental retardation living with family caregivers. *American Journal on Mental Retardation, 96,* 163–176.

Heller, T., & Factor, A. (2008). Family support and intergenerational caregiving: Report for the State of the Science in Aging with Developmental Disabilities Conference. *Disability and Health Journal, 1,* 131–135.

Heller, T., Hsieh, K., & Rimmer, J. (2004). Attitudinal and psychological outcomes of a fitness and health education program on adults with Down syndrome. *American Journal on Mental Retardation, 109,* 175–185.

Heller, T., Janicki, M., Hammel, J., & Factor, A. (2002). *Promoting healthy aging, family support and age-friendly communities for persons aging with developmental disabilities: Report of the 2001 Invitational Research Symposium on Aging with Developmental Disabilities.* Chicago, IL: Rehabilitation Research and Training Center on Aging with Developmental Disabilities, Department of Disability and Human Development, University of Illinois at Chicago.

Herr, S. S., & Weber, G. (1999). Prospects for ensuring rights, quality supports and a good old age. In S. S. Herr & G. Weber (Eds.), *Aging, rights and quality of life: Prospects for older people with developmental disabilities* (pp. 343–370). Baltimore, MD: Brookes.

Hewitt, A., Lightfoot, E., Bogenschutz, M., McCormack, K., Sedlezky, L., & Doljanic, R. (2010). Parental caregivers' desires for lifetime assistance planning for future supports for their children with intellectual and developmental disabilities. *Journal of Family Social Work, 13,* 420–434. doi:10.1080/105 22158.2010.514678.

Janicki, M., Dalton, A., Henderson, C., & Davidson, P. (1999). Mortality and morbidity among older adults with intellectual disability: Health services considerations. *Disability and Rehabilitation, 21,* 284–294.

Janicki, M., McCallion, P., & Dalton, A. (2002). Dementia-related care decision-making in group homes for persons with intellectual disabilities. *Journal of Gerontological Social Work, 38,* 179–195. doi:10.1300/J083v38n01_04

Judge, J., Walley, R., Anderson, B., & Young, R. (2010). Activity, aging, and retirement: The views of a group of Scottish people with intellectual disabilities. *Journal of Policy and Practice in Intellectual Disabilities, 7,* 295–301. doi:10.1111/j.1741-1130.2010.00279.x

Levitz, M. (1999). Self-advocacy for a good life in our older years. In S. S. Herr & G. Weber (Eds.), *Aging, rights and quality of life: Prospects for older people with developmental disabilities* (pp. 279–287). Baltimore, MD: Brookes.

Lightfoot, E., Hewitt, A., & Sauer, J. (2004). Organizational change and restructuring to provide consumer directed supports. In S. Larson & A. Hewitt (Eds.), *Effective recruitment, retention and training: Strategies for human services organizations.* Baltimore, MD: Brookes.

Lum, T., & Lightfoot, E. (2005). The effects of volunteering on the physical and mental health of older people. *Research on Aging, 27,* 31–55, doi:10.1177/0164027504271349

Mackelprang, R., & Salsgiver, R. (1996). People with disabilities and social work: Historical and contemporary issues. *Social Work, 41,* 7–14.

Mahon, M., & Mactavish, J. (2000). A sense of belonging: Older adults' perspectives on social integration. In M. Janicki & E. Ansello (Eds.), *Community supports for aging adults with lifelong disabilities* (pp. 41–53). Baltimore, MD: Brookes,

McCallion, P., & Grant-Griffin, L. (2000). Redesigning services to meet the needs of multi-cultural families. In M. P. Janicki, & E. Ansello, (Eds.), *Aging and developmental disabilities* (pp. 97–108). Baltimore, MD: Brookes.

McCallion, P., & Kolomer, S. R. (2003). Aging persons with developmental disabilities and their aging caregivers. In B. Berkman & L Harootyan (Eds.), *Social work and health care in an aging world* (pp. 201–225). New York, NY: Springer.

McCallion, P., & McCarron, M. (2004) Aging and intellectual disabilities: A review of recent literature. *Current Opinion in Psychiatry*, *17*, 349–352. doi. org/10.1097/01.yco.0000139968.14695.95

McCallion, P., McCarron, M., Fahey-McCarthy, E., & Connaire, K. (2012). Meeting the end of life needs of older adults with intellectual disabilities. In E. Chang & A Johnson (Eds.), *Contemporary and innovative practice in palliative care*. Rijeka, Croatia: Intech.

McCallion, P., Nickle, T., & McCarron, M. (2005). A comparison of reports of caregiver burden between foster family care providers and staff caregivers of persons in other settings. *Dementia*, *4*, 401–412.

McCallion, P., & Toseland, R. W. (1993). An empowered model for social work services to families of adolescents and adults with developmental disabilities. *Families in Society*, *74*, 579–589.

McCarron, M., Swinburne, J., Burke, E., McGlinchey, E., Carroll, R., & McCallion, P. (2013). Patterns of multimorbidity in an older population of persons with an intellectual disability: Results from the intellectual disability supplement to the Irish Longitudinal Study on Ageing (IDS-TILDA). *Research in Developmental Disabilities*, *34*, 521–527. doi.org/10.1016/j.ridd. 2012.07.029

McGlinchey, E., McCallion, P., Burke, E., Carrol, R., & McCarron, M. (2013). Examining the area of employment in older adults with an intellectual disability in Ireland. *Journal of Applied Research in Intellectual Disabilities*, *26*, 335–343.

Messinger-Rapport, B., & Rapport, D. (1997). Primary care for the developmentally disabled adult. *Journal of General Internal Medicine*, *12*, 629–636. 10.1046/j.1 525-1497.1997.07123.x

National Association of Social Workers. (2008). *Code of ethics of the National Association of Social Workers*. Retrieved from https://www.socialworkers.org/ pubs/code/code.asp

National Council on Disability. (2011). *Rising expectations: The Developmental Disabilities Act revisited*. Washington, DC: Author. www.ncd.gov/policy/ long_term_services

National Work Group on Disability and Transplantation. (2004). *Summary report of individual and family disability survey*. Washington, DC: National Work Group on Disability and Transplantation, American Association on Mental Retardation.

Ng, J., & Li, S. (2003). A survey exploring the educational needs of care practitioners in learning disability settings in relation to death, dying and people with learning disabilities. *European Journal of Cancer Care*, *12*, 12–19.

O'Brien, J., & O'Brien, C. L. (1998). *A little book about person centered planning*. Toronto, Canada: Inclusion Press.

Olmstead et al. v. L.C. et al., 527 U.S. 581 (1999).

Perez, T. E. (2012). *Testimony: The thirteenth anniversary of the* Olmstead *decision*. US Senate Committee on Health, Education, Labor and Pensions. Washington, DC: US Senate.

Perkins, E. A., & Moran, J. A. (2010). Aging adults with intellectual disabilities. *Journal of the American Medical Association*, *304*, 91–92. doi:10.1001/ jama.2010.906

Ryan, K., & McQuillan, R. (2005). Palliative care for disadvantaged groups: People with intellectual disabilities. *Progress in Palliative Care*, *13*, 70–74. doi. org/10.1179/096992605X42431

Scheepers, M., Kerr, M., O'Hara, D., Bainbridge, D., Cooper, S., Davis, R., . . . Wehmeyer, M. (2005). Reducing health disparity in intellectual disabilities: A report from the Health Issues Special Interest Research Group of the International Association for the Scientific Study of Intellectual Disabilities. *Journal of Policy and Practice in Intellectual Disabilities*, *2*, 249–255, doi:10.1111/ j.1741-1130.2005.00037.x

Sutton, E., Sterns, A., & Schwartz-Park, L. (1993). Realities of retirement and preretirement planning. In E. Sutton, A. Factor, B. Hawkins, T. Heller, & G. Geltzer (Eds.), *Older adults with developmental disabilities: Optimizing choice and change* (pp. 95–106). Baltimore, MD: Brookes.

Todd, S. (2007). Silenced grief: Living with the death of a child with intellectual disabilities. *Journal of Intellectual Disability Research*, *51*, 637–648. doi. org/10.1111/j.1365-2788.2007.00949.x

US Department of Health and Human Services. (2002) *Health centers: America's primary care safety net reflections on success, 2002–2007*. US Department of Health and Human Services. Health Resources and Services Administration, Bureau of Primary Health Care USA.

Wilkinson, H., Janicki, M. P., & Edinburgh Working Group on Dementia Care Practices (EWGDCP). (2002). The Edinburgh principles with accompanying guidelines and recommendations. *Journal of Intellectual Disabilities Research*, *46*, 279–284.

vanSchrojenstein L. D. V. H. M., Metsemakers, J. F., Haveman, M. J., & Crebolder, H. F. (2000). Health problems in people with intellectual disability in general practice: A comparative study. *Family Practice, 17,* 405–407.

Yanok, J., & Beifus, J. A. (1993). Communicating about loss and mourning: Death education for individuals with mental retardation. *Mental Retardation, 31,* 144–147.

Zendell, A. (2010). *Decision-making among siblings of adults with intellectual or developmental disabilities.* Unpublished dissertation. Albany, NY: University at Albany.

LETHA A. CHADIHA
PHILIP A. ROZARIO
MARIA P. ARANDA
ANDREA S. FIELDING

SECTION **IV**

Older Adults from Diverse Cultures

OVERVIEW

Gerontologists and demographers agree that population aging is a global phenomenon, which Burnette and Sun's chapter (Chapter 53) underscores, particularly in non-Western nations. While population aging will yield "prospects, challenges, and directions for action" for all nations, Burnette and Sun caution that we have to pay special attention to older adults living in developing nations. Due to reasons they carefully delineate in their chapter, these nations may be challenged especially in their capacity to provide, balance, and prioritize resources necessary to meet the health and functional needs of a rapidly expanding population of older adults.

Together, the chapters in this section, which focus on the intersections of racial/ethnic, religious, geographic, and/or sexual diversity with health and aging, share a common theme—all recognize an increasingly diverse older adult population particularly in the United States. Even though these chapters individually deal with a particular identity group, the respective authors of each chapter remind us that these groups are heterogeneous and, as such, members may face different levels of challenges and opportunities depending on their intersectionality. Indeed, Min and Moon's chapter highlights the diversity of Asian Americans along key demographic indicators as well as their national origins, immigration status, and English-language proficiency (Chapter 47). Patterns of variations and heterogeneity are also evident among older Black; Latino; Native American; lesbian, gay, bisexual, and transgender (LGBT); Jewish; Muslim; immigrant; and refugee elders discussed in this section.

A second theme that emerges from the disparate groups of older adults is the health disparities faced by members of these groups. In her chapter on older Latino Americans (Chapter 48), Aranda calls attention to the disparity between the elevated rates of depression among this group in comparison with the general older population and their low mental health service utilization rates. Additionally, Richardson and Browne's chapter points to the significance of acculturation in the level of depression and isolation faced by Muslim Americans (Chapter 50). Moon and Hoang (Chapter 52) pinpoint acculturation as well as isolation from extended family and low mental health service use as risk factors contributing to poor mental health among more recent waves of immigrant and refugee elders. In particular, elders immigrating

as refugees, as Moon and Hoang emphasize, face the risk of poor mental health due to extensive trauma in their country of origin or en route to the United States.

The lifecourse perspective, though not always explicitly articulated by various contributors to this section, remains an important framework to understand the opportunities and constraints faced by older adults from underrepresented groups. A key principle is the recognition of the interconnectedness of lives across generations (Bengtson, Elder, & Norella, 2005). For instance, Chadiha, Rozario, Aranda, and Fielding (Chapter 46) report that current generations of older Blacks are similar to prior generations of older Blacks as regards informal social support and the care they receive from the kinship system in addition to the role of the church and religion as a source of psychological support. The principle of linked lives is further emphasized in Richardson and Browne's review of older adults in the Appalachian regions. These older adults are separated from their younger kin because of economic out-migration and are unable to receive the necessary instrumental supports in the absence of these kinfolk (Chapter 50). Older American Indians similarly experience this geographical isolation because their adult children have left the community in pursuit of a better life elsewhere (see Chapter 49, "American Indians/Alaska Native Elders," by Tovar, Patterson, and Lewis). In contrast to older adults living in the United States, a western nation, older adults living in non-Western or developing nations, according to Burnette and Sun (Chapter 53), tend to live in multigenerational households or near their children—a fact suggesting these older adults may live in an environment that fosters interconnectedness or linked lives across generations.

Regarding the usefulness of the lifecourse perspective as a framework to understand the challenges facing older LGBT people in terms of coming out and hiding their true identities as strategies of survival, Butler and Zodikoff reinforce the principle that recognizes the influence of social and historical context in shaping individual lives (Chapter 51). Similarly Tovar et al. (Chapter 49) point to the intergenerational impact of the legacy of governmental genocidal efforts to eradicate native language and cultural practices among American Indians.

A number of strides have been made in the availability of empirical literature on minority aging since the publication of the first edition of the

Handbook. For example, contributors to this edition, as well as contributors to the section "Social Work and Minority Aging" of the *Handbook of Minority Aging* (Rozario & Chadiha, 2014), were able to cite many more empirical sources that included nationally and regionally representative research studies to better understand the health and mental health disparities experienced by members of these underrepresented groups. Still, a dearth of empirical literature remains in some specific areas. For example, Aranda reports that there were only seven published empirical articles of depression treatment outcomes for older adults by racial/ethnic groups between 1990 and 2010. Similarly, Tovar et al.'s chapter on American Indians and Butler and Zodikoff's chapter on LGBT elders underscore the dearth of nationally representative research on health disparities among these seriously underrepresented groups.

Altogether the chapters in this section further underscore the notion that population diversity should not result in disparities faced by underrepresented groups (see Min and Moon's chapter). To that end, contributors to this section underline the importance of social workers embracing culturally competent practice in their work with these underrepresented groups. Despite this repeated call for cultural competency, Chadiha and her colleagues highlight the unavailability of accurate measures in social work to effectively measure cultural competency. To that end, Garroutte, Sarkinian, and Karamnov's (2012) research might provide social work researchers with some tools for such inquiry. In their study of older American Indians' health service use, Garroutte et al. (2012) underscore the importance of expressing empathy and building rapport while demonstrating respect in situations of high discordance between provider and clients. Additionally, they advocate the need to diversify the professional and paraprofessional workforce in health, mental health, and community-based agencies serving these groups.

We recognize the difficulty facing social work practitioners in knowing everything about a particular historically underrepresented group. Indeed, such a recipe-approach to cultural competence is unrealistic and impossible to achieve because, as previously mentioned, these groups are not monoliths. To be effectively culturally competent, social workers have to be open to both self-reflection and challenge their beliefs and assumptions. Indeed, it is also important that social workers recognize the resiliency and strengths that members from these groups have exhibited in the face of oppressive structures. Finally, social workers have to be comfortable in admitting that they hold internalized stereotypes that stem from racist, anti-Semitic, Islamophobic, classist, homophobic, heterosexist, and transphobic ideologies while being open to nonoppressive ideas.

REFERENCES

Bengtson, V. L., Elder, G. H., Jr., & Norella, M.P. (2005). The lifecourse perspective on ageing: Linked lives, timing, and history. In M. L. Johnson (Ed.), *The Cambridge Handbook of Age and Ageing* (pp. 493–501). Cambridge, UK: Cambridge University Press.

Garroutte, E. M., Sarkisian, N., & Karamnov, S. (2012). Active interactions in medical visits: Ethnic differences among American Indian older adults. *Journal of Aging and Health*, *24*, 1224–1251. doi: 10.1177/0898264312457410

Rozario, P. A., & Chadiha, L. A. (2014). Introduction: Social work and minority aging. In K. E. Whitfield & T. A. Baker (Eds.), *Handbook of minority aging* (pp. 257–263). New York, NY: Springer.

The Black older population, comprising native-born African Americans and Black immigrants primarily from the Caribbean Islands, forms the largest group of elders of color in the United States. In this chapter, we address the growth and heterogeneity of the Black population aged 65 and older; social, demographic, and economic characteristics; health characteristics; informal sources of support; and informal caregiving. We end with implications for social work practice and research with this population.

Throughout this chapter, we follow the revised Standards for the Classification of Federal Data on Race and Ethnicity set forth by the Office of Management and Budget (1997) in referencing racial and ethnic groups. We use the terms "Black" and "African American," race categories, interchangeably in referencing native Blacks and nonnative Blacks (e.g., Caribbean immigrants) of African descent. When reporting comparative data on ethnicity, we use the terms "Hispanic" or "Latino," ethnic categories, in reference to persons who self-report their race as "White" or "Black" or "African American," whereas the term "non-Hispanic" refers to persons who do not self-report as "Hispanic" or "Latino."

GROWTH AND HETEROGENEITY OF THE BLACK OLDER ADULT POPULATION

Ethnic or racial minorities constituted 21% of the population in 2011; almost half of that percentage (9% vs. 12% for all other groups) identified as Black (US Department of Health and Human Services [DHHS], 2012), and this percentage is expected to grow to 11% by 2050 (Administration on Aging [AOA], 2010). Data in Figure 46.1 shows past, present, and projected growth of the Black older adult population between 1980 and 2050.

Growth of the Black older adult population is attributed mainly to the rising longevity of native-born Blacks rather than to immigration (Gerst-Emerson & Burr, 2014). This population is diverse in national origins and cultural backgrounds (Kent, 2007). Toward the end of the 20th century, new Black immigrants made up 17% of the growth in the US Black population, and from the early to middle of the 21st century they are expected to contribute to 20% of the growth in this population (Kent, 2007), portending a diverse landscape of Black older adults.

LETHA A. CHADIHA
PHILIP A. ROZARIO
MARÍA P. ARANDA
ANDREA S. FIELDING

Older African Americans and Other Black Populations

46

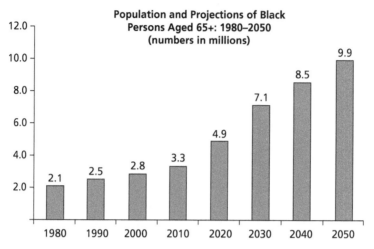

FIGURE 46.1 Population and Projections of Black Persons Aged 65+: 1980–2050.
Source: AOA (2010).

Sex Ratio

Females outnumber males in old age because of women's lower mortality risk across the life span (Howden & Meyer, 2011); however, this gap has narrowed slightly since the early-2000s. Among Black older adults in 2000, the sex ratio was 70 males per 100 females 65–74 years old (Angel & Hogan, 2004); this increased to 74 males in 2011 (Gerst-Emerson & Burr, 2014). Scholars have explained the imbalanced sex ratio for Blacks as due partly to a higher male mortality rate in the early years of life (Gerst-Emerson & Burr, 2014).

Educational and Poverty Levels

Over time, levels of education and income have risen and poverty levels have declined within the Black older adult population. In 2008, more than 60% of Blacks aged 65 and older had a high school education; in 1970 that figure was only 9% (AOA, 2010). Similarly, an increasing number of Black older adults had completed 4 years of college or more by 2008 (AOA, 2010). Roughly half (48%) of the Black older adult population aged 65 and older lived in poverty in 1968; 40 years later, in 2008, the figure was down to 20% (AOA, 2010), but this rate was more than twice that for older adults overall (9.7%).

Following national trends, older minority women are more likely to live in households falling below the poverty line, with a poverty rate of 10.7% in 2011

compared with 6.2% for older minority men (DHHS, 2012). Women living alone in later life are highly susceptible to impoverishment; Black and Hispanic older women living alone experience the highest poverty rates, 38.8% and 32.2% respectively (DHHS, 2012).

Marital Status and Living Arrangements

Using data from the 2006–2010 American Community Survey, Gerst-Emerson and Burr (2014) found that the prevalence of being married was lowest (34.4%) and living alone was highest (32.9%) among Black older adults compared with older adults of other racial and ethnic groups. Gerst-Emerson and Burr explain that the observed variations in marital status and living arrangement across racial and ethnic groups are "due in part to variation in life expectancy, availability of kin (especially adult children), socioeconomic resources, and cultural norms" (p. 394).

HEALTH CHARACTERISTICS

Health includes physical, mental, and social well-being (Johnson & Misra, 2001). Non-Hispanic Blacks and Hispanics, age 65 and older, are less likely to report good to excellent health status (63% respectively) than their non-Hispanic White peers (78%) (Federal Interagency Forum on Aging-Related Statistics [FIFA], 2012). Lucas,

Barr-Anderson, and Kington (2003) report that after adjusting for age and socioeconomic status, non-native-born Black men were less likely to report fair or poor health and functional limitations than native-born Black men. Further, the health status of non-native-born Black men was more similar to, or even better than, that of native-born White men.

Life Expectancy

Despite significant increases in life expectancy in the United States, Blacks (75.1 years at birth) still lag behind non-Hispanic Whites (78.8 years at birth) (Population Reference Bureau, 2013). Gender and race shape life expectancy: Women outlive men, and Whites outlive Blacks (National Center for Health Statistics, 2013). An important exception to this pattern is the "Black-White mortality crossover" among the oldest old, whereby the Black mortality curve crosses over the White mortality curve in later life. This phenomenon remains controversial; however, it may be that adaptation and selection processes predispose Blacks to longer lives (Hummer, Benjamins, & Rogers, 2004).

Chronic Health Conditions, Risk Factors, Morbidity, and Mortality

Chronic health conditions among persons age 65 years and older vary by race and ethnicity. For instance, non-Hispanic Whites age 65 and older are more likely to report heart disease and arthritis than non-Hispanic Blacks or Hispanics age 65 and older; non-Hispanic Blacks and Hispanics age 65 and older are more likely to report diabetes and hypertension than non-Hispanic Whites age 65 and older; and non-Hispanic Blacks age 65 and older are more likely to report stroke than either non-Hispanic Whites or Hispanics age 65 and older (FIFA, 2012).

Risk factors of heart disease and stroke, such as hypertension, obesity, and high cholesterol, also differ by racial group. The Behavioral Risk Factor Surveillance System survey shows that older Blacks are more likely than Whites to report two or more of these risk factors, with the greatest risk among those with less than a high school diploma (Centers for Disease Control and Prevention [CDC], 2005). People of low socioeconomic status (SES) are also

more likely to have chronic diseases and to be affected by these diseases at an earlier age (Crimmins, Hayward, & Seeman, 2004). Drawing on work by House and colleagues, D. R. Williams and Wilson (2001) note a curvilinear relationship between SES and health that is "small in early adulthood, increases markedly in middle and early old age, and decreases in late old age" (p. 165). D. R. Williams and Wilson contend that racial disparities in access and quality of medical care for Black older adults play a critical role in the continuing racial disparity in health, a contention corroborated by Schneider, Zaslavsky, and Epstein's (2002) research that indicates the existence of racial disparities in the quality of healthcare received by Medicare enrollees.

Regarding mortality and chronic health conditions, Black older adults are more likely than Whites to die from heart disease and stroke, particularly among those between 65 and 84 years of age (Rooks & Whitfield, 2004). Death rates due to cancer are highest among Black men and women (US Cancer Statistics Working Group, 2013). Prostate cancer strikes disproportionate numbers of older African American men, and more of them die than men of any other racial/ethnic group (Pierce, Chadiha, Vargas, & Mosley, 2003). Despite lower breast cancer incidence rates overall, for every 100 breast cancers diagnosed, Black women had nine more deaths than White women, 27 deaths versus 18 deaths respectively (CDC, 2012).

Physical Functioning and Disability

With increasing age and chronic conditions, people may experience disability associated with a decline in functional limitations in activities of daily living (ADLs, such as bathing and grooming) and instrumental activities of daily living (IADLs, such as shopping and preparing meals). Disability rates for both older males and females have declined in the United States (FIFA, 2012); yet Black-White differences continue throughout the life span (Nuru-Jeter, Thorpe, & Fuller-Thomson, 2011). Among women age 65 and over, more non-Hispanic Black women (33.4%) and Hispanic (33.6%) women than non-Hispanic White women (28.6%) were unable to perform any one of five physical functions: stooping/kneeling, reaching over the head, writing/grasping small objects, walking 2–3 blocks, and lifting 10 pounds (FIFA, 2012).

Cognitive Health

Evidence suggests that fewer years in school and a poorer quality education can be risks for developing the most prevalent form of late-life dementia, Alzheimer's disease (AD) (Mehta et al., 2009). Whether Blacks have higher rates of dementia and cognitive impairment than other racial or ethnic groups remains equivocal (Potter et al., 2009), but any differences found could be related to low education and socioeconomic status, vascular disease, cultural differences, lifestyle, and genetic factors (Tang et al., 1998).

Mental Health and Subjective Well-Being

A study using data from the National Survey of American Life (NSAL) reported 8.5% of Blacks 55 and older met criteria for a 12-month disorder. Alcohol abuse, PTSD, and major depression were the most prevalent conditions, but prevalence declined with age (Ford et al., 2007). In race comparative analysis based on NSAL data, older non-Hispanic Whites and Latinos had significantly greater odds of meeting criteria for a mood or an anxiety disorder than Blacks (Jimenez, Alegría, Chen, Chan, & Laderman, 2010; Woodward et al., 2012); older African Americans have lower rates of major depressive disorder (MDD) and dysthymia than older non-Hispanic Whites and Black Caribbeans (Woodward et al., 2012). Having an MDD has been shown to be associated with other psychiatric disorders and high overall mental illness severity among older African Americans and Black Caribbeans; older Black Caribbean men had particularly high rates of MDD (Woodward, Taylor, Abelson, & Matusko, 2013). Aranda et al. (2012) speculate the lower prevalence of MDD among African Americans may indicate differential symptom expression; protective factors such as religion and family support; displacement of distress into physical symptoms and disorders; and protective psychological resources.

Another study using data from the NSAL reports lifetime prevalence of suicidal ideation and attempts among older Blacks age 55 and older are 6.1% and 2.1%, respectively (Joe, Ford, Taylor, & Chatters, 2013). Older Black men reported attempting suicide and seriously considering taking their own lives more often than older Black women. A more recent study examined subjective well-being among African Americans age 55 and older in the NSAL with at least one psychiatric disorder: Almost one-third of them reported being very satisfied with their lives, while an equal portion indicated that they were very happy overall (Peterson, Chatters, Taylor, & Nguyen, 2014). This study's findings suggest older African Americans experiencing poor mental health also may report positive subjective well-being.

INFORMAL SOCIAL SUPPORT

Social support, defined as "a process of interaction or exchange between individuals and significant others" (Lincoln, 2014, p. 26), underscores the importance of social relationships. Early studies indicated that Black older adults received social support from kin and nonkin and engaged in social relationships involving exchanges of emotional and instrumental support (Barker, Morrow, & Mitteness, 1998; Chatters, Taylor, & Neighbors, 1989). Later studies using a race comparative approach have not been totally consensual. For example, Silverstein and Waite (1993) reported no significant differences between races in instrumental support, although there were gender differences, with older Black women more likely than older White women to receive instrumental support than emotional support but similar to older White women in providing instrumental support.

Citing studies from the 1980s up to the early 2000s, Taylor, Hernandez, Nicklett, Taylor, and Chatters (2014) concluded that Black older adults received assistance from kin, particularly their adult children, and nonkin, and few Black older adults were socially isolated or lacked a social support network. Woodward, Chatters, Taylor, Neighbors, and Jackson (2010) found that when Black older adults aged 55 years and older faced a serious problem, they were more likely to turn to informal network members for help than to professional providers. Lincoln, Taylor, and Chatters (2003) reported that Black older adults aged 55 and older exchanged emotional support with kin and friends and reported fewer negative social interactions.

Religion and the church community are sources of inspiration and assistance to Black Americans, providing invaluable psychological resources in the form of informal support from church members (Taylor, Chatters, & Levin, 2004). Religious and spiritual coping also serve as a resource for Black older adults, helping them manage stressful life events and life problems (Chatters, Taylor, Jackson, & Lincoln, 2008). Religious coping has its downsides, such as potentially promoting avoidance and acceptance rather than a proactive or problem-solving approach (Taylor et al., 2004). A heavier reliance on informal systems of social support may place older Blacks at risk of poor health outcomes (S. W. Williams & Dilworth-Anderson, 2002). Acknowledging these contradictions does not negate the overwhelming evidence that the church and religion have a significant positive impact on the lives of elderly Blacks.

CAREGIVING

According to a national survey of caregivers in the United States from 2009, Black caregivers are predominantly female, tend to be younger, and are more likely to be single or never married than their White counterparts (National Alliance for Caregiving [NAC] & AARP, 2009a). Black caregivers report significantly lower household incomes than White caregivers (61% of Black caregivers reporting less than $50,000 versus 35% of White caregivers), even though they are just as likely as White caregivers to be employed full-time (NAC & AARP, 2009b).

Literature reviews have concluded that minority elders are more likely than White elders to receive informal care from family and friends (Dilworth-Anderson, Williams, & Gibson, 2002; Pinquart & Sörensen, 2005). Black caregivers are less likely than White caregivers to have the help of other caregivers (NAC & AARP, 2009a), whether paid (29% vs. 43%) or unpaid (58% vs. 72%); and 57% of Black caregivers report they are the primary caregiver for their care recipient (NAC & AARP, 2009b). Scharlach and colleagues (2006) found many Black focus group participants felt they had to provide for all their care recipient's needs regardless of the extent of those needs or their own circumstances.

In their meta-analysis of research on minority caregivers, Pinquart and Sörensen (2005) found that Black care recipients were more physically and cognitively impaired than their White counterparts. Dilworth-Anderson and colleagues (2002) report that DHHS data indicate that the prevalence of severe functional limitations is higher for all minority elders, including Black Americans, than for White elders. Although older Blacks have the highest rate of disability and chronic illnesses, regardless of their health status, they are less likely than older Whites

to live in an institutional setting or alone (Dilworth-Anderson et al., 2002; Gelman, Tompkins, & Ihara, 2014), suggesting greater care challenges for their caregivers.

Challenges Facing African American Caregivers: Contextual Considerations

Researchers and practitioners alike agree that caregiving can be stressful, although individual caregivers will respond differently to these challenges. Much of the research on caregiving has relied on the stress process model, which posits that stressors emerging from the conditions of caregiving and caregivers' responses to those conditions influence their well-being (Pinquart & Sörensen, 2005). The availability of internal and external resources including the caregiver's coping strategies and quality of social supports may help explain differences in caregiving experiences and outcomes (Gelman et al., 2014).

Recognizing that racial and ethnic differences are layered on the ethnic minority caregiver's access to and availability of resources, researchers have argued that when exploring the experiences and outcomes for Black caregivers, contextual differences need to be considered (Aranda & Knight, 1997; Dilworth-Anderson & Anderson, 1994). Different contexts may provide caregivers with strengths and vulnerabilities that could impact their caregiving experiences (Gelman et al., 2014). For example, Aranda and Knight (1997) argue that ethnic minorities face greater risks for certain diseases and disability at a younger age, suggesting minority caregivers may have to deal with their own failing health while providing care to someone else. Dilworth-Anderson and colleagues (1999) posit the sociocultural context of caregiving may influence caregivers' beliefs about their obligations to their older relatives. Although aging in place among minority older adults is jeopardized by the social and economic strains they face, Herrera, George, Angel, Markides, and Torres-Gil (2013) found that the ability to live independently did not predict the use of services funded by the Older Americans Act for Black older adults and their caregivers, but having more education was a predictor. Ecological contexts, such as geographic location, might further explain differences in experience and outcomes for Black family caregivers. For instance, Chadiha, Feld, and Rafferty (2011) found that in comparison with their rural counterparts, a significantly larger proportion of urban Black caregivers reported reliance on secondary caregivers.

The symptoms of cognitive impairment can further complicate the caregiving experience and negatively impact outcomes. Sink and colleagues (as cited in Gelman et al., 2014) found that Black older adults with AD are more likely than their White counterparts to present with problems difficult for caregivers, such as wandering and combativeness.

Caregiver Health and Mental Health Outcomes

In a national survey, about 20% of Black caregivers reported fair to poor health in comparison with 13% of the general adult population (NAC & AARP, 2009a, 2009b), while significantly fewer Black caregivers reported that caregiving made their health worse compared with their White counterparts (NAC & AARP, 2009b). In their meta-analyses, Pinquart and Sörensen (2005) found that, compared with non-Hispanic White caregivers, Black caregivers reported lower levels of burden and depression despite often elevated levels of stressors. The researchers attributed these differences to intrinsic motivation to provide care, greater informal support, and cognitive coping strategies that facilitated finding personal and spiritual meaning in the caregiving experience. Haley and colleagues (2004) found White caregivers of older adults with AD were more bothered by their caregiving experience, while Black caregivers were more positive.

Dilworth-Anderson and colleagues (2002) found that Black caregivers were either less depressed than or not significantly different from their White counterparts; spirituality and religiosity were linked to lower levels of depression and burden in the caregiving role. In a study by Haley and colleagues (2004), Black caregivers of older adults with AD reported greater religiosity than their White counterparts. Rozario and DeRienzis (2008) found that more traditional beliefs about caregiving were related to more depressive symptoms.

IMPLICATIONS FOR SOCIAL WORK

The growth and heterogeneity of the Black population, due to immigration, geographic location, and socioeconomic differences, has necessitated the recognition "of barriers that prevent access to our social systems and building a broader community infrastructure" (Yee, 2002, p. 6). The challenge for social work professionals is the delivery of culturally appropriate and inclusive services to older adults (Capitman, 2002), including hiring more professional and paraprofessional staff from the community and training all staff to be culturally competent. Unfortunately, neither the field of aging nor social work has developed an accurate measure that would allow social work professionals to assess the effectiveness of culturally competent social work practice (Geron, 2002).

To address the health and well-being of Black older adults, we refer professionals to Ford and Hatchett's (2002) three levels of intervention: promoting the social, economic, and health-related well-being of Black older adults; increasing social workers' knowledge of help-seeking barriers (e.g., stigma, gaps in healthcare); and mitigating the effects of chronic disease and disability on older Black adults and their families. These researchers also consider case management to be essential, such as linking Black older adults to appropriate community resources and advocating for them.

Professionals need to be aware of the importance of informal social support for Black older adults, and assess the natural system's capacity to support their needs. They should be informed of the social inequalities and racial disparities that can add further risks and challenges to family caregivers. Chadiha, Adams, Biegel, Auslander, and Gutierrez (2004) suggest that social workers adopt the empowerment approach in their work with these caregivers.

Research that focuses on experiences of Black older adults and their caregivers is needed. Studies of older adults' caregivers have tended to focus on non-Hispanic Whites or make comparisons between them and Black caregivers (Gelman et al., 2014). While it is necessary to focus on the similarities and differences between race and ethnic groups (Pinquart & Sörensen, 2005), it is also important to identify and explain the sources of within-group heterogeneity; often cross-comparison research fails to capture the diversity within an ethnic group (Rozario & DeRienzis, 2008). Dilworth-Anderson and colleagues (2002) stress the importance of cultural relevancy in regard to cultural frameworks and theoretical perspectives.

Finally, unprecedented numbers of older Black Americans are living longer. Social work and other healthcare professionals face challenges and opportunities to deliver culturally appropriate services to ensure their well-being and health. Indeed Haley and colleagues (2004) argue that if culturally competent interventions are effective, professionals will be more likely to employ them. Caregiver support services and policies that address the needs of Black caregivers and their care recipients are especially important and should be expanded (Gelman et al., 2014).

ACKNOWLEDGMENTS

We thank Jennifer Hopson, Danyelle Okesanjo, and Phyllis Kreger Stillman for assistance with this chapter.

REFERENCES

Administration on Aging (AOA). (2010). *A statistical profile of Black older Americans aged 65+*. Retrieved from http://www.aoa.gov/

Angel, J. L., & Hogan, D. P. (2004). Population aging and diversity in a new era. In K. Whitfield (Ed.), *Closing the gap: Improving the health of minority elders in the new millennium* (pp. 1–12). Washington, DC: Gerontological Society of America.

Aranda, M. P., Chae, D. H., Lincoln, K. D., Taylor, R. J., Woodward, A. T., & Chatters, L. M. (2012). Demographic correlates of DSM-IV major depressive disorder among older African Americans, Black Caribbeans, and non-Hispanic Whites: Results from the National Survey of American Life. *International Journal of Geriatric Psychiatry, 27*, 940–947. doi:10.1002/gps.2805

Aranda, M. P., & Knight, B. G. (1997). The influence of ethnicity and culture on the caregiver stress and coping process: A sociocultural review and analysis. *The Gerontologist, 37*, 342–354. doi:10.1093/geront/37.3.342

Barker, J. C., Morrow, J., & Mitteness, L. S. (1998). Gender, informal social support networks, and elderly urban African Americans. *Journal of Aging Studies, 12*, 199–222. doi:10.1016/S0890-4065(98)90015-9

Capitman, J. (2002). Defining diversity: A primer and a review. *Generations, 26*(3), 8–14. Retrieved from http://asaging.org/publications

Centers for Disease Control and Prevention (CDC). (2005). Racial/ethnic and socioeconomic disparities in multiple risk factors for heart disease and stroke—United States, 2003. *Morbidity and Mortality Weekly Report, 54*, 113–117. Retrieved from http://www.cdc.gov/mmwr

Centers for Disease Control and Prevention (CDC). (2012). Vital signs: Racial disparities in breast cancer severity—United States, 2005–2009. *Morbidity and Mortality Weekly Report, 61*, 922–926. Retrieved from http://www.cdc.gov/mmwr

Chadiha, L. A., Adams, P., Biegel, D. E., Auslander, W., & Gutierrez, L. (2004). Empowering African American women informal caregivers: A literature synthesis and practice strategies. *Social Work, 49*, 97–108. doi:10.1093/sw/49.1.97

Chadiha, L. A., Feld, S., & Rafferty, J. (2011). Likelihood of African American primary caregivers and care recipients receiving assistance from secondary caregivers: A rural-urban comparison. *Journal of Applied Gerontology, 30*, 422–442. doi:10.1177/0733464810371099

Chatters, L. M., Taylor, R. J., Jackson, J. S., & Lincoln, K. D. (2008). Religious coping among African Americans, Caribbean Blacks and Non-Hispanic Whites. *Journal of Community Psychology, 36*, 371–386. doi:10.1002/jcop.20202

Chatters, L. M., Taylor, R. J., & Neighbors, H. W. (1989). Size of informal helper network mobilized during a serious personal problem among Black Americans. *Journal of Marriage and Family, 51*, 667–676. doi:10.2307/352166

Crimmins, E. M., Hayward, M. D., & Seeman, T. E. (2004). Race/ethnicity, socioeconomic status, and health. In N. Anderson, R. Bulatao, & B. Cohen (Eds.), *Critical perspectives on racial and ethnic differences in health in late life* (pp. 310–352). Washington, DC: National Academies Press.

Dilworth-Anderson, P., & Anderson, N. B. (1994). Dementia caregiving in Blacks: A contextual approach to research. In E. Light, G. Nierderche, & B. D. Lebowitz (Eds.), *Stress effects on family caregivers of Alzheimer's patients: Research and interventions* (pp. 385–409). New York, NY: Springer.

Dilworth-Anderson, P., Wallace Williams, S., & Cooper, T. (1999). The contexts of experiencing emotional distress among family caregivers to elderly African Americans. *Family Relations, 48*, 391–396. Retrieved from http://dx.doi.org/10.2307/585246

Dilworth-Anderson, P., Williams, I. C., & Gibson, B. E. (2002). Issues of race, ethnicity, and culture in caregiving research: A 20-year review (1980–2000). *The Gerontologist, 42*, 237–272. doi:10.1093/geront/42.2.237

Federal Interagency Forum on Aging-Related Statistics (FIFA). (2012). *Older Americans 2012: Key indicators of well-being*. Washington, DC: US Government

Printing Office. Retrieved from http://www.aging-stats.gov/Main_Site/Data/2012_Documents/docs/EntireChartbook.pdf

Ford, B. C., Bullard, K. M., Taylor, R. J., Toler, A. K., Neighbors, H. W., & Jackson, J. S. (2007). Lifetime and 12-month prevalence of Diagnostic and Statistical Manual of Mental Disorders, Fourth Edition disorders among older African Americans: Findings from the National Survey of American Life. *American Journal of Geriatric Psychiatry*, 15, 652–659. doi:10.1097/JGP.0b013e3180437d9e

Ford, M. E., & Hatchett, B. (2002). Gerontological social work with older African American adults. *Journal of Gerontological Social Work*, 36, 141–155. doi:10.1300/J083v36n03_11

Gelman, C. R., Tompkins, C. J., & Ihara, E. S. (2014). The complexities of caregiving for minority older adults: Rewards and challenges. In K. E. Whitfield & T. A. Baker (Eds.), *Handbook of minority aging* (pp. 313–328). New York, NY: Springer.

Geron, S. M. (2002). Cultural competency: How is it measured? Does it make a difference? *Generations*, 26, 39–45. Retrieved from http://asaging.org/generations-journal-american-society-aging

Gerst-Emerson, K., & Burr, J. A. (2014). The demography of minority aging. In K. E. Whitfield & T. A. Baker (Eds.), *Handbook of minority aging* (pp. 387–404). New York, NY: Springer.

Haley, W. E., Gitlin, L. N., Wisniewski, S. R., Feeney Mahoney, D., Coon, D. W., Winter, L. . . . Ory, M. (2004). Well-being, appraisal, and coping in African-American and Caucasian dementia caregivers: Findings from the REACH study. *Aging and Mental Health*, 8, 316–329. doi:10.1080/13607860410001728998

Herrera, A. P., George, R., Angel, J. L., Markides, K., & Torres-Gil, F. (2013). Variation in Older Americans Act caregiver service use, unmet hours of care, and independence among Hispanics, African Americans, and Whites. *Home Health Services Quarterly*, 32, 35–56. doi:10.1080/01621424.2012.755143

Howden, L. M., & Meyer, J. A. (2011). *Age and sex composition: 2010.* Retrieved from http://www.census.gov/prod/cen2010/briefs/c2010br-03.pdf

Hummer, R. A., Benjamins, M. R., & Rogers, R. G. (2004). Racial and ethnic disparities in health and mortality among the U.S. elderly population. In N. B. Anderson & B. Cohen (Eds.), *Critical perspectives on racial and ethnic differences in health in late life* (pp. 53–94). Washington, DC: National Academies Press.

Jimenez, D. E., Alegría, M., Chen, C. N., Chan, D., & Laderman, M. (2010). Prevalence of psychiatric illnesses in older ethnic minority adults. *Journal of American Geriatrics Society*, 58, 256–264. doi:10.1111/j.1532-5415.2009.02685.x

Joe, S., Ford, B. C., Taylor, R. J., & Chatters, L. M. (2013). Prevalence of suicide ideation and attempts among Black Americans in later life. *Transcultural Psychiatry*, 51, 190–208. doi:10.1177/1363461513503381

Johnson, C. D., & Misra, D. (2001). Mental health. In D. Misra (Ed.), *The women's health data book: A profile of women's health in the United States* (3rd ed., pp. 104–115). Menlo Park, CA: Jacobs Institute of Women's Health and the Henry J. Kaiser Family Foundation.

Kent, M. M. (2007). Immigration and America's black population. *Population Bulletin*, 62(4), 1–16. Retrieved from: htpp://www.prb.org/pdf07/62.4immigration.pdf

Lincoln, K. D. (2014). Social relationships and health among minority older adults. In K. E. Whitfield & T. A. Baker (Eds.), *Handbook of minority aging* (pp. 25–46). New York, NY: Springer.

Lincoln, K. D., Taylor, R. J., & Chatters, L. M. (2003). Correlates of emotional support and negative interaction among older Black Americans. *Journals of Gerontology, Series B: Psychological Sciences and Social Sciences*, 58, S225–S233. doi:10.1093/geronb/58.4.S225

Lucas, J. W., Barr-Anderson, D. J., & Kington, R. S. (2003). Health status, health insurance, and health care utilization patterns of immigrant Black men. *American Journal of Public Health*, 93, 1740–1747. doi:10.2105/AJPH.93.10.1740

Mehta, K. M., Stewart, A. L., Langa, K. M., Yaffe, K., Moody-Ayers, S., Williams, B. A., & Covinsky, K. E. (2009). "Below average" self-assessed school performance and Alzheimer's Disease in the Aging, Demographics and Memory Study. *Alzheimer's and Dementia*, 5, 380–387. doi:10.1016/j.jalz.2009.07.039

National Alliance for Caregiving (NAC) & AARP. (2009a). *Caregiving in the US 2009.* Bethesda, MD: Authors. Retrieved from http://www.caregiving.org/pdf/research/Caregiving_in_the_US_2009_full_report.pdf

National Alliance for Caregiving (NAC) & AARP. (2009b). *Caregiving in the US: A focused look at the ethnicity of those caring for someone age 50 or older* [Executive Summary]. Bethesda, MD: Authors. Retrieved from http://www.caregiving.org/pdf/research/FINAL_EthnicExSum_formatted_w_toc.pdf

National Center for Health Statistics. (2013). *Health, United States, 2012: With special feature on emergency care.* Hyattsville, MD: National Center for Health Statistics.

Nuru-Jeter, A. M., Thorpe, R. J., Jr., & Fuller-Thomson, E. (2011). Black-White differences in self-reported disability outcomes in the U.S.: Early childhood to older adulthood. *Public Health Reports, 126*, 834–843. Retrieved from http://www.publichealthreports.org/issueopen.cfm?articleID=2750

Office of Management and Budget. (1997). Revisions to the standards for the classification of federal date on race and ethnicity. *Federal Register, 62*(210), 1–9. Washington, D.C.: OMB Publications Office. Retrieved from http://www.Whitehouse.gov/omb/fedreg_1997standards

Peterson, T., Chatters, L. M., Taylor, R. J., & Nguyen, A. (2014). Subjective well-being of older African Americans with DSM IV psychiatric disorders. *Journal of Happiness Studies, 15*, 1179–1196. doi:10.1007/s10902-013-9470-7

Pierce, R., Chadiha, L. A., Vargas, A., & Mosley, M. (2003). Prostate cancer and psychosocial concerns in African American men: Literature synthesis and recommendations. *Health and Social Work, 28*, 302–311. doi:10.1093/hsw/28.4.302

Pinquart, M., & Sörensen, S. (2005). Ethnic differences in stressors, resources, and psychological outcomes of family caregiving: A meta-analysis. *The Gerontologist, 45*, 90–106. doi:10.1093/geront/45.1.90

Population Reference Bureau. (2013). The health and life expectancy of older Blacks and Hispanics in the United States. *Today's Research on Aging, 28*, 1–8. Washington, DC. Retrieved from http://www.prb.org/Publications.aspx

Potter, G. G., Plassman, B. L., Burke, J. R., Kabeto, M. U., Langa, K. M., Llewellyn, D. J., . . . Steffens, D. C. (2009). Cognitive performance and informant reports in the diagnosis of cognitive impairment and dementia in African Americans and Whites. *Alzheimers and Dementia, 5*, 445–453. doi:10.1016/j.jalz.2009.04.1234

Rooks, R. N., & Whitfield, K. E. (2004) Health disparities among older African Americans: Past, present, and future perspectives. In K. Whitfield (Ed.), *Closing the gap: Improving the health of minority elders in the new millennium* (pp. 45–54). Washington, DC: Gerontological Society of America.

Rozario, P. A., & DeRienzis, D. (2008). Familism beliefs and psychological distress among African American women caregivers. *The Gerontologist, 48*, 772–780. doi:10.1093/geront/48.6.772

Scharlach, A. E., Kellam, R., Ong, N., Baskin, A., Goldstein, C., & Fox, P. J. (2006). Cultural attitudes and caregiver service use: Lessons from focus groups with racially and ethnically diverse family caregivers. *Journal of Gerontological Social Work, 47*, 133–156. doi:10.1300/JO83v47n01_09

Schneider, E. C., Zaslavsky, A. M., & Epstein, A. M. (2002). Racial disparities in the quality of care for enrollees in Medicare managed care. *Journal of the American Medical Association, 287*, 1288–1294. doi:10.1001/jama.287.10.1288

Silverstein, M., & Waite, L. J. (1993). Are blacks more likely than whites to receive and provide social support in middle and old age? Yes, no, and maybe so. *Journal of Gerontology, 48*, S212–S222. doi:10.1093/geronj/48.4.S212

Tang, M., Stern, Y., Marder, K., Bell, K., Gurland, B., Lantigua, R., . . . Mayeux, R. (1998). The APOE-epsilon 4 allele and the risk of Alzheimer's disease among African Americans, Whites, and Hispanics. *Journal of the American Medical Association, 279*, 751–755. doi:10.1001/jama.279.10.751

Taylor, R. J., Chatters, L. M., & Levin, J. (2004). *Religion in the lives of African Americans: Social, psychological, and health perspectives.* Thousand Oaks, CA: Sage.

Taylor, R. J., Hernandez, E., Nicklett, E. J., Taylor, H. O., & Chatters, L. M. (2014). Informal social support networks of African American, Latino, Asian American, and Native American older adults. In K. E. Whitfield & T. A. Baker (Eds.), *Handbook of minority aging* (pp. 417–435). New York, NY: Springer.

US Cancer Statistics Working Group. (2013). *United States cancer statistics: 1999–2009 Incidence and mortality web-based report.* Atlanta, GA: Department of Health and Human Services, Centers for Disease Control and Prevention and National Cancer Institute. Retrieved from www.cdc.gov/uscs

US Department of Health and Human Services (DHHS). (2012). *A profile of older Americans: 2012.* Washington, DC: Administration on Aging. Retrieved from http://www.aoa.gov/Aging_Statistics/Profile/2012/3.aspx

Williams, D. R., & Wilson, C. M. (2001). Race, ethnicity, and aging. In R. H. Binstock & L. K. George (Eds.), *Handbook of aging and the social sciences* (pp.160–178). San Diego, CA: Academic Press. doi:10.1097/00019442-200207000-00018

Williams, S. W., & Dilworth-Anderson, P. (2002). Systems of social support in families who care for dependent African American elders. *The Gerontologist, 42*, 224. doi:10.1093/geront/42.2.224

Woodward, A. T., Chatters, L. M., Taylor, R. J., Neighbors, H. W., & Jackson, J. S. (2010). Differences in professional and informal help seeking among older African Americans, Black Caribbeans and Non-Hispanic Whites. *Journal of the Society for Social Work and Research, 1*, 124–139. doi:10.5243/jsswr.2010.10

Woodward, A. T., Taylor, R. J., Abelson, J. M., & Matusko, N. (2013). Major depressive disorder among older African Americans, Caribbean Blacks, and Non-Hispanic Whites: Secondary analysis of the National Survey of American Life. *Depression and Anxiety, 30*, 589–597. doi:10.1002/da.22041

Woodward, A. T., Taylor, R. J., Bullard, K. M., Aranda, M. P., Lincoln, K. D., & Chatters, L. M. (2012). Prevalence of lifetime DSM-IV affective disorders among Older African Americans, Black Caribbeans, Latinos, Asians and Non-Hispanic Whites. *International Journal of Geriatric Psychiatry, 27*, 816–827. doi:10.1002/gps.2790

Yee, D. (2002). Introduction: Recognizing diversity, moving toward cultural competence. *Generations, 26*(3), 5–7. Retrieved from: http://asaging.org/publications

Comprising at least 24 detailed groups in the United States (Hoeffel, Rastogi, Kim, & Shahid, 2011), an estimated 18.8 million Asians, alone or in combination, accounted for 5.8% of the nation's population (US Census Bureau, 2013). The fastest growing population in the United States, the number of Asians grew by 43% from 2000 to 2010 compared with a 9.7% increase of the total population (Hoeffel, Rastogi, Kim, & Shahid, 2011).

Building on the chapter in the first edition, we present an overview of major issues of physical health, disability, mental health, long-term care and caregiving, and end-of-life care relevant to older Asian Americans. In doing so, we primarily draw from the literature published since 2006.

DEMOGRAPHIC, SOCIOECONOMIC, AND HEALTH PROFILES

As shown in Table 47.1, the older population in the United States increased by 18.3% between 2000 and 2011 (US Census Bureau, 2011). During the same time period, the Asian American population (those who identified as "Asian alone") aged 65 and older grew by 101.8% from 782,994 to 1,579,696, representing approximately five times greater rate of increase than the US older population.

Among older Asian Americans, Chinese Americans (416,429) constituted the largest group in 2011, followed by those of Filipino origins. Yet, Vietnamese and Indian Americans continue to show substantial growth from 2000 to 2011, 153.7% and 204.9% respectively. Similarly, older Korean-, Filipino-, and Chinese American groups also showed steady increases. In contrast, older Japanese grew by 9.1%, representing the smallest increase among Asian American groups. As for age subgroups, while approximately two-thirds of Filipino, Korean, and Vietnamese populations were in the 65–74 years age group, the proportions of Chinese and Japanese populations who were 85 and older were much higher at 13.3% and 19.8% respectively. Table 47.2 presents immigration and socioeconomic characteristics of older Asian Americans. The overwhelming majority of five groups (91.6% to 98.8%) were foreign-born, except Japanese Americans. Nearly 60% of older Asian Americans reported limitations in their English proficiency (LEP), ranging from 23.6% for Japanese- to 87.0% for Vietnamese Americans.

JONG WON MIN

AILEE MOON

Older Asian Americans

TABLE 47.1 Demographic Characteristics of Six Major Older Asian Americans in the United States, 2000 and 2011: Weighted Percent[a]

Older Adults (65+)	Population Size (65+)			% of 65+ per Total Population		Age Subgroup (%) in 2011		
	2000	2011	Increase (%)	2000	2011	65–74	75–84	85 +
US Population	34,978,972	41,387,956	18.3	12.4	13.3	54.4	31.8	13.8
Asian Americans (alone)	782,994	1,579,696	101.8	7.7	8.9	59.7	30.0	10.3
Asian Indian	62,089	189,329	204.9	3.8	6.5	68.6	25.5	6.3
Chinese	231,903	416,429	79.6	9.6	11.7	53.8	33.0	13.3
Filipino	162,809	308,620	89.6	8.7	12.1	63.9	27.4	8.7
Japanese	162,551	177,291	9.1	20.4	23.5	38.0	42.2	19.8
Korean	66,254	149,686	125.9	6.2	10.3	66.9	27.1	6.0
Vietnamese	55,057	139,684	153.7	5.0	8.5	66.6	27.2	6.2

Source: US Census Bureau (2011); Ruggles et al. (2010).
[a] All the figures were obtained by applying personal weights provided in the data.

As an aggregate, 28% of older Asian Americans had less than a high school education while 27.7% finished high school; and 44.3% had some college or more education, which is higher than the general older population. A larger proportion of Asian Americans lived in poverty in 2011, compared with the general older population, showing a bimodal pattern. While Japanese-, Filipino-, and Indian Americans reported relatively lower rates of poverty, older Chinese-, Korean-, and Vietnamese Americans reported much higher rates of poverty between 18% and 20%. The projected increase in absolute numbers of Asian Americans in general and older adults in particular, coupled with their longer life expectancy (Social Security Administration, 2013), underscores the importance of their late-life economic security (Insight Center for Community Economic Development, 2011). Fewer Asian Americans (27%) were reported to have retirement savings and pension income than Whites (44%).

Table 47.3 presents the disability status of older Asian Americans in the areas of cognition, ambulation, independent living, and self-care. In comparison with older Americans, Asian Americans generally reported fewer ambulatory and self-care difficulties. However, more Asian Americans reported cognitive and independent living difficulties than the general American elders. Among the Asian subgroups, Vietnamese Americans reported the poorest disability status on all types of the difficulties. On the other hand, Korean Americans showed the lowest level of difficulties with cognition, ambulation, self-care, and independent living.

PHYSICAL HEALTH

In general, Asian American adults continue to report better health status, compared with non-Hispanic Whites and other racial/ethnic groups in the United States (Barnes, Adams, & Powell-Griner, 2008; Bauer, Chen, & Alegría, 2012). For older Asian Americans, limited national-level health data in the past decades have hampered reliable estimates of disease prevalence and accurate understanding of their health status (LaVeist, 1995). However, the availability of the California Health Interview Survey (CHIS), a statewide population-representative survey in the state of California (UCLA Center for Health Policy Research, http://www.chis.ucla.edu) allows for the systematic examination of health status among older Asian Americans, although limited to those in California.

Health Status of Older Asian Americans

Analysis of the 2005 CHIS showed that older Asian Americans were less likely to rate their health

TABLE 47.2 Immigration and Socioeconomic Characteristics of Six Major Older Asian Americans in the United States, 2011: Weighted Percent[a]

Older Adults (65+)	Foreign-Born (%)	Limited English Proficiency (LEP)[b] (%)	Educational Attainment (%)				Poverty Status (%)	
			Less than High School education	High School Diploma	Some college, Bachelor's degree	Graduate/professional degree	2000	2011
US Population	13.0	8.5	19.0	42.6	28.6	9.9	9.9	9.3
Asian Americans (alone)	87.5	60.3	28.0	27.7	32.4	12.1	12.3	13.3
Asian Indian	96.7	48.1	26.0	20.9	26.5	26.7	9.8	7.5
Chinese	91.6	74.8	34.5	23.2	29.5	12.8	19.4	19.3
Filipino	93.6	46.4	18.0	24.8	48.0	8.4	6.3	7.1
Japanese	34.8	23.6	11.1	46.9	33.4	8.7	9.7	6.0
Korean	97.4	77.0	24.3	34.1	31.1	10.5	14.8	19.6
Vietnamese	98.8	87.0	43.9	32.0	19.7	4.4	16.0	18.1

Source: US Census Bureau (2011); Ruggles et al. (2010).
[a] All the figures were obtained by applying personal weights provided in the data.
[b] Limited English Proficiency indicates the level of English proficiency less than "well."

TABLE 47.3 Disability Status of Six Major Older Asian Americans in the United States, 2011: Weighted Percent [a]

Older Adults (65+)	Have Cognitive Difficulty [b] (%)	Have Ambulatory Difficulty [c] (%)	Have Independent LIVING Difficulty [d] (%)	Have Self-Care Difficulty [e] (%)
US Population	11.1	25.6	18.5	11.0
Asian American (alone)	11.5	20.7	20.2	9.8
Asian Indian	9.0	19.6	18.7	7.5
Chinese	11.0	19.3	20.4	10.8
Filipino	10.7	21.5	20.0	9.3
Japanese	12.2	21.0	18.2	9.2
Korean	8.3	17.3	16.2	8.2
Vietnamese	15.4	23.0	23.1	11.1

Source: US Census Bureau (2011); Ruggles et al. (2010).
[a] All the figures were obtained by applying personal weights provided in the data.
[b] Cognitive difficulty indicates whether the respondent has cognitive difficulties (such as learning, remembering, concentrating, or making decisions) because of a physical, mental, or emotional condition.
[c] Ambulatory difficulty indicates whether the respondent has a condition that substantially limits one or more basic physical activities, such as walking, climbing stairs, reaching, lifting, or carrying.
[d] Independent living difficulty indicates whether the respondent has any physical, mental, or emotional condition lasting 6 months or more that makes it difficult or impossible to perform basic activities outside the home alone. This does not include temporary health problems, such as broken bones or pregnancies.
[e] Self-care difficulty indicates whether respondents have any physical or mental health condition that has lasted at least 6 months and makes it difficult for them to take care of their own personal needs, such as bathing, dressing, or getting around inside the home. This does not include temporary health conditions, such as broken bones or pregnancies.

positively than non-Hispanic Whites (54.8% vs. 73.9%) (Min, Rhee, Lee, Rhee, & Tran, 2013), even though they reported lower prevalence rates of arthritis and any types of cancer. Data from 2001 and 2007 showed that Vietnamese Americans disclosed the lowest self-rated health, and Japanese Americans the highest. Filipino- and Vietnamese Americans were more likely than other older Asian Americans to have chronic diseases and disability (G. Kim et al., 2010; Kagawa-Singer et al., 2008). Compared with older Chinese Americans, older Japanese Americans were less likely to report poor or fair health ratings, but older Vietnamese Americans were more likely to report poor health ratings, along with limitations in activities of daily living (ADLs) and major chronic conditions (Sorkin, Tan, Hays, Mangione, & Ngo-Metzger, 2008). Consequently, older Vietnamese were 1.77 times more likely than older Chinese to report that they did less than they wanted in the past 4 weeks because of physical limitation. Older Filipinos were 2.27 times more likely than older Chinese to report limitations from any chronic conditions.

Health Service Use and Access to Care

Results from 2005 and 2007 CHIS showed that health insurance coverage increased the likelihood of physician use by about five times, while controlling for other variables (Nguyen, Bernstein, & Goel, 2012). For Chinese Americans, advanced age was associated with a *decreased* likelihood of seeing a physician in the last 12 months, indicating their unique and diverse help-seeking patterns shaped by their health beliefs and distrust of and misconceptions about care. Furthermore, using 2003 and 2005 CHIS, Nguyen (2012) found that Vietnamese Americans were more likely than Chinese to have a usual source of care. Fewer Korean Americans reported having a usual source of care than other Asian American groups. These differences were found to be related to lower levels of English proficiency. In another study of 100 older Indian Americans in New York City, Shibusawa and Mui (2010) found differential predictors of health service use, in that the number of medical conditions was a significant predictor of physician visits, while age and having medical insurance were significantly associated with length of hospital stay. Finally, medical insurance coverage was a significant predictor of the use of emergency rooms, while those with poor English proficiency more likely to turn to traditional medicine. Lastly, G. Kim, Ford, Chiriboga, and Sorkin (2012), using data from the 2009 CHIS, found that Asians were significantly less likely than Whites to regularly test their blood glucose or have a foot examination.

FUNCTIONAL HEALTH AND DISABILITY

In the past several years, with continued interest in physical health status among older Asian Americans as previously discussed, more researchers have given their attention to studying the prevalence of disability or functional health of the population. Until the early 21st century, we had no national- or state-level estimates of the disability rate for older Asian Americans. More recently, three nationally representative studies—the 5% Public Use Microdata Sample (PUMS) of the 2000 Census (Mutchler, Prakash, & Burr, 2007), the pooled data from the NHIS 2001–2003 (Coustasse, Bae, Arvidson, & Singh, 2008), and the US Census Bureau American Community Survey (ACS) 2006 (Fuller-Thomson, Brennenstuhl, & Hurd, 2011)—have addressed this empirical gap.

Mutchler, Prakash, and Burr (2007) used 5% PUMS of the 2000 Census to examine the disability profiles of community-dwelling older Asian populations (both foreign-born and US-born) in comparison with their non-Hispanic White counterparts aged 65 or older. Both US-born and foreign-born Asians (predicted probability of .15 and .18 respectively) were less likely than non-Hispanic Whites (predicted probability = .21) to report physical limitations. However, foreign-born Asians were more likely than the other groups to report difficulty performing self-care tasks or difficulty going outside alone, a finding that conflicts with previous findings of health advantage of older Asian Americans. Using pooled data from the NHIS 2001–2003, Coustasse, Bae, Arvidson and Singh (2008) estimated a prevalence rate of the disability of any type for the overall population (13.5%). Older Asians as a group showed a similar rate at 13%, which was lower than that of non-Hispanic Whites (17.8%). When examined by subgroups, Chinese

elders disclosed the highest rate of ADL limitations among all racial/ethnic groups (11.6%), even higher than that rate for non-Hispanic Blacks (10.2%). The Indian American subgroup, in contrast, reported the lowest ADL (4.6%) and instrumental ADL (IADL) (9.1%) disability rates. Relying on 2006 ACS data, Fuller-Thomson, Brennenstuhl and Hurd (2011) found that Asian American as a group had lower levels of disability in all four areas (i.e., functional limitations, limitations in ADLs, cognitive problems, and blindness or deafness) than Whites in both total and community-dwelling samples, except cognitive problems for the community sample. Within-group analysis revealed variations, in that Japanese respondents had significantly higher odds of ADL limitations and cognitive problems than did the Chinese respondents. The Vietnamese reported higher rates of disability than did other subgroups. Based on the 2006 ACS, De Souza and Fuller-Thomson (2013) found that higher level of acculturation was associated with greater odds of disabilities among Filipino men. Culturally prescribed roles and gender-specific experiences might have led Filipino men to be more sensitive to acculturation-effects than females at the time of immigration.

MENTAL HEALTH

Until recently, we had no national estimates of prevalence data on mental health disorders for older Asian Americans. Information on mental healthcare needs among Asian American elderly has remained limited and fragmented. However, the National Latino and Asian American Study (NLAAS) 2002–2003 (Alegría et al., 2004) and subsequent research based on the survey have filled the substantial data gaps on mental health for older and younger Asian American adults. The NLAAS data have established national-level estimates on the lifetime and the 12-month prevalence rates of DSM-IV-based psychiatric and mental disorders and mental health service use among Asian Americans (Abe-Kim, Takeuchi, & Hong, 2007; Takeuchi, Zane, & Hong, 2007).

Prevalence of Mental Disorders Among Older Asian Americans

Using data from the NLASS 2002–2003, J. Kim and Choi (2010) found that the 12-month prevalence rate of mental disorders for Asian Americans was 13.6% among all age groups combined. The age group–specific rates ranged from 7.4% in the 60 or older group to 20.1% in the 18–29 group. The prevalence rates for Asian Americans were lower than those for non-Hispanic Whites and Hispanics/Latinos. At the state-level, Sorkin, Nguyen, and Ngo-Metzger (2011) found that except for Japanese Americans, all Asian subgroups reported greater levels of mental distress (12% to 20.3%) than non-Hispanic Whites (9.7%) in California. Specifically, Filipino and Korean Americans had approximately two-times the odds of reporting mental distress symptoms compared with non-Hispanic whites. In a regional probability sample ($n = 407$) of six groups of Asian immigrant elders in New York City, Mui and Kang (2006) found that nearly 40% of their sample were depressed, which is a much higher rate than reported in previous studies. Higher acculturation stress and poor perceived health was strongly associated with higher depression among all the subgroups. Similar associations between acculturation and mental distress were examined in other studies of older Korean Americans (Han, Kim, Lee, Pistulka, & Kim, 2007; Jang & Chiriboga, 2010; Jang, Kim, & Chiriboga, 2006). Moreover, Jang and Chiriboga (2010) found that acculturative stress mediated the relationship between the acculturation and mental distress among 472 Korean American elders in Florida. Jang, Kim and Chiriboga (2006) also highlighted the mediating role of health perception in the linkages between physical and mental health.

Mental Health Service Use Among Older Asian Americans

Based on the 2007 CHIS, Sorkin, Nguyen, and Ngo-Metzger (2011) found that while Filipino and Korean Americans reported higher level of mental distress than non-Hispanic Whites, they were significantly less likely to use any mental health services (i.e., seeing a primary care provider or other professional or taking a prescription medication). G. Kim et al. (2010) reported that while 2.8% of the older Asian immigrants in the NLAAS survey reported having mood disorders and 6.2% reported anxiety disorders, only 4.7% of those with the disorders reported seeing psychiatrists, psychologists, or other mental health professional or using a hotline for problems with their emotions. The underuse of care has been attributed to cultural and structural barriers. The structural barriers, such as a lack of awareness of available services, lack of insurance, and lack of language proficiency, may pose great challenges for older adults to get the care they need. Also, cultural barriers such as stigma, the loss of face, shame, denial, and unique patterns of help-seeking have been known to be associated with low mental health service use (Abe-Kim et al., 2007; Jang, Chiriboga, & Okazaki, 2009). Finally, Nguyen (2011) found that Asians (50 and older) with limited English proficiency were three times more likely than those with better English proficiency to perceive mental health need. This study showed that acculturation in older Asian American affected perception of mental health need, in turn influencing their help-seeking behaviors regarding mental health professionals.

LONG-TERM CARE AND CAREGIVING

The field of long-term care for older Asian Americans has been in great need of any reliable estimates of long-term care service use of either home- and community-based services (HCBS) or the institutions. The majority of the available studies have shown underuse of long-term care services by older Asian Americans. However, as more research becomes available, we are able to shed some light on the institutionalization rate and nursing home use, based on the national data. Analyzing the 2006 ACS, Fuller-Thomson and Chi (2012) found that the national prevalence of institutionalization among those with ADL limitations ranged from 4.7% of Indian Americans to 18.8% of Korean Americans. These rates among the Asian subgroups, however, were significantly lower than that of non-Hispanic Whites (23.8%). One the other hand, Feng, Fennell, Tyler, Clark, and Mor (2011) found that while there was a decline of 6.1% in the national nursing home population, the relative share of Asian nursing home residents changed from 1.0% in 1999 to 1.6% in 2008, representing a 54.1% increase. The growth of the Asian residents was shown in both the absolute numbers and the relative proportions of nursing home residents. This was in contrast to declining trends for White residents. The authors attributed the increase in nursing home use by older Asian Americans to unavailability of or access barriers to preferred HCBS, which serves as an alternative to nursing homes for older Asian populations. Similar barriers to HCBS were reported for older Korean and Japanese Americans (Casado & Lee, 2012; Lau, Machizawa, & Doi, 2012).

Caregivers and Caregiving

Recent research focusing primarily on Korean caregivers (Casado & Sacco, 2012; Han, Choi, Kim, Lee, & Kim, 2008; Yoo & Kim, 2010) and Chinese and Vietnamese caregivers (Liu, Hinton, Tran, Hinton, & Barker, 2008) continue to highlight the centrality of family responsibilities and filial piety, which emphasizes collectivism and interdependence. These values often need to be balanced with American social norms of individualism and independence, requiring the families to seek new opportunities and resources the American society provides for the care of their older family members. Yoo and Kim (2010) and Han, Choi, Kim, Lee and Kim (2008) highlighted that a major motivation among Korean Americans for their caregiving was their sense of filial piety and traditional cultural value of family obligation. Adult children considered caregiving as repayment for the nurture, care, and support that their parents provided earlier in their lives. They expressed reluctance to send older family members into nursing homes, which would be stigmatizing. And yet, they found it challenging to balance employment and maintenance of their traditional role. Often feeling trapped because of caregiving responsibilities, Korean caregivers were at high risk of negative experiences and adverse consequences for their own well-being. Casado and Sacco (2012) found that caregiver burden was higher when there were lower levels of agreement, higher levels of dependency by care-recipients, and lower levels of self-efficacy in care management.

END-OF LIFE CARE AND HOSPICE CARE

Older Asian Americans are underrepresented in hospice care (Ngo-Metzger, McCarthy, Burns, Davis, Li, & Phillips, 2003), as are other ethnic minority communities. Relying on the Surveillance, Epidemiology, and End Results (SEER) Program between 1988 and 1998, Ngo-Metzger, Phillips, and McCarthy (2008) found that Asian American patients had lower rates of hospice use than White patients. Of those who enrolled in hospice (approximately 20% of the total

sample), Japanese patients had a shorter median length of stay (21 days), and Filipinos had a longer median length of stay (32 days) than White patients (26 days).

Factors in Use of Hospice Care

Three explanations are available for the underuse of hospice care by Asians. First, the lack of awareness or knowledge of, or the misconception of, hospice care may be one of the primary barriers to hospice enrollment of minority populations. A couple of studies revealed the prevalence of a lack of knowledge or misconceptions about end-of-life care among older adults and caregivers in the Korean American community (Kwak & Salmon, 2007; Jang, Chiriboga, Allen, Kwak, & Haley, 2010). Additionally, Jang, Chiriboga, Allen, Kwak and Haley (2010) found that the awareness of hospice was associated with a willingness to use hospice among older Korean Americans. Similarly, in a qualitative study of older Chinese adults, Enguidanos Yonashiro-Cho, and Cote (2013) found that only 11.8% of older Chinese adults knew someone who had received hospice care, and some of them were confused about the difference between hospice care and assisted suicide. A second explanation may be related to cultural values and beliefs specific to Asian groups. Western health practice emphasizes autonomy, self-determination, and individualistic decision-making styles as pillars of the Patient Self-Determination Act, which is inconsistent with the collectivistic values of Asians regarding healthcare decision-making (Blackhall, Murphy, Frank, Michel, & Azen, 1995). Kwak and Salmon (2007) found that older Korean Americans preferred indirect, implicit, or nonverbal methods of communication about end-of-life care treatments and showed more family-based or collective decision-making style. Studies of older Korean Americans in New York City also showed that although they considered disclosure and advance directives as helpful to decision-making and preparation, some of them perceived such disclosures as causing emotional distress and hastening death (Berkman & Ko, 2010; Ko & Berkman, 2012). Third, the lower rates of hospice use by Asian groups could be attributed to systemic barriers. For example, the Medicare Hospice Benefit legislation requires the presence of a full-time caregiver and the provision of informed consent, which may be inconsistent with family-centered model of decision-making for older Asians and their family (Kwak & Salmon, 2007; Ngo-Metzger, Phillips, & McCarthy, 2008).

CONCLUSION

Older adults in general experience and adjust to changes in their biological, psychological, and social functioning. Aging policy, intervention, and programs may mitigate losses associated with these changes. However, older Asian Americans may be at greater risk of experiencing multiple and compounding issues in their aging process due to their unique experiences of historical oppression, discrimination, and immigration-related characteristics.

Research on older Asian Americans continues to grow not only in the number of published studies but also in the range of topics and subjects. The national and statewide estimates of prevalence rates of major physical and mental health indicators have been established, gradually filling the wide data gap that existed for a long time in the United States These encouraging efforts allow researchers and policy makers to begin to understand the level of health conditions, healthcare quality, and healthcare access of the population and to compare the health status of Asian Americans with that of other racial/ethnic groups. It is critical to continue to secure representative data on Asian American populations to make it possible for researchers to describe patterns and the nature of changes or shifts in health status and service use of older Asian Americans over time and to identify significant factors affecting their health status. Such information is essential to developing and testing any programs or interventions[1] aimed at improving the population's quality of life.

The fast-growing diversity in the older age groups should not result in widening health disparities. Instead we need to recognize diversity and cultural differences as an integral and natural part of service design and social work practice. As such, we suggest that future investigations on older Asian Americans be framed within the perspective of health disparities (August & Sorkin, 2010; Min, Rhee, Lee, Rhee, & Tran, 2013). Monitoring and tackling health disparities has been an important national agenda in the United States since the late 1990s, as seen in the federal initiatives *Healthy*

People 2000, 2010, and *2020*. Despite practice and policy efforts, health disparities, defined as "particular type[s] of health difference[s ...] closely linked with social, economic, and/or environmental disadvantage" (US Department of Health and Human Services [US DHHS], n.d.), still persist in health status, healthcare quality, and access to healthcare among racial/ethnic groups in the United States (US DHHS, 2013). However, research focusing on older Asian Americans remains sparse (Braveman, Cubbin, Egerter, Williams, & Pamuk, 2010). Notwithstanding health advantages of Asians over other racial/ethnic groups on some health indicators, there is evidence of health disparities *within* and *among* Asian Americans in their underuse of health, mental health, long-term care, and hospice services (De Souza & Fuller-Thomson, 2013; G. Kim, Ford, Chiriboga, & Sorkin, 2012; Min, Rhee, Lee, Rhee, & Tran, 2013; Mutchler, Prakash, & Burr, 2007; Sorkin, Nguyen, & Ngo-Metzger, 2011). The recent report (US DHHS, 2013) showed that Asians as an aggregate had worse care than Whites for 37 measures of healthcare quality and access. Further, the report indicated that older Asian hospice patients did not receive the right amount of help for feelings of anxiety or sadness.

We recommend that future research on the health of older Asian Americans could benefit if the conceptualization of the approaches are considered in three areas specified in the *Healthy People 2020*: individual behavioral determinants, social environment determinants, and health services–related determinants of health in older adults. This recommendation is informed by the increase of older Asians in nursing homes due to barriers to accessing home- and community-based alternatives (Feng, Fennel, Tyler, Clark, & Mor, 2011) related to the lack of culturally appropriate services for minority elders (Casado & Lee, 2012). Other relevant issues such as care coordination and self-care management should also be investigated for older Asian Americans. As a part of the Affordable Care Act of 2010 (Section 4302), data collection standards on race, ethnicity, sex, primary language, and disability status have been established by the US DHSS since 2011. We hope that disaggregated racial and ethnic categories would lead to more consistent efforts in monitoring, analyzing, and tracking health disparities, especially for the Asian American population.

NOTE

1. For more information on social work practice in this area, please refer to the first edition of the *Handbook of Social Work in Health and Aging*.

REFERENCES

Abe-Kim, J., Takeuchi, D. T., Hong, S., Zane, N., Sue, S., Spencer, M. S., . . . Alegria, M. (2007). Use of mental health-related services among immigrant and US-born Asian Americans: results from the National Latino and Asian American Study. *American Journal of Public Health, 97*, 91–98. doi:10.2105/AJPH.2006.098541

Alegría, M., Takeuchi, D. T., Canino, G., Duan, N., Shrout, P., Meng, X. L., . . . Gong, F. (2004). Considering context, place, and culture: The National Latino and Asian American Study. *International Journal of Methods in Psychiatric Research, 13*, 208–220. doi:10.1002/mpr.178

August, K. J., & Sorkin, D. H. (2010). Racial and ethnic disparities in indicators of physical health status: Do they still exist throughout later life? *Journal of the American Geriatric Society, 58*, 2009–2015. doi:10.1111/j.1532-5415.2010.03033.x

Barnes, P. M., Adams, P. F., & Powell-Griner, E. (2008). Health characteristics of the Asian adult population: United States, 2004–2006. *Advanced Data, 394*, 1–22. Centers for Disease Control and Prevention, National Center for Health Statistics.

Bauer, A. M., Chen, C., & Alegría, M. (2012). Prevalence of physical symptoms and their association with race/ethnicity and acculturation in the United States. *General Hospital Psychiatry, 34*, 323–331. doi:10.1016/j.genhosppsych.2012.02.007

Berkman, C. S., & Ko, E. (2010). What and when Korean American older adults want to know about serious illness? *Journal of Psychosocial Oncology, 28*, 244–259. doi:10.1080/07347331003689029

Blackhall L. J., Murphy S. T., Frank G., Michel, V., & Azen, S. (1995). Ethnicity and attitudes toward patient autonomy. *Journal of the American Medical Association, 274*, 820–825. doi:10.1001/jama.1995.03530100060035

Braveman, P. A., Cubbin, C. C., Egerter, S., Williams, D. R., & Pamuk, E. (2010). Socioeconomic disparities in health in the United States: What the patterns tell us. *American Journal of Public Health, 100*, S186–S196. doi:10.2105/AJPH.2009.166082

Casado, B., & Lee, S. (2012). Access barriers to and unmet needs for home- and community-based services among older Korean Americans. *Home Health Care Services Quarterly, 31*, 219–242. doi:10.1080/01621424.2012.703540

Casado, B., & Sacco, P. (2012). Correlates of caregiver burden among family caregivers of older Korean Americans. *Journals of Gerontology, Series B: Psychological Sciences and Social Sciences, 67*, 331–336. doi:10.1093/geronb/gbr115

Coustasse, A., Bae, S., Arvidson, C. J., & Singh, K. P. (2008). Disparities in self-reported activities of daily living and instrumental activities of daily living disability among Asian American subgroups in the United States: Results from the National Health Interview Survey 2001–2003. *Disability and Health Journal, 1*, 150–156. doi:10.1016/j.dhjo.2008.04.005

De Souza, L. R., & Fuller-Thomson, E. (2013). Acculturation and disability rates among Filipino-Americans. *Journal of Immigrant and Minority Health, 15*, 462–471. doi:10.1007/s10903-012-9708-1

Enguidanos, S., Yonashiro-Cho, J., & Cote, S. (2013). Knowledge and perceptions of hospice care of Chinese older adults. *Journal of the American Geriatrics Society, 61*, 993–998. doi:10.1111/jgs.12280

Feng. Z., Fennell, M. L., Tyler, D. A., Clark, M., & Mor, V. (2011). Growth of racial and ethnic minorities in US nursing homes driven by demographics and possible disparities in options. *Health Affairs, 30*, 1358–1365. doi:10.1377/hlthaff.2011.0126

Fuller-Thomson, E., Brennenstuhl, S., & Hurd, M. (2011). Comparison of disability rates among older adults in aggregated and separate Asian American/Pacific Islander subpopulations. *American Journal of Public Health, 101*, 94–100. doi:10.2105/AJPH.2009.176784

Fuller-Thomson, E., & Chi, M. (2012). Older Asian Americans and Pacific Islanders with activities of daily living (ADL) limitations: Immigration and other factors associated with institutionalization. *International Journal of Environmental Research and Public Health, 9*, 3264–3279. doi:10.3390/ijerph9093264

Han, H., Choi, Y. J., Kim, M. T., Lee, J. E., & Kim, K. B. (2008). Experiences and challenges of informal caregiving for Korean immigrants. *Journal of Advanced Nursing, 63*, 517–526. doi:10.1111/j.1365-2648.2008.04746.x

Han, H., Kim, M., Lee, H., Pistulka, G., & Kim, K. B. (2007). Correlates of depression in the Korean American elderly: Focusing on personal resources of social support. *Journal of Cross-Cultural Gerontology, 22*, 115–127. doi:10.1007/s10823-006-9022-2

Hoeffel, E., Rastogi, S., Kim, M., & Shahid, H. (2011). *The Asian population: 2010, 2010 census briefs*. C2010BR-11. Retrieved from http://www.census.gov/prod/cen2010/briefs/c2010br-11.pdf

Insight Center for Community Economic Development. (2011). *Asian Americans, Pacific Islanders and Social Security: A primer*. Retrieved from http://www.insightcced.org/uploads/CRWG/APASocialSecurityPrimer.pdf

Jang, Y., & Chiriboga, D. A. (2010). Living in a different world: Acculturative stress among Korean American elders. *Journal of Gerontology: Psychological Sciences, 65B*, 14–21. doi:10.1093/geronb/gbp019

Jang, Y., Chiriboga, D. A., Allen, J. Y., Kwak, J., & Haley, W. E. (2010). Willingness of older Korean-American adults to use hospice. *Journal of the American Geriatrics Society, 58*, 352–356.

Jang, Y., Chiriboga, D. A., & Okazaki, S. (2009). Attitudes toward mental health services: Age-group differences in Korean American adults. *Aging and Mental Health, 13*, 127–134. doi:10.1080/13607860802591070

Jang, Y., Kim, G., & Chiriboga, D. (2006). Health perception and depressive symptoms among older Korean Americans. *Journal of Cross-Cultural Gerontology, 21*, 91–102. doi:10.1007/s10823-006-9026-y

Kagawa-Singer, M., Min, J. W., Rhee, S., Phan, P., Rhee, J., & Tran, T. (2008). Health of older Asian Americans in California: Findings from California Health Interview Survey (CHIS). *UCLA AAPI Nexus: Journal of Policy, Research and Practice, 6*(2), 17–44.

Kim, G., Chiriboga, D. A., Jang, Y., Lee, S., Huang, C. H., & Parmalee, P. (2010). Health status of older Asian Americans in California. *Journal of the American Geriatrics Society, 58*, 2003–2008. doi:10.1111/j.1532-5415.2010.03034.x

Kim, G., Ford, K. L., Chiriboga, D. A., & Sorkin, D. H. (2012). Racial and ethnic disparities in healthcare use, delayed care, and management of diabetes mellitus in older adults in California. *Journal of the American Geriatrics Society, 60*, 2319–2325. doi:10.1111/jgs.12003

Kim, G., Jang, Y., Chiriboga, D. A., Ma, G. X., & Schonfeld, L. (2010). Factors associated with mental health service use in Latino and Asian immigrant elders. *Aging and Mental Health, 14*, 535–542. doi:10.1080/13607860903311758

Kim, J., & Choi, N. G. (2010). Twelve-month prevalence of DSM-IV mental disorders among older Asian Americans: Comparison with younger groups. *Aging and Mental Health, 14*, 90–99. doi:10.1080/13607860903046461

Ko, E., & Berkman, C. S. (2012). Advance directives among Korean American older adults: Knowledge, attitudes, and behavior. *Journal of Gerontological Social Work, 55*, 484–502. doi:10.1080/01634372.2012.714705

Kwak, J., & Salmon, J. R. (2007). Attitudes and preferences of Korean-American older adults and caregivers on end-of-life care. *Journal of the American Geriatric Society, 55*, 1867–1872. doi:10.1111/j.1532-5415.2007.01394.x

Lau, D. T., Machizawa, S., & Doi, M. (2012). Informal and formal support among community-dwelling Japanese American elders living alone in Chicagoland: An in-depth qualitative study. *Journal of Cross-Cultural Gerontology, 27*, 149–161. doi:10.1007/s10823-012-9166-1

LaVeist, T. A. (1995). Data sources for aging research on racial and ethnic groups. *The Gerontologist, 35*, 328–339. doi:10.1093/geront/35.3.328

Liu, D., Hinton, L., Tran, C., Hinton, D., & Barker, J. C. (2008). Reexamining the relationships among dementia, stigma, and aging in immigrant Chinese and Vietnamese family caregivers. *Journal of Cross-Cultural Gerontology, 23*, 283–299. doi:10.1007/s10823-008-9075-5

Min, J. W., Rhee, S., Lee. S. E., Rhee, J., & Tran, T. (2013). Comparative analysis on determinants of self-rated health among non-Hispanic White, Hispanic, and Asian American older adults. *Journal of Immigrant and Minority Health*. doi:10.1007/s10903-013-9852-2.

Mui, A. C., & Kang, S. (2006). Acculturation stress and depression among Asian immigrant elders. *Social Work, 51*, 243–255. doi:10.1093/sw/51.3.243

Mutchler, J. E., Prakash, A., & Burr, J. A. (2007). The demography of disability and the effects of immigrant history: Older Asians in the United States. *Demography, 44*, 251–263.

Ngo-Metzger, Q., McCarthy, E. P., Burns, R. B., Davis, R. B., Li, F. P., & Phillips, R. S. (2003). Older Asian Americans and pacific islanders dying of cancer use hospice less frequently than older White patients. *American Journal of Medicine, 115*, 47. doi:10.1016/S0002-9343(03)00258-4

Ngo-Metzger, Q., Phillips, R. S., & McCarthy, E. (2008). Ethnic disparities in hospice use among Asian-American and Pacific Islander patients dying with cancer. *Journal of the American Geriatrics Society, 56*, 139–144. doi:10.1111/j.1532-5415.2007.01510.x

Nguyen, D. (2011). Acculturation and perceived mental health need among older Asian immigrants. *Journal of Behavioral Health Services and Research, 38*, 526–533. doi:10.1007/s11414-011-9245-z

Nguyen, D. (2012). The effects of sociocultural factors on older Asian Americans' access to care. *Journal of Gerontological Social Work, 55*, 55–71. doi:10.1080/01634372.2011.618525

Nguyen, D., Bernstein, L. J., & Goel, M. (2012). Asian-American elders' health and physician use: An examination of social determinants and lifespan influences. *Health, 4*, 1106–1115. doi:10.4236/health.2012.411168

Ruggles, S. J., Alexander, T., Genadek, K., Goeken, R., Schroeder, M. B., & Sobek, M. (2010). *Integrated Public Use Microdata Series: Version 5.0*. Machine-readable database. Minneapolis: University of Minnesota. Retrieved from http://www.ipumgs.org

Shibusawa, T., & Mui, A. (2010). Health status and health services utilization among older Asian Indian immigrants. *Journal of Immigrant and Minority Health, 12*, 527–533. doi:10.1007/s10903-008-9199-2

Social Security Administration. (2013). *Social Security is important to Asian Americans and Pacific Islanders*. Retrieved from http://www.ssa.gov/pressoffice/factsheets/asian.htm

Sorkin, D. H., Nguyen, H., & Ngo-Metzger, Q. (2011). Assessing the mental health needs and barriers to care among a diverse sample of Asian American older adults. *Journal of General Internal Medicine, 26*, 595–602. doi:10.1007/s11606-010-1612-6

Sorkin, D. H., Tan, A., Hays, R. D., Mangione, C. M., & Ngo-Metzger, Q. (2008). Self-reported health status of older Vietnamese and non-Hispanic white older adults in California. *Journal of the American Geriatrics Society, 56*, 1543–1548. doi:10.1111/j.1532-5415.2008.01805.x

Takeuchi, D. T., Zane, N., Hong, S., Chae, D. H., Gong, F., Gee, G. C., ... Alegria, M. (2007). Immigration-related factors and mental disorders among Asian Americans. *American Journal of Public Health, 97*, 84–90. doi:10.2105/AJPH.2006.088401

US Census Bureau. (2008). *An older and more diverse nation by midcentury*. Retrieved from http://www.census.gov/newsroom/releases/archives/population/cb08-123.html.

US Census Bureau. (2011). *American Community Survey 2011 (1-year estimate)*. Retrieved from http://www.ipums.org

US Census Bureau. (2013). *Annual estimates of the resident population by sex, race alone or in combination, and Hispanic origin for the United States, states, and counties: April 1, 2010 to July 1, 2012*. Retrieved from http://www.census.gov/popest/data/national/asrh/2012/index.html

US Department of Health and Human Services (US DHHS). (n.d.). *The Secretary's Advisory Committee on National Health Promotion and Disease Prevention Objectives for 2020; Phase I report: Recommendations for the framework and format of Healthy People 2020*. Retrieved from http://www.healthypeople.gov/hp2020/advisory/PhaseI/sec4.htm#_Toc211942917

US Department of Health and Human Services (US DHHS). (2013). *2012 National Healthcare Disparities Report*. Agency for Healthcare Research and Quality. AHRQ Publication No. 13-0003. Retrieved from www.ahrq.gov/research/findings/nhqrdr/index.html

Yoo, G., & Kim, B. (2010). Remembering sacrifices: Attitude and beliefs among second-generation Korean Americans regarding family support. *Journal of Cross-Cultural Gerontology, 25*, 165–181. doi:10.1007/s10823-010-9116-8

INTRODUCTION

The US Latino[1] population is relatively young, yet is experiencing steady population growth in the 65 years and older subgroup. In 2010, the older Latino 65+ population numbered 3 million, and that number is expected to grow to 17.5 million by the year 2050 (Federal Interagency Forum on Aging-Related Statistics [FIFARS], 2012). By 2028, Latinos will constitute the largest racial/ethnic historically underrepresented group over age 65 in the United States (Administration on Aging, 2012).

The purpose of this chapter is to discuss selected sociodemographic, health, and cultural indicators relevant to social work practice from a mental health perspective. To frame the discussion, the material will be applied to the case of late-life depressive illness. This chapter attempts to narrow the gap in the mental health literature specifically in terms of social work practice with older adults from historically underrepresented groups in the United States. Such information has important implications for practice because social workers are typically the "front-line" providers of mental health services in the United States (Substance Abuse and Mental Health Services Association, 2010).

LATE-LIFE DEPRESSION

Depression is one of the most prevalent mental disorders among older adults, including ethnic and racial historically underrepresented groups, and is considered a leading cause of disease burden and disability (Alexopoulos, 2005). Late-life depression is defined as clinically diagnosable unipolar depressive syndromes that affect older people such as major depression, dysthymic disorder, adjustment disorder with depressive features, and clinically significant depressive symptoms, or minor depression. Unipolar depressive syndromes affect about 15% to 20% of older adults depending on the case definitions used (Alexopoulos, 2005; Aranda, Lee, & Wilson, 2001; Blazer, 2002, 2003; Lebowitz, 1996; Scott, Von Korff, Alonso, et al., 2008). Except for one study (Swenson, Baxter, Shetterly, Scarbro, & Hamman, 2000), previous work indicates that older Latinos have elevated rates of clinically significant depression compared with the general older adult population (females—25.6% and 25.4% vs. males—10% and 15.1%, respectively; Black, Markides, & Miller, 1998;

MARÍA P. ARANDA

Social Work Practice with Older Latinos in the United States: A Mental Health Perspective

Blazer, Hughes, & George, 1987; González, Haan, & Hinton, 2001; Kemp, Staples, & López-Aqueres, 1987; Mendes de Leon & Markides, 1988; White, Kohout, Evans, Cornoni-Huntley, & Ostfeld, 1986).

Effective and safe pharmacological and nonpharmacological treatments for late-life depression exist. A systematic review by Fuentes and Aranda (2012) found that while there is strong evidence in support of pharmacological and psychosocial depression treatments overall, much less evidence is available with regard to older racial and ethnic minority populations. For example, they found that between 1990 and 2010, only seven published research articles addressed depression treatment outcomes for older adults by racial/ethnic group. This finding is in light of the fact that racial and ethnic minorities with depression report higher levels of impairment and are more persistently ill than non-Hispanic White older adults, yet have lower use of mental healthcare (Alegría et al., 2008; Brown, Schulberg, Madonia, Shear, & Houck, 1996; Garrido, Kane, Kass, & Kane, 2011; González, Tarraf, Whitfield, et al., 2010; González, Vega, Williams, et al., 2010; Williams et al., 2007).

Although older Latinos may be at risk for depressive disorders, they also tend to be low users of specialty mental healthcare (Jimenez, Alegría, Chen, Chan, & Laderman, 2010). Significant barriers exist leading to limited access to mental health services by older Latinos. System-level barriers—such as insufficient (or inaccessible) mental health resources, lack of bilingual/bicultural providers, long waiting times, inadequate outreach, lack of transportation, lack of information on services, service fragmentation, lack of health insurance, and low level of Medicare and Medicaid reimbursement—are often the most important barriers to mental health service use (Abramson, Trejo, & Lai, 2002; Aranda & Torres, 1999; Biegel, Farkas, & Song, 1997; Padgett, Burns, & Grau, 1998; Pew Hispanic Center/Kaiser Family Foundation, 2002; Unützer et al., 2003). Thus, older Latinos wait until their condition worsens before seeking care or following up with their treatment regimens, which may lead to more chronic disease trajectories. This is unfortunate, given the emerging work indicating that low-income Latinos are able to respond favorably to depression treatment, even with modest linguistic and cultural adaptations (Ell et al., 2011; Miranda et al., 2003), and in some cases supersede the positive effects found among Whites (Unützer et al., 2003).

SOCIODEMOGRAPHIC INDICATORS

Latinos, like other adults, look forward to living a healthy and productive life in their later years. To what degree this comes to fruition is in part dependent on the person's ability to accumulate a "three-pronged" retirement income profile consisting of Social Security benefits, private pensions, and savings and investment income (Villa & Aranda, 2000).

Having confronted significant cumulative educational and employment disadvantages during their earlier years, many Latinos have been unable to accumulate sufficient financial resources to sustain themselves during retirement. For example, baby boomers of Mexican origin, who make up the largest numbers of Latino baby boomers in the United States, may not share the same advantages of health, income, and educational attainment as seen among US-born non-Hispanic Whites (Villa, Wallace, Bagdasaryan, & Aranda, 2012). Older Latinos are more likely to either *never* receive Social Security benefits (Whitman, Reznik, & Shoffner, 2011), or receive Social Security benefits as their *primary* source of income (Caldera, 2010; Villa & Aranda, 2000), have the lowest median annual income, and are least likely to receive pension and asset income (Social Security Administration, 2012). Thus, it comes as no surprise that the poverty rate for Latino older adults 65 years and older is twice that of the total older population (18% vs. 9%; Social Security Administration, 2012) with older Hispanic women reporting poverty rates upward of 21% (FIFARS, 2012), compared with 14.2% of their male counterparts, and 6.8% of the non-Hispanic White 65 and older population (US Census Bureau, 2011).

Poverty and restricted lifetime accumulation of wealth have significant implications related to depression risk and limited access to quality mental health services. One implication is the association between depression and lower income status, which has been well supported regardless of a person's race or ethnicity, thus underscoring the higher prevalence of depression among persons of limited financial means, financial strain, and income inequality (Blazer, 2003; Cornoni-Huntley et al., 1990; Dunlop, Song, Lyons, Manheim, & Chang, 2003; Lorant et al., 2003; Messias, Eaton, & Grooms, 2011; Zimmerman & Katon, 2005).

Older Latinos with higher levels of financial strain are twice as likely to report clinically depressive symptomatology as their national counterparts

(Angel, Frisco, Angel, & Chiriboga, 2003; Black et al., 1998), with one out of two Mexican Americans over the age of 65 reporting not having enough money at the end of the month to make ends meet (Chiriboga, Black, Aranda, & Markides, 2002). In sum, older Latinos are overrepresented in terms of low-income status, with older Latinas and immigrants being most at risk of developing depressive symptomatology.

Another issue is the complex interaction between depression, chronic illness, and medication adherence. For example, patients with serious chronic illnesses experience adverse and reoccurring health events when they restrict their use of prescription drugs due to cost factors (Heisler et al., 2004). Those who restricted buying medications are more likely to have lower annual income and educational levels, to have no insurance, or to have insurance without full prescription medication coverage (Heisler et al., 2004). In sum, being uninsured or underinsured could result in poor adherence to guideline-concordant pharmacological treatments, which in turn can exert deleterious effects on mental health and physical outcomes.

Educational Attainment and Literacy

Lower education attainment presents a challenge to practitioners to the degree that evidence-based depression interventions are developed based on an expectation of proficient health literacy, that is, the ability to obtain and understand basic health information to make appropriate healthcare decisions. Although educational attainment among older Americans has increased in the last few decades, large educational differences exist among older Latinos and their non-Latino counterparts. About 49% of older Hispanics completed high school compared with 81% of the overall older adult population (Administration on Aging, 2012).

This is especially problematic for US Latinos, Spanish speakers, and adults 65 years of age and older who tend to have below basic or basic health literacy skills (White, 2008). Social workers need to consider that clients with low literacy may need longer treatment encounters, diverse formats of psychoeducational materials, and family or caregiver involvement in the management of their depression.

HEALTH AND CULTURAL INDICATORS

Depression coexists with physical illness and functional disability in older adults (Alexopoulos, 2005; Blazer, 2002, 2003). Moreover, depression not only is associated with the presence of disease but also is implicated in the development of disease and disability over time. Older adults with impairments in at least two domains of activities of daily living are at highest risk for major depression (up to 31.5%; Aranda, Chae, Lincoln et al., Taylor, Woodward, & Chatters, 2011). While mortality for certain conditions is equivalent to—and in some cases better than—that of non-Latino Whites, Latinos are disadvantaged for certain chronic medical conditions and have higher rates of disability than non-Latino Whites (Eschbach, Al-Snih, Markides, & Goodwin, 2007).

Chronic disease burden is greater for older people and people from disadvantaged backgrounds, who suffer from higher rates of illness, functional impairments, and poorer health outcomes (Hummer, Benjamins, & Rogers, 2004; Raphael et al., 2003). Although advancements have been made in the area of life expectancy (Zhang, Hayward, & Lu, 2012), health disparities among older Latinos persist. Compared with non-Hispanic Whites, older Mexican Americans have a higher incidence of diabetes and obesity (Ostir, Markides, Freeman, & Goodwin, 2000; Stern, Patterson, Mitchell, Haffner, & Hazuda, 1990), have lower access to primary care services (Gornick, Eggers, Reilly, et al., 1996), are more functionally impaired (Markides, Eschbach, Ray, & Peek, 2007), have lower rates of physical activity and report more disabilities (Markides, 2007), and report higher numbers of risk factors for impaired cognitive functioning (Alzheimer's Association, 2004; Zhang et al., 2012). Taken together, these factors influence the onset, nature, and outcomes of disability and depression in older Latinos. In developing depression care, it is important to address the roles that physical illness and disability play in the etiology of depression as well as in the ways providers tailor treatment modalities that acknowledge this mind–body connection. Thus, depression care necessitates an integrated behavioral care approach that emphasizes social work knowledge and practice behaviors intended to reduce health and mental health disparities alike (Williams, Chapa, & Des Marais, 2013).

Culture and Language

Positive outcomes in mental health encounters are predicted to a substantial degree by the consumer–provider relationship or alliance, regardless of the treatment orientation of the providers or service provided (Hepworth, Rooney, Dewberry Rooney, & Strom-Gottfried, 2013). A precursor to developing the therapeutic alliance is the ability of the consumer to express her or his situation in a way that the provider can comprehend—not only the spoken word but also culturally laden idioms, patterns of communication, and nonverbal gestures and cues (Aranda, 1999; Aranda & Morano, 2007). Thus, the language and ethnicity of both consumer and provider play a key role in the communication between both parties and the ability to formulate a helping relationship. Communication is enhanced by improving our understanding of the cultural expressions of mental health and illness, cultural explanatory models or notions of the etiology of psychological distress, and personal and sociocentric beliefs regarding treatment responsibility, which may impact older Latinos in their help-seeking behaviors and acceptance of interventions (Cabassa & Baumann, 2013; Fuentes & Aranda, 2012; Lewis-Fernàndez & Díaz, 2002). Social workers are positioned to embrace these cultural indicators, given their historical commitment to issues of diversity, social justice, and cultural competency (Council on Social Work Education, 2008). Yet, the integration of cultural knowledge and competencies in social work training with older persons from underrepresented racial and ethnic communities is sorely needed.

Delaying treatment or inappropriate treatment may have adverse effects in that low income, older Latinos may accommodate to the symptoms of depressive illness and appear more fatalistic in their perceptions about being able to get better. Sometimes this sense of fatalism is misperceived as a cultural value, when in reality it is an accommodation and survival strategy in the face of chronic strain (Aranda & Knight, 1997). Thus, social workers and other providers are faced with real-life situations that are at a crisis—or near crisis level—that have gone unnoticed or ignored for many years. This increases the likelihood that the social work practitioner will be involved in providing therapeutic services as well as intensive case management and other forms of resource-enhancing, crisis mitigating activities.

SUMMARY

This chapter addressed a selected set of sociodemographic, health, and cultural indicators and their implications for social work practice with older Latinos with mental health needs. Personalized and culturally congruent psychosocial care should include the following: (1) ensuring treatment encounters are provided in the clients' language of preference; (2) assessing culture-specific beliefs and traditions related to mind-body-soul wellness; (3) discussing medication effects and side effects; (4) involving family and caregivers in treatment goals; (5) providing case management and community-based services; (6) incorporating empirically supported depression care; (7) integrating behavioral healthcare to include chronic disease self-management; and (8) using diverse formats of psychoeducation materials that address variations in literacy levels. With the aging of subsequent cohorts of US Latinos, we can expect social workers to play a significant role in the delivery of services to older US Latinos and their families.

NOTE

1. According to the US Census Bureau, the definition of Hispanic or Latino origin used in the 2010 Census "refers to a person of Cuban, Mexican, Puerto Rican, South or Central American, or other Spanish culture or origin regardless of race" (Ennis, Rios-Vargas, & Albert, 2011, p. 2).

REFERENCES

Abramson, T. A., Trejo, L., & Lai, D. W. L. (2002). Culture and mental health: Providing appropriate services for a diverse older population. *Generations*, 26, 21–27.

Administration on Aging. (2012). *A profile of older Americans: 2012.* Retrieved from http://www.aoa.gov

Alegría, M., Chatterji, P., Wells, K., Cao, Z., Chen, C.-N., Takeuchi, D., . . . Meng, X. L. (2008). Disparity in depression treatment among racial and ethnic minority populations in the United States. *Psychiatric Services, 59*, 1264–1272. doi: 10.1176/appi.ps.59.11.1264

Alexopoulos, G. S. (2005). Depression in the elderly. *Lancet, 365*, 1961–1970. doi: 10.1016/S0140-6736(05)66665-2

Alzheimer's Association. (2004). *Hispanics/Latinos and Alzheimer's disease*. Retrieved from http://www.alz.org/national/documents/report_hispanic.pdf

Angel, R. J., Frisco, M., Angel, J. L., & Chiriboga, D. A. (2003). Financial strain and health among elderly Mexican-origin individuals. *Journal of Health and Social Behavior, 44*, 536–551.

Aranda, M. P. (1999). Cultural issues and Alzheimer's disease: Lessons from the Latino community. *Geriatric Case Management Journal, 9*, 13–18.

Aranda, M. P., Chae, D. H., Lincoln, K. D., Taylor, R. J., Woodward, A. T., & Chatters, L. M. (2011). Demographic correlates of DSM-IV major depressive disorder among older African Americans, Black Caribbeans, and non-Hispanic Whites: Results from the National Survey of American Life. *International Journal of Geriatric Psychiatry, 27*, 940–947. doi: 10.1002/gps.2805

Aranda, M. P., & Knight, B. G. (1997). The influence of ethnicity and culture on the caregiver stress and coping process: A sociocultural review and analysis. *The Gerontologist, 37*, 342–354. doi: 10.1093/geront/37.3.342

Aranda, M. P., Lee, P. J., & Wilson, S. (2001). Correlates of depression in older Latinos. *Home Health and Community Care Services Quarterly, 20*, 1–20. doi: 10.1300/J027v20n01_01

Aranda, M. P., & Morano, C. (2007). Psychoeducational strategies for Latino caregivers. In C. B. Cox (Ed.), *Dementia and social work practice: Research and interventions* (pp. 189–204). New York, NY: Springer.

Aranda, M. P., & Torres, M. S. (1999). Self-reported barriers to the use of community-based, long-term care services: A comparative study of elderly and disadvantaged Mexican Americans and Non-Latino Whites. In M. Sotomayor & A. Garcia (Eds.), *La familia: Traditions and realities* (pp. 45–66). Washington, DC: Family Service Association.

Biegel, D., Farkas, K., & Song, L. (1997). Barriers to the use of mental health services by African-American and Hispanic elderly persons. *Journal of Gerontological Social Work, 29*, 23–44. doi: 10.1300/J083v29n01_03

Black, S. A., Markides, K. S., & Miller, T. Q. (1998). Correlates of depressive symptomatology among older community-dwelling Mexican Americans: The Hispanic EPESE. *Journal of Gerontology: Social Sciences, 53B*, S198–S208. doi: 10.1093/geronb/53B.4.S198

Blazer, D. G. (2002). *Depression in late life* (3rd ed.). New York, NY: Springer.

Blazer, D. G. (2003). Depression in late life: Review and commentary. *Journals of* Gerontology Series A: Biological Sciences and Medical Sciences, 58, 249–265. doi: 10.1093/gerona/58.3.M249

Blazer, D., Hughes, D. C., & George, L. K. (1987). The epidemiology of depression in an elderly community population. *The Gerontologist, 16*, 118–124. doi: 10.1093/geront/27.3.281

Brown, C., Schulberg, H. C., Madonia, M. J., Shear, M. K., & Houck, P. R. (1996). Treatment outcomes for primary care patients with major depression and lifetime anxiety disorders. *American Journal of Psychiatry, 153*, 1293–1300.

Cabassa, L. J., & Baumann, A. A. (2013). A two-way street: Bridging implementation science and cultural adaptation of mental health treatments. *Implementation Science, 8*(90), 1–14. doi: 10.1186/1748-5908-8-90

Caldera, S. (2010). *Fact sheet 201: Social Security: A key retirement income source for minorities*. Washington, DC: AARP Public Policy Institute.

Chiriboga, D. A., Black, S. A., Aranda, M. P., & Markides, K. S. (2002). Stress and depressive symptoms among Mexican American elderly. *Journal of Gerontology: Social Sciences, 57B*, P559–P568. doi: 10.1093/geronb/57.6.P559

Cornoni-Huntley, J., Blazer, D. C, Lafferty, M. E., Everett, D. F., Brock, D. B., & Farmer, M. E. (1990). *Established populations for epidemiologic studies of the elderly: Vol. 11. Resource data book*. Washington, DC: US Department of Health and Human Services, National Institutes of Health, National Institute on Aging (NIH Publication No. 90-495).

Council on Social Work Education. (2008). *Code of Ethics of the National Association of Social Workers*. Washington, DC: Author.

Dunlop, D. D., Song, J., Lyons, J. S., Manheim, L. M., & Chang, R. W. (2003). Racial/ethnic differences in rates of depression among preretirement adults. *American Journal of Public Health, 93*, 1945–1952.

Ell, K., Xie, B., Quinn, D., Kapetanovik, S., Lee, P. J., Wells, A., & Chou, C.P. (2011). Collaborative depression care among low-income, minority cancer patients: 1-year post-intervention sustained depression improvement or recurrence and trial attrition. *Psychiatric Services, 62*, 162–170.

Ennis, S. R., Rios-Vargas, M., & Albert, N. G. (2011). *The Hispanic population: 2010*. US Census Bureau. Retrieved from http://www.census.gov/prod/cen2010/briefs/c2010br-04.pdf

Eschbach, K., Al-Snih, S., Markides, K. S., & Goodwin, J. S. (2007). Disability and active life expectancy of older U.S.- and foreign-born Mexican Americans. In J. L. Angel & K. E. Whitfield (Eds.), *The health of aging Hispanics: The Mexican-origin population* (pp. 40–49). Medford, MA: Springer Science+Business Media.

Federal Interagency Forum on Aging-Related Statistics (FIFARS). (2012). *Older Americans 2012: Key indicators of well-being*. Washington, DC: US Government Printing Office.

Fuentes, D., & Aranda, M. P. (2012). Depression interventions among racial and ethnic minority older adults: A systematic review across 20 years. *American Journal of Geriatric Psychiatry, 20*, 915–931. doi: 10.1097/JGP.0b013e31825d091a

Garrido, M. M., Kane, R. L., Kaas, M., & Kane, R. A. (2011). Use of mental health care by community-dwelling older adults. *Journal of the American Geriatrics Society, 59*, 50–56. doi:10.1111/j.1532-5415.2010.03220.x

González, H. M., Haan, M. N., & Hinton, L. (2001). Acculturation and the prevalence of depression in older Mexican-Americans: Baseline results of the Sacramento Area Latino Study on Aging. *Journal of the American Geriatrics Society, 49*, 948–953. doi: 10.1046/j.1532-5415.2001.49186.x

González, H. M., Tarraf, W., Whitfield, K. E., & Vega, W. A. (2010). The epidemiology of major depression and ethnicity in the United States. *Journal of Psychiatric Research, 44*, 1043–1051.

González, H. M., Vega, W. A., Williams, D. R., Tarraf, W., West, B. T., & Neighbors, H. W. (2010). Depression care in the United States: Too little for too few. *Archives of General Psychiatry, 67*, 37–46.

Gornick, M. E., Eggers, P. W., Reilly, T. W., Mentnech, R. M., Fitterman, L. K., Kucken, L. E., & Vladeck, B. C. (1996). Effects of race and income on mortality and use of services among Medicare beneficiaries. *New England Journal of Medicine, 335*, 791–799.

Heisler, M., Langa, K. M., Eby, E. L., Fendrick, A. M., Kabeto, M. U., & Piette, J. D. (2004). The health effects of restricting prescription medication use because of cost. *Medical Care, 42*, 626–634.

Hepworth, D. H., Rooney, R. H., Dewberry Rooney, G., & Strom-Gottfried, K. (2013). *Direct social work practice: Theory and skills* (9th ed.). Belmont, CA: Brooks/Cole.

Hummer, R. A., Benjamins, M. R., & Rogers, R. G. (2004). Racial and ethnic disparities in health and mortality among the U.S. Elderly Population. In N. B. Anderson, R. A. Bulatao, & B. Cohen (Eds.), *Critical perspectives on racial and ethnic differences in health in late life*. Washington, DC: National Academies Press.

Jimenez, D., Alegría, M., Chen, C.-N., Chan, D., & Laderman, M. (2010). Prevalence of psychiatric illnesses in older ethnic minority adults. *Journal of the American Geriatrics Society, 58*, 256–264. doi: 10.1111/j.1532-5415.2009.02685.x

Kemp, B. J., Staples, F., & López-Aqueres, W. (1984). Epidemiology of depression and dysphoria in an elderly Hispanic population. *American Geriatrics Society, 35*, 920–926.

Lebowitz, B. D. (1996). Depression and treatment of depression in late life: An overview of the NIH consensus statement. *American Journal of Geriatrics Psychiatry, 4*, S3–S6.

Lewis-Fernàndez, R., & Díaz, N. (2002). The cultural formulation: A method for assessing cultural factors affecting the clinical encounter. *Psychiatric Quarterly, 73*, 271–295. doi: 10.1023/A:102041200018

Lorant, V., Deliege, D., Eaton, W., Robert, A., Philippot, P., & Ansseau, M. (2003). Socioeconomic inequalities in depression: A meta-analysis. *American Journal of Epidemiology, 157*, 98–112.

Markides, K. S. (2007). *Encyclopedia of health and aging*. Los Angeles, CA: Sage.

Markides, K. S., Eschbach, K., Ray, L., & Peek, K. (2007). Census disability rates among older people by race/ethnicity and type of Hispanic origin. In J. L. Angel & K. E. Whitfield (Eds.), *The health of aging Hispanics: The Mexican-origin population* (pp. 26–39). Medford, MA: Springer Science+Business Media.

Mendes de Leon, C., & Markides, K. (1988). Depressive symptoms among Mexican Americans: A three generation study. *Journal of Epidemiology, 127*, 150–160.

Messias, E., Eaton, W. W., & Grooms, A. N. (2011). Economic grand rounds: Income inequality and depression prevalence across the United States: An ecological study. *Psychiatric Services, 62*, 710–712. doi: 10.1176/appi.ps.62.7.710

Miranda, J., Duan, N., Sherbourne, C., Schoenbaum, M., Lagomasino, I., Jackson-Triche, M., & Wells, K. B. (2003). Improving care for minorities: Can quality improvement interventions improve care and outcome for depressed minorities? Results of a randomized, controlled trial. *Health Services Research, 38*, 613–630. doi: 10.1111/1475-6773.00136

Ostir, G., Markides, K., Freeman, D. J., & Goodwin, J. (2000). Obesity and health conditions in Elderly Mexican Americans: The Hispanic EPESE: Established Population for Epidemiologic Studies of the Elderly. *Ethnicity and Disease, 10*, 31–38.

Padgett, D., Burns, B., & Grau, L. (1998). Risk factors and resilience: Mental health needs and service use of older women. In B. Levin, K. Blanch, & A. Jennings (Eds.), *Women's mental health services: A public health perspective* (pp. 390–413). Thousand Oaks, CA: Sage.

Pew Hispanic Center/Kaiser Family Foundation. (2002). *National Survey of Latinos.* Washington, DC: Henry J. Kaiser Family Foundation.

Raphael, D., Anstice, S., Raine, K., McGannon, K., Rizvi, S., & Yu, V. (2003). The social determinants of the incidence and management of type 2 diabetes mellitus: Are we prepared to rethink our questions and redirect our research activities? *International Journal of Health Care Quality Assurance, 16,* 10–20.

Scott, K. M., Von Korff, M., Alonso, J., Angermeyer, M., Bromet, E. J., Bruffaerts, R., . . . Williams, D. (2008). Age patterns in the prevalence of DSM-IV depressive/anxiety disorders with and without physical co-morbidity. *Psychol Med, 38,* 1659–1669. doi: 10.1017/S0033291708003413

Social Security Administration. (2012). *Income of the aged chartbook, 2010.* SSA Publication No. 13-11727. Retrieved from http://www.ssa.gov/policy/docs/chartbooks/income_aged/2010/iac10.pdf

Stern, M. P., Patterson, J. K., Mitchell, B. D., Haffner, S. M., & Hazuda, H. P. (1990). Overweight and mortality in Mexican Americans. *International Journal of Obesity and Related Metabolic Disorders, 14,* 623–629.

Substance Abuse and Mental Health Services Administration. (2010). *Mental health, United States, 2010.* Washington, DC: USDHHS. Retrieved from http://www.samhsa.gov/data/2k12/MHUS2010/MHUS-2010.pdf

Swenson, C. J., Baxter, J., Shetterly, S. M., Scarbro, S. L., & Hamman, R. F. (2000). Depressive symptoms in Hispanic and non-Hispanic White rural elderly: The San Luis Valley Health and Aging Study. *American Journal of Epidemiology, 152,* 1048–1055.

Unützer, J., Katon, W., Callahan, C. M., Williams, J. W. Jr, Hunkeler, E., Harpole, L., . . . Oishi, S. (2003). Depression treatment in a sample of 1,801 depressed older adults in primary care. *Journal of American Geriatrics Society, 51,* 505–514. doi: 10.1046/j.1532-5415.2003.51159.x

US Census Bureau. (2011). *Table 26. Poverty status of the population by sex, age, Hispanic origin, and race: 2010.* Current Population Survey, Annual Social and Economic Supplement. Retrieved from http://www.census.gov/hhes/www/cpstables/032012/pov/toc.htm

Villa, V. M., & Aranda, M. P. (2000). The demographic, economic, and health profile of older Latinos: Implications for health and long-term care policy and the Family. *Journal of Health and Human Services Administration, 23,* 161–180.

Villa, V. M., Wallace, S. P., Bagdasaryan, S., & Aranda, M. P. (2012). Hispanic baby boomers: Health inequities likely to persist in old age. *The Gerontologist, 52,* 166–176. doi: 10.1093/geront/GNS002

Williams, D. R., González, H. M., Neighbors, H., Nesse, R., Abelson, J. M., Sweetman, J., & Jackson, J. S. (2007). Prevalence and distribution of major depressive disorder in African Americans, Caribbean Blacks, and non-Hispanic Whites: Results from the National Survey of American Life. *Archives of General Psychiatry, 64,* 305–315 doi: 10.1001/archpsyc.64.3.305

Williams, J. H., Chapa, T., & Des Marais, E. A. (2013). *Advanced social work practice behaviors to address behavioral health disparities.* Washington, DC: National Association of Deans and Directors of Social Work. Retrieved from http://www.naddssw.org/pages/wp-content/uploads/2013/10/Behavioral-Health-Disparities-e-pub.pdf

White, L. R., Kohout, F., Evans, D. A., Cornoni-Huntley, J., & Ostfeld, A. M. (1986). Related health problems. In J. C. Coroni-Huntley, D. B. Brock, A. M. Ostfeld, J. O. Taylor, & R. B. Wallace (Eds.), *Established populations for epidemiologic studies of the elderly: Resources data book* (pp. 129–165). US Department of Health and Human Services. NIH Pub No. 862443.

White, S. (2008). *Assessing the nation's health literacy: Key concepts and findings of the National Assessment of Adult Literacy.* American Medical Association Foundation. Retrieved from http://www.ama-assn.org/ama1/pub/upload/mm/367/hl_report_2008.pdf

Whitman, K., Reznik, G. L., & Schoffner, D. (2011). Who never receives social security benefits? *Social Security Bulletin, 71,* 17–24.

Zhang, Z., Hayward, M. D., & Lu, C. (2012). Is there a Hispanic epidemiologic paradox in later life? A closer look at chronic morbidity. *Research on Aging, 34,* 548–571.

Zimmerman, F. J., & Katon, W. (2005). Socioeconomic status, depression disparities, and financial strain: What lies behind the income-depression relationship? *Health Economics, 14,* 1197–1215. doi: 10.1002/hec.1011

MOLLY TOVAR

DAVID PATTERSON

JORDAN LEWIS

American Indian/Alaska Native Elders

INTRODUCTION

The term "American Indians/Alaska Natives" (AI/AN) refers to people with heritage from any of the original peoples of North America, South America, and Central America who maintain tribal affiliation or some level of community attachment, and who are sometimes identified as Native Americans or Indigenous Peoples. In the 2010 US Census, approximately 3 million people reported their sole race as AI/AN and 2.3 million people reported their race as combined AI/AN and one or more other races (US Census Bureau, 2012). With a combined total of more than 6 million people in 2012, AI/ANs make up about 2% of the US population. For the purposes of this chapter, we will use "American Indian/Alaska Native" (AI/AN) to include all AI/AN peoples.

Currently, 566 federally recognized AI/AN tribes and more than 100 state-recognized tribes exist in the United States. Also, some tribes exist without any state or federal recognition. Figure 49.1 shows that the distribution of AI/AN population varies across regions of the United States, with most AI/ANs residing in the western and southern regions (Norris, Vines, & Hoeffel, 2012). Although many people perceive AI/ANs as residents of remote reservations, separated from the rest of America, the majority live in urban areas; only about one-third live on reservations and tribal trust lands (US Census Bureau, 2012).

Like American elders from other racial and ethnic groups, the AI/AN elder population continues to grow. The US Department of Health and Human Services, Administration on Aging, provided a statistical profile of AI/ANs living in the United States and Alaska in 2009 (Administration on Aging [AOA], 2013). There were just over 200,000 elders who identified as AI/AN in 2009, and by 2050, that number is expected to increase to over 900,000 (Vincent & Velkoff, 2010). Fifty percent of AI/AN elderly lived in only six states (see Figure 49.2) (AOA, 2013).

HEALTH AND WELLNESS

Health, according to the *Constitution of the World Health Organization*, is "a state of complete physical, mental and social well-being and not merely the absence of disease or infirmity" (World Health Organization, 2006, p. 1). Compared with other racial/ethnic groups, AI/AN adults tend to experience

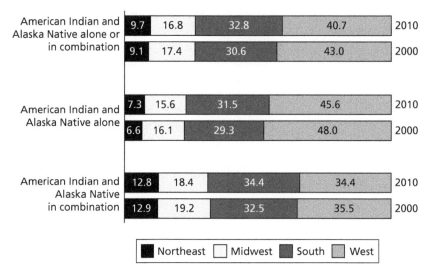

FIGURE 49.1 Percentage Distribution of the American Indian and Alaska Native Population by Region: 2000 and 2010.

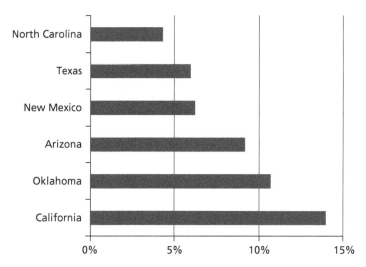

FIGURE 49.2 Percentage of AI/AN Elders in Six States.

more health problems. Diseases of the heart, malignant neoplasm, unintentional injuries, and diabetes mellitus are leading causes of death in AI/AN communities (Centers for Disease Control and Prevention [CDC], 2010). Natives Americans who are born today have a life expectancy that is 4.1 years less than all races in the United States' population. Along with the growing number of AI/AN elders, these health problems are also expected to increase concomitantly (US Census Bureau, 2002). Despite poor health indicators in AI/AN populations, the resiliency within these communities can be linked to

improved health and mental conditions, specifically among elders. American Indian/Alaska Native elders are the ideal representatives of resiliency, defined as the ability to successfully alter one's life despite risks and hardships (Grandbois & Sanders, 2009).

HISTORICAL VIEW OF BOARDING SCHOOLS AND EFFECTS ON ELDERS

Boarding schools are one aspect of colonization that played a significant role in the lives of young indigenous children, the scars of which many elders still carry today. During the "boarding school era" (between 1880 and 1930), systematic assimilation of AI/AN children increased as children were removed to residential schools, often hundreds of miles away from their tribes (Charbonneau-Dahlen, 2011). In 1920, school attendance became compulsory, but even before that, children as young as 4 were often forcibly removed from their parents. At the start of a new school year, community members recall police and even soldiers "kid catching" (Barrett & Britton, 1997, p. 11), a term used for the rounding up of children to be sent to residential schools (Juneau & Montana State Office of Public Instruction, 2001; Reyhner & Eder, 2004). By 1930, over half of all Native children who attended school did so in such institutions (Evans-Campbell, Walters, Pearson, & Campbell, 2012; Charbonneau-Dahlen, 2011).

The beliefs that colonizing nations held about AI/AN peoples were rooted in stereotypical ideas that Natives were "savages" without "real" languages (Ridgeway & Pewewardy, 2004, p. 29). Indian education was for the purpose of converting these "savages" into patriotic American citizens (Barrett & Britton, 1997, p. 29). The methods for doing so were cultural genocide: ridding the younger generation of their "barbarous dialects" and traditions and assimilating them into the "civilized" norms and religions of Anglo society (Ridgeway & Pewewardy, 2004, p. 30).

Mission and government boarding schools were designed to eradicate Native language, culture, and religion and followed a military model, using authoritarian discipline, gender segregation, manual labor, and rote memorization (Lomawaima, 1999). Education in these schools mandated English only (Barrett & Britton, 1997; Ridgeway & Pewewardy, 2004) and emphasized basic academic skills. Students spent part of each day in instruction and the other part in manual labor as a function of the education process, under the guise of vocational training (Barrett & Britton, 1997; McDade, 2008). The dual concept of "Christianizing and civilizing" flourished in boarding schools, where Native practices were regarded as "barbaric and pagan" (Barrett & Britton, 1997, p. 23). Some AI/AN adults who survived the boarding schools remember being given a Christian name and others recall being called only by a number (Barrett & Britton, 1997; Reyhner & Eder, 2004). Christian holidays were honored, but Native ceremonies were outlawed and could not even be discussed. One elder felt that "the pressure was so

great that you didn't dare try to be Indian" (Barrett & Britton, 1997, p.15).

Health issues plagued these schools, often due to dormitory-style living, where contagious diseases spread quickly. In addition, many students suffered from malnutrition due to a lack of food, poor food variety, and poor food quality (Barrett & Britton, 1997; Reyhner & Eder, 2004). Poor sanitation, crowded conditions, and inadequate heat and ventilation all contributed to health issues (Reyhner & Eder, 2004).

Community massacres, forced relocation, and prohibition of and punishment for cultural practices make up the experiences of successive generations of AI/AN peoples. The at-risk behaviors and damaging patterns of victims, who continue to carry their pain throughout their lives and themselves become abusers is due, in part, to historical trauma. Historical trauma is a "cumulative emotional and psychological wounding, over the lifespan and across generations" (Brave Heart, 2003, p. 7).

Research shows that the impact of boarding schools may result in "intergenerational trauma," a term used to indicate the generational persistence of traumatic events that can manifest in such mental issues as depression, suicidal thoughts, and PTSD symptoms, as well as physical health issues in future generations (Evans-Campbell et al., 2012, p. 425; Gone, 2009, p. 752). The physical, sexual, and cultural assaults felt by the generations who attended boarding schools have yielded a legacy of distress and disability for contemporary AI/ANs, so prevalent that the term "residential school syndrome" (Gone, 2009, p. 755) has been proposed to contextualize these symptoms. A common thread that elders expressed was that the boarding school took their identity. One elder said, "I lost my culture," and another claimed that "our people . . . were brainwashed . . . to believe that . . . traditional practices were evil . . ." (Gone, 2009, p. 758). Many AI/AN intergenerational health outcomes, such as poor mental health, anxiety, and substance abuse, undoubtedly stem from the "soul wound" inflicted by colonization (Gone, 2009, p. 752).

Overall, boarding school experiences have important implications for the provision of culturally relevant services for American Indian and Alaska Native elders. In working with boarding school "survivors," counselors have found that those in need of therapy are dealing with past personal pain (Gone, 2009, p. 755). Historical trauma may manifest itself in survivors' self-destructive behavior, anger, and difficulty with expressing emotions; therefore, health and social work practitioners need to consider the implications of historical trauma. Healing must involve personal treatment, but also must take into account the entire community. Programs that teach and reestablish Native practices and culture as well as rebuild individual and collective strength and heritage are essential (Evans-Campbell et al., 2012; Gone, 2009). Such programs will assist in the healing of the soul wound.

CULTURAL UNDERSTANDINGS OF ELDERS

Unlike mainstream American society, which tends to define age chronologically, traditional AI/AN concepts of tribal elders disregard numerical age and focus on the significance of the elder in the community (Baldridge, 2001; Graves, Shavings, & Rose, 2009). Within Indian communities, there is a distinction made between an elder and an elderly person. An Indian elder is not necessarily an old person. Status is more often related to a person's ability to function and to be productive and demonstrate leadership (Weibel-Orlando, 1989; Williams, 1976; Varcoe, Bottorff, Carey, Sullivan, & Williams, 2010). In general, older persons are respected and Native children are taught to care for the elderly (Day, 2007).

In the past, elders were vital to Indian life, serving as mentors and counselors, keeping alive the traditions, roles, and values within families and the community. As part of an extended family, elders worked in gardens, maintained households, and raised the children of working parents (Baldridge, 2001; Williams, 1976). Even though urbanization and assimilation seem to have weakened the role of elders today, elders are still acknowledged for their wisdom, knowledge of history and tradition, and accumulated experiences as they relate to the tribal community (Cooke-Dallin, Rosborough, & Underwood, 2000; Day, 2007). The communities in which elders were raised instilled their values and social norms. Through daily interaction with the children and youth, elders use oral communication and example to transmit and reinforce their wisdom until it becomes internalized in the next generation (Cooke-Dallin et al., 2000; Jackson, 2002).

While every tribe is different, research shows that individuals viewed as elders must earn that position.

For example, in Alaska Native communities, to be an elder means that one has maintained a healthy lifestyle, has extensive cultural knowledge, and uses good judgment (Graves et al., 2009). The position demands selflessness and a willingness to help others. Elders earn respect by teaching and helping others and realize how important their roles are to the communities ("Elders Begin to Realize," 2004). Some elders may be "chosen" because of family heritage, but not all are willing to be immersed in the traditional ways or comfortable sharing their teachings. Others may have the desire but have not earned the respect and trust afforded to an elder ("Age not only," 1993; Cooke-Dallin et al., 2000).

Elders demonstrate the core tribal values of reciprocity and responsibility by maintaining and sharing the teachings and traditions (Christensen & Poupart, 2012). The role of the elder is specifically to pass on this knowledge, which Erikson coined as "Generativity" among his eight stages of human development (Slater, 2003). These teachings are messages about how to act, how to perform a task, how to comprehend—all with an appropriate attitude (Cooke-Dallin, Rosborough, & Underwood, 2000). While children learn age-appropriate physical skills, adolescents and young adults are taught the cultural values by those most equipped to teach: the elders. Because Native communities are steeped in oral tradition, teachings are emphasized through repetition and modeling. The interaction between the one who shares and the one who listens builds intergenerational relationships as well as cognitive skills, self-discipline, and respect (Cooke-Dallin et al., 2000; Graves et al., 2009).

Elders must demonstrate a willingness to be approached by others; they prepare through practice and through practice they feel prepared when they are sought out. As a role model, the elder behaves in a manner that is consistent with the teachings about being "right with the universe." An elder's personal life is ideally one of humbleness, honesty, and integrity. It is important that elders show a deep understanding of social and spiritual awareness and model respect and adherence to cultural traditions (Cooke-Dallin et al., 2000; Graves et al., 2009).

The underlying belief of Native culture is that elders supply the balance and harmony within the community through their ancestral connections to the past. Generations are strengthened through the elders, and that interdependency ensures that the people will retain their identity and that the culture will survive (Cooke-Dallin et al., 2000; Graves et al., 2009). Because the accumulation of teachings is considered a lifelong undertaking, chronological age becomes valued, as it signifies increased knowledge and wisdom from which others will benefit. The proceeding section highlights respectful practices to use when interacting and working with AI/AN elders and their families. These examples/recommendations are also relevant when working with other racial and ethnic minority elders in the United States. They are only examples and will not apply to every AI/AN individual but can serve as an example of how to work with AI/AN elders.

CULTURALLY COMPETENT PRACTICES WITH AI/AN OLDER ADULTS

Social workers serving AI/AN older adults should aspire to build respectful relationships and establish effective communications with this population.

Ways to Show Respect and Establish Rapport

Social workers can show respect to older adults by greeting them first and then greeting others who are present. Social workers should use the elder's formal address initially but should later ask if the elder prefers a different way of being addressed (Hendrix, 2001). To build rapport, social workers may consider sharing something about themselves, such as information about their family.

Language and Literacy Assessment

Social workers are advised to ascertain the older adult's proficiency with the English language, as many older AI/AN adults may not speak English fluently and some do not speak English at all. In those situations, the social worker should work with an interpreter. Social workers should not assume a lack of understanding when an older AI/AN adult speaks indirectly through stories.

Communication

To enhance the quality of interactions between AI/AN older adults and social workers, one should establish a calm demeanor. It is important for social workers to slow down when communicating, especially during initial visits and when healthcare decisions are being made. An AI/AN older adult may speak with a specific cadence. Social workers should match their conversational pace with that of the older adult. This improves the flow of information and builds stronger trust and rapport (LaFramboise, Trimble, & Mohatt, 1990; Thomason, 1991). This also gives older adults enough time to express themselves without interruptions. Social workers should listen more than they talk. They should give the older adult their total attention.

Nonverbal Communication

When some AI/AN older adults nod their heads, they are indicating that they hear what is being said. Raised eyebrows may indicate agreement. They may furrow their brow to indicate they disagree. When they hold their arms tightly, that may indicate that they want to maintain a distance. Some AI/AN elders may avoid eye contact to indicate respect for the person (J. T. Garrett & Garrett, 1994; LaFramboise & Dixon, 1981). Because healthcare providers are held in high regard, it is customary for elders to not look directly at the social workers even though they are listening to what is being said. This practice comes from the belief that healthcare providers have the gift of healing.

How They See the World/ Decision-Making

Many AI/AN older adults have a holistic view of the world, viewing themselves as connected to their family, community, and environment. They put others' needs before their own and engage in activities and practices that promote the health and well-being of their family (Graves, Smith, Easley, & Charles, 2004). Numerous AI/AN older adults feel a sense of purpose to transmit their knowledge to the younger generations. They realize that once they pass away, their knowledge is no longer available. Transmitting knowledge contributes to their sense of purpose, which affects their health and well-being. This AI/AN proverb sums up the importance of learning from our elders: "When an elder dies, a library burns."

LONG-TERM SUPPORTS AND SERVICES FOR INDIAN COUNTRY

As more AI/ANs live to adulthood and old age, the elderly population (age 55 and older) is projected to increase from 5.5% of the total US population in 1990 to 12.6% in 2050 (Satter & Wallace, 2010). According to Goins, Moss, Buchwald, and Guralnik (2007), the number of AI/ANs aged 75 years or older who will need long-term care will double in the next 25 years. It is customary in Indian Country for the extended family to take care of an elder. It is estimated that family members provide 90% of long-term care in Indian Country (Goins, Moss, Buchwald, & Guralnik, 2007). Their tradition is now colliding with Western society, as more AI/AN people live off their reservations and are less connected with tribal values of caring for their elders.

Long-term supports and services (LTSS) are limited in rural areas and do not reach many of the isolated elders across Indian Country. A majority of the Alaska Native villages are isolated and only accessible by boat or airplane when weather permits. According to M. D. Garrett (2002), AI/AN elders are most often located in rural areas, while younger family members have moved to urban areas for employment. The lack of younger family members' support creates challenges for providing AI/AN elders' care.

Younger people are migrating out of tribal communities because of lack of jobs or to pursue education. This leaves fewer caregivers for the growing population of older adults in AI/AN communities. We also have to look at the dysfunction of young people: high rates of alcoholism and substance abuse (Lowe, Liang, Riggs, & Henson, 2012). Caregivers are not as healthy and are less able to take care of the elder family members. Another important consideration is that baby boomers grew up more acculturated than previous generations, which has shaped their values and expectations for care.

Who Funds Long-Term Supports and Services?

Medicaid is the single largest payer for virtually all forms of LTSS. These supports and services, where available, are financed by Medicaid, the Older Americans Act (OAA) programs, state or tribal programs, or individuals. Very few individuals in the United States, including Indian Country, have the resources to pay for their own LTSS. Research indicates that home healthcare is the most frequently needed service among AI/ANs. However, 88% of AI/AN communities surveyed by the US AOA are not able to meet that demand for home healthcare (Jervis, Jackson, & Manson, 2002).

Administration on Aging

The AOA is a major funding source for LTSS in Indian Country. Under Title VI of the OAA, the AOA awards grants directly to tribes and tribal organizations for supportive and nutritional services for older AI/ANs. Services may include congregate and home-delivered meals, senior centers, homemaker services, and other assistance that helps to keep elders living at home. Title VI programs continue to form the foundation of tribal elder programs. These programs are also important sources of socialization and supportive services. Examples of such programs include traditional craft activities, physical fitness classes, and various dance programs (AOA, 2013).

As part of the OAA, Title VI-C is the National Family Caregiver Support Program of 2000, which provides grants to tribal communities for the implementation of caregiver support programs for those caring for someone with a chronic illness or disability. However, the funding for these programs is limited. In regard to LTSS, supporting the overall family is equivalent to caring for older adults.

Medicaid and Medicare

Medicaid has been moving away from facility-based care toward more home- and community-based care (Aldrich & Benson, 2010), which is the preference of tribal communities and AI/AN elders (Goins & Spencer, 2005). States can provide in-home services to help an older person through Medicaid services. The first is through a Medicaid service called "Personal Care" (Wallace, Satter, & Zubiate, 2003). Most, but not all, states provide personal care services as part of the regular Medicaid program, called "state plan" services. They can also offer personal care and related services through a special program called a "1915c waiver." This is a special program that allows states to provide services in the home and community to help Medicaid recipients stay out of nursing homes. Most, but not all, states have waiver programs that cover elderly and disabled people (Wallace et al., 2003).

Each state administers its own Medicaid program and establishes eligibility standards, scope of service, and rates. States must meet federal requirements in order to receive federal matching funds. Medicaid pays health programs for medical assistance provided to elders, including nursing home care and home- and community-based health and social services, for those who meet the eligibility criteria. Eligibility for Medicaid coverage is primarily based on income levels, and individuals can apply for coverage in each state.

Medicare is a health insurance program for people age 65+, people under age 65 with certain disabilities, and people of all ages with end-stage renal disease. The other critical piece for Medicare eligibility that is often a concern in Indian Country is the fact that recipients must have paid into the system. For example, one must have worked for a wage for at least 40 quarters and had Medicare tax deducted from one's pay. In general many AI/AN older adults do not meet this criteria. Medicare will pay for LTSS for a maximum of 100 days as necessary for rehabilitation or skilled nursing care after a 3-day hospitalization (National Indian Health Board, 2009). In-home services are available, but the recipients must be home-bound or need intermittent skilled nursing or therapy services. Additionally, recipients must be under the care of a physician who prescribes their plan of care.

TRIBAL PROGRAMS AND SERVICES

According to the 2013 Center for Medicare and Medicaid Services (CMS) report, "only 2–13% of tribes had access to assisted living, nursing homes, adult care, and hospice care compared to 84%–92% of tribes that had access to home-delivered meals and nutrition site programs" (p. 10). According to R. T. Goins and Spencer (2005), nursing homes are the least favored care options for AI/AN elders. The CMMS report also indicated that "logistical, financial, and cultural factors have served as barriers" (p. 10) for LTSS for AI/ANs. Also, AI/AN elders may also be reluctant to seek LTSS because of cultural barriers, such as the belief that the needs of family members or the community are more important. Moreover, some AI/AN elders may believe that spiritual needs are more important than physical needs (Goins & Spencer, 2005).

The Indian Health Service (IHS), an agency within the Department of Health and Human Services, is responsible for providing federal health services to American Indians and Alaska Natives in the United States. The provision of health services to members of federally- recognized tribes grew out of the special government-to-government relationship between the federal government and Indian tribes.... The IHS is the principal federal health care provider and health advocate for Indian people, and its goal is to raise their health status to the highest possible level. The IHS provides a comprehensive health service delivery system, not including LTSS, for approximately 1.9 million AI/AN who belong to 566 federally recognized tribes in 35 states. (Indian Health Service, n.d., para. 4)

The Indian Health Service is working in partnership with Tribes and Urban Indian Organizations to increase access to LTSS for elders and younger individuals with disabilities. With the passage of the Affordable Care Act of 2010, the need for culturally appropriate LTSS provided by tribal communities has become the focus of Indian Country. The challenge with this legislative mandate is the lack of funding allocated to the IHS. One of the challenges facing the tribal healthcare system in Alaska and throughout Indian Country is that the IHS does not directly fund LTSS for elders. Meanwhile the demand for these services is increasing (Lewis & Boyd, 2012).

Program of All-Inclusive Care for the Elderly (PACE)

Programs of All-Inclusive Care for the Elderly (PACE) is a federal program designed to keep elders living in their homes, connected with their communities. PACE provides an all-inclusive and comprehensive continuum of care. It is designed to improve the quality of life for our older adults. One example of a successful PACE program in Indian Country is the Cherokee Nation Elder Care (CNEC) program. The CNEC program is "the first PACE program in the state of Oklahoma and the first PACE program to be sponsored by a Native American tribe" (Johns, 2009, p. 20). The CNEC program provides to elders a physician, clinical nurses, physical and occupational therapists, speech therapists, activities director, a social worker, adult home care coordinators, adult day center nurses, personal care aides, and a dietician. For participants who can no longer drive, transportation is provided to and from participants' homes. The center also offers a noon meal; morning and afternoon snacks; and a full-service clinic. These services allow the center to provide a primary care physician and physical and mental activities to AIAN older adults. This extensive program is not found among most tribal communities. Tribes provide healthcare for their members, and many have been successful in contracting their healthcare services to address the needs unmet by IHS (Johns, 2009).

CONCLUSION

The United States, as well as the world, is facing a global aging boom and with this comes the need for community-driven strategies. As social workers, we understand the value of community engagement when tackling complex and important issues such as the growing elderly population. Social workers should advocate for a shift in the way LTSS are delivered and should support more home-based, culturally responsive services for AI/AN elders. Indian Country should consider strategies to increase funding for the training of home healthcare workers and the expansion of home healthcare for the elderly AI/AN population.

REFERENCES

Administration on Aging (AOA). (2013). *Facts: American Indian, Alaska Native, and Native Hawaiian programs*. Retrieved from http://www.aoa.gov/aoaroot/Press_Room/Products_Materials/fact/pdf/Native_American_Program.pdf

Aldrich, N., & Benson, W. (2010). *Caregiving in Indian Country: Tribes supporting family traditions*. National Association of Chronic Disease Directors. CDC Healthy Aging Program. Retrieved from http://c.ymcdn.com/sites/www.chronicdisease.org/resource/resmgr/healthy_aging_critical_issues_brief/ha_cib_indiancaregiving.pdf

Baldridge, D. (2001). Indian elders: Family traditions in crisis. *American Behavioral Scientist, 44*, 1515–1527. doi: 10.1177/00027640121956953

Barrett, C., & Britton, M. W. (1997). "You didn't dare try to be Indian": Oral histories of former Indian boarding school students. *North Dakota History, 64*(2), 4–25. Retrieved from http://search.ebscohost.com/login.aspx?direct=true&db=ahl&AN=45883310&site=ehost-live&scope=site

Brave Heart, M. (2003). The historical trauma response among natives and its relationship with substance abuse: A Lakota illustration. *Journal of Psychoactive Drugs, 35*, 7–13.

Centers for Disease Control and Prevention (CDC). (2010). *American Indians and Alaska Natives*. Retrieved August 3, 2013, from http://www.cdc.gov/minorityhealth/populations/REMP/aian.html#10

Charbonneau-Dahlen, B. (2011). Giving voice to historical trauma through storytelling: The impact of boarding school experience on American Indians. *Dissertation Abstracts International: Section B: The Sciences and Engineering, 72*. Retrieved from http://search.ebscohost.com/login.aspx?direct=true&db=psyh&AN=2011-99180-216&site=ehost-live&scope=site. (2011-99180-216)

Christensen, R., & Poupart, L. M. (2012). Elder teachers gather at Manitou Api, Manitoba: Igniting the fire, gathering wisdom from all nations. *International Journal of Qualitative Studies in Education, 25*, 933–949. doi: 10.1080/09518398.2012.720733

Cooke-Dallin, B., Rosborough, T., & Underwood, L. (2000). The role of elders in child and youth care education. *Canadian Journal of Native Education, 24*, 82–91.

Day, P. A. (2007). American Indian elders. In P. J. Kolb (Ed.), *Social work practice with ethnically and racially diverse nursing home residents and their families* (pp. 1–48). New York, NY: Columbia University Press.

Evans-Campbell, T., Walters, K. L., Pearson, C. R., & Campbell, C. D. (2012). Indian boarding school experience, substance use, and mental health among urban two-spirit American Indian/Alaska natives. *American Journal of Drug and Alcohol Abuse, 38*, 421–427. doi: 10.3109/00952990.2012.701358

Garrett, J. T., & Garrett, M. W. (1994). The path of good medicine: Understanding and counseling Native American Indians. *Journal of Multicultural Counseling and Development, 22*, 134–144.

Garrett, M. D. (2002). Census information on American Indian and Alaska Natives: Implications for long term care. In *American Indian and Alaska Native Roundtable on Long Term Care: Final Report*. Albuquerque, NM: National Indian Council on Aging.

Goins, R. T., Moss, M., Buchwald, D., & Guralnik, J. M. (2007). Disability among older American Indians and Alaska Natives: An analysis of the 2000 Census

Public Use Microdata Sample. *The Gerontologist, 47,* 690–696. doi:10.1093/geront/47.5.690

Goins, R. T., & Spencer, S. M. (2005). Public health issues among older American Indians and Alaska Natives. *Generations, 29*(2), 30–35.

Gone, J. P. (2009). A community-based treatment for Native American historical trauma: Prospects for evidence-based practice. *Journal of Consulting and Clinical Psychology, 77,* 751–762. doi: 10.1037/a0015390

Grandbois, D. M., & Sanders, G. F. (2009). The resilience of Native American Elders. *Issues in Mental Health Nursing, 30,* 569–580. doi:10.1080/01612840902916151

Graves, K., Shavings, L., & Rose, E. (2009). Alaska native elders' views of abuse: The tradition of harmony, respect, and listening. *Alaska Journal of Anthropology, 7,* 71–88.

Graves, K., & Smith, S. L., Easley, C., & Charles, G. P. (2004). *Conferences on Alaska Native elders: Our view of dignified aging.* Anchorage, AK: National Resource Center for American Indian, Alaska Native, and Native Hawaiian Elders.

Hendrix, L. R. (2001). *Health and health care of American Indians and Alaska Native elders.* Ethnogeriatric Curriculum Module. Stanford Geriatric Education Center. Retrieved from http://sgec.stanford.edu/ethnomed/index.html

Indian Health Service. (n.d.). *About IHS.* Retrieved from http://www.ihs.gov/aboutihs/

Jackson, D. D. (2002). Introduction. In *Our elders lived it: American Indian identity in the city* (pp. 3–18). DeKalb: Northern Illinois University Press.

Jervis, L., Jackson, M., & Manson, S. (2002). Need for availability of and barriers to the provision of long term care services for older American Indians. *Journal of Cross-Cultural Gerontology, 17,* 295–311.

Johns, J. (2009). *Overview of long term care in Indian Country.* Centers for Medicare and Medicaid Tribal Technical Advisory Group and National Indian Health Board. Washington, DC: National Indian Health Board.

Juneau, S., & Montana State Office of Public Instruction. (2001). *A history and foundation of American Indian education policy* Retrieved from http://search.ebscohost.com/login.aspx?direct=true&db=eric&AN=ED456945&site=ehost-live&scope=site

LaFramboise, T. D., & Dixon, D. N. (1981). American Indian perceptions of trustworthiness in a counseling interview. *Journal of Counseling Psychology, 28,* 135–139.

LaFramboise, T. D., Trimble, J. E., & Mohatt, G. V. (1990). Counseling intervention and American Indian

tradition: An integrative approach. *Counseling Psychologist, 18,* 628–654.

Lazaruk, S. (1993). Age not only criteria for elders: Position demands selflessness, willingness to help others. *Windspeaker, 11*(8), 12.

Lewis, J., & Boyd, K. (2012). Reconceptualizing long term care in rural Alaska. *IHS Primary Care Provider, 37*(2), 12–44.

Lomawaima, K. T. (1999). The unnatural history of American Indian education. In K. G. Swisher & J. W. Tippeconnie III (Eds.), *Next steps: Research and practice to advance Indian education* (pp. 3–39). Charlestown, WV: ERIC Clearinghouse on Rural Education and Small Schools.

Lowe, J., Liang, H., Riggs, C., & Henson, J. (2012). Community partnership to affect substance abuse among Native American adolescents. *American Journal of Drug and Alcohol Abuse, 38,* 450–455. doi: 10.3109/00952990.2012.694534

McDade, J. R. (2008). *The birth of American Indian manual labor boarding schools: Social control through culture destruction, 1820–1850.* Lewiston, NY: Mellen Press.

National Indian Health Board. (2009). *Long term supports and services report.* Retrieved from http://www.nihb.org

Norris, T., Vines, P. L., & Hoeffel, M. E. (2012). Percentage distribution of the American Indian and Alaska Native population by region: 2000 and 2010. United States Census Bureau. Washington, DC: US Department of Commerce. Economics and Statistics Administration.

Parker, A. (2004). Elders begin to realize the importance of their role. *Windspeaker, 22*(6), 23.

Reyhner, J. A., & Eder, J. M. (2004). *American Indian education.* Norman: University of Oklahoma Press.

Ridgeway, M., & Pewewardy, C. (2004). Linguistic imperialism in the United States: The historical eradication of American Indian languages and the English-only movement. *Multicultural Review, 13*(2), 28–34. Retrieved from http://search.ebscohost.com/login.aspx?direct=true&db=eft&AN=507920733&site=ehost-live&scope=site

Satter, D. E., & Wallace, S. P. (2010). American Indian Elder health: Critical information for researchers and policymakers. Los Angeles, CA: UCLA Center for Health Policy Research.

Slater, C. L. (2003). Generativity versus stagnation: An elaboration of Erikson's adult stage of human development. *Journal of Adult Development, 10,* 53–65.

Thomason, T. C. (1991). Counseling Native Americans: An introduction for non-Native

American counselors. *Journal of Counseling and Development, 69,* 321–327.

US Census Bureau. (2002). *Statistical abstract of the United States: 2002* (122nd ed.). Washington, DC: US Census Bureau.

US Census Bureau. (2012). *The American Indian and Alaska Native Population: 2010.* Retrieved October 30, 2011, from http://www.census.gov/prod/cen2010/briefs/c2010br-10.pdf

Varcoe, C., Bottorff, J., Carey, J., Sullivan, D., & Williams, W. (2010). Wisdom and influence of Elders: Possibilities for health promotion and decreasing tobacco exposure in First Nations Communities. *Canadian Public Health Association, Revue Canadienne de Santé Publique, 101,* 154–158.

Vincent, G., & Velkoff, V. (2010). *The next four decades: The older population in the United States: 2010 to 2050.* US Census Bureau, Economic and Statistics Administration. Retrieved from http://www.census.gov/prod/2010pubs/p25-1138.pdf.

Wallace, S. P., Satter, D. E., & Zubiate, A. (2003). *Medicaid home care and tribal health services: A tool kit for developing new programs: Final Report.* Los Angeles, CA: UCLA Center for Health Policy Research.

Weibel-Orlando, J. (1989). Elders and elderlies: Well-being in Indian old age. *American Indian Culture and Research Journal, 13,* 149–170.

Williams, G. C. (1976). Changing roles and status of the Indian elderly. *Papers in Anthropology, 17,* 75–80.

World Health Organization. (2006). *Constitution of the World Health Organization: Basic documents* (45th ed.). Supplement, October 2006. Geneva: Switzerland. Retrieved from http://www.who.int/governance/eb/who_constitution_en.pdf.

Members of minority groups share a common identity and collectively experience marginalization relative to the dominant culture. We typically define minority groups according to such criteria as race, gender, ethnicity, sexual orientation, religion, and national origin in the United States. Other chapters in this section have addressed the most common minority groups along the lines of race, ethnicity, gender, and sexual orientation. This chapter focuses on older adults from "other minority groups," specifically those from marginal religions and regions. Our intent is to raise social workers' understanding of older minority persons who have received limited attention from the social work profession, highlight salient issues that social workers must address with these older adults, and suggest innovative interventions. First, we discuss older adults from Jewish and Muslim religions; second, we consider older Appalachians and Native Hawaiians and other Pacific Islanders.

RELIGION AND OLDER PERSONS

Religion is a central issue for many older persons (Kosmin & Keysar, 2009). It provides people with meaning, support, and guidance in daily life, at work, and in relationships with family, friends, and colleagues. Most older adults (90) describe themselves as religious, while only 67% of younger adults describe themselves this way (Pew Research, 2012). Although national census data exclude gathering information on Americans' religious preferences, other organizations and research centers have conducted surveys that shed light on people's religious affiliations. One such survey, the American Religious Identification Survey (ARIS), used random-digit dialing to collect data from over 50,000 Americans in 2008. The survey revealed that although most Americans identify with the Christian denominations, this has declined since 1990, while the percentage of those stating no religious preference has increased. People within religious groups vary in their views. The Jewish and Muslim populations are especially diverse; they include individuals from different countries and various ethnic backgrounds.

Jewish Older Adults

The American Jewish population includes between 6 and 9 million adults (depending on how this is

VIRGINIA E. RICHARDSON
COLETTE V. BROWNE

Social Work Practice with Older Adults in Other Minority Groups

estimated), including Holocaust survivors, Jews from the former Soviet Union who recently immigrated to the United States, and those unaffiliated with Jewish organizations (Sheskin & Dashefsky, 2012; Pew Research, 2013). The percentage of US adults who say they are Jewish is declining, while those who describe themselves as having no religion is rising (Pew Research, 2013). Most older Jewish persons are US born while others are first-generation immigrants. Jewish identity varies by generation; about 93% of the oldest cohort identifies themselves as Jewish in contrast to 68% of those born after 1980 (Pew Research, 2013).

The Jewish population is older than the non-Jewish population in the United States (Sheskin & Dashefsy, 2012). Between 19% and 25% of the Jewish population is over the age of 65; 18% is over the age of 70 (Kosmin, 2009). The percentage of American Jewish elderly is expected to increase over the next 15 years (Sheskin, 2010).

Physical and Mental Health

Most older Jewish persons are in good health, but they are more likely than younger Jewish persons to report poor or fair health, have lower incomes, and live alone. Compared with younger Jewish persons, older Jewish adults more often participate in their Jewish communities. They more closely identify with their Jewish heritage and tend to have more Jewish friends, feel more emotionally attached to Israel, and more frequently regard being Jewish as important than their younger counterparts (Sheskin, 2010; Pew Research, 2013). Like older Muslim adults, Orthodox Jews may observe strict food restrictions.

Elderly Soviet Jews, many of whom are non-English speaking, minimally acculturated, and without adequate economic support, are especially in need of social work services (UJA-Federation of New York, 2012). These older Jewish persons and their offspring account for about 10% of the US Jewish population (Pew Research, 2013). Older Holocaust survivors also require special attention. They have experienced anti-Semitism throughout their lives and sometimes have lingering trauma associated with their Holocaust experiences. Caregivers of Holocaust survivors often are reluctant to seek assistance (Anderson, Fields, & Dobb, 2013).

Cultural Values and Social Work Interventions

Many organizations provide support to older Jewish and increasingly to non-Jewish persons and their caregivers, although this varies by region. These include the Jewish Association for Services for the Aged in New York (https://jasa.org/), the Council for the Jewish Elderly in Chicago (http://cje.net/), and the Jewish Council for the Aging in Washington, DC (http://www.accessjca.org/) along with Jewish agencies such as the Association of Jewish Aging Services, Jewish Family and Community Services, and Jewish Retirement Homes, which are excellent resources for these older adults. These programs offer adult day programs and other respite services for caregivers, congregate meal sites and meals on wheels (including hot kosher meals), various group programs, and home- and community-based services. Jewish Home Lifecare offers resources for elders and their caregivers. Some, such as the Jewish Child and Family Services, provide Holocaust Community Services for aging survivors of Nazi persecution, which many caregivers might use when moving a Holocaust survivor into a long-term care facility (Anderson, Fields, & Dobb, 2011). Many Jewish communities are building Jewish assisted living facilities and nursing homes. Several organizations, such as The Jewish Federations of North America, actively advocate for national, state, and local aging policies and services.

Culturally Competent Social Work Interventions

As social workers increase their knowledge of older Jewish adults, they will more effectively help these older minority persons get the services they need. Cultural competence involves several components including (1) knowledge and skills that are compatible with culturally diverse populations (2) attitudes and values that honor diversity and (3) a dual focus on the responsibilities of the provider to improve practice, policy, and research related to the culturally diverse (Mokuau, 2011). The Office of Minority Health has published standards for cultural and linguistic competence that emphasize culturally competent care, language access services, and organizational supports (Office of Minority Health [OMH], 2001). New revisions to the National Standard for Cultural and Linguistic Appropriate Services (CLAS), also developed by the OMH, provide a useful framework for social workers and other professionals to follow (OMH, 2013). Literature related to cultural competence and older populations supports these general concepts (Mokuau, 2011).

Muslim Older Adults

Less than 1% of adults (2.6 million) identify with the Muslim/Islamic religion in the United States, although this may be underestimated due to reluctance of many older Muslims to respond to questions about their religion (Pew Research, 2012; Kosmin & Keysar, 2009). The Muslim population is expected to double in the next 20 years. The majority of Arab Americans are not Muslims, and the majority of Muslims are not Arab Americans (Ajrouch, 2007). There are at least three categories of older Muslims. The first group includes those who immigrated to the United States at the turn of the century and live with younger family members. Intergenerational differences sometimes arise in these families. The second category includes the parents of younger family members who accompanied them to America. The third and smallest group includes those who converted to Islam. The majority of US Muslims (64.5%) were born in another country, with the greatest numbers of immigrations coming from Pakistan, Bangladesh, or Somalia. Of the 35.5% who were born in the United States about half are African Americans; the rest are second- or third-generation immigrants (Pew Research, 2011). Although in 2010 those over the age of 60 represented about 13% of the US population, a smaller proportion (9.5%) will be age 60 and over in 2030 due to immigration and high fertility rates (Pew Research, 2011).

Caring for older relatives is an emerging concern for many Muslim Americans, who have until recently belonged to a relatively younger population. As older Muslims increase in the population, health practitioners need to better understand important cultural values that affect these care recipients and caregivers.

Physical and Mental Health

Most Muslim Americans adhere to a holistic conception of health that links religious, physical, and mental components (Padela, Gunter, & Killawi, 2011). Health practitioners must understand these older persons' views about healing to effectively establish trust and rapport. Given the heterogeneity within the Muslim population, holistic assessments that allow for tailored interventions are essential. Older Muslim immigrants are at higher risk for depression and social isolation than their US-born counterparts who have acculturated to the mainstream culture (Ajrouch, 2007). In addition, older Muslim immigrants who maintain their own heritage culture more often become depressed compared with those who are more integrated in the American culture (Abu-Bader, Tirmazi, & Ross-Sheriff, 2011). Social interactions with family members and peers presumably can buffer these effects, but this can be difficult when adult children and grandchildren are more assimilated. Following the events of September 11, 2001, Muslims have experienced increased apprehension from other Americans. Muslims who dress in their traditional garments or speak English with a foreign accent are harassed more often than older Muslim adults who conceal their cultural or ethnic identities (Abu-Bader et al., 2011). Social workers must advocate against such hostility and discriminatory practices and educate others about Muslims to eradicate stereotypical attitudes.

Culturally Competent Social Work Interventions

Helping others is central to Muslim daily life. The help is usually informal and family based, but increasing numbers of social service agencies, such as Muslim Family Services, are emerging. Many older Muslim families eschew formal help because of the stigma associated with seeking professional guidance. Although most Muslim caregivers report they find "immense satisfaction" caring for their parents, many are unable to find nursing homes and assisted living facilities that will maintain their parents' "way of life" (Stabiner, 2011). Social workers who practice culturally sensitive approaches with Muslim traditions and rituals may become more appealing to older Muslims. Many older Muslims also feel more comfortable talking to social workers who share the same religious background. In addition, social workers who partner with the natural, informal support systems in Muslim communities will lessen the stigma for these older adults.

The oldest and largest Muslim social service agency is the Arab Community Center for Economic and Social Services (ACCESS) in Dearborn, Michigan, created in the mid-1970s. Organizations devoted to helping caregivers are also emerging. These include the American Muslim Women's

Association (http://www.amwaaz.org) and the Islamic Social Services Association USA, based in Phoenix (http://www.issausa.org/). These programs are organized around participants' ethnic and religious values and provide culturally competent assistance, including requirements for diet and space to pray. Based on an in-depth study using focus groups with American Muslims ranging in age from 18 to 75 in southeastern Michigan study, Padela et al. (2011) identified three healthcare accommodations that should be top priorities: (1) gender-concordant care to accommodate Islamic conceptions of modesty and privacy, (2) Halal food (prepared according to Islamic law), and (3) prayer space to allow for a ritual five-time-daily prayer routine. They also recommended that health facilities offer imams for American Muslim persons who seek such spiritual assistance.

REGIONAL MINORITIES

Some older adults become members of other minority groups as a result of living in certain areas, such as in Appalachia or on one of the Pacific Islands. Older persons from Appalachia and the Pacific Islands represent distinct social and economic characteristics and need support in various ways.

Appalachian Older Persons

The Appalachian Mountains are a major mountain chain in the northeastern United States, covering 1,500 miles of land from the Canadian province of Quebec to northern Alabama. It is organized into several distinct subregions: Central Appalachia, which remains the poorest of the Appalachian subregions and has suffered more from the recent recession than the rest of the nation; Northern Appalachia, which includes the highest percentage of older adults; North Central Appalachia; South Central Appalachia; and Southern Appalachia, which overlaps with the nation's "Sun Belt." (Appalachian Regional Commission [ARC], 2013); see the ARC website for more information on these regions at http://www.arc.gov. Older persons constitute about 15% of the population in Appalachia, and they have increased in number at a slightly faster pace than they have in the rest of the country. The median age (40 years) is more than two-and-a-half years older than that of the US population as a whole and will continue to rise (Pollard & Jacobsen, 2013).

The demographic shifts in the Appalachian population are due mostly to out-migration of young adults seeking jobs elsewhere because of unemployment and other economic pressures. Few older persons, especially those in poor health, leave the area in part because they maintain stronger attachments to the land and their communities than younger persons (Pollard & Jacobsen, 2013).

Physical and Mental Health

Older Appalachian persons, especially Appalachian women, have high disability rates, as measured by their abilities to perform activities of daily living and instrumental activities of daily living. Relative to older non-Appalachians, they also tend to have more chronic illnesses. In general, Appalachian adults have higher mortality and morbidity than non-Appalachian adults with respect to heart disease, cancer, stroke, chronic obstructive pulmonary disease, and diabetes (Ludke, Obermiller, & Horner, 2012). One reason for these high rates of disability is the lack of access to preventive care (Ludke & Obermiller, 2012). Many older persons live at great distances from hospitals and other clinics, and transportation to these places is often difficult.

Although many researchers have investigated the physical health problems of Appalachians, few have studied their mental health. Keefe and Curtin (2012) found especially high rates of depression in the economically distressed Central Appalachian coal mining regions, and these rates are much higher than the national average. Those at greatest risk for depression and suicide in this region are military veterans returning home to rural areas and those who are homebound and socially isolated (Keefe & Curtin, 2012). Many older rural Appalachians experience mental illness through somatization.

Traditionally, older Appalachian adults have relied on friends and family members to assist them in their later years. However, the out-migration of younger Appalachians who would otherwise provide informal assistance to their older relatives often lead older persons to rely more on friends and neighbors for support (Glasgow, 2000).

Culturally Competent Social Work Interventions

Although cultural variations exist in these subregions, older Appalachians share many common values and lifestyles. For example, older Appalachians emphasize self-reliance and hard work, and maintain strong religious beliefs (Keefe & Curtin, 2012). In addition, these older persons are remarkably resilient despite the adversity associated with economic impoverishment. Self-reliance is such a strong value that many rural Appalachians eschew using formal services, including placing family members in nursing homes. Rural Appalachian communities "tend to be anchored on kinship and rely on a moral economy at the local level" (Keefe, 2009, p. 18). Social workers can empower older clients in these communities by recognizing these existing strengths in the communities, empowering families, and implementing participatory development interventions that include older residents.

Keefe (2009) recommended the creation of flexible services to accommodate the needs of low-income people. For example, home-based mental health interventions have been found to be effective in these communities. Home visitations decrease the stigma associated with mental health treatment. Telehealth (e.g., virtual visits via videophone or the Internet) is an attractive alternative that can provide more unobtrusive support for these families. Family treatment also might work better with these older persons than psychotherapy that emphasizes the individual (Keefe & Curtin, 2012). In addition, mutual self-help groups work well with these older adults. Keefe and Curtin (2012) recommend that health practitioners incorporate an ethnomedical model that is grounded in ethnic groups' assumptions about the causes of their problems yet recognizes individual differences.

Advocacy is especially important when assisting older Appalachian persons (Keefe, 2009). This includes campaigning on behalf of older Appalachians to: (1) increase their economic resources, (2) expand physical and mental healthcare, (3) strengthen social resources, (4) implement community-based interventions and community-academic partnerships, (5) employ evidenced-based approaches, and (6) improve transportation and other community services assistance. Further, Keefe (2009) encouraged more research on the interaction between mental and physical health that will lead to the most effective interventions for these individuals and their families.

Keefe (2009) suggested that social workers learn more about community norms, involve residents, partner with other professionals, incorporate a "collectivist" perspective, and tailor interventions that are sensitive to these older persons' cultural and religious preferences. These suggestions are consistent with the recent application of the strength perspective with older adults that emphasizes, "discovering, developing, and building on the person's internal and external resources" (Nelson-Becker, Chapin, & Fast, 2013, p. 164).

Older Native Hawaiian and Other Pacific Islanders

Native Hawaiian and Other Pacific Islanders (NHOPI) make up 0.3% of the total population, totaling 1.4 million persons. This category of people is most concentrated in Hawaii, with 26% of the total state population reporting being NHOPI. According to the US Census Bureau, the Native Hawaiian and Other Pacific Islander population category includes those who indicated their race(s) as Native Hawaiian, Guamanian or Chomorro, Samoan, or Other Pacific Islander, or reported entries such as Polynesian (e.g., Tahitian, Tongan, and Tokelauan), Micronesian (e.g., Marshallese, Palauan, and Chuukese) and Melanesian (e.g., Fijian, Guinean, and Soloman Islander). In addition to the state of Hawaii, NHOPI primarily come from the US-associated Pacific Island Jurisdictions that comprise American Samoa, the Commonwealth of the Northern Marianas Islands and Guam, and three freely associated states: the Federated States of Micronesia, the Republic of the Marshall Islands, and the Republic of Palau. Overall, the NHOPIs are a young population with a median age of 35.2 (US Census Bureau, 2010), and only 5% are over the age of 65. Nearly three-fourths of the NHOPI residing in the United States and its territories live in the western states, and more than half live in two states, California and Hawaii. Ten states—California, Hawaii, Washington, Texas, New York, Florida, Utah, Nevada, Oregon, and Arizona—account for 80% of the nation's NHOPI population.

Native Hawaiians are the largest NHOPI group, including 518,000 persons or 46% of the NHOPI population. The next two largest groups are Samoans (either alone or in combination with other races), comprising 174,000 people and making up 15% of the NHOPI population, and Guamanian/Chamorro (either alone or in combination), consisting of 108,000 persons or 11% of the population. Five percent of the Samoans and 2% of Guamanian/Chamorro are people over the age of 65. For various historical reasons, these NHOPI had a much higher proportion of respondents reporting two or more races compared with all other races (US Census Bureau, 2010).

Older NHOPI differ from the overall older adult population in the United States in several ways. For example, the median household income and the per capita incomes for older NHOPI are significantly lower than the incomes of older US persons in general, although nearly the same proportion (10%) of NHOPI and US elders lives in poverty (US Census Bureau, 2010). Nearly 30% of NHOPI elders do not list English as their first language, and 28% of these older persons report not speaking English well or at all. In contrast, less than 1% of US-born elders state that English is not their first language, with only 12.4% of this group reporting they do not speak English well or at all. Additionally, NHOPI elders rarely live alone compared with US elders, with the average household and family sizes consequently larger for NHOPI than Americans. Contrary to popular opinion, NHOPI families are less likely than the general population to live in rural areas (US Census Bureau, 2010).

Older Pacific Islanders represent numerous cultures unique in language, values, lifestyles, history and patterns of adaptation to the United States (Srinivisan & Guillermo, 2000). The increased awareness of the heterogeneity of Asian Americans and Pacific Islanders in culture, language, and origin is one reason the US Census separated Asian Americans from NHOPI and created two distinct racial categories (US Census Bureau, 2010). This change aimed to correct the ways in which aggregated data tended to mask rather than illuminate the differences in mental and physical health issues among the NHOPI population (Srinivisan & Guillermo, 2000).

Physical and Mental Health

Although the leading causes of death for NHOPI mirror those of other Americans—heart disease, stroke, and cancer—Native Hawaiians have one of the nation's shortest life expectancies, and have significantly higher death rates for these three diseases (Kaopua, Braun, Mokuau, Browne, & Park, 2011). Also, NHOPI have higher cancer death rates and higher rates of diabetes than non-Hispanic Whites (Centers for Disease Control [CDC], 2013). They also have a disproportionately high prevalence of asthma, alcohol, smoking and tobacco use, Hepatitis B, HIV/AIDS, and tuberculosis (CDC, 2013). Many researchers have linked increased morbidity and mortality from chronic diseases among NHOPI to changes in lifestyle in the last century (Lassetter, 2011). Contrary to the traditional Pacific Islander diet of low-fat, high fiber foods and active lifestyles, today's NHOPIs have adopted a Western diet high in fats and refined food and a sedentary lifestyle (Englberger, Marks, & Fitzgerald, 2003). Others have suggested that the forced colonization of Pacific Islanders with the resultant loss of land and spiritual well-being, together with high rates of poverty, are the chief culprits for their poor health (Kaholokula, Iwane, & Nacapoy 2010; Ka`opua et al. 2011; Mokuau, 2011).

Additionally, several studies have suggested that Pacific Islanders are at greater risk for mental health problems compared with Whites, due to stressors such as immigration, adjustment to living in an alien culture, discrimination and prejudice, language barriers, economics, and education/occupation stresses and diseases (Asian and Pacific Islander American Health Forum, 2010). Scholars have linked the internalization of discriminatory attitudes felt by many NHOPI populations to feelings of social alienation and disenfranchisement (Kaholokula et al., 2010; Mokuau, 2011). The NHOPI also exhibit more psychological symptoms than the overall population, although few researchers have examined the mental health issues in the older NHOPI population (Braun & Browne, 1998).

Culturally Competent Social Work Interventions

Numerous sociohistorical factors have adversely affected NHOPI mental and physical health (Braun, Yee, Browne, & Mokuau, 2004; Browne, Mokuau, & Braun, 2009). These include international trade, military strategies, and missionary influences that were imposed on NHOPIs and resulted in the replacement of local traditions and rituals with Western norms and practices (Braun et al., 2004; Mokuau, 2011). Other forces, such as diseases, migrations, economic ruins, and intermarriages of NHOPI and non-NHOPI have exacerbated these trends. Cultural values and social structures also contribute to many health disparities among NHOPI and how easily—or not easily—older NHOPI access and participate in various social services (Mokuau, Browne & Braun, 1998).

Nonetheless, older NHOPI are resilient, and like many older minority persons, older NHOPI have many strengths that have sustained them during difficult times. For example, the majority of NHOPI maintains strong spiritual beliefs and revere nature and spiritual realism. They tend to value collective over individual needs (Braun et al., 2004; Mokuau, 2011). In addition, most NHOPI, especially Native Hawaiians, Samoans, and Chamorros, value reciprocity and helpfulness with their families and community (Braun et al., 2004; Mokuau & Tauili'ili, 2011). Similar to many traditional cultures, NHOPI also respect elders for their strength, wisdom, and courage. They appreciate their older adults for their skills as arbitrators and for the knowledge they share with younger generations. Despite varying levels of acculturation, many older NHOPI are leaders in their family, church, and communities (Browne et al., 2009; Mokuau, 2011). However, elders' roles and status in their families are undermined when poverty, discrimination, and poor health persist in their communities (Browne et al., 2009)

One approach that aims for culturally competent social work practice with these populations is to focus on the many strengths of NHOPI and learn more about NHOPI culture, history, and demographics. Social workers will avoid stereotyping older NHOPI and more effectively tailor interventions to these older persons' unique circumstances by respecting the diversity within NHOPI cultures. This knowledge will keep social workers abreast of cultural and demographic changes that will inevitably impact older NHOPI families in the next century. Through practice, policy-making, and research, social workers must work to alleviate the social and health disparities that too often characterize these populations and compromise their physical and mental health.

Social workers will appeal to older NHOPI, who typically underuse social workers, by integrating the strengths perspective with culturally competent practice and with the incorporation and use of indigenous practices (Braun, Browne, Ka'opua, Kim, & Mokuau, 2013). Social workers can and should work collaboratively to solve problems and empower NHOPI elders by teaching them both change and coping strategies that may be used in various contexts. Nonhierarchical interactions, a belief in bidirectional professional–community learning, and a commitment to community-based participatory approaches in practice and research are essential with NHOPI clients, who have long histories of oppression and unwelcome interventions (Browne et al., 2009).

Social workers face numerous challenges when working with older adults from other minority groups who encounter universal barriers, such as rising healthcare costs, that are common to all older persons. They must recognize culturally specific barriers that different ethnic minority elders face. For example, older NHOPI may struggle with English as a second language, with critical implications for health literacy interventions (Braun & Browne, 1998; Braun, Takamura, Forman, Sasaki, & Meininger, 1995; Nishita & Browne, 2013). The anticipated increase in older persons from these other minority populations underscores the need for social work training in culturally competent practice that takes into account older minority persons' diverse and special strengths as well as sociohistorical influences (Browne, Braun, Mokuau, & McLaughlin, 2002). These demographic trends support the need for research that evaluates competent and culturally tailored interventions that can guide practice and policy-making. Social workers must ensure that all older persons have access to quality care and services, and this requires the adoption of interventions that are indigenous to the culture (Braun et al., 2013). As the older cohorts become increasingly heterogeneous, social workers must recommit themselves to the values of social justice and actively engage in work with older adults from various geographical, and sociohistorical, and cultural backgrounds.

REFERENCES

Abu-Bader, S. H., Tirmazi, M. T., & Ross-Sheriff, F. (2011). The impact of acculturation on depression among older Muslim immigrants in the United States. *Journal of Gerontological Social Work, 54,* 425–448. doi: 10.1080/01634372.2011.560928

Ajrouch, K. J. (2007). Resources and well-being among Arab-American elders. *Journal of Cross Cultural Gerontology, 22,* 167–182. doi: 10.1007/s10823-007-903505

Anderson, K. A., Fields, N. L., & Dobb, L. A. (2011) Understanding the impact of early-life trauma in nursing home residents. *Journal of Gerontological Social Work, 54,* 755–767. doi: 10.1080/01634372.2011.5969.17

Anderson, K. A., Fields, N. L., & Dobb, L. A. (2013). Caregiving and early life trauma: Exploring the experiences of family caregivers to aging Holocaust survivors. *Family Relations, 62*, 366–377. doi: 10.1111/fare.12000

Appalachian Regional Commission (ARC). (2013). *The Appalachian region*. Retrieved from http://www.arc.gov/appalachian_region/TheAppalachianRegion.asp

Asian and Pacific Islander American Health Forum. (2010). *Native Hawaiian and Pacific Islander heath disparities*. San Francisco, CA: Asian and Pacific Islander American Health Forum. Retrieved from http://www.cdc.gov/minorityhealthpopulations/REMP/nhopi.html

Braun, K., & Browne, C. (1998). Perceptions of dementia, caregiving, and help seeking among Asian and Pacific Islander Americans. *Health and Social Work, 23*, 262–274. doi: 10.1093/hsw/23.4.262

Braun, K., Browne, C., Ka`opua, L. S., Kim, B. J., & Mokuau, N. (2014). Research on indigenous elders: From positivistic to decolonizing methodologies. *The Gerontologist 54*, 117–126. doi: 10.1093/geront/gnt067

Braun, K., Takamura, J., Forman, S., Sasaki, P., & Meininger, L. (1995). Developing and testing outreach materials on Alzheimer's Disease for Asian and Pacific Islander Americans. *The Gerontologist, 35*, 122–126. doi: 10.1093/geront/35.1.122

Braun, K., Yee, B., Browne, C., & Mokuau, N. (2004). Native Hawaiian and Pacific Island Elders: Health status, health disparities, and culturally competent services. In K. Whitfield (Ed.), *Closing the gap*. Washington, DC: Gerontological Society of America.

Browne, C., Braun, K., Mokuau, N., & McLaughlin, L. (2002). Developing a multisite project in geriatric and/or gerontological education with emphases in interdisciplinary practice and cultural competence. *The Gerontologist, 42*, 698–704. doi: 10.1093/geront/42.5/698

Browne, C., Mokuau, N., & Braun, K. (2009). Adversities and resiliencies in the lives of Native Hawaiians. *Social Work, 54*, 253–261. doi: 10.1093/sw/54.3.253

Centers for Disease Control (CDC). (2013). *Native Hawaiian and other Pacific Islander populations*. Retrieved from http://www.cdc.gov/minorityhealth/populations/REMP/nhopi.html

Englberger, L., Marks, G. C., & Fitzgerald, M. H. (2003). Insights on food and nutrition in the Federated States of Micronesia: A review of the literature. *Public Health Nutrition, 6*, 5–17. doi: 10.1079/PHN20022364

Glasgow, N. (2000). Rural/urban patterns of aging and caregiving in the United States. *Journal of Family Issues, 21*, 611–631. doi.org/10.1177/019251300021005005

Kaopua, L., Braun, K., Browne, C., Mokuau, N., & Park, C. B. (2011). Why are Native Hawaiians underrepresented in Hawaii's older adult population? Exploring social and behavioral factors of longevity. *Journal of Aging Research*, July 2011, 1–8. Article #701232. doi: 10.4061/2011/701232

Kaholokula, J. K., Iwane, M. K., & Nacapoy, A. (2010). Effects of perceived racism and acculturation on hypertension in Native Hawaiians. *Hawaii Medical Journal, 69*(5), 11–15. doi: 10.1007/s10865-011-933-z. PMCID:PMC3158444PMID:20544603

Keefe, S. E. (2009). *Participatory development in Appalachia*. Knoxville: University of Tennessee Press.

Keefe, S. E., & Curtin, L. (2012). Mental health. In R. L. Ludke & P. J. Obermiller (Eds.), *Appalachian health and well-being*. Lexington: University Press of Kentucky. [Kindle version].

Kosmin, B. A. (2009). *ARIS presentation: The changing population profile of American Jews 1990–2008*. ARIS Publications. Retrieved from http://commons.trincoll.edu/aris/

Kosmin, B. A., & Keysar, A. (2009). *American religious identification survey*. ARIS Publications. Retrieved from http://commons.trincoll.edu/aris/

Lassetter, J. H. (2011). The integral role of food in Native Hawaiian migrants' perceptions of health and well-being. *Journal of Transcultural Nursing, 22*, 63–70. doi: 10.1177/1043659610387153

Ludke, R. L., & Obermiller, P. J. (2012). *Appalachian health and well-being*. Lexington: University Press of Kentucky. [Kindle version].

Ludke, R. L., Obermiller, P. J., & Horner, R. D. (2012). The health status and health determinants of urban Appalachian adults and children. In R. L. Ludke & P. J. Obermiller (Eds.), *Appalachian health and well-being*. Lexington, KY: University Press of Kentucky. [Kindle version].

Mokuau, N. (2011). Culturally-based solutions to preserve the health of Native Hawaiians. *Journal of Ethnic and Cultural Diversity in Social Work, 20*, 98–113. doi: 10.1080/153/3204.2011.570119

Mokuau, N., Browne, C., & Braun, K. (1998). Na Kupuna in Hawai`i: A Review of social and health status, service use, and the importance of value-based intervention of Native Hawaiian elders. *Pacific Health Dialogue Journal of Community Health and Clinical Medicine for the Pacific, 5*, 282–289.

Mokuau, N., & Tauili'ili, P. (2011). Families with Native Hawaiian and Samoan roots. In E. W. Lynch & M. J. Hanson (Eds.), *Developing cross-cultural competence* (4th ed., pp. 365–391). Baltimore. MD: Brookes.

Nelson-Becker, H., Chapin, R., & Fast, B. (2013). The strengths model with older adults. In D. Saleebey (Ed.), *The strengths perspective in social work practice* (6th ed., pp. 161–181). Boston: Pearson. [Kindle version.]

Nishita, C., & Browne, C. (2013). Advancing research in transitional care: Challenges of culture, language and health literacy in Asian Americans and Native Hawaiian elders. *Journal of Health Care for the Poor and Underserved, 24,* 404–418. doi: 10.1353/hpu.2013.0025

Office of Minority Health. (2001). *Closing the gap.* Washington, DC: US Department of Health and Human Services, Office of Minority Health.

Office of Minority Health (OMH). (2013). *The national CLAS standards.* Washington, DC: US Department of Health and Human Services, Office of Minority Health.

Padela, A., Gunter, K., & Killawi, A. (2011). *Meeting the health care needs of American Muslims: Challenges and strategies for healthcare settings.* Washington, DC: Institute for Social Policy and Understanding. Retrieved from http://www.ispuorg/pdfs/620_ispu_report_aasim%20padela_final.pdf

Pew Research. (2011). *Religion and Public Life Project: The future of the global Muslim population.* Retrieved from http://www.pewforum.org/2011/01/27/the-future-of-the-global-muslim-population/

Pew Research. (2012). *Nones on the rise.* Pew Research: Religion and Public Life Project. Retrieved from http://www.pewforum.org/2012/10/09/nones-on-the-rise/

Pew Research. (2013). *A portrait of Jewish Americans: Findings from a Pew Research Center Survey of U.S. Jews.* Retrieved from http://www.perforum.org/2013/10/01/jewish-american-beliefs-attitudes-culture-survey/

Pollard, K., & Jacobsen, L. A. (2013). *The Appalachian region: A data overview from the 2007–2011 American Community Survey Chartbook.* Washington, DC: Population Reference Bureau. Retrieved from http://www.arc.gov/research/researchreportdetails.asp?REPORT_ID=103

Sheskin, I. (2010). *Elderly Jews: An increasing priority for the American Jewish community.* Jerusalem Center for Public Affairs: Jerusalem Issue Briefs. Retrieved from http://jcpa.org/article/elderly-jews-an-increasing-priority-for-the-American-jewish-community/

Sheskin, I., & Dashefsky, A. (2012). *Jewish population in the United States, 2011.* Berman Institute-North American Jewish Data Bank University of Connecticut. Retrieved from http://www.jewishdatabank.org/studies/downloadRile.cfm?FileID=2917

Srinivisan, S., & Guillermo, T. (2000). Toward improved health: Disaggregating Asian American and Native Hawaiian Pacific Islander data. *American Journal of Public Health, 90,* 1731. Retrieved from http://dx.doi/10.2105/AJPH.90.11.1731

Stabiner, K. (2011, March 15). For elderly Muslims, few care options outside the home. *New York Times.* Retrieved from http://newoldage.blogs.nytimes.com/2011/03/15/for-elderly-muslims-few-care-options-outside-the-home/

UJA-Federation of New York. (2012). *Jewish Community Study of New York: 2011.* Retrieved from http://www.ujafedny.org/jewish-community-study-of-new-york-2011/

US Census Bureau. (2010). *The Native Hawaiian and other Pacific Islander population: 2010.* Retrieved from http://www.census.gov/prod/cen2010/briefs/c2010br-12.pdf

BRADLEY D. ZODIKOFF

SANDRA S. BUTLER

Social Work with Lesbian, Gay, Bisexual, and Transgender Older Adults

INTRODUCTION

Lesbian, gay, bisexual, and transgender (LGBT) older persons are diverse in terms of race, ethnicity, culture, physical ability, income, education, marital or relationship status, household composition, and geographical location. For many elders, LGBT identities are central to their sense of self-definition and affiliation with LGBT persons, organizations, and communities. However, this is not true for all LGBT older adults. The current cohort of LGBT elders has shared experiences of stigma, discrimination, rejection, and violence over the life course. The degree to which oppression has affected this cohort in terms of health, mental health, and quality of life outcomes is only beginning to be studied and understood. Though societal attitudes toward LGBT persons of all ages have evolved dramatically in the past few decades, there is evidence to suggest that LGBT older adults continue to confront transphobia, homophobia, and discrimination in health, mental health, and long-term care settings. This chapter provides an introductory overview of research on LGBT older adults, followed by a discussion of gay-affirmative policy and practice relevant to gerontological social work.

OLDER LGBT POPULATION ESTIMATES

The proportion of LGBT older persons in the United States remains difficult to estimate accurately because most population-based national surveys have failed to include questions about sexual orientation or gender identity (Cantor, Brennan, & Shippy, 2004). In fact, the Institute of Medicine (2011) recently called on the National Institutes of Health (NIH) to support the inclusion of sexual orientation and gender identity measures in health survey research and to encourage NIH grant applicants to address sexual minorities in their samples. Citing probability-based surveys that have included such measures, Fredriksen-Goldsen & Muraco (2010) report an estimate that 2% to 8% of the US population is lesbian, gay or bisexual (LGB). Currently, at least 1 to 3 million persons are LGB older adults. By 2030, with an expected 20% growth rate in the older population age 65 and over, the number of persons who are LGB adults will expand to at least 2 to 7 million in the United States (Grant, 2009).

APPROACHES TO UNDERSTANDING LGBT OLDER ADULTS

Fredriksen-Goldsen and Muraco (2010) identify the life-course perspective as a valuable approach to understanding LGBT aging. Informed by Elder (1994) and others, the life-course perspective suggests that individuals interact with one another over time and embedded within distinct social and historical contexts. In order to appreciate the lives of LGBT older adults, one needs to consider individuals' life trajectories as moving through the changing historical worlds in which LGBT elders came of age, matured, and grew old (Fredriksen-Goldsen & Muraco, 2010). Many LGBT older adults learned to cope with discrimination throughout their lifetimes by choosing to hide their sexual orientation in specific settings as a means of survival (Barranti & Cohen, 2000; Brotman, Ryan, & Cormier, 2003; Kochman, 1997). Brotman et al. (2003) emphasize that LGBT older adults' strategy of "hiding" may be understood as an adaptive, long-term coping mechanism for dealing with ongoing discrimination. Many individuals from the current cohort of LGBT older adults came to terms with their LGBT identities long before the modern gay liberation movement began in the early 1970s or before the American Psychiatric Association decided in 1973 to remove "homosexuality" from its list of mental disorders in its *Diagnostic and Statistical Manual* (Barranti & Cohen, 2000). Such individuals were faced with the extraordinary challenge of sustaining adult lives during whole decades in which familial, social, and cultural institutions remained intensely homophobic and repressive. Some LGBT older persons were subjected to treatments that attempted to "cure" their homosexuality using electroshock therapy, aversion therapy, or other means now scientifically discredited (Brotman et al., 2003). A deep sense of shame and stigma, particularly with respect to interacting with health professionals and institutions, remains acute for some LGBT older adults today (Brotman et al., 2003). Yet at the same time, professionals must recognize the remarkable resilience of this diverse population, as many LGBT older adults have reached old age with affirmative self-identities, and armed with effective coping skills honed from surviving years of discrimination and oppression.

Definition of Terms

The term "homosexual" has largely been dismissed by the gay community because of its link to pathological diagnosis. These days the preferred term "gay," which came into favor after the 1969 Stonewall riots, is used to refer to men whose primary emotional and sexual connections are with other men. Although "gay" is an overarching term for homosexuality, it is generally used to refer particularly to men. The term "lesbian," which came out of the feminist movement of the 1970s as a substitute for the word "gay," refers to women whose primary emotional and sexual connections are with other women. Some elder lesbians may refer to themselves as gay rather than lesbian. "Bisexual" refers to men and women who have sexual attractions to both sexes. And "transgender," which came into usage in the 1990s, applies to people who resist gender stereotypes or who transgress sex-gender norms. Transgender individuals may identify as either gay or "straight" (i.e., heterosexual; Hunter & Hickerson, 2003).

WHAT IS KNOWN ABOUT LGBT OLDER ADULTS?

Research literature on LGBT aging has evolved over the past two decades due to an increasing number of studies conducted in the domains of health, mental health, social support, caregiving and care receiving, community-based services, and long-term care. Many studies have relied on nonprobability samples of predominantly White, self-identified LGBT older adults often recruited through LGBT-identified organizations, thereby limiting generalizability to broader populations inclusive of LGBT older persons of color, for example. For a comprehensive review of the literature on aging and sexual orientation over a 2-decade span, see Fredriksen-Goldsen and Muraco (2010). A key theme over time is documented evidence that many lesbian, gay, and bisexual older adults demonstrate positive psychosocial functioning even in the face of structural discrimination over the life course.

In the domain of health and mental health, a number of recent studies have identified health disparities among LGBT older adults, as well as risk and protective factors associated with specific health outcomes. For a comprehensive treatment of this emerging literature, see the Institute of Medicine (2011) report on LGBT health, which includes an informative chapter on later adulthood. Scientific literature reviewed in the Institute of Medicine (2011) report includes categories on mental health, sexual/reproductive health, cancer, cardiovascular disease, obesity, HIV/AIDS, disability, and transgender-specific mental and physical health issues. Wallace, Cochran, Durazo, and Ford (2011), using California statewide data, found that older gay and bisexual men were more likely to report hypertension, diabetes, psychological distress, physical disability, or fair/poor health status compared with their heterosexual counterparts. They also found that older lesbian and bisexual women reported with more frequency psychological distress, physical disability, or fair/poor health status compared with heterosexual older women. Fredriksen-Goldsen and coauthors (2013) in a large-scale national survey examined factors associated with health, disability, and depression among LGB older adults. Fredriksen-Goldsen and coauthors found that lifetime victimization, financial barriers, obesity, and lack of physical activity correlated with poor health, disability, and depression among LGB older adults. Notably, the authors further identified internalized stigma as predictive of disability and depression. Disproportionately high levels of poor health, disability, depression, and stress among transgender older adults compared with their non-transgender counterparts remain an underresearched public health concern (Witten, 2014). For a review of literature on transgender aging and findings from the first large-scale survey of transgender-identified individuals, see Witten (2014).

The needs of LGBT elders with respect to long-term care have emerged as a notable research focus in the past decade. Several studies identify specific concerns of older LGBT adults faced with the prospect of entering long-term care. For example, older gay and lesbian adults express fears related to discrimination they anticipate facing in entering mainstream long-term care facilities (Stein, Beckerman, & Sherman, 2010). The potential need to "retreat to the closet" in old age as a survival strategy in institutional settings has been expressed as a recurrent concern (Jackson, Johnson, & Roberts, 2008). The management of sexual identity disclosure in long-term care is a complex phenomenon, informed not solely by individuals' perceptions of vulnerability

but also by dimensions of resiliency (Jenkins, Walker, Cohen, & Curry, 2010). However, evidence of negative attitudes of long-term care personnel toward same-sex relationships (Hinrichs & Vacha-Haase, 2010) and lack of training of nursing home administrators and other staff (Bell, Bern-Klug, Kramer, & Saunders, 2010; Dickey, 2013) suggest a pressing need to equip long-term care providers with knowledge, skills, and attitudes to support gay-affirmative practices. Resources for such training can be found on the website of the National Resource Center on LGBT Aging (http://www.lgbtagingcenter.org). The need for LGBT-sensitive training extends to aging providers across the spectrum of care (Hughes, Harold, & Boyer, 2011; Knochel, Croghan, Moone, & Quam, 2012; Knochel, Quam, & Croghan, 2011).

CAREGIVING

The caregiving needs of LGBT older adults constitute another focal point of recent research. Caregiving to older adults is provided predominantly by biological kin. Grossman, D'Augelli, and Dragowski (2007) explain that many older gay and lesbian persons moved away from places and families of origin earlier in their lives to seek acceptance in newly adopted communities and in the context of newly formed social relationships far removed from biological kin. Some gay and lesbian elders, despite evidence of strong social support networks in later life (Grossman, D'Augelli, & Hershberger, 2000), nevertheless lack primary caregivers to assist with personal care. Older LGBT persons serve in both caregiver and care-receiving roles. Shippy (2007) found that many older LGB adults provided caregiving assistance to biological kin in addition to family members of choice. Coon (2007) describes interventions specifically framed for an LGBT sociological context given obstacles encountered by LGBT caregivers and care receivers throughout the service system.

CIVIL RIGHTS POLICIES AFFECTING LGBT OLDER ADULTS: A CHANGING LANDSCAPE

The policy context for LGBT individuals of all ages is in a rapid state of change. The speed of policy change is captured in the Lambda Legal YouTube video "From Criminals to Newlyweds" (available at lambdalegal.org) referring to two historic Supreme Court decisions with an exact 10-year span between them: *Lawrence v. Texas* on June 26, 2003, and *United States v. Windsor* on June 26, 2013. The first decision finally struck down the sodomy laws that still existed in 14 states at that time, and one decade later the court ruled that parts of the Defense of the Marriage Act (DOMA) were unconstitutional.

Sodomy laws were a harsh reality for many years for the current cohort of elder LGBT individuals. These laws, originally existing throughout the country, essentially made gay sex illegal. Some states repealed their sodomy laws in the 1960s and 1970s, but in 1986, the Supreme Court upheld Georgia's sodomy law in *Bowers v. Hardwick*, reminding all LGBT individuals that their lives were not acceptable to society and that they needed to hide who they were (American Civil Liberties Union [ACLU], 2003). Fortunately, much has changed in the quarter-century since *Bowers v. Hardwick*, with the recent decision on DOMA dramatically illustrating the shift toward increased acceptance.

Earlier efforts to change marriage laws in Hawaii had led to a conservative backlash and the passage of DOMA by Congress in 1996. This law defined marriage as a contract between one man and one woman and allowed states to refuse to recognize same-sex marriages performed in other states (Porche & Purvin, 2008). In the same year that *Lawrence v. Texas* was decided—2003—Massachusetts became the first state to establish legal same-sex marriage in the United States. By 2013, when *United States v. Windsor* struck down sections of DOMA—that is, the court ruled that the federal government could not withhold spousal benefits from same-sex couples who had been legally married under state statutes—13 states and the District of Columbia allowed same-sex marriage.

The situation facing widowed Edith Windsor, the 84-year-old plaintiff in the 2013 Supreme Court case, was like that of so many LGBT elders in committed relationships. She and her partner of 40 years, Thea Spyer, married in Toronto in 2007. After Spyer's death in 2009, Windsor realized she was faced with a $363,053 bill for inheritance taxes because Spyer was legally considered a friend rather than a spouse. Windsor's anger at this situation fueled her to take her case to court, and she eventually won (Gabatt, 2013). More recently, the Supreme Court ruled on June 26, 2015, in Obergefell vs. Hodges, that the Constitution's guarantees of due process and equal protection under the law mean that states can no longer ban same-sex marriages (Hurley, 2015). This was indeed a historic moment for all advocates of LGBT rights.

Despite these historic advances, there are activists and scholars who have criticized the recent focus on marriage. For example, some feminists have labeled same-sex marriage as a "capitulation to an inherently patriarchal institution" (Porche & Purvin, 2008, p. 15) and do not believe it can be saved from "heteropatriarchy" to become a neutral, egalitarian institution (Jeffreys, 2004). LaSala (2007) suggests that too much energy has been placed on marriage at the expense of other civil rights. Legal scholar, Nancy Polikoff (2009) argues that the current Social Security system continues to privilege an outdated family structure—a single-earner married couple—that was popular when the system was established. She submits that rather than fighting for spousal benefits, LGBT advocacy would be better directed at creating a base level benefit for all older Americans; the many low-income LGBT older adults who are not in committed relationships would be better served by such a change.

Despite these thoughtful criticisms, the demise of DOMA will allow same-sex couples to access many previously unavailable federal benefits (see Grant, 2009, for a thorough discussion of this inequality). The administration of President Obama has moved quickly since the decision to implement the required changes. For example, just 2 months after the decision, the Internal Revenue Service announced that it would fully recognize marriage equality for all married LGBT taxpayers, even those living in states without marriage equality. Simultaneously, the Department of Health and Human Services announced that married LGBT elders enrolled in the Medicare Advantage Program—that is, Medicare Part C, private health plans that contract with Medicare to provide both Part A and Part B benefits and often prescription drug coverage—will be able to access benefits for their spouses in skilled nursing facilities that were previously unavailable. Prior to this time, LGBT elders had to choose between being in a nursing home away from their spouse or paying more money to be together (Carey, 2013).

A group of 11 progressive organizations have collaborated to produce a series of fact sheets called After DOMA: What It Means For You. The fact sheets cover topics such as Social Security spousal benefits and protections, veteran and military spousal benefits, Medicare spousal protections, immigration, federal taxes, and the Family and Medical Leave Act. These can be accessed at www.lamdalegal.org/publications or on the websites of any of the following contributing organizations:

- American Civil Liberties Union: aclu.org/lgbt
- Center for American Progress: americanprogress.org
- Family Equality Council: familyequality.org
- Freedom to Marry: freedomtomarry.org
- Gay & Lesbian Advocates & Defenders: glad.org
- Human Rights Campaign: hrc.org
- Immigration Equality: immigrationequality.org
- Lambda Legal: lambdalegal.org
- National Center for Lesbian Rights: nclrights.org
- National Gay and Lesbian Taskforce: thetaskforce.org
- Outserve-SLDN: outserve-sldn.org

While same-sex marriage has been in the media spotlight and LGBT advocates have devoted considerable time and resources to the cause, the issue of discrimination has received less attention (LaSala, 2007). Although 89% of Americans believe it is illegal under federal law to be fired for being gay or transgender (Hunt, 2012), in reality, there is no federal law prohibiting such discrimination. Seventeen states and the District of Columbia ban discrimination based on sexual orientation and gender identity and another four states ban discrimination based on sexual orientation, but not gender identity, leaving 29 states where such discrimination is perfectly legal.

The Employment Non-Discrimination Act (ENDA), first introduced in Congress nearly 20 years ago in 1994, would make it illegal under federal law to discriminate against LGBT individuals in any aspect of employment. This bill is narrower than state laws, which also protect against discrimination in housing and public accommodations. The bill has been introduced in every Congress since 1994, except one (the 109th), and gender identity was added in 2007. As of this writing, it has yet to be introduced in the 114th Congress that began in January 2015 (Human Rights Campaign, 2015a). In most sessions, the bill has died in committee before reaching a floor vote, although it did pass the house in 2007 (Hunt, 2011). The ENDA bill was introduced in the 113th Congress in April 2013 and was approved by the Senate Health, Education, Labor and Pensions Committee by a bipartisan vote of 15 to 7 It ultimately passed in the Senate with a strong bipartisan vote of 64 to 32, though the House version did not pass before the session ended in December 2014 (Human Rights Campaign, 2015b). With the June 2015 historic ruling by the Supreme Court protecting same-sex marriage in all states (Hurley, 2015), perhaps the time is ripe for Congress to finally vote to also protect LGBT individuals from employment discrimination. Such a victory would have both symbolic and practical implications for LGBT elders. For those still employed, it would provide a previously unknown federal protection against unfair employment practices resulting from homophobia and transphobia. For those who have retired, the passage of ENDA would indicate that our country has taken one more step toward accepting who they are.

Today's LGBT elders have lived through years of legalized oppression and discrimination. Although their numbers are significant, they are not always visible, having spent many years protecting their private lives, sexual orientation, and/or gender identity from public view. Social worker practitioners can be at the forefront of improving the quality of life for today's LGBT elders and for the elder generations to follow by advocating for increased civil rights at the federal and state levels. For example, at the federal level, social workers should be at the forefront of pressuring their members of Congress to finally pass ENDA. At the state level, advocacy is needed to enact antidiscrimination, enforce marriage equality laws in those states which have previously banned same-sex marriage, and to counter ongoing efforts to prevent LGBT individuals from having full civil rights, such as the recently proposed bill in Kansas legislature blatantly allowing such discrimination (Stern, 2014).

Forms of Oppression That Affect LGBT Elders

Homophobia refers to the irrational fear of homosexuals and the hatred of LGB individuals based solely on their sexual orientation.

Heterosexism, an ideological system that denies, denigrates, and stigmatizes any nonheterosexual form of behavior, identity, relationship, or community, refers to beliefs and attitudes that favor opposite-sex over same-sex partnerships (Cahill, South, & Spade, 2000; Kochman, 1997).

Transphobia refers to social prejudice against transgender persons, which can be even more intense than homophobia (Cook-Daniels, 1997)

PRACTICE CONSIDERATIONS FOR WORKING WITH LGBT OLDER ADULTS

All social workers in the field of gerontology must be prepared to work with LGBT older adults, as LGBT older adults present for assistance and support across the full spectrum of aging service programs. Bergh and Crisp (2004) propose a framework for defining cultural competence with sexual minorities of all ages in the domains of attitudes, knowledge, and skills, drawing on the gay-affirmative practice model described by Appleby and Anastas (1998). Bergh and Crisp (2004) encourage practitioners to develop self-awareness regarding their own potentially negative attitudes about LGBT clients and to actively pursue practice knowledge relevant to LGBT populations through continuing education, in-service trainings, and clinical supervision. They also suggest practical ideas for communicating a safe, inclusive, and gay-affirmative environment within a service setting, such as making literature or events on LGBT-related topics publicly available to all clients or placing a rainbow flag (a widely recognized symbol of LGBT community diversity) in a noticeable place within the service setting (Bergh & Crisp, 2004).

Community-based agencies should become better aware that they communicate attitudes toward LGBT older clients through the psychosocial assessment process. Several authors highlight the need for agencies to review outreach and intake procedures (Brotman et al., 2003; Humphreys & Quam, 1998; Metz, 1997). Prospective older LGBT clients, by virtue of their life-course experience, are highly attuned to subtle and overt forms of heterosexism in agency settings and may interpret heterosexist attitudes as an indication that they are not welcome as clients (Metz, 1997). At intake, social workers should assess, rather than assume, a client's sexual orientation (Bergh & Crisp, 2004). Consider one of the most common intake questions: "What is your marital status?" or "Are you married?" Though recently achieved federal and state legal recognition of same-sex marriages increases the likelihood that this question will apply to a growing number of LGBT elders in relationships now and in the future, it is important to recognize that for many elders in the current cohort, marriage may not have been a legal option, choice, or preference during their life course, so this question may still resonate as heterocentric or exclusionary based on one's individual experience. Services and Advocacy for GLBT Elders [SAGE] and the National Resource Center on LGBT Aging (2013) suggest a number of effective strategies to design intake forms and clinical interviews that are inclusive of LGBT elders. For example, in asking clients about their marital status, response options should include "partner," "spouse," "life partner," "primary caregiver," and "domestic partner." SAGE and the National Resource Center on LGBT Aging (2013) further recommend changing the category "marital status" to "relationship status," wherever possible. Similarly, Metz (1997) suggests that social workers might consider phrasing a marital status question in a more neutral way. For example: "Please describe those relationships that are or have been most important to you" (Metz, 1997, p. 37). The alternative wording of this question demonstrates sensitivity to a prospective LGBT older adult client, who may now feel more comfortable describing to the worker the significant same-sex relationships (past and present) in his or her life.

For an overview of knowledge, skills, and attitudes at the intersection of age-competent and gay-affirmative practice, see Crisp, Wayland, and Gordon (2008). The following broad practice guidelines offer strategies to increase sensitivity and competence regarding working with older LGBT adults (Berger, 1985; Connolly, 1996; Cook-Daniels, 1997; Grant, 2009; Healy, 2002; Humphreys & Quam, 1998; Morrow, 2001).

- Engage in self-reflection and work through your own heterosexism and homophobia.
- Recognize diversity within the LGBT community.
- Respect a client's right to privacy and confidentiality.
- Listen especially carefully and strive to connect with your client.
- Recognize that all presenting problems are not due to being old or being LGBT.
- Honor relationships and treat identified family as family.
- Use inclusive language and plan activities that are neutral with respect to sexual orientation.
- Educate yourself about special issues facing LGBT older adults, respectful service providers, and resources in the community.
- Assist the client in connecting to the LGBT community.

- Work to develop more LGBT-friendly resources.
- Include LGBT elders in program planning.
- Advocate changing heterosexist organizational, local, state, and federal policies.

A number of useful Web-based resources are available. The National Resource Center on LGBT Aging (http://www.lgbtagingcenter.org) is a project of Services and Advocacy for Gay, Lesbian, Bisexual, and Transgender Elders (SAGE) launched with a grant from the US Department of Health and Human Services, Administration on Aging. This landmark federally funded initiative offers training, technical assistance, and educational resources for aging service providers, LGBT organizations, and LGBT older adults. Practitioners, program planners, and advocates will find a wealth of information on this site relevant to developing culturally competent practices with LGBT elders. Services and Advocacy for GLBT Elders operates its own organization website (http://www.sageusa.org), offering another useful Web portal on a range of issues affecting LGBT elders in practice and policy. The LGBT Aging Issues Network (http://www.asaging.org/lain) of the American Society on Aging administers an LGBT aging resources clearinghouse and sponsors Web seminars on many LGBT aging topics in addition to promoting LGBT aging through its publications and conference programs.

The following brief case vignette describes a presenting concern of an older gay male referred to an LGBT-identified social service program. The vignette illustrates the relationship between the uniquely experienced aspects of an individual client's sexual orientation and his use of mainstream and LGBT-specific health and social services. The vignette further demonstrates the practitioner's use of a gay-affirmative practice approach to address the client's presenting concern.

Z, a 69-year-old single gay African American male with end-stage renal disease, lives alone in an apartment in the city and goes to dialysis three times a week. Due to declining health and increasing frailty, the dialysis treatment team recommended home care to assist Z with activities of daily living. Z repeatedly refuses home care help, even though his insurance and financial resources cover the expense. Z will not disclose to any health care staff the "real" reason why he does not want a home care worker in his home. Finally, a social worker from an LGBT-identified organization (whom Z contacted independently) learned during the first home visit that Z is extremely afraid to hire an unknown home care worker. He fears that upon entering his home and seeing his personal collection of art, books, and photography on the walls of his apartment, the home care worker would learn he is gay. He fears the home care worker might say or do something harmful to him because he is a gay man. Z said he did not want to feel vulnerable and self-conscious within the comfort of his own home, especially in such weak physical condition. The social workers from an LGBT organization, in coordination with Z and his dialysis team, helped arrange the hiring of a home care worker from an agency that had undergone sensitivity training working with LGBT older clients. Z found this to be an acceptable plan and then agreed to hire the home care worker.

Lesbian, gay, bisexual, and transgender older adults encounter the same range of problems in aging as heterosexual older adults do. However, LGBT older adults face additional challenges in accessing health and social services that are responsive to their individual needs. Gerontological social workers must understand LGBT older adults as consumers of the full spectrum of aging services and must work to develop sensitive and inclusive approaches to address the needs of this underserved population.

REFERENCES

American Civil Liberties Union (ACLU). (2013). *History of sodomy laws and the strategy that led to today's decision*. Retrieved from www.aclu.org

Appleby, G. A., & Anastas, J. W. (1998). *Not just a passing phase: Social work with gay, lesbian, and bisexual people*. New York, NY: Columbian University Press.

Barranti, C., & Cohen. H. (2000). Lesbian and gay elders: An invisible minority. In R. Schneider, N. Kropf, & A. Kisor (Eds.), *Gerontological social work: Knowledge, service settings and special populations* (2nd ed., pp. 343–367). Belmont, CA: Wadsworth.

Bell, S. A., Bern-Klug, M., Kramer, K. W. O., & Saunders, J. B. (2010). Most nursing home social service directors lack training in working with lesbian, gay, and bisexual residents. *Social Work in Health Care, 49,* 814–831. doi: 10.1080/00981389.2010.494561

Berger, R. M. (1985). Rewriting a bad script: Older lesbians and gays. In H. Hidalgo, T. L. Peterson, & N. J. Woodman (Eds.), *Lesbian and gay issues: A resource manual for social workers* (pp. 53–59). Silver Spring, MD: National Association of Social Workers.

Bergh, N. V. D., & Crisp, C. (2004). Defining culturally competent practice with sexual minorities: Implications for social work education and practice. *Journal of Social Work Education, 40,* 221–238. Retrieved from www.cswe.org/Publications/JSWE.aspx

Brotman, S., Ryan, B., & Cormier, R. (2003). The health and social service needs of gay and lesbian elders and their families in Canada. *Gerontologist, 43,* 192–202. Retrieved from http://dx.doi.org/10.1093/geront/43.2.192

Cahill, S., South, K., & Spade, J. (2000). *Outing age: Public policy issues affecting gay, lesbian, bisexual and transgender elders.* Washington, DC: Policy Institute, National Gay and Lesbian Task Force.

Cantor, M. H., Brennan, M., & Shippy, R. A. (2004). *Caregiving among older lesbian, gay, bisexual, and transgender elders.* New York, NY: National Gay and Lesbian Task Force Policy Institute.

Carey, R. (2013, August 30). *Big news for LGBT taxpayers and LGBT seniors.* E-mail alert from the National Gay and Lesbian Task Force. Retrieved from theTaskForce@theTaskForce.org

Connolly, L. (1996). Long-term care and hospice: The special needs of older gay men and lesbians. *Journal of Gay and Lesbian Social Services, 5,* 77–91. Retrieved from http://dxdoi.org/10.1300/J041v05n01_06

Cook-Daniels, L. (1997). Lesbian, gay male, bisexual, and transgendered elders: Elder abuse and neglect issues. *Journal of Elder Abuse and Neglect, 9,* 35–49. Retrieved from http://dx.doi.org/10.1300/J084v09n02_04

Coon, D. W. (2007). Exploring interventions for LGBT caregivers: Issues and examples. *Journal of Gay and Lesbian Social Services, 18,* 109–128. doi: 10.1300/J041v18n03_07

Crisp, C., Wayland, S., & Gordon, T. (2008). Older gay, lesbian, and bisexual adults: Tools for age-competent and gay affirmative practice. *Journal of Gay and Lesbian Social Services, 20,* 5–29. doi: 10.1080/10538720802178890

Dickey, G. (2013). Survey of homophobia: Views on sexual orientation from certified nurse assistants who work in long-term care. *Research on Aging, 35,* 563–570. doi: 10.1177/0164027512447823

Elder, G. H. (1994). Time, human agency, and social change: Perspective on the life course. *Social Psychology Quarterly, 57,* 4–15. Retrieved from spq.sagepub.com

Fredriksen-Goldsen, K. I., Emlet, C. A., Kim, H.-J., Muraco, A., Erosheva, E., Goldsen, J., & Hoy-Ellis, C. (2013). The physical and mental health of lesbian, gay male, and bisexual (LGB) older adults: The role of key health indicators and risk and protective factors. *Gerontologist, 53,* 664–675. doi: 10.1093/geront/gns123

Fredriksen-Goldsen, K. I., & Muraco, A. (2010). Aging and sexual orientation: A 25-year review of the literature. *Research on Aging, 32,* 372–413. doi: 10.1177/0164027509360355

Gabatt, A. (2013, June 26). Edith Windsor and Thea Spyer: "A love affair that just kept on and on and on." *The Guardian.* Retrieved from www.theguardian.com

Grant, J. M. (2009). *Outing Age 2010: Public policy issues affecting gay, lesbian, bisexual and transgender elders.* Washington, DC: Policy Institute, National Gay and Lesbian Task Force.

Grossman, A. H., D'Augelli, A. R., & Dragowski, E. A. (2007). Caregiving and care receiving among older lesbian, gay, and bisexual adults. *Journal of Gay and Lesbian Social Services, 18,* 15–38. doi: 10.1300/J041v18n03_02

Grossman, A. H., D'Augelli, A. R., & Hershberger, S. L. (2000). Social support networks of lesbian, gay, and bisexual adults 60 years of age and older. *Journals of Gerontology: Series B. Psychological Sciences and Social Sciences, 55,* P171–P179. Retrieved from http://dx.doi.org/10.1093/geronb/55.3.P171

Healy, T. (2002). Culturally competent practice with elderly lesbians. *Geriatric Care Management Journal, 12,* 9–13. Retrieved from http://www.care-manager.org/members-only/member resources/gcm-journal/

Hinrichs, K. L. M., & Vacha-Haase, T. (2010). Staff perceptions of same-gender sexual contacts in long-term care facilities. *Journal of Homosexuality, 57,* 776–789. doi:10.1080/00918369.2010.485877

Hughes, A. K., Harold, R. D., & Boyer, J. M. (2011). Awareness of LGBT aging issues among aging services network providers. *Journal of Gerontological Social Work, 54,* 659–677. doi: 10.1080/01634372.2011.585392

Human Rights Campaign (HRC). (2015a). *Employment Non-Discrimination Act*. Retrieved from www.hrc.org

Human Rights Campaign (HRC). (2015b). *Employment Non-Discrimination Act: Legislative Timeline*. Retrieved from www.hrc.org

Humphreys, N., & Quam, J. (1998). Middle-aged and old gay, lesbian and bisexual adults. In G. A. Appleby & J. W. Anastas (Eds.), *Not just a passing phase: Social work with gay, lesbian and bisexual people* (pp. 245–267). New York, NY: Columbia University Press.

Hunt, J. (2011). *A history of the Employment Non-Discrimination Act: It's past time to pass the law*. Center for American Progress Action Fund. Retrieved from www.americanprogressaction.org

Hunt, J. (2012). *A state-by-state examination of nondiscrimination laws and policies: State nondiscrimination policies fill the void but federal protections are still needed*. Retrieved from www.americanprogressaction.org/wp-content/uploads/issues/2012/06/pdf/state_nondiscrimination.pdf

Hunter, S., & Hickerson, J. C. (2003). *Affirmative practice: Understanding and working with lesbian, gay, bisexual and transgender persons*. Washington, DC: NASW Press.

Hurley, L. (2015, June 27–28). High court upholds gay marriage. *Bangor Daily News*, p. A1.

Institute of Medicine. (2011). *The health of lesbian, gay, bisexual, and transgender people: Building a foundation for better understanding*. Washington, DC: National Academies Press.

Jackson, N. C., Johnson, M. J., & Roberts, R. (2008). The potential impact of discrimination fears of older gays, lesbians, bisexuals and transgender individuals living in small- to moderate-sized cities on long-term health care. *Journal of Homosexuality, 54*, 325–339. doi: 10.1080/00918360801982298

Jeffreys, S. (2004). The need to abolish marriage. *Feminism and Psychology, 14*, 327–331. Retrieved from http://dx.doi.org/10.1177/0959-353504040314

Jenkins, D., Walker, C., Cohen, H., & Curry, L. (2010). A lesbian older adult managing identity disclosure: A case study. *Journal of Gerontological Social Work, 53*, 402–420. doi: 10.1080/01634372.2010.488280

Knochel, K. A., Croghan, C. F., Moone, R. P., & Quam, J. K. (2012). Training, geography, and provision of aging services to lesbian, gay, bisexual, and transgender older adults. *Journal of Gerontological Social Work, 55*, 426–443. doi: 10.1080/01634372.2012.665158

Knochel, K. A., Quam, J. K., & Croghan, C. F. (2011). Are old lesbian and gay people well served? Understanding the perceptions, preparation, and experiences of aging services providers. *Journal of Applied Gerontology, 30*, 370–389. doi: 10.1177/0733464810369809

Kochman, A. (1997). Gay and lesbian elderly: Historical overview and implications for social work practice. *Journal of Gay and Lesbian Social Services, 6*, 1–10.

LaSala, M. C. (2007). Too many eggs in the wrong basket: A queer critique of the same-sex marriage movement. *Social Work, 52*, 181–183. Retrieved from http://dx.doi.org/10.1093/sw/52.2181

Metz, P. (1997). Staff development for working with lesbian and gay elders. *Journal of Gay and Lesbian Social Services, 6*, 35–45. Retrieved from http://dx.doi.org/10.1300/J041v06n01_04

Morrow, D. F. (2001). Older gays and lesbians: Surviving a generation of hate and violence. *Journal of Gay and Lesbian Social Services, 13*, 151–169.

Polikoff, N. (2009). *Beyond (straight or gay) marriage: Valuing all families under the law*. Boston, MA: Beacon Press.

Porche, M. V., & Purvin, D. M. (2008). "Never in our lifetime": Legal marriage for same-sex couples in long-term relationships. *Family Relations, 57*, 144–159. Retrieved from http://dx.doi.org/10.1111/j.1741-3729.2008.00490.x

Services and Advocacy for GLBT Elders (SAGE) and National Resource Center on LGBT Aging. (2013). *Inclusive questions for older adults: A practical guide to collecting data on sexual orientation and gender identity*. New York: Author. Retrieved from http://www.lgbtagingcenter.org/resources/pdfs/InclusiveQuestionsOlder%20Adults_Guidebook.pdf

Shippy, R. A. (2007). We cannot go it alone: The impact of informal support and stressors in older gay, lesbian and bisexual caregivers. *Journal of Gay and Lesbian Social Services, 18*, 39–51. doi: 10.1300/J041v18n03_03

Stein, G. L., Beckerman, N. L., & Sherman, P. A. (2010). Lesbian and gay elders and long-term care: Identifying the unique psychosocial perspectives and challenges. *Journal of Gerontological Social Work, 53*, 421–435. doi : 10.1080/01634372.2010.496478

Stern, M. (2014, February 13). Kansas' anti-gay segregation bill is an abomination. *Slate*. Retrieved from www.slate.com

Wallace, S. P., Cochran, S. D., Durazo, E. M., & Ford, C. L. (2011). *The health of aging lesbian, gay and bisexual adults in California*. Health Policy Research Brief. UCLA Center for Health Policy Research. Retrieved from http://escholarship.org/uc/item/9gv99494.pdf

Witten, T. (2014). It's not all darkness: Robustness, resilience, and successful transgender aging. *LGBT Health, 1*, 24–33. doi: 10.1089/lgbt.2013.0017

IMMIGRATION HISTORY AND PATTERNS

As a nation of immigrants, the United States has admitted about 79 million immigrants, including refugees and asylum seekers, between 1820 and 2012 (US Department of Homeland Security, 2013). In 2010, the number of the foreign-born population hit a record of 40 million, or 13% of the total US population, with an average of 19 years of residence in the United States (Camarota, 2012). Sixty-two percent of them came to live in the United States in 1990 or later, including 35% who came in 2000 or later (US Census Bureau, 2012). Whereas immigrants in the late 19th century and early 20th century were mostly from European countries, the past 6 decades have seen rising numbers of immigrants from Mexico, Central and South Americas, and Asia. Beginning with the Displaced Persons Act of 1948, over 700,000 people came from Eastern Europe and what were then "Iron Curtain" countries. The Immigration and Naturalization Act of 1965 opened the door to several million Asians, Mexicans, and Central and South Americans. Following the fall of South Vietnam in 1975, about 1.5 million Vietnamese, Hmong, Laotians, and Cambodians came to the United States between 1975 and 2012 (Niedzwiecki & Duong, 2004; US Department of Homeland Security, 2013).

Of 10.5 million new immigrants between 2003 and 2012, 42% were from the Americas, particularly Mexico, Cuba, and El Salvador; 38% from Asia, including China, India, the Philippines, Korea, and Vietnam; and the remaining 20% from Africa, Europe, and Oceania (US Department of Homeland Security, 2013, Table 3). One-fourth of this foreign-born population lived in California in 2010, while New York, Texas, and Florida were home to 30.4% combined (US Census Bureau, 2012).

The immigrant population age 65 years or older increased by 70% during the last two decades, from 2.7 million in 1990 to 4.6 million in 2010 (Population Reference Bureau, 2013). In 2012, 13.1% of new legal immigrants to the United States were 55 years or older, including 5.4% of those who were 65 years or older (US Department of Homeland Security, 2013, Table 8).

GROWING DIVERSITY AND ITS IMPLICATIONS

The continued influx of older immigrants/refugees from more than 200 countries together with the

AILEE MOON

TRANG HOANG

Older Immigrants and Refugees

aging younger immigrants of past decades has meant that the older immigrant/refugee population in the United States has become increasingly diverse. This diversity includes not only racial and ethnic background but also reasons for immigration (e.g., family reunification, economic opportunities, fleeing from war, fear of persecution, or political turmoil in the country of origin), age at the time of immigration, length of residence in the United States, and acculturation level, including English proficiency. Besides historical and demographic diversity, one finds expanding diversity in cultural norms and values governing the family, its role as caregiver for older relatives, living arrangements, family relations, interpersonal behavior, health beliefs, the role of religion and spirituality, and attitudes toward and use of health and social services (Hue, Davies, & Hansen, 2004; Treas, 2009).

The immigration history, cultural norms and values, and socioeconomic background of immigrants have significant effects on their well-being and on the process of adjustment in the new environment. These factors may vary not only among older immigrant groups from different regions or countries but also within the same ethnic group. For example, ethnic Chinese elders from the People's Republic of China, Hong Kong, Singapore, and Taiwan may have different values and ideologies, different educational and economic backgrounds, different levels of acculturation and English proficiency, and different service needs. Older Muslim war refugees who recently came from Kosovo and Bosnia may experience different levels and types of war-related trauma than Afghan elders, who came in the 1970s, when they were in their 40s, fleeing the war with Russia. On the other hand, the importance of religious and spiritual coping and healing may be similar among predominantly Christian Korean, Buddhist Cambodian and Laotian, and Muslim Indonesian immigrant elderly.

Indeed, it is difficult to generalize the life experiences and issues of increasingly heterogeneous immigrant/refugee older populations, not only because they all have different backgrounds but also because their experiences and expectations change in the process of adjustment and settlement in the United States.

Although immigration may have a varied impact on individuals, most older immigrants/refugees, especially during the early period of adjustment to their new environment, experience stresses. These stresses include migratory grief, attachment to their home country, language and mobility difficulties, social isolation, limited social support, unfamiliarity with health and social services, increased dependency on children and their families, lowered status within the family and the society, and barriers to participating in mainstream social and political activities (Hsu, Davies, & Hansen, 2004; Kirmayer et al., 2011; Morioka-Douglas, Sacks, & Yeo, 2004).

FAMILY AND CAREGIVING

From a general perspective, the family, in all cultures, is the main source of support, and many of the issues and challenges faced by older immigrants/refugees and their families may be more similar than different among different cultures and ethnic groups. However, the specific problems and needs of older immigrants/refugees, and their perception of issues and approach to problem solving, can vary substantially depending on the cultural norms, available economic and social resources, and special circumstances in which the family and the older person are situated.

Families have played a critical role in caring for and assisting with needs of their older members in most immigrant/refugee populations. As reflected in *familismo*, a strong tie to immediate and extended family members, immigrant Latino families can mobilize a large network of relatives and friends in order to provide needed care and support for their older relatives (Ayon, Marsiglia, & Bermudez-Parsai, 2010). Similarly, many Asian immigrant families practice the traditional norm of filial responsibility, perceiving elder care as a moral duty. A study of 118 Asian Indians in Dallas, Texas, for example, found that many family caregivers strongly believed in elder care as a moral duty and experienced lower levels of caregiver burden than the other respondents (Gupta & Pillai, 2012). In another study of 339 Canadian-Chinese family caregivers, caregivers' belief in filial piety lowered the negative effects of caregiving stressors and enhanced the positive appraisal of caregiving, thereby contributing to reducing perceived caregiving burden (Lai, 2010).

Many older immigrants, on the other hand, provide emotional and other support for their children, including advice, household chores, and caring for their grandchildren. For many Chinese who immigrated to the United States in their old age, for example, family reunion and caring for their young grandchildren were the most common reasons for immigration (Chiang-Hanisko, 2010; Lin, Bryant, Boldero, & Dow, 2014). In fact, about 14.4% of all immigrants 65 and older, compared with only 3.6% of US-born elders, lived with at least one grandchild under age 18 in 2007 (Terrazas, 2009). Gurak and Kritz (2010) noted that while 12% of US-born older White people lived in extended households in 2000, the percentages for older Asian and Hispanic immigrants were significantly higher at 44% and 39%, respectively. Family may be an even more important source of care for the older immigrants in rural areas, where supportive services in general, and culturally and linguistically tailored services in particular, may be less available than in urban areas. In such areas, the family may be almost the exclusive source of help with language issues, loneliness, and internal family problems.

The likelihood of older immigrants' living with children or others is also significantly influenced by their reduced socioeconomic resources; lack of English skills; shorter durations of residence in the United States; noncitizenship, which disqualifies them for a full range of public income and medical assistance, such as Supplemental Security Income and the combined Medicare and Medicaid benefits; and demand for caring for grandchildren and assistance with domestic work (Treas, 2008). Therefore, a multigenerational living arrangement may not necessarily be indicative of strong family ties or practice of filial responsibility for care of the elderly person. Indeed, issues and challenges faced by family caregivers of older immigrants may vary depending on the intensity of care needed, availability of economic and other resources, and quality of the relationship with the older relative as well as culturally expected roles of family caregivers.

HEALTH, MENTAL HEALTH, AND SERVICE USE

Research shows that older immigrants/refugees, especially among those recently arrived from non-English-speaking, less developed, and/or war-torn countries, report poor physical and mental health and underuse needed services. Using a national representative sample of the US-born and three older immigrant groups (Black, Hispanic, and White), Lum and Vanderaa (2010) found that older immigrants reported poorer self-rated health, higher levels of depression, and more IADL (instrumental activity of daily living) difficulties than the US-born. Furthermore, older Black and Hispanic immigrants reported poorer self-reported health status and higher depression levels and were less likely to have both Medicare and other health insurance coverage but more likely to have Medicaid coverage than White older immigrants even after adjusting for the effects of age, gender, education, and income. Among the three older immigrant groups, the Hispanic immigrants reported significantly higher levels of depression than the Black or White immigrant groups.

Using national survey data, Williams and his colleagues (2007) found that the prevalence rate of a major depressive disorder, 10%, among Caribbean Black older participants (65% of whom were immigrants) was significantly higher than that of 7.1% for African Americans or 6% for non-Hispanic Whites. A comparative study of physical and mental health status of four mostly immigrant Asian groups (Chinese, Filipino, Korean, and Vietnamese) and mostly US-born Japanese Americans aged 60 and older in California found substantial variation among the groups (Kim, Chiriboga, et al., 2010): The Vietnamese reported the poorest self-rated health and the highest disability rates, and Filipinos showed the highest number of chronic diseases. While Koreans reported fewest chronic diseases and the least evidence of comorbidity, they reported the highest level of serious psychological distress. While an average of only 5.8% of the total sample did not have health insurance, the Korean sample reported the highest uninsured rate at 20.7%.

The prevalence rate of depression among older Asian immigrants/refugees varies considerably depending on the location of research; methodology, including sampling and measurement tool used; and sample size (Kuo, Chong, & Joseph, 2008). Mui and Kang (2006) reported that the prevalence rate of depression using the Geriatric Depression Scale (GDS) ranged from 76% for older Japanese to 64% for Vietnamese, 50% for Asian Indians, 46% for Chinese, 24% for Korean, and 15% for Filipino in New York. Suen and Morris (2006) found depression prevalence of 16% among older Taiwanese immigrants. The GDS prevalence rate for older Korean immigrants in Tampa, Florida, was 24% (Jang, Kim, & Chiriboga, 2005), while the depression prevalence for older Korean immigrants in Los Angeles, California, in a two-wave panel study using the Center for Epidemiological Studies Depression (CES-D) Scale and a probability sampling method, was significantly lower—12.9% and 11.9% at both waves—but higher than those of non-Hispanic Whites (7.6% and 7.1%) (Min, Moon, & Lubben, 2005). Using a national sample, Lam, Yip, and Gee (2012) reported the joint effects of age and age of immigration in health and mental health outcomes: Older Asian immigrants/refugees who came to the United States later in life reported the worst physical health outcomes but no effects on mental health.

For both Asian and Latino older immigrants, poor self-rated mental health was a significant predictor of greater mental health service use, which implies the importance of understanding how older immigrants assess their own mental health status (Kim, Jang, Chiriboga, Ma, & Schonfeld, 2010). Furthermore, Asian and Latino immigrants aged 60 and older with limited English proficiency, compared with those with English proficiency and those with English only, had poorer self-rated health and higher psychological distress and were more likely to experience barriers to service use and inadequate healthcare (Kim et al., 2011). In addition to poor health, language, and acculturation issues, Kirmayer and colleagues (2011), in their extensive literature review, further identified decreased social support and isolation, increased dependency on others due to language and mobility difficulties, lack of meaningful work, and loss of status as a respected elder in the family as risk factors for psychological distress among newly arrived older immigrants/refugees (p. E962).

Older immigrants/refugees may not seek help with mental health problems for several reasons, including unfamiliarity with formal mental health services; skepticism about the treatability of mental illness; institutional barriers such as lack of mental health professionals from the same culture or class; and fear of shame and stigma attached to mental illness (Moon & Cho, 2011). Furthermore, in many cultures of older immigrants/refugees, religious and spiritual beliefs seem to influence their views of illness, methods of coping, and use of formal services. Among them, it is still common practice to seek advice and help from religious and spiritual leaders for their family problems and emotional support.

Older immigrants/refugees are more susceptible to a broad range of symptoms associated with culture-bound folk illnesses and beliefs (Jackson, 2006; Paniagua & Yamada, 2013). Physical complaints or somatization of psychological or emotional problems are relatively common among many immigrant/refugee groups. For example, *Hwa-Byung* (HB), literally anger syndrome, is a widely perceived folk illness among elderly immigrant Korean women who endured feelings of victimization within their oppressive patriarchal family structure and experienced suppressed anger for an extensive period of time in life (Choi & Yeom, 2011). Many of those experiencing HB report a variety of somatic, as well as psychological, symptoms, such as headache, sensations of heat, oppressed sensations in the chest, presence of epigastric mass, diminished concentration, and anxiety). *Ataque de nervios* among Latinos is considered out-of-consciousness state resulting from evil spirits or in response to a severe stressful event, and its symptoms include attacks of uncontrollable crying, shouting, physical or verbal aggression, and intense heat in the chest moving to the head that are often associated with major stressful events (Hovey, 2006).

As a result of their tendency to experience the body and mind as a unitary system and to communicate psychosocial distress and other stressful life events through somatic symptoms and complaints, older immigrants/refugees are more likely to seek medical care for physical symptomatology than to seek mental health services. Among the Afghan immigrant elders, for example, the most frequently reported "health" complaint was mental health problems, particularly depression and physical symptoms related to stress from refugee trauma and loss, occupational and economic problems, cultural conflict, and social isolation (Morioka-Douglas et al., 2004). The non-Western traditional causes of mental or even physical illness may be strongly rooted in traditional spiritual and religious beliefs, such as punishment for sins committed in one's previous life among some Buddhist elders from Asian countries or failure to adhere to the principles of Islam and the will of God and possession by evil spirits among Muslim elders.

IMPLICATIONS FOR SOCIAL WORK PRACTICE

In consideration of the characteristics, major issues, and service needs of older immigrants/refugees and their families, we suggest the following social work practice implications within an evidence-based generalist perspective: that social workers recognize the intergroup and intragroup diversity among older immigrants/refugees including language, religious and spiritual beliefs and practice, attitudes toward health, behavioral health and wellness, help-seeking behaviors, and trust in formal social service institutions. Given these differences, it behooves social work practitioners to approach service delivery with a blend of sensitivity of the unique individual situation within the sociohistorical context of migration or adjustment and cultural variations.

At the outreach and engagement level, practitioners are faced with cultural stigma associated with vulnerability, helplessness, and need for self-efficacy. These notions determine the individual's problem definition and tolerance of severity, which decide when the situation is deemed at the crisis level requiring outside help. An example of cultural and social influences is seen in the Southeast Asian community and concepts of trauma and associated symptoms and help-seeking. Despite the experience of war and immigration-related trauma, the individual expression of pain and suffering are in the forms of somatic concerns. For the individual to accept their emotional response to the experience, community and family admission of trauma is necessary, because the public recognition of pain allows the individual to accept their vulnerability within the larger context. This expression and need for cultural and social acceptance of helplessness is consistent with the interdependent and collectivistic philosophy. For the social work practitioner, this implies that outreach efforts be addressed not only at the individual level but also at multiple systemic levels. Stigma reduction efforts should start at the community level, aimed at identifying how geopolitical forces have shaped the specific immigrant communities. This public recognition of distress, trauma, and resilience allows families to reduce the shame associated with behavioral and emotional symptomatology. At the individual level, use of familiar health and wellness concepts and terminology reduces the fear and increases trust in the service delivery.

Collaboratively, the practitioner determines with the client and their family to what extent is the problem within the cultural norm and how is it considered dysfunctional. In order to engage individuals into service use, consideration of family involvement and/or endorsement is dependent on living arrangements and family caregiving practices (Liu, Hinton, Tran, Hinton, & Barker, 2010). Family endorsement may be essential for some older people, yet for

others it is inappropriate to involve adult children and caregivers in an open discussion or in service planning. The induction process to introduce health, behavioral, and wellness services can include concrete services, such as transportation and resources for learning English, for performing basic tasks of daily living, and for accessing the community health and social service systems. These opportunities for socialization and skill development are part of an empowerment process that can increase self-efficacy as well as build trust with an unknown source of support (Kally, Cherry, Howland, & Villarruel, 2013).

Service use is dependent on access to service both at the practical as well as at the psychosocial levels. The case management type services can lower dependence on the family and reduce isolation and loneliness while increasing self-esteem and life satisfaction of the older client. Information about legal and other eligibility requirements of financial, medical, and other benefit programs that are applicable to different immigrants/refugees can reduce the ambivalence and/or reluctance to use services or confusion with procedures.

To ensure that services are relevant and appropriate, they need to be available in culturally and linguistically sensitive ways. If spiritual faith is an important component of the older client, support and participation of community and religious leaders in the outreach effort enhances trust building and validates the help-seeking behavior. Use of ethnic media and organizations also provide community-level education and recognition of specific health, behavioral health, and wellness needs and issues prevalent in the ethnic communities.

At the individual engagement level, an effective approach to relationship formation with an older client includes a congenial, personal manner rather than an impersonal, businesslike one. Lu, Organista, Manzo, Wong, and Phung (2008) found that clinicians'cultural competence and matching personal styles enhanced the relationship between clinicians and the Latino clients. Because most older immigrants/refugees are not familiar or comfortable with the existing service system, it is especially important for the practitioner to show a personal interest and empathy with the client's problems and to be warm, friendly, and reassuring. Dong, Chang, and Simon (2011) presented a model using cultural humility to build rapport with Chinese older adults with depression. This model calls for the worker to engage in self-reflection and self-critique in order to "learn from the patients" in a partnership that evolves over the course of the collaborative process with the clients. From another standpoint, Delgado (2007) presented a cultural assets model that incorporates natural support systems from the client and the ethnic community. The stages start from precontact understanding and research of resources in the client's community, assets identification and mapping of cultural assets, relationship building and sustaining, intervention, and ongoing evaluation of resources and assets toward solutions.

With increasing emphasis on evidence-based practice (EBP) in the social work field, application of EBP with refugee and immigrant communities requires that these practice models be tested and modified to accommodate the very specific needs related to aging, socioeconomic, cultural, and linguistic diversity. For example, Hodges and Oei (2006) provided a discussion of conceptual compatibility between cognitive-behavioral therapy and some common values of Chinese culture. They noted that while the use of CBT is found to be useful with Chinese clients, the cognitive reframing process in CBT contradicts somewhat with the Chinese client's acceptance of norms and hierarchy. Furthermore, Hodge and Nadir (2008) noted that in using cognitive therapy for Muslim clients, secular self-statements need to be packaged to be consistent with Islamic teachings and values. To be relevant, the practitioner needs to allow the individual to articulate pertinent components of their spiritual beliefs, and specific restructuring is coached within the appropriate cognitive style of their value system. Foulk, Ingersoll-Dayton, Cavanagh, Robinson, and Kales (2014) found efficacy of the mindfulness-based stress reduction (MBSR) model with older adults with depression and anxiety. They also noted that the group format of MBSR enhances the support network of the isolated older adult. This type of treatment can be culturally familiar for Asian clients who practice meditation.

Another dimension of practice that is influenced by cultural factors is the target of intervention. Indeed, mental health services targeting older immigrants/refugees should employ treatment strategies designed to facilitate support from family members. For example, the use of multisystemic family therapy with a Korean American family needs to account for the living arrangements and family caregiving practices while acknowledging

the potential variability in the actual roles the elderly client's family is willing and able to perform in meeting the needs of the client. These intergenerational dynamics determine the type of intervention and the level where it should be addressed. Another example is the understanding of intergenerational transfer of trauma among the refugee and immigrant families and the impact on conflict between older adults and their caregivers, mutual understanding across generations, or generational gaps and isolation. Intervention efforts in these instances need to account for the varying degree and expression of trauma among the family's generations in order to target intervention at multiple family members rather than just the individual. In this sense, services are provided for more than just the individual older adult. Collateral family work is necessary in order to enhance protective factors for the identified client as well as involved family members. Family interdependence can be construed as resilience rather than a barrier among immediate and extended family members in refugee and immigrant communities.

With increasing understanding of diversity among refugee and immigrant communities, there is recognition for practices that emerge from the informal as well as formal community settings, that show optimal treatment effects, and that include indigenous beliefs about the cause as well as healing practices of physical and mental health problems. These practices are incorporated as an essential part of a holistic treatment plan while addressing the gap between traditional and Western methods of treatment.

CONCLUSION

Social work practice with older immigrant/refugee populations requires cultural competence and the ability to understand the target population's special issues and needs in service delivery, as well as an understanding of their cultural and immigration/refugee background. Special service delivery arrangements to overcome the language and cultural barriers, acknowledgment of the traditional methods of coping and healing, and demonstration of culturally appropriate interpersonal skills, in both verbal communication and behavioral aspects of interaction, can significantly increase effectiveness in meeting the service needs and thereby improving the well-being of older immigrants/refugees. For example, the practitioner's effort to show respect for the client's culture and special needs, such as expressing an interest in and appreciation of the client's cultural background during the initial stage of relation formation, and speaking clearly and slowly and sometimes repeatedly, with patience, to clients with limited English can make a difference in gaining the client's acceptance and trust of the practitioner.

Considering the growing heterogeneity not only among different older immigrant/refugee populations but also within the same ethnic group, practitioners must be cautioned against overgeneralizing and stereotyping groups and individuals solely based on their immigrant/refugee and ethnic background. Multiplicity and complexity of ethnicity and culture demand a multidimensional approach to social work practice with the immigrant and refugee populations, whose culture and immigration-related factors are only some of the numerous factors to be considered in practice. Nevertheless, cultural competency enables practitioners to better understand "where the client is" and how best to meet the client's needs.

REFERENCES

Ayon, C., Marsiglia, F., & Bermudez-Parsai, M. (2010). Latino family mental health: Exploring the role of discrimination and familismo. *Journal of Community Psychology, 38,* 742–756. doi: 10.1002/jcop.20392

Camarota, S. A. (2012). *Immigrants in the United States: A Profile of America's Foreign-Born Population.* Center for Immigration Studies. Retrieved September 24, 2013, from http://heartland.org/sites/default/files/immigrants-in-the-united-states-2012.pdf

Chiang-Hanisko, L. (2010). Paradise lost: How older adult Taiwanese immigrants make decisions about their living arrangements. *Journal of Cultural Diversity, 17,* 99–104. Retrieved from http://euro-pepmc.org/abstract/MED/20860334

Choi, M., & Yeom, H. A. (2011). Identifying and treating the culture-bound syndrome of Hwa-Byung among older Korean immigrant women: Recommendations for practitioners. *Journal of the American Academy of Nurse Practitioners, 23,* 226–232. doi: 10.1111/j.1745-7599.2011.00607.x

Delgado, M. (2007). *Social work with Latinos: A cultural assets paradigm.* New York, NY: Oxford University Press.

Dong, X., Chang, E., & Simon, M. (2011). Depression in the Chinese aging population: Leveraging cultural humility to improve the quality of care of a vulnerable population. *Aging Health, 7,* 849. doi: 10.2217/ahe.11.77

Foulk, M., Ingersoll-Dayton, B., Kavanagh, J., Robinson, E., & Kales, H. (2014). Mindfulness-based cognitive therapy with older adults: An exploratory study. *Journal of Gerontological Social Work, 57,* 498–520. doi: 10.1080/01634372.2013.869787

Gupta, R., & Pillai, V. K. (2012). Elder caregiving in South-Asian families in the United States and India. *Social Work and Society, 10,* International online journal. ISSN 1613-8953. Retrieved from http://nbn-resolving.de/urn:nbn:de:hbz:464-sws-260 http://www.socwork.net/sws/article/viewFile/339/692

Gurak, D. T., & Kritz, M. M. (2010). Elderly Asian and Hispanic foreign and native-born living arrangement: Accounting for differences. *Research on Aging, 32,* 567–594. doi: 10.1177/0164027510377160

Hodge, D., & Nadir, A. (2008). Moving toward culturally competent practice with Muslims: Modifying cognitive therapy with Islamic tenets. *Social Work, 53,* 31–40. doi: 10.1093/sw/53.1.31

Hodges, J., & Oei, T. P. S. (2006). Would Confucius benefit from psychotherapy? The compatibility of cognitive behavior therapy and Chinese values. *Behaviour Research and Therapy, 45,* 901–914. doi: 10.1016/j.brat.2006.08.015

Hovey, J. (2006). *Ataque de nervios.* In K. Jackson (Ed.), *Encyclopedia of multicultural psychology* (p. 133). Thousand Oaks, CA: Sage.

Hsu, E., Davies, C., & Hansen, D. (2004). Understanding mental health needs of Southeast Asian refugees: Historical, cultural, and contextual challenges. *Clinical Psychology Review, 24,* 193–213. doi: 10.1016/j.cpr.2003.10.003

Jackson, K. (Ed.) (2006). *Encyclopedia of multicultural psychology.* Thousand Oaks, CA: Sage.

Jang, Y., Kim, G., & Chiriboga, D. (2005). Acculturation and manifestation of depressive symptoms among Korean American older adults. *Aging and Mental Health, 9,* 500–507. doi: 10.1080/13607860500193021

Kally, Z., Cherry, D., Howland, S., & Villarruel, M. (2013). Asian Pacific Islander dementia care network: A model of care for underserved communities. *Journal of Gerontological Social Work, 57,* 710–727. doi: 10.1080/01634372.2013.854856

Kim, G., Chiriboga, D. A., Jang, Y., Lee, S., Huang, C., & Parmelee, P. (2010). Health status of older Asian Americans in California. *Journal of American Geriatric Society, 58,* 2003–2008. doi: 10.1111/j.1532-5415.2010.03034.x

Kim, G., Jang, Y., Chiriboga, D. A., Ma, G. X., & Schonfeld, L. (2010). Factors associated with mental health service use in Latino and Asian immigrant elders. *Aging and Mental Health, 14*, 535–542. doi: 10.1080/13607860903311758

Kim, G., Worley, C. Allen, R., Vinson, L., Crowther, M., Parmelee, P., & Chiriboga, D. (2011). Vulnerability of older Latino and Asian immigrants with limited English proficiency. *Journal of American Geriatric Society, 59*, 1246–1252. doi: 10.1111/j.1532-5415.2011.03 483.x

Kirmayer, L. J., Narasiah, L., Munoz, M., Rashid, M., Ryder, A. G., Guzder, J., . . . Pottie, K. (2011). Common mental health problems in immigrants and refugees: General approach in primary care. *Canadian Medical Association Journal, 183*, E959–E967. doi: 10.1503/cmaj.090292

Kuo, B. C., Chong, B., & Joseph, J. (2008). Depression and its psychological correlates among older Asian immigrants in North America: A critical review of two decades of research. *Journal of Aging and Health, 20*, 615–652. doi: 10.1177/0898264308321001

Lai, D. W. L. (2010). Filial piety, caregiving appraisal, and caregiving burden. *Research on Aging, 32*, 200–223. doi: 10.1177/0164027509351475

Lam, J., Yip, T., & Gee, G. (2012). The physical and mental health effects of age of immigration, age, and perceived difference in social status among first generation Asian Americans. *Asian American Journal of Psychology, 3*, 29–43. doi: 10.1037/a0027428

Lin, X., Bryant, C., Boldero, J., & Dow, B. (2014). Older Chinese immigrants' relationships with their children: A literature review from a solidarity-conflict perspective. *The Gerontologist*. Advance access published February 17, 2014. doi: 10.1093/geront/gnu004

Liu, D., Hinton, L., Tran, C., Hinton, D., & Barker, J. C. (2010). Re-examining the relationships among dementia, stigma and aging in immigrant Chinese and Vietnamese family caregivers. *Journal of Cross-Cultural Gerontology, 23*, 283–299. doi: 10.1007/s10823-008-9075-5

Lu, Y., Organista, K., Manzon, S., Wong, L., & Phung, J. (2008). Exploring dimensions of culturally sensitive clinical styles with Latinos. *Journal of Ethnic and Cultural Diversity in Social Work, 10*, 45–66. doi: 10.1300/J051v10n02_04

Lum, T. Y., & Vanderaa, J. P. (2010). Health disparities among immigrant and non-immigrant elders: The association of acculturation and education. *Journal of Immigrant Minority Health, 12*, 743–753. doi: 10.1007/s10903-008-9225-4

Min, J., Moon, A., & Lubben, J. (2005). Determinants of psychological distress over time among older Korean Americans and non-Hispanic White elders: Evidence from a two-wave panel study. *Journal of Mental Health and Aging, 9*, 210–222. doi: 10.1080/13607860500090011

Moon, A., & Cho, I. (2011). Psychology of Asian American older adults: Status, challenges, and strengths. In E. C. Chang & C. A. Downey (Eds.), *Handbook of race and development in mental health* (pp. 189–206). New York, NY: Springer.

Morioka-Douglas, N., Sacks, T., & Yeo, G. (2004). Issues in caring for Afghan American elders: Insights from literature and a focus group. *Journal of Cross-Cultural Gerontology, 19*, 27–40. doi: 10.1023/B:JCCG.0000015015.63501.db

Mui, A. C., & Kang, S. Y. (2006). Acculturation stress and depression among Asian immigrant elders. *Social Work, 51*, 243–255. doi: 10.1093/sw/51.3.243

Niedzwiecki, M., & Duong, T. C. (2004). *Southeast Asian American statistical profile*. Washington, DC: Southeast Asia Resource Action Center (SEARAC). Retrieved from http://www.lana-usa.org/uploads/SEARAC-seaStatProfileMay04.pdf

Paniagua, F. A., & Yamada, A. (Eds). (2013). *Culture-bound syndromes, cultural variations, and psychopathology* (2nd ed.). San Diego, CA: Academic Press.

Population Reference Bureau. (2013). *Elderly immigrants in the United States*. Retrieved November 2, 2013, from http://www.prb.org/Publications/Reports/2013/us-elderly-immigrants.aspx,

Suen, L. J., & Morris, D. L. (2006). Depression and gender differences: Focus on Taiwanese American older adults. *Journal of Gerontological Nursing, 32*, 28–36.

Terrazas, A. (2009). *Older immigrants in the United States*. Migration Policy Institute Spotlight. Retrieved October 11, 2013, from http://www.migrationpolicy.org/article/older-immigrants-united-states

Treas, J. (2008). Four myths about older adults in America's immigrant families. *Generations, 32*(4), 40–45.

US Census Bureau. (2012). *The foreign-born population in the United States: 2010, American Community Survey*. Survey report, May 2012, p. 5. Retrieved October 11, 2013, from https://www.census.gov/prod/2012pubs/acs-19.pdf

US Department of Homeland Security. (2013). *Yearbook of immigration statistics: 2012 legal permanent residents*. Retrieved October 22, 2013, from http://www.dhs.gov/yearbook-immigration-statistics-2012-legal-permanent-residents

Williams, D. R., Gonzales, H. M., Neighbors, H., Nesse, R., Abelson, J. M, Sweetman, J., & Jackson, J. S. (2007). Prevalence and distribution of major depressive disorder in African Americans, Caribbean Blacks, and Non-Hispanic Whites: Results from the National Survey of American Life. *Archives of General Psychiatry, 64,* 305–315. doi: 10.1001/archpsyc.64.3.305

DENISE BURNETTE

FEI SUN

Global Aging in the Twenty-First Century: Prospects, Challenges, and Directions for Action

Chronological demarcations of old age are disputed, as they fail to adequately account for variations in human aging. Developed countries conventionally use Bismarck's retirement criterion of age 65 years, but many are now gradually pushing that threshold upward. The World Health Organization (WHO) defines older persons as aged 50 years and over, reflecting lower life expectancy in many less developed countries, while the United Nations (UN) benchmark old age is 60 years. We use age 60 as the referent herein.

Regardless of how old age is defined, human populations are aging (Palacious, 2002). In 2010, the number of persons aged 60 years and over was estimated at 765 million, 11% of the global population. Life expectancy at 60 is between 18.5 to 21.6 years; by 2050, we can expect more than 2 billion older adults, or one in five people, and the number will for the first time exceed that of children (United Nations Population Fund [UNFPA], 2012; HelpAge International, 2010). Further, the older population itself is aging. People aged 85 and over now constitute 8% of the 65-and-over population—12% in more developed countries and 6% in less developed countries. Between 2010 and 2050, this "oldest-old" sector is projected to increase by 351%, compared with 188% for persons aged 65 and over and 22% for those under age 65. Moreover, the number of centenarians, a subgroup of the "oldest old," is expected to increase 10-fold.

The most rapid and extensive population aging is now and will continue to be in less developed countries, undergoing demographic transition, where the number of older adults is projected to increase by more than 250% between 2010 and 2050, compared with 71% increase in developed countries. Presently, Asia accounts for more than half of all older persons (414 million, including 166 million in China and 92 million in India), followed by Europe (nearly 161 million), Northern America (65 million), Latin America and the Caribbean (59 million), Africa (55 million), and Oceania (6 million) (United Nations Department of Economic and Social Affairs [UNDESA], 2013).

Multiple factors interact over time to shape changes in population age structure. To demonstrate the *process* and *variability* of population aging, we begin with a brief overview of the classic demographic transition model (DTM). Drawing on the underlying principles of the 2002

Second World Assembly on Ageing in Madrid and the World Health Organization (WHO) concept of *active ageing* (WHO, 2002a), we then discuss *conditions* that contribute to the shared and variable experiences of aging in a globalizing world and produce different *pathways* and *outcomes* for people who age in different times and places. Such distinctions often engender and embody disparities in opportunities and outcomes throughout the life course. We conclude with a discussion of the need for policies and legal structures, evidence-informed and culturally grounded practices, and a strong research base that will help achieve longer, better lives for all.

DEMOGRAPHIC TRANSITION

The classic DTM holds that birth and death rates decline, albeit at different rates, as countries progress toward industrialized economies. This process begins with a stationary period of high birth rates and high death rates, followed in stage 2 by a relatively precipitous decline in mortality. Longer lives then lead to population expansion until the birth rate drops off in stage 3, producing a low stationary population in stage 4.

The DTM lacks explanatory and predictive power and is thus best viewed as a heuristic for conceptualizing demographic history. There is considerable speculation about a fifth phase of transition, as the development agendas of many developing nations are currently producing unsustainable rates of population growth that will not await industrialization and modernization to adequately reduce fertility. Making clear that demography is *not* destiny, the interactions of population dynamics with current forces such as macroeconomic strains, shifting disease profiles, transnational migration, urbanization, and emergent technologies are influencing the pace, extent, and experience of population aging. These and other evolving contextual factors must be balanced with resources, constraints, and competing demands when determining and prioritizing needs.

PRIORITIES FOR THE AGING TRANSFORMATION

The *Madrid International Plan of Action on Ageing* (UNDESA, Social Policy and Development Division,

2002) lists three priority directions: mainstreaming older persons in development, advancing health and well-being into old age, and ensuring enabling and supportive environments. In conjunction with the Madrid Assembly, the WHO (2002a) adopted a policy framework on active aging, with a goal to help people realize their potential for physical, social, and mental well-being throughout the life course and to participate in society while receiving adequate protection, security, and care when they need it. The framework is grounded in the UN principles of independence, participation, dignity, care, and self-fulfillment; acknowledges the salience of gender, earlier life experiences, and culture on individual aging; and recognizes the impact of lifelong biological, psychological, behavioral, economic, social, and environmental factors on late-life health and well-being.

Health and Physical Functioning: Advancing Health into Old Age

The demographic transition from high to low fertility and mortality also created major shifts in causes of disease and death, with infectious and acute diseases of childhood being replaced by chronic and degenerative noncommunicable diseases (NCDs) that typically affect adults and increase dramatically as a function of age. Noncommunicable diseases now represent the single greatest burden on global human health and are a major barrier to development and economic growth. These conditions account for 63% of all deaths, 80% of which are in low- and middle-income countries (LMICs), and half of persons who die of NCDs are in their prime productive years. Bloom and colleagues (2011) project the cost of NCDs will exceed $30 trillion, or 48% of the 2010 global GDP, over the next 20 years, depleting workforces and family resources and pushing millions into poverty. Likewise, the WHO's analysis in 23 LMICs estimated that without intervention, the economic losses from heart disease, stroke, and diabetes would total US$83 billion between 2006 and 2015 (Abegunde, Mathers, Adam, Ortegon, & Strong, 2007).

Cardiovascular diseases, cancer, chronic respiratory diseases, and diabetes account for about 80% of the total burden of chronic disease mortality in developing countries. For older adults, ischemic heart disease, stroke, and chronic lung disease are the chief causes of mortality, while visual and hearing impairment, dementia, and osteoarthritis lead to most of the disability. Older adults in the developing world compared with those in developed countries lose five times as many years from chronic lung disease and twice as many years from stroke and bear almost three times the burden of visual impairment. Such disparities are even more marked when comparing older adults in poorest and richest countries. In addition to the many challenges posed by NCDs in aging populations, older people also account for a growing share of *communicable diseases* in low-income countries. Increasing evidence indicates that persons in this age group, especially those who have an existing chronic or infectious disease, are highly susceptible to other infectious diseases due to processes such as immunosenescence and frailty. Tuberculosis, a common comorbid risk factor, has serious health outcomes for older people.

The global HIV and AIDS epidemic is also aging, as the availability of highly active antiretroviral therapy (ART) enables more people with HIV/AIDS to survive to older ages. At the end of 2011, 8% of 34 million people living with HIV infection were aged 50 years or older (Negin & Cumming, 2010). Further, an estimated two-thirds of the more than 16 million children under age 18 who are orphaned by AIDS are being raised by their grandparents, whose number has doubled in the last 10 years (AVERT, 2013). This trend is most striking in industrialized countries with concentrated epidemics and greater access to treatment. The number of older Americans with HIV rose 77% between 2001 and 2005 and will represent half of all HIV cases by 2015 (Effros et al., 2008). Similarly, 13% of new cases in western Europe in 2007 were for people aged 50 and over, up from 10% in 2003 (Lazarus & Nielsen, 2010).

The populations of sub-Saharan Africa (SSA) are young, but the number of persons aged 60+ years in the region is expected to quadruple between 2010 and 2050, from 40 million to nearly 160 million, exceeding the pace of aging in all other regions. In 2007, 14.3% of the 21 million people aged 15+ years and living with HIV in SSA were at least 50 years old. Prevalence for this group was 4%, compared with 5% for persons aged 15–49 (Negin & Cumming, 2010). Since HIV prevalence peaks in the mid-40s in most countries, this peak will shift upward as future cohorts age with ART. This shift, coupled with the diffuse nature of the epidemic in SSA and a serious lack of knowledge about older persons who either acquire the infection later in life or age into the status, suggests that population aging in SSA is likely to worsen the HIV situation and further impede social development.

Mental Health and Aging Populations

Under the WHO banner "no health without mental health" (Prince et al., 2007), attention to the extensive and growing burden of mental, neurological, and substance use (MNS) disorders has risen dramatically during the past decade. The lifetime prevalence of MNS disorders is estimated at between 12.2% and 48.6%, and they account for 13% of the global burden of disease, surpassing both cardiovascular disease and cancer (WHO, 2008). Depression is the third leading contributor to the global burden of disease; and it is estimated that someone develops dementia every 7 seconds (Ferri et al., 2005), costing up to $609 billion in 2009 (Collins et al., 2011). Abegunde et al. (2007) estimate that mental health conditions, which have a major impact of productivity and quality of life, will account for loss of another $16.1 trillion.

Over 20% of adults aged 60 and over suffer from a mental or neurological disorder, and 6.6% of all disability among over 60s is attributed to neurological and mental disorders (Institute for Health Metrics and Evaluation, 2010). Social isolation and poverty affect health and mental health, and common health problems such as stroke, hypertension, and diabetes increase the risk of mental disorder. Moreover, the burden of poor mental health among older persons is likely underestimated due to poor understanding of the association of mental disorders and other health conditions, and the fact that many mental problems go undetected and untreated owing to barriers such as stigma and lack of awareness, knowledge, and services. Nevertheless, attention to the mental health needs of older people is gaining ground. A major call for global scaling-up mental healthcare as public health, human rights, and development priorities specifies the care and services across the life course (Patel & Prince, 2010), for example, and the World Federation for Mental Health (2013) Mental Health Day focused on older people.

Social Well-Being and Enabling Environments

Rapidly modernizing societies and industrializing economies are driving the changing patterns of social organization worldwide. This fast-paced change is eroding the social status of older people and the long-standing protective and supportive functions of traditional family structures in developing countries (Aboderin, 2005).

Realistic options for meaningful inclusion and participation of older adults in social and civic life are lacking, especially when there is competition for scarce resources. Intergenerational solidarity also appears to be declining, especially in high-income countries, and shifts to nuclear, and in the West, alternative family forms, together with transnational and urban migration are changing the nature of family ties and traditions of family care. Multigenerational households have thus been declining in more developed countries, and increasing numbers of older adults are living alone by choice. In less developed countries, two-generation and three-generation households remain the norm and older people tend to prefer to live either with or close to their children for economic and cultural reasons (Kinsella & Phillips, 2005; UNDESA Population Division, 2005).

By mid-2010, an estimated 31 million international migrants were aged 60 years or over, accounting for 14% of all migrants worldwide. Older people are less likely than young adults to move in any given year, but many find it necessary due to circumstances such as retirement, widowhood, or poor health. Older persons are also affected when children migrate out and may later move to join them (UNDESA, 2013). Such a move can assuage some difficulties, but may create others, including social, cultural, and linguistic isolation (Lai, 2009; Wong, Yoo, & Stewart, 2007). With respect to internal migration, the number of older urban residents nearly quadrupled between 1975 and 2005, and most of the future growth of older populations will be in urban areas of developing countries (UNDESA, 2010). Yet the proportion of populations aged 60 years and over is now higher in rural than in urban areas, as young adult migration to cities in search of employment has left many rural areas with high numbers of children and older persons relative to working-age persons (UNDESA, 2013). These migration patterns, with economic pressures and social health conditions such as the HIV and AIDS epidemic, have produced a dramatic increase in the number of "skipped generation" households, comprising only grandparents and grandchildren, in LMICs (Burnette, Sun, & Sun, 2013).

Changing family structures in contemporary societies may also contribute to increased elder mistreatment, already a significant social problem worldwide (Lachs & Pillemer, 2004). The WHO (2008) defines elder abuse as "a single, or repeated act, or lack of appropriate action, occurring within any relationship where there is an expectation of trust which causes harm or distress to an older person." Despite sociocultural subtleties, most identified abuse consists of physical, financial, emotional, and sexual abuse and neglect (WHO, 2002b). Forging an older relative's signature is an example of a common financial abuse in some more developed countries, while scapegoating and then expelling an older person from the tribe presents an example of elder abuse in some less developed societies (Lachs & Pillemer, 2004).

In a systematic review of the prevalence of elder abuse in community settings around the world, Sooryanarayana, Choo, and Hairi (2013) reported established rates for the United States, United Kingdom, Finland, the Netherlands, Ireland, Spain, Israel, South Korea, Turkey, Russia, Thailand, India, Taiwan, Hong Kong, and mainland China. Overall rates ranged from 1.1% in the United States to 44.6% in Spain, depending on definitions, measurement, and sampling strategy. Studies that used the Conflict Tactics Scale (Straus, 1979) to assess elder abuse found rates ranging from 3.2% in the United States to 27.5% in Hong Kong. Prevalence rates are lowest in the United States and highest in Asian countries. Risk factors for abuse included attributes of older adults (e.g., minority status, disability) and their perpetrators (e.g., substance abuse), social support (e.g., small network), cultural factors (e.g., violation of filial piety norms in Chinese culture), and social variables (e.g., economic instability in a country).

Social engagement and personal security can be substantially enhanced by an age-friendly physical environment that promotes inclusion, development and use of communication and assistive technologies, especially for mobility and sensory impairments, as people age (WHO, 2007a). Affordable housing and accessible transportation are also essential to aging in place while maintaining independence and involvement. Active promotion of the human rights of older persons would lend further support to these and other environmental initiatives.

There is progress toward the development of international human rights instruments that specifically address older persons (Fredvang & Biggs, 2012). A report of the secretary-general to the United Nations General Assembly (2013) notes four main areas of concerns in the rights of older persons: (1) discrimination, fueled by ageism and worsened due to gender, race, ethnicity, religion, disability, and poverty; (2) poverty, which encompasses homelessness, malnutrition, untreated health conditions, lack of access to safe drinking water and sanitation, unaffordable medicines and treatments, and income insecurity; (3) violence and abuse; and (4) lack of services, especially specialized services, to meet the growing demand of older adults and their families.

Economic Security

Along with healthcare, both older adults and governments consider income security the most urgent and challenging concerns of aging populations. Pension systems are among the most significant means of ensuring economic independence and reducing poverty in later life; they benefit entire families and, in times of crisis, may be the primary or sole source of household income. Yet only one-third of all countries have comprehensive social protection schemes. Of these, most only cover persons in formal employment, or less than half of the economically active population worldwide (UNFPA & HelpAge International, 2012). The recent global economic crisis has caused developed nations to question the sustainability of current pension systems, while less-developed countries struggle with basic social protection and an inability to develop pension schemes due to the outsized labor market in the informal sector (see National Institutes of Health, 2007). The development and revision of public pension schemes should aim to provide adequate and reliable income to older people, reduce poverty in this age sector, and promote equal treatment of men and women in retirement, even when lifetime earnings and average life expectancy differ greatly (Bloom & McKinnon, 2013).

DISCUSSION AND CONCLUSIONS

Global aging is unprecedented, pervasive, and enduring and has profound implications for human life at all levels. Policy, practice, and research with and for older adults will help determine whether these added years of life are characterized by good health, mental well-being, social engagement, and productivity or by illness, disability, and increased dependency.

The development and implementation of effective public policy requires broad public support and strong political will. An important initial and ongoing strategy in policy-making is thus to increase public awareness of and favorable attitudes toward the strengths as well as needs of older adults, including their vital family, social, and civic roles. This would require shifting from a needs-based to a rights-based culture and the translation of international human rights instruments into national laws and regulations, and affirmative measures to challenge age discrimination and recognize the autonomy and capacities of older adults (UNFPA & HelpAge International, 2012).

Policies should aim to strengthen the capacity of national and local governments to adapt to the demands of population aging through social and economic reforms that support access, equity, and quality in health and social services and that foster personal dignity and economic security. Health and mental health policies should aim to maximize functioning and quality of life by ensuring access to basic prevention, intervention, and restorative services. There are vast variations in healthcare for older persons around the world. Those in developed countries have more access to acute and long-term care services (National Institutes of Health, 2011). Most European countries have universal healthcare systems; in the United States, Medicare and Medicaid target the medical needs of the older population; and China is launching healthcare reform that is intended to incorporate "left-behind" rural older adults (National Institutes of Health, 2007). Despite healthcare coverage, financial expenses including health insurance premiums, prescription drug cost, and copayment can be proportionally higher for older adults.

Home- and community-based service systems and institutional care are rarely available in developing countries, while marginalized groups tend to have less access to such services in developed countries (Min, 2005; Rooks et al., 2008). Older immigrants experience tremendous stress associated with immigration, acculturation, discrimination, and prejudice (Kuo, Chong, & Joseph, 2008) and face cultural barriers such as feelings of shame, distrust, and misunderstanding of the service system; limited financial and transportation resources; and language difficulties (Choi & Gonzalez, 2005). Another example is indigenous Aboriginal and Torres Strait Islanders in Australia, for whom services are often not compatible with their needs or their social and cultural beliefs, behaviors, and values (Ranzijn, 2010).

Social and environmental policies should provide opportunities and supports for social integration and participation, which confer immediate and long-range benefits on society and directly and indirectly affect physical and mental health status (Morrow-Howell, Hinterlong & Sherraden, 2001). Intergenerational policies can further consolidate and maximize resources and long-term gain, while social protection floors and other social investments can promote independence and aging in place, guarantee income security, and provide a safety net that will help postpone disability and prevent impoverishment. National humanitarian responses, climate change mitigation and adaptation plans, and disaster management and preparedness programs should also include older adults (UNFPA & HelpAge International, 2012). Lastly, policies for older adults will fare better if mainstreamed into broader social and legal structures that promote, build, and use their capabilities. Aging policies should be integrated in gender policies and in national development policies, for example, and should be clearly specified and indicated in the post-2015 development agenda (United Nations System Task Force on the Post-2015 UN Development Agenda, 2013).

Since the 2002 Madrid Conference, aging policies have been enacted in many countries, however their implementation and enforcement have been slow, especially in resource-constrained settings. Mainstreaming and consolidating resources in broad, nonaging specific arenas can move these efforts forward while promoting access, equity, and quality in practice. Unless otherwise indicated, the delivery of health and mental healthcare in community primary care clinics would improve access and affordability and may also diminish social stigma associated with conditions such as HIV and AIDS and mental disorders (Beaglehole et al., 2008).

One major challenge for practice is the severe shortage of nonageist health and mental health professionals, both generalists and specialists, who are knowledgeable about and competent in geriatrics. All professional and continuing education programs should require training in this body of knowledge, skills, and values. There is also growing evidence that shifting or sharing less skilled elements of screening and treatment with well-trained, supervised lay health workers can yield comparable outcomes. Diligent monitoring and stringent accountability of policy implementation will also allow for necessary course corrections and will promote effective, equitable, and responsible use of available resources.

The UNFPA (2012) advises that all policy and practice for older people should be based on a long-term vision, supported by a strong political commitment and a budget secured against crises and governmental changes. This vision requires the availability of up-to-date, scientifically sound, and readily implementable research. Significant gains in human longevity have led to rapid advances in knowledge about human development. Mapping of the human genome, strides in neurobiology and brain studies, and advances in epigenetics hold great promise, especially for NCDs, and scientific and technological advances confirm that these broad areas of human life are closely intermeshed and mutually reinforcing, simultaneously and longitudinally (Bengtson, Silverstein, Putney, & Gans, 2009). An example is the emergent field of biodemography, which integrates demographic and biological theory and methods to understand the impact of aging on health and longevity and the biological and demographic determinants of and interactions between birth and death processes that shape individuals, cohorts, and populations.

There are growing numbers of single- and multicountry studies on aging (National Institute on Aging, 2013a). An example is the longitudinal WHO Study on Global AGEing and Adult Health, which addresses the gap in reliable data and scientific knowledge on aging and health in LMICs with nationally representative samples of persons aged 50 years and over in China, Ghana, India, Mexico, Russia, and South Africa (Kowal et al., 2012). Cross-cultural research must particularly address the need to develop uniform indicators that permit meaningful comparisons. Careful translation procedures to establish linguistic, metric, and cultural equivalency can be augmented through use and, when appropriate, integration of qualitative and quantitative methods and through interdisciplinary research teams.

In tandem with advances in empirical research, innovative approaches to disciplinary, interdisciplinary, and transdisciplinary studies are enriching theory on the experience of human aging across the life course and in social, cultural, and historical context. Innovative use of multilevel approaches to research is increasing awareness that personal agency and actions; social constraints, such as class, race, gender, and culture; and systems of healthcare and state pensions are central to the causes and consequences of aging. As Bengtson and colleagues (2009) note, "although difficult to orchestrate and expensive to develop, theory-driven interdisciplinary investigations of aging are nevertheless the wave of the future" (p. 23).

In closing, we reiterate that aging is situated within complex societies and social and political agendas. Though often implicit, these and other issues related to aging persons and populations are evident in social development and social work agendas and must be supported and advanced. The WHO, for example, lists health, mental health, changing roles of the family, quality of life, human rights, social inclusion, and productive roles as major topics in aging. Early findings from the UN Development Group's consultation program to develop post-Millennium Development Goals suggest that moving from vulnerability to empowerment, inclusion and fairness, environmental sustainability, security, and growing and moving populations merit more attention in future development agendas. Likewise, the *Global Agenda for Work and Social Development Commitment to Action*, issued jointly by the International Federation of Social Workers, International Association of Schools of Social Work, and the International Council on Social Welfare (2012), has pledged to focus efforts during 2012–2016 on social and economic equality, promoting dignity and worth of peoples, working toward environmental sustainability, and strengthening recognition of the importance of human relationships. In recognizing and supporting the work of these and other organizations with similar purposes, we endorse and advance a commitment to longer, better lives for older people worldwide, now and in the future.

RESOURCES

Aging and Society: http://agingandsociety.com/
Aging Portfolio: http://www.agingportfolio.org/
Center for Strategic and International Studies: http://csis.org/program/global-aging-initiative

Gerontological Global Aging: http://www.geron.org/component/content/article/519
Global Action on Aging: http://www.globalaging.org
Global Aging Research Network: http://www.garn-network.org/
Global Coalition on Aging: http://www.globalcoalition-onaging.com/
Help Age International: http://www.helpage.org/
International Federation on Aging: http://www.ifa-fiv.org/
International Association of Homes and Services for the Aging: http://www.iahsa.net/
International Network on Healthy Life Expectancy (REVES) www.prw.le.ac.uk/reves/
Program on the Global Demography of Aging: http://www.hsph.harvard.edu/pgda/
UN Department of Economic and Social Affairs Population Division
http://www.un.org/esa/population/publications/worldageing19502050/
US Census Bureau, International Data Base www.census.gov/ipc/www/idbnew.htm.
WHO Ageing and Life Course Programme ww.who.int/hpr/ageing/index.htm

REFERENCES

Abegunde, D. O., Mathers, C. D., Adam, T., Ortegon M., & Strong, K. (2007). The burden and costs of chronic diseases in low-income and middle-income countries. *Lancet, 370*, 1929–1938. doi: 10.1016/S0140-6736(07)61696-1

Aboderin, I. (2005). Changing family relationships in developing nations. In M. L. Johnson, V. L. Bengtson, P. Coleman, & T. Kirkwood (Eds.), *The Cambridge handbook of age and ageing* (pp. 469–475). Cambridge, UK: Cambridge University Press.

AVERT. (2013). *Children orphaned by HIV and AIDS*. Retrieved from http://www.avert.org/children-orphaned-hiv-and-aids.htm

Beaglehole, R., Epping-Jordan, J., Patel, V., Chopra, M., Ebrahim, S., Kidd, M., & Haines, A. (2008). Improving the prevention and management of chronic disease in low-income and middle-income countries: A priority for primary health care. *Lancet, 372*, 940–949. doi: 10.1016/S0140-6736(08)61404-X

Bengtson, V. L., Silverstein, M., Putney, N. M., & Gans, D. (Eds.). (2009). *Handbook of theories of aging*. New York, NY: Springer.

Bloom, D. E., Cafiero, E. T., Jané-Llopis, E., Abrahams-Gessel, S., Bloom, L. R., Fathima, S., . . . Weinstein, C. (2011). *The global economic* burden of noncommunicable diseases. Geneva, Switzerland: World Economic Forum.

Bloom, D. E., & McKinnon, R. (2013). *The design and implementation of public pension systems in developing countries: Issues and options*. Program on the Global Demography of Aging. Working Paper No. 102. Retrieved from http://www.hsph.harvard.edu/program-on-the-global-demography-of-aging/WorkingPapers/2013/PGDA_WP_102.pdf

Burnette, D., Sun, J., & Sun, F. (2013). A comparative review of grandparent care of children in the U.S. and China. *Ageing International, 38*, 43–57. doi: 10.1007/s12126-012-9174-z

Choi, N., & Gonzalez, J. (2005). Barriers and contributors to minority older adult's access to mental health treatment: Perceptions of geriatric mental health clinicians. *Journal of Gerontological Social Work, 44*, 115–135. doi: 10.1300/J083v44n03_08

Collins, P. Y., Patel, V., Joestl, S. S., March, D., Insel, T. R. . . . Daar, A. S. (2011). Grand challenges in global mental health. *Nature, 475*, 27–30. doi: 10.1038/475027a

Effros, R. B., Fletcher, C. V., Gebo, K., Halter, J. B., Hazzard, W. R., Horne, F. M., . . . High, K. P. (2008). Aging and infectious diseases: Workshop on HIV infection and aging: What is known and future research directions. *Clinical Infectious Disease, 47*, 542–553. doi: 10.1086/590150

Ferri, C. P., Prince, M., Brayne, C., Brodaty, H., Fratiglioni, L., Ganguli, M., . . . Alzheimer's Disease International. (2005). Global prevalence of dementia: A Delphi consensus study. *Lancet, 366*, 2112–2117. doi: 10.1016/S0140-6736(05)67889-0

Fredvang, M., & Biggs, S. (2012). *The rights of older persons: Protection and gaps under human rights law*. Melbourne, Australia: Centre for Public Policy, University of Melbourne.

HelpAge International. (2010). *Strengthening older people's rights: Towards a UN convention*. Retrieved from http://social.un.org/ageing-working group/documents/Coalition%20to%20Strengthen%20the%20Rights%20of%20Older%20People.pdf

Institute for Health, Metrics and Evaluation. (2010). *Global burden of disease study*. Retrieved from http://ghdx.healthmetricsandevaluation.org/global-burden-disease-study-2010-gbd-2010-data-downloads

International Federation of Social Workers, International Association of Schools of Social Work, and International Council on Social Welfare. (2012). *The global agenda for social work and social development: Commitment to action*. Retrieved from http://cdn.ifsw.org/assets/globalagenda2012.pdf

Kinsella, K., & Phillips, D. R. (2005). Global aging: The challenge of success. *Population Bulletin, 60*(10), 5–42. Retrieved from www.prb.org

Kowal, P., Chatterji, S., Naidoo, N., Biritwum, R., Fan, W., Ridaura, R. L., . . . the SAGE Collaborators. (2012). Data resource profile: The World Health Organization Study on global AGEing and adult health (SAGE). *International Journal of Epidemiology, 41*, 1639–1649. doi: 10.1093/ije/dys210

Kuo, B. C. H., Chong, V., & Joseph, J. (2008). Depression and its psychosocial correlates among older Asian immigrants in North America: A critical review of two decades' research. *Journal of Aging and Health, 20*, 615–652. doi: 10.1177/0898264308321001

Lachs, M. S., & Pillemer, K. (2004). Elder abuse. *Lancet, 364*, 1263–1272. doi: 10.1016/S0140-6736(04)17144-4

Lai, D. W. L. (2009). Filial piety, caregiving appraisal, and caregiving burden. *Research on Aging, 32*, 200–223. doi: 10.1177/0164027509351475

Lazarus, J. V., & Nielsen, K. K. (2010). HIV and people over 50 years old in Europe. *HIV Medicine, 11*, 479–481. doi: 10.1111/j.1468-1293.2009.00810.x

Min, J. W. (2005). Cultural competency: A key to effective future social work with racially and ethnically diverse elders. *Families in Society, 86*, 347–357. doi: 10.1606/1044-3894.3432

Morrow-Howell, N., Hinterlong, J., & Sherraden, M. (Eds.). (2001). *Productive aging: Concepts and challenges*. Baltimore: Johns Hopkins University Press.

National Institute on Aging. (2013a). *Global health and aging: New data on health and aging*. Retrieved from http://www.nia.nih.gov/research/publication/global-health-and-aging/new-data-aging-and-health#.UnfWYFNHKYk

National Institute on Aging. (2013b). *Initiative on global aging*. Retrieved from http://www.nia.nih.gov/research/dbsr/initiative-global-aging

National Institutes of Health. (2007). *Why population aging matters: A global perspective*. Retrieved from http://www.nia.nih.gov/research/publication/why-population-aging-matters-global-perspective

National Institutes of Health. (2011). *Global health and aging*. Retrieved from http://www.nia.nih.gov/sites/default/files/global_health_and_aging.pdf

Negin, J., & Cumming, R. G. (2010). HIV infection in older adult in sub-Saharan Africa: Extrapolating prevalence from existing data. *Bulletin of the World Health Organization, 88*, 847–853. doi: 10.2471/BLT.10.076349

Palacious, R. (2002). The future of global ageing. *International Journal of Epidemiology, 31*, 786–791. doi: 10.1093/ije/31.4.786

Patel, V., & Prince, M. (2010). Global mental health: A new global health field comes of age. *JAMA, 303*, 1976–1977. doi: 10.1001/jama.2010.616

Prince, M., Patel, V., Saxena, S., Maj, M., Maselko, J., Phillips, M. R., & Rahman, A. (2007). No health without mental health. *Lancet, 370*, 859–877. doi: 10.1016/S0140-6736(07)61238-0

Ranzijn, R. (2010). Active ageing: Another way to oppress marginalized and disadvantaged elders? Aboriginal elders as a case study. *Journal of Health Psychology, 15*, 716–723. doi: 10.1177/1359105310368181

Rooks, R. N., Simonsick, E. M., Klesges, L. M., Newman, A. B., Ayonayon, H. N., & Harris, T. B. (2008). Racial disparities in health care access and cardiovascular disease indicators in black and white older adults in the Health ABC Study. *Journal of Aging and Health, 20*, 599–614. doi: 10.1177/0898264308321023

Sooryanarayana, R., Choo, W., & Hairi, N. N. (2013). A review on the prevalence and measurement of elder abuse in the community. *Trauma, Violence, and Abuse, 14*, 316. doi: 10.1177/1524838013495963

Straus, M. A. (1979). Measuring intrafamily conflict and violence: The conflict tactics (CT) scales. *Journal of Marriage and the Family, 41*, 75–88.

United Nations, Department of Economic and Social Affairs (UNDESA). (2010). *World population ageing 2009. ESA/P/WP/212*. Retrieved from http://www.un.org/esa/population/publications/WPA2009/WPA2009_WorkingPaper.pdf

United Nations, Department of Economic and Social Affairs (UNDESA), Population Division. (2005). *Living arrangements of older persons around the world*. New York. Retrieved from http://www.un.org/esa/population/publications/livingarrangement/report.htm

United Nations, Department of Economic and Social Affairs (UNDESA), Population Division, Population Estimates and Projections Section. (2013). *World population prospects: The 2012 revision*. Retrieved from http://esa.un.org/wpp/

United Nations, Department of Economic and Social Affairs (UNDESA), Social Policy and Development Division. (2002). *Madrid International Plan of Action*. Retrieved from http://undesadspd.org/Ageing/Resources/MadridInternationalPlanofActiononAgeing.aspx

United Nations General Assembly. (2013). Follow-up to the International year of Older Persons: Second world assembly on ageing. Report of the secretary-general. Third Committee (Social, Humanitarian & Cultural). 68th session, Item 27(c), A/68/167. New York, NY: United Nations.

United Nations Population Fund (UNFPA) and HelpAge International. (2012). *Ageing in the twenty-first century: A celebration and a challenge*. Retrieved from http://www.unfpa.org/public/home/publications/pid/11584

United Nations System Task Team on the Post-2015 UN Development Agenda. (2013). *Statistics and indicators for the post-2015 development agenda*. New York, NY. Retrieved from http://www.un.org/en/development/desa/policy/untaskteam_undf/them_tp2.shtml

Wong, S. T., Yoo, G. J., & Stewart, A. L. (2007). An empirical evaluation of social support and psychological well-being in older Chinese and Korean immigrants. *Ethnicity and Health, 12*, 43–67. doi: 10.1080/13557850600824104

World Federation for Mental Health. (2013). *Mental Health Day focused on older people*. Retrieved from http://www.wfmh.com/00WorldMentalHealthDay.htm

World Health Organization (WHO). (2002a). *Active ageing: A policy framework*. Retrieved from http://whqlibdoc.who.int/hq/2002/WHO_NMH_NPH_02.8.pdf

World Health Organization (WHO). (2002b). *Missing voices: Views of older person on elder abuse*. Geneva, Switzerland: WHO Press.

World Health Organization (WHO). (2007a). *Global age-friendly cities: A guide*. Retrieved from http://www.who.int/ageing/age_friendly_cities_guide/en/index.html

World Health Organization (WHO). (2007b). *Global network of age-friendly cities and communities*. Retrieved from http://www.who.int/ageing/projects/age_friendly_cities_network/en/index.html

World Health Organization (WHO). (2008). *Mental Health Gap Action Programme (mhGAP): Scaling up care for mental, neurological, and substance use disorders*. Retrieved from http://www.who.int/mental_health/mhgap_final_english.pdf

LOUISA DARATSOS
JUDITH L. HOWE

SECTION V

Older Adults in Palliative and End-of-Life Care

OVERVIEW

The importance of the social worker's role in providing palliative and end-of-life care is well documented in the literature. Social workers are in a unique position to work with clients and their families and caregivers because of the profession's focus on psychosocial issues, group and individual counseling, advocacy, knowledge of healthcare policies and the identification of community resources. The chapters contained in this section examine social work's important and expanding involvement in palliative and end-of-life care with respect to assessment, interventions, skills, roles, legal and ethical issues, and bereavement support.

In this section of the *Handbook of Social Work in Health and Aging*, we are pleased to include three chapters that introduce micro, mezzo, and macro levels of practice in the realm of palliative and end-of-life care. In the first chapter, the section editors (Daratsos and Howe) present the landscape of palliative and end-of-life care, as well as key constructs and definitions. The chapter also addresses the numerous settings of care in which social workers practice and the array of roles that social workers undertake in the field. The second chapter, by Raveis and Waldrop, discusses the history and development of end-of life care. This chapter helps us understand how social workers helped launch the specialty of palliative and end-of-life care out of their observations and experiences working with their sickest patients. The chapter explains that while some medical consumers and their families welcome innovations that extend life, there are many people who

advocate for interventions that ease suffering and facilitate peaceful deaths. Also addressed is the cost of healthcare in an increasingly expensive technologically complex system and how this relates to issues of medical decision-making in our aging population. The third chapter, by Souza and Gutheil, discusses the psychosocial aspects of dying. This chapter is important because it offers social workers guidance about how to work with clients who may be at the end of their lives, and underscores the need for palliative care social work expertise early in the disease process or when the aging process challenges physical and mental functioning. The chapter addresses the important areas of assessment, education, and intervention, such as advance care planning, and uses case examples to demonstrate how social workers elicit and facilitate choices in end-of-life planning and their valuable role in helping clients achieve their personal choices.

Social work contributions to palliative and end-of-life care are significant and have been expanded and defined since the first Handbook was published in 2006. When one of us (Howe) wrote the section overview in 2005 she predicted that the social worker's role would be increasingly articulated in the upcoming decade, similar to the roles of medicine and nursing. This has in fact occurred, as the three section chapters demonstrate, with social work having a more solid footing in the field. However, as the field continues to transform, with new communication tools (e.g., online support communities and telehealth) to disseminate information, provide support, and deliver care, the role of social work will continue to evolve and expand.

LOUISA DARATSOS
JUDITH L. HOWE

Social Work Practice in Palliative and End-of-Life Care

CONTEXT OF PALLIATIVE AND END-OF-LIFE CARE AND THE ROLE OF SOCIAL WORK PRACTICE

There continues to be an international movement to provide greater access to palliative and end-of-life care for patients and families. The movement was catalyzed by an influential conference at Yale University School of Nursing in 1966, which brought together thought leaders who eventually developed and sustained palliative care throughout their careers (Daratsos & Howe, 2007; Foster & Corliss, 1999). The momentum was fueled by factors such as increasing government and private support, heightened media attention, public awareness about the need for compassionate care at the end of life, and large numbers of baby boomers confronting the aging and death of their parents. The National Association of Social Work recognized palliative care in social work practice with both masters- and bachelors-level credentials jointly awarded with the National Hospice and Palliative Care Organization. The Social Work Summit on End-of-Life and Palliative Care held in March 2002 aimed at developing a national consortium of social work leaders and organizations to shape an agenda for social work and end-of-life care and develop programs in practice, education, and research (Gwyther et al., 2005). Since then, there have been many opportunities for social workers to learn about and contribute to this specialty. For example, there is a professional organization called Social Work in Palliative and Hospice Network (SWPHN), and in 2011, the *Oxford Textbook of Social Work in Palliative Care* was published.

Although not all social workers practice in settings devoted to palliative or end-of-life care, all social workers will eventually work with clients experiencing life-threatening illnesses and family members who are grieving (Kramer, 1998; Kramer, Hovland-Scafe, & Pacourek 2003). Competent care for those facing life-threatening, serious illness is recognized to be multifaceted and holistic. By its nature, palliative care is an interdisciplinary area of practice, and hence the psychosocial domains of a client's well-being must be addressed in a comprehensive manner (National Consensus Project for Quality Palliative Care, 2013).

As noted by Steinhauser et al. (2000), "whereas physicians tend to focus on physical aspects, patients and families tend to view the end of life with a broader psychosocial and spiritual meaning, shaped by a lifetime of experiences" (p. 2482). Efforts over the last decade have focused on educating all team members about the role of others on the team, but in fact each profession has a core function and orientation based on its training (Nadicksbernd, Thornberry, & von Gunten, 2011). The social worker is often the health-care team member who assists patients, families, and caregivers with the emotional, psychological, social, cultural, financial, and environmental aspects of care (Saunders, 2011). Palliative care social workers have a particularly important role in working with clients and families coping with impending loss of life. This impending loss is often experienced as yet another loss layered on a series of prior losses.

In this chapter we discuss the landscape of palliative and end-of-life care and key constructs and definitions in the field. This chapter also addresses the settings of care for social work practice in palliative care, and the many roles of the palliative care social worker.

SETTINGS OF CARE

Social workers practice in a range of settings in palliative and end-of-life care, including the hospital, nursing home, home, outpatient clinic or practice, and hospice. Although 90% of all individuals state their wish to die at home, in fact only about one in five individuals actually die at home. The National Mortality Followback Survey found that 56% die in the hospital, 19% in a nursing home, 21% at home, and 4% in other settings (National Vital Statistics System, 2010).

Social workers are key individuals on the palliative care team in assuring smooth transitions from setting to setting along the care continuum. Individuals with life-threatening illnesses may move frequently from setting to setting, and the social worker is often the team member who recognizes crisis points in the illness trajectory. These crisis points represent opportunities for effective social work intervention. Social workers are the team members with the expertise and training in community resources and referrals. They apply the tasks associated with discharge planning and merge it with their counseling skills to assist the individual and his or her support system in attaining the best available setting for palliative and end-of-life care. Table 54.1 lists websites that can assist social workers, their teams, and patients with pertinent information

TABLE 54.1 Useful Websites

www.aahpm.org

American Academy of Hospice and Palliative Medicine

www.abcd-caring.org

Americans for Better Care of the Dying

www.americanhospice.org

American Hospice Foundation

www.aoa.gov

Administration on Aging

www.aosw.org

Association of Oncology Social Work

www.beliefnet.org

An online community for religion and spirituality

www.cancer.org

American Cancer Society

www.cancercare.org

Help for patients and caregivers living with a diagnosis of cancer

www.capc.org

Center to Advance Palliative Care

www.caringinfo.org/i4a/pages/index.cfm?pageid=1

Caring Connections, information and support regarding living with advanced illness

www.eperc.mcw.edu

End of life/Palliative Education Resource Center

www.growthhouse.org

An online community for End of Life Care

www.hospicefoundation.org

Hospice Foundation of America

www.hpna.org

Hospice and Palliative Care Nurses Association

www.lls.org

The Leukemia and Lymphoma Society

www.medicaring.org

The Washington Home, Center for Palliative Care Studies

http://www.painpolicy.wisc.edu/

University of Wisconsin Pain and Policy Studies Group

www.naswdc.org

National Association of Social Workers

www.nationalconsensusproject.org/

Recent Clinical Practice Guidelines for Quality Palliative Care

www.nhpco.org

(continued)

TBLE 54.1 Continued

National Hospice and Palliative Care Organization

www.ssa.gov

US Social Security Administration

www.stoppain.org

Beth Israel Medical Center, Department of Pain Medicine
and Palliative Care

www.smith.edu/ssw/acad_cont_graduate_elc.php

Smith College School for Social Work Certificate in
End-of-Life Care

http://socialwork.nyu.edu/academics/zelda-foster-studies.
html

New York University, Silver School of Social Work, Zelda
Foster Studies in Palliative and End-of-Life Care

http://www.va.gov/oaa/fellowships/palliative.asp

Veterans Health Administration, Interprofessional
Palliative Care Fellowship Program

and resources about palliative and end-of-life care.
The National Priorities Partnership (November,
2010) argues for a "seamless palliative care experience for patients and their families" (p. 4). This
argument is supported by Temel et al. (2010), whose
research finds that patients with advanced small-cell
lung cancer who had palliative care integrated in
their care had significant improvements in quality of
life and mood at the end of life.

The common organizational delivery models
of palliative care, including hospice programs, are
delineated in Table 54.2.

Hospitals

The hospital is frequently the host site for palliative and hospice care. There are a variety of
models for care delivery, including freestanding
hospice or supportive care units and palliative care

consultation teams. Often, facilities have inpatient
units, consultation teams, and outpatient clinics.
These teams work in conjunction with intensive
care unit and emergency department teams and are
charged with a variety of functions aimed at promoting patient and family choices of care, increasing patient and family satisfaction with the quality
of care and decreasing the cost of medical care,
particularly when the inevitability of death is present (Lawson, 2011; McCormick, 2011; Mulkerin,
2011). Computerized medical records, such as
used in the Veterans Health Administration, allow
for automated case finding to identify patients
requiring palliative and end-of-life care. The
social worker is an instrumental team member
in ascertaining when a transfer is appropriate for
nonmedical reasons such as caregiver functioning
and changes in the patient/family/caregiver triad
(Mulkerin, 2011).

Nursing Homes

Nationwide, one-quarter to one-third of nursing home discharges are the result of death
(Administration on Aging [AOA], 2013). Among
people with dementia, 70% die in a nursing home
(Bern-Klug & Simons, 2011; Sefcik, Rao, & Ersek,
2013). The Administration on Aging projects a 57%
increase in the number of elders in nursing homes
by the year 2030 as compared with the nursing home
population in the late 1980s (AOA, 2013). It is further projected that 3.4% of people over the age of 65,
and nearly 17% of those over the age of 85, will be in
a nursing home by 2030. For social workers working in nursing homes, end-of-life care is an integral
and day-to-day part of practice. Social workers are
often the only trained mental health professionals on nursing home staffs and are in a unique role
to identify and address the range of practical and

TABLE 54.2 Palliative Care and Hospice Settings

Hospital (acute and rehabilitation)	Nursing Home	Home/Outpatient Practice or Clinic
Consultation Team	Consultation Team	Private Practice based
Inpatient Unit	Inpatient Unit	Home-Based Primary Care
Combined with Freestanding Inpatient Hospice	Combined with Freestanding Inpatient Hospice	Hospice-Based Consultation Team
Combined Consultation Team, Inpatient Unit, and Outpatient Clinic	Combined Consultation Team, Inpatient Unit, and Outpatient Clinic	Hospice-Based Palliative Care

emotional end-of-life issues (Bern-Klug & Simons, 2011). Increasingly, nursing homes have palliative care teams and have contractual relationships with hospice programs to provide hospice care on site (Aldridge Carlson, & Twaddle, 2013). These teams, of course, include social work (Sefcik et al., 2013).

Home-Based and Outpatient Care

For patients whose palliative care needs are just beginning to be identified, the outpatient clinic functions as a transitional care setting in which symptoms can be assessed and managed. When it becomes necessary, more intensive interventions can be identified and arranged (Rabow, 2013). The outpatient setting can function as the provider of record for patients receiving hospice care at home. In this case, the outpatient clinic team, including social workers, works collaboratively with the hospice team to care for patients primarily in the home in order to minimize travel to and from the clinic. This is an advantageous arrangement because it allows the patients to have their care managed by their providers of choice and, at the same time, it integrates the expertise of the hospice team.

Home-based palliative care for people with life-limiting illnesses has increased in the last decade in part because of more favorable reimbursement rates and the aging of the population with multiple chronic medical conditions including dementia (Zhang et al., 2013). The roles of social workers in home-based palliative care programs include assessment, interventions, psychoeducation, developing goals of care, and caregiver support (Davis-Stenhouse, Moore, & Niemeyer, 2011). As highlighted by Zhang et al. (2013), the home-based primary care model affords team members the ability to integrate principles of palliative care for chronically ill, homebound patients and to coordinate care among specialized services.

Hospice may be defined as a model for quality and compassionate care for individuals with terminal illness. It provides interdisciplinary care for patients with serious illness for whom curative treatments are no longer effective or desired (Aldridge et al., 2013). While often provided in the patient's home, hospice services are also provided in a variety of residential settings including hospitals, nursing homes, assisted living facilities, and prisons.

THE ROLE OF THE SOCIAL WORKER AND SCOPE OF PRACTICE

Care at the end of life is highly individualized and should be achieved through a process of shared decision-making and clear communication that acknowledges the values and preferences of patients, caregivers, and families (National Priorities Partnership, 2010). Social workers carry out multiple roles in palliative and end-of-life care, often in the context of the interdisciplinary team. These roles include:

Clinician. The social worker provides counseling to patients and families to help them confront changes in physical, cognitive, and emotional functioning and to cope with the anticipated death. The social work clinician often facilitates development of goals of care and advanced directives. The team social worker links patients and families to needed resources, frequently even after the patient's death, such as assisting with funeral planning and bereavement (Wiesenfluh, 2011). He or she may identify potential ethical issues such as truth telling and confidentiality (O'Donnell, 2011).

Educator. The social worker, with an interdisciplinary educational foundation, can play a significant role in curriculum development and teaching in end-of-life and palliative care to other social workers and to other professionals. Social workers' specific strengths include educating about cultural diversity, health literacy, and economic distress. There are increasing opportunities for leadership in this area with the emergence of advanced training programs for social workers. For instance, New York University Silver School of Social Work sponsors the Zelda Foster Post-Masters Certificate and the Post-Masters Leadership Fellowship (http://socialwork.nyu.edu/academics/zelda-foster-studies.html) and Smith College hosts a Post-Masters End-of-Life Care Certificate (http://www.smith.edu/ssw/acad_cont_graduate_elc.php).

Researcher. Over the last decade there has been an increased need for social workers who are competent researchers and can participate in interdisciplinary collaboration (Palos, 2011). Social work practitioners, with their unique, day-to-day perspectives, can also bring frontline

experience to the identification and conceptu-
alization of research problems (Kramer, Christ,
Bern-Klug, & Francoeur, 2005; Parker-Oliver &
Washington, 2011).

Organizational Leadership. Social workers often
hold key positions in healthcare and social service agencies and on national committees focusing on palliative care. They provide leadership in
program and policy development, system redesign, fundraising, grant writing, outreach, and
advocacy.

Liaison. The social worker often provides the link
between the patient and family and the professional community. This function is particularly
important when family members are separated
by distance. In addition, the social worker often
coordinates communication between the clinical
service providers and other community agencies.

Advocate. Social workers are trained to advocate
for scarce resources and to overcome obstacles
to treatment and entitlements for patients and
families. This skill serves social workers well in
other arenas such as legislative advocacy.

Team Member. The social worker, having advanced
communication and facilitation skills, can play
an important role on the interdisciplinary team
in the areas of leadership, problem-solving, and
other team-building and maintenance tasks so
critical to effective teamwork.

Social Work Practice and Interdisciplinary Teamwork

Optimal care for patients with life-limiting illnesses
is ideally provided by a well-functioning interdisciplinary healthcare team that recognizes the knowledge and skills of each team member. Team members
exchange information with respect and shared leadership in case discussions and care plan development
(Sherman & Howe, 2006). However, interdisciplinary teamwork is often challenged by factors such as
poor communication, lack of cohesion, and insufficient role clarity. The role of social work on the
team is often a source of some confusion, because
other disciplines do not always understand the scope
of practice of social work and may view the social
worker's role in a more limited fashion (e.g., discharge planning, resource identification). There have
been initiatives in schools of social work to prepare

recent graduates to work effectively on interdisciplinary teams and have the tools and confidence to "have
a seat at the table." For instance, the John A. Hartford
Foundation–funded Geriatric Interdisciplinary Team
Training program developed materials to describe the
role of social work on healthcare teams and curriculum materials for teaching teamwork skills to social
work students (Howe, Hyer, Mellor, Lindeman, &
Luptak, 2001). It is important that social workers,
with their specialized training and skills in human
relationships, communication, and engagement are
given the opportunity to play a key role in managing
team dynamics on palliative care teams.

CONCLUSION

As the World War II and baby boomer generations
age, social work practice in the area of palliative and
end-of-life care is becoming increasingly complex.
Social workers are involved in palliative care no
matter what setting they work in or what population they help, because death and dying are universal
experiences. The social work contribution to palliative care touches on many domains, from interdisciplinary team member, to administrator, to educator,
to therapist, to researcher, to peer support leader.
Social workers who have an interest in this work are
encouraged to share their experiences and lessons
learned with their colleagues on their teams, within
their practice settings, and beyond in regional and
national venues. It is exactly this sharing that will
continue to deepen the knowledge base, improve the
level of practice, and promote the leadership role of
the social worker in all areas of practice.

REFERENCES

Administration on Aging (AOA). (2013). *Aging into the
21st century*. Retrieved from http://www.aoa.gov/
AoARoot/Aging_Statistics/future_growth/aging21/
health.aspx

Aldridge Carlson, M., & Twaddle, M. (2013). In what
settings can hospice be provided? In N. Goldstein &
R. S. Morrison (Eds.), *Evidence-based practice of
palliative medicine* (pp. 448–449). Philadelphia,
PA: Elsevier.

Bern-Klug, M., & Simons, K. (2011). Palliative care in
long term settings. In T. Altillio & S. Otis-Green
(Eds.), *Oxford textbook of palliative social work* (pp.
103–114). New York, NY: Oxford University Press.

Daratsos, L., & Howe, J. (2007). The development of palliative programs in the Veterans Administration. *Journal of Social Work in End-of-Life and Palliative Care, 3*, 29–40. doi: 10.1300/J457v03n01_07

Davis-Stenhouse, E., Moore, K., & Niemeyer, B. (2011). Home based palliative care. In T. Altillio & S. Otis-Green (Eds.), *Oxford textbook of palliative social work* (pp. 87–102). New York, NY: Oxford University Press.

Foster, Z., & Corliss, I. (1999). Origins: An American perspective. In I. Corless & Z. Foster (Eds.), *The hospice heritage: Celebrating our future* (pp. 9–14). Binghamton, NY: Haworth Press.

Gwyther, L. P., Altillio, T., Blacker, S., Christ, G., Csikai, E. L., Hooyman, N., . . . Howe, J. L. (2005). Social work competencies in palliative and end-of-life care. *Journal of Social Work in End-of-Life Care, 1*, 87–119.

Howe, J. L., Hyer, K., Mellor, J., Lindeman, D., & Luptak, M. (2001). Educational approaches for preparing social work students for interdisciplinary teamwork on geriatric health care teams. *Social Work in Health Care, 32*(4), 19–42. doi: 10.1300/J010v32n04_02

Kramer, B. J. (1998). Preparing social workers for the inevitable: A preliminary investigation of a course on grief, death, and loss. *Journal of Social Work Education, 34*, 211–277.

Kramer, B. J., Christ, G., Bern-Klug, M., & Francoeur, R. (2005). A national agenda for social work research in palliative and end-of-life care. *Journal of Palliative Medicine, 8*, 418–431. doi: 10.1089/jpm.2005.8.418

Kramer, B. J., Hovland-Scafe, C., & Pacourek, L. (2003). Analysis of end of life content in social work textbooks. *Journal of Social Work Education, 39*, 299–320.

Lawson, R. (2011). Palliative social work in the emergency room. In T. Altillio & S. Otis-Green (Eds.), *Oxford textbook of palliative social work* (pp. 63–70). New York, NY: Oxford University Press.

McCormick, A. (2011). Palliative social work in the intensive care unit. In T. Altillio & S. Otis-Green (Eds.), *Oxford textbook of palliative social work* (pp. 53–62). New York, NY: Oxford University Press.

Mulkerin, C. (2011). Palliative care consultation. In T. Altillio & S. Otis-Green (Eds.), *Oxford textbook of palliative social work* (pp. 43–52). New York, NY: Oxford University Press.

Nadicksbernd, J., Thornberry, K., & von Gunten, C. (2011.) Social work and physician collaboration in palliative care. In T. Altillio & S. Otis-Green (Eds.), *Oxford textbook of palliative social work* (pp. 471–476). New York, NY: Oxford University Press.

National Consensus Project for Quality Palliative Care. (2013). *Clinical practice guidelines for quality palliative care* (3rd ed.). Retrieved from http://www.nationalconsensusproject.org/NCP_Clinical_Practice_Guidelines_3rd_Edition.pdf

National Priorities Partnership. (2010). *Improving health and healthcare.* Retrieved March 17, 2014, from https://www.qualityforum.org/Topics/Improving_Health_and_Healthcare.aspx

National Vital Statistics System. (2010). *Deaths: Final data for 2010.* Retrieved March 17, 2014, from http://www.cdc.gov/nchs/data/nvsr/nvsr61/nvsr61_04.pdf

O'Donnell, P. (2011). Ethical considerations in palliative care. In T. Altillio & S. Otis-Green (Eds.), *Oxford textbook of palliative social work* (pp. 603–614). New York, NY: Oxford University Press.

Palos, G. (2011). Social work research agenda in palliative and end-of-life care. In T. Altillio & S. Otis-Green (Eds.), *Oxford textbook of palliative social work* (pp. 719–734). New York, NY: Oxford University Press.

Parker-Oliver, D., & Washington, K. (2011). Merging research and clinical practice. In T. Altillio & S. Otis-Green (Eds.), *Oxford textbook of palliative social work* (pp. 735–744). New York, NY: Oxford University Press.

Rabow, M. (2013). What new models exist for ambulatory palliative care? In N. Goldstein & R. S. Morrison (Eds.), *Evidence-based practice of palliative medicine* (pp. 468–473). Philadelphia, PA: Elsevier.

Saunders, C. (2011). Social work and palliative care: The early history. In T. Altillio & S. Otis-Green (Eds.), *Oxford textbook of palliative social work* (pp. 5–10). New York, NY: Oxford University Press.

Sefcik, J., Rao, A., & Ersek, M. (2013). What models exist for delivering palliative care in nursing homes? In N. Goldstein & R. S. Morrison (Eds.), *Evidence-based practice of palliative medicine* (pp. 450–457). Philadelphia, PA: Elsevier.

Sherman, D. W., & Howe, J. L. (2006). Interdisciplinary educational approaches to promote team-based geriatrics and palliative care. *Gerontology and Geriatrics Education, 26*(3), 1–16. doi: 10.1300/J021v26n03_01

Steinhauser, K. E., Christakis, N. A., Clipp, E. C., McNeilly, M., McIntyre, L., & Tulsky, J. A. (2000). Factors considered important at the end of life by patients, family, physicians, and other care providers. *JAMA, 284*, 2476–2482. doi: 10.1001/jama.284.19.2476

Temel, J., Greer, J., Muzikansky, A., Gallagher, E., Admane, S., Jackson, V., . . . Lynch, T. (2010). Early palliative care of patients with metastatic non-small-cell lung cancer. *New England Journal of Medicine, 363*, 733–742. doi: 10. 1056/NEJMoa10678

Wiesenfluh, S. (2011). Social work and palliative care in hospice. In T. Altillio & S. Otis-Green (Eds.), *Oxford textbook of palliative social work* (pp. 71–78). New York, NY: Oxford University Press.

Zhang, M., Smith, K., Cook-Mack, J., Wajnberg, A., DeCherrie, L., & Soriano, T. (2013) How can palliative care be integrated into home-based primary care programs? In S. Morrison & N. Goldstein (Eds.), *Evidence-based practice of palliative medicine* (pp. 458–467). Philadelphia, PA: Elsevier.

INTRODUCTION AND OVERVIEW

In the 1900s the leading causes of death in the United States were infectious diseases; today they are chronic conditions. Medical advances have transformed the context of dying and end-of-life care developed in response to growing recognition of the needs that occur at life's end. This chapter describes the hospice and death and dying movements, as well as legislative and historic events in end-of life care. Tragic landmark deaths that influenced policy development, current political and social context, the cost of care, and advance care planning are discussed. The chapter closes with a look at the influence of online communication and visions of the future.

THE HOSPICE MOVEMENT

The origins of the modern hospice movement can be traced back to the later half of the 20th century and the work of Dame Cicely Saunders. Although hospices have existed since the Middle Ages, as a place of shelter and rest for weary or ill travelers on a long journey (Saunders, 2000), the model of hospice in contemporary society reflects provision of quality compassionate care that does not hasten or postpone death but reduces pain and suffering at the end-of-life. Dame Cicely, who was trained as a social worker, nurse, and physician, recognized the inadequacy of care of the dying that was offered in hospitals. She saw the importance in combining quality medical and nursing care with holistic support that acknowledged practical, emotional, social, and spiritual need and promoted this philosophy of compassionate care, with a primary mission to reduce suffering and pain at the end of life.

Dame Cicely lectured widely on this philosophy, introducing the concept and approach firsthand to the US healthcare community in a 1966 conference convened at Yale University by Florence Wald, dean of the Yale School of Nursing. By 1967, Dame Cicely had founded the first modern hospice, St. Christopher's Hospice in London. St. Christopher's combined quality pain and symptom control with compassionate care, teaching, and clinical research. It remains a leader in the field of palliative medicine (St. Christopher's Hospice, n.d.).

The 1970s saw the initiation of hospice initiatives in the United States. In 1974, Florence Wald founded the first hospice program in Branford, Connecticut.

VICTORIA H. RAVEIS
DEBORAH P. WALDROP

The History and Development of End-of-Life Care

Box 55.1
Overview of Medicare Hospice Benefit

Eligibility:

- Beneficiary is eligible for Medicare Part A (Hospital insurance)
- Beneficiary's physician and hospice medical director certify terminal illness and 6-month life expectancy
- Beneficiary agrees to forgo all Medicare-covered, nonhospice benefits for the terminal illness

Hospice Care Team:

- Physicians
- Nurses or nurse practitioners
- Mental health counselors (e.g., psychologists, pastoral counselors)
- Social workers
- Physical and occupational therapists
- Speech/language pathologists
- Hospice aides
- Homemakers
- Volunteers

Services Provided:

- Physician services
- Nursing care
- Durable medical equipment (e.g., wheelchairs, walkers)
- Medical supplies
- Drugs and biologicals for symptom management and pain control
- Home health aide and homemaker services
- Physical and occupational therapy
- Speech therapy
- Social work services
- Nutrition and dietary counseling
- Grief and loss counseling to beneficiary and family
- Inpatient respite care in a Medicare-approved hospital or nursing home, up to 5 days per episode
- Physician and nurse on call 24/7

Other Key Features

- Hospice care must be provided by a Medicare-approved hospice program
- Beneficiary can change hospice provider only once during each 90- or 60-day certification period
- Beneficiary can be recertified indefinitely, initially two 90-day periods, then every 60 days
- Beneficiary can elect to leave hospice, reselect prior Medicare health plan's nonhospice coverage for his/her condition, and at some future time reselect the hospice benefit
- Beneficiary can use Medicare health plan to receive care for unrelated conditions

Costs to Beneficiary—Gaps and Limitations in Care

- Beneficiary pays part of the cost for outpatient drugs for terminal illness, co-pay $5 per prescription in 2013
- Beneficiary pays part of inpatient respite care, 5% of the Medicare payment amount in 2013
- Medicare does not cover costs of room and board, exception is inpatient or respite care
- Hospice in the home requires informal/familial caregiving
- Hospice programs vary in range of palliative care services provided

For further information see Centers for Medicare and Medicaid Services (2013).

By the latter part of the decade, the Health Care Financing Administration (HCFA) initiated demonstration programs at 26 hospices nationwide. The Medicare hospice benefit (MHB), signed into law as a healthcare benefit in 1982, was made permanent in 1986.

As the nation's largest integrated healthcare system, the US Department of Veterans Affairs (VA) has had a broad impact on palliative care and the hospice movement, initiating innovative training and service programs to address the health needs of aging veterans that are replicated in other settings (Daratsos & Howe, 2007). By 1978, the VA had initiated policies and procedures for delivering quality compassionate care at the end of life (Olsen & Wilson, 1982). Establishment of a Hospice Consultation Team was mandated for all VA facilities by 1992 (Abrahm, Callahan, Rossetti, & Pierre, 1996). The VA Hospice and Palliative Care Initiative (VAHPC), issued in 2001, in combination with a series of VA directives in 2002 and 2003, ensures provision of evidence-based palliative care services and hospice programs that meet the needs of dying veterans whether received in VA or in community settings (Daratsos & Howe, 2007). In 2010, over 40% of veterans were 65 and older (US Census Bureau, 2012), many living with chronic conditions.

With the selection of hospice as the standard for end-of-life care in the United States, an increasing number of terminally ill elders have accepted this care option. The hospice movement has grown and changed, being influenced by demographics, advancing medical technology, and healthcare financing. Currently, the National Hospice and Palliative Care Organization (NHPCO) reports that there are over 5,300 programs. The majority, 58%, are independent, freestanding agencies. The programs are either part of a hospital system (20%), home health agency (17%), or nursing home (5%) (NHPCO, 2012). The Medicare hospice benefit (see Box 55.1 for eligibility and covered services) pays for the majority (84%) of hospice care in the United States (NHPCO, 2012).

Current estimates by NHPCO indicate that about 45% of all deaths in the United States in 2011 were under the care of a hospice program (NHPCO, 2012). In the 1970s when hospice was initiated in the United States, the majority of hospice admissions were cancer patients. In 2011, cancer diagnoses represented 38% of the admissions. The top noncancer primary diagnoses were debility unspecified (14%), dementia (13%), heart disease (11%), and lung disease (9%) (NHPCO, 2012). Although growing numbers of hospice patients demonstrate an increasing societal awareness of hospice, the average length of stay (LOS) remains at about 69 days, with the median LOS at 19 days. Considered together with the fact that 36% of all hospice patients die or are discharged within seven days of admission, these statistics indicate a large number of short stays (NHPCO, 2012).

THE DEATH AND DYING MOVEMENT

The philosophy underlying the current US hospice model of care is grounded in the death and dying movement. Beginning in the later half of the 20th century, this grassroots movement ushered in a foundational change in the culture of end-of-life care. Elizabeth Kubler-Ross's treatise, *On Death and Dying* (Kubler-Ross, 1969), provided firsthand accounts of how imminent death affects the dying, their family, and the healthcare team. This work helped coalesce the growing awareness that both quality of care and quality of life, regardless of the time left, were important to the experience of dying and put forth the basic tenet that the dying should have a voice in their own care (see Box 55.2). The standard for a good death, "one that is free from avoidable distress

---

Box 55.2
Zelda Foster, CSW—Visionary and Champion

Zelda Foster stands out as an exemplar of the early clinical leaders whose vision and support of palliative care and the hospice philosophy helped shape and define current end-of-life practice in the United States (Daratsos & Howe, 2007). An early champion of end-of-life care, Foster published a seminal article in the journal *Social Work* (Foster, 1965) that delineated a fundamental role for social work in the care of the terminally ill and presaged the contemporary interdisciplinary hospice practice model. This publication led to her participation in 1966 in a conference of experts in the hospice movement at Yale University, where she formed a long-standing relationship with Dame Cicely Saunders. In the 2 decades that she served as chief of social work services at the Brooklyn Veterans Affairs (VA) Hospital, she was a central figure in the US Department of Veterans Affairs' development and implementation of hospice and palliative care workers (Daratsos & Howe, 2007), while also advancing educational and training resources in end-of-life care for social workers (Davidson & Bullock, 2007). She was cofounder and first president of the New York State Hospice Association.

and suffering for patients, families, and caregivers; in general accord with patients' and families wishes; and reasonably consistent with clinical, cultural, and ethical standards" (Field & Cassel, 1997, p. 4), was put forward. As different fatal conditions present distinct dying trajectories (Lunney, Lynn, & Hogan, 2002), this necessitates that the physical, psychological, social, cultural, spiritual, religious, and existential aspects of care at the end of life be appropriate to these different dying trajectories (Field & Cassel, 1997).

With the evolution and expansion of end-of-life care in the United States, the National Consensus Project (NCP), composed of representatives of the leading hospice and palliative care organizations, put forth *Clinical Practice Guidelines for Quality Palliative Care* to serve as a manual to guide developing programs. These guidelines were adopted by the National Quality Forum (NQF) within the document *A National Framework and Preferred Practices for Palliative and Hospice Care Quality: A Consensus Report* (National Quality Forum, 2006). In 2013, the NCP released revised and updated practice guidelines to reflect the growth and maturation in the field, the diverse array of models and approaches to care, and the increasing presence in ambulatory care, nursing homes, and community home programs (National Consensus Project for Quality Palliative Care, 2013). Social work practice in end-of-life care settings has also come of age (Blacker, Christ, & Lynch, 2005). The National Association of Social Workers (NASW), developed standards for the core elements of social work functions in palliative and end-of-life care, spearheaded by a collaborative effort that involved the Project on Death in America's Social Work Leadership Development Program, and the Social Work Section of the National Council of Hospice and Palliative Professionals (NCHPP) (National Association of Social Workers [NASW], 2004).

LEGISLATIVE EVENTS IMPACTING END OF LIFE

A number of key legislative events over the last 4 decades have shaped in important ways the current situation in end-of-life care for the elderly. These developments, detailed in Box 55.3, include Congress's 1982 act authorizing MHB. The Patient Self-Determination Act (PSDA) of 1990 reaffirmed an individual's right to self-determination. The PSDA promoted the use of advance directives (AD) to guide care after a patient has lost decision-making capacity.

This led to the introduction of Physician or Medical Orders for Life Sustaining Treatment (POLST or MOLST) protocols. In New York State, since 2008, the MOLST form can be used to issue nonhospital do-not-resuscitate (DNR) and do-not-intubate (DNI) orders that must be honored by emergency medical services and other healthcare personnel. Similar legislation exists in other states. The passage of PSDA also sparked an ongoing legal and ethical debate about euthanasia and physician-assisted suicide (PAS). Ultimately, this social movement led to Oregon's landmark policy in legalizing physician-assisted suicide (PAS) in 1994, followed by similar legislation in Washington and Vermont. Initiation of Medicare coverage for prescription drugs in 2006 redefined end-of-life care options for the elderly. By providing access to low-cost drugs, the economic burden of symptom management was reduced. The Patient Protection and Affordable Care Act (PPACA) of 2010 included a provision to implement a multisite Medicare demonstration project of concurrent care. If shown to be cost-effective and feasible, this benefit could redefine end-of-life care in the United States.

PUBLIC DEATHS, PRIVATE TRAGEDIES

Advancements in medical technology made it possible to extend life and prompted a "technological imperative," or the expectation that these technologies should be used at every opportunity (Brown, 2012; Mahon, 2010). Life-sustaining treatments can have unintended consequences such as extended suffering and diminished or no consciousness. Chronic disorders of consciousness (CDCs) such as an irreversible coma and persistent vegetative state (PVS) disconnect biological life, which continues, from psychological life, which ceases (Racine, Amaram, Seidler, Karczewska, & Illes, 2008). Laws that are based on the notion that a person is either alive or not alive became outdated by life-prolonging treatment (Belling, 2010). The stories of Karen Ann Quinlan, Nancy Cruzan, and Terri Schiavo, each of whom were treated with life-prolonging measures and died very public deaths, highlighted the limitations of clinical decision-making at the time and precipitated discussions about the use and discontinuation of life-sustaining treatment.

In 1975, Karen Ann Quinlan was 21 years old when she stopped breathing and was resuscitated

Box 55.3
Legislative Events Impacting End-of-life Care

1976 California Natural Death Act passed, enacted the first "living will" statute.

1982 Congress authorized Medicare to provide end-of-life care to terminally ill beneficiaries. Medicare hospice benefit (MHB) included in Part A in 1983, made permanent in 1986.

1984 Advance directives (ADs) recognized in 22 states and District of Columbia. By 1994 some type of AD recognized in all states.

1990 Congress passed the Patient Self-Determination Act (PSDA). Instituted in 1991, PSDA required healthcare agencies receiving Medicare and Medicaid reimbursement to recognize the living will and power of attorney for healthcare as ADs, inform patients about ADs, and incorporate ADs into patients' medical records.

1994 Oregon voters approved the Death with Dignity Act. Went into effect in 1998. Oregon first state to legalize physician-assisted suicide (PAS). Death with Dignity Acts passed in Washington and Vermont in 2008 and 2013.

1997 Balanced Budget Act of 1997 (PL 105-33) amended MHB, established differential benefit periods.

2003 Congress approved the Medicare Prescription Drug, Improvement, and Modernization Act, authorizing the Part D Prescription Drug Plan, providing prescription drug benefits to all enrollees by 2006, and covering consultation with hospice physicians to discuss hospice care options and referrals.

2010 Patient Protection and Affordable Care Act (PPACA), commonly called the Affordable Care Act (ACA), signed into law by President Obama, and designed to overhaul the US healthcare system. Among the provisions was a requirement for Medicaid to pay for concurrent care (joint hospice and curative treatments) for children. It also created the Centers for Medicare and Medicaid (CMS) Innovations to institute pilot programs and demonstration projects, including demonstration of concurrent care for Medicare patients.

2010 Family Health Care Decision Act (FHDA) went into effect in New York State. It specified a prioritized surrogate list of who has legal authority to make healthcare decisions in the event a patient loses the capacity to do so and does not have a legal guardian or healthcare proxy.

2011 Palliative Care Information Act required the attending healthcare practitioner in New York State to provide terminally ill patients with information and counseling regarding palliative care and end-of-life options.

---

after mixing alcohol and drugs. She was eventually diagnosed as being in a PVS and kept on life support against the wishes of her parents, who sought to have the ventilator removed. Quinlan did not meet the Harvard Brain Death Criteria, so one argument was that withdrawing the ventilator would constitute murder. The alternate argument was that because PVS was a permanent, neurologically devastating condition in which she could not perceive or interact with the environment it was disrespectful to continue breathing for her (Mahon, 2010). The ventilator was eventually removed, but Quinlan continued to breathe for almost 10 years. Central to this case was deep public concern about

the determination of death (Belling, 2010), and it became a catalyst for discussions about prolonging life (Kenny, 2005).

In 1983, Nancy Cruzan, age 25, was anoxic for 20 minutes following a car accident. She was resuscitated but suffered substantial brain damage. She eventually began breathing on her own and was diagnosed as being in a PVS. Her parents wanted her feeding tube removed, and the Missouri State Trial Court affirmed the right to refuse treatment, but the decision was reversed by the Missouri State Supreme Court, countering that the state was interested in the preservation of life and that substituted judgment was inadequate. The US Supreme Court supported the right of competent patients to refuse decisions and decided that states could apply the "clear and convincing" evidence standard when a guardian sought to discontinue nutrition and hydration for a person who was in a PVS. Absent any documentation of her wishes, the central question was what Cruzan would have wanted. Two friends described conversations with her about the Quinlan case and their statements met the standard, so the tube was removed (Mahon, 2010). This case became a catalyst for the development of advance directives.

In 1990, Terri Schiavo, age 26, suffered a cardiac arrest, prolonged anoxia, and brain damage and was in a PVS. Schiavo's husband wanted her feeding tube removed, but her parents wanted it to remain. Twelve years of legal disputes followed. Ultimately, the Florida House of Representatives wrote Terri's Law in an effort to prolong her life. Central to this case was the question of how the government should be involved in family disputes about artificial hydration and nutrition (Snead, 2005). This case became a catalyst for the completion of advance directives.

These stories highlighted the importance of end-of-life decision-making. Each portrayed existence in two liminal zones: (1) between life and death and (2) between medical and lay authority over end-of-life decision-making (Mahon, 2010). The Quinlan case brought increased recognition of the need for decision-making for people without capacity. Right-to-die movements and the origin of hospital ethics committees have both been attributed to the Quinlan case (Kenny, 2005). Both the Quinlan and Cruzan cases illuminated the right to refuse nonbeneficial treatments (Mahon, 2010). The Cruzan case has been attributed to the development of PSDA, which legislated advance directives. The Schiavo case challenged the "err on the side of life" principle, because her interests were violated without her awareness (Merrell, 2009). These cases illustrated that the distinction between killing and letting die can be inferred only by understanding both the present and future state of a condition.

THE POLITICAL AND SOCIAL CONTEXT OF END-OF-LIFE CARE

Public policy ensures—in principle—that no American need be at the mercy of unwanted life-extending medical intervention. Congress took an important step in passing PSDA and while advance

directives slowly became more common; they remain underused (Holley, 2011). The reasons for limited use of the available means for documenting end-of-life wishes are not well understood. Discerning patients' preferences and goals of care is arguably one of the most important elements of end-of-life care.

During the development of PPACA, a proposal was made to authorize reimbursement of one advance care planning consultation every 5 years (Kennelley, 2009). The provision had widespread bipartisan support until the summer of 2009, when former Alaska governor Sarah Palin and other public figures transformed end-of-life discussions into rhetoric about "death panels," igniting fears about the government's role in healthcare (Brown, 2012). The provision was removed from the pending legislation in reaction to resulting political turmoil (Hoefler, 2010; Tinetti, 2012).

Subsequently, voluntary advance care planning during annual wellness visits was included in the draft of a Centers for Medicare and Medicaid (CMS) rule in 2010, and commentary was positive but media coverage rekindled the controversy and the provision was removed (Holley, 2011; Tinetti, 2012). No subsequent CMS rules or regulations address end-of-life planning (Conway & Berwick, 2011). The discussion of death panels politicized conversations about the end of life and slowed the momentum of the advance care planning movement (Tinetti, 2012). The United States has made only incremental progress in establishing end-of-life options that honor the preferences of people who are dying (Brown, 2012).

The US Supreme Court has evaluated myriad end-of-life cases and determined that the choice between life and death is a deeply personal decision with finality. The law has firmly established that a competent adult patient has the right to refuse treatment. Conversely, a patient has the right to choose from appropriate treatments offered by physicians and what happens to his/her body (Holley, 2011). The issue of choice in dying has been operationalized in the PAS movement. In 2013, three states (Oregon, Washington, Vermont) allowed PAS, and one allows it by a court ruling (Montana), while 46 consider it illegal (ProCon.org., 2013). Active euthanasia, assisted dying, or the desire to hasten death have been heavily debated within the academic and medical communities and dominated by struggles over morality (Brown, 2012).

ADVANCE CARE PLANNING: A PUBLIC HEALTH IMPERATIVE

In 1900, only 4% of Americans were over age 65, and most died relatively soon after becoming fatally ill. By 2050, projections indicate that one in five will be 65 or older and the majority will live for months and sometimes years with chronic disabling conditions (Hoefler, 2010). With the aging of the population and growth in the number of people who are facing life's end, the need for attention to advance care planning has become an urgent public health concern (Tilden et al., 2011). The development of written advance directives, DNR, DNI, POLST, or MOLST protocols are important mechanisms for helping people express, document, and actualize their wishes. Patient-family-provider communication about end-of-life options and desired treatment occurs infrequently and is often poor in quality. In the absence of completed directives, people continue to have unwanted and nonbeneficial disease-focused treatment (Waldrop & Meeker, 2012).

THE COST OF CARE AT LIFE'S END

The Congressional Budget Office estimates that total US spending on healthcare will reach 25% of the gross domestic product (GDP) in 2025 and 49% by 2082. End-of-life care accounts for a high proportion of total healthcare costs. The percentage of Medicare payments attributable to patients in their last year of life was 25% in 2006 (Donley & Danis, 2011). Medicare payments in the last year of life average between $24,000 and $28,000, and hospital expenses range from $53,432 to $105,000 in the last 2 years of life (Lin, Levine, & Scanlan, 2012). Little progress has been made in reducing these costs.

Hospice programs provided care for 1.65 million people who were dying in 2011, and 83.2% were over age 65 (NHPCO, 2012). The hospice movement began as holistic, multidisciplinary care for people who are dying and their families. In the 31 years since the authorization of MHB, hospice has become a multimillion dollar industry in which nonprofits compete with for-profit providers, which are often publicly traded, managed by business-trained executives, and governed by corporate boards (Perry & Stone, 2011). There has been dramatic growth in the number of hospices in the United States—41% since 2000. Yet, only 39% of all people who die in the United States received hospice care and there

is disparate use by race, ethnicity, income, and education (Carlson, Bradley, Du, & Morrison, 2010). Between the years of 1999 and 2009, 40% of the Medicare-certified hospices had experienced one or more changes in ownership; the most prominent trend was moving from nonprofit to for-profit status (Thompson, Carlson, & Bradley, 2012). The extent to which MHB and the increase of hospice providers has resulted in cost savings in the end-of-life care remains contested (Perry & Stone, 2011).

Hospice care costs for nursing home patients jumped nearly 70% between 2005 and 2009, while the number of hospice patients in nursing homes increased only 40%. Hospices with a large share of patients in nursing homes were typically for profit and appeared to seek out patients with a longer life expectancy and lower demand for care (Hellander & Bhargavan, 2012). Gandhi (2012) compared the responses of for-profit and nonprofit hospices to financial incentives that were created by MHB and found evidence that they influence their patient mix and referral networks to increase profits (Gandhi, 2012). Chronically ill Medicare patients spent fewer days in the hospital and received more hospice care in 2007 than in 2003, but there was also an increase in the intensity of hospital care. While Medicare patients who are diagnosed with severe chronic illness were less likely to die in a hospital and more likely to receive hospice care at the same time, they also had more physician visits and spent more days in intensive care units. Higher use of intensive care and medical specialists can lead to increased aggressiveness of care, which is associated with higher cost. The rate of hospitalization in the last 6 months of life was 10.9 days per patient in 2007, and 36% saw 10 or more physicians (Goodman, Esty, Fisher, & Chang, 2011). Hospital-based palliative care teams have been established in more than 60% of hospitals (Morrison, Maroney-Galin, Kralovec, & Meier, 2005) and are estimated to save $1.2 billion per year (Meier, 2011). Hospice and palliative care teams help patients shift care from the hospital to the home or community, thus reducing spending for the sickest people for whom care is the costliest (Meier, 2011).

INFLUENCE OF THE INTERNET AND ONLINE COMMUNICATION ON END-OF-LIFE CARE

The Internet has changed communication, information dissemination, and support resources for the dying and their families. It is being used by the terminally ill to communicate "in person" with others via webcams and Skype and permits distant family members to be present at the death (Moore, 2012). Virtual communities of support provide resources and bereavement support to families dealing with loss (Lynn & Rath, 2012). Grief therapy and psychotherapeutic grief interventions are also being delivered through this medium (Neimeyer & Noppe-Brandon, 2012; Wagner & Maercher, 2007). The Internet is also beginning to be used for health communication and decision-making. Begun in 2010, the Blue Button initiative is an online patient portal, supported by the VA and Medicare on My HealtheVet and MyMedicare.gov (HealthIT.gov, n.d.). It enables individuals to download and access their health records and, in some instances, add personal data, such as the Universal Advance Digital Directive (uADD), an all-digital universal directive that enables individuals to create, update, and store their advance directive online for 24/7 access by healthcare personnel worldwide (MyDirectives.com, 2012).

HISTORY PREDICTS THE FUTURE: VISIONS OF WHAT IS AHEAD

Psychosocial support for patients and families as a unit of care continues to be a key element of the hospice and palliative care movements. Historic events have informed policy developments and underscored the importance of conversations about surrogate decision-making at the end of life. Understanding of the important influence of quality end-of-life care on family adaptation in bereavement is growing. The importance of choice about how one faces life's end has emerged as a recent phenomenon that is transforming end-of-life care. The social work profession has had a central role in the field's development and continued transformation.

REFERENCES

Abrahm, J., Callahan, J., Rossetti, K., & Pierre, L. (1996). The impact of a hospice consultation team on the care of veterans with advanced cancer. *Journal of Pain and Symptom Management, 12,* 23–31. doi: http://dx.doi.org/10.1016/0885-3924(96)00045-0

Belling, C. (2010). The living dead: Fiction, horror, and bioethics. *Perspectives in Biology and Medicine, 53,* 439–451. doi: 10.1353pbm.0.0168

Blacker, S., Christ, G. H., & Lynch, S. (2005). *Charting the course for the future of social work in end-of-life and palliative care.* A special report of The Social Work in Hospice and Palliative Care Network. Retrieved from http://www.swhpn.org/monograph.pdf

Brown, L. D. (2012). Stealing on insensibly: End of life politics in the United States. *Health Economics, Policy, and Law, 7,* 467–483. doi: 10.1017/s1744133112000254

Carlson, M. D. A., Bradley, E. H., Du, Q., & Morrison, R. S. (2010). Geographic access to hospice in the United States. *Journal of Palliative Medicine, 13,* 1331–1338. doi: 10.1089jpm.2010.0209

Centers for Medicare and Medicaid Services. (2013). *Medicare hospice benefits.* CMS Product No. 02155, Revised August, 2013. Retrieved September 26, 2013, from http://www.medicare.gov/

Conway, P. H., & Berwick, D. M. (2011). Improving the rules for hospital participation in Medicare and Medicaid. *Journal of the American Medical Association, 306,* 2256–2257. doi: 10.1001/jama.2011.1611

Daratsos, L., & Howe, J. L. (2007). The development of palliative care programs in the Veterans Administration. *Journal of Social Work in End-of-Life and Palliative Care, 3,* 29–39. doi: 10.1300/J457v03n01_05

Davidson, K., & Bullock, K. (2007). Zelda Foster and her contributions to social work in end-of-life care. *Journal of Social Work in End-of-Life and Palliative Care, 3,* 69–82. doi: 10.1300/J457v03n01_11

Donley, G., & Danis, M. (2011). Making the case for talking to patients about the costs of end-of-life care. *Journal of Law, Medicine, and Ethics, 39,* 183–193. doi: 10.1111/j.1748-720X.2011.00587.x

Field, M. J., & Cassel, C. K. (Eds.). (1997). *Approaching death: Improving care at the end of life.* Washington, DC: National Academy Press, Institute of Medicine.

Foster, Z. (1965). How social work can influence hospital management of fatal illness. *Social Work, 10*(4), 30–35. doi: 10.1093/sw/10.4.30

Gandhi, S. O. (2012). Differences between non-profit and for-profit hospices: Patient selection and quality. *International Journal of Health Care Finance and Economics, 12,* 107–127. doi: 10.1007/s10754-012-9109-y

Goodman, D. C., Esty, A. R., Fisher, E. S., & Chang, C. H. (2011). *Trends and variation in end-of-life care for Medicare beneficiaries with severe chronic illness.* A report of the Dartmouth Atlas Project. Retrieved from http://www.dartmouthatlas.org/downloads/reports/EOL_Trend_Report_0411.pdf

HealthIT.gov. (n.d.). *About Blue Button.* Retrieved October 7, 2013, from http://www.healthit.gov/patients-families/blue-button/about-blue-button

Hellander, I., & Bhargavan, R. (2012). Report from the United States: The U.S. health crisis deepens amid rising inequality: A review of data, Fall 2011. *International Journal of Health Services*, 42, 161–175. doi: http://dx.doi.org/10.2190/HS.42.2.a

Hoefler, J. M. (2010). United States lags on palliative care at the end of life. [Letter]. *Journal of Pain and Symptom Management*, 40, e1–e3. doi: 10.1016/j.jpainsymman.2010.08.007

Holley, D. (2011). CMS rule reversal: Understanding the impact on advance care planning. *ABA Health eSource*, 7(7). Retrieved from http://www.americanbar.org/content/newsletter/publications/aba_health_esource_home.html

Kennelley, B. M. (2009). *Sick to death of Medicare "death panel" propaganda*. Retrieved from http://www.ncpssm.org/EntitledtoKnow/entryid/1651/Sick-to-death-of-Medicare-Death-Panel-Propaganda

Kenny, R. W. (2005). A cycle of terms implicit in the idea of medicine: Karen Ann Quinlan as a rhetorical icon and the transvaluation of the ethics of euthanasia. *Health Communication*, 17, 17–39. doi: 10.1207/s15327027hc1701_2

Kubler-Ross, E. (1969). *On death and dying*. New York, NY: Collier Books, Macmillan.

Lin, R. Y., Levine, R. J., & Scanlan, B. C. (2012). Evolution of end-of-life care at United States hospitals in the new millennium. *Journal of Palliative Medicine*, 15, 592–601. doi:10.1089/jpm.2011.0432

Lunney, J., Lynn, J., & Hogan, C. (2002). Profiles of older Medicare decedents. *Journal of the American Geriatrics Society*, 50, 1108–1112. doi: http://dx.doi.org/10.1046/j.1532-5415.2002.50268.x

Lynn, C., & Rath, A. (2012). GriefNet: Creating and maintaining an Internet bereavement community. In C. J. Sofka, I. N. Cupit, & K. R. Gilbert (Eds.), *Dying, death, and grief in an online universe: For counselors and educators* (pp. 87–102). New York, NY: Springer.

Mahon, M. M. (2010). Clinical decision making in palliative care and end of life care. *Nursing Clinics of North America*, 45, 345–362. doi: 10.1016/j.cnur.2010.03.002

Meier, D. E. (2011). Increased access to palliative care and hospice services: Opportunities to improve value in health care. *Milbank Quarterly*, 89, 343–380. doi: 10.1111/j.1468-0009.2011.00632.x

Merrell, D. A. (2009). Erring on the side of life: The case of Terri Schiavo. *Journal of Medical Ethics*, 35, 323–325. doi: http://dx.doi.org/10.1136/jme.2007.023002

Moore, J. (2012). Being there: Technology at the end-of-life. In C. J. Sofka, I. N. Cupit, & K. R. Gilbert (Eds.), *Dying, death, and grief in an online universe: For*

counselors and educators (pp. 78–86). New York, NY: Springer.

Morrison, R. S., Maroney-Galin, C., Kralovec, P. D., & Meier, D. E. (2005). The growth of palliative care programs in United States hospitals. *Journal of Palliative Medicine*, 8, 1127–1134. doi: 10.1089/jpm.2005.8.1127

MyDirectives.com. (2012). *Advance planning healthcare start-up recognized by HHS*. Retrieved September 27, 2013, from http://www.mydirectives.com/en/news/advance-planning-healthcare-start-up-recognized-by-hhs/

National Association of Social Workers (NASW). (2004). *NASW standards for palliative and end of life care*. Retrieved from http://www.naswdc.org/practice/bereavement/standards/default.asp

National Consensus Project for Quality Palliative Care. (2013). *Clinical practice guidelines for quality palliative care* (3rd ed.). Retrieved from http://www.nationalconsensusproject.org/NCP_Clinical_Practice_Guidelines_3rd_Edition.pdf

National Hospice and Palliative Care Organization (NHPCO). (2012). *NHPCO facts and figures: Hospice care in America*. Retrieved from http://www.nhpco.org/sites/default/files/public/Statistics_Research/2012_Facts_Figures.pdf

National Quality Forum. (2006). *A national framework and preferred practices for palliative and hospice care quality*. Retrieved from http://www.qualityforum.org/Publications/2006/12/A_National_Framework_and_Preferred_Practices_for_Palliative_and_Hospice_Care_Quality.aspx

Neimeyer, R. A., & Noppe-Brandon, G. (2012). Attachment at distance: Grief therapy in the virtual world. In C. J. Sofka, I. N. Cupit, & K. R. Gilbert (Eds.), *Dying, death, and grief in an online universe: For counselors and educators* (pp. 103–118). New York, NY: Springer.

Olsen, E., & Wilson, D. (1982). Hospice: Within the VA hospital system. *Family and Community Health*, 5(3), 21–29. doi: http://dx.doi.org/10.1097/00003727-198211000-00006

Perry, J. E., & Stone, R. C. (2011). In the business of dying: Questioning the commercialization of hospice. *Journal of Law, Medicine, and Ethics*, 39, 224–234. doi: 10.1111/j.1748-720X.2011.00591.x

ProCon.org. (2013). *Euthanasia*. Retrieved September 26, 2013, from http://euthanasia.procon.org/view.resource.php?resourceID=000132

Racine, E., Amaram, R., Seidler, M., Karczewska, M., & Illes, J. (2008). Media coverage of the persistent vegetative state and end-of-life decision-making. *Neurology*, 71, 1027–1032. doi: 10.1212/WNL.0b013e3181afobfb

Saunders, C. (2000). The evolution of palliative care. *Patient Education and Counseling, 41,* 7–13. doi: 10.1093/acprof:oso/9780198570530.003.0040

Snead, O. C. (2005). Dynamic complementarity: Terri's law and separation of powers principles in the end-of-life context. *Florida Law Review, 57,* 53–89. http://www.floridalawreview.com/

St. Christopher's Hospice. (n.d.). *Dame Cicely Saunders: Her life and work.* Retrieved September 13, 2013, from http://www.stchristophers.org.uk/about/damecicelysaunders

Thompson, J. W., Carlson, M. D. A., & Bradley, E. H. (2012). US hospice industry experienced considerable turbulence from changes in ownership, growth, and shift to for-profit status. *Health Affairs, 31,* 1286–1293. doi: 10.1377/hlthaff.2011.1247

Tilden, V., Corless, I., Dahlin, C., Ferrell, B., Gibson, R., & Lentz, J. (2011). Advance care planning as an urgent public health concern. *Nursing Outlook, 59,* 55–56. doi: http://dx.doi.org/10.1016/j.outlook.2010.12.001

Tinetti, M. E. (2012). The retreat from advanced care planning. *Journal of the American Medical Association, 307,* 915–916. doi: 10.1001/jama.2012.229

US Census Bureau. (2012). Table 521: Veterans living by period of service, age, and sex: 2010. In *Statistical Abstract of the United States: 2012.* Retrieved from www.census.gov/compendia/statab/2012/tables/12s0521.pdf

Wagner, B., & Maercher, A. (2007). A 1.5-year follow-up of an Internet-based intervention for complicated grief. *Journal of Traumatic Stress, 20,* 625–629. doi: http://dx.doi.org/10.1002/jts.20230

Waldrop, D. P., & Meeker, M. A. (2012). Communication and advanced care planning in palliative and end-of-life care. *Nursing Outlook, 60,* 365–369. doi: 10.1016/j.outlook.2012.08.012

Dying has become a medical and legal issue, but will always be a profoundly personal event. Social workers focus on psychosocial issues and are trained to work with individuals, families, and larger systems, thus they are uniquely capable to work in end-of-life care. Social workers view people from a holistic perspective and have expertise in facilitating communication, addressing taboo topics, and mediating between individuals and organizations. All of these skills are essential to effective end-of-life care. Social workers have been identified as critical to the healthcare team (Csikai, 2004), involved in patient education (Baker, 1995; Christ & Sormanti, 1999), and active in working with family members in end-of-life planning (Werner & Carmel, 2001) and care (Weisenfluh & Csikai, 2013).

Case Example

Hattie was referred to the palliative care social worker because she had a recurrence of cancer. She had breast cancer and surgery 6 years prior to this hospitalization, but because of a lack of health insurance Hattie was not provided any other interventions or follow-up after her surgery. The social worker met with Hattie regularly to discuss her health concerns while she remained in the hospital for radiation. Considering that Hattie understood her reoccurrence of cancer as a failure of the healthcare system, she needed time to verbalize her concerns and fears. The social worker encouraged such dialogue and continued to assess Hattie's psychosocial well-being and unmet needs. One day Hattie told the social worker that she urgently needed to return home, saying she had to go "to see my grans, I just have that feeling." The social worker, who was familiar with the importance of responding immediately to an urgent request from a person with a terminal diagnosis, quickly informed the physician of Hattie's wishes and worked with the unit staff to expedite her discharge.

Late in the afternoon, when Hattie was expected to leave, the social worker happened on the ambulance drivers waiting at the elevator. They were leaving without Hattie and said that she was not ready for discharge. The social worker insisted they return and coordinated with the unit staff to assure the necessary steps were taken to guarantee a successful discharge, including

MARGARET M. SOUZA
IRENE A. GUTHEIL

Providing Services at the End of Life: Focusing on the Psychosocial Aspects of Dying

56

finalizing her prescriptions, setting an appointment for radiation therapy for the following day, and teaching the daughter how to give insulin. Once again, the ambulance drivers refused to transport Hattie, claiming that her blood pressure was too low for them to take her home. The social worker asserted herself and informed them that Hattie was going home to die, not because she was medically stable. Coordination and advocacy enabled the transfer to occur.

The following day the social worker was informed by the unit staff that Hattie had died at 2:00 in the morning at her home. Staff members were grateful they had enabled her to go home to die. The social worker was able to successfully coordinate this rapid care transition because of her strong rapport with Hattie, dedication to ongoing assessment, understanding of the importance of urgently responding to Hattie's changing wishes, willingness to address the barriers met within the organization, and skillful use of cooperative teamwork. ▨

This chapter addresses general guidelines for social work practice in hospice, palliative care, and end-of-life care settings and services. Paramount to this type of practice is an understanding of the concept that dying is a personal event related to the choices and values of the persons involved, especially the dying person[1] and her family.[2] The setting in which the social worker intersects with the dying person affects the roles assumed and interventions offered. Within this context it is the responsibility of the clinician to listen for and to elicit the needs of the client and seek to respond to these needs as much as possible. The social work roles of broker, teacher, mediator, enabler, and advocate (Compton & Galaway, 1999) provide a framework for the actions of the social worker in successfully responding to the needs and wishes of all involved.

DYING IN OLD AGE

The diversity and widening age range among older persons complicate discussions with older adults about the end of life. A terminally ill grandmother at 67, who is raising her grandchildren and is still employed, has vastly different needs than a 90-year-old infirm and demented resident who has spent the last 5 years in a nursing home. Both persons and their families may require professional but different types of assistance in dealing with and coming to terms with the finality of a terminal illness. Regardless of the age or condition of the older person, death represents a finality and loss to the person and to those who are connected to him.

Death in older adults is thought to be the natural progression of the life cycle and, therefore, inevitable. Care providers may minimize the intensity and importance of the experience, diminishing the centrality of long-standing companionships and neglecting the significance of family ties. While death for some older persons may be welcomed, for many others and their families, death remains a dreaded experience.

When death is understood simply as the "natural" next step in old age, unrealistic expectations of acceptance may result. Often clients who are grieving reveal that other family members or friends try to soothe their grief by indicating they should be grateful that the person had a "long and good life." For example, at a viewing for his recently deceased mother, who died in her mid-80s after a difficult adjustment to dementia and nursing home placement, a physician stood by her coffin and began to recite reasons to believe that she had a good, long life. But then he sat in a chair, put his head down, and said "So why do I feel so bad?" In discussing her mother's death, Reeve Lindbergh (2002) indicates that even though her mother had several strokes and was in a compromised state for a long period of time, the moment of her death was unexpected. She goes on to explain that in the reading of one of her mother's poems at the funeral service, the opening line described how all those in the room felt—"But how can I live without you . . .?" This sense of loss at the time of death, regardless of the condition of the person who has died, impacts the loved ones left to grieve (Souza, 2014).

SOCIAL WORK ASSESSMENT

Palliative care and hospice services acknowledge and validate the holistic needs of dying persons. At times, these programs may focus on nursing and medical needs, seeking to provide comfort and symptom control from what may be perceived as painful and difficult physical processes that occur in long-term illness. This approach to comfort can be essential to dying persons and their families, but it must not obscure other, less visible needs that at times may have greater significance. Emotional distress can intensify physical pain, and relief from stress can lessen it. Assessment in end-of-life care considers relevant biopsychosocial factors as well as the needs of the dying person and the family (National Association of Social Workers [NASW], 2004).

Identification of the Client

The foremost assessment task of social workers in end-of-life care is identification of the different clients. The social worker's primary clients are generally the dying person and the family. The social worker is challenged to listen to ways in which the dying person verbally and nonverbally expresses his needs and to the needs expressed by family and staff members. These can be put together with a focus on the dying person as the central client. Although the needs of the dying person and family may be compatible, social workers must also be attuned to discrepancies that may exist. The needs of the family and the terminally ill person may differ.

The social worker may work with family members to help them accept the primacy of the dying person's needs. Yet discomfort around death and the difficulties involved in communicating with dying persons may result in work with the family inappropriately taking precedence over work with the dying person. If the dying person is unable to assert or articulate his needs, the needs of the family may appropriately become the primary focus of social work interventions. In addition, staff members and other professional colleagues may need help in letting go of their desire to manage the situation.

Capacity

In helping individuals complete the healthcare proxy and advance directive documents, social workers need to evaluate an older person's ability to complete this document when cognitive impairment is diagnosed or suspected. All adults are presumed to be legally competent to make decisions on their own behalf unless a court has officially supported the determination of incompetence. Unlike competency, which is legally defined, capacity is a concept that is clinically determined through observation and interview.

The presence of mild cognitive impairment does not necessarily disqualify a person from making informed decisions or knowingly signing contracts and other legally binding documents. Social workers must carefully assess cognitive capacity, as well as

the degree of understanding of the options and likely outcomes of a decision. Dementia symptom severity can vary throughout the day, so the social worker should investigate whether the individual is more lucid at certain times. When in doubt, the social worker may obtain a medical or psychiatric consultation to determine capacity. Because the completion of a healthcare proxy does not require the same level of capacity as other documents with legal standing, it is important to assure that an individual who is capable of choosing an agent be given the opportunity to do so.

One's Own Perceptions of Death and Dying

A critical step for social workers in end-of-life care is awareness of the losses in their own lives and the meaning death has for them. Social workers must be aware of their beliefs, values, and their own needs to ensure these do not influence their work with the dying person and his family. Although self-reflection is an essential component of social work practice, working with people who are dying raises particular challenges because of the larger social and cultural environment that seeks to keep death at a distance. Although modern society is exposed to more death through the media there still remains a fear of it (Noys, 2005). In addition to self-knowledge, social workers in end-of-life care have a responsibility to be knowledgeable about the dying process, illness-related issues, manifestations of pain, advance directives, and the range of settings and resources for end of life (NASW, 2004).

Interactions with Other Providers

Death is usually the result of a deteriorating condition that may have a continual and rapid downward spiral or have continuing acute episodes that leave the individual in an increasingly debilitated condition. Dying persons may become objectified as the process of disengagement is promoted by healthcare professionals. Consequently, it is essential that the social worker constantly be aware of the context of care for the dying person and family. The social worker must understand the functioning of the organization providing services and how this impacts on care to the individual and attention to the concerns of family members.

Each member of the team operates from a different perspective. The social worker's viewpoint should be to represent the personal and social concerns of the dying person and family. Social workers may need to use all of their skills to provide other well-intentioned care providers with the perspective of the dying person and, if necessary, act as mediators between their clients and the health care team. Because of their focus on the emotional and social aspects of care and human need, social workers can also be a resource for the medical team whose training and practice may limit their ability to recognize or validate their own personal responses to the dying process.

A woman with dementia who lived in a nursing home was going to be transferred to the hospital because of an acute episode. When the ambulance team tried to move her from her chair to the stretcher she held on to the arms of the chair tightly, resisting their attempts. The team asked the social worker to assist, but she refused, indicating that she believed the woman was communicating quite clearly her refusal to be transferred. Although on this occasion the social worker was ultimately unable to convince the other providers to honor what she believed to be the woman's wishes, she eventually coordinated with the family and the nursing home team to create a plan that enabled the woman to die at the nursing home without multiple high-tech interventions. Education for direct care staff and other professional colleagues will help them understand how the words and behaviors of older persons, particularly when referring to interventions for themselves or others, can provide insight into their choices.

Emotional Loss

The assessment of the needs of the dying person and his family generally begins at a basic level with a focus on concrete tasks that the social worker can perform. These needs may include access to information, help with advance directive completion, or assistance with brokering the arrangement of services. Yet even these needs often have emotional components. If assessment prematurely ends at this concrete level, other critical needs may be overlooked. Loss is a component of dying for all persons involved. The dying person faces the loss of a future and continued participation in the life cycle. The family is diminished

as well. Even when the dying person is not a highly regarded member of the family or when the person was significantly impaired long ago due to dementia, the family members still face the physical absence of that person. When a family member provides care for the older adult, there is also a loss of the caregiver role. These experiences of loss, while universal, are experienced in each family and by each family member in a unique way. One of the challenges the social worker faces is assessing the meaning of loss to all involved. Death reveals our own mortality, and the social worker must be accepting of these feelings and recognize that everyone will react differently. Some people may not be saddened by the loss of their family member, and others will not be able to communicate their sadness.

Social Support

Assessment of the social resources of the dying person is critical. Some older persons have no family or are estranged from loved ones. Unless they have others intimately involved in their lives, they may be bereft of social resources and face the end of their life alone. When family is present, there may be strong interfamilial support or there may be discord. The discord may be long-standing, or may be the result of differences in how to best deal with the current situation. The head of an intensive care unit commented that he often sees family members who were not actively involved in elder caregiving suddenly show up at the hospital demanding ongoing care and interventions.

Finally, it is important to understand the support available from outside the family. Many families have strong connections to individuals or organizations in the community, such as churches, that can serve as resources to them. Death is a time when families may benefit from being encouraged to avail themselves of their informal resources in order to meet their own needs and those of the dying person. Social workers can empower the dying person and family by having a well-developed list of resources, and may need to use advocacy to help families access these resources.

Financial Resources

Financial concerns are an unwelcome but powerful influence on healthcare provision. Funding sources and family finances often determine what care is available and where care is provided. Financial concerns also may influence decision-making by dying persons, families, or care providers. Social workers need to be attentive to the power of financial concerns, even when they are unspoken. At times family members advocating for hastening end of life may be concerned about the cost of care for the dying person or the financial resources that will be used providing care. Alternatively a person may seem to be ineligible for needed direct care services. The social worker creatively can recognize the way in which to access them. A 60-year-old man was going home with a feeding tube after his surgery for throat cancer. Home care rejected his case because they deemed the apartment unsafe despite the fact that he had lived there with his leg in a cast for an extended period of time. The social worker recommended the physician request hospice benefits for him knowing that the hospice service would accept him. She underscored how his cancer diagnosis could be recognized as a terminal condition within the following 6 months albeit the man was not actively dying. The hospice support he received provided him with nursing care while his feeding tube was in place. He was eventually able to have the tube removed, hospice suspended, and managed to live for another year, after which hospice care was restored until his death.

In addition church and fraternal organizations as well as disease-specific foundations often provide some financial or care support to chronically ill and/or dying individuals. Working with families to find out what resources they could benefit from and how to request them is a valuable intervention. It also can free them to spend quality time with their dying family member.

Religious and Spiritual Beliefs

Social workers also need to evaluate whether there are any unmet religious or spiritual needs. While often a source of strength, the importance of religion differs among families. These differences must be recognized and respected. Death can cause a spiritual crisis for the dying person and family members. The social worker needs to evaluate whether religious assistance is needed. She can help broker the connection as necessary. However, social workers also need to be willing to discuss spiritual concerns and issues, and recognize when the spiritual aspect

of an individual's life is a source of strength in the absence of religious beliefs. The dying person or family may want a safe place to talk about the meaning life has for them and how to find strength in the face of death. These essential conversations do not necessarily require the assistance of a spiritual person.

Culture

Social workers understand the importance of sensitivity to the cultural differences of dying persons and their families and the need to adhere to specific customs and traditions that bring meaning to the dying process. Equally important is the particular way the dying person believes how the world should work and the need for consistency with the values he holds concerning life. When discussing the dying process and available interventions, the individual's and family's culturally informed beliefs need to be recognized. Understanding that there are differences in the ways individuals accept or reject particular aspects of their culture will enable a sensitive response without mistaken assumptions about cultural adherence. In end-of-life literature, much research has focused on cultural variations in relation to issues of advance care planning and directives (Blackhall et al., 1999; Bullock, 2011; Hofmann et al., 1997). While the focus is on the completion of these documents, there is recognition that a variety of approaches are helpful in assisting with completion. This cultural sensitivity must be extended to the context of the dying process and the larger issues of role expectation, dependency, and other areas in which values vary.

Quality of Life and Death

Every effort must be made to ensure that the quality of life of the dying person, as she understands it to be, is maintained up to the end. Some dying persons choose to forgo optimal pain medication in order to be able to remain as alert and involved with life as possible. Others may make a different choice. The important task is to create an environment where the choice can be heard and will be respected. For quality of life to be maintained, the social worker must see and deal with the older individual as a person and respond to her needs and preferences in a manner that accepts physical and mental losses without having those losses diminish personhood. When a dying person is unable to clearly articulate her wishes, the individual's behavior may illustrate choices. Resistance to particular interventions may be a non-verbal way of communicating treatment preferences. Social workers can provide a model of behavior and an approach to the dying person for the family and other staff members to emulate.

When a woman was actively dying, her husband and daughter sat at the end of the bed watching. The social worker when she spoke to the family and dying woman stood next to her and gently stroked her arm. Later in the afternoon when the social worker returned the husband and daughter were doing the same.

SOCIAL WORK INTERVENTIONS

While death is a time of loss and pain for most people, the process of dying can give a person a sense of completion if the person's life is recognized and affirmed. Hopefully, with appropriate support and assistance, the dying person and her family can experience death under the best possible conditions considering their particular circumstances. For this to occur, the full range of psychosocial needs of dying persons and their families must be addressed. Social work interventions may take a range of forms including individual counseling, family counseling, group modalities, case management, and system advocacy (NASW, 2004). Since each individual and family is unique, the choice of intervention is based on the needs of the dying person and his family. The social worker may be challenged to be creative when the needs call for help that is not readily available. For example, it may be necessary to develop a support group specifically for healthcare agents who have made decisions to withdraw life-sustaining treatment and are struggling to deal with the awesome responsibility this decision entails.

Social Work Roles

In supporting clients in end-of-life and palliative care settings, social workers may assume any of five interventional roles, as outlined by Compton and Galaway (1999), including the roles of teacher, enabler, broker, mediator, or advocate (Table 56.1).

As a teacher, the social worker may focus on helping people to understand the dying process and anticipate feelings that may arise can help to normalize experiences. As an enabler, the social worker supports the creation of an environment where the dying individual and his family can talk freely about concerns and fears, which may help to reduce angered or blaming interactions that are hurtful at a time of great vulnerability. The mediating social worker understands the ways in which families communicate, both through direct dialogue and through more coded dialogue. The social worker serving as a broker assists the dying person and his family to prepare for the death and burial arrangements (Jenkins, 2002), and can empower the client through achieving a sense of control. The social work profession has a long history of advocacy in partnership with clients, and practitioners. Working with people at the end of life provides an opportunity to use advocacy skills to achieve a number of important goals. Assuring respectful interactions with dying persons and their families is essential. This includes honoring their preferred language for discussing death and dying instead of defaulting to the jargon-loaded terminology so often employed by medical providers. Fostering ongoing communication between the healthcare team and dying individuals and their families is critical. However, social workers may need to represent the views of the dying individual during team conferences when the client cannot be there in person.

Teaching and enabling are essential skills for assisting persons in the completion of advance care planning tools. Broker, mediator, and enabler roles are used to assist individuals with terminal illness and their families with concrete care needs. A broker can make connections to the services that persons need. A mediator assists them with acceptance of health decline and losses in functioning, appetite, and energy. An enabler helps by assisting family members to accept increased care needs and provide or supervise the care. These are all essential social work tasks. Helping a family to deal with the losses they experience as their loved one's condition deteriorates enables them to be present and to respond to care needs. When death occurs, although it is still painful, guilt may be lessened.

At some point in the trajectory of long-term illness, decisions may need to be made about limiting treatment. At times, particularly when treatment has already continued for multiple medical issues and functional decline, persons may decide that comfort is more appropriate than continued pursuit of curative medicine. Social workers need to evaluate

TABLE 56.1 Social Work Interventions in End-of- Life Care

Broker

- Locating the services that meet the specific needs of families and dying persons
- Arranging for both formal and informal care services as needed
- Negotiating with various systems to honor the expressed wishes of the families and dying persons
- Helping families to request emotional support and needed assistance from their informal networks
- Assisting in operationalizing advance directives
- Connecting families and dying persons to spiritual resources as requested

Teacher

- Educating about advance care planning
- Educating about illnesses
- Educating about the right to pursue or reject medical interventions
- Providing information about the dying process
- Assisting persons to articulate their health concerns
- Discussing ways in which to communicate with the healthcare team
- Teaching clients to prepare written lists of questions for the healthcare team
- Modeling styles of communication for families to use with different team members
- Modeling styles of communication for healthcare teams to use with families and dying persons
- Informing clients and colleagues about available resources and services
- Educating the healthcare team about cultural differences
- Helping the healthcare team to understand the particular psychosocial needs of clients
- Helping families to identify meaningful ways to interact and communicate with the dying person

Mediator

- Negotiating with families to best meet the needs of the dying person with available resources
- Facilitating communication between dying persons and healthcare providers
- Facilitating communication between family members and healthcare providers
- Encouraging open communication among family members to achieve mutual support and understanding
- Assisting in the resolution of long-standing and recent family conflicts and tensions

Enabler

- Empowering dying persons
- Empowering family members
- Collaborating with the healthcare team to assess and respond appropriately to changing health needs, client preferences, and systemic barriers
- Affirming the emotional needs of healthcare providers in responding to death
- Assisting dying persons to feel socially alive and connected for as long as possible
- Supporting families and dying persons in the expression of multiple and mixed emotional responses to the dying process
- Encouraging families to communicate with the dying person through verbal and physical means during the dying process
- Providing bereavement services that support survivors in continuing to honor the person who has died, including through the use of personally meaningful rituals of memorialization
- Normalizing the diverse feelings of family members after the loss of a loved one

(continued)

TABLE 56.1 Continued

Advocate
• Interceding with the organizations providing services on behalf of the dying person and family
• Advocating with members of the healthcare team on behalf of the dying person and family
• Vocalizing the dying person's needs and wishes when the client is unable to do so
• Overcoming barriers to mobilizing needed services and resources
• Assuring that medical practitioners and families understand and comply with dying persons' expressed or documented wishes regarding end-of-life care and surrogate decision-makers
• Assisting families and healthcare teams to recognize the social needs of dying persons

whether depression is present and is causing an individual to give up, whether untreated pain is the cause of the depression, and whether the person understands the situation and chooses to focus on comfort recognizing that these choices may hasten death. At times, medical practitioners pursue interventions based on assumptions of the hopefulness of the person. Social workers in these situations need to be cognizant of potential changes in treatment preferences, help clients to consider their needs, and assist medical staff in understanding these evolving issues. If clients choose comfort over treatment they may need a mediator and, in some cases, an advocate. On the other hand, if clients want to pursue treatment against the advice of medical personnel they may also need an advocate.

Social Work Support of Advance Directives

The increased use of technology in medicine has resulted in persons with increased disabilities and multiple illnesses living longer, at times resulting in long and difficult deaths. While imperfect and often fraught with difficulties, advance care planning is essential if the choices of the elderly person are to be recognized. Recently, attention has focused on the importance of communication between older persons and their potential agents (Gutheil & Heyman, 2005). Communication about healthcare planning is essential, but it is imperative that social workers understand the reluctance some individuals have in completing the documentation and being able to discuss their concerns, fears, and wishes with family, with the individual they will name as their agent, and with their healthcare providers. Social workers may recognize that the rationale for refusal has profound implications for the family and may need to

communicate with other providers about the importance of supporting the family through this process. Social workers must also be alert to the possibility of dying persons wanting to change their decisions about end-of-life care, even if refusing an intervention seems counterintuitive.

Another key issue is the way individuals speak about end-of-life care. If providers focus only on the medical and legal language of advance directives, they may fail to hear important messages regarding the ways people think about such choices. For example, when older persons observe life-sustaining care being given to another, and they respond by saying that they would not want something similar to be done to them, there is a need to follow up. Social workers should remain alert to these types of communications as indications of care preferences, but should also instruct and support direct care staff to be alert for remarks that indicate a person's thoughts about specific treatments and interventions. Documenting these types of communications can provide evidence of the person's wishes.

Although documentation of advanced directives may have been completed, problems may still develop. Family members may disagree with the agent's choice of actions, or healthcare providers may fail to act on the agent's decisions. Social workers need to bear in mind that advance directives also can become a means to protect medical providers from litigious concerns (Souza, 2004). Acting as a mediator or advocate, the social worker can help the healthcare agent carry out what at times can seem like emotionally overwhelming responsibilities. Clinical support and the empowerment of patients, families, and other providers are essential at these times.

A mistaken notion may exist that because dying persons and their families remain hopeful in their communications and plans for the future, they have not accepted the terminal condition or impending death. Most persons aware of impending death do maintain a hopeful demeanor despite their understanding of the proximity of death and the choices they have made regarding refusal for aggressive treatments. When an oncologist informed the social worker that an elderly woman would be going to an in-patient hospice, he was troubled because the patient continued to speak about going home and getting better. He felt that a DNR order would be appropriate, but was uncomfortable trying to obtain it in the face of such optimism. The social worker led him into the woman's room and said to her "if your heart stopped beating and you were unable to breathe would you want a doctor to try and restart your heart or give you something to help you breathe?" She looked at the two of them in wonder and said, "I have gone to glory and you want to bring me back. Are you crazy?"

Expressions of hope among dying persons do not impede their understanding of impending death or their preferences regarding end-of-life care. Using clear, understandable language that describes the purpose and process of advance care planning can assist in eliciting the dying person's perspective.

Since medical decisions can be complex and an agent may struggle to ensure that she is following the wishes of the individual, the social worker can help by providing cues that may jog her memory concerning prior conversations and utterances made about how people die. A helpful question is: "When family members died, did your mother remark on the type of death that occurred and did she say how she felt about it or what she thought about it?" Another approach is bringing up nationally known figures, such as by asking "When Terri Schiavo was in the news, did your father say what his opinion was and what he felt should occur?" These informal conversations may reveal end-of-life preferences more clearly than relying only on the formal language of an advance directive document.

Since many older adults have multiple illnesses for which they have continued to receive treatment for a long period of time, the decision to discontinue, stop, or not pursue a particular treatment makes visible the reality that death is expected and a treatment choice is made. Knowing the correct time to prepare for death is a difficult challenge. Often intervention options are presented as a yes/no dichotomy, where you choose to have a particular intervention or nothing (Battin, 2005). The roles of enabler, mediator, and advocate are essential in this context, as social workers use their listening skills accompanied by supportive techniques to help older persons and their families reject or request interventions according to their wishes and after considering all available options. Advance care planning usually focuses on the cessation or omission of treatment, but it is essential to remember that it also is meant to inform the provision of treatments that patients and families prefer.

CONCLUSION

The role of the social worker in end-of-life care starts before the final stage of illness and continues after death occurs. Social workers may enter this continuum at various points, depending on the practice setting. This chapter, in highlighting the range of psychosocial issues to assess and intervention roles to adopt, underscores the valuable and diverse services that social workers provide in working with dying persons and their families.

RESOURCES

AARP Caregiving Resource Center
http://www.aarp.org/home-family/caregiving/
Association of Oncology Social Work
http://aosw.org/
Center to Advance Palliative Care (CAPC)
http://www.capc.org/
Growth House, Inc.—Improving Care for the Dying
growthhouse.org
Medical Orders for Life-Sustaining Treatment (MOLST)
http://www.health.ny.gov/professionals/patients/
   patient_rights/molst/
National   Hospice   and   Palliative   Care
   Organization—End-of-Life Care Resources
http://www.nhpco.org/resources/end-life-care—
   resources
USA.gov—Government Made Easy
http://www.usa.gov/Topics/Seniors.shtml

NOTES

1. We use the term "person" for those who are dying to clearly demarcate that dying is a human act. If dying persons are understood as patients, it is easy to respond to them and their needs within a medical model.

2. The term "family" is used to denote a closeness of relationship and refers to biological or fictive kin.

REFERENCES

Baker, M. E. (1995). *Advance directives: An examination of the knowledge, attitudes and behavior of health care social workers toward end-of-life decision making.* Unpublished doctoral dissertation. Ohio State University, Columbus, OH.

Battin, M. P. (2005). *Ending life: Ethics and the way we die.* New York, NY: Oxford University Press.

Blackhall, L. J., Frank, G., Murphy, S. T, Michel, V., Palmer, J. M., & Azen, S. P. (1999). Ethnicity and attitudes towards life sustaining technology. *Social Science and Medicine, 48,* 1779–1789. doi: 10.1016/S0277-9536(99)00077-5

Bullock, K. (2011). The influence of culture on end of life decision making. *Journal of Social Work in End of-Life and Palliative Care, 7,* 83–98. doi: 10.1080/155 24256.2011.548048

Christ, G., & Sormanti, M. (1999). Advancing social work practice in end-of-life care. *Social Work in Health Care, 30,* 81–99. doi: 10.1300/J010v30n02_05

Compton, B. R., & Galaway, B. (1999). *Social work processes* (6th ed.) Belmont, CA: Wadsworth.

Csikai, E. L. (2004). Social workers' participation in the resolution of ethical dilemmas in hospice care. *Health and Social Work, 29,* 67–76. doi: 10.1093/hsw/29.1.67

Gutheil, I. A., & Heyman, J. C. (2005). Communication between older persons and their health care agents: Results of an intervention. *Health and Social Work, 30,* 107–116.

Hofmann, J., Wenger, N. S., Davis, R. B., Teno, J., Connors, A. F., Desbiens, N., . . . Phillips, R. S. (1997). Patients preferences for communication with physicians about end-of life decisions. *Annals of Internal Medicine, 127,* 1–12. doi: 10.7326/0003-4819-127-1-199707010-00001

Jenkins, M. (2002). *You only die once: Preparing for the end of life with grace and gusto.* Nashville, TN: Integrity.

Lindbergh, R. (2002). *No more words: A journal of my mother: Anne Marie Lindbergh.* New York, NY: Simon and Schuster.

National Association of Social Workers (NASW). (2004). *NASW standards for social work practice in palliative and end of life care.* Retrieved from http://www.socialworkers.org/practice/bereavement/standards/default/asp

Noys, B. (2005). *The culture of death.* New York, NY: Berg.

Souza, M. (2004). *Multiple voices in the new medicalization of dying: The case for palliative care.* Doctoral dissertation. New School University, New York, NY.

Souza, M. (2014). Dying persons and their families. In C. Staudt & J. H. Ellens, *Our changing journey to the end: Reshaping death, dying, and grief in America* (pp. 45–57). New York, NY: Praeger.

Weisenfluh, S., & Csikai, E. (2013). Professional and educational needs of hospice and palliative care social workers. *Journal of Social Work in End-of-Life and Palliative Care, 9,* 58–73. doi: 10.1080/15524256.2012.758604

Werner, P., & Carmel, S. (2001). End-of-life decision making: Practices, beliefs and knowledge of social workers in health care settings. *Educational Gerontology, 27,* 387–398. doi: 10.1080/03601270152053410

NAMKEE CHOI

Policies and Regulations in Health and Aging

OVERVIEW

This section of the *Handbook* discusses social policies that most directly affect older adults and their families. Social workers working with diverse groups of older adults and their families should not only understand policies and regulations at multiple system levels but also have expert skills for evaluating the impact of these policies at micro, mezzo, and macro levels. The chapters in this section are intended to provide practitioners and students with a critical overview of key policies and serve as a foundation for advanced policy analysis and advocacy in the following areas: income maintenance; healthcare; protection of the rights and support for families/informal caregivers; social service, housing, and transportation; and decisional capacity. There have been some significant changes and updates in each of these key policy arenas over the past decade, and each chapter provides information on significant changes, challenges facing the future, and the implications for social work practice.

In Chapter 57, Hudson and DiNitto first review the place of private pensions in the overall retirement income picture, recent trends in private pension coverage, and the inadequacy of private pensions in helping to meet the retirement needs of vulnerable populations. The authors point out that private pension coverage and participation remain low and uneven, with more than one-half of workers and retirees uncovered or only minimally covered. The second half of the chapter provides a comprehensive overview of the Social Security system and the challenges in maintaining its solvency in the years ahead with declining birth rates and increasing life expectancy. The chapter concludes with a discussion of the role of social workers in educating the public about income security especially for low-income older adults and advocating for ways to expand private pension coverage and keep Social Security viable.

In chapter 58, Lee provides an overview of Medicare and new policy developments brought forth by the Patient Protection and Affordable Care Act (PPACA), signed into law by President Barack Obama on March 23, 2010. New policy developments that Lee describes include preventive services and yearly "wellness" visits, the hospital readmission reductions policy, the patient-centered medical home, and expansions of mental health and substance use disorder coverage. Lee further discusses Medicare long-term care benefits and the various

roles that social workers can play in the post-PPACA era. The chapter concludes with a discussion of the challenges in keeping Medicare financially secure, while providing affordable, quality healthcare to increasing numbers of older and disabled persons.

Chapter 59, authored by Galambos and Jun, provides an overview of the policies and programs in Medicaid that support older adults. Emphasis is on long-term care programs and community care programs. Historical antecedents to the programs are explored and standards and guidelines for Medicaid services are explained. A detailed discussion of specific Medicaid policies and programs for older adults is provided, including Medicare and Medicaid dual eligibility and state buy-ins for dual eligibles, Programs of All-Inclusive Care for the Elderly (PACE), managed long-term services and supports, Medicaid waiver and innovation programs, home- and community-based services, and the Money Follows the Person program. The chapter highlights the impact of long-term care financing issues and the Patient Protection and Affordable Care Act on Medicaid services for older adults.

Chapter 60, written by Thomas, provides a comprehensive overview of key social policies related to social services, housing, and transportation that are designed to help older adults age in place in their own housing and to ensure the health and quality of life older adults in the community and reduce long-term care costs by preventing premature institutionalization. Most adults prefer to age in place and need to access to a range of services to address the opportunities, challenges, and limitations associated with aging. Although there are a patchwork of policies and programs at federal, state, and local levels, this chapter includes only federal-level policies, including provisions and mandates of the Older Americans Act, the Medicaid home- and community-based services waiver programs, the Social Services Block Grant (Title XX of the Social Security Act), and the Americans with Disabilities Act. With respect to federal housing policies and programs, the author discusses different types of subsidized housing programs, home equity conversion mortgage programs, and federal tax policies that provide direct and indirect benefits to older adults. The chapter concludes with the discussion of various federal transportation policies for an aging society.

In Chapter 61, Wilber, Yonashiro-Cho, Navarro, and Alkema discuss the ethical, legal, economic, and civil rights issues of older persons' competency and proxy determination and provide a review of the complicated but fragmented policies governing protective services and supportive and surrogate decision-making policies. Social workers can look to a repertoire of services that support older adults with diminished decisional capacity, including preplanned powers of attorney, representative payeeship, and legal guardianship. Choosing the right blend of services can be challenging and that blend may vary over time as circumstances change. Older adults engaged in any decision-making arrangements that transfer some level of authority to informal or formal service providers are vulnerable to mistreatment, malfeasance, and exploitation. Several core values provide ethical guidelines to guide treatment decisions when applying supportive and surrogate policies and programs. Social workers can be instrumental in providing critical insights, thereby helping to sort through the array of policies, programs, and services relevant in their state.

In the last chapter in this section, Davitt, Li, and Rastigue summarize and critically analyze select policies that protect the rights of older adults and support their families/informal caregivers. The chapter begins with a critical examination of policies that prohibit discrimination based on age or disability, including the Age Discrimination in Employment Act, the Americans with Disabilities Act, the Fair Housing Act Amendments, and the Olmstead decision. Policies to protect the rights of vulnerable older adults are then analyzed, including those which address elder abuse, neglect, and exploitation, such as the Older Americans Act and the Elder Justice Act. The chapter concludes with an exploration of policies and programs that support informal caregivers and families of older adults with care needs, including the Family and Medical Leave Act (FMLA), the National Family Caregiver Support Program (NFCSP), and the Lifespan Respite Care Program (LRCP).

The "fear of outliving one's income" has long stood as the principal economic concern facing people in old age. Adequate income is a necessary condition for ensuring well-being at every stage of life. The Social Security program, administered by the US government's Social Security Administration (SSA), has been described as the foundation of retirement income (DeWitt, 1996). Also important for a decent standard of living in retirement is a pension or private retirement plan, often secured through employment. However, half of US workers have no private pension coverage (Social Security Administration [SSA], 2013). Personal savings are also important in retirement, but 57% of Americans have less than $25,000 in savings and investments (not counting the value of their home or any defined [guaranteed] retirement benefit plan they may have) (Helman, Greenwald & Associates, Adams, Copeland, & VanDerhei, 2013). This chapter first reviews the place of private pensions in the overall retirement income picture, recent trends in private pension coverage, and the adequacy of private pensions in helping to meet the retirement needs of vulnerable populations. The second half of the chapter provides a comprehensive overview of the Social Security system. These issues are of special importance to geriatric social workers, who must be knowledgeable about the income adequacy and security challenges that their clients are facing.

PRIVATE RETIREMENT BENEFITS

ROBERT B. HUDSON

DIANA M. DINITTO

Private Retirement and Social Security Programs

The American Express Company established the first private pension plan in the United States in 1875, although most of the initial plans were concentrated in the railroad industry (Sass, 1997). The number of workers covered under these defined benefit plans (DBPs) grew slowly over the next several decades (roughly 3 million workers covered by the time of Social Security's enactment in 1935); grew dramatically in the years during and after World War II (coverage growing from roughly 4 million in the late 1930s to 10 million by 1950); and climbed to 31 million workers by 1975, having since leveled off more recently at roughly 40 million participants (US Department of Labor [DOL], 2012). The early plans, especially in the railroad industry, were justified (to shareholders) as a way of increasing workers' loyalty and to reduce strikes and high turnover, which plagued the industry in those years. While pensions proved ineffective in meeting these objectives, they

57

did play a role in supporting mandatory retirement provisions directed at older workers who were deemed less productive.

By the late-1960s a number of problems had emerged involving both worker protection and plan solvency. When companies went bankrupt (e.g., Studebaker Automobile Company in 1963) or fraud was rampant (Teamsters' Union Pension Fund in 1964), workers were left unprotected. Long vesting periods also left many workers at risk should they be laid off or fired after years of service. These concerns led in 1974 to the passage of the nation's principal private pension legislation—the Employee Retirement Income Security Act (ERISA). Among other provisions, ERISA:

- established pension plan termination insurance through the newly created Pension Benefit Guarantee Corporation
- set minimum vesting standards (number of years required for pension benefits)
- strengthened funding and fiduciary standards within plans
- required plans to report to participants their accrued benefits and vesting status
- permitted employees, upon job separation, to transfer their pension rights on a tax-free basis from one plan to another.
- created tax-deferred individual retirement accounts (IRAs)

As Schulz (1988) pointed out, however, ERISA did not address all private pension problems. Employers were not required to offer a plan, only to adhere to these regulations if they do offer one. As well, state and local government plans were excluded from coverage, survivors' provisions were weak, and—unlike Social Security—pension benefits were not indexed to increases in the cost of living.

The post-1970s period has been marked by a leveling off in the expansion of private pension coverage among workers and by a dramatic shift in the *type* of private pension coverage being offered to workers. Well into the 1970s, there was hope that expansion—coverage had tripled between the early 1950s and the mid-1970s—would continue. Yet, economic stagnation, changes in the domestic and international competitive marketplace, and employers' perceived needs for more flexible labor force policies precluded this further expansion in coverage. The number of DBP private plans declined precipitously from 170,000 in 1985 to 47,000 in 2010, while the number of defined contribution plans (DCPs), made possible by ERISA provisions, escalated dramatically, rising from only 208,000 in 1975 to 660,000 in 2010 (DOL, 2012).

These two trends are somewhat offsetting, but the overall reality is that pension coverage has been in slow decline. Well under one-half of workers continue to be without any private pension coverage, including the growing proportion who are subject to the vagaries of their investment decisions inherent in DCP design.

Types of Private Pensions

Defined benefit plans (DBP) and defined contribution plans (DCP) constitute the two principal types of employer-sponsored pension plans available in the United States These do not include two other well-known retirement vehicles: individual retirement accounts (available generally to workers with no employer-sponsored plan) and Keogh Plans (available to the self-employed or small business owners). Public sector plans may also be categorized as DBPs (Social Security is the world's largest defined benefit plan) or DCPs (employees of the federal government now contribute to such plans), but the discussion here is confined to private sector plans only.

In a DBP, employers promise employees a given ("guaranteed") benefit amount upon retirement in accordance with a benefit formula stated in the plan. The three principal types of DBPs are:

1. Flat-benefit formula—a flat dollar amount is paid for each year of service recognized under the plan;
2. Career-average formulas—employees earn a percentage of the pay recognized for each year they are plan participants, or the formula averages the participant's earnings over the period of plan participation. At retirement, the benefit equals a percentage of the career-average pay, multiplied by the participant's number of years of service;
3. Final-pay formulas—benefits are based on average earnings during a specified number of years (presumably the time period when earnings are the highest) at the end of a participant's career. This plan has the effect of providing preretirement inflation protection to the employee, but it can represent a higher cost to the employer (Employee Benefit Research Institute [EBRI], 1997a).

In the case of DCPs, employers make provision for contributions to an account established for each participating employee. The final retirement benefit equals the total of employer contributions, employee contributions (if any), and investment gains and losses. Employer contributions are often based on a specific formula, such as a percentage of employee salary or company profits. Because of these features, future benefits of a DCP cannot be calculated in advance (EBRI, 1997a). Strictly speaking, only DBPs are "pensions" by virtue of their paying a monthly benefit that is based on a formula tied to length of service and earnings; DCPs should be understood as tax-deferred savings plans providing benefits that are based on underlying assets, interest, dividends, and capital appreciation (Friedland, 1996). There are several types of DCPs, the most common being money-purchase plans (mandatory employer contributions as a percentage of worker salary), profit-sharing plans (amount derived from company profits), a thrift or savings plan (essentially an employee savings account, often with employer matching contributions), and 401(k) plans (a qualified deferral arrangement under this section of the tax code, which allows an employee to have a portion of compensation—otherwise payable in cash—contributed to a plan such as those immediately above; these contributions are most commonly treated as a pretax reduction in salary) (EBRI, 1997a, 1997b).

Data in Table 57.1 shows that the number of DBPs has declined notably since the early-1980s; the number of DCP plans has risen significantly; the number of individuals covered under DBPs has stagnated;

and the number of participants covered under DCPs has grown enormously.

Within the DCP category, assets grew from $74 billion in 1975 to $3.8 trillion in 2010. Finally, the move toward DCPs grew to the point where by 1997, DCP assets exceeded DBP assets for the first time (DOL, 2012).

The Employee Retirement Income Security Act of 1974 also established IRAs to give workers who did not have employer-based pensions an opportunity to save for retirement on a tax-deferred basis. Legislation in 1981 dramatically liberalized IRA eligibility to include workers who also had employer-based coverage. In 1986, restrictions for the latter group were again imposed, restricting the tax-deferral provision to those families with relatively low incomes. While considerable assets are held in IRA accounts (VanDerhei, 2001), much of this results from contributions made by middle- and upper-income workers in the early 1980s when deductibility extended across both income and pension-covered groups. The percentage of workers contributing to IRAs has remained consistently low since the 1990s, with the percentage ranging only from 6% in 1997 to 7% in 2003 and again in 2006 (US Congressional Budget Office [CBO], 2006).

Between 1997 and 2006, participation rates in all types of tax-favored retirement plans have ranged only from 50% to 52% (including public sector workers, whose pension coverage has been much higher than private sector workers), with no discernible trend over time; participation rates in employment-based plans for all workers—wage earners and the self-employed alike—ranged from

TABLE 57.1 Private Pension Plans and Participants

Number of Private Plans					
	1975	1985	1995	2005	2010
DBP (thousands)	103	170	69	48	47
DCP (thousands)	208	462	624	631	660
DCP (as % of Total)	67%	73%	90%	93%	93%
Number of Private Plan Participants					
DBP Participants (millions)	33	40	40	42	41
DCP Participants (millions)	12	35	48	75	88
DCP as % of Total	27%	47%	54%	50%	64%

Source: DOL (2012).

46% to 48%; and IRA participation ranged from 6% to 8% (CBO, 2006).

Private Pension Coverage

Although private pensions have developed over more than a century, a significant proportion of individuals and families have had no pension coverage or insufficient coverage. The "second leg of the retirement income stool" (Social Security being the first leg and individual savings being the third leg) is either too short or nonexistent. Not surprisingly, many of these same individuals are those toward whom social workers direct many of their service efforts: low-income individuals, women, populations of color, part-time workers, employees of small firms, and many—to use Barbara Ehrenreich's (2001) term—in sectors where workers are "nickeled and dimed." The contrast between these workers and the workers who are White, male, full-time, highly educated, and working in traditional main-line or emerging high-technology fields is stark.

Since the late 1970s, the percentage of private sector workers aged 25–64 who are participating in employer-based plans has remained essentially constant, although it has declined somewhat recently. However, there are important dynamics within this overall pattern of constancy. Female workers participate in retirement plans at a lower rate than males; however, among full-time, full-year workers, females had a higher rate of participation. Since 2001, women were more likely than men to participate in a retirement plan than males. Furthermore, when examining participation by earnings level, the proportion of women participating in a plan was higher at all but the lowest earnings level. This seeming disparity from the aggregate figures appears to result from women workers' overall lower earnings and/or lower rates of full-time work, categories in which participation rates are disproportionately low (EBRI, 2012; see Table 57.2).

Despite these relative improvements in private pension coverage for women, the proportion of older (age 65 and older) women who receive pension income remains decidedly lower than that of older men; this pattern cuts across education and marital status as well. The median pension income for older women also remains much lower than the median pension income for older men. For example, in 1976 and 2006, 35% and 44% of older men had a pension coverage, and the incomes they received were $6,515 and $9,855, whereas in those same years, only 9% and 28% of older women had a pension coverage, and the incomes they received were $4,236 and $4,501 (Women's Institute for a Secure Retirement [WISER], 2008).

Marked differences in participation are also seen by race and ethnicity. Most notably, Hispanic workers were significantly less likely to participate in a retirement plan than either Black or White workers. This gap persists at all earnings levels, whereas the Black and White rates remain comparable across incomes, in fact, with Blacks having slightly higher rates than Whites at the higher income levels. Table 57.3 shows the relative effects of race/ethnicity and income on plan participation.

The more dramatic picture painted by these data shows the critical place of income and employment status in determining pension coverage. There are greater similarities by income across race and ethnic groups than there are by race and ethnicity within income groups. Consistent with these findings is a trend reported by Snyder (1993) showing a 66% increase in the number of retired Black men receiving pension income between 1982 and 1990, and a 250% increase between 1970 and 1990. However, as with the comparison between men and women, pension incomes by race and ethnicity have not improved as much as has pension plan coverage. Thus, among retirees age 65 or over receiving pension income, Whites receive $560, Blacks $507, Hispanics $375, and "Other" $416 (EBRI, 2003).

Overall, there have been notable improvements in recent years in the numbers of women and people of color covered by private pension plans. The more

TABLE 57.2 Percentage of Wage and Salary Workers Ages 21–64 Who Participated in an Employment-Based Retirement Plan, by Annual Earnings and Gender, 2011

	Male	Female
Less than $10K	8.8	8.6
$10-$19K	13.8	20.4
$20-$29K	29.0	39.1
$30-$39K	42.5	54.1
$40-$49K	52.9	64.2
$50-$75K	62.3	70.3
$75K or more	68.9	72.4

Source: EBRI (2012, Figure 5).

TABLE 57.3 Percentage of Wage and Salary Workers Ages 21–64 Who Participated in an Employment-Based Retirement Plan, by Race/Ethnicity and Annual Earnings

	White	Black	Hispanic	Other
>$20K	16.4	14.0	7.9	11.1
$20-$39K	45.2	44.0	27.5	37.5
$40-$75K	65.0	64	50.5	55.9
$75K>	70.5	71.3	62.7	69.1

Source: EBRI (2012, Figure 9).

sobering finding is that coverage declines markedly with decreasing income, and there are notably higher proportions of women and people of color earning low wages who thus remain disproportionately underprotected. Also, the improvements seen in pension coverage and income among the Black population are largely not the case among Hispanic workers and retirees.

SOCIAL SECURITY

The stock market crash of 1929 and the widespread indigence that followed prompted the federal government to make its first major forays into social welfare, once considered the domain of local and state governments. On August 14, 1935, President Franklin D. Roosevelt signed the Social Security Act. This watershed event established the Social Security retirement program and a number of other social welfare programs. Although Congress and the president could have structured this federally operated retirement program for the masses in a number of ways, they chose to do so in the tradition of social insurance programs first established under the regime of conservative German Chancellor Otto von Bismarck in the late 1800s. Social insurance may be considered a conservative approach because it protects the government and taxpayers from having to support people due to indigence.

Originally, Social Security was intended to be a self-financing program. Funds would be kept in trust and would earn interest, and these monies would be used to pay benefits. However, it did not take long to realize that these funds were needed to help boost the country's ailing economy. Social Security became a "pay as you go" program in which current generations of workers pay for the retirement benefits of previous generations of workers.

During the first decades of the Social Security program, the emphasis was on increasing the program's scope. More workers were covered under the program (today 91% of workers pay into the program; SSA, 2013). Benefits were increased substantially. While initially designed to pay benefits only to retirees, in 1939, dependents of retired workers and survivors of workers who died before age 65 were added to the program. Beginning in the 1950s, disabled workers were added to the program, and workers were allowed to retire, albeit with lower benefits, beginning at age 62.

As (1) the number of Social Security retirees continued to grow and their life spans increased, (2) fertility rates dropped resulting in fewer workers available to support the Social Security program, and (3) Congress increased benefits paid to retirees, it became clear that steps were needed to ensure that Social Security remained solvent. In an important bipartisan effort in 1983 under the Reagan administration, Congress took action to strengthen the program's actuarial position, such as making the benefit inflation adjustment factor more conservative, gradually raising from 65 to 67 the age at which full retirement benefits can be received, and gradually reducing benefits that can be received at age 62 from 80% to 70% of full retirement benefits (Social Security Advisory Board, 2010). Though it was once unthinkable to consider taxing Social Security benefits, in 1993, as part of President Clinton's deficit reduction plan, a portion of the benefits of some retirees with additional income became subject to taxation.

How the Social Security Program Works

Under the Social Security program, workers and their employers both contribute to the program during the employee's working years. Rather than deposit these funds into a separate account for each worker (like a bank account), the Social Security Administration maintains a record of each worker's contributions, and the government promises to pay benefits when a worker meets the requirements for retirement or disability. Spouses and dependents (usually minor or older disabled children) of retired, disabled, and deceased workers may also receive benefits.

Workers and their employers each contribute 6.2% (a total of 12.4) of the employee's income to

Social Security: 5.35% goes to the pay for Old Age and Survivors Insurance (OASI), the retirement portion of the program, and .85 goes to pay for Disability Insurance (DI). These contributions, often called Social Security or payroll taxes, are deducted directly from workers' paychecks. Self-employed individuals pay 12.4% of their income (in essence both the employer and employee share). Another 1.45% is assessed to both employees and employers for the health insurance program known as Medicare; the self-employed are taxed at 2.9%. Medicare is discussed in Chapter 58. Here we focus on OASI and DI, known as Old Age, Survivors, and Disability Insurance (OASDI).

Workers qualify for Social Security retirement or disability benefits once they have earned sufficient credits (usually equivalent to 10 years of work for retirement benefits; the number of credits varies by age for disability benefits). Beginning at age 62, the spouse of a retired worker can claim benefits of 50% of the amount the retired worker receives. Widows and widowers (generally beginning at age 60 or at age 50 if they are disabled) are also entitled to benefits based on their spouse's earnings, though widows and widowers caring for children under age 16 can receive benefits at any age. Minor children are also entitled to benefits.

The Concept of Social Insurance

Social insurance programs like Social Security differ from private insurance in a number of ways. Private insurance is self-financed, risk is greater and is spread over a smaller group of people, and people are generally not required to participate. Social insurance benefits are supported by others' contributions, there is less risk and risk is spread over a very large group of participants, and most workers are required to participate. Since 1972, Social Security benefits are automatically adjusted for inflation, while private insurance benefits are generally not adjusted for inflation. Social Security follows workers from job to job while workers may not benefit from private pension programs if they do not remain with the same employer for a specified period of time.

Social insurance is also different from public assistance programs. Social Security is considered a universal program, because the vast majority of the population participates in it regardless of their

wealth, based on the contributions they have made. Public assistance is considered residual, because only people who are poor participate in it. Although public assistance recipients may have paid income taxes, which are used to finance public assistance, there are no required contributions and no accounts earmarked with their names. Public assistance recipients often experience the stigma associated with receiving "welfare," while most people feel entitled to receive Social Security benefits because they have paid directly into the program.

Adequacy, equity, and efficiency are major goals of social insurance programs like Social Security (Social Security Advisory Board, 2010). It is important that Social Security benefits be sufficiently adequate to assist Americans in retirement or if they become disabled prior to retirement age. Social Security can be said to meet this goal, because of all the federal government's social welfare programs, it has the greatest affect in reducing poverty. In 2012, Social Security lifted 15.3 million individuals aged 65 and older out of poverty and reduced the poverty rate from just over 44% of this age group to just under 9% (Van de Water, Sherman, & Ruffing, 2013). Social Security accounts for at least 90% of the income of 23% of older married couples and 46% of those who are not married and at least 50% of the income of 53% of older married couples and 74% of those who are not married (SSA, 2013). In June of 2013, the average monthly payment was $1,269 for a retired worker and $1,129 for a disabled worker (SSA, 2013). The maximum monthly payment a retiree could receive was $2,533 (SSA, n.d.).

Equity refers to treating Social Security participants fairly, both those who earn lower wages and pay Social Security taxes at the same rate as higher-income workers, and higher-income workers who pay Social Security taxes on a greater amount of income than lower-income workers. The OASDI taxes are considered regressive because they are assessed on all the worker's earnings up to prescribed limits but not on income above this level or on other income sources (e.g., interest on savings or income from investments) that those in higher income brackets are more likely to receive. Social Security taxes are also considered regressive because unlike the federal personal income tax, they are assessed at a flat rate without consideration of factors such as the number of dependents a worker is supporting. At Social Security's inception the payroll tax was 1%, and the taxable wage base was $3,000 so that employees and employers paid no more than an annual tax of $30. In 2013, workers and employers paid OASDI taxes of 6.2% on income up to $113,700. While the Social Security payroll tax is regressive, benefits paid on retirement or disability are progressive. In 2013, Social Security replaced wages at about 56% for low earners, 42% for medium earners, and about 35% for high earners.

Gender equity also raises concerns. For example, although women's labor force participation has increased over the years, women often earn less than men; therefore, their Social Security benefits are lower, and they are more likely to be in poverty (Government Accountability Office [GAO], 2012). Also of concern is that a divorced individual can collect benefits based on her or his former spouse's earnings only if the marriage lasted at least 10 years. It is usually former wives rather than former husbands who collect on their spouses' earnings record following divorce. In addition, it is usually the wife who stays at home to care for children or elderly family members. Spouses who stay at home can collect Social Security benefits based on their spouse's earning record, but they accrue no Social Security credits of their own when not in the paid labor force (GAO, 2007). While remaining out of the paid labor force may be considered a personal choice, others have suggested that giving Social Security credits to the spouse who remained at home to perform essential caregiving roles might serve them better in retirement. Other options to address gender inequities include providing additional Social Security benefits to those in greatest economic need (GAO, 2012).

Race and ethnicity have also been debated as equity issues in Social Security for several reasons. For example, some argue that Social Security treats African Americans unfairly because they have shorter life spans than Whites and therefore collect Social Security retirement benefits for shorter periods even though they paid into the program at the same rates as Whites (Tanner, 2001). Hispanics as a group are considerably younger than Whites, while the retired population is disproportionately White and more affluent. Both African Americans and Hispanics tend to earn less than Whites, and they are more likely to work at physically demanding jobs that may cause them to retire earlier, also resulting in lower benefits at retirement. However, analyses indicate that African Americans' overall rate of return

on their Social Security contributions is the same or slightly higher than that of Whites for retirement and survivors' benefits and higher for disability benefits (Spriggs & Furman, 2006). Hispanics also have higher rates of disability but longer life expectancies than Whites (Center on Budget and Policy Priorities, 2012), and they, too, receive higher rates of return on their tax contributions (Torres-Gil, Greenstein, & Kamin, 2005).

Intergenerational equity is another concern. The number of workers now supporting each retired worker has dropped substantially, placing a greater burden on the current workforce. Any adjustments to the program must be considered in light of what is fair to current and future generations of retirees and workers.

Efficiency means that the program should be administered in a way that provides good service to beneficiaries while also conserving the amount spent on administrative functions. Slightly less than one cent per dollar goes to program administration, but concerns are that staff may be too few to provide timely help to the growing numbers of individuals participating in Social Security (SSA, 2010).

Challenges Facing Social Security

Today, 90% of adults aged 65 and older receive Social Security benefits (SSA, 2013). In 2013, more than 57 million Americans received Social Security benefits totaling $816 billion. Most (37 million) were retired workers, 8.9 million were disabled workers, and the remaining 11.2 million were their survivors or dependents. With such broad participation, it is no wonder that the Social Security program enjoys strong bipartisan support. Conservatives often support social insurance as a form of thrift, and liberals support it because it redistributes income. But confidence that the Social Security program will be able to provide benefits at today's level has waned (Helman et al., 2013). Projections are that in 2021 the combined OASDI trust funds plus interest will pay out more than collected, and in 2033, the combined OASDI trust funds will be depleted (there will not be enough to pay the benefits due) (Social Security and Medicare Boards of Trustees, 2013).

Social Security faces challenges in maintaining solvency in the years ahead for two primary reasons.

One is that declining birth (fertility) rates mean that there are fewer workers per retiree to support the program. In 1950, there were 16.5 workers for each retiree. Today, that figure has dropped to 2.8 workers, and by 2033, the figure will drop further to 2.1 workers (SSA, 2013). Second, as life expectancy increases, retirees are collecting Social Security benefits over a longer period of time. In 1940 an individual who was 65 years old could expect to live another 14 years to age 79. Today, a 65-year-old can expect to live until age 85 (SSA). Those eligible to receive Social Security retirement benefits have been encouraged to stay in the workforce longer with the promise of increased benefits for delaying retirement, but most people begin collecting benefits before they reach their full retirement age. The amount retirees can earn while collecting Social Security benefits has also been increased because these earnings are subject to Social Security taxes, which also help to fund the Social Security program. In fact, since 2000, individuals can earn as much as they wish after reaching full retirement age with no loss of Social Security benefits (though a portion of benefits may be subject to taxes depending on the type and amount of any additional income).

To keep the program solvent, Congress must raise more revenues, reduce benefits, or do both (Social Security Advisory Board, 2010). Over the years, Congress has made adjustments, such as raising the payroll tax rate. Each year the taxable wage base is also adjusted according to the national average wage index, and most years this figure increases. Congress could again raise the payroll tax rate; escalate the rate at which the taxable wage base rises or collect Social Security taxes on all earned income; increase the full retirement age, perhaps to age 70; tax a greater proportion of Social Security benefits or tax the benefits of higher income retirees at higher rates; reduce benefits for all but the most needy; employ a combination of these options; or adopt a variety of other approaches. One option that received a good deal of attention during the George W. Bush administration was to adopt some form of privatization. This would allow the government to invest the funds not currently being used to make benefit payments in investments that would be somewhat riskier than the low-risk, low-interest bonds currently used. Since the market failures of 2008, enthusiasm for this option has waned. Another option is a prefunded system where each generation would fund its own retirement rather than today's system in which the

current generations of workers support those who are retired; however, the cost to make this conversion comes with a hefty initial price tag.

The Social Security Advisory Board (2010) has advised that action to ensure Social Security solvency be taken sooner rather than later. This will allow changes to be phased in more gradually, economic stability to be maintained, and confidence in Social Security to be enhanced and will give workers and employers more time to make the necessary adjustments.

CONCLUSION

The Social Security retirement and disability programs are vitally important components of the US social welfare system. Federal law requires that most Americans participate in this US government–administered social insurance program. They pay Social Security taxes during their working years and receive benefits upon retirement or disability. Others receive benefits as a dependent of a retired or disabled worker or as a survivor of a deceased worker. The nearly universal, mandatory participation in Social Security is a hallmark of the program and also distinguishes Social Security from voluntary and private retirement programs. Because so many Americans rely on Social Security as a main source of retirement income and because it the country's most effective antipoverty program, Americans must think carefully about how to preserve this social contract for future generations.

Though Social Security rules and benefits are the same throughout the United States and the program is efficiently administered, social workers help many vulnerable clients and their family members interface with the Social Security system. Social workers help ensure that individuals and families understand how the program works and that they receive the benefits to which they are entitled. Social workers also know about Social Security because they, too, participate in it. Social workers also educate the public about the Social Security programs and advocate for ways to keep Social Security viable. This includes careful analysis of the array of alternatives proposed to maintain solvency in order to be fair to all groups (men and women, people of all racial and ethnic groups, and members of each generation) who participate in the system. Given longer life spans, there are now many fewer workers available to support the growing retired population, and there are no easy solutions to ensuring that Social Security will remain financially healthy in the years ahead. Likely several strategies will be adopted to ensure that the burdens and benefits of keeping Social Security viable are widely distributed. To maintain strong bipartisan support, Social Security must maintain its character as a social insurance program for all Americans. Social workers and many others are also concerned that Social Security never loses sight of its role in helping to alleviate poverty among those who have paid into the system in order to support previous generations.

In addition, most of the data and trends portrayed in this chapter paint a troubling picture of the United States' private pension system. Coverage and participation remain low and uneven. By various measures more than one-half of workers and retirees are uncovered or only minimally covered. The move from defined benefit to defined contribution programs creates investment risks for many workers, especially because the level of "financial illiteracy" among workers is distressingly high. Good news is seen in women's coverage increasing notably in recent years (with men's declining, however). However, disparity in asset accumulation by gender (and by race and ethnicity) remains troublingly large. That participation and accumulation is highly correlated by income across gender and ethnic lines is positive in that rising incomes may raise all demographic clusters, but in the absence of rising incomes and with growing levels of income inequality in the current period it appears as more than an offsetting weight to whatever grounds for optimism there might be.

The workings of the private pension system in the United States and the patterns of participation in these plans have major implications for geriatric social workers. Not surprisingly, these private sector vehicles—sweetened with inversely redistributive tax benefits—work to the advantage of relatively privileged groups in American society. Whether by gender, race, income, or education, the privileged tend to prevail.

Two implications in particular emerge for geriatric social work. The first is to be cognizant of the ways in which the workings of the system—notably which employers offer plans—work to the advantage of the better-off. It is imperative that social workers involved with low-income individuals and communities work to modify seeming inequities and, more immediately, to encourage clients—where they are

able—to participate in plans in order to prepare for their retirement years.

The second implication is for geriatric social workers themselves. A growing body of literature is predicting that alarming numbers of Americans will be forced to rely too heavily on Social Security benefits in their retirement years. Since the maximum retirement benefit available under Social Security is about $30,000 (and the average benefit is $13,000), large numbers of workers approaching retirement will find their standard of living in major jeopardy. And, as research by Martha Ozawa (1993) has documented, social workers are less financially prepared for retirement than professionals in either nursing or education. Not only is the personal professional; here, the professional is personal.

REFERENCES

Center on Budget and Policy Priorities. (2012). *Policy basics: Top ten facts about Social Security*. Washington, DC: Author. Retrieved December 6, 2013, from http://www.cbpp.org/cms/?fa=view&id=3261

DeWitt, L. (1996). *Research Note #1: Origins of the three-legged stool metaphor for Social Security*. Baltimore, MD: Social Security Administration. Retrieved December 4, 2013, from http://www.ssa.gov/history/stool.html

Ehrenreich, B. (2001). *Nickeled and dimed: On (not) getting by in America*. New York, NY: Metropolitan Books.

Employee Benefit Research Institute (EBRI). (1997a). Pension plans. In *Fundamentals of employee benefit programs* (5th ed., Ch. 4). Washington, DC: Author.

Employee Benefit Research Institute (EBRI). (1997b). Defined benefit and defined contribution plans: Understanding the differences. In *Fundamentals of employee benefit programs* (5th ed., Ch. 5). Washington, DC: Author.

Employee Benefit Research Institute (EBRI). (2003). *EBRI notes*. Washington, DC: Author.

Employee Benefit Research Institute (EBRI). (2012). *Issue brief, #378*. Washington, DC: Author.

Friedland, R. (1996). Privatizing social insurance. *Public Policy and Aging Report, 7*(4), 11–15.

Government Accountability Office (GAO). (2007). *Retirement security: Women face challenges in ensuring financial security in retirement*. Washington, DC: Author. Retrieved December 5, 2013, from http://www.gao.gov/new.items/d08105.pdf

Government Accountability Office (GAO). (2012). *Retirement security: Women still face challenges.*

Washington, DC: Author. Retrieved December 5, 2013, from http://www.gao.gov/assets/600/592726.pdf

Helman, R., Greenwald, M., and Associates, Adams, N., Copeland, C., & VanDerhei, J. (2013). *The 2013 retirement confidence survey: Perceived savings needs outpace reality for many.* Issue Brief 384. Washington, DC: Employee Benefit Research Institute–Education and Research Fund. Retrieved December 3, 2013, from http://www.ebri.org/pdf/briefspdf/EBRI_IB_03-13.No384.RCS2.pdf

Ozawa, M. N. (1993). Earnings history of social workers: A comparison to other professional groups. *Social Work, 38,* 542–551.

Sass, S. A. (1997). *The promise of private pensions.* Cambridge, MA: Harvard University Press.

Schulz, J. A. (1988). *The economics of aging* (4th ed.). New York, NY: Auburn House.

Snyder, D. C. (1993). The economic well-being of retired workers by race and Hispanic origin. In R. V. Burkhauser & D. L. Salisbury (Eds.), *Pensions in a changing economy.* Washington, DC: National Academy on Aging.

Social Security Administration (SSA). (n.d.). *2013 Social Security changes.* Baltimore, MD: Author. Retrieved December 5, 2013, from http://www.ssa.gov/pressoffice/factsheets/colafacts2013.pdf

Social Security Administration (SSA). (2010). Administering Social Security: Challenges yesterday and today. *Social Security Bulletin, 70,* 27–78. Retreived December 6, 2013, from http://www.ssa.gov/policy/docs/ssb/v70n3/v70n3p27.html

Social Security Administration (SSA). (2013). *Social Security basic facts.* Washington, DC: Author. Retrieved December 5, 2013, from http://www.ssa.gov/pressoffice/basicfact.htm

Social Security Advisory Board. (2010). *Social Security: Why action should be taken soon.* Retrieved December 3, 2013, from http://www.ssab.gov/Documents/Sooner_Later_2010.pdf

Social Security and Medicare Boards of Trustees. (2013). *Status of the Social Security and Medicare programs: A summary of the 2012 annual reports.* Retrieved September 28, 2013, from http://www.ssa.gov/oact/trsum/index.html

Spriggs, W., & Furman, J. (2006). *African Americans and Social Security: The implications of reform proposals.* Washington, DC: Center on Budget and Policy Priorities. Retrieved December 5, 2013, from http://www.cbpp.org/cms/?fa=view&id=885

Tanner, M. (2001). *Disparate impact: Social Security and African Americans.* Washington, DC: Cato Institute. Retrieved December 5, 2013, from http://object.cato.org/sites/cato.org/files/pubs/pdf/bp61.pdf

Torres-Gil, F., Greenstien, R., & Kamin, D. (2005). *The importance of Social Security to the Hispanic community.* Washington, DC: Center on Budget and Policy Priorities. Retrieved December 5, 2013, from http://www.cbpp.org/cms/?fa=view&id=436

US Congressional Budget Office (CBO). (2006). *Use of tax incentives for retirement saving in 2006.* Washington, DC: CBO.

US Department of Labor (DOL). (2012). *Private pension plan bulletin historical tables and graphs: Tables E1, E5.* Washington, DC: US Dept. of Labor, Employee Benefits Security Administration.

VanDerhei, J. (2001). *The changing face of retirement.* Issue Brief #232. Washington, DC: Employee Benefit Research Institute.

Van de Water, P. N., Sherman, A., & Ruffing, K. (2013). *Social Security keeps 22 million Americans out of poverty: A State-by-state analysis.* Washington, DC: Center on Budget and Policy Priorities. Retrieved December 5, 2013, from http://www.cbpp.org/files/10-25-13ss.pdf

Women's Institute for a Secure Retirement (WISER). (2008). *Minority women and retirement income.* Washington, DC: WISER.

This chapter provides an overview of Medicare, which was enacted as part of Title XVIII of the Social Security Act of 1965. It also discusses Medicare's new policy developments and its effects on older adults.

OVERVIEW OF MEDICARE

Medicare is a federal health insurance program for older persons and persons with disabilities enacted under Title XVIII of the Social Security Act of 1965. It is an entitlement program and covers persons regardless of income or prior health condition. The program currently covers more than 50 million Americans (Kaiser Family Foundation, 2012a). In 2012, Medicare spending accounted for 16% of the total federal spending and 21% of total national health spending (Kaiser Family Foundation, 2012c).

Medicare consists of four parts (Figure 58.1): (1) Part A—Hospital insurance program; (2) Part B—Supplementary Medical insurance; (3) Part C—Medicare Advantage; and (4) Part D—Outpatient prescription drugs program. General revenues, payroll tax contributions, beneficiary premiums, and other sources finance Medicare.

Almost any person age 65 and over is entitled to Part A if either the person or the person's spouse is eligible for Social Security payments. Persons who are 65 and under who receive Social Security disability payments are also generally covered after a 2-year waiting period. All persons regardless of age who have end-stage renal disease (ESRD) are entitled to Part A. Persons who are not automatically entitled to enroll in Part A can voluntarily obtain coverage by paying full actuarial cost.

Medicare Part B is voluntary. All persons age 65 and over who are enrolled in Part A are eligible to enroll in Part B by paying a monthly premium. About 95% of Part A beneficiaries voluntarily enroll in Part B. Persons who voluntarily enroll in Part A must enroll in Part B.

All beneficiaries who have Medicare Part A and Part B must participate in Part D (prescription drug plan) unless they can document that they have prescription drug plan coverage from another source.

Medicare Part A is a hospital insurance program. It covers inpatient hospital stays, skilled nursing facility stays, home health visits (also covered under Part B), and hospice care. Part A is financed mainly through 1.45% of payroll tax paid by each the employee and employer (total 2.9%),

JI SEON LEE

Policies Affecting Health, Mental Health, and Caregiving: Medicare

58

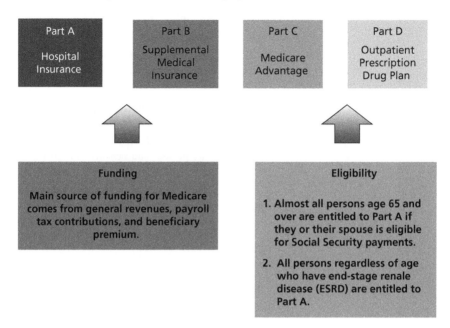

FIGURE 58.1 STRUCTURE OF MEDICARE.

which is deposited into the Hospital Insurance Trust Fund. Starting in 2013, the payroll tax increased by 0.9% for high-income earners (more than $200,000 for an individual or $250,000 as a couple).

Medicare Part B is a supplementary medical insurance program. It covers physician and outpatient hospital care, preventative services, lab tests, medical supplies, and home healthcare (for those not covered under Part A). Part B is primarily financed through beneficiary premiums and general revenues. The monthly Part B premium was $104.90 in 2013. Higher income earners ($85,000 for individual or $170,000 for couples) pay higher monthly premiums ranging from $146.90 to $335.70 a month (Kaiser Family Foundation, 2012c).

There are two major types of Medicare plans beneficiaries can choose from: (1) Original Medicare and (2) Medicare Advantage. Regardless of which type of Medicare plan a person is enrolled in, as long as one has Medicare Part A and Part B, that person has a right to the same basic benefits. The Original Medicare plan is structured as a traditional fee for service plan offered by the federal government. A person eligible to enroll in Medicare will be automatically enrolled in this plan. The pros to this plan include access to one's choice of any doctor or hospital. The cons to this plan include the large out-of-pocket cost stemming from large hospital

deductibles, annual deductibles for doctor's visits, and copayments for most outpatient medical care. It also has limited coverage.

Medicare Part C, also called Medicare Advantage, is a private Medicare managed care plan. To participate in a Medicare Advantage plan, beneficiaries must have both Medicare Part A and Part B. Health maintenance organizations (HMOs) have been an option under Medicare since the 1970s. But the role of these private plans expanded greatly under the Balanced Budget Act (BBA) of 1997 by including other plans such as preferred provider organizations (PPOs), private fee for service plans (PFFS), provider-sponsored organizations (PSOs), and medical savings accounts. The Medicare Prescription Drug, Improvement, and Moderation Act of 2003 created another option, called regional PPOs. The pros of participating in a Medicare Advantage plan include that it is more affordable than the Original Medicare plan with lower monthly premiums and deductibles. It also covers all benefits traditional Medicare plans cover and provides additional coverage that is not available in the traditional plan. Furthermore, beneficiaries do not need to file paperwork to Medicare directly. However, the cons to this plan include that it provides access only to plan-participating providers and restricts access to specialists and services.

Medicare Part D is an outpatient prescription drug plan. Enacted through the

Medicare Prescription Drug, Improvement, and Modernization Act of 2003, it was implemented in 2006. Each beneficiary pays a deductible for the first $250 in drug costs; pays 25% of total drug costs between $250 and $2,970; and pays 47.5% of total brand-name drug costs if the beneficiary spends more than $2,970 in prescription drugs in a given year. The beneficiary who spends between $2,970 and $6,733 is in what is called a "doughnut hole," that is, benefits paid to the beneficiary under Part D are limited. However, once spending surpasses $6,733 the beneficiary receives benefits under Part D catastrophic coverage and pays 5% of cost.

There is a penalty for late enrollment in Part D. Beneficiaries will owe a late enrollment penalty if at any time the initial enrollment period is over and there is a period of 63 days or more in row without Part D or other credible prescription drug coverage. The cost of the late enrollment penalty depends on how long the beneficiary went without credible prescription drug coverage. The penalty is calculated by multiplying 1% of the "national base beneficiary premium" times the number of full, uncovered months.

Beneficiary premiums, general revenues, and state payments finance Part D. The average premium for a prescription drug plan is about $40 a month. In 2013, high-income beneficiaries paid a premium surcharge ranging from $11.60 to $66.60 a month.

As of 2012, 63% of all Medicare beneficiaries were enrolled in Medicare Part D plans. Of this total, 37% were enrolled in Medicare Advantage drug plans. Another 30% of Medicare beneficiaries had drug coverage through employer plans, retiree plans in which their employers received subsidies, or plans through Veterans Affairs. However, an estimated 10% of the Medicare beneficiaries still did not have credible coverage as of 2010 (Kaiser Family Foundation, 2012b).

Choosing Medicare Coverage

There are two main ways to get Medicare coverage: Original Medicare or a Medicare Advantage plan. See Figure 58.2 for pathways to coverage.

Supplemental Coverage to Medicare

Medicare beneficiaries rely on some form of public or private supplemental insurance to cover the gaps in Medicare's coverage and to reduce out-of-pocket costs. This supplemental coverage may be obtained through Medigap policies, Medicaid, Medicare Advantage, or employer-sponsored health insurance. A "Medicare Supplement Insurance" policy (also called Medigap) is private health insurance that's

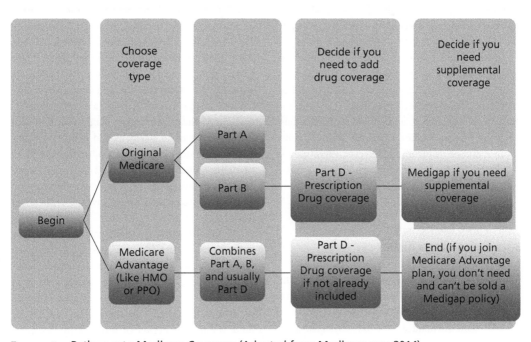

FIGURE 58.2 Pathways to Medicare Coverage (Adapted from Medicare.gov, 2014).

designed to supplement Original Medicare. This means it helps pay some of the healthcare costs that Original Medicare does not cover, like copayments, coinsurance, and deductibles. Generally, Medigap policies do not cover long-term care (like care in a nursing home), vision or dental care, hearing aids, eyeglasses, or private-duty nursing.

According to Jacobson, Huang, and Neuman (2014), in 2010, 86% of Medicare beneficiaries had some additional coverage to supplement Medicare. Twenty-three percent had coverage from Medigap policies, 26% from employer-sponsored plans, 14% from Medicaid only, and 13% from Medicare Advantage.

Nationwide, nearly one in four of all Medicare beneficiaries had a Medigap policy in 2010. In some states, enrollment was much higher than the national average. About half of all beneficiaries in five states had a Medigap policy (Iowa, Kansas, North Dakota, Nebraska, and South Dakota). Most Medigap enrollees live on incomes below $40,000 per person, and nearly half have incomes below $20,000 per person (Jacobson, Huang, & Newman, 2014).

Medicaid also provides supplemental coverage for Medicare beneficiaries. Low-income and disabled Medicare beneficiaries are entitled to partial or full coverage under Medicaid. Some beneficiaries are dual-eligible for Medicare and Medicaid. Medicare is typically the payer of first choice when both Medicare and Medicaid provide benefits, then Medicaid picks up the portions not covered by Medicare (typically the long-term care benefits). Prescription drugs are also covered under Medicaid. There are also certain groups, based on income, who receive other limited benefits from Medicaid. They are called Qualified Medicare Beneficiaries, Specified Low-Income Medicare Beneficiaries, and Qualified Individuals. For these groups, Medicaid typically pays for coinsurance and/or deductibles. However, these groups do not qualify for prescription drug benefits under Medicaid.

MEDICARE SPENDING AND FINANCIAL CRISIS

Spending on Medicare accounts for 16% of the federal budget. Of Medicare spending in 2012, 26% was spent on hospital inpatient services, 23% on Medicare Advantage, 13% on physician payments, 10% on outpatient prescription drugs, 6%

on hospital outpatient services, 5% on skilled nursing faculties, 4% on home health care, and 13% on other services. Medicare spending per beneficiary is highly skewed—10% of beneficiaries from the traditional Medicare plan accounted for more than 50% of spending in 2009 (Kaiser Family Foundation, 2012c).

According to the Congressional Budget Office (CBO, 2013), total Medicare spending is projected to double from $551 billion in 2012 to $1 trillion in 2023 due to the growth in the Medicare population and rising healthcare costs. Between 2012 and 2023, Medicare's share of the federal budget is projected to increase by almost 3%, while Medicare spending as a share of GDP is projected to grow from 3.5% to 4.1%. To address the financial problems of Medicare, Congress adopted a prospective payment system (PPS) to replace a retrospective payment for hospitals in 1983. The PPS is a method of reimbursement in which Medicare payment is made based on a predetermined and fixed amount. Payment amounts for services are determined by the classification system for each particular service, such as diagnosis-related groups (DRGs) for inpatient hospital services. Though the Balanced Budget Act (BBA) of 1997, the PPS expanded from acute hospital payments to home health agencies, hospital outpatient, hospice, hospital outpatient, inpatient psychiatric facilities, inpatient rehabilitation facilities, long-term care hospitals, and skilled nursing facilities in 2000, each with their own specific rate. However, the financial burden of Medicare has not lessened, and the Affordable Care Act (ACA) was designed in part to reduce Medicare costs. The ACA includes $716 billion in net Medicare spending reductions over the next 10 years by reducing annual payments to hospitals, other providers, and Medicare Advantage plans. The ACA also includes reforms in payment and delivery systems aimed at reducing costs and improving quality of care. The Independent Payment Advisory Board established through the ACA reports to Congress on whether projected spending growth exceeds target levels.

Medicare's predicted financial crisis has long been discussed. Between 1994 and 1996, the trustees of Medicare projected that the hospital insurance (HI) fund would become insolvent by 2001 (Kaiser Family Foundation, 2005). By 2001, however, the trustees projected a 28-year solvency for the HI fund, the longest period of solvency in Medicare's history. In 2013, the trustees projected depletion by

2026—that is, in only 13 years (Medicare Boards of Trustees, 2012).

Why is there such fluctuation in projections of the health of Medicare funds? There are three main factors. The first factor is how the HI fund is financed—mainly through payroll taxes. Like social security's OASDI fund, the HI fund is a pay-as-you-go system, where current employees pay for the HI fund for the current Medicare beneficiaries. As a result, the aging of the country's population coupled with a lower number of workers supporting a beneficiary through their payrolls directly affects the health of the HI fund. According to the Medicare trustee report (Medicare Boards of Trustees, 2012), there were 3.3 workers per Medicare beneficiary in 2011. By 2030, the number of workers supporting a Medicare beneficiary was expected to fall to 2.3. Given these parameters, theoretically, the HI fund could become insolvent. In contrast, the Supplementary Medical Insurance (SMI) fund cannot be insolvent because its revenues come from premiums paid by beneficiaries and general tax revenues. Furthermore, Medicare requires general revenues and beneficiary premiums to be automatically adjusted to cover the cost for Medicare Part B. However, SMI costs are growing faster than those of the HI fund. To keep up with the rising costs, both beneficiaries' premiums and contributions from general revenues must increase. Therefore, the insolvency of the HI fund has become a proxy to the overall financial health of Medicare. The second factor is rising medical costs. Medicare's spending is projected to grow at a faster rate than that of the overall economy. According to the Centers for Medicare and Medicaid Services (CMS, 2012), health spending is projected to grow at an average rate of 5.8% from 2012 to 2022, 1 percentage point faster than the expected average annual growth in the GDP. Improving economic conditions, the ACA coverage expansions, and the aging of the population drive faster projected growth in health spending. The third factor is related to the economy. The better the economy, the higher the availability of general tax revenues. This potentially gives Medicare more funds to add to the trust fund.

NEW POLICY DEVELOPMENTS

The ACA protects Medicare coverage, because beneficiaries do not participate in the health insurance marketplace established by the Act. Whether Medicare beneficiaries participate in the Original Medicare or Medicare Advantage plan, they still have the same benefits as before the implementation of the ACA.

The ACA actually strengthens Medicare. The new law provides more preventive services, such as mammograms or colonoscopies, without charging beneficiaries for the Part B coinsurance or deductible. It also covers free annual wellness visits. Furthermore, beneficiaries can save money on brand-name prescription drugs. If the beneficiary is in the doughnut hole, they will receive a 50% discount when buying Part D–covered brand-name prescription drugs. This discount will increase every year until 2020, when the doughnut hole in Part D will be completely closed. It also supports physicians with new initiatives to support care coordination. Lastly, it helps build in financial protections for Medicare by providing savings on premiums and coinsurance. The ACA includes new fees for people on Medicare with relatively high incomes. If a beneficiary is single and has an annual income more than $85,000 or is married and has an annual income of more than $170,000, the beneficiary may pay higher premiums. Implementation of these new measures extended the life of the Medicare Trust Fund by 12 years (Medicare.gov, 2013).

Medicare's Hospital Readmission Reduction Program

The ACA required the Department of Health and Human Services to establish a hospital readmission reduction program. In 2012, about 20% Medicare patients were readmitted to the hospital within 1 month of discharge. The CMS (2013b) believed this number was too high and considered readmission an indicator of lack of quality of care. To reduce the number of costly and unnecessary hospital readmissions, the CMS, effective October 1, 2012, implemented a new program tied to Medicare payment to hospitals. This program is part of the CMS's efforts to paying for care based on quality not just on quantity.

The new program seeks to improve quality and lower costs for Medicare patients. Its intent is to ensure patients are discharged from hospitals when they are fully prepared and safe for continued care in the home or in a lesser care environment. The new program will provide hospitals with incentives to reduce the number of readmissions by better care coordination during transitions and increase the quality of care provided to Medicare beneficiaries. The incentive is a higher penalty that decreases the hospital's payments for all of its Medicare cases when the hospital is deemed to have "excessive readmissions" for acute myocardial infarction (AMI), congestive heart failure (CHF), and pneumonia patients. The "excessive readmissions" are adjusted for clinical factors and patient fragility. Hospital readmission is defined as an admission to a subsection of a hospital within 30 days of discharge from the same or another subsection hospital, including short-term inpatient acute care hospitals. The penalty started at 1% of Medicare payments in 2012. It went up to 2% of Medicare payments for a hospital that was determined to have "excessive readmissions." This increased to 3% in 2014. In 2015, additional penalties for conditions other than AMI, CHF, or pneumonia were added. These penalties affect only hospitals and not payment for physician services ("Health Policy Brief," 2013).

Hospitals are responding to these new programs by implementing new strategies to reduce readmissions such as better coordination of care, improved discharge planning, patient education, and follow-up with discharged patients. These efforts also include the use of electronic medical records to allow sharing of information and better coordination of care among providers.

Medicare Payment for Patient-Centered Medical Home

The patient-centered medical home (PCMH) model is being showcased as a way to improve healthcare by transforming primary care. The PCMH is not a physical place but rather a model that organizes delivery of primary healthcare. The concept was first introduced in 1967 by the American Academy of Pediatrics (AAP), which focused on medical records for children with special healthcare needs. Today's model expands on this foundation: The PCMH focuses on the patient and the family and is not only for patients with special healthcare needs but also for all who need healthcare. According to the Agency for Healthcare Research and Quality (AHRQ, 2013a), the PCMH has five functions and attributes:

1. Comprehensive Care –The PCMH is accountable for a large part of the patient's physical and mental healthcare needs. This includes prevention, wellness, acute care, and chronic care. The model requires a team of care providers. It is not considered a "gatekeeper" model.

2. Patient Centered—The model views the PCMH as a place that emphasizes care of the whole person. It recognizes the patient and the patient's family as part of the core care team.

3. Coordinated Care—The model coordinates care across the broader healthcare system including specialty care, hospitals, home healthcare, and community services. It emphasizes the proper and efficient care during transitions of systems.

4. Accessible Services—The model seeks to make primary care more accessible through lower wait times, enhanced office hours, and after hours care through telephone or e-mail.

5. Quality and Safety—The model is committed to providing safe clinical care through evidence-based care, performance measurement, and population health management.

The PCMH model is built on three major supports. First, the PCMH model seeks to use health information technology (IT), in particular, electronic medical records. Health information collected and managed through health IT can improve the healthcare process and outcomes of patients. Second, the PCMH model seeks to build a strong primary care workforce. This includes physician assistants, nurses, medical assistants, social workers, nutritionists, and care managers who are considered part of the core care team. Third, the PCMH model seeks to reform payment structures to achieve its goals. The current fee structure often does not reimburse for enhanced access, care coordination, or the contributions of the full team. It also has no incentive to reduce duplication of services across the continuum of care (AHRQ, 2013a). The new 2014 payment rates for physicians outlined by CMS change the current fee structure to include separate payments to providers who manage a patient's care outside of a face-to-face visit. This shows the CMS's support and recognition of the critical role of primary care in providing care to Medicare beneficiaries with multiple chronic illnesses (CMS, 2013a).

The promise of the PCMH model to increase access and quality and decrease the rate of growth in healthcare costs has gained attention from many. Health maintenance organizations, medical providers, community health centers, private integrated delivery systems, and the Veterans Health Administration use the PCMH model. In 2008, there were only 28 PCMH sites recognized by the National Committee on Quality Assurance (NCQA); by May 2013, there were more than 5,700 sites across the country (NCQA, 2013). In particular, for the 50 million older adults who have Medicare, the PCMH model can provide better care, especially for people with chronic illness and/or complex healthcare needs. Although PCMH is gaining rapid recognition, according to the results of the national demonstration conducted by the American Academy of Family Physicians (Nutting, et al., 2009), the transformation to a PCMH from a physician-centered care model requires continuous commitment on the part of the medical practice and all members of the care team. Substantial investments in funds, technology, and physician support are required for transformation to the PCMH to take place.

Medicare and Mental Health Benefits

The ACA provides for one of the largest expansions of mental health and substance use disorder coverage in a generation. The ACA builds on the Mental Health Parity and Addiction Equity Act of 2008 (MHPAEA, or the federal parity law), which requires group health plans and insurers that offer mental health and substance use disorder benefits to provide coverage that is comparable to coverage for general medical and surgical care.

There are three ways that the ACA increases access to mental health and substance abuse services. First, ACA expands coverage of mental health and substance abuse benefits and parity. All new small group and individual market plans are required to cover the 10 essential health benefit categories including mental health and substance use disorder services and are required to cover them at parity with medical and surgical benefits (Beronio, Po, Skopec, & Glied, 2013). Second, health plans must now cover preventive services such as depression screening for adults and behavioral assessments for children at no cost. Third, plans are not able to deny coverage for those with preexisting conditions such as mental illness.

Through the ACA, 32.1 million Americans were expected to gain access to coverage that includes mental health and/or substance use disorder benefits

that comply with federal parity requirements. In addition, 30.4 million Americans already receiving some mental health and substance abuse benefits would benefit from the federal parity protections. In total, 62 million people were poised to receive mental health and substance abuse coverage (Beronio et al., 2013).

LONG-TERM CARE AND MEDICARE

Long-term care comprises a variety of services including medical and nonmedical care for people who have a chronic illness or a disability. Many people who need long-term care services receive support services such as help with activities of daily living (e.g. bathing, dressing, and toileting). Long-term care is provided in various settings including but not limited to the home, the community, and assisted living and nursing homes. Medicare does not pay the largest part of long-term care services or personal or custodial care.

Medicare was not originally conceived to provide long-term care services but rather was created to provide basic healthcare services to seniors. Medicare pays for only medically necessary services in skilled nursing facilities and home healthcare, and only on a short-term or "intermittent" basis. Most people who need long-term care services, however, need support services (nonskilled care) for help with activities of daily living. Medicare does not pay for this type of support service. Furthermore, Medicare's approach to healthcare is medically oriented and does not fully incorporate the psychosocial aspect of healthcare that can influence a patient's treatment outcomes. As a result, social workers who can provide vital psychological and social services to older patients have played a minimal role in providing care in skilled nursing facilities and home healthcare.

According to the Kaiser Family Foundation (2013), 7 out of 10 older adults will need long-term care services, with an average time of needing assistance with activities of daily living of 3 years. In 2010, 12 million Americans needed long-term care. By 2050, these numbers will increase to 27 million. Given the large number of older persons potentially needing long-term care services coupled with its high cost of care, many older adults will be financially vulnerable. They may have to pay out of pocket for long-term care services through long-term care insurance or private pay. Ultimately, many older adults needing long-term care services may use up all their financial resources and qualify for Medicaid, which pays for support services and nursing home care.

Currently, there are about 9.6 million dual-enrolled beneficiaries in Medicare and Medicaid (Young, Garfield, Musumeci, Clemans-Cope, & Lawton, 2013). Dual-eligibles account for 33% of Medicare spending in 2009. Dual-eligible beneficiaries are different in many ways from other Medicare beneficiaries. They are among the sickest and poorest individuals covered by either Medicare or Medicaid. In 2009, 15% of dual-eligible beneficiaries received care in a long-term care facility. Forty-three percent had difficulty with at least one activity of daily living. Dual-eligible beneficiaries are more likely to have serious health conditions such as depression, diabetes, and cognitive impairments (Young et al., 2013).

For these dual-enrollees, coverage of services is the key to their healthcare. While Medicare covers basic healthcare services, Medicaid will pay for Medicare's premiums and cost sharing and cover other benefits that Medicare does not cover, such as nonskilled long-term care services. For dual-eligible beneficiaries, coverage of nonskilled long-term care services such as home care and nursing home care is critical. For many older persons in the United States, being dually enrolled is the only way to receive coverage for long-term care service.

SOCIAL WORK AND MEDICARE

Social work services have been a vital part of patient care for Medicare beneficiaries, who are often in need of mental health services and other social services. Historically, before PPS was introduced in skilled nursing facilities and home healthcare, social work was reimbursed independently. The Balanced Budget Act of 1997 changed this to include social work services under a consolidated bill. This unintentionally discouraged the use of social workers in these settings, although social workers have been the primary mental healthcare providers in skilled nursing facilities, because psychologist and psychiatrist payments were not included in the consolidated billing and could be used to seek additional reimbursement.

Provision of medical social service has been a part of Medicare home health since the start of the program. Medicare requires that social work services be available to the patients (Health Care Financing Administration, 1992). But there is no requirement that social workers see patients or participate in the planning of their care (Dhooper, 1997). Under Medicare, social work services are not considered a primary service like skilled nursing and physical and speech therapy. Therefore, social work services cannot be the only services provided to a patient in home healthcare. For that reason, the traditional pathway for a patient to receive social work services under Medicare is to receive a referral from a nurse or a physical or speech therapist.

For home health agencies to get reimbursed for social work visits, Medicare requires that social work visits be justified by "a clear and specific link between the social and emotional needs of the beneficiary and the beneficiary's medical condition or rate of recovery" (Medicare Benefit Policy Manual, 2014).

The Clinical Social Work Medicare Equity Act of 2003 changed the reimbursement for clinical social work services and excluded these services from the consolidated billing under PPS. These changes mark an important point in Medicare, creating equity among mental health providers in Medicare payments.

There are many new opportunities under the ACA for social workers (Andrews, Darnell, McBride, & Gehlert, 2013). To improve patient care coordination, the ACA established PCMHs for patients with complex healthcare needs. The ACA also established accountable care organizations (ACOs), for Medicare beneficiaries. It is less structured than the PCMH, but supports providers to develop new ways to provide more cost-effective and quality care. Social workers are well trained and positioned to assist in both PCMHs and ACOs. Social workers have specialized knowledge in case management and working with various systems. Although the social worker can be a major contributor to these models, it is yet to be seen how many social workers will be actively engaged in working in these models. It will depend on the reimbursement structure of social work services.

Another opportunity for social workers under ACA is in the area of behavioral health treatment. Under ACA, the Mental Health Parity and Addiction Equity Act (MHPAEA) is expanded to increase coverage to about 30 million people (Beronio et al., 2013). This growth in coverage will bring growth in demand for services. Most professionals in behavioral health area are already social workers (Bureau of Labor Statistics, 2012).

FUTURE CHALLENGES

Medicare is an important program that has provided health insurance to millions of older adults and disabled. The major challenge of Medicare is to provide affordable, quality healthcare to Medicare beneficiaries while keeping the program financially secure. The ACA took steps to improve benefits and also slow the growth of spending. However, for the long-term viability of the program, changes in Medicare should be part of an overall effort to reduce the federal deficit.

REFERENCES

Agency for Health Care Research and Quality (AHRQ). (2013a). *Defining the patient centered medical home (PCMH)*. Retrieved from http://pcmh.ahrq.gov/page/defining-pcmh

Agency for Health Care Research and Quality (AHRQ). (2013b). *Tools and Resources PCMH*. Retrieved from http://pcmh.ahrq.gov/page/tools-resources

Andrews, C. M., Darnell, J. S., McBride, T. D., & Gehlert, S. (2013). Social work and implementation of the Affordable Care Act. *Health and Social Work, 38*, 67–71. http://dx.doi.org/10.1093/hsw/hlt002

Beronio, K., Po, R., Skopec, L., & Glied, S. (2013). ASPE research brief: Affordable Care Act will expand mental health and substance use disorder benefits and parity protections for 62 million Americans. Washington, DC: US Department of Health and Human Services. Retrieved from http://aspe.hhs.gov/health/reports/2013/mental/rb_mental.pdf

Bureau of Labor Statistics. (2012). *Occupational outlook handbook, 2012–2013*. Retrieved from http://www.bls.gov/ooh

Centers for Medicare and Medicaid Services (CMS). (2012). *National expenditure projection 2012–2022*. Retrieved from http://www.cms.gov/Research-Statistics-Data-and-Systems/Statistics-Trends-and-Reports/NationalHealthExpendData/Downloads/Proj2012.pdf

Centers for Medicare and Medicaid Services (CMS). (2013a). *CMS finalizes physician payment rate for 2014*. Retrieved from http://cms.gov/Newsroom/MediaReleaseDatabase/Press-Releases/2013-Press-Releases-Items/2013-11-27-2.html

Centers for Medicare and Medicaid Services (CMS). (2013b). *Readmissions reduction program*. Retrieved from http://www.cms.gov/Medicare/Medicare-Fee-for-Service-Payment/AcuteInpatientPPS/Readmissions-Reduction-Program.html

Centers for Medicare and Medicaid Services (CMS) and the National Association of Insurance Commissioners (NAIC). (2015). *Choosing a Medigap policy: A guide to health insurance for people with Medicare*. Retrieved from http://www.medicare.gov/Pubs/pdf/02110.pdf

Congressional Budget Office (CBO). (2013). *Medicare May 2013 baseline*. Retrieved from http://www.cbo.gov/sites/default/files/cbofiles/attachments/44205_Medicare_0.pdf

Dhooper, S. S. (1997). *Social work in health care in the 21st century*. Thousand Oaks, CA: Sage.

Health Care Financing Administration (1992). Medicare home health agency manual. Washington, DC: U.S. Government Printing Office.

Health policy brief: Medicare hospital readmissions reduction program. (2013). *Health Affairs, November 12, 2013*, 1–5.

Jacobson, G. A., Huang, J. T., & Neuman, T. (2014). *Medigap Reform: Setting the Context for Understanding Recent Proposals*. Kaiser Family Foundation. Retrieved from http://kff.org/medicare/issue-brief/medigap-reform-setting-the-context/

Kaiser Family Foundation. (2005). *Medicare Chartbook, Third Edition*. Retrieved from https://kaiserfamily-foundation.files.wordpress.com/2013/01/medicare-chart-book-3rd-edition-summer-2005-report.pdf

Kaiser Family Foundation. (2012a). *Medicare at a glance*. Retrieved from http://www.kff.org/medicare/fact-sheet/medicare-at-a-glance-fact-sheet/

Kaiser Family Foundation. (2012b). *The Medicare prescription drug benefit fact sheet*. Retrieved from http://www.kff.org/medicare/fact-sheet/the-medicare-prescription-drug-benefit-fact-sheet/

Kaiser Family Foundation. (2012c). *Medicare spending and financing fact sheet*. Retrieved from http://kff.org/medicare/fact-sheet/medicare-spending-and-financing-fact-sheet/

Kaiser Family Foundation. (2013). A short look at long-term care for seniors. *Journal of the American Medical Association, 310*, 786. doi: 10.1001/jama.2013.17676

Medicare Benefit Policy Manual. (2014). *Chapter 7: Home health services*. Retrieved from https://www.cms.gov/Regulations-and-Guidance/Guidance/Manuals/downloads/bp102c07.pdf

Medicare Boards of Trustees. (2012). *2012 annual report of the boards of trustees of the Federal Hospital Insurance and Federal Supplementary Medical Insurance Trust Funds*. Retrieved from http://www.cms.gov/Research-Statistics-Data-and-Systems/

Statistics-Trends-and-Reports/ReportsTrustFunds/downloads/tr2012.pdf

Medicare.gov. (2013). *The Affordable Care Act and Medicare*. Retrieved from http://www.medicare.gov/about-us/affordable-care-act/affordable-care-act.html

Medicare.gov. (2014). *Your Medicare coverage choices*. Retrieved from http://www.medicare.gov/sign-up-change-plans/decide-how-to-get-medicare/your-medicare-coverage-choices.html

National Committee on Quality Assurance (NCQA). (2013). *Patient centered medical homes*. Retrieved from http://www.ncqa.org/Portals/0/Public%20Policy/2013%20PDFS/pcmh%202011%20fact%20sheet.pdf

Nutting, P. A., Miller, W. L., Crabtree B. F., Jean, C. R., Stewart, E. E., & Stange, K. C. (2009). Initial lessons from the first national demonstration project on practice transformation to a patient-centered medical home. *Annals of Family Medicine, 7*, 254–260. doi: 10.1370/afa.1002

Young, K., Garfield, R., Musumeci, M., Clemans-Cope, L., & Lawton, E. (2013). *Medicaid's role for dual eligible beneficiaries*. Retrieved from http://kaiserfamilyfoundation.files.wordpress.com/2013/08/7846-04-medicaids-role-for-dual-eligible-beneficiaries.pdf

Title XIX of the Social Security Act (SSA), commonly referred to as Medicaid, became law in 1965. Prior to its enactment, healthcare services for the poor were provided piecemeal through an arrangement of services offered by state and local programs, charities, and hospitals (Provost & Hughes, 2000). Modeled on the 1960 Kerr-Mills Act, Medical Assistance for the Aged, and the Social Security Amendments of 1950, it was designed as a cooperative program, funded jointly by the federal and state governments, including the District of Columbia and the Territories (Grogan & Patashnik, 2003; Provost & Hughes, 2000). Its purpose was to furnish medical assistance to needy persons. It is an entitlement program that pays for medical care for certain individuals and families that demonstrate low income and limited resources (Klees, Wolfe, & Curtis, 2011). Originally established as a program to subsidize medical care for the poor, its particular emphasis is on dependent children and their mothers, the disabled, and older persons. In 2014, the Affordable Care Act (ACA) expanded Medicaid eligibility offering more coverage to low-income individuals; projections estimate a growth of 20 million enrollees by 2019 (Truffer, Klemm, Wolfe, & Rennie, 2010).

MEDICAID: STANDARDS AND GUIDELINES

Using broad national guidelines that are established by federal regulations, each state shapes and administers its own Medicaid program and develops its own standards. These standards include eligibility requirements; type, amount, duration, and scope of services; and rate of payment for services. Due to state-developed standards, there is great variability in Medicaid policies throughout the country.

Medicaid is not designed to provide medical assistance for all poor persons. Low income is one test for Medicaid eligibility. In addition, resources and assets are tested against threshold levels. These threshold levels are determined by each state, using federal guidelines. States have discretion in the determination of the financial criteria for Medicaid eligibility and which groups of individuals will be covered in their Medicaid program. States may also develop a type of program called a state-only program that provides medical assistance for designated poor persons who do not qualify for Medicaid. These state-only programs are optional, and each state varies in the

COLLEEN GALAMBOS
JUNG SIM JUN

Policies Affecting Health, Mental Health, and Caregiving: Medicaid

amount and type of state-only programs offered in an area (Klees et al., 2011).

As part of the cooperative venture with the federal government, states are required to provide Medicaid coverage for particular individuals who receive federally assisted income-maintenance payments and for related groups who are not receiving cash payments. Table 59.1 outlines the mandatory Medicaid categorically needy eligibility groups for which the federal government provides matching

funds. In addition to these mandatory related groups, States have the option of providing Medicaid coverage for other categorically related groups. These groups fall within defined categories, but the eligibility criteria are more liberal. Table 59.1 outlines these categorically related groups.

Certain provisions of these optional and mandatory categorically related groups have particular relevance for older Americans, such as the medically needy option (MNO). The MNO contains provisions

TABLE 59.1 Medicaid Categorically Needy Eligibility Groups

Medicaid Categorically Needy Eligibility Groups—Federal Matching Funds Are Provided	
• Individuals are generally eligible if they meet the requirement for the Aid to Families with Dependent Children (AFDC) program in effect in their State on July 16, 1996, or, at state option, more liberal criteria.	• All children born after September 30, 1983, who are under age 19, in families with incomes at or below the FPL
• Children < age 6 whose family income is at or below 133% of the federal poverty level (FPL).	• Supplemental Security Income (SSI) recipients in most states (some use more restrictive Medicaid eligibility requirements that predate SSI).
• Pregnant women whose family income is below 133% of the FPL (services limited to those related to pregnancy, complications of pregnancy, delivery, and postpartum care).	• Special protected groups (typically individuals who lose their cash assistance due to earnings from work or from increased Social Security benefits, but who may keep Medicaid for a period of time).
• Recipients of adoption or foster care assistance under Title IV of the Social Security Act.	• Certain Medicare beneficiaries.

State Options—Medicaid Coverage for Other Categorically Related Groups (The broadest optional groups for which states will receive federal matching funds for coverage under the Medicaid program include those listed here.)	
• Infants up to age 1 and pregnant women not covered under the mandatory rules whose family income is no more than 185% of the FPL (the percentage amount is set by each state).	• TB-infected persons financially eligible for Medicaid at the SSI income level if they were within a Medicaid covered category (limited to TB-related ambulatory services and TB drugs).
• Children under age 21 who meet the AFDC income and resources requirements in effect in their state on July 16, 1996.	• Certain aged, blind, or disabled adults who have incomes above those requiring mandatory coverage, but below the FPL.
• Institutionalized individuals and individuals in home- and community-based waiver programs eligible under a special income level (states set the amount—up to 300% of the SSI federal benefit rate).	• Certain working-and-disabled persons with family income less than 250% of the FPL who would qualify for SSI if they did not work.
• Aged, blind, or disabled recipients of state supplementary income payments.	• Optional targeted low-income children included within the Children's Health Insurance Program (CHIP; formerly SCHIP) established by the BBA
• Individuals who would be eligible if institutionalized, but who are receiving care under HCBS waivers	• Medically needy (MN) persons.
	• Certain uninsured or low-income women who are screened for breast or cervical cancer through a program administered by the Centers for Disease Control and Prevention.

Source: Adapted from Klees et al. (2011, pp. 23–24).

that broaden eligibility requirements to persons who are eligible for Medicaid under one of the mandatory or optional groups with the exception that their income and/or resources exceed the eligibility level set by the state in which they reside. Under these circumstances, persons may qualify immediately or may be required to spend down their resources through incurring medical expenses that reduce their income to or below the level set for medically needy persons as outlined by individual state requirements. Under spend-down requirements, individuals are eligible for Medicaid coverage after expenditures exceed assets. Starting in 2014, states are required to use the modified adjusted gross income for eligibility determination for applicants. This method uses an adjusted gross income, modified by applying a 5% disregard, and replaces resource testing. This provision essentially raises Medicaid eligibility to individuals under the age of 65 in families with income below 138% of the federal poverty line (Klees et al., 2011; National Conference of State Legislatures, 2011).

Eligibility for Medicaid and benefit provisions for the medically needy are not required to be as extensive as those required for the categorically needy; in fact, regulations may be fairly restrictive. While federal matching funds are available for medically needy programs (MNPs), states are expected to follow specific federal requirements including the inclusion of certain groups and services. In addition to these mandated requirements, states may elect to extend the medically needy eligibility to other additional groups and to provide supplementary services. In 2009, the number of states offering MNPs dropped slightly from 38 states in 2000, to 33 states. Those states that have not opted for MNPs may use the special income level option to extend Medicaid to the near poor in medical institutional settings (Klees et al., 2011).

Although Title XIX of the SSA allows flexibility for states to craft their own Medicaid plan, there are some federal requirements mandatory for states to follow in order to receive federal matching funds. States are required to offer medical assistance for basic services to the categorically needy group as outlined by federal guidelines. Mandated services particularly germane to older adults include nursing facility services for persons age 21 and over, home healthcare for persons eligible for skilled nursing services (in addition to inpatient and outpatient hospital services), rural health clinic services, physician services, and laboratory and X-ray services. In addition

to these mandatory services, states may provide some optional services for which they receive a federal match. Examples of approved optional Medicaid services include diagnostic services, clinic services, prescription drugs, prosthetic devices, optometry and eyeglasses, transportation, rehabilitation and physical therapy, and home- and community-based care for certain persons with chronic impairments. In 2009, the elderly accounted for 25% of medically needy enrollment and 50% of total medically needy spending (Kaiser Commission on Medicaid and the Uninsured [KCMU], 2012a). Beneficiaries who are dual-eligible make up 28% of medically needy enrollees and 68% of medically needy spending (KCMU, 2012a). Under section 1902 (a)(10)(C) of the ACA, current requirements for medically needy eligibility did not change.

The Personal Responsibility and Work Opportunity Reconciliation Act of 1996 (PRWORA), introduced restrictive changes to eligibility standards for Supplemental Security Income (SSI) coverage. This law had an impact on the Medicaid program, as one eligibility category is SSI recipients. The law imposed restrictions on SSI eligibility among legal resident aliens and other qualified aliens who entered the United States on or after August 22, 1996. The law requires a 5-year waiting period before these individuals can be eligible for SSI. States can exercise the option to provide Medicaid coverage for aliens who entered before that date and for alien individuals after the 5-year waiting period. Emergency services continue to be mandatory for alien groups. For those aliens who lost SSI benefits due to the new restrictions imposed by PRWORA, coverage can be provided only under another eligibility status outlined within Medicaid regulations (Klees et al., 2011).

HISTORICAL ANTECEDENTS IN COVERAGE OF OLDER ADULTS

Within its almost 50-year history, Medicaid has evolved as an assistance program for low-income older adults and the disabled. A 1972 amendment to the SSA established a federal program for cash assistance for the aged, blind, and disabled. This program, known as Supplemental Security Income (SSI), set uniform national minimum eligibility standards and benefits (Rowland & Garfield, 2000). Within this legislation, optional benefits eligible for federal matching funds included services provided by intermediate care facilities and intermediate care facilities for the mentally retarded. Further legislation in the 1980s assured Medicaid coverage to some Medicare beneficiaries who had not met the eligibility requirements for any cash assistance program. Additionally, in the 1980s, changes to the Medicaid benefits package expanded options for home- and community-based long-term care (LTC), increasing the role these programs have for low-income older adults. These legislative changes also emphasized increased access to services, quality of care, improved outreach programs, specific benefits, and fewer limits on services (Rowland & Garfield, 2000).

Older adults have larger per-person Medicaid expenditures than other population groups. National data for 2008 indicate that Medicaid payment for services for 22.8 million children, or 49% of all Medicaid beneficiaries, averages $2,643 per child. In that same period, Medicaid payment for 4.6 million aged, or 10% of all Medicaid beneficiaries, averaged $15,869 per person (Klees et al, 2011). Additionally, it is predicted that the need for the LTC provision in Medicaid will increase as the aging population expands.

THE RELATIONSHIP BETWEEN MEDICAID AND MEDICARE: STATE BUY–INS FOR "DUAL-ELIGIBLES"

For low-income individuals with limited assets who receive Medicare, dual enrollment in Medicaid is an option. For these dual-eligible beneficiaries, Medicare healthcare coverage is supplemented by programs and services available through the state Medicaid program, if eligibility categories are met. Low-income older adults may be eligible for Medicaid under the following four categories:

- Recipients of the federal SSI program
- Older adults with excessive medical or LTC expenses in proportion to their income and assets
- Older adults whose income levels are below the federal poverty threshold, and who have limited financial assets
- Older adults who have incomes between 100% and 120% of the federal poverty threshold and who have limited financial assets.

Services provided under the dual enrollment program include such items as prescription drugs,

eyeglasses, hearing aids, and nursing home care that extends beyond the 100-day limit allowed by Medicare. Assistance may also be provided in covering Medicare premiums and cost-sharing payments through the state Medicaid program. For all eligible services, Medicare is billed as the first payer, and Medicaid is considered the payer of last resort.

In 2006, a new Medicare prescription drug benefit began providing drug coverage for Medicare recipients and older adults who receive coverage from Medicaid. The dual-eligible receive a low-income subsidy for the Medicare drug plan premium and assistance with cost sharing for prescriptions. Medicaid coverage no longer includes prescription drug benefits for Medicare recipients (Klees et al., 2011). Since 1965, Medicaid has covered the Medicare premiums and the cost sharing of additional benefits not covered by Medicare for SSI recipients. Additionally, Medicaid's role in financing low-income Medicare beneficiaries expanded through a series of incremental legislative changes. One expansion is the development of Medicaid into a Medicare supplement. In 2011, 19.7% of Medicare enrollees were dually eligible for Medicaid (Medicare-Medicaid Coordination Office, 2013).

PROGRAMS OF ALL-INCLUSIVE CARE FOR THE ELDERLY

One state option for older adults is Programs of All-inclusive Care for the Elderly (PACE). Initially, started as a demonstration project, which gained program status through the 1997 Balanced Budget Act (Mollica, 2003), PACE is designed to provide an alternative to institutional care for persons age 55 and older deemed as needing nursing facility level of care (Mehdizadeh, Applebaum, Kunkel, & Faust, 2012; Mollica, 2003). A federal program option under both Medicare and Medicaid, PACE allows for an integrated model of acute and LTC services for dual-eligible individuals (Mehdizadeh et al., 2012; Mollica, 2003). It is designed to serve a relatively small number of people with a high level of services. Currently, 30 states operate PACE sites under the Section 1934 State Plan amendment (O'Keeffe et al., 2010). While managing the health, medical, and social services of participants enrolled in the program, PACE is also responsible for coordinating the use of other needed services for rehabilitation, prevention, and psychosocial needs, including day health centers, homes, hospitals, and nursing homes. Providers in the PACE program receive payment for services through predeveloped PACE agreements. In exchange for a monthly capitated Medicaid payment and Medicare support, PACE providers assumes full financial risk for participant care (Medizadeh et al., 2012; US Department of Health and Human Services [DHHS], 2010). Providers must make available items and services covered under both Titles XVIII and XIX. These services must be rendered without amount, duration, or scope limitations, and without requiring deductibles, copayments, or other forms of cost sharing. Outcome studies conducted on PACE consistently find that the program has a positive impact on mortality, functional status, and quality of life. For the most part, the program is cost-effective for the Medicare program, but Medicaid expenditures for participants exceed expenditures incurred by comparison groups (Medizadeh et al., 2012).

MEDICAID AND MANAGED CARE

In response to rising Medicaid costs, state Medicaid programs turned to managed care to provide an accessible, cost-effective approach to healthcare service delivery. Under the managed care system, health maintenance organizations, prepaid health plans, and other forms of managed care contract with states to provide an agreed on set of services to Medicaid enrollees. In return, the provider system receives a predetermined payment per enrollee for a specific period of time.

Since the 1980s, states have continued to experiment with various managed care approaches in an attempt to contain costs, reduce redundancy of services, and strive for better coordination and continuity of care. The Balanced Budget Act (BBA) of 1997, provides states with the option of setting up Medicaid managed care programs without the prior waivers required in the past (Hoffman, Klees, & Curtis, 2000). The proportion of Medicaid enrollees participating in managed care increased from 14% of enrollees in 1993 to 58% in 2002 to 74% in 2011 (CMS, 2003a, 2011). Most state Medicaid managed care enrollees consist of children and nondisabled adults. As of July 2011, 47 states were using Medicaid managed care programs including risk-based arrangements and primary care case management (CMS, 2011). In the past, older adults and the disabled were considered a high-risk

population group for managed care arrangements due to the charge to deliver comprehensive services to a high need group while controlling costs (Provost & Hughes, 2000). However, through managed care waivers some states are providing LTC services. As of 2009, 12 states were providing such services and supports through risk-based managed care arrangements, showing slow adoptions of these programs at the state level.

Managed long-term services and supports (MLTSS) include the delivery of LTC services, which include both home- and community-based services (HCBS) and institution-based services. These services are provided through Medicaid managed care programs. Designed to be flexible, MLTSS may be used to support such initiatives as Money Follows the Person and the Balancing Incentive Program. The number of states with MLTSS programs increased from 8 in 2004 to 16 in 2012 (CMS, 2013a). It is expected that as MLTSS expands, older adults and adults with chronic disabilities will transition into these programs.

MEDICAID WAIVER AND INNOVATION PROGRAMS

Some HCBS are funded through the Medicaid waiver programs. The legislative change that allowed for the development of Medicaid waiver programs was Section 2176 of the Omnibus Reconciliation Act of 1981. Under HCBS waiver programs, states are permitted to waive certain federal and state requirements in order to provide HCBS to people who would otherwise receive institutional care reimbursable through Medicaid.

To be eligible for waiver services, individuals must first meet eligibility criteria such as age and diagnosis. States may have waiver programs that target different groups, for example people age 65 or older, persons with AIDS, and persons with traumatic brain injury. Individuals who meet the eligibility or targeting criteria must meet service criteria, which for HCBS waiver programs are the level-of-care criteria states use to determine eligibility for institutional care.

Since its establishment, three mechanisms have allowed states to test Medicaid program innovations: (1) Section 1915(b) or Freedom of Choice Waivers; (2) Section 1115 Research and Demonstration Projects; and (3) Section 1915(c) HCBS.

Section 1915(b) Freedom of Choice Waivers refer to programs that enroll beneficiaries in managed care programs on a mandatory basis. Additional services are provided through savings produced from managed care, and carve-out systems are provided for specialty care such as mental health. (Provost & Hughes, 2000).

Section 1115 Research and Demonstration Projects provide a mechanism for states to test new ideas. Under this initiative, states investigate program innovations, such as small-scale pilots of new benefits, various financing mechanisms, and major restructuring of state Medicaid funding (Provost & Hughes, 2000).

The HCBS waiver program or Section 1915 (c) allows states flexibility to develop and implement alternatives to institutionalization through the development of a network of healthcare and social services that allows individuals to remain in the community and avoid institutionalization (Klees et al., 2011; Provost & Hughes, 2000).

There are seven specific services outlined under the regulation that may be offered as part of a HCBS waiver. These services are case management services, homemaker services, home health aide services, personal care services, adult day healthcare services, habilitation services, and respite care services (Duckett & Guy, 2000; Health Care Financing Administration, 1996). In addition to these specific services, other services may be provided if they are state requested and approved by the Health Care Financing Administration. They must be cost-effective and demonstrated to be necessary to avoid institutionalization. Examples of additional services include transportation, in-home support services, meal services, special communication services, minor home modifications, and adult daycare (Duckett & Guy, 2000; Health Care Financing Administration, 1996). Under the HCBS waiver program, a capitation device allows plans to provide services that are not otherwise available through Medicaid. In capitation arrangements, providers receive from the state a monthly reimbursement rate for each Medicaid managed care enrollee. Within that reimbursement, the providers are at full risk to pay for all services covered by the managed care plan (Fisher & Raphael, 2003).

The HCBS program has experienced tremendous growth since its development in 1981. Under the ACA, the development and expansion of HCBS in lieu of institutional care is a national priority (KCMU, 2012c).

The ACA of 2010 also establishes a new state plan optional benefit—the Community First Choice Option, effective October 2011. To be eligible for services, individuals must require hands-on assistance, supervision, or cueing with activities of daily living, instrumental activities of daily living, and/or health-related tasks and meet income requirements. The Deficit Reduction Act (DRA) of 2005 added §1915(i) to the SSA, which allows states, at their option, to provide HCBS under the Medicaid State Plan without a waiver. Section 1915(i) was subsequently amended by the Patient Protection and ACA of 2010.

HOME- AND COMMUNITY-BASED SERVICES PROGRAMS

The shifting of funds away from institutional care to home- and- community-based settings was a direct policy response to the disproportionate amount of Medicaid expenditures that were being used within that system (Grannemann & Pauly, 1983; Provost & Hughes, 2000). Part of the inappropriate use of nursing facilities was linked to an institutional bias in the Medicaid benefit and eligibility structure (Grannemann & Pauly, 1983; Holahan, 1975). In addition, studies indicated that there were people residing in nursing homes who were receiving Medicaid funding that were capable of living in the community (Fox & Clauser, 1980; Kraus et al., 1976; Pegels, 1980; Weissert, 1986). Under the influence of the ACA, there are increased efforts to develop and expand home- and community-based alternatives to institutional care. The national percentage of Medicaid spending on HCBS has grown from 20% in 1995 to 45% in 2010. In terms of cost growth, from 2000 to 2009, total Medicaid spending on HCBS increased by more than $32 billion. This increase in spending moved expenditures closer to the level of spending for institutional services over this period. States can provide Medicaid HCBS in three ways: through (1) the mandatory home health services state plan benefit, (2) the optional personal care services state plan benefit, and (3) optional Section 1915(c) HCBS waivers (KCMU, 2012c).

One program, home health services, is a mandatory benefit for individuals entitled to nursing facility care under a Medicaid State Plan—that is, for categorically eligible persons age 21 or older. To be covered, home health services must be ordered by a physician as part of a written plan of care and reviewed every 60 days. There are mandatory services, and states may also select to expand coverage to include optional home health services. Mandatory state plan home health services include the following:

1. Nursing services provided on a part-time or intermittent basis by a home health agency that meets requirements for participation in Medicare;
2. Home health aide services provided by a home health agency that meets requirements for participation in Medicare; and
3. Medical supplies, equipment, and appliances suitable for use in the home.

Optional home health services are available and include physical therapy, occupational therapy, speech pathology, and audiology services. States are required to make available the same home health benefit services to all Medicaid beneficiaries who are entitled to such services. States are allowed to place coverage limits on home health services as they relate to medical necessity and/or utilization control. Service eligibility is not dependent on a discharge from institutional care or need for skilled services (O'Keeffe et al., 2010).

Personal care services are another HCBS option, available since the mid-1970s. The first program was medically oriented, was provided in a person's place of residence, and required a physician's prescription. These services were supervised by a registered nurse, who developed and carried out a care plan.

In 1993, Congress formally incorporated personal care into federal Medicaid law. Changes were made to allow personal care to occur outside a person's home. In 1994, changes were made that broadened who was allowed to provide supervision and removed the physician prescription. Additional changes occurred in 1999, broadening personal care services to include activities of daily living and instrumental activities of daily living. Personal care was expanded to include cueing and supervision of tasks for persons with cognitive impairments. One of the most empowering changes was to permit the care receiver to direct and supervise the personal care. In 2005, 36 states covered personal care services under their Medicaid state plans (DHHS, 2010).

MONEY FOLLOWS THE PERSON PROGRAM

Authorized under the DRA, the Money Follows the Person (MFP) demonstration grant provides states with federal matching funds for Medicaid beneficiaries who transition from institutions to community-based settings. Its aim is to reduce reliance on institutional care for individuals needing LTC and supports and to expand options for individuals with disabilities and older adults who wish to remain in the community.

Through the federal MFP demonstration grant, 45 states and the District of Columbia have worked with Medicaid beneficiaries in transitioning from institutions to community-based placements. Many MFP participants have made significant strides, increasing transitions from 8,902 in 2010 to 25,100 in 2012. The DRA and the ACA strengthen and expand the MFP program extending it through September 2016, with an allocation of $2.25 billion, allowing more states to take part in the program (KCMU, 2013a)

LONG-TERM CARE FINANCING ISSUES

Medicaid is the primary source of LTC insurance for the older adults and people with disabilities (KCMU, 2012b). Over 10 million people needed LTC services and supports, and about 50% of them are over age 65. In 2009, $240 billion were used for LTC services including community and institutional care. Medicaid paid for 43% of total LTC expenditures (KCMU, 2012b). National data indicated that Medicaid financed the nursing home care of over 63% residents in nursing facilities in 2011 (KCMU, 2013b). Medicaid covers skilled nursing facility care, intermediate facility nursing care, intermediate care for the mentally retarded and developmentally disabled, and HCBS. Medicaid finances nursing home care after an individual's savings and income are depleted or spent down (Klees et al., 2011).

Recent data indicate some declines in numbers of residents in nursing home care. In fiscal year 2002, a total of $93,219 billion dollars was spent on nursing home care, or about 37.5% of total Medicaid expenditures for 1.7 million persons (CMS, 2003b). In fiscal year 2011, about 41.5% of total Medicaid expenditures (around $169.18 billion dollars) were spent for 1.4 million persons (CMS, 2013b; KCMU, 2011). It is noted that Medicaid's expanded role in the financing of LTC services has contributed to the development of quality standards for this industry (Rowland & Garfield, 2000). Key influences include implementation of comprehensive nursing home reform that raised standards for quality nursing home care and protections offered to spouses of nursing home residents outlined in the Spousal Impoverishment Act (Rowland & Garfield, 2000). Also, the home- and community-based initiatives for older adults provide less costly care options while allowing individuals to remain in the least restrictive setting. The ACA will continue to expand home- and community-based options for low-income older adults.

CONCLUSIONS

President Johnson signed the Medicaid legislation into law on July 30, 1965, at the Truman Library in Independence, Missouri. The House Ways and Means Committee chairperson Wilbur Mills crafted the legislation as a federal matching program so that states would have the ability to provide additional health insurance to low-income parents and dependent children, older adults, and people with disabilities. This program established the principle that the government would take responsibility for the provision of healthcare to low-income individuals (Min DeParle, 2000). Today, the ACA has the potential to shape Medicaid and the program's effectiveness in providing coverage for low-income individuals (National Conference of State Legislatures, 2011).

Challenges for the future of the financing of healthcare services for older Americans through Medicaid center around the question of how to provide comprehensive care to a growing population of persons in the most efficient and effective manner possible. This nation is confronted with larger numbers of older adults who are living longer. Use of health services will increase tremendously as the baby boomers age. This increase in use will challenge Medicaid's ability to provide needed services to older adults. Will America keep pace with the changes, or will a portion of the aging population go unserved? Only time will tell.

REFERENCES

Centers for Medicare and Medicaid Services. (2003a). *Home and community based services*. Retrieved from http://www.cms.hhs.gov/publications/overview-medicare-medicaid

Centers for Medicare and Medicaid Services. (2003b). *Medicaid: A brief summary*. Retrieved from http://www.cms.hhs.gov/publications/overview-medicare-medicaid/default4.asp

Centers for Medicare and Medicaid Services. (2011). *Medicaid-managed care enrollment report*. Retrieved from http://www.cms.gov/Research-Statistics-Data-and-Systems/Computer-Data-and-Systems/MedicaidDataSourcesGenInfo/MdManCrEnrllRep.html.

Centers for Medicare and Medicaid Services. (2013a). *Medicaid managed long term services and supports*. Retrieved from www.medicaid.gov/Medicaid-CHIP-Program-Information/By-Topics/Delivery-Systems/Medicaid-Managed-Long-Term-Services-and-Supports-MLTSS.html

Centers for Medicare and Medicaid Services. (2013b). *Nursing facilities (NF)*. Retrieved from www.medicaid.gov/Medicaid-CHIP-Program-Information/By-Topics/Delivery-Systems/Institutional-Care/Nursing-Facilities-NF.html

Duckett, M. J., & Guy, M. R. (2000). Home and community based services waivers. *Health Care Financing Review*, 22, 123–125.

Fisher, H. M., & Raphael, T. G. (2003). Managed long term care: Care integration through care coordination. *Journal of Aging and Health*, 15, 223–245.

Fox, P. D., & Clauser, S. B. (1980). Trends in nursing home expenditures: Implications for aging. *Health Care Financing Review*, 2, 65–70.

Grannemann, T. W., & Pauly, M. V. (1983). *Controlling Medicaid costs*. Washington, DC: American Enterprise Institute for Public Policy Research.

Grogan, C. M., & Patashnik, E. M. (2003). Universalism within targeting: Nursing home care, the middle class, and the politics of the Medicaid program. *Social Service Review, March*, 51–71.

Health Care Financing Administration. (1996). *Health care financing review: Medicare and Medicaid statistical supplement, 1996*. Washington, DC: US Government Printing Office.

Hoffman, E. D., Klees, B. S., & Curtis, C. A. (2000). Overview of the Medicare and Medicaid programs. *Health Care Financing Review*, 22, 175–183.

Holahan, J. (1975). *Financing health care to the poor*. Lexington, MA: Urban Institute.

Kaiser Commission on Medicaid and the Uninsured (KCMU). (2011). *Medicaid's long-term care users: Spending patterns across institutional and community-based settings*. Retrieved from http://kaiserfamilyfoundation.files.wordpress.com/2013/01/7576-02.pdf

Kaiser Commission on Medicaid and the Uninsured (KCMU). (2012a). *The Medicaid medically needy program: Spending and enrollment update.* Retrieved from http://kaiserfamilyfoundation.files.wordpress.com/2013/01/4096.pdf

Kaiser Commission on Medicaid and the Uninsured (KCMU). (2012b). *Medicaid and long-term care services and supports.* Retrieved from http://kaiserfamilyfoundation.files.wordpress.com/2013/01/2186-09.pdf

Kaiser Commission on Medicaid and the Uninsured (KCMU). (2012c). *Medicaid home and community-based services programs: 2009 data update.* Retrieved from http://kaiserfamilyfoundation.files.wordpress.com/2013/01/7720-06.pdf

Kaiser Commission on Medicaid and the Uninsured (KCMU). (2013a). *Money follows the person: A 2012 survey of transitions, services and costs.* Retrieved from http://kff.org/medicaid/issue-brief/money-follows-the-person-a-2012-survey-of-transitions-services-and-costs/

Kaiser Commission on Medicaid and the Uninsured (KCMU). (2013b). *Overview of nursing facility financing and ownership in the United States in 2011.* Retrieved from http://kaiserfamilyfoundation.files.wordpress.com/2013/06/8456-overview-of-nursing-facility-capacity.pdf

Klees, B. S., Wolfe, C. J., & Curtis, C. A. (2011). *Brief summaries of Medicare and Medicaid: Title XVIII and Title XIX of the Social Security Act.* Baltimore, MD: Centers for Medicare and Medicaid Services.

Kraus, A. S., Spasoff, R. A., Beattie, E. J., Holden, D. E., Lawson, J. S., Rodenburg, M., & Woodcock, G. M. (1976). Elderly applications to long term care institutions: The application process: Placement and care needs. *Journal of the American Geriatric Society, 24,* 165–172. doi: 10.1111/(ISSN)1532-5415

Medicare-Medicaid Coordination Office. (2013). *Data analysis brief Medicare-Medicaid dual enrollment from 2006–2011.* Retrieved from http: www.cms.gov/Medicare-Medicaid/Dual_Enrollment_2006-2011_Final_Document.pdf

Mehdizadeh S., Applebaum, R., Kunkel, S., & Faust, P. (2012). *Evaluation of Ohio's program of all inclusive care for the elderly (PACE).* Oxford, OH: Scripps Gerontology Center, Miami University.

Min DeParle, N. A. (2000). Celebrating 35 years of Medicare and Medicaid. *Health Care Financing Review, 22,* 1–7.

Mollica, R. (2003). Coordinating services across the continuum of health, housing, and supportive services. *Journal of Aging and Health, 15,* 165–188. doi: 10.1177/0898264302239022

National Conference of State Legislatures. (2011). *Medicaid and the Affordable Care Act.* Retrieved from http://www.ncsl.org/documents/health/HRMedicaid.pdf

O'Keeffe, J., Saucier, P., Jackson, B., Cooper, R., McKenney, E., Crisp, S., & Moseley, C. (2010). *Understanding Medicaid home and community services: A primer.* Washington, DC: US Department of Health and Human Services.

Pegels, C. C. (1980). Institutional versus noninstitutional care for the elderly. *Journal of Health Politics Policy Law, 5,* 205–212.

Provost, C., & Hughes, P. (2000). Medicaid: 35 years of service. *Health Care Financing Review, 22,* 141–174.

Rowland, D., & Garfield, R. (2000). Health care for the poor: Medicaid at 35. *Health Care Financing Review, 22,* 23–34.

Truffer, C. J., Klemm, J. D., Wolfe, C. J., & Rennie, K. E. (2010). *2010 actuarial report on the financial outlook for Medicaid.* Washington, DC: Department of Health and Human Services.

US Department of Health and Human Services (DHHS). (2010). *Understanding Medicaid home and community services: A primer.* Washington, DC: Office of the Assistant Secretary for Planning and Evaluation.

Weissert, W. C. (1986): Hard choices: Targeting long-term care to the "at-risk" aged. *Journal of Health Politics Policy Law, 11,* 463–481.

The Older Americans Act (OAA; P.L. 89-73) and the Social Security Act (P.L. 74-271) form the core of the nation's aging policy. The specific provisions under these acts are augmented by other federal, state, and local policies that focus specifically on older Americans or on special needs like disability that overlap with an aging population. Increasingly, these policy stalwarts focus on helping older adults age at home and in community-based settings of their choice. Both original and more recent provisions of the OAA and Medicaid emphasize programs that serve individuals in the community and prevent long-term institutionalization. These policy provisions reflect the demographic reality of an aging population, concerns about the costs of long-term institutionalization, and the expressed preferences of older adults. Only 2.4% of the over 60 million adults aged 60 and over live in nursing homes or other institutions (US Census Bureau, 2012), and most adults ages 45 and over indicate that they prefer to age in their own housing (AARP, 2010).

The desire to age at home is threatened by the challenges that can accompany aging and the absence of environmental supports that facilitate aging in place. Over one-quarter of the households in which the oldest member is 65–74 years old include someone with a disability, and nearly one-half of those households in which the oldest member is 75–84, and two-thirds of those households in which the oldest member is 85 and over include a member with a disability (Center for Housing Policy, 2012). For households that are economically disadvantaged, the rate of disability is higher. Available social services, housing, and transportation become crucial to ensure the health and quality of life older adults in the community.

This chapter describes key aging policies that provide these services for older adults. The first section highlights the mandates of the OAA and other federal policy provisions that support community-based social services. The second section discusses federal housing and related tax policies that benefit older Americans. The third section highlights federal transportation programs that enable seniors to access necessary services and engage in their communities.

M. LORI THOMAS

Policies Affecting Community-Based Social Services, Housing, and Transportation

COMMUNITY-BASED SOCIAL SERVICES FOR OLDER PERSONS

Social services and the community infrastructure to support the health and well-being of older adults are

60

ensured principally through the OAA. Additional provisions, however, are provided through several federal policies, including the Medicaid and Social Services Block Grant titles of the Social Security Act, the Americans with Disability Act (ADA), and, most recently, the Patient Protection and Affordable Care Act (ACA).

The Older Americans Act

The OAA is the nation's primary vehicle for organizing, coordinating, and delivering services and protections for older Americans and their families. The original act made its services universally available to persons aged 60 and over, while requiring states to target assistance to persons with the "greatest social or economic need." The OAA facilitates the provision of home care, congregate and home-delivered meals, transportation, caregiver supports, information and assistance, health promotion and disease prevention, other community activities, and advocacy for persons aged 60 and over. Through the OAA, every state has a comprehensive information, counseling, education, and assistance system linking consumers to resources and services needed to remain safe in their homes and communities (Administration on Aging, US Department of Health and Human Services [AOA], n.d.).

The OAA establishes the administrative structure and funding mechanisms for the federal Administration on Aging (AOA), 56 State and territory Units on Aging (SUAs), and 629 local Area Agencies on Aging (AAAs). These entities plus 244 tribal organizations, 2 Hawaiian tribal organizations representing 400 tribes, and about 20,000 local community-based service providers and their volunteers form a nationwide collaboration of federal, state, and local partners known as the Aging Service Network (AOA, n.d.). The SUAs designate planning and service areas (PSAs) within which AAAs coordinate and arrange for service delivery, typically through contracts with local governments and private agencies. Forty-six SUAs have multiple PSAs; 10 operate a single PSA serving the entire state or territory. Most states and territories also use their own general revenue to expand these programs beyond the provisions of the OAA (AOA, n.d.).

Each title of the OAA authorizes specific programs and service. The purpose of each title is described briefly in Table 60.1. Title III defines a number of services particularly relevant for social workers and crucial for the well-being of older adults residing in community settings. These social and nutrition services reached over 11 million seniors in fiscal year 2011 (AOA, 2012). Title III also provides grants to states to support mental and physical health through disease prevention, health promotion, and chronic disease self-management programs and activities.

The OAA is typically reauthorized by Congress every 7 years, most recently in 2006. The legislation

TABLE 60.1 Titles and Descriptions of the Older Americans Act (OAA)

Title	Purpose
Title I—Declaration of Objectives, Definitions	Defines key terms and describes the objectives of the OAA
Title II—Administration on Aging (AOA)	Establishes AOA within DHHS and the duties of its executive, the assistant secretary for aging
Title III—Grants for State and Community Programs on Aging	Establishes a state and local framework for a comprehensive and coordinated system on aging, including the provision of nutrition services and an array of supportive services
Title IV—Activities for Health, Independence, and Longevity	Supports education, research, planning, and workforce development to address the needs of an aging population
Title V—Community Service Senior Opportunities Act	Establishes a program to offer employment and training opportunities for adults ages 55 and over.
Title VI—Grants for Native Americans	Promotes the delivery of nutrition and supportive services to American Indians, Alaskan Natives, and Native Hawaiians
Title VII—Allotments for Vulnerable Elder Rights Protection Activities	Establishes a system to prevent elder abuse, neglect, and exploitation including legal assistance and the ombudsman program

was due for reauthorization in 2011. With the exception of cuts mandated by sequestration in 2013, it was funded at previous levels as negotiations for reauthorization continued. Current proposed bipartisan legislation (S 1562) "does no harm" to the OAA and rejects proposed reductions to funding levels (National Council on Aging [NCOA], 2013). Nevertheless, as costs to provide services and the number of older Americans eligible to receive services increase, current funding levels are insufficient to meet the needs of an aging population. While over 11 million seniors were served in 2011, over 60 million were eligible for services and over 23 million were economically insecure (NCOA, 2013).

The Social Security Act

The Social Security Act also provides community-based social services, principally through Medicaid (Title VII) but also through Social Services Block Grants (Title XX). The Medicaid waiver programs, including the home- and community-based services (HCBS) waiver program, added to Medicaid through the Omnibus Reconciliation Act of 1981, help address the needs of low-income older adults and adults with disabilities. The HCBS waiver program, Section 1915(c) of the Social Security Act, allows states to apply for funds to develop and implement health and social service programs that enable individuals to remain in the community and prevent institutionalization. Waiver programs can provide one or more of seven specific services including case management, homemaker services, home health aide services, personal care services, adult day health services, habilitation services, and respite care services (Duckett & Guy, 2000). According to the Centers for Medicare and Medicaid Services, US Department of Health and Human Services (CMS, n.d.), 47 states and the District of Columbia offer at least one HCBS waiver program.

Another addition to Medicaid that impacts community-based social services for low-income older adults was made in the Deficit Reduction Act of 2005. The Money Follows the Person (MFP) demonstration grants provided up to $1.44 billion in reimbursement funding for states to move Medicaid-enrolled individuals from institutions back to the community and rebalance the "institutional bias" of Medicaid expenditures (Coffey, 2008). When formerly institutionalized persons move back

into the community they receive HCBS as outlined in Section 1915 (c) and/or other supplemental services as necessary to facilitate the successful transition into the community. At the end of 2012, 37 states were operating MFP programs, 6 were in planning stages, and over 30,000 transitions had occurred (Irvin et al., 2013). The demonstration program was extended to 2016 through the ACA.

Title XX, Social Services Block Grants (SSBG), was added to the Social Security Act in 1975 to provide supportive services to complement federal Community Development Block Grants (CDBG) to low-income communities. Title XX provides flexible funding to each state to address the needs of children and families, persons with disabilities, at-risk youth and young adults, and older adults. Programs using SSBG funding must provide services in one of 29 service categories ranging from foster care and adoption services for children and youth to various services for older adults including protective services, home-delivered and congregate meals, adult daycare, case management, legal services, and transportation. In 2010, 24 million Americans received SSBG services. Among the 39 states that reported the known ages of their service recipients, only 7% of services were provided to recipients aged 60 and older (Office of Community Service [OCS], 2010).

The Americans with Disabilities Act

Federal legislation concerning community-based social services for older adults and the programs implemented through the legislation have been significantly influenced by the passage of the Americans with Disabilities Act of 1990 and the Supreme Court's ruling in *Olmstead v. L.C. and E.W.* Department of Justice regulations concerning Title II of the ADA required that public entities should provide services "in the most integrated setting appropriate to the needs of qualified individuals with disabilities" (28 C.F.R.§ 35.130(d)). The case was brought in 1995 by the Atlanta Legal Aid Society on behalf of two women with developmental disabilities. The suit claimed the women's rights were violated under Title II of the ADA because they were held in a state psychiatric hospital although treating professionals agreed that a community-based setting would be better for them. The 11th Circuit Court agreed stating that when a state "confines an individual with a disability in an institutional setting when a community placement is appropriate, the State has violated the core principle underlying the ADA's integration mandate." The Supreme Court upheld the circuit court ruling and set a high standard for states to serve disabled persons in least restrictive community settings. The *Olmstead* decision was a key impetus toward increased emphasis on community-based support services and the development of the concept of consumer direction in care (Benjamin, 2001). In 2001, President George W. Bush announced the New Freedom Initiative, an executive order promoting the "full participation of people with disabilities in all areas of society" (Bush, 2001). The initiative piloted a number of demonstration grants through various policy mechanisms and included funding nursing home transition, personal assistance services, Money Follows the Person, quality assurance/improvement, transportation services, and broader systems change grants.

The Patient Accountability and Affordable Care Act

In 2010, President Barack Obama signed the ACA, restructuring the nation's healthcare system to ensure access to affordable healthcare, to improve healthcare delivery systems, and to manage healthcare costs (Kaiser Family Foundation, 2013). Of particular relevance to the community-based care of older adults and adults age 50–64, the Act initially extended Medicaid to 138% of the federal poverty level, making more adults eligible for HBCS; amended Medicaid to further incentivize HCBS for long-term care; extended the Money Follows the Person Demonstration Program; and established additional options for HCBS through state plans rather than waivers. The Act also established the Community First Choice Option in Medicaid to provide community-based supports such as assistance with activities of daily living and health-related tasks to individuals with disabilities who would otherwise qualify for institutionalization. In addition, the ACA created the State Balancing Incentive Program, which provides financial incentives to states to increase the number of noninstitutional long-term care services and supports (Harrington, Ng, LaPlante, & Kaye, 2012) and it included the community living assistance services and supports (CLASS) program to

provide cash payments to offset the costs of services that help older adults and persons with a disability remain in the community.

Despite provisions to strengthen HBCS, changes in the ACA since its initial passage have impacted its capacity to do so. The CLASS program was repealed by the American Taxpayer Relief Act of 2012. In addition, in the 2012 decision in *National Federation of Independent Business v. Sebelius*, the Supreme Court struck down the ACA requirement that states expand Medicaid to 138% federal poverty level, allowing a coverage gap that will impact economically vulnerable older adults. As of March 2014, 19 states had decided not to expand Medicaid and 5 additional states were still debating expansion (Kaiser Family Foundation, 2014).

HOUSING POLICIES FOR ELDERS

In addition to federal policies that facilitate community-based social services for elders, a variety of "environmental" policies ensure the well-being of elders in the community, including policies that ensure housing and transportation. Housing not only provides shelter, a basic human need, but is also the immediate context for individual identity, health, and a platform for "ontological security" (Padgett, 2007). As individuals age, particularly those who are economically insecure, the loss or absence of "home" exacerbates the decline of physical and mental health (Spillman, Biess, & MacDonald, 2012).

In 2011, 25.1 million households were headed by adults aged 65 and older. Of those households, 81% owned and 19% rented their residences (AOA, 2012). For older homeowners, the home is their primary and sometimes only asset, an asset threatened by economic disadvantage and the homeowners' inability to pay rising property taxes, continue paying a mortgage, or make repairs and afford structural modifications to meet needs associated with aging. From 2000 to 2009, the number of mortgage-free homeowners ages 50 and over fell from 40% to 36% (AARP, 2010). Older adults with mortgages face deepening affordability crises as the cost of housing requires a greater portion of income and yet few resources are available to help maintain stable housing.

For older renters, the need for affordable housing continues to grow while the number of affordable, available, and adequate units declines. The US

Department of Housing and Urban Development (HUD) categorizes households as extremely low income if household income falls at 30% or below the area median income (AMI), roughly $15,000 or the income from a full-time minimum-wage job; very low income if the income is 31%–50% AMI; and low income if the household earns 51%–80% AMI (HUD, n.d.d.). For every 100 extremely low-income rental households, there are only 30 affordable, available, and adequate housing units. For every 100 very low-income rental households, there are only 57 units (Joint Center for Housing Studies [JCHS], 2013). While the protections of the Social Security Act and the OAA have ensured that only a small percentage of older households are in poverty, 40% of households with a member aged 65 and older have incomes at less than 50% AMI (Center for Housing Policy, 2012).

This section describes the major programs in a range of policy provisions created through federal housing and tax policy that assist elders in finding, obtaining, and maintaining accessible, affordable, and safe housing. A report by the US Government Accountability Office (GAO, 2005) notes 23 federal housing programs that either target older adults directly or make specific provisions for an aging population.

Federal Housing Policy

A series of federal housing and tax acts have established the infrastructure for addressing the nation's housing needs. The acts build on the Home Owners' Loan Act of 1933 and the National Housing Act of 1934, New Deal legislation that marked the country's first efforts to support long-term home mortgages, develop low-income housing, and make housing more affordable. In addition to the programs discussed below, additional housing or housing-related programs may help older adults secure and maintain housing, including the Section 811 program for persons with disabilities, the Section 521 rural housing program, and the Low-Income Home Energy Assistance Program (LIHEAP). In addition, LIHEAP (P.L. 105-185) helps low-income renters and homeowners pay for energy-related housing costs. States may use the funds for assistance in paying heating and cooling bills, low-cost weatherization projects, and other related services for households with incomes up to 150% of the federal poverty level (Perl, 2013).

Public Housing

Established by the Housing Act of 1937, the first federal public housing program included construction for low-income elderly and nonelderly persons. Public housing remains the largest source of subsidized housing for economically disadvantaged elders. Of the 1.1 million households living in public housing units, approximately one-third are headed by those 62 years and older (Schwartz, 2010). Tenants must have very low incomes and pay 30% of their income for rent. This housing is owned, operated, and maintained by approximately 3,300 local nonprofit public housing authorities (PHAs), typically governed by community members appointed by local governments (Schwartz, 2010).

Funding for public housing decreased 12% between 2008 and 2012 (JCHS, 2013), and few new PHA-owned and -operated units have been produced since 1994, when PHAs began to focus on mixed-income developments through public–private partnerships. Between 1994 and 2008, the nation lost nearly 270,000 public housing units (Schwartz, 2010), and the supply of public housing is decreasing at a rate of 10,000 units per year (JCHS, 2013).

Section 202 Housing

First enacted as part of the Housing Act of 1959, Section 202 is the largest federal housing program primarily for older adults (ages 62+). Section 202 provides capital grants to nonprofit developers to cover acquisition, construction, or rehabilitation costs. As long as the property remains affordable to older adults for 40 years, grants do not have to be repaid. Additional resources are available to provide assisted living services to residents in existing developments, and the Assisted Living Conversion Program allows nonprofit owners of Section 202 and other subsidized housing to convert some or all of their units into an assisted living facility. Tenants of Section 202 projects pay 30% of their income for rent. The program produces approximately 5,000 units annually, down from 9,000 units between the 1970s and 1990s. In 2009, there were about 300,000 units, 85% of which were occupied by older adults and 15% by disabled younger adults (Schwartz, 2010).

Housing Choice Vouchers

The Housing and Community Development Act (HCDA) of 1974 created the Section 8 rental program to serve all ages, including older adults. Section 8 vouchers, now called Housing Choice Vouchers, are used by individuals to supplement their rent on units in the private market. Landlords must agree to accept the vouchers and the units must meet Housing Quality Standards. In 1989, approximately 48% (1,152,000) of the 2.4 million apartments subsidized by Section 8 vouchers were occupied by older adults (US Senate, Special Committee on Aging, 1990). In 2009, only 16.5% (334,445) of the 2 million apartments subsidized by vouchers were occupied by older adults (Schwartz, 2010). A HUD (2001) study found that voucher success rates decline for seniors, perhaps because mobility challenges make it more difficult to search the private market for available housing.

Block Grants

The HCDA of 1974 also addressed the need for housing and broader community development concerns through the Community Development Block Grant (CDBG) program and in 1990 the HOME Investment Partnerships program (HOME). The CDBG provides funding to states and localities to develop urban communities through housing, "suitable living environments," and economic development (HUD, n.d.a). In 2008, approximately $1.3 billion or 25% of CDBG allocations went to housing (Schwartz, 2010). The HOME program focuses exclusively on housing activities to benefit low-income renters and homeowners. The HOME funding may be used to acquire, build, or renovate housing or provide direct rental assistance to low-income households (HUD, n.d.b). In 2009, funding for HOME totaled $1.8 billion, assisting 1.1 million low-income renters and homeowners (Schwartz, 2010).

Home Equity Conversion Mortgage Program

Home equity conversion mortgages, also known as reverse mortgages, allow older homeowners who need cash for living expenses or home repairs to borrow against the equity in their home. The mortgages are offered by private lenders, but the federally insured Home Equity Conversion Mortgage (HECM) program, established by the HCDA of 1987 allows the largest loan advances and the greatest choice in how to receive the cash. The funds received from an HECM can be used for any purpose, and although costly, they are less so than private reverse mortgages. The HECM loans must be paid in full when the last surviving borrower dies, cannot live in the home for 12 consecutive months, or sells the home (HUD, n.d.c).

Federal Tax Policy

The federal housing programs discussed above provide direct expenditures to subsidize housing-related costs in the United States. While these are the most recognized form of subsidized housing, the largest form of housing assistance comes through tax expenditures. In fiscal 2009, federal tax expenditures totaled $181.7 billion (Schwartz, 2010). Tax expenditures primarily benefit homeowners, but many of the housing programs discussed above are also supported by tax expenditures that benefit private investors.

The largest government housing program is the federal tax deduction allowed on mortgage interest: 84% of federal tax expenditures in fiscal 2009, or $151.2 billion (Schwartz, 2010). Mortgage interest deductions allow homeowners to reduce their income when calculating federal income tax. Homeowners are also able to deduct their property taxes on their principal residence. The value of the tax credit increases with income, so high- and middle-income households benefit more than low-income households. Potential deductions for low-income families are typically lower than the standard deduction, so the tax credit is usually of little or no value (Schwartz, 2010).

Tax incentives also encourage investors to finance the development of affordable housing. In 2009, tax expenditures for investments in affordable rental housing totaled over $29.5 billion (Schwartz, 2010). Among investor tax expenditures, the Low Income Housing Tax Credit (LIHTC) is the largest subsidy for low-income rental housing and totaled nearly $5.8 billion in fiscal 2009 (Schwartz, 2010). The LIHTC program was established by the Tax Reform Act of 1986. For every $1 tax credit received, the developer can reduce federal taxes by $1. Developers can receive the tax credit for 10 years as long as the property is occupied by low-income households for at least 15 years. The LIHTCs are often combined with other programs, like Section 202 grants, to fund affordable housing for seniors, which can extend the period of time the property remains affordable. Developers who receive LIHTC can "sell" them to private investors or join with investors to form limited partnerships or limited liability corporations, a process called syndication. Syndication provides additional funding for acquisition, construction, and development costs and provides additional incentive for private developers to participate in the development of affordable housing.

TRANSPORTATION FOR AN AGING SOCIETY

Available and accessible transportation enables older adults to stay in their homes and communities and access the services they need to avoid institutionalization. According to the AARP, more than 8 million adults aged 65 and older do not drive, and that number is expected to grow (Lynott & Figueiredo, 2011). Like community-based social services and housing programs, federal policy provides for the transportation of older adults through multiple policy mechanisms. Programs use existing fixed-route public transportation in addition to specialized and assisted transportation to meet the needs of those who have barriers to accessing existing public and private transportation. Assisted transportation includes door-to-door service and door-through-door services, where passengers may be assisted with personal items (e.g., groceries) (Lynott, Fox-Grage, & Guzman, 2013).

The Older Americans Act

Transportation services are funded through Title III-B programs of the OAA and offered to adults ages 60 and above typically through AAAs and Aging and Disability Resource Centers. Over 25.6 million rides were provided in 2010 (Robinson, Lucado, & Schur, 2012), transporting seniors to doctor's appointments, pharmacies, grocery stores, congregate meal cites, senior centers, and other necessary daily activities. Robinson and colleagues (2012) recently found that the seniors who use transportation services have poor self-rated health, live alone in a nonmetro area, are female, and need regular assistance with activities

of daily living, suggesting that services are vital for the most vulnerable seniors.

The Social Security Act

Both Medicare and Medicaid legislation provide transportation assistance to ensure that older adults and adults with disabilities have access to medically necessary services. Medicare primarily funds emergency ambulance services for older adults. Medicare also funds some ambulance transportation for regular nonemergency medical purposes, like routine dialysis, and periodical medical visits, like primary care or other doctor's office visits (Lynott et al., 2013).

Medicaid funds emergency medical transport as well as nonemergency medical transportation (NEMT). Medicaid state plans must assure transportation to all medically necessary services, although as a part of the 2006 Deficit Reduction Act, states have the option of implementing "benchmark" plans that can eliminate or reduce NEMT transportation benefits. While NEMT is a relatively small portion of Medicaid spending, it is the second-largest federal payment system for transportation, second only to the spending of the Department of Transportation (Rosenbaum, Lopez, Morris, & Simon, 2009). State Medicaid plans often use transportation brokers to assure the availability of NEMT through a competitive bidding process. (Lynott et al., 2013). Optional Medicaid waivers can support additional transportation options to services in home- and community-based settings. Section 1915(c) waivers may be used to fund transportation to and from traditional HCBS services and other waiver services not typically covered by Medicaid. States who choose to expand Medicaid through the ACA will be able to extend HCBS-related transportation services to additional elders. The ACA also indirectly incentivizes transportation services through comprehensive discharge planning and the Community Based Collaborative Care Network Program (Lynott et al., 2013).

The Federal Transit Administration

The Federal Transit Administration (FTA), formerly the Urban Mass Transit Administration was created by the Urban Mass Transportation Act of 1964 and renamed the FTA in 1991. The FTA provides financial and technical assistance to local public transit authorities (US Department of Transportation, n.d.), including assistance for specialized transportation. Many of the FTA's programs were updated and consolidated under the 2012 reauthorization entitled Moving Ahead for Progress in the 21st Century (MAP-21) (US Department of Transportation, n.d.).

Enhanced Mobility for Seniors and Individuals with Disabilities Program (Section 5310)

The MAP-21 reauthorization consolidated and enhanced two previous FTA programs that targeted seniors and individuals with disabilities, the Elderly Individuals and Individuals with Disabilities program and the New Freedom Program. The new MAP-21 program provides capital and operating expenses to states to support the transportation needs of seniors and individuals with disabilities when existing public transportation does not sufficiently address these needs. Most funding (55%) must be used to address capital projects. The remaining funding can be used for projects that exceed the requirements of the ADA, provide greater access to fixed-routes for seniors and individuals with disabilities, or provide them public transportation alternatives (FTA, 2012). A typical project under the Elderly Individuals and Individuals with Disabilities program would include the purchase of state vehicles for use by nonprofits and local government entities to meet the transportation needs of seniors and individuals with disabilities (Lynott et al., 2013).

The Urbanized Area (Section 5307) and Rural Area (Section 5311) Formula Programs

The Urbanized Area and Rural Area Formula programs of MAP-21 both incorporate the former Job Access and Reverse Commute (JARC) program. The JARC program, while not specifically targeted toward seniors, provides for trip-based services, information-based services, capital investment projects, and planning activities to support access to employment opportunities for low-income individuals (Lynott et al., 2013). Such services and capital investments are important for individuals ages 50–64 as they approach retirement age and for seniors who must continue to work because their retirement income is insufficient to meet their needs.

CONCLUSION

Federal, state, and local entities tasked with ensuring the health and well-being of older adults must navigate numerous policies and programs to create a patchwork of community-based social service, housing, and transportation opportunities to help seniors remain at home and avoid long-term institutionalization. In addition to the sheer complexity of the system, those who work with older adults face other challenges that threaten programs and the ability to address the complex needs of an aging population. First, federal funding levels are not adequate to meet the needs of a rapidly aging population. Whether it is the continued reduction of funding for subsidized housing or the level funding of the programs of OAA as the landmark legislation awaits reauthorization, the nation's current and future capacity is inadequate for a society where the population 65 and over will double by 2060 (AOA, 2012). Second, the success of many federal programs depends on the willingness and financial capacity of states to participate. Few programs are fully funded by federal government, others, like Medicaid HCBS, are dependent on state contributions during a time when many states are reducing their own budgets and when nearly half of the states have chosen not to expand Medicaid. Finally, partisan politics resulting in the sequestration of 2013 and the stalled reauthorization of the OAA threaten to undermine efforts to respond to and plan for demographic changes currently well underway. In order to ensure the viability of community-based social services, housing, and transportation programs, social workers and allied disciplines must continue to advocate for the preservation of the nation's aging policies.

RESOURCES

AARP—Public Policy Institute
http://www.aarp.org/research/ppi/

Community-Based Social Services
National Association of State Units on Aging
http://www.nasuad.org
Administration on Aging—Older Americans Act
    Programs
http://www.aoa.gov/AOA_programs/OAA/index.aspx

Social Services Block Grants
http://www.acf.hhs.gov/programs/ocs/programs/ssbg
HCBS waiver program
http://www.medicaid.gov/Medicaid-CHIP-
Program-Information/By-Topics/Waivers/
Home-and-Community-Based-1915-c-Waivers.html

Housing
Public Housing
http://portal.hud.gov/hudportal/HUD?src=/program_
offices/public_indian_housing/programs/ph
Section811
http://portal.hud.gov/hudportal/HUD?src=/program_
offices/housing/mfh/progdesc/disab811
LIHEAP
http://www.acf.hhs.gov/programs/ocs/programs/liheap
Housing Choice Vouchers
http://portal.hud.gov/hudportal/HUD?src=/topics/
housing_choice_voucher_program_section_8
Community Development Block Grant http://portal.
hud.gov/hudportal/HUD?src=/program_offices/
comm_planning/communitydevelopment/
programs
HOME Program
http://portal.hud.gov/hudportal/HUD?src=/hud
programs/home-program
HECM
http://portal.hud.gov/hudportal/HUD?src=/
program_offices/housing/sfh/hecm/hecmabou
LIHTC   http://portal.hud.gov/hudportal/HUD?src=/
program_offices/comm_planning/affordable
housing/training/web/lihtc/basics

Transportation
MAP-21
http://www.fmcsa.dot.gov/map-21-moving-ahead-
progress-21st-century-act
Section 5310 Program
http://www.fta.dot.gov/grants/13093_3556.html
Section 5311
http://www.fta.dot.gov/grants/13093_3555.html
Section 5307
http://www.fta.dot.gov/grants/13093_3561.html
JARC
http://www.fta.dot.gov/grants/13093_3550.html

REFERENCES

AARP. (2010). *Home and community preferences of the 45+population.* Washington, DC: Author. Retrieved from http://www.aarp.org/livable-communities/learn/research-trends/info-12-2012/aarp-home-community-preferences.html

Administration on Aging, US Department of Health and Human Services (AOA). (n.d.). *Older Americans Act and aging network.* Washington, DC: Author. Retrieved from http://www.aoa.gov/AoA_Programs/OAA/introduction.aspx

Administration on Aging, US Department of Health and Human Services (AOA). (2012). *A profile of older Americans: 2012.* Washington, DC: Author. Retrieved from http://www.aoa.gov/Aging_Statistics/Profile/2012/docs/2012profile.pdf

Benjamin, A. E. (2001). Consumer-directed services at home: A new model for persons with disabilities. *Health Affairs, 20,* 80–95.

Bush, G. W. (2001). *Executive Order 13217: Community-based alternatives for individuals with disabilities.* Retrieved from http://www.gpo.gov/fdsys/pkg/FR-2001-06-21/pdf/01-15758.pdf

Center for Housing Policy. (2012). *Housing an aging population: Are we prepared?* Washington, DC: Author. Retrieved from http://www.nhc.org/media/files/AgingReport2012.pdf

Centers for Medicare and Medicaid Services, US Department of Health and Human Services (CMS). (n.d.). (2015). *Home and community based services.* Washington, DC: Author. Retrieved from http://www.medicaid.gov/Medicaid-CHIP-Program-Information/By-Topics/Long-Term-Services-and-Support/Home-and-Community-Based-Services/Home-and-Community-Based-Services.html

Coffey, G. (2008). *Money follows the person 101.* Washington, DC: National Senior Citizens Law Center. Retrieved from http://www.nsclc.org/wp-content/uploads/2011/08/Money-Follows-the-Person-101.pdf

Duckett, M. J., & Guy, M. R. (2000). Home and community based services waivers. *Health Care Financing Review, 22,* 123–125.

Federal Transit Administration (FTA). (2012). *Moving ahead for progress in the 21st Century Act (MAP-21): A summary of public transportation provisions.* Washington, DC: Author. Retrieved from http://www.fta.dot.gov/documents/MAP21_essay_style_summary_v5_MASTER.pdf

Harrington, C., Ng, T., LaPlante, M., & Kaye, H. S. (2012). Medicaid home-and community-based services: impact of the affordable care act. *Journal of Aging and Social Policy, 24,* 169–187.

Irvin, C. V., Denny-Brown, N., Kehn, M., Lester, R. S., Lipson, D., Lim, W., . . . Stone, C. (2013). *Money Follows the Person 2012 annual evaluation report.* Cambridge, MA: Mathematica Policy Research. Retrieved from http://www.mathematica-mpr.com/publications/pdfs/health/MFP_2012_Annual.pdf

Joint Center for Housing Studies (JCHS). (2013). *The state of the nation's housing 2013*. Cambridge, MA: Joint Center for Housing Studies of Harvard University. Retrieved from http://www.jchs.harvard.edu/research/publications/state-nations-housing-2013

Kaiser Family Foundation. (2013). *Summary of the Affordable Care Act*. Washington, DC: Author. Retrieved from http://kaiserfamilyfoundation.files.wordpress.com/2011/04/8061-021.pdf

Kaiser Family Foundation. (2014). *Status of state action on the Medicaid expansion decision, 2014*. Washington, DC: Author. Retrieved from http://kff.org/health-reform/state-indicator/state-activity-around-expanding-medicaid-under-the-affordable-care-act/

Lynott, J., & Figueiredo, C. (2011). *How the Travel Patterns of Older Adults Are Changing: Highlights from the 2009 National Household Travel Survey*. Washington, DC: AARP Public Policy Institute. Retrieved from http://www.aarp.org/home-garden/transportation/info-04-2011/fs218-transportation.html

Lynott, J., Fox-Grage, W., & Guzman, S. (2013). *Weaving it together: A tapestry of transportation funding older adults*. Washington, DC: AARP Public Policy Institute. Retrieved from http://www.aarp.org/content/dam/aarp/research/public_policy_institute/liv_com/2013/weaving-it-together-report-transportation-funding-for-older-adults-AARP-ppi-liv-com.pdf

National Council on Aging (NCOA). (2013). *Older Americans Act reauthorization*. Washington, DC: Author. Retrieved from http://www.ncoa.org/public-policy-action/older-americans-act/

Office of Community Services, Administration for Children and Families, US Department of Health and Human Services (OCS). (2010). *Social Services Block Grant annual report 2010*. Washington, DC: Author. Retrieved from http://www.acf.hhs.gov/sites/default/files/ocs/ssbg_annual_report_2010_finalv2.pdf

Older Americans Act of 1965 (42 U.S.C. 3001 note Enacted July 14, 1965, P.L. 89-73, sec 1, 79 Stat. 219)

Padgett, D. K. (2007). There's no place like (a) home: Ontological security among persons with serious mental illness in the United States. *Social Science and Medicine, 64*, 1925–1936.

Perl, L. (2013). *LIHEAP: Program and funding*. Washington, DC: Congressional Research Service. Retrieved from http://neada.org/wp-content/uploads/2013/08/CRSLIHEAPProgramRL31865.1.pdf

Robinson, K., Lucado, J., & Schur, C. (2012). *Use of transportation services among OAA Title III program participants*. Research Brief Number 6. Washington, DC: Administration on Aging, US Department of Health and Human Services. Retrieved from http://www.aoa.gov/aoaroot/program_results/docs/2012/AoA_6th_xation_Brief_Oct_2012.pdf

Rosenbaum, S., Lopez, N., Morris, M. J., & Simon, M. (2009). *Medicaid's medical transportation assurance: Origins, evolution, current trends, and implications for health reform*. Washington, DC: George Washington University School of Public Health and Health Services.

Schwartz, A. F. (2010). *Housing policy in the United States* (2nd ed.). New York, NY: Routledge.

Spillman, B.C., Biess, J., & MacDonald, G. (2012). *Housing as a platform for improving outcomes for older renters*. Washington, DC: Urban Institute.

US Census Bureau. (2012). *The older adult population estimates: 2012*. Washington, DC: US Government Printing Office. Retrieved from http://www.census.gov/population/age/data/2012.html

US Department of Transportation. (n.d.). *About FTA and our history*. Washington, DC: Author. Retrieved from http://www.fta.dot.gov/about/14103.html

US Government Accountability Office (GAO). (2005). *Elderly housing: Federal programs that offer assistance for the elderly*. Washington, DC: Author. Retrieved from http://www.gao.gov/newitems/d05795t.pdf

US Housing and Urban Development (HUD). (n.d.a). *Community Development Block Grant program (CDBG)*. Washington, DC: Author. Retrieved from http://portal.hud.gov/hudportal/HUD?src=/program_offices/comm_planning/communitydevelopment/programs

US Housing and Urban Development (HUD). (n.d.b). *HOME Investment Partnerships Program*. Washington, DC: Author. Retrieved from http://portal.hud.gov/hudportal/HUD?src=/program_offices/comm_planning/affordablehousing/programs/home

US Housing and Urban Development (HUD). (n.d.c). *Home equity conversion mortgages for seniors*. Washington, DC: Author. Retrieved from http://portal.hud.gov/hudportal/HUD?src=/program_offices/housing/sfh/hecm/hecmhome

US Housing and Urban Development (HUD). (n.d.d). *Income limits*. Washington, DC: Author. Retrieved from http://www.huduser.org/portal/datasets/il.html

US Housing and Urban Development (HUD). (2001). *Study on Section 8 voucher success rates*. Washington, DC: Author. Retrieved from http://www.huduser.org/Publications/pdf/sec8success.pdf

US Senate, Special Committee on Aging. (1990). *Developments on aging, 1989*. Washington, DC: US Government Printing Office.

This chapter discusses decision-making policies and proxy issues affecting the lives of older adults. The topic is challenging because of a lack of national policy on guardianship and the variety of "guardianship alternatives." Each state develops its own protective service policies, which are carried out by professionals at the local level, including probate judges, Adult Protective Services (APS) workers, and health and social service providers. To help clarify the complex needs of vulnerable adults and sort through the confusing array of policies, programs, and services available to social workers, we begin with a case study.

> ▪ Mrs. C., aged 86 and recently widowed, has been diagnosed with diabetes and congestive heart failure. A neighbor, concerned that Mrs. C has difficulty paying her bills and keeping her apartment clean, calls a local Aging and Disability Resource Center, linked with APS. The APS visit reveals a filthy, malodorous, and trash-filled home. Mrs. C. is unkempt and dirty; she is unable to accurately answer questions about her age, birth date, or where she lives. Her phone is disconnected; there is no food in her house, and she remembers eating little in recent days. Her companions are two birds and a dog.
>
> Mrs. C. appears to have little social support, few if any links to the formal service delivery system, and several complex problems that compromise her daily functioning and safety. It is unclear whether her apparent confusion stems from an immediately treatable condition (e.g., dehydration, unstable blood sugar, urinary tract infection), or a progressive dementing illness. Regardless, she needs immediate and probably long-term assistance. Social workers are likely to be key participants in her treatment if Mrs. C is hospitalized, at discharge or after she has returned home. ▪

KATHLEEN H. WILBER
JEANINE YONASHIRO-CHO
ADRIA E. NAVARRO
GRETCHEN E. ALKEMA

Policies Related to Competency and Proxy Issues

61

CORE VALUES GUIDING SERVICE DELIVERY TO OLDER ADULTS

One of the major challenges is providing Mrs. C. with appropriate support without inappropriately restricting her rights to autonomy and self-determination. To ensure that safety does not inappropriately trump individual freedom, several core values can guide treatment decisions (Wilber, 2000). These include (1) striving to offer the least restrictive appropriate alternative, (2) marshalling services to support aging in place whenever possible, (3) centering decisions to the greatest extent possible around client preferences and expressed needs, (4) drawing from the repertoire of available interventions to develop an individualized care plan, (5) supporting informal caregivers, and (6) interdisciplinary communication to clinically integrate medical, social, and housing services. Ideally core values are operationalized in the context of self-determination and person–environment fit, offering social workers the tools to balance respect for the client's personal freedom with legitimate concerns about personal safety.

Daily money management (DMM), shown in Table 61.1, is the umbrella term for services designed to assist people with meeting their everyday needs, using a variety of approaches that can include (1) offering education and advice on how to manage financial affairs; (2) ensuring that clients receive entitled benefits, and (3) providing hands-on assistance in budgeting, bill-paying, balancing the checkbook, completing medical claim forms and following up with insurance carriers, setting up direct deposits, arranging automatic bill payments, and identifying unknown assets such as retirement investments. Daily money management services also include future planning to ensure that client wishes are carried out if they no longer have the capacity to make decisions. Planning could include establishing a power of attorney (discussed later); setting-up joint

TABLE 61.1 Characteristics of Financial and Health-Related Services Available to Older Persons

Service	Capacity		Appropriateness to address risk of older person			Complexity
	Required for execution	Survives incapacity	Personal risk; high, medium, low	Financial risk; high, medium, low	Oversight/ recourse	Ability to address complex financial/ medical issues
Power of attorney	Yes	No	Low	Medium	Oversight by family; legal action	Medium
Bill-paying services	Yes	Not usually	Low	Medium	Agency audit; legal action	Low
Joint accounts/ joint tenancy	Yes	Yes	Low	Medium	Virtually none; legal action	Low
Durable power of attorney	Yes	Yes	Low	High	Oversight by family; legal action	Medium
Durable power of attorney for healthcare	Yes	Yes	Medium	Low	Oversight by family; legal action	Medium
Representative payee	No	Yes	Medium	Medium	Virtually none by federal governmental agency	Low
Personal trusts	Yes	Yes, if drawn properly	Medium	High	Internal audit, banking commissioner, legal action	High
Limited guardianship	No	Yes	High	High	Court; legal action	High
Plenary guardianship	No	Yes	High	High	Court; legal action	High

Note: *These criteria assume the availability of an appropriate social support network.*
Source: Wilber and Reynolds (1995).

accounts or joint tenancy by adding a trusted friend or family member to bank accounts, nonretirement investments, and property; designating a representative payee for federal benefits; or developing a trust to include all assets and naming a trusted individual as a trustee to act on one's behalf (for more information on various financial planning transactions see Quinn, 2005). Finally, in the event that a client lacks the capacity to engage in future planning, DMM services also include the use of court-sanctioned guardianships (discussed later).

WHAT IS CAPACITY?

In the United States, all adults aged 18 and older are assumed to have capacity unless a court of law determines otherwise. An adult's capacity and related legal decision-making authority, however, can be challenged in court by filing a guardianship petition.

A legal determination of capacity is quite specific in that a court of law determines whether or not someone has capacity to make "reasoned decisions." The American Bar Association (ABA), American Psychological Association (APA), and National College of Probate Judges (NCPJ) (2006) recommend that courts (1) screen cases for appropriateness, degree of need, and level and immediacy of risk to the client and community; (2) gather and review relevant information, requesting additional investigation, reports, and documentation as necessary; (3) conduct guardianship hearings to take judicial note of relevant reports, obtain relevant testimonies, and allow the older adult to be present and self-advocate through testimony or cross-examination; (4) implement the least restrictive action possible, considering denial of guardianship petitions, enactment of limited rather than plenary guardianships, limitations on guardian powers and preservation of itemized individual powers, and protection of individual civil and human rights. If the guardianship petition is enacted, (5) ensure oversight of guardians through training and monitoring, and when appropriate, reassess the continued need for guardianship.

The ABA, APA, and NCPJ (2006) recommend that court evaluations include "six pillars" of capacity assessment: (1) medical condition; (2) cognition; (3) everyday functioning; (4) values and preferences; (5) risk and level of supervision; and (6) means to enhance capacity, which are discussed below.

Capacity as a psychological construct is more ambiguous than its codified legal definition. In this context, capacity may be decision-specific and fluctuating (ABA & APA, 2008). For example, Mrs. C might be able to make decisions about her living arrangements but not her finances. She may be clear about her affairs one day yet confused the next. Psychologists have identified domains of capacity that require different levels and types of cognitive and functional abilities (ABA & APA, 2008; Sabatino & Wood, 2012). Physicians and psychologists may be asked to assess and determine capacity. Some jurisdictions use interdisciplinary teams, including physicians, psychologists, and social workers, to evaluate capacity and appropriateness for guardianship (Gibson, 2011; Skelton, Kunik, Regev, & Naik, 2010). Within these disciplines, capacity assessments are becoming a specialized area that requires additional training and expertise. The ABA and APA (2008) recommend a nine-item framework to assess capacities: (1) jurisdiction-specific legal standards; (2) functional elements, including ability to complete activities of daily living (ADLs), instrumental activities of daily living (IADLs), and other client-specific daily tasks; (3) relevant cognitive or mental health diagnoses, the client's expected prognosis and disease trajectory, and the possibility of improvement or reversibility and the possible timetable for such changes; (4) cognitive underpinnings and functioning; (5) psychological or emotional factors, including current function and relevant treatment interventions that may improve future function; (6) values, including personal beliefs and approaches; (7) the level of risk to the client and community; (8) clinical recommendations for treatment or accommodations to enhance or improve capacity; and, finally, (9) clinical judgment of capacities.

In situations where an individual is assessed to have capacity, undue influence can lead to compromised decisions. Undue influence occurs when a trusted person exploits a personal relationship to exert their personal influence over the will of the individual (ABA & APA, 2008). Perpetrators may try to create dependent relationships through manipulation and isolation of the victim (ABA & APA, 2008).

Social Worker's Role in Capacity Assessments

Social workers provide critical insight that can inform judicial and psychological capacity assessments.

Participating on interdisciplinary capacity assessment teams, social workers provide the court with a comprehensive, balanced assessment of client capacity including strengths, important components in evaluating the least restrictive appropriate alternative (Gibson, 2011). Even when social workers do not formally assess and document client capacity, they play a critical role in identifying client values, beliefs, practices, and approaches. These are essential to the assessment process and offer insight into the client's decision-making and behavior, particularly if a diversion from long-standing norms is observed (ABA & APA, 2008). Social workers may also provide counseling and support for individuals undergoing capacity assessments and facing judicial proceedings.

APPLYING SUPPORTIVE AND SURROGATE POLICIES AND PROGRAMS

Identification of Mrs. C.'s needs involves assessing the types of decisions she must make, what type of support is appropriate and available, and how and by whom decisions will be carried out. Collopy (1988) and Smyer (1993) distinguish between decisional capacity, the ability *to make* a reasoned choice, and executional capacity, the ability *to act* on the choice. This distinction is important for choosing the appropriate level of intervention, supportive decision-making or surrogate decision-making. Individuals who retain decisional capacity but need support to act on their decisions can be served through *supportive decision-making* interventions. In contrast, *surrogate decision-making* support is most appropriate for those who have lost the capacity to make reasoned decisions based on the legal criteria and need a proxy to make decisions on their behalf (Wilber & Reynolds, 1995).

Supportive Decision-Making

It is possible that once Mrs. C.'s health is stabilized she will be able to make and execute her own decisions. However, if ongoing help is needed, supportive decision-making services help Mrs. C implement her decisions through assistance with everyday tasks. For example, if Mrs. C.'s husband managed the finances, Mrs. C. might not know how to organize and pay her bills. With *support*, she can agree on the amount she wants to pay for each item, sign checks, and mail payments. Mrs. C. might also decide that her home needs cleaning but may be physically unable to complete the task. With her permission, housecleaning can be provided, allowing her to return home.

In assessing Mrs. C.'s strengths and need for support, a social worker is often in a position to identify and assess the informal support available. If Mrs. C. does not have help from a trusted family member or friend, a social worker can assist her with finding and setting up locally available DMM services (shown in Table 61.1), such as help with bill paying or hiring professional representative payee services.

International efforts under the United Nations Convention on the Rights of Persons with Disabilities have focused on implementing supportive, rather than surrogate decision-making practices where possible, to protect individual human rights to personhood and legal decision-making (Sabatino & Wood, 2012). Recognizing the continued decision-making rights of incapacitated individuals, countries have sought to pair them with third-party supportive decision-makers who serve to approve decisions, and to represent or take action on behalf of the incapacitated adult with their permission and/or consultation (Sabatino & Wood, 2012).

Social Worker's Role in Supportive Decision-Making

Social workers and other gerontological professionals function in a variety of supportive decision-making roles. A social worker could facilitate communication between Mrs. C. and her niece by explaining Mrs. C.'s current physical and cognitive state, detailing current and future needs upon discharge from the hospital, and helping her assume responsibility of her aunt's financial matters. The social worker could assist the niece with locating needed resources that would generally not be covered by insured services, such as attendant care, durable medical equipment, or home modifications. Additionally, a social worker could provide psychosocial support to Mrs. C. during this transition period. If Mrs. C. had not planned for incapacity, a social worker could assist her by referral to a community agency for DMM or by providing DMM to her under the auspices of a community agency's defined protocols.

Surrogate Decision-Making

Although Mrs. C might experience improved functioning after receiving care for a treatable condition, it is possible that she has a progressive degenerative disease that has caused irreversible cognitive impairment and lacks the capacity to make decisions about her care and her finances. In this case, a social worker's most appropriate intervention might be activating surrogate decision-making tools on her behalf, including determining whether there are powers of attorney that are preplanned and triggered by incapacity, as well as representative payeeship or legal guardianship, in which decisions facing Mrs. C. are formally transferred to another party.

Powers of Attorney

Powers of attorney (POAs) delineate surrogate decision-making arrangements ahead of time so that if Mrs. C. loses capacity, her wishes about daily living and preferences for end-of-life care can be effectively carried out. The POA delegates authority to an "agent" to carry out specific or general tasks. Typically, because of this delegated authority, a POA is in effect only as long as the person who is delegating the authority, the "principal," has capacity. However, durable powers of attorney (DPAs) may be developed to allow the agent to make decisions for the principal (Mrs. C.) if she has lost decision-making capacity. The two important types of DPA are durable power of attorney for healthcare (DPAHC) and DPA for finances. By enacting a DPAHC prior to incapacity, Mrs. C. can make her healthcare wishes known and then designate an agent to carry out those wishes if she loses capacity. For example, she might specify that she wants to have a "do not resuscitate" order, in the event that her breathing and/or heart stop. Likewise, Mrs. C. can spell out how she wants her finances managed through a DPA for finances, and designate an agent to administer her affairs. Because it is a private arrangement, however, it offers little external oversight to protect against fraud and/or abuse (Dessin, 2003). States may have some variation in policies related to POAs. Different institutions also may have different requirements for managing POAs, with some financial institutions requiring that their own proxy forms be used. When establishing a DPAHC, physicians should be involved and provided with a copy because they will have a critical role in carrying out decisions that the proxy makes once the DPAHC is activated.

Representative Payee

Representative payeeship, a tool to manage public benefits such as Social Security, Social Security Disability Insurance (SSDI), Supplemental Security Income (SSI), and Veteran's Affairs (VA) benefits, is the only nationally based surrogate decision-making policy. The US Government Accountability Office (GAO, 2011) reported growing rates of representative payeeship for older adult Social Security and VA beneficiaries. The federal government authorizes "rep payees" for beneficiaries who lack the capacity to manage their government-provided funds based on physician certification reporting physical and/or mental impairment (Social Security Administration, 2004). Beneficiaries with a rep payee retain their civil liberties, including decision-making rights (GAO, 2011). Rep payees can be individuals or previously authorized organizations that agree to accept this responsibility. Beneficiaries can request this service and name a friend or family member to become rep payee, or without the beneficiaries' consent, the federal government may determine that the beneficiary lacks capacity and requires a rep payee before funds are disbursed.

Rep payees undergo screening prior to appointment to ensure that they are appropriate and have no history of prior mismanagement or criminal activity (GAO, 2011). Once approved, they are responsible for providing for the clients' necessities (food, clothing, and shelter, personal care items, and healthcare expenses) and maintaining separate accounting receipts for expenses incurred (GAO, 2011; Social Security Administration, 2012). Organizations that serve as rep payees for multiple beneficiaries and meet other requirements may apply for designation as fee-for-service payee and receive up to $76 per month for their services (Social Security Administration, 2013b). However, if Mrs. C. had few resources or received only SSI, even this small amount could significantly reduce the amount available for her necessities. Although agencies provide periodic monitoring of rep payees, recent reports have called for greater oversight and supervision to guard against abuses (GAO, 2011).

Rep payeeship is the only recognized means for dispersal of federal funds; existing POAs, guardians, authorized representatives, and those with joint accounts must be established as rep payees before receiving funds on behalf of a beneficiary (Social Security Administration, 2013a). Conversely, rep payee designees are restricted to managing only public benefits. Therefore, if Mrs. C. received Social Security and a pension, the rep payee would oversee the Social Security payment, and Mrs. C. would still need another mechanism to manage her private pension.

Guardianship

If Mrs. C. lacks capacity, and alternatives are not available or do not adequately meet her needs, guardianship may be the only option. Guardianship is intended to protect vulnerable, dependent persons who are at high risk for personal injury or financial loss or those who require a legal decision-maker for treatment decisions and/or to authorize financial transactions. Considered the "court of last resort" (Schmidt, 1995), guardianship, called conservatorship in some states, is a legal arrangement in which a guardian—an individual or legal entity—is appointed by the court to manage the affairs of an adult who becomes a "ward." If Mrs. C. were placed under legal guardianship she would effectively lose civil liberties, reducing her legal status to that of a minor (GAO, 2004; Quinn, 2005).

To initiate guardianship a petitioner makes a formal request to the court. While some jurisdictions allow the use of elder mediation to determine proceedings (Crampton, 2013), most guardianship cases require a court hearing involving a judge, the petitioner who requests the hearing, and the respondent—Mrs. C. in this case. The petitioner, who may or not be appointed guardian, can be a family member, friend, private professional (a private agency or individual such as an attorney or accountant), or public guardian. Forty-nine states have a public guardian program which typically serves as the last alternative of protective care for wards that lack willing or qualified caregivers and do not have resources to pay for a private guardian (Teaster, Schmidt, Wood, Lawrence, & Mendiondo, 2010). Family members are most likely to act as petitioners and subsequent guardians, often after a specific triggering event or critical incident, such as physical health emergency, acute mental health problem, financial mismanagement, or the need for nursing home placement (Keith & Wacker, 1994). If the court finds Mrs. C. lacks the capacity to manage her affairs, a guardian is appointed. Most hearings are brief, with the vast majority—more than 90%—resulting in guardianship (Lisi & Barinaga-Burch, 1995).

Once guardianship is granted, the decision is essentially permanent because the ward lacks the legal authority to contest.

Although guardianships may be full (plenary) or partial (limited), most are plenary, in that the guardian is given responsibility for all aspects of the ward's life, including determining living arrangements, medical treatment, and financial expenditures and managing all assets (Quinn, 2005). Sometimes this is referred to as guardianship of both the "person" and the "estate" because it encompasses powers over both personal care and financial matters. In some instances, the court may limit the guardian's authority to specific areas. For example, if Mrs. C. has a rep payee and no other assets to be managed, the court might appoint a limited guardianship for healthcare decisions. Or if Mrs. C. had a complex estate but was able to make decisions about her personal affairs, the court may appoint a guardian of the estate to manage financial matters only.

Ethics and Realities of Guardianship

Guardianship operates under the state's *parens patriae* authority, which obligates government to safeguard individuals who lack the capacity to protect themselves even when they do not consent. The guardian is expected to manage the ward's affairs with care and diligence based on the ward's best interests (Friedman & Savage, 1988). Because guardianship is a draconian intervention that removes constitutionally guaranteed liberties and decision-making authority from wards, it should be used only as a last resort and only after due process safeguards have been followed. Unfortunately, some older adults receive substandard due process arising from professional biases, unreliable or inadequate capacity assessments, and perfunctory decision-making (Gavisk & Greene, 2007; Moye & Marson, 2007). A lack of knowledge and training in capacity assessment and documentation may result in the generation of poor quality reports (Moye & Naik, 2011), including those that primarily focus on clinical diagnoses rather than functional abilities, strengths, or reasons for the guardianship petition, which may thus result in inappropriate guardianships, especially plenary guardianships when less restrictive alternatives are overlooked (Gibson, 2011; Dudley & Goins, 2003). Nevertheless, despite inadequately documented legal need, courts grant guardianship petitions (Dudley & Goins, 2003).

Elder mediation, another method to determine need for support, is designed to reach amicable nonjudicial solutions through consensus-building and decision-making facilitated by a third party. This approach should be used cautiously in guardianship cases, because results may not always be in the best interest of the older adult and processes can be called into question when clients possess questionable decision-making capacity (Crampton, 2013).

In addition to ensuring due process safeguards in the establishment of guardianship, adequate court monitoring is needed to ensure that guardianship benefits vulnerable adults (GAO, 2011; Karp & Wood, 2007). Although all but two states require annual written reports and accounting, courts vary by jurisdiction in their guardian-monitoring policies and procedures. Unfortunately, conducting regular monitoring of guardians requires funding that is not available in all jurisdictions (GAO, 2004, 2011; Karp & Wood, 2007; Teaster et al., 2010). For this and other reasons, many courts do not review monitoring documents, verify the information provided, or conduct in-person monitoring visits (Karp & Wood, 2007; GAO, 2004).

Currently, the entities responsible for creating and enforcing guardianship laws and regulations are states and US territories. In the absence of a mandated national policy, each state's laws and regulations determine legal processes, duties and responsibilities of the court and legal guardians, and the terminology used. In 1997, the National Conference of Commissioners on Uniform State Laws (NCCUSL), a nonpartisan group of legal experts that develops uniform legislative templates for states to frame their own laws, adopted an updated version of the Uniform Guardianship and Protective Proceedings Act (UGPPA) proposing standardized guardianship rights including the right to due process; use of limited guardianships and the least restrictive means possible; appropriate guardian roles, duties, and responsibilities; oversight of guardians; and efforts to maximize individual rights while ensuring safety (National Conference of Commissioners on Uniform State Laws [NCCUSL], 2013a). Unfortunately, few jurisdictions have adopted the statute (NCCUSL, 2013c). Efforts to standardize responses to interstate jurisdictional disputes have yielded more demonstrable success with 37 states, the District of Columbia, and one territory adopting the NCCUSL's Uniform Adult Guardianship and Protective Proceedings

Jurisdiction Act (UAGPPJA), which proposes legislative language to establish rules for guardianship transfers, determination of guardianship jurisdiction in disputed cases, and interstate enforcement of court orders (NCCUSL, 2013b, 2013d).

There is a similar lack of public guardianship uniformity across states. Public guardianship programs, generally implemented at the county level, are housed in a variety of administrative units, including aging, adult services, mental health, and developmental disabilities, and district attorneys' offices. Differences in statutory authority, participant eligibility, and program oversight make it difficult to gauge the level of support available for vulnerable incapacitated adults.

A number of states have built on guardianship reform efforts to enact more enlightened guardianship laws, yet the immediate impact of these reforms may be limited implementation (Karp & Wood, 2007; Teaster et al., 2010). Media exposés and government reports have identified serious problems in guardianship, yet a study on the quality of care and estate management found that most guardians provide adequate services (AARP, 1990). In direct interviews with wards, Wilber, Reiser, and Harter (2001) found that the most frequently expressed problems were feelings of loneliness and isolation rather than concerns about guardianship. This research suggests the need to enhance quality of life by encouraging the ward's involvement in everyday decision-making and opportunities for socialization. If Mrs. C. were placed under guardianship, she should be encouraged to make and participate in decisions to the extent practically possible. For example, the guardian would strive to honor her preference to live in her home with her pets, if at all feasible.

The Role of Social Workers in Surrogate Decision-Making

As interventions become more restrictive, so too does the importance of practitioners' clinical effectiveness in working with older adults with profoundly diminished capacity. In particular, social workers have a professional ethical responsibility to protect and promote their older adult clients' interests and right to self-determination (National Association of Social Workers [NASW], 2008). Surrogate decision-making is the most intrusive step toward the removal of personal liberties. Therefore, social workers possess responsibilities to discuss opportunities for maximizing client choice by planning for surrogate decision-making using legal tools such as the DPA, advocate for respect of client preferences to the greatest extent possible, and when necessary intervene cautiously and judiciously with those who need unplanned surrogate decision-making assistance via rep payee and/or guardianship. These roles require fundamental social work skills of direct counseling, client education, and advocacy to ensure that a client's rights and best interests are appropriately safeguarded (NASW, 2008).

THE MISCHIEF FACTOR: VULNERABILITY TO MISTREATMENT

Older adults engaged in any decision-making arrangements that transfer some level of authority to informal or formal service providers are vulnerable to mistreatment, malfeasance, and exploitation. A GAO report (2010) found that such allegations of abuse are numerous and widespread and can involve multiple types of mistreatment including physical abuse, neglect, and financial exploitation. Part of this dilemma is due to the limited external oversight for most alternatives to guardianship (GAO, 2010; Wilber & Reynolds, 1995). The Elder Justice Act of 2009, which was passed but not funded by Congress, includes provisions for the establishment of an Elder Justice Coordinating Council, funding for Adult Protective Services and Long-Term Care Ombudsman Programs, and the formation of Elder Abuse Forensic Centers (Elder Justice Act, 2010).

Currently all states have procedures in place to report elder abuse and most have mandatory reporting laws that require social workers and other professionals to report abuse. Because the range of behaviors constituting elder and/or dependent adult abuse vary from state to state (Wilber & McNeilly, 2001), social workers must know their state's elder abuse definitions and reporting guidelines. Social workers must carefully distinguish between family tensions or control issues involving a dependent older adult and his or her caregivers and legitimate complaints about financial mismanagement or exploitation. Comprehensive assessment including person-in-environment fit requires astute clinical knowledge and judgment and often teamwork from other invested professionals.

Social workers are ethically bound to work in the best interests of their clients, and preventing role conflicts through appropriate professional boundaries is a key component of this principle (NASW, 2008). One potential conflict that might arise is when a social worker is asked to assume a supportive or a surrogate decision-making role. For example, Mrs. C. might report "feeling comfortable" with her community social worker, John, and ask him to be her agent on a DPA for finance because "he's like the son I never had." This request could be honored if John's agency provides DMM to older adults and these services are performed as part of a formal program with written protocols and procedures and clearly defined limits of responsibility. Lack of a formal program, however, can put the agency, the social worker, and the client at risk. John would have an ethical duty to inform Mrs. C. how their therapeutic relationship would change in the event that the DPA was activated. It is also essential that John garner the support of his supervisor and management on the appropriateness of this arrangement based on Mrs. C.'s current situation, her mental capacity to make this decision, and agency policies and protocols. Whatever the outcome, John and his agency must use appropriate and clear documentation of all transactions to shield against the potential accusation of impropriety by Mrs. C. or other parties (e.g., friends, family members, external regulatory agencies).

CONCLUSION

Social workers have a repertoire of services to choose from when supporting older adults with diminished decisional and/or executional capacity. These services are guided by state policies and operational definitions of capacity. Choosing the right blend of services can be challenging, and needs may vary over time as circumstances change. A set of core values provides ethical guidelines to assist social workers when choices are not clear. In addition to understanding practice issues and applying these core values, it is imperative that social workers know and operate from the relevant state statutes and regulations in place in the communities in which they practice.

REFERENCES

AARP. (1990). *National guardianship monitoring project.* Washington, DC: Author.
American Bar Association (ABA) & American Psychological Association (APA). (2008).

Assessment of older adults with diminished capacity: A handbook for psychologists. Retrieved from http://www.apa.org/pi/aging/programs/assessment/capacity-psychologist-handbook.pdf

American Bar Association (ABA), American Psychological Association (APA), & National College of Probate Judges (NCPJ). (2006). *Judicial determination of capacity of older adults in guardianship proceedings.* American Bar Association. Retrieved from http://www.americanbar.org/content/dam/aba/uncategorized/2011/2011_aging_bk_judges_capacity.authcheckdam.pdf

Collopy, B. J. (1988). Autonomy in long term care: Some crucial distinctions. *The Gerontologist, 28*(Suppl), 10–17. doi: 10.1093/geront/28.Suppl.10

Crampton, A. (2013). Elder mediation in theory and practice: Study results from a national caregiver mediation demonstration project. *Journal of Gerontological Social Work, 56*, 423–437. doi: 10.1080/01634372.2013.777684

Dessin, C. L. (2003). Financial abuse of the elderly: Is the solution a problem? *McGeorge Law Review, 34*, 267.

Dudley, K. C., & Goins, R. T. (2003). Guardianship capacity evaluations of older adults: Comparing current practice to legal standards in two states. *Journal of Aging and Social Policy, 15*, 97–115. doi: 10.1300/J031v15n01_06

Elder Justice Act of 2009, 42 U.S.C. §§ 1320b-25, 1395i-3a, and 1397j-1397m-5. (2010).

Friedman, L., & Savage, M. (1988). Taking care: The law of conservatorship in California. *Southern California Law Review, 61*, 273–290.

Gavisk, M., & Greene, E. (2007). Guardianship determinations by judges, attorneys and guardians. *Behavioral Sciences and the Law, 25*, 339–353. doi: 10.1002/bsl.772

Gibson, L. (2011). Giving courts the information necessary to implement limited guardianships: Are we there yet? *Journal of Gerontological Social Work, 54*, 803–818. doi: 10.1080/01634372.2011.604668

Karp, N., & Wood, E. F. (2007). Guardianship monitoring: A national survey of court practices. *Stetson Law Review, 37*, 143–192.

Keith, P. M., & Wacker, R. R. (1994). *Older wards and their guardians.* Westport, CT: Praeger.

Lisi, L. B., & Barinaga-Burch, S. (1995). National study of guardianship systems: Summary of findings and recommendations. *Clearinghouse Review, 29*, 643.

Moye, J., & Marson, D. C. (2007). Assessment of decision-making capacity in older adults: An emerging area of practice and research. *Journals of Gerontology Series B: Psychological Sciences and Social Sciences, 62*, P3–P11.

Moye, J., & Naik, A. D. (2011). Preserving rights for individuals facing guardianship. *Journal of the American Medical Association, 305*, 936–937. doi: 10.1001/jama.2011.247

National Association of Social Workers (NASW). (2008). *Code of ethics of the National Association of Social Workers.* Retrieved from http:///www.socialworkers.org/pubs/code/code.asp

National Conference of Commissioners on Uniform State Laws (NCCUSL). (2013a). *Guardianship and Protective Proceedings Act summary.* Retrieved from http://www.uniformlaws.org/ActSummary.aspx?title=Guardianship%20and%20Protective%20Proceedings%20Act

National Conference of Commissioners on Uniform State Laws (NCCUSL). (2013b). *Adult Guardianship and Protective Proceedings Jursidiction Act summary.* Retrieved from http://www.uniformlaws.org/ActSummary.aspx?title=Adult%20Guardianship%20and%20Protective%20Proceedings%20Jurisdiction%20Act

National Conference of Commissioners on Uniform State Laws (NCCUSL). (2013c). *Legislative fact sheet: Guardianship and Protective Proceedings Act.* Retrieved from http://www.uniformlaws.org/LegislativeFactSheet.aspx?title=Guardianship%20and%20Protective%20Proceedings%20Act

National Conference of Commissioners on Uniform State Laws (NCCUSL). (2013d). *Legislative fact sheet: Guardianship and Protective Proceedings Jurisdiction Act.* Retrieved from http://www.uniformlaws.org/LegislativeFactSheet.aspx?title=Adult%20Guardianship%20and%20Protective%20Proceedings%20Jurisdiction%20Act

Quinn, J. B. (2005). *Guardianship of adults: Achieving justice, autonomy, and safety.* New York, NY: Springer.

Sabatino, C. P., & Wood, E. (2012). The conceptualization of legal capacity of older persons in Western law. In I. Doron & A. M. Soden (Eds.), *Beyond elder law* (pp. 35–55). New York, NY: Springer-Verlag. doi: 10.1007/978-3-642-25972-2_3

Schmidt, W. C. (1995). *Guardianship: The court of last resort.* Durham, NC: Carolina Academic Press.

Skelton, F., Kunik, M. E., Regev, T., & Naik, A. D. (2010). Determining if an older adult can make and execute decisions to live safely at home: A capacity assessment and intervention model. *Archives of Gerontology and Geriatrics, 50*, 300–305. doi: 10.1016/j.archger.2009.04.016

Smyer, M. (1993). Aging and decision-making capacity. *Generations, 17*, 51–56.

Social Security Administration. (2004). *Representative payee program*. Retrieved from http://www.ssa.gov/payee.index.htm

Social Security Administration. (2012). *When a representative payee manages your money*. SSA Publication No. 05-10097. Retrieved from http://www.ssa.gov/pubs/EN-05-10097.pdf

Social Security Administration. (2013a). *FAQs for representative payees*. Retrieved from http://www.socialsecurity.gov/payee/faqrep.htm

Social Security Administration. (2013b). *Fee for service fact sheet*. Retrieved from http://www.ssa.gov/payee/fee_fact_sheet.htm#ao=3&sb=1

Teaster, P. B., Schimdt, W. C., Wood, E. F., Lawrence, S. A., & Mendiondo, M. S. (2010). *Public guardianship: In the best interests of incapacitated people?* Santa Barbara, CA: Praeger.

US Government Accountability Office (GAO). (2004). *Collaboration needed to protect incapacitated elderly people*. GAO-04-655. Retrieved from http://www.gao.gov/assets/250/243297.pdf

US Government Accountability Office. (2010). *Guardianships: Cases of financial exploitation, neglect and abuse of seniors*. GAO-10-1046. Retrieved from http://www.gao.gov/assets/320/310741.pdf

US Government Accountability Office. (2011). *Incapacitated adults: Oversight of federal fiduciaries and court-appointed guardians needs improvement*. GAO-11-678. Retrieved from http://www.gao.gov/products/GAO-11-678

Wilber, K. H. (2000). Aging. In R. J. Patti (Ed.), *The handbook of social welfare management* (pp. 521–533). Thousand Oaks, CA: Sage.

Wilber, K. H., & McNeilly, D. P. (2001). Elder abuse and victimization. In J. E. Birren & K. W. Schaie (Eds.), *The handbook of the psychology of aging* (pp. 569–591). San Diego, CA: Academic Press.

Wilber, K., Reiser, T., & Harter, K. (2001). New perspectives on conservatorship: The views of older adult conservatees and their conservators. *Aging, Neuropsychology, and Cognition, 8*, 225–240. doi: 10.1076/anec.8.3.225.831

Wilber, K. H., & Reynolds, S. L. (1995). Rethinking alternatives to guardianship. *The Gerontologist, 35*, 248–257. doi: 10.1093/geront/35.2.248

This chapter focuses on explicating select policies that protect the rights of older adults and support their families/informal caregivers. We begin by discussing those policies that prohibit discrimination based on age or disability, including the Age Discrimination in Employment Act (ADEA), the Americans with Disabilities Act (ADA), the Fair Housing Act Amendments (FHAA), and the *Olmstead* decision. Then we discuss policy to address elder abuse, neglect, and exploitation, including the Older Americans Act (OAA) and the Elder Justice Act (EJA). Finally, the chapter reviews policies and programs that support families of older adults with care needs, including the Family and Medical Leave Act (FMLA); the National Family Caregiver Support Program (NFCSP); and the Lifespan Respite Care Program (LRCP).

Policies to Protect Older Adults

Ageism is defined as "the process of systematic stereotyping of and discrimination against people because they are old" (Butler, 1969, p. 243). The key to ageism is that older adults are judged not as individuals but as members of a social category with certain traits that are perceived negatively (Quadagno, 2002). Older adults may encounter discrimination in employment, public services, and housing, as well as mistreatment, neglect or abuse perpetrated by children, spouses and other family members, or staff at nursing homes, assisted living, and other facilities. Knowledge of policies to protect older adults from such discrimination and mistreatment is essential for competent social work practice.

Discrimination Based on Age: Employment

Age discrimination in employment was the norm in the late 1960s (US Department of Labor, 1965). Congress thus enacted the ADEA (P.L. 90-202, 29 U.S.C. §§ 621-634, regulations at 29 C.F.R. § 1625) in 1967 to prohibit *arbitrary* age discrimination in hiring, termination, promotion, compensation, terms/ conditions, and privileges (Querry, 1995–1996). The ADEA makes employment discrimination against employees age 40 and older illegal (Tichy, 1991). Private employers with more than 20 employees, employment agencies, and labor unions, as well

JOAN K. DAVITT
LYDIA W. LI
KERRY A. RASTIGUE

Policies to Protect the Rights of Older Adults and Support Family Caregivers

62

as federal employers are covered under this Act (Kapp, 2001).

Employers can assert the following exemptions against an age discrimination claim: (1) where age is a "bona fide occupational qualification" (BFOQ) reasonably necessary to the normal operation of a particular business; (2) where the action is based on "reasonable factors other than age" (RFOA); (3) to observe the terms of a bona fide seniority system; (4) to observe the terms of a bona fide employee benefit plan; or (5) to discharge or otherwise discipline an individual for good cause (29 U.S.C. @ 623 (f)) (Koff & Park 1999; Tichy, 1991). In some cases age may be a factor in one's ability to safely perform the job, such as police officer or firefighter and can thus be used as a qualifying criterion (Kapp, 2001). Also employers can require medical exams for applicants over age 40, but only when it is directly related to the specific work to be performed and when exams are required for all applicants regardless of age (Tichy, 1991). Likewise, employers can promote a younger employee over an older employee due to greater seniority of the younger employee. In addition, the employer cannot establish a mandatory retirement system, but can legally offer a retirement incentive as long as it is voluntary (Kapp, 2001; Tichy, 1991). An employer is allowed to fire or refuse to hire/promote based on an individual's qualifications or actual job performance, but cannot use chronological age as a proxy for job performance.

A plaintiff presents a prima facie case of age discrimination to the Equal Employment Opportunity Commission (EEOC) by showing that the plaintiff was a member of the protected group (e.g., over age 40), the plaintiff was qualified for the job, the plaintiff was adversely affected, and the employer hired/promoted someone else for the same position (Tichy, 1991). The alleged aggrieved employee also does not have to provide direct evidence of the employer's unlawful intent, rather they merely have to provide evidence to refute any reasons for rejecting an applicant (for hire, promotion, etc.) put forward by the employer (Kapp, 2001). In addition, some states have their own versions of the ADEA, some of which provide broader protections (Kapp, 2001).

Problems with ADEA abound. First, the act does not clarify the term *arbitrary* (Querry, 1995–1996). Second, ADEA has had little effect on hiring decisions, as such discrimination can be very difficult

to prove (Jolls, 1996). Third, Harper (1993) contends that ADEA does little to protect workers in relation to retirement incentives. Employers offer retirement incentives as a way to reduce the workforce through attrition rather than forced layoffs. Older workers in most cases cost employers more for a variety of reasons (service time, higher healthcare costs, etc.). Thus it benefits the company more to reduce the number of older workers (regardless of productivity levels) than to reduce the number of younger workers (Frolik, 1999; Harper, 1993). "Conditional age-based exit incentives can be used to achieve precisely what the ADEA seeks to eradicate: the age-based elimination of productive older workers who would prefer continued employment to retirement" (Harper, 1993, p. 69).

Americans with Disabilities Act and Employment Discrimination

Until 1990 older employees who had adverse action taken against them (firing, failure to promote, etc.) due to "reasonable factors other than age" (RFOAs) had little recourse (Hood, 1998). However, in 1990 Congress passed the ADA (P.L. 101-336, 104 Stat. 327 [1990], 42 U.S.C. 12101-12213 [1994]), and this may help those older workers who are terminated for health reasons (Kapp, 2001).

The ADA (specifically Title I) prohibits public and private employers with 25 or more employees from discriminating "against a qualified individual with a disability . . . in regard to job application procedures, the hiring, advancement or discharge of employees, employee compensation, job training, and other terms, conditions, and privileges of employment" (42 U.S.C. § 12112 (a)). A disabled person is defined under the Act as one who "(1) has an actual physical or mental impairment that substantially limits one or more major life activities; (2) has a record or past history of an impairment . . .; (3) is regarded as having an impairment" (42 U.S.C. § 12102(2)(A, B, C)). A qualified individual with a disability is defined as a person "who can perform the essential functions of the job with or without reasonable accommodations" (42 U.S.C. § 12111(8)). Such accommodations can include reassignment or restructuring of the job, providing special aids or training and access to employer-provided facilities such as cafeterias, lounges, and fitness centers (42 U.S.C. § 12111(8)). The employer must provide these accommodations unless they can show that it would "impose an undue hardship on the employer" (Kapp, 2001; Hood, 1998).

According to Kapp (2001) and Hood (1998) an older worker with arthritis prior to ADA could be terminated under the RFOA exemption of the ADEA. "Now, however, that same employer may be liable under the ADA if it could reasonably accommodate her arthritis on the job" (Hood, 1998, p. 8). (See www.eeoc.gov/docs/accommodation for further guidelines on the ADA.)

Discrimination in Public Services: The Americans with Disabilities Act and Older Adults

Title II of the ADA also protects individuals with disabilities in relation to discrimination in public services. Title II states, "no qualified individual with a disability shall by reason of such disability, be excluded from participation in or be denied the benefits of the services, programs, or activities of a public entity or be subjected to discrimination by such an entity" (42 U.S.C. § 12131(1)). A qualified individual is defined as "an individual with a disability who, with or without reasonable modifications to rules, policies, or practices, the removal of architectural, communication, or transportation barriers, or the provision of auxiliary aids and services, meets the essential eligibility requirements for the receipt of services or the participation in programs or activities provided by a public entity" (42 U.S.C. § 12131 (2)).

The Supreme Court in *Olmstead v. L.C.* (119 S.Ct. 2176 [1999]) further interpreted Title II of the ADA. The court held that "unjustified isolation ... is properly regarded as discrimination based on disability." The court noted that "institutional placement of persons who can handle and benefit from community settings perpetuates unwarranted assumptions that persons so isolated are incapable or unworthy of participating in community life [and] confinement in an institution severely diminishes the everyday life activities of individuals, including family relations, social contacts, work options, economic independence, educational advancement, and cultural enrichment" (Olmstead v. L.C., 1999, at 2176). Under this decision, states are now required to provide community-based services or less restrictive service settings when a professional determination indicates that such placement is appropriate,

the affected person does not oppose the placement, and the placement can be reasonably accommodated (Fried, 2001; Kapp, 2001).

Many states have made ample progress toward implementation of the *Olmstead* decision by refocusing their energy on community-based care options. However, this has been a very slow process, with community-based care still lagging behind institutional care options. For example, 56% of Medicaid spending on long-term services and supports was earmarked for institutional care, while 44% was spent on community-based care in 2009 (Eiken, Sredl, Burwell, & Gold, 2012). Such structural lag erodes the ability to promote the rights of older adults to engage in community life (Hudson, 2009).

Discrimination in Housing: The Americans with Disabilities Act and Fair Housing Amendments

Persons with disabilities housing rights are protected via the ADA (Titles II public services, and III public accommodations), Section 504 of the Rehabilitation Act (29 U.S.C. § 794), and the FHAA of 1988 (P.L. 100-430, 102 Stat.1619 [1988] 42 U.S.C. §. 3601-3619). Section 504 of the Rehabilitation Act prohibits organizations and employers that receive federal funding from excluding or denying individuals with disabilities equal access to benefits and services. The FHAA make it illegal to discriminate in the sale, rental, terms, conditions, or privileges of sale/rental or in the provision of services or facilities because of a handicap of the buyer/renter, someone intended to live in the property, or someone connected with that buyer/renter (Kapp, 2001).

Of note is the fact that the Act covers renters and buyers who live or are associated with a person with a disability. Thus, families wishing to take in an elderly, disabled relative, older adults caring for mentally/physically disabled adult children, or grandparents caring for a disabled grandchild would fall under these protections. Also, the FHAA may be applicable in cases where independent living complexes or communities refuse to rent to a senior in a wheelchair or with other disabilities (Ziaja, 2001). Providers may be exempt from this policy if they can show that the discriminatory policy is fundamental to the nature of the facility and such a change would instill an undue burden related to accommodation on the facility. Finally, the FHAA may also prohibit certain state or local regulations (e.g., zoning and fire safety codes) that restrict certain types of housing operators from admitting residents with certain disabilities (*Cason v. Rochester Housing Auth.*, 748 F. Supp. 1002 [W.D.N.Y. 1990]).

Protection from Abuse, Neglect, and Exploitation

Policy related to elder abuse, neglect, and exploitation is found at both the federal and state levels. The OAA defines these terms in the following ways:

> Abuse is the willful infliction of injury, unreasonable confinement, intimidation, or cruel punishment with resulting physical harm, pain, or mental anguish; or deprivation by . . . a caregiver of goods or services . . . necessary to avoid physical harm, mental anguish, or mental illness. (42 U.S.C. § 3002(13)(A-B))
>
> Neglect is the failure to provide for oneself goods or services necessary to avoid physical harm, mental anguish or mental illness . . . [or] failure of a caretaker to provide such goods or services. (42 U.S.C. § 3002(37)(A-B))
>
> Exploitation means the illegal or improper act or process of an individual, including a caregiver, using the resources of an older individual for monetary or personal benefit, profit, or gain. (42 U.S.C. § 3002 (26))

These definitions provide guidelines for the states. However, the OAA does not stipulate penalties for the commission of abuse/neglect.

In 2010 the EJA was passed as part of the Patient Protection and Affordable Care Act, providing further federal guidance on elder abuse. The EJA established subtitle B under Title XX of the Social Security Act, authorizing appropriations for a variety of initiatives to address elder abuse, neglect, and exploitation. The act also defines elder justice activities to include prevention, detection, treatment, and prosecution while recognizing older adults' autonomy. The EJA focuses on training of long-term care workers and enhanced capacity within state Adult Protective Services departments, state surveying authorities, and the Long-Term Care Ombudsman Program. The law also established a National Elder Justice Coordinating Council within the Department of Health and Human Services and mandates reporting of crimes committed against residents living in federally funded facilities. Unfortunately, the act does not establish uniform standards for investigating or addressing elder abuse reports (O'Shaughnessy, 2010). Thus the policy in this area still consists of a hodge-podge of state laws.

Every state has enacted elder abuse legislation that defines abuse. Most states have the equivalent of an Adult Protective Services unit that is responsible for investigating and substantiating cases of abuse or neglect as well as providing protection from further mistreatment. Most state statutes provide for criminal liability for care omission or willful acts of elder mistreatment (Kapp, 2001). Most statutes include family as well as formal care providers under the definition of "caregiver." Finally, some statutes mandate certain professionals to report elder abuse/neglect, while other statutes provide for voluntary reporting of abuse/neglect (Kapp, 1999). All states protect the reporter of abuse; as long as they have made a report in good faith, they are immune from subsequent charges of harm or defamation (Kapp, 1999).

POLICIES TO SUPPORT FAMILIES OF OLDER ADULTS WITH CARE NEEDS

The growth of the elderly population and the increased likelihood of chronic illness, degenerative neurocognitive disorders/dementia, and disability with age have made elder care one of the major challenges faced by the United States. Currently, the bulk of elder care is unpaid assistance provided by families of older persons. Policy makers have begun to realize that family caregiving cannot be taken for granted. In this section, we describe three federal policies and programs that support family caregivers.

The Family and Medical Leave Act (FMLA)

The FMLA was signed into law by President Clinton in February 1993. From its inception, the policy had few changes until 2008, when it was amended to provide military-related leave protection (US Department of Labor, 2013a). The Act requires companies with 50 or more employees and all public-sector employers to provide eligible employees with up to 12 weeks of unpaid leave per year for the following reasons:

- care for self, a child, spouse, or parent due to a serious health problem;
- care for a newborn, newly adopted, or foster child;
- to address "qualifying exigencies" arising out of the military deployment of a spouse, child, or parent; or
- care for a spouse, child, parent, or next of kin who is an injured military service member (26 weeks for military caregiver leave).

Eligible employees are those who have worked for the company for at least 1 year and for 1,250 hours over the previous 12 months. The unpaid leave comes with two protections: job security and maintenance of health benefits. An employee is entitled to return to the same or an equivalent position after the leave and to receive the same health benefits while on leave as received while working. Employees are required to notify their employers prior to taking leave, and employers can request medical certifications to justify the absence (National Partnership for Women and Families, 2013).

Approximately two-thirds of the US labor force worked for employers covered by the FMLA in 2012 (Klerman, Daley, & Pozniak, 2012). However, among the covered companies, not all employees are eligible because of the Act's requirements for length of employment and hours worked. Combining employees in public and private sectors, about 59.2% are both covered and eligible. Workers who are unable to benefit from the FMLA tend to be young (< 25 years old) or old (> 64 years old), never married, low-educated (< high school education), and hourly paid and tend to have low family incomes.

Studies have shown that most employees who had taken an FMLA leave viewed the leave positively (Cantor et al., 2000;Commission on Leave, 1996; Klerman et al., 2012). A majority indicated that taking the leave had a positive effect on their ability to care for a family member and on the emotional well-being and/or physical health of their family members or themselves. Employers generally felt that the law was a minimum burden (Klerman et al., 2012; Wisensale, 2001).

While the FMLA is an important step in supporting family caregivers, it has significant limitations. First, many employed caregivers cannot take advantage of the Act, such as those working for smaller companies and those who are hired as part-time, seasonal, or temporary workers. Second, the definition of family is narrow and does not include individuals such as same- or opposite-sex domestic partners, in-laws, grandparents, siblings, aunts, and uncles. Finally, the FMLA does not require employers to pay employees while on leave, which is a strong deterrent to taking FMLA leave.

Despite numerous attempts by some members of Congress to expand the FMLA, all such proposals have failed (Wisensale, 2003). In response, many states have taken matters into their own hands and adopted legislation that expands the rights of their residents to take leave (US Department of Labor, 2013b). For example:

- California, Washington, and New Jersey provide *paid FMLA leave*.
- Maine, Minnesota, Oregon, Rhode Island, Vermont, Washington, and Washington, DC, have *lowered the employee threshold* below 50.
- California, Connecticut, Hawaii, Maine, New Jersey, Oregon, Rhode Island, Vermont, Wisconsin, and Washington, DC, *have expanded the definition of family* to *include domestic partners, grandparents, and parents-in-law.*

The federal law has yet to follow these state initiatives to expand the coverage to a broader workforce (e.g., workers in smaller companies, and in part-time, seasonal, or temporary positions), update the definition of family (e.g., including siblings, domestic partners, parents-in-law, and grandparents), and most importantly, promote access to paid family leave.

The National Family Caregiver Support Program

The NFCSP was established in 2000 under the OAA Amendments and was reauthorized in 2006. The program, administered by the Administration on Aging (AOA) within the Department of Health and Human Services, is the first national program for which the family caregiver rather than the older adult is the focus. The NFCSP calls for all states, in partnership with Area Agencies on Aging (AAAs) and local community-service providers, to provide direct support services to meet the range of family caregiver needs. There are five basic service categories (US Administration on Aging [AOA], 2013a):

- *Information* about services available to caregivers;
- *Assistance* to caregivers in gaining access to services;
- *Individual counseling, support groups, and training* to caregivers;
- *Respite care* to caregivers;
- *Supplemental services* to complement caregiver assistance.

Federal grants are allocated to states based on a proportionate rate of the population 70 years of age or older, to implement the program. Eligible service recipients include:

- Adult family or other informal caregivers of older adults age 60 or over;
- Adult family or other informal caregivers of persons with Alzheimer's disease or related disorders;
- Grandparents or other relative caregivers, age 55 or older, of children under 18;
- Grandparent or other relative caregivers, age 55 or older, of disabled adults age 18–59.

States are to give priority consideration to those with greatest social and economic needs, especially low-income individuals and older adults caring for persons with severe disabilities.

Congress appropriated $153–$154 million a year for the NFCSP from 2008 to 2011. States have used this funding to provide a wide array of services to family caregivers, including respite care (the most common service offered), home modifications, assistive technology, emergency alarm response systems, information and assistance, education and training, care management, personal care, and counseling (AOA, 2013a). Some of the more innovative services offered by states are family meetings to help resolve caregiver issues and improve communication among family members; cash grants to purchase goods (e.g., incontinence products, ramps, grab bars) and/or services (e.g., respite care); and eHealth applications (e.g., telemedicine, interactive websites) (Feinberg, Newman, Gray, Kolb, & Fox-Grage, 2004). Consumer-directed approaches, such as making direct payments to family caregivers or providing a voucher for goods and services, are gaining significant traction among the states and are viewed by

the AOA as a promising approach to strengthening caregiver support services and dealing with problems of direct care worker shortage (Feinberg et al., 2004).

According to the most recent data from the AOA, significant progress has been made in implementing the NFCSP (AOA, 2013a). For instance, the AOA reported that in 2010, over 700,000 caregivers received services through the NFCSP to help them manage their caregiving responsibilities, including almost 125,000 caregivers receiving counseling and training and over 64,000 receiving respite care, with a total of 6.8 million hours of temporary relief. The program also provided assistance to 1 million caregivers in accessing services.

Data from the 2012 national survey of OAA participants suggest that the NFCSP has had a positive effect on caregivers and their families (AOA, 2013b). For example, 82% of caregivers reported that services enabled them to provide care longer than otherwise would have been possible, and 74% said that they experienced less stress because of receiving services. Despite positive outcomes, significant work is still needed before the NFCSP can have a meaningful impact on family caregivers nationwide. Insufficient funding is the biggest challenge. The funding for the NFCSP has been flat for several years, and the modest level of funding is inadequate to meet the multifaceted needs of family caregivers. A second challenge is outreach to caregivers who are unaware of available services. Although caregiver awareness has increased, many caregivers fail to identify themselves and therefore do not seek services until it is too late (Feinberg, Wolkwitz, & Goldstein, 2006). A third challenge is the shortage of direct care workers, which has hampered the delivery of quality services to caregiving families, especially those in rural areas (Feinberg, Newman, & Steenberg, 2002). In addition, to increase the program's effectiveness, more efforts are needed to improve caregiver assessment and integration and coordination of services (Feinberg et al., 2006). Finally, the lack of standardized requirements on the collection of outcome data makes it difficult to assess the effectiveness of the NFCSP.

The Lifespan Respite Care Program

Respite care is one of the most frequently requested services by family caregivers, but quality respite care is often unaffordable and inaccessible to them

(Feinberg et al., 2002). The LRCP, administered by the Administration for Community Living (ACL)/ AOA, was authorized in 2006 under the Public Health Service Act. Its purpose is to improve the delivery and quality of respite services available to family caregivers. Competitive grants are awarded to states to implement lifespan respite care, which is defined as "coordinated systems of accessible, community-based respite care services for family caregivers of children and adults of all ages with special needs" (US Administration for Community Living (ACL), 2013). The LRCP has the following objectives:

- Expand and enhance respite services;
- Improve coordination and dissemination of respite services funded through different sources;
- Streamline access to various respite programs;
- Fill gaps in service;
- Improve the quality of respite services.

Since 2009, Congress has appropriated approximately $2.5 million per year to implement the LRCP. As of 2012, grants of up to $200,000 were awarded to eligible agencies in 30 states and Washington, DC. States have used these grants in a variety of ways, including needs assessment and environmental scans to understand respite programs available in the state; outreach to and education for family caregivers about respite and how to access services; recruiting, training, and retaining volunteer and paid respite providers; and partnering with faith-based organizations to develop respite options (ACL/AOA, 2013).

The LRCP defines family caregivers broadly, including any unpaid adults caring for someone across all ages and disability groups at home. While recognizing family caregiving occurs over the life span and in various conditions, it is challenging to meet the respite care needs of such a diverse population of family caregivers, especially when the funding level of the LRCP is so low. Some states have yet to receive any federal funds to implement the LRCP, as the distribution of funds is through competitive grants. The amount of the award is relatively small, which limits the scale and the impact of activities.

CONCLUSION

The rights of older adults and their caregivers are protected via a hodgepodge of policies generated by case law, executive order, or legislation. This chapter simply touches the tip of the proverbial iceberg in relation to these areas. The several policies described here to protect the rights of older adults support the following OAA objectives:

- an opportunity for employment with no discrimination based on age;
- obtaining and maintaining suitable housing, independently selected, designed and located with reference to special needs and available at costs which older citizens can afford;
- participating in and contributing to meaningful activity within . . . civic, cultural, educational, training and recreational opportunities;
- efficient community services . . . with emphasis on maintaining a continuum of care for vulnerable older individuals;
- a comprehensive array of community-based, long term care services adequate to appropriately sustain older people in their communities and in their homes;
- Freedom, independence and the free exercise of individual initiative in . . . managing their own lives . . . and
- protection from abuse, neglect and exploitation. (OAA, 1965)

The ADEA, ADA, and other policies continue to promote the rights of older adults to actively participate in societal institutions unencumbered by age discrimination. The EJA and the various state elder abuse laws continue to promote both the well-being and autonomy of older adults. However, inadequate funding, cultural lag, and this policy patchwork continue to challenge our ability as a society to promote the rights and interests of older adults and their caregivers.

The FMLA, NFCSP, and LRCP represent a formal recognition of the importance of family caregivers. The FMLA has provided job protection and its associated health benefit protection to employed caregivers, and the NFCSP and LRCP have increased public awareness of caregivers, spurred innovative support services, and provided assistance to numerous family caregivers. A major limitation of the FMLA is that the leave is unpaid; additionally, its coverage and eligibility criteria exclude many family caregivers in the workforce. The NFCSP and LRCP both are constrained by low funding levels, which are insufficient to match the demand for services. Lack of standardized procedures and criteria also hamper these programs' ability to evaluate effectiveness, which might support increased funding.

Older adults, their families, and social worker advocates must understand that federal legislation is important, but equally important are state statutes, court decisions interpreting these laws, and the regulations that guide implementation. Thus, social workers not only need to be informed about new legislation but also must be aware of changes made in all areas of policy creation. The OAA objectives provide guidelines for those key areas that we, as a society, have identified as crucial to the health and well-being of older adults. However, as advocates, social workers must go beyond these guidelines to continue to enhance and expand the rights of older adults.

REFERENCES

Butler, R. (1969). Ageism: Another form of bigotry. *The Gerontologist, 9*, 243–246. Retrieved from www.os.dhhs.gov/news/press/1999pres/990412.html doi: 10.1093/geront/9.4_Part_1.243

Cantor, D., Waldfogel, J., Kerwin, J., McKinley Wright, M., Levin, K., Rauch, J., … Stapleton Kudela, M. (2000). *Balancing the needs of families and employers: Family and Medical Leave surveys.* Retrieved September 10, 2013, from www.dol.gov/whd/fmla/toc.pdf

Commission on Leave. (1996). *A workable balance: Report to Congress on family and medical leave policies.* Retrieved September 10, 2013, from http://www.dol.gov/whd/fmla/1995Report/family.htm

Eiken, S., Sredl, K., Burwell, B., & Gold, L. (2012). *Medicaid expenditures for long term services and supports: 2011 update.* Cambridge, MA: Thomson Reuters. Retrieved from www.thescanfoundation.org

Feinberg, L. F., Newman, S. L., Gray, L., Kolb, K. N., & Fox-Grage, W. (2004). *State of the states in family caregiver support: A 50-state study.* San Francisco, CA: Family Caregiver Alliance. Retrieved September 19, 2013, from http://www.caregiver.org/caregiver/jsp/content/pdfs/50_state_report_complete.pdf

Feinberg, L. F., Newman, S. L., & Steenberg, C. V. (2002). *Family caregiver support: Policies, perceptions and practices in 10 states since passage of the National Family Caregiver Support Program.* San Francisco, CA: Family Caregiver Alliance. Retrieved August 23, 2013, from http://www.caregiver.org/jsp/content/pdfs/op_200211_10_state_full.pdf

Feinberg, L. F., Wolkwitz, K., & Goldstein, C. (2006). *Ahead of the curve: Emerging trends and practice in family caregiver support.* Washington, DC: AARP. Retrieved August 26, 2013, from http://assets.aarp.org/rgcenter/il/2006_09_caregiver.pdf

Fried, L. B. (2001). Olmstead: Catalyst to expand services for the elderly. *Bifocal, 22*(3), 6, 8–9.

Frolik, L. A. (1999). *Aging and the law: An interdisciplinary reader.* Philadelphia, PA: Temple University Press.

Harper, M. C. (1993). The effect of conditional age-based exit incentives, coercion, and the prospective waiver of ADEA Rights: The failure of the Older Workers Benefit Protection Act. *Virginia Law Review, 79*, 1271.

Hood, C. K. (1998). Age discrimination in employment and the Americans with Disabilities Act: A second bite at the apple. *Elder Law Journal, 6*, 1.

Hudson, R. (2009). Analysis and advocacy in home and community based care: An approach in three parts. *Journal of Gerontological Social Work, 53*, 3–20. doi: 10.1080/01634370903425832

Jolls, C. (1996). Hands-tying and the Age Discrimination in Employment Act. *Texas Law Review, 74*, 1813.

Kapp, M. B. (1999) *Geriatrics and the law* (3rd ed.). New York, NY: Springer.

Kapp, M. B. (2001). *Lessons in law and aging.* New York, NY: Springer.

Klerman, J., Daley, K., & Pozniak, A. (2012). *Family and medical leave in 2012.* Retrieved September 10, 2013, from http://www.dol.gov/asp/evaluation/fmla/fmla2012.htm

Koff, T. H., & Park, R. W. (1999). *Aging public policy bonding the generations* (2nd ed.). Amityville, NY: Baywood.

National Partnership for Women and Families. (2013). *Guide to the Family and Medical Leave Act (FMLA): Questions and answers.* Retrieved September 10, 2013, from http://www.nationalpartnership.org/research-library/work-family/fmla/guide-to-fmla.pdf

Older Americans Act of 1965, Pub. L. No. 89–73, title I, § 101 (1965).

O'Shaughnessy, C. V. (2010). *The basics- The Elder Justice Act: Addressing elder abuse, neglect, and exploitation.* Washington, DC: National Health Policy Forum. Retrieved from http://www.nhpf.org/library/the-basics/Basics_ElderJustice_11-30-10.pdf

Quadagno, J. (2002). *Aging and the life course: An introduction to social gerontology.* Boston, MA: McGraw Hill.

Querry, T. J. (1995–1996). Note: A rose by an other name no longer smells sweet: Disparate treatment discrimination and the age proxy doctrine after Hazen Paper Co. v. Biggins. *Cornell Law Review, 81*, 530.

Tichy, G. J. (1991). The Age Discrimination in Employment Act of 1967. *Catholic Lawyer, 34*, 373.

US Administration for Community Living (ACL). (2013). *Lifespan Respite Care Program.* Retrieved September 1, 2013, from http://www.acl.gov/Programs/CDAP/OIP/LifespanRespite/index.aspx

US Administration for Community Living & Administration on Aging (ACL/AOA) (2013). *Lifespan Respite Care Program: Building integrated and sustainable lifespan respite care programs.* Retrieved September 16, 2013, from http://www.acl.gov/Funding_Opportunities/ Announcements/docs/2013/FY2013_LifespanRespite Program_Pre-ApplTeleconferenceTranscript_IntegrationAnd Sustainability.pdf

US Administration on Aging (AOA). (2013a). *National Family Caregiver Support Program (OAA Title IIIE).* Retrieved September 5, 2013, from http://aoa.gov/aoa_programs/hcltc/caregiver/

US Administration on Aging (AOA). (2013b). *Aging integrated database.* Retrieved September 9, 2013, from http://www.agidnet.org/CustomTables/

US Department of Labor. (1965). *The older American worker: Age discrimination in employment.* Washington, DC: Author.

US Department of Labor. (2013a). *Leave benefit: Medical and family leave.* Retrieved September 5, 2013, from http://www.dol.gov/dol/topic/benefits-leave/fmla.htm

US Department of Labor. (2013b). *Federal vs. state family and medical leave laws.* Retrieved September 20, 2013, from http://www.dol.gov/whd/state/fmla/

Wisensale, S. (2001). *Family leave policy: The political economy of work and family in America.* Armonk, NY: Sharpe.

Wisensale, S. (2003). Two steps forward, one step back: The Family and Medical Leave Act as retrenchment policy. *Review for Policy Research, 20*, 135–151. doi: 10.1111/1541-1338.00008

Ziaja, E. (2001). Do independent and assisted living communities violate the Fair Housing Amendments Act and the Americans with Disabilities Act? *Elder Law Journal, 9*, 313.

Index

intellectual and developmental disabilities (*continued*)
person-centered care for, 489–90
residential options, 492–93
rights and advocacy, 495–96
social work practice, 491–92, 494–96
types of, 489
inter-assessor reliability, 20
interdisciplinary team member, 230
for GCM, 196
for palliative and end-of-life care, 593
intergenerational family interventions
ecological perspective, 45
functional age model, 46–47
systems theory, 45
intermittent, progressive frailty, Fahey concept of, 243
Intermodal Surface Transportation Efficiency Act (Federal Transit Act), 186
internal scale reliability, 20
International Association of Schools of Social Work, 581
International Council on Social Welfare, 581
International Federation of Social Workers, 581
Internet, end-of-life care and, 603–4
interpersonal therapy, 209
intra-assessor reliability, 20
intrinsic ability, 227
IOM. *See* Institute of Medicine
IRAs. *See* individual retirement accounts
Islamic Social Services Association USA, 547

JARC. *See* Job Access and Reverse Commute
Jewish Home for Aging Parents, 284
Jewish older adults, 545
culturally competent social work interventions, 546–47
cultural values and social work interventions, 546
physical and mental health, 546
Job Access and Reverse Commute (JARC) program, 658
John A. Hartford Foundation
Geriatric Interdisciplinary Team Training program, 593
PPS in HHC study by, 126
social work education and healthcare practice study, 126
Johnson, Lyndon B., 185
The Joint Commission (TJC), 109
Joint Commission on Mental Illness and Health, *Action for Mental Health* report, 142

Kaiser Permanent, 165
Kane, Rosalie A., 175, 241, 284
Kennedy, John F., 142
Kitwood, Tom, 282
Kubler-Ross, Elisabeth, 307, 599
Kuhn, Maggie, 280, 379

Language Bank, hospitals use of, 114
Late Life Social Roles, 44*t*
late onset stress symptomology (LOSS), 56, 209
Latinos, 503
cancer, 337
counseling and support services, 203
CVD, 344
dementia, 378
depression, 375, 387, 388, 527–28, 567

diabetes and, 357*t*, 507
disability prevalence, 322, 507, 627
disease and disability rates, 300
dual sensory impairment and, 304
educational attainment, 529
family and, 356
HBP, 507
health characteristics, 506, 507, 529–30
HIV/AIDS, 364
home care, 120
homeownership and, 225
immigrant/refugee elders, 567
income of, 528
language issues and, 529, 530
life expectancy, 436
literacy, 529
mental health issues and, 391, 520, 528
as nursing home residents, 259
oldest old, 431
pension plans and, 624–25
population growth and diversity, 132
poverty of, 224, 433, 468, 506, 528
Social Security and, 528, 627
sociodemographic indicators, 528–29
vision impairment and, 302, 303
Lawrence v. Texas, 558
learning circles, 281
length of stay (LOS), 115
lesbian, gay, bisexual, and transgender (LGBT), 503–4, 555–63
approaches to understanding, 556
caregiving roles, 367, 557
civil rights policies, 557–60
counseling and support services, 209
culturally sensitive GCM services, 195
hospitals and, 114
knowledge about, 556–57
Medicare and, 558
mental health disorders treatment, 208–9
oppression, 559
population estimates, 555–56
SAGE senior center for, 156, 560, 561
social work practice considerations, 560–61
Web-based resources, 559, 561
licensed practitioner nurses (LPNs), 185
life challenges interview, for surgery or medical procedures anxiety, 58–59
Life Long Learning Institutes (LLIs), 206
life review, 5
dementia patients and, 382
for depression, 58, 389
effectiveness of, 55
group interventions, 47, 48–49, 59, 209
for one-to-one interactions, 54
outcomes focus, 55
reminisce compared to, 54
veterans and, 56, 59
Life Review and Experiencing Form (LREF), 48–49, 58
Life Satisfaction Index, 24
Lifespan Respite Care Program (LRCP), 620, 671
life transitions, life review for, 58

persons with dementia (PWD) (*continued*)
  cognitive stimulation programs, 382
  communication guidelines, 383*t*
  depression and, 375, 379–80
  Gwyther on, 284
  HD and, 408
  hospitalizations and, 113
  IADLs and, 379
  intervention strategies, 381–83
  Kitwood pioneering work on, 282
  memory albums and charts, 382
  NH services and, 135
  oldest old, 437, 438
  racial and ethnic status, 378
  religion and spirituality role, 380
  SCUs, 240
  strength-based perspective and, 65
  women, 375, 378
pharmacological interventions, 364–65
for anxiety, 375, 391
  for depression, 375, 390, 528
  medication nonadherence, 390, 398
  for PWD, 380, 381–82
Philadelphia Geriatric Center Morale Scale, 24
phobias, 391
PHQ-9. *See* Patient Health Questionnaire
physical environments, community aging initiatives
  and, 215
physician-assisted suicide (PAS), 600
Physician or Medical Orders for Life Sustaining Treatment
  (POLST or MOLST) protocols, 600, 603
physician practice case management, 183
Pioneer Network for Culture Change, 236, 239, 243, 285
PLST. *See* progressively lowered stress threshold
PMPM. *See* per member per month
pneumonia, hospital readmission penalties for, 164
POAs. *See* powers of attorney
point-of-service (POS) financing, 165
policy, 100*t*, 619
  ACA on healthcare, 164
  affecting LTSS, 99
  disabilities, 99, 100*t*, 326
  in global aging, 579–80
  healthy aging and, 326
  for healthy aging factors, 326
  housing, 228, 655, 656–57
  legislative actions change to, 99
  LGBT civil rights, 557–60
  Medicaid and Medicare disability, 326
  Medicare overview, 631–33
  of NAPGCM on client grievances, 193–94
  for prison inmates, 453–54, 456
  public, AL and, 241
Polikoff, Nancy, 558
political influence, of older population, 133
POLST. *See* Physician or Medical Orders for Life
  Sustaining Treatment
population growth, of older adults, 132
population health management focus, of ACA, 167
POS. *See* point-of-service
positive core memories, 57

positive psychology movement, 65, 69
postacute case management, 183, 184
post-traumatic stress disorder (PTSD), 58, 209
poverty
  African Americans/Blacks, 132, 224, 433, 435, 468, 506
    Asian Americans, 132, 224, 433, 468, 516
    elderly women, 468, 474
    extent of, 467–68
    functional disabilities and, 322
    heterogeneity of, 468, 470
    Latinos, 224, 433, 468, 506, 528
    mental health and, 577
    near poor elders, 468
    oldest old and, 433
    practice and service delivery recommendations, 472–75
    racial and ethnic minorities, 468, 469–70*t*, 474
    ratio by race, 469–70*t*
    rural elderly, 470, 474–75
    service delivery barriers, 419, 472, 473*t*
    Social Security and, 467, 626
powers of attorney (POAs), 665
PPOs. *See* preferred provider organizations
PPS. *See* prospective payment system
predictive validity, 20
Preferences for Everyday Life Inventory (PELI), 21
preferred provider organizations (PPOs), 165
presbyopia, 302
President's Fiscal Year 2015 budget and Appropriations
  bill, Elder Justice Initiative of, 132
President's New Freedom Commission on Mental Health,
  Older Adults Subcommittee, 375
preventive health services
  ACA on, 103
  Advisory Committee on Immunization Practices, 103–4
  Medicare and, 103
Preventive Services Task Force, US, 103–4
primary care homes
  collaborative care models for depression in, 389
  counseling services, 204
primary stressors, for caregivers, 45
prison inmates, 284, 453–64
  aging in place, 462*f*
  building bridges, 460
  community reintegration, 457
  compassionate policies and laws, 456
  dementia care for, 458
  diversity among, 454–56
  elder offender definition, 454
  end-of-life issues for, 458
  integrated health and justice response, 456
  intervention plan, 461*t*
  medical issues for, 455
  mental health issues for, 455
  online resources, 463
  population, 453–54
  practice innovations, 457–60
  programs for, 459
  punishment policies high cost, 453–54
  recidivism of, 460
  recommendations, 460–61
  social worker role expansion and, 462–63

Printed in the USA/Agawam, MA

July 29, 2022

796359.005